John Willis and Ben Hodges
THEATRE WORLD®

Volume 62
2005 – 2006

APPLAUSE
THEATRE & CINEMA BOOKS

AN IMPRINT OF HAL LEONARD CORPORATION
NEW YORK

THEATRE WORLD
Volume 62

Published in 2008 by **Applause Theatre & Cinema Books**
An Imprint of Hal Leonard Corporation
7777 West Bluemound Road
Milwaukee, WI 53213

Trade Book Division Editorial Offices
19 West 21st Street, New York, NY 10010

Printed in the United States of America

Book Composition by Kristina Rolander

ISBN 978-1-55783-708-0
ISSN 1088-4564

www.applausepub.com

DEDICATION

Over the sixty-two-year history of this publication, many famous people have graced the dedication pages of this series, from the indefatigable Carol Channing to the consummate Hal Prince to the ubiquitous Bernadette Peters. They, as well as the other personalities and organizations who have been honored here, however, would be the first to acknowledge that they have not gotten as far as they have all by themselves. Nor have we who are dedicated to the history and preservation of the American theatre engaged in our pursuit alone.

John Willis, an editor of this volume for more than 40 years, often speaks of his college drama teacher, Ms. Dimple Hart Christian, who played an influential role in his early appreciation of the theatre—her inspiration led to a dedication here 40 years ago. Mr. Willis's late sister, Aileen Willis, was for decades an unheralded benefactress of the Theatre World Awards for Outstanding Broadway and Off-Broadway Debuts; her devotion and commitment to her brother were largely responsible early on for the continuation of the now venerable ceremony. (The Theatre World Awards are now a fully incorporated 501(c)(3) nonprofit organization.)

We who currently edit these volumes could not accomplish the increasingly challenging job of documenting theatre in America without the encouragement and support of those who have selflessly sustained us in doing so. They are no less responsible for the record published here and referenced by students, professionals, educators, and theatre devotees worldwide than are we.

To my late grandfather, James L. "Zeke" Cosson (June 29, 1924–March 31, 1999); grandmother, Flora Sue Cosson; aunt, Patricia Cosson Henderson; and mother, Susan Cosson.

With eternal gratitude—

Ben Hodges
New York City

CONTENTS

PAST EDITOR

Daniel Blum (1945–1963)

CO-EDITORS

John Willis (1964–present)

Ben Hodges (1998–present)

ASSOCIATE EDITORS

Scott Denny

Allison Graham

ACKNOWLEDGMENTS

Assistant Editors: Shane Frampton Wolters, Lisa Kuhnen, Caitlin Thomson
Staff Photographers: Henry Grossman, Michael Riordan, Laura Viade, Michael Viade, Jack Williams
Applause Books Staff: Michael Messina, Gail Siragusa, Bernadette Malavarca,
Marybeth Keating, Kristina Rolander

SPECIAL THANKS

Epitacio Arganza; Seth Barrish, Lee Brock, Eric Paeper, and The Barrow Group Theater Company/The Barrow Group School; Nicole Boyd; Helen Guditis and the Broadway Theater Museum; Fred Cantor; Fred Caruso; Michael Che; Jason Cicci, Monday Morning Productions, and Summer Stage New York; Christopher Cohen; Sue Cosson, Susan Cosson, Robert Dean Davis; Carol and Nick Dawson; Carmen Diaz; Diane Dixon; Craig Dudley; Ben Feldman, Amy Luce, and Epstein, Levinsohn, Bodine, Hurwitz & Weinstein; Emily Feldman; Stanley Morton Ackert III and Gersen, Blakeman, and Ackert; Yvonne Ghareeb; the estates of the late Charles J. Grant Jr. and Zan Van Antwerp; Brad Hampton; Laura and Tommy Hanson; Esther Harriot; Richard M. Henderson Jr. and Jennifer Henderson; Richard M. Henderson Sr. and Patricia Lynn Henderson; Al and Sherry Hodges; Leonard Jacobs; Gretchen, Aaron, Eli, and Max Kerr; Jane, Lynn, and Kris Kircher; Tim Deak, Kim Spanjol, and The Learning Theatre, Inc.; David Lowry; Cecelia McCarton and the staff of the McCarton Center/The McCarton School; Barry Monush and Screen World; Virginia Moraweck; Lucy Nathanson; Jason Bowcutt, Shay Gines, Nick Micozzi, and the staff and respective voting committees of the New York Innovative Theatre Awards; Petie Dodrill, Craig Johnson, Rob Johnson, Dennis Romer, Katie Robbins, Dean Jo Ann VanSant, Ed Vaughan, the late Dr. Charles O. Dodrill and the staff of Otterbein College/Otterbein College Department of Theatre and Dance, Kathie Packer; Hugo Uys and the staff of Paris Commune and Shag; David Plank; Angie and Drew Powell; Carolyn, David, and Glenna Rapp; Robert Rems; Ric Wanetik, David Hagans, Steven Gelston, Kim Jackson, and Mollie Levin at Ricochet, LLC; Jeutan Dobbs, Sydney Davalos, Todd Haimes, and Roundabout Theatre Company; Kate Rushing; Bill Schaap; William Jack Sibley, Hannah Richman Slosberg, and Jason Slosberg; Susan Stoller; Jamie deRoy, Patricia Elliott, Peter Filichia, Leigh Giroux, Doug Holmes, Tom Lynch, Kati Meister, Matthew Murray, and the board of The Theatre World Awards, Inc.; Bob Ost and Theater Resources Unlimited; Harry Haun, Howard Kissel, Frank Scheck, Michael Sommers, Doug Watt, Linda Winer, and the voting committee of The Theatre World Awards, Inc.; Renée Isely Tobin and Bob, Kate, Eric, Laura, Anna, Foster, and Lucky Tobin; Adam Blanshay, Emily Erstling, Liz Frankel, and Waxman Williams Entertainment; Wilson Valentin; Jack Williams, Barbara Dewey, and the staff of the University of Tennessee at Knoxville; Sarah and Bill Willis.

HIGHLIGHTS

RABBIT HOLE

Above: John Slattery, Cynthia Nixon,
Tyne Daly, Mary Catherine Garrison

PHOTO BY JOAN MARCUS

THE COLOR PURPLE

Right: Felicia P. Fields and La Chanze

PHOTO BY PAUL KOLNIK

THE ODD COUPLE

Above: Nathan Lane and Matthew Broderick

PHOTO BY CAROL ROSEGG

THREE DAYS OF RAIN

Top Left: Paul Rudd and Julia Roberts

PHOTO BY JOAN MARCUS

THE TRIP TO BOUNTIFUL

Left: Lois Smith

PHOTO BY CAROL ROSEGG

THE PAJAMA GAME
Above: The Company
PHOTO BY JOAN MARCUS

[TITLE OF SHOW]
Right: Heidi Blickenstaff (top, left),
Jeff Bowen (bottom, left), Susan Blackwell
(top, right), Hunter Bell (bottom, right)
PHOTO BY CAROL ROSEGG

JERSEY BOYS
Left: J. Robert Spencer, John Lloyd Young,
Daniel Reichard, Christian Hoff
PHOTO BY JOAN MARCUS

SWEENEY TODD
Below: The Company
PHOTO BY PAUL KOLNIK

THE WEDDING SINGER
Above: Stephen Lynch and Laura Benanti

PHOTO BY JOAN MARCUS

GREY GARDENS
Top Right: Christine Ebersole (seated on bench) with
(left to right) Audrey Twitchell, Sarah Hyland, Bob Stillman,
John McMartin, Michael Potts, Sara Gettelfinger

PHOTO BY JOAN MARCUS

THE LIEUTENANT OF INISHMORE
Right: David Wilmot and Alison Pill

PHOTO BY MONIQUE CARBONI

THE DROWSY CHAPERONE
Above: Sutton Foster and Company
PHOTO BY JOAN MARCUS

AWAKE AND SING!
Left: Ned Eisenberg, Zoe Wanamaker,
Jonathan Hadary, Richard Topol, Lauren Ambrose
PHOTO BY PAUL KOLNIK

ABIGAIL'S PARTY
Above: Lisa Emery,
Jennifer Jason Leigh, Elizabeth Jasicki
PHOTO BY CAROL ROSEGG

THE HISTORY BOYS
Right: Richard Griffiths
PHOTO BY JOAN MARCUS

John Willis and Ben Hodges
THEATRE WORLD®

Volume 62
2005 – 2006

BROADWAY

Productions That Opened **June 1, 2005 – May 31, 2006**

AFTER THE NIGHT AND THE MUSIC

Biltmore Theatre; First Preview: April 28, 2005 2004; Opening Night: June 1, 2005; Closed July 3, 2005; 39 previews and 28 performances

Manhattan Theatre Club (Lynne Meadow, Artistic Director; Barry Grove, Executive Producer) production of three new plays by Elaine May; produced by special arrangement with Julian Schlossberg and Roy Furman; Dance Arrangements by Randy Skinner, Brad Ross, and Wayne Barker; Director, Daniel Sullivan, Choreography, Randy Skinner; Scenery, John Lee Beatty; Costumes, Michael Krass; Lighting, Peter Kaczorowski; Original Music and Sound, John Gromada; Production Stage Manager, Roy Harris; Stage Manager, Denise Yaney; Casting, Nancy Piccione and David Caparelliotis; Director of Artistic Operations, Mandy Greenfield; Production Manager, Ryan McMahon; Director of Development, Jill Turner Lloyd; Director of Marketing, Debra A. Waxman; General Manager, Florie Seery; Director of Artistic Development, Paige Evans; Director of Artistic Production, Michael Bush; Assistant Director, Jeremy Lewitt; Associate General Manager, Seth Shepsle; Technical Director, William Mohney; Assistant Choreographer, Sara Brians; Associate Scenic Design, Eric Renschler; Company Manager, Denise Cooper; Fight Consultant, Brent Langdon; Marketing, Marketing Consultants; Advertising, SPOTCo, Inc.; Press, Boneau/Bryan-Brown

Brian Kerwin, J. Smith-Cameron, Jeannie Berlin PHOTOS BY JOAN MARCUS

Jere Burns and J. Smith-Cameron

Cast: Act 1-*Curtain Raiser:* Keith **Eddie Korbich**; Brittany **Deirdre Madigan**; Gloria **J. Smith-Cameron**; Bartender **Jere Burns**; Another Man **Brian Kerwin**; Another Woman **Joanna Glushak**. *Giving Up Smoking:* Kathleen **J. Smith-Cameron**; Sherman **Jere Burns**; Joanne **Jeannie Berlin**; Mel **Brian Kerwin**. Act 2-*Swing Time:* Gail **Jeannie Berlin**; Darryl Grade **Jere Burns**; Ron **Brian Kerwin**; Mitzi Grade **J. Smith-Cameron**

Understudies: Joel Blum (Keith), Joanna Glushak (Brittany, Gail), Deirdre Madigan (Gloria, Joanne, Kathleen, Mitzi Grade), Peter Marx (Another Man, Bartender, Darryl Grade, Mel, Ron, Sherman)

World premiere of three one-act comedies presented with one intermission.

Synopsis: Three new plays about life in the new millennium, including middle-aged men longing to dance, married couples longing for sex, and aging singles looking for love.

J. Smith-Cameron and Eddie Korbich

MARK TWAIN TONIGHT!

Brooks Atkinson Theatre; First Preview: June 6, 2005; Opening Night: June 9, 2005; Closed June 26, 2004; 3 previews and 15 performances

Revival of the solo performance play created by Hal Holbrook from the works of Samuel Clemens; Produced by Ira Pittelman, Jeffrey Sine, Scott Rudin, Max Cooper, Ben Sprecher, William P. Miller, Michael Moore, Elliot Martin, Eve Holbrook and Emanuel Azenberg; General Manager, Abbie M. Strassler; Company Manager, Sean Free; Production Supervisor, Richard Costabile; Technical Supervisor, Theatretech, Inc., Brian Lynch; Sound, Wally Flores; Light Board, Manuel Becker; Wardrobe, Kelly Saxon; Assistant to Mr. Holbrook, Joyce Cohen; Management Staff, Eduardo Castro, Shelley Ott, and Michael Salonia; Carpenter, Thomas A Lavaia; Properties, Joseph P. DePaulo; Production Assistant, Betty Tung; Press, Advertising, Serino Coyne, Inc.; Press, Bill Evans & Associates

Cast: Mark Twain **Hal Holbrook**

Return engagement of a solo performance piece presented with intermission. Originally produced on Broadway at the Longacre Theatre, March 23, 1966 (See *Theatre World* Volume 22, page 70) and revived at the Imperial Theatre, March 15, 1977 (See *Theatre World* Volume 33, page 58).

Synopsis: Hal Holbrook reprises award-winning performance of humorist and author Mark Twain through excerpts from Twain's letters, autobiography, speeches, essays, and fiction.

Hal Holbrook PHOTOS BY CHUCK STEWART

Hal Holbrook

THE CONSTANT WIFE

American Airlines Theatre; First Preview: May 27, 2005; Opening Night: June 16, 2005; Closed August 21, 2005; 23 previews and 77 performances

Roundabout Theatre Company (Todd Haimes, Artistic Director; Harold Wolpert, Managing Director; Julia C. Levy, Executive Director); revival of a play by W. Somerset Maugham; Director, Mark Brokaw; Scenery, Allen Moyer; Costumes, Michael Krass; Lighting, Mary Louise Geiger; Sound, David Van Tieghem and Jill BC Du Boff; Original Music, David Van Tieghem; Hair and Wigs, Paul Huntley; Assistant Director, Kip Fagan; Production Stage Manager, Lisa Buxbaum; Stage Manager, Leslie C. Lyter, Jonathan Donahue; Dialect Coach, Deborah Hecht; Casting, Jim Carnahan and Mele Nagler; Technical Supervisor, Steve Beers; General Manager, Sydney Beers and Nichole Larson; Founding Director, Gene Feist; Associate Artistic Director, Scott Ellis; Marketing, David B. Steffen; Director of Development, Jeffory Lawson; Company Manager, Denys Baker; Advertising, The Eliran Murphy Group; Press, Boneau/Bryan-Brown: Adrian Bryan-Brown, Matt Polk, Jessica Johnson, Joe Perotta

Lynn Redgrave, Michael Cumpsty, Kate Burton PHOTOS BY JOAN MARCUS

Cast: Mrs. Culver, Constance Middleton's mother **Lynn Redgrave**; Bentley, the butler **Denis Holmes**; Martha, Constance's sister **Enid Graham**; Barbara Fawcett, a friend **Kathleen McNenny**; Constance Middleton **Kate Burton**; Marie-Louise, a friend **Kathyrn Meisle**; John Middleton, F.R.C.S., Constance's husband **Michael Cumpsty**; Bernared Kersal, a friend **John Dossett**; Mortimer Durham, Marie-Louise's husband **John Ellison Conlee**

Understudies/Standbys: Robert Ari (Bentley, Mortimer Durham), Tony Carlin (Bernard Kersal, John Middleton, F.R.C.S.), Tara Falk (Marie-Louise Durham, Martha Culver), Lucy Martin (Barbara Fawcett, Mrs. Culver), Kathleen McNenney (Constance Middleton)

Setting: The Middleton's house in Harley Street, London, 1926. A comedy presented in two acts; originally produced on Broadway November 29, 1926 at Maxine Elliot's Theatre where it played for 296 performances. This production was the fourth Broadway revival.

Synopsis: *The Constant Wife* follows the marriage of a top surgeon and his wife. The comedy of manners delivers a twist after a seemingly secret affair between the husband and his wife's friend is revealed.

(Seated) Lynn Redgrave and John Dossett. (Standing) Kate Burton and Michael Cumpsty

Kate Burton, John Dossett, Lynn Redgrave

PRIMO

Music Box Theatre; First Preview: July 8, 2005; Opening Night: July 17, 2005; Closed August 14, 2005; 4 previews and 35 performances

The National Theatre of Great Britain (Sir Hayden Phillips, Chairman of the Board; Nicholas Hytner, Director; Nick Starr, Executive Director) production of a new play with music adapted by Antony Sher, based on *If This Is A Man* by Primo Levi; Produced by Bill Kenwright and Thelma Holt; Director, Richard Wilson; Scenery and Costumes, Hildegard Bechtler; Original Lighting, Paul Pyant; Lighting Recreated by David Howe; Sound, Rich Walsh; Music, Jonathan Goldstein; Technical Supervisor, Larry Morley; General Management, David R. Richards and Tamar Climan; Stage Managers, David Hyslop and Thomas Vowles; Company Manager, Brig Berney; Press, Philip Rinaldi and Barbara Carroll

Antony Sher PHOTOS BY IVAN KYNCL

Antony Sher

Antony Sher

Antony Sher

Cast: Primo Levi **Antony Sher**

Musicians: Robin Thompson-Clarke (cello), Paul Beniston (trumpet), Andy Findon (piccolo), Tristan Fry (percussion), Oren Marshall (tuba), Ian Watson (accordion)

2005–2006 Awards: Drama Desk Award: Outstanding Solo Performance (Antony Sher)

A drama presented without intermission. Originally presented at the National's Cottesloe Theatre, fall, 2004, subsequently playing Cape Town, South Africa, and returning to London's Hampstead Theatre.

Synopsis: *Primo* features Antony Sher as Italian chemist and Holocaust survivor Primo Levi. Levi's 1947 memoir chronicles the time he spent in a concentration camp during the final year of World War II.

Suzanne Somers PHOTOS BY PAUL PARKS

THE BLONDE IN THE THUNDERBIRD

Brooks Atkinson Theatre; First Preview: July 8, 2005; Opening Night: July 17, 2005; Closed July 23, 2005; 10 previews and 9 performances

A new play with music by Mitzie and Ken Welch, conceived by Suzanne Somers, based on her autobiographies *Keeping Secrets* and *After the Fall*; Produced by Alan Hamel; Directors Mitzie and Ken Welch; Scenery and Lighting, Roger Ball; Sound, Robert Ludwig; Technical Supervisor, Overlap Production/Tony Hauser; Music Direction/Orchestrations, Doug Walter; Music Coordinator, John Miller; Original Music and Lyrics, Ken and Mitzie Welch; Production Stage Manager, Robert Bennett; General Manager, The Sprecher Organization (Ben Sprecher and Peter Bogyo); Press, The Publicity Office, Bob Fennell, Marc Thibodeau, Michael S. Borowski, and Candi Adams

Performed by **Suzanne Somers**

Suzanne Somers

Musical Numbers: The Blonde in the Thunderbird, Fifty Percent, How Do I Say I Love You, If I Could Live It All Over Again, If I Only Had Brain, If You Knew Susie, Inventory, Johnny's Theme, No More Secrets, Pick Yourself Up, Repartee, Self Portrait, She Loves Me, Take Back Your Mink, That Face, Wake Up Little Susie

A solo performance play with music presented without intermission. Originally presented at the Spreckels Theatre in San Diego, California, January 2004.

Synopsis: A chronicle of hardship, pain, and conflict that blossoms into a great love story. Somers shares openly and honestly in this musical autobiography about her journey to become the successful and well-known performer/entrepreneur she is today, mixing stories with well-known songs and tunes of her own composition.

Suzanne Somers

LENNON

Broadhurst Theatre; First Preview: July 7, 2005. Opening Night: August 14, 2005; Closed September 24, 2005; 42 previews and 49 performances

A new musical conceived by Don Scardino with music and lyrics by John Lennon, book by Don Scardino, and with special thanks to Yoko Ono Lennon; Produced by Allan McKeown, Edgar Lansbury, Clear Channel Entertainment, and Jeffrey A. Sine; Director, Don Scardino; Scenery and Projections, John Arnone; Costumes, Jane Greenwood; Lighting, Natasha Katz; Sound, Bobby Aitken; Music Coordinator, John Miller; Music Director, Jeffrey Klitz; Orchestrator, Harold Wheeler; Music Supervisor/Arranger, Lon Hoyt; Creative Consultants, Bob Eaton and Brian Hendel; Marketing, TMG-The Marketing Group; General Management, NLA/Maggie Edelman; Executive Producer, Nina Lannan; Associate Producer, Louise Forlenza; Special Effects, Chic Silber; Production Manager, Arthur Siccardi; Production Stage Manager, Arthur Gaffin; Stage Manager, Laurie Goldfeder; Assistant Stage Manager, Justin Scribner; Associate Director, Dianne Trulock; Assistant Director, Ellie Dvorkin; Assistant Choreographer, Allison Leo; Dance Captain, Marcy Harriell; Associate Costumes, Wade Laboissonniere; Associate Projections, Michael Clark; Scenic Associate, Brian Webb; Company Manager, Chris Morey; Associate Company Manager, Shaun W. Moorman; Music Copying, Emily Grishman Music Preparation; Casting, Janet Foster; Press, Boneau/Bryan-Brown, Chris Boneau, Susanne Tighe, Juliana Hannett

Cast: Will Chase; **Chuck Cooper**; **Julie Danao-Salkin**; **Mandy Gonzalez**; **Marcy Harriell**; **Chad Kimball**; **Terrence Mann**; **Julia Murney**; **Michael Potts**

Standbys: Rona Figueroa (Julie and Mandy), Mark Richard Ford (Chuck, Terrence, and Michael), Nicole Lewis (Marcy and Julia), Darin Murphy (Will, Chad, and Terrence)

Orchestra: Jeffrey Klitz (Music Director/keyboards), Dave Keyes (Associate Music Director/keyboards), John Benthal and Jack Cavari (guitars), David Anderson (bass), Warren Odze (drums), Dave Yee (percussion), Tom Murray (reeds), Tony Kadleck (trumpet), Larry Dean Farrell (trombone)

Musical Numbers: New York City, Mother, Look At Me, Money, Twist and Shout, Instant Karma, India India, Real Love (Boys and Girls), Mind Games, The Ballad of John and Yoko, How Do You Sleep, God, Give Peace a Chance, Power to the People, Woman Is the Nigger of the World, Attica State, Gimme Some Truth, I'm Losing You/I'm Moving On, I'm Stepping Out, I Don't Want to Lose You, Whatever Gets You Through the Night, Woman, Beautiful Boy, Watching the Wheels, (Just Like) Starting Over, Grow Old With Me, Imagine

A new musical presented in two acts. World premiere at the Orpheum Theatre in San Francisco prior to its Broadway engagement.

Synopsis: A musical biography, concert, and celebration of life, *Lennon* takes audiences on a magical, mythical journey behind the greatest rock legacy with words, images, and some of the best pop songs ever written. The nine-member ensemble replays Lennon's life from his childhood, the Beatles, anti-war activism, his love story with Yoko Ono, and to the fateful day at the Dakota in New York.

Will Chase PHOTOS BY JOAN MARCUS

The Cast of *Lennon*

Julia Murney, Marcy Harriell, Julie Danao-Salkin, Mandy Gonzalez

A NAKED GIRL ON THE APPIAN WAY

American Airlines Theatre; First Preview: September 13, 2005; Opening Night: October 6, 2005; Closed December 4, 2005; 27 previews and 69 performances

Roundabout Theatre Company (Todd Haimes, Artistic Director; Harold Wolpert, Managing Director; Julia C. Levy, Executive Director) production of a play by Richard Greenberg; Director, Doug Hughes; Scenery, John Lee Beatty; Costumes, Catherine Zuber; Lighting, Peter Kaczorowski; Original Music and Sound, David Van Tieghem; Production Stage Manager, Leslie C. Lyter; Stage Manager, Amy Patricia Stern; Casting, Jim Carnahan and Mele Nagler; Technical Supervisor, Steve Beers; General Manager, Sydney Beers and Nichole Larson; Founding Director, Gene Feist; Associate Artistic Director, Scott Ellis; Marketing, David B. Steffen; Director of Development, Jeffory Lawson; Company Manager, Denys Baker; Assistant Director, Mark Schneider; Assistant Scenic, Eric Renschler and Yoshi Tanokura; Assistant Costume, David Newell; Assistant Lighting, Aaron Spivey; Associate Sound, Jill B.C. Du Boff; Dialect Consultant, Kate Mare; Advertising, The Eliran Murphy Group; Press, Boneau/Bryan-Brown: Adrian Bryan-Brown, Matt Polk, Jessica Johnson, Joe Perotta

Matthew Morrison and Susan Kelechi Watson PHOTOS BY JOAN MARCUS

Richard Thomas

James Yaegashi, Jill Clayburgh

Cast: Bess Lapin **Jill Clayburgh**; Jeffrey Lapin **Richard Thomas**; Sadie **Ann Guilbert**; Elaine **Leslie Ayvazian**; Juliet Lapin **Susan Kelechi Watson**; Thad Lapin **Matthew Morrison**; Bill Lapin **James Yaegashi**

Understudies/Standbys: Nancy Franklin (Sadie), Phyllis Johnson (Juliet Lapin), Charlotte Maier (Bess Lapin, Elaine), Terrence Riordan (Thad Lapin), James Seol (Bill Lapin), Ray Virta (Jeffrey Lapin)

Setting: Present day, a beautiful house in some Hampton; early June. New York premiere of a new comedy presented without intermission; commissioned and premiered at the South Coast Repertory Theatre, Costa Mesa, California.

Synopsis: A chain reaction of revelations is unearthed in a neighborhood when two children of a successful author/cooking-show host and an eccentric genius return to their American home following a year-long excursion in Europe.

Jill Clayburgh, Susan Kelechi Watson, Richard Thomas, Matthew Morrison

LATINOLOGUES

Helen Hayes Theatre; First Preview: September 13, 2005; Opening Night: October 13, 2005; Closed December 31, 2005; 34 previews and 93 performances

A collection of monologues created and written by Rick Najera; Produced by Tate Entertainment Group, Inc. (Robin Tate: President); Produced in association with AEG Live, Icon Entertainment and TATI Incorporated; Associate Producer, Kevin Benson; Director, Cheech Marin; Lighting Design, Kevin Adams; Sound Design, T. Richard Fitzgerald; Costume Design, Santiago; General Manager, Morer/Bowman Productions; Company Manager, Jill Bowman; Production Stage Manager, Arabella Powell; Stage Manager, Pat Sosnow; Video Design, Dennis Diamond; Associate Video Design, Kevin Frech and Marc Gamboa; Assistant Lighting Design, Aaron Sporer; Assistant Costume Design, Jonathan Solari; Advertising, Jim Weiner and Weiner Associates; Marketing, Jim Weiner and Weiner Associates; Graphic Design, Claudia Hernandez; Casting, Elsie Stark and Stark Naked Productions; Press, Jim Randolph, Bill Evans & Associates, Susie Albin and Trina Bardusco

Cast: Eugenio Derbez; **Rick Najera**; **Rene Lavan**; **Shirley A. Rumierk**

Understudies: Carlo D'Amore, Ivette Sosa

Replacement: Jamie Camil (December 6–31, 2005)

An evening of monologues presented without intermission.

Synopsis: *Latinologues* is a collection of comedic and poignant monologues, performed in English, revealing the Latino experience in America. Cast members take on everything from beauty pageants to immigration, shattering Latino stereotypes with hilarious results.

Eugenio Derbez PHOTOS BY JOAN MARCUS

Rick Najera, Eugenio Derbez, Rene Lavan, Shirley Rumierk

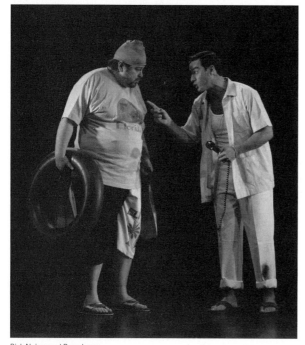

Rick Najera and Rene Lavan

Rick Najera

ABSURD PERSON SINGULAR

Biltmore Theatre; First Preview: September 22, 2005; Opening Night: October 18, 2005; Closed December 4, 2005; 29 previews and 56 performances

Manhattan Theatre Club (Lynne Meadow, Artistic Director; Barry Grove, Executive Producer) revival of a play by Alan Ayckbourn; Director, John Tillinger; Scenery, John Lee Beatty; Costumes, Jane Greenwood; Lighting, Brian MacDevitt; Sound, Bruce Ellman; Production Stage Manager, Diane DiVita; Casting, Nancy Piccione and David Caparelliotis; Director of Artistic Operations, Mandy Greenfield; Production Manager, Ryan McMahon; Director of Development, Jill Turner Lloyd; Director of Marketing, Debra A. Waxman; General Manager, Florie Seery; Director of Artistic Development, Paige Evans; Director of Artistic Production, Michael Bush; Stage Manager, Neil Krasnow; Technical Director, William Mohney; Company Manager, Denise Cooper; Fight Direction, Rick Sordelet; Dialect Coach, Charlotte Fleck; Assistant Director, Henry Wishcamper; Advertising, SPOTCo., Inc.; Press, Boneau/Bryan-Brown

Cast: Jane **Clea Lewis**; Sidney **Alan Ruck**; Ronald **Paxton Whitehead**; Marion **Deborah Rush**; Eva **Mirelle Enos**; Geoffrey **Sam Robards**

Understudies: Mark H Dold (Geoffrey, Sidney), John Christopher Jones (Ronald), Leslie Lyles (Marion), Crista Moore (Eva, Jane)

Deborah Rush and Mirelle Enos PHOTOS BY JOAN MARCUS

Sam Robards and Mirelle Enos

Setting: England, 1970s. Last Christmas: Sidney and Jane's kitchen; This Christmas: Geoffrey and Eva's kitchen; Next Christmas: Ronald and Marion's kitchen. Revival of a comedy presented in three acts. Originally produced on Broadway at the Music Box Theatre, October 8, 1974, where it ran for 591 performances (see *Theatre World* Volume 31, page 12).

Synopsis: Three couples, three kitchens, three successive Christmas Eves: welcome to the world of Alan Ayckbourn's comedy about social class and splendid cocktails.

Paxton Whitehead

Clea Lewis and Alan Ruck

IN MY LIFE

Music Box Theatre; First Preview: September 30, 2005; Opening Night: October 20, 2005; Closed December 11, 2005; 23 previews and 61 performances

A new musical with book, music, and lyrics by Joseph Brooks; Produced by Watch Hill Productions and TBF Music Corp.; Director, Joseph Brooks; Music Director, Henry Aronson; Musical Staging, Richard Stafford; Scenery, Allen Moyer; Costumes, Catherine Zuber; Lighting, Christopher Akerlind; Sound, John H. Shivers; Projections, Wendall K. Harrington; Hair and Wigs, Tom Watson; Associate Director, Dan Fields; Production Manager, Arthur Siccardi; Production Stage Manager, Jane Grey; Orchestrations, Kinny Landrum; Music Coordinator, Michael Keller; Stage Manager, Nancy Wernick; Assistant Stage Manager, Jason J. Carroll; General Manager, Nina Lannan Associates, Devin Keudell; Company Manager, Edward Nelson; Associate Company Manager, Shaun Moorman; Aerial Staging, Rob Besserer; Dance Captain, Jonathan Groff; Make-up, Angelina Avallone; Casting, Dave Clemmons Casting; Marketing, HHC Marketing; Advertising, Serino Coyne, Inc.; Press, Richard Kornberg & Associates, Don Summa, Laura Kaplo-Goldman

Cast: Vera **Chiara Navarra**; J.T. **Christopher J. Hanke**; Jenny **Jessica Boevers**; Winston **David Turner**; Al **Michael J. Farina**; Samantha **Laura Jordan**; Liz **Roberta Gumbel**; Nick **Michael Halling**; Ensemble **Courtney Balan, Carmen Keels, Kilty Reidy, Brynn Williams**

Chiara Navarra and Michael Farina

Christopher J. Hanke

Christopher J. Hanke and Jessica Boevers PHOTOS BY JOAN MARCUS

Swing: Jonathan Groff

Understudies: Courtney Balan (Jenny, Samantha), Jonathan Groff (J.T., Nick), Michael Halling (J.T.), Laura Jordan (Jenny), Carmen Keels (Liz, Samantha), Kilty Reidy (Al, Nick, Winston), Brynn Williams (Vera)

Musicians: Henry Aronson (Conductor), Gregory Dlugos (Associate Conductor, keyboards), Ted Kooshian, Maggie Torres, Fran Minarik (keyboards), Bruce Uchitel, J.J. McGeehan (guitar), Randy Landau (bass), Brian Blake (drums), Andrew Barrett (synthesizer programmer)

Musical Numbers: Life Turns on a Dime, It Almost Feels Like Love, Perfect for an Opera, What a Strange Life We Live, Doomed, What a Strange Life We Live (reprise), Sempre Mio Rimani, I Am My Mother's Son, Volkswagen, What a Strange Life We Live (reprise), Headaches, When I Sing, Secrets #1, In My Life, A Ride on the Wheel, Perfect for an Opera (reprise), Didn't Have to Love You, When She Danced, Volkswagen (reprise), Not This Day, Floating on Air, Not This Day (reprise), On This Day, In My Life (reprise), Life Turns on a Dime (reprise)

Setting: New York and Heaven, now. World premiere of a new musical presented without intermission.

Synopsis: A romantic musical comedy about two young lovers who are unwitting participants in God's first reality opera.

THE ODD COUPLE

Brooks Atkinson Theatre; First Preview: October 4, 2005; Opening Night: October 27, 2005; still running as of May 31, 2006

Revival of a play by Neil Simon; Produced by Ira Pittelman, Jeffrey Sine, Ben Sprecher, Max Cooper, Scott E. Nederlander, and Emanuel Azenberg; Director, Joe Mantello; Scenery, John Lee Beatty; Costumes, Ann Roth; Lighting, Kenneth Posner; Sound, Peter Fitzgerald; Original Music, Marc Shaiman; Casting, Bernard Telsey Casting; Hair, David Brian Brown; Production Stage Manager, William Joseph Barnes, (succeeded by Jill Cordle); Stage Manager, Jill Cordle (succeeded by Richard Costabile); Technical Supervisor, Brian Lynch; Associate Producers, Roy Furman and Jay Binder; General Manager, Abbie M. Strassler; Company Manager, John E. Gendron; Assistant Director, Lisa Leguillou; Production Supervisor, William Joseph Barnes; Props, Chuck Dague; Associate Scenery, Eric Renschler; Associate Lighting, Philip Rosenberg; Associate Sound, Jill BC DeBoff; Advertising, Serino Coyne, Inc./Angelo Desimini; Press, Bill Evans and Associates, Jim Randolph

Cast: Speed **Rob Bartlett**; Murray **Brad Garrett***1; Roy **Peter Frechette**; Vinnie **Lee Wilkof**; Oscar Madison **Nathan Lane***2; Felix Ungar **Matthew Broderick**; Gwendolyn Pigeon **Olivia d'Abo**; Cecily Pigeon **Jessica Stone**

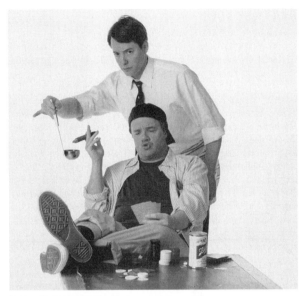

Matthew Broderick and Nathan Lane PHOTO BY CHRIS CALLAS

Nathan Lane, Lee Wilkof, Rob Bartlett, Matthew Broderick, Brad Garrett, Peter Frechette
PHOTO BY CAROL ROSEGG

Nathan Lane and Matthew Broderick PHOTO BY CAROL ROSEGG

Understudies: Peter Frechette (Felix Ungar), Gene Gabriel (Murray, Oscar Madison, Roy, Speed, Vinnie), Marc Grapey (Felix Ungar, Murray, Roy, Speed, Vinnie), Christy Pusz (Cecily Pigeon, Gwendolyn Pigeon)

Setting: Oscar Madison's Riverside Drive apartment, Summer, 1965. A comedy in three acts and four scenes presented with one intermission; originally produced on Broadway at the Plymouth Theatre and later the Eugene O'Neill Theatre, March 10, 1965, running for 966 performances (see *Theatre World* Volume 21, page 84); a revised "female version" of the play was produced at the Broadhurst Theatre, June 11, 1985 (see *Theatre World* Volume 42, page 6).

Synopsis: In one of Neil Simon's most popular comedies, two divorced men, sportswriter/slob Oscar Madison and fastidious photographer Felix Unger, share an apartment with hilarious results.

Matthew Broderick, Nathan Lane, Jessica Stone, Olivia d'Abo PHOTO BY CAROL ROSEGG

*Succeeded by: 1.Mike Starr (1/3/06) 2. Brad Garrett returned to play "Oscar" January 20–22, 2006 for an ailing Mr. Lane

SWEENEY TODD
The Demon Barber of Fleet Street

Eugene O'Neill Theatre; First Preview: October 3, 2005; Opening Night: November 3, 2005; still running as of May 31, 2006

Revival of the musical with music and lyrics by Stephen Sondheim, book by Hugh Wheeler, from an adaptation by Christopher Bond; Originally directed on Broadway by Harold Prince; Produced by Tom Viertel, Steven Baruch, Marc Routh, Richard Frankel, Ambassador Theatre Group, Adam Kenwright, Tulchin/Bartner/Bagert; Director/Scenery/Costumes, John Doyle; Music Supervision and Orchestrations, Sarah Travis; Lighting, Richard G. Jones; Sound, Dan Moses Schreier; Wigs and Hair, Paul Huntley; Resident Music Supervisor, David Loud; Casting, Bernard Telsey Casting; Music Coordinator, John Miller; General Management, Richard Frankel Productions, Inc., Jo Porter; Production Stage Manager, Adam John Hunter; Company Manager, Sammy Ledbetter; Stage Manager, Julia P. Jones (succeeded by Newton Cole); Assistant Stage Manager, David Redman Scott (succeeded by Aja Kane); Assistant Company Manager, Jason Pelusio; Production Management, Showman Fabricators, Inc.; Associate Scenery, Ted LeFevre; Associate Costumes, Patrick Chevillot; Make-up, Angelina Avallone; Associate Lighting, Paul Miller; Associate Sound, David Bullard; Advertising, Serino Coyne, Inc.; Press, Barlow-Hartman, John Barlow, Michael Hartman, Rick Miramontez, Leslie Baden; Cast recording: Nonesuch 79946-2

The Cast of *Sweeney Todd* PHOTOS BY PAUL KOLNIK

Manoel Felciano and Patti LuPone

Cast: Mrs. Lovett (Tuba, Orchestra Bells, Percussion) **Patti LuPone**; Sweeney Todd (Guitar, Orchestra Bells, Percussion) **Michael Cerveris**; Judge Turpin (Trumpet, Orchestra Bells, Percussion) **Mark Jacoby**; Pirelli (Accordion, Keyboard, Flute) **Donna Lynne Champlin**; Tobias Ragg (Violin, Clarinet, Keyboard) **Manoel Felciano**; The Beadle (Keyboard, Trumpet) **Alexander Gemignani**; Jonas Fogg (Bass) **John Arbo**; Beggar Woman (Clarinet) **Diana Dimarzio**; Anthony Hope (Cello, Keyboard) **Benjamin Magnuson**; Joanna (Cello, Penny Whistle) **Lauren Molina**

Standbys: Benjamin Eakeley (Anthony Hope, The Beadle, Tobias Ragg), Merwin Foard (Judge Turpin, Sweeney Todd), Dorothy Stanley (Mrs. Lovett, Pirelli), Elisa Winter (Beggar Woman, Johanna); Replacement standbys: David Hess (Jonas Fogg, Judge Turpin, Sweeney Todd, The Beadle), Stephen McIntyre (Jonas Fogg), Jessica Wright (Beggar Woman, Pirelli)

Musical Numbers: The Ballad of Sweeney Todd, No Place Like London, The Barber and His Wife, The Worst Pies in London, Poor Thing, My Friends, Green Finch and Linnet Bird, Ah Miss, Johanna, Pirelli's Miracle Elixir, The Contest, Johanna, Wait, Kiss Me, Ladies in Their Sensitivities, Quartet, Pretty Women, Epiphany, A Little Priest, God That's Good!, Johanna, By the Sea, Not While I'm Around, Parlor Songs, City on Fire!, Final Sequence, The Ballad of Sweeney Todd

Michael Cerveris and Patti LuPone

Michael Cerveris and Patti LuPone

2005–2006 Awards: Tony Award: Direction of Musical (John Doyle), Orchestrations (Sarah Travis); Drama Desk Award: Revival of a Musical, Director of a Musical (John Doyle), Orchestrations (Sarah Travis), Lighting Design (Richard G. Jones); Drama League Award: Revival of a Musical, Distinguished Achievement in Musical Theatre (Patti LuPone); Outer Critics Circle Award: Revival of a Musical, Direction of a Musical (John Doyle); New York Drama Critics Circle Award: Special Citation to John Doyle, Sarah Travis, and the cast.

A musical presented in two acts. This version was originally presented at the Watermill Theatre, Berkshire, Great Britain. Originally produced on Broadway at the Uris (Gershwin) Theatre, March 1, 1979, by Richard Barr, Charles Woodward, Robert Fryer, Mary Leah Johnson, Martin Richards, in association with Dean and Judy Manos, where it ran for 557 performances (see *Theatre World* Volume 35, page 32). Revived on Broadway at Circle in the Square, September 14, 1989 (see *Theatre World* Volume 46, page 8).

Synopsis: Stephen Sondheim's award-winning musical about a murderous barber, hell-bent on revenge, who takes up with his enterprising neighbor in a delicious plot to slice their way through England's upper crust. This unique reinvention of the show utilizes the ten-member cast as the musicians.

(Top, clockwise) Patti LuPone, Donna Lynne Champlin, Manoel Felciano, Michael Cerveris

(Foreground) Michael Cerveris, Donna Lynne Champlin. (Background) Manoel Felciano, Diana Di Marzio, Mark Jacoby

Michael Cerveris and Patti LuPone

JERSEY BOYS

August Wilson Theatre; First Preview: October 4, 2005; Opening Night: November 6, 2005; still running as of May 31, 2006

A new musical with book by Marshall Brickman and Rick Elice; music by Bob Gaudio; and lyrics by Bob Crewe; Produced by Dodger Theatricals (Michael David, Edward Strong, Rocco Landesman, Des McAnuff), Joseph J. Grano, Pelican Group, Tamara Kinsella and Kevin Kinsella; Produced in association with Latitude Link, Rick Steiner and Osher/Staton/Bell/Mayerson Group; Director, Des McAnuff; Choreography, Sergio Trujillo; Musical Director, Vocal Arrangements, Incidental Music, Ron Melrose; Scenery, Klara Zieglerova; Costumes, Jess Goldstein; Lighting, Howell Binkley; Sound, Steve Canyon Kennedy; Projections, Michael Clark; Hair and Wigs, Charles LaPointe; Fight Director, Steve Rankin; Production Stage Manager, Richard Hester; Orchestrations, Steve Orich; Music Coordinator, John Miller; Technical Supervisor, Peter Fulbright; East Coast Casting, Tara Rubin Casting; West Coast Casting, Sharon Bialy and Sherry Thomas; Company Manager, Sandra Carlson; Associate Producers, Lauren Mitchell and Rhoda Mayerson; Executive Producer, Sally Campbell Morse; Promotions, HHC Marketing; Stage Manager, Michelle Bosch; Assistant Stage Manager, Michael T. Clarkston; Dialect Coach, Stephen Gabis; Dance Captain, Peter Gregus; Fight Captain, Peter Gregus; Music Technical Design, Deborah Hurwitz; Associate Scenery, Nancy Thun and Todd Ivins; Associate Costumes, Alejo Vietti; Associate Lighting, Patricia Nichols; Associate Sound, Andrew Keister; Assistant Projection Design, Jason Thompson and Chris Kateff; Associate General Manager, Jennifer F. Vaughan; Assistant Company Manager, Tim Sulka; Assistant Directors, Holly-Anne Ruggiero and Alex Timbers; Assistant Choreographer, Kelly Devine; Marketing, Dodger Marketing; Advertising, Serino Coyne, Inc.; Press, Boneau/Bryan-Brown; Adrian Bryan-Brown, Susanne Tighe, Heath Schwartz; Cast recording: Rhino R2 73271

Cast: French Rap Star/Detective #1/Hal Miller/Barry Belson/Police Officer/Davis **Tituss Burgess**; Stanley/Hank Majewski/Crewe's PA/Joe Long **Steve Gouveia**; Bob Crewe/others **Peter Gregus**; Tommy DeVito **Christian Hoff**; Nick DeVito/Stosh/Billy Dixon/Norman Waxman/Charlie Calello/others **Donnie Kehr**; Joey/Recording Studio Engineer/others **Michael Longoria**; Gyp De Carlo/others **Mark Lotito**; Mary Delgado/Angel/others **Jennifer Naimo**; Church Lady/Miss Frankie Nolan/Bob's Party Girl/Angel/Lorraine/others **Erica Piccininni**; Bob Gaudio **Daniel Reichard**; Frankie's Mother/Nick's Date/Angel/Francine/others **Sara Schmidt**; Nick Massi **J. Robert Spencer**; Frankie Valli **John Lloyd Young**; Thugs **Ken Dow, Joe Payne**

John Lloyd Young , Daniel Reichard, Christian Hoff, J. Robert Spencer PHOTO BY JOAN MARCUS

Daniel Reichard, John Lloyd Young, Christian Hoff, J. Robert Spencer PHOTO BY CHRIS CALLIS

Understudies: Steve Gouveia (Bob Gaudio, Nick Massi), Donnie Kehr (Gyp De Carlo, Tommy DeVito), John Leone (Gyp De Carlo, Nick Massi, Tommy DeVito), Michael Longoria (Frankie Valli), Dominic Nolfi (Bob Gaudio, Frankie Valli)

Swings: Heather Ferguson, John Leone, Dominic Nolfi

Replacement Swing/Understudy: Matthew Scott (Tommy DeVito, Frankie Valli, Bob Gaudio)

Musicians: Ron Melrose (Conductor/keyboards), Deborah Hurwitz (Associate Conductor/ keyboards), Stephen "Hoops" Snyder (keyboards), Joe Payne (guitars), Ken Dow (bass), Kevin Dow (drums), Matt Hong and Ben Kono (reeds), David Spier (trumpet)

Christian Hoff, John Lloyd Young, Daniel Reichard, J. Robert Spencer PHOTO BY JOAN MARCUS

J. Robert Spencer, John Lloyd Young, Daniel Reichard, Christian Hoff PHOTO BY JOAN MARCUS

Christian Hoff, J. Robert Spencer, John Lloyd Young, Steve Gouveia, Peter Gregus, Daniel Reichard PHOTO BY JOAN MARCUS

Robert Spencer, John Lloyd Young, Daniel Reichard, Christian Hoff PHOTO BY JOAN MARCUS

Musical Numbers: Ces Soirées-La (Oh What a Night), Silhouettes, You're the Apple of My Eye, I Can't Give You Anything But Love, Earth Angel, Sunday Kind of Love, My Mother's Eyes, I Go Ape, (Who Wears) Short Shorts, I'm in the Mood for Love/Moody's Mood for Love, Cry for Me, An Angel Cried, I Still Care, Trance, Sherry, Big Girls Don't Cry, Walk Like a Man, December, 1963 (Oh What a Night), My Boyfriend's Back, My Eyes Adored You, Dawn (Go Away), Walk Like a Man (Reprise), Big Man in Town, Beggin', Stay, Let's Hang On (To What We've Got), Opus 17 (Don't You Worry 'Bout Me), Bye Bye Baby, C'mon Marianne, Can't Take My Eyes Off of You, Working My Way Back to You, Fallen Angel, Rag Doll, Who Loves You

J. Robert Spencer, John Lloyd Young, Daniel Reichard, Christian Hoff PHOTO BY JOAN MARCUS

Daniel Reichard, Christian Hoff, J. Robert Spencer, John Lloyd Young PHOTO BY JOAN MARCUS

2005–2006 Awards: Tony Awards: Best Musical, Best Actor in a Musical (John Lloyd Young), Best Featured Actor in a Musical (Christian Hoff), Best Lighting Design (Howell Binkley); Drama Desk Awards: Actor in a Musical (John Lloyd Young), Sound (Steve Canyon Kennedy); Outer Critics Circle Awards: Broadway Musical, Actor in a Musical (John Lloyd Young), Lighting (Howell Binkley); Drama League Awards: Distinguished Production of a Musical, Julia Hansen Award for Excellence in Directing (Des McAnuff); **Theatre World Award:** John Lloyd Young

Setting: New Jersey, New York, and across the U.S., 1950s-now. A new musical presented in two acts. World Premiere produced by La Jolla Playhouse (Des McAnuff, Artistic Director; Steven B. Libman, Managing Director), October 5, 2004.

Synopsis: "How did four blue-collar kids become one of the greatest successes in pop music history? You ask four guys, you get four different answers." *Jersey Boys* is the story of the legendary Four Seasons, blue-collar boys who formed a singing group and reached the heights of rock 'n' roll stardom.

SOUVENIR

Lyceum Theatre; First Preview: October 28, 2005; Opening Night: November 10, 2005; Closed January 8, 2005; 14 previews and 68 performances

A new play with music by Stephen Temperley; Produced by Ted Snowdon in association with Janice Montana, by arrangement with the York Theatre Company (James Morgan, Artistic Director); Director, Vivian Matalon; Scenery, R. Michael Miller; Costumes, Tracy Christensen; Lighting, Ann G. Wrightson; Sound, David Burdries; Musical Supervision, Tom Helm; Wigs, David H. Lawrence; Casting, Barry Moss, Bob Kale; Production Stage Manager, Jack Gianino; Production Manager, Showman Fabricators (Kai Brothers, Annie Jacobs); Marketing, HHC Marketing; General Manager, Roy Gabay; Company Manager, Bruce Klinger; Stage Manager, Alex Finch; Advertising, The Eliran Murphy Group, Ltd.; Press, Richard Kornberg & Associates, Tom D'Ambrosio, Laura Kaplow-Goldman

Donald Corren and Judy Kaye PHOTOS BY CAROL ROSEGG

Donald Corren and Judy Kaye

Judy Kaye

Cast: Florence Foster Jenkins **Judy Kaye**; Cosme McMoon **Donald Corren**

Standbys: Meg Bussert, Bob Stillman

Setting: A supper club with resident pianist somewhere in Greenwich Village, New York City, 1964. A play with music presented in two acts; originally played Off Broadway at the York Theatre Company, December 1, 2004 (see *Theatre World* Volume 61, page 204).

Synopsis: *Souvenir* tells the story of Florence Foster Jenkins through the eyes of her accompanist. Jenkins, an eccentric society woman, believed she was a great soprano, although the opposite was true. Despite her lack of talent, Jenkins' charity recitals brought her much fame. Jenkins often mistook audiences' muffled laughter for cheers, and over 2,000 people were turned away from her Carnegie Hall concert in the mid-1940s.

THE WOMAN IN WHITE

Marquis Theatre; First Preview: October 28, 2005; Opening Night: November 11, 2005; Closed February 19, 2006; 20 previews and 109 performances

A new musical with music by Andrew Lloyd Webber, lyrics by David Zippel, and book by Charlotte Jones, freely adapted from the novel by Wilke Collins; Produced by Boyett Ostar Productions, Nederlander Presentations, Inc., Sonia Friedman Productions, Ltd., The Really Useful White Company, Inc., Lawrence Horowitz/Jon Avnet, Ralph Guild/Bill Rollinick, Clear Channel Entertainment/ PIA, Thomas L. Miller; Director, Trevor Nunn; Set, Costume, and Video Design, William Dudley; Lighting, Paul Pyant; Sound, Mick Potter; Orchestrations, David Cullen; Orchestrations Supervisor, Andrew Lloyd Webber; Musical Supervisor, Simon Lee; Movement Director, Wayne McGregor; Associate Musical Supervisor/Music Director, Kristen Blodgette; Music Copying, Emily Grishman Music Preparation; Technical Supervisor, David Benken; Projection Realization and System Design, Mesmer, Dick Straker/Sven Ortel; Casting, Jim Carnahan; Music Coordinator, David Lai; Production Stage Manager, Rick Steiger; Marketing, HHC Marketing; General Management, 101 Productions, Ltd.; Associate Producers, Stage Entertainment BV; Illusionist, Paul Kieve; Fight Director, Tom Schall; Dialect and Vocal Coach, Deborah Hecht; Animal Trainer, William Berloni Theatrical Animals; Stage Manager, Lisa Dawn Cave; Assistant Stage Managers, Kevin Bertolacci, Jennifer Marik; Company Manager, Penelope Dalton; Assistant Company Manager, Megan Trice; Dance/Fight Captain, Greg Mills; Advertising, Serino Coyne; Press, Barlow-Harman, John Barlow, Michael Hartman, Dennis Crowley, Ryan Ratelle; London Cast recording: EMI International

Cast: Walter Hartright **Adam Brazier**; Signalman **Norman Large**; Anne Catherick **Angela Christian**; Coachman **Greg Mills**; Marian Halcombe **Maria Friedman**; Mr. Fairlie **Walter Charles**; Mr. Fairlie's Servant **John Dewar**; Laura Fairlie **Jill Paice**; A Village Girl **Justis Bolding**; Sir Percival Glyde **Ron Bohmer**; Count Fosco **Michael Ball**; Priest **Daniel Marcus**; A Pawnbroker **Norman Large**; A Con Man **Richard Todd Adams**; Prostitute **Lisa Brescia**; The Warden **Patty Goble**; The Company **Richard Todd Adams, Justis Bolding, Lisa Brescia, John Dewar, Courtney Glass, Patty Goble, Norman Large, Michael Shawn Lewis, Elizabeth Loyacano, Daniel Marcus, Greg Mills, Elena Shaddow, Daniel Torres**

Swings: Laura Dekkers, Roger E. DeWitt, Leah Horowitz, Sean MacLaughlin.

Maria Friedman and Michael Ball

Angela Christian   PHOTOS BY PAUL KOLNIK

Understudies: Richard Todd Adams (Sir Percival Glyde), Lisa Brescia (Marian Halcombe), Laura Dekkers (Laura Fairlie), John Dewar (Mr. Fairlie, Signal Man), Roger E. DeWitt (Mr. Fairlie, Signal Man), Courtney Glass (Anne Catherick), Leah Horowitz (Marian Halcombe), Norman Large (Count Fosco), Michael Shawn Lewis (Walter Hartright), Elizabeth Loyacano (Anne Catherick), Daniel Marcus (Count Fosco), Greg Mills (Sir Percival Glyde), Elena Shaddow (Laura Fairlie), Daniel Torres (Walter Hartright), Replacement: Laura Hope Wills (Ensemble, u.s. Laura)

Orchestra: Kristen Blodgette (Conductor), Milton Granger (Associate Conductor/keyboard), Mat Eisenstein (Assistant Conductor/keyboard), Ann Gerschefski (keyboard), Debra Shufelt-Dine, David Blinn (viola), Sarah J. Seiver, Dorothy Lawson (cello), Jeff Cooper (acoustic bass/electric bass), Russ Rizner, Shelagh Abate (French horn), Kathleen Nester (flute/ piccolo/alto flute/bass flute), David Young (oboe/English horn), Paul Garment (clarinet/bass clarinet), Michael Green (bassoon), Daniel Haskins (percussion)

Musical Numbers: I Hope You'll Like It Here, Perspective, Trying Not to Notice, I Believe My Heart, Lammastide, You See I Am No Ghost, A Gift for Living Well, The Holly and the Ivy, All for Laura, The Document, Act I Finale, If I Could Only Dream This World Away, The Nightmare, Evermore Without You, Lost Souls, You Can Get Away With Anything, The Seduction

2005–2006 Awards: Theatre World Award: Maria Friedman

Setting: Limmeridge, Cumberland and the Blackwater House, Hampshire, England, late 1800s. American premiere of a musical drama presented in two acts; originally opened in London at the Palace Theatre, September 16, 2004, and closed a week after the Broadway production closed.

Synopsis: A dashing young man, employed as the art tutor to two devoted sisters, is stranded at a remote railway station. Out of the darkness looms a woman, a mysterious figure dressed in white, desperate to share a chilling secret. He and the sisters soon find themselves trapped in a web of betrayal and greed, the victims of a seemingly flawless crime. Together they use their resourcefulness and courage to outwit a hugely charismatic and ingenious villain.

SEASCAPE

Booth Theatre; First Preview: October 28, 2005; Opening Night: November 21, 2005; Closed January 8, 2006; 27 previews and 55 performances

Lincoln Center Theatre (André Bishop, Artistic Director; Bernard Gersten, Executive Producer) revival of a play by Edward Albee; Director, Mark Lamos; Scenery, Michael Yeargan; Costumes, Catherine Zuber; Lighting, Peter Kaczorowski; Sound, Aural Fixation; Movement Coordinator, Rick Sordelet; Stage Manager, Michael McGoff; Assistant Stage Manager, Elizabeth Miller; Casting, Daniel Swee; Company Manager, Brig Berney; Assistant Director, Evan Cabnet; Fight Captain, Michael McGoff; Props, Faye Armon; Make-up Design, Angelina Avallone; Hair, Susan Schectar; Technical Supervisor, Walter Murphy and Patrick Merryman; Associate Sound, Tony Smolenski, IV; LCT Director of Development, Hattie Jutagir; LCT Director of Marketing, Linda Mason Ross; LCT General Manager, Adam Siegel; LCT Production Manager, Jeff Hamlin; Poster Art, James McMullan; Press, Philip Rinaldi, Barbara Carroll

Cast: Nancy **Frances Sternhagen**; Charlie **George Grizzard**; Leslie **Frederick Weller**; Sarah **Elizabeth Marvel**

Understudies: Jack Davidson (Charlie), Jennifer Harmon (Nancy), Steve Kazee and Baylen Thomas (Leslie), Jennifer Ikeda (Sarah)

Elizabeth Marvel, Frederick Weller, Frances Sternhagen, George Grizzard

Elizabeth Marvel and Frances Sternhagen

Frederick Weller, Elizabeth Marvel, George Grizzard, Frances Sternhagen

Setting: The present time, on a beach. A drama presented in two acts. Originally produced on Broadway at the Shubert Theatre, January 26, 1975 (see *Theatre World* Volume 31, page 38).

Synopsis: A starkly expressionistic drama set on a deserted stretch of beach, where retired couple Charlie and Nancy are strolling and talking about their future. With the arrival of another duo, Leslie and Sarah—who happen to be green, cold-blooded quadrupeds—the conversation takes on a more far-reaching tenor.

George Grizzard and Frances Sternhagen PHOTOS BY JOAN MARCUS

THE COLOR PURPLE

Broadway Theatre; First Preview: November 1, 2005; Opening Night: December 1, 2005; still running as of May 31, 2006

A new musical with book by Marsha Norman, music and lyrics by Brenda Russell, Allee Willis, and Stephen Bray; based upon the novel by Alice Walker and the Warner Brothers/Amblin Entertainment 1986 motion picture directed by Stephen Spielberg; Presented by Oprah Winfrey, Scott Sanders, Roy Furman, Quincy Jones, Creative Battery, Anna Fantaci & Cheryl Lachowicz, Independent Presenters Network, David Lowy, Stephanie P. McClelland, Gary Winnick, Jan Kallish, Nederlander Presentations, Inc., Bob & Harvey Weinstein, Andrew Asnes & Adam Zotovich, Todd Johnson; Director, Gary Griffin; Scenery, John Lee Beatty, Costumes, Paul Tazewell; Lighting, Brian MacDevitt; Sound, Jon Weston; Choreography, Donald Byrd, Music Supervisor and Incidental Music Arrangements, Kevin Stites; Music Director, Linda Twine; Dance Music Arrangements, Daryl Waters; Additional Arrangements, Joseph Joubert; Music Coordinator, Seymour Red Press; Orchestrations, Jonathan Tunick; Casting, Bernard Telsey; Hair, Charles G. LaPointe; Production Managers, Arthur Siccardi, Patrick Sullivan; Production Stage Manager, Kristen Harris; General Management, NLA/Amy Jacobs; Marketing, TM — The Marketing Group; Company Manager, Kimberly Kelly; Assistant Company Manager, Doug Gaeta; Associate Director, Nona Lloyd; Assistant to the Choreographer, Ruthlyn Salomons; Stage Manager, Glynn David Turner; Assistant Stage Manager, Neveen Mahmoud; Fight Director, J. Steven White; Fight Captain, James Brown III; Dialect Coach, Deborah Hecht; Make-up, Angelina Avallone; Dance Captain, Stephanie Guiland-Brown; Assistant Dance Captain, Jamal Story; Music Copyists, Emily Grishman Music Preparation; Associate Designers, Eric L. Renschler (scenery), Michael F. McAleer (costumes), Mark T. Simpson, Jennifer M Schriever, David Arch (lighting), Jason Strangfeld; Advertising, SPOTCo, Inc.; Press, Barlow-Hartman, Carol Fineman, Leslie Baden; Cast recording: Angel Records /EMI 0946 3 42954 2 0

Renee Elise Goldsberry and LaChanze PHOTOS BY PAUL KOLNIK

Cast: Young Nettie, Mister Daughter **Chantylla Johnson**; Young Celie, Mister Daughter, Young Olivia, Henrietta **Zipporah G. Gatling**; Church Soloist **Carol Dennis**; Church Lady/Doris **Kimberly Ann Harris**; Church Lady/Darlene **Virginia Ann Woodruff**; Church Lady/Jarenne, Daisy **Maia Nkenge Wilson**; Preacher, Prison Guard **Doug Eskew**; Pa **JC Montgomery**; Nettie **Renée Elise Goldsberry**[*1]; Celie **LaChanze**; Mister **Kingley Leggs**; Young Harpo/Young Adam **Leon G. Thomas III**[*2]; Harpo **Brandon Victor Dixon**; Sofia **Felicia P. Fields**; Squeak **Krisha Marcano**; Shug Avery **Elisabeth Withers-Mendes**; Ol' Mister **Lou Myers**; Buster, Chief **Nathaniel Stampley**[*3]; Grady **JC Montgomery**; Bobby **James Brown III**; Older Olivia **Bahiyah Sayyed Gaines**; Older Adam **Grasan Kingsberry**

Ensemble: James Brown III, LaTrisa A. Coleman, Carol Dennis, Anika Ellis, Doug Eskew, Bahiyah Sayyed Gaines, Zipporah G. Gatling, Charles Gray, James Harkness, Francesca Harper, Kimberly Ann Harris, Chantylla Johnson, Grasan Kingsberry, JC Montgomery, Lou Myers, Angela Robinson, Nathaniel Stampley, Jamal Story, Leon G. Thomas III, Maia Nkenge Wilson, Virginia Ann Woodruff; Replacement ensemble: Stephanie Guiland-Brown

Swings: Jeannette I. Bayardelle, Eric L. Christian, Bobby Daye, Stephanie Guiland-Brown , Corinne McFarlane; Replacement swing: Kemba Shannon

LaChanze

Zipporah G. Gatling, LaChanze, Leon G. Thomas III, Renee Elise Goldsberry

Understudies: Jeannette I. Bayardelle (Celie, Nettie), James Brown III (Harpo), Carol Dennis (Sofia), Anika Ellis (Shug Avery), Charles Gray (Mister), Francesca Harper (Squeak), Kimberly Ann Harris (Sofia), Kenita R. Miller (Celie, Nettie), JC Montgomery (Mister), Angela Robinson (Shug Avery), Nathaniel Stampley (Harpo)

Orchestra: Linda Twine (Conductor), Joseph Joubert, (Associate Conductor), Barry Danielian, Brian O'Flaherty, Kamau Adilifu (trumpets), Larry Farrell, Jason Jackson (trombones), Les Scott, Lawrence Feldman, Jay Brandford (woodwinds), Joseph Joubert, Shelton Becton (keyboards), Buddy Williams, Damien Bassman (drums/percussion), Steve Bargonetti (guitar), Ben Brown (bass), Paul Woodiel, Mineko Yajima (violins), David Creswell (viola), Clay C. Ruede (cello), Bruce Samuels (synthesizer programmer)

Musical Numbers: Huckleberry Pie, Mysterious Ways, Somebody Gonna Love You, Our Prayer, Big Dog, Hell No!, Brown Betty, Shug Avery Comin' to Town, Too Beautiful for Words, Push Da Button, Uh-Oh!, What About Love?, African Homeland, The Color Purple, Mister's Song, Miss Celie's Pants, Any Little Thing, I'm Here, The Color Purple (Reprise)

2005–2006 Awards: Tony Award: Actress in a Musical (LaChanze); **Theatre World Awards:** Felicia P. Fields and Elisabeth Withers-Mendes

Setting: The story takes place in Georgia between 1909 and 1949. A musical presented in two acts; originally produced by the Alliance Theatre, Atlanta, Georgia in 2004 (Susan Booth, Artistic Director, Thomas Pechar, Managing Director).

Synopsis: An inspiring and unforgettable story of a woman, who, through love, finds the strength to triumph over adversity and discover her unique voice in the world. With a moving book and a score featuring gospel, jazz, pop, and the blues, *The Color Purple* is about hope, a testament to the healing power of love and a celebration of life.

*Succeeded by 1. Darlesia Cearcy 2. Ricky Smith 3. Ga.vin Gregory

LaChanze and Elisabeth Withers-Mendes

Kimberly Ann Harris, Virginia Ann Woodruff, Maia Nkenge Wilson

Brandon Victor Dixon and Felicia P. Fields

The Cast of *The Color Purple*

A TOUCH OF THE POET

Studio 54; First Preview: November 11, 2005; Opening Night: December 8, 2005; Closed January 29, 2006; 32 previews and 50 performances

Roundabout Theatre Company (Todd Haimes, Artistic Director; Harold Wolpert, Managing Director; Julia C. Levy, Executive Director) revival of a play by Eugene O'Neill; Director, Doug Hughes; Scenery and Costumes, Santo Loquasto; Lighting, Christopher Akerlind; Original Music and Sound, David Van Tieghem; Hair and Wigs, Tom Watson; Production Stage Manager, Peter Hanson; Dialect Coach, Stephen Gabis; Fight Director, Rick Sordelet; Casting, Jim Carnahan; Technical Supervisor, Steve Beers; General Manager, Sydney Beers; Founding Director, Gene Feist; Associate Artistic Director, Scott Ellis; Marketing, David B. Steffen; Director of Development, Jeffory Lawson; Company Manager, Nichole Larson; Stage Manager, Rachel S. McCutchen; Associate Director, Mark Schneider; Associate Costumes, Mitchell Bloom; Associate Sound, Jill BC DuBoff; Make-up, Angelina Avallone; Consulting Dramaturg, Robert Scanlon; Movement Consultant, Barry McNabb; Period Movement Coach, Thomas Baird; Advertising, The Eliran Murphy Group, Ltd.; Press, Boneau/Bryan-Brown, Adrian Bryan-Brown, Matt Polk, Jessica Johnson, Joe Perotta

Dearbhla Molloy and Emily Bergl PHOTOS BY JOAN MARCUS

Gabriel Byrne, Ciaran O'Reilly, David Power, Randall Newsome

Cast: Mickey Maloy **Daniel Stewart Sherman**; Jamie Cregan **Byron Jennings**; Sara Melody **Emily Bergl**; Nora Melody **Dearbhla Molloy**; Cornelius Melody **Gabriel Byrne**; Dan Roche **Ciaran O'Reilly**; Paddy O'Dowd **Randall Newsome**; Deborah (Mrs. Henry Harford) **Kathyrn Meisle**; Nicholas Gadsby **John Horton**

Musician: Kevin McHugh (Uilleann pipes)

Understudies: Kristen Bush (Sara), Colin Lane (Cornelius), Kevin McHugh (Roche, O'Dowd), Randall Newsome (Cregan, Maloy), Elizabeth Norment (Nora, Deborah)

2005–2006 Awards: Outer Critics Circle Awards: Actor in a Play (Gabriel Byrne)

Setting: The dining room of Melody's Tavern, in a village a few miles from Boston. July 27, 1828. A drama presented in four scenes in two acts; originally produced at the Helen Hayes Theatre, October 2, 1958 (see *Theatre World* Volume 15, page 12) where it ran for 284 performances. Revived on Broadway May 2, 1967 (Volume 23, page 63), and again at the Helen Hayes Theatre, December 28, 1977 (Volume 34, page 26).

Synopsis: A down-on-his luck Irish immigrant tavern owner, who thinks himself a distinguished gentleman (though evidence to the contrary is overwhelming) finds himself in a quandary when his daughter falls for the son of a wealthy American.

Gabriel Byrne and Emily Bergl

CHITA RIVERA: A DANCER'S LIFE

Gerard Schoenfeld Theatre; First Preview: November 23, 2005; Opening Night: December 11, 2005; Closed February 19, 2006; 20 previews and 72 performances

A new musical written by Terrence McNally, musical concepts, arrangements, music direction by Mark Hummel; with original songs by Lynn Ahrens and Stephen Flaherty; Featuring songs with lyrics by Milton Leeds, James Taylor, Irving Berlin, Lawrence Holofcener, Sheldon Harnick, Cole Porter, Stephen Sondheim, Lee Adams, Fred Ebb, Dorothy Fields, Edward Eliscu, Stella Unger and Jerry Bock; Featuring songs by Victor Young, Alberto Domingues, James Taylor, Irving Berlin, Jerry Bock, Sheldon Harnick, Cole Porter, Leonard Bernstein, Charles Strouse, John Kander, Cy Coleman, Astor Piazzolla, Billy Rose and Lawrence Holofcener; Produced by Marty Bell, Aldo Scrofani, Martin Richards, Chase Mishkin, Bernard Abrams, Michael Speyer, Tracy Aron and Joe McGinnis; Produced in association with Stefany Bergson, Scott Prisand, Jennifer Maloney, G. Marlyne Sexton, Judith Ann Abrams, Jamie DeRoy, Pat Addiss, Robert Rittereiser and Bernard Carragher; Director and Choreographer, Graciela Daniele; Orchestrations, Danny Troob; Scenery, Loy Arcenas, Costumes, Toni-Leslie James; Lighting, Jules Fisher and Peggy Eisenhauer; Sound, Scott Lehrer; Hair, David Brian Brown; Jerome Robbins Choreography Reproduced by Alan Johnson; Bob Fosse Choreography Reproduced by Tony Stevens, Biographical Research, Patrick Pacheco; Production Stage Manager, Arturo E. Porazzi; Associate Choreographer, Madeleine Kelly; Production Manager, Aurora Productions; Marketing, TMG-The Marketing Group; Casting, Mark Simon; Executive Producers, Marty Bell and Aldo Scrofani; Associate Producers, Dan Gallagher and Michael Milton; General Management, Alan Wasser Associates; Music Coordinator, Michael Keller; Additional Orchestrations, Larry Hochman; Synthesizer Programmer, Andrew Barrett; Music Copying, Kay-Houston Music; Company Manager, Judi Wilfore; Stage Manager, Gary Mickelson; Assistant Stage Manager; David M. Beris; Dance Captain: Madeleine Kelly, Assistant Dance Captain, Cleve Asbury; Associate Scenery, Christine Peters; Associate Costume, Neno Russell; Associate Lighting, Scott Davis; Moving Lights Programmer, Thomas Celner; Associate Sound, Leon Rothenberg; Ms. Rivera's Assistant, Rosie Bentinck; Ms. Rivera's Publicist, Merle Frimark; Make-up and Stylist for Ms. Rivera, Kate Best; Company Make-up, Patrick Eichler/MAC; Advertising, SPOTCo, Inc.; Press, Barlow-Hartman, Rick Miramontez, Jon Dimond

Chita Rivera PHOTOS BY PAUL KOLNIK

Cast: Chita Rivera **Chita Rivera**; Little Chita Rivera/Lisa **Liana Ortiz**. *Mi Familia Loca* scene ("Dancing on the Kitchen Table"): Pedro Julio **Richard Montoya**; Armando Modesto **Edgard Gallardo**; Carmen Maria **Allyson Tucker**; Lola **Lainie Sakakura**; Mother **Malinda Farrington**; Daddy **Richard Amaro** *Ballet Class* scene **Malinda Farrington, Deidre Goodwin, Lainie Sakakura, Allyson Tucker.** *The Gypsy Life* scene: Dance Partner in "Something to Dance About" **Richard Montoya**; Colette in "Camille, Colette, Fifi" **Allyson Tucker**; Camille in "Camille, Colette, Fifi" **Deirdre Goodwin**; Chita's *"West Side Story"* Partner **Edgard Gallardo**; "Can-Can" Dancers **Allyson Tucker, Malinda Farrington, Lainie Sakakura, Deidre Goodwin.** *Co-Stars* scene: "Put on a Happy Face"/ "Rosie" partner **Lloyd Culbreath***; "Big Spender" Shadow **Deidre Goodwin**; *The Audition* scene Choreographer **Lloyd Culbreath**; *The Men* scene with **Richard Amaro, Liana Ortiz**; *The White House "All that Jazz"* scene with **Liana Ortiz**

Ensemble: Richard Amaro, Lloyd Culbreath, Malinda Farrington, Edgard Gallardo, Deirdre Goodwin, Richard Montoya, Lainie Sakakura, Alex Sanchez, Allyson Tucker

*Special Guest Star: **Dick Van Dyke** (January 24–26, 2006)

Swings: Cleve Asbury, Madeleine Kelly

Understudies: Richard Amaro (Chita's West Side Story Partner), Malinda Farrington (Camille, Colette), Edgard Gallardo (Chita's Father/Tango Partner), Jasmine Perri (Little Chita Rivera/Lisa), Lainie Sakakura (Camille, Colette), Allyson Tucker (Big Spender Shadow)

Lainie Sakakura, Lloyd Culbreath, Alex Sanchez, Chita Rivera, Edgard Gallardo, Richard Montoya, Deirdre Goodwin, Allyson Tucker

Orchestra: Mark Hummel (Conductor/piano), Gary Adler (Associate Conductor/keyboard 2), Entcho Todorov (violin), Wolfram Koessel (cello), Ted Nash and Mark Phaneuf (reeds), Jeffrey Kievit (lead trumpet), John Chudoba (trumpet), Randy Andos (trombones/tuba), Jim Donica (bass), Michael Croiter (drums), Bill Hayes (percussion)

Musical Numbers: Perfidia, Secret o' Life, Dancing on the Kitchen Table, Something to Dance About (*Call Me Madam*), I'm Available *(Mr. Wonderful)*, Camille, Colette, Fifi *(Seventh Heaven)*, Garbage *(The Shoestring Revue)*, Can-Can *(Can-Can)*, Mr. Wonderful *(Mr. Wonderful)*, A Boy Like That/Dance at the Gym (Mambo)/Somewhere *(West Side Story)*, Put On a Happy Face/Rosie *(Bye Bye Birdie)*, Don't Ah Ma' Me *(The Rink)*, Big Spender *(Sweet Charity)*, Nowadays *(Chicago)*, Tangos: Adios Noñino/ Detresse/ Calambre, More Than You Know, A Woman the World Has Never Seen (original song by Ahrens and Flaherty), Class *(Chicago)*, Chief Cook & Bottle Washer *(The Rink)*, Kiss of the Spider Woman/ Where Are You *(Kiss of the Spider Woman)*, All That Jazz: *(Chicago)*

A biographical musical review presented in two acts. Originally presented at the Old Globe Theatre, San Diego, California (Jack O'Brien, Artistic Director; Louis G. Spisto, Executive Director).

Synopsis: Chita Rivera shares her landmark life from aspiring ballerina to Broadway legend. As she relives her life in story and song and recreates some of her greatest show biz numbers, she shares her experiences with some of the greatest talents, from her leading men to her legendary creative mentors such as Jerome Robbins, Leonard Bernstein, Bob Fosse, Gower Champion, and Michael Kidd.

Llana Ortiz and Chita Rivera

Chita Rivera

Chita Rivera

Richard Montoya, Chita Rivera, Edgard Gallardo

BRIDGE AND TUNNEL

Helen Hayes Theatre; First Preview: January 12, 2006; Opening Night: January 26, 2006; still running as of May 31, 2006

A solo performance play written by Sarah Jones; Produced by Eric Falkenstein, Michael Alden, and Boyett Ostar Productions; Director, Tony Taccone; Scenery, David Korins; Lighting, Howell Binkley; Sound, Christopher Cronin; Music, DJ Rekha, Asa Taccone; Marketing, Nancy Richards and Marcia Pendelton; Assistant Director, Steve Colman; Production Stage Manager, Laurie Goldfeder; Technical Supervisor, Aurora Productions; Associate Producer, Tom Wirtshafter, Pat Flicker Addiss, Jayson Jackson/Judith Aidoo, Mark Marmer, Marcia Roberts; General Management, Richards/Climan, Inc.; Company Manager, Chris Morey (succeeded by Jolie Gabler); Associate Scenery, Rod Lemmond; Assistant Scenery, Lawrence Hutcheson; Associate Lighting, Sarah Maines; Vocal Coach, Andrea Haring; Advertising, Serino Coyne, Inc.; Press, The Pete Sanders Group, Glenna Freedman, Shane Marshall Brown

Sarah Jones PHOTOS BY PAUL KOLNIK

Performed by **Sarah Jones**

Setting: Onstage at a Queens, New York poetry slam, now. A solo performance play presented without intermission; originally produced Off Broadway at the Culture Project (Allan Buchman, founding director) February 19, 2004 (see *Theatre World* Volume 60, page 114); developed at the Berkeley Repertory Theatre.

Synopsis: Jones transforms into more than a dozen characters of various ethnicities through slight changes in voice and costume. The actress weaves together a community, with each character dealing with assimilation in modern urban America, and delves into portraits of a certain few. Among her melting pot of personae include a Pakistani accountant, an Eastern European Jewish woman, a young Vietnamese male slam poet, a wheelchair-bound Mexican labor organizer, an Australian artist, a Haitian social worker, a Chinese mother, and a young Latina. Jones earned an honorary Theatre World Award for this performance in 2004.

Sarah Jones

RABBIT HOLE

Biltmore Theatre; First Preview: January 12, 2006; Opening Night: February 2, 2006; Closed April 9, 2006; 23 previews and 77 performances

Manhattan Theatre Club (Lynne Meadow, Artistic Director; Barry Grove, Executive Producer) production of a new play by David Lindsay-Abaire; Director, Daniel Sullivan; Scenery, John Lee Beatty; Costumes, Jennifer Von Mayrhauser; Lighting, Christopher Akerlind; Original Music and Sound, John Gromada; Production Stage Manager, Roy Harris; Casting, Nancy Piccione/David Caparelliotis; Director of Artistic Operations, Mandy Greenfield; Production Manager, Ryan McMahon; Director of Development, Jill Turner Lloyd; Director of Marketing, Debra A. Waxman; General Manager, Florie Seery; Director of Artistic Development, Paige Evans; Director of Artistic Production, Michael Bush; Associate General Manager, Seth Shepsle, Lindsey T. Brooks; Company Manager, Denise Cooper; Stage Manager, Bruce A. Hoover; Dialect Coach, Deborah Hecht; Associate Scenery, Eric Renschler; Technical Director, William Mohney; Advertising, SPOTCo, Inc.; Press, Boneau/Bryan-Brown

Cynthia Nixon and John Slattery

(Clockwise, left) Mary Catherine Garrison, John Slattery, John Gallagher, Jr., Tyne Daly, Cynthia Nixon   PHOTOS BY JOAN MARCUS

Cast: Becca **Cynthia Nixon**; Izzy **Mary Catherine Garrison**; Howie **John Slattery**; Nat **Tyne Daly**; Jason **John Gallagher, Jr.**

Understudies: Cynthia Darlow (Nat), Troy Deutsch (Jason), Erika Rolfsrud (Becca, Izzy)

2005–2006 Awards: Tony Awards: Actress in a Play (Cynthia Nixon)

Setting: The home of Becca and Howie, present. World premiere of a drama presented in two acts; originally developed at the South Coast Repertory Theatre.

Synopsis: Becca and Howie Corbett have everything they could want, until a life-shattering accident turns their world upside down, leaving the couple to drift perilously apart. Becca, who must also cope with the distractions of her reckless sister and their opinionated mother, takes solace in her unlikely friendship with a neighborhood teenager, Jason, who might provide the key to lead her back from the darkest of places.

Tyne Daly, Cynthia Nixon, John Slattery, Mary Catherine Garrison

BAREFOOT IN THE PARK

Cort Theatre; First Preview: January 24, 2006; Opening Night: February 16, 2006; Closed May 21, 2006; 27 previews and 108 performances

Revival of a play by Neil Simon; Produced by Robyn Goodman, Roy Gabay, Walt Grossman, Geoff Rich, Danzansky Partners, Ergo Entertainment, Ruth Hendel, in association with Paramount Pictures; Director, Scott Elliot; Scenery, Derek McLane; Costumes, Isaac Mizrahi; Lighting, Jason Lyons; Sound, Ken Travis; Production Stage Manager, Valerie A. Peterson; Casting, Judy Henderson; Marketing, Margery Singer; Props Coordinator, Kathy Fabian; Production Manager, Showman Fabricators; General Manager, Roy Gabay; Associate Producers, Leah and Ed Frankel, Oliver Dow, CJ Entertainment/URL Productions, Stephen Kocis; Assistant Director, Marie Masters; Stage Manager, Neil Krasnow; Company Manager, Cheryl Dennis; Associate Scenery, Todd Potter; Associate Lighting, Rachel Einhorn; Associate Sound, Shannon Slaton; Advertising, SPOTCo, Inc.; Press, Richard Kornberg & Associates, Tom D'Ambrosio, Don Summa, Carrie Friedman; Laura Kaplow-Goldman

Cast: Corie Bratter **Amanda Peet**; Telephone Repairman **Adam Sietz**; Deliveryman **Sullivan Walker**; Paul Bratter **Patrick Wilson**; Corie's Mother, Mrs. Banks **Jill Clayburgh**; Victor Velasco **Tony Roberts**

Understudies: Benim Foster (Paul, Repairman, Deliveryman), Erin Fritch (Corie), Jennifer Harmon (Mrs. Banks), Sullivan Walker (Victor Velasco)

Setting: The Bratter's apartment, New York City, 1963. A comedy presented in two acts; originally produced on Broadway at the Biltmore Theatre, October 23, 1963 (see *Theatre World* Volume 20, page 40).

Synopsis: A hilarious and heart-warming chronicle of the trials and tribulation of newlyweds Paul and Corie, who have just moved into their first apartment, a fifth-floor walk-up, in New York's Greenwich Village.

Amanda Peet PHOTOS BY CAROL ROSEGG

Tony Roberts, Jill Clayburgh, Amanda Peet, Patrick Wilson

Tony Roberts, Jill Clayburgh, Amanda Peet

Amanda Peet and Jill Clayburgh

THE PAJAMA GAME

American Airlines Theatre; First Preview: January 27, 2006; Opening Night: March 2, 2006; still running as of May 31, 2006

Roundabout Theatre Company (Todd Haimes, Artistic Director; Harold Wolpert, Managing Director; Julia C. Levy, Executive Director); revival of the musical with book by George Abbott and Richard Bissell, music and lyrics by Richard Adler and Jerry Ross, based on the novel *7½ Cents* by Richard Bissell, and book revisions for this production by Peter Ackerman; Produced by special arrangement with Jeffrey Richards, James Fuld, Jr., and Scott Landis; Director and Choreographer, Kathleen Marshall; Musical Supervisor and Vocal and Dance Arranger, David Chase; Orchestrations, Dick Lieb and Danny Troob; Scenery, Derek McLane; Costumes, Martin Pakledinaz; Lighting, Peter Kaczorowski; Sound, Brian Ronan; Production Stage Manager, David O'Brien; Hair and Wigs, Paul Huntley; Music Coordinator, Seymour Red Press; Casting, Jim Carnahan; Associate Director, Marc Bruni; Associate Choreographer, Musical Director, Rob Berman; Technical Supervisor, Steve Beers; General Manager, Sydney Beers; Founding Director, Gene Feist; Associate Artistic Director, Scott Ellis; Marketing, David B. Steffen; Director of Development, Jeffory Lawson; Company Manager, Denys Baker; Assistant Stage Managers, Stephen R. Gruse, Leslie C. Lyter; Assistant to the Director, Jenny Hogan; Dance Captain, Jenny Hogue; Synthesizer Programmer, Andrew Barrett; Associate Designers, Shoko Kambara (sets), Karen Spahn (lighting), Make-up, Angelina Avallone; Advertising, The Eliran Murphy Group; Press, Boneau/Bryan-Brown: Adrian Bryan-Brown, Matt Polk, Jessica Johnson, Shanna Marcus; Cast recording: Columbia Records CK 99035:

The Cast of *The Pajama Game* PHOTOS BY JOAN MARCUS

Michael McKean and the Company

Cast: Factory Workers: Prez **Peter Benson**; Mae **Joyce Chittick**; Virginia **Bridget Berger**; Charlie **Stephen Berger**; Martha **Kate Chapman**; Brenda **Paula Leggett Chase**; Poopsie **Jennifer Cody**; Lewie **David Eggers**; Cyrus **Michael Halling**; Carmen **Bianca Marroquin**; Jake **Vince Pesce**; Joe **Devin Richards**; Ralph **Jeffrey Schecter**; Shirley **Debra Walton**; Hines **Michael McKean**; Mr. Hasler **Richard Poe**; Gladys **Megan Lawrence**; Mabel **Roz Ryan**; Granzenlicker/Pop **Michael McCormick**; Sid Sorokin **Harry Connick, Jr.**; Babe Williams **Kelli O'Hara**

Swings: Michael O'Donnell, Amber Stone.

Understudies: Bridget Berger (Babe Williams), Stephen Berger (Granzenlicker, Hasler, Pop), Kate Chapman (Mabel), Jennifer Cody (Gladys), Michael Halling (Sid Sorokin), Michael McCormick (Hines), Jeffrey Howard Schecter (Prez), Debra Walton (Mae).

Orchestra: Rob Berman (Conductor), Chris Fenwick (Associate Conductor/piano), Marilyn Reynolds (violin), Beth Sturdevant (cello), Steven Kenyon, John Winder (reeds), Roger Ingram (trumpet), John Allred, Joe Barati (trombone), Jim Hershman (guitar) Neal Caine (Bass), Paul Pizutti (drums)

Kelli O'Hara and Harry Connick, Jr.

Musical Numbers: Racing With the Clock, A New Town Is a Blue Town, I'm Not At All in Love, I'll Never Be Jealous Again, Hey There, Racing With the Clock (Reprise), Sleep-Tite, Her Is, Once a Year Day, Her Is (Reprise), Small Talk, There Once Was a Man, Hey There (Reprise), Steam Heat, The World Around Us, Hey There (Reprise), If You Win, You Lose, Think of the Time I Save, Hernando's Hideaway, The Three of Us, 7 1/2 Cents, There Once Was a Man (Reprise), The Pajama Game

2005–2006 Awards: Tony Awards: Best Revival of a Musical, Best Choreography (Kathleen Marshall), Drama Desk Awards: Outstanding Choreography (Kathleen Marshall); **Theatre World Award:** Harry Connick, Jr.; Outer Critics Circle Award: Outstanding Choreography (Kathleen Marshall)

Setting: 1954. The Sleep-Tite Pajama Factory, Cedar Rapids, Iowa. A musical presented in two acts; originally produced on Broadway at the St. James Theatre, May 13, 1954 (see *Theatre World* Volume 10, page 100) then transferred to the Shubert Theatre where it ran for 1063 performances. The show was first revived at the Lunt-Fontanne Theatre on December 9, 1973, for a limited engagement (see *Theatre World* Volume 30, page 26).

Synopsis: Labor trouble and love go head-to-head at the Sleep-Tite pajama factory, where worker demands for a seven-and-a-half-cent raise are going unheeded. In the midst of a looming strike, an unlikely romance blossoms between Babe Williams, head of the workers' Grievance Committee, and Sid, the new factory superintendent, in this classic musical about love, sex, labor unions, and the workplace.

Michael McKean and the Company

Kelli O'Hara and Harry Connick, Jr.

RING OF FIRE
The Johnny Cash Musical Show

Barrymore Theatre; First Preview: February 8, 2006 Opening Night: March 12, 2006; Closed April 30, 2006; 37 previews and 57 performances

A new musical revue created by Richard Maltby, Jr., conceived by William Meade, featuring the music of Johnny Cash; Produced by William Meade, CTM Productions, Bob Cuillo and GFour Productions; Director, Richard Maltby, Jr.; Choreography, Lisa Shriver; Scenic Production, Neil Patel; Costumes, David C. Woolard; Lighting, Ken Billington; Sound, Peter Fitzgerald and Carl Casella; Projection Design, Michael Clark; Musical Director, Jeff Lisenby; Technical Director, Brian Lynch; Associate Technical Supervisor, Matt Maraffi; Marketing, HHC Marketing; Producing Associate, Doug MacArthur; Production Stage Manager, Mark Dobrow; Casting, Dave Clemmons; Associate Producer, IDT Entertainment, Tamlyn Freund Yerkes, David Maltby; Company Manager, Susan Bell; General Management, Snug Harbor Productions (Steven Chaikelson & Brannon Wiles); Associate Company Manager, Adam J. Miller; Executive Producer, James B. Freydberg; Associate/Resident Choreographer, Michelle Weber; Associate Musical Director, August Eriksmoen; Stage Manager, Beverly Jenkins; Assistant Stage Manager, Nancy Elizabeth Vest; Associate General Manager, Jamie Tyrol; Associate Designers, Tim Mackabee (scenic), Kevin Brainerd (costumes), John Demous (lighting), Domonic Sack (sound); Associate Casting, Sara Schatz; Moving Lights Programmer, David Arch; Projection Programmer, Paul Vershbow; Advertising, SPOTCo, Inc.; Press, Boneau/Bryan-Brown, Matt Polk, Jessica Johnson, Shanna Marcus

Jason Edwards, Cass Morgan, Jeb Brown, Lari White, Beth Malone, Jarrod Emick

Cast: Jeb Brown; **Jason Edwards**; **Jarrod Emick**; **Beth Malone**; **Cass Morgan**; **Lari White**; **David M. Lutken** (banjo/dobro/evoharp/guitar/harmonica/mandolin); **Randy Redd** (keyboards/mandolin); **Jeff Lisenby** (Conductor, accordion, keyboards); **Eric Anthony** (electric guitar/mandolin); **Laurie Canaan** (fiddle/mandolin); **Dan Immel** (bass); **Ron Krasinski** (drums); **Brent Moyer** (guitar/cornet)

Understudies: Rod Weber, Jim Price (Jeb); Scott Wakefield, David M. Lutken, Jim Price (Jason); Mark Luna, Rod Weber (Jarrod); Sherrié Austin (Beth); Melanie Vaughan, Gail Bliss (Cass); Gail Bliss, Sherrié Austin (Lari); Scott Wakefield, Jim Price (David); August Eriksmoen (Jeff); Eric Anthony, Miles Aubrey, August Eriksmoen (Randy); Miles Aubrey (Eric and Brent); DeAnn Whalen (Laurie); Eric Anthony, Scott Wakefield (Dan); Steve Bartosik (Ron)

Musical Numbers: Let the Train Blow the Whistle, Hurt *(Music and Lyrics By Michael Trent Reznor)*, Country Boy, Thing Called Love *(Music and Lyrics By Jerry Hubbard)*, There You Go, While I've Got It on My Mind, My Old Faded Rose *(Music and Lyrics By June Carter Cash and John R. Cash)*, Daddy Sang Bass *(Music and Lyrics By Carl L. Perkins and John R. Cash)*, Straight A's in Love, Big River, I Still Miss Someone *(Music and Lyrics By Roy Cash Jr. and John R. Cash)*, Five Feet High and Rising, Flesh and Blood, Look at Them Beans *(Music and Lyrics By Joseph Arrington, Jr.)*, Get Rhythm, Flushed *(Music and Lyrics By Jack H. Clement)*, Dirty Old Egg Sucking Dog *(Music and Lyrics By Jack H. Clement)*, Angel Band, If I Were a Carpenter *(Music and Lyrics By James Timothy Hardin)*, Ring of Fire *(Music and Lyrics By June Carter Cash and Merle Kilgore)*, Jackson *(Music and Lyrics By Jerry Leiber and Billy Edd Wheeler)*, Big River (Reprise), I've Been Everywhere *(Music and Lyrics By Geoff Mack)*, Sunday Mornin' Comin' Down *(Music and Lyrics By Kris Kristofferson)*, Temptation *(Music and Lyrics By Arthur Freed and Nacio Herb Brown)*, I Feel Better All Over *(Music and Lyrics By Ken Rogers and Ferlin Husky)*, A Boy Named Sue *(Music and Lyrics By Shel Silverstein)*, Going to Memphis, Delia's Gone *(Music and Lyrics By Karl M. Silbersdorf, Richard Toops and John R. Cash)*, Austin Prison, Orleans Parish Prison *(Music and Lyrics By Dick Feller)*, Folsom Prison Blues, Man in Black, All Over Again, I Walk the Line, The Man Comes Around, Waiting on the Far Side Banks of Jordan *(Music and Lyrics By Terry Smith)*, Why Me *(Music and Lyrics By Kris Kristofferson)*, Hey Porter

A musical review presented in two acts. Originally presented at the Studio Arena Theatre in Buffalo, New York.

Synopsis: Life, love, loss, and faith as experienced by "The Man in Black." With more than 40 songs composed by Johnny and June Carter Cash and other composers, the review follows three couples whose lives are intertwined with story lines from the Cash song cycle, as well as interaction with the eight-member onstage band.

Cass Morgan, Jason Edwards, Beth Malone, Jarrod Emick, Lari White, Jeb Brown

WELL

Longacre Theatre; First Preview: March 10, 2006; Opening Night: March 30, 2006; Closed May 14, 2006; 23 previews and 53 performances

A new play by Lisa Kron; Produced by Elizabeth Ireland McCann, Scott Rudin, Boyett Ostar Productions, True Love Productions, Inc., Terry Allen Kramer, Roger Berlind, Carole Shorenstein Hays and John Dias; Produced in association with Larry Hirschhorn, The Public Theater (Oskar Eustis, Artistic Director; Mara Manus, Executive Director) and The American Conservatory Theatre; Director, Leigh Silverman; Scenery, Tony Walton; Costumes, Miranda Hoffman; Lighting, Christopher Akerlind; Original Music and Sound, John Gromada; Hair & Wigs, Tom Watson; Production Stage Manager, Susie Cordon; Casting, Jay Binder, Jack Bowdan; Executive Producer/General Manager, Joey Parnes; Company Manger/Associate General Manager, Elizabeth M. Blitzer; Stage Manager, Allison Sommers; Assistant Stage Manager, Brian Rardin; Dramaturg, John Dias; Assistant Producer, S.D. Wagner; Assistant to the Director, Katherine Peter Kovner; Associate Scenery, Kelly Hanson; Associate Lighting, Michael J. Spadaro; Associate Costume, Brian J. Bustos; Associate Sound, Christopher Cronin; Marketing, TMG-The Marketing Group; Advertising, SPOTCo, Inc.; Press, Boneau/Bryan-Brown, Chris Boneau, Jackie Green, Susanne Tighe, Matt Ross

Cast: Lisa **Lisa Kron**; Ann **Jayne Houdyshell**; Nurse/others **John Hoffman**; Kay/others **Saidah Arrika Ekulona**; Jim/others **Daniel Breaker**; Joy/others **Christina Kirk**

Standbys: Randy Danson (Ann, Joy/others), Cindy Katz (Lisa)

Understudies: Colman Domingo (Jim/others), Donnetta Lavinia Grays (Kay/others), Joel Van Liew (Nurse/others)

Lisa Kron and Jayne Houdyshell PHOTOS BY JOAN MARCUS

2005–2006 Awards: Theatre World Award: Jane Houdyshell

Setting: Lansing, Michigan, the past and present. A new autobiographical play presented without intermission; originally produced Off Broadway at the Public Theatre, March 28, 2004 (see *Theatre World* Volume 60, page 119).

Synopsis: "A solo show with other people in it." Writer/performer Lisa Kron explores issues of health, family, and community in relation to her mother's struggle to heal a changing neighborhood, and in turn explores her own past and uneasy relationship with her mother.

Lisa Kron and the cast of *Well*

FESTEN

Music Box Theatre; First Preview: March 23, 2006; Opening Night: April 9, 2006; Closed May 20, 2006; 20 previews and 49 performances

The Almeida Theatre Company production of a dramatization by David Eldridge; Based on the *Dogme* film and play by Thomas Vinterberg, Mogens Rukov and Bo Hr. Hansen; Produced by Bill Kenwright and Marla Rubin; Director, Rufus Norris; Scenery, Ian MacNeil; Costumes, Joan Wadge; Lighting, Jean Kalman; Music, Orlando Gough; Sound, Paul Arditti; Casting, Jim Carnahan; Fight Director Terry King; Technical Supervisor, Larry Morley; General Manager, Alan Wasser Associates, Jim Brandeberry; Production Stage Manager, Michael McGoff; Stage Manager, Richard Rauscher; Company Manager, Brig Berney; Vocal Coach, Deborah Hecht; Associate Costumes, Mitchell Bloom; Associate Lighting, Fiona Simpson; Associate Sound, Christopher Cronin; Fight Coordinator, Michael G. Chin; Advertising, The Eliran Murphy Group, Ltd.; Marketing, Hugh Hysell Communications; Press Representative, The Publicity Office, Bob Fennell, Marc Thibodeau, Candi Adams, Michael S. Borowski

The Cast of *Festen*

Julianna Margulies and Michael Hayden PHOTOS BY JOAN MARCUS

Cast: Christian **Michael Hayden**; Michael **Jeremy Sisto**; Little Girl **Meredith Lipson/Ryan Simpkins** (alternating); Mette **Carrie Preston**; Lars **Stephen Kunken**; Helene **Julianna Margulies**; Else **Ali MacGraw**; Helge **Larry Bryggman**; Pia **Diane Davis**; Helmut **Christopher Evan Welch**; Grandfather **John Carter**; Poul **David Patrick Kelly**; Kim **C. J. Wilson**; Gbatokai **Keith Davis**

Understudies: Michael Bakkensen (Christian, Helmut, Kim, Michael), Natalie Gold (Else, Helene, Mette, Pia), Edward James Hyland (Grandfather, Helge, Lars, Poul), Ezra Knight (Gbatokai, Kim, Lars)

Setting: The home of Helge and Else Klingenfelt, Denmark. American premiere of a drama presented in two acts; originally produced in London at the Almeida Theatre in 2004.

Synopsis: A beloved patriarch, surrounded by family and friends, is celebrating his sixtieth birthday at his country home. As the evening progresses, the man's eldest son, Christian, breaks the silence surrounding a family secret. Standing to propose a toast, he offers his father an amusing yet simple choice. The games begin, revelations and accusations tumble across the dinner table, paving the way for a celebration that no one will ever forget.

Julianna Margulies, Stephen Kunken, Jeremy Sisto

AWAKE AND SING!

Belasco Theatre; First Preview: March 23, 2006; Opening Night: April 17, 2006; still running as of May 31, 2006

Lincoln Center Theatre (André Bishop, Artistic Director; Bernard Gersten, Executive Producer) revival of a play by Clifford Odets; Director, Bartlett Sher; Scenery, Michael Yeargan; Costumes, Catherine Zuber; Lighting, Christopher Akerlind; Sound, Peter John Still and Marc Salzberg; Stage Manager, Robert Bennett; Assistant Stage Manager, Denise Yaney; Casting, Daniel Swee; LCT Director of Development, Hattie Jutagir; LCT Director of Marketing, Linda Mason Ross; LCT General Manager, Adam Siegel; LCT Production Manager, Jeff Hamlin; Company Manager, Matthew Markoff; Assistant Director, Sarna Lapine; Props Coordinator, Christopher Schneider; Dialect Coach, Ralph Zito; Wig Design, Tom Watson; Make-up, Angelina Avallone; Animal Trainer, William Berloni; Advertising, Serino Coyne; Technical Supervision, Walter Murphy and Patrick Merryman; Poster Art, James McMullan; Press, Philip Rinaldi, Barbara Carroll

Zoe Wanamaker and Ned Eisenberg PHOTOS BY PAUL KOLNIK

Mark Ruffalo

Ned Eisenberg, Zoe Wanamaker, Jonathan Hadary, Richard Topol, Lauren Ambrose

Cast: Ralph Berger **Pablo Schreiber**; Myron Berger **Jonathan Hadary**; Hennie Berger **Lauren Ambrose**; Jacob **Ben Gazzara**; Bessie Berger **Zoe Wanamaker**; Schlosser **Peter Kybart**; Moe Axelrod **Mark Ruffalo**; Uncle Morty **Ned Eisenberg**; Sam Feinschreiber **Richard Topol**

Understudies: Tony Campisi (Myron Berger, Uncle Morty), Stan Lachow (Jacob Berger, Schlosser), Annie Purcell (Hennie Berger), Charles Socarides (Ralph Berger), Ed Vassallo (Moe Axelrod, Sam Feinschreiber), Lori Wilner (Bessie Berger)

2005–2006 Awards: Tony Awards: Revival of a Play, Costume Design of a Play (Catherine Zuber); Drama Desk Awards; Revival of a Play, Set Design of a Play (Michael Yeargan), Outstanding Ensemble Performance; Outer Critics Circle Award: Revival of a Play

Setting: The mid-1930s. An apartment in the Bronx, New York City. A drama in three acts and four scenes presented with two intermissions. Originally produced at the Belasco Theatre February 19, 1935. This production was the fourth Broadway revival, with the first two revivals running simultaneously in 1939 at Daly's 63rd Street Theatre and the Windsor Theatre, and a third at Circle in the Square on March 8, 1984 (see *Theatre World* Volume 40, page 30).

Synopsis: Clifford Odets' classic tragicomedy details the struggles of three generations of a Depression-era Jewish family in the Bronx.

THREE DAYS OF RAIN

Bernard Jacobs Theatre; First Preview: March 28, 2006; Opening Night: April 19, 2006; still running as of May 31, 2006

A play by Richard Greenberg; Produced by Marc Platt, David Stone, and The Shubert Organization; Director, Joe Mantello; Scenery and Costumes, Santo Loquasto; Lighting, Paul Gallo; Original Music and Sound, David Van Tieghem; Casting, Bernard Telsey Casting; Rain, Jauchem & Meeh; Hair, Lyndell Quiyou; Production Stage Manager, William Joseph Barnes; Production Management, Aurora Productions; General Management, Stuart Thompson Productions/ James Triner; Stage Manager, Timothy R. Semon; Assistant Director, Michael Silverstone, Associate Scenery, Jenny Sawyers; Associate Lighting, Paul Miller; Associate Sound, Jill BC DuBoff; Advertising, Serino Coyne, Inc.; Press, The Publicity Office, Bob Fennell, Marc Thibodeau, Candi Adams, Michael S. Borowski

Cast: Walker/Ned **Paul Rudd**; Nan/Lina **Julia Roberts**; Pip/Theo **Bradley Cooper**

Understudies: Michael Dempsey (Walker/Ned, Pip/Theo), Michelle Federer (Nan/Lina)

Bradley Cooper and Julia Roberts

Paul Rudd and Bradley Cooper   PHOTOS BY JOAN MARCUS

Bradley Cooper and Julia Roberts

Paul Rudd and Julia Roberts

Setting: Act 1-An unoccupied loft space in downtown Manhattan, 1995. Act 2-The same space, 1960. A play presented in two acts; originally produced Off Broadway by the Manhattan Theatre Club, October 21, 1997 (see *Theatre World* Volume 54, page 90); commissioned and first produced by South Coast Repertory Theatre.

Synopsis: Brought together for the reading of a will, three young adults — sister, brother, and a longtime friend — unwittingly replay their parents' tangled relationships. The themes of love, friendship, ambition, and betrayal expand exponentially in Act Two, when the same actors play youthful versions of the parents, business partners in love with the same woman.

THE THREEPENNY OPERA

Studio 54; First Preview: March 24, 2006; Opening Night: April 20, 2006; still running as of May 31, 2006

Roundabout Theatre Company (Todd Haimes, Artistic Director; Harold Wolpert, Managing Director; Julia C. Levy, Executive Director) revival of the musical with book and lyrics by Bertolt Brecht and music by Kurt Weill, in a new translation by Wallace Shawn; based on Elisabeth Hauptmann's German translation of John Gay's *The Beggar's Opera*; Director, Scott Elliott; Choreography, Aszure Barton; Music Director, Kevin Stites; Scenery, Derek McLane; Costumes, Isaac Mizrahi; Lighting, Jason Lyons; Sound, Ken Travis; Hair and Wigs, Paul Huntley; Original Orchestrations, Kurt Weill; Music Coordinator; John Miller; Production Stage Manager, Peter Hanson; Casting, Jim Carnahan; Technical Supervisor, Steve Beers; General Manager, Sydney Beers; Founding Director, Gene Feist; Associate Artistic Director, Scott Ellis; Marketing, David B. Steffen; Director of Development, Jeffory Lawson; Company Manager, Nichole Larson; Stage Manager, Jon Krause; Assistant Director, Marie Masters; Assistant Choreographer, William Briscoe; Associate Music Director, Paul Raiman; Associate Lighting, Jennifer Schriever; Associate Sound, Tony Smolenski; Make up, Chantel Miller; Music Copying, Emily Grishman Music Preparation; Advertising, The Eliran Murphy Group; Press, Boneau/Bryan-Brown: Adrian Bryan-Brown, Matt Polk, Jessica Johnson, Joe Perotta

Cast: Jenny **Cyndi Lauper**; Smith **John Herrera**; Walter/Betty **Maureen Moore**; Jimmy/Dolly **Brooke Sunny Moriber**; Rev. Kimball/Eunice **Terry Burrell**; Robert **Romain Frugé**; Vixen **Deborah Lew**; Matthew **David Cale**; Macheath **Alan Cumming**; Mr. Peachum **Jim Dale**; Beggar/Beatrice **Brian Butterick**; Filch **Carlos Leon**; Mrs. Peachum **Ana Gasteyer**; Polly Peachum **Nellie McKay**; Jacob **Adam Alexi-Malle**; Eddie **Kevin Rennard**; Tiger Brown **Christopher Innvar**; Bruno/Molly **Christopher Kenney**; Harry/Velma **Lucas Steele**; Lucy Brown **Brian Charles Rooney**; Policeman and Beggars: **Maureen Moore, Brooke Sunny Moriber, Terry Burrell, Romain Frugé, Deborah Lew, Brian Butterick, Carlos Leon, Adam Alexi-Malle, Kevin Rennard, Christopher Kenney, Lucas Steel**

Swings: Nehal Joshi, Valisia Lekae Little

Understudies: Romain Frugé (Mac), Maureen Moore (Jenny), Brooke Sunny Moriber (Polly), Terry Burrell (Mrs. Peachum), David Cale (Mr. Peachum), Lucas Steele (Lucy) Adam Alexi-Malle (Filch), John Herrera (Tiger)

Orchestra: Kevin Stites (Conductor), Paul Raiman (Associate Conductor/piano-harmonium-Celeste), Eddie Salkin and Roger Rosenberg (reeds), Tim Schadt and Matt Peterson (trumpets), Mike Christianson (tenor trombone), Charles du-Chateau (cello/accordion), Greg Utzig (guitar/Hawaiian guitar/banjo/mandolin), Charles Descarfino (percussion/drums), Richard Sarpola (bass)

Musical Numbers: Overture, Song of the Extraordinary Crimes of Mac the Knife, Peachum's Morning Hymn, The 'Rather Than' Song, Wedding Song, Pirate Jenny, The Army Song, Wedding Song (reprise), Love Song, The 'No' Song, Certain Things Make Our Life Impossible, Goodbye, Polly's Song, The Ballad of the Overwhelming Power of Sex, The Ballad of the Pimp, The Ballad of the Happy Life, The Jealously Duet, How Do Humans Live?, The Ballad of the Overwhelming Power of Sex (reprise), The Song of Inadequacy of Human Striving, The Song of Inadequacy of Human Striving (reprise), Lucy's Aria, Cry from the Grave, The Ballad in which Macheath asks Everyone's Forgiveness, Finale

Cyndi Lauper PHOTOS BY JOAN MARCUS

Jim Dale, Ana Gasteyer, Alan Cumming, Nellie McKay, Cyndi Lauper

2005–2006 Awards: Drama Desk Award: Featured Actor in a Musical (Jim Dale); **Theatre World Award:** Nellie McKay

Setting: London, 1837. A musical presented in two acts; originally produced at the Empire Theatre on April 13, 1933. The show was revived previously in 1954 and 1955–1961 at Theater de Lys (Off Broadway), 1966 at the Billy Rose Theatre, 1976–1977 at the Vivian Beaumont, and in 1989 at the Lunt-Fontanne.

Synopsis: A notorious bandit marries a girl, much to the chagrin of her father. The peeved patriarch does everything in his power to imprison his son-in-law in this updated version of the political and social satire, directed by Shawn with a nod to Brecht's style.

Richard Griffiths, Frances de la Tour, Stephen Campbell Moore

Jamie Parker, Andrew Knott, Dominic Cooper, James Corden

Stephen Campbell Moore and Dominic Cooper PHOTOS BY PHOTOS BY JOAN MARCUS

THE HISTORY BOYS

Broadhurst Theatre; First Preview: April 14, 2006; Opening Night: April 23, 2006; still running as of May 31, 2006

American premiere of The National Theatre of Great Britain (Sir Hayden Phillips, Chairman of the Board; Nicholas Hytner, Director; Nick Starr, Executive Director) production of a new play by Alan Bennett; Produced by Boyett Ostar Productions, Roger Berlind, Debra Black, Eric Falkenstein, Roy Furman, Jam Theatricals, Stephanie P. McClelland, Judith Resnick, Scott Rudin, Jon Avnet/Ralph Guild, Dede Harris/Mort Swinsky; Director, Nicholas Hytner; Scenery and Costumes, Bob Crowley; Lighting, Mark Henderson; Music, Richard Sisson; Video, Ben Taylor; Sound, Colin Pink; Casting Toby Whale (UK), Tara Rubin (US); General Management, 101 Productions, Ltd.; Production Stage Manager, Michael J. Passaro; Marketing, HHC Marketing; Technical Supervisor, David Benken; Company Manager, Gregg Arst; Stage Manager, Charlie Underhill; UK Musical Director, Tom Attwood; Associate Lighting, Daniel Walker; UK Associate Production Manager, Andy Ward; Assistant Technical Supervisor, Rosemarie Palombo; Movement Director, Jack Murphy; Moving Lights, Bobby Harrell; Press, Boneau/Bryan-Brown, Adrian Bryan-Brown, Jim Byk, Juliana Hannett

Cast: The Boys: Akthar **Sacha Dhawan**; Crowther **Samuel Anderson**; Dakin **Dominic Cooper**; Lockwood **Andrew Knott**; Posner **Samuel Barnett**; Rudge **Russell Tove**; Scripps **Jamie Parker**; Timms **James Corden. The Teachers:** Headmaster **Clive Merrison**; Mrs. Lintott **Frances de la Tour**; Hector **Richard Griffiths**; Irwin **Stephen Campbell Moore.** TV Director **Colin Haigh**; Make-up Lady **Pamela Merrick**; Other Boys **Joseph Attenborough, Tom Attwood, Rudi Dharmalingam**

Understudies: Joseph Attenborough (Lockwood, Rudge, Timms, TV Director), Tom Attwood (Crowther, Posner, Scripps), Rudi Dharmalingam (Akthar, Crowther, Dakin), Colin Haigh (Headmaster, Hector), Pamela Merrick (Mrs. Lintott)

2005–2006 Awards: Tony Awards: Best Play, Actor in a Play (Richard Griffiths), Featured Actress in a Play (Frances de la Tour), Direction of a Play (Nicholas Hytner), Scenic Design of a Play (Bob Crowley); Lighting Design of a Play (Mark Henderson); Drama Desk Awards: Outstanding Play, Actor in a Play (Richard Griffiths), Featured Actor in a Play (Samuel Barnett), Featured Actress in a Play (Frances de la Tour), Director (Nicholas Hytner); **Theatre World Award:** Richard Griffiths; Outer Critics Circle Awards: Outstanding Play, Featured Actor in a Play (Richard Griffiths), Featured Actress in a Play (Frances de la Tour), Director of a Play (Nicholas Hytner); New York Drama Critics Circle Award: Best Play; Drama League Award: Distinguished Production of a Play

Setting: The mid-1980s at a grammar school (English equivalent of high school) in the north of England. A comedy/drama with music presented in two acts; originally produced at the Lyttelton Theatre, May 5, 2004, and subsequently a world tour before coming to New York.

Synopsis: A rambunctious group of smart and funny sixth-form boys are in pursuit of sex, sport, and a place at university as they prepare for their A-level examinations. Led by a headmaster obsessed with results, a history teacher whose methods are untraditional, and another whose practices are by the book, the eight students experience the school year that would forever change their lives. Bennett examines rivalry, adolescence, and education with wit and precision in the season's most awarded play.

LESTAT

Palace Theatre; First Preview: March 25, 2006; Opening Night: April 25, 2006; Closed May 28, 2006; 33 previews and 39 performances

A new musical with music by Elton John, lyrics by Bernie Taupin, and book by Linda Woolverton; based on the *The Vampire Chronicles* by Anne Rice; produced by Warner Brothers Theatre Ventures (Raymond Wu, Laura Valan, Mark Corker, Maria Gonzalez, Carol Wood, Jennifer Kim); Director, Robert Jess Roth; Musical Staging, Matt West; Scenery, Derek McLane; Costumes, Susan Hilferty; Lighting, Kenneth Posner; Sound, Jonathan Deans; Visual Concept, Dave McKean; Wigs and Hair, Tom Watson; Make-up, Angelina Avallone; Fight Director, Rick Sordelet; Projections Coordinator, Howard Werner; Musical Supervisor, Guy Babylon; Orchestrations, Steve Margoshes & Guy Babylon; Additional Orchestrations, Bruce Coughlin; Music Direction, Incidental Music and Additional Vocal Arrangements, Brad Haak; Vocal Arrangements, Todd Ellison; Casting, Jay Binder, Mark Brandon; Production Stage Manager, Bonnie L. Becker; Music Coordinator, John Miller; Associate Director, Sam Scalamoni; Associate Scenic Design, Bryan Johnson; General Management, Alan Wasser Associates and Allan Williams; Technical Supervision, Juniper Street Productions; Company Manager, Mark Shacket; Associate Company Manager, Maria Mazza; Stage Manager, J. Philip Bassett; Assistant Stage Manager, Kimberly Russell; Associate General Manager, Aaron Lustbader; Dance Captain, Sarah Solie; Fight Captain, Steve Wilson; Associate Lighting, Philip Rosenberg; Associate Costumes, Maiko Matsushima, Nancy Palmatier; Music Preparation, Paul Holderbaum/ Chelsea Music; Marketing, TMG-The Marketing Group; Press, Barlow-Hartman, Wayne Wolfe, Andrew Snyder

Allison Fischer, Jim Stanek, Hugh Panaro PHOTOS BY PAUL KOLNIK

Cast: Lestat **Hugh Panaro**; Gabrielle **Carolee Carmello**; Armand **Drew Sarich**; Louis **Jim Stanek**; Nicolas **Roderick Hill**; Marius **Michael Genet**; Claudia **Allison Fischer**; Magnus **Joseph Dellger**; Marquis/Laurent **Will Swenson**; Beautiful Woman **Megan Reinking**

Ensemble: Rachel Coloff, Nikki Renée Daniels, Joseph Dellger, Colleen Fitzpatrick, Patrick Mellen, Chris Peluso, Dominique Plaisant, Megan Reinking, Will Swenson, Tommar Wilson

Swings: Sean MacLaughlin, Sarah Solie, Steve Wilson

Standby for Claudia: Amy Sparrow

Understudies: Drew Sarich, Will Swenson (Lestat), Rachel Coloff, Colleen Fitzpatrick (Gabrielle), Sean MacLaughlin, Will Swenson (Armand), Chris Peluso, Tommar Wilson (Nicholas and Louis), Joe Dellger, Steve Wilson (Marius)

Orchestra: Brad Haak (Conductor), Andy Grobengieser (Associate Conductor/ keyboard 2), Martin Agee (Concertmaster), Natalie Cenovia Cummins and Cecelia Hobbs Gardner (violin), Maxine L. Roach (viola), Stephanie L. Cummins and Chungsun Kim (celli), Chuck Wilson (flute/clarinet), Lynne A Cohen (oboe/English horn), Chris Komer and Bradley C. Gemeinhardt (French horn), Matt Ingman (trombone/euphonium), Jason DeBord (keyboard 1), Jose Simbulan (keyboard 3), Bruce Uchitel (guitars), Brad Hamm (bass), Dave Ratajczak (percussion/drums), Thad Wheeler (percussion/Associate Conductor)

Musical Numbers: From the Dead, Beautiful Boy, In Paris, The Thirst, Right Before My Eyes, Make Me As You Are, To Live Like This, Morality Play, The Crimson Kiss, Welcome to the New World, Embrace It, I Want More, I'll Never Have That Chance, Sail Me Away, To Kill Your Kind, Embrace It (reprise), After All This Time, Finale

Setting: France, 1700s and New Orleans, 1800s. A musical presented in two acts; world premiere presented December 17, 2005 at the Curran Theatre, San Francisco.

Synopsis: The romantic and heartbreaking story of the extraordinary journey of one man who escapes the tyranny of his oppressive family only to have his life taken from him. Thrust into the seductive and sensual world of an immortal vampire, Lestat sets out on a road of adventures in a quest for everlasting love and companionship but is forced to reconcile his innate sense of good with his primal need to exist.

Hugh Panaro

THE WEDDING SINGER

Al Hirschfeld Theatre; First Preview: March 30, 2006; Opening Night: April 27, 2006; still running as of May 31, 2006

A new musical with music by Matthew Sklar, book by Chad Beguelin and Tim Herlihy, and lyrics by Chad Beguelin; based upon the New Line Cinema film written by Tim Herlihy; additional music and lyrics by Adam Sandler and Tim Herlihy; Produced by Margo Lion, New Line Cinema, The Araca Group, Roy Furman, Douglas L. Meyer/James D. Stern Productions, Rick Steiner/The Staton Bell Osher Mayerson Group, JAM Theatricals; Produced in association with Jujamcyn Theatres, Jay Furman, Michael Gill, Dr. Lawrence Horowitz, Marisa Sechrest, Gary Winnick, Élan V. McAllister/Allan S. Gordon/Adam Epstein; Director, John Rando; Choreography, Rob Ashford; Scenery, Scott Pask; Costumes, Gregory Gale; Lighting, Brian Macdevitt; Sound, Peter Hylenski; Casting, Bernard Telsey; Hair, David Brian Brown; Make-up, Joe Dulude II; Orchestrations, Irwin Fisch; Incidental & Dance Music Arranger, David Chase; Music Director, James Sampliner; Music Coordinator, John Miller; Executive Producer, Mark Kaufman; Production Manager, Juniper Street Productions; Associate Choreography, JoAnn M. Hunter; Production Stage Manger, Rolt Smith; Marketing, The Araca Group; General Management; Wilcox Company; Company Manager, Edward Nelson; Associate Company Manager, Beverly Edwards; Stage Manager, Julie Balduff; Assistant Stage Manager, Janet Takami; Dance Captains, Angelique Ilo and Michael McGurk; Assistant Director, Jen Bender; Associate Scenery, Orit Jacoby Carroll; Associate Costumes, Janine Marie McCabe; Associate Lighting, Charles Pennebaker; Associate Hair/Wigs, Josh Marquette; Press, Richard Kornberg, Don Summa; Cast recording: Sony Classical/BMG: 82876-82095-2

Amy Spanger and Matthew Saldivar PHOTOS BY JOAN MARCUS

Peter Kapetan, Eric Lajuan Summers, Matthew Saldivar, Kevin Cahoon, (background) Stephen Lynch

Cast: Robbie Hart **Stephen Lynch**; Sammy **Matthew Saldivar**; George **Kevin Cahoon**; Julia Sullivan **Laura Benanti**; Holly **Amy Spanger**; Glen Guglia **Richard H. Blake**; Rosie **Rita Gardner**; Linda **Felicia Finley**; Imposters **Tracee Beazer, Cara Cooper, Peter Kapetan, J. Elaine Marcos, T. Oliver Reid, Christina Sivrich, Matthew Stocke**

Ensemble: Adinah Alexander, Matt Allen, Tracee Beazer, Cara Cooper, Ashley Amber Haase, Nicolette Hart, David Josefsberg, Peter Kapetan, Spencer Liff, J. Elaine Marcos, T. Oliver Reid, Christina Sivrich, Matthew Stocke, Eric Lajuan Summers

Swings: Angelique Ilo, Kevin Kern, Joanne Manning, Michael McGurk, Adam Zotovich

Standby for Julia Sullivan: Tina Madigan

Understudies: Matthew Stocke (Robbie Hart), Cara Cooper (Holly), Matthew Stocke (George, Glen Guglia), David Josefsberg (Sammy), Nicolette Hart (Linda), Christina Sivrich (Rosie)

Stephen Lynch

Orchestra: James Sampliner (Conductor/keyboards); John Samorian (Associate Conductor/keyboards); Larry Saltzman, Stephen Lynch, John Putnam, Gary Sieger (guitar); Jon Working (keyboards); Irio O'Farrill, Matthew Saldivar (bass); Warren Odze (drums); Clifford Lyones, Jack Bashkow (reeds); Trevor Neumann (trumpet); James Saporito (percussion)

Musical Numbers: It's Your Wedding Day, Right on Time, Awesome, It's Your Wedding Day (reprise), Right on Time (reprise), A Note From Linda, Pop, Somebody Kill Me, Rosie's Note, Casualty of Love, Come Out of the Dumpster, Today You Are a Man, George's Prayer, Not That Kind of Thing, Saturday Night in the City, All About the Green, Right in Front of Your Eyes, Single, If I Told You, Let Me Come Home, If I Told You (reprise), Move That Thang, Grow Old With You, It's Your Wedding Day (Finale)

Setting: Ridgefield, New Jersey, 1985. A musical presented in two acts; world premiere presented February 9, 2006 at the 5th Avenue Theatre, Seattle, Washington (David Armstrong, Producing Artistic Director; Marilynn Sheldon, Managing Director).

Synopsis: Rock-star wannabe Robbie Hart, New Jersey's favorite wedding singer, is the life of the party—until his own fiancée leaves him at the altar. Shot through the heart, Robbie makes every wedding he plays as disastrous as his own. Enter Julia, a winsome waitress who wins his affection, but Julia is about to be married to a Wall Street shark. Unless Robbie can pull off the performance of the decade, the girl of his dreams will be gone forever. *The Wedding Singer* takes us back to a time when hair was big, greed was good, collars were up, and a wedding singer just might be the coolest guy in the room.

Felicia Finley

Rita Gardner and Kevin Cahoon

Stephen Lynch and Laura Benanti

HOT FEET

Hilton Theatre; First Preview: April 15, 2006; Opening Night: April 30, 2006; still running as of May 31, 2006

A new dance musical conceived by Maurice Hines, book by Heru Ptah, music and lyrics by Maurice White, with additional music and lyrics by Philip Bailey, Reginald Burke, Valerie Carter, William B Champlin, Peter Cor, Eddie Del Barrio, Larry Dunn, David Foster, Garry Glenn, Jay Graydon, James N. Howard, Jonathan G. Lind, Al McKay, Skip Scarbrough, Skylark, Charles Stepney, Beloyd Taylor, Wayne Vaughn, Wanda Vaughn, Verdine White, and Allee Willis; new songs additional music and lyrics by Cat Gray, Brett Laurence, Bill Meyers, Heru Ptah, and Allee Willis; Produced by Transamerica, Rudy Durand, in association with Laliba Entertainment, Inc, Meir A & Eli C, LLC, Polymer Global Holdings, and Godley Morris Group, LLC; Director and Choreography, Maurice Hines; Scenery, James Noone, Costumes, Paul Tazewell; Lighting, Clifton Taylor; Sound, Acme Sound Partners; Hair, Qodi Armstrong; Music Director and Conductor, Jeffrey Klitz; Arrangements and Orchestrations, Bill Meyers; Music Coordinator, John Miller; Production Manager, Arthur Siccardi; Casting, Stuart Howard, Amy Schecter, and Paul Hardt; Assistant Director, Ricardo Khan; Production Stage Manager, Michael E. Harrod; Marketing, HHC Marketing; General Management, Leonard Soloway, Steven M. Levy; Company Manager, Alexandra Gushin; Stage Manager, Dan Shaheen; Assistant Stage Manager, Frances W. Falcone; Assistant Choreographer, Danita Salamida, Duane Lee Holland; Assistant Company Manager, Sara Jane Baldwin; Associate Designers, Dennis Ballard (costumes), Ed McCarthy (lighting); Automated Lighting, Paul J. Sonnleitner; Music Copyist, Robert Nowak and Associates; Press, Springer Associates, Joe Trentacosta

Hot Feet ensemble in "Dirty" with Daryl Spiers (center) PHOTOS BY PAUL KOLNIK

Cast: Louie **Allan Hidalgo**; Emma **Samantha Pollino** (evenings)/**Sarah Livingston** (matinees); Kalimba **Vivian Nixon**; Mom **Ann Duquesnay**; Anthony **Michael Balderrama**; Victor **Keith David**; Naomi **Wynonna Smith**; Rahim **Daryl Spiers**

Ensemble: Kevin Aubin, Gerrard Carter, Dionne Figgins, Ramón Flowers, Karla Puno Garcia, Nakia Henry, Duane Lee Holland, Iquail S. Johnson, Dominique Kelley, Steve Konopelski, Sumie Maeda, Jon-Paul Mateo, Vasthy Mompoint, Tera-Lee Pollin, Monique Smith, Daryl Spiers, Felicity Stiverson, Hollie E. Wright

Swings: Jessica Hope Cohen, Dana Marie Ingraham, Terace Jones, Matthew Warner Kiernan, Danita Salamida

Band Vocalists: Brent Carter, Keith Anthony Fluitt, Theresa Thomason

Band Vocalist Swings: Marvel J. Allen, John A. James

Standbys: Adrian Bailey (Victor), Sandra Reaves-Phillips (Mom), Caesar Samayoa (Louie), Sarah Livingston (Emma)

Understudies: Dionne Figgins (Kalimba), Daryl Spiers (Anthony), Nakia Henry (Naomi), Jon-Paul Mateo (Rahim)

Orchestra: Jeffrey Klitz (Conductor/synthesizer); Andy Ezrin (Associate Conductor/synthesizer); Keith Robinson, Bernd Schoenhart (guitar); Artie C. Reynolds, III (electric bass/bass synthesizer); Brian Dunne (drums); Errol Crusher Bennett (percussion); Dave Keys (synthesizer); Scott Kreitzer (saxophones); Don Downs, David Trigg (trumpets); Keith O'Quinn (trombone)

Musical Numbers: Overture, In the Stone, Rock That/Boogie Wonderland, When I Dance, Dearest Heart, September, Turn It Into Something Good, Ponta de Areia, Thinking of You, Mighty Mighty, Serpentine Fire, Fantasy, Louie's Welcome, Getaway, Dirty, After the Love Has Gone, Can't Hide Love, You Don't Know, Kali, Hot Feet Ballet (Intro, Let Your Feelings Show, System of Survival, Saturday Night, Africano, Star, Faces), Kali (reprise), Mega Mix, September, Shining Star, Gratitude

Setting: New York City, now. A dance musical presented in two acts.

Synopsis: A modern-day version of *The Red Shoes* using the music of the pop group Earth, Wind, and Fire, *Hot Feet* tells the story of Kalimba, a beautiful young dancer, who gets involved in a Faustian bargain when she is persuaded to dance in a pair of enchanted red shoes.

Michael Balderrama and Vivian Nixon

THE DROWSY CHAPERONE

Marquis Theatre; First Preview: April 3, 2006; Opening Night: May 1, 2006; still running as of May 31, 2006

A new musical with music and lyrics by Lisa Lambert and Greg Morrison, book by Bob Martin and Don McKellar, by special arrangement with Paul Mack; Produced by Kevin McCollum, Roy Miller, Boyett Ostar Productions, Stephanie McClelland, Barbara Freitag, Jill Furman; Director and Choreography, Casey Nicholaw; Scenery, David Gallo; Costumes, Gregg Barnes; Lighting, Ken Billington and Brian Monahan; Sound, Acme Sound Partners; Casting, Bernard Telsey; Hair, Josh Marquette; Make-up, Justen M. Brosnan; Orchestrations, Larry Blank; Dance and Incidental Music Arrangements, Glen Kelly; Music Director and Vocal Arrangements, Phil Reno; Music Coordinator, John Miller; Production Supervisors, Brian Lynch and Chris Kluth; Production Stage Manager, Karen Moore; Associate Producers; Sonny Everett, Mariano Tolentino, Jr.; Marketing, TMG — The Marketing Group; General Management, The Charlotte Wilcox Company; Company Manager, Seth Marquette; Assistant Company Manager, Robert E. Jones; Stage Manager, Josh Halperin; Assistant Stage Manager, Rachel S. McCutchen; Assistant Director, Josh Rhodes; Dance Captain, Angela Pupello; Associate Designers, Charlie Smith (scenery), Sky Switser (costumes), Stephen N. Boulmetis (lighting); Properties, George Wagner; Music Preparation, Hotstave, Ltd.; Press, Boneau/Bryan Brown; Cast recording: Sh-K-Boom Records/Ghostlight 7915584411-2

Bob Martin PHOTOS BY JOAN MARCUS

Bob Martin and Beth Leavel

The Cast of *The Drowsy Chaperone*

Cast: Man in Chair **Bob Martin**; Mrs. Tottendale **Georgia Engel**; Underling **Edward Hibbert**; Robert Martin **Troy Britton Johnson**; George **Eddie Korbich**; Feldzieg **Lenny Wolpe**; Kitty **Jennifer Smith**; Gangster #1 **Jason Kravits**; Gangster #2 **Garth Kravits**; Aldolpho **Danny Burstein**; Janet Van De Graaff **Sutton Foster**; The Drowsy Chaperone **Beth Leavel**; Trix **Kecia Lewis-Evans**; Ensemble **Linda Griffin, Angela Pupello, Joey Sorge, Patrick Wetzel**

Swings: Andrea Chamberlain, Jay Douglas, Stacia Fernandez, Kilty Reidy

Understudies: Patrick Wetzel, Jay Douglas (Man in Chair/Feldzieg); Angela Pupello, Andrea Chamberlain (Janet/Kitty); Joey Sorge, Jay Douglas (Robert/Aldolpho) Linda Griffin, Stacia Fernandez (The Drowsy Chaperone/Mrs. Tottendale/Trix); Patrick Wetzel, Kilty Reidy (Underling/George); Joey Sorge, Kilty Reidy (Gangster 1 & 2)

Orchestra: Phil Reno (Conductor); Lawrence Goldberg (Associate Conductor/keyboards); Matt Perri (keyboards); Edward Joffe, Tom Murray, Tom Christensen, Ron Jannelli (reeds); Dave Stahl, Glenn Drewes, Jeremy Miloszewicz (trumpet); Steve Armour, Jeff Nelson (trombone); Ed Hamilton (guitar); Michael Keunnen (bass); Perry Cavari (drums); Bill Hayes (percussion)

Musical Numbers: Overture, Fancy Dress, Cold Feets, Show Off, As We Stumble Along, I Am Aldolpho, Accident Waiting Happen, Toledo Surprise; Message From a Nightingale, Bride's Lament, Love Is Always Lovely, I Do I Do in the Sky, As We Stumble Along (reprise)

2005–2006 Awards: Tony Awards: Best Book of a Musical, Best Score of a Musical, Best Featured Actress in a Musical (Beth Leavel), Scenic Design of a Musical (David Gallo), Costume Design of a Musical (Gregg Barnes); Drama Desk Awards: Outstanding Musical, Outstanding Book of a Musical, Outstanding Featured Actress in a Musical (Beth Leavel), Outstanding Lyrics, Outstanding Music, Outstanding Set Design of a Musical (David Gallo); Outstanding Costume Design (Gregg Barnes); **Theatre World Award**: Bob Martin

Setting: The New York apartment and in the mind of Man in Chair; current. A musical presented without intermission; American premiere produced at the Ahmanson Theatre Center by Center Theatre Group, Los Angeles, California.

Synopsis: To chase his blues away, a modern-day musical theatre addict, Man in Chair, drops the needle on his favorite LP—the 1928 musical comedy *The Drowsy Chaperone*. From the crackle of his hi-fi, the uproariously funny musical magically bursts to life in his living room, telling the tale of a pampered Broadway starlet who wants to give up show business to get married. Enter her producer who sets out to sabotage the nuptials, the "drowsy" chaperone, the debonair groom, a dizzy chorine, a Latin lover, a couple of gangsters, and ruses are played, hi-jinks occur, and the plot spins completely out of control.

Danny Burstein and Beth Leavel

Joey Sorge, Linda Griffin, Angela Pupello, Sutton Foster, Patrick Wetzel, Jennifer Smith, Lenny Wolpe, Beth Leavel, Jason Kravits, Garth Kravits

THE LIEUTENANT OF INISHMORE

Lyceum Theatre; First Preview: April 18, 2006; Opening Night: May 3, 2006; still running as of May 31, 2006

Off Broadway transfer of the Atlantic Theater Company (Neil Pepe, Artistic Director; Andrew D. Hamingson, Managing Director) production of a new play by Martin McDonagh; Produced by Randall L. Wreghitt, Dede Harris, Atlantic Theater Company, David Lehrer, Harriet Newman Leve & Ron Nicynski, Zavelson Meyrelles Greiner Group, Mort Swinsky & Redfern Goldman Productions, and Ruth Hendel; Director, Wilson Milam; Scenery, Scott Pask; Costumes, Theresa Squire; Lighting, Michael Chybowski; Sound, Obadiah Eaves; Music, Matt McKenzie; Arrangements, Andrew Ranken; Casting, Pat McCorkle; Fight Director, J. David Brimmer; Dialect Coach, Stephen Gabis; Production Stage Manager, James Harker; Stage Manager, Freda Farrell; Production Management, Aurora Productions; General Management, Richards/Climan, Inc.; Associate Producer, Braun-McFarlane Productions; Company Manager, Thom Clay; Assistant to the Director, Nick Leavens; Associate Scenery, Nancy Thun; Production Properties Supervisor, Anmaree Rodibaugh; Fight Captain, Jeff Binder; Marketing, HHC Marketing; Advertising, SPOTCo, Inc.; Press, Boneau/Bryan Brown, Chris Boneau, Susanne Tighe, Heath Schwartz

David Wilmot and Alison Pill PHOTOS BY MONIQUE CARBONI

Peter Gerety and Domhnall Gleeson

Jeff Binder and David Wilmot

Domhnall Gleeson and Peter Gerety

Cast: Davey **Domhnall Gleeson**; Donny **Peter Gerety**; Padraic **David Wilmot**; James **Jeff Binder**; Mairead **Alison Pill**; Christy **Andrew Connolly**; Joey **Dashiell Eaves**; Brendan **Brian d'Arcy James**

Understudies: John Ahlin (Donny, Christy), Brian Avers (Davey, Padraic, James, and Christy), Cristin Milioti (Mairead)

2005–2006 Awards: Theatre World Award: David Wilmot; Lucille Lortel Award: Best Play, Best Actor (David Wilmot); Obie Award: Playwriting (Martin McDonagh)

Setting: The play is set in 1993 on the island of Inishmore, County Galway, Ireland. A comedy presented in two acts. Opened at the Atlantic Theater Company February 27, 2006 (see Off Broadway Company Series in this volume). The play was originally produced at the Royal Shakespeare Company, Stratford, England, in June, 2002.

Synopsis: Described as Monty Python meets Quentin Tarantino, this wicked black comedy is about a ruthless, violent Irish liberation army enforcer and the one thing he loves more than anything…his black cat. Shocking, gory, yet farcical and hilarious, the play examines the absurdity of political and gun violence in our society.

Cherry Jones   PHOTO BY JOAN MARCUS

FAITH HEALER

Booth Theatre; First Preview: April 18, 2006; Opening Night: May 4, 2006; still running as of May 31, 2006

The Gate Theatre Dublin production of the revival of a play by Brian Friel; Produced by Michael Colgan & Sonia Friedman Productions, The Shubert Organization, Robert Bartner, Roger Berlind, Scott Rudin, and Spring Sirkin; Director, Jonathan Kent; Scenery and Costumes, Jonathan Fensom; Lighting, Mark Henderson; Sound, Christopher Cronin; Video, Sven Ortel; U.S. Casting, Jim Carnahan; Production Stage Manager, Jane Grey; Production Management, Aurora Productions; General Management, Stuart Thompson Productions, James Triner; Associate Producer, Lauren Doll; Company Manager, Shawn M. Fertitta; Stage Manager, Sid King; Assistant to the Director, Will MacAdams; Associate Lighting, Kristina Kloss; Advertising, SPOTCo, Inc.; Press, Barlow-Hartman, John Barlow, Michael Hartman, Dennis Crowley, Ryan Ratelle

Cast: Frank Hardy **Ralph Fiennes**; Grace Hardy **Cherry Jones**; Teddy **Ian McDiarmid**

Standbys: Patrick Boll (Frank), Jarlath Conroy (Teddy), Robin Moseley (Grace)

2005 – 2006 Awards: Tony Awards: Featured Actor in a Play (Ian McDiarmid); **Theatre World Award:** Ian McDiarmid

A drama presented in four scenes in two acts. Part 1: Freddie, Part 2: Grace, Part 3: Teddy, Part 4: Frank. Originally produced on Broadway at the Longacre Theatre, April 5, 1979 (see *Theatre World* Volume 35, page 39). This production was presented at the Dublin Gate Theatre, Dublin, Ireland, from February 6 – March 31, 2006 with Mr. Fiennes and Mr. McDiarmid in the cast.

Synopsis: Told in a series of four monologues, *Faith Healer* looks at mystic experiences and the fine line between artists and con men. A dissolute, charismatic healer, his longtime lover, and his devoted manager travel the back roads of Scotland and Wales peddling miracles. As they wrestle with Frank's genuine but elusive gift for healing, they ask potent questions about who we trust, what we know, and why we believe.

Ralph Fiennes   PHOTOS BY ANTHONY WOODS

Ian McDiarmid   PHOTO BY ANTHONY WOODS

THE CAINE MUTINY COURT-MARTIAL

Gerald Schoenfeld Theatre; First Preview: April 14, 2006; Opening Night: May 7, 2006; Closed May 21, 2006; 27 previews and 17 performances

Revival of a play by Herman Wouk; Produced by Jeffrey Richards, Jerry Frankel, Debra Black, Roger Berlind, Ronald Frankel, Terry E. Schnuck, Sheldon Stein, Barry Weisbord, in association with Roy Furman; Director, Jerry Zaks; Scenery, John Lee Beatty; Costumes, William Ivey Long; Lighting, Paul Gallo; Sound, Dan Moses Schreier; Company Manager, Bruce Klinger; Production Stage Manager, Steven Beckler; Casting, Stuart Howard, Amy Schecter, and Paul Hardt; Marketing, Irene Gandy; Stage Manager, Lisa Dawn Cave; General Management, Albert Poland; Technical Supervisor, Neil Mazzella; Assistant Director, Jamibeth Margolis; Assistant Producer, Alana Karpoff; Advertising, SPOTCo, Inc.; Press, Jeffrey Richards Associates/Irene Gandy, Adam Farabee, Alana Karpoff, Eric Sanders

Zeljko Ivanek (seated), David Schwimmer, Tim Daly PHOTOS BY CAROL ROSEGG

Zeljko Ivanek and David Schwimmer

David Schwimmer

Cast: Lt. Barney Greenwald **David Schwimmer**; Lt. Stephen Maryk **Joe Sikora**; Lt. Com. John Challee **Timothy Daly**; Lt. Com. Philip Francis Queeg **Željko Ivanek**; Captain Blakely **Terry Beaver**; Lt. Thomas Keefer **Geoffrey Nauffts**; Signalman Third Class Junius Urban **Paul David Story**; Lt. (Jr. Grade) Willis Seward Keith **Ben Fox**; Captain Randolph Southard **Murphy Guyer**; Dr. Forrest Lundeen **Brian Reddy**; Dr. Bird **Tom Nelis**; Stenographer **Tom Gottlieb**; Orderly **Robert L. Devaney**; Members of the Court **Peter Bradbury, Michael Quinlan, Brian Russell, Doug Stender**; Party Guests **Denis Butkus, Greg McFadden**

Understudies: Brian Russell (Bird, Lundeen, Orderly), Michael Quinlan (Blakely, Southard), Denis Butkus (Urban, Keith, Stenographer), Robert L. Devaney (Challee, Maryk, Keefer), Doug Stender (Blakely, Southard, Lundeen), Peter Bradbury (Challee, Queeg), Greg McFadden (Keefer, Members of the Court, Stenographer), Tom Gottlieb (Bird, Keith, Urban)

Setting: February, 1945. The General Court Martial room of the Twelfth Naval District, then the Private Dining Room at the Fairmont Hotel, San Francisco. A court room drama presented in three scenes in two acts. Originally produced on Broadway at the Plymouth (former name of the Schoenfeld Theatre) on January 20, 1954, where it ran for 415 performances (see *Theatre World*, Volume 10).

Synopsis: A young naval lieutenant (Maryk) is on trial for deposing his commanding officer, (Queeg) whom he believed to be insane. The idealistic attorney (Greenwald) set out to defend him and his fellow deposer (Keefer) is faced with an ethical dilemma as he sympathizes with the man he is prosecuting and believes his defendants to be guilty. The classic court-room drama builds to a surprise ending.

SHINING CITY

Biltmore Theatre; First Preview: April 20, 2006 Opening Night: May 9, 2006; still running as of May 31, 2006

Manhattan Theatre Club (Lynne Meadow, Artistic Director; Barry Grove, Executive Producer) production of a new play by Conor McPherson; Produced by special arrangement with Scott Rudin, Roger Berlind, and Debra Black; Director, Robert Falls; Scenery, Santo Loquasto; Costumes, Kaye Voyce; Lighting, Christopher Akerlind; Sound, Obadiah Eaves; Dialect Coach, Deborah Hecht; Production Stage Manager, Barclay Stiff; Casting, Nancy Piccione/David Caparelliotis; Director of Artistic Operations, Mandy Greenfield; Production Manager, Ryan McMahon; Director of Development, Jill Turner Lloyd; Director of Marketing, Debra A. Waxman; General Manager, Florie Seery; Director of Artistic Development, Paige Evans; Director of Artistic Production, Michael Bush; Associate General Manager, Lindsey T. Brooks; Company Manager, Denise Cooper; Stage Manager, Francesca Russell; Assistant Director, Henry Wishcamper; Associate Scenery, Jenny B. Sawyers; Technical Director, William Mohney; Advertising, SPOTCo, Inc.; Press, Boneau/Bryan-Brown, Chris Boneau, Jim Byk, Aaron Meier, Heath Schwartz

Brían F. O'Byrne PHOTOS BY JOAN MARCUS

Peter Scanavino and Brían F. O'Byrne

Martha Plimpton and Brían F. O'Byrne

Oliver Platt

Cast: Ian **Brían F. O'Byrne**; John **Oliver Platt**; Neasa **Martha Plimpton**; Laurence **Peter Scanavino**

Understudies: Chris Genebach (Ian, Laurence), Fiana Toiban (Neasa)

Setting: An office in Dublin, present. Roughly two months separate each scene. American premiere of a drama presented without intermission; originally produced at the Royal Court Theatre, London, and the Gate Theatre, Dublin, on June 4, 2004.

Synopsis: A supernatural tale that concerns a widower who visits a first-time therapist, claiming to have seen the ghost of his recently deceased wife. The therapist is confronted with his own demons, and the visits between the two become a gripping struggle to survive. A "coup de theatre" thrilling ending leaves them changed for the rest of their lives.

TARZAN

Richard Rodgers Theatre; First Preview: March 24, 2006; Opening Night: May 10, 2006; still running as of May 31, 2006

A new musical with music and lyrics by Phil Collins, book by David Henry Hwang; Produced by Disney Theatrical Productions (under the direction of Thomas Schumacher); based on the 1999 Disney animated feature film *Tarzan* (screenplay by Tab Murphy, Bob Tzudiker and Noni White; directed by Kevin Lima and Chris Buck); Based on the story "Tarzan of the Apes" by Edgar Rice Burroughs; Director/Scenery/Costumes, Bob Crowley; Choreography, Meryl Tankard; Musical Production and Vocal Arrangements, Paul Bogaev; Aerial Design, Pichoón Baldinu; Lighting, Natasha Katz; Sound, John Shivers; Hair, David Brian Brown; Make Up, Naomi Donne; Soundscape, Lon Bender; Special Creatures; Ivo Coveney; Fight Director, Rick Sordelet; Music Director and Dance Arrangements, Jim Abbott; Orchestrations, Doug Besterman; Music Coordinator, Michael Keller; Casting, Bernard Telsey Casting; Production Supervisor, Clifford Schwartz; Technical Supervisor, Tom Shane Bussey; Associate Director, Jeff Lee; Associate Producer, Marshall B. Purdy; Project Manager, Lizbeth Cone; Company Manager, Randy Meyer; Associate Company Manager, Eduardo Castro; Assistant Choreographer, Leonora Stapleton; Assistant Aerial Designer, Angela Phillips; Animated Sequence, Little Airplane Productions; Stage Manager, Frank Lombardi; Assistant Stage Managers, Julia P. Jones, Tanya Gillette, Robert Armitage; Dance Captain, Marlyn Ortiz; Fight Captain/ Assistant Dance Captain, Stefan Raulston; Associate Designers, Brian Webb, Rosalind Coombes (scenery), Mary Peterson (costumes), Yael Lubetzky (lighting), David Partridge (sound); Automated Lighting, Aland Henderson, Jesse Belsky; Technical Supervisor, Tom Shane Bussey; Music Copyist, Russell Anixter, Donald Rice; Dialogue and Vocal Coach, Deborah Hecht; Advertising, Serino Coyne, Inc.; Press, Boneau/Bryan-Brown, Jim Byk, Matt Polk, Juliana Hannett; Cast recording: Disney Records 61541-7

Cast: Kerchak **Shuler Hensley**; Kala **Merle Dandridge**; Young Tarzan **Daniel Manche/Alex Rutherford**; Terk **Chester Gregory II**; Tarzan **Josh Strickland**; Jane Porter **Jenn Gambatese**; Professor Porter **Tim Jerome**; Mr. Clayton **Donnie Keshawarz**; Snipes **Horace V. Rogers**

Ensemble: Marcus Bellamy, Celina Carvajal, Dwayne Clark, Kearran Giovann, Michael Hollick, Kara Madrid, Kevin Massey, Anastacia McCleskey, Rika Okamoto, Marlyn Ortiz, John Elliott Oyzon, Andy Pellick, Stefan Raulston, Horace V. Rogers, Sean Samuels, Niki Scalera

Michael Hollick and Rika Okamoto

Jenn Gambatese and Josh Strickland PHOTOS BY JOAN MARCUS

Swings: Veronica deSoyza, Joshua Kobak, Whitney Osentoski, Angela Phillips, Nick Sanchez, Natalie Silverlieb, JD Aubrey Smith, Rachel Stern

Standby: Darrin Baker (Kerchak and Porter)

Understudies: Joshua Kobak, Kevin Massey (Tarzan); Celina Carvajal, Niki Scalera (Jane); Michael Hollick, Horace V. Rogers (Kerchak); Kearran Giovanni, Natalie Silverlieb (Kala); Dwayne Clark, Nick Sanchez (Terk); Michael Hollick, Joshua Kobak (Clayton); Michael Hollick (Porter)

Orchestra: Jim Abbott (Conductor/keyboard 1); Ethan Popp (Associate Conductor/keyboard 2); Andrew Barrett (synthesizer programmer); Martyn Axe (keyboard 3); Gary Seligson (drums); Roger Squitero, Javier Diaz (percussion); Hugh Mason (bass); JJ McGeehan (guitar); Leanne LeBlanc (cello); Anders Boström (flutes); Charles Pillow (reeds); Anthony Kadleck (trumpet); Bruce Eidem (trombone); Theresa MacDonnell (French horn)

Musical Numbers: Two Worlds, You'll Be in My Heart, Jungle Funk, Who Better Than Me, No Other Way, I Need to Know, Son of Man, Son of Man (reprise), Sure As Sun Turns to Moon, Waiting for This Moment, Different, Trashin' the Camp, Like No Man I've Ever Seen, Strangers Like Me, Who Better Than Me (reprise), Everything That I Am, You'll Be in My Heart (reprise), Sure As Sun Turns to Moon (reprise), Two Worlds (Finale)

Setting: The Coast of Africa, early 1900s. World premiere of a musical presented in two acts.

Synopsis: Tarzan, a shipwrecked baby who was raised in an African jungle by apes, has his first encounter with humans (including the beautiful Jane) and must choose where he belongs—the "civilized" human world or the "wild" one that nurtured him.

BROADWAY

Productions from Past Seasons That **Played Through This Season**

AVENUE Q

Golden Theatre; First Preview: July 10, 2003; Opening Night: July 31, 2003 (see *Theatre World* Volume 60, page 25); Performances as of May 31, 2006: 1,182

Transfer of the Off Broadway musical with music and lyrics by Robert Lopez and Jeff Marx, book by Jeff Whitty; Produced by Kevin McCollum, Robyn Goodman, Jeffrey Seller, Vineyard Theatre and The New Group; Director, Jason Moore; Choreography, Ken Roberson; Music Supervision, Orchestrations, and Arrangements, Stephen Oremus; Puppets Conception and Design, Rick Lyon; Scenery, Anna Louizos; Costumes, Mirena Rada; Lighting, Howell Binkley; Sound, Acme Sound Partners; Animation, Robert Lopez; Music Director/Incidental Music, Gary Adler; Music Coordinator, Michael Keller; Casting, Cindy Tolan; Technical Supervisor, Brian Lynch; Marketing, TMG-The Marketing Group; General Manager, John Corker; Production Stage Manager/Resident Director, Evan Ensign; Associate Producers, Sonny Everett, Walter Grossman, Morton Swinsky; Company Manager, Mary K. Witte; Dance Captain, Natalie Venetia Belcon; Associate Conductor, Mark Hartman; Stage Manager, Christine M. Daly; Assistant Director, Jen Bender; Assistant Stage Manager, Aymee Garcia; Associate Scenery, Todd Potter; Associate Lighting, Timothy F. Rogers; Music Copying, Emily Grishman and Alex Lacamoire; Animation and Video Production, Noodle Soup Production, Jeremy Rosenberg; Sound and Video Design Effects, Brett Jarvis; Advertising, SPOTCo, Inc.; Press, Sam Rudy Media Relations; Cast recording: RCA 82876-55923-2.

Opening Night Cast: Princeton/Rod **John Tartaglia**[1]; Brian **Jordan Gelber**[2]; Kate Monster/Lucy the Slut **Stephanie D'Abruzzo**[3]; Nicky/Trekkie Monster/Bad Idea Bear **Rick Lyon**[4]; Christmas Eve **Ann Harada**[5]; Gary Coleman **Natalie Venetia Belcon**[6]; Mrs. T./Bad Idea Bear/Others **Jennifer Barnhart**; Ensemble **Jodi Eichelberger, Peter Linz**[7]

Understudies: Jodi Eichelberger, Peter Linz (Princeton, Rod), Peter Linz (Brian), Jennifer Barnhart, Aymee Garcia (Kate Monster, Lucy the Slut, Others), Jodi Eichelberger, Peter Linz (Nicky, Trekkie Monster, Bear, Others), Aymee Garcia (Mrs. T, Bear, Others), Erin Quill (Christmas Eve), Carmen Ruby Floyd (Gary Coleman)[8]

Mary Faber and Lucy the Slut   PHOTOS BY CAROL ROSEGG

Orchestra: Gary Adler (Conductor, keyboard), Mark Hartman (Associate Conductor, keyboard), Maryann McSweeney (bass), Brian Koonin (guitar), Patience Higgins (reeds), Michael Croiter (drums).

Musical Numbers: Avenue Q Theme, What Do You Do With a BA in English?/It Sucks to be Me, If You Were Gay, Purpose, Everyone's a Little Bit Racist, The Internet Is for Porn, Mix Tape, I'm Not Wearing Underwear Today, Special, You Can Be as Loud as the Hell You Want (When You're Making Love), Fantasies Come True, My Girlfriend, Who Lives in Canada, There's a Fine, Fine Line, There Is Life Outside Your Apartment, The More You Ruv Someone, Schadenfreude, I Wish I Could Go Back to College, The Money Song, For Now

Setting: The present. An outer borough of New York City. A musical presented in two acts; originally produced at the Vineyard Theatre, February 20, 2003, and previously at the 2002 O'Neill Music Theatre Conference, Waterford, Connecticut. Awards: 2004 Tony Awards (Best Musical, Best Score, and Best Book of a Musical); 2004 Theatre World Awards: John Tartaglia and Stephanie D'Abruzzo; 2004 Outer Critics Circle Award: Special Achievement for Ensemble Performance and Puppetry Artistry; 2004 Clarence Derwent Award: John Tartaglia; 2003 Lortel Award: Best Musical.

Synopsis: *Avenue Q* is about real life: finding a job, losing a job, learning about racism, getting an apartment, getting kicked out of your apartment, being different, falling in love, promiscuity, avoiding commitment, and internet porn. Twenty and thirty-something puppets and humans survive life in the big city and search for their purpose in this naughty but timely musical that features "full puppet nudity!"

Princeton and Howie Michael Smith

Succeeded by: 1. Barrett Foa (2/1/05), Howie Michael Smith (7/3/06) 2. Evan Harrington (1/24/06) 3. Mary Faber (2/26/06) 4. Christian Anderson (7/5/05), Rick Lyon (5/30/06) 5. Ann Sanders (10/26/04), Ann Harada (1/25/05), Sala Iwamatsu (11/30/05), Ann Harada (12/24/05), Ann Sanders (2/27/06) 6. Haneefah Wood (11/30/05), Natalie Venetia Belcon (12/24/05) 7. Barrett Foa, Carmen Ruby Floyd, Leo Daignault, Matt Schreiber, Howie Michael Smith 8. Angela Ai (Christmas Eve), Becca Ayers (Bear, Kate Monster, Lucy the Slut, Mrs. T), Minglie Chen (Bear, Christmas Eve, Mrs. T), Leo Daignault (Bear, Brian, Nicky, Trekkie Monster), Carmen Ruby Floyd (Bear, Mrs. T), Barrett Foa (Nicky, Princeton, Rod), Ann Sanders (Christmas Eve), Howie Michael Smith (Bear, Nicky, Princeton, Rod, Trekkie Monster), Jasmin Walker and Chandra Wilson (Gary Coleman), Darryl D. Winslow (Brian)

BEAUTY AND THE BEAST

Palace Theatre*; First Preview: Wednesday, March 9, 1994; Opening Night: Monday, April 18, 1994 (see *Theatre World* Volume 50, page 55); Performances as of May 31, 2006: 4,978

A new musical with music by Alan Menken, lyrics by Howard Ashman, Tim Rice, book by Linda Woolverton; Produced by Walt Disney Productions (Ron Logan, President, Walt Disney Theatrical Productions; Robert McTyre, Vice President and Producer, Walt Disney Theatrical Productions); Associate Producer: Donald Frantz; Director, Robert Jess Roth; Orchestrations, Danny Troob; Musical Supervision/Vocal Arrangements, David Friedman; Musical Director/Incidental Arrangements, Michael Kosarin; Choreography, Matt West; Scenery, Stan Meyer; Costumes, Ann Hould-Ward; Lighting, Natasha Katz; Sound, T. Richard Fitzgerald; Hair, David H. Lawrence; Illusions, Jim Steinmeyer, John Gaughan; Prosthetics, John Dods; Fight Director, Rick Sordelet; General Manager, Dodger Productions; Production Supervisor, Jeremiah J. Harris; Company Manager, Kim Sellon; Stage Managers, James Harker, John M. Atherlay, Pat Sosnow, Kim Vernace; Press, Chris Boneau/Adrian Bryan-Brown, Amy Jacobs, Steven Padla; Cast recording: Walt Disney 60861.

Opening Night Cast: Enchantress **Wendy Oliver**; Young Prince **Harrison Beal**; Beast **Terrence Mann***1; Belle **Susan Egan***2; Lefou **Kenny Raskin***3; Gaston **Burke Moses***4; Three Silly Girls **Paige Price, Sarah Solie Shannon, Linda Talcott**; Maurice **Tom Bosley***5; Cogsworth **Heath Lamberts***6; Lumiere **Gary Beach***7; Babette **Stacey Logan***8; Mrs. Potts **Beth Fowler***9; Chip **Brian Press***10; Madame de la Grande Bouche **Eleanor Glockner***11; Monsieur D'Arque **Gordon Stanley***12; Prologue Narrator **David Ogden Stiers**

Townspeople/Enchanted Objects: Joan Barber, Roxane Barlow, Harrison Beal, Michael-Demby Cain, Kate Dowe, David Elder, Merwin Foard, Gregory Garrison, Jack Hayes, Kim Huber, Elmore James, Rob Lorey, Patrick Loy, Barbara Marineau, Joanne McHugh, Anna McNeely, Bill Nabel, Wendy Oliver, Vince Pesce, Paige Price, Sarah Solie Shannon, Gordon Stanley, Linda Talcott, Wysandria Woolsey*13

Swings: Joan Barber, Kate Dowe, Gregory Garrison, Alisa Klein, Rob Lorey, Dan Mojica.

Standby: Chuck Wagner (Beast).

Understudies: Harrison Beal (Lefou), Kate Dowe (Enchantress, Silly Girl), David Elder (Beast), Merwin Foard (Gaston), Gregory Garrison (Young Prince), Kim Huber (Belle), Alisa Klein (Enchantress, Silly Girl), Rob Lorey (Monsieur D'Arque), Barbara Marineau (Madame de la Grande Bouche, Mrs. Potts), Joanne McHugh (Babette), Anna McNeely (Madame de la Grande Bouche, Mrs. Potts), Dan Mojica (Young Prince), Bill Nabel (Cogsworth, Lumiere, Maurice), Vince Pesce (Lefou), Paige Price (Belle), Sarah Solie Shannon (Babette), Gordon Stanley (Cogsworth, Lumiere, Maurice), Linda Talcott (Chip), Chuck Wagner (Gaston).

Musical Numbers: Overture, Prologue (Enchantress), Belle, No Matter What, Me, Home, Gaston, How Long Must This Go On?, Be Our Guest, If I Can't Love Her, Entr'acte/Wolf Chase, Something There, Human Again, Maison des Lunes, Beauty and the Beast, Mob Song, The Battle, Transformation, Finale

A musical presented in two acts. 1994 Tony Award: Best Costume Design.

Jacob Young PHOTO BY JOAN MARCUS

Synopsis: A stage adaptation of the animated Walt Disney film about a strong-willed young woman who breaks the spell that turned a handsome prince into a monstrous beast. Trying to save her beloved father from the Beast's clutches, Belle agrees to become his prisoner forever. But once she is inside the Beast's enchanted castle, the members of his court, who have been transformed into household objects like clocks and candlesticks, decide to play matchmakers. As the Beast begins to fall in love with Belle, he becomes progressively less beastly. But the spell can be broken only if the Beast can get her to love him in return.

*Moved to the Lunt-Fontanne Theatre on November 12, 1999

*Succeeded by: 1. Jeff McCarthy, Chuck Wagner, James Barbour, Steve Blanchard, Jeff McCarthy, Steve Blanchard 2. Sarah Uriarte Berry, Christianne Tisdale, Kerry Butler, Deborah Gibson, Kim Huber, Toni Braxton, Andrea McArdle, Sarah Litzsinger, Jamie-Lynn Sigler, Sarah Litzsinger, Megan McGinnis, Christy Carlson Romano, Brooke Tansley, Ashley Brown, Sarah Litzsinger 3. Harrison Beal, Jamie Torcellini, Jeffrey Howard Schecter, Jay Brian Winnick, Gerard McIsaac, Brad Aspel, Steve Lavner, Aldrin Gonzalez 4. Marc Kudisch, Steve Blanchard, Patrick Ryan Sullivan, Christopher Sieber, Chris Hoch, Grant Norman 5. MacIntyre Dixon, Tom Bosley, Kurt Knudson, Timothy Jerome, J.B. Adams, Jamie Ross 6. Peter Bartlett, Robert Gibby Brand, John Christopher Jones, Jeff Brooks, Christopher Duva 7. Lee Roy Reams, Patrick Quinn, Gary Beach, Meshach Taylor, Patrick Page, Paul Schoeffler, Patrick Page, Bryan Batt, Rob Lorey, David DeVries, Peter Flynn, Jacob Young 8. Pamela Winslow, Leslie Castay, Pam Klinger, Louisa Kendrick, Pam Klinger, Meredith Inglesby 9. Cass Morgan, Beth Fowler, Barbara Marineau, Beth Flower, Cass Morgan, Alma Cuervo, Jeanne Lehman 10. Pierce Cravens, Jonathan Andrew Bleicher, Joseph DiConcetto, Andrew Keenan-Bolger, Adam Casner, Rick Ashley, Matthew Dotzman, Harrison Chad, William Ullrich, Zachary Grill, Nicholas Jonas, Jeremy Bergman, Joey Caravaglio, Henry Hodges, Alex Rutherford, Matthew Gumley, Patrick O'Neil Henney, Marlon Sherman, Trevor Braun, Alexander Scheitinger, 11. Judith Moore, Gina Ferrall, Marguerite Willbanks, Mary Stout, Sherry Anderson, Mary Stout 12. Glenn Rainey, Denny Paschal, Glenn Rainey 13. (in alphabetical order) 1994–1999: Ana Maria Andricain, Steven Ted Beckler, Kevin Berdini, Andrea Burns, Kevin M. Burrows, Christophe Caballero, Michael Clowers, Karl duHoffmann, Sally Mae Dunn, Stacia Fernandez, Barbara Folts, Robert H. Fowler, Teri Furr, Jerry Godfrey, Lauren Goler-Kosarin, Jennifer Hampton, Ellen Hoffman, Alisa Klein, Pam Klinger, Michael Lang, Linda Talcott Lee, Sarah E. Litzsinger, Lisa Mayer, Ken McMullen, Beth McVey, Tom Pardoe, Angela Piccinni, Elizabeth Polito, Glenn Rainey, Graham Rowat, Raymond Sage, Joseph Savant, Matthew Shepard, Steven Sofia, Amanda Watkins, David A. Wood, 1999–2006: Ana Arvia, Kevin Berdini, Andrea Burns, Christophe Caballero, Gina Carlette, Karl Christian, Brian Collier, Christopher Deangelis, Sally Mae Dunn, Barbara Folts, Keith Fortner, Tracey Generalovich, Lauren Goler-Kosarin, Jill Hayman, Michael Lang, David E. Liddell, Michelle Lookadoo, Stephanie Lynge, Michelle Mallardi, Jennifer Marcum, Anna McNeely, Garrett Miller, Christopher Monteleone, Bill Nabel, Brian O'Brien, Brynn O'Malley, Patrick Page, Denny Paschall, Rod Roberts, John Salvatore, Ann Sanders, Daria Lynn Scatton, Marguerite Shannon, Sarah Solie Shannon, Jennifer Shrader, Billy Sprague, Jr, Erin Stoddard, Rob Sutton, James Tabeek, Linda Talcott-Lee, Marguerite Willbanks, Brek William, Jennifer Hope Wills, Tia Marie Zorne.

CHICAGO

Richard Rodgers Theatre*; First Preview: October 23, 1996; Opening Night: November 14, 1996 (see *Theatre World* Volume 53, page 14); Performances as of May 31, 2006: 3,964

Revival of the musical with music by John Kander, lyrics by Fred Ebb, and book by Fred Ebb and Bob Fosse; Script Adaptation, David Thompson; Based on the play by Maurine Dallas Watkins; Original Production Directed and Choreographed by Bob Fosse; Produced by Barry & Fran Weissler in association with Kardana Productions; Director, Walter Bobbie; Choreography, Ann Reinking in the style of Bob Fosse; Music Director, Rob Fisher; Orchestrations, Ralph Burns; Scenery, John Lee Beatty; Costumes, William Ivey Long; Lighting, Ken Billington; Sound, Scott Lehrer; Dance Arrangements, Peter Howard; General Manager, Darwell Associates and Maria Di Dia; Company Manager, Scott A. Moore; Stage Managers, Clifford Schwartz, Terrence J. Witter; Press, Pete Sanders/Helene Davis, Clint Bond Jr., Glenna Freedman, Bridget Klapinski; Cast recording: RCA 68727-2.

Opening Night Cast: Velma Kelly **Bebe Neuwirth***1; Roxie Hart **Ann Reinking***2; Fred Casely **Michael Berresse**; Sergeant Fogarty **Michael Kubala**; Amos Hart **Joel Grey***3; Liz **Denise Faye**; Annie **Mamie Duncan-Gibbs**; June **Mary Ann Lamb**; Hunyak **Tina Paul**; Mona **Caitlin Carter**; Matron "Mama" Morton **Marcia Lewis***4; Billy Flynn **James Naughton***5; Mary Sunshine **D. Sabella***6; Go-To-Hell-Kitty **Leigh Zimmerman**; Harry **Rocker Verastique**; Aaron **David Warren-Gibson**; Judge **Jim Borstelmann**; Martin Harrison/Doctor **Bruce Anthony Davis**; Court Clerk **John Mineo**; Juror **Michael Kubala**

Brooke Shields PHOTO BY CAROL ROSEGG

Understudies/Standbys: Michael Berresse (Billy Flynn), Mamie Duncan-Gibbs (Matron), Nancy Hess (Roxie Hart, Velma Kelly), J. Loeffelholz (Mary Sunshine), John Mineo (Amos Hart)

Musical Numbers: All That Jazz, Funny Honey, Cell Block Tango, When You're Good to Mama, Tap Dance, All I Care About, A Little Bit of Good, We Both Reached for the Gun, Roxie, I Can't Do It Alone, My Own Best Friend, Entr'acte, I Know a Girl, Me and My Baby, Mister Cellophane, When Velma Takes the Stand, Razzle Dazzle, Class, Nowadays, Hot Honey Rag, Finale.

Setting: Chicago, late 1920s; a new production of the 1975 musical presented in two acts. 1997 Tony Awards: Revival of a Musical, Leading Actor in a Musical (James Naughton), Leading Actress in a Musical (Bebe Neuwirth), Direction of a Musical, Choreography, and Lighting. Originally produced on Broadway June 3, 1975 at the 46th Street Theatre (now the Richard Rodgers Theatre where this revival first opened) with Gwen Verdon, Chita Rivera, and Jerry Orbach (see *Theatre World* Volume 32, page 8.)

Synopsis: Murder, media circus, vaudeville, and celebrity meet in this 1920's tale of two of the Windy City's most celebrated felons and their rise to fame amidst a razzle-dazzle trial. This production is based on the staged concert version presented by City Center Encores.

*Moved to the Shubert Theatre on February 12, 1997; moved to the Ambassador Theatre on January 29, 2003.

*Succeeded by: 1. Nancy Hess, Ute Lemper, Bebe Neuwirth, Ruthie Henshall, Mamie Duncan-Gibbs, Bebe Neuwirth, Donna Marie Asbury, Sharon Lawrence, Vicki Lewis, Jasmine Guy, Bebe Neuwirth, Donna Marie Asbury, Vicki Lewis, Deidre Goodwin, Anna Montanero, Deidre Goodwin, Donna Marie Asbury, Roxane Carrasco, Deidre Goodwin, Stephanie Pope, Roxane Carraasco, Caroline O'Connor, Brenda Braxton, Deidre Goodwin, Reva Rice, Brenda Braxton, Pia Dowes, Brenda Braxton, Terra C MacLeod, Brenda Braxton, Luba Mason 2. Marilu Henner, Karen Ziemba, Belle Calaway, Charlotte d'Amboise, Sandy Duncan, Belle Calaway, Charlotte d'Amboise, Belle Calaway, Nana Visitor, Petra Nielsen, Nana Visitor, Belle Callaway, Denise Van Outen, Belle Calaway, Bianca Marroquin, Amy Spanger, Charlotte d'Amboise, Belle Calaway, Tracy Shayne, Melanie Griffith, Charlotte d'Amboise, Bianca Marroquin, Charlotte d'Amboise, Gretchen Mol, Charlotte d'Amboise, Tracy Shayne, Paige Davis, Charlotte d'Amboise, Tracy Shayne, Charlotte D'Amboise, Michelle DeJean, Charlotte D'Amboise, Brooke Shields, Charlotte D'Amboise, Robin Givens, Tracy Shane, Charlotte D'Amboise 3. Ernie Sabella, Tom McGowan, P.J. Benjamin, Ernie Sabella, P.J. Benjamin, Tom McGowan, P.J. Benjamin, Raymond Bokhour, P.J. Benjamin, Rob Bartlett, P.J. Benjamin, Bruce Winant, Raymond Bokhour, Kevin Chamberlin 4. Roz Ryan, Marcia Lewis, Roz Ryan, Marcia Lewis, Roz Ryan, Marcia Lewis, Jennifer Holliday, Marcia Lewis, Michele Pawk, Alix Korey, B.J. Crosby, Angie Stone, Carmille Saviola, Debbie Gravitte, Roz Ryan, Anne L. Nathan, Mary Testa, Debra Monk, Lillias White 5. Gregory Jbara, Hinton Battle, Alan Thicke, Michael Berresse, Brent Barrett, Robert Urich, Clarke Peters, Brent Barrett, Chuck Cooper, Brent Barret, Chuck Cooper, George Hamilton, Eric Jordan Young, Ron Raines, George Hamilton, Michael C. Hall, Destan Owens, Taye Diggs, Billy Zane, Kevin Richardson, Clarke Peters, Gregory Harrison, Brent Barrett, Patrick Swayze, James Naughton, Norm Lewis, Christopher Sieber, Tom Wopat, Wayne Brady, Tom Wopat, Brent Barrett, Bernard Dotson, Christopher McDonald, Huey Lewis, John O'Hurley, Obba Babatundé 6. J. Loeffelholz, R. Bean, A. Saunders, J. Maldonado, R. Bean, A. Saunders, R. Bean, M. Agnes, D. Sabella, R. Bean, D. Sabella-Mills, R Bean, R Lowe. Replacement ensemble: (in alphabetical order) Timothy J. Alex, Shaun Amyot, Michael Arnold, Donna Marie Asbury, Mark Bove, Gregory Butler, Marc Calamia, Roxane Carrasco, Mindy Paige Davis, Michelle DeJean, Bernard Dotson, Bryn Dowling, Jennifer MacKensie Dunne, Shawn Emamjomeh, Jennifer Frankel, Gabriela Garcia, Greg Graham, Deidre Goodwin, Suzanne Harrer, Mary Ann Hermansen, Mike Jackson, Denis Jones, Sebastian LaCause, Lisa Leguillou, Dan LoBuono, Gregory Mitchell, James Mitchell, Dana Moore, Sharon Moore, Denny Paschall, Michelle Potterf, Angel Reda, Josh Rhodes, Krissy Richmond, Matthew Risch, Michelle M. Robinson, Solange Sandy, Randy Slovacek, Steven Sofia, Amy Spanger, Mark Anthony Taylor, David Warren-Gibson, Jennifer West, Darlene Wilson, Eric Jordan Young; Replacement Swings: (in alphabetical order) Christine Brooks, Rosa Curry, David Eggers, Gabriela Garcia, JoAnn M. Hunter, Kevin Neil McCready, James Patric Moran, Mark Price, Greg Reuter, Dante A. Sciarra, Jeff Shade, Lillie Kae Stevens

DIRTY ROTTEN SCOUNDRELS

Imperial Theatre; First Preview: January 31, 2004. Opening Night: March 3, 2005 (see *Theatre World* Volume 61, page 52); Performances as of May 31, 2006: 518

A new musical with book by Jeffrey Lane; music and lyrics by David Yazbek; based on the film "Dirty Rotten Scoundrels" written by Dale Launer, Stanley Shapiro and Paul Henning; Produced by Marty Bell, David Brown, Aldo Scrofani, Roy Furman, Dede Harris, Amanda Lipitz, Greg Smith, Ruth Hendel, Chase Mishkin, Barry and Susan Tatelman, Debra Black, Sharon Karmazin, Joyce Schweickert, Bernie Abrams/Michael Speyer, David Belasco+, Barbara Whitman, Weissberger Theater Group/Jay Harris, Cheryl Wiesenfeld/Jean Cheever, Florenz Ziegfeld+, Clear Channel Entertainment and Harvey Weinstein; Produced in association with MGM On Stage/Darcie Denkert and Dean Stolber, and the entire Prussian Army;+ Executive Producers, Marty Bell and Aldo Scrofani. Director, Jack O'Brien, Choreography, Jerry Mitchell; Music Direction and Incidental Music Arrangements, Ted Sperling; Scenery, David Rockwell; Costumes, Gregg Barnes; Lighting, Kenneth Posner; Sound, Acme Sound Partners; Casting, Bernard Telsey Casting; Associate Choreographer, Denis Jones; Orchestrations, Harold Wheeler; Vocal Music Arrangements, Ted Sperling and David Yazbek; Dance Music Arrangements, Zane Mark; Music Coordinator, Howard Jones; Technical Supervisor, Christopher Smith; Production Stage Manager, Michael Brunner; Marketing, Margery Singer Company; General Management, The Charlotte Wilcox Company; Company Manager, Matthew Lambert; Stage Manager, Daniel S. Rosokoff; Assistant Company Manager, Dina Steinberg; Assistant Stage Manager, Dana Williams; Dance Captain, Greg Graham; Assistant Director, Benjamin Klein; Associate Scenery, Richard Jaris; Associate Costumes, Sky Switser; Associate Lighting, Philip Rosenberg; Make-up, Jorge Vargas; Music Copying, Emily Grishman; Advertising, SPOTCo, Inc.; Press, Barlow-Hartman; Cast recording: Sh-K-Boom/Ghostlight Records, RTADV84406-2.

Opening Night Cast: Freddy Benson **Norbert Leo Butz***1; Lawrence Jameson **John Lithgow***2; Christine Colgate **Sherie René Scott***3; Jolene Oakes **Sara Gettelfinger***4; Muriel Eubanks **Joanna Gleason***5; Andre Thibault **Gregory Jbara***6

Ensemble: Timothy J. Alex, Andrew Asnes, Roxane Barlow, Stephen Campanella, Joe Cassidy, Julie Connors, Rachel deBenedet, Laura Marie Duncan, Sally Mae Dunn, Tom Galantich, Jason Gillman, Amy Heggins, Grasan Kingsberry, Michael Paternostro, Rachelle Rak*7

Norbert Leo Butz, Mylinda Hull, Jonathan Pryce PHOTOS BY CAROL ROSEGG

Swings: Jeremy Davis, Nina Goldman, Greg Graham, Gina Lamparella, Chuck Saculla.*8

Standby: Nick Wyman (Lawrence Jameson)*9

Understudies: Joe Cassidy (Andre, Freddy), Julie Connors (Jolene), Rachel deBenedet (Muriel), Laura Marie Duncan (Christine, Muriel), Tom Galantich (Lawrence), Jason Gillman (Freddy), Gina Lamparella (Christine), Michael Paternostro (Andre, Freddy), Rachelle Rak (Jolene).*10

Orchestra: Fred Lassen (Conductor), Jan Rosenberg (Associate Conductor, keyboards), Howard Joines (Assistant Conductor, Musical Coordinator, percussion), Antoine Silverman (Concert Master), Michael Nicholas and Claire Chan (violin), Anja Wood (cello), Andrew Sterman, Dan Willis and Mark Thrasher (woodwinds), Kevin Bryan and Hollis Burridge (trumpet), Mike Boschen (trombone), Theresa MacDonnell horn), Dan Lipton (keyboards), Erik Della Penna (guitar), Mike DuClos (bass), Dean Sharenow (drums).

Musical Numbers: Overture, Give Them What They Want, What Was a Woman to Do?, Great Big Stuff, Chimp in a Suit, Oklahoma?, All About Ruprecht, What Was a Woman to Do? (Reprise), Here I Am, Nothing Is Too Wonderful to Be True, The Miracle (Act I Finale), Entr'acte, Rüffhousin' mit Shüffhausen, Like Zis/Like Zat, The More We Dance, Love Is My Legs, Love Sneaks In, Like Zis/Like Zat (Reprise), Son of Great Big Stuff, The Reckoning, Dirty Rotten Number, Finale.

Setting: The French Rivera, the present. A musical presented in two acts; originally produced at the Old Globe Theatre, San Diego, California (Jack O'Brien, Artistic Director; Louis G. Spisto Executive Director); 2005 Awards: Tony Award: Leading Actor in a Musical (Norbert Leo Butz); Drama Desk Award: Actor in a Musical (Norbert Leo Butz); Drama League Awards: Distinguished Production of a Musical, Distinguished Performance (Norbert Leo Butz); Outer Critics Circle Award: Actor in a Musical (Norbert Leo Butz).

Synopsis: Based on the 1988 film. Two con men living on the French Riviera unsuccessfully attempt to work together, only to find the town isn't big enough for both of them. They agree on a settlement: the first to extract $50,000 from a young heiress wins, and the other has to leave town. A battle of cons ensues, and an unexpected twist leaves the audience laughing and guessing until the end.

+Not actual Producers of the show, but listed as a joke in all publicity material.

*Succeeded by: 1. Brian d'Arcy James (7/21/06) 2. Jonathan Pryce (1/1/06), Keith Carradine (7/21/06) 3. Rachel York (2/5/06), Sherie René Scott (6/20/06) 4. Mylinda Hull (1/17/06), Sara Gettelfinger (3/28/06) 5. Rachel deBenedet (5/2–21/06), Lucie Arnaz (5/23/06) 6. Richard Kind (8/3/06) 7. Jacqueline Bayne, Will Erat, Tom Galantich, Joan Hess, Chuck Saculla, Dennis Stowe, Matt Wall 8. Christine Bokhour, Julie Connors, Jenifer Foote 9. Dennis Parlato 10. Timothy J. Alex (Andre, Freddy), Paula Leggett Chase (Muriel), Julie Connors (Christine), Rachel deBenedet (Muriel), Joan Hess (Christine, Muriel), Dennis Parlato (Andre)

Jonathan Pryce, Rachel York, Norbert Leo Butz

DOUBT

Walter Kerr Theatre; First Preview: March 9, 2005; Opening Night: March 31, 2005; (see *Theatre World* Volume 61, page 64); Performances as of May 31, 2006: 488

Transfer of the Off Broadway play by John Patrick Shanley; Produced by Carole Shorenstein Hays, Manhattan Theatre Club (Lynne Meadow, Artistic Director; Barry Grove, Executive Producer), Roger Berlind and Scott Rudin. Director, Doug Hughes; Scenic Design, John Lee Beatty; Costume Design, Catherine Zuber; Lighting Design, Pat Collins; Original Music and Sound Design, David Van Tieghem; Production Stage Manager, Charles Means; Casting, Nancy Piccione and David Caparelliotis; Production Manager, Aurora Productions (Gene O'Donovan, W. Benjamin Heller II, Elise Hanley, Bethany Weinstein); Marketing, TMG - The Marketing Group; General Manager, Stuart Thompson Productions/ James Triner; Executive Producer, Greg Holland; Company Manager, Bobby Driggers; Stage Manager, Elizabeth Moloney; Dialect Coach, Stephen Gabis; Assistant Company Manager, Laura Penney; Assistant Director, Mark Schneider; Associate Scenic Design, Eric Renschler; Assistant Scenic Design, Yoshinori Tanakura; Associate Lighting Design, D. M. Wood; Assistant Sound Design, Walter Trarbach; Advertising, SPOTCo, Inc.; Press, Boneau/Bryan-Brown

Adriane Lenox PHOTOS BY JOAN MARCUS

Opening Night Cast: Sister Aloysius **Cherry Jones***1; Father Flynn **Brían F. O'Byrne***2; Sister James **Heather Goldenhersh***3; Mrs. Muller **Adriane Lenox**

Standbys: Nadia Bowers (Sister James), Caroline Stefanie Clay (Mrs. Muller), Chris McGarry (Father Flynn).

Setting: St. Nicholas Church School in the Bronx. Autumn 1964; a play presented without intermission; originally produced by the Manhattan Theatre Club on November 23, 2004 (see *Theatre World* Volume 61, page 185). 2005 Awards: Pulitzer Prize for Drama ; Tony Awards: Best Play, Leading Actress in a Play (Cherry Jones), Featured Actress in a Play (Adriane Lenox), Director of a Play (Doug Hughes); Outer Critics Circle Awards: Best Play, Leading Actress in a Play (Cherry Jones), Leading Actor in a Play (Brían F. O'Byrne), Director of a Play (Doug Hughes); Drama League Award: Outstanding Production of a Play; Drama Critics Circle Award: Best Play; Drama Desk Awards: Best Play, Leading Actress in a Play (Cherry Jones), Leading Actor in a Play (Brían F. O'Byrne), Featured Actress in a Play (Adriane Lenox), Director of a Play (Doug Hughes); Theatre World Award: Heather Goldenhersh.

Synopsis: Set against the backdrop of a Bronx Catholic school in 1964, *Doubt* is the story of a strong-minded woman faced with a difficult decision. Should she voice concerns about one of her male colleagues even if she's not entirely certain of the truth?

Ron Eldard and Eileen Atkins

*Succeeded by: 1. Eileen Atkins 2. Ron Eldard 3. Jena Malone

HAIRSPRAY

Neil Simon Theatre; First Preview: July 18, 2002; Opening Night: August 15, 2002 (see *Theatre World* Volume 59, page 25); Performances as of May 31, 2006: 1,571

A new musical with book by Mark O'Donnell and Thomas Meehan; music by Marc Shaiman; lyrics by Marc Shaiman and Scott Wittman; based on the 1988 film written and directed by John Waters; Produced by Margo Lion, Adam Epstein the Baruch-Viertel-Routh-Frankel Group, James D. Stern/Douglas L. Meyer, Rick Steiner, Frederic H. Mayerson, SEL and GFO, New Line Cinema, in association with Clear Channel Entertainment, Allan S. Gordon, Elan V. McAllister, Dede Harris, Morton Swinsky, John and Bonnie Osher; Director, Jack O'Brien, Choreography, Jerry Mitchell; Scenery, David Rockwell; Costumes, William Ivey Long; Lighting, Kenneth Posner; Sound, Steve C. Kennedy; Orchestrations, Harold Wheeler, Music Direction, Lon Hoyt, Music Coordinator, John Miller, Assistant Director, Matt Lenz, Associate Choreographer, Michele Lynch; Associate Producers, Rhoda Mayerson, the Aspen Group, Daniel C. Staton; Casting, Bernard Telsey Casting; Production Stage Manager, Steven Beckler; Stage Manager, J. Philip Bassett; Press, Richard Kornberg and Associates, Richard Kornberg, Don Summa, Tom D'Ambrosio, Carrie Friedman; Cast recording: Sony SK 87708.

Opening Night Cast: Tracy Turnblad **Marissa Jaret Winokur***[1]; Corny Collins **Clarke Thorell***[2]; Amber Von Tussle **Laura Bell Bundy***[3]; Brad **Peter Matthew Smith***[4]; Tammy **Hollie Howard***[5]; Fender **John Hill***[6]; Brenda **Jennifer Gambatese***[7]; Sketch **Adam Fleming***[8]; Shelley **Shoshana Bean***[9]; IQ **Todd Michel Smith**; Lou Ann **Katharine Leonard***[10]; Link Larkin **Matthew Morrison***[11]; Prudy Pingleton, Gym Teacher, Matron **Jackie Hoffman***[12]; Edna Turnblad **Harvey Fierstein***[13]; Penny Pingleton **Kerry Butler***[14]; Velma Von Tussle **Linda Hart***[15]; Harriman F. Spritzer, Principal, Mr. Pinky, Guard **Joel Vig***[16]; Wilbur Turnblad **Dick Latessa***[17]; Seaweed J. Stubbs **Corey Reynolds***[18]; Duane **Eric Anthony***[19]; Gilbert **Eric Dysart***[20]; Lorraine **Danielle Lee Greaves***[21]; Thad **Rashad Naylor***[22]; The Dynamites **Kamilah Martin, Judine Richard, Shayna Steele***[23]; Little Inez **Danelle Eugenia Wilson***[24]; Motormouth Maybelle **Mary Bond Davis***[25]

Diana DeGarmo PHOTO BY PAUL KOLNIK

Denizens of Baltimore: Eric Anthony, Shoshana Bean, Eric Dysart, Adam Fleming, Jennifer Gambatese, Danielle Lee Greaves, John Hill, Jackie Hoffman, Hollie Howard, Katharine Leonard, Kamilah Martin, Rashad Naylor, Judine Richard, Peter Matthew Smith, Todd Michel Smith, Shayna Steele, Joel Vig

Swings: Joshua Bergasse, Greg Graham, Brooke Tansley*[26]

Onstage Musicians: Matthew Morrison, guitar; Linda Hart, keyboard; Joel Vig, glockenspiel; Kerry Butler, harmonica

Understudies: Eric Anthony (Seaweed J. Stubbs), Shoshana Bean (Tracy Turnblad, Velma Von Tussle), Eric Dysart (Seaweed J. Stubbs), Adam Fleming (Link Larkin), Jennifer Gambatese (Penny Pingleton), Danielle Lee Greaves (Motormouth Maybelle), David Greenspan (Edna Turnblad, Wilbur Turnblad), Katy Grenfell (Tracy Turnblad), John Hill (Corny Collins, Link Larkin), Jackie Hoffman (Velma Von Tussle), Hollie Howard (Amber Von Tussle, Penny Pingleton), Katharine Leonard (Amber Von Tussle), Kamilah Martin (Motormouth Maybelle), Judine Richárd (Little Inez), Peter Matthew Smith (Corny Collins), Shayna Steele (Little Inez), Joel Vig (Edna Turnblad, Wilbur Turnblad)

Orchestra: Lon Hoyt (Conductor/keyboard), Keith Cotton (Associate conductor/keyboard), Seth Farber (assistant conductor/keyboard), David Spinozza and Peter Calo (guitars), Francisco Centeno (electric bass), Clint de Ganon (drums), Walter "Wally" Usiatynski (percussion), David Mann and Dave Rickenberg (reeds), Danny Cahn (trumpet), Birch Johnson (trombone), Rob Shaw and Carol Pool (violins), Sarah Hewitt Roth (cello)

Musical Numbers: Good Morning Baltimore, The Nicest Kids in Town, Mama I'm a Big Girl Now, I Can Hear the Bells, The Legend of Miss Baltimore Crabs, The Madison, The Nicest Kids in Town (Reprise), Welcome to the '60s, Run and Tell That, Big, Blond and Beautiful, The Big Dollhouse, Good Morning Baltimore, Timeless to Me, Without Love, I Know Where I've Been, Hairspray, Cooties, You Can't Stop the Beat

Setting: 1962. Baltimore. A musical presented in two acts. Winner of Eight 2003 Tony Awards: Best Musical, Best Score, Best Book of a Musical, Best Director of a Musical, Leading Actor in a Musical, Leading Actress in a Musical, Featured Actor in a Musical, Costume Design. Winner of Ten 2003 Drama Desk Awards: Outstanding New Musical, Outstanding Book of a Musical, Outstanding Actor in a Musical, Outstanding Actress in a Musical, Outstanding Featured Actor in a Musical, Outstanding Director of a Musical, Outstanding Orchestrations, Outstanding Lyrics, Outstanding Music, Outstanding Costume Design. 2003 Theatre World Awards: Marissa Jaret Winokur and Jackie Hoffman.

Synopsis: *Hairspray* is the story of Tracy Turnblad, who is going to do whatever it takes to dance her way onto TV's most popular show. Can a big girl with big dreams—and even bigger hair—turn the whole town around?

*Succeeded by: 1. Kathy Brier, Carly Jibson, Marissa Jaret Winokur, Shannon Durig 2. Jonathan Dokuchitz 3. Tracy Jai Edwards, Jordan Ballard, Becky Gulsvig 4. Michael Cunio 5. Lindsay Nichole Chambers 6. Andrew Rannells, Serge Kushnier 7. Cameron Adams, Leslie Goddard 8. Bryan West 9. Leslie Kritzer, Donna Vivino 10. Becky Gulsvig, Anne Warren 11. Richard H. Blake, Andrew Rannells 12. Liz Larsen, Julie Halston 13. Michael McKean, Bruce Vilanch, John Pinette 14. Jennifer Gambatese, Brooke Tansley, Jennifer Gambatese, Tracy Miller, Diana DeGarmo, Caissie Levy 15. Liz Larsen (vacation), Linda Hart, Barbara Walsh, Leah Hocking, Barbara Walsh, Leah Hocking, Liz Larsen, Leah Hocking 16. Jim J Bullock, Kevin Meany, Blake Hammond 17. Peter Scolari (vacation), Todd Susman, Stephen DeRosa 18. Chester Gregory II, Tevin Campbell 19. Tyrick Wiltez Jones 20. Eric L. Christian, Arbender J Robinson 21. Terita R. Redd 22. Tommar Wilson, Rashad Naylor 23. Carla J. Hargrove, Nicole Powell, Candice Marie Woods, Judine Richard Somerville 24. Aja Maria Johnson, Nia Imani Soyemi, Chloe Smith 25. Darlene Love 26. Joe Abraham, Clyde Alves, Denosh Bennett, Gretchen Bieber, Jennie Ford, Leslie Goddard, Michelle Kittrell, Abdul Latif, Michael Longoria, Rusty Mowery, CJay Hardy Philip, Nicole Powell, Willis White.

THE LIGHT IN THE PIAZZA

Vivian Beaumont Theatre; First Preview: March 17, 2005; Opening Night: April 18, 2005 (see *Theatre World* Volume 61, page 71); performances as of May 31, 2006: 471

Lincoln Center Theatre (André Bishop, Artistic Director; Bernard Gersten, Executive Producer) presentation of a new musical with book by Craig Lucas, music and lyrics by Adam Guettel, based on the novel by Elizabeth Spencer; Produced by arrangement with Turner Entertainment Co., owner of the original motion picture "Light in the Piazza." Director, Bartlett Sher; Scenery, Michael Yeargan; Costumes, Catherine Zuber; Lighting, Christopher Akerlind; Sound, Acme Sound Partners; Orchestrations, Ted Sperling and Adam Guettel; Casting, Janet Foster; Stage Manager, Thom Widmann; Musical Theater Associate Producer, Ira Weitzman; General Manager, Adam Siegel; Production Manager, Jeff Hamlin; Director of Development, Hattie K. Jutagir; Director of Marketing, Linda Mason Ross; Company Manager: Matthew Markoff; Associate Company Manager, Josh Lowenthal; Assistant Director, Sarna Lapine; Assistant to Mr. Lucas, Troy Miller; Assistant Stage Manager, Claudia Lynch; Dance Captain, Laura Griffith; Additional Orchestrations, Bruce Coughlin; Music Copyist, Emily Grishman Music Preparation, Katherine Edmonds; Properties, Christopher Schneider; Dialect Coach, Ralph Zito; Hair and Wigs, Jerry Altenburg; Musical Coordinator, Seymour "Red" Press; Poster Art, James McMullan; Advertising, Serino Coyne, Inc.; Press, Philip Rinaldi; Cast recording: Nonesuch Records, 79829-2.

Aaron Lazar and Katie Clark PHOTO BY JOAN MARCUS

Opening Night Cast: Margaret Johnson **Victoria Clark***; Clara Johnson, her daughter **Kelli O'Hara***[1]; Fabrizio Naccarelli **Matthew Morrison***[2]; Signor Naccarelli, Fabrizio's father **Mark Harelik***[3]; Giuseppe Naccarelli, Fabrizio's brother **Michael Berresse**; Franca Naccarelli, Giuseppe's wife **Sarah Uriarte Berry**; Signora Naccarelli, Fabrizio's mother **Patti Cohenour ***; Roy Johnson, Margaret's husband **Beau Gravitte**; Tour Guide **Felicity LaFortune**; Priest **Joseph Siravo**

Ensemble: David Bonanno, David Burnham, Laura Griffith, Prudence Wright Holmes, Jennifer Hughes, Felicity LaFortune, Michel Moinot, Joseph Siravo.

Swings: Glenn Seven Allen, Catherine LaValle*[4]

Understudies: Glenn Seven Allen (Priest), David Bonanno (Giuseppe Naccarelli), David Burnham (Fabrizio Naccarelli), Patti Cohenour (Margaret Johnson), Laura Griffith (Franca Naccarelli), Jennifer Hughes (Clara Johnson), Felicity LaFortune (Signora Naccarelli), Catherine LaValle (Tour Guide), Joseph Siravo (Roy Johnson, Signor Naccarelli).

Orchestra: Ted Sperling (Conductor), Dan Riddle (Associate Conductor, piano, celesta), Christian Hebel (Concertmaster), Matthew Lehmann, Sylvia D'Avanzo, James Tsao, Lisa Matricardi, Katherine Livolsi-Stern (violin), Peter Sachon, Ariane Lallemand (celli), Victoria Drake (harp), Richard Heckman (clarinet/English horn/oboe), Gili Sharett (bassoon), Willard Miller (percussion), Andrew Schwartz (guitar/mandolin).

Musical Numbers: Statues and Stories, The Beauty Is, Il Mondo Era Vuoto, Passeggiata, The Joy You Feel, Dividing Day, Hysteria, Say It Somehow, Aiutami, The Light in the Piazza, Octet, Tirade, Octet (Reprise), The Beauty Is (Reprise), Let's Walk, Love to Me, Fable.

Setting: Florence and Rome in the summer of 1953, with occasional side trips to America; a musical performed in two acts; premiered at Intiman Theatre Company and The Goodman Theatre (Robert Falls, Artistic Director; Roche Schulfer, Executive Director); developed with the assistance of The Sundance Theatre Laboratory; 2005 Awards: Tony Awards: Leading Actress in a Musical (Victoria Clark), Original Score Written for the Theatre (Adam Guettel), Scenic Design of a Musical (Michael Yeargan), Lighting Design of a Musical (Christopher Akerlind), Costume Design of a Musical (Catherine Zuber), Orchestrations (Ted Sperling, Adam Guettel, and Bruce Coughlin); Drama Desk Awards: Actress in a Musical (Victoria Clark), Orchestrations (Ted Sperling, Adam Guettel, and Bruce Coughlin), Scenic Design of a Musical (Michael Yeargan); Outer Critics Circle Awards: Actress in a Musical (Victoria Clark), Lighting Design (Christopher Akerlind).

Synopsis: Margaret and Clara Johnson, a North Carolinian mother and daughter, are traveling through Italy in the summer of 1953, and Clara finds romance with a handsome, high-spirited Florentine, Fabrizio. Margaret's determined efforts to keep the two apart and hide Clara's secret from him and his family are not enough to thwart their true love.

*Succeeded by: 1. Jennifer Hughes (12/6/05), Katie Clark (12/17/05) 2. Aaron Lazar (9/2/05) 3. Chris Sarandon (9/13/05) 4. Adam Overett, Peter Samuel

*Patti Cohenour played Margaret at select Friday evening and Saturday Matinee performances. Diane Sutherland played Signora Naccarelli at those performances.

THE LION KING

New Amsterdam Theatre; First Preview: October 15, 1997; Opening Night: November 13, 1997 (see *Theatre World* Volume 54, page 20); Performances as of May 31, 2006: 3,596

A musical with music by Elton John, lyrics by Tim Rice, additional music and lyrics by Lebo M, Mark Mancina, Jay Rifkin, Julie Taymor and Hans Zimmer, book by Roger Allers and Irene Mecchi adapted from screenplay by Ms. Mecchi, Jonathan Roberts and Linda Woolverton; Produced by Walt Disney Theatrical Productions (Peter Schneider, President; Thomas Schumacher, Executive VP); Director, Julie Taymor; Choreography, Garth Fagan; Orchestrations, Robert Elhai, David Metzger, Bruce Fowler; Music Director, Joseph Church; Scenery, Richard Hudson; Costumes, Julie Taymor; Lighting, Donald Holder; Masks/Puppets, Julie Taymor, Michael Curry; Sound, Tony Meola; Vocal Arrangements/Choral Director, Lebo M; Company Manager, Steven Chaikelson; Stage Manager, Jeff Lee; Press, Boneau/Bryan-Brown, Jackie Green, Cast recording: Walt Disney 60802-7.

Opening Night Cast: Rafiki **Tsidii Le Loka**[1]; Mufasa **Samuel E. Wright**[2]; Sarabi **Gina Breedlove**[3]; Zazu **Geoff Hoyle**[4]; Scar **John Vickery**[5]; Young Simba **Scott Irby-Ranniar**[6]; Young Nala **Kajuana Shuford**[7]; Shenzi **Tracy Nicole Chapman**[8]; Banzai **Stanley Wayne Mathis**[9]; Ed **Kevin Cahoon**[10]; Timon **Max Casella**[11]; Pumbaa **Tom Alan Robbins**; Simba **Jason Raize**[12]; Nala **Heather Headley**[13]

Ensemble Singers: Eugene Barry-Hill, Gina Breedlove, Ntomb'khona Dlamini, Sheila Gibbs, Lindiwe Hlengwa, Christopher Jackson, Vanessa A. Jones, Faca Kulu, Ron Kunene, Anthony Manough, Philip Dorian McAdoo, Sam McKelton, Lebo M, Nandi Morake, Rachel Tecora Tucker[14]

Josh Tower and Company PHOTO BY JOAN MARCUS

Ensemble Dancers: Camille M. Brown, Iresol Cardona, Mark Allan Davis, Lana Gordon, Timothy Hunter, Michael Joy, Aubrey Lynch II, Karine Plantadit-Bageot, Endalyn Taylor-Shellman, Levensky Smith, Ashi K. Smythe, Christine Yasunaga[14]

Understudies/Swings: Kevin Bailey (Scar), Eugene Barry-Hill (Mufasa), Camille M. Brown (Sarabi), Kevin Cahoon (Timon, Zazu), Alberto Cruz Jr. (Young Simba), Sheila Gibbs (Rafiki), Lana Gordon (Shenzi), Lindiwe Hlengwa (Nala, Rafiki), Tim Hunter (Simba), Christopher Jackson (Simba), Vanessa A. Jones (Sarabi, Shenzi), Jennifer Josephs (Young Nala), Sonya Leslie (Nala), Philip Dorian McAdoo (Banzai, Mufasa, Pumbaa), Danny Rutigliano (Pumbaa, Timon, Zazu), Levensky Smith (Banzai), Frank Wright II[15]

Musical Numbers: Circle of Life, Morning Report, I Just Can't Wait to Be King, Chow Down, They Live in You, Be Prepared, Hakuna Matata, One by One, Madness of King Scar, Shadowland, Endless Night, Can You Feel the Love Tonight, King of Pride Rock/Finale

A musical presented in two acts; 1998 Tony Awards: Best Musical, Direction of a Musical (Julie Taymor), Scenic Design (Richard Hudson), Costume Design (Julie Taymor), Lighting Design (Donald Holder), and Choreography (Garth Fagan).

Synopsis: Based on the Disney animated feature film, *The Lion King* tells the story of the epic adventures of a young lion cub named Simba as he struggles to accept the responsibilities of adulthood and his destined role as king.

*Succeeded by: 1. Thuli Dumakude, Sheila Gibbs, Nomvula Dlamini, Tshidi Manye 2. Alton Fitzgerald White 3. Meena T. Jahi, Denise Marie Williams, Meena T. Jahi, Robyn Payne, Jean Michelle Grier 4. Bill Bowers, Robert Dorfman, Tony Freeman, Adam Stein, Jeffrey Binder, Tony Freeman 5. Tom Hewitt, Derek Smith, Patrick Page, Derek Smith, Patrick Page 6. (in alphabetical order) Caleb Archer, Alexio K. Barboza, Mykel Bath, Kai Braithwaite, Jeremy Chu, Aaron D. Conley, Ruben L. Delvalle, Jr., Danny Fetter, Rajonie Hammond, Alexander Mitchell, Ashley Renee Jordan, Justin Martin, David "Dakota" Sanchez, Jarrell J. Singleton 7. (in alphabetical order) Alex de Castro, Kailani M. Coba, Tiana Coles, Zipporah G. Gatling, Natalie Guerrero, Netousha N. Harris, Tra 'Lynn Husbands, Ashley Renee Jordan, Tristin Mays, Jordan Puryear, Imani Parks, Ashley Perry 8. Vanessa S. Jones, Lana Gordon, Marlayna Sims, Bonita J. Hamilton 9. Keith Bennett, Leonard Joseph, Curtis I' Cook, Rodrick Covington, Benjamin Sterling Cannon 10. Jeff Skowron, Jeff Gurner, Timothy Gulan, Thom Christopher Warren, Enrique Segura 11. Danny Rutigliano, John E. Brady, Danny Rutigliano 12. Christopher Jackson, Josh Tower 13. Mary Randle, Heather Headley, Bashirrah Cresswell, Sharon L. Young, Renée Elise Goldsberry, Kissy Simmons 14. Michelle Aguilar Camaya, Sandy Alvarez, Kristina Michelle Bethel, Terron Brooks, LaMae Caparas, E. Clayton Cornelious, Gabriel A. Croom, Bobby Daye, Michelle Dorant, Christopher Freeman, Ian Yuri Gardner, Jean Michelle Grier, Rod Harrelson, Michael A. Henry, Charles Holt, Nikki Long, Marque Lynch, Jr., Brandon Louis Matthieus, Sheryl McCallum, Ray Mercer, S'bu Ngema, Brandon O'Neal, Dawn Noe Pignuola, Jacqueline Rene, Angelo Rivera, Keena Smith, Sophia N. Stephens, L. Steven Taylor, Torya, Kenny Redell Williams, Kyle Wrentz, Felipe Abrigo, Kyle R. Banks, Don Bellamy, Kylin Brady, Eric L. Christian, LaTrisa A. Coleman, Ramón Flowers, Gregory A. King, Nkosi Kress, Lisa Lewis, Ian Vincent McGinnis, Jeremiah Tatum, Ryan Brooke Taylor, Shonte Walker, Steven Evan Washington, Valencia Yearwood, Lindiwe Dlamini, Bongi Duma, Leslie Elliard, Andrea Frierson-Toney, Meena T. Jahi, Keswa, Brian M. Love, Evan Dexter Parke, Cinda RamSeur, Mpume Sikakane, Rema Webb, Leonard Wooldridge, Zulu-Lava 15. Swings: Kyle R. Banks, Sophina Brown, Garland Days, Michelle Dorant, C. Ross Edwards, Ross Edwards, Angelica Edwards Patterson, Christopher Freeman, Ian Yuri Gardner, Rod Harrelson, Jennifer Harrison Newman, Dameka Hayes, Duane Lee Holland, Christine Hollingsworth, Tony James, Dennis Johnston, Cornelius Jones Jr., Erika LaVonn, Abdul Latif, Gary Lewis, Dennis Lue, Anthony Manough, Sinclair Mitchell, Leonora Stapleton, Sophia N. Stephens, Torya. Standbys: Mark Deklin (Pumbaa, Scar), Mel Johnson, Jr. (Mufasa), Jack Koenig (Pumbaa, Scar), Thom Christopher Warren (Pumbaa, Scar, Timon, Zazu). Understudies: Jeff Binder (Scar), John E. Brady (Pumbaa, Timon, Zazu), Kylin Brady (Nala), C.C. Brown (Mufasa, Scar), Eric L. Christian (Simba), Bashirrah Cresswell (Nala), Garland Days (Banzai), Michelle Dorant (Shenzi), Ross Edwards (Shenzi), Angelica Edwards Patterson (Shenzi), Tony Freeman (Scar), Andrea Frierson-Toney (Rafiki), Ian Yuri Gardner (Ed), Lana Gordon (Nala), Jean Michelle Grier (Sarabi), Jeff Gurner (Timon, Zazu), Rod Harrelson (Simba), Michael A. Henry (Mufasa, Scar), Marva Hicks (Rafiki), Timothy Hunter (Ed), Dennis Johnston (Ed, Simba), Cornelius Jones Jr. (Banzai, Ed, Simba), Martin Kildare (Scar), Erika LaVonn (Nala), Brian M. Love (Simba), Anthony Manough (Banzai), Brandon Louis Matthieus (Simba), Sheryl McCallum (Rafiki, Sarabi), Evan Dexter Parke (Mufasa, Scar), Jacqueline Rene (Nala), Enrique Segura (Timon, Zazu), Mpume Sikakane (Rafiki), Jeff Skowron (Timon, Zazu), Sophia N. Stephens (Nala, Shenzi), L. Steven Taylor (Mufasa), Torya (Sarabi), Rick Wasserman (Pumbaa, Timon, Zazu), Rema Webb (Nala, Rafiki, Shenzi), Kenny Redell Williams (Banzai), Leonard Wooldridge (Ed), Frank Wright II (Mufasa).

MAMMA MIA!

Cadillac Winter Garden Theatre; First Preview: October 5, 2001: Opening Night: October 18, 2001 (see *Theatre World* Volume 58, page 27); Performances as of May 31, 2006: 1,934

A new musical with book by Catherine Johnson, music, lyrics, and orchestrations by Benny Andersson, Björn Ulvaeus, some songs with Stig Anderson; Produced by Judy Craymer, Richard East and Björn Ulvaeus, For Littlestar in Association with Universal; Director, Phyllida Lloyd; Scenery and Costumes, Mark Thompson; Lighting, Howard Harrison; Sound, Andrew Bruce, Bobby Aitken; Wigs, Paul Huntley Choreography, Anthony Van Laast; Musical Supervision/Orchestrations, Martin Koch; Musical Direction, David Holcenberg; Musical Coordination, Michael Keller; Associate Director, Robert McQueen; Associate Choreographer, Nichola Treherne; Technical Supervisor, Arthur Siccardi; Production Supervisor, Tom Capps; General Manager, Nina Lannan & Associates; Company Manager, Devin M. Keudell; Stage Managers, Sherry Cohen, Dean R. Greer; Dance Captain, Janet Rothermel; Casting, Tara Rubin; Press, Boneau/Bryan-Brown, Steven Padla, Jackie Green, Karalee Dawn; Original London Cast recording: Polydor 543 115 2.

Opening Night Cast: Sophie Sheridan **Tina Maddigan**[*1]; Ali **Sara Inbar**[*2]; Lisa **Tonya Doran**[*3]; Tanya **Karen Mason**[*4]; Rosie **Judy Kaye**[*5]; Donna Sheridan **Louise Pitre**[*6]; Sky **Joe Machota**[*7]; Pepper **Mark Price**[*8]; Eddie **Michael Benjamin Washington**[*9]; Harry Bright **Dean Nolan**[*10]; Bill Austin **Ken Marks**[*11]; Sam Carmicheal **David W. Keeley**[*12]; Father Alexandrios **Bill Carmichael**[*13]

Ensemble: Meredith Akins, Leslie Alexander, Stephan Alexander, Kim-E J. Balmilero, Robin Baxter, Brent Black, Tony Carlin, Bill Carmichael, Meghann Dreyfuss, Somer Lee Graham, Kristin McDonald, Adam Monley, Chris Prinzo, Peter Matthew Smith, Yuka Takara, Marsha Waterbury[*14]

Swings: Barrett Foa, Jon-Erik Goldberg, Hollie Howard, Janet Rothermel[*15]

Understudies: Meredith Akins (Lisa), Leslie Alexander (Tanya), Stephan Alexander (Pepper), Kim-E J. Balmilero (Ali), Robin Baxter (Rosie), Brent Black (Bill Austin, Sam Carmicheal), Tony Carlin (Bill Austin, Harry Bright, Sam Carmicheal), Bill Carmichael (Harry Bright), Meghann Dreyfuss (Sophie Sheridan), Jon-Erik Goldberg (Pepper), Somer Lee Graham (Sophie Sheridan), Kristin McDonald (Ali), Adam Monley (Sky), Chris Prinzo (Eddie), Peter Matthew Smith (Eddie, Sky), Yuka Takara (Lisa), Marsha Waterbury (Donna Sheridan, Rosie, Tanya)

Ben Gettinger and Judy McLane PHOTOS BY JOAN MARCUS

Orchestra: David Holcenberg (Conductor, keyboard), Rob Preuss (Associate Conductor, keyboard 3), Steve Marzullo (keyboard 2), Myles Chase (keyboard 4), Doug Quinn (guitar 1), Jeff Campbell (guitar 2), Paul Adamy (bass), Gary Tillman (drums), David Nyberg (percussion)

Musical Numbers: Chiquitita, Dancing Queen, Does Your Mother Know?, Gimme! Gimmie! Gimmie!, Honey, Honey, I Do, I Do, I Do, I Do, I Have a Dream, Knowing Me Knowing You, Lay All Your Love on Me, Mamma Mia, Money Money Money, One of Us, Our Last Summer, Slipping Through My Fingers, S.O.S., Super Trouper, Take a Chance on Me, Thank You For the Music, The Name of the Game, The Winner Takes All, Under Attack, Voulez-Vous

Setting: A wedding weekend. A tiny Greek island. A musical presented in two acts.

Synopsis: Songs of the 1970s group ABBA strung together in a story of baby boomer wistfulness and a girl's search for her unknown father.

*Succeeded by: 1. Jenny Fellner, Sara Kramer, Carey Anderson 2.Veronica J. Kuehn, Rebecca Kasper, Joi Danielle Price, Olivia Oguma 3. Keisha T. Fraser, Samantha Eggers 4. Jeanine Morick, Tamara Bernier, Judy McLane 5. Harriett D. Foy, Liz McCartney, Robin Baxter, Olga Merediz 6. Dee Hoty, Carolee Carmello, Carol Linnea Johnson, Michele Pawk, Laura Mufson, Michelle Pawk, Corinne Melancon 7. Aaron Stanton, Andy Kelso 8. Jason Weston, Chris Prinzo, Ben Gettinger 9. Michael James Scott, Albert Guerzon, Raymond J. Lee 10. Richard Binsley, Michael Winther, David Beach 11. Adam LeFevre, Mark L. Montgomery, Bryan Scott Johnson 12. John Hillner, David W. Keeley, John Hillner, Daniel McDonald, Peter Kelly Gaudreault, John Dossett 13. Timothy Booth, Bryan Scott Johnson 14. Timothy Booth, Jen Burleigh-Bentz, Samantha Eggers, Lori Haley Fox, Amber Kryzs, Erica Mansfield, Whitney Osentoski, Angela Ara Brown, David Ayers, Isaac Calpito, Christopher Carl, Carlos L. Encinias, Shakiem Evans, Kelly Fletcher, Tom Galantich, Kurt Andrew Hansen, Bryan Scott Johnson, Carol Linnea Johnson, Corinne Melançon, Steve Morgan, Jeanine Morick, Jesse Nager, Megan Osterhaus, Joi Danielle Price, Sandy Rosenberg, Gerard Salvador, Patrick Sarb, Darryl Semira, Ryan-Michael Shaw, Britt Shubow, Collette Simmons, Natasha Tabandera, Mackenzie Thomas, Leah Zepel 15. Jerad Bortz, Rachel Bress, Lanene Charters, Joanna Chozen, Matthew Farver, Tyler Maynard, Ryan Sander, Britt Shubow

The current cast of *Mamma Mia!*

MONTY PYTHON'S SPAMALOT

Shubert Theatre; First Preview: February 14, 2004; Opening Night: March 17, 2005 (see *Theatre World* Volume 61, page 55); Performances as of May 31, 2006: 504

A new with book and lyrics by Eric Idle, music by John DuPrez and Eric Idle; based on the screenplay of the motion picture "Monty Python and the Holy Grail" written by Eric Idle, John Cleese, Terry Gilliam, Terry Jones, Michael Palin and Graham Chapman; Produced by Boyett Ostar Productions, The Shubert Organization (Gerald Schoenfeld: Chairman; Philip J. Smith: President; Robert E. Wankel: Executive Vice President), Arielle Tepper, Stephanie McClelland, Lawrence Horowitz, Élan V. McAllister, Allan S. Gordon, Independent Presenters Network, Roy Furman, GRS Associates, JAM Theatricals, TGA Entertainment, Ltd. and Clear Channel Entertainment; Associate Producer, Randi Grossman and Tisch/Avnet Financial; Director, Mike Nichols; Choreography, Casey Nicholaw; Scenery and Costumes, Tim Hatley; Lighting, Hugh Vanstone; Sound, Acme Sound Partners; Hair and Wigs, David Brian Brown; Special Effects, Gregory Meeh; Projections, Elaine J. McCarthy; Music Director/Vocal Arrangements, Todd Ellison; Orchestrations, Larry Hochman; Music Arrangements, Glen Kelly; Music Coordinator, Michael Keller; Casting, Tara Rubin; Associate Director/Production Stage Manager, Peter Lawrence; Associate Choreography, Darlene Wilson; Production Management, Gene O'Donovan; General Management, 101 Productions, Ltd. (Jeff Wilson, Wendy Orshan; Dave Auster); Marketing, HHC Marketing; Company Manager, Elie Lindaue; Production Management, Aurora Productions, Inc. (Gene O'Donovan, W. Benjamin Heller II, Elise Hanley, Bethany Weinstein); Fight Director, David DeBesse; Make-up Designer, Joseph A. Campayno; Stage Managers, Mahlon Kruse, Jim Woolley and Rachel Wolff; Assistant Company Manager, Nathan Gehan; Dance Captain, Pamela Remler and Scott Taylor; Fight Captain, Greg Reuter; Vocal Coach, Kate Wilson; Assistant to Mike Nichols, Jane Levy; Associate Scenery, Paul Weimer; Assistant Scenery Raul Abrego and Derek Stenborg; UK Assistant Designer, Andy Edwards; Associate Costumes, Scott Traugott; Costume Associate, Ilona Somogyi; Costume Assistants, Cory Ching and Robert J. Martin; Associate Lighting, Philip Rosenberg; Magic Consultant, Marshall Magoon Puppetry Consultant, Michael Curry; Associate Special Effects, Vivien Leone; Assistant Lighting, John Viesta;

Asmeret Ghebremichael, Brad Bradley, Greg Reuter, Martin Moran, Christian Borle
PHOTO BY JOAN MARCUS

Moving Light Programmer, Laura Frank; Assistant Sound, Sten Severson; Associate Projections, Gareth Smith; Assistant Projections, Ariel Sachter-Zeltzer and Jacob Daniel Pinholster; Music Copying, Emily Grishman Music Preparation; Production Associate, Lisa Gilbar; Production Assistants, Chad Lewis and Mary Kathryn Flynt; Advertising, Serino Coyne, Inc. Press, Boneau/Bryan-Brown; Cast recording: Decca Broadway, B0004265-02.

Opening Night Cast: Historian/Not Dead Fred/French Guard/Minstrel/Prince Herbert **Christian Borle**; Mayor/Patsy/Guard 2 **Michael McGrath**; King Arthur **Tim Curry***1; Sir Robin/Guard 1/Brother Maynard **David Hyde Pierce***2; Sir Lancelot/The French Taunter/Knight of Ni/Tim the Enchanter **Hank Azaria***3; Sir Dennis Galahad/The Black Knight/Prince Herbert's Father **Christopher Sieber***4; Dennis' Mother/Sir Bedevere Concorde **Steve Rosen**; The Lady of the Lake **Sara Ramirez***5; Sir Not Appearing **Kevin Covert**; God **John Cleese**; French Guards **Thomas Cannizzaro, Greg Reuter**; Minstrels **Brad Bradley, Emily Hsu, Greg Reuter**; Sir Bors **Brad Bradley**

Ensemble: Brad Bradley, Thomas Cannizzaro, Kevin Covert, Jennifer Frankel, Lisa Gajda, Jenny Hill, Emily Hsu, Abbey O'Brien, Ariel Reid, Greg Reuter, Brian Shepard, Scott Taylor*6

Standbys: John Bolton (Arthur, Lancelot, Galahad, Robin, Bedevere), James Ludwig (Robin, Bedevere, Patsy, Historian, Not Dead Fred, Prince Herbert, Lancelot), Darlene Wilson (Lady of the Lake).*7

Swings: Pamela Remler, Rick Spans*8

Understudies: Brad Bradley, Thomas Cannizzaro, Emily Hsu*9, Greg Reuter, Brian Shepard

Orchestra: Todd Ellison (Conductor), Ethyl Will (Associate Conductor, keyboard), Ann Labin (Concertmaster), Maura Giannini and Ming Yeh (violin), Richard Brice (viola), Diane Barere (cello), Ken Dybisz and Alden Banta (reeds), John Chudoba (lead trumpet), Anthony Gorruso (trumpet), Mark Patterson (trombone), Zohar Schondorf (French horn), Antony Geralis (keyboard 2), Scott Kuney (guitars), Dave Kuhn (bass), Sean McDaniel (drums), Dave Mancuso (percussion).

Musical Numbers: Fisch Schlapping Song, King Arthur's Song, I Am Not Dead Yet, Come With Me, The Song That Goes Like This, All for One, Knights of the Round Table, The Song That Goes Like This (Reprise), Find Your Grail, Run Away, Always Look on the Bright Side of Life, Brave Sir Robin, You Won't Succeed on Broadway, The Diva's Lament, Where Are You?, Here Are You, His Name Is Lancelot, I'm All Alone, The Song That Goes Like This (Reprise), The Holy Grail, Find Your Grail Finale—Medley.

A musical presented in two acts; 2005 Awards: Tony Awards: Best Musical, Direction of a Musical (Mike Nichols), Featured Actress in a Musical (Sara Ramirez); Drama Desk Awards: Outstanding Musical Lyrics (Eric Idle), Costume Design (Tim Hatley); Outer Critics Circle Awards: Best Musical, Direction of a Musical (Mike Nichols), Featured Actress in a Musical (Sara Ramirez), Costume Design (Tim Hatley); Theatre World Award: Hank Azaria.

Synopsis: Telling the legendary tale of King Arthur and the Knights of the Round Table, and their quest for the Holy Grail, *Monty Python's Spamalot* features a chorus line of dancing divas and knights, flatulent Frenchmen, killer rabbits, and one legless knight.

*Succeeded by: 1. (John Bolton for Tim Curry's vacation 7/22/05–8/7/05); Simon Russell Beale (12/20/05), Harry Groener (4/25/06) 2. Martin Moran (4/4/06) 3. Alan Tudyk (7/7/05), Hank Azaria (12/5/05), Steve Kazee (4/4/06) 4. Lewis Cleale (7/5/06) 5. Lauren Kennedy (12/20/05) 6. Asmeret Ghebremichael, Kristie Kerwin 7. Beth Johnson, Lee A. Wilkins 8. Rosena M. Hill (Lady of the Lake), Drew McVety (Arthur, Bedevere, Galahad, Lancelot, Robin) 9. Asmeret Ghebremichael

THE PHANTOM OF THE OPERA

Majestic Theatre; First Preview: January 9, 1988. Opening Night: January 26, 1988 (see *Theatre World* Volume 44, page 20); Performances as of May 31, 2006: 7,648

A musical with music by Andrew Lloyd Webber, lyrics by Charles Hart; additional lyrics and book by Richard Stilgoe; book by Mr. Lloyd Webber, based on the novel by Gaston Leroux; Produced by Cameron Mackintosh and The Really Useful Theatre Co.; Director, Harold Prince; Musical Staging/Choreography, Gillian Lynne; Orchestrations, David Cullen, Mr. Lloyd Webber; Design, Maria Björnson; Lighting, Andrew Bridge; Sound, Martin Levan; Musical Director and Supervisor, David Caddick; Casting, Johnson-Liff & Zerman; General Manager, Alan Wasser; Company Manager, Michael Gill; Stage Managers, Steve McCorkle, Bethe Ward, Richard Hester, Barbara-Mae Phillips; Press, The Publicity Office, Michael Borowski, Merle Frimark, Marc Thibodeau; Original London Cast recording: Polydor 831273.

Opening Night Cast: The Phantom of the Opera **Michael Crawford**[*1]; Christine Daae **Sarah Brightman**[*2]; Christine Daae (alt.) **Patti Cohenour**[*3]; Raoul, Vicomte de Chagny **Steve Barton**[*4]; Carlotta Giudicelli **Judy Kaye**[*5]; Monsieur Andre **Cris Groenendaal**[*6]; Monsieur Firmin **Nicholas Wyman**[*7]; Madame Giry **Leila Martin**[*8]; Ubaldo Piangi **David Romano**[*9]; Meg Giry **Elisa Heinsohn**[*10]; Monsieur Reyer **Peter Kevoian**[*11]; Auctioneer **Richard Warren Pugh**[*12]; Porter/Marksman **Jeff Keller**[*13]; Monsieur Lefevre **Kenneth H. Waller**[*14]; Joseph Buquet **Philip Steele**[*15]; Don Attilio/Passarino **George Lee Andrews**[*16]; Slave Master **Luis Perez**[*17]; Solo Dancer/Flunky/Stagehand **Barry McNabb**[*18]; Hairdresser/Marksman/Policeman **Charles Rule**[*19]; Page (Don Juan) **Olga Talyn**[*20]; Porter/Fireman **William Scott Brown**[*21]; Page (Don Juan)/Spanish Lady **Candace Rogers-Adler**[*22]; Wardrobe Mistress/Confidante **Mary Leigh Stahl**[*23]; Princess **Rebecca Luker**[*24]; Madame Firmin **Beth McVey**[*25]; Innkeeper's Wife **Jan Horvath**[*26]; Ballet Chorus of the Opera Populaire **Irene Cho**, **Nicole Fosse**, **Lisa Lockwood**, **Lori MacPherson**, **Dodie Pettit**, **Catherine Ulissey**[*27]; Ballet Swing **Denny Berry**[*28]

Swings Frank Mastrone, Alba Quezada[*29]

Understudies: George Lee Andrews (Monsieur André, Monsieur Firmin), William Scott Brown (Ubaldo Piangi), Cris Groenendaal (Raoul), Jan Horvath (Carlotta Guidicelli), Jeff Keller (Phantom of the Opera), Peter Kevoian (Monsieur André, Monsieur Firmin), Rebecca Luker (Christine Daaé), Barry McNabb (Slave Master), Beth McVey (Carlotta Guidicelli), Dodie Pettit (Meg Giry), Richard Warren Pugh (Ubaldo Piangi), Mary Leigh Stahl (Madame Giry), Olga Talyn (Madame Giry), Catherine Ulissey (Meg Giry)

Musical Numbers: Think of Me, Angel of Music, Little Lotte/The Mirror, Phantom of the Opera, Music of the Night, I Remember/Stranger Than You Dreamt It, Magical Lasso, Notes/Prima Donna, Poor Fool He Makes Me Laugh, Why Have You Brought Me Here?/Raoul I've Been There, All I Ask of You, Masquerade/Why So Silent?, Twisted Every Way, Wishing You Were Somehow Here Again, Wandering Child/Bravo Bravo, Point of No Return, Down Once More/Track Down This Murderer, Finale

The complete current cast of the *The Phantom of the Opera* which played performance #7,486 on January 9, 2006, breaking the record held by *Cats* to become the longest-running show in Broadway history. Included in the center of the front row are stars Howard McGillin, Sandra Joseph and Tim Martin Gleason.

Setting: In and around the Paris Opera House, 1881–1911. A musical presented in two acts with nineteen scenes and a prologue. Winner of 1988 Tony Awards for Best Musical, Leading Actor in a Musical, Featured Actress in a Musical, Direction of a Musical, Scenic Design, and Lighting Design.

Synopsis: A disfigured musical genius haunts the catacombs beneath the Paris Opera and exerts strange control over a lovely young soprano.

On January 9, 2006, *Phantom of the Opera* played its 7,486th performance to become Broadway's longest running musical, breaking the record previously held by *Cats*. The occasion was marked by assemblies of past actors who have portrayed the roles of "Christine" and "The Phantom" and speeches by some members of the creative team, including composer Andrew Lloyd Webber, director Hal Prince, choreographer Gillian Lynne, and producer Cameron Macintosh.

Sandra Joseph and Howard McGillin

Succeeded by: 1. Timothy Nolen, Cris Groenendaal, Steve Barton, Kevin Gray, Mark Jacoby, Marcus Lovett, Davis Gaines, Thomas James O'Leary, Howard McGillin, Hugh Panaro, Brad Little, Howard McGillin, Hugh Panaro, Howard McGillin, Hugh Panaro, Howard McGillin 2. Patti Cohenour, Rebecca Luker, Dale Kirsten, Karen Culliver, Mary D'Arcy, Tracy Shane, Adrienne McEwan, Sarah Pfisterer, Sandra Joseph, Lisa Vroman, Sandra Joseph, Rebecca Pitcher 3. Katharine Buffaloe, Luann Aronson, Laurie Gayle Stephenson, Adrienne McEwan, Teri Bibb, Sarah Pfisterer, Adrienne McEwan, Lisa Vroman, Adrienne McEwan, Julie Hanson, Rebecca Pitcher, Jennifer Hope Wills 4. Kevin Gray, Davis Gaines, Hugh Panaro, Ciaran Sheehan, Brad Little, Gary Mauer, Jim Weitzer, Michael Shawn Lewis, John Cudia, Tim Martin Gleason, Michael Shawn Lewis 5. Marilyn Caskey, Elana Jeanne Batman, Geena Jeffries, Liz McCartney, Patricia Hurd, Kelly Ellenwood, Leigh Munro, Julie Schmidt, Patricia Phillips, Anne Runolfsson 6. Jeff Keller, George Lee Andrews 7. George Lee Andrews, Jeff Keller, Paul Harmon, Kenneth Kantor, Timothy Jerome ,David Cryer 8. Kristina Marie Guiguet, Leila Martin, Sally Williams, Rebecca Judd, Marilyn Caskey 9. John Horton Murray, Gary Rideout, Nicholas F. Saverine, John McMaster, Patrick Jones, David Gaschen, Erick Bukley, Frederic Heringes, Larry Wayne Morbitt, Roland Rusinek 10. Catherine Ulissey, Tener Brown, Geralyn Del Corso, Joelle Gates, Heather McFadden, Kara Klein, Heather McFadden 11. Frank Mastrone, Gary Barker, Thomas James O'Leary, Ted Kegan, Richard Poole 12. Scott Mikita, Carrington Vilmont 13. David Cleveland, Gary Lindemann, Maurizio Corbino, John Schroeder,, Michael Shawn Lewis, Stephen R. Buntrock, Carrington Vilmont 14. John Jellison 15. Joe Gustern, Chris Huddleston, Richard Warren Pugh 16. Thomas Sandri, Peter Atherton, (roles split) Craig A. Benham/Thomas Sandri, John Kuether/ Thomas Sandri, Scott Watanabe, Gregory Emanuel Rahming, Kenneth Kantor/Carrington Vilmont 17. David Loring, Thomas Terry, Paul B. Sadler, Jr., Daniel Rychlec, Wesley Robinson, Jack Hayes, Eric Otte, David A. Scamardo, John J. Todd, Daniel Rychlec 18. Jeff Siebert, (roles split) Wesley Robinson/Thomas Terry, Paul Sadler Jr./Jack Hayes, Gary Giffune, Shaun R. Parry/Richard Toda, Cornel Crabtree/Jack Hayes 19. Stacey Robinson, Paul Laureano, Thomas Sandri, (roles split) Gary Lindemann/Thomas Sandri, John Schroeder, Michael Shawn Lewis, Scott Watanabe, Carrington Vilmont,, Stephen R. Buntrock 20. Patrice Pickering, Sharon Wheatley 21. Maurizio Corbino, John Jellison, Torrance Blaisdell, Stephen R. Buntrock, Aaron Lazar, Scott Mikita, John Wasiniak 22. Rhonda Dillon, Elana Jeanne Batman, Diane Ketchie, Marci DeGonge-Manfredi, Wren Marie Harrington 23. Janet Saia 24. Raissa Katona, Elizabeth Southard, Kimilee Bryant, Virginia Croskery, Marie Danvers, Susan Facer, Megan Starr-Levitt, Rebecca Pitcher Julie Hanson, Susan Owen 25. Dawn Leigh Stone, Melody Johnson, Patty Goble, Melody Rubie 26. Wysandria Woolsey, Lorian Stein, Rebecca Eichenberger, Teresa Eldh, Johanna Wiseman, Megan Starr-Levitt, Wren Marie Harrington 27. Tener Brown, Alina Hernandez, Natasha MacAller, Tania Philip, Kate Solmssen, Christine Spizzo, Harriet M. Clark, Cherylyn Jones, Emily Addona, Marisa Cerevis, Elizabeth Nackley, Teresa DeRose, Nina Goldman, Erin Brooke Reiter, Katerine Wray, Annemarie Lucania, Dara Adler, Deanne Albert, Polly Baird, Victoria Born, Geralyn Del Corso, Charlene Gehm, Susan Gladstone, Diana Gonzalez, Careen Hobart, Anita Intrieri, Susannah Israel, Leslie Judge, Kara Klein, Laurie LeBlanc, Wendi Lees Smart, Sabra Lewis, Gianna Loungway, Laura Martin, Heather McFadden, Jessica Radetsky, Susan Russell, Carly Blake Sebouhian, Kitty Skillman Hilsobeck, Dana Stackpole, Joan Tsao, Dianna Warren 28. Lori MacPherson, Susan Gladstone, Laurie LeBlanc, Harriet Clark 29. Keith Buterbaugh, Paul Laureano, James Romick, Suzanne Ishee, David Cleveland, Laurie Gayle Stevenson, Matthew R. Jones, Linda Poser, Jim Weitzer, Susan Russell, DC Anderson, Michael Babin, D.B. Bonds, Amick Byram, Marie Danvers, John Dewar, Louise Edeiken, Ray Gabbard, Michael Gerhart, Leslie Giammanco, Brad Little, Gary Mauer, Michael McCoy, Scott Mikita, Brian Noonan, Grant Norman, Fred Rose, Janet Saia, Julie Schmidt, Sharon Wheatley

Tim Jerome, George Lee Andrews, Anne Runolfsson

THE PRODUCERS

St. James Theatre; First Preview: March 21, 2001; Opening Night: Thursday, April 19, 2001 (see *Theatre World* Volume 57, page 40); Performances as of May 31, 2006: 2,129

A new musical with music and lyrics by Mel Brooks, book by Mel Brooks and Thomas Meehan; based on the 1967 film of the same name, written and directed by Mel Brooks. Produced by Rocco Landesman, SFX Theatrical Group, The Frankel-Baruch-Viertel-Routh Group, Bob and Harvey Weinstein, Rick Steiner, Robert F.X. Sillerman and Mel Brooks, in association with James D. Stern/Douglas L. Meyer; Director and Choreography, Susan Stroman; Musical Director and Vocal Arrangements, Patrick S. Brady; Musical Arrangements/Supervision, Glen Kelly; Orchestrations, Douglas Besterman, Larry Blank (uncredited); Set, Robin Wagner; Costumes, William Ivey Long; Lighting, Peter Kaczorowski; Sound, Steve Canyon Kennedy; Hair/Wigs, Paul Huntley; General Manager, Richard Frankel/Laura Green; Company Manager, Kathy Lowe; Production Stage Manager, Steven Zweigbaum; Stage Manager, Ira Mont; Cast recording, Sony; Casting, Johnson-Liff Associates; Advertising, Serino Coyne, Inc.; Press, John Barlow–Michael Hartman/Bill Coyle, Shellie Schovanec. Cast recording: Sony SK 89646.

Opening Night Cast: The Usherettes **Bryn Dowling, Jennifer Smith***1; Max Bialystock **Nathan Lane***2; Leo Bloom **Matthew Broderick***3; Hold-me Touch-me **Madeleine Doherty***4; Mr. Marks **Ray Wills***5; Franz Liebkind **Brad Oscar***6; Carmen Ghia **Roger Bart***7; Roger De Bris **Gary Beach***8; Bryan; Judge; Jack Lepidus **Peter Marinos**; Scott; Guard; Donald Dinsmore **Jeffry Denman***9; Ulla **Cady Huffman***10; Lick-me Bite-me **Jennifer Smith***11; Shirley; Kiss-me Feel-me; Jury Foreman **Kathy Fitzgerald***12; Kevin; Jason Green; Trustee **Ray Wills***5; Lead Tenor **Eric Gunhus**; O'Rourke; Baliff **Abe Sylvia***13; O'Riley **Matt Loehr***14; O'Houlihan **Robert H. Fowler***15

John Treacy Egan and the Cast of *The Producers*

Hunter Foster, John Treacy Egan, Gary Beach, Jai Rodriguez PHOTOS BY PAUL KOLNIK

Ensemble: Jeffry Denman, Madeleine Doherty, Bryn Dowling, Kathy Fitzgerald, Robert H. Fowler, Ida Gilliams, Eric Gunhus, Kimberly Hester, Naomi Kakuk, Matt Loehr, Peter Marinos, Angie L. Schworer, Jennifer Smith, Abe Sylvia, Tracy Terstriep, Ray Wills*16

Understudies: Jim Borstelmann (Franz Liebkind, Roger De Bris); Jeffry Denman (Franz Liebkind, Leo Bloom); Ida Gilliams, Angie L. Schworer (Ulla); Jamie LaVerdiere (Carmen Ghia, Leo Bloom); Brad Musgrove (Carmen Ghia, Roger De Bris); Brad Oscar (Max Bialystock, Roger De Bris); Ray Wills (Max Bialystock)

Swings: Jim Borstelmann, Adrienne Gibbons, Jamie LaVerdiere, Brad Musgrove, Christina Marie Norrup

Musical Numbers: Opening Night, The King of Broadway, We Can Do It, I Wanna Be a Producer, In Old Bavaria, Der Guten Tag Hop Clop, Keep It Gay, When You Got It Flaunt It, Along Came Bialy, Act One Finale, That Face, Haben Sie Gehoert das Deutsche Band?, You Never Say "Good Luck" On Opening Night, Springtime for Hitler, Where Did We Go Right?, Betrayed, 'Til Him, Prisoners of Love, Leo and Max, Goodbye!

Setting: New York City, 1959; a musical comedy presented in two acts; 2001 Tony Awards: Best Musical, Score of a Musical, Book of a Musical, Actor in a Musical (Nathan Lane), Featured Actor in a Musical (Gary Beach), Featured Actress in a Musical (Cady Huffman), Director of a Musical, Choreography, Sets, Costumes, Lighting, Orchestrations.

Synopsis: A theatrical producer and his accountant hatch a surefire scheme to make money: raise more cash than you need for a surefire Broadway flop entitled *Springtime for Hitler*. Adapted from the 1968 film written by Mel Brooks, *The Producers* is the most awarded show in Broadway history, and a film version of the musical was made in 2005 featuring many of the original cast members, and directed by Susan Stroman.

*Succeeded by: 1. Jennifer Clippinger, Courtney Young, Christina Marie Norrup, Ashley Yeater 2. Henry Goodman, Brad Oscar, Lewis J. Stadlen, Fred Applegate, Nathan Lane, Brad Oscar, John Treacy Egan, Richard Kind, John Treacy Egan 3. Steven Weber, Roger Bart, Don Stephenson, Matthew Broderick, Roger Bart, Hunter Foster, Alan Ruck, Roger Bart, Hunter Foster, Roger Bart 4. Lisa Rothauser, Madeleine Doherty 5. Mark Lotito, Kevin Ligon 6. Jim Borstelmann, John Treacy Egan, Peter Samuel, John Treacy Egan, Bill Nolte 7. Sam Harris, Brad Musgrove, Roger Bart, Brooks Ashmankas, Jai Rodriguez 8. John Treacy Egan, Gary Beach, Jonathan Freeman, Gary Beach 9. Jim Borstelmann 10. Sarah Cornell, Angie L. Schworer 11. Christina Marie Norrup 12. Pamela Dayton, Kathy Fitzgerald 13. James Gray, Mike McGowan, Jason Patrick Sands, Will Taylor 14. Justin Bohon, Chris Holly, Chris Klink 15. Andre Ward, Robert H. Fowler 16. Jennifer Paige Chambers, Jennifer Clippinger, Ida Leigh Curtis, Robert H. Fowler, James Gray, Chris Holly, Shauna Hoskin, Kimberly Jones, Charley Izabella King, Renée Klapmeyer, Chris Klink, Kevin Ligon, Mark Lotito, Melissa Rae Mahon, Mike McGowan, Christina Marie Norrup, Jessica Perrizo, Lisa Rothauser, Jason Patrick Sands, Jenny-Lynn Suckling, Andre Ward, Ashley Yeater, Courtney Young

RENT

Nederlander Theatre; First Preview: April 16, 1996; Opening Night: April 29, 1996 (see *Theatre World* Volume 52, page 58); Performances as of May 31, 2006: 4,211

A musical with book, music, and lyrics by Jonathan Larson; Produced by Jeffrey Seller, Kevin McCollum, Allan S. Gordon, and New York Theatre Workshop; Director, Michael Greif; Arrangements, Steve Skinner; Musical Supervision and Additional Arrangements, Tim Weill; Choreography, Marlies Yearby; Original Concept and Additional Lyrics, Billy Aronson; Scenery, Paul Clay; Costumes, Angela Wendt; Lighting, Blake Burba; Sound, Kurt Fischer; Wig, Hair and Make-up, David Santana; Film, Tony Gerber; General Management, Emanuel Azenberg, John Corker; Company Manager, Brig Berney; Production Stage Manager, John Vivian; Stage Manager, Crystal Huntington; Dramaturg, Lynn M. Thompson, Production Coordinator, Susan White; Technical Supervision, Unitech Productions, Inc; Advertising, Serino Coyne, Inc.; Press, Richard Kornberg, Don Summa, Ian Rand; Cast recording: Dreamworks 50003.

Opening Night Cast: Roger Davis **Adam Pascal**[*1]; Mark Cohen **Anthony Rapp**[*2]; Tom Collins **Jesse L. Martin**[*3]; Benjamin Coffin III **Taye Diggs**[*4]; Joanne Jefferson **Fredi Walker**[*5]; Angel Schunard **Wilson Jermaine Heredia**[*6]; Mimi Marquez **Daphne Rubin-Vega**[*7]; Maureen Johnson **Idina Menzel**[*8]; Mark's Mom/Alison/Others **Kristen Lee Kelly**[*9]; Christmas Caroler/Mr. Jefferson/Pastor/Others **Byron Utley**[*10]; Mrs. Jefferson/Woman with Bags/Others **Gwen Stewart**[*11]; Gordon/The Man/Mr. Grey/Others **Timothy Britten Parker**[*12]; Steve/Man with Squeegee/Waiter/Others **Gilles Chiasson**[*13]; Paul/Cop/Others **Rodney Hicks**[*14]; Alexi Darling/Roger's Mom/Others **Aiko Nakasone**[*15]

Swings: Yassmin Alers, Darius de Haas, Shelley Dickinson, David Driver, Mark Setlock, Simone[*16]

Understudies: Yassmin Alers (Maureen Johnson, Mimi Marquez), Gilles Chiasson (Mark Cohen, Roger Davis), Darius de Haas (Angel Schunard, Benjamin Coffin III, Tom Collins), Shelley Dickinson (Joanne Jefferson), David Driver (Mark Cohen, Roger Davis), Rodney Hicks (Benjamin Coffin III), Kristen Lee Kelly (Maureen Johnson), Mark Setlock (Angel Schunard), Simone (Joanne Jefferson, Mimi Marquez), Byron Utley (Tom Collins)[*17]

Musical Numbers: Tune Up, Voice Mail (#1-#5), Rent, You Okay Honey?, One Song Glory, Light My Candle, Today 4 U, You'll See, Tango: Maureen, Life Support, Out Tonight, Another Day, Will I?, On the Street, Santa Fe, We're Okay, I'll Cover You, Christmas Bells, Over the Moon, La Vie Boheme/I Should Tell You, Seasons of Love, Happy New Year, Take Me or Leave Me, Without You, Contact, Halloween, Goodbye Love, What You Own, Finale/Your Eyes

Musicians: Tim Weil (Conductor/keyboards), Steve Mack (bass), Kenny Brescia (guitar) Daniel A. Weiss (Associate Conductor, guitar), Jeffrey Potter (drums)

Setting: New York City's East Village, 1990; a musical presented in two acts; originally presented Off Broadway at the New York Theatre Workshop on February 13, 1996. Tragedy occurred when the 35-year-old author, Jonathan Larson, died of an aortic aneurysm after watching the final dress rehearsal of his show on January 24, 1996.

The 2005–2006 Company of *Rent* PHOTO BY JOAN MARCUS

Synopsis: Based on Puccini's opera *La Boheme*, the musical centers on a group of impoverished young artists and musicians struggling to survive and create in New York's Alphabet City in the early 1990s, under the shadow of AIDS.

Rent celebrated its 10th Anniversary on April 24, 2006, its 4,157th performance (five days before its official anniversary) with a one night only benefit concert of the show, dubbed *Rent 10*, which featured members of the original cast and directed by Michael Grief and musical directed by Tim Weil. The reunion concert benefited three organizations associated with late lyricist-librettist-composer Jonathan Larson: Friends In Deed (which supports those facing illness), The New York Theatre Workshop (where *Rent* was launched), and The Jonathan Larson Performing Arts Foundation (created in Larson's memory to encourage writers of musical theatre).

*Succeeded by: 1. Norbert Leo Butz, Richard H. Blake (alt.), Manley Pope, Sebastian Arcelus, Ryan Link, Jeremy Kushnier, Cary Shields, Tim Howar 2. Jim Poulos, Trey Ellett, Matt Caplan, Joey Fatone, Matt Caplan, Drew Lachey, Matt Caplan 3. Michael McElroy, Rufus Bonds Jr., Alan Mingo Jr., Mark Leroy Jackson, Mark Richard Ford, Destan Owens 4. Jacques C. Smith, Stu James, D'Monroe 5. Gwen Stewart, Alia Leon, Kenna J. Ramsey, Danielle Lee Greaves, Natalie Venetia Belcon, Myiia Watson-Davis, Merle Dandridge, Kenna J. Ramsey, Merle Dandridge, Danielle Lee Greaves, Kenna J. Ramsey 6. Wilson Cruz, Shaun Earl, Jose Llana, Jai Rodriguez, Andy Señor, Jai Rodriguez, Andy Señor, Justin Johnston 7. Marcy Harriell, Krysten Cummings, Maya Days, Loraine Velez, Karmine Alers, Krystal L. Washington, Melanie Brown, Karmine Alers, Antonique Smith 8. Sherie René Scott, Kristen Lee Kelly, Tamara Podemski, Cristina Fadale, Maggie Benjamin, Cristina Fadale, Maggie Benjamin, Kelly Karbacz, Ava Guadet 9. Jessica Boevers, Haven Burton, Jodi Carmeli, Amy Ehrlich, Kristen Lee Kelly, Tracey Langran, Caren Lyn Manuel, Carly Thomas 10. Marcus Paul James, Destan Owens, Todd E. Pettiford 11. Aisha de Haas, Shelley Dickinson, Maia Nkenge Wilson, Catrice Joseph, Frenchie Davis 12. Peter Matthew Smith, Chad Richardson, Mark Setlock 13. Will Chase, Robin De Jesus, Scott Hunt, Justin Johnston, Owen Johnston II, Matthew Murphy, Enrico Rodriguez 14. Robert Glean, Darryl Ordell, Nick Sanchez 15. Mayumi Ando, Sala Iwamatsu, Tina Ou, Kim Varhola 16. Karmine Alers, Sebastian Arcelus, Dean Armstrong, Richard H. Blake, Justin Brill, Mario Burrell, Matt Caplan, Julie Danao, Juan Carlos Gonzalez, Calvin Grant, Scott Hunt, Owen Johnston II, Catrice Joseph, Diana Kaarina, Kendra Kassebaum, Joshua Kobak, Joshua Kobak, Tracey Langran, Sharon Leal, Philip Dorian McAdoo, Moeisha McGill, Crystal Monee Hall, Matthew Murphy, Karen Olivo, John Eric Parker, Jai Rodriguez, Dominique Roy, Antonique Smith, Peter Matthew Smith, Shayna Steele, Robin S. Walker, Jay Wilkison, Haneefah Wood

THE 25TH ANNUAL PUTNAM COUNTY SPELLING BEE

Circle in the Square; First Preview: April 15, 2005; Opening Night: May 20, 2005 (see *Theatre World* Volume 61, page 80); Performances as of May 31, 2006: 450

Transfer of the Second Stage Theatre's Off Broadway musical with music and lyrics by William Finn, book by Rachel Sheinkin, conceived by Rebecca Feldman, and additional material by Jay Reiss; Based on "C-R-E-P-U-S-C-U-L-E," an original play by The Farm; Produced by David Stone, James L. Nederlander, Barbara Whitman, Patrick Catullo, Barrington Stage Company and Second Stage Theatre (Carole Rothman, Artistic Director; Timothy J. McClimon, Executive Director). Director, James Lapine, Choreography, Dan Knechtges; Set and Lobby Design, Beowulf Boritt; Costumes, Jennifer Caprio; Lighting, Natasha Katz; Sound, Dan Moses Schreier; Orchestrations, Michael Starobin; Music Director, Vadim Feichtner; Vocal Arrangements, Carmel Dean; Music Coordinator, Michael Keller; Casting, Tara Rubin; Production Stage Manager, Andrea "Spook" Testani; Production Manager, Kai Brothers; General Management, 321 Theatrical Management (Nancy Nagel Gibbs, Nina Essman, Marcia Goldberg); Marketing, The Araca Group; Company Manager, Seth Marquette; Resident Director, Darren Katz; Stage Manager, Kelly Hance; Dance Captain, Derrick Baskin; Assistant Stage Manager, Lisa Yuen; Assistant Choreographer, DJ Gray; Hair and Wig Design, Marty Kapulsky; Associate Lighting, Philip Rosenberg; Associate Sound, David Bullard; Associate Production Manager, Jason Block; Music Preparation, Emily Grishman; Advertising, Serino Coyne, Inc.; Press, The Publicity Office; Cast recording: Sh-K-Boom/Ghostlight Records 7915584407-2.

Opening Night Cast: Mitch Mahoney **Derrick Baskin**; Marcy Park **Deborah S. Craig**; Leaf Coneybear **Jesse Tyler Ferguson**[1]; William Barfee **Dan Fogler**[2]; Rona Lisa Peretti **Lisa Howard**; Olive Ostrovsky **Celia Keenan-Bolger**; Chip Tolentino **Jose Llana**; Douglas Panch **Jay Reiss**[3]; Logainne Schwartzandgrubenierre **Sarah Saltzberg**

Understudies: Todd Buonopane (Douglas, Leaf, Mitch, William) Kate Wetherhead (Logainne, Marcy, Olive), Willis White (Chip, Douglas, Mahoney), Lisa Yuen (Marcy, Olive, Rona Lisa)[4]

Musicians: Vadim Feichtner (Conductor/piano), Carmel Dean (Associate Conductor/ synthesizer), Rick Henderson (reed), Amy Ralske (cello), Glenn Rhian (drums/percussion).

Musical Numbers: The 25th Annual Putnam County Spelling Bee, The Spelling Bee Rules/My Favorite Moment Of The Bee 1, My Friend, The Dictionary, The First Goodbye, Pandemonium, I'm Not That Smart, The Second Goodbye, Magic Foot, Pandemonium Reprise/My Favorite Moment Of The Bee 2, Prayer Of The Comfort Counselor, My Unfortunate Erection (Chip's Lament), Woe Is Me, I'm Not That Smart (Reprise), I Speak Six Languages, The I Love You Song, Woe Is Me (Reprise), My Favorite Moment Of The Bee 3/Second, Finale, The Last Goodbye.

Setting: Now. The Putnam County Junior High School Gymnasium. A musical presented without intermission; originally produced at Second Stage in January, 2005 and at the Barrington Stage Company, Sheffield, Massachusetts, July, 2004. 2005 Awards: Tony Awards: Featured Actor in a Musical (Dan Fogler); Book of a Musical (Rachel Sheinkin); Drama Desk Awards: Outstanding Ensemble Performance (Cast), Book of a Musical (Rachel Sheinkin), Director of a Musical (James Lapine); Outer Critics Circle Award: Featured Actor in a Musical (Dan Fogler); Theatre World Awards: Dan Fogler and Celia Keenan-Bolger.

Synopsis: Four audience participants and six young people experience the anxiety and pressure of a regional spelling bee. The six kids in the throes of puberty, overseen by grown-ups who barely managed to escape childhood themselves, learn that winning isn't everything and that losing doesn't necessarily make you a loser.

*Succeeded by: 1. Barrett Foa (6/25/06) 2. Josh Gad (1/31/06) 3. Greg Stuhr (10/25/05) 4. Todd Buonopane (Chip), Maurice Murphy (Chip, Douglas, Mitch), Lee Zarrett (Leaf, William)

The Cast of *The 25th Annual Putnam County Spelling Bee* PHOTO BY JOAN MARCUS

WICKED

Gershwin Theatre; First Preview: October 8, 2003; Opening Night: October 30, 2003 (see *Theatre World* Volume 60, page 34); Performances as of May 31, 2006: 1,079

Musical with book by Winnie Holzman, music and lyrics by Stephen Schwartz; Based on a novel by Gregory Maguire; Produced by Marc Platt, Universal Pictures, The Araca Group, Jon B. Platt and David Stone; Director, Joe Mantello; Choreography, Wayne Cilento; Scenery, Eugene Lee; Costumes, Susan Hilferty; Lighting, Kenneth Posner; Sound, Tony Meola; Projections, Elanie J. McCarthy; Special Effects, Chic Silber; Flying Sequences, Paul Rubin/ZFX Inc.; Wigs and Hair, Tom Watson; Orchestrations, William David Brohn; Music Arrangements, Alex Lacamoire and Stephen Oremus; Music Director, Stephen Oremus; Music Coordinator, Michael Keller; Dance Arrangements, James Lynn Abbott; Executive Producers, Marcia Goldberg and Nina Essman; Casting, Bernard Telsey Casting; Production Stage Manager, Steven Beckler; Stage Manager, Erica Schwartz; Press, The Publicity Office, Bob Fennell, Marc Thibodeau, Michael S. Borowski; Cast recording: Decca B 0001 682-02.

Opening Night Cast: Glinda **Kristin Chenoweth***1; Witch's Father **Sean McCourt***2; Witch's Mother **Cristy Candler***3; Midwife **Jan Neuberger***4; Elphaba **Idina Menzel***5; Nessarose **Michelle Federer***6; Boq **Christopher Fitzgerald***7; Madame Morrible **Carole Shelley***8; Doctor Dillamond **William Youmans***9; Fiyero **Norbert Leo Butz***10; Ozian Official **Sean McCourt***2; The Wonderful Wizard of Oz **Joel Grey***11; Chistery **Manuel Herrera***12

Ensemble: Ioana Alfonso, Ben Cameron, Cristy Candler, Kristy Cates, Melissa Bell Chait, Marcus Choi, Kristoffer Cusick, Kathy Deitch, Melissa Fahn, Rhett G. George, Manuel Herrera, Kisha Howard, LJ Jellison, Sean McCourt, Corrine McFadden, Jan Neuberger, Walter Winston O'Neil, Andrew Palermo, Andy Pellick, Michael Seelbach, Lorna Ventura, Derrick Williams*13

Standbys: Laura Bell Bundy (Glinda), Eden Espinosa (Elphaba)*14

Understudies: Melissa Bell Chait (Glinda), Kristy Cates (Elphaba), Kristoffer Cusick (Fiyero), Sean McCourt (The Wonderful Wizard of Oz, Doctor Dillamond), Jan Neuberger, and Lorna Ventura (Madame Morrible), Andrew Palermo (Boq), Cristy Candler and Eden Espinosa (Nessarose), Kristen Lee Gorski (Witch's Mother)*15

Swings: Adinah Alexander; Kristen Lee Gorski, Eddie Korbich, Mark Myars*16

Orchestra: Stephen Oremus (Conductor), Alex Lacamoire (Associate Conductor, piano, synthesizer); Christian Hebel (Concertmaster), Victor Schultz (violin), Kevin Roy (viola), Dan Miller (cello), Konrad Adderly (bass), Greg Skaff (guitar), John Moses(clarinet/soprano sax), John Campo (bassoon/ baritone sax/clarinet), Tuck Lee (oboe), Helen Campo (flute), Jon Owens (lead trumpet), Tom Hoyt (trumpet), Dale Kirkland, Douglas Purviance (trombone), Theo Primis, Kelly Dent (French horn), Paul Loesel, David Evans (keyboards), Ric Molina, Andy Jones (percussion), Gary Seligson (drums), Laura Sherman (harp)

Musical Numbers: No One Mourns the Wicked, Dear Old Shiz, The Wizard and I, What Is This Feeling?, Something Bad, Dancing Through Life, Popular, I'm Not That Girl, One Short Day, A Sentimental Man, Defying Gravity, No One Mourns the Wicked (Reprise), Thank Goodness, The Wicked Witch of the East, Wonderful, I'm Not That Girl (Reprise), As Long as You're Mine, No Good Deed, March of the Witch Hunters, For Good, Finale

Setting: The Land of Oz; a musical presented in two acts; world premiere presented in San Francisco at the Curran Theatre May 28 – June 29, 2003; 2004 Awards: Tony Awards: Leading Actress in a Musical (Idina Menzel), Scenic Design, Costume Design; Drama Desk Awards: Outstanding Musical, Director of a Musical (Joe Mantello), Book (Winnie Holzman), Lyrics (Stephen Schwartz), Costume Design, Set Design; Outer Critics Circle Awards: Outstanding Broadway Musical, Director of a Musical (Joe Mantello), Set Design, Costume Design; Drama League Awards: Outstanding Production of a Musical; Grammy Award: Best Musical Show Album.

Synopsis: *Wicked* explores the early life of the witches of Oz, Glinda and Elphaba, who meet at Shiz University. Glinda is madly popular and Elphaba is green. After an initial period of mutual loathing, the roommates begin to learn something about each other. Their life paths continue to intersect, and eventually their choices and convictions take them on widely different paths.

*Succeeded by: 1. Jennifer Laura Thompson (6/20/04), Megan Hilty (5/31/05), Kate Reinders (5/30/06) 2. Michael DeVries 3. Katie Webber 4. Adinah Alexander, Kathy Santen 5. Shoshana Bean (1/11/05), Eden Espinosa (1/10/06) 6. Cristy Candler (1/10/06), Jenna Leigh Green (3/17/06) 7. Randy Harrison (6/22/07), Christopher Fitzgerald (7/27/04), Jeffrey Kuhn (1/11/05), Rob Sapp (10/11/05) 8. Rue McClanahan (5/31/05), Carol Kane (1/10/06) 9. Sean McCourt (1/26/05) 10. Kristoffer Cusick (11/25/03), Taye Diggs (12/22/03), Norbert Leo Butz (1/20/04), Joey McIntyre (1/20/04), David Ayers (1/11/05), Derrick Williams (1/10/06) 11. Sean McCourt (1/20/04), George Hearn (5/31/05), Gene Weygandt (8/30/05), Ben Vereen (9/4/05), George Hearn (1/17/06), Ben Vereen (2/3/06), David Garrison (4/4/06) 12. Phillip Spaeth 13. Adinah Alexander, Ionna Alfonso, Clyde Alves (Swing, Assistant Dance Captain), Kevin Aubin, Jerad Bortz, James Brown, III, Michael DeVries, Lori Ann Ferrari, Adam Fleming, Anthony Galde, Asmeret Ghebremichael, Lauren Gibbs, Gaelen Gilliland, Zach Hensler, Dominique Kelley, Reed Kelly, Kenway Hon Wai K. Kua, Stacie Morgain Lewis, Brandi Chavonne Massey, Brandon Mattieus, Clifton Oliver, Adam Sanford, Rob Sapp, Megan Sikora, Heather Spore, Phillip Spaeth, Marty Thomas, Shanna VanDerwerker, Jennifer Waldman, Katie Webber, Briana Yacavone 14. Megan Hilty (Glinda), Saycon Sengbloh (Elphaba), Katie Adams (Glinda), Shoshana Bean (Elphaba) 15. Adinah Alexander (Madame Morrible), Clyde Alves (Boq), Jerad Bortz (Fiyero, Ozian Official, Witch's Father), Ben Cameron (Ozian Official, Witch's Father), Michael DeVries (Doctor Dillamond, The Wonderful Wizard of Oz), Melissa Fahn (Glinda), Lori Ann Ferrari (Nessarose, Witch's Mother), Adam Fleming (Boq), Anthony Galde (Doctor Dillamond, Ozian Official, The Wonderful Wizard of Oz, Witch's Father), Gaelen Gilliland (Madame Morrible), Tiffany Haas (Nessarose), Reed Kelly (Chistery), Eddie Korbich (Doctor Dillamond, The Wonderful Wizard of Oz), Stacie Morgain Lewis (Nessarose), Brandi Chavonne Massey (Elphaba), Brandon Mattieus (Fiyero), Mark Myars (Boq, Chistery), Clifton Oliver (Fiyero), Walter Winston Oneil (Boq), Adam Sanford (Boq), Robb Sapp (Boq), Megan Sikora (Glinda, Nessarose), Heather Spore (Glinda), Charlie Sutton (Chistery), Marty Thomas (Boq), Derrick Williams (Fiyero) 16. Clyde Alves, Angela Brydon, Alexis Ann Carra, Anthony Galde, Eric Stretch, Charlie Sutton, Marty Thomas, Shanna VanDerwerker

BROADWAY

Productions from Past Seasons That **Closed During This Season**

Denzel Washington in *Julius Caesar* PHOTO BY JOAN MARCUS

Robert Goulet and the Cagelles in *La Cage Aux Folles* PHOTO BY CAROL ROSEGG

Sarah Paulson and Josh Lucas in *The Glass Menagerie* PHOTO BY PAUL KOLNIK

700 SUNDAYS
Broadhurst Theatre
First Preview: November 12, 2004
Opened: December 5, 2004; Closed: June 5, 2005
21 previews, 166 performances

JULIUS CAESAR
Belasco Theatre
First Preview: March 8, 2005
Opened: April 3, 2005; Closed: June 12, 2005
31 previews, 81 performances

BROOKLYN, THE MUSICAL
Gerald Schoenfeld Theatre
First Preview: September 23, 2004
Opened: October 21, 2004; Closed: June 26, 2005
27 previews, 284 performances

LA CAGE AUX FOLLES
Marquis Theatre
First Preview: November 11, 2004
Opened: December 9, 2004; Closed: June 26, 2005
31 previews, 229 performances

ON GOLDEN POND
Cort Theatre
First Preview: March 22, 2005
Opened: April 7, 2005; Closed: June 26, 2005
19 previews, 93 performances

A STREETCAR NAMED DESIRE
Studio 54
First Preview: March 26, 2005
Opened: April 26, 2005; Closed: July 3, 2005
33 previews, 73 performances

THE GLASS MENAGERIE
Barrymore Theatre
First Preview: February 24, 2005
Opened: March 22, 2005; Closed: July 3, 2005
29 previews, 120 performances

STEEL MAGNOLIAS
Lyceum Theatre
First Preview: March 15, 2005
Opened: April 4, 2005; Closed: July 31, 2005
23 previews, 136 performances

GLENGARRY GLEN ROSS
Bernard Jacobs Theatre
First Preview: April 8, 2005
Opened: May 1, 2005; Closed: August 28, 2005
27 previews, 137 performances

Alan Alda and Liev Schreiber in *Glengarry Glen Ross* PHOTO BY SCOTT LANDIS

Michael Cavanaugh in *Movin' Out* PHOTO BY JOAN MARCUS

Harvey Fierstein and Rosie O'Donnell in *Fiddler on the Roof* PHOTO BY CAROL ROSEGG

JACKIE MASON: FRESHLY SQUEEZED
Helen Hayes Theatre
First Preview: March 8, 2005
Opened: March 23, 2005; Closed: September 4, 2005
14 previews, 172 performances

WHO'S AFRAID OF VIRGINIA WOOLF?
Longacre Theatre
First Preview: March 12, 2005
Opened: March 20, 2005; Closed: September 4, 2005
8 previews, 177 performances

THE PILLOWMAN
Booth Theatre
First Preview: March 21, 2005
Opened: April 10, 2005; Closed: September 18, 2005
23 previews, 185 performances

ALL SHOOK UP
Palace Theatre
First Preview: February 20, 2005
Opened: March 24, 2005; Closed: September 25, 2005
33 previews, 213 performances

MOVIN' OUT
Richard Rodgers Theatre
First Preview: September 30, 2002
Opened: October 24, 2002; Closed: December 11, 2005
28 previews, 1303 performances

SWEET CHARITY
Al Hirschfeld Theatre
First Preview: April 11, 2005
Opened: May 4, 2005; Closed: December 31, 2005
25 previews, 279 performances

CHITTY CHITTY BANG BANG
Hilton Theatre
First Preview: March 27, 2005
Opened: April 28, 2005; Closed: December 31, 2005
34 previews, 285 performances

FIDDLER ON THE ROOF
Minskoff Theatre
First Preview: January 23, 2004
Opened: February 26, 2004; Closed: January 8, 2006
36 previews, 781 performances

OFF-BROADWAY

Productions That Opened **June 1, 2005 – May 31, 2006**

THE PULL OF NEGATIVE GRAVITY

59E59 Theatre A; First preview: May 11, 2005; Opening Night: May 15, 2005; Closed June 5, 2005

A new play by Jonathan Lichtenstein; Presented by The Mercury Theatre Colchester (Dee Evans, Artistic Director) as part of the Brits Off Broadway 2005; Director, Gregory Thompson; Scenery and Costumes, Ellen Cairns; Lighting, Robin Carter; Sound, Andrea J. Cox; Movement Director, Nicola Roswewarne; Company Stage Manager, Patricia Davenport; AEA Stage Manager, Jenny Deady; Press, Karen Greco

Cast: Vi Williams **Joanne Howarth**; Bethan **Louise Collins**; Rhys Williams **Daniel Hawksford**; Dai Williams **Lee Haven-Jones**

Setting: A farm in Wales, UK. 2004. New York premiere of a play presented without intermission. (Due to editorial error, this listing was accidentally omitted from *Theatre World* Volume 61.)

Synopsis: A wounded soldier returns to his Welsh farm home to his family and fiancée and copes with the grim realities and fallout from the war in Iraq.

MORTAL LADIES POSSESSED

59E59 Theatre C; First preview May 17, 2005; Opening Night: May 19, 2005; Closed June 5, 2005

A new play by Matthew Hurt, adapted from the short stories of Tennessee Williams; Produced by Linda Marlowe Productions in association with Guildford's Yvonne Arnaud Theatre as part of the Brits Off Broadway 2005; Director, Stuart Mullins; Scenery, Rachana Jadhav; Lighting, Phil Hewitt; Sound, Simon McCorry; Stage Manager, Kathryn Hayzer; Company Manager, Mishi L B; Assistant Director/Stage Manager, Meriel Baistow-Clare; Press, Karen Greco

Cast: Widow Holly/others **Linda Marlowe**

Setting: A New Orleans boarding house. A solo performance play presented without intermission. (Due to editorial error, this listing was accidentally omitted from *Theatre World* Volume 61.)

Synopsis: Widow Holly (from the short story "The Coming of Something to Widow Holly") conjures the exotic female guests that have passed through her doors. Colorful characters from Tennessee Williams' little known works — including "The Interval," "Man Bring This Up Road," "In Memory of an Aristocrat," and "Oriflamme" — make memorable appearances in this sometimes haunting, often hilarious, and extremely passionate theatrical re-imagination.

A SINGLE WOMAN

45 Below Bleecker; Opening Night: May 24, 2005; Closed June 19, 2005; 28 performances

Nevada Shakespeare Company's production of a play written and directed by Jeanmarie Simpson; Stage Manager, Jason A. Quinn; Dramaturg, Rick Foster

Cast: Jeannette Rankin **Claudia Schneider**; Everyman **Neal Mayer**

New York premiere of a new play presented in two acts. (Due to editorial error, this listing was accidentally omitted from *Theatre World* Volume 61.)

Synopsis: *A Single Woman* is an exploration of the genius and courage of the career of Jeannette Rankin, the first U.S. congresswoman, as an activist and advocate for women, workers, and children.

TABLOID CALIGULA

59E59 Theatre B; First preview: May 24, 2005; Opening Night: May 26, 2005; Closed June 12, 2005

A play by Darren Murphy; Produced by Tror Taa and Kay Ellen Consolver for KLN Productions Limited as part of the Brits Off Broadway 2005; Director, Lisa Forrell; Scenery and Costumes, Rachel Payne; Lighting, David W. Kidd; Sound, Shock Productions; General Manager, Harold Sanditen; Deputy Stage Manager- London, Russell Young; AEA Stage Manager, Terri K. Kohler; Press, Karen Greco

Cast: Robert **Peter Tate**; Mary **Suzanne Sylvester**; Joe **Chris Harper**

Setting: A basement below a tailor shop, London. American premiere of a new play presented without intermission. (Due to editorial error, this listing was accidentally omitted from *Theatre World* Volume 61.)

Synopsis: *Tabloid Caligula* centers on Robert, an aging criminal and wannabe businessman. Part mentor, part historian, part psychopath, he strides about his storeroom like a low-rent Godfather, filling his young protégé, Joe, with tales of underworld glamour and ancient historical conquests. Joe dreams of being just like Robert. But Robert's not telling Joe everything he knows. Then in walks Mary, and Robert's game is up.

LAZER VAUDEVILLE

Lambs Theatre; June 9 – August 21, 2005; 84 performances. This production previously ran at the John Houseman Theatre March 9 – May 14, 2005 prior to that theatre's demolition.

A juggling, magic, and acrobat show created by Carter Brown, Cindy Marvell, and Nicholas Flair; Director, Carter Brown; Scenery, Maia Robbins-Zust; Laser Design, Cory Simpson; Costumes; Jennifer Johanos; Musical Director, Jesse Manno; Choreography, Cindy Marvell; Production Stage Manager, Seth Allshouse; Press, Keith Sherman and Associates

Cast: Carter Brown; **Cindy Marvell**; **Nicholas Flair**

A theatrical event presented in two parts

Synopsis: A juggler's take on the vaudeville era. Hand-painted, fluorescent clubs and ropes spin through the backlight. Century-old bicycle rims roll around the juggler's body and circle the stage as if by magic. Hand drums are used as taiko-style tennis rackets, ultra-light indoor stunt kites fly over the audience, and twirling L.E.D. staffs put a high-tech spin on an ancient art form.

SOUTH PACIFIC

Isaac Stern Auditorium at Carnegie Hall, June 9, 2005, 1 performance

Music by Richard Rodgers, lyrics by Oscar Hammerstein II, Book by Joshua Logan and Oscar Hammerstein II adapted from James Michener's *Tales of the South Pacific*; Concert Adaptation, David Ives; Director, Walter Bobbie; Musical Director/Conductor, Paul Gemignani; Orchestra: Orchestra of St. Luke's; Orchestrations, Robert Russell Bennett; Dance and Instrumental Music, Trude Rittmann; Musical Staging, Casey Nicholaw; Scenic Consultant, John Lee Beatty; Costume Consultant, Catherine Zuber; Lighting, Aland Adelman; Sound, Nevin Steinberg; Stage Manager, Hank Neimark; Assistant Stage Manager, Leigh Boone; Music Coordinator, Kristen Sonntag; Casting, Jay Binder; Recording: DVD- PBS Great Performances and CD-Decca Broadway

Cast: Ensign Nellie Forbush **Reba McEntire**; Emile de Becque **Brian Stokes Mitchell**; Lt. Joseph Cable **Jason Danieley**; Bloody Mary **Lillias White**; Capt. George Brackett **Conrad John Schuck**; Cmdr. William Harbison **Dylan Baker**; Luther Billis **Alec Baldwin**; Jerome **Alexio Barboza**; Ngana **Alex de Castro**; Liat **Renita Croney**; Stewpot **Alexander Gemignani**; Professor **Tom Deckman**

Ensemble: Mark Aldrich, Nancy Anderson, Stephanie Bast, Rebecca Baxter, Hunter Bell, Tim Breese, Tony Capone, Carson Church, Alvin Crawford, Nikki Renée Daniels, Tom Deckman, Colleen Fitzpatrick, David Frye, Gaelen Gilliland, Alexander Gemignani, Patty Goble, Gregg Goodbrod, Tim Gulan, LaTanya Hall, Steve Hogle, Elmore James, Jessica Kostival, Ian Knauer, Tony Lawson, Mark Ledbetter, C. Mingo Long, Rob Lorey, David Lowenstein, Benjamin Magnuson, Frank Mastrone, David Masenheimer, Jason Mills, Adam Overett, Kilty Reidy, Devin Richards, Vale Rideout, Robert Rokicki, Graham Rowat, Tim Salamandyk, Matthew Shepard, Trevor Southworth, Lawrence Street, Christianne Tisdale, Andrew Varela, Victor Wallace, J.D. Webster, Sally Wilfert, Laurie Williamson, Tony Yazbeck, Peter Yonka

Setting: World War II, an island in the South Pacific. Concert version of the musical presented in two acts.

Synopsis: *South Pacific* follows parallel love stories that are threatened by the dangers of prejudice and war. Ensign Nellie Forbush, a Navy nurse from Little Rock, falls in love with the distinguished Emile de Becque, a French planter who for some years has been living on the island paradise. Meanwhile, Lt. Joe Cable falls in love with the bawdy Bloody Mary's daughter, Liat.

Tim Phillips, Victoria Moseley, Will Adamsdale, Ferdy Roberts in *Faster* PHOTO BY NIGEL ROBERTS

FASTER

59E59 Theatre C; First preview: June 7, 2005; Opening Night: June 12, 2005; Closed June 26, 2005

Scripted by Stephen Brown; inspired by the book *Faster: The Acceleration of Just About Everything* by James Gleick; Producer, Emma Stenning; Devised by Filter (Will Adamsdale, Chris Branh, Oliver Dimsdale, Rachel Edwards, Tom Haines, Victoria Moseley, Tim Phillips, Guy Retallack, Ferdy Roberts, Gemma Saunders, Wole Sawyerr) as part of Brits Off Broadway 2005; Director, Guy Retallack; Dramaturgy, Kate McGrath; Music and Sound, Chris Branch, Tom Haines, Tim Phillips; Lighting, Guy Kornetzki; Photography, Talula Sheppard; Original Script, Dawn King and Oliver Wilkinson; Company Manager, Elke Laleman; AEA Stage Manager, Kathryn "China" Hayzer; Financial Manager, Daniel Morgenstern; Press, Karen Greco

Cast: Will **William Adamsdale**; Vic **Victoria Moseley**; Ben **Ferdy Roberts**

Musicians: Chris Branch and Tim Phillips

World premiere of a multi media play presented without intermission

Synopsis: A love triangle where multitasking and alienation are playfully but poignantly explored through jump cuts, sound design, movement, and non-linear storytelling.

JACKSON'S WAY

59E59 Theatre C; First preview: June 9, 2005; Opening Night: June 12, 2005; Closed June 26, 2005

Created and written by Will Adamsdale; Presented by Underbelly Productions, Fuel Theatre, and Will Adamsdale; Dramaturg, Kate McGrath; Press, Karen Greco

Cast: Chris John Jackson **Will Adamsdale**; New York premiere of a solo performance play presented without intermission

Synopsis: Part theatre, part comedy, *Jackson's Way* is a modern-day parody of American motivational speakers and a satire on the world of self-help and corporate jargon.

Will Adamsdale in *Jackson's Way* PHOTO BY BARNEY BRITTON

CHRISTINE JORGENSEN REVEALS

59E59 Theatre B; Opening Night: June 12, 2005; Closed June 28, 2005; 6 performances; Dodger Stages Theatre 5; Re-Opening Night: December 29, 2005; Closed January 21, 2006; 14 performances; Extended at Theatre Row Studio Theatre; February 16 – April 1, 2006; 28 performances

Conceived by Bradford Louryk; Produced by The Splinter Group, Highbrow Entertainment, Sterling Bridge Productions and Sandra Garner; Director, Josh Hecht; Scenery, Wilson Chin; Costumes, Mary Ping; Lighting, Josh Bradford; Sound, Rob Kaplowitz; Wigs, Jason P. Hayes; Video/Projections; Kevin Frech; Stage Manager, Frank Ramirez; Dramaturg; Christie Evangelisto; Properties, Jung Griffin; Press, Judy Jacksina

Cast: Christine Jorgensen **Bradford Louryk**; Interviewer (Mr. Russell) **Rob Grace**

Setting: New York recording studio, 1957. A biographical play presented without intermission.

Synopsis: Bradford Louryk portrays and lip-synchs Christine Jorgensen, one of the first spokespersons for transgendered people, in actual interview in this unique theatrical experience, featuring press clips and newsreels from the past of the real Christine Jorgensen.

MANUSCRIPT

Daryl Roth Theatre; First preview: June 1, 2005; Opening Night: June 12, 2005; Closed August 14, 2005; 13 previews, 72 performances

By Paul Grellon; Produced by Daryl Roth and Scott Rudin; Director, Bob Balaban; Scenery, David Swayze; Costumes, Sara Tosetti; Lighting, David Weiner; Sound, Peter Fitzgerald; Production Stage Manager, Donald Fried; Production Manager, Shannon Case; General Manager, Adam Hess; Marketing, HHC Marketing; Press, Pete Sanders

Cast: Chris Fernando **Jeffrey Carlson**; Elizabeth Hawkins **Marin Ireland** David Lewis **Pablo Schreiber**

Setting: David's apartment in Brooklyn Heights, Christmastime. New York premiere of a new play presented without intermission.

Synopsis: When a manuscript is discovered that can guarantee success, three ambitious people set into motion a manipulative quest for vengeance and fame in this calculating comedy.

OEDIPUS

Mint Theatre Space; First preview: June 3, 2005; Opening Night: June 12, 2005; Closed June 26, 2005; 25 performances

Theatre By the Blind (George Ashiotis and Ike Schambelan, Co Artistic Directors) production of the play by Sophocles, adapted by Ted Hughes; Director, Ike Schambelan; Scenery, Merope Vachlioti; Costumes, Christine Field; Lighting, Bert Scott; Sound, Nicholas Viselli; Production Manager, Nicholas Lazzaro; Stage Manager, Ann Marie Morelli; Assistant Stage Manager, Sarah Locke; Company Manager, Terry Jackson; Marketing, Michelle Brandon; Press; Shirley Herz

Cast: Player 1-Creon/Slave/Chorus **Nicholas Viselli**; Player 2-Jocasta/Chorus **Melanie Boland**; Player 3-Oedipus/Chorus **George Ashiotis**; Player4-Manto/Chorus **Pamela Sabaugh**; Player 5-Tiresias/Messenger/Chorus **J. M. McDonough**

Setting: An Oval Office, present day. Revival of the play presented without intermission.

Synopsis: Theatre by the Blind presents a modern spin on the classic tale of the Theban king who murders his father, marries his mother, brings a plague to his kingdom, and finds truths underneath.

PRIVATE FEARS IN PUBLIC PLACES

59E59 Theatre A; First preview: June 9, 2005; Opening Night: June 14, 2005; Closed July 3, 2005

Written and directed by Alan Ayckbourn; Presented by the Stephen Joseph Theater, Scarborough, England as part of the Brits Off Broadway 2005; Designer, Pip Leckenby; Lighting, Mick Hughes; Costumes; Christine Wall; Original Music; John Pattison; Company Stage Manager, Emily Vickers; SJT Senior Technician, Ben Vickers; Assistant Stage Manager, Holly Hill; AEA Stage Manager, Jenny Deady; Touring and Programming Director, Amada Saunders; Production Manager, Alison Fowler, Master Carpenter, Frank Matthews; Press, Karen Greco

Cast: Nicola **Melanie Gutteridge**; Stewart **Paul Kemp**; Ambrose **Adrian McLoughlin**; Charlotte **Alexandra Mathie**; Imogen **Sarah Moyle**; Dan **Paul Thornley**

Setting: London, present day. American premiere of a new play presented without intermission.

Synopsis: Six lives intertwined through complex circumstance; Ayckbourn's 67th play paints heartrending portraits of lonely people who attempt to make connections to those around them with inevitable isolation resulting.

UNSUSPECTING SUSAN

59E59 Theatre B; First preview June 14, 2005; Opening Night: June 15, 2005; Closed July 3, 2005

A play by Stewart Permutt; Produced by Sandpiper Productions as part of Brits Off Broadway 2005; Director, Lisa Forrell; Scenery and Costumes, Nigel Hook; Lighting, David W. Kidd; Sound, Edmund Butt; Assistant Director; Adam Barnard; Deputy Stage Manager London, Rusell Young; AEA Stage Manager, Terri K. Kohler; Press, Karen Greco

Cast: Susan Chester **Celia Imrie**; Policeman **Gus Danowski**; Policewoman **Frankie Shaw**

Setting: a village in Hampshire, UK. American premiere of a new play presented without intermission.

Synopsis: Susan is an insensitive, petty-minded queen bee of a smart Hampshire village. Then her son commits an unspeakable crime that shakes the entire world.

BORDER/CLASH: A LITANY OF DESIRES

45 Bleecker; First preview: June 3, 2005; Opening Night: June 16, 2005; Closed August 7, 2005; 11 previews, 49 performances

Culture Project (Ira Pittelman, Executive Producer; Allan Buchman, Artistic Director) production of a play written by Staceyann Chinn; Director, Rob Urbinati; Scenery and Lighting, Garin Marschall; Sound, Emily Wright; Consultant, Carolyn Allen; Press, Origlio Public Relations

Performed by **Staceyann Chinn**

A solo performance play presented without intermission

Synopsis: *Border/Clash* blends slam poetry, autobiographical story-telling, and political commentary as Chin paints the journey from her Jamaican childhood through the discovery of her sexual identity and political voice to New York.

DRUMSTRUCK

Dodger Stages Theatre 2; First preview: May 12, 2005; Opening Night: June 16, 2005; Still running as of May 31, 2006

An interactive drum-theatre experience conceived by Warren Lieberman, co-created by Kathy-Jo Ross; Presented by Drum Café, Dodger Theatricals, Visual Spirit, in association with Amy J. Moore; Director, David Warren; Sets, Neil Patel; Lighting, Jeff Croiter; Sound, Tom Morse; Dance Consultant, Moving Into Dance; Technical Supervisor, Tech Production Services, Inc.; Production Stage Manager, Bernita Robinson; Promotions, HHC Marketing; Press, Boneau/Bryan-Brown; Executive Producers, Sally Campbell Morse, James Sinclair (VSI); Company Management, Wendeen Lieberman, Bill Schaeffer

Cast: Nicholas Africa Djanie, Vuyelwa Booi, Sebone Dzwanyudzwanyu Rangata, Enock Bafana Mahlangu, Tiny Modise, Kevin Brubaker, Richard Carter, Themba Kubheka, Ronald Thabo Medupe, Molutsi Mogami, Molebedi Sponch Mogapi, LeeAnét Noble

A performance piece presented without intermission. Originally produced in Johannesburg, South Africa by Drum Café, directed by Kathy-Jo Ross.

Synopsis: A South African drumming event gives each audience member a drum and makes them part of the show.

The Company of *Drumstruck* PHOTO BY JOAN MARCUS

Staceyann Chin in *Border/Clash* PHOTO BY BRIAN MICHAEL THOMAS

MY SWEETHEART'S THE MAN IN THE MOON

14th Street Y; Opening Night: June 16, 2005; Closed July 10, 2005; 32 performances

The Hypothetical Theatre Company production of a play by Don Nigro; Produced by Lauren Stevens; Director, Amy Feinberg; Scenery, Mark Symczak; Costumes, Chris Lione; Lighting, Randy Glickman; Sound, Tim Kramer; Stage Manager, Sarah Izzo; Assistant Stage Manager, Daniel Nelson; Press, Ron Lasko

Cast: Evelyn Nesbit **Kit Paquin**; Stanford White **Mark Pinter**; Harry Thaw **Tim Altmeyer**; Mrs. Nesbit **Catherine Lynn Dowling**; Mrs. Thaw **Annette Hunt**

Accompanist: Tom Berger

Setting: New York City, 1906. New York premiere of a new play with music presented in two acts.

Synopsis: *My Sweetheart's the Man in the Moon* explores the explosive love triangle between the girl on the red velvet swing, Evelyn Nesbit; the famous NY architect Stanford White; and Harry K. Thaw of Pittsburgh that led to the "Crime of the Century."

PEOPLE ARE LIVING THERE

Peter Norton Space; First preview: June 8, 2005; Opening Night: June 16, 2005; Closed July 24, 2005

Specific Theatre Company (John Thomas Gorsk, Producer/Artistic Director; Larry Silverberg, Artistic Director) production of a play by Athol Fugard; Director, Suzanne Shepherd; Scenery, Roger Mooney; Lighting, Beth Turomsha; Costumes/Props, Brenna McGuire; Fight Director, Carroll C. Calkins; Production Stage Manager,

Alexis Prussack; General Manager, Frank Ravis; Assistant Producer, Tara Fogarty; Advertising, Triton; Press, Origlio Public Relations

Cast: Millie **O'Mara Leary**; Don **Larry Silverberg**; Shorty **Ben Rauch**; Sissy **Emma Myles**

Setting: Elizabeth, New Jersey. Revival of a play presented in two acts.

Synopsis: A feisty landlady of a sleazy boarding house, celebrating her 50th birthday, is looking forward to a nice romantic evening at home until she finds out her lover has run off with a younger woman. Stuck at home with her three downbeat lodgers, she is determined to celebrate and have her revenge as she persuades her guests to join her for a party none of them will forget.

FOOLS IN LOVE

MET Theatre at 55 Mercer; First preview: June 10, 2005; Opening Night: June 23, 2005; Still running as of May 31, 2006

Millennium Talent Group in association with Manhattan Ensemble Theatre production of a play adapted from *A Midsummer Night's Dream* by William Shakespeare, conceived by Sarah Rosenberg and Louis Reyes Cardenas; Director, Sarah Rosenberg; Choreography, Amelia Campbell; Scenery, Bruce Dean; Costumes, Adriana Desier Durantt; Lighting, Sean Linehan; Sound, Stephanie Palmer; Props, Faye Armon; Production Stage Manager, Chelsea Morgan Hoffmann; Press, Max Eisen

Cast: Hermia **Erika Villalba**; Helena **Breeda Wool**; Lysander **Matt Schuneman**; Demetrius **Antony Raymond**; Peter Quince **Tom Falborn**; Bottom **Ryan Knowles**; Flute **Louis Reyes Cardenas**; Snug **Anthony Gallucio**; Tom Snout **Joseph Desantis**; Titania **Margaret Curry**; Oberon **Andy Langton**; Puck **Brandy Wykes**; Peaseblossom **Taylor Stockdale**; Ensemble **Jacqueline Algarin, Amelia Campbell, Laura Cloutier, Simone Galon, Laura Gosheff, Mike Gomez, Frank Kelly, Nova Mejia, D.J. Paris, Jacqueline Raposo, Eunhye Grace Sakong**; Doo Wop Group **Trevor Allen, Lauren Haughton, Misti Vara, Johanna Bon, D.J. Paris**

Setting: 1962, Duke's Diner, California. A play with music presented without intermission.

Synopsis: In this new version of the Shakespeare classic geared toward younger audiences, *Fools in Love* uses classic songs from the 50s and 60s as fairies on roller skates explode from the juke box and dance their magic.

Louis Butelli, Marwa Bernstein, Andrew Schwartz, Lincoln Hudson (standing) in *Twelfth Night* PHOTOS (C) 2005 LOIS GREENFIELD

THE HOLLOW MEN

Village Theatre; Opening Night: June 24, 2006; Closed July 16, 2005

Created by David Armand, Rupert Russell, Sam Spedding and Nick Tanner; Presented by WestBeth Entertainment (Arnold Engelman, President); Robin Reardon, Producer; Chris Petrelli, Producing Associate; Press, Boneau/Bryan-Brown, Heath Schwartz

Cast: David Armand; Rupert Russell; Sam Spedding; Nick Tanner

Sketch comedy and skits presented in two acts.

Synopsis: Four Cambridge University alumni take sketch comedy to places it's never dared to go — sex, death, madness, all in a lovable knockout fashion.

TWELFTH NIGHT

Baruch Performing Arts Center Nagelberg Theatre; First preview: June 17, 2005; Opening Night: June 25, 2005; Closed August 21, 2005; 9 previews, 34 performances

Aquila Theatre Company (Peter Meineck, Artistic Director) production of the play by William Shakespeare adapted by Robert Richmond; Created, Designed and Directed by Peter Meineck and Robert Richmond; Composer/Musical Director, Anthony Cochrane; Lighting, Peter Meineck; Costumes, Megan Bowers; General Manager, Nate Terracio; Assistant Producer, Todd Batstone; Graphics, Brown Cathell

Cast: Feste, the Clown **Louis Butelli**; Viola, Sebastian's twin sister later disguised as Cesario **Lindsay Rae Taylor**; Orsino, Duke of Illyria **Andrew Schwartz**; Sir Toby Belch, Olivia's uncle **Anthony Cochrane**; Maria, Olivia's Lady-in-Waiting **Natasha Piletich**; Olivia, a noblewoman of Illyria **Lisa Carter**; Sir Andrew Aguecheek, Olivia's suitor **Lincoln Hudson**; Malvolio, Olivia's steward **Kenn Sabberton**; Antonio, a Sea Captain **Andrew Schwartz**; Sebastian, Viola's twin brother **Stephen Stout**

Revival of the play presented in two acts

Synopsis: This story of identical twins and mistaken identity explores the universal themes of love and all its ambiguous effects on human behavior. In the tradition of Aquila's Shakespearean comedies, *Twelfth Night* promises more than a little eyebrow raising when Elizabethan dance moves meet techno music and cool contemporary staging.

DRIVING ON THE LEFT SIDE

TBG Theatre Space; First preview: June 25, 2005; Opening Night: June 30, 2005; Closed July 31, 2005

A play by Amy Merrill; Produced by Blackbird Productions; Director, Florante Gavez; Scenery, Carlo Adinofi; Costumes, Ali Turns; Lighting, Federico Restrepo; Sound, Andrew Fremont Smith; Original Music, Mark Shine/Chillup Publishing; Music Director, Aljam Smith; Production Stage Manager, Amy Lee; Producer/General Manager, Rita A. Fucillo

Cast: Serena **Jennifer McCabe**; Cowboy **Postell Pringle**; Celia **Sharon Tsahai King**; George **Paul Navarra**

The Band: Reggaelution-Al "Aljam" Smith (Bandleader/vocals/guitar), Delroy Campbell (vocals/percussion), Bunny Cunningham (keyboard/vocals), George Ricketts (bass/writer/arranger).

Setting: Jamaica, the present. A new play presented in two acts.

Synopsis: The story of four people each at their own personal and professional crossroads. An American schoolteacher left stranded at the altar impulsively goes on her Jamaican honeymoon alone and falls in love with the lead vocalist in a reggae beach band. Complications arise when the bride's concerned father arrives and promptly falls in love with the singer's alluring mother.

FATAL ATTRACTION: A GREEK TRAGEDY

East 13th Street Theatre; First preview: July 1, 2005; Opening Night: July 10, 2005; Closed August 27, 2005; 8 previews, 58 performances

A new play by Alana McNair and Kate Wilkinson, with text from Euripides, C.H. Fowler, and W.H. DePuy; Produced by Gorilla Productions; Director, Timothy Haskell; Scenery, Paul Smithyman; Costumes, Wendy Yang; Lighting, Tyler Micoleau; Sound, Vincent Olivieri; Props, Faye Armon; Stage Manager, Denyse Owens; Fight Director, Rod Kinter; Dance Choreography, Rebeca Ramirez; General Management, Cris Buchner; Company Manager, John Hume; Production Management, The Murmur Machine; Press; Publicity Outfitters

Cast: Ellen Hamilton Latzen **Aaron Haskell**; Michael Douglas **Corey Feldman**; Anne Archer **Kate Wilkinson**; Glenn Close **Alana McNair**; Chorus 2 (Zoltan) **Nick Arens**; Chorus 3 (Octavius Maximus) **Sergio Lobito**; Chorus 4 (Persimmon Walters) **Kellie Arens**; Chorus 1 (Phaedra McQueen) **Ebony A. Cross**

Setting: New York, NY in the 80's... of any century future or past. A new play presented without intermission.

Synopsis: A loose parody of the 1987 thriller *Fatal Attraction* concerns a bigtime corporate lawyer who has a one-night stand with a no-nonsense businesswoman while his wife is away. The mistress becomes obsessed and all hell breaks loose. Skewering the film's blatant fear of the successful businesswoman and celebration of traditional family values, this Greek tragedy adopts a chorus that comments on the action by using texts from the Greek tragedy oeuvre, as well as from turn-of-the-century home etiquette propaganda.

MELBA MOORE: SWEET SONGS OF THE SOUL

Harry De Jour Playhouse; Opening Night: July 10, 2005; Closed July 30, 2005

Conceived by Melba Moore; Produced by the New Federal Theatre (Woodie King Jr., Artistic Director); Director, Rhonda Passion Hansome; Scenery and Lighting, Antoinette Tynes; Sound; Sean O'Halloran; Production Stage Manager, John Eric Scutchins; Assistant Stage Manger, Anne Skeete; Company Manager, Patricia White; Press, Max Eisen

Performed by **Melba Moore**

Musical Numbers: The Other Side of the Rainbow, Don't Mean a Thing, Stormy Weather, Rock of Ages, Air Mail Special, Hair Medley, Purlie, I Got Love,

Rock Me Tonight, Do Me Baby, You Give Good Love, Ain't No Stoppin' Us Now, Love Come Down, Falling, Lean On Me, Praise Him

Revival of an autobiographical solo performance play with music presented in two acts; originally produced April 2005 for a limited engagement.

Synopsis: Melba Moore, Tony-Award, winning star of the musical *Purlie*, shares her life story, from growing up poor in rural Alabama through the ups and downs of her musical career, with a mix of gospel, jazz, and Broadway songs.

GOLF: THE MUSICAL

Clubhouse at Sofia's; Opening Night: July 13, 2005, Closed August 31, 2005; 16 performances

Book, music and lyrics by Michael Roberts, based on a concept by Eric Krebs; Produced by Eric Krebs; Director and Choreographer, Christopher Scott; Musical Directors/Accompanist (rotating), Michael Roberts, Ken Lundie, Rachel Kaufman; Scenery, James Joughin; Costumes, Bernard Grenier; Lighting, Aaron Spivey; Musical Director, Ken Lundie; General Manager, Jonathan Shulman; Casting, Stephanie Klapper; Press; Terence Womble and Jeffrey Kurtz.

Cast (Rotating): **Joel Blum**; **Angela Madaline**; **Trisha Rapier**; **Christopher Sutton**; **Tom Gamblin**; **Robin Haynes**; **Lyn Philistine**

Musical Numbers: A Show About Golf, The History of Golf, Who Plays Celebrity Golf?, Scratch Golfer, Plaid, The Golfer's Psalm, Tiger Woods, A Great Lady Golfer, Let's Bring Golf to the Gulf, My Husband's Playing Around, The Golfing Museum, The Road to Heaven, No Blacks, No Chicks, No Jews, The Ballad of Casey Martin, Pro Shop Polyphony, Golf's Such a Naughty Game, Presidents and Golf, The Beautiful Time, I'm Going Golfing Tomorrow

Revival of a musical revue presented in two acts; originally produced at the John Houseman Theatre November 19, 2003 where it ran for 136 performances (See *Theatre World* Volume 60, page 107).

Synopsis: A quirky revue about the players and people passionate about the game of golf.

WALK TWO MOONS

Lucille Lortel Theatre; First preview: July 7, 2005; Opening Night: July 13, 2005; Closed August 14, 2005; 38 performances

A Theatreworks/NYC (Barbara Pasternack, Artistic Director; Ken Arthur, Managing Director) presentation of a play by Julia Jordan, adapted from the book by Sharon Creech; Produced by special arrangement with The Lucille Lortel Theatre Foundation; Director, Melissa Kievman; Sets, Louisa Thompson; Costumes, Anne Kennedy; Lighting, Paul Hackenmueller; Original Music, Lucas Papaelias; Sound, Eric Shim; Production Stage Manager, Sara Jaramillo; Production Coordinator, B.D. White; Assistant Director, Courtney Phelps; Casting, Robin D. Carus; Press; Rubenstein Communications, Andy Shearer

Cast: Salamanca Hiddle **Sarah Lord**, Potential Lunatic/Ben/John Hiddle **Lucas Papaelias**, Sheriff/Mrs. Winterbottom, Mrs. Cadaver **Heather Dilly**, Phoebe Winterbottom **Susan Louise O'Connor**, Grandpa Hiddle **Charles H. Hyman**, Gram **Peggy Scott**; **Understudies:** Kenneth Boys (Grandpa Hiddle), Craig

McEldoway (Potential Lunatic), Carolyn McDermott (Gram/Mrs. Cadaver), Greta Storace (Salamanca/Phoebe)

World premiere of a new play for young audiences presented without intermission.

Synopsis: *Walk Two Moons* follows a girl on a road trip across the country with her eccentric grandparents. Her tales of life back home, by turns hilarious and touching, create a journey within a journey as she and her know-it-all best friend discover that things aren't always what they seem.

THE CAPITOL STEPS: FOUR MORE YEARS IN THE BUSH LEAGUES

The Supper Club; Opening Night: July 26, 2005 Closed August 13, 2005; 15 performances

Musical revue by Bill Strauss, Elaina Newport and Mark Eaton; Produced by Eric Krebs and Capitol Steps; Directors, Bill Strauss, Elaina Newport and Mark Eaton; Press Secretary General, Bill Hurd

Cast (alternating): **Kevin Corbett**; **Jack Rowles**; **Mike Thornton**; **Mike Tilford**; **Elaina Newport**; **Ann Schmitt**; **Michael Forrest**; **Morgan Duncan**; **Mike Carruthers**; **Bari Biern**; **Tracey Stephens**; **Mark Eaton**

Pianists: Marc Irwin, Howard Breitbart

Musical Numbers: What a Difference Delay Makes, Embraceable Jew, Wouldn't It Be Hillary, Sunni Side of Tikrit, Someone Dumber Might, I Like Big Cuts and I Cannot Lie, There Is Nothing Like Ukraine, How Do You Solve a Problem Like Korea?, Fakey Purple Hearts, I've Taken Stands on Both Sides Now, Candidates' Debate, Der Nadermouth, It Don't Mean a Thing (If It Ain't Got That Swing), Electile Dysfunction, He Works Hard for the Country, If Only I Had a Plan, Impossible Dean, Sunni & Cher, This Land's Not Your Land,. Detective Story, Supremes, Help Rwanda, Ain't No Surplus, Now It's Gone, Deep Throat by Dr. Seuss, Lirty Dies

Newest edition of the political musical revue presented in two acts.

Synopsis: Armed and hilarious with new songs and numbers, *The Capitol Steps* brings its timely and irreverent spoof of the headlines to the New York stage and promises to bring down the entire house — and Senate.

"Wouldn't It Be Hilary" performed by Capitol Steps   PHOTO BY KEITH STANLEY)

ONE-MAN STAR WARS TRILOGY

Lamb's Theatre; First preview: August 2, 2005; Opening Night: August 9, 2005; Closed December 31, 2005; 184 performances*

Written by Charles Ross; Produced by Dan Roche in association with Carolyn Rossi Copeland Productions; Director, TJ Dawe; Lighting, Mike Schaldmose; General Manager, Big Leap Productions; Technical Director, Tom Mackey; Stage Manager Christine Fisichella; Press, Keith Sherman

Performed by **Charles Ross**

New York premiere of a solo performance play presented without intermission

Synopsis: Charles Ross distills the original *Star Wars* trilogy, episodes IV, V, and VI, and plays all the characters, recreates the effects, sings the music, flies the ships, wields the swords, and fights both sides of the battles.

*The show was on hiatus from November 1 – 22, 2005.

ONCE AROUND THE SUN

Zipper Theatre; First preview: July 27, 2005; Opening Night: August 11, 2005; Closed: October 7, 2005: 17 previews, 64 performances

Music and lyrics by Robert Morris, Steven Morris, and Joe Shane, book by Kellie Overbey; Produced by URL Productions LLC, Sibling Entertainment Inc, in association with Maffei Productions LLC; Associate Producers, Ed and Leah Frankel, Valer and Zuzana Guhr, James V. Johnson, Maria Jannace Spinozza, and David Spinozza; Director, Jace Alexander; Choreography, Taro Alexander; Scenery, Beowulf Boritt; Costumes, Daniel Lawson; Lighting, Jason Lyons; Sound, T. Richard Fitzgerald and Carl Casella; Orchestrations/Musical Supervisor, David Spinozza; Music Director, Henry Aronson; Music Coordinator, John Miller; Arrangements, David Spinozza and the Borough Boys; Casting, Victoria Pettibone; Marketing, HHC Marketing; Advertising, Maxim Creative Group; General Manager, Brent Peek; Production Stage Manager, Renée Rimland; Company Manager, Scott Newsome; Assistant Stage Manager, Lisa Gavaletz; Press, Keith Sherman and Associates

Cast: Kevin **Asa Somers**; Skye **Caren Lyn Manuel**; Ray **Kevin Mambo**; Dave **Jesse Lenat**; Richie **Wes Little**; Lane **John Hickok**; Nona **Maya Days**; **Standbys:** Daniel Cooney, Risa Benson

Musicians: Henry Aronson (Conductor/keyboard), Gillian Berkowitz (Associate Conductor/synthesizer), Chris Biesterfeldt, Tony Di Lullo (guitars), Steve Count (bass), Wes Little (drums), Frank Pagano (percussion)

Musical Numbers: It's All Music, First Dance, Life Is What You Make of It, You're My Lullaby, Let Go, And That's Your Life, Fool Like Me, Once Around the Sun, Lucky Day, G-I-R-L, Missing You My Friend, Something Sentimental, Love and Live On, Just Another Year

Setting: New York, the present. World premiere of a new musical presented in two acts.

Synopsis: An invitation from a beautiful stranger offers a struggling New York musician the opportunity to escape his disappointments and take a leap of faith into his dream, but at the risk of betraying family, lifelong friends, and true love. Seduced by his desire to finally be heard, he makes some unexpected choices and ultimately discovers the flight to glory is like nothing he could have ever imagined.

JOY

Actors' Playhouse; First Preview: July 31, 2005; Opening Night: August 14, 2005; Closed: September 25, 2005; 17 previews, 49 performances.

A new play by John Fisher; Produced by Sean Mackey, Eva Price, and Ben Rimalower; Director, Ben Rimalower; Scenery, Wilson Chin; Costumes, David Kaley; Lighting, Ben Stanton; Sound, Zach Williamson; Executive Producer, Phillip D. Gibson; General Manager, Maria Di Dia and Robert E. Schneider; Casting, Michael Cassara; Marketing, HHC Marketing; Production Stage Manager, Jennifer Noterman; Music Director and Arrangements, Mark Hartman; Choreography, James Deforte; Production Manager, Scott H. Schneider; Company Manager, Robert E Schneider; Assistant Stage Manager, Carla L. Muniz; Press, Shaffer-Coyle Public Relations

Cast: Gabriel **Christopher Sloan**; Paul **Paul Whitthorne**; Corey **Ken Barnett**; Kegan **January LaVoy**; Christian **Ben Curtis**; Elsa **Ryan Kelly**; Darryl **Michael Busillo**

Understudies: Scott Evan Davis (Paul, Corey), Julia Krohn (Kegan, Elsa), Jake Manabat (Gabriel, Christian, Darryl)

Setting: San Francisco, mid 1990s and the present. New York premiere of a play presented in two acts; originally produced as *The Joys of Gay Sex* in San Francisco.

Synopsis: *Joy* follows a group of college friends as they fall in and out of love in San Francisco over the course of a year.

Brian Morvant and Drew Hildebrand in *Screenplay* PHOTO BY MAX RUBY

SIDES: THE FEAR IS REAL...

45 Bleecker; First preview: August 18, 2005; Opening Night: August 25, 2005; Closed October 27, 2005; 86 performances

Written by Sekiya Billman, Cindy Cheung, Paul H. Juhn, Peter Kim, Hoon Lee, and Rodney To; Produced by Mr. Miyagi's Theatre Company in association with the Culture Project and Rel2 Productions; Director, Anne Kauffman; Scenery, David Korins; Costumes, Elizabeth Flauto; Lighting, John-Paul Szczepanski; Sound/Video, Jamie McElhinney; Production Manager, Garin Marschall; Production Stage Manager, Daryn Brown; Assistant Stage Manager, Cyrille Blackburn; General Manager/Company Manager, The Culture Project; Production Manager-Technical Director, Garin Marschall

Cast: Sunny Kenai'Apuni/Guinevere/Stephani/Stripper Girl **Sekiya Billman**; Tracy Cheung/Joan/Darlene/Japanese Girl **Jane Cho**; Chip Kim/Downtown Guy **Paul H. Juhn**; Pete Suh/Patrick/MFA Guy **Peter Kim**; Johnny Fantastiko/Shakespeare Guy **Hoon Lee**; Danbury Brackenbury III/Ghetto Boy/Ding Ding/Choreographer **Rodney To**

Standbys: Eileen Rivera, Jonathan Salkin

Setting: Various waiting rooms, casting offices, and rehearsal studios in New York. A series of scenes and vignettes presented without intermission; originally presented at the 2003 New York International Fringe Festival and off-off Broadway at P.S. 122.

Synopsis: Six hopeful actors seek entertainment employment through true-life audition nightmares. Terrible scripts, psychotic casting directors, and competitive colleagues all stand in their way. In a series of comedic vignettes and scenes, these brave actors face their fears and almost triumph.

SCREENPLAY

Flea Theatre; Opening Night: September 8, 2005; Closed September 30, 2005. The production previously ran at the Flea Theatre as an off-off Broadway production May 27 – July 30, 2005.

Flea Theatre (Jim Simpson, Artistic Director; Carol Ostrow, Producing Director) production of a play by A.R. Gurney; Director, Jim Simpson; Costumes, Melissa Schlachtmeyer; Lighting, Joe Novak; Sound, Greg Duffin; Musical Director, Kris Kukul; Assistant to the Director, Deborah Wolfson; Press, Spin Cycle-Ron Lasko

Cast: Charley Washington **Dave McKeel**; Senator Abner Patch **John Fico**; Sally **Meredith Holzman**; Nick **Drew Hildebrand**; The Swing Actor **Kevin T. Moore**; Walter Wellman **Brian Morvant**; Narrator **Nedra McClyde**

Setting: 2015, just before the election. World premiere of a political satire performed without intermission.

Synopsis: Liberally based on a classic 1942 film, *Screen Play* is a tale of politics, history, the city of Buffalo, and a love ruined by the Bush-Gore election of 2000. In an America ruled by a conservative religious majority, the economy is sagging, wars are raging, and culture is in decay.

PATIENCE

State Theatre at Lincoln Center; September 10 – October 5, 2005; 8 performances

New York City Opera (Paul Kellogg, General and Artistic Director) presentation of the light opera with music by W.S Gilbert, libretto by Arthur Sullivan; Director, Tazewell Thompson; Conductor/Musical Director, Gary Thor Wedow; Scenery, Donald Eastman; Costumes, Merrily Murray-Walsh; Lighting, Robert Wiezel; Chorus Masters, Anthony Piccolo, Charles Frederic Prestinari; Associate Conductor, Brian DeMaris; Musical Preparation, Lynn Baker, Liora Maurer, Marijo Newman; Assistant Directors, Lawrence Edelson, Albert Sherman; Stage Managers, Rachel Stern, Lisa Jean Lewis, Jenny Lazar; Diction Coach, Kathryn LaBouff; Casting, Mark Simon; Press, Susan Woelzl

Cast: The Lady Angela **Jennifer Roderer**; The Lady Ella **Kathleen Magee**; The Lady Saphir **Heather Johnson**; The Lady Jane **Myrna Paris**; Patience **Tonna Miller**; Colonel Calverley **Timothy Nolen**; The Duke of Dunstable **Christopher Jackson**; Major Murgatroyd **Matthew Burns**; Reginald Bunthorne **Michael Ball**; Archibald Grosvenor **Kevin Burdette**; Bunthorne's Solicitor **Keith Partington**

Revival of an operetta presented in two acts

Synopsis: Twenty maidens are lovesick for two pretentious poets, but the bards are vying for Patience, the simple village milkmaid who cares nothing for their verses. Ultimately, they all learn that the key to winning in love is not to play any games at all.

BUKOWSKI FROM BEYOND

SoHo Playhouse; Opening Night: September 11, 2005; Closed January 1, 2006; 60 performances

Adapted for the stage by Leo Farley and Steve Payne from the writings of Charles Bukowski; Presented by LSMFT Productions and Darren Lee Cole; Director, Leo Farley; Scenery, Mark Symczak; Lighting Design/ Production Stage Manager, Cesar Malantic; House Manager, James Smith; Graphic Design, Orianne Cosentino; Photography, Fouad Salloum

Cast: Charles Bukowski **Steve Payne**; Pianist: Carl Riehl

A solo performance play presented without intermission. Originally presented off-off Broadway at the SoHo Playhouse on Monday evenings August 8–30, 2005

Synopsis: 29th Street Rep company member Steve Payne brings the extraordinary writings and spirit of Charles Bukowski to the stage for a visceral evening of poetry and prose. Bukowski, one of America's best-known contemporary writers, was a low-life drifter, prophet of the unemployed, who didn't start writing until he was 35, after quitting his job at the post office.

SILK STOCKINGS

Lost Musicals US Inc. and The Lost Musicals Charitable Trust (UK) presentation of the musical with music and lyrics by Cole Porter, book by George S. Kaufman, Leueen MacGrath, and Abe Burrows; suggested by the screenplay *Ninotchka* by Charles Brackett, Billy Wilder, Walter Reisch, and Ernst Lubitsch, based on

an original story by Melchior Lengyel; Director/Design/ Lighting, Ian Marshall Fisher; Music Director, Lawrence Yurman; Press, Boneau/Bryan-Brown

Florence Gould Hall; September 11 – October 3, 2005; 4 performances

Cast: Boroff **Mitchell Greenberg**; Doorman **Brian Kenneth**; Maurice **Bill Galarno**; Flower Girl **Sarajean Devenport**; Babinski **Tom Mardirosian**; Ivanov **Robert Ari**; Brankov **Wally Dunn**; Canfield **Daniel Gerroll**; Choreographer **Philip Deyesso**; Markovitch **Peter van Wagner**; Vera **Anne Rothenberg**; Ninotchka **Valerie Cutko**; Reporters **Jeffrey Stern**, **Philip Deyesso**; Janice Dayton **Nina Hennessey**; Saleslady **Meghann Babo**; Fabour Model **Jean McCormick**; M Fabour **Ryan Brunton**; Bookstall Owner **Sarajean Devenport**; Sonia **Jean McCormick**

Setting: Paris, 1939. Staged concert of the musical presented in two acts.

Synopsis: Special envoy Nina Yaschenko is dispatched from the Soviet Union to rescue three foolish commissars who have been seduced by the pleasures of Paris. She is romanced by theatrical agent Steven Canfield and eventually comes to recognize the viruses of capitalist indulgence.

THE BLOWIN OF BAILE GALL

Donaghy Theater at the Irish Arts Center, First preview: September 8, 2005; Opening Night: September 13, 2005; Closed October 30, 2005; 6 previews, 42 performances

Written by Ronan Noone; Presented by Julian Pelenur and Aidan Connolly, in association with the Irish Arts Center and Gabriel Byrne; Director, David Sullivan; Scenery, Richard Chambers; Costumes, Jennifer Caprio; Lighting, Daniel Meeker; Original Music, Haddon Kime; Sound, Julie Pittman; Fight Choreography, D. C. Wright; Production Stage Manager, Elizabeth Cheslock; Casting, Stephanie Klapper; Press, Karen Greco

Cast: Eamon Collins **Colin Hamell**; Stephen O'Gorman **Ciaran Crawford**; Samuel Carson **George C. Heslin**; Molly Black **Susan B. McConnell**; Laurence **Ato Essandoh**

Setting: Baile Gall, Ireland. New York premiere of a new play presented in two acts.

Synopsis: Set on a construction site. Four workers struggle to build futures in a small Irish town. But when the General Contractor hires an African refugee (a "blowin") instead of a local, generations of grudges are unearthed with tragic results. As the workers fight to hold on to their history, dignity, and the soil beneath them, they are torn apart by their need for money, acceptance, and ultimately revenge.

THE LADIES OF THE CORRIDOR

East 13th Street Theatre; First preview: September 7, 2005; Opening Night: September 14, 2005; Closed October 23, 2005; 58 performances

Peccadillo Theater Company production of the play by Dorothy Parker and Arnaud d'Usseau; Artistic Director/Director, Dan Wackerman; Scenery, Chris Jones; Costumes, Amy C. Bradshaw; Lighting, Tyler Micoleau; Graphics, Dick Larson; Dramaturg, William M, Peterson; Production Stage Manager, Michael Gianakos;

Assistant Stage Manager, Kristen Dreger; General Manager, Tim Hurley; Press, Brett Singer and Associates

Cast: Mrs. Gordon/Mary Linscott **Libby George;** Mr. Humphries/Tom Linscott **Hal Blankenship;** Mrs. Lauterbach **Carolyn Seiff;** Charles Nichols **Ron Bagden;** Grace Nichols **Peggy Cowles;** Harry **Garth T. Mark;** Lulu Ames **Susan Jeffries;** Mildred Tynan **Domenica Cameron-Scorsese;** Robert Ames **Patrick Boyd;** Betsy Ames **Dawn Evans;** Connie Mercer **Jo Ann Cunningham;** Irma **Susan Varon;** Paul Osgood **Kelly AuCoin;** Casey **Andy Phelan**

Setting: Hotel Marlow, New York City, 1950's. Revival of a play presented in two acts. Originally produced on Broadway at the Longacre Theatre, October 21, 1953 where it ran for 45 performances (See *Theatre World* Volume 10.)

Synopsis: *The Ladies of the Corridor* is a funny and sympathetic look behind the closed doors of New York City's seedy Hotel Marlow. Lulu Ames, a widow carrying on with a much younger man; Mildred Tynan, who flees an abusive husband only to partner with an alcoholic; and Grace Nichols, who intends to keep her son close at all costs, along with several other colorful characters, cross paths in the corridor of this genteel establishment, where a skeleton is hung in every closet.

*Succeeded by Tom Biglin

Javier Rivera and Andres Munar in *Kissing Fidel* PHOTOS BY CAROL ROSEGG

KISSING FIDEL

Kirk Theatre; First preview: September 6, 2005; Opening Night: September 20, 2005; Closed October 23, 2005; 45 performances

INTAR (Edward Machado, Artistic Director, Editha Rosario, Executive Director) production of a new play by Eduardo Machado; Director, Michael John Garcés; Scenery, Mikiko Suzuki; Costumes, Meghan Healey; Lighting, Paul Whitaker; Sound, David M. Lawson; Production Manager, Sergio Cruz; Production Stage Manager, Michael Alifanz; Casting, Orpheus Group; Press, Richard Kornberg & Associates

Cast: Oscar **Bryant Mason;** Miriam **Karen Kondazian;** Daniel **Javier Rivera;** Osvaldo Marques **Lazaro Perez;** Yolanda **Judith Delgado;** Ismael **Andres Munar**

Setting: Miami, Florida. 1994. World premiere of a new play presented in two acts.

Synopsis: In the back room of a Miami funeral parlor, the Cuban-American Marques family has gathered for the final rites of its matriarch. Shattered by Castro but utterly gouged by family skeletons and the "fictional" tell-all novels of grandson Oscar, the Marques family is consumed with alternately exhuming and obliterating the past;\ tasks which become even more difficult when Oscar announces his plan to kiss and forgive Fidel Castro.

RED BEADS

Jack H. Skirball Center for the Performing Arts; September 20 – 24, 2005; 5 performances

Mabou Mines production of an experimental theatre piece created by Lee Breuer and Basil Twist; based on an original story by Plina Klimovitskaya; produced in association with the Skirball Center; Director, Lee Breuer; Music/Arrangements, Ushio Torikai; Animated Design/Wind Puppetry, Basil Twist; Performance Poem, Lee Breuer; Lighting, Jennifer Tipton, M. L. Geiger; Projections, Julie Archer; Costumes, Meganne George; Sound, Ken Travis; Produced for Mabou Mines by Sharon Fogarty; Production Manager, Juniper Street Productions, Inc., John Paull

Cast: The Girl **Clove Galilee;** The Father **Rob Besserer;** The Mother **Ruth Maleczech**

Setting: Edwardian New England. World premiere of a performance piece presented without intermission.

Synopsis: *Red Beads,* combining the disparate arts of performance, movement, opera, and puppetry, is a gothic coming-of-age fairy-tale/opera, choreographed aerially. Lee Breuer's performance poem explores the eerie family dynamic of a daughter's transition into womanhood and the "gift," from mother to daughter, of the red beads, a metaphor for the passage of power and sexuality.

THE PAVILION

Rattlestick Theatre 224 Waverly; First preview: September 9, 2005; Opening Night: September 20, 2005; Closed October 23, 2005; 9 previews, 27 performances

Rattlestick Playwrights Theatre (Artistic Director, David Van Asselt; Managing Director, Sandra Coudert) production of a play by Craig Wright; Casting, Jodi

Collins; Associate Artistic Director, Lou Moreno; Director, Lucie Tiberghien; Composer/Accompanist, Christopher Tiberghien; Scenery, Takeshi Kata; Costumes, Mimi O'Donnell; Lighting, Matt Richards; Production Stage Manager, Paige Van Den Burg; Assistant Stage Manager, Libby Steiner; Press, Origlio Public Relations

Cast: Peter **Brian d'Arcy James**; Kari **Jennifer Mudge**; Narrator **Stephen Bogardus**

Setting: Pine City, Minnesota. New York premiere of a play presented in two acts.

Synopsis: In the titular 100-year-old dance hall, the lives of ex-sweethearts Peter Mollberg and Kari Hermanson — and dozens of other characters — intertwine once more to form a pattern of love and loss.

*Succeeded by Tasha Lawrence (October 5, 2005)

DR. SEX

Peter Norton Space; First Preview: August 26, 2005; Opening Night: September 21, 2005; Closed: October 9, 2005; 24 previews, 22 performances

Music and lyrics by Larry Bortniker, book by Larry Bortniker and Sally Deering; Produced by Richard Ericson and Greg Young; Production Supervisor/Production Stage Manager, Greg Hirsch; Choreography, Mark Esposito; Music Supervision and Arrangements, Patrick Vaccariello; Scenery, Rob Bissinger; Costumes, John Carver Sullivan; Lighting, Richard Winkler; Sound, Michael Ward, Tony Smolenski IV; Orchestrations, Larry Hochman, David Siegel, Ned Ginsburg; Conductor, Alan Bukowiecki; Dance Music Arrangements, Sam Davis; Associate Producers, Jann Cobler, Tom Wilson; General Manager, Ideal Theatricals, Jeffrey Chrzczon; Consulting Producers, Jay Bernzweig, Jerry Felix, Casting, Carol Hanzel; Stage Manager, Sarah A. Tschirpke; Dance Captain, Colleen Hawks; Music Copying, Anne Kaye, Doug Houston; Press, David Gersten and Associates

Cast: Alfred C. Kinsey **Brian Noonan**; Clara Kinsey **Jennifer Simard**; Wally **Christopher Corts**; IU Student/George/Bar Patron/American **Jared Bradshaw**; Miss Baxter/Mrs. Cavendish/Bar Patron/Miss Loretta Rockefeller/Operator **Linda Cameron**; IU Student/Dean Howell/Mr. Cavendish/Dr. Wilhelm Hoffstedter **David Edwards**; IU Student/Daphne/Brenda **Christy Faber**; IU Student/Phoebe **Colleen Hawks**; IU Student/Jack/Edgar Stevens **Benjie Randall**; The Kinsey Players/Americans **Jared Bradshaw, Linda Cameron, David Edwards, Christy Faber, Colleen Hawks, Benjie Randall**; Understudies: Brian Ogilvie, Dana Winkle

Marya Grandy, Leslie Kritzer, Linda Hart in *The Great American Trailer Park Musical*

Musicians: Alan Bukowiecki (Conductor/piano), John Meyers (drums/percussion), William Sloat (bass), Trevor Neumann (trumpet), Mike Seltzer (trombone), Scott Shachter (woodwinds)

Musical Numbers: 1 2 3 4 5 6, Rah Rah Rah Rah, I'm in Love With My Zoology Professor, Here in a Bog, Gall Wasp Wedding, Honeymoon Dance, The Call of the Wild, Angelface, Dr. Sex, What People Really Do When the Lights Are Low, Pharaoh's Tomb, Swingin' for Science, John D. Rockefeller, They'll Tell You Everything, The Doctor's Wife, A Simple Rotational System, I'm Still in Love With My Zoology Professor, That Dirty Book, Kinsey in the Eleventh Hour

Setting: Indiana University, Bloomington, Chicago, and New York, 1930's-1940's. New York premiere of a musical presented in two acts.

Synopsis: *Dr. Sex* explores the loving relationship between Dr. Alfred Kinsey, his wife, Clara ... and their handsome boyfriend (and lab assistant), Wally Matthews. When Professor Kinsey, tired of cataloguing American gall wasps, discovers his life's work in human sexual research, Bloomington becomes a hotbed of science and sex.

THE GREAT AMERICAN TRAILER PARK MUSICAL

Dodger Stages Theatre 1; First preview: August 20, 2005; Opening Night: September 27, 2005; Closed December 4, 2005: 121 performances

Music and lyrics, David Nehls, book by Betsy Kelso; Produced by Jean Doumanuan and Jeffrey Richards in association with Janet Pailet; Director, Betsy Kelso; Music Director, David Nehls; Choreography, Sergio Trujillo; Scenery, Derek McLane; Lighting, Donald Holder, Costumes, Markas Henry; Sound, Peter Fitzgerald; Technical Supervision, Rob Conover; Hair, Josh Marquette; Casting, Dave Caparelliotis; General Manager, Laura Heller; Production Stage Manager; Marketing, HHC Marketing; Associate Producer, George S. Kaufman; Production Stage Manager, Richard C Rauscher; Stage Manager, Francesca Russell; Dance Captain, Marya Grandy; Press, Irene Gandy; Cast Recording: Sh-K-Boom 91558605129

Cast: Betty **Linda Hart**; Linoleum **Marya Grandy**; Pickles **Leslie Kritzer**; Norbert **Shuler Hensley**; Jeannie **Kaitlin Hopkins**; Pippi **Orfeh**; Leo/Duke **Wayne Wilcox**

Musicians: David Nehls (Conductor/keyboard), David Matos (guitar), Paul Panieri (bass), Damien Bassman (drums)

Musical Numbers: This Side of the Tracks, Immobile in My Mobile Home, Do Nuthin' Day, It Doesn't Take a Genius, Owner of My Heart, The Great American TV Show, Flushed Down the Pipes, Storm's-A-Brewin', This Side of the Tracks (reprise), Road Kill, But He's Mine/It's Never Easy, That's Why I Love My Man, Panic, Big Billy's No-Tell Motel, Finale

Setting: A Trailer Park in Starke, Florida. A new musical presented in two acts (during the run the intermission was eliminated). Originally produced at the 2004 New York Musical Theatre Festival.

Synopsis: A country-rock and blues musical about agoraphobia, adultery, '80s nostalgia, spray cheese, road kill, hysterical pregnancy, a broken electric chair, kleptomania, strippers, flan, and disco, *The Great American Trailer Park Musical* centers around regular guy Norbert and his agoraphobic wife, Jeannie, whose marriage is threatened by Armadillo Acres' newcomer, the hot young stripper Pippi. The trailer park also plays home to a Greek-chorus-like trio of women Linoleum, Betty and Pickles, each dysfunctional in her own right.

MEDEA

HSA Theatre; First preview: September 15, 2005; Opening Night: September 23, 2005; Closed October 23, 2005; 29 performances

Classic Theatre of Harlem (Alfred Preisser, Co-Founder and Artistic Director; Christopher McElroen, Co-Founder and Executive Director) production of the play by Euripides; Director/Adaptation, Alfred Preisser; Musical Director, Kelvyn Bell; Choreography, Tracy Jack, Scenery, Christopher Thomas; Costumes, Kimberly Glennon; Lighting, K.J. Hardy; Sound, Stefan Jacobs; Original Music and Songs, Kelvyn Bell and David Red Harrington; Stage Manger, Niki Spruill; Development Associate, Michelle Y. Hodges; Press, Brett Singer

Cast: Kreon **Earle Hyman**; Nurse **Juanita Howard**; Fates **Shamika Cotton, Tisza Cher-rie Evans, Ebbe Bassey**; Choral Leader/Death **Zainab Jah**; Medea **April Yvette Thompson**; Jason **Lawrence Winslow**; Messenger **Yoki Brown**; Medea Children **Brian Gilbert, Laron Griffin**; Princess Glauke **Zora Howard**; Soldier **Messiyah McGinnest**; Chorus **E. Donisha Brown, Monique Brown, Julianne Hamburgo, Caran L. Harris, Althea Alexis Vyfhuis**

Understudy: Alethea Alexis Vyfhuis (Medea)

Musician: Shayshahn Macpherson (drums, viola)

Revival of the play with original music presented without intermission; CTH previously presented this adaptation in 2002.

Synopsis: Using live, original music, chant, dance, and a highly theatrical treatment of text emphasizing contemporary speech, Classical Theatre of Harlem creates a vital present-tense *Medea*. The all-black cast features a chorus of tattooed, body-painted Corinthian women, who employ dance and song to reinvent the choral passages as the ritualistic counterpoint to the dramatic story line they were originally intended to be.

Peter Scolari, Brian Henderson, Marilyn Sokol, Josh Prince, Lisa Datz in *In The Wings*
PHOTO BY CAROL ROSEGG

NO FOREIGNERS BEYOND THIS POINT

Ma-Yi Theatre Company (Ralph B. Peña, Artistic Director; Jorge Z. Ortoll, Executive Director) production of a new play by Warren Leight; Produced by in association with Swingline Productions; Director/Scenery, Loy Arcenas; Costumes, Carol Bailey; Lighting Japhy Wiedeman; Sound, Fabian Obispo; Assistant Director, Michael Lew; Stage Manager, April Kline; Production Manager, Jamie Smith; Properties; Winnie Lok; Press, Sam Rudy Media Relations

45 Bleecker-Below; First preview: September 17, 2005; Opening Night: September 25, 2005; Closed October 16, 2005; 30 performances

Cast: Xiao Wan/Xiao Da **Laura Kai Chen**; Sherman/Worker Ying **Ron Domingo**; Widow Wan/Teacher Ming **Wai Ching Ho**; Vice Principal Huang/Lincoln **Francis Jue**; Teacher Chen/Pearl **Karen Tsen Lee**; Paula Wheaton **Abby Royle**; Andrew Baker **Ean Sheehy**; Principal Wang/Customs Officer **Henry Yuk**

Setting: Guangdong, China. 1980. A new play presented in two acts.

Synopsis: After the horrors of the Cultural Revolution, two idealistic Americans become the first foreign instructors at a small isolated trade school. Their students crave access to everything Western; the school's bureaucrats are desperate to control that access; and the Americans soon find themselves living under virtual house arrest. In a world where betrayal is necessary for survival, the students and teachers struggle to overcome cultural, political, and personal barriers to intimacy and identity.

IN THE WINGS

Promenade Theatre; First preview: September 9, 2005; Opening Night: September 28, 2005: Closed October 16, 2005; 21 previews, 21 performances.

A new play by Stewart F. Lane; Produced by Bonnie Comley and Stellar Productions Int'l, Inc.; Songs by Michael Garin; Director, Jeremy Dobrish; Musical Direction, Edward Straus; Additional Music, Doug Maxwell and Peter Scolari; Scenery, William Barclay; Costumes, Mattie Ullrich; Lighting, Phil Monat; Sound, Jill B C Deboff; Orchestrations, Martin Erskine, Doug Maxwell; Production Manager, PRF Productions; Production Stage Manager, Pamela Edington; General Management, Roger Alan Gindi; Casting, Liz Lewis and Elizabeth Bunnell; Marketing, HHC Marketing; Company Manager, A. Scott Falk; Stage Manager, Gerald Cosgrove; Press; Keith Sherman Associates

Cast: Melinda Donahugh **Lisa Batz**; Nicky Sanders **Brian Henderson**; Steve Leonards **Josh Prince**; Bernardo **Peter Scolari**; Martha Leonards **Marilyn Sokol**

Understudies: Carrie Keranen (Melinda), John Michael Coppola (Nicky), Brian Henderson (Steve), Mitchell Greenberg (Bernardo), Maria Cellario (Martha)

Setting: New York City, 1977. World premiere of a new play presented in two acts.

Synopsis: A young couple, both actors, is cast in a new musical titled *I Married a Communist*, but one gets left behind when the show moves to Broadway.

BUSH IS BAD: THE MUSICAL CURE FOR THE BLUE-STATE BLUES

Triad Theatre; First preview: September 15, 2005; Opening Night: September 29, 2005; Still running as of May 31, 2006

Concept, music and lyrics by Joshua Rosenblum; Produced by Tim Peierls and Shrubbery Productions; Director and Choreographer, Gary Slavin; Graphic Design, Colin Stokes; Costumes, Anne Auberjonois; Lighting and Sound, Tonya Pierre; Musical Director, Joshua Rosenblum; Assistant Director/Assistant Choreographer, Janet Bushor; Props, Julian Brightman; Creative Consultant, Joanne Lessner; Production Coordinator, Ayelet Arbuckle; Marketing, Gary Shaffer; Digital Imaging, Julian Rosenblum; Graphic Design/Design Adaptation, Michael Holmes; Press, Kevin McAnarney; Cast Recording: Original Cast Records 837101 123426

Cast: Kate Baldwin*1; **Neal Mayer**; **Michael McCoy***2

Pianist: Joshua Rosenblum

Musical Numbers: How Can 59 Million People Be So Dumb?, Bush is Bad, New Hope for the Fabulously Wealthy, Das Busch Ist Schlecht, Good Conservative Values, The Gay Agenda, I May Be Gay, I'm Losing You, Karl, Love Song of W. Mark Felt , John Bolton Has Feelings, Too, Crazy Ann Coulter, Lying Liars, Survivor: Beltway Scumbag Edition, The "I" Word , Get Real, The Inauguration Was Marvelous, Good Conservative Values II, Culture of Life,. Beaten by a Dead Man, Sure You Betcha, Georgie, In His Own Words, On Our Way to Guantonamo Bay

A musical revue presented without intermission

Synopsis: Described as a cross between *Forbidden Broadway* and *The Daily Show*, *Bush Is Bad* is a left-eyed look at the current sorry state of affairs in American government.

Succeeded by: 1. Jill Abramovitz, Kate Baldwin, Janet Dickinson 2. Tom Treadwell, Michael McCoy

CYCLING PAST THE MATTERHORN

Clurman Theatre; First preview: September 18, 2005; Opening Night: September 26, 2005; Closed November 6, 2005; 11 previews, 45 performances

A new play by Deborah Grimberg; Produced by Farm Avenue Productions, Joseph Smith; Director, Eleanor Holdridge; Scenery, Beowulf Boritt; Costumes, Kiki Smith; Lighting, Les Dickert; Original Music and Sound, Scott Killian; Production Stage Manager, Wesley Apfel; Dialect Coach, Gilliam Lane-Plescia; Casting, Carrie Gardner; Company Manager, Stephen Rebolledo; General Manager, Louis Salamone, Toy; Advertising, Chuck Marks; Press, Shaffer-Coyle

Cast: Amy **Carrie Preston**; Joanne **Nina Jacques**; Esther **Shirley Knight**; Anita **Brenda Wehle**; Doug **Ben Fox**

Setting: London, the present. A new play presented in two acts.

Synopsis: Amy, a young sidewalk psychic (with mediocre abilities) and her eccentric mother, Esther, are at a crossroads. Esther has recently been left by her husband and has just discovered she is slowly going blind. Amy, fearing being stuck as Esther's caretaker, considers marrying her American boyfriend to escape the predicament while Esther decides to forge ahead with her life and joins a cycling excursion in Switzerland to see the mountains while she still can.

LATE FRAGMENT

Studio Dante; First preview: September 28, 2005; Opening Night: October 1, 2005; Closed October 22, 2005; 16 performances

Studio Dante (Michael and Victoria Imperioli, Artistic Directors) production of a play by Francine Volpe; Produced by Mr. and Mrs. Imperioli, Tina Thor, Howard Axel; Directors, Michael Imperioli and Zetna Fuentes; Scenery and Costumes, Victoria Imperioli; Lighting, Tony Giovannetti; Painter, Richard Cerullo; Master Carpenter, Ryczard Chlebowski; Stage Manager, Darren Rosen; Assistant Stage Manager, Brigid Harmon; Casting, Cindi Rush; Press, The Karpel Group

Cast: Cameraman **Ken Forman**; Brian **Dean Harrison**; Dorian **Michael Mosley**; Matthew **Nick Sandow**; Marta **Jenna Stern**

Setting: New York City, September 11, 2001. A new play presented in two acts.

Synopsis: Michael, a white-collar worker, comes home covered in soot, having survived the attacks on the World Trade Center to face an impatient wife, their manipulative lawyer, and reporters desperate to spin his ordeal into a hero story.

SLUT

American Theatre of Actors, Chernuchin Theatre; First preview: September 13, 2005; Opening Night: October 1, 2005; Closed November 13, 2005; 19 previews, 50 performances

Book and lyrics by Ben H. Winters, music and additional lyrics by Stephen Sislen; Produced by Dena Hammerstein and Pam Pariseau for James Hammerstein Productions; Director, Gordon Greenberg; Choreography, Warren Carlyle; Music Director and Orchestrations, Eric Svejcar; Scenery, Beowulf Boritt; Costumes, Anne Kennedy; Lighting, Jane Cox; Sound, Peter Hylenski; Casting, Eric Woodall/Tara Rubin Casting; Production Manager, Shannon Nicole Case; Production Stage Manager, Sara Jaramillo; General Management, Theatre Production Group, LLC; Company Manager, Tegan Meyer; Assistant Stage Manager, Benjamin J. Shuman; Dance Captain, Amanda Watkins; Press, Bill Evans and Associates, Jim Randolph

Cast: Adam **Andy Karl**; Yesterday's News/Veronica, etc **Mary Faber**; Doug/Sea Captain/Janey's Father/ etc **Kevin Pariseau**; Lilly/Janey's Mother/etc **Harriett D. Foy**; Janey/etc **Amanda Watkins**; J-Dogg/Buddy Pendleton/etc **David Josefsberg**; Dan **Jim Stanek**; Delia **Jenn Colella**

Standbys: Rich Affannato, Sara Chase

Musicians: Eric Svejcar (keyboards), Brad Carbone (drums), Joe Brent (guitar), Steve Gilewski (bass)

Musical Numbers: I'm Probably Not Gonna Call, Fuel for the Fire; Tiny Little Pieces, Slutterday Night, The Bravest Little Boat, A Girl That You Meet in a Bar, Tiny Little Pieces (reprise), Lower the Bar, True Love, The Slut of the World, J-Dogg's Lament, Janey's Song, I Wouldn't Change a Thing, One Adam at a Time, A Girl That You Meet in a Bar (reprise), Slutterday Night (reprise)

Setting: New York City, the East Village, and around the world. A musical presented in two acts; originally produced at the 2004 New York Fringe Festival.

Synopsis: *Slut* tells the story of Adam, a single dude on a lifelong quest for one-night stands; his best friend, the brilliant Doctor Dan; and the sexy rocker Delia who comes between them. Set in the East Village and around the world, this highly improbable, irreverent adventure comes with singing, dancing, partying, and raspberry margaritas.

A WOMAN OF WILL

Daryl Roth Theatre; First preview: September 17, 2005; Opening Night: October 2, 2005; Closed October 9, 2005; 16 previews, 9 performances

Book and lyrics by Amanda McBroom, music, book and direction by Joel Silberman, additional music by Michele Bourman; Produced by David A. Braun, Jack Nadel, and Julie Nadel; Musical Director, Sam Davis; Choreography, Thommie Walsh; Scenery/Lighting/Projections, Trefoni Michael Rizzi; Costumes, Tobin Ost; Sound, Lewis Mead; Orchestrations, Larry Hochman; Music Coordinator, Michael Keller; General Managers, Ken Denison and Carol Fishman; Production Stage Manager, Jane Pole; Technical Supervisor, TheatreSmith Inc.; Press, Shaffer-Coyle

Cast: Kate McNall **Amanda McBroom**; Voice of the Husband **George Ball**; Voice of the Boyfriend **Patrick Cassidy**; Voice of the Playwright **Jim Dale**; Voice of the Director **Andre DeShields**; Voice of the Agent **Alix Korey**; Voice of the Composer **Jay Rogers**

Musicians: Sam Davis (Conductor/keyboards), James Mironchik (keyboards/synthesizer), Jimmie Young (percussion), Charles Pillow (woodwinds)

Christa Scott-Reed, Henny Russell, Susan Louise O'Connor in *Marion Bridge*
PHOTO BY PAVEL ANTONOV

Musical Numbers: Cleveland, Screen, Words, Tomorrow Was Born Tonight, The Bitch Is Out, Ophelia, Stand Up, Suddenly Love. Lady Macbeth Sings the Blues, In His Hands, The Hard to Be a Fairy Blues, True to My Heart, Is It Love?, The Merchant of Havana, Hello, The Road Not Taken, I Choose To Love

Setting: A Holiday Inn in Cleveland, Ohio. A solo performance musical presented in two acts.

Synopsis: Hired to finish the lyrics of a Broadway-bound musical version of *The Merchant of Venice,* Kate faces the demands of an unrelenting deadline in addition to important decisions about her marriage and future. In desperation, she reaches out to Shakespeare's leading ladies for guidance.

EINSTEIN'S GIFT

Acorn Theatre; First preview: October 1, 2005; Opening Night: October 6, 2005; Closed November 6, 2005; 40 performances

Epic Theatre Center production of a new play by Vern Thiessen; Director, Ron Russell; Scenery, John McDermott; Costumes, Margaret E. Weedon; Lighting, Elizabeth Gaines, Jeremy Morris Burke; Production Stage Manager, Jana Llynn; Press, Barlow-Hartman, Jon Dimond, Rick Miramontez

Cast: Albert Einstein **Shawn Elliott;** F.J. Haber **Aasif Mandvi;** Clara Immerwahr **Melissa Friedman;** Otto **James Wallert;** Deacon Auffarth/Peterson/Gestapo **Godfrey L. Simmons Jr.;** Deimling/Bernhard Rust **Glenn Fleshler;** Soldier/Singer **Nilaja Sun;** Lotta Haber **Sarah Winkler;** American premiere of a new play presented in two acts

Synopsis: *Einstein's Gift* centers on the relationship between Albert Einstein and Friedrich Haber, two-world-famous scientists who shared little in common, but witnessed their great discoveries used for massive destruction.

MARION BRIDGE

Urban Stages; First preview: October 1, 2005; Opening Night: October 6, 2005; Closed November 27, 2005; 56 performances

Urban Stages (Frances Hill, Artistic Director, Sonia Kozlova, Managing Director; Lori Laster, Program Director) production of a play by Daniel MacIvor; Director, Susan Fenichell; produced by special arrangement with Sonny Everett and Ashley Gates; Scenery and Costumes, Carol Bailey; Lighting, Jorge Arroyo; Original Music and Sound, Eric Shim; Stage Manager, Keleigh Eisen; Assistant Stage Manager, Stephen Risciaca; Technical Director, Joe Powell; Props, Tim Domack; Make-up, Anthea King; Marketing, Michelle Brandon; Casting, Stephanie Clapper; Press, Brett Singer

Cast: Theresa MacKeigan **Christa Scott-Reed**; Agnes MacKeigan **Henny Russell**; Louise MacKeigan **Susan Louise O'Connor**; TV Voices **Victor Slezak, Jennifer Ferrin**

Setting: The Present. Cape Breton, Nova Scotia. American premiere of a new play presented in two acts.

Synopsis: *Marion Bridge* is the humorous and touching story of three sisters who return home to care for their mother. Trapped by life choices and unfulfilled expectations that have left them isolated, the three women search for the courage to create a new family from the remnants of the old.

FIVE COURSE LOVE

Minetta Lane Theatre; First preview: October 1, 2005; Opening Night: October 16, 2005; Closed December 31, 2005; 16 previews, 70 performances

Book, music and lyrics by Gregg Coffin; Produced by Geva Theatre Center and Five Course Love, LLC; Director, Emma Griffin; Choreography, Mindy Cooper; Scenery and Costumes, G.W. Mercier; Lighting, Mark Barton; Sound, Rob Kaplowitz; Music Director, Fred Tessler; Orchestrations, David Labman; Dramaturg, Marge Betley; General Manager, Roy Gabay; Production Manager, Showman Fabricators; Production Stage Manager, Martha Donaldson; Casting, Paul Fouquet and Elissa Myers; Press, Origlio Public Relations

Cast: Matt/Gino/Klaus/Guillermo/Clutch **John Bolton**; Barbie/Sofia/Gretchen/ Rosalinda/Kitty **Heather Ayers**; Dean/Carlo/Heimlich/Ernesto/Pops **Jeff Gurner**; **Understudies/Off Stage Singers:** Erin Maguire, Billy Sharpe

Musicians: Fred Tessler (Conductor/keyboards), Carl Haan (keyboards), Taylor Price (guitar/bass), Steve McKeown (percussion)

Musical Numbers: Five-Course Love Overture, A Very Single Man, Jumpin' the Gun, Dean's Old Fashioned All-American Down Home Bar-B-Que Texas Eats, I Loved You When I Thought Your Name Was Ken, Morning Light, If Nicky Knew, Give Me This Night, Nicky Knows, Shelter-Lied, "No" Is a Word I Don't Fear, Der Bumsen-Kratzentanz, Risk Love, Gretchen's Lament, The Ballad of Guillermo, Come Be My Love, Pick Me, The Blue Flame, True Love at the Star-Lite Tonight, It's A Mystery, Medley, Love Looking Back at Me

Setting: Dean's Old Fashioned All-American Down Home Bar-B-Que Texas Eats, La Trattoria Pericola, Der Schlupfwinkel Speiseplatz, Ernesto's Cantina, and The Star-Lite Diner. New York premiere of a new musical presented without intermission.

Synopsis: Five dates. Five restaurants. Endless sidesplitting laughs. The endearing and often elusive search for love is played out through the love lives of fifteen characters played by three actors in this high-energy screwball musical comedy.

IN THE AIR

Theatre 315; First preview: October 12, 2005; Opening Night October 20, 2005; Closed December 3, 2005; 40 performances

Stageplays Theatre Company (Tom Ferriter, Producer) production of a play by Paul Enger; Director, Tom Ferriter; Scenery, Zhanna Gurvich; Costumes, Kristine Koury; Lighting, Jeffrey Koger; Sound, Guy Sherman/Aural Fixation; Original Music, Cindy O'Connor; Choreography, Daniel Haley; Stage Manager; Elizabeth Paige; Assistant Stage Manager, Jamie Rose Thoma; Casting, Laura Dragomir; Press, Pete Sanders

Cast: Ellen **Jeanine Bartel**; Clara **Nisis Sturgis**; Ben **Preston Dane**; Mrs. Ames **Celia Howard**

Setting: Mayville, North Dakota, 1918. World premiere of a new drama presented in two acts.

Synopsis: *In the Air* is the story of two sisters and a pioneering aviator who experience first love while confronting the ravages to their community by the Great Flu Epidemic of 1918. The drama explores the epidemic's devastating effects on the young and is a metaphor for the incurable diseases of our own time.

Heather Ayers and John Bolton in *Five Course Love*   PHOTO BY RICHARD TERMINE

ASHLEY MONTANA GOES ASHORE IN THE CAICOS … OR WHAT AM I DOING HERE?

Flea Theatre; First preview: October 6, 2005; Opening Night: October 20, 2005; Closed November 19, 2005; 36 performances

Written by Roger Rosenblatt; Produced by the Flea Theatre (Jim Simpson, Artistic Director; Carol Ostrow, Managing Director); Director, Jim Simpson; Scenery, Kyle Chepulis; Costumes, Melissa Schlachtmeyer; Lighting, Brian Aldous; Choreography, Mimi Quillin; Production Graphics, David Prittie; Music, Peter Weissman, Lyrics, Roger Rosenblatt; Musical Director, Kris Kukul; Percussionist, Christopher Lipton; Managing Director, Todd Rosen; Stage Manager, Yvonne Perez; Press, Spin Cycle-Ron Lasko

Cast: Woman 1 **Bebe Neuwirth**; Man 1 **Jeffrey DeMunn**; Woman 2 **Jenn Harris**; Man 2 **James Waterston**

World premiere of a series of vignettes with music presented without intermission

Synopsis: A series of piercingly funny vignettes about aging, angst, missed opportunities, New York, New Age, the next big thing, and the last hurrah.

ON SECOND AVENUE

Godman-Sonnenfeldt Theatre; First preview: October 22, 2005; Opening Night: October 27, 2005; Closed January 1, 2006; 6 previews, 63 performances.

Created by Moishe Rosenfed and Zalmen Mlotek; Produced by Folksbiene Yiddish Theatre in association with the Dora Wasserman Yiddish Theatre of Montreal; Director, Bryna Wasserman; Scenery, J.C. Olivier; Costumes, Kate Whitehead, Lighting, Jacques-Olivier Dupuis; Sound, Kevin Brubaker; Musical Director, Zalmen Mlotek; Choreography/Assistant Director, Lorna Wayne; Managing Director, Jennifer Dumas; Production Supervisor, Mary Botosan; Stage Manager, Marci Skolnick; Assistant Stage Manager/Dance Captain/Swing, Penny Ayn Maas; Orchestrations, Peter Sokolow; Press, Beck Lee, Media Blitz

Cast: Mike Burstyn; **Joanne Borts**; **Lisa Fishman**; **Robert Abelson**; **Elan Kunin**; **Lisa Rubin**

Musicians: Jeff Buchsbaum (Conductor/piano), Dave Braynard (bass), Dave Chamberlain (trombone), Larry Gillespie (trumpet), Rachel Golub (violin), Matt Temkin (drums), Howie Leshaw (flute/clarinet/saxophone)

Revival of a musical review presented in two acts. This production was produced with this cast February 20–April 10, 2005. Due to editorial error, this listing was accidentally omitted from *Theatre World* Volume 61. The show was originally produced Off Broadway in 1986.

Synopsis: *On Second Avenue* is a review filled with authentic period songs and comedy sketches spanning the Yiddish theatre's origins in Jassy Romania to its heyday in New York.

THE INVISIBLE MAN

Baruch Performing Arts Center Nagelberg Theatre; First preview: October 21, 2005; Opening Night: October 27, 2005; Closed November 6, 2005; 8 previews, 10 performances

Aquila Theatre Company (Peter Meineck, Artistic Director) production of a play adapted from the H.G. Wells novel; Created by Anthony Cochrane, Peter Meineck, Robert Richmond and Doug Varone; Director/Choreographer, Doug Varone; Original Music, Anthony Cochrane; Choreography, Doug Varone; Scenery, Peter Meineck and Robert Richmond; Costumes, Megan Bowers; Lighting, Jane Cox; Associate Producer, Todd Batstone; Production Manager, Nate Terracio; Associate Lighting, Travis I. Walker; Graphics, Brown Cathell; Press, The Karpel Group

Cast: Mrs. Hall **Peggy Baker**; Dr. Cuss **John Beasant III**; Griffen (The Stranger) **Daniel Charon**; Dr. Kemp **Anthony Cochrane**; Nurse 1 **Natalie Desch**; Nurse 2 **Catherine Miller**; Nurse 3 **Adriane Fang**; The Janitor **Larry Hahn**; Candy Striper **Stephanie Liapis**; The Orderly **Edward Taketa**

Setting: A private clinic in the rural North East some time in the past, winter. A play with dance presented without intermission.

Synopsis: Griffin, a talented young scientist, makes a startling discovery. In the midst of experimentation putting his radical theories into practice, he renders himself invisible, which proves to be a curse, as he suffers total isolation and lack of human contact. Though removed from society, he profoundly affects all who encounter him. The stranger becomes the outcast, reviled, hated, and feared and responding with pain, madness, and terror.

CAPTAIN LOUIE

Little Shubert Theatre; First preview: October 28, 2005; Opening Night: October 31, 2005; Closed November 13, 2005; 6 previews, 16 performances

Book by Anthony Stein, music and lyrics by Stephen Schwartz, based on the children's book *The Trip* by Ezra Jack Keats; Produced by Meridee Stein, Kurt Peterson, and Bob Reich; Director, Meridee Stein; Music Director, Ray Fellman; Choreography, Joshua Bergasse; Multi-Media, the Joshua Light Show; Lighting, Jason Lyons; Sound, Shannon Slaton; Sets, Jeff Subik, based on the illustrations of Ezra Jack Keats; Costumes, Elizabeth Flauto, based on the illustrations of Ezra Jack Keats; Graphic Design, Frank Dain, based on the illustrations of

Ezra Jack Keats; Casting, Sara Schatz, Dave Clemmons; Orchestrations, Alex Lacamoire; Production Stage Managers, Chad Lewis, Pam Edington; Assistant Stage Manager, Larry Hamilton; Production Management, Aurora Productions; General Management, R. Erin Craig, La Vie Productions; Press, The Publicity Office; Studio Cast Recording: PS Classics.

Cast: Louie **Douglas Fabian**; Amy/Broom **Sara Kapner**; Roberta/Mouse **Katelyn Pippy**; Ziggy **Paul Pontrelli**; Archie **Ricky Smith**; Julio **Ronny Mercedes**; New Kids/Ensemble **Ryan Appleby, Rachel Cantor, Noemi Del Rio, Remy Zaken**

Understudies: Ryan Appleby (Julio), Noemi Del Rio (Amy/Broom), Remy Zaken (Roberta/Mouse), Larry Hamilton (Ziggy)

Musicians: Ray Fellman (Conductor/keyboard 1), Daniel Feyer (keyboard 2), Bruce Doctor (drums/percussion), Craig Wilson (guitar

Musical Numbers: New Kid in the Neighborhood, Big Red Plane, A Welcome for Louie, Shadows, Trick or Treat, Looza on the Block, Spiffin' Up Ziggy's, Captain Louie, Home Again, Finale

Setting: Halloween night. New York City; a new musical presented without intermission; originally presented at the York Theatre this season (see Off-Broadway Company Series in this volume).

A MOTHER, A DAUGHTER, AND A GUN

Dodger Stages Theatre 3; First preview: October 15, 2005; Opening Night: November 1, 2005; Closed November 27, 2005; 19 previews, 30 performances

A new comedy by Barra Grant; Produced by Brian Reilly and Nelle Nugent; Director, Jonathan Lynn; Scenery, Jesse Poleshuck; Costumes, David C. Woolard; Lighting, Beverly Emmons; Sound, T. Richard Fitzgerald and Carl Casella; Wigs, Paul Huntley; Production Supervision, Rob Conover, PRF Productions; Dialect Coach, Sam Chwat; Fight Director, Rick Sordelet; Associate Producer, Kenneth Teaton; Production Stage Manager, Donald Fried; Stage Manager, Robert. M. Armitage; General Manager, Peter Bogyo; Casting, Paul Hardt, Stuart Howard, Amy Schecter; Press, The Publicity Office

Cast: Beatrice **Olympia Dukakis**; Jess **Veanne Cox**; Alvin **George S. Irving**; Paul **David Bishins**; Juan **Mario Campanaro**; David **Matthew Greer**; Fran **Laura Heisler**; Cheryl/Elanor **Stephanie Kurtzuba**; Bob/Stefan **Daniel Pearce**

Understudies: David Bishins (Alvin), Mario Campanaro (Bob/Stefan), Katrina Ferguson (Jess/Fran/Cheryl/Eleanor), Stephanie Kurtzuba (Jess), Marilyn Pasekoff (Beatice/Fran), Daniel Pearce (David/Paul)

Setting: Upper West Side, New York City. New York premiere of a play presented in two acts. The production premiered at the Helen Hayes Theatre, Nyack, NY, prior to opening Off Broadway.

Synopsis: Jess has just been left by her husband, David, for a young woman and has also just learned she is pregnant. At her wit's end, she buys a gun and sets out to kill her husband. Unfortunately, her plans go awry when her controlling mother Beatrice shows up with a house full of strangers for an impromptu dinner party.

INFERTILITY: THE MUSICAL THAT'S HARD TO CONCEIVE

Dillon's; First preview: October 14, 2005; Opening Night: November 4, 2005; Closed February 25, 2006

Book, music and lyrics by Chris Neuner; Produced by Kathryn Frawley and Chris Neuner; Director, Dan Foster; Musical Director/Pianist, Albert Ahronheim; Choreography, Michelle Yaroshko; Scenery, Victor Whitehurst; Lighting, Andrew Gmoser; Costumes, Zinda Williams; Stage Manager, Olivia Tsang; General Manager, Jamie Cesa; Executive Producer, Jonathan C. Herzog, Esq.; Press, Shaffer-Coyle

Cast: April **Erin Davie**; Zusu **Jenni Frost**; Jane **Cadden Jones**; Doctor **Larry Picard**; Dick **Kurt Robbins**

Understudies: Amy Justman, Michael Deleget

Musical Numbers: Love Song, You've Got Parts; All Ya' Gotta Do Is, The Donor Dating Game, Cricket, Infertile Love Song, I've Got Sperm in my Pocket and I'm Talkin' to Eileen; Adoption Interrogation; Ain't It Great to Have a Kid?, The Color of Your Eyes, Infertile Love Song (continued), Big Dogs Run, When I Have You,

A musical presented without intermission

Synopsis: *Infertility* follows the trials and tribulations of five would-be parents as they try to beat an uncooperative stork.

BINGO

Theatre at St. Luke's Church; First preview: October 24, 2005; Opening Night: November 7, 2005; Closed February 25, 2006; 19 previews, 92 performances

Music and lyrics by Michael Heitzman, Ilene Reid, David Holcenberg; book by Michael Heitzman and Ilene Reid; Produced by Aruba Production, Buddy & Sally Productions, in association with Sharleen Cooper Cohen, Corsican Summer Productions, and Elizabeth Frankel; Director, Thomas Caruso; Music Director/Orchestrations, Steven Bishop; Choreography, Lisa Stevens; Scenery, Eric Renschler; Costumes, Carol Brys; Lighting, John Viesta; Sound, Lewis Mead; General Manager, Ken Denison, Carol Fishman; Production Stage Manager, Gregory Covert; Technical Director, Robert G. Mahon III, Casting, Dave Clemmons; Vocal Arrangements, Susan Draus; Press; Shaffer-Coyle Public Relations; Cast recording: BINGO Records

Cast: Bernice/Marilyn **Klea Blackhurst**; Minnie **Chevi Colton**; Honey **Liz Larsen**; Alison **Beth Malone**[*1]; Vern **Liz McCartney**; Patsy **Janet Metz**; Sam/Frank **Patrick Ryan Sullivan**

Understudies: Debra Cardona (Bernice/Marilyn/Patsy/Minnie/Vern), Michael Pemberton (Sam/Frank), J.B. Wing (Honey/Alison/Patsy/Minnie)

Musicians: Steven Bishop (Conductor/keyboards), Bill Stanley (keyboards), Aaron Russell (percussion)

Musical Numbers: Overture, Girls' Night Out, Anyone Can Play Bingo, I Still Believe in You, I've Made Up My Mind, Under My Wing, Gentleman Caller, The Birth of Bingo, Ratched's Lament, Swell, Gentleman Caller (reprise), I Still Believe in You (reprise), B4, I've Made Up My Mind (reprise), Finale

Setting: Basement of St Luke's Church, Hamerin County. New York premiere of an environmental musical comedy presented in two acts.

Synopsis: The audience gets to join in the *Bingo* game where they will meet Vern, Honey, and Patsy, three pals who have driven through a terrible thunderstorm in the name of their weekly obsession. In between the number calling, strange rituals, and fierce competitions, love blossoms and estranged friends reunite, sending everyone home a winner.

Succeeded by: 1. Jessica Snow Wilson

ALMOST HEAVEN: THE SONGS OF JOHN DENVER

Promenade Theatre; First preview: October 28, 2005; Opening Night: November 9, 2005; Closed December 31, 2005; 12 previews, 61 performances

Conceived by Harold Thau and adapted by Peter Glazer from Denver's autobiography, *Take Me Home*; Produced by Harold Thau in association with Lexie Potamkin, R.H. and Ann Crossland, Lawrence J. Winnerman and Robert Courson; Director, Randal Myler; Musical Director/Additional Arrangements, Charlie Alterman; Scenery, Kelly Tighe; Costumes, Tobin Ost; Lighting, Don Darnutzer; Sound, Lewis Mead; Projection Consultant, Jan Hartley; Music Supervisor/Orchestrations/Vocal Arrangements, Jeff Waxman; Music Coordinator, John Miller; Associate Producer/General Manager, Ken Denison; Production Stage Manager, Jane Pole; Assistant Stage Manager, Bonnie Brady; Company Manager, Charlissa Jackson; Technical Supervisor, TheatreSmith Inc.; Casting, Mungioli Theatricals; Press, Shaffer-Coyle

Cast: Jennifer Allen; Terry Burrell; Valisia Lekae Little; Lee Morgan; Jim Newman; Nicholas Rodriguez

Understudies: Colin Donnell, Myjah Moore Westbrooks

Musicians: Musicians: Charlie Alterman (Conductor/piano), Chris Biesterfeldt (guitar), Steve Count (bass), Bob Green (fiddle/ mandolin/acoustic guitar), Frank Pagano (percussion)

Musical Numbers: All of My Memories, For Bobbie, Rhymes and Reasons, Draft Dodger Rag, I Wish I Could've Been There (Woodstock), Take Me Home, Country Roads, Fly Away, I Guess He'd Rather Be in Colorado, Rocky Mountain High, Let Us Begin (What Are We Making Weapons For?), Calypso, This Old Guitar, Thank God I'm a Country Boy, Grandma's Feather Bed, Annie's Song , Goodbye Again, How Can I Leave You Again, Back Home Again, Leaving on a Jet Plane, For You, I'm Sorry, Sunshine on My Shoulders, Looking for Space, Wild Montana Skies, Songs Of, Poems, Prayers and Promises, Yellowstone

New York premiere of a musical revue presented in two acts.

Synopsis: *Almost Heaven* weaves together the songs of John Denver to create a theatrical narrative that reflects upon the country during the years in which he wrote them. Denver's songs are rediscovered and reinvented, performed by six singers and five musicians against a backdrop of stunning visual images of America in the late '60s and early '70s, a time of social unrest and political protest. Denver's music captures the noble yet earthy quality of the American soul, and how it has carved an indelible mark in the heart of the country.

JUNIE B. JONES

Lucile Lortel Theatre; First preview: November 4, 2005; Opening Night: November 9, 2005; Closed December 3, 2005; 38 performances

TheatreWorks NYC (Barbara Pasternack, Artistic Director; Ken Arthur Managing Director) production of a musical for young audiences with book and lyrics by Marcy Heisler and music by Zina Goldrich, based on the books by Barbara Park; Produced by special arrangement with the Lucille Lortel Theatre Foundation; Director, Peter Flynn; Music Director, Kimberly Grigsby; Choreography, Devanand Janki; Scenery, Luke Hegel-Cantarella; Costumes, Lora LaVon; Lighting, Jeff Croiter; Sound, Eric Shim; Orchestrations, Jesse Vargas; Associate Musical Director, Brian Lowdermilk; Stage Manager, Jeff Davolt; Technical Coordinator, B.D. White; Assistant Director, Tract Generalovich; Marketing, M/K Advertising Partners; Casting, Robin D. Carus; Press, Rubenstein Communications, Andy Schearer

Cast: Junie B. Jones **Russell Arden Koplin**; Mr. Scary & others **Michael McCoy**; May & others **Jill Abramovitz**; Lucille & others **Yasmeen Sulieman**; Herb & others **Adam Overett**; Sheldon & others **Randy Aaron**

Understudies: Jonathan Monk (Mr. Scary/Herb/Sheldon), Kiera O'Neil (Junie B. Jones/May/Lucille)

Russell Arden Koplin in *Junie B. Jones* PHOTO BY JOAN MARCUS

Orchestra: Brian Lowdermilk (Conductor/piano) David Berger (percussion)

Musical Numbers: Top Secret Personal Beeswax, Lucille Camille Chenille, You Can Be My Friend, Time to Make a Drawing, Show and Tell, Now I See, Lunch Box, Gladys Gutzman, Recess Hullabaloo, Kickball Tournament, Sheldon Potts' Halftime Show, When Life Gives You Lemons, Kickball Tournament (reprise), When Life Gives You Lemons (reprise), Writing Down the Story of My Life

Revival of the musical with presented in two acts; originally presented at the Lortel Theatre July 21, 2004 (See *Theatre World* Volume 61, page 118). This production contained new scenes and songs from the original version.

Synopsis: Junie B. Jones adjusts to a new group of friends, a new teacher, new eyeglasses, and various other first-grade angst-ridden situations.

THE ARK

37 Arts; First preview: October 14, 2005; Opening Night: November 14, 2005; Closed November 20, 2005; 36 previews, 8 performances

Music by Michael McLean, lyrics and book by Michael McLean and Kevin Kelly; Produced by Erik Orton and Karen Walter Goodwin, in association with Suzanne Ross and D. Keith Ross Jr.; Director/Choreographer, Ray Roderick; Music Director/Orchestrations/Arrangements, Joseph Baker; Scenery, Beowulf Boritt; Costumes, Lisa L. Zinni; Lighting, Eric T. Haugen; Sound, Ryan Powers; Production Stage Manager, Bryan Landrine; General Manager, Richards/Climan; Production Manager, Aurora Productions; Press, Origlio/Miramontez Company; Cast recording: Deseret Book 4975650; Original Studio Recording: Shadow Mountain 51982

Cast: Noah **Adrian Zmed**; Eliza **Annie Golden**; Egyptus **Janeece Aisha Freeman**; Martha **Marie-France Arcilla**; Ham **D.B. Bonds**; Shem **Justin Brill**; Sariah **Jacquelyn Piro**; Japeth **Rob Sutton**

Understudies: Julie Foldesi (Eliza/Egyptus/Sariah/Martha), Marie-France Arcilla (Egyptus), Chuck Ragsdale (Noah/Ham/Japeth/Shem), Rob Sutton (Noah)

Musical Numbers: What a Sight, Ship Without an Ocean, More Than I Asked For, Noah's Prayer, Whenever He Needs a Miracle, It Takes Two, Lift Me Up, Rain Song #1, You Cannot Be a Beauty Queen Forever, Rain Song #2, Rain Song #3, I Got a Man Who Loves Me, I Got a Man Who Loves Me (reprise), Oh Yeah, Rain Song #4, Song of Praise, Why Can't We?, Couple of Questions, Couple of Questions (reprise), In a Perfect World, Eliza's Breakdown-Hold On, Dinner, You Must Believe in Miracles #1, You Must Believe in Miracles #2, You Must Believe in Miracles #3, You Must Believe in Miracles #4, So Much More Than I Asked For (reprise), Lift Me Up/Hold On (reprise), I Thought I Was Alone, Lift Me Up (reprise), Song of Praise (reprise)

New York premiere of a new musical presented in two acts; originally presented at Seattle's Village Theatre, September 2003.

Synopsis: A fresh, contemporary look at the classic story of Noah that shows the backstory of his family. Living inside the floating community to escape a drowning world, we see that when facing the challenges of life, we're all in the same boat. The animals come two by two, and a family's story of hope, love, and strength is brought to life.

HILDA

59E59 Theatre A; First preview: November 11, 2005; Opening Night: November 15, 2005; Closed December 11, 2005; 4 previews, 28 performances

A new play by Marie Ndiaye; Produced by the Laura Pels International Foundation in association with the American Conservatory Theatre and Studio Theatre; Presented as part of the Act French Festival; Director, Carey Perloff; English translation, Erika Rundle; Scenery, Donald Eastman; Costumes, David F. Draper; Lighting, Nancy Schertler; Original music, David Lang; Sound, Cliff Caruthers; Assistant Director, Marco Baricelli; General Manager, Maria Di Dia; Stage Manager, Karen Storms; Production Manager, Lester Grant, Jee Han; Casting, Ellen Novack; Press, Springer Associates

Cast: Mrs. Lemarchand **Ellen Karas**; Frank **Michael Earle**; Corinne **Brandy Burre**

New York premiere of a new play presented without intermission

Synopsis: *Hilda* tells the haunting story of an upper-class woman's consuming obsession with the woman she hires to care for her children. With stark cinematic undertones, *Hilda* is a potent and provocative look at the seductiveness of control.

RFK

45 Bleecker; First preview: November 5, 2005; Opening Night: November 15, 2005; Closed February 26, 2006; 84 performances

The Culture Project (Allan Buchman, Artistic Director, David S. Singer, Executive Director) production of a play by Jack Holmes; Produced by special arrangement with Winship Cook, Arleen Sorkin, and Martin Davich; Director, Larry Moss; Scenery, Neil Patel; Lighting, David Weiner; Sound, Philip Lojo; General Manager, Ideal Theatricals; Associate Producer, Duane Baughman; Production Stage Manager, Greg Hirsch; Press, Origlio Public Relations

Cast: Robert F. Kennedy **Jack Holmes**

New York premiere of a solo performance play performed without intermission

Synopsis: Robert Kennedy's words, struggles and ideals come to life in this dramatic telling of the short, inspirational life of the would-be President.

WAITING FOR GODOT

Theatre at St. Clement's Church; First preview: November 8, 2005; Opening Night: November 16, 2005; Closed January 1, 2006; 8 previews, 48 performances.

By Samuel Beckett; Developed at the Actors Studio; Presented by Petina Cole, Red Horse Productions, LLC, Leonard Soloway, Steven M. Levy, and Rock and a Hard Place Productions, LLC; D Director, Alan Hruska; Scenery, Ken Foy; Costumes, Ann Hould-Ward; Lighting, Paul Miller; Sound, Matthew Burton; Hair and Wigs, Robert-Charles Vallance; Production Stage Manager, Alan Fox; General Manager, Steven M. Levy and Leonard Soloway; Technical Supervisor, Rob Conover; Press, Boneau/Bryan-Brown

Cast: Vladimir **Sam Coppola**; Estragon **Joseph Ragno**; Pozzo **Ed Setrakian**; Lucky **Martin Shakar**; Boy **Tanner Rich**

Understudies: Howard Green (Estragon/Lucky), Richmond Hoxie (Vladimir/Pozzo), Chris Nolan (Boy), Dallas Snoderly (Boy)

Setting: A country road. A tree. Evening. 50th Anniversary revival of the tragicomedy presented in two acts.

Synopsis: Vladimir and Estragon, two dilapidated bums, fill their days as painlessly as they can as they wait for Godot, a personage who will explain their interminable insignificance or put an end to it.

THE RAT PACK IS BACK!

The Supper Club; First preview: November 17, 2005; Closed in previews December 12, 2005; 8 performances.

Book by Don Reo and David Cassidy; Produced by The Supper Club, in association with Rachlin Entertainment and Dave Clemens; Director, David Cassidy

Cast: Frank **Michael Cisca**; Dean **Julian Rebolledo**; Joey **Mark Cohen**; Sammy **Eric Jordan Young**; Bobby **David Cassidy**

A musical play presented without intermission.

Synopsis: *The Rat Pack Is Back;* a tribute to Frank Sinatra, Sammy Davis, Jr., Joey Bishop, Jr., and Dean Martin, is a fast-paced theatrical musical play based on a night at the Sands Hotel in Las Vegas, circa 1961.

PETER PAN

Theatre at Madison Square Garden; Opening Night: November 30, 2005; Closed December 30, 2005; 39 performances

The national touring production of the musical play by Sir James Barrie; lyrics by Carolyn Leigh; music by Moose Charlap; additional lyrics by Betty Comden and Adolph Green; additional music by Jule Styne; Produced by McCoy Rigby Entertainment (Tom and Cathy Rigby McCoy, Producing Artistic Directors), the Nederlander Organization and La Mirada Theater for the Performing Arts, in association with Albert Nocciolino, Larry Payton and J. Lynn Singleton, Director, Glenn Casale; Choreography, Patti Colombo; Musical Direction/Vocal and Dance Arrangements, Craig Barna; Scenery, John Iacovelli; Costumes, Shigeru Yaji; Lighting, Martin Aronstein; Sound, Francois Bergeron; Flying, ZFX; Wigs, Robert Cybula; Associate Choreographer, John Charron

Cast: Mrs. Darling/Grown up Wendy/Mermaid Tracy Lore**;** Wendy Darling **Elisa Sagardia**; John Darling **Gavin Leatherwood**; Michael Darling **Abigail Taylor/Victoria Wood**; Liza/Tiger Lily **Dana Solimando**; Nana/Bill Jukes/Indian **Jonathan Warren**; Mr. Darling/Captain Hook **James Clow**; Peter Pan **Cathy Rigby**; Curly **Jordan Bass**; 1st Twin **Sarah Marie Jenkins**; 2nd Twin/Jane **Theresa McCoy**; Slightly **Omar D. Brancato**; Tootles **Tiffany Barrett**; Mr. Smee **Patrick Richwood**; Cecco/Crocodile **Tony Spinosa**; Gentleman Starkey **Noel Douglas Orput**; Noodler/Indian **Nathan Balser**; Mermaid **Tiffany Helland**; Pirates and Indians **Tim Fournier, Seth Hampton, Luis Villabon, Tiffany Helland, John B. Williford**

Swings: Gail Bianchi, Cameron Henderson

Touring Musicians: Craig Barna (Conductor), Bruce Barnes (keyboard 1/Assistant Conductor), Anne Shuttlesworth (keyboard 2); Keith Levenson (keyboard 3), Richard Henry Grant (drums/percussion)

Musical Numbers: Overture, Prologue, Tender Shepherd. I've Gotta Crow, Neverland, I'm Flying, Pirate March, A Princely Scheme, Indians!, Wendy, I Won't Grow Up, Another Princely Scheme, Ugg-A-Wugg, Distant Melody, Captain Hook's Waltz, I Gotta Crow (reprise), Tender Shepherd (reprise), I Won't Grow Up (reprise), Neverland (reprise)

Setting: The Darling Nursery, London, and Neverland. Revival of the musical presented in two acts.

Synopsis: In her farewell performance as Peter Pan, Tony Award nominee Cathy Rigby takes flight in the 100th anniversary of the immortal James M. Barrie tale *Peter Pan*. This timeless musical masterpiece, complete with evil Captain Hook, a crafty crocodile and the enchantment of Neverland, will touch, inspire, dazzle, and charm every generation.

IN THE CONTINUUM

Perry Street Theatre; First preview: November 18, 2005; Opening Night: December 1, 2005; Closed January 14, 2006

A new play by Danai Gurira and Nikkole Salter; Produced by Primary Stages (Casey Childs, Executive Producer; Andrew Leynse, Artistic Director; Elliot Fox, Managing Director) in association with the Perry Street Theatre (David Elliott and Martin Platt, Co-Directors), Patrick Blake and Cheryl Wiesenfeld; Director, Robert O'Hara; Scenery, Peter R. Feuchtwanger; Costumes, Sarah Hillard; Lighting, Colin Young; Original Music and Sound, Lindsay Jones

Cast: Abigail/Others **Danai Gurira**; Nia/Others **Nikkole Salter**

Setting: The present, Los Angeles, California and Harare, Zimbabwe. Transfer of the play presented without intermission; previously made it's world premiere debut at 59E59 as part of Primary Stage's season (See "Off Broadway Company Series" in this volume).

Synopsis: *In the Continuum* dramatizes the devastating problem of AIDS among African and African-American women. Living worlds apart—California and Africa—two young women experience a kaleidoscopic weekend of darkly comic life-changing revelations. With the two playwright/actors playing dozens of roles, *In the Continuum* envelopes the audience in its story of parallel denials and self-discoveries.

A BROADWAY DIVA CHRISTMAS

Julia Miles Theatre; First preview: November 23, 2005; Opening Night: December 4, 2005; Closed December 31, 2005; 15 previews, 33 performances

A musical revue presented by Parker Russell Productions, Tom D'Angora and Michael Duling; Music Director/Arrangements, Brian Nash; Press, Maya Public Relations, Penny Landau

Cast: Kathy Brier; Maya Days; Ellen Greene; Christine Pedi; Marla Schaffel

Jingle Babes: Tedi Marsh, Kate Pazakis, Sally Schwab, N'Kenge Simpson-Hoffman

Band: Brian Nash (Conductor/piano), Ben Zwein (bass), Benn Trigg (cello), Christian Linsey (percussion)

A musical revue presented without intermission.

Synopsis: A new holiday show featuring Broadway's most talented women performing the most popular Christmas music of all time, along with new songs and new arrangements of old favorites.

APPARITION

Connelly Theater; First preview: November 28, 2005; Opening Night: December 4, 2005; Closed January 7, 2005; 8 previews, 38 performances

A play by Anne Washburn; Produced by Apparition Off-Broadway, LLC; Director, Les Waters; Scenery, Andromache Chalfant; Costumes, Christal Weatherly; Lighting, Jane Cox; Sound, Darron L. West; Production Stage Manager, Elizabeth Moreau; Assistant Stage Manager, Elizabeth Kegley; Production Manager, Shannon Nicole Case; Assistant Director, Isaac Butler; General Manager, The Splinter Group; Press, Shaffer-Coyle

Cast: Maria Dizzia; Emily Donahoe; David Andrew McMahon; Garrett Neergaard; T. Ryder Smith

Understudies: Shawn Fagan, Makela Spielman

A play performed without intermission. Previously workshopped at SoHo Rep in 2001 and presented Off-Off Broadway at Chashama in 2003.

Synopsis: *Apparition*, a nonlinear play, combines whispers of dread, slivers of *Macbeth*, dining demons, and a murder that may or may not have happened. *Apparition* is about the feeling that something is coming to get you, and there is nowhere to hide.

Nikkole Salter and Danai Gurira in *In the Continuum* PHOTO BY JAMES LEYNSE

ROPE

Zipper Theatre; First preview: November 21, 2005; Opening Night: December 4, 2005; Closed, December 23, 2005; 14 previews, 23 performances

A play by Patrick Hamilton; Produced by the Highbrow Entertainment, The Zipper, True Love Productions, and the Drama Department (Douglas Carter Beane, Artistic Director; Michael S. Rosenberg, Executive Director); Director, David Warren; Scenery, James Youmans; Costumes, Gregory Gale; Lighting, Jeff Croiter; Sound Kai Harada; Fight Director; Rick Sordelet; Production Stage Manager, Adam Grosswirth; Assistant Stage Manager, Annette Verga-Lagier; Production Manager, George Gountas; Casting, Jodi Collins; Dialect Coach, Shane Ann Younts; Press, Shaffer-Coyle

Cast: Sabot **Christopher Duva**; Lelia **Ginifer King**; Kenneth Raglan **John Lavelle**; Mrs. Debenham **Lois Markle**; Rupert Cadell **Zak Orth**; Brandon **Sam Trammell**; Sir Johnstone Kentley **Neil Vipond**; Granillo **Chandler Williams**

Setting: An apartment in Mayfair, London, in the 1920s. Revival of the thriller presented in three acts.

Synopsis: *Rope* tells the story of two young Oxford men who attempt 'the perfect murder' to prove that they are above ordinary people.

KLONSKY & SCHWARTZ

Ensemble Studio Theatre; First preview: November 28, 2005; Opening Night: December 5, 2005; Closed December 23, 2005

A new play by Romulus Linney; Produced by Ensemble Studio Theatre (Curt Dempster, Artistic Director); Director, Jamie Richards; Scenery and Lighting, Maruti Evans; Costumes, Amela Baksic; Sound, Graham Johnson; Press, David Gersten

Cast: Delmore Schwartz **Bill Wise**; Milton Klonsky **Chris Ceraso**

Setting: 1966 and before, New York City. A new play presented without intermission.

Synopsis: *Klonsky and Schwartz* evokes the creative life of the mercurial and gifted poet Delmore Schwartz, who rose to fame during the mid-20th-century artistic and political ferment in New York City. Milton Klonsky, Delmore Schwartz's lifelong partner and protégé, fights to rescue his troubled mentor and friend in the turbulent 1960s.

TIGHT EMBRACE

Kirk Theatre; First preview: November 22, 2005; Opening Night: December 6, 2005; Closed December 30, 2005; 34 performances

INTAR (Edward Machado, Artistic Director, Editha Rosario, Executive Director) production of a new play by Jorgé Ignacio Cortiñas; Director, Lisa Peterson; Scenery, Mikiko Suzuki; Costumes, Meghan E. Healey; Lighting, Paul Whitaker; Sound, David M. Lawson; Production Manager, Sergio Cruz; Production Stage Manager, Michael Alifanz; Casting, Orpheus Group; Press, Richard Kornberg and Associates

The Company of *Disney Live! Winnie the Pooh*

Cast: Adalina **Mia Katigbak;** Claudia **Zabryna Guevara**; Zero **Robert Jiménez**; Barquin **Andres Munar**; Young Girl **Marisa Echeverria**

Setting: A Safe house in a Latin country. World premiere of a new play presented in two acts.

Synopsis: Two kidnap victims, an elderly woman and a pregnant woman, negotiate the boundaries of reality and memory as they try to survive with each other and the two men assigned to guard them. A haunting examination of the consequences of political violence, the play speaks to a world where violence is a part of our daily landscape.

DISNEY LIVE! WINNIE THE POOH

Beacon Theatre; Opening Night: December 8, 2005; Closed December 28, 2005; 35 performances

Limited engagement of an interactive theatrical production; Produced by Feld Entertainment, (Kenneth Feld, CEO; Nicole Feld, Assistant Producer; Jerry Bilik, Creative Director) and the Walt Disney Company; Director, B.T. McNicholl; Music Director, David Loud; Choreography, Christopher Gattelli; Scenery and Production Design, Anna Louizos; Costumes, Gregg Barnes; Lighting, Patrick Dierson; Character Development Director; Production Coordinator, Rick Papineau; Production Support, Mark Freddes, Todd Kauchick, Scott Dickerson; Company Manager, Mitch Matsunaga; Production Stage Manager, Adam Quick; Press, Telescope Public Relations

Cast: Efrain Baez; **Derek Baxter**; **Brandon Bolden**; **Joey Daysog**; **Tracie Franklin**; **Richard Jagodzinski**; **Sheleena Jones**; **Keiko Kano**; **Aliele Nurse**; **Sallie Palmieri**; **Gregory Parks**; **Kevin Rego**; **Tony Robinette**; **Matthew Santorelli**; **Cheon Son**

A musical entertainment presented without intermission

Synopsis: *Disney Live! Winnie the Pooh* brings the characters of the Hundred Acre Wood to stage in a charming story of friendship. This all-new touring production, narrated by Tracie and his "hunny helpers," features the hunny-loving Winnie the Pooh and his friends Tigger, Piglet, Eeyore, Rabbit, Kanga, Roo, and Owl, who embark on a journey of fun and surprise as they plan a surprise party for Winnie the Pooh.

A CHRISTMAS CAROL

Lucille Lortel Theatre; First preview: December 10, 2005; Opening Night: December 15, 2005; Closed December 31, 2005; 32 performances

TheatreWorks NYC (Barbara Pasternack, Artistic Director; Ken Arthur, Managing Director) production of a musical with book by David Armstrong, lyrics by Mark Waldrop, and music by Dick Gallagher, based on the story by Charles Dickens; Produced by special arrangement with the Lucille Lortel Theatre Foundation; Director/Choreographer, David Armstrong; Musical Director, Rick Hip-Flores; Scenery, James Wolk; Costumes, Gregory A. Poplyk; Lighting, Jeff Carnevale, Jeff Croiter; Sound, Eric Shim; Stage Manager, Bradford West; Technical Supervisor, B.D. White; Orchestrations, Greg Pliska; Casting, Robin D. Carus; Press, Rubenstein Communications, Andy Shearer

Cast: Marley/Fezziwig/Others **Kevin Del Aguila**; Ghost of Christmas Future **Stewart Gregory**; Bob Cratchit/Dick Wilkins/Others **Christopher Guilmet**; Boy Scrooge/Tiny Tim/Others **Miles Kath**; Scrooge **Herndon Lackey**; Ghost of Christmas Past/Mrs. Cratchit/Others **Meghan McGeary**; Fan/Abigail/Others **Margaret Nichols**; Fred/Young Scrooge/Others **Tom Plotkin**

Understudies: Carole J. Bufford (Fan/Mrs. Cratchit), Lee James Falco (Tiny Tim), Stewart Gregory (Bob Cratchit/Fezziwig/Fred/Scrooge)

Musicians: Rick Hip-Flores (Conductor/piano), David Berger (percussion), Eric Kay (woodwinds)

Musical Numbers: Once a Year, Break the Chain, I Have No Time for Christmas, Christmas Shines a Light to Guide Us Home, Fezziwig's Annual Christmas Ball; The Ghost of Christmas Present, Christmas Is Coming, Here With You, Christmas Shines A Light to Guide Us Home (reprise), Guess Who Kicked the Bucket Last Night, Here With You (reprise), Scrooge's Pledge, It's a Gift, Finale

A musical for young audiences presented without in two acts

Synopsis: The classic story of Scrooge, Tiny Tim, and Bob Cratchit geared for younger audiences featuring an original score.

DOG SEES GOD
CONFESSIONS OF A TEENAGE BLOCKHEAD

Century Center for the Performing Arts; First Preview: December 1, 2005; Opening Night: December 15, 2005; Closed February 20, 2006; 12 previews, 86 performances

A new play by Bert V. Royal; Produced by Dede Harris, Martian Entertainment, in association with Sharon Karmazin/Michelle Schneider/Mort Swinsky; Director, Trip Cullman; Scenery, David Korins; Costumes, Jenny Mannis; Lighting, Brian MacDevitt; Sound, Darron L. West; Wigs and Make-up, Erin Kennedy Lunsford; Fight Director, Rick Sordelet; Production Stage Manager, Lori Ann Zepp; Production Manager, Randall Etheredge; Casting, Bernard Telsey; Marketing, Martian Media; General Manager, Roy Gabay; Associate Producer, Sorrel Tomlinson; Company Manager, Daniel Kuney; Assistant Stage Manager, Tammy Scozzafava; Assistant Director, Teddy Bergman; Press, Sam Rudy Media Relations

Cast: CB **Eddie Kaye Thomas**; CB's Sister **America Ferrera**; Van **Keith Nobbs**; Matt **Ian Somerhalder**[*1]; Beethoven **Logan Marshall-Green**; Tricia **Kelli Garner**; Marcy **Ari Graynor**; Van's Sister **Eliza Dushku**[*2]

Understudies: Karen DiConcetto, Colby Chambers

A new play presented without intermission. Originally presented and the New York International Fringe Festival, 2004.

Synopsis: *Dog Sees God* follows the original gang from the Charles Schulz "Peanuts" comic strip a decade later, soon after their beloved beagle companion dies. Impending adulthood has now resulted in new identities: a once popular boy in an existential dilemma, an abused pianist, a pyromaniac ex-girlfriend, two drunken cheerleaders, a homophobic quarterback, a burnt out Buddhist, and a drama queen sister.

*Replaced by: 1. Brian Patrick Murphy 2. Melissa Picarello

NEWSICAL 2006: THE NEXT EDITION

Village Theatre; December 17–31, 2005; 20 performances

A new musical revue with music and lyrics by Rick Crom, Presented by Fred Caruso; Director/Choreographer, Donna Drake; Musical Director, Ed Goldschneider; Scenery, Peter P. Allburn; Costumes, David Kaley; Lighting, Michael Flink; Wigs and Make-up, Jason Hayes; Production Stage Manager, Mark Harborth; Casting, Margolis-Seay Casting; Assistant General Manager, A. Scott Falk; Marketing, HHC Marketing; Associate Producers, Gary Maffei, Jacki Barila-Florin, Barry Fisher, and Jesse Adelaar; Press, Publicity Outfitters, Timothy Haskell; Cast Recording: Original Cast Record B00081920A.

Cast: Stephanie Kurtzuba; **Trish Rapier**; **Jamison Stern**; **John Tartaglia**

Limited return engagement of a musical revue presented in two acts. Originally produced at Upstairs at 54 during the previous theatre season (see *Theatre World* Volume 61, page 125).

Synopsis: A revised version of the ever-changing new topical musical comedy, *Newsical* plucks its material from the wealth of current events and constant headliners. The evolving work features updated songs and material every week, making the show almost a completely new experience within months, depending on how celebrities and politicians have been making asses of themselves.

MEASURE FOR MEASURE

St. Ann's Warehouse; First preview: December 20, 2005; Opening Night: December 22, 2005; Closed January 1, 2006; 3 previews, 10 performances

Shakespeare's Globe Theatre of London's production of the play by William Shakespeare; Presented by Theatre for a New Audience and Arts at St. Ann's, in association with 2Luck Concepts; Shakespeare's Globe Theatre; Artistic Director, Mark Rylance; Executive Producer, Greg Ripley-Duggan; Master of Play, John Dove; Master of Clothing, Properties and Hangings, Jennifer Tiramani; Master of Theater Music, Claire van Kampen; Master of Dance, Siân Williams; Master of Historical Music, Research and Arrangements, Keith McGowan; Master of Light, Stan Pressner; Master of the Words, Giles Block; Master of Movement, Glynn MacDonald; Master of Voice, Stewart Pearce; Musical Director, Keith Thompson; Globe Production Manager, Richard Howey; U.S.A. Production Manager, Tony Schondel

Cast: Vincentio **Mark Rylance**; Angelo **Liam Brennan**; Claudio **David Stur-zaker**; Isabella **Edward Hogg**; Mariana/Francisca **Michael Brown**; Mistress Overdone/Justice **Peter Shorey**; Lucio **Colin Hurley**; Escalus **Bill Stewart**; Provost **Terry McGinity**; Friar Thomas/Elbow/Abhorson **Roger Watkins**; Friar Peter/Second Gentleman **Thomas Padden**; Froth, First Gentleman and Barnadine **Roger McKern**; Pompey **John Dougall**; Varrius and Juliet **David Hartley**

New York premiere of this touring version of the play presented in two acts.

Synopsis: Love and lust, justice and mercy, purity and villainy, all lock horns in Shakespeare's famously troubling comedy of a man sentenced to death and his sister, a nun, who can save his life only at the cost of her virtue.

ANOMAL

Chernuchin Theatre at the American Theatre of Actors; Opening Night: January 2, 2006; Closed January 29, 2006; 36 performances

A new play by Ehud Segev; Director, Glory Bowen; Original Music, Nir Graf; Scenery, Roy Nachum; Lighting, James Bedell; Consultants, Asi Wind, Michael Ziegfeld, Yafit Hallely, Eric Walton; Press, Keith Sherman and Associates

Performed by **Ehud Segev**

A solo performance supernatural play presented without intermission

Synopsis: Ehud Segev aka "The Mentalizer" shares his unusual life story and his inspiring perspective on life by telling the amazing story of a young man who developed supernatural abilities. Segev offers a rare opportunity to take a brief view into the life of a psychic entertainer, displaying his relationships with others and showing the highlights and downfalls of possessing such abilities.

Ehud Segev in *Anomal*

THE REVENGER'S TRAGEDY

45 Bleecker Below; January 6 – 22, 2006; 18 performances; previously ran as an Off Off Broadway production November 27 – December 18, 2005

Off Broadway extension of the play by Thomas Middleton, Adapted and directed by Jesse Berger; Presented by Red Bull Theatre; Producing Director, Jessica Niebanck; Lighting, Peter West; Original Music, Daniel Levy; Scenery, Evan O'Brient; Costumes, Clint Ramos; Choreography, Tracy Bersley; Fight Director, J. David Brimmer; Masks, Emily deCola; Make-up, Hair, and Wigs, Erin Kennedy Lunsford; Production Stage Manager, Renee Blinkwolf; Associate Producer, Dylan McCullough; Press, Publicity Outfitters

Cast: Vindice **Matthew Rauch**; Hippolito **Haynes Thigpen**; Castiza **Naomi Peters**; Gratiana **Petronia Paley**; Duke of Venice **Christopher Oden**; Duchess of Venice **Claire Lautier**; Lussurioso **Michael Urie**; Spurio **Jason C. Brown**; Ambitioso **Daniel Talbott**; Supervacuo **Ryan Farley**; Flaminio **Russ Salmon**; Antonio **Paul Niebanck**; Lucretia **Saudia Davis**; Pietro **Ty Jones**; Nencio **Daryl Lathon**; Sordido **Aaron Clayton**; Antonio's Lord **Yaegel Welch**; Spurio's Servant **Russ Salmon**; First Officer **Denis Butkus**; Second Officer **William Peden**

Setting: Venice, 1600s; a play presented in two acts.

Synopsis: The Duke's son rapes and kills a virtuous woman, Gloriana; her death prompts her betrothed Vindice to swear revenge on the Duke's family. His plots are aided by the lusts and ambition of the various members of the family; most of them die flamboyantly before Vindice is led off to face justice.

H.M.S. PINAFORE

New York City Center; Opening Night: January 6, 2006; Closed January 15, 2006; 4 performances

New York Gilbert and Sullivan Players revival of the operetta with libretto by Sir William S. Gilbert, music by Sir Arthur Sullivan; Original Staging, Kristen Garver; Director/Conductor, Albert Bergeret; Choreography, Bill Fabris; Scenery, Albere; Costumes, Gail J. Wofford; Lighting, Sally Small; Production Stage Mangers, Jan Holland, David Sigafoose; Dance Captain, Michael Levesque; Assistant Music Director, Andrea Stryker-Rodda; Press, Peter Cromarty and Company

Cast: The Rt. Hon. Sir Joseph Porter, K.C.B. (First Lord of the Admiralty) **Stephen O'Brien**; Captain Corcoran (Commander of H.M.S. Pinafore) **Richard Alan Holmes, Keith Jurosko**; Ralph Rackstraw (Able Seaman) **Brian Kuchta**; Dick Deadeye (Able Seaman) **Louis Dall'Ava**; Bill Bobstay (Boatswain's Mate) **William Whitefield**; Bob Becket (Carpenter's Mate) **David Wannen**; Josephine (The Captain's Daughter) **Charlotte Detrick**; Cousin Hebe (Sir Joseph's First Cousin) **Erika Person**; Little Buttercup (A Portsmouth Bumboat Woman) **Angela Smith**; Sergeant of Marines **Paul Sigrist**; Tom Tucker (Midshipmite) **Jeremy Senie**; The Sailors of the H.M.S. Pinafore: Derrick Cobey, Dan Debenport, Michael Galante, Alan Hill, Michael Levesque, David Macaluso, Lance Olds, Chris-Ian Sanchez, Paul Sigrist, Matthew Trombetta; Sisters, Cousins and Aunts Robin Bartunek, Kimberly Deana Bennett, Meredith Borden, Susan Case, Kathleen Glauber, Katie Hall, Debra Joyal, Megan Loomis, Rebecca O'Sullivan, Kirsten Witsman; **Ensemble Swings:** Michael Connolly, Lauren Wenegrat

Musicians: Violins: Robert Lawrence (concertmaster), Andrea Andros, Valerie Levy, Peter Van de Water, Eleanor Schiller, William Zinn, Paula Flatow; Viola: Carol Benner, Carol Landon; Cello: Daniele Doctorow, Amy Camus; Bass: Deborah Spohnheimer; Flute: Laura George, Melanie Bradford; Oboe: Nancy Ranger; Clarinets: Larry Tietze, Joan Porter; Bassoon: Susan Shaw; French Horns: Stephen M. Quint, Peter Hirsch; Trumpets: Terry Szor, Richard Titone; Trombones: Steve Shulman, Paul Geidel; Percussion: Mike Osrowitz

Setting: Late 1800s, Quarterdeck of H.M.S. Pinafore, off Portsmouth. Revival of an operetta presented in two acts.

Synopsis: In *HMS Pinafore* or *The Lass That Loved a Sailor,* the lowly sailor, Ralph Rackstraw, has fallen in love with Josephine, daughter of the repressed but ever polite Captain Corcoran, whose social climbing ambitions have caused him to promise Josephine in marriage to the insufferable Sir Joseph Porter. Josephine promises not to follow her heart in returning Ralph's affection, and the Captain reveals his own attraction to the lowly peddler woman, Little Buttercup.

THE MIKADO

New York City Center; Opening Night: January 7, 2006; Closed January 15, 2006; 5 performances

New York Gilbert and Sullivan Players revival of the operetta with libretto by Sir William S. Gilbert, music by Sir Arthur Sullivan; Director/Conductor, Albert Bergeret; Scenery, Albere; Costumes, Gail J. Wofford and Kayko Nakamura; Lighting, Sally Small; Production Stage Manager, Jan Holland, David Sigafoose; Assistant Music Director, Andrea Stryker-Rodda; Press, Peter Cromarty and Company

Cast: The Mikado of Japan **Keith Jurosko**; Nanki-Poo (his son, disguised as a wandering minstrel) **Michael Scott Harris**; Ko-Ko (Lord High Executioner of Titipu) **Stephen Quint**; Pooh-Bah (Lord High Everything Else) **Louis Dall'Ava**; Pish-Tush (A Noble Lord) **Edward Prostak**; Yum-Yum (Ward of Ko-Ko) **Laurelyn Watson**; Pitti-Sing (Ward of Ko-Ko) **Melissa Attebury**; Peep-Bo (Ward of Ko-Ko) **Robin Bartunek**; Katisha (an elderly lady in love with Nanki-Poo) **Diana Dollman**; Noblemen, Coolies, Schoolgirls, and Townspeople: **Kimberly Deana Bennett, Ted Bouton, Michael Connolly, Katie Hall, Alan Hill, Michael Levesque, Daniel Lockwood, Megan Loomis, David Macaluso, Rebecca O'Sullivan, Erika Person, Jennifer Piacenti, Julie Price, Paul Sigrist, Angela Smith, Matthew Trombetta, David Wannen, Lauren Wenegrat, William Whitefield, Kirsten Witsman**

Ensemble Swings: Michael Galante, Kathleen Glauber

Understudies: Nanki-Poo: Daniel Lockwood, Pish-Tush: David Macaluso, Yum-Yum: Jennifer Piacenti, Pitti-Sing: Erika Person, Peep-Bo: Megan Loomis, Katisha: Angela Smith

Musicians: Violins: Robert Lawrence (concertmaster), Andrea Andros, Valerie Levy, Peter Van de Water, Eleanor Schiller, William Zinn, Paula Flatow; Viola: Carol Benner, Carol Landon; Cello: Daniele Doctorow, Amy Camus; Bass: Deborah Spohnheimer; Flute: Laura George, Melanie Bradford; Oboe: Nancy Ranger; Clarinets: Larry Tietze, Joan Porter; Bassoon: Susan Shaw; French Horns: Stephen M. Quint, Peter Hirsch; Trumpets: Terry Szor, Richard Titone; Trombones: Steve Shulman, Paul Geidel; Percussion: Mike Osrowitz

Setting: A Japanese Garden. Revival of the operetta presented in two acts.

Synopsis: In *The Mikado, or The Town of Titipu,* Yum-Yum loves Nanki-Poo but is engaged to Ko-Ko the executioner. The romantic triangle takes the usual course of thwarted romance, until the arrival of the fearsome Katisha, claiming Nanki-Poo as her perjured lover, and later of the Mikado with his own list of punishments to fit the crime. Ko-Ko must use his wits to convince the unattractive Katisha to marry him.

ALMOST, MAINE

Daryl Roth Theatre; First preview: December 15, 2005; Opening Night: January 12, 2006; Closed February 10, 2006; 30 previews, 37 previews

A new play by John Cariani; Produced by Jack Thomas/Bulldog Theatrical and Bruce Payne; Director, Gabriel Barre; Scenery, James Youmans; Costumes, Pamela Scofield; Lighting, Jeff Croiter; Sound, Tony Smolenski IV and Walter Trarbach; Original Music, Julian Fleisher; Associated Producers, Kathy Hogg, Andrew Polk, Haviland Stillwell; Production Management, Showman Fabricators; Casting, Pat McCorkle; Marketing HHC Marketing; Stage Manager, Karyn Meek; General Management, Snug Harbor Productions, Steven Chaikelson/Brannon Wiles; Company Manager, Lauren P. Yates, Stage Manager, Marti McIntosh; Associate General Manager, Jamie Tyrol; Press, The Pete Sanders Group

Cast: Pete/Steve/Lendall/Randy/Man **Todd Cerveris**; East/Jimmy/Chad/Phil/Dave **Justin Hagan**; Sandrine/Marvalyn/Marci/Rhonda **Miriam Shor**; Ginette/Glory/Waitress/Gayle/Woman **Finnerty Steeves**

Understudies: Patrick Noonan and Colleen Quinlan

Setting: Various locales in Almost, Maine, a small township in Northern Maine; nine o'clock on a Friday night in the middle of winter. New York premiere of a new play presented in ten scenes in two acts. Developed by the Cape Cod Theatre Project and premiered at Portland Stage Company (Anita Stewart, Artistic Director).

Synopsis: This romantic comedy is about the residents of a small northern town who are falling in and out of love at an alarming rate. Love is discovered; hearts are broken and mended—almost—in this midwinter's night's dream.

THE FEAR PROJECT

TBG Theatre; First preview: January 11, 2006; Opening Night: January 16, 2006; Closed February 13, 2006; 6 previews, 29 performances

The Barrow Group (Seth Barrish and Lee Brock, Artistic Directors; Eric Paeper, Executive Director) production of new plays by Trish Alexandro (*Vichie*), Joshua James (*Extreme Eugene*), K. Lorell Manning (*A & J Rule the Universe*), Scott Organ (*Afraid.Yes.Of*), Eric Paeper (*Heads in the Sand*), and Stefanie Zadravec (*Haunted* and *Leaving*); Director, Eric Paeper; Scenery, Andrew Cavanaugh Holland, Costumes, James P. Hammer; Lighting, Tyler Micoleau; Sound, David Herman; Video, Emory van Cleve; Stage Manager, Alison Dingle; Technical Supervisor, Vincent Burich; Production Coordinator, Vincent DeMarco; Assistant Director, Tony Capone; Assistant Stage Manager, Melanie T. Morgan; Press, Shirley Herz Associates, Dan Demello

Cast: Jeremy Folmer; J. Garrett Glaser; DeAnna Lenhart; Amy Loughead; Porter Pickard; Dan McCabe; Taylor Ruckel; Brant Spencer; Emory van Cleve; Stefanie Zadravec

Seven new short plays presented in two acts

Synopsis: Fear-based media, politics, and personal choices fuel *The Fear Project*. Original footage and compiled media images link seven provocative short plays, each begging the question: can one find balance between being informed and staying functional? Fear surrounds us in the media, in politics, in advertising. Everywhere you look something or someone is exploiting our fears.

FUNNYHOUSE OF A NEGRO

HSA Theatre; First preview: January 11, 2006; Opening Night: January 20, 2006; Closed February 16, 2005; 26 performances

Classic Theatre of Harlem (Alfred Preisser, Co-Founder and Artistic Director; Christopher McElroen, Co-Founder and Executive Director) revival of a play by Adrienne Kennedy; Director, Billie Allen; Scenery, Tony Hourie; Costumes, Kimberly Glennon; Lighting, Aaron Black; Sound, Michael Messer; Assistant Director/Stage Manager, Stacy Waring; Dramaturg, Debra Cardona; Development Director, Michelle Y. Hodges; Press, Brett Singer

Cast: Negro Sarah **Suzette Gunn**; Duchess of Hapsburg **Monica Stith**; Queen Victoria Regina **Trish McCall**; Patrice Lumumba **Willie E. Teacher**; Jesus **Lincoln Brown**; Raymond **Danny Camiel**; Mother **Kellie McCants**; Landlady **Alice Spivak**

Revival of a play presented without intermission. The original OBIE winning production was produced in 1964.

Synopsis: The play chronicles the last hours in the life of Sarah, a young black woman troubled by race and identity, struggling with self-hatred and alienation from the mainstream culture.

(I AM) NOBODY'S LUNCH

59E59 Theatre B, First preview: January 15, 2006; Opening Night: January 21, 2006; Closed February 5, 2005; 21 performances

A cabaret-theatre piece written and directed by Steven Cosson from interviews written by the company; music and lyrics by Michael Friedman; Presented by the Civilians (Steve Cosson, artistic director; Kyle Gorden, producing director); Scenery, Andromache Chalfant; Costumes, Sarah Beers; Sound, Shane Rettig; Lighting, Marcus Doshi; Stage Manager, Catherine Bloch; Assistant Stage Manager, Robert Signom III; Choreographer, Karinne Keithley; Associate Producer, Kirsten Bowen; Assistant Director, Dyana Kimball; Technical Directors, Ray Harold, Josh Helman; Production Assistant, Paul Trinh; Additional interviews, Jennifer Gillespie, Jen Taher, Amy Waschke, Chris Wells; Created with Andy Boroson, Daoud Heidami, Christina Kirk, Alix Lambert, Matt Maher, Caitlin Miller, Peter Morris, and KJ Sanchez

Cast: Quincy Tyler Bernstine; **Matt Dellapina**; **Brad Heberlee**; **Daoud Heidami**; **Caitlin Miller**; **Jennifer R. Morris**

Pianist: Andy Boroson

Musical Numbers: The Telephone Song, Someone to Keep Me Warm, It's Scary How Easy It Is, Watch Out Ladies, Supersecret Places, Song of Progressive Disenchantment, America, Schrödinger's Cat

A political cabaret presented without intermission. Previously ran off-off Broadway at P.S. 122 September 24 – October 17, 2004

Synopsis: *(I Am) Nobody's Lunch* is an eccentric evening of cabaret-theatre combining original music and text from interviews. This lively show about the politics of information attempts to answer how we know what we know when nobody knows if everyone else is lying or when someone or something wants to have you for lunch.

BUSH WARS

Collective: Unconscious Theatre; First preview: January 12, 2006; Opening Night: January 22, 2006; Closed February 19, 2006; 23 performances*

Created and directed by Nancy Holson; Produced and Conceived by Jim Russek; Co-Director/Choreography, Jay Falzone; Scenery/Props, Patrice Escandon; Costumes, Elizabeth Payne; Lighting, Scott Borowka Musical Director, Alexander Rovang; Production Stage Manager, Jeanne-Marie Fisichella; General Management, CESA Entertainment; Company Manager, Townsend Teague; Press, Peter Cromarty and Company

Cast: Satan/Bill Frist/Barbara Bush/Jesus **Jay Falzone**; George W. Bush **Jason Levinson**; Eve/Hallie Burton/Betsy Ross/Professor of Republican Sociology 101 **Andrea McCormick**; Blue State Blues Singer/Condoleezza Rice/Supreme Court Justice **Abigail Nessen**; Osama bin Laden/Thomas Jefferson/Border Patrol **Chris Van Hoy**

Pianist: Alex Rovang

A new political musical revue presented without intermission

Synopsis: Told through 16 musical parodies and dozens of costume changes, *Bush Wars* is a compassionate counterattack on what its creators view as the disgraceful agenda of the Bush administration.

*Reopened at the Rattlestick Theatre, March 17 – April 23, 2006 where it played an additional 27 performances

LOVELY DAY

Beckett Theatre; First preview: January 12, 2006; Opening Night: January 22, 2006; Closed February 12, 2006

The Play Company (Kate Loewald, Founding Producer; Lauren Weigel, Managing Producer) production of a play by Leslie Ayvazian; Director, Blair Brown; Scenery, David Korins; Costumes, Michael Krass; Lighting, Paul Whitaker; Sound, Darron L. West; Production Stage Manager, Lisa Iacucci; Production Manager, Lester Grant; Associate Producer, Linda Barthaolomai; Guitar Music, Ivan Anderson, Joel Hoekstra, Joe Satriani; Casting, Judy Henderson; Press, The Karpel Group

Cast: Fran **Deirdre O'Connell**; Martin **David Rasche**; Brian **Javier Picayo**

New York premiere of a new play presented without intermission

Synopsis: As Fran and Martin are celebrating their wedding anniversary, they learn of a military recruiter's visit to their only son's high school. Suddenly, they find themselves on opposite sides of one of the most profound questions any mother or father can face. A detailed portrait of a marriage, *Lovely Day* goes to the heart of what it means to be a parent as well as a patriot.

MAJOR BANG, OR HOW I LEARNED TO STOP WORRYING AND LOVE THE DIRTY BOMB

St. Ann's Warehouse; First preview: January 18, 2006; Opening Night: January 23, 2006; Closed February 19, 2006; 9 previews, 25 performances

Foundry Theatre (Melanie Joseph, Artistic Director) production of a suspense comedy with magic by Kirk Lynn; conceived and created by Steve Cuiffo, Kirk Lynn and Melanie Joseph; Producers, Chris Kam and Anne Erbe, Sunder Ganglani; Director, Paul Lazar; Scenery, Michael Casselli; Costumes, Wendy Meiling Yang; Lighting, David Moodey; Video, Marilys Ernst; Sound, Raul Vincent Enriquez; Dramaturg, Melanie Joseph; Choreography, Chris Giarmo and Annie-B Parson; Magic Consultant, the Amazing Russello; Magic Assistant, James Kroener; Additional Music, Andy Gillis; Stage Manager, Jill Beckman; Production Manager, Jacob Heinrichs; Press, Blake Zidell, Sacks & Co.

Cast: Steve Cuiffo; Maggie Hoffman

A thriller with comedy and magic presented without intermission

Synopsis: Part suspense thriller, part magic act, part instructional seminar, *Major Bang* is a dark and comic take on our new era of global (in)security. Sprung from the contents of a backpack left on the subway, the piece samples Kubrick's *Dr. Strangelove* and the true story of David Hahn, a Boy Scout who built a nuclear reactor in his parents' garage to earn his Atomic Energy Badge. The result is a 75-minute ride through 21st century concepts of fear — both real and manufactured.

Maggie Hoffman and Steve Cuiffo in *Major Bang* PHOTO BY RICHARD TERMINE

25 QUESTIONS FOR A JEWISH MOTHER

Ars Nova Theatre; First preview: January 18, 2006; Opening Night: January 25, 2006; Closed March 19, 2006; 49 performances

A solo performance play by Kate Moira Ryan, with additional material by Judy Gold; Director, Karen Kohlhaas; Scenery and Costumes, Louisa Thompson; Lighting, Jennifer Tipton; Sound, Jorge Muelle; Production Stage Manager, Ain Rashida Sykes; Press, The Publicity Office

Performed by **Judy Gold**

A new solo performance play presented without intermission

Synopsis: Actress/comedienne Gold and playwright Ryan interviewed over 50 Jewish women of different ages, ethnicities, and occupations across the U.S. to assemble this moving and humorous portrait of what makes a Jewish mother a Jewish mother.

ZOMBOID! (FILM/PERFORMANCE PROJECT #1)

Ontological Theatre at St. Marks Church; First preview: January 12, 2006; Opening Night: January 25, 2006; Closed April 9, 2006; 65 performances

Ontological-Hysteric Theater live theatrical and film production written, directed, sound, lights and design by Richard Foreman; Managing director/production manager, Morgan von Prelle Pecelli; Technical Director, Paul DiPietro; Assistant Director, Anthony Cerrato; Costumes, Oana Botez-Ban; Video, Vivian Wenli Lin; Sound Engineer, Daniel Allen Nelson; Props Engineer, Meghan Buchanan; Lighting Engineer, Joshua Briggs; Press, Manny Igrejas

Cast: Katherine Brook; Temple Crocker; Ben Horner; Caitlin McDonough Thayer; Stephanie Silver

Melbourne Film Cast: Gorkem Acaroglu, Margaret Cameron, Tayla Chalef, Martyn Coutts, Olivia Crang, Tara Daniel, Sue Ingleton, Kibby McKinnon, Joe Mitchell, Merfyn Owens, Rochelle Whyte, Tom Papathanassiou, Kelly Somes, Sam Strong, Willoh Weiland, Lucy Wilson

World premiere of a live theatre and film performance piece presented without intermission.

Synopsis: *Zomboid! (Film-Performance Project #1)* marks the advent of a series of performances dominated by projected tableaux vivants against which live actors (and in the case of Zomboid!, multiple transcendental donkeys) appear and disappear. *Zomboid!* marks the space of a new and uniquely Foreman kind of philosophically oriented performance which lives in the heretofore unfathomable territory between projected image and on-stage corporality.

LENNY BRUCE ... IN HIS OWN WORDS

Zipper Theatre; First preview: January 30, 2006; Opening Night: February 1, 2006; Closed February 25, 2006; 2 previews, 28 performances

A new play written and directed by Joan Worth and Alan Sacks; Produced by Ron Delsener and Marvin Worth Productions; Sound, Worth and Sacks; Press, Sam Rudy Media Relations

Cast: Lenny Bruce **Jason Fisher**

New York premiere of a new solo performance play presented without intermission. Previously played in Los Angeles prior to this engagement.

Synopsis: *Lenny Bruce…In His Own Words* is a play created verbatim from the controversial satirist's most unforgettable routines.

MOSCOW CATS THEATRE

Lambs Theatre; Opening Night: February 3, 2006; Closed May 28, 2006; 118 performances

Created by Yuri Kuklachev; Produced by Gelfman International Enterprises;, Mark Gelfman; Director, Jace Alexander; Scenery, Beowulf Boritt; Lighting, Jason Lyons; Sound, T. Richard Fitzgerald; Production Stage Manager, Renée Rimland; Assistant Stage Manager, Lisa Gavaletz; Associate Stage Manager, Melissa Spengler; Technical Director, George Gountas; Director Assistant, Tony Speciale; General Manager, Yanis Gelfman; Marketing, HHC Marketing; Press, Lika Gelfman; Keith Sherman and Associates

Cast: Yuri Kuklachev; **Yelena Kuklachev**; **Inga Gerasimova**; **Lioudmila Smirnova**; **Alexander Gerasimov**; **Eugeny Lazarev**

A family entertainment performed without intermission. This production previously played off-off Broadway at the Tribeca Performing Arts Center September 17–December 29, 2005.

Synopsis: 20 cats, 2 dogs, and 6 clowns! Walking tightropes! Death-defying Balancing acts! Dancing! Acrobatics! The international family smash hit from Russia—the only entertainment of its kind in the world—features non-stop action by a group of talented felines performing original and astounding acrobatic feats, integrated into a non-verbal, colorful, and fun-filled family show.

CONFESSIONS OF A MORMON BOY

SoHo Playhouse; First preview: January 27, 2006; Opening Night: February 5, 2006; Closed: April 16, 2006; 12 previews, 80 performances

A solo performance play by Steven Fales; Produced by MB Productions, in association with James Fales, Kyle Kimoto and Carleton and Sharon Spaulding; Director, Jack Hofsiss; Scenery and Lighting, Tim Saternow; Costumes, Ellis Tillman; Sound, Robert Kaplowitz; Graphic Design, CHMajor; Marketing, HHC Marketing; Assistant Director, Ken Daigle; General Management, The Splinter Group; Production Management, Aurora Productions; Production Stage Manager, Charles M. Turner III; Acting Coach, Holly Villaire; Voice/Dialect Coach, David Alan Stern; Press, Sam Rudy Media Relations

Performed by **Steven Fales**

An autobiographical solo play performed without intermission. Previously presented at the Coconut Grove Playhouse, Miami, Florida, and at the New York International Fringe Festival, presented by The Present Company, August 2005.

Synopsis: *Confessions of a Mormon Boy* explores one young man's captivating journey through excommunication, divorce, prostitution, and drugs, as he struggles to reclaim himself, his children, and his "Donny Osmond" smile.

THE BLACK & WHITE BLUES

Laurie Beechman Theatre; First preview: January 18, 2006; Opening Night: February 9, 2006; Closed March 18, 2006; 33 performances

Music by Harry Mayronne, book and lyrics by Ricky Graham; Produced by Martian Entertainment, Some People Productions, and Loeber Entertainment; Directors, Ricky Graham and Heidi P. Junius; Musical Director, Harry Mayronne; Choreography, Heidi P. Junius; Costumes, Cecile Casey Covert; Sound, Jason Knobloch; Production Stage Manager, Renee Blinkwolt; General Manager, Martian Entertainment (Tom Smedes, Carl D. White, Peter R. Stern); Press, David Gersten; Original Cast Recording, Trylon Music

Cast: Bob Edes Jr.; **Heidi P. Junius**; **Harry Mayronne, Jr.**; **Jessie Terrebonne**; **Chris Wecklein**

Musical Numbers: Tonight in Black & White, I've Always Dreamed, Waiter Lingo, Fairy Godwaitress, Four-Course Nightmare, The Cocktail Conga, Waiting Around, Pork Sushi, Cookin' on TV, The Black & White Blues, Finale

Setting: A New Orleans restaurant; New York premiere of the New Orleans Restaurant Musical Revue presented in two acts. The show had been running in New Orleans since 2003 and relocated to New York after Hurricane Katrina devastated the city in the fall of 2005.

Synopsis: *The Black & White Blues* takes place in a restaurant purgatory where four waiters sing and dance their way through bitchy customers, while conquering the waiter lingo, working under the watchful eye of "management," and having visions of The Fairy God-Waitress, complete with big hair, magic wand, and order pad.

RED LIGHT WINTER

Barrow Street Theatre; First preview: January 20, 2006; Opening Night: February 9, 2006; Still running as of May 31, 2006

The Steppenwolf Theatre Company production of a play by Adam Rapp; Produced by Scott Rudin/Paramount Pictures, Robyn Goodman, Roger Berlind, and Stuart Thompson; Director, Adam Rapp; Scenery, Todd Rosenthal; Costumes, Michelle Tesdall; Lighting, Keith Parham; Sound, Eric Shim; Production Stage Manager, Richard A. Hodge; Original Casting, Erica Daniels; New York Casting, David Caparelliotis; Production Management, Aurora Productions; General Management, James Triner; Associate Producers, Ruth Hendel, Stephen Kocis; Assistant Stage Manager, Monica West; Press, Boneau/Bryan-Brown, Jim Byk, Julianna Hannett, Matt Ross

Cast: Matt **Christopher Denham**; Davis **Gary Wilmes**; Christina **Lisa Joyce**

Standbys: Jason Fleitz, Monica West

Setting: A hotel room in Amsterdam, Red Light District, and a small apartment in the East Village. New York premiere of a new play presented in two acts; originally produced at the Steppenwolf Theatre Company, Chicago, Illinois.

Synopsis: Two college friends spend a wild, unforgettable evening in Amsterdam's Red Light District with a beautiful young prostitute. They find that their lives have changed forever when their bizarre love triangle plays out in unexpected ways a year later in the East Village.

ALL'S WELL THAT ENDS WELL

Duke on 42nd Street; First preview: February 4, 2006; Opening Night: February 12, 2006; Closed March 19, 2006; 40 performances

Theatre for a New Audience (Jeffrey Horowitz; Founding Artistic Director, Dorothy Ryan, Managing Director) production of the play by William Shakespeare; Director Darko Tresnjak; Scenery, David P. Gordon; Costumes, Linda Cho; Lighting, Rui Rita; Sound, Aural Fixation; Musical Arranger, Michael Friedman; Dramaturg, Michael Feingold; Voice and Speech Consultant, Robert Neff Williams; Production Stage Manager, Renee Lutz; Assistant Stage Manager, Lisa Bracigliano; Production Manager, Len Larson; General Manager, Theresa Von Klug; Casting, Deborah Brown, Press, Bruce Cohen Group

Cast: Lafew **Tom Bloom**; Italian Soldier **William Connell**; Helena **Kate Forbes**; Bertram **Lucas Hall**; Lord of the Court/Italian Soldier **Jonathan Hammond**; Elder Lord Dumaine **Thomas Michael Hammond**; Lavatch **John Christopher Jones**; Countess of Rossillion **Laurie Kennedy**; Diana/Lady of the Court **Nicole Lowarnce**; The King of France **George Morfogen**; Younger Lord Dumaine **Paul Niebanck**; Reynaldo/Street Singer **Gordon Stanley**; Parolles **Adam Stein**; Widow/Lady of the Court **Myra Lucretia Taylor**; Isbel/Mariana **Lisa Velten**; King's Attendant/Duke of Florence/Street Singer **Price Waldman**

Setting: Rossillion, Paris, Florence, Marseilles. Revival of the play presented in two acts.

Synopsis: What does a woman do when the only man she wants to marry won't have her, even when the king commands it? Shakespeare's fascinating, problematic romance pits the wise and witty woman doctor Helena against the haughty, hotheaded courtier Bertram in a clash of wills, filled with comic surprises and gems of passionate poetry.

I LOVE YOU BECAUSE

Village Theatre; First preview: January 19, 2006; Opening Night: February 14, 2006; Closed May 21, 2006; 30 previews, 111 performances

Music by Joshua Salzman, book and lyrics by Ryan Cunningham; Produced by Jennifer Maloney, Fred M. Caruso, Robert Cuillo and GFour Productions, in association with Jana Robbins and Saron Carr; Director, Daniel Kutner; Choreography, Christopher Gattelli; Music Director, Jana Zielonka; Scenery, Beowulf Boritt and Jo Winiarski; Lighting, Jeff Croiter; Sound, Tony Smolenski IV and Walter Trarbach; Costumes, Millie B. Hiibel; Production Stage Manager, Brian Meister; Production Manager, Shannon Case; Marketing, HHC Marketing; Associate Producer, Jeffrey Kent; General Manager, Fred M. Caruso; Associate General Manager, Scott Newsome; Music Contractor, Michael Keller; Orchestrations, Larry Hochman; Vocal and Music Arrangements, Joshua Salzman; Press, Shaffer-Coyle Public Relations; Dance Captain, Barrett Hall; Cast Recording: PS Classics

Cast: Austin Bennet **Colin Hanlon**; Jeff Bennet **David A. Austin**; Marcy Fitzwilliams **Farah Alvin**; Diana Bingley **Stephanie D'Abruzzo**; NYC Man **Jordan Leeds**; NYC Woman **Courtney Balan**

Understudies: Courtney Balan (Marcy), Barrett Hall, Jaclyn Huberman

The Band: Jana Zielonka (Musical Director/keyboard 1), Brian Cimmet (keyboard 2), Fred Dechristofaro (reeds), Brad Russell (bass), Sean Dolan (drums/percussion)

Musical Numbers: Another Saturday Night in New York, Oh What a Difference, The Actuary Song, But I Don't Want to Talk About Her, Coffee, The Perfect Romance, Because of You, We're Just Friends, Maybe We Just Made Love, Just Not Now, Alone, That's What's Gonna Happen, Even Though, But I Do, What Do We Do It For, Marcy's Yours, Goodbye, I Love You Because

Setting: New York City, the present day. World premiere of a new musical presented in two acts.

Synopsis: In this modern-day *Jane Austin*, Austin Bennet, a structured greeting card writer who finds his girlfriend in bed with another man, is sent back out into the treacherous New York dating scene. He meets Marcy, whose spontaneity is matched only by her ability to drive Austin insane. What ensues is a comedy about love that explores the rules and nuances of dating, and how sometimes love is learning to love someone not in spite of their differences, but because of them.

CLEAN ALTERNATIVES

59E59 Theatre C; First preview: February 9, 2006; Opening Night: February 15, 2006; Closed March 12, 2006; 33 performances

A new play by Brian Dykstra; Produced by Fresh Ice Productions in association with Jack Batman and Greg Shaffert; Director, Margarett Perry; Scenery and Lighting, Maruti Evans; Costumes, Jennifer R. Halpern; Production manager/Sound, Ken Hypes; Production Stage Manager, Paige van den Burg; Press, Origlio/Miramontez Company

Cast: Mr. Cutter **Brian Dykstra**; Mr. Slate **Mark Boyett**; Jackie **Sue-Anne Morrow**

World premiere of a new play presented in two acts

Synopsis: *Clean Alternatives* is a no-holds-barred satire on corporate America about an environmentalist's fight against a toxin-spreading mega-corporation. Brian Dykstra's signature style crackles in this scathing, tightlywound comedy about the elusiveness of enlightenment in this dark age of the almighty dollar. Dykstra's impassioned characters wage war on each other with the most powerful weapons in their arsenal. But do words have a chance against all that cash?

ACTS OF MERCY: PASSION-PLAY

Rattlestick Playwrights Theatre 224 Waverly; First preview: February 8, 2006; Opening Night: February 16, 2006; Closed March 19, 2006; 6 previews, 24 performances

Rattlestick Playwrights Theatre (David Van Asselt, Artistic Director; Sandra Coudert; Managing Director) production of a new play by Michael John Garcés; Director, Gia Forakis; Sets, Robin Vest; Costumes, Elizabeth Hope Clancy; Lighting, Peter West; Sound, Daniel Baker; Original Music, Matthew Sutter and Broken Chord Collective; Fight Director, Rick Sordelet; Production Stage Manager, Anne Michelson; Press, Origlio/Miramontez Company

Cast: Arabella **Veronica Cruz;** Nestor **Jose Febus;** Kathleen **Jenny Maguire;** Jaime **Bryant Mason;** Eladio **Andres Munar;** T.J. **Tommy Schrider;** Ricky **Ivan Quintanilla**

World premiere of a new play presented in two acts

Synopsis: During the course of one sweltering summer night, two sons must reconcile themselves to their dying brutal father, hoping to gain redemption through small but life-giving acts of mercy.

RETZACH

59E59 Theatre B; First preview: February 9, 2006; Opening Night: February 15, 2006; Closed March 12, 2006

A play by Hanoch Levin, translated by Liat Glick, Shauna Kanter, and Tzahi Moskovitz; Produced by Crooked Timber Productions in association with VOICETheatre; Director, Shauna Kanter; Scenery, Casey Smith; Costumes, Amelia Dombrowski; Lighting, Graham Kindred; Original Music and Sound, Joseph T LaBarbera; Videographer, Sean Weiner; Additional Music, Kiril D'Jajkovski; Puppets, Serra Hirsch; Dramaturg, Deidre O'Keefe; Technical Director, Travis Walker; General Manager, Angrette McCloskey; Marketing, Shorey Walker; Press, Timothy Haskell/Publicity Outfitters

Cast: Flushed Soldier/Passer By/Soldier **Gili Getz**; Girl/Purple Whore/Child/Ensemble **Christel Halliburton**; Tanned Soldier/Guest/Neighbor/Officer/UN Aid Worker/Groom's Brother **Simon MacLean**; Soldier/Ensemble **Joseph Mancuso**; Messenger **Stephen Medwid**; Father/Cracked Whore **Tony Naumovski**; Wrecked Worker/Ensemble **Raj Pannu**; Pale Soldier/Bridegroom/Neighbor **Andrew Russell**; Bride/Pink Whore/Ensemble **Jelena Stupljanin**; Mother of the Bride/Orange Whore/Ensemble **Arley Tapirian**; Arab Boy/Boy/Ensemble **Morteza Tavakoli**.

Ensemble/Understudies: Sarah Imes, Amy Kovalchick, Chris Paolucci, Emily Shapiro, Hadar Shemesh

World premiere of a new translation of the play presented in three acts without intermission

Synopsis: *Retzach* portrays the dark forces that drive the escalation of human conflict. Staged in three acts, the play begins with a father's grisly discovery of the death of his child at the hands of three young soldiers amidst the chaos of war. This ignites successive acts of vengeance leading to a senseless cycle of brutality. This poetic allegory which uses puppetry, dance, and original music, puts a human face on the players who commit acts of violence, and illuminates the causes that turn victims into victimizers.

INDOOR/OUTDOOR

DR2 Theater; First preview: February 2, 2006; Opening Night: February 22, 2006; Closed March 19, 2006; 23 previews, 29 performances

A new play by Kenny Finkle; Produced by Margo Lion, Hal Luftig, and Daryl Roth in association with Lily Hung; Director, Daniel Goldstein; Scenery, David Korins; Costumes, Michael Krass; Lighting, Ben Stanton; Sound, Walter Trarbach and Tony Smolenski IV; General Manager, Adam Hess; Associate General Manager, Erika Happel; Production Stage Manager, Brian Maschka; Production Manager, Shannon Case; Assistant Stage Manager, Richard Morrison; Casting, Stephanie Klapper; Marketing, HHC Marketing; Press, Pete Sanders, Glenna Freedman

Cast: Oscar and others **Mario Campanaro**; Shuman **Brian Hutchison**; Samantha **Emily Cass McDonnell**; Matilda/Mom/Sister **Keira Naughton**

Standbys: Mark Alhadeff, Susan Louise O'Connor

A romantic comedy presented without intermission; originally produced at the Summer Play Festival 2004

Synopsis: Samantha, a feisty house cat, dreams of adventure and risks everything to find true unconditional love. But will she find it in the home of her quirky owner Shuman or with the sexy alley cat Oscar in the great outdoors? With help from Matilda, a neurotic pet therapist, life, love, and relationships are explored in this romantic comedy filled with warmth, emotion, and the journey from codependence to independence.

DARKLING

East 13th Street Theatre; First preview: February 26, 2006; Opening Night: February 28, 2006; Closed March 18, 2006; 14 performances

Adapted and directed by Michael Comlish from the book "Darkling: A Poem" by Anna Rabinowitz; Produced by American Opera Projects (Charles Jarden, Executive Director and Producer); Original Music by Stefan Weisman; "The Darkling Thrush" song by Lee Hoiby; Vocal Soundscape, Thomas Hamilton; Music Director, J. David Jackson; Conductor, Brian DeMaris; Scenery, Glenn Reed; Costumes, Anna Kiraly; Lighting, Brian Scott; Sound, Zachary Williamson; Projections/Video Editing, Gregory King; Props/Assistant Set Design, Claire Falkenberg; Production Management, Scott Schneider; Stage Manager, Sara Bancroft; Assistant Director, Crystal M Manich; Movement Coach, Hillary Spector; Makeup/Hair, Daniella Shachter; Dramaturg/Press, Matt Gray

Cast: Lead Singers **Jon Garrison, Marcus DeLoach**; Actors **Sid Williams, Elzbieta Czyzewska, Hillary Spector, Carol Monda, Julie Lockhart, Perri Yaniv**; Ensemble **Jody Sheinbaum, Hai-Ting Chinn, Mark Uhlemann**; Soundscape voices **Elzbieta Czyzewska, Yuval David, Peter Kazaras, Mikel Sarah Lambert, Julie Lockhart, Carol Monda, Yehuda Nir, Anna Rabinowitz, Dina Rose Rivera, Lois C. Schwartz, Hillary Spector, Mark Uhlemann, Sid Williams, Perri Yaniv**

Musicians: FLUX Quartet- Tom Chiu (violin 1), Conrad Harris (violin 2), Max Mandel (viola), Raman Ramakrishnan (cello)

World premiere of an experimental opera-theatre piece presented

Synopsis: *Darkling* assembles narratives of the Holocaust through the turbulence of multiple voices in the act of finding themselves. The production recasts opera in a contemporary form by overlaying poetry with live music, interweaving the drama with a landscape of projected films and images, collages of spoken text and pre-recorded soundscapes.

TRANSATLANTIC LIAISON

Clurman Theatre; First preview: February 20, 2006; Opening Night: March 1, 2006; Closed April 15, 2006

A new play by Fabrice Rozié; Produced by Treetop Productions; Director, John McLean; Scenery and Lighting, David Lovett; Costumes, Joanna Zischang; Original Music, Areski Belkacem; Sound, Jeff Benish; Production Stage Manager, Wes Apfel; Press, Sam Rudy Media Relations

Cast: Simone de Beauvoir **Elizabeth Rothan**; Nelson Algren **Matthew S. Tompkins**

Cellist: Camilla Boatright

Setting: Chicago, New York, and Mexico, late 1940's. A new play presented without intermission.

Synopsis: *Transatlantic Liaison*, a drama about the love affair between the French existentialist writer and her unlikely American lover, provides insights into how Beauvoir forged her identity as an artist, intellectual, and woman of passion. This new play is Beauvoir's story of love beyond conventions of marriage, or of adultery, sifting details from her published letters to Algren and her novel inspired by their relationship, *The Mandarins*.

SAKE WITH THE HAIKU GEISHA

Perry Street Theatre; First preview: February 24, 2005; Opening Night: March 2, 2006; Closed April 8, 2006; 43 performances

Gotham Theatre Company (Michael Barra, Executive Director; Peter H. Smith, Director of Artistic Production; Julia Haubner Smith, Director of Artistic Operations, Katie Dietz, Director of Programming) production of a new play by Randall David Cook; Director, Alex Lippard; Scenery, David Newell; Costumes, Charlene Alexis Gross; Original Compositions and Sound, Allison Leyton-Brown; Lighting, Lucas Benjaminh Krech; Choreography, Alex Tressor; Movement, Miho Imoto, Yumiko Niimi; Production Stage Manager, Marci Skolnick; Assistant Stage Manager, Alison DeSantis; Casting, Dani Super; Press, Spin Cycle-Ron Lasko

The Company of *The Most Happy Fella*   PHOTO BY CAROL ROSEGG

Cast: Ichihiro/Hashimoto/Mr. Moriguchi/Mr. Omori **David Shih**; Charlotte Linscott/Rosalind **Emma Bowers**[*1]; Granny/Brianna MacInnis/Virgin Queen **Fiona Gallagher**[*2]; Parker Hamilton/The Ghost of Caleb/Jim **Jeremy Hollingsworth**; Haiku Geisha/Sumiko Matsushita **Angela Lin**; Mrs. Noriko/Tomoko Yamashita-Sensei/Mother/Mrs. Matsushita **Sala Iwamatsu**[*3]; Ke Ohta/Michi/Father **Ikuma Isaac**

Setting: A Japanese Lodge, the present. World premiere of a new play presented in two acts; this play was the inaugural full fledged production for Gotham Theatre Company.

Synopsis: In *Sake with the Haiku Geisha*, a trio of foreign teachers attends a party hosted by a mysterious Geisha who only speaks in Haiku. Sake flows, secrets are revealed, and hearts are opened in an evening that weaves together five interconnected tales of sexual mishaps, romance, and cross-cultural miscommunication.

Succeeded by: 1. Liz Morton 2. Julia Haubner Smith 3. Ako

THE MOST HAPPY FELLA

State Theatre; First preview: March 4, 2006; Opening Night: March 7, 2006; Closed March 25, 2006; 3 previews, 11 performances

New York City Opera production of the musical with music, lyrics, and book by Frank Loesser, based on the play *They Knew What They Wanted* by Sidney Howard; Director, Phillip Wm. McKinley; Musical Director/Conductor, George Manahan; Choreography, Peggy Hickey; Scenery, Micahel Anania; Costumes, Ann Hould Ward; Lighting, Robert Wierzel; Sound, Abe Jacob; Orchestrations, Don Walker; Casting, Mark Simon; Chorus Master, Charles F. Prestinari; Associate Conductor, Braden Toan; Stage Managers, Peggy Imbire, Cindy Knight, Anne Dechêne, Samantha Greene

Cast: Cashier/Postman **William Ryall**; Cleo **Leah Hocking**; Amy (Rosabella) **Lisa Vroman**; Waitress **Kelly Crandall**; Tony **Paul Sorvino**; Marie **Karen Murphy**; Max **Boyd Schlaefer**; Herman **John Scherer**; Clem **Matt Bailey**; Jake **Paul Castree**; Al **Ryan Silverman**; Joe **Ivan Hernandez**; Pasquale **Bruce Winant**; Giuseppe **Matthew Surapine**; Ciccio **Andrew Drost**; Doctor **Eddie Korbich**; Priest **Gregory Hostetler**

Musical Numbers: Overture, Ooh! My Feet!, Somebody Somewhere, The Most Happy Fella, Nobody's Ever Gonna Love You Like I Love You, Standing on the Corner, Joey Joey Joey, Rosabella, Abbondanza, Sposalizio, Benvenuta, Eyes Like a Stranger, Don't Cry, Fresno Beauties, Happy to Make Your Acquaintance, Big D, How Beautiful the Days, Warm All Over, I Like Ev'rybody, My Heart Is So Full of You, Mamma, Mamma, I Like Ev'rybody (reprise), Song of a Summer Night, Please Let Me Tell You, Finale

Setting: 1934, San Francisco and Napa, California. Revival of the musical performed in two acts.

Synopsis: An aging vineyard owner, Tony, courts Amy (whom he calls "Rosabella"), a lonely waitress, through mail correspondence and wins her over in a marriage proposal. Afraid of rejection, he encloses a photograph of his handsome ranch hand, Joe. Despite this deception, Tony and Rosabella find love and, eventually, forgiveness and acceptance. Herman (Tony's gentle-natured employee) and Cleo (Rosabella's smart, tart-tongued friend) also find a playful romance.

FAMILY SECRETS

37 Arts Theatre B; First preview: February 22, 2006; Opening Night: March 8, 2006; Closed April 9, 2006; 15 previews, 39 performances

A play by Sherry Glaser and Greg Howell; Produced by Harriet Newman Leve in association with Dan Markley, Mike Skipper and Bisno/Shapiro/Finewill Entertainment; Director, Bob Balaban; Scenery, Rob Odorisio; Lighting, John-Paul Szczepanski (based on the original design by Brian MacDevitt); Sound, Ryan Powers; Production Stage Manager, Pamela Edington; Associate Producers, Bernhard-Borden Productions, Healthy Living Management, Ron Nicynski, Redfern Goldman Productions, Morty Swinsky, and Laura Wagner; General Manager, Richard Frankel; Production Managers, Terry Jackson, Murmur Machine; Press, Barlow-Hartman

Cast: Mort/Bev/Fern/Kahari/Sandra/Rose **Sherry Glaser**

Revival of the solo performance play presented without intermission; originally produced at the Westside Theatre/Downstairs September 28, 1993–January 11, 1995, garnering a Theatre World Award for Ms. Glaser (See *Theatre World* Volume 50, page 96).

Synopsis: *Family Secrets* is an intimate portrait of five members of a Jewish family transplanted from the Bronx to Southern California. Glaser plays all five members of the family.

BULRUSHER

Urban Stages; First preview: March 7, 2006; Opening Night: March 11 2006; Closed April 9, 2006; 35 performances

Urban Stages (Frances Hill, Artistic Director, Sonia Kozlova, Managing Director; Lori Laster, Program Director) production of a new play by Eisa Davis; Director, Leah C. Gardiner; Scenery/ Video/Projections, Dustin O'Neill; Costumes, Kimberly Ann Glennon; Lighting, Sarah Sidman; Sound, Jill BC Du Boff; Original Songs, Eisa Davis and Robert Beitzel; Original Score Composer, Daniel T. Denver; Original Score Performed by Daniel T. Denver, Manoel Felciano, Robert Beitzel; Choreography, Jennifer Harrison Newman; Fight Choreography, Denise Hurd; Assistant Director, Ronald Francis Brescio; Production Stage Manager, Jana Llynn; Assistant Stage Manager/Props, Stephen Riscica; Marketing, Michelle Brandon; Graphic Design, Sondra Graff, Pentacle; Casting, Stephanie Klapper, Press, Brett Singer & Associates

Cast: Bulrusher **Zabryna Guevara**; Madame **Charlotte Colavin**; Logger **Guiesseppe Jones**; Schoolch **Peter Bradbury**; Boy **Robert Beitzel**; Vera **Tinashe Kajese**

Setting: 1955 Boonville, California, north of San Francisco. World premiere of a play presented in two acts.

Synopsis: This poetic, evocative play is set at the dawn of the Civil Rights movement in the year Emmett Till was murdered. In a small town in California, a young African-American girl begins to understand what race means when a stranger from Alabama arrives. Set in a brothel with its own unique homespun language (Boontling), *Bulrusher* tests our assumptions about race, sexuality, and love.

THE EMPEROR JONES

St. Ann's Warehouse; First preview: Opening Night: March 11, 2006; Closed April 2, 2006; 25 performances

The Wooster Group production of the play by Eugene O'Neill; Director, Elizabeth LeCompte; Scenery, Jim Clayburgh; Costumes, Wooster Group; Lighting, Jennifer Tipton; Original Music, David Linton; Video, Christopher Kondek; Sound, John Collins, Geoff Abbas; Production Stage Manager, Teresa Hartmann; Assistant Director, Clay Hapaz; Video/Master Electrician; Gabe Maxson; Video/Stage Assistant, Margaret Mann; Production Manager, Bozkurt Karasu; Technical Director, Ruud van den Akker

Cast: Brutus Jones **Kate Valk;** Smithers **Scott Shepherd, Ari Fliakos;** Stage Assistant **Ari Fliakos, Scott Shepherd**

Revival of the play presented without intermission; previously presented by the Wooster Group in 1993 and again in 1998.

Synopsis: O'Neill's controversial play is scaled down for three actors in this hypnotic story of Brutus Jones, a venal black train porter with a criminal past who sets himself up as a ruthless dictator of a tiny Caribbean nation and is forced to flee from both the natives he has exploited and from his own haunted past.

HARD RIGHT

Players Theatre; First preview: March 7, 2006; Opening Night: March 12, 2006; Closed, April 16, 2006

A new play written and directed by David Barth; Produced by Billy Humphreys and Dieter Weihl; Scenery, Mark Cruzan; Costumes, Jodi B.; Dramaturg/Assistant Producer, Zachary Barton; Stage Manager, Billy Humphreys; Assistant Stage Manager, Bia Parente; Press, Spin Cycle-Ron Lasko

Cast: Henry **Jeremy Beck**; Greta **Shayne Dukevitch**; Barbara **Susan Engbrecht**; Bob **Dylan Price**; Phil **Stacy Shane**

New York premiere of a play presented without intermission

Synopsis: A slacker college student brings his girlfriend home for a visit with the folks, but family tensions turn into family trauma when a "counselor" conducting a dubious field study pays them visit. The timeless conflict between liberty and absolute power is reexamined in this darkly comic parable set on the eve of the age of terror.

SIDD

Dodger (New World) Stages Theatre 5; First preview: February 23, 2006; Opening Night: March 15, 2006; Closed March 26, 2006; 23 previews, 13 performances

A new musical with book and lyrics by Andrew Frank, music and lyrics by Doug Silver, based on the novel *Siddhartha* by Hermann Hesse; Produced by Always on the Way, LLC, Fran Kirmser Sharma, Executive Producer; Director, Andrew Frank; Musical Director, Ned Paul Ginsburg; Choreography, Fran Kirmser Sharma; Orchestrations, Doug Silver and Ned Paul Ginsburg; Scenery,

Maruti Evans; Costumes, Michael Bevins; Lighting, Chris Dallos; Sound, Andrew Bellware; Production Stage Manager, Kate Hefel; Production Associate, Meryl Schonfeld; Associate Producer, Joel Schonfeld; Production Manager, Avancy, Inc., Neil Creedon; General Management, CESA Entertainment, Jamie Cesa; Associate General Manager, Rick L. Stevens; Casting, Alan Filderman; Assistant Stage Manager, Misha Siegel Rivers; Press, The Karpel Group

Cast: Valerie/others **Marie-France Arcilla;** Mala/others **Natalie Cortez;** Willie/others **Dann Fink;** Traveler/others **Nicole Lewis;** Buddha/others **Arthur W. Marks;** Father/Ferryman/others **Gerry McIntyre;** Sidd **Manu Narayan**

Understudies: John-Andrew Morrison, Carly Hughes

Musicians: Ned Paul Ginsburg (Conductor/piano), Stefan Schatz (drums/percussion), Mary Wooten (cello)

Musical Numbers: Bravest of All, You Will Do Great Things, It's Time, Valerie's Decision, Standing and Waiting, The Map Song, Let it Go, Two Villagers, Borders, Buddha's Song, Everybody Needs Something, Happy Shop, That's Business; Teach Me How to Move, Act One Finale, Working Man's Shuffle, It Ain't Good, Here's the Thing, Something Going On, Fifteen Years, Always On the Way, You Are Here, Lessons (Part One: Moving, Part Two: Changing, Part Three: Voices, Part Four: Hello Ferryman?), Is There Anything I Can Do, He Is My Son, Sidd's Enlightenment, Finale

A new musical presented in two acts

Synopsis: The story follows the travails of a young man as he journeys from his small hometown to the big city and eventually an encounter with Buddha.

A NIGHT IN NOVEMBER

Irish Arts Center; First preview: March 14, 2006; Opening Night: March 17, 2006; Closed April 15, 2006; 29 performances

A play by Marie Jones; Produced by the Irish Arts Center in association with Georganne Aldrich Heller and Ed Burke; Director, Tim Byron Owen; Scenery, Robert Ballagh; Lighting, Peter Strauss; Stage Manager, Nicole Press; Master Carpenter, Angrette McCloskey; Press, Karen Greco

Cast: Kenneth McAllister/others **Marty Maguire**

Setting: November 1993–June 1994. Belfast, Dublin, and New York City. Revival of a solo performance play presented in two acts

Synopsis: Marty Maguire plays over 26 characters in this one-man tour de force that tells the story of a Belfast Protestant clerk who embarks on a journey to free himself from the shackles of hatred and bigotry after witnessing the Republic of Ireland-Northern Ireland soccer match *One Night in November.*

HEINER MÜLLER: A MAN WITHOUT A BEHIND

Castillo Theatre; Opening Night: March 17, 2006; Closed April 22, 2006

Castillo Theatre (Diane Stiles, Managing Director) and All Stars Project Inc. production of a variety show with texts and interviews with Heiner Müller, texts translated by Carl Weber, conceived by Dan Friedman, music and lyrics by Fred Newman Director, Gabrielle L. Kurlander; Music Design, Fred Newman; Music Arrangements, David Belmont; Music Director, Michael Walsh; Scenery, Joseph

Spirito; Costumes, Sylvia Grieser; Lighting, Julie Kinnett; Producer, Jim Horton; Assistant Director, Marian Rich; Assistant Stage Manager, Michelle Cramer; Assistant to the Producer, Connie Byrne; Choreography, Gail Bloom; Rap Dance, Nekia Wise; Percussionist, Arnie Wise; Casting, Kenneth Hughes; Press, Roger Grunwald

Cast: Madelyn Chapman; Belinda Fervier; Roger Grunwald; Kenneth Hughes; Ellen Korner; David Nackman; Anne Suddaby; Vicky Wallace

Musical Numbers: Müller's Behind, Outta My Head, A Dead Father, I Wish My Father Were a Shark, She Was Dead, Yesterday on a Sunny Afternoon, Heiner's Note, Finale- Müller's Behind

An avant garde variety show presented in two acts

Synopsis: *Heiner Müller: A Man Without a Behind* is a moving theatrical mosaic featuring texts by—and interviews of—Heiner Müller, Germany's most poetic and controversial playwright since Brecht. Staged to commemorate the 10th anniversary of his death, the show features original music, sketch comedy, and video to explore the complex connections between Müller's life, politics and poetry.

CYCLONE

Studio Dante; First preview: March 15, 2006; Opening Night: March 18, 2006; Closed April 15, 2006; 20 performances

Studio Dante (Michael and Victoria Imperioli, Artistic Directors) production of a play by Ron Fitzgerald; Produced by Mr. and Mrs. Imperioli, Tina Thor and Howard Axel; Director, Brian Mertes; Scenery and Costumes, Victoria Imperioli; Lighting, Tony Giovannetti; Sound, David Thomas; Painter, Richard Cerullo; Master Carpenter, Ryczard Chlebowski; Fight Director, Felix Ivanov; Stage Manager, Darren Rosen; Assistant Stage Manager, Carrie Tongarm; Casting, Vince Liebhart; Press, The Karpel Group

Cast: Joe **Michael Cullen;** Martin **Jeremy Davidson;** Jim **James Hendricks;** Erin **Marin Ireland;** Mitch **Hamish Linklater;** Bob **Lucas Papelias;** Steve **Matthew Stadelmann**

Setting: New Jersey, the present. World premiere of a new play presented in two acts.

Synopsis: A dark comedy, *Cyclone* centers on a young man searching for his life's worth after the death of his estranged father. Strapped with a pack of cigarettes and his father's remains, he takes his quest along a New Jersey landscape dotted with an eccentric cast of characters who, like him, are wrestling with absurdity on the outskirts of the American Dream.

POINTS OF DEPARTURE

Kirk Theatre; First preview: March 7, 2006; Opening Night: March 19, 2006; Closed April 16, 2006; 26 performances

INTAR (Edward Machado, Artistic Director, Editha Rosario, Executive Director) production of a new play by Michael John Garcés; Director, Ron Daniel; Scenery, Mikiko Suzuki; Costumes, Meghan Healey; Lighting, Paul Whitaker; Sound, David M. Lawson; Original Music/Guitarist, Cristian Amigo; Production Manager, Sergio Cruz; Production Stage Manager, Michael Alifanz; Casting, Judy Bowman; Press, Richard Kornberg and Associates

Cast: Marquez **Alfredo Narciso**; Cruz **David Anzuelo**; Vargas **Mateo Gomez**; Petrona **Sandra Delgado**; Leti **Marisa Echeverría;** Xun/Papa/Tumin **Antonio Suarez**

World premiere of a new play presented in two acts

Synopsis: This eloquent political thriller recounts the dangers and difficulties of returning to, and leaving from, a country where a passport might not always be a valid document, the government forbids indigenous groups to speak their native tongues, and alliances and identities constantly shift. As one man tries to return to his village in Central America and another woman tries to embark to the U.S., they experience turmoil which contends that if an immigrant's journey to the U.S. is difficult, the journey back home is almost impossible.

WALK THE MOUNTAIN

59E59 Theatre B; First preview: March 16, 2006; Opening Night: March 19, 2006; Closed April 9, 2006; 23 performances

A new play by Jude Narita; Produced by Cobi Narita, Jazz Center of New York, and Paul and Sam Ash Music Stores; Director, Darling Narita; Scenery/Lighting, Jerry Browning; Photo slides, Vivian Rothstein; Text slides, Dan Kwong; Technical Director, Michael Ou; Assistant Technical Director, Eric Cronlund; Press, Karen Greco

Performed by **Jude Narita**

New York premiere of a solo performance play presented without intermission

Synopsis: *Walk the Mountain* is a one-woman play about Vietnamese and Cambodian women, and the effects of the Vietnam War (or as it's called in Vietnam, the American War) on the people in those countries. Through it we can begin to see how history is distorted by the media and actually re-written by Hollywood movies.

LIVING ROOM IN AFRICA

Beckett Theatre: First preview: March 13, 2006; Opening Night: March 20, 2006; Closed April 15, 2006; 30 performances

Edge Theatre (Carolyn Cantor, Artistic Director/Co-Founder, David Korins, Co-Founder/Producer; Ted Rounsaville, General Manager) production of a play by Bathsheba Doran; Director, Carolyn Cantor; Scenery, David Korins; Costumes, Jenny Mannis; Lighting, Matt Richards; Original Music, Michael Friedman; Sound, Eric Shim; Props, Kathy Fabian; Assistant Director, Michael F. Goldberg; Stage Manager, Jeff Meyers; Assistant Stage Manager, Dustin Tucker; Press, The Karpel Group

Cast: Marie **Ana Reeder**; Edward **Rob Campbell**; Mark **Michael Chernus**; Nsugo **Marsha Stephanie Blake**; Anthony **Maduka Steady**; Michael Lee **Guy Boyd**

World premiere of a new play presented in two acts

Synopsis: Edward and Marie, who move from the UK to a remote African village to open an art museum, realize soon after arriving that they are in the middle of an area beset with poverty and AIDS, and are faced with some troubling questions about personal and political responsibilities. *Living Room in Africa* takes an unflinching look at the notion of individual and global responsibility in the face of human crisis.

FAHRENHEIT 451

59E59 Theatre C; First preview: March 16, 2006; Opening Night: March 21, 2006; Closed April 23, 2006

Godlight Theatre Company (Joe Tantalo, Artistic Director) production of a play by Ray Bradbury, adapted from his 1953 novel; Director, Joe Tantalo; Scenery and Lighting, Maruti Evans; Original Music and Sound, Andrew Recinos; Associate Design, Aaron Paternoster; Productions Stage Manager, Jenny Deady; Assistant Stage Manager, Amy Acorn; Fight Choreography, Josh Renfree; Movement Choreography, HaChi Yu; Press, Karen Greco

Cast: Guy Montag **Ken King**; Clarice **Teal Wicks**; Mildred **Gracy Kaye**; 1st Paramedic/Voices/Aristotle **David Bartlett**; 2nd Paramedic/Voices/Fire Fighter Black/Book Person **Cyrus Roxas**; Captain Beatty **Gregory Konow;** Fire Fighter Holden/Voices/Book Person **Sam Whitten**; Mrs. Hudson/Voices/Alice/Book Person **Kristen Rozanski**; Faber/Voices **Mike Roche;** Helen/Voices/Book Person **Jessica Rider**

New York premiere of a play presented without intermission.

Synopsis: In Bradbury's futuristic world, books are banned and television rules. Firemen set the fires, burning books along with the homes in which they were hidden. When young firefighter Guy Montag learns of a past when people were not afraid, and glimpses a future in which people can think, he realizes what he has to do to attain intellectual freedom.

MERCY ON THE DOORSTEP

Flea Theatre; First preview: March 14, 2006; Opening Night: March 23, 2006; Closed May 6, 2006; 48 performances

Flea Theatre (Jim Simpson, Artistic Director; Carol Ostrow, Producing Director) production of a play by Gip Hoppe; produced by special arrangement with Nicholas Paleologos, Peg McFeeley Golden and Robert Mirmingham; Director, Jim Simpson; Scenery, Susan Zeeman Rogers; Costumes, Eric Elizabeth Murphy and Nathalie Ferrier; Music, Rick Arnoldi; Choreography, Mimi Quillin; Technical Director, Gary Levinson; Stage Manager, Jennifer Noterman; Assistant Director, Jason Podplesky; Props, Michael Goldsheft; Graphics, David Prittie; Press, Spin Cycle, Ron Lasko

Cast: Corrine **Laura Esterman**; Rena **Jenn Harris**; Mark **Mark Rosenthal**

Setting: Mark and Rena's living room, New York premiere of a new play presented.

Synopsis: The play tells the story of Corrine and Rena, an alcoholic widow and her born-again, right-wing stepdaughter. This mismatched pair must learn to co-exist in the house that Corrine's husband left behind.

THE PROPERTY KNOWN AS GARLAND

Actors' Playhouse; First preview: March 13, 2005; Opening Night: March 23, 2005; Closed May 21, 2005; 12 previews, 68 performances.

A play by Billy Van Zandt; Produced by Barry Krost, Sally V. Winters, Mark Fleming and Jane Milmore; Director, Glenn Casale; Scenery, Charlie Smith; Costumes, Cynthia Nordstrom; Lighting, Richard Winkler; Sound, Jill BC DuBoff; Production Stage Manager, Thom Schilling; Wigs, David H. Lawrence; Marketing, HHC Marketing; General Management, 321 Theatrical Management; Executive Producer, Billy Van Zandt; Company Manager, Lauren P. Yates; Assistant Stage Manager, Jonathan E Shultz; Make-up, Stacey Panepinto; Press, Keith Sherman & Associates

Cast: Judy Garland **Adrienne Barbeau**; Ed **Kerby Joe Grubb**; Standby: Jonathan E Shultz (Ed)

Setting: Copenhagen, Denmark, March 25, 1969. World premiere of a new play presented without intermission.

Synopsis: *The Property Known as Garland* is a fictional backstage account of Judy Garland's final concert appearance at the Falkoner Center in Denmark. Ms. Garland passed away three months after this performance.

SARAH PLAIN AND TALL

Lucille Lortel Theatre; First preview: March 19, 2006; Opening Night: March 23, 2006; Closed: April 30, 2006; 57 performances

TheatreWorks NYC (Barbara Pasternack, Artistic Director; Ken Arthur Managing Director) production of a musical with book by Julia Jordan, lyrics by Nell Benjamin; music by, Laurence O'Keefe, based on the book by Patricia MacLachlan; Produced by special arrangement with the Lucille Lortel Theatre Foundation; Director, Joe Calarco; Scenery, Michael Fagin; Costumes, Anne Kennedy; Lighting, Chris Lee; Sound, Eric Shim; Orchestrations, Laurence O'Keefe; Music Director, Jono Mainelli; Casting, Robin D. Carus, Technical Coordinator, B.D. White; Stage Manager, Emily N. Wells; Marketing, M/K Advertising Partners, Ltd.; Press, Rubenstein Communications, Inc, Andy Shearer

Cast: Anna **Kate Wetherhead**; Caleb **Gene Biscontini**; Jacob **Herndon Lackey**; Matthew/William **Kenneth Boys**; Sarah **Becca Ayers**; Estelle/Maggie **Heather Ayers**

Understudies: Kate Fahrner (Anna, Caleb), Mika Duncan (Jacob, Matthew/William), Lani Shipman (Sarah, Estelle/Maggie)

Orchestra: Jono Mainelli (Conductor/piano), Greg Joseph, Tom Partington (percussion), Peter Sachon (cello)

Musical Numbers: Lady of the House, Letters, Sarah Plain and Tall, Would You Miss Me?, Don't Miss the Sea, Sixty Cents, Make It Through Tonight, Something Better, Is It Me You Want to Kiss, Sing You to Sleep

Setting: Late 1800s, Kansas and Maine. A theatre for young audiences musical presented without intermission.

Synopsis: Jacob, a widowed farmer with two small children, places an ad in a paper for a new wife. Sarah, a spinster in Maine, answers the ad and journeys to the plains to become a part of this new family.

TRIAL BY WATER

45 Bleecker-Below; First preview: March 14, 2006; Opening Night: March 26, 2006; Closed April 9, 2006; 28 performances

Ma-Yi Theatre Company (Ralph B. Peña, Artistic Director; Jorge Z. Ortoll, Executive Director) production of a new play by Qui Nguyen; Produced in association with Queens Theater in the Park; Director, John Gould Rubin; Scenery and Costumes, Clint Ramos; Puppets, Jane Stein; Lighting, Nicole Pearce; Sound, Elizabeth Rhodes; Assistant Director, Don Nguyen; Choreography, Qui Nguyen; Dramaturg, Mallory Catlett; Press, Sam Rudy Media Relations

Cast: Hung Tran **Dinh Q. Doan**; Huy Tran **Genevieve DeVeyra**; Pham Tran/Tong **Karen Tsen Lee**; Khue Tran **Jojo Gonzalez**; Tien **Arthur Acuña**; Puppeteers **Timothy McCown Reynolds, Jessica Chanly Smith**

Setting: 1988, The South China Sea. World premiere of a drama featuring puppet theatre presented in two acts.

Synopsis: *Trial By Water* is a searing account of the odyssey of two Vietnamese teenage brothers who are forced to escape their homeland in the middle of the night. As they set off for America by boat, with the dream of a better life, their voyage at sea becomes an allegory of desperate choices. When the boat's engine breaks down, their journey turns into a nightmare. Faced with unthinkable acts of survival, each brother confronts his own issues of mortality and morality.

JACQUES BREL IS ALIVE AND WELL AND LIVING IN PARIS

Zipper Theatre; First preview: March 5, 2006; Opening Night: March 27, 2006; Still running as of May 31, 2006

Production conception, English lyrics and additional material by Eric Blau and Mort Shuman, based on Jacques Brel's lyrics and commentary; music by Jacques Brel; Produced by Dan Whitten, Bob and Rhonda Silver, Ken Grossman, in association with Tiger Theatricals; Director, Gordon Greenberg; Music Director/Arrangements, Eric Svejcar; Choreography, Mark Dendy; Scenery, Robert Bissinger; Costumes, Mattie Ullrich; Lighting, Jeff Croiter; Sound, Peter Fitzgerald; Production Manager, Aurora Productions; Production Stage Manager, Sara Jaramillo; Creative Consultant, Howard Bateman; Associate Producer, Kathleen Brochin; General Manager, Richards/Climan, Inc.; Assistant Director, Ryan J. Davis; Marketing, HHC Marketing; Casting, Cindi Rush; Press, Origlio/Miramontez Company; Cast Recording: Sh-K-Boom/Ghostlight Records 7915584416-2

Cast: Robert Cuccioli; **Natascia A. Diaz**; **Rodney Hicks**; **Gay Marshall**;

Understudies: Kevin Del Aguila, Jayne Paterson

Musicians: Eric Svejcar (Conductor/piano/accordion/acoustic guitar/French Horn/Trumpet/Hammond B-3), Stephen Gilewski (acoustic and electric bass), Brad Gorilla Carbone (drums and percussion)

Musical Numbers: Le Diable (Ça Va), If We Only Have Love, Alone, I Loved, Jackie, My Childhood, Madeleine, Bachelor's Dance, Fanette, Le Moribond/Goodbye My Friends/My Last Supper, The Desperate Ones, Timid Frieda, Girls and Dogs, The Statue, Sons Of, Amsterdam, The Bulls, Brussels, Ne Me Quitte Pas, The Middle Class, Old Folks, Funeral Tango, My Death, Marieke, Song For Old Lovers, Next, No Love You're Not Alone, Carousel, If We Only Have Love

Revival of a musical revue presented in two acts. Originally produced Off Broadway at the Astor Place Theatre May 17 – September 1, 1974, where it ran for 125 performances (see *Theatre World* Volume 30, page 92).

Synopsis: Brel's timeless relevance and enduring passions are celebrated in this diverse revue featuring ballads, tangos, boleros, rock, and classics. With raw human emotion, each piece tells a story, examining themes of love, war, adventure, broken dreams, people from all classes, being young, growing old, and death — but never forgetting that life with all its complexities shows much humor.

THE GOD COMMITTEE

Lamb's Theatre; First preview: March 11, 2006; Opening Night: March 29, 2006; Closed April 16, 2006; 22 previews, 21 performances

A new play by Mark St. Germain; Produced by Carolyn Rossi Copeland in association with Robert Stillman; Director, Kevin Moriarty; Scenery, Beowulf Boritt; Costumes, David Murin; Lighting, Tyler Micoleau; Sound, Robert Kaplowitz; General Manager, Mary Kickel, The Lamb's Theatre Company, Production Stage Manager, Marc Eardley; Assistant Stage Manager, Cherene Snow; Production Supervisor, Thom Schilling; Associate Producer, Dan Roche; Company Manager, Chris Cragin Day; Casting, Pat McCorkle; Press, Keith Sherman & Associates, Brett Oberman

Cast: Dr. Ann Ross **Amy Van Nostrand**; Dr. Keira Banks **Maha Chehlaoui**; Dominick Piero **Ron Orbach**; Dr. Alex Gorman **Peter Jay Fernandez**; Nella Larkin R.N. **Brenda Thomas**; Father Charles Dunbar **Michael Mulheren**; Dr. Jack Klee **Larry Keith**

Understudies: Gannon McHale, Cherene Snow

A new play presented without intermission

Synopsis: A life-and-death suspense drama, *The God Committee* places the audience in the boardroom of the St. Patrick's Hospital transplant selection committee. Medicine, money, and morality clash as just one heart becomes suddenly available for one of four candidates.

MEN OF CLAY

June Havoc Theatre; First preview: March 30, 2006; Opening Night: April 2, 2006; Closed April 23, 2006; 25 performances

A new play written and directed by Jeff Cohen; Produced by The Theatre Outlet of Allentown, Pennsylvania (John Moletress Producing Artistic Director), and the Dog-Run Repertory Theatre; Produced in association with Ruth Marder and Elayne and Benno Hurwitz; Scenery and Technical Supervision, Dynamic Construction; Costumes, Kim Gill; Lighting, Ku'uipo Curry; Sound, Cherry Herring Entertainment Company; Production Stage Manager, Michal V. Mendelson; Set Dressing, Betty-Ann Thomas; Painter, Scott Aranow; Casting, Mark Simon, Fiona Horrigan; Graphics, Scott Menchin; Dramaturg, Abigail Katz; Assistant Director/ Assistant Stage Manager, Maxwell Zener; Production Assistant, Grey Garrett; Press, Shaffer-Coyle Public Relations, Bill Coyle

Cast: Arnold Dickler **Matthew Arkin**; Nate Askin **Daniel Ahearn**; Danny Dickler **Victor Barbella**; Rachel "Rocky" Gorelick **Gabrielle Maisels**; Ira Farber **Steve Rattazzi**; Stan "Squeaky" Cohen **Danton Stone**

Setting: Baltimore, 1970s. World premiere of a new comedy presented in two acts.

Synopsis: *Men of Clay* captures summers on the red clay tennis courts of Druid Hill Park and the camaraderie between Squeaky Cohn and his buddies Ira Farber, Danny Dickler, and Nate Askin — along with the era's Jewish culture and racial tensions and the men's penny-pinching schemes and stubborn resistance to change.

THE MENTALIZER SHOW

The Paradox Space; Opening Night: April 2, 2006; Closed May 21, 2006

Created by Ehud Segev; Produced by Jessica Sara; Original Music, Jason Rosen; Advisor, Asi Wind; Technician, Jonathan Rosen; Publicity Manager, Marie V. Press, Keith Sherman and Associates, Guido Goetz

Performed by **Ehud Segev**

A theatrical experience presented without intermission. Previously presented at the Clurman Theatre, June 2004, TBG Theatre space and at the Paradox Space in 2005.

Synopsis: Ehud Segev, The Mentalizer, performs his critically acclaimed supernatural experience. In *The Mentalizer Show*, Segev talks about spirituality and shares his spiritual journey along with his special abilities of telekinesis, telepathy, future predictions, and metal bending.

MACRUNE'S GUEVARA

Theatre at St. Clement's Church; First preview: March 29, 2006; Opening Night: April 4, 2006; Closed May 10, 2006; 56 performances

Mirror Repertory Company and Young Mirror (Sabra Jones McAteer, Artistic Director) production of a play by John Spurling; Co-Produced by the Mirror Rep Board (Donna Ward, Chairman), Leila Maw Straus, and Jann Leeming; Director, Anthony Nelson; Scenery, Maruti Evans; Costumes, Gail Cooper-Hecht; Lighting/Technical Director, Beau Kennedy; Stage Manager, Carol A. Sullivan; Assistant Director, Mark Defrancis; Dramaturg, Jose Bolivar; Press, Shirley Herz and Associates

Cast: Edward Hotel **Rob O'Hare**; Che Guevara **Max Shulman**; Juan Wolf MacRune; Angelique/Surgeon/Dissenter **Sophia Bushong**; Serapio/Felipe/the Manager/Marco **Matthew Naclerio**; Tania **Mariessa Portelance**; Joaquin/ Rolando **Rich Hollman**; Isabella/Mrs. Rent **Rachel Evans**; Raimundo/Sore **Joseph Varca**; Macrune/Black Jacques **MacAdam Smith**; Karl Marx/Coque Lope/Benjamin/2nd Peasant **Dominic Tancredi**; Rosaura/Pablo **Joanna Simmons**; Coco Peredo/The Lieutenant/Frank le Blanc/Loro/1st Peasant **DeVon Jackson**

American premiere of a new adaptation of the play presented in two acts

Synopsis: *MacRune's Guevara* tells the story of MacRune, a Scottish painter who covers his apartment in pictures of Che Guevara, and then dies. The next man to enter his apartment is the art critic Edward Hotel, who explores the life of Che, the man MacRune, and his own ambition in scenes comedic, tragic, and even musical.

SANDRA BERNHARD: EVERYTHING BAD & BEAUTIFUL

Daryl Roth Theatre; First preview: March 29, 2006; Opening Night: April 5, 2006; Still running as of May 31, 2006

An extravaganza written by Sandra Bernhard; Produced by Daryl Roth; Musical Director, LaFrea Sci; Scenery, David Swayze; Lighting, Ben Stanton; Sound, Walter Trarbach and Tony Smolenski IV; Production Manager, Shannon Nicole Case; General Manager, Adam Hess; Associate Producer, Joe Watson; Press, Pete Sanders; Show recording: Breaking Records

Cast: Sandra Bernhard; The Rebellious Jezebels- La Frae Sci, John Pahmer, Eric Jayk, Mark Vanderpoel, Matt Aronoff, Stefani Lippman

New York premiere of a solo performance theatrical extravaganza presented without intermission

Synopsis: Sandra Bernhard, accompanied the Rebellious Jezebels, performs her brand of wild comedy, reckless rock and roll, and trademark social commentary in her newest work, ripping apart celebrity culture while commenting on events of the time, including Britney Spears, Laura Bush, Condoleezza Rice, Bob Dylan, Mariah Carey, and the war on terror.

Amelia Campbell and Maxwell Caulfield in *Tryst* PHOTO BY PAUL KOLNIK

TRYST

Promenade Theatre; First preview: March 21, 2006; Opening Night: April 6, 2006; Still running as of May 31, 2006

A play by Karoline Leach; Produced by Morton Wolkowitz, Suitz LLC, and Barbara Freitag; Director, Joe Brancato; Scenery, David Korins; Costumes, Alejo Vietti; Lighting, Jeff Nellis; Sound, Johnna Doty; Wigs, Paul Huntley; Casting, Laura Stanczyk; Production Stage Manager, David H. Lurie; General Management, Richard Frankel Productions, Rod Kaats; Production Manager, Theatresmith Inc.; Company Manager, Kim Sellon; General Management Associate, Leslie Anne Pinney; Dialect Coach, Deborah Hecht; Props, Propstar/Kathy Fabian; Make-up, Angelina Avallone; Press, Cromarty & Company

Cast: George Love **Maxwell Caulfield**; Adelaide Pinchon **Amelia Campbell**

Standbys: Brent Harris, Emma Bowers

Setting: London and Weston Super Mare, 1910. World premiere of a romance/thriller presented in two acts.

Synopsis: George Love, a handsome con man who woos loved-starved women, meets Adelaide Pinchon, a desperate woman who dreams beyond her mundane world at the local millinery store. Mr. Love has a history of illicit affairs, but after meeting the fantasizing shop-girl ... there is a twist of fate.

AIN'T SUPPOSED TO DIE A NATURAL DEATH

Club T New York; Opening Night: April 7, 2006; Still running as of May 31, 2006

Classic Theatre of Harlem (Alfred Preisser, Co-Founder and Artistic Director; Christopher McElroen, Co-Founder and Executive Director) production of the musical with music and lyrics by Melvin Van Peebles; Produced in association with AIN'T LLC.; Director, Alfred Preisser; Press, Brett Singer and Associates

Cast: Sunshine **Jordan Brown;** Tomboy **Chudney Sykes;** Country **Taharaq Patterson;** Fattso **John-Andrew Morrison;** Missy **Robyn Landiss Walker;** Sweet Daddy/Cop **Willie Teacher;** Big Titties **April McCants;** Barmaid **Althea Vyfhuis;** Blindman/Con **J. Kyle Manzay;** Junebug **Charles Rueben;** Wino/Frog **Glenn Turner;** Funky Girl **Neil Dawson;** The Dyke **Tracy Jack;** Postman **James Tolbert;** Lily **Mo Brown;** Scavenger Lady **Kimberlee Monroe**

Revival of the musical with music presented without intermission. CT Harlem revived this show October 2004. The original production opened October 20, 1971 at the Barrymore Theatre, transferring to the Ambassador, playing for 325 performances (See *Theatre World* Volume 28, page 15)

Synopsis: A totally unique fiction form, *Ain't Supposed to Die a Natural Death* is a gutsy, lusty narrative of black street life that explores every aspect of ghetto agony. Peopled by junkies, whores, pimps, lesbians, drag queens, sweating workers, crooked cops, prisoners, lovers, and dreamers, Van Peebles' play is considered a tradition-shattering and trend-setting work that spawned the choreopoem, spoken word, and rap music.

Jake Ehrenreich and the Band in *A Jew Grows in Brooklyn* PHOTO BY CAROL ROSEGG

LOS BIG NAMES

47th Street Theatre; First preview: April 1, 2006; Opening Night: April 9, 2006; Closed May 14, 2006; 10 previews, 41 performances

A play by Marga Gomez; Produced by Johnathan Reinis and The Puerto Rican Traveling Theatre (Miriam Colón Valle, Producer); Director, David Schweizer; Scenery and Lighting, Alexander V. Nichols; Sound, Mark O'Brien; General Manager/Associate Producer, Jamie Cesa; Associate Producer, Eva Price, Adam Friedson; Press, Peter Cromarty and Company

Performed by **Marga Gomez**

A solo performance play presented without intermission

Synopsis: *Los Big Names* is an autobiographical play set in two eras: the New York Latin show business world of the '60s and Hollywood of the '90s. It follows the lives of an unconventional Latino family of three pursuing their dreams of fame and fortune. Ms. Gomez portrays her mom, dad, the bodega busybody, Queen Latifah, Kathleen Turner, and all of the vivid characters in this wild but true tale interweaving a moving family saga with an all-out skewering of celebrity.

A JEW GROWS IN BROOKLYN

Chernuchin Theatre at the American Theatre of Actors; First preview: March 28, 2006; Opening Night: April 10, 2006; Still running as of May 31, 2006*

A solo performance musical by Jake Ehrenreich; Produced by Growing Up in America, LP, Dana Matthew, Philip Roger Roy and Second Generation Productions; Director, Jon Huberth; Scenery, Joseph Egan; Costumes, Lisa Ehrenreich; Lighting, Anjeanette Stokes; Sound, David Ferdinand and One Dream Sound; Musical Director, Elysa Sunshine; Press, Keith Sherman and Associates

Performed by **Jake Ehrenreich**

Musicians: Todd Isler, Zvi Klein, Mark Muller, Elysa Sunshine

A solo performance musical presented with intermission

Synopsis: *A Jew Grows in Brooklyn* is the story of a young man, who as a son of survivors growing up in Brooklyn in the 1960s, wanted nothing more than to be an American. While his Yiddish-speaking parents may have failed to understand the game of baseball, or make sense of rock music, they did more than he may have realized growing up to teach him the lessons of life and to help him appreciate how music, culture, and creativity are truly wellsprings of renewal.

*The show closed May 29 – June 6 to transfer to the Lamb's Theatre June 7, 2006

GUARDIANS

45 Bleecker; First preview: April 1, 2006; Opening Night: April 11, 2006; Closed May 25, 2006; 56 performances

The Culture Project (Allan Buchman, Artistic Director, David S. Singer, Executive Director) production of a play by Peter Morris; Director, Jason Moore; Scenery, Richard Hoover; Costumes, Michelle R. Phillips; Lighting, Garin Marschall; Production Stage Manager, Thomas J. Gates; Dialect Coach, Stephen Gabis; Casting, David Caparelliotis; Press, Origlio/Miramontez Company

Cast: English Boy **Lee Pace**; American Girl **Katherine Moennig**

American premiere of a new play presented without intermission. The play won the Fringe First Award at the 2005 Edinburgh Fringe Festival.

Synopsis: *Guardians*, a two-character monologue play, is a fictional account inspired by the true stories of the Abu Ghraib/Lynndie England affair and the resignation of the editor of the British paper The Daily Mirror for publishing fake torture pictures. This twin scandal and the eerie collision of Britain and America raise troubling questions about torture and accountability in the U.S. Army and the responsibility of journalists during wartime.

ON THE LINE

Cherry Lane Theatre; First preview: April 4, 2006; Opening Night: April 11, 2006; Closed April 23, 2006; 24 performances

A new play by Joe Roland; Produced by Mike Nichols, Jill Furman, Boyett Ostar Productions; Director, Peter Sampieri in association with Rachel Neuburger; Scenery, Michael McGarty; Costumes, Robin L. McGee, Lighting, Brian J. Lilienthal; Sound, Peter Hurowitz; General Management, 101 Productions, LTD, Stage Manager, Jennifer Rogers; Technical Supervisor, Aurora Productions, Inc; Company Manager, Heidi Neven; Props, Rob Presley; Development, Jan Gura; Wardrobe, Robin L. McGee; Marketing, HHC Marketing; Press, Pete Sanders Group

Cast: Dev **Joe Roland**; Mikey **David Prete**; Jimmy **John Zibell**

Setting: Now. A working class town not too far from here. World premiere of a new play presented in two acts.

Synopsis: Three lifelong friends take on management, the union, and ultimately each other when a strike wreaks havoc on their working-class town. Along the way they have to negotiate mobs of angry first-graders, bat-wielding bartenders, no-neck corporate shills, and the North American Free Trade Agreement. Lines are drawn, crossed, and double-crossed in this raw, powerful, and often hilarious story about loyalty, love, and the crippling power of unbending principles.

THE CONTRAST

Theatre at St. Clement's Church; First preview: April 9, 2006; Opening Night: April 15, 2006; Closed May 27, 2006; 52 performances

Mirror Repertory Company (Sabra Jones McAteer, Artistic Director) production of a play by Royall Tyler; Co-Produced by the Donna Ward, Leila Maw Straus, Jann Leeming, and the Mirror Rep Board; Director, Peter Bloch; Scenery, Maruti Evans; Costumes, Gail Cooper-Hecht; Lighting, Malcolm Sturchio; Technical Director, Beau Kennedy; Stage Manager, Emileena Pedigo; Press, Shirley Herz and Associates

Cast: Charlotte **Cate Campbell**; Letitia **Emily Hartford**; Maria **Lindsey Andersen**; Van Rough **Mathew Cowles**; Manly **Kyle T. Jones**; Jessamy **Jessie May**; Jonathan **Nicholas Uber Leonard**; Dimple **Zachary Green**; Jenny **Brigette Hayes**; Musician/Servant/Betty **Charles McAteer**

Setting: New England, mid 1780s. A play presented in two acts.

Synopsis: *The Contrast* is a comedy/satire that explores the differences between the vital American colonists and the fashionable people of the Old World. First produced in 1787, it was the first American play ever performed in public by a company of professional actors. Its success was one of the powerful influences sparking a national revolution of sentiment with respect to drama and theatrical amusements.

THE MISTAKES MADELINE MADE

45 Bleecker-Below; First preview: April 15, 2006; Opening Night: April 23, 2006; Closed May 13, 2006; 24 performances

Naked Angels production of a new play by Elizabeth Meriwether; Director, Evan Cabnet; Scenery, Lauren Helpern; Costumes, Jessica Wegener; Lighting, Tyler Micoleau; Sound, Drew Levy; Props, Faye Armon; Production Stage Manager, Hannah Cohen; Production Manager, Dynamic Productions, Craig Sanogueira, Brian Rosenblum; Press, Sacks & Company, Blake Zidell

Cast: Wilson **Ian Brennan**; Edna **Laura Heisler**; Drake/Jake/Blake **Brian Henderson**; Buddy **Tom Sadoski**; Beth **Colleen Werthmann**

Setting: New York, the present. A new play presented without intermission.

Synopsis: *The Mistakes Madeline Made* is about a girl who develops ablutophobia, the fear of bathing. Mourning the loss of her brother and struggling with a soul-crushing job, she wages a war against personal hygiene and all things complacent and clean. As her smell starts to overwhelm her co-workers and casual lovers, the play raises the questions: Is dirty living a political act? And is clean living even possible in these times of unrest?

RELATIVITY

Ensemble Studio Theatre; Opening Night: April 30, 2006; Closed May 13, 2006

Ensemble Studio Theatre (Curt Dempster, Artistic Director) production of a new play by Cassandra Medley; Produced by Carlos Armesto and Elizabeth Van Dyke and presented as the Mainstage of the First Light 2006 Festival; Director, Talvin Wilks; Scenery and Lighting, Maruti Evans; Costumes, Clint Ramos, Sound, Graham Johnson; Multi-Media; Maya Ciarrocchi; Press, David Gersten and Associates

Cast: Dan **Tony Crane**; Claire **Elain Graham**; Kalima **Melanie Nicholls-King**; Iris Preston **Petronia Paley**; Malik **Kim Sullivan**

New York premiere of a new play presented in two acts

Synopsis: For Claire, a lifetime of work and dedication as a leading melanin scientist (those who believe people of color are genetically superior due to higher concentrations of melanin) is culminating in a new book: a collaboration with her daughter Kalima. But Kalima's research in molecular genetics is leading her away from her mother's theories—and to greater success. Forced to choose between science and family, Kalima must decide where her loyalty lies.

SORE THROATS

Duke on 42nd Street; First preview: April 22, 2006; Opening Night: April 30, 2006; Closed May 21, 2006; 30 performances

Theatre for a New Audience (Jeffrey Horowitz, Artistic Director; Dorothy Ryan, Managing Director) production of a play by Howard Brenton; Director, Evan Yionoulis; Scenery, Adam Stockhausen; Costumes, Katherine Roth; Lighting, Donald Holder; Sound, Mike Yionoulis; Dialect Consultant, Elizabeth Smith; Fight Director, J. David Brimmer; Production Stage Manager, Linda Marvel; Assistant Stage Manager, Heather Prince; General Manager, Theresa Von Klug; Production Manager, Ken Larson; Casting, Deborah Brown; Press, The Bruce Cohen Group

Cast: Jack **Bill Camp**; Judy **Laila Robins**; Sally **Meredith Zinner**

Setting: A flat in South London, 1979–1980. New York premiere of a play presented in two acts.

Synopsis: Marriage, sex, and money collide in this powerful study of what happens to Judy when her 20-year-old marriage crashes and burns. Haunted by Jack, her alternately brutal and tender ex-husband, and experimenting with booze, drugs, and sex with Sally, her new-younger-generation roommate, Judy begins a riveting trajectory with a wholly unpredictable end.

J.A.P. CHRONICLES, THE MUSICAL

Perry Street Theatre; First preview: April 17, 2006; Opening Night: May 3, 2006; Closed May 28, 2006; 42 performances

Written and composed by Isabel Rose, based on her novel *The J.A.P Chronicles*; Produced by Keith Sherman; Director, Carl Andress; Musical Director/Arrangements/Orchestrations, Jesse Vargas; Musical Staging, Denis Jones; Creative Consultant, Julian Fleisher; Scenery, Michael Anania; Costumes, Dona Granata; Lighting, Kirk Bookman; Sound, Ryan Powers; Marketing, Leanne Schanzer Productions, Inc., General Manager, Richards/Climan, Inc.; Production Manager, Aurora Productions, Production Stage Manager, Donald William Myers; Press, Keith Sherman and Associates

Cast: Ali/Arden/Jessica/Beth/Dafna/Wendy **Isabel Rose**

Musicians: Jesse Vargas (Conductor/keyboard), Marshall Keating (Associate Conductor), Dave Nolad (flute/clarinet/saxophone), John Lang (bass), Jeff Barone (guitar), Jeffrey Roberts (drums/percussion)

Musical Numbers: Thank God I'm Not One of Them, If Anyone Knew, If Anyone Knew (reprise), You'll Get Yours, J.A.P.P.Y Rhymes with Happy, Wedding Planning Is Such Fun, Revenge, Jewish American Powerhouse (the J.A.P. Rap),

My Name is Jessica Bloom, The Plot Always Thickens, How Can I Get Wendy, Ski Trip, Revenge (reprise), Looking, Palm Beach, Take the Garden Path, The Victory Song, I Was Born For More, The Camera Doesn't Lie

World premiere of a new solo performance musical presented without intermission

Synopsis: Six former bunkmates (all performed by Rose) reunite at Willow Lake Camp's 100th anniversary. Ali Cohen, the former "ugly duckling" turned self-made swan, secretly hopes her teenage tormentors have grown into adult losers. As each woman steps into focus, however, she discovers that things are not quite so simple. Her expectations hilariously undermined, Ali reconsiders her subjects (not to mention herself) as whole, flawed and, finally, very human beings.

CIRQUE DE SOLEIL: CORTEO

Grand Chapiteu at Randall's Island; First preview: April 25, 2006; Opening Night: May 4, 2006; Still running as of May 31, 2006

Created and directed by Daniele Finzi Pascal; Produced by Cirque de Soleil (Guy Laliberté, Founder and CEO); Director of Creation, Line Tremblay; Scenery, Jean Rabasse; Lighting, Martin Labrecque; Costumes, Dominique Lemieux; Sound, Jonathan Deans; Acrobatic Rigging, Danny Zen; Make up, Nathalie Gagné; Composer/Music Director, Phillippe Leduc, Maria Bonzanigo, Michel Smith; Acting Coaches, Hugo Gargiulo, Antonio Vergamini; Dramaturgical Analyst, Dolores Heredia

Cast: The Dead Clown **Jeff Raz**; The Loyal Whistler **Robert Stemmons**; The White Clown **Taras Shevchenko**; The Clowness **Valentyna Paylevanyan**; The Little Clown **Grigor Paylevanyan**; The Giant Clown **Victorino Antonio Lujan**

Musicians: Roger Hewett (Bandleader, keyboards), Gérard Cyr (keyboards), Michel Vaillancourt (guitar), Buddy Mohmed (bass/double bass), Suzie Gagnon (accordion), Kit Chatham (percussion), Gale Hess (violin/clarinet), Paul Bisson and Marie-Michelle Faber (singers)

A theatrical event with music, juggling, acrobats, gymnastics, dance and more presented in two acts

Synopsis: *Corteo* (which means "cortege" in Italian) combines the craft of the actor with the prowess of the acrobat, plunging the audience into a world of playfulness and spontaneity situated in a mysterious region between heaven and earth. In the show, a clown pictures his own funeral taking place in a carnival atmosphere, watched over by quietly caring angels.

LOOK MA … NO EARS!

Laurie Beechman Theatre; First preview: April 29, 2006; Opening Night: May 6, 2006; Still running as of May 31, 2006

Book by Stephen Winer and Lindsey Alley, music and lyrics by Bob Stein; Produced by Eva Price; Director, Ben Rimalower; Lighting, Allison Greaker and Joey Pieragowski; Costumes, Michael H. Woll; Choreography, James Deportee; Music Director, Bob Stein; Press, Shaffer-Coyle

Performed by **Lindsey Alley**

Musicians: Bob Stein (Conductor/piano), Mark Wade (bass), Brian Czach and Michael Klopp (drums)

An auto-biographical solo performance musical presented without intermission

Synopsis: When she was a child, Alley spent seven seasons as a Mousketeer on *All New Mickey Mouse Club* alongside Keri Russell, Britney Spears, Justin Timberlake, and Christina Aguilera. She then moved to New York to pursue her Broadway dreams. The show is a hilarious musical memoir and an honest, touching tale of a small-town girl making it in the big city — with, of course, her mother to thank.

DEFYING HITLER

59E59 Theatre C; First preview: May 2, 2006; Opening Night: May 7, 2006; Closed May 21, 2006

Adapted for the stage by Rupert Wickham from the book by Sebastian Haffner; Presented by Theatre Unlimited as part of the Brits Off Broadway 2006; Director, Peter Symonds; AEA Stage Manager, Terri K. Kohler

Performed by **Rupert Wickham**

New York premiere of a solo performance play presented without intermission. Played in rep with *The Bogus Woman*

Synopsis: *Defying Hitler* is an absorbing and chilling adaptation of the candid, witty, and heart-wrenching memoirs of Sebastian Haffner, a young German growing up in Berlin between the two world wars.

THE BOGUS WOMAN

59E59 Theatre C; First preview: May 2, 2006; Opening Night: May 7, 2006; Closed May 21, 2006

A solo performance play by Kay Adshead; Produced by Leicester Haymarket Theatre and Daniel Clarke as part of the Brits Off Broadway 2006; Director, Kully Thiarai; Scenery and Costumes, Kate Unwin; Lighting, Ciaran Bagnall; Sound, Ben Harrison; Stage Manager, Lyndsey Owen; AEA Stage Manager, Terri K. Kohler; Drummer, Wolde Salessl; Press, Karen Greco

Performed by **Sarah Niles**

New York premiere of a solo performance play presented without intermission. Played in rep with *Defying Hitler*

Synopsis: *The Bogus Woman* is the story of a young African woman who flees her own country following the mass murder of her family to seek asylum in England. Following her interrogation at Heathrow Airport, she is locked up in the UK's national refugee detention center, Campsfield House, near Oxford.

ALL DOLLED UP

Acorn Theatre; First preview: April 29, 2006; Opening Night: May 7, 2006; Still running as of May 31, 2006

A new play with music by Bobby Spillane; Produced by Colin Quinn and Working Stiff Productions; Director, Susan Campanaro; Scenery, Kenny McDonough and Chris Wiggins; Lighting, Dana Giangrande and Tim Stephenson; Original Music and Sound, Alex Jost; Video, Billy Delace; Press, Shaffer-Coyle

Cast: Sally **Michael Basile**; Frankie/Conductor/Spider **Tomm Bauer**; News-women **Jennifer Blood**; Patti **Jamie Bonelli**; Ricky **Matt Gallagher**; Vince/Tom Kelly **John F. O'Donohue**; John **Rocco Parente**; Joey/Bartender **Christo Parenti**; Karen/Jody **Alyssa Truppelli**

Setting: 1960s, New York City. A new play with music presented without intermission. Originally presented at The Producers Club April, 2005.

Synopsis: Based on the story of a real-life cross-dressing mobster, *All Dolled Up* tells the story of Salvatore, a wiseguy from Bensonhurst who is trying to keep his newly discovered dressing fetish a secret from his associates. When his secret is out, the Italian Mafia and Greenwich Village's gay community come together in a hilarious scheme to keep "Sally" alive.

THE THREE MUSKETEERS

Baruch Performing Arts Center Nagelberg Theatre; May 9–20, 2006; 9 performances

The Acting Company (Margot Harley, Producing Artistic Director) production of the play adapted from the Alexadre Dumas novel by Linda Alper, Dorothy Langworthy, and Penny Metropulos; Director, Casey Biggs; Scenery, Efren Delgadillo, Jr.; Costumes, Jared Aswegan; Lighting, Michael Chybowski; Original Music, Ray Leslee; Sound, Jeremy Wilson; Voice Coach, Deborah Hecht; Assistant Director, Pamela Nyberg; Casting, Liz Woodman; Production Manager, Rick Berger; Assistant Production Manager, Steve Lorick; Production Stage Manager, Michaella K. McCoy; Assistant Stage Manager, Michele Harms; Stage Management Intern, Devan Hibbard; Fight Director and Movement, Felix Ivanov; Development/Communications, Gerry Cornez; General Manager, Ishanee DeVas; Associate Producing Director, Douglas Mercer; Production Manager, Rick Berger; Press, Judy Katz

Cast: Captain Treville/Bonacieux **Keith Eric Chappelle**; Athos **Timothy Carter**; Aramis **David Foubert**; Porthos **Cedric Hayman**; D'Artagnan **Chad Hoeppner**; Rochefort **Spencer Aste**; Jussac/Buckingham **William Brock**; Planchet **Matt Steiner**; Constance **Megan McQuillan**; King/Felton **Henry Vick**; Queen/Abbess **Deb Heinig**; Cardinal Richelieu/Coquenard **Matt Bradford Sullivan**; D'Astree/Kitty **Carine Montbertrand**; Milady de Winter **Kaitlin O'Neal**

David Foubert, Cedric Hayman, Chad Hoeppner, Timothy Carter in *The Three Musketeers*
PHOTO BY RICHARD TERMINE

Musicians: Jack Bashkow (piccolo, flute, oboe, English horn), Stew Cutler (electric and acoustic guitars), Ray Leslee (keyboards/drum programming), Garo Yellin (cello), Frances Rowell (cello in prologue)

New York premiere of a new adaptation of the play with music presented in two acts

Synopsis: Alexander Duma's romantic, swashbuckling adventure gets an entertaining new stage adaptation. This classic tale follows the brave young d'Artagnan as he changes from country boy to daring hero, not only rescuing the kidnapped Constance but also preserving the honor of the Queen herself. His journey toward maturity is enabled by Athos, Porthos, and Aramis, famously known as the Three Musketeers.

NO CHILD...

Beckett Theatre; First preview: April 29, 2006; Opening Night: May 10, 2006; Still running as of May 31, 2006

Epic Theatre Center production of a new play by Nilaja Sun; Director, Hal Brooks; Scenery, Narelle Sissons; Costumes, Jessica Gaffney, Lighting, Mark Barton; Sound, Ron Russell; Stage Manager, Tom Taylor; Press, Origlio/Miramontez Company

Performed by **Nilaja Sun**

World premiere of a new solo performance play presented without intermission

Synopsis: *No Child* is an unflinching look into the New York City Public Education system. Sun transforms herself into the teachers, students, parents, administrators, janitors, and security guards who inhabit our public schools every day and are shaping the future of America.

MACBETH

Baruch Performing Arts Center Nagelberg Theatre; May 11–13, 2006; 4 performances

The Acting Company (Margot Harley, Producing Artistic Director) production of the play by William Shakespeare; Director, Eve Shapiro; Scenery, Christopher Barreca; Costumes, James Scott; Lighting, Michael Chybowski; Sound, Fitz Patton; Voice and Text Consultant, Wendy Waterman; Fight Director, Felix Ivanov; Casting, Liz Woodman; Production Manager, Rick Berger; Production Stage Manager, Michaella K. McCoy; Assistant Stage Manager, Michele Harms; Stage Management Intern, Devan Hibbard; Development/Communications, Gerry Cornez; General Manager, Ishanee DeVas; Associate Producing Director, Douglas Mercer; Production Manager, Rick Berger; Company Manager, Daniel A. Finney; Press, Judy Katz

Cast: Witches **Deb Heinig, Megan McQuillan, Kaitlin O'Neal**; Duncan, King of Scotland **William Brock**; Malcolm, his elder son **Henry Vick**; Donalbain, his younger son/Attendant at Macbeth's Castle **Matt Steiner**; Captain/Second Murderer/Soldier **Keith Eric Chappelle**; Lennox **Timothy Carter**; Ross **David Foubert**; Macbeth **Matt Bradford Sullivan**; Banquo **Cedric Hayman**; Lady Macbeth **Carine Montbertrand**; Fleance, son to Banquo **Megan McQuillan**; Macduff **Chad Hoeppner**; Porter/First Murderer/Seyton **Spencer Aste**; Third Murderer **William Brock**; Lady Macduff **Kaitlin O'Neal**; Macduff's son **Matt Steiner**; Doctor, of physic **William Brock**; Gentlewoman **Deb Heinig**

Revival of the play presented in two acts

Synopsis: Combining swift action and soaring poetry, we follow one man's rash power-play for the crown. Ambition infects Macbeth's brain like a virus upon hearing three witches predict that he will one day be king. Spurred on by his equally ambitious wife, he murders the good King Duncan. One evil deed leads to the next, unleashing an escalating cascade of violence, guilt, sleeplessness, paranoia, and madness.

BILLY CONNOLLY LIVE!

37 Arts Theatre A; First preview: May 9, 2006; Opening Night: May 11, 2006; Still running as of May 31, 2006

Written and performed by **Billy Connolly**; Presented by WestBeth Entertainment (Arnold Engelman, President)

New York premiere of a solo comedy show performed without intermission

Synopsis: The well known British comedian brings his uncensored, uncut, and unpredictable stand-up to New York. Billy Connolly has been described as "a genius", his stand-up "otherworldly", and his honesty "terrifyingly insightful." Billy is poised to conquer America alone on stage with a microphone, bringing his oxygen-depriving take on all things taboo.

BEAU BRUMMELL

59E59 Theatre B; First preview: May 9, 2006; Opening Night: May 12, 2006; Still running as of May 31, 2006

A play by Ron Hutchinson; Presented by The Ideas Foundry (Paul Savident, Executive Producer) as part of the Brits Off Broadway 2006; Director, Simon Green; Scenery and Costumes, Tom Rand; Lighting, Adam H. Greene; Sound, Mike Walker; Original Music, George Taylor; AEA Stage Manager, Mandy Berry; Press, Karen Greco

Cast: Beau Brummell **Ian Kelly**; Austin **Ryan Early**

Setting: 1821, on the day King George IV passed through Northern France en route to Hanover; New York premiere of a play presented without intermission. Played in rep with *Cooking for Kings.*

Synopsis: Beau Brummell is about the legendary British dandy who cut a swathe through late Georgian society by redefining men's fashion and masculinity. The play traces his final precipitous fall into poverty and madness.

COOKING FOR KINGS

59E59 Theatre B; First preview: May 10, 2006; Opening Night: May 13, 2006; Still running as of May 31, 2006

A play by Ian Kelly, based on his biography of Antonin Carême; Presented by The Ideas Foundry (Paul Savident, Executive Producer) as part of the Brits Off Broadway 2006; Director, Simon Green; Scenery and Costumes, Tom Rand; Lighting, Adam H. Greene; Sound, Scott George; Original Music, George Taylor; AEA Stage Manager, Mandy Berry; Press, Karen Greco

Cast: Antonin Carême **Ian Kelly**

Setting: The kitchens of the Royal Pavilion in Brighton, the Romanov Pavlovsk Palace, and Antonin Carême. Revival of the solo performance play presented without intermission. This production previously played the Brits Off Broadway 2004. Played in Rep with *Beau Brummell.*

Synopsis: *Cooking for Kings* is based on the life of Antonin Carême, the first celebrity chef, and follows his rise to become a chef for Napoleon, the Prince Regent, Tsar Alexander I, and others.

ANNULLA

Theatre at St. Luke's; First preview: May 4, 2006; Opening Night: May 14, 2006; Still running as of May 31, 2006

A new play by Emily Mann; Produced by Edmund Gaynes and the West End Artists Company; Director, Pamela Hall; Scenery, Josh Iacovelli, Costumes, Elizabeth Flores, Lighting, Kimberly Jade Tompkins; General Manager, Jessimeg Productions; Production Stage Manager, Josh Iacovelli; Press, David Gersten & Associates

Cast: Annulla Allen **Eileen DeFelitta**; Voice of Emily **Neva Small**

Setting: 1974, Annulla's London kitchen. New York premiere of a new play presented without intermission.

Synopsis: In this "interview" play, Annulla Allen, a vibrant woman who had a fascinating history of living as a Polish Jew posing as an Aryan in Nazi Germany, tells a treasure trove of stories how she managed to elude authorities and get her Austrian Jewish husband out of Dauchau.

CAGELOVE

Rattlestick Playwrights Theatre 224 Waverly; First preview: May 10, 2006; Opening Night: May 15, 2006; Still running as of May 31, 2006

Rattlestick Playwrights Theatre (Artistic Director, David Van Asselt; Managing Director, Sandra Coudert) production of a play by Christopher Denham; Director, Adam Rapp; Scenery, John McDermott; Costumes, Erika Munro; Lighting, Ed McCarthy; Sound, Eric Shim; Fight Direction, Rick Sordelet; Production Stage Manager, Paige Van Den Burg; Make up, Pamela May; Press, Origlio/Miramontez Company

Cast: Sam **Daniel Eric Gold**; Katie **Gillian Jacobs**; Ellen **Emily Cass McDonnell**

Setting: Sam's apartment, Chicago, Illinois; the present. A new play presented without intermission.

Synopsis: In *cagelove*, Sam's fiancée Katie has been raped by a former lover. Or has she? With a wedding date looming, Sam fights to save their now fragile relationship, even while undertaking a desperate search to uncover Katie's secret past. Whispers become certainty, certainty becomes obsession, and Sam must decide: How far is too far for love?

NOT A GENUINE BLACK MAN

DR2 Theatre; First preview: May 10, 2006; Opening Night: May 17, 2006; Still running as of May 31, 2006

Written by Brian Copeland, developed by Brian Copeland and David Ford; Produced by Daryl Roth; Director, Bob Balaban; Lighting/Stage Manager, David Hines; Wardrobe Consultant, Sara Tosetti; General Manager, Adam Hess; Production Manager, Ray Harold; Associate General Manager, Erika Happel; Development, Marcia Pendelton; Company Manager, Steven M. Garcia; Marketing, HHC Marketing and Marcia Pendelton; Press, Pete Sanders

Performed by **Brian Copeland**

Setting: New York premiere of a solo performance play presented without intermission. The play holds the record for the longest running solo show in the Bay Area.

Synopsis: The well-known San Francisco radio talk show host and comic explores how surrounding's make us who we are. Brian tells of defining himself as black after growing up in the 1970s in San Leandro, California, one of the most notoriously racist white communities in the U.S.

Nathalie Nicole Paulding, Patricia Randell, Laura Breckenridge in *Suicide Club*

PHOTO BY GERRY GOODSTEIN

YOUNG PLAYWRIGHTS FESTIVAL XXIV

Peter Jay Sharp Theatre; First preview May 9, 2006; Opening Night: May 17, 2006; Closed May 27, 2006; 6 previews, 18 performances

Three new plays by Kit Steinkellner, Miriam Eichenbaum, and Deborah Yarchun; Produced by Young Playwrights Inc (Stephen Sondheim, Founder; Sherry Goldhirsch, Artistic Director; Alfred Uhry, Chairman; Janet Brenner Maltby, President); Directors, Richard Caliban and Valentina Fratti; Lighting, Mike Riggs; Costumes, Joanne M. Haas; Sound, Jill BC DuBoff; Dramaturgs, Brooke Berman, Paul Selig, Crystal Skillman; Production Stage Manager, Dan Zittel; Assistant Stage Manager Lisa Bracigliano; Press, Shaffer-Coyle

LOS ANGELES LULLABY by Kit Steinkellner

Cast: Sonia **Laura Breckenridge**; Abbott **Mike Hartman**; Chazz **James Miles**

SUICIDE CLUB by Miriam Eichenbaum

Cast: Brigitte **Laura Breckenridge**; Lucy **Nathalie Nicole Paulding**; Sister Grace **Patricia Randell**; Mary **Janine Barris**; Priest **Mike Hartman**; Boy **James Miles**

FREEZE FRAME by Deborah Yarchun

Cast: Paul **Teddy Eck**; Mark **Jedadiah Schultz**; Brianna **Janine Barris**; Aliyah **Nathalie Nicole Paulding**

World premiere of three short plays presented in two acts; all playwrights were 18 at the time of play submissions. The festival also included a reading of *Qualis Vita* by Alexandria Symonds on May 21–23 for three performances

Synopsis: In *Los Angeles Lullaby,* a young woman struggling to mother her new baby girl finds herself becoming a little girl again when forced to confront her brilliant yet emotionally absent father. In *Suicide Club,* after an uncharacteristic attempted suicide in a Catholic girls' school bathroom, Brigitte—the witty "good girl"—ends up in the contradictory world of the so-called "bad girls". Set at a Philadelphia college, *Freeze Frame* is an electrically-charged techno-pop drama that focuses on how to freeze a man's soul and the apocalyptic reversal of the Earth's magnetic poles.

THE RACE

59E59 Theatre A; First preview: May 16, 2006; Opening Night: May 18, 2006; Still running as of May 31, 2006

Created and Devised by Gecko (Amit Lahav and Al Nedjari, Co-Artistic Directors; James Flynn, and Katharine Markee, Devisors); Produced by Fuel (Louise Blackwell, Kate McGrath and Sarah Quelch, Founders) as part of the Brits Off Broadway 2006; Directors, Amit Lahav and Al Nedjari; Technician, Joseph White; Assistant Director, Helen Baggett; Production Manager, Stuart Heyes; Technician, Rachel Bowen; Costumes, Ellen Parry and Gecko; Lighting, Kristina Hjelm and Gecko; Props, Torben Schact and Gecko; Press, Karen Greco

Cast: Amit Lahav; **Al Nedjari**; **James Flynn**; **Katharine Markee**; **Natalie Ayton**

Off Stage Performer: Joseph White

Understudy: Helen Baggett

New York premiere of a theatrical experience presented without intermission

Synopsis: One man is on a collision course with his future, sprinting toward the most important moment of his life. But will he be ready? How can a man prepare to meet his first child? *The Race* chronicles a man trying to reconnect his feelings and truly live.

MACBETH

Theatre at St. Clement's Church; Opening Night: May 18, 2006; Closed May 27, 2006; 12 performances

Mirror Repertory Company (Sabra Jones McAteer, Artistic Director) production of the play by William Shakespeare; Co Produced by Donna Ward, Lelia Maw Straus, Jann Leeming and the Mirror Rep Board; Director, Alex Harvey; Press, Shirley Herz and Associates

Cast: Macbeth, etc. **Erik Hellman**; Lady Macbeth, etc. **Molly Brennan**; Macduff, etc. **Anthony Nelson**; Lady Macduff, etc. **Erika Ratcliffe**; Banquo, etc. **Jono Waldman**

Setting: Castle Inverness, Scotland, the Eleventh Century. Revival of the play presented in two acts.

Synopsis: Mirror Repertory offers an imaginative take on Shakespeare's classic in the style of ACTER ACTER, developed by Patrick Stewart and Homer Swindon, which utilizes five actors—three men and two women—to strip bare Shakespeare's play and expose its deepest themes. This style of performance sidesteps the distractions of scenery and "setting" in order to bring what is most important in the play directly to the surface.

Kyle Manzay and Wendell Pierce in *Waiting for Godot* PHOTO BY MICHAEL MESSER

LEE EVANS: SAME WORLD DIFFERENT PLANET

37 Arts Theatre C; Opening Night: May 19, 2006; Closed June 3, 2006; 12 performances

Written and performed by **Lee Evans**

New York debut of a solo performance comedy show presented without intermission

Synopsis: Lee Evans, one of the biggest stand-up comedy stars in the UK, started out as a boxer and has used his unique comedy and irrepressible physicality to create an eclectic career that includes working with Ben Stiller, Christopher Walken, Nathan Lane, and *Stomp*. He received an Olivier Award nomination for his performance as Leo Bloom in the London production of *The Producers* opposite Lane.

WAITING FOR GODOT

HSA Theatre; First preview: May 18, 2006; Opening Night: May 21, 2006; Still running as of May 31, 2006

Classic Theatre of Harlem (Alfred Preisser, Co-Founder and Artistic Director; Christopher McElroen, Co-Founder and Executive Director) production of the play by Samuel Beckett; Director, Christopher McElroen; Scenery, Troy Hourie; Costumes, Kimberly Glennon; Lighting, Aaron Black; Stage Manager, Joan H. Cappello; Dramaturg, Debra Cardona; Press, Brett Singer

Cast: Vladimir **Wendell Pierce**; Estragon **J. Kyle Manzay**; Pozzo **Chris McKinney**; Lucky **Billy Eugene Jones**; Boy **Tanner Rich**

Setting: A country road. A tree. Evening. Revival of the tragicomedy presented in two acts. Tanner Rich also played "Boy" in the earlier revival of *Godot* this season at St. Clement's.

Synopsis: Vladimir and Estragon, two dilapidated bums, fill their days as painlessly as they can as they wait for Godot, a personage who will explain their interminable insignificance, or put an end to it.

HAMLET

Theatre 5; First preview: May 16, 2006; Opening Night: May 21, 2006; Still running as of May 31, 2006

Theatre By The Blind (George Ashiotis and Ike Schambelan, Co Artistic Directors) production of the play by William Shakespeare, Director, Ike Schambelan; Scenery, Merope Vachlioti; Costumes, Christine Field; Lighting, Bert Scott; Sound, Nicholas Viselli and Ann Marie Morelli; Production Manager, Nicholas Lazzaro; Fight Director, Matt Opatrny; Stage Manager, Ann Marie Morelli; Assistant Stage Manager, Francis Eric Montesa; Marketing, Michelle Brandon; Press; Shirley Herz

Cast: Guardian: Marcellus/Polonius/Gentleman/Gravedigger/Osric **John Little**; King: Ghost/Claudius/Player King **George Ashiotis**; Queen: Gertrude/Reynaldo/Player Queen/Second Gravedigger **Melanie Boland**; Prince: Francisco/Hamlet/Sailor **Nicholas Viselli**; Lover: Horatio/Ophelia/Rosencrantz **Pamela Sabaugh**; Friend: Bernardo/Laertes/Guildenstern/Player **Nick Cordileone**

Revival of the play presented in two acts

Synopsis: In this sleek, visceral production, a prince receives a charge to avenge his father's murder and wonders if he really saw a ghost or unjustly suspects his uncle. *Hamlet* is about playing, seeming, acting, fired by showmanship, flauntingly theatrical. Theater By The Blind strips the artifice and veneer, to reveal the meat, bones, and life—leaping back over 400 years of encrusted tradition to Shakespeare's rules.

TEMPEST TOSSED FOOLS

MET Theatre at 55 Mercer; First preview: May 18, 2006; Opening Night: May 25, 2006; Still running as of May 31, 2006

Millennium Talent Group in association with Manhattan Ensemble Theatre production of a play adapted by Sarah Rosenberg, based on *The Tempest* by William Shakespeare, conceived and directed by Sarah Rosenberg and Louis Reyes Cardenas; Music, Eric Luke, Louis Reyes Cardenas, and Stephanie Bailey; Scenery, Bruce Dean; Costumes, Martina Melendez; Lighting, Sean Linehan; Choreography, Robert Gonzalez Jr., Press, Max Eisen

Cast: Prospero **Kevin Barry**; Antonio **Nick Denning**; Ariel **Anna Chlumsky**; Caliban **Robert Gonzales Jr.**; Ferdinand **John Buxton**; Trinculo **Brian W. Seibert**; Stephano **Tommy Dickie**; Alonso **Diego Kelman Ajuz**; Miranda **Rebecca Navarro**; Antonio **Brett Berkly**; Sprites **Stephanie Bentley, Stephanie Leigh Coren, Nichole Azalee-DSuczek**

A play with music for young audiences performed without intermission. Running in repertory with *Fools in Love*

Synopsis: A new musical re-imagining of Shakespeare's *The Tempest*, a tale of magic, revenge, romance, and a comedy involving a magical island filled with sprites, a storm-wrecked ship coming to shore, and a creature called Caliban.

DARK YELLOW

Studio Dante; First preview: May 24, 2006; Opening Night: May 27, 2006; Still running as of May 31, 2006

Studio Dante (Michael and Victoria Imperioli, Artistic Directors) production of a play by Julia Jordan; Produced by Mr. and Mrs. Imperioli, Tina Thor, Howard Axel; Director, Nick Sandow; Scenery and Costumes, Victoria Imperioli; Lighting, Tony Giovannetti; Sound, David Margolin Lawson; Painter, Richard Cerullo; Master Carpenter, Ryczard Chlebowski; Stage Manager, Carrie Tongarm; Assistant Stage Manager, Emily Park Smith; Assistant Director, Zetna Fuentes; Casting, Jack Doulin; Press, The Karpel Group

Cast: Bob **Elias Koteas**; Jenny **Tina Benko**; Tommy **Max Kaplan**

Setting: A rural place, somewhere in America. World premiere of a new noir play presented without intermission.

Synopsis: A murder in a cornfield becomes the focus of an unusual encounter between a local woman and a stranger she meets at the small town bar. As they engage in a game of questions, wordplay, and sexual intrigue, both strive for a connection while identities and motives remain hidden. In the end, the truth about the murder is unearthed in this exploration of crime, human nature, vengeance, and redemption.

Graeme Hawley in *cloud:burst*

CLOUD:BURST

59E59 Theatre C; First preview: May 23, 2006; Opening Night: May 30, 2006; Still running as of May 31, 2006

Written and Directed by Chris O'Connell; Presented by Theatre Absolute, Coventry (Julie Negus, Producer) as part of the Brits Off Broadway 2006; Scenery and Costumes, Janet Vaughan; Lighting, James Farncombe; Soundscape, Andy Garbi; Company Stage Manager, Lizzie Wiggs; AEA Stage Manager, Terri K. Kohler; Marketing and Press, Champberlain AMPR, Karen Greco

Cast: Dominic **Graeme Hawley**

New York premiere of a solo performance play presented without intermission. Performed in rep with *Private Peaceful*

Synopsis: Dominic is an ordinary man who is consumed by the glare of the media after his daughter is murdered. When the press attention moves elsewhere, he is left to pick up the pieces.

PRIVATE PEACEFUL

59E59 Theatre C; First preview: May 24, 2006; Opening Night: May 30, 2006; Still running as of May 31, 2006

Adapted by Simon Reade from the novel by Michael Morpurgo; Presented by the Bristol Old Vic and Scamp Theatre (Louise Callow and Jennifer Sutherland, Founders) as part of the Brits Off Broadway 2006; Director, Simon Reade; Scenery and Costumes, Bill Talbot; Lighting, Tim Streader, Sound, Jason Barnes; AEA Stage Manager, Terri K. Kohler; Press, Karen Greco

Cast: Tommo Peaceful **Alexander Campbell**

American premiere of a solo performance play presented without intermission. Performed in rep with *cloud:burst*

Synopsis: *Private Peaceful* is the story of the final hours of a 16-year-old First World War soldier as he awaits a dawn execution by firing squad. Peaceful looks back at his short but joyful past growing up in rural Devon; his exciting first days of school; the accident in the forest that killed his father; his adventures with Molly, the love of his life; and the battles and injustices of war that brought him to the front line.

OFF-BROADWAY

Productions from Past Seasons That **Played Through This Season**

ALTAR BOYZ

Dodger Stages, Theatre IV*; First Preview: February 15, 2005; Opening Night: March 1, 2005; (See *Theatre World* Volume 61, page 142); 522 performances as of May 31, 2006

A new musical with Book by Kevin Del Aguila, Music, Lyrics, and Vocal Arrangements by Gary Adler and Michael Patrick Walker, Conceived by Marc Kessler and Ken Davenport; Produced by Ken Davenport and Robyn Goodman, in association with Walt Grossman, Ruth Hendel, Sharon Karmazin, Matt Murphy, and Mark Shacket; Director, Stafford Arima; Musical Director/Dance Music and Additional Arrangements, Lynne Shankel; Choreography, Christopher Gattelli; Scenery, Anna Louizos; Lighting, Natasha Katz; Costumes, Gail Brassard; Sound, Simon Matthews; Orchestrations, Doug Katsaros and Lynne Shankel; Casting, David Caparelliotis; Production Stage Manager, Pat Sosnow; Hair, Josh Marquette; Production Manager, Andrew Cappelli; Associate Producer, Stephen Kocis; Press; David Gersten and Associates; General Manager, Roy Gabay; Stage Manager, Laurie Silipigno; Associate Choreographer, Tammy Colucci; Cast Recording: Sh-K-Boom Records 7915586050-2.

Opening Night Cast: Matthew **Scott Porter***1; Mark **Tyler Maynard***2; Luke **Andy Karl***3; Juan **Ryan Duncan***4; Abraham **David Josefsberg***5; Voice of GOD **Shadoe Stevens**

Understudies: Kevin Kern, Daniel Torres

Altar Boyz Band: Lynne Shankel (Conductor/keyboard), Matt Gallagher (keyboard), David Matos (guitar), Clayton Craddock (drums), Doug Katsaros (music programmer).

Musical Numbers: We Are the Altar Boyz, Rhythm in Me, Church Rulz, The Calling, The Miracle Song, Everybody Fits, Something About You, Body Mind & Soul, La Vida Eternal, Epiphany, Number 918, Finale: I Believe

Setting: Here and Now. A musical presented without intermission. Originally produced at the New York Musical Theatre Festival, September, 2004.

Synopsis: A struggling Christian boy band (with one nice Jewish boy), trying to save the world one screaming fan at a time, perform their last tour date at the Dodger Stages. Their pious pop act worked wonders on the home state Ohio bingo-hall-and-pancake breakfast circuit, but will temptation for solo record deals threaten to split the Boyz as they take a bite out of the forbidden Big Apple?

*Succeeded by: 1. James Royce Edwards, Corey Boardman, Jason Celaya 2. Danny Calvert, Tyler Maynard 3. James Royce Edwards, Andrew C. Call 4. Daniel Torres, Nick Sanchez, Clyde Alves, Ryan Duncan 5. Dennis Moench

*Renamed New World Stages March 13, 2006

Jason Celaya, Ryan Duncan, Andrew C. Call, Tyler Maynard, Dennis Moench in *Altar Boyz*
PHOTO BY CAROL ROSEGG

Jenna Pace and Noah Weisberg in *The Awesome 80's Prom* PHOTO BY DREW GERACI

THE AWESOME 80'S PROM

Webster Hall; First Performance: July 23, 2004 (Friday evenings only); Opening Night: September 10, 2004-Fridays and Saturdays (See *Theatre World* Volume 61, page 21); Still running as of May 31, 2006 (Saturday evening performances only)

Written and produced by Ken Davenport; Co-Authored by The Class of '89 (Sheila Berzan, Alex Black, Adam Bloom, Anne Bobby, Courtney Balan, Mary Faber, Emily McNamara, Troy Metcalf, Jenna Pace, Amanda Ryan Paige, Mark Shunock, Josh Walden, Noah Weisberg, Brandon Williams, Simon Wong and Fletcher Young); Director, Ken Davenport; Choreography, Drew Geraci; Costumes, Randall E. Klein; Lighting, Martin Postma; Production Stage Manger, Matthew Ashman; Associate Producers, Amanda Dubois, Jennifer Manocherian; Company Manager, Matt Kovich; Assistant Stage Manager, Kathryn Galloway; Casting, Dave Clemmons; Press, David Gersten & Associates

Opening Night Cast: Johnny Hughes/the DJ **Rye Mullis***1; Lloyd Parker/the photographer **Tom Dooley***2; Dickie Harrington/the drama queen **Stephen Guarino***3; Michael Jay/the class president **Jeff Hiller***4; Mr. Snelgrove/the principal **Fletcher Young***5; Molly Parker/the freshman **Regina Peluso***6; Inga Swanson/the swedish exchange student **Emily McNamara***7; Joshua "Beef" Beefarowski/a football player **Troy Metcalf***8; Whitley Whitiker/the head cheerleader **Jenna Pace***9; Fender/the rebel **Brian Peterson***10; Heather #1-a cheerleader **Sarah Katherine Mason***11; Heather #2-the other cheerleader **Jessica West Regan***12; Kerrie Kowalski/the spaz **Kathy Searle**; Missy Martin/the head of the prom committee **Nicole Cicchella***13; Louis Fensterpock-the nerd **Noah Weisberg**; Blake Williams/the captain of the football team **Brandon Williams***14; Mrs. Lascalzo/the drama teacher **Anne Bobby***15; Feung Schwey/the asian exchange student **Simon Wong***16; the mystery guest **CP Lacey**

An interactive theatrical experience presented without intermission

Synopsis: Wanaget High's Senior Prom-1989. The Captain of the Football Team, the Asian Exchange Student, the Geek, the Head Cheerleader are all competing for Prom King and Queen. The audience decides who wins, all while moonwalking to retro hits from the decade.

*Succeeded by: 1. Philip Burke 2. Jaron Vesely 3. Bennett Leak 4. James Heslop, Jake Mosser 5.Edward Kelly, Robert Neal Marshall, Fletcher Young 6.Lauren Schafler 7. Kate Riley, Emily McNamara 8. David Surkin 9. Julie Kotarides, Jessica West Regan 10. Sean Attebury 11. Sheila Berezan (previews), Megan Gerlach, Jessica West Reagan 12. Susan Rader, Megan Gerlach 13. Keri Setaro, Angie Blocher, Brooke Engen 14. Major Dodge 15. Jennifer Winegardner, Jennifer Miller 16. Anderson Lim.

BLUE MAN GROUP

Astor Place Theatre; Opening Night: November 7, 1991 (See *Theatre World* Volume 48, page 90); 7,126 performances as of May 31, 2006

Created and written by Matt Goldman, Phil Stanton, Chris Wink; Director, Marlene Swartz and Blue Man Group; Artistic Directors, Caryl Glaab, Michael Quinn; Artistic/Musical Collaborators, Larry Heinemann, Ian Pai; Set, Kevin Joseph Roach; Costumes, Lydia Tanji, Patricia Murphy; Lighting, Brian Aldous, Matthew McCarthy; Sound, Raymond Schilke, Jon Weston; Computer Graphics, Kurisu-Chan; Video Design, Caryl Glaab, Dennis Diamond; Stage Manager, Patti McCabe; Executive Director/North American Theatrical Productions, Maureen Moynihan; Resident General Manager, Leslie Witthohn; Senior General Manager, Colin Lewellyn; Associate Artistic Director, Marcus Miller; Senior Performing Director, Chris Bowen; Performing Directors, Chris Bowen, Michael Dahlen, Randall Jaynes, Jeffrey Doornbos, Biran Scott; Presented by Blue Man Productions; Original Executive Producer, Maria Di Dia; Casting, Deb Burton; Press, Manuel Igrejas, Ian Allen

Opening Night Cast: Matt Goldman; Phil Stanton; Chris Wink

2005–2006 Cast: Gideon Banner, Wes Day, Matt Goldman, Colin Hurd, Michael Rahhal, Matt Ramsey, Pete Simpson, Phil Stanton, Steve White and Chris Wink

Musicians: Tom Shad, Geoff Gersh, Clem Waldmann, Dan Dobson, Jeff Lipstein, Byron Estep, Matt Hankle, Dave Corter

An evening of performance art presented without intermission

Synopsis: The three-man new-vaudeville Blue Man Group combines comedy, music, art, and multimedia to produce a unique form of entertainment.

*Succeeding Cast Members 1992–2005: Chris Bowen, Michael Cates, Wes Day, Jeffrey Doornbos, Gen. Fermon Judd Jr., Matt Goldman, John Grady, Colin Hurd, Randall Jaynes, Michael Rahhal, Matt Ramsey, Pete Simpson, Phil Stanton, Pete Starrett, Steve White, Chris Wink

Blue Man Group PHOTO BY DAVID HAWE

Jared Bradshaw (left), Jeanne Montano (center), Michael West in *Forbidden Broadway: SVU* CAROL ROSEGG PHOTO

FORBIDDEN BROADWAY: SPECIAL VICTIMS UNIT

Douglas Fairbanks Theatre*; First Preview: October 16, 2004; Opening Night: December 16, 2004 (See *Theatre World* Volume 61, page 134); 504 performances as of May 31, 2006**

Created and written by Gerard Alessandrini; Produced by John Freedson, Jon B. Platt, Harriet Yellin; Directors, Gerard Alessandrini and Phillip George; Music Director, David Caldwell; Scenery, Megan K. Halpern; Costumes, Alvin Colt; Lighting, Marc Janowitz; Production Consultant, Pete Blue; Associate Producers, Gary Hoffman, Jerry Kravat, Masakazu Shibaoka; General Manager, Ellen Rusconi; Production Stage Manager, Jim Griffith; Marketing, SRO Marketing; Press, The Pete Sanders Group, Glenna Freedman; Original Cast Recording: DRG 12629

Opening Night Cast: Ron Bohmer[1]**; Megan Lewis**[2]**; Jason Mills**[3]**; Jennifer Simard**[4]**; David Caldwell** (Piano)

Understudies: Gina Kreiezmeir, William Selby

A musical revue of Broadway parodies presented in two acts.

Synopsis: Off-Broadway's longest-running revue reopens in this latest version, spoofing not only America's obsession with crime drama, but the latest crop of Broadway shows and stars, including *Avenue Q, Wicked, Sweet Charity, Sweeney Todd, Jersey Boys, The Pajama Game,* Kathleen Turner, Chita Rivera, Rita Moreno, Julie Andrews, Harvey Fierstein, Bernadette Peters, and as always, Ethyl Merman.

*The show transferred to the 47th Street Theatre May 29, 2005

**The show went on hiatus from March 27–June 9, 2006 and performed in San Diego to allow resident company Puerto Rican Traveling Theatre to use the theatre.

*Succeeded by: 1. David Benoit, Jerry Chritakos, Jared Bradshaw, James Sasser, Edward Staudenmeyer, Michael West 2. Donna English, Felicia Finley, Valerie Fagan 3. Michael West, Jared Bradshaw 4. Valerie Fagan, Jeanne Montano

I LOVE YOU, YOU'RE PERFECT, NOW CHANGE

Westside Theatre/Upstairs; First preview: July 15, 1996; Opening Night: August 1, 1996 (See *Theatre World* Volume 53, page 116); 4,090 performances as of May 31, 2006

Music and Arrangements by Jimmy Roberts; Lyrics and Book, by Joe DiPietro; Presented by James Hammerstein, Bernie Kukoff, Jonathan Pollard; Director, Joel Bishoff; Musical Director, Tom Fay; Set, Neil Peter Jampolis; Costumes, Candice Donnelly; Lighting, Mary Louise Geiger; Sound, Duncan Edwards; Production Supervisor, Matthew G. Marholin; Stage Manager, William H. Lang; Company Manager, Adam Levi; Press, Bill Evans and Jim Randolph; Cast Recording, Varese Sarabande VSD-5771.

Opening Night Cast: Jordan Leeds[*1]; **Robert Roznowski**[*2]; **Jennifer Simard**[*3]; **Melissa Weil**[*4]

Standbys: Thomas Michael Allen, Jill Geddes, Kevin Pariseau, Cheryl Stern

Musical Numbers: Cantata for a First Date, Stud and a Babe, Single Man Drought, Why Cause I'm a Guy, Tear Jerk, I Will Be Loved Tonight, Hey There Single Guy/Gal, He Called Me, Wedding Vows, Always a Bridesmaid, Baby Song, Marriage Tango, On the Highway of Love, Waiting Trio, Shouldn't I Be Less in Love with You?, I Can Live with That, I Love You You're Perfect Now Change

A musical revue presented in two acts. On January 7, 2001, the production played its 1,848th performance and became the longest running musical revue in Off-Broadway history (besting *Jacques Brel Is Alive and Well and Living in Paris*).

Synopsis: A musical comedy with everything you ever secretly thought about dating, romance, marriage, lovers, husbands, wives and in-laws, but were afraid to admit.

*Succeeded by: 1. Danny Burstein, Adam Grupper, Gary Imhoff, Adam Grupper, Jordan Leeds, Bob Walton, Jordan Leeds, Darrin Baker, Danny Burstein, Jordan Leeds 2. Kevin Pariseau, Adam Hunter, Sean Arbuckle, Frank Baiocchi, Colin Stokes 3. Erin Leigh Peck, Kelly Anne Clark, Andrea Chamberlain, Lori Hammel, Andrea Chamberlain, Amanda Watkins, Karyn Quackenbush, Marissa Burgoyne, Andrea Chamberlain, Karyn Quackenbush, Sandy Rustin, Andrea Chamberlain, Jodie Langel 4. Cheryl Stern, Mylinda Hull, Melissa Weil, Evy O'Rourke, Marylee Graffeo, Cheryl Stern, Marylee Graffeo, Janet Metz, Anne Bobby, Janet Metz, Anne Bobby

Jordan Leeds and Janet Metz in *I Love You, You're Perfect, Now Change* CAROL ROSEGG PHOTOS

Sam Wolfson, Bryan Fogel, Lorry Goldman in *Jewtopia* CAROL ROSEGG PHOTO

JEWTOPIA

Westside Theatre (Downstairs); First Preview: September 28, 2004; Opening Night: October 21, 2004 (See *Theatre World* Volume 61, page 126); 698 performances as of May 31, 2006

Written by Bryan Fogel and Sam Wolfson; Produced by WEJ Production LLC, William I Franzblau, Jenkay LLC, and Jay H. Harris; Director, John Tillinger; Scenery, Patrick Fahey; Costumes, Cynthia Nordstrom; Lighting, Mike Baldassari; Sound, Kevin Lacy; Stage Manager, Jeff Benish; Associate Producers, John Ballard, Steve Boulay, David Elzer, Epstein/Robers, Martha R. Gasparian, Kanar/Dickler, Brian Melzer, Elsa Daspin Suisman, Lawrence S. Toppall, Helaine Weissman; General Manager, Richards/Climan, Inc.; Production Manager, Terry Jackson; Casting, Arnold Mungioli; Marketing, Leanne Schanzer; Press, Keith Sherman & Associates

Cast: Marcy Cohen/Arlene Lipschitz **Cheryl David**[*1]; Chris O'Connell **Bryan Fogel**; Dennis Lipschitz/Party Guy **Lorry Goldman**; Rachel **Irina Pantaeva**[*2]; Bad Dates/Jill/Nurse/Allison Cohen **Jackie Tohn**[*3]; Rabbi Schlomo/Irving **Gerry Vichi**[*4]; Adam Lipschitz **Sam Wolfson**

Understudies: Adam Ludwig (Chris/Adam)[*5], D.L. Schroder (Rabbi Schlomo/Irving/ Dennis/Party Guy), Christine Delaine (Women's roles and Assistant Stage Manager)

A play presented in two acts.

Synopsis: Adam Lipschitz, 29 and single, is obsessed with dating gentile girls because they don't remind him of his mother. One night at a mixer, he meets Chris O'Connell, a single gentile man in search of "jewtopia," where all his decisions will be made for him. In exchange for some coaching on Jewish culture, Chris offers to set Adam up with the perfect girl.

*Succeeded by: 1. Becky London, Glynis Bell 2. Deborah Teng, Rosanne Ma 3. Vanessa Lemonides, Samantha Daniel 4. Larry Black, David Rogers, Joel Rooks 5. David L. Townsend

Naked Boys Singing

NAKED BOYS SINGING

Actor's Playhouse*; First Preview: July 2, 1999; Opening Night: July 22, 1999 (See *Theatre World* Volume 56, page 114); 2,398 performances as of May 31, 2006 (Weekend performances only)

By Stephen Bates, Marie Cain, Perry Hart, Shelly Markham, Jim Morgan, David Pevsner, Rayme Sciaroni, Mark Savage, Ben Schaechter, Robert Schrock, Trance Thompson, Bruce Vilanch, Mark Winkler; Conceived and Directed by Robert Schrock; Choreography, Jeffry Denman; Musical Direction/Arrangements, Stephen Bates; Set/Costumes, Carl D. White; Lighting, Aaron Copp; Stage Manager, Christine Catti; Presented by Jamie Cesa, Carl D. White, Hugh Hayes, Tom Smedes, Jennifer Dumas; Press, Peter Cromarty.

Opening Night Cast: Glenn Allen; **Jonathan Brody**; **Tim Burke**; **Tom Gualtieri**; **Daniel C. Levine**; **Sean McNally**; **Adam Michaels**; **Trance Thompson**

Pianist: Stephen Bates; Substitute Pianists: William Johnson and Jono Mainelli

2005–2006 Cast: Jarrod Cafaro, Gavin Esham, Frank Galgano, Timothy John, Scott McLean, Eric Sand, Phil Simmons, Trevor Southworth, Gregory Stockbridge, Mickey Toogood, Jeffrey Biering (piano)

Musical Numbers: Gratuitous Nudity, Naked Maid, Bliss, Window to Window, Fight the Urge, Robert Mitchum, Jack's Song, Members Only, Perky Little Porn Star, Kris Look What You've Missed, Muscle Addiction, Nothin' but the Radio on, The Entertainer, Window to the Soul, Finale/Naked Boys Singing!

A musical revue presented in two acts.

Synopsis: The title says it all! Caution and costumes are thrown to the wind in this all-new musical revue featuring an original score and a handful of hunks displaying their special charms as they celebrate the splendors of male nudity in comedy, song, and dance.

*Naked Boys Singing played at The Actors' Playhouse to March 7, 2004; Theatre Four from March 17, 2004 through September 5, 2004; the John Houseman Theater September 17–October 31, 2004; the 47th Street Theatre November 12, 2004–April 29, 2005; the Julia Miles Theatre May 6, 2005; and Dodger Stages (subsequently renamed New World Stages) October 14, 2005.

Succeeding Cast Members 2000–2005: Timothy Connell, Eric Dean Davis, Trevor Richardson, Charlie Duff, Richard Lear, David Macaluso, Steven Spraragen, Patrick Boyd, William DiPaola, Scott McLean, Kristopher Kelly, Ryan Lowe, Jeffrey Todd , Gavin Esham, George Livengood, Billy Briggs, Robert McGown, John Serchrist, Trevor Southworth, Cannon Starnes, Gregory D. Stockbridge, Luis Villabon, Patrick Herwood, Timothy John , Stephan Alexander, Brian M. Golub, Eric Potter, Dennis Stowe, Phil Simons, Bruce Linser, Mickey Toogood, Frang Galagno

PERFECT CRIME

Courtyard Playhouse*; Opening Night: April 18, 1987 (see *Theatre World* Volume 43, page 96); 7,774 performances as of May 31, 2006

Written by Warren Manzi; Director, Jeffrey Hyatt; Set, Jay Stone, Mr. Manzi; Costumes, Nancy Bush; Lighting, Jeff Fontaine; Sound, David Lawson; Stage Manager, Julia Murphy; Presented by The Actors Collective in association with the Methuen Company; Press, Debenham Smythe/Michelle Vincents, Paul Lewis, Jeffrey Clarke.

Opening Night Cast: Margaret Thorne Brent **Catherine Russell**; Inspector James Ascher **Perry Pirkkanen***[1]; W. Harrison Brent **Warren Manzi***[2]; Lionel McAuley **Marc Lutsky***[3]; David Breuer **W. MacGregor King***[4]

Understudies: Lauren Lovett (Females); J.R. Robinson (Males)

Setting: Windsor Locks, Connecticut. A mystery presented in two acts. Catherine Russell has only missed four performances since the show opened in 1987.

Synopsis: Murder mystery about a psychiatrist who is accused of killing her husband by a detective who can't quite pin the murder on her. The complication is that the psychiatrist and the detective are in love.

*Transferred to the Second Stage, 47th St. Playhouse, Intar 53 Theater, Harold Clurman Theatre, Theatre Four, The Duffy Theatre, and currently the Snapple Theatre Center

*Succeeded by: 1. Warren Manzi, Jim O'Malley, David Breitbarth, Craig Mathers, Dana Scott Galloway, David Valcin, Dennis Pfister, Jack Davis, Gene Terinoni, Mark Hoffmaier, Carl Palmer, Joseph Adams, James Farrell, Michael Wilson, Jay Potter, Michael Minor, Paul Coufos,Terence Schappert, Laurence Lau, David McDonald, Jay Nickerson, James Kiberd, Vasili Bogazianos, Richard Shoberg 2. Warren Manzi, Jim O'Malley, David Breitbarth, Craig Mathers, Dana Scott Galloway, David Valcin, Dennis Pfister, Jack Davis, Gene Terinoni, Mark Hoffmaier, Carl Palmer, Joseph Adams, James Farrell, Michael Wilson, Jay Potter, Michael Minor, Paul Coufos,Terence Schappert, Laurence Lau, David McDonald, Jay Nickerson, James Kiberd, Vasili Bogazianos, Richard Shoberg 3. John Sellars, Brian Dowd, Doug DeLauder, Jim Shankman, Trip Hamilton, David Chapman, Jay Nelson, Zenon Zelenich, Terry Londeree, Carter Inskeep, John O'Creagh, Richard Gang, Gerald Anthony, Walter Cline, Chris Lutkin, Brian Hotaling, Charles Geyer, Michael Minor, Matt Landers, Victor Talmadge, Ed Sala, Stephen Clarke, Robin Haynes, Philip Hoffman 4. Lionel Chute, Dean Gardner, Patrick Robustelli

Catherine Russell in *Perfect Crime* PHOTO BY FRAN COLLIN

Slava Polunin in *Slava's Snowshow*

SLAVA'S SNOWSHOW

Union Square Theatre; First preview: August 24, 2004; Opening Night: September 8, 2004 (See *Theatre World* Volume 61, page 121); 742 performances as of May 31, 2006

Created and staged by Slava Polunin by arrangement with SLAVA and Gwenael Allan; Produced by David J. Foster and Ross Mallison; Co-Producer, Tom Lightburn and Jared Geller; Scenery and Costumes, Anna Hannikaninen; Lighting, Oleg Iline; Sound, Rastyam Dubinnikov; General Manager, Simon Bryce; Production Managers, Carolyn Kelson and Jason Janicki; Company Manager, Ginger Dzerk; Advertising, Eliran Murphy Group; Press, Marc Thibodeau, The Publicity Office

Opening Night Cast: Yelllow **Slava Polunin, Derek Scott, Robert Saralp. Fyodar Makarov**; Green Clowns **Ivan Polunin. Nikolai Terentiev. Alexandre Frish, Onofrio Colucci, Boris Hybner. Jason Janicki, Aelita Loukhaeva, Yury Musatov, Elena Ushakova, Stanislav Varkki**

Replacements: Richard Crawford, Oleg Lugovskoy, Aelita Ioukhaeve, Georgiy Deliyev, Artem Zhimolokhov, Spencer Chandler

An Eastern European clown show presented without intermission

Synopsis: Russians greatest clown strings together a series of breathtaking images performed to popular music. A giant cobweb stretches over the entire audience; a raging blizzard coats the audience in snow; giant helium-filled beach balls are kept afloat by the viewers. Lyrical, hilarious, poignant, and brilliant.

STOMP

Orpheum Theatre; First Preview: February 18, 1994; Opening Night: February 27, 1994 (See *Theatre World* Volume 50, page 113); 5,149 performances as of May 31, 2006

Created/Directed by Luke Cresswell and Steve McNicholas; Lighting, Mr. McNicholas, Neil Tiplady; Production Manager, Pete Donno; General Management, Richard Frankel/Marc Routh; Presented by Columbia Artists Management, Harriet Newman Leve, James D. Stren, Morton Wolkowitz, Schuster/Maxwell, Galin/Sandler, and Markley/Manocherian; Press, Chris Boneau/Adrian Bryan-Brown, Jackie Green, Bob Fennell.

Opening Night Cast: Luke Cresswell; Nick Dwyer; Sarah Eddy; Theseus Gerard; Fraser Morrison; David Olrod; Carl Smith; Fiona Wilekes

Swings: Everett Bradley, Allison Easter

2005–2006 Cast: Marivaldo Dos Santos, Sean Edwards, Fritzlyn Hector-Opare, Brad Holland, Stephanie Marshall, Keith Middleton, Yako Miyamoto, Raymond Poitier, Camille Shuford, Carlos Thomas, Nicholas V. Young

A percussive performance art piece presented with an intermission

Synopsis: *Stomp* is a high-energy, percussive symphony, coupled with dance, played entirely on non-traditional instruments, such as garbage can lids, buckets, brooms and sticks.

Succeeding Cast Members 1995–2005: Quami Adams, Shaneca Adams, Vincent Adams, Taro Alexander, Morris Anthony, Harold "Kekoa" Bayang, Ahmed Best, Michael Bove, Maria Emilia Breyer, E. Donisha Brown, Hallie Bulleit, David Cox, Miles Crawford, Sean Curran, Steven Dean Davis, Ivan Delaforce, Kwame Densu, Jeremy Dolan, Paulo Dos Santos, Michael Duvert, Jr., Dashiell Eaves, James Joseph Englund, Dan Finnerty, Rory Flores, Darren Frazier, Khalid Freeman, Thomas Fujiwara, Richard Giddens, Coralissa Gines, Ann Hairston, Mindy Haywood, Dave Heilman, Jim Holdridge, Elizabeth Homer-Smith, Raquel Horsford, Tonya Kay Linebrink, Tony James, Anthony Johnson, Ameenah Kaplan, Konrad Kendrick, Chad Kukahiko, Elton 'Boom' Laron, Kirk Leggett, Mina Liccione, Jarred Lillis, Patrick Lovejoy, Kimmarie Lynchy, Peter Michael Marino, Stephanie Marshall, Mignon Mason, Hillel Meltzer, Keith Middleton, Jason Mills, Sean M. Mullins, Cameron Parker Newlin, Michael Oakley, John Elliott Oyzon, Steven Palmer, Michael Paris, Andrew Patrick, Samantha 'Soda' Persi, Raymond Poitier, Ana Sofia Pomales, Randi Rader, Dannielle Reddick, Warren L. Richardson, Walter Rodriquez, Jason Rogoff, Ray Rodriquez Rosa, R.J. Samson, John Sawicki, Matthew Scanlon, David Schommer, Sophie Sharp, Harry W. Shead, Jr., Columbus Keith Short, Elec Simon, Kamal Sinclair-Steele, Anthony and Anita Dasiell-Sparks, Vickie Tanner, Doug Thoms, Marcia Thompson, Michael Tiger, Mario Torress, Seth Ullian, Elizabeth Vidos, Davi Vieira, Sherilynn Wactor, Dan Weiner, Fiona Wilkes, Rick Willett, Ejoe Wilson

The Cast of *Stomp* PHOTO BY OLEG MICHEYEV

THE TALK OF THE TOWN

The Oak Room; Opening Night: May 23, 2005 (See *Theatre World* Volume 61, page 152); Still running as of May 31, 2006 (Sunday and Monday performances only)

Transfer of the Off Off Broadway musical with Book, Lyrics and Music by Ginny Redington and Tom Dawes; Presented by The Peccadillo Theatre Company (Dan Wackerman, Artistic Director; Kevin Kennedy, Managing Director) and the Algonquin Hotel; Director, Dan Wackerman, Musical Director, Mark Janas; Movement Consultant, Mercedes Ellington; Assistant Director/Stage Manager, Michael Gianakos; Scenery and Lighting, Chris Jones; Costumes, Amy C. Bradshaw; Arrangements and Orchestrations, Jeffrey Biering; Dramaturge, William M. Peterson, PhD.; General Manager, Jamie Cesa; Associate General Manager, Rick L. Stevens; Company Manager, Townsend Teague; Press, Brett Singer & Associates, Peter Cromarty

Opening Night Cast: Dorothy Parker **Kristin Maloney**; Robert Benchley **Jared Bradshaw**; Alexander Woolcott **Chris Weikel**; Robert Sherwood **Adam J. MacDonald**; Edna Ferber **Donna Coney Island**; Marc Connelly **Stephen Wilde**; George S. Kaufman **Jeffrey Biering**

Musicians: Mark Janas (Piano/Conductor), Justin Depuyt (Keyboard)

Musical Numbers: The Restorative Lunch, Work Is a Four-Letter Word, The Restorative Lunch II, Because It's There, The Restorative Lunch III, Two Heads Are Better Than One, The Restorative Lunch IV, Never Tell the One You Love, The Talk of the Town, Through a Writer's Eyes, The Critic, Robert It Should Have Been You, Robbie Sherwood's Merrie Band of Friends, And the Circle Goes Round and Round, Behind the Velvet Rope, Say Something Funny, Sink or Swim, I'm All Out of Words, The Man I Might Have Been, Doin' the Breakaway, The Restorative Lunch (reprise), The Toast, And The Circle Goes Round and Round (reprise), The Talk of the Town (reprise).

Setting: The action takes place in New York City over a ten year period beginning in 1920. A musical presented in two acts. Originally presented in association with William Repicci at the Bank Street Theatre on November 4 – December 19, 2004. During the run there it officially became an Off Broadway production from December 5 – 19.

Synopsis: *The Talk of the Town* tells the story of the ten-year friendship of the wittiest literary lights of the 1920's. Loaded with their legendary quips, critiques, and put-downs, this delightful period musical traces the legendary skirmishes (both romantic and otherwise) around the famed Algonquin Round Table.

TONY 'N TINA'S WEDDING

Washington Square Church/Carmelita's; Opening Night: February 6, 1988 (See *Theatre World* Volume 44, page 63); 5,402 performances as of May 31, 2006.*

Created by Artificial Intelligence (Core Group- James Altuner, Mark Campbell, Chris Fracchiolla, Jack Fris, Larry Pellegrini); Executive Producers, Joseph and Daniel Corcoran; Producer, Mark Campbell; Conception and Artistic Director, Nancy Cassaro; Director, Larry Pelligrini; Choreography, Hal Simons; Costumes/ Hair/Make-Up, Cake Design & Construction, Randal Thropp; Original Press, David Rothenberg, Terence Womble, Todd Lundgren; Press, 1992 – 2003, David Gersten.

Opening Night Cast: Valentina Lynne Vitale Nunzio, the bride **Nancy Cassaro**[1]; Anthony Angelo Nunzio, the groom **Mark Nassar**[2]; Connie Mocogni, maid of honor **Moira Wilson**[3]; Barry Wheeler, best man **Mark Campbell**[4]; Donna Marsala, bridesmaid **Elizabeth Dennehy**[5]; Dominick Fabrizzi, usher **James Altuner**[6]; Marina Gulino, bridesmaid **Patricia Cregan**[7]; Johnny Nunzio, usher/brother of the groom **Eli Ganias**[8]; Josephine Vitale, mother of the bride **Susan Varon**[9]; Joseph Vitale, brother of the bride **Thomas Michael Allen**[10]; Luigi Domenico, great uncle of the bride **Jacob Harran**[11]; Rose Domenico, aunt of the bride **Jennifer Heftler**[12]; Sister Albert Maria, cousin of the bride **Elizabeth Herring**[13]; Anthony Angelo Nunzio, Sr., father of the groom **Chris Fracchiolla**[14]; Madeline Monore, Mr. Nunzio's girlfriend **Jennie Moreau**[15]; Grandma Nunzio, grandmother to the groom **Denise Moses**[16]; Michael Just, Tina's ex-boyfriend **Jack Fris**[17]; Father Mark, parish priest **Phil Rosenthal**[18]; Vinnie Black, the caterer **Kevin A. Leonidas**[19]; Loretta Black, his wife **Joanna Cocca**[20]; Mick Black, his brother **Gary Schneider/ William Marsilii**[21]; Mikie Black, his son **Mickey Abbate**[22]; Nikki Black, his daughter **Judy Sheehan/Cathryn de Prume**[23]; Mitzi Black, his sister (subsequently written out) **Carrie Gordon**; Pat Black, other sister of the caterer (added second year) **Mari Biechler**[24]; Timothy Sullivan, the video man (subsequently became Rick DeMarco) **Tom Hogan**; Rick DeMarco, the video man **Neil Monaco/Patrick Smith**[25]; Sal Antonucci, the photographer **Victor Floriani**[26]; Donny Dolce, the bandleader **Michael Winther**[27]; Celeste Romano, keyboards **Kia Colton/Debra Barsha**; Carlo Cannoli, bass **Charlie Terrat/Jim Dillman**; Rocco Caruso, drums **Towner Gallaher**

An interactive environmental theatre production. The action takes place at Tony and Tina's wedding and reception.

Synopsis: Tony and Tina are getting hitched. Audience members become part of the exuberant Italian family — attending the ceremony, mingling with relatives and friends, eating, drinking and dancing to the band.

*After opening, the production transferred to St. John's Church (wedding ceremony) and Vinnie Black's Coliseum (reception) until August, 1988, and then transferred to St. Luke's Church and Vinnie Black's Vegas Room Coliseum in the Edison Hotel. The production closed May 18, 2003, then reopened on October 3, 2003. It closed again May 1, 2004, reopened under new co-producers (Raphael Berko and Jeff Gitlin) on May 15th, 2004.

*Succeeded by: 1. Kelly Cinnate, Sharon Angela, Justine Rossi, Shanna Keller, Susan Campanaro, Domenica Cameron Scorsese, Kelly Cinnante 2. Ron Eldard, David Dundara, Robert Cea, Rick Pasqualone, Lee Mazzilli, Tony Meola, Patrick Buckley, Scott Bielecky 3. Chase Winton, Judy Sheehan, Dina Losito, Doma Villella, Susan Laurenzi, Sophia Antonini 4. Bruce Kronenberg, Keith Primi, Timothy Monagan, Joe Dallo 5. Patty Granau, Debi Toni, Lisa Casillo, Susan Campanaro, Lisa Casillo 6. George Shifini, Lou Martini, Jr., Joesph Barbara, Sal Marino 7. Aida Turturro, Celeste Russi, Cheryl Giuliano, Susan Ann Davis 8. James Duont, James Georgiades, Michael Creo, Ken Garito, Nick Gambella, Michael Perri 9. Rosanna Mineo, Louise Drevers, Nancy Timpanero, Victoria Barone, Jacqueline Carol 10. Billy Joe Young, Paul Spencer, Richard Falzone, Michael Gargani 11. Kirk Duncan, Allen Lewis Rickman, Stan Winston, Frankie Waters 12. Kelly Ebsary, Wendy Caplan, Cayte Thorpe, Susan Varon 13. Jean Synodinos, Fran Gennuso, Renae Patti 14. Rick Shapiro, Dan Grimaldi, Mark Nasser 15. Leila Kenzle, Liliane DuRae, Georgienne Millen, Karen Cellini, Denise Fennell, 16. Bonnie Rose Marcus, Elaine Unnold, Letty Serra 17. Eric Cadora, Anthony T. Lauria, Patrick Holder 18. Vincent Florianai, David Carr, Gary Schneider, James J. Hendricks 19. Tom Karlya, Henry Caplan 20. Victoria Constan, Rebecca Weitman 21. Joe Bacino, Tony Palellis, Robert R. Oliver, Matthew Bonifacio 22. John Allen Groffedo, Paul Maisano, Anthony Luongo, John Walter, Eric Gutman 23. Sharon Angela, Jodi Grant, Maria Gentile, Jodi Grant, Alyson Silverman 24. Donna Villella, Jody Oliver, Maria Gentile, Joanne Newborn 25. Marc Romero, Kerry Logan Anthony Barone 26. Daniel Maher, John Fulweiler, Patrick Smith, Glenn Taranto, Tony Patellis, Tony DiBenedetto 27. Tony Dowdy, Michael Visconti, Ken Phillips

OFF-BROADWAY

Productions from Past Seasons That **Closed During This Season**

Stuart Zagnit and June Gable in *Picon Pie*   PHOTO BY CAROL ROSEGG

The Cast of *Captain Louie*   PHOTO BY CAROL ROSEGG

Brian d'Arcy James, Gregg Edelman, and Kerry O'Malley in *Flight*

PICON PIE
Lamb's Theatre
First Preview January 29, 2005
Opened February 17, 2005; Closed June 2, 2005
24 previews, 137 performances

SCORE
Peter Jay Sharp Theatre at Playwrights Horizons
First Preview April 26, 2005
Opened May 1, 2005; Closed June 9, 2005
40 performances

BFE
Peter Jay Sharp Theatre at Playwrights Horizons
First Preview May 17, 2005
Opened May 31, 2005; Closed June 12, 2005
29 performances

CAPTAIN LOUIE
Theatre at St. Peter's Church- York Theatre Company
First Preview May 4, 2005
Opened May 8, 2005; Closed June 12, 2005
50 performances

DESIGNER GENES
Pelican Studio Theatre
First Preview May 10, 2005
Opened May 18, 2005; Closed June 12, 2005
24 performances

WOMAN BEFORE A GLASS
Promenade Theatre
First Preview February 18, 2005
Opened March 10, 2005; Closed June 12, 2005
22 previews, 110 performances

THE ARGUMENT
Gertrude and Irving Dimson Theatre - Vineyard Theatre
First Preview May 14, 2005
Opened May 25, 2005; Closed June 19, 2005
36 performances

FLIGHT
Lucille Lortel Theatre
First Preview May 8, 2005
Opened May 16, 2005; Closed June 19, 2005

SONGS FROM AN UNMADE BED
New York Theatre Workshop
First Preview May 12, 2005
Opened May 24, 2005; Closed June 19, 2005
31 performances

MISS JULIE
Theatre 224 Waverly – Rattlestick Playwrights Theatre
First Preview May 12, 2005
Opened May 19, 2005; Closed June 19, 2005
4 previews, 35 performances

DISCONNECT
East 13th Street Theatre
First Preview May 27, 2005
Opened May 31, 2005; Closed June 25, 2005

SHE STOOPS TO CONQUER
Irish Repertory Theatre
First Preview May 5, 2005
Opened May 12, 2005; Closed June 26, 2006
54 performances

TERRORISM
Harold Clurman Theatre – The New Group
First Preview May 9, 2005
Opened May 23, 2005; Closed June 26, 2005
49 performances

HURLYBURLY
37 Arts
First Preview April 11, 2005
Opened May 20, 2005; Closed July 2, 2005
83 performances

THE DONKEY SHOW
Club El Flamingo
Opened August 18, 1999; Closed July 16, 2005
1,717 performances

Joy Lynn Matthews, Lynn Eldredge, Mary Jo McConnell, Megan Thomas in *Menopause: The Musical* PHOTO BY BEN STROTHMAN

TROLLS
Actors Playhouse
First Preview May 4, 2005
Opened May 19, 2005; Closed July 17, 2005
71 performances

BEAST ON THE MOON
Century Center for the Performing Arts
Opened March 7, 2004; Closed August 7, 2005
120 performances

COOKIN'
Minetta Lane Theatre
Opened March 7, 2004; Closed August 7, 2005
632 performances

THRILL ME
Theatre as St. Peter's Church – York Theatre Company
First Preview May 16, 2005
Opened May 26, 2005; Closed August 21, 2005
10 previews, 73 performances

THE MUSICAL OF MUSICALS — THE MUSICAL!
Dodger Stages Theatre 5
First Preview: February 2, 2005
Opened February 10, 2005; Closed November 13, 2005
9 previews, 327 performances

THOM PAINE (BASED ON NOTHING)
DR2 Theatre
First Preview January 25, 2005
Opened February 1, 2005; Closed December 24, 2005

ORSON'S SHADOW
Barrow Street Theatre
First Preview March 1, 2005
Opened March 13, 2005; Closed December 31, 2005
349 performances

ORGASMS
SoHo Playhouse
First Preview April 8, 2005
Opened April 21, 2005; Closed January 1, 2006
220 performances

MENOPAUSE: THE MUSICAL
Playhouse 91
Opened April 4, 2002; Closed May 14, 2006
1,712 performances

Off-Broadway Company Series

ABINGDON THEATRE COMPANY

THIRTEENTH SEASON

Jan Buttram and Pamela Paul; Co-Artistic Directors; Samuel Bellinger, Managing Director

Associate Artistic Director/Literary Manager, Kim T. Sharp; Director of Marketing, Jessica M. Sher; Director of Development, Edward J. McKeaney; Development Associate, Lori Gardner; Business & Box Office Manager, Rob Weinstein; Theatre Rental Manager/Facilities Manager, Bill Ellis/Stephen Squibb; Production Manager, Gabriel Evansohn; Casting, William Schill; Resident Dramaturg, Julie Hegner; Press, Shirley Herz, Dan Demello

WAR IN PARAMUS by Barbara Dana; Director, Austin Pendleton; Scenery, Michael Schweikardt; Costumes, Wade Laboissonniere; Lighting, David Castaneda; Sound, David Margolin Lawson; Fight Choreography, Rick Sordelet; Production Stage Manager, Mary E. Leach; Assistant Stage Manager, Eric Houston; Assistant to the Director, Kira Simring; **Cast:** Matthew Arkin (William Gardner, Jr.); Jeremy Beiler (Kevin Parnell), Kate Bushmann (Violet Gardner), Gene Gallerano (Harry Tonto), David Holmes (Philip Riser), Anne Letscher (Thelma Gardner), Lisa McCormick (Jennifer Gardner)

Setting: 1970. The Garndner home, Paramus, NJ. World premiere of a new play presented in two acts; June Havoc Theatre; October 7 – November 6, 2005 (Opening Night October 11, 2005); 32 performances.

Matthew Arkin and Anne Letscher in *War In Paramus* PHOTOS BY KIM T. SHARP

DECEMBER FOOLS by Sherman Yellen; Director, Donald Brenner; Music by Wally Harper; Scenery, James F. Wolk; Costumes, Susan Scherer; Lighting, Matthew McCarthy; Arrangements, William Cox; Production Stage Manager, Mary E. Leach; Assistant Stage Manager, Julie Griffith; **Cast:** Eric Michael Gillett (Mr. Parker-Benton/Dr. Asher/Maurice/Dr. Lewitt), Celia Howard (Mrs. Hogan), Mikel Sarah Lambert (Mildred), Carole Monferdini (Vivian), Arleigh Richards (Marcie Temple Sklar), Elizabeth Shepherd (Gloria Temple)

Setting: New York City, the early 1980s. Gloria Temples Fifth Avenue apartment in the Sherry Netherland. World premiere of a new play presented in two acts; June Havoc Theatre; January 27 – February 26, 2006 (Opening Night February 1, 2006); 32 performances.

ELVIS AND JULIET by Mary Willard; Director Yvonne Conybeare; Scenery, Ray Recht; Costumes, Ingrid Maurer; Lighting, David Castaneda; Sound, Ken Hypes; Production Stage Manager, Eric Selk; Assistant Stage Managers, Greg LoProto, Amy L. Smith; Dramaturg, Rob Kendt; **Cast:** Bridget Clark (Clancy Austen Jones), Lori Gardner (Juliet Bronte Jones), Warren Kelley (Owen Heathcliff Jones), Haskell King (Elvis Aaron Lesley), Christy McIntosh (Lisa Marie Lesley), Carole Monferdini (Nancy Clancy Jones), Pamela Paul (Becky Godfrey Lesley), David Rasche (Joey Francis Lesley), Justin Schultz (Roberto Clemente Jones), Fred Willard (Arthur Julius Lesley)

Setting: May 1989. A Yale University dorm room, the Lesleys' house in Las Vegas, Nevada, and the Jones's house in New Haven Connecticut. World premiere of a new play presented in two acts; June Havoc Theatre; June 2 – July 2, 2006 (Opening Night June 7, 2006); 32 performances.

David Rasche and Christy McIntosh in *Elvis and Juliet*

ATLANTIC THEATER COMPANY

TWENTIETH SEASON

Neil Pepe, Artistic Director; Andrew D. Hamingson, Executive Director

School Executive Director, Mary McCann; General Manager, Melinda Berk; Associate Artistic Director, Christian Parker; Development Director, Erika Mallin; Production Manager, Lester Grant; Marketing Director, Jodi Sheeler; Membership Coordinator, Sara Montgomery; Company Manager, Christopher Richardson; School Director, Steven Hawley; School Administrative Director, Kate Blumberg; Business Manager, Diana Ascher; Education Director, Frances Tarr; School Production Director, Freda Farrell; School Production Manager, Eric Southern; Casting, Bernard Telsey; Press Representative, Boneau/Bryan-Brown, Joe Perotta

THE CHERRY ORCHARD by Anton Chekov, adapted by Tom Donaghy; Director, Scott Zigler; Choreography, Ted Morin; Scenery, Orit Jacoby Carrol, Scott Pask; Costumes, Theresa Squire; Lighting, Howard Werner; Sound and Original Music, Fitz Patton; Hair and Wigs; Robert-Charles Vallance; Magic Effects, Peter Maloney; Production Stage Manager, Jennifer Grutza; Assistant Stage Manager; Elizabeth Kegley; Production Manager, Kurt Gardner; Dramaturg, Christian Parker; **Cast:** Brooke Adams (Lyubov Andreyevna Ranevskaya), Pepper Binkley (Dunyasha), Laura Breckenridge (Anya), Larry Bryggman (Leonid Andreyevich Gayev), Dan Domingues (Footman/Homeless Man/Station Master), Alvin Epstein (Firs), Scott Foley (Pyotr Sergeyevich Trofimov), Erin Gann (Yasha), Peter Maloney (Boris Borisovich Semyonov-Pishchik) , Mary McCann (Charlotta Ivanova), Charlie Rose (Charlotta's Dog), Diana Ruppe (Varya), Todd Weeks (Semyon Panteleyevich Yepikhodov), Isiah Whitlock, Jr. (Yermolai Alekaseyevich Lopakhin)

Revival of a play presented in two acts; Atlantic Mainstage; May 25–July 3, 2005 (Opening night:, June 15, 2005); 41 performances. (This production was the final show of the 19th Season).

Remy Auberjonois in *The Intelligent Design of Jenny Chow* PHOTO BY CAROL ROSEGG

THE INTELLIGENT DESIGN OF JENNY CHOW by Rolin Jones; Director, Jackson Gay; Scenery, Takeshi Kata; Costumes, Jenny Mannis; Lighting, Tyler Micoleau; Sound, Daniel Baker; Composer, Matthew Suttor; Dramaturg, Christian Parker; Production Stage Manager, Robyn Henry; Assistant Stage Manager, Nicole Bouclier; **Cast:** Julienne Hanzelka Kim (Jennifer Marcus), Michael Cullen (Mr. Marcus/Mr. Zhang), Remy Auberjonois (Preston/Terrence/Dr. Yakunin/Col. Hubbard), Linda Gehringer (Adele Hartwick/Su Yang), Ryan King (Todd/Boy), Eunice Wong (Jenny Chow)

Understudies: Marcia Saunders

Setting: A second-story bedroom, Calabasas, CA. Now. Right now. A play presented in two acts; Atlantic Mainstage; August 31–October 16, 2005 (Opening Night September 19, 2005); 48 performances.

CELEBRATION AND THE ROOM by Harold Pinter; Director, Neil Pepe; Scenery, Walt Spangler; Costumes, Ilona Somogyi; Lighting, David Weiner; Sound Obadiah Eaves; Fight Director, Rick Sordelet; Production Stage Manager, Darcy Stephens; Assistant Stage Manager, Lauren Stoler; Company Manager, Nick Leavens; Wigs, Chuck LaPointe; Dialect Coach, Stephen Gabis; **Cast:** *The Room:* Thomas Jay Ryan (Bert Hudd), Mary Beth Peil (Rose), Peter Maloney (Mr. Kidd), Kate Blumberg (Mrs. Sands), David Pittu (Mr. Sands), Earle Hyman (Riley); *Celebration:* David Pittu (Waiter), Patrick Breen (Lambert), Betsy Aidem (Julie), Thomas Jay Ryan (Matt), Carolyn McCormick (Prue), Brennan Brown (Russell), Kate Blumberg (Suki), Philip Goodwin (Richard), Christa Scott-Reed (Sonia)

Laura Breckenridge and Scott Foley in *The Cherry Orchard* PHOTO BY CAROL ROSEGG

Two one act plays presented with intermission; Atlantic Mainstage; November 16 2005–Januray 21, 2006 (Opening Night December 5, 2005); 71 performances.

THE LIEUTENANT OF INISHMORE by Martin McDonagh; Director, Wilson Milam; Scenery, Scott Pask; Costumes, Theresa Squire; Lighting, Michael Chybowski; Sound, Obadiah Eaves; Music, Matt McKenzie; Arrangements, Andrew Rankin; Casting, Pat McCorkle; Fight Director, J. David Brimmer; Production Stage Manager, James Harker; Assistant Stage Manager, Freda Farrell; Company Manager, Nick Leavens; Special Effects, Anthony Giordano; Wigs, Charles LaPointe; **Cast:** Domhnall Gleeson (Davey), Peter Gerety (Donny), David Wilmot (Padraic), Jeff Binder (James), Kerry Condon (Mairead), Andrew Connolly (Christy), Dashiell Eaves (Joey), Brian d'Arcy James (Brendan); Replacements (4/4/06): Alison Pill (Mairead)

Setting: 1993, Island of Inishmore, County Galway, Ireland. A play presented in two acts; February 5–April 9, 2006 (Opening Night February 27, 2006); 71 performances. This production transferred to the Lyceum Theatre April 19, 2006 (see Broadway Plays that Opened in this volume).

(Seated) Carolyn McCormick, Thomas Jay Ryan, Betsy Aidem; standing: Patrick Breen, Kate Blumberg, Brennan Brown in *Celebration* PHOTO BY MONIQUE CARBONI

David Wilmot and Kerry Condon in *The Lieutenant of Inishmore* PHOTO BY MONIQUE CARBONI

SPRING AWAKENING based on the play by Frank Wedekind, book and lyrics by Steven Sater, music by Duncan Sheik; Director, Michael Mayer; Choreography, Bill T. Jones; Music Director, Kim Grigsby; Scenery, Christine Jones; Costumes, Susan Hilferty; Lighting, Kevin Adams; Sound, Brian Ronan; Vocal Arrangements, AnnMarie Milazzo; Additional Arrangements, Simon Hale; Casting, Jim Carnahan, Carrie Gardner; Fight Director, J. David Brimmer; Production Stage Manager, Allison Sommers; Assistant Stage Manager, Bethany Russell; Company Manager, Nick Leavens; **Cast:** Lea Michele (Wendla), Mary McCann (The Adult Women), Lilli Cooper (Martha), Lauren Pritchard (Ilse), Phoebe Strole (Anna), Remy Zaken (Thea), Frank Wood (The Adult Men), Brian Johnson (Otto/Student), Jonathan B. Wright (Hanschen/Student), Gideon Glick (Ernst/Student), Skylar Astin (Georg/Student), John Gallagher Jr. (Moritz), Jonathan Groff (Melchior); Band: Thad de Brock (guitar), George Farmer (bass), Trey Files (drums), Ben Kalb (cello)

Musical Numbers: Mama Who Bore Me, Mama Who Bore Me (reprise), All That's Known, The Bitch of Living, My Junk, Touch Me, The Word of Your Body, The Dark I Know Well, And Then There Were None, The Mirror-Blue Night, I Believe, There Once Was a Pirate, Don't Do Sadness, Blue Wind, Left Behind, Totally Fucked, Word of Your Body (reprise), Whispering, Mama Who Bore Me/Touch Me (reprise), Those You've Known/The Northern Wind, The Song of Purple Summer

Setting: 1890s, a provincial German town. A musical presented in two acts; Atlantic Mainstage; May 19–August 5, 2006 (Opening Night June 15, 2006); 79 performances. This production was slated to transfer to Broadway fall, 2006.

Jonathan Groff, Mary McCann, John Gallagher, Jr., Frank Wood in *Spring Awakening* PHOTO BY MONIQUE CARBONI

BROOKLYN ACADEMY OF MUSIC

FOUNDED IN 1861

Alan H. Fishman, Chairman of the Board; Karen Brooks Hopkins, President; Joseph V. Melillo, Executive Producer

HECUBA by Euripides; adaptation and direction by Tony Harrison; Presented by the Royal Shakespeare Company; Scenery and Costumes, Es Devlin; Lighting, Adam Silverman; Composer, Mick Sands; Sound, Fergus O'Hare; Movement, Gary Sefton; Choreography, Heather Habens; Music Director, Bruce O'Neill; Production Stage Manager, Laura Deards; **Cast:** Vanessa Redgrave (Hecuba), Alan Dobie (Talthybius), Darrell D'Silva (Odysseus/Polymestor), Lydia Leonard (Polyxena), Matthew Douglas (Polydorus), Christopher Terry (Guard), Malcolm Tierney (Agamemnon); Charlotte Allam, Jane Arden, Rosalie Craig, Maisie Dimbleby, Barbara Gellhorn, Aileen Gonsalves, Michele Moran, Sasha Oakley, Katherine O'Shea, Judith Paris, Natalie Turner-Jones, Sarah Quist (Chorus)

Revival of a play presented without intermission; Howard Gilman Opera House; June 17–26, 2005; 11 performances

2005 NEXT WAVE FESTIVAL

TALL HORSE by Khephra Burns; Presented by Handspring & Sogolon Puppet Companies; Director, Marthinus Basson; Puppet Design, Yaya Coulibaly and Adrian Kohler; Scenery and Costumes, Adrian Kohler; Lighting, Wesley France; Music, Warrick Sony; Choreography, Koffi Kôkô; Video Animation, Jaco Bouwer; a play with puppetry presented in two acts; Harvey Theater; October 4–9, 2005; 6 performances

EMILIA GALOTTI by Gotthold Ephraim Lessing; Presented by Deutsches Theatre Berlin; Director, Michael Thalheimer; Scenery and Costumes, Olaf Altmann; Music, Bert Wrede; **Cast:** Sven Lehmann , Regine Zimmermann; a play presented in two acts; Harvey Theatre; Oct 12–15, 2005; 4 performances

4.48 PSYCHOSE by Sarah Kane, translated by Evelyne Pieiller; Director, Claude Régy; Scenery, Daniel Jeanneteau; Lighting, Dominique Bruguière; Costumes, Ann Williams; Sound, Philippe Cachia; **Cast:** Isabelle Huppert, Gérard Watkins; a play presented without intermission; Harvey Theatre; October 19–30, 2005; 11 performances

THE WINTER'S TALE by William Shakespeare; Presented by the Watermill Theatre (UK); Director, Edward Hall; Designer, Michael Pavelka; Lighting, Ben Ormerod; Music, Tony Bell, Richard Clothier, Dugald Bruce Lockhart and Jules Werner; **Cast:** Bob Barrett, Jason Baughan, Jamie Beamish, William Buckhurst, Alistair Craig, Matthew Flynn, Vincent Leigh, Adam Levy, Chris Myles, Simon Scardifield, James Tucker, Tam Williams; revival of a play presented in two acts; Harvey Theatre; November 2–6, 2005; 6 performances

BRIGHT ABYSS Written and directed by James Thiérrée; Produced by La Compagnie du Hanneton; Costumes, Victoria Thiérrée and Cidalia Da Costa; Lighting, Jérôme Sabre; Sound, Thomas Delot; **Cast:** James Thiérrée, Una Ysamat (Singer/Actress), Raphaëlle Boitel (Contortionist), Niklas Ek (Dancer/Actor), Thiago Martins (Acrobat/Dancer); a theatrical piece with acrobats, dance, mime, and music; Harvey Theatre, November 9–13, 2005; 5 performances

SUPER VISION Conceived and created by The Builders Association and dbox; Conception by James Gibbs, Marianne Weems, Matthew Bannister, Charles d'Autrement, Dan Dobson, Jeff Webster; Text by Constance deJong; Executive Producer, Kim Whitener; Director, Marianne Weems; Scenery and Costumes, Stewart Laing; Lighting, Jennifer Tipton; Virtual Design, dbox; Video design, Peter Flaherty; Sound and Original Music, Dan Dobson; Production Manager, Neal Wilkinson; Technical Director, Joseph Silovsky; Stage Manager, Ela Orleans; Managing Director, Lexi Robertson; Company and Marketing Manager, Claire Hallereau; **Cast:** Moe Angelos (Grandmother), Kyle decamp (Carol), Rizwan Mirza (Traveller), David Pence/Harry Sinclair (John Sr.), Tnaya Selvaratnam (Jen/The Voice of Claritas), Joseph Silovsky (Border Agent); a multi media theatrical piece presented without intermission; November 29–December 3, 2005; 5 performances

HEDDA GABLER by Henrik Ibsen, adapted by Andrew Upton; Presented by the Sydney Theatre Company; Director, Robyn Nevin; Scenery, Fiona Crombie; Costumes, Kristian Fredrikson; Lighting, Nick Schlieper; Music, Alan John; Sound, Paul Charlier; Production Stage Manager, Mary Macrae; **Cast:** Cate Blanchett (Hedda Gabler), Hugo Weaving (Judge Brack), Annie Byron (Berte), Justine Clark (Thea Elvsted), Julie Hamilton (Julie Tesman), Anthony Weigh (Jorgen Tesman), Aden Young (Ejlert Lovborg)

Revival of a play with music presented in two acts; Harvey Theatre; February 28–March 26, 2006; 28 performances.

Vanessa Redgrave and chorus in *Hecuba* PHOTO BY MANUEL HARLAN

Sven Lehmann and Regine Zimmermann in *Emilia Galotti* PHOTO BY RICHARD TERMINE

(Left to Right) Rizwan Mirza, Joseph Silovsky in *Super Vision* PHOTO BY STEPHANIE BERGER

PEER GYNT by Henrik Ibsen, adapted, directed, scenery and lighting by Robert Wilson; music by Michael Galass; Co Production of The National Theatre of Bergen, Norway and the Norwegian Theatre, Oslo; Co-director, Ann-Christin Rommen; Dramaturg, Monica Ohlsson; Production Stage Manager, Per Berg Nilsen; **Cast:** Henrik Rafaelsen (Peer as a young man), Endre Hellestveit (Peer as a grown man), Sverre Bentzen (Peer as an old man), Wenche Medboe (Ase), Kjersti Sandal (Solveig), Gjertrud Jynge (Anitra)

Revival of a play presented in two acts; Howard Gillman Opera House; April 11–16, 2006; 5 performances.

THE IMPORTANCE OF BEING EARNEST by Oscar Wilde; Presented by the Theatre Royal Bath/Peter Hall Company; (Danny Moar, Producer); Director, Sir Peter Hall; Production Design, Kevin and Trish Rigdon; Sound, Rob Milburn and Michael Bodeen; Associate Director/Producer, Trish Rigdon; Casting, Deborah Brown; Production Stage Manager, John McNamara; Company Manager/Assistant Stage Manager, Brian J. L'Ecuyer; **Cast:** James A. Stephens (Lane), Robert Petkoff (Algernon Moncrieff), James Waterston (Jack Worthing), Lynn Redgrave (Lady Bracknell), Bianca Amato (Gwendolyn Fairfax), Miriam Margolyes (Miss Prism), Charlotte Parry (Cecily Cardew), Terence Rigby (Reverend Canon Chasuble), Geddeth Smith (Merriman), Greg Felden (Footman); **Understudies:** Margaret Daly, Greg Felden, Diane Landers, Geddeth Smith

Revival of a play in three acts presented with one intermission; Harvey Theatre; April 18–May 14, 2006; 28 performances.

CITY CENTER ENCORES!

THIRTEENTH SEASON

Arlene Shuler, President and CEO, City Center; Mark Litvin, Senior Vice President and Managing Director, City Center; Jack Viertel, Artistic Director; Paul Gemignani, Music Director

Scenic Consultant, John Lee Beatty; Sound, Dan Moses Schreier; Concert Adaptation, David Ives; Music Coordinator, Seymour Red Press; Company Manager, Michael Zande; Casting; Jay Binder and Jack Bowdan; Press, Helene Davis; Encores Artistic Associates: John Lee Beatty, Jay Binder, Walter Bobbie, David Ives, Kathleen Marshall; Conductor, Paul Gemignani; Associate Conductor/piano-Annbritt duChateau;

KISMET Book by Charles Lederer and Luther Davis (founded on a play by Edward Knoblock), music and lyrics by Robert Wright and George Forrest (from themes by Borodin); Director, Lonny Price; Choreography, Sergio Trujillo; Costume Consultant, Tracy Christensen; Lighting, Kevin Adams; Production Stage Manager, Tripp Phillips; Original Orchestrations, Arthur Kay; Production Consultant, Elias EL-Hage; **Cast:** Tom Aldredge (Jawan, the Master Brigand), Dennis Blackwell (Pearl Merchant), Jane Brockman (Widow Yussef/Ayah), Liza Bugarin (Princess of Ababu), Michelle Camaya (Princess of Ababu), Scott Dispensa (Muezzin/Brigand/Orange Merchant), Tony Falcon (Muezzin/Fig Seller/Slave Merchant), Danny Gurwin (The Caliph), Venus Hall (Slave Girl/Princess Samahris of Turkestan), Marcy Harriell (Marsinah), Randall Duk Kim (Omar Khayyam), Jay Lusteck (Policeman), Sumie Maeda (Princess of Ababu), Michael X. Martin (Chief Policeman), Frank Mastrone (Inam of the Mosque), Marin Mazzie (Lalume, Wife of Wives to the Wazir), Justin Lee Miller (Hassan-Ben, a Brigand), Brian Stokes Mitchell (A Public Poet, sometime called Hajj), Marcus Nance (Brigand), Elizabeth Parkinson (Nedeb, a genie/Princess Zubbediya of Zanzibar), Rachelle Rak (Slave Girl), Roland Rusinek (Silk Merchant/Policeman), Danny Rutigliano (The Wazir of Police), Tim Salamandyk (First Beggar), Jennifer Savelli (Slave Girl) ,Scott Watanabe (Muezzin/Silk Merchant); **Ensemble:** Christine Arand, Michael Balderrama, Dennis Blackwell, Jane Brockman, Liza Bugarin, Michelle Camaya, Marcus Choi, Christine Clemmons-McCune, Scott Dispensa, Tony Falcon, Venus Hall, Keith Kuhl, Jay Lusteck, Sumie Maeda, Frank Mastrone, André McRae, Justin Lee Miller, Marcus Nance, Nina Negri, Elizabeth Parkinson, Robyn Payne, Rachelle Rak, Joe Aaron Reid, Roland Rusinek, Tim Salamandyk, Jennifer Savelli, Larry Beale Small, Laura Yen Solito, Scott Watanabe

Musical Numbers: Sands Of Time, Rhymes Have I, Fate, Fate (reprise), Bazaar of The Caravans, Ababu Dance, Not Since Nineveh, Baubles, Bangles And Beads, Stranger In Paradise, He's In Love!, Gesticulate, Bored, Finale Act One, Night Of My Nights, Stranger in Paradise (reprise), Baubles, Bangles and Beads (reprise), Night of My Nights (reprise), Was I Wazir, The Olive Tree, Rahadlakum, And This Is My Beloved, Finale Act Two

Setting: One day in Baghdad, capital of the Abbasid Caliphate, 1071 A.D. Concert version of the musical presented in two acts; City Center; February 9–12, 2006; 5 performances. The original production of *Kismet* opened in New York at the Ziegfeld Theatre on December 3, 1953 and played for 583 performances (See *Theatre World* Volume 10).

70 GIRLS, 70 Book by Fred Ebb and Norman L. Martin, music by John Kander, lyrics by Fred Ebb; based on the play *Breath of Spring* by Peter Coke, adaptation by Joe Masteroff; Director and Choreography, Kathleen Marshall; Costume

Consultant; William Ivey Long; Lighting, Peter Kaczorowski; Sound, Brian Ronan; Production Stage Manager, Tripp Phillips; Original Orchestions, Don Walker; Associate Director, Marc Bruni; Associate Choreography, Carol Lee Meadows; **Cast:** Lalan Parrott (Lorraine), Tina Fabrique (Melba Jones), Mary Jo Catlett (Fritzi Clews), George S. Irving (Harry Hardwick), Carole Cook (Gert Appleby), Bob Dishy (Walter Hatfield), Anita Gillette (Eunice Miller), Olympia Dukakis (Ida Dodd), Mark Price (Eddie), Charlotte Rae (Sadie), Susan Lehman (Mrs. McIlhenny), Carleton Carpenter (Mr. McIlhenny), Ronn Carroll (Pete), Ira Hawkins (Moe/Minister), Robert Fitch (Charlie/Officer Kowalski), Gerry Vichi (Jack/Detective Callahan), Patti Karr (Old Lady), Harvey Evans (Guard), Merwin Goldsmith (Policeman One), Bob Freschi (Policeman Two); Residents of the Sussex Arms Hotel: Mary Jane Ashley, Carleton Carpenter, Ronn Carroll, Harvey Evans, Diane J. Findlay, Robert Fitch, Bob Freschi, Merwin Goldsmith, Ira Hawkins, Patti Karr, Susan Lehman, Joan Marshall, Gerry Vichi

Musical Numbers: Old Folks, Home, Broadway My Street, The Caper, Coffee in a Cardboard Cup, You and I, Hit It Lorraine; Do We? The Caper (reprise), See the Light, Entr'acte, Boom Ditty Boom, Believe, Go Visit Your Grandmother, The Elephant Song, Boom Ditty Boom (reprise), 70, Girls, 70, Yes

Setting: New York City. The Cornucopia Tea Room; the Broadhurst Theatre; Ida's room; Sadie's fur salon; lobby of Sussex Arms; Arctic Cold Storage Co.; the Coliseum; a chapel. Concert version of the musical presented in two acts; City Center; March 30 – April 2, 2006; 5 performances. The original production of 70, Girls, 70 opened in New York at the Broadhurst Theatre on April 15, 1971 and played for 35 performances (See Theatre World Volume 27, page 45).

Marin Mazzie and Brian Stokes Mitchell in Kismet

Victor Garber and Jennifer Laura Thompson in Of Thee I Sing PHOTOS BY JOAN MARCUS

OF THEE I SING Music and lyrics by Ira Gershwin, book by George S. Kaufman and Morrie Ryskind; Director, John Rando; Choreography, Randy Skinner; Lighting, Paul Miller; Costume Consultant, Toni-Leslie James; Production Stage Manager, Tripp Phillips; Original Orcehstrations, Robert Russell Bennett, William Daly, George Gershwin; Stage Manager, Patty Lyons; Associate Choreogoraphy, Kelli Barclay; General Management Associate, Stephenie Overton; Music Associate, Joshua Clayton; **Cast:** Lewis J Stadlen (Louis Lippman), Wayne Duvall (Francis X. Gilhooley), Michael Mulheren (Matthew Arnold Fulton), Jonathan Freeman (Senator Robert E. Lyons), Erick Devine (Senator Carver Jones), Jefferson Mays (Alexander Throttlebottom), Victor Garber (John P. Wintergreen), Jacqueline Thompson (Chambermaid), Jeffry Denman (Sam Jenkins), Jenny Powers (Diana Devereaux), Jennifer Laura Thompson (Mary Turner), Raymond Jaramillo McLeod (Vladimir Vidovitch), Todd A. Horman (Yussef Yussevitch/Senate Clerk), Mara Davi (Miss Benson), Bob Sheppard (Eric Michael Gillett (The Chief Justice), Patty Goble (White House Guide), David Pittu (The French Ambassador), Jay Lusteck (Stagehand), Fred Inckley (The Senator from Massachusetts), Todd Latimore (Chief Flunky); **Ensemble:** David Baum, Sara Edwards, Eric Michael Gillett, Patty Goble, Blythe Gruda, Holly Holcomb, Todd A. Horman, Drew Humphrey, Fred Inkley, Cara Kjellman, Ian Knauer, Todd Lattimore, Mark Ledbetter, Jay Lusteck, Raymond Jaramillo McLeod, Marcus Nance, Nina Negri, Shannon Marie O'Bryan, Greg Stone, Kelly Sullivan, Jacqueline Thompson, Anna A. White

Musical Numbers: Wintergreen for President, Who Is the Lucky Girl to Be?, The Dimple on My Knee, Because Because, Who Is the Lucky Girl to Be? (reprise), As the Chairman of the Committee, How Beautiful, Never Was There a Girl So Fair, Some Girls Can Bake a Pie, Love Is Sweeping the Country, Of Thee I Sing, Wintergreen for President (reprise), Entrance of the Supreme Court Judges, A Kiss for Cinderella, I Was the Most Beautiful Blossom, Some Girls Can Bake a Pie (reprise), Of Thee I Sing (reprise), Hello Good Morning, Who Cares?, Garcon S'il Vous Plait, Entrance of the French Ambassador, The Illegitimate Daughter, Because Because (reprise), We'll Impeach Him, Who Cares (reprise), Senatorial Roll Call, The Impeachment Proceeding, Garcon, S'il Vous Plait (reprise), The Illegitimate Daughter (reprise), Jilted, Senatorial Roll Call, I'm About to Be a Mother, I Was the Most Beautiful Blossom (reprise), Posterity Is Just Around the Corner, Trumpeter Blow Your Golden Horn, Finale Ultimo: On That Matter No One Budges/Of Thee I Sing (reprise)

Concert version of the musical presented in two acts; City Center; May 11 – 15, 2006; 6 performances. The original production of Of Thee I Sing opened in New York at the Music Box Theatre on December 26, 1931 and played for 441 performances.

CLASSIC STAGE COMPANY

THIRTY-EIGHTH SEASON

Brian Kulick, Artistic Director, Jessica R. Jenen, Executive Director

General Manager, Lisa Barnes; Director of Development, Megan Condit; Artistic Associates, Jeff Janisheski and Daisy Walker; Casting, James Calleri; Press, The Publicity Office: Michael Borowski, Marc Thibodeau, Candi Adams

HAMLET by William Shakespeare; Director, Brian Kulick; Scenery, Mark Wendland Costumes, Oana Botez-Ban; Lighting, Brian Scott; Sound, Jorge Muelle; **Cast:** Michael Cumpsty (Hamlet), Jon DeVries (Ghost, Player King), Robert Dorfman (Claudius), Herb Foster (Polonius), Karl Kenzler (Bernardo/Laertes/Guildenstern), Caroline Lagerfelt (Gertrude), Jason Ma (Marcellus/Rosencrantz), Kellie Overbey (Ophelia) and Graham Winton (Horatio)

Revival of the play presented in two acts: CSC East 13th Street Theatre; November 3–December 11, 2005 (Opening night: November 13, 2005); 40 performances

CLASSICKIDS: TELL ME MORE STORIES told by Pennylyn White "Wizards, Witches and Spells" November 5–6, 2005; "Magic, Mystery and Mayhem" November 12–13, 2005; Secrets and Sorcery November 19–20, 2005

FIRST LOOK FESTIVAL

One night only staged reading and workshop productions of rarely seen classics

THE SPANISH TRAGEDY by Thomas Kyd; **Cast:** Mia Barron, Vivienne Benesch, Bill Camp, Paul Lazar, Melissa Miller , Tom Nelis, Michael Potts, Matt Saldivar, Mauricio Tafur Salgado, Adam Stein, David L. Townsend; November 21, 2005

ANTONIO'S REVENGE by John Marston; **Cast:** David Chandler, Lynn Cohen, Robert Dorfman, Jessica Hecht, Marin Ireland, Trey Lyford, Jesse Pennington, Steven Rattazzi, Michael Stuhlbarg, Sam Tsoutsouvas; November 28, 2005

THE ROMAN ACTOR by Phillip Messinger; **Cast:** Mark Blum, Sanjit De Silva, Jennifer Ikeda, Jacob Ming-Trent, Armin Parsanejad, Michael Potts, Steven Rattazzi, Matt Saldivar, Ruben Santiago-Hudson, Shrimani Senay, Jeremy Shamos, Myra Lucretia Taylor, Reginald Veneziano, Janet Zarish; December 5, 2005

Will Badgett and David Greenspan in *Faust Parts I and II* PHOTO BY JILL JONES

Tony Torn, Juliana Francis, Zachary Oberzan in *Fragment* PHOTO BY JOAN MARCUS

FRAGMENT Drawn from the lost plays of Sophocles and Euripides , text assembled by Kelly Copper; Director, Pavol Liska; **Cast:** Zachary Oberzan, Tony Torn, Juliana Francis

A new play presented without intermission; CSC East 13th Street Theatre; March 22–April 9, 2006; 20 performances

COLUMBIA STAGES PRODUCTION OF THE YOUNG COMPANY

Columbia MFA Acting students in three productions by Molière: *Scapin* Director, Niky Wolcz; *The Misanthrope* Director Michael Sexton; *Tartuffe* Director, Brian Kulick; January 3–15, 2006

FAUST, PARTS I AND II Target Margin Theater's production of the plays by Johann Wolfgang von Goethe, translated by Douglas Langworthy; Director, David Herskovits; Original Music, Katie Down, Additional Music, John King; Set Design, Carol Bailey; Costumes, Kaye Voyce; Lighting, Lenore Doxsee; Sound, John Collins, Production Manager, Monica Moore; Production Stage Manager, Brenna St. George Jones; Assistant Stage Manager, D.J. Potter; Production Coordinator, Joe Novak; Technical Director, Ian Grunes; **Cast:** Will Badgett (Faust/Ensemble), Aysan Celik (Martha/Galatea/Ensemble), Daphne Gaines (Producer/Helena/Ensemble), David Greenspan (Mephistopheles), George Hannah (Scholar/Nereus/Ensemble), Lian-Marie Holmes (Liesl/Homunculus/Ensemble), Ty Jones (Young Faust/Ensemble), E.C. Kelly (Witch/Thales/Ensemble), Wayne Alon Scott (Wagner/Valentine/Ensemble), Eunice Wong (Gretchen/Ensemble)

Revival of the play presented in two parts running in repertory, each part presented in two acts; CSC East 13th Street Theatre; April 21–May 20, 2006 (Opening night: April 30, 2006); Part I: 19 performances; Part II: 16 performances

MONDAY NIGHT LEAR

Open rehearsals of Shakespeare's magisterial play; April 17, 2006: F. Murray Abraham as Lear, Director, Brian Kulick; May 1, 2006: Ron Leibman as Lear, Director, Brian Kulick; May 8, 2006: Richard Easton as Lear, Director, Michael Sexton; May 15, 2006: Kristin Linklater as Lear, Director, Diane Paulus

IRISH REPERTORY THEATRE

EIGHTEENTH SEASON

Ciarán O'Reilly, Producing Director; Charlotte Moore, Artistic Director

Managing Director, Patrick A. Kelsey; Director of Development, Molly Murray; Membership Manager, Eric Scott; Literary Manager, Philip Levie; Dialect Coach, Stephen Gabis; Box Office Manager, Jeffrey Wingfield; Casting, Laura Maxwell-Scott; Press, Shirley Herz Associates, Dan Demello

PHILADELPHIA, HERE I COME! By Brian Friel; Scenery, David Raphael; Costumes, David Toser; Lighting, Brian Nason; Sound, Murmod, Inc.; Hair and Wigs; Robert-Charles Vallance; Production Stage Manager, John Handy; Stage Manager, Bethany Russell; **Cast:** Joe Berlangero (Tom), Helena Carroll (Lizzy Sweeney), Darren Connolly (Joe), Paddy Croft (Madge), Michael Fitzgerald (Gareth O'Donnell in public), James Kennedy (Gareth O'Donnell in private), Tessa Klein (Kate Doogan), John Leighton (Con Sweeney), Leo Leyden (Canon Mick O'Byrne), Edwin C. Owens (S.B. O'Donnell), Gil Rogers (Senator Doogan), Tim Ruddy (Ned), Geddeth Smith (Ben Burton), James A. Stephens (Master Boyle)

Setting: 1964. The small village of Ballybeg in County Donegal, Ireland. Revival of a play presented in two acts; Irish Repertory Theatre Mainstage; July 14–September 25, 2005 (Opening night July 21, 2005); 77 performances. (This production was the final production of the seventeenth season).

BEOWULF Adaptation and lyrics by Lindsey Turner, music and lyrics by Lenny Pickett; Director, Charlotte Moore; Music Director, Mark Janus; Scenery, Akira Yoshimura; Costumes, Randall Klein; Lighting, Brian Nason; Sound, Zachary Williamson; Puppets and Masks, Bob Flanagan; Production Stage Manager, Pamela Brusoski; Stage Manager, Rebecca Goldstein-Glaze; **Cast:** Richard Barth (Beowulf), Edwin Cahill (Wiglaf), David Garry (Hrothgar), Bill Gross (Grendel's Mother/King), John Halbach (Hrethric), Jay Lusteck (Grendel/King), Shaun R. Parry (Unferth); **Musicians:** Mark Janas (Conductor/harmonium), Erin Hill (Harp)

Setting: Early Sixth Century A.D. Denmark and Geatland. World premiere of a rock opera of the epic poem presented without intermission; Irish Repertory Theatre Mainstage; October 7–November 27, 2005 (Opening night October 16, 2005); 53 performances.

Malachy Cleary and Paddy Croft in *The Field* PHOTOS BY CAROL ROSEGG

Dana Ivey in *Mrs. Warren's Profession*

THE BELLS OF CHRISTMAS Arranged and Directed by Ciarán O'Reilly; Scenery, Jean Moore; Lighting, Paul Jones; Music Director, Mary Feinsinger; **Cast:** Clo Bowyer, Keith Merrill, Jay Lusteck, Julie Price

An evening of music, poetry, story, and song presented without intermission; W Scott McLucas Theatre; December 9–31, 2005; 23 performances

MRS. WARREN'S PROFESSION by George Bernard Shaw; Director, Charlotte Moore; Scenery, Dan Kuchar; Costumes, David Toser; Lighting, Mary Jo Dondlinger, Sound, Murmod, Inc.; Hair and Wigs, Robert-Charles Vallance; Production Stage Manager, Elis C. Arroyo; Stage Manager, Rebecca Goldstein-Glaze; **Cast:** Kevin Collins (Frank Gardner), Kenneth Garner (Rev. Samuel Gardner), Dana Ivey (Mrs. Warren), Laura Odeh (Vivie), David Staller (Mr. Praed), Sam Tsoutsouvas (Sir George Crofts)

Setting: 1894. Haslemer in Surrey. Revival of a play presented in two acts; December 9, 2005–February 19, 2006 (Opening night December 18, 2005); 74 performances.

GEORGE M. COHAN TONIGHT! by Chip Deffaa; music and lyrics by George M. Cohan; Director/Musical Arrangements, Chip Deffaa; Additional Musical Arrangements, D.J. Bradley, Broc Hempel; Music Director/Additional Musical Arrangements, Sterling Price-McKinney; Choreography, Jon Peterson; Scenery, James Morgan; Costumes, David Toser; Lighting, Mary Jo Dondlinger; Production Stage Manager, Pamela Brusoski, Rachel S. McCutchen; **Cast:** Jon Peterson (George M. Cohan); **Musicians:** Sterling Price-McKinney (Conductor/piano), Vince Giordano (bass), Rob Garcia (drums); Cast recording: Sh-K-Boom/Ghostlight Records

Musical Numbers: Hello Broadway/Give My Regards To Broadway, The Man Who Owns Broadway, Night Time, Musical Moon, Ireland, My Land Of Dreams, I'm Saving Up To Buy A Home For My Mother, Josephine/Oh, You Wonderful Girl, The Hinkey Dee, Thank You, Harrigan, You Won't Do Any Business If You Haven't Got A Band, If I'm Going To Die I'm Going To Have Some Fun, My Father Told Me, Forty-Five Minutes From Broadway, Oh, You Beautiful Girl/I Want The World To Know, Goodbye Flo, I Want To Hear A Yankee Doodle Tune, The Fatal Curse Of Drink, The Yankee Doodle Boy, Mary, You're A Grand Old Flag, Over There, Sweet Popularity/I'm A Popular Man, Drink With Me/Did Ya Ever Have One Of Those Days?, I Love Everyone In The Wide, Wide World/I'm True To Them All, All-American Sweetheart, I Won't Be An Actor No More, Life's A Funny Proposition After All, All Aboard For Broadway/Give My Regards To Broadway

A solo performance musical presented in two acts; Irish Repertory Theatre Mainstage; March 3 – May 14, 2006 (Opening night March 9, 2006); 84 performances

THE FIELD by John B. Keane; Director, Ciarán O'Reilly; Scenery, Charlie Corcoran; Costumes, Martha Hally; Lighting, Jason Lyons, Sound, Zachary Williamson; Wigs and Hair, Robert-Charles Vallance; Casting, Laura Maxwell-Scott; Fight Director, Rick Sordelet; Production Stage Manager, Elis C. Arroyo; Stage Manager, Janice M. Brandine; **Cast:** Craig Baldwin (Father Murphy), Orlagh Cassidy (Maimie Flanagan), Malachy Cleary (Mick Flanagan), Paddy Croft (Maggie Butler), Karen Lynn Gorney (Mrs. Dandy McCabe), Ken Jennings ("The Bird" O'Donnell), Laurence Lowry (Sergeant Leahy), Marty Maguire ("The Bull" McCabe), Paul Nugent (Leamy Flanagan), John O'Creagh (Dandy McCabe), Tim Ruddy (Tadgh McCabe), Chandler Williams (William Dee)

Setting: 1965. Flanagan's Bar, Carriagthomond, Ireland. American premiere of a new play presented in two acts; Irish Repertory Theatre Mainstage; May 23 – August 6, 2006 (Opening night June 1, 2006); 77 performances.

Jon Peterson in *George M. Cohan Tonight!*

JEAN COCTEAU REPERTORY

THIRTY-FIFTH SEASON

Ernest Johns, Artistic Director; Ryan Teller, Managing Director

General Manager, Lynn Marie Macy; Marketing and Publicity Director, Rachel Macklin; Box Office Manager, Brooke Barlow; Technical Director, Evan Schlossberg; Production Associate, Chris Connolly; Artistic Associates, Judith Jarosz, Adam Shive, Dan Zisson; Education Diretor, Jay Nickerson

THE MAIDS by Jean Genet, Director, Ernest Johns; Sets, Roman Tatarowicz; Lighting, Richard Dunham; Costumes, Nicole Frachiseur; Fight Director, Dan Zisson; Production Stage Manager, Allison R. Smith; Assistant Stage Manager, Julie Dulude; Assistant Director, Rachel Macklin; **Cast:** Amanda Jones (Solange), Kate Holland (Claire), Natalie Ballesteros (Madame)

Extension of the play presented without intermission; Bouwerie Lane Theatre; July15 – July 30, 2005; 14 performances. This production was previously presented April 8 – June 5, 2005.

MOTHER COURAGE by Bertolt Brecht; Translated by Marc Blitzstein, with original music by Paul Dessau and additional arrangements by Jason Wynn; Director, David Fuller; Music Director/Accompanist, Jason Wynn; Scenery, Roman Tatarowicz; Costumes, Viviane Galloway; Lighting, Giles Hogya; Assistant Director/Dramaturg, Ryan Mark Weible; Production Stage Manager, Andrea Cibelli; **Cast:** Lorinda Lisitza (Mother Courage), Danaher Dempsey (Eilif/Regimental Clerk/Soldier), Timothy McDonough (Holey Cheese/Soldier/Peasant), Sara Jeanne Asselin (Kattrin), Angus Hepburn (The Chaplain/Peasant), Seth Duerr (The Cook), Lynn Marie Macy (Yvette/Peasant), Mickey Ryan (Storyteller), Taylor Wilcox (Storyteller)

A play presented in three acts; Bouwerie Lane Theatre; September 4 – October 8, 2005 (Opening night August 26, 2005).

MEDEA by Euripides, adapted by Joseph Goodrich; Director, Ernest Johns; Scenery and Lighting, David Kniep; Costumes, Nicole Frachiseur; **Cast:** Ramona Floyd (Medea), Pascal Beauboeuf (Jason), Angus Hepburn (Creon), Mickey Ryan (Aegeus), Lynn Marie Macy (Chorus), Elsie James (The Nanny), Taylor Wilcox (The Messenger)

A play presented in two acts; Bouwerie Lane Theatre; October – December 3, 2005 (Opening night October 30, 2005).

CANDIDA by George Bernard Shaw; Director, Michael Halberstam; Scenery, Sidney Bembridge; Costumes, Sean Sullivan; Lighting, Joel Moritz; Sound, Josh Schmidt; Production Stage Manger, Allen Hale; **Cast:** Amanda Jones (Candida), David Tillistrand (Rev. James Morell), Danaher Dempsey (Marchbanks), Seth Duerr (Lexy), Kate Holland (Miss Prossy), Angus Hepburn (Burgess)

A play presented in three acts; Bouwerie Lane Theatre; December -February 11, 2006 (Opening night December 28, 2005)

THE MISER by Moliere, adapted and updated by the Company; Director, Dan Zisson; Scenery, Roman Tatarowicz; Costumes, Timothy Alan Church; Lighting, Richard Dunham; Wigs, David Zimmerman; Production Stage Manager, **Cast:** Melanie Hopkins (Mariane), Lorinda Lisitza, Seth Duerr (Cléante), Taylor Wilcox (Elise), Angus Hepburn (Harpagon), Albert Aeed (Valère), Mickey Ryan (Maître Jacques)

A play presented in two acts; Bouwerie Lane Theatre; February – March 15, 2006 (Opening night February 23, 2006).

THE MAIDS X 2 by Jean Genet; An EgoPo/Cocteau Repertory Ensemble co-production; Director, Lane Savadove; Scenery, Nick Lopez and Lane Savadove; Costumes, Mattie Olson; Lighting, Lopez; Production Stage Manager, Ed Farrell; **Cast:** Part 1-Leah Loftin (Solange), Alejandra Cejudo (Claire), Taylor Wilcox (Madame), Part 2-Kevin V. Smith (Solange), J.J. Brennan (Claire), Nick Lopez (Madam)

A one act play presented twice with an intermission; Bouwerie Lane Theatre; March 21 – April 23, 2006 (Opening night March 31, 2006).

LINCOLN CENTER THEATER

TWENTY-FIRST SEASON

André Bishop, Artistic Director; Bernard Gersten, Executive Producer

General Manager, Adam Siegel; Production Manager, Jeff Hamlin; Director of Development, Hattie K. Jutagir; Director of Finance, David S. Brown; Director of Marketing, Linda Mason Ross; Director of Education, Kati Koerner; Musical Theatre Associate Producer, Ira Weitzman; Dramaturg and Director of the LCT Directors Lab, Anne Cattaneo; Casting, Daniel Swee; Press, Philip Rinaldi and Barbara Carroll

THIRD by Wendy Wasserstein; Director, Daniel Sullivan; Scenery, Thomas Lynch; Costumes, Jennifer von Mayrhauser; Sound, Scott Stauffer; Stage Manager, Roy Harris; Assistant Stage Manager, Denise Yaney; Company Manager, Matthew Markoff; **Cast:** Dianne Wiest (Laurie Jameson), Jason Ritter (Woodson Bull, III), Gaby Hoffmann (Emily Imbrie), Charles Durning (Jack Jameson), Amy Aquino (Nancy Gordon); **Understudies/Recorded voices:** William Cain (Jack), Josh Heine (Woodson), Stephanie Nava (Emily), Caitlin O'Connell (Laurie/Nancy)

Setting: A small New England college. Academic year 2002–2003. World premiere of a new play presented in two acts; Mitzi E. Newhouse Theatre; September 29–December 18, 2005 (Opening Night October 24, 2005); 24 previews, 64 performances.

Jason Ritter in *Third* PHOTO BY JOAN MARCUS

Phylicia Rashad in *Bernarda Alba* PHOTO BY PAUL KOLNIK

BERNARDA ALBA Music and lyrics by Michael John LaChiusa, based on the play *The House of Bernarda Alba* by Federico Garciá Lorca; Director and Choreography, Graciela Daniele; Scenery, Christopher Barreca; Costumes, Toni-Leslie James; Lighting, Stephen Strawbridge; Sound, Scott Stauffer; Orchestrations, Michael Starobin; Music Director, Deborah Abramson; Music Coordinator, Seymour Red Press; Stage Manager, Jennifer Rae Moore; Assistant Stage Manager, Julie C. Miller; Company Manger, Josh Lowenthal; **Cast:** Phylicia Rashad (Bernarda Alba), Saundra Santiago (Angustias), Judith Blazer (Magdalena), Sally Murphy (Amelia), Daphne Rubin-Vega (Martirio), Nikki M. James (Adela), Yolande Bavan (Maria Josepha), Candy Buckley (Poncia), Laura Shoop (Young Maid), Nancy Ticotin (Servant/Prudencia); **Understudies:** Cheryl Alexander (Bernarda Alba), Bertilla Baker (Maria Josepha/Poncia), Stephanie Pope Caffey (Angustias/Magdalena/ Prudencia/Servant), Betsy Morgan (Amelia/Martirio), Diane Veronica Phelan (Adela/Maid); **Orchestra:** Deborah Abramson (Conductor/synthesizer), Larry Spivack (Associate Conductor/ percussion), Stephen Benson (guitar), Sarah Davol (woodwinds), Joseph Gottesman (viola), Benjamin Wyatt, Katie Schlaikjer (celli), Raymond Kilday (bass), Jennifer Hoult (harp)

Musical Numbers: Prologue, The Funeral, On the Day That I Marry/Prayer, Love Let Me Sing You, Let Me Go to the Sea, Madalena, Angustias, Amelia, Martirio, Adela, I Will Dream of What I Saw, Thirty Odd Years, Limbrada's Daughter, One Moorish Girl, The Smallest Stream, The Stallion, Lullaby, Open the Door, Finale

Setting: A house in a small village in rural Spain, 1930s. A musical presented in three acts with no intermission; Mitzi E. Newhouse Theatre; February 11–April 9, 2006 (Opening Night March 6, 2006); 25 previews, 40 performances.

MCC THEATRE

TWENTIETH SEASON

Robert LuPone and Bernard Telsey, Artistic Directors; William Cantler, Associate Artistic Director; John G. Schultz, Executive Director

General Manager, Barbara L. Auld; Literary Manager/Resident Dramaturg, Stephen Willems; Director of Development, John W. Fichtel; Sales Manager, Anne Love; Director of Marketing, Shanta Mali; Director of Education and Outreach, Katie Miller; Production Manager, B.D. White; Resident Director, Doug Hughes; Office Manager, Eric Bornemann; Casting, Bernard Telsey; Press, Richard Kornberg (*Colder Than Here*); Shaffer-Coyle Public Relations, Adriana Douzos (*The Wooden Breeks/Some Girl(s)*)

COLDER THAN HERE By Laura Wade; Director, Abigail Morris; Scenery, Jeff Cowie; Costumes, Candice Donnelly; Lighting, Michael Chybowski; Sound, Bill Grady; Sound consultant, John Leonard; Projections, Brian H. Kim; Dialect Coach, Stephen Gabis; Production Stage Manager, Amy McCraney; Assistant Stage Manager, Catherine Connington; **Cast:** Judith Light (Myra), Lily Rabe (Jenna), Sarah Paulson (Harriet) and Brian Murray (Alec)

American premiere of a new play presented without intermission; Lucille Lortel Theater, 121 September 7–October 15, 2005 (Opening night: September 28, 2005), 40 performances.

Sarah Paulson and Lily Rabe in *Colder Than Here* PHOTOS BY JOAN MARCUS

Maria Dizzia and Louis Cancelmi in *The Wooden Breeks*

THE WOODEN BREEKS by Glen Berger; Director, Trip Cullman; Scenery, Beowulf Boritt; Costumes, Anita Yavich; Lighting, Paul Whitaker; Original Music/Sound, Fitz Patton; Fight Director, Rick Sordelet; Dialect Coach, Stephen Gabis; Production Stage Manager, Hannah Cohen; Assistant Stage Manager, Emily Roberts; Movement, Amy Klewitz; **Cast:** Adam Rothenberg (Tom Bosch), Ana Reeder (Hetty Grigs/Anna Livia Spoon), Jaymie Dornan (Wicker Grigs), T. Ryder Smith (Jarl von Hoother), Steve Mellor (Enry Leap), Ron Cephas Jones (Toom the Stoup), Veanne Cox (Mrs. Nelles), Maria Dizzia (Tricity Tiara), Louis Cancelmi (Armitage Shanks)

A new play presented in two acts; Lucille Lortel Theater; February 2–March 11, 2006 (Opening night: February 21, 2006); 39 performances

SOME GIRL(S) By Neil LaBute; Director, Jo Bonney; Scenery, Neil Patel; Costumes, Mimi O'Donnell; Lighting, David Weiner; Sound, Robert Kaplowitz; Production Stage Manager, Kevin Bertolacci; Assistant Stage Manager, Carmen I. Abrazado; Properties, Jeremy Chernick; **Cast:** Fran Drescher (Lindsay), Eric McCormack (Guy), Judy Reyes (Tyler), Brooke Smith (Sam), Maura Tierney (Bobbi)

American premiere of a new play presented without intermission; Lucille Lortel Theater; May 17–July 8, 2006 (Opening night: June 8, 2006), 62 performances

Eric McCormack and Fran Drescher in *Some Girl(s)*

MANHATTAN THEATRE CLUB

THIRTY-FOURTH SEASON

Lynne Meadow, Artistic Director; Barry Grove, Executive Producer

General Manager, Florie Seery; Director of Artistic Production, Michael Bush; Director of Artistic Development, Paige Evans; Director of Artistic Operations, Mandy Greenfield; Director of Casting, Nancy Piccione; Casting Director, David Caparelliotis; Literary Manager, Emily Shooltz; Director of Musical Theatre, Clifford Lee Johnson III; Director of Development, Jill Turner Lloyd; Director of Marketing, Debra A. Waxman; Director of Finance, Jeffrey Bledsoe; Associate General Manager, Seth Shepsle; Company Manager/NY City Center, Lindsey T. Brooks; Director of Education, David Shookhoff; Director of Subscriber Services, Robert Allenberg; Production Manager, Ryan McMahon; Technical Director, William Mohney; Press, Boneau/Bryan-Brown, Jim Byk, Aaron Meier

THE OTHER SIDE by Ariel Dorfman; Director, Blanka Zizka; Scenery, Beowulf Boritt; Costumes, Linda Cho; Lighting, Russell H. Champa; Sound, Scott Killian; Production Stage Manager, James Fitzsimmons; Stage Manager, Thea Bradshaw Gilles; **Cast:** John Cullum (Atom Roma), Gene Farber (Guard), Rosemary Harris (Levan Julak); **Understudies:** Bev Appleton (Atom), Darrie Lawrence Levana), Chris Genebach (Guard)

New York premiere of a play presented without intermission; City Center Stage I; December 13, 2005–January 15, 2006 (Opening Night November 10, 2005); 32 previews, 38 performances.

BEAUTY OF THE FATHER by Nilo Cruz; Director, Michael Greif; Scenery, Mark Wendland; Costumes, Miranda Hoffman; Lighting, James F. Ingalls; Sound, Darron L. West; Dialect Coach, Deborah Hecht; Production Stage Manager, Barclay Stiff; Stage Manager, David H. Lurie; **Cast:** Ritchie Coster (Emiliano), Oscar Isaac (Federico Garcia Lorca), Priscilla Lopez (Paquita), Pedro Pascal (Karim), Elizabeth Rodriguez (Marina); **Understudies:** Joaquin Torres (Lorca/Karim), Marnia Squerciati (Marina/Paquita)

New York Premiere of a play presented in two acts; City Center Stage II; January 10–February 19, 2006 (Opening Night December 15, 2005); 28 previews, 48 performances.

Rosemary Harris and Gene Farber in *The Other Side* PHOTO BY JOAN MARCUS

DEFIANCE by John Patrick Shanley; Director, Doug Hughes; Scenery, John Lee Beatty; Costumes, Catherine Zuber, Lighting, Pat Collins; Original Music and Sound, David Van Tieghem; Production Stage Manager, James Fitzsimmons; Stage Manager, Thea Bradshaw Gillies, Elizabeth Wiesner Paige; **Cast:** Chris Bauer (Chaplain White), Chris Chalk (Captain Lee King), Margaret Colin (Margaret Littlefield), Stephen Lang (Lt. Colonel Littlefield), Trevor Long (Gunnery Sergeant), Jeremy Strong (P.F.C. Evan Davis); Replacements: Chris McGarry (Chaplain White); **Understudies:** Royce Johnson (King), Christopher McHale (Littlefield/White/Gunnery Sergeant), Trevor Oswalt (Davis), Rita Rehn (Margaret)

Setting: Spring, 1971. Camp Lejeune, North Carolina. World premiere of a new play presented without intermission; City Center Stage I; February 28–June 4, 2006 (Opening Night February 9, 2006); 21 previews, 115 performances.

BASED ON A TOTALLY TRUE STORY by Robert Aguirre-Sacasa; Director, Michael Bush; Scenery, Anna Louizos; Costumes, Linda Cho; Lighting, Traci Klainer; Sound, Ryan Rumery; Production Stage Manager, Gail Eve Malatesta; Stage Manager, Diane M. Ballering; **Cast:** Carson Elrod (Ethan Keene); Erik Heger (Tyler/Apple Boy/Kim's Guy/Hot LA Guy), Kristine Nielsen (Mary Ellen), Pedro Pascal (Michael Sullivan), Michael Tucker (Ethan's Dad); **Understudies:** Mitchell Greenberg (Ethan's Dad), Linda Marie Larson (Mary Ellen), Carter Roy (Ethan/Michael/Tyler)

Setting: New York, Philadelphia, Los Angeles. Right now. World premiere of a new play presented in two acts; City Center Stage II; April 11–May 28, 2006 (Opening Night March 23, 2006); 21 previews, 56 performances.

Chris Chalk, Stephen Lang, Chris Bauer in *Defiance* PHOTO BY JOAN MARCUS

MINT THEATER COMPANY

FOURTEENTH SEASON

Jonathan Bank, Artistic Director

General Manager, Sherri Kotimsky; Associate Director, Ted Altschuler; Box Office Manager, Toni Anita Hull; Casting, Stuart Howard, Amy Schecter & Paul Hardt; Graphic Design, Jude Dvorak; Press, David Gersten and Associates

THE SKIN GAME by John Galsworthy; Director, Eleanor Reissa; Scenery, Vicki R. Davis; Costumes, Tracy Christensen; Lighting, Traci Klainer; Sound, Bruce Ellman; **Cast:** John C. Vennema (Hillcrist), Nicole Lowrance (Jill Hillcrist), Richard Waddingham (Fellows/Solicitor), Carl Palmer (Mr Jackman), Pat Nesbit (Mrs. Jackman), Stephen Rowe (Dawker), Monique Fowler (Amy Hillcrist), James Gale (Hornblower), Leo Kittay (Charles Hornblower), Diana LaMar (Chloe), Denis Butkus (Rolf Hornblower), Nick Berg Barnes (Auctioneer/Stranger)

A play presented in two acts; Mint Theater; June 21–August 14, 2005 (Opening Night July 10, 2005); 52 performances.

IVANOV by Anton Chekhov, translated by Paul Schmidt; Presented by the National Asian American Theatre Company (Mia Katigbak, Artistic Director); Director, Jonathan Bank; Scenery, Sarah Lambert; Costumes, Elly van Horne; Lighting , Stephen Petrilli; Sound, Jane Shaw; Stage Manager, Karen Hergesheimer; Artistic Associate: Nancy Kim; Technical Director: Evan Scholssberg; **Cast:** Joel de la Fuente (Ivanov), Orville Mendoza (Borkin), Thom Sesma (Count Shabelsky), Deepti Gupta (Anna), Arthur Acuna (Doctor Lvov), Mia Katigbak (Zinaida), Rochele Tillman (Martha Babakina)Mel Duane Gionson (Kosykh), C.S. Lee (Lebedev), Virginia Wing (Avdotya Nozarovna), Michi Barall (Sasha)

A play presented in two acts; Mint Theatre; August 2–September 4, 2005; 28 performances. This production was previously presented at the Baruch Performing Arts Center's Bernie West Theatre May 20–June 8, 2005.

WALKING DOWN BROADWAY by Dawn Powell; Director, Steven Williford; Scenery, Roger Hanna; Costumes, Brenda Turpin; Lighting, Stephen Petrilli; Sound, Jane Shaw; **Cast:** Christine Albright (Marge), Denis Butkus (Chick), Antony Hagopian (Mac), Carol Halstead, (Eva Elman) Amanda Jones (Elsie), Emily Moment (Librarian #1), Stacy Parker (Librarian #2), Ben Roberts (Dewey), Cherene Snow (Isabel), Sammy Tunis (Ginger)

Setting: Upper West Side, New York City, 1931. World premiere of a 1931 never produced play presented in three acts; Mint Theatre; September 15–November 6, 2005 (Opening Night September 25, 2005); 54 performances.

SOLDIER'S WIFE by Rose Franken; Director, Eleanor Reissa; Scenery, Nathan Heverin; Costumes, Clint Ramos; Lighting, Josh Bradford; Sound, Elizabeth Rhodes; Dramaturg, Amy Stoller; Production Stage Manager, Karen Hergesheimer; **Cast:** Angela Pierce (Katherine Rogers), Judith Hawking (Florence Lane), Michael Polak (John Rogers), Jordan Lage (Alexander Craig), Kate Levy (Peter Gray)

Setting: The Roger's apartment on Riverside Drive, New York City, 1944. A play presented in three acts; Mint Theatre; February 7–April 2, 2006 (Opening Night: February 23, 2006); 55 performances.

James Gale, Monique Fowler, John C. Vennema in *The Skin Game* PHOTO BY RAHAV SEGEV

Carol Halstead and Christine Albright in *Walking Down Broadway* PHOTO BY RICHARD TERMINE

Judith Hawking and Angela Pierce in *Soldier's Wife* PHOTO BY RICHARD TERMINE

THE NEW GROUP

TENTH SEASON

Scott Elliott, Artistic Director; Geoffrey Rich, Executive Director

Associate Producer, Jill Bowman; Director of Corporate and External Affairs, Oliver Dow; Associate Artistic Director, Ian Morgan; Associate Executive Director, Wren Longno; General Manager, Amanda Brandes; Production Supervisor, Peter R. Feuchtwanger/PRF Productions; Business and Company Manager, Theodore Hall; Casting, Judy Henderson; Press, The Karpel Group, Bridget Klapinski and Billy Zavelson

ABIGAIL'S PARTY by Mike Leigh; Director, Scott Elliott; Scenery, Derek McLane; Costumes, Eric Becker; Lighting, Jason Lyons; Sound, Ken Travis; Hair, Jeff Francis; Make up, Angela Di Carlo; Production Stage Manager, Valerie A. Peterson; Assistant Stage Manager, Fran Rubinstein; Prop Master, Tessa Dunning; Dialect Coach, Stephen Gabis; Assistant Director, Marie Masters; **Cast:** Max Baker (Laurence), Lisa Emery (Susan), Darren Goldstein (Tony), Elizabeth Jasicki (Angela), Jennifer Jason Leigh (Beverly); Replacement: Gayton Scott (Beverly-March 13, 2006)

Revival of the play presented in two acts; Acorn Theatre; November 14 – April 8, 2006 (Opening night: December 1, 2006); 144 performances

Sarah Wolfson, Lauren Jelencovich, Kristin Knutson, Elisa Cordova, Rebecca Robbins in *The Music Teacher* PHOTOS BY CAROL ROSEGG

THE MUSIC TEACHER by Wallace Shawn, Music by Wallace Shawn; Director and Scenery, Tom Cairns; Musical Director, Timothy Long; Choreography, David Neumann; Costumes, Kaye Voyce; Lighting, Matt Frey; Sound, Shane Rettig; Video, Greg Emetaz; Production Stage Manager, Cat Domiano; Additional Casting, Kimberly Graham; Assistant Director, Kevin Newbury; Associate Producers, Ian Morgan, Beatrix Ost; **Cast:** Ross Benoliel and Jason Forbach (alternate the roles of Jim/Chronilos), Mark Blum (Smith), Elisa Cordova (Nadine/Greek Chorus), Wayne Hobbs (Young Smith/Alcimedes), Lauren Jelencovich (Angelique/Greek Chorus), Kristin Knutson (Janet/Greek Chorus), Stefanie Nava (Alice & Waitress), Kellie Overbey (Jane), Jeffrey Picon (Young Smith/Alcimedes), Rebecca Robbins (Vocalist/Greek Chorus), Kathryn Skemp (Young Jane/Aeola), Bobby Steggert (Rupert/Bellman), Kristina Valada-Viars, (Ellen/Stewardess), Sarah Wolfson (Young Jane/Aeola); **Understudies:** Elisa Cordova (Vocalist)

World premiere of a play/opera presented in two acts; Minetta Lane Theatre; February 21 – April 8, 2006 (Opening night: March 6, 2006); 47 performances

NEW YORK THEATRE WORKSHOP

TWENTY-SIXTH SEASON

James C. Nicola, Artistic Director; Lynn Moffat, Managing Director

Associate Artistic Director, Linda S. Chapman; Director of Communications, Robert Marlin; Director of Planning and Development, Carl M. Sylvestre; Director of Finance and Administration, Robert Wayne; Director of Marketing, Harry J. McFadden; General Manager, Harry J. McFadden; Production Manager, Michael Casselli, Associate Production Manager, Laura Mroczkowski; Operations Manager, William-Kevin Young; Technical Director, Efren Delgadillo, Jr.; Casting, Jack Doulin; Press, Richard Kornberg, Don Summa

OEDIPUS AT PALM SPRINGS by the Five Lesbian Brothers; Director, Leigh Silverman; Scenery, David Korins; Costumes, Miranda Hoffman; Lighting, M.L. Geiger; Sound, John Gromada; Production Stage Manager, Martha Donaldson; **Cast:** Babs Davy (Joni), Lisa Kron (Con), Maureen Angelos (Fran), Dominique Dibbell (Prin), Peg Healey (Terri)

Setting: A Palm Springs resort, the Present. A new play presented in two acts; July 20 – August 28, 2005 (Opening Night August 3, 2005); 46 performances.

SPIRIT Created by Arlene Audergon, Julian Crouch, Guy Dartnell, Phelim McDermott, Lee Simpson; Co-Produced by the Royal Court Theatre; Directors, Arlene Audergon, Julian Crouch; Lighting, Colin Grenfell; Sound, Andrew Paine; Designer Realization, Julian Crouch, Graeme Gilmour, Helen Maguire, Rob Thirtle; Production Manager, Helen Maguire; **Cast:** Guy Dartnell, Phelim McDermott, Lee Simpson

An improvised performance piece presented without intermission; September 13 – October 9, 2005 (Opening Night September 15, 2005); 32 performances.

BACH AT LEIPZIG by Itamar Moses; Director, Pam MacKinnon; Scenery, David Zinn; Costumes, Mathew J. LeFebvre; Lighting, David Lander; Sound, John Gromada; Production Stage Management, C.A. Clark; Fight Choreography, Felix Ivanov; Assistant Stage Manager, Jonathan Donahue; **Cast:** Jeffrey Carlson (Johann Martin Steindorf), Richard Easton (Georg Friedrich Kaufmann), Michael Emerson (Georg Bathasar Schott), Boyd Gaines (Johann Friedrich Fasch), Reg Rogers (Georg Lenck), Andrew Weekms (Johann Christoph Graupner)

Setting: Leipzig, German, 1772. A play presented in two acts; October 28 – December 18, 2005 (Opening Night November 14, 2005); 57 performances.

Lee Simpson, Phelim McDermott, Guy Dartnell in *Spirit* PHOTOS BY CAROL ROSEGG

Benton Greene, Jamyl Dobson, Edwin Lee Gibson (above) in *The Seven*

THE SEVEN Text and Composition by Will Power; Director/Development, Jo Bonney; Choreography, Bill T. Jones; Scenery, Richard Hoover; Costumes, Emilio Sosa; Lighting, David Weiner; Sound, Darron L. West; Music Production/Additional Composition, Justin Ellington; Additional Composition, Will Hammond; Music Director, Daryl Waters; Production Stage Manager, Wendy Ouellette; Rehearsal Stage Manager, Judith Schoenfeld; Company Manager, Katy Savard; **Cast:** Uzo Aduba (Second Woman/Amphiarus), Shawtane Monroe Bowen (Third Man/Hippomedon), Jamyl Dobson (Polynices), Amber Efé (DJ/Dance Captain), Edwin Lee Gibson (Oedipus/Laius), Benton Greene (Eteolcles), Manuel Herrera (Eteoclus/First Man), Flaco Navaja (Tydeus), Tom Nelis (Right Hand), Postell Pringle (Greek Hip-Hop Chorus/Capennus/Second Man), Pearl Sun (First Woman/Parthenopaeus), Charles Turner (Recorded Voice/Aeschylus)

World premiere of a hip-hop play with music and dance; January 18–March 12, 2006 (Opening Night February 12, 2006); 57 performances.

COLUMBINUS by The United States Theatre Project; Text by Stephen Karam and PJ Paparelli; Director/Conception, PJ Paparelli; Dramaturgy, Patricia Hersch; Scenery, Tony Cisek; Costumes, Miranda Hoffman; Lighting, Dan Covey; Sound, Martin Desjardins; Projections, JJ Kaczynski; Production Stage Manager, Amy McCraney; **Cast:** Anna Camp, Joaquín Pérez-Campbell, James Flanagan, Carmen Herlihy, Nicole Lowrance, Karl Miller, Will Rogers, Bobby Steggert

Setting: Littleton, Colorado, 1999. After the Columbine High School shootings. New York premiere of a "theatrical discussion" play presented in two acts; May 5–June 11, 2006 (Opening Night May 22, 2006); 40 performances.

PAN ASIAN REPERTORY THEATRE

TWENTY-NINTH SEASON

Tisa Chang, Artistic Producing Director

Artistic Associate, Ron Nakahara; Communications Director, Sylvie H. Fan; Producing Associate, June Prager; Resident Workshop Instructor, Ernest Abuba; Marketing Consultant, Reva Cooper; Bookeeper, Rosemary Khan; Technical Director, Richard Hodge; Master Electrician, Paul Jones; Photo Archivist, Corky Lee; Press, Keith Sherman and Associates

CAMBODIA AGONISTES Text and lyrics by Ernest Abuba; music by Louis Stewart; Director and Musical Staging, Tisa Chang; Cambodian Ballets, Sam-Ouem Tes; NOTION tm Orchestrations, Jack Jarrett; Scenery, Kaori Akazawa; Costumes, Carol Ann Pelletier; Masks, Tom Lee; Lighting, Victor En Yu Tan; Stage Manager, Elis C. Arroyo; Assistant Stage Manager, April Klein; **Cast:** Lydia Gaston (The Dancer), John Baray (Politician/Opthamologist/ElderBodhi), Ariel Estrada (Politician/Chinese Dance Solo/Intruder), Rebecca Lee Lerman (Politician/Mit Neary), Virginia Wing (Politician/Social Worker 1), Ron Nakahara (Child Who Becomes a Dictator/Factory Worker), Derek Wong (Mit/Social Worker 2)

Musical Numbers: Remembering When, Whatever Happened to Angkor Wat, Khmer Rouge Anthem, Songs of Devastation, Splendors of Cambodia Long Ago, I Cannot See, Who's Child Are You? I'll Plant You, From Phnom Penh We Marched, The Soul is a Nail, Wisdom Is A Sin Against the State, Legend of the Black Lady Ballet, Little Basket That Is So Round, The Eleventh American Winter, My Son Was Three/Your Eyes May Look Like Mine, Finale

Setting: New York and the Khmer Rouge camps in Cambodia, now and the mid 70s; Revival of a new musical presented in two acts; West End Theatre; November 2–20, 2005 (Opening Night October 29, 2005); 2 previews, 18 performances.

PAN ASIAN FESTIVAL OF NEW WORKS
"Recollections" written and perfomed by Kendra Ware
"Elevator Sex" written and performed by Lan Tran
"ABC (American Born Chinese)" written and performed by John Quincy Lee
"38th Parallels" written and performed by Terry Park

Four new solo performance plays/performance pieces presented in repertory, West End Theatre; May 3–28, 2006 (Opening Night May 10, 2006); 7 previews, 20 performances

Kendra Ware, Lan Tran, John Quincy Lee, Terry Park in *Spring Festival of New Works*

PHOTOS BY CAROL ROSEGG AND DIANA TOSHIKO

PEARL THEATRE COMPANY

TWENTY-SECOND SEASON

Shepard Sobel, Artistic Director; Joanne Camp, Associate Director; Amy Kaiser; Managing Director

Development Director, Leah Maddrie; Marketing and Press Director, Matt Schicker, Associate Marketing Director, Matthew Shane Coleman; Audience Services Manager, Tricia Smith; Assistant to the Managing Director, Leigh Goldenberg; Development Assistant, Raelyn Richards; Education Director, Christopher Moore; Speech and Text Coach, Robert Neff Williams; Casting, Rachel Botchan, Joanne Camp; Season Stage Designer, Susan Zeeman Rogers; Season Lighting Design, Stephen Petrilli

THE MASTER BUILDER by Henrik Ibsen, translated by Nichols Rudall; Director, Shepard Sobel; Costumes, Sam Fleming; Sound, Jane Shaw; Properties, Melanie Mulder; Stage Manager, Lisa Ledwich; **Cast:** Robert Hock (Knut Brovik), Marsha Stephanie Blake (Kaja Fosli), Sean McNall (Ragnar Brovik), Dan Daily (Halvard Solness), Robin Leslie Brown (Aline Solness), Arthur French (Doctor Herdal), Michele Vazquez (Miss Hilde Wangel)

Setting: Norway, late 1800's. New York premiere of the translation of the play presented in two acts; Theatre 80; September 22 – October 30, 2005 (Opening Night October 2, 2005) 11 previews, 27 performances.

THE GENTLEMAN DANCING-MASTER by William Wycherley; Director, Gus Kaikkonen; Costomes, Devon Painter; Sound and Original Music, Jane Shaw; Properties, Melanie Mulder; Choreography, Rachel List; Fight Director, David DeBesse; Stage Manager, Dale Smallwood; **Cast:** Marsha Stephanie Blake (Hippolita), Michele Vazquez (Prue), Sean McNall (Mr. Paris), Robin Leslie Brown (Mrs. Caution), John Livingstone Rolle (Mr. Martin), Bradford Cover (Mr. Gerrard), Ryland Blackinton (Waiter/Parson/Musician), Heather Girardi (Mrs. Flounce), Rachel Botchan (Mrs. Flirt), Dan Daily (Mr. James Formal or Don Diego)

Setting: London, 1672, the residence of Mr. James Formal and The French House. New York premiere of a play presented in two acts; 80 St Marks Place; November 10 – December 18, 2005 (Opening night November 20, 2005); 11 previews, 26 performances.

Marsha Stephanie Blake, Sean McNall, Bradford Cover in *The Gentleman Dancing Master*

Kelli Holsopple, Susan Hunt, Joanne Camp, and Rocelyn Halili in *Hecuba*

HECUBA by Euripides, translated by Janet Lembke and Kenneth J. Reckford; Director, Shepard Sobel; Costumes, Devon Painter; Sound and Original Music, Jane Shaw; Properties, Melanie Mulder; Dramaturge, Kate Farrington; Mask Design, James Seffens; Mask Consultant, Jim Calder; Stage Manager, Lisa Ledwich; **Cast:** Carolyn Ratteray (Ghost of Polydorus/Polyxena), Joanne Camp (Hecuba), Rachel Botchan (Chorus), Vinie Burrows (Chorus), Carol Schultz (Chorus), John Livingstone Rolle (Odysseus/Agamemnon), Dominic Cuskern (Talthybius/Polymestor), Rocelyn Halili (Hecuba's Attendant), Kelli Holsopple (Hecuba's Attendant), Susan Hunt (Hecuba's Attendant), Mel England (Guard), Bashir Solebo (Guard)

Setting: The coast of Thrace, shortly after the Greek victory over Troy. Revival of a play presented without intermission; 80 St Marks Place; January 5 – February 12, 2006 (Opening Night January 15, 2006); 11 previews, 27 performances.

MEASURE FOR MEASURE by William Shakespeare; Director, Beatrice Terry; Costumes, Frank Champa; Sound Design and Original Music, Jane Shaw; Properties, Melanie Mulder; Stage Manager, Dale Smallwood; **Cast:** Ron Simons (Duke Vincentio), Robert Hock (Escalus), Sean McNall (Angelo), Carol Schultz (Mistress Overdone/Sister Francisca), Dominic Cuskern (Lucio), Edward Seamon (Pompey), Noel Vélez (Claudio), Raphel Peacock (Provost), T.J. Edwards (Friar Peter/Elbow/Abhorson), Rachel Botchan (Isabella), Romel Jamison (Froth/Servant/Guard), Holley Fain (Juliet), Kelli Holsopple (Mariana), John Mazurek (Barnadine)

Setting: Vienna, 1604. Revival of a play presented in two acts; 80 St Marks Place; February 23 – April 9, 2006 (Opening Night March 5, 2006); 11 previews, 34 performances.

MARY STUART by Friedrich Schiller, translated by Michael Feingold; Director, Eleanor Holdridge; Costumes, Jessica Ford; Sound, Jane Shaw; Properties, Melanie Mulder; Assistant Director, Kim Martin-Cotton; Wigs, Ashley Ryan; Stage Manager, Amy Patricia Stern; **Cast:** Beth Dixon (Hannah Kennedy), Edward Seamon (Sir Amyas Paulet), Tyler Woods (Drudgeon Drury), Joanne Camp (Mary Stuart), Sean McNall (Mortimer), Dominic Cuskern (William Cecil), Noel Vélez (William Davison), Carol Schultz (Elizabeth I), T.J. Edwards (Count Aubespine/Melvil), Raphael Peacock (Count Bellievre/Burgoyne), Robert Hock (George Talbot), Bryan Hicks (Robert Dudley), Clester Rich (Page/Guard), Kenric Green (Guard/O'Kelley)

Setting: 1587, Fotherinhay Castle and Westminster, London. New York premiere of a new translation of the play presented in two acts; 80 St Marks Place; April 20 – May 21, 2006 (Opening Night April 30, 2006); 11 previews, 20 performances.

PLAYWRIGHTS HORIZONS

THIRTY-FIFTH SEASON

Tim Sanford, Artistic Director; Leslie Marcus, Managing Director; William Russo, General Manager

Literary Manager, Lisa Timmel; Casting, James Calleri and Alaine Alldaffer; Production Manager, Christopher Boll; Director of Development, Jill Garland; Controller, Daniel C. Smith; Director of Marketing, Eric Winick; Director of Ticket Central, Mike Rafael; Playwrights Horizons Theatre School Director, Helen R. Cook; Press, The Publicity Office: Bob Fennell, Marc Thibodeau, Michael S. Borowski, Candi Adams; General Management Associate, Sandra Gardner; Assistant to the Artistic Director, Julie Foh; Assistant to the Managing Director/Production Company Manager, Caroline Aquino; Associate Production Manager, Shannon Nicole Case; Technical Director, Brian Coleman

FRAN'S BED Written and Directed by James Lapine; Scenery, Derek McLane (based on an original design by Douglas Stein); Costumes, Susan Hilferty; Lighting, David Lander; Original Music and Sound, Fitz Patton; Projections, Elaine J. McCarthy; Production Stage Manager, Scott Taylor Rollison; Assistant Stage Manager, Sid King; **Cast:** Mia Farrow (Fran), Heather Burns (Vicky), Brenda Pressley (Dolly), Harris Yulin (Hank), Julia Stiles (Birdie), Marcia DeBonis (Lynne/Doctor), Jonathan Walker (Eddie, Doctor)

Setting: The present and the past. Arizona and Michigan. New York premiere new play presented without intermission; Mainstage Theater; August 30–October 9, 2005 (Opening night September 25, 2006); 45 performances.

Brenda Pressley, Mia Farrow, Heather Burns in *Fran's Bed* PHOTOS BY JOAN MARCUS

Jeremy Shamos, Kristine Nielsen, Colleen Werthmann in *Miss Witherspoon*

MISS WITHERSPOON by Christopher Durang; Produced in association with The McCarter Theatre (Emily Mann, Artistic Director; Mara Isaacs, Producing Director; Jeffrey Woodward, Managing Director; Janice Paran, Dramaturg); Director, Emily Mann; Scenery, David Korins; Costumes, Jess Goldstein; Lighting, Jeff Croiter; Soundscape, Darron L. West; Production Manager McCarter Theatre, David York; Production Stage Manager, Alison Cote; Assistant Stage Manager, Christine Whalen; **Cast:** Kristine Nielsen (Veronica), Mahira Kakkar (Maryamma), Colleen Werthmann (Mother 1 and 2), Jeremy Shamos (Father 1 and 2/Man in the Playground/Dog Owner/Wise Man), Lynda Gravátt (Teacher, Woman in a Hat)

Setting: Recent past, foreseeable future. Earth and not earth. New York premiere of a new play presented without intermission; Mainstage Theater; November 11, 2005–January 1, 2006 (Opening night November 29, 2005); 60 performances.

Deirdre O'Connell and Molly Price in *Manic Flight Reaction*

MANIC FLIGHT REACTION by Sarah Schulman; Scenery, Louisa Thompson; Costumes, Jenny Mannis; Lighting, Paul Whitaker; Sound, Fitz Patton; Harris Skibell; Production Manager, Joshua Helman; Production Stage Manager, Marion Friedman; Assistant Stage Manager, Stephanie Gatton; **Cast:** Jessica Collins (Grace), Angel Desai (Susan), Michael Esper (Luke), Austin Lysy (Albert), Deirdre O'Connell (Marge), Molly Price (Cookie/Claire)

Setting: The present. Outside Champaign-Urbana, Illinois. World premiere of a new play presented in two acts; Peter Jay Sharp Theater; October 20–November 20, 2005 (Opening night October 30, 2005); 37 performances.

GREY GARDENS Book by Doug Wright, music by Scott Frankel; lyrics by Michael Korie; based on the film *Grey Gardens* by David and Albert Maysles, Ellen Hovde, Muffie Myer and Susan Froemke; Director, Michael Greif; Musical Staging, Jeff Calhoun; Scenery, Allen Moyer; Costumes, William Ivey Long; Lighting, Peter Kaczorowski; Sound, Brian Ronan; Projections, Wendall K. Harrington; Hair and Wigs,

Paul Huntley; Orchestrations, Bruce Coughlin; Music Director, Lawrence Yurman; Music Coordinator, John Miller; Additional Casting, Alan Filderman; Production Stage Manager, Judith Schoenfeld; Assistant Stage Manager, Carrie Meconis; Dialect Coach, Stephen Gabis; Associate Choreography, Jodi Moccia; Music Copying, Emily Grishman, Katherine Edmonds; **Cast:** Mary Louise Wilson (Edith Bouvier Beale Act 2), Christine Ebersole (Edith Bouvier Beale-Act 1/"Little" Edie Beale-Act 2); Bob Stillman (George Gould Strong); Michael Potts (Brooks Sr./ Brooks Jr.) Sarah Hyland (Jacqueline Bouvier); Audrey Twitchell (Lee Bouvier), Sara Gettelfinger ("Little" Edie Bouvier-Act 1), Matt Cavenaugh (Joseph Patrick Kennedy, Jr./Jerry), John McMartin (J.V. "Major" Bouvier/Norman Vincent Peale); **Understudies:** Barbara Broughton, Ryan Hilliard, Russell Arden Koplin, Mike McGowan, Chelsea Meyers; **Musicians:** Lawrence Yurman (Conductor), Karl Mansfield (Associate Conductor/synthesizer), Eric DeGioia (violin), Anik Oulianene (cello), Ken Hitchcock and Tom Murray (reeds), Jeremy Miloszewicz (trumpet/flugelhorn), Patrick Pridemore (French horn), Bill Sloat (acoustic bass), Tim McLafferty (percussion/drums)

Musical Numbers: Toyland, The Five-Fifteen, Body Beautiful Beale, Mother Darling, Better Fall Out of Love, Being Bouvier, Hominy Grits, Peas in a Pod, Drift Away, The Five-Fifteen (reprise), Tomorrow's Woman, Daddy's Girl, The Telegram, Being Bouvier (reprise), Will You?, The Revolutionary Costume for Today, The Cake I Had, Entering Grey Gardens, The House We Live In, Jerry Likes My Corn, Around the World, Will You (reprise), Choose to Be Happy, Another Winter in a Summer Town, Peas in a Pod (reprise)

Setting: Grey Gardens, East Hampton, Long Island, NY. Act 1: July 1941, Act 2: 1979. World premiere of a new musical presented in two acts, Peter J. Sharp Theatre; February 10–April 30, 2006 (Opening Night March 7, 2006); 92 performances. This production was scheduled to transfer to the Walter Kerr Theatre fall, 2006.

Christine Ebersole in *Grey Gardens*

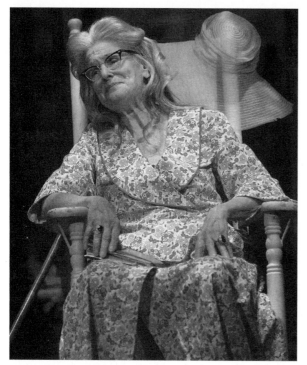

Mary Louise Wilson in *Grey Gardens* PHOTOS BY JOAN MARCUS

PEN by David Marshall Grant; Director, Will Frears; Scenery, Robin Vest; Costumes, Jenny Mannis; Lighting, Matthew Richards; Sound, Obadiah Eaves; Production Stage Manager, Carmen I. Abrazado; Assistant Stage Manager, Alexander Libby; **Cast:** Reed Birney (Jerry), Dan McCabe (Matt), J. Smith-Cameron (Helen)

Setting: 1969. Long Island. World premiere of a new play presented in two acts; Peter Jay Sharp Theater; March 23–April 16, 2006 (Opening Night April 2, 2006); 29 performances.

THE BUSY WORLD IS HUSHED by Keith Bunin; Director, Mark Brokaw; Scenery, Allen Moyer; Costumes, Michael Krass; Lighting, Mary Louise Geiger; Original Music and Sound, Lewis Flinn; Production Stage Manager, David Sugarman; Assistant Stage Manager, Mary Kathryn Flynt; **Cast:** Hamish Linklater (Brandt), Jill Clayburgh (Hannah), Luke Macfarlane (Thomas)

Setting: The library of an apartment on West 122nd Street in New York City, the present. World premiere of a new play presented in two acts; Mainstage Theater; June 5–July 9, 2006 (Opening Night June 25, 2006); 40 performances.

PRIMARY STAGES

TWENTY-FIRST SEASON

Casey Childs, Executive Producer; Andrew Leynse, Artistic Director; Elliot Fox, Managing Director

Associate Artistic Director, Tyler Marchant; Director of Marketing, Louis Bavaro, Director of Development, Erica Raven; Business Manager, Stephanie Coulombe; Company Manager/Artistic Associate, Michelle Bossy; Production Manager, Lester P. Grant; Marketing Assistant, Jill Simon; IT Manager/Development Assistant, David Goldsmith; Associate to the Artistic Director, Lucy McMichael; Literary Manager, Kathryn Moroney; Casting, Stephanie Klapper; Press, OPR/Origlio Public Relations, Philip Carrubba

Nathan Lane and Marian Seldes in *Dedication or the Stuff of Dreams* PHOTOS BY JAMES LEYNSE

DEDICATION OR THE STUFF OF DREAMS by Terrence McNally; Director, Michael Morris; Scenery, Narelle Sissons; Costumes, Laura Crow; Lighting, Jeff Croiter; Original Music and Sound, Lindsay Jones; Props, R. Jay Duckworth; Wigs, Paul Huntley; Fight Director, B.H. Barry; Production Stage Manager, Emily N. Wells; Assistant Stage Manager, Talia Krispel; Produced in association with Norma Langworthy, Jamie deRoy, and Michael Filerman; **Cast:** Nathan Lane (Lou Nuncie); Alison Fraser (Jessie, his partner), Miriam Shor (Ida Head, Jessie's daughter), Darren Pettie (Toby Cassidy, Ida's boyfriend), Michael Countryman (Arnold Chalk), Marian Seldes (Annabelle Willard), R.E. Rodgers (Edward, her driver); Replacement for show extension: Don Amendolia (Lou Nuncie)

Setting: A theatre. Now. New York premiere of a new play presented in two acts, 59E59 Theatre A; July 26–October 16, 2005 (Opening Night August 18, 2005); 24 previews, 60 performances.

The Cast of *The Right Kind of People*

THE RIGHT KIND OF PEOPLE by Charles Grodin; Director, Chris Smith; Scenery, Annie Smart; Costumes, Jenny Mannis; Lighiting, Russell Champa; Sound, Fabian Obispo; Production Stage Manager, Emily Wells; **Cast:** Doris Belack (Betty Butler/Mrs. Goldberg), Stephen Bradbury (Bill Hayes), Fred Burrell (Bruce Delson), Mitch Greenberg (Doug Bernstein), Keith Jochim (Jack Carmichael/Mr. Goldberg), Katherine Leask (Claire Wilson), Ed Owens (Frank Rashman), Robert Stanton (Tom Rashman), Evan Thompson (Coles Lang), John C. Vennema (Craig Hutto)

Setting: Fifth Avenue Co Op building, New York. Now. New York premiere of a new play presented; 59E59 Theatre A; January 24–March 5, 2006 (Opening Night February 9, 2006); 16 previews, 26 performances.

Danai Gurira and Nikkole Salter in *In the Continuum*

IN THE CONTINUUM by Danai Gurira and Nikkole Salter; Director, Robert O'Hara; **Cast:** Danai Gurira and Nikkole Salter

A new play presented without intermission; 59E59 Theatre A; Sunday and Wednesday evenings September 11–October 30, 2005 (Opening Night October 2, 2006); 6 previews, 9 performances. This production subsequently transferred to the Perry Street Theatre (see "Off Broadway Plays That Opened This Season" in this volume.

A SAFE HARBOR FOR ELIZABETH BISHOP by Marta Góes; Director, Richard Jay-Alexander; Scenery, Jeff Cowie; Costumes, Ilona Somogyi; Lighting, Russell Champa; Original Composition and Sound, Fitz Patton; Projections, Zachary Borovay; Wigs, Paul Huntley; Props, Hillary M. Baldwin; Production Stage Manager, Darcy Stephens; Assistant Stage Manager, Jonathan Donahue; Production Supervision, PRF Productions; Produced in association with Mahega Productions; **Cast:** Amy Irving (Elizabeth Bishop)

Setting: The port of Santos, Brazil, 1952. New York premiere of a new solo performance play presented without intermission; 59E59 Theatre A; March 21–April 30, 2006 (Opening Night March 30, 2006) 9 previews, 33 performances.

THE PUBLIC THEATER

FIFTIETH SEASON

Oskar Eustis, Producer; Mara Manus, Executive Director

Managing Director, Michael Hurst; Associate Producers, Peter Dubois, Steven Tabakin, Heidi Griffiths; Director of Institutional Development, Anne M. Scott; Director of Marketing, Tom Michel; Director of Production, Ruth E Sternberg; Director of Communications, Arlene R. Kriv; Casting, Jordan Thaler and Heidi Griffiths; Press, Sam Neuman

AS YOU LIKE IT by William Shakespeare; Original music by Vadim Feichtner and William Finn; Director, Mark Lamos; Choreography, Sean Curran; Scenery, Riccardo Hernández; Costumes, Candice Donnelly; Lighting, Peter Kaczorowski; Sound, Acme Sound Partners; Production Stage Manager, Michael McGoff; Assistant Stage Manager, Francesca Russell; Vocal Coach, Liz Smith; Orchestrations, Michael Starobin; **Cast:** Vanessa Aspillaga (Audrey), Alec Beard (Ensemble), Brian Bedford (Jaques), Kristen Bush (Ensemble), Lynn Collins (Rosalind), Helmar Augustus Cooper (Corin), David Cromwell (Duke Frederick/Duke Senior), Jordan Dean (Ensemble), Gregory Derelian (Charles/Ensemble), Jennifer Dundas (Phoebe), Michael Esper (Silvius/Ensemble), Al Espinosa (Oliver), Danny Fetter (Boy), Herb Foster (Adam), Enver Gjokaj (Jacques de Boys/Ensemble), Jocelyn Green (Ensemble), Brian Henderson (Ensemble), Dale Ho (Lord/Ensemble), Chad Hoeppner (Ensemble), Andre Holland (Ensemble), Jennifer Ikeda (Celia), Steve Kazee (Ensemble), Philip Kerr (Le Beau), John G. Preston (First Lord), Bob Stillman (Sir Oliver Martext), Richard Thomas (Touchstone), Reynaldo Valentin (Lord/Ensemble), James Waterston (Orlando)

Setting: Oliver's Orchard, Duke Frederick's Court, and the Forest of Arden. Revival of the play presented in two acts; Delacorte Theatre; June 12 – July 17, 2005 (Opening Night June 25, 2005); 18 performances.

Richard Thomas, Brian Bedford in *As You Like It* PHOTO BY MICHAL DANIEL

TWO GENTLEMEN OF VERONA Adapted by John Guare and Mel Shapiro, lyrics by John Guare, music by Galt MacDermot, based on the play by William Shakespeare; Director and Choreography, Kathleen Marshall; Scenery, Riccardo Hernández; Costumes, Martin Pakledinaz; Lighting, Peter Kaczorowski; Sound, Acme Sound Partners; Music Director/Conductor, Kimberly Grigsby; Music Supervisor, Rob Fisher; Music Coordinator, Seymour Red Press; Animal Trainer, William Berloni; Production Stage Manager, Lori Lundquist; Assistant Director, Marc Bruni; Assistant Choreography, David Eggers; Music Copying, Emily Grishman; Assistant Stage Manager, Buzz Cohen; **Cast:** Don Stephenson (Vissi D'Amore Boy/Thurio),John Cariani (Speed), Norm Lewis (Valentine), Oscar Isaac (Proteus), Rosario Dawson (Julia), Megan Lawrence (Lucetta), David Costabile (Launce), Kate Chapman (Vissi D'Amore Girl), Richard Ruiz (Antonio), Mel Johnson, Jr. (Duke of Milan), Renee Elise Goldsberry (Silvia), Paolo Montalban (Eglamour), Danielle Lee Greaves (Milkmaid); Buster (Crab, Launce's dog); Tracee Beazer, Bridget Berger, Kate Chapman, Shakiem Evans, Danielle Lee Greaves, Joanne Javien, Raymond J. Lee, Dequina Moore, Maurice Murphy, Richard Ruiz, Stacey Sargeant, Amber Stone, Will Swenson, JD Webster, Noah Weisberg (Citzens of Verona and Milan); Swings: Christine DiGiallonardo, Rubén Flores; **Musicians:** Kimberly Grigsby (Conductor/keyboard), Allen Won (woodwinds), Christian Jaudes and Elaine Burt (trumpets), Wayne Goodman (trombone), Steve Bargonetti (guitar/mandolin), Wilbur Bascomb (bass), Brian Brake (drums), Joseph Cardello (percussion)

Musical Numbers: Love, Is That You?, Summer, Summer, I Love My Father, That's A Very Interesting Question, I'd Like To Be A Rose, Thou Julia, Thou Has Metamorphosed Me, Symphony, I Am Not Interested In Love, Love, Is That You? (reprise), Thou, Proteus, Thou Has Metamorphosed Me, What Does A Lover Pack?, Pearls, I Love My Father (reprise), Two Gentlemen Of Verona, Follow The Rainbow, Where's North?, Bring All The Boys Back Home, Who is Sylvia?, Love's Revenge, To Whom It May Concern, Night Letter, Love's Revenge (reprise), Calla Lily Lady, Land Of Betrayal, Thurio's Samba, Hot Lover, What A Nice Idea, Who is Sylvia? (reprise), Love Me, Eglamour, Kidnapped, Eglamour (reprise), Mansion, What's A Nice Girl Like Her, Don't Have the Baby, Love, Is That You? (reprise), Milkmaid, I Love My Father (reprise), Love Has Driven Me Sane

Setting: Verona, Milan, and a Forest. Revival of the musical presented in two acts; Delacorte Theatre; August 16 – September 25, 2005 (Opening Night August 28, 2005); 24 performances. Originally produced by the New York Shakespeare Festival at the St. James Theatre December 1, 1971 where it ran for 613 performances (see *Theatre World* Volume 28, page 24).

SEE WHAT I WANNA SEE Book, music and lyrics by Michael John LaChiusa, suggested by the stories of Ryunosuke Akutagawa as translated by Takashi Kojimo; Director, Ted Sperling; Music Director, Chris Fenwick; Choreography, Jonathan Butterell; Scenery, Tom Lynch; Costumes, Elizabeth Caitlin Ward; Lighting, Christopher Akerlind; Sound, Acme Sound Partners; Orchestrations, Bruce Coughlin; Music Coordinator, Seymour Red Press; Production Stage Manager, Heather Cousens; Company Manager, Steve Showalter; Assistant Stage Manager, Sharika Niles; **Cast:** Marc Kudisch (Morito/The Husband/ A CPA), Aaron Lohr (A Thief/A Reporter), Idina Menzel (Kesa/The Wife/An Actress), Henry Stram (The Janitor/A Priest), Mary Testa (A Medium/Aunt Monica); **Musicians:** Chris Fenwick (Conductor/piano), Todd Groves (reed 1), John Winder (reed 2), Diana Herold and Mark Sherman (percussion), Mark Vanderpoel (bass), Norbert Goldberg (drums); Cast recording: Sh-K-Boom/Ghostlight Records 7915584408-2

Musical Numbers: Act One: (Kesa and Morito) Kesa; (R Shoman): The Janitor's Statement, The Thief's Statement/She Looked at Me, See What I Wanna See, Big Money, The Park/You'll Go Away With Me, Murder, Best Not to Get Involved,

The Wife's Statement, Louie, The Medium and Husband's Statement, You'll Go Away With Me (Quartet), No More, Simple As This, Janitor's Statement, Light in the East, Finale Act 1; Act Two: (*Kesa and Morito*) Morito; (*Gloryday*) Confession/Last Year, The Greatest Practical Joke, First Message, Central Park, Second Message, Coffee, Gloryday, Curiosity/Prayer, Third Message/Feed the Lions, There Will Be a Miracle, Prayer (reprise), Rising Up/Finale Act 2

Setting: *Kesa and Morito:* Medieval Japan. *R Shoman:* New York City, 1951. *Gloryday:* New York City, the present. New York premiere of a new musical of three tales presented in two acts; Anspacher Theater; October 11–December 4, 2005 (Opening Night October 30, 2005); 60 performances.

THE RUBY SUNRISE by Rinne Groff; Director, Oskar Eustis; Scenery, Eugene Lee; Costumes, Deborah Newhall; Lighting, Deb Sullivan; Sound, Bray Poor; Production Stage Manager, Buzz Cohen; **Cast:** Audra Blaser (Suzie Tyrone), Patch Darragh (Henry/Paul Benjamin), Jason Butler Harner (Tad Rose), Marin Ireland (Ruby/Elizabeth Hunter), Richard Masur (Martin Marcus), Anne Scurria (Lois Haver/ Ethel Reed), Maggie Siff (Lulu)

Setting: Kokomo, Indiana, 1927 and New York City, 1952. New York premiere of a new play in three parts presented in two acts; Martinson Hall; November 1–December 4, 2005 (Opening Night November 16, 2006); 37 performances.

Sandra Oh in *Satellites*

The Company of *Stuff Happens* PHOTOS BY MICHAL DANIEL

MEASURE FOR PLEASURE by David Grimm; Director, Peter DuBois; Scenery, Alexander Dodge; Costumes, Anita Yavich; Lighting, Christopher Akerlind; Sound, Tony Smolenski IV and Walter Trarbach; Music, Peter Golub; Style Consultant, B.H. Barry; Production Stage Manager, Jane Pole; **Cast:** Michael Stuhlbarg (Will Blunt), Wayne Knight (Sir Peter Lustforth), Saxon Palmer (Capt. Dick Dashwood), Euan Morton (Molly Tawdry), Suzanne Bertish (Lady Vanity Lustforth), Susan Blommaert (Dame Stickle), Emily Swallow (Hermione Goode), Frederick Hamilton (Foorman), Ryan Tresser (Footman)

Setting: England, 1751. World premiere of a new play presented in two acts; Anspacher Theatre; February 21–March 26, 2006 (Opening night March 6, 2006); 39 performances.

STUFF HAPPENS by David Hare; Director, Daniel Sullivan; Scenery, Riccardo Hernández; Costumes, Jess Goldstein; Lighting, Pat Collins; Sound, Dan Moses Schreier; Production Stage Manager, James Latus; **Cast:** George Bartenieff (Hans Blix/Jack Straw), Jeffrey DeMunn (Donald Rumsfeld), Glenn Fleshler (George Tenet), Zach Grenier (Dick Cheney), Lameece Issaq (Palestinian Academic), Peter Francis James (Colin Powell), Byron Jennings (Tony Blair), Ken Marks (David Manning/Michael Gerson), David Pittu (Paul Wolfowitz/Sir Richard Dearlove), Gloria Reuben (Condoleezza Rice), Jay O. Sanders (George W. Bush), Thomas Schall (Alastair Campbell/Jeremy Greenstock), Armand Schultz (Jonathan Powell/Robin Cook), Robert Sella (Angry Journalist/Dominique De Villepin), Brenda Wehle (New Labour Politician/ Laura Bush), Waleed F. Zuaiter (Iraqi Exile/Trevor Mac); Extension Replacements: Reed Birney (Tony Blair); Tony Carlin (Jonathan Powell/Robin Cook); and Larry Pine (Donald Rumsfeld)

Setting: Washington D.C., 2003. New York premiere of a new play presented in two acts; Newman Theatre; March 28–June 25, 2006 (Opening Night April 13, 2006); 103 performances.

SATELLITES by Diana Son; Director, Michael Greif; Scenery, Mark Wendland; Costumes, Miranda Hoffman; Lighting, Kenneth Posner; Sound, Tony Smolenski IV and Walter Trarbach; Music, Michael Friedman; Production Stage Manager, Martha Donaldson; **Cast:** Ron Brice (Walter), Kevin Carroll (Miles), Johanna Day (Kit), Ron Cephas Jones (Reggie), Satya Lee (Mrs. Chae), Sandra Oh (Nina), Clarke Thorell (Eric)

Setting: Brooklyn, New York, the present. World premiere of a new play presented without intermission; Martinson Hall; May 30–July 2, 2006 (Opening Night June 18, 2006); 39 performances.

LABYRINTH THEATRE

IN RESIDENCE AT THE PUBLIC THEATER

FOURTEENTH SEASON

Philip Seymour Hoffman and John Ortiz, Artistic Directors; Steve Asher, Executive Director

Associate Artistic Director, Florencia Lozano; Associate Producer, Marieke Gaboury; Marketing Director, Siobhan Foley; Director of Development, Veronica R. Bainbridge; Company Manager, Kristina Poe; Marketing Associate, Lyssa Mandel; Literary Manager, Andrea Ciannavei; Press, Boneau/Bryan-Brown, Juliana Hannett, Matt Ross

MASSACRE (SING TO YOUR CHILDREN) by José Rivera; Director, Kate Whoriskey; Scenery, Cameron Anderson; Costumes, Mattie Ullrich; Lighting, Jason Lyons; Music Composition and Sound, David Meschter; Production Stage Manager, Betsy Ayer; **Cast:** Julian Acosta, Elizabeth Canavan, Ron Cephas Jones, Florencia Lozano, Adrian Martinez, Jason Manuel Olazábal, Matt Saldívar and Sona Tatoyan

Setting: Granville, New Hampshire. A new play presented in two acts; Shiva Theatre; October 5–23, 2005; 15 performances.

ALL THE BAD THINGS by Cusi Cram; Director, Paula Pizzi; Scenery, Andromache Chalfant; Costumes, Maggie Dick; Lighting, Sarah Sidman; Composer and Sound, Rob Kaplowitz; Production Stage Manager, Marc Eardley; **Cast:** Vanessa Aspillaga (Sue), Jennifer Lauren Grant (Lianne), Peter Hirsch (David), Justin Reinsilber (Mike), Alexa Scott-Flaherty (Fernanda), Phyllis Somerville (Elsabeth)

Setting: West Village apartment, New York, now. A new play presented in two acts; Shiva Theatre; February 15–March 5, 2006; 15 performances.

SCHOOL OF THE AMERICAS by José Rivera; Director, Mark Wing-Davey; Produced in association with The Public Theater; Scenery, Andromache Chalfant; Costumes, Mimi O'Donnell; Lighting, David Weiner; Sound, Rob Kaplowitz; Production Stage Manager, Damon W. Arrington; Animal Trainer, William Berloni; **Cast:** Karina Arroyave (Lucila Cortes), Raul Castillo (Guard), Nathan LeBron (Guard), John Ortiz (Che Guevara), Felix Solis (Felix Rodriguez), Patricia Velasquez (Julia Cortes)

World premiere of a new play presented in two acts; Shiva Theatre; June 20–July 23, 2006 (Opening Night July 6, 2006); 40 performances.

Florencia Lozano and Julian Acosta in *Massacre (Sing to Your Children)* PHOTOS BY MONIQUE CARBONI

Justin Reinsilber and Vanessa Aspillaga in *All The Bad Things*

John Ortiz and Patricia Velasquez in *School of the Americas*

ROUNDABOUT THEATRE COMPANY

FORTIETH SEASON

Todd Haimes, Artistic Director; Harold Wolpert, Managing Director; Julia C. Levy, Executive Director of External Affairs; Scott Ellis, Associate Artistic Director

Founding Director, Gene Feist; Director of Artistic Development/Casting, Jim Carnahan; Education Director, Megan Kirkpatrick; General Manager, Sydney Beers; General Manager Steinberg Center, Don-Scott Cooper; Director of Marketing, David B. Steffen; Director of Development, Jeffory Lawson; Director of Sales, Jim Seggelink; Production Manager, Kai Brothers; Casting, Mele Nagler; Press, Boneau/Bryan-Brown

THE PARIS LETTER by Jon Robin Baitz; Director, Doug Hughes; Scenery, John Lee Beatty; Costumes, Catherine Zuber; Lighting, Peter Kaczorowski; Original Music and Sound, David Van Tieghem; Production Stage Manager, Diane DiVita; Stage Manager, Rachel S. McCutchen; **Cast:** Jason Butler Harner (Burt Sarris/Young Anton), Ron Rifkin (Sandy Sonnenberg/Dr. Moritz Schiffman), John Glover (Anton Kilgallen), Michele Pawk (Katie Arlen/Lillian Sonnenberg), Daniel Eric Gold (Sam Arlen/Young Sandy), Christopher Czyz (Waiter); Understudies/Standbys: Michael Bakkensen, Len Kliban, Martin LaPlatney, Susan Pellegrino.

Setting: 1962–2002. New York and Paris. A play presented in two acts; Laura Pels Theatre, May 13–August 7, 2005 (Opening Night June 12, 2005); 100 performances.

John Ellison Conlee and Denis O'Hare in *Pig Farm*

MR. MARMALADE by Noah Haidle; Director, Michael Greif; Scenery, Allen Moyer; Costumes, Constance Hoffman; Lighting, Kevin Adams; Original Compositions, Michael Friedman; Sound, Walter Trarbach and Tony Smolenski IV; Production Stage Manager, Lori M. Doyle; Stage Manager, Dyanne M. McNamara; **Cast:** Mamie Gummer (Lucy), Michael C. Hall (Mr. Marmalade), Virginia Louise Smith (Sookie/Emily/Sunflower), David Costabile (Bradley), Brian Hutchison (George/Cactus/Bob), Pablo Schreiber (Larry); Understudies/Standbys: Julie Jesneck, Frances Mercanti-Anthony, Alex Cranmer, Quincy Dunn-Baker.

Setting: The Present. A living room in New Jersey. A play presented without intermission; Laura Pels Theatre, November 1, 2005–January 29, 2006 (Opening Night November 20, 2005); 101 performances.

Michael C. Hall, Mamie Gummer, David Costabile in *Mr. Marmalade* PHOTOS BY JOAN MARCUS

ENTERTAINING MR. SLOAN by Joe Orton; Director, Scott Ellis; Scenery, Allen Moyer; Costumes, Michael Krass; Lighting, Kenneth Posner; Sound, John Gromada; Hair and Wigs, Paul Huntley; Production Stage Manager, Diane DiVita; Dialect Coach, Kate Maré; Fight Director, Rick Sordelet; Stage Manager, Megan Smith; **Cast:** Jan Maxwell (Kath), Chris Carmack (Sloane), Richard Easton (Kemp), Alec Baldwin (Ed); Replacements: Barbara Sims (Kath); Understudies/Standbys: Tony Carlin, Kate Guyton, Philip LeStrange, Richard Short.

Setting: September and March, mid-1960s. Outside of London. A play presented in two acts; Laura Pels Theatre; February 17–May 21, 2006 (Opening Night March 16, 2006); 106 performances.

PIG FARM by Greg Kotis; Produced in collaboration with the Old Globe Theatre, San Diego; Director, John Rando; Scenery, Scott Pask; Costumes, Gregory Gale; Lighting, Brian MacDevitt; Original Music and Sound, John Gromada; Fight Director, Steve Rankin; Hair and Make Up, Josh Marquette; Production Stage Manager, Pat Sosnow; **Cast:** John Ellison Conlee (Tom), Katie Finneran (Tina), Logan Marshall-Green (Tim), Denis O'Hare (Teddy); Replacement: Nicholas Heck (Tim)

Setting: A farm somewhere in America. World premiere of a new play presented in two acts; Laura Pels Theatre; June 9–September 3, 2006 (Opening Night June 27, 2006); 96 performances.

Chris Carmack, Alec Baldwin in *Entertaining Mr. Sloan*

SECOND STAGE THEATRE

TWENTY-SIXTH/TWENTY-SEVENTH SEASON*

Carole Rothman, Artistic Director; Executive Director, Timothy J. McClimon, C. Barrack Evans, General Manager

Associate Artistic Director, Christopher Burney; Director of Development, Sarah Bordy; Director of Marketing, Melissa Skinner; Ticket Services Manager, Kathleen Grace; Production Manager, Jeff Wild; Technical Director, Robert G. Mahon III; Literary Manager, Elizabeth Bennett; Casting, Tara Rubin Casting; Press, Richard Kornberg and Associates, Tom D'Ambrosio, Don Summa, Rick Miramontez, Carrie Friedman

BIRDIE BLUE by Cheryl L. West; Director, Seret Scott; Scenery, Anna Louizos; Costumes, Emilio Sousa; Lighting, Don Holder; Sound, Obadiah Eaves; Production Stage Manager, Lisa J. Snodgrass; Stage Manager, Jennifer O'Byrne; Casting Director, Eric Woddall; **Cast:** S. Epatha Merkerson (Birdie), Billy Porter (Bam/Little Pimp/Sook/Minerva), Charles Weldon (Jackson)

New York premiere of a play presented without intermission; June 2 – July 17, 2005 (Opening Night June 23, 2005); 61 performances.

SWIMMING IN THE SHALLOWS by Adam Bock; Director, Trip Cullman; Scenery, David Korins; Lighting, Paul Whitaker; Sound, Bart Fasbender; Production Stage Manager, Lori Ann Zepp; Stage Manager, Diane M. Ballering; **Cast:** Michael Arden (Nick), Rosemarie DeWitt (Donna), Murphy Guyer (Bob), Logan Marshall-Green (Shark), Susan Pourfar (Carla Carla), Mary Shultz (Barb)

Setting: The present. Twig, Rhode Island. New York premiere of a new play presented without intermission; McGinn/Cazele Theatre; June 21 – July 17, 2005 (Opening Night June 28, 2005); 28 performances.

Billy Porter and S. Epatha Merkerson (Birdie) in *Birdie Blue* PHOTOS BY JOAN MARCUS

Taye Diggs in *A Soldier's Play*

THE DEAR BOY by Dan O'Brien; Director, Michael John Garces; Scenery, Wilson Chin; Costumes, Amela Baksic; Lighting, Ben Stanton; Sound, Sunil Rajan; Production Stage Manager, Rachel J. Perlman; Stage Manager, Stephanie Gatton; **Cast:** T. Scott Cunningham (Richard Purdy); Danny Gerroll (James Flanagan); Dan McCabe (James Doyle); Susan Pourfar (Elise Sanger)

Setting: December, 1990. Scarsdale Public High School and various locations in New York City. World premiere of a new play presented without intermission; McGinn/Cazele Theatre; August 1 – 27, 2005 (Opening Night August 8, 2005); 28 performances.

A SOLDIER'S PLAY by Charles Fuller; Director, Jo Bonney; Scenery, Neil Patel; Costumes, David Zinn; Lighting, David Weiner; Sound, Fitz Patton; Production Stage Manager, C. Randall White; Stage Manager, Rachel J. Perlman; Fight Director, Rick Sordelet; Dialect Coach, Deborah Hecht; Music Supervisor, Steven Bargonetti; **Cast:** Teagle F. Bougere (Private Tony Smalls), Joaquin Perez Campbell (Lieutenant Byrd), Mike Colter (Private C.J. Memphis), Taye Diggs (Captain Richard Davenport), Nelsan Ellis (Corporal Bernard Cobb), Joe Forbrich (Captain Wilcox), Michael Genet (Private James Wilkie), Royce Johnson (Corporal Ellis), Anthony Mackie (Private First Class Melvin Peterson), James McDaniel (Tech Sergeant Vernon C. Waters), Dorian Missick (Private Louis Henson), Steven Pasquale (Captain Charles Taylor)

Setting: 1944. Fort Neal, Louisiana. Revival of a play presented in two acts; September 20 – November 27, 2005 (Opening Night October 17, 2005); 82 performances. Originally produced by the Negro Ensemble Company at Theatre Four November 10, 1981 (See *Theatre World* Volume 38, page 88). Recipient of the 1982 Pulitzer Prize.

Julie White and Neal Huff in *The Little Dog Laughed* PHOTO BY JOAN MARCUS

Debra Monk and Judy Greer in *Show People* PHOTO BY JOAN MARCUS

THE LITTLE DOG LAUGHED by Douglas Carter Beane; Director, Scott Ellis; Scenery, Allen Moyer; Costumes, Jeff Mahshie; Lighting, Don Holder; Original Music and Sound, Lewis Flinn; Production Stage Manager, Linda Marvel; Stage Manager, Heather Prince; **Cast:** Johnny Galecki (Alex), Neal Huff (Mitchell), Zoe Lister-Jones (Ellen), Julie White (Diane)

Setting: New York and Los Angeles. Now. World premiere of a new play presented in two acts; December 13, 2005–February 26, 2006 (Opening Night January 9, 2006); 81 performances.

SHOW PEOPLE by Paul Weitz; Director, Peter Askin; Scenery, Heidi Ettinger; Costumes, Jeff Mahshie; Lighting, Jeff Croiter; Original Music and Sound, Lewis Flinn; Production Stage Manager, Rachel J. Perlman; Stage Manager, Kit Ingui; **Cast:** Ty Burrell (Tom), Judy Greer (Natalie), Debra Monk (Marnie), Lawrence Pressman (Jerry)

Setting: The Present. Montauk. World premiere of a new play presented in two acts; March 16–April 30, 2006 (Opening Night April 6, 2006); 55 performances.

THE WATER'S EDGE by Theresa Rebeck; Director, Will Frears; Scenery, Alexander Dodge; Costumes, Junghyun Georgia Lee; Lighting, Frances Aronson; Sound, Vincent Olivieri; Original Music, Michael Friedman; Production Stage Manager, Roy Harris; Stage Manager, Shanna Spinello; **Cast:** Kate Burton (Helen), Tony Goldwyn (Richard), Mamie Gummer (Erica), Austin Lysy (Nate), Katharine Powell (Lucy)

New York premiere of a play presented in two acts; May 23–July 9, 2006 (Opening Night June 14, 2006); 56 performances.

GETTING HOME by Anton Dudley; Director, David Schweizer; Scenery Andrew Lieberman; Costumes, Erin Chianani; Lighting, Aaron Black; Sound, Ryan Rumery; Production Stage Manager, Rachel J. Perlman; Stage Manager, Stephanie Atlan; **Cast:** Marcy Harriell (Jen/Kadeeshya), Brian Henderson (Tristan/Viktor/Laser), Manu Narayan (Cab Driver/Craig/Nalesh)

Setting: Present day NYC and other places of the human imagination. World premiere of a new play presented without intermission; McGinn/Cazele Theatre; June 5–July 1, 2006 (Opening Night June 14, 2006); 28 performances.

ALL THIS INTIMACY by Rajiv Joseph; Director, Giovanna Sardelli; Scenery, David Newell; Costumes, Amy Landecker; Lighting, Rie Ono; Sound, Bart Fasbender; Production Stage Manager, Rachel J. Perlman; Stage Manager, Stephanie Atlan; **Cast:** Gretchen Egolf (Jen), Adam Green (Seth), Amy Landecker (Maureen), Kate Nowlin (Franny), Krysten Ritter (Becca), Thomas Sadoski (Ty)

Setting: Present. Brooklyn and Manhattan. A new play presented in two acts; McGinn/Cazale Theatre; July 17–August 12, 2006 (Opening Night July 27, 2006); 28 performances.

*Second Stage Theatre's season runs from September to September; thus, the first three entries above mark the end of their twenty-sixth season and the remaining shows were a part of their twenty-seventh season.

Manu Narayan, Marcy Harriell, Brian Henderson in *Getting Home* PHOTO BY CAROL ROSEGG

SIGNATURE THEATRE COMPANY

FIFTEENTH SEASON—PART ONE: INAUGURAL SIGNATURE SERIES

James Houghton, Founding Artistic Director; Kathryn M. Lipuma, Executive Director

Transition and Capital Projects Director, Jodi Schoenbrun Carter; Artistic Associate, Beth Whitaker; Production Manager, Chris Moses, Marketing Manger, Nella Vera; Associate General Manager, Adam Bernstein; Grants Coordinator, Brooke McCartny; Transition and Capital Projects Administrator, Dara Ann Prushansky; Casting, Bernard Telsey; Press, The Publicity Office, Bob Fennell, Michael Borowski, Candi Adams; Playwrights in residence: Horton Foote and John Guare

THE TRIP TO BOUNTIFUL by Horton Foote; Director, Harris Yulin; Scenery, E. David Cosier; Costumes, Martin Pakledinaz; Lighting, Frank Griadeau; Original Music and Sound, Brett R. Jarvis, Loren Toolajian; Additional Music and Sound, Fitz Patton, Harris Skibell; Production Stage Manager, Coel Bonenberger; **Cast:** Lois Smith (Carrie Watts), Hallie Foote (Jessie Mae Watts), Devon Abner (Ludie), Meghan Andrews (Thelma), Jim Demares (Sheriff), Gene Jones (Houston Ticket Man #1), Sam Kitchen (Houston Ticket Man #2), Frank Giradeau (Harrison Ticket Man)

Setting: A Houston Apartment; The Trip, A Country Place, 1950's. Revival of a play presented without intermission; Peter Norton Space; November 15, 2005 – March 11, 2006 (Opening night: December 4, 2005); 128 performances.

Lois Smith in *A Trip to Bountiful* PHOTOS BY CAROL ROSEGG

Sherie René Scott and Lili Taylor in *Landscape of the Body*

LANDSCAPE OF THE BODY Text and songs by John Guare; Director, Michael Greif; Additional Music/Music Director, Michael Friedman; Scenery, Allen Moyer; Costumes, Miranda Hoffman; Lighting, Howell Binkley; Sound, Brett R. Jarvis; Fight Director, Rick Sordelet; Dialect Coach, Stephen Gabis; Production Stage Manager, Cole Bonenberger; Assistant Stage Manager, Winnie Y. Lok; **Cast:** Lili Taylor (Betty), Paul Sparks (Capt. Marvin Holahan), Sherie Rene Scott (Rosalie), Bernard White (Raulito), Stephen Scott Scarpulla (Bert), Paul Iacono (Donny), Jill Shackner (Joanne), Colby Minifie (Margie), Brian Sgambati (Masked Man/Dope King of Providence/Bank Teller), Jonathan Fried (Durwood Peach)

Setting: Greenwich Village, New York, mid-1970s. Revival of the play presented in two acts; Peter Norton Space; March 28 – May 28, 2006 (Opening night: April 16, 2006); 69 performances.

VINEYARD THEATRE

TWENTY-FIFTH SEASON

Douglas Aibel, Artistic Director; Jennifer Garvey-Blackwell, Executive Director

Director of Production & Finance, Reed Ridgley; General Manager, Rebecca Habel; Associate Artistic Director, Sarah Stern; Director of Marketing & Audience Development, Shane Guiter; Production Manager, Ben Morris; Company Manager, Rachel E. Ayers; Marketing Associate, Y. Angel Wuellner; Development Associate, Allison Geffner; Box Office Manager, Dennis Hruska; Casting, Cindy Tolan; Press, Sam Rudy, Bob Lasko, Dale Heller

MIRACLE BROTHERS Book, music, lyrics, arrangements by Kristen Childs; Director, Tina Landau, Music Director, Fred Carl; Choreography, Mark Dendy; Scenery, G.W. Mercier; Costumes, Anita Yavich; Lighting, Scott Zielinski; Sound, Brett Jarvis; Orchestrations, Daryl Waters; Projection Design, Jan Hartley; Fight Director, Rick Sordelet; Capoeira Consultant, Jelon Viera; Production Stage Manager, Bret Torbeck; Stage Manager, Kit Ingui; Additional Casting, Dave Clemmons; Associate Music Directors John DiPinto and Carl Haan; Music Copying, Emily Grishman and Katharine Edmonds; **Cast:** Kerry Butler (Isabel), Cheryl Freeman (Felicidade), Jay Goede (Lascivio/Xavier), Anika Larsen (Juan), Nicole Leach (Ginga), Tyler Maynard (Fernando), Darrell Moultrie (Pato), Clifton Oliver (Green Eyes), Karen Olivo (Jeca), Devin Richards (Henrique), Gregory Treco (Maroto), William Youmans (Rancor); **Orchestra:** John DePinto (keyboards), Carl Haan (keyboards), Roland Guerero (percussion), Manny Moreira (guitars), Roger Squitero (percussion)

Musical Numbers: Botos in Brazil, Tell Me Your Tale, The World Belongs To Me, Mundo Paraiso, A Mother's Lament, Tonight You Learn Capoeira; Cuckold, Tears Of Blood, All We Were Doing, Tell Me Your Tale (reprise), Saudade (Homesickness), Bandeirantes!, It's Really All Right With Me, I Gotta Get Ta Palmares, My True, True Love, Pirate Orientation/Query, You Bring Me Rain, Green Eyes, Mundo Paraiso Reprise (Finale)

Setting: Bahia, Brazil. The Present and the Past. World premiere of a new musical presented in two acts; Gertrude and Irving Dimson Theatre; August 26–October 16, 2005 (Opening Night September 18, 2005); 56 performances.

Mary Pat Gleason in *Stopping Traffic* PHOTOS BY CAROL ROSEGG

Darrell Moultrie, Gregory Treco, Karen Olivo in *Miracle Brothers*

[TITLE OF SHOW] Music and lyrics By Jeff Bowen, book by Hunter Bell; Director and Choreography, Michael Berresse; Music Director and Arrangements, Larry Pressgrove; Scenery, Neil Patel; Costumes, Chase Tyler; Lighting, Ken Billington and Jason Kantrowitz; Sound, ACME Sound Partners, LLC.; Production Stage Manager, Martha Donaldson; Assistant Stage Manager, Tom Reynolds; **Cast:** Hunter Bell (Hunter), Susan Blackwell (Susan), Heidi Blickenstaff (Heidi), Jeff Bowen (Jeff); **Musician:** Larry Pressgrove (Piano)

Musical Numbers: Untitled Opening Number, Two Nobodies in New York, An Original Musical, Monkeys and Playbills, Part of It All, I Am Playing Me, What Kind of Girl is She?, Die Vampire, Die, Filling Out the Form, September Song (Festival Medley), Secondary Characters, Montage/Photo Shoot, A Way Back to Then, Nine People's Favorite Thing

Setting: [place]. [time]. A new musical presented without intermission; Gertrude and Irving Dimson Theatre; February 15–April 30, 2006 (Opening Night February 25, 2006); 68 performances.

STOPPING TRAFFIC by Mary Pat Gleason; Director, Lonny Price; Scenery, Neil Patel, Costumes, Tracy Christensen; Lighting, David Weiner; Sound, Obadiah Eaves; Stage Manager, Kate Hefel; **Cast:** Mary Pat Gleason (Herself)

A solo autobiographical performance play presented without intermission; Gertrude and Irving Dimson Theatre; May 24–July 2, 2006 (Opening Night June 7, 2006) 30 performances.

Jeff Bowen and Hunter Bell in *[title of show]*

WOMEN'S PROJECT

TWENTY-EIGHTH SEASON

Loretta Greco, Producing Artistic Director; Julie Crosby, PhD., Managing Director

Associate Artistic Director, Lisa McNulty; General Manager, Wei-Jie Chou; Development Consultants, Paul Slee, Kat Williams; Development Associate, Maagan Lesperance; Artistic Programs Administrator, Heather Honnold; Financial Services, Patricia Taylor; Education Director, Frances Tarr; Production Manager, Dynamic Productions (Brian Rosenblum and Craig Sanoguiera, Allison Bond); Press, Barlow-Hartman, Carol Fineman and Leslie Baden

WOMEN'S WORK
Annual festival of new and contemporary work by women

YELLOW by Cybele Pascal, directed by Lisa Rothe; November 7, 2005

IMAGINARY FRIENDS by Karen Hartman, Laura Flanagan, Chris Wells; November 7, 2005

BECHNYA by Saviana Stanescu; directed by Suzanne Agins; November 8, 2005

THE RICH SILK OF IT by Deb Margolin, directed by Suzanne Agins; November 8, 2005

GOING AFTER ALICE by Megan Mostyn-Brown, directed by Meredith McDonough; November 9th

KILLING WOMEN by Marisa Wegrzyn; directed by Elyse Singer, Co-sponsored by the Hourglass Group; November 14th, 2005

LAS MENINAS by Lynn Nottage, directed by Kate Whoriskey; November 15, 2005

STILL LIFE by Emily Mann, directed by Tamsen Wolff; November 16, 2005

VICTORIA MARTIN: MATH QUEEN by Kate Walat, directed by Loretta Greco; November 17, 2005

(Top) Barnaby Carpenter, Kelly McAndrew (Bottom) Vanessa Aspillaga, Tug Coker in *The Cataract* PHOTOS BY T. CHARLES ERICKSON

JUMP/CUT by Neena Beber; Director, Leigh Silverman; Scenery, Narelle Sissons; Costumes, Miranda Hoffman; Lighting, Mary Louise Geiger; Original Music and Sound, Jill BC DuBoff; Projection Design, Brian Beasley; Production Stage Manager, Leigh Boone; Dramaturg, Jamee Freedus; **Cast:** Michi Barall (Karen), Luke Kirby (Dave), Thomas Sadoski (Paul)

New York premiere of a new play presented in two acts; Julia Miles Theatre; February 1–26, 2006 (Opening Night February 12, 2006); 26 performances.

THE CATARACT by Lisa D'Amour; Director, Katie Pearl; Scenery, Rachel Hauck; Costumes, Sarah Beers; Lighting, Sarah Sidman; Sound, Daniel Baker; Original Music, The Chord Collective; Production Stage Manager, Leigh Boone; Technical Director, John Martinez; Assistant Stage Manager, Colleen Danaher; **Cast:** Vanessa Aspillaga (Dinah), Barnaby Carpenter (Cyrus), Tug Coker (Dan), Kelly McAndrew (Lottie)

New York premiere of a new play presented in two acts; Julia Miles Theatre; March 22–April 15, 2006 (Opening Night April 2, 2006); 26 performances.

Luke Kirby, Michi Barall, Thomas Sadoski in *Jump/Cut*

YORK THEATRE COMPANY

THIRTY-SEVENTH SEASON

James Morgan, Artistic Director; David McCoy, Chairman of the Board; Founding Director, Janet Hayes Walker

Associate Artistic Director, Brian Blythe; Director of Development, Nancy P. Barry; Company Administrator, Alyssa Seiden; Production Manager, Chris Robinson; Marketing Director, Sol Lieberman; Technical Director, Scott F. Dela Cruz; Developmental Reading Series Coordinator, Jeff Landsman; Casting, Norman Meranus; Press, Helene Davis, Shaffer-Coyle Public Relations

MUSICALS IN MUFTI (NINETEENTH SEASON)

Musical Theatre Gems in Staged Concert Performances

I CAN GET IT FOR YOU WHOLESALE Book by Jerome Weidman, music and lyrics by Harold Rome, Director, Richard Sabellico; Music Director, Danny Percefull; Lighting, Chris Robinson; Production Stage Manager, Allison Deutsch; Assistant Stage Manager, Andrea Jo Martin; **Cast:** Anne Torsiglieri (Miss Marmelstein), Ray DeMattis (Maurice Pulvermacher), Josh Prince (Harry Bogen), Christopher Totten (Tootsie Maltz), Rena Strober (Ruthie Rifkin), Jana Robbins (Mrs. Bogen), Jodi Stevens (Martha Mills), Andréa Burns (Blanche Bushkin), Chris Hoch (Meyer Bushkin), Jonathan Hammond (Teddy Asch), Christopher Totten (Sheldon Bogen)

Musical Numbers: The Way Things Are, When Gemini Meets Capricorn, Momma, Momma, Momma, The Sound Of Money, The Family Way, Too Soon, Who Knows?, Ballad of the Garment Trade, A Gift Today, Miss Marmelstein, The Sound of Money (reprise), On My Way to Love, What Are They Doing To Us Now?, Eat a Little Something

A musical presented in two acts; Theatre at St. Peter's Church; October 21 – 23, 2005; 5 performances

Christiane Noll and Glen Seven Allen in *A Fine and Private Place* PHOTOS BY CAROL ROSEGG

THE GREAT BIG RADIO SHOW! Book by Philip Glassborow and Nick McIvor, music and lyrics by Philip Glassborow; Director, David Glenn Armstrong; Music Director, Ken Clifton; Tap Choreographer, Paul Liberti; Arrangements and Dance Music, David Rhind-Tutt; Lighting, Chris Robinson; Wardrobe Advisor, Cheryl Mc Caron; Production Stage Manager, Allison Deutsch; Assistant Stage Manager, Andrea Jo Martin; Assistant Director, Shana Solomon; **Cast:** Tyler Maynard (Jerry), Lexy Fridell (Polly), David Staller (Blue), Nancy Anderson (Myrtle), Robert Ari (Bernstein), Ed Dixon (Professor Zannenberg), Seth Rudetsky (Stanley), Ruth Gottschall (Freckles), Dan Sharkey (Big Louie), Wally Dunn (Two Gun), Lynne Wintersteller (Olga)

Musical Numbers: Unmistakably, She Ain't Here Yet, Surprises, What Can I Do for You?, Radio in My Mind, No Matter What, Where Have I Seen You Before?, Pretty as a Picture, Suddenly I'm Singing, You Came By, I Felt Myself Falling, Then I Bumped Into You, You Take My Breath Away, Your Turn for a Rainbow, The Balalaika, Tomorrow is Another Day, Unmistakably, Me and My Stradivarius, You Came By

A musical presented in two acts; Theatre at St. Peter's Church; October 28 – 30, 2005; 5 performances

IS THERE LIFE AFTER HIGH SCHOOL? Book by Jeffrey Kindley, music and lyrics by Craig Carnelia, based on the book by Ralph Keyes; Director, Craig Carnelia; Music Director, Bryan Perri; Lighting, Chris Robinson; Production Stage Manager, Andrea Jo Martin; Assistant Stage Manager, Jack McDowell; Assistant Director, Adam Wagner; Assistant Musical Director, Albin Konopka; **Cast:** Stephanie Bast, Jedidiah Cohen, Holly Davis, Jeffrey Doornbos, Chris Fuller, Stacie Morgain Lewis, Garrett Long, Greg Roderick, Caesar Samayoa

Adam Monley and Nancy Anderson in *Fanny Hill*

Musical Numbers: The Kid Inside, Things I Learned in High School, Second Thoughts, Nothing Really Happened, Beer, For Them, Diary of a Homecoming Queen, Reunion, High School All Over Again, Fran & Janie, I'm Glad You Didn't Know Me, Reunion (reprise), The School Song

A musical presented in two acts: Theatre at St. Peter's Church; November 4–6, 2005; 5 performances

THEDA BARA AND THE RABBI FRONTIER Music and lyrics by Bob Johnston, book and lyrics by Jeff Hochhauser, Director, Lynne Taylor-Corbett; Music Director, Caryl Ginsburg Fantel; Lighting, Chris Robinson; Casting, Carol Hanzel; Production Stage Manager, Andrea Jo Martin; Assistant Stage Manager, Jack McDowell; **Cast:** Jonathan Brody (Adolph Zukor/Morris), Patrick Boll (Gordon Edwards/Sammy Goldfish), Tom Lucca (D.W. Griffith), Rena Strober (Theda Bara), Susan J. Jacks (Fanny/Foremother), Fred Berman (Isaac Birnbaum), Allen Lewis Rickman (Selwyn Farp), Alison Cimmet (Irene/Foremother), Alicia Irving (Rachel Birnbaum), Lois Hart (Foremother)

Musical Numbers: Father, I Have Sinned, Frontier Rabbi, There Are So Many Things that a Vampire Can't Do, It's Like a Movie, Velcome to Shul, Bolt of Love, The Sermon, The Scene with the Grapes, Another Rabbit Outta the Hat, There Are So Many Things that a Vampire Can Do, If She Came Back Again, Waiting for the Kiss to Come, Oh Succubus, Finale

A musical presented in two acts: Theatre at St. Peter's Church; December 2–4, 2005; 5 performances

MISS LIBERTY Book by Robert E. Sherwood, music and lyrics by Irving Berlin; Director, Michael Montel; Music Director, Zachary Dietz; Lighting, Chris Robinson, Production Stage Manager, Andrea Jo Martin; Assistant Stage Manager, Jack McDowell; **Cast:** Jerry Christakos (Ambassador/Ensemble), Erick Devine (James Gordon Bennett/Ensemble), David Garry (Cartwright/Ensemble), Nikki M. James (Monique DuPont), Julie Kotarides (Maisie Dell), David Larsen (Horace Miller), Patricia O'Connell (Countess), Fred Rose (Barholdi/Ensemble), Roland Rusinek (Pulitzer/Ensemble), Deborah Jean Templin (Maid/Ensemble), Tom Treadwell (Mayor/Ensemble), Nick Verina (Lamplighter/Ensemble), Carla Woods (Model/Ensemble)

Musical Numbers: Extra, Extra, What Do I Have to Do to Get My Picture Took?, The Most Expensive Statue in the World, A Little Fish in a Big Pond, Let's Take and Old-Fashioned Walk, Homework, Paris Wakes Up and Smiles, Only for Americans, Just One Way to Say I Love You, Miss Liberty, You Can Have Him, The Policeman's Ball, Homework (reprise), Me and My Bundle, Falling Out of Love Can Be Fun, Give Me Your Tired, Your Poor

A musical presented in two acts: Theatre at St. Peter's Church; December 9–11, 2005; 5 performances

MIRETTE Book by Elizabeth Diggs, music by Harvey Schmidt, lyrics by Tom Jones, based on the picture book *Mirette on the High Wire* by Emily Arnold McCully; Director, Drew Scott Harris; Music Director, Matt Castle; Lighting, Chris Robinson; Production Stage Manager, Andrea Jo Martin; Assistant Stage Manager, Jack McDowell; **Cast:** Sue Cella (Madame Gateau), Joy Franz (Mme. Rouspenskaya, Russian singer) Davis Duffield (Tabac, a juggler), David Garry (Clouk, an acrobat), Patti Murin (Claire, an acrobat), Kelly Sullivan (Gaby, a dancer/mime), Anthony Santelmo Jr (Camembert, a clown), Maggie Watts (Mirette), Robert Cuccioli (Bellini), Ed Dixon (Max)

Musical Numbers: Madame Gateau's Colorful Hotel, Maybe, A Tiny Little Room, Irkutsk, Practicing, Learning Who You Are, The Show Goes On, Feet Upon the Ground, Learning Who You Are (reprise), If You Choose to Walk Upon the Wire, The Great Bellini, Sometimes You Just Need Someone, Madame Gateau's Desolate Hotel, Finale

Setting: Paris in the 1890's. A musical presented without intermission; Theatre at St. Peter's Church; December 16–18, 2005; 5 performances.

FANNY HILL Book, music, music, and lyrics by Ed Dixon; based on the novel by John Cleland; Presented by Dennis Grimaldi Productions and Nick Cavarra; Associate Produced by Maffei Productions LLC, Jacki Barlia Florin; Director, James Brennan, Music Director, Stan Tucker; Scenery and Costumes, Michael Bottari and Ronald Cast; Lighting, Phil Monat; Wigs and Hair, Gerard Kelly; Orchestrations, Nick DeGregorio; Casting, Dave Clemmons; Production Stage Manager, Jack McDowell; Assistant Stage Manager, Andrea Jo Martin; **Cast:** Nancy Anderson (Fanny Hill), Christianne Tisdale (Phoebe Davis), Patti Allison (Mrs. Brown), Emily Skinner (Martha), Gina Ferrall (Esther/Count Brodski), David Cromwell (The Honorable Mister Croft/Lord Hereford/Father Norbert), Tony Yazbeck (Charles Waneigh), Adam Monley (Will Plenty), Michael J. Farina (Mr. Sneed/Mr. Barville); Replacement: Marla Schaffel (Martha); **Orchestra:** Stan Tucker (piano/keyboard), Tara Chambers (cello), Jeff Nichols (reeds)

Musical Numbers: Overture, Lancashire, On the Road, Seeing London, Going to Mrs. Brown's, House of Joy, Croft's Serenade, Welcome to London, Sailor's Song, The Most Heavenly Creature, I Have Never Been So Happy, Marriage Song, Phoebe's Song, The Weeping Song, Entr'acte, The Card Game, Tea Service, Honor Lost, A Little House in the Country, My Only Love, Every Man in London, Big, I Came to London, Pleasure Dance, Goodbye, Storm, Finale

Setting: England 1750, Lancashire, London and Environs. New York Premiere of a new musical presented in two acts; Theatre at St. Peter's Church; February 1–March 12, 2006 (Opening Night February 14, 2006); 46 performances.

A FINE AND PRIVATE PLACE Book and lyrics by Erik Haagensen, music by Richard Isen; based on the novel by Peter S. Beagle; Director, Gabriel Barre; Musical Director, Milton Granger; Scenery, James Morgan, Costumes, Pamela Scofield; Lighting, Jeff Croiter; Sound, Eric McMiller; Projections, Scott Dela-Cruz; Orchestrations, Richard Isen; Casting, Mark Simon; Production Stage Manager, Allison Deutsch; **Cast:** Joe Kolinski (Jonathan Rebeck), Glenn Seven Allen (Michael Morgan), Evalyn Baron (Gertrude Klapper), Christiane Noll (Laura Durand), Gabriel Barre (The Raven), Larri Rebega (Campos); Replacements: Gary Littman (The Raven); **Orchestra:** Milton Granger (piano), David Wolfson (keyboards), Barbara Merjan (percussion), Alan Brady (reeds), Suzy Perelman (violin)

Musical Numbers: Prologue, I'm Not Going Gently, Much More Alive, You Know What I Mean, A Fine and Private Place, As Long As I Can, Stop Kidding Yourself, The Telepathetique, What Did You Expect? Let Me Explain, It's None of My Business, Quartet, What Should I Do, Close Your Eyes, Argument, No One Ever Knows, Because of Them All, Do Something, How Can I Leave Here?, Finale

Setting: Yorkchester Cemetery, Bronx, New York. New York premiere of a musical presented in two acts; Theatre at St. Peter's; April 11–May 21, 2006 (Opening Night April 27, 2006); 45 performances.

OFF-OFF-BROADWAY

Productions That Opened **June 1, 2005 – May 31, 2006**

14TH STREET THEATER

SAVING THE GREEKS: ONE TRAGEDY AT A TIME by Jason Pizzarello; Produced by Bay Bridge Productions, Push Productions, and The Grift; Director, Michael Kimmel; Scenery, Kerry Chipman; Costumes, Marija Djordjevic; Lighting, Andrew Hill and Pahu Van Riel; Sound, Scott O'Brien; Video, Aaron Rhyne; Stage Manager, Ana Mari de Quesada; Executive Producer, J. Edward Cecala; **Cast:** Valerie Clift, Matt DeVriendt, Tom Escovar, Carey Evans, Eric Forand, William Jackson Harper, Alan Jestice, Pete Mele, Carrie McCrossen, Brian Normant, Season Oglesby, Eva Patton, Brian Reilly; September 8–25, 2005

SUNDAY ON THE ROCKS by Theresa Rebeck; Presented by On Our Own Productions; Director, Sherrie Ahlin; **Cast:** Lisa Lamoth, Hilary Mann, Lauren Shannon, Caroline Renner; October 6–30, 2005

MOTHER TERESA GIRL Written and performed by Aviva Jane Carlin; Presented by the Hypothetical Theatre Company; January 4–14, 2006

LOVE IS IN THE AIR Based on the film by Harold Stimple; Produced by the Pig Brooch Theatre Company (Aurélia Fisher, Justin Tyler, Aaron Wilton); Director, Paul Peers, Dramaturg, Jamee Freedus; Costumes, Amelia Dombrowski; Lighting, Chris Hoyt; **Cast:** Dustin Helmer, Justin Tyler, Jennie Smith, Seth Powers, Anna Moore, Marty Keiser, Jordan Wishner, Genevieve Gearhart, Alden Ford, Laura Blau, Mason Chapple, Jonny Tyler, Jen Datka; April 20–May 6, 2006

440 STUDIOS

ON THE VERGE New music and lyrics from up and coming songwriting teams of Brian Lowdermilk and Kait Kerrigan, Daniel S. Acquisto and Sammy Buck, Ryan Cunningham and Joshua Salzman, Carla Rose Arnone and Barbara J. Anselmi, Joe Iconis, and Robert Jay Cronin; Director, Judy Blazer; Presented by the New Heights Theatre Company; **Cast:** Brad Bass, Dana Hart, Matt Hinkley, Robyn Elizabeth Lee, Andrea Scott, Kristina Teschner, and Nathan Watson; July 10–11, 2005

THINGS BEYOND OUR CONTROL by Jesse Kellerman; Presented by Grid Theater Company; Director, Justin Ball; Design, Leighton Mitchell, Campbell Ringel, Michael O'Connor, Brittany O'Neill; Stage Manager, Angrette McCloskey; **Cast:** Annie Armstrong, Birgit Huppuch, Matthew Johnson, Jennifer Lafleur, Preston Martin, Matthew J. Nichols, Ross Partridge, Andrew Zimmerman; Linhart Theater; January 17–28, 2006

SEASCAPE WITH SHARKS AND DANCER by Don Nigro; Director, Mike McKee; Produced by Marksman Theatre Group; Stage Manager, Charlotte Miller; **Cast:** Bryna Alderman, Lucas Beck; February 3–6, 2006

THE SIBLINGS Written and directed by Edward Elefterioun; Produced by Rabbit Hole Ensemble; February 13–19, 2006

TESTIFY Dramatizations of Congressional Transcripts; Part 3: The Security Consequences of Outing a Covert Intelligence Officer; Presented by breedinggroundartists (Tomi Tsunoda, Douglas Paulson, Kate Rogers); **Cast:** Michele Naumann Carlstrom, Todd Carlstrom, Doug Paulson, Justin Steeve; April 14–15, 2006

I'D LEAVE YOU … BUT WE HAVE RESERVATIONS 4 short plays produced by Peter Marsh, Mia Vaculik, Jesse RosBrow and Alex Lincoln: *Past the Teeth* by Robert Askins, directed by Marco Jo Clate; *Lunch* by Jacqueline Christy, directed by Marco Jo Clate; *Nice Is For Dogs* by Stephanie Rabinowitz, directed by Chris Schraufnagel; and *Club Justice* written and directed by Maria Gabriele; Design, Brent Barkhaus, Angrette McCloskey, Wilburn Bonnell, Graham Johnson; Stage Manager, Treasa O'Neill; **Cast:** Mia Aden, Greg Oliver Bodine, Brooke Chirone, Heather Collis, Rose Courtney, Erin Kukla, Alexandra Linxoln, Peter Marsh, Kyle Masteller, Shelley McPherson, Joseph Tomasini; Linhart Theatre; May 11–28, 2006

45 BLEECKER — THE CULTURE PROJECT

DAVID & JODI & DAVID & JACKIE adapted from the screenplay "Bob & Carol & Ted & Alice"; Director, Michael Schiralli; **Cast:** Jackie Hoffman, David Rakoff, David Ilku, Jodi Lennon; June 10–25, 2005

WOMEN CENTER STAGE 2005 July 29–August 31, 2005; Presented by Culture Project; Series included: "Baghdad Burning" adapted by Kimberly Kefgen and Loren Novek, directed by Ken Rus Schmoll; *Nightingale* written and performed by Lynn Redgrave; *The Scarlet Letter* adapted by Carol Gilligan, directed by Wier Harman, starring Marisa Tomei; *Women Rebel-The Words of Margaret Sanger* adapted by Katherine Creel, directed by Mallory Catlett, starring Lynn Cohen; *Saviour* by Timothy Cooper, directed by Ian Morgan; *The Speed Queen* adapted and performed by Anne Stockton from Stewart O'Nan's novel, directed by Austin Pendleton

REVELATION READINGS Presented by Red Bull Theatre; September 9–November 2, 2005 and December 11–13, 2005

KARLA by Steve Earle; Director, Bruce Kronenberg; Produced by Caney Creek Productions; Design, Allison Keating, Kip Marsh; Stage Manager, Alison Dingle; **Cast:** Jodie Markell, Linda Marie Larson, Jeremy Schwartz, E. Jason Liebrecht; 45 Below; October 20–November 13, 2005

THE REVENGER'S TRAGEDY by Thomas Middleton; Adapted and directed by Jesse Berger; Presented by Red Bull Theatre; November 27, 2005–December 18, 2005; Extended January 6–22nd under an Off Broadway Contract (For full credits please see listing in "Off Broadways Plays That Opened' in this volume)

AJAX: 100% FUN adapted from Sophocles; Presented by LightBox (formerly EB&C); **Cast:** Melody Bates, Justin Badger, Brian Deneen, Margot Ebling, Shawn Fagan, Robert M. Johanson, Fletcher Liegerot, Chris Oden; 45 Below; February 22–March 5, 2006

TROUT STANLEY by Claudia Dey; Director, Jen Wineman; Design, Tim Mackabee, Tse Wei Lim, Caitlin O'Connor, Elizabeth Coleman; Music, Andrew Shapiro; Stage Manager, Molly Eustis; **Cast:** Kelly McAndrew, Erika Rolfsrud, Warren Sulatycky; Presented by Renaissant Arts; 45 Below; May 22–June 11, 2006

45TH STREET THEATRE

MERRILY WE ROLL ALONG Music and lyrics by Stephen Sondheim, book by George Furth; Director, Steve Velardi; Choreography, Tony Montenieri; Musical Director, Seth Bisen-Hersh; Scenery, Bill Wood; Costumes, Renee M. Bell; Lighting, Robert J. Weinstein; Orchestrations, Danny Percefull; **Cast:** James Archer, Jason Beaubien, Holden Berryman, Charles Bonnin, Kelley Calpin, Felicity Claire, Robert J. Cross, Angela Donovan, Jason Alan Edward, Meredith Ellis, Laurice Alicia Farrell, Kristen Florio, Jenny Gattone, Joshua William Gelb, Heather Gladis, Eoghan Broderick Greely, Anna Kirkland, Chazmond J. Peacock, Steve Velardi, Lisa Villalobos; July 15–August 7, 2005

ONE FESTIVAL Presented by Double Helix Theatre Company; November 16–20, 2005; Series included: *Creation* conceived and performed by Lucas Caleb Rooney, directed by Orlando Pabotoy; *Jazz Desert* written and performed by Rebecca Hart; *Accidental Pervert* written and performed by Andrew Goffman; *Soul to Keep* written and performed by Joyia Bradley; *Wild Rice* written and performed by Scarlett Lam; *I Need a Guy Who Blinks* written and performed by Janine Squillari; *Pentecostal Wisconsin* written and performed by Ryan Paulson, directed by Virginia Scott

GROWN UPS by Jules Feiffer; Presented by The Roundtable Ensemble; Director, Frank Blake; Design, Nick Francone, Liam O'Brien, Matt Stine; Stage Manager, Andrea Ghersetich; **Cast:** David Berent, Lawrence Frank, Joy Keaton, Kelly Ann Moore, Cai Tanikawa Oglesby, Kate Tellers; January 12–February 4, 2006

THE BLACKBIRD RETURNS by Alexis Kozak and Barbara Panas; Presented by The Roundtable Ensemble and KoPan Productions; Director, Alexis Kozak; Design, Nick Francone, Kimberly Klearman, Justin Kennedy-Grant; Stage Manager, Cara DeCiccio; **Cast:** Julie Jensen, Douglas Lally, Barbara Panas, David Lloyd Walters; January 15–31, 2006

OFFSPRING by Jimmy Barden; Director, Stacy Waring; Design, Christophe Pierre, Antoine Jermaine Thrower, Jesse Harris; Presented by Negro Ensemble Company (Charles Weldon, Artistic Director); **Cast:** Janice Marie, Brad Holbrook, Hisham Tawfiq, Maryann Myika Day, March 3–19, 2006

SODOM'S WIFE Conceived and directed by Erin Brindley and Maximillian Davis; Produced by Ripple Productions, Katherine Jaeger and Michael Patrick, co-produced by Eric Krebs; Scenery and Sound, Erin Brindley and Michael Patrick, Costumes, Can Coskunes; Lighting, Andrew Lu; Stage Manager, Laura Schlachtmeyer; **Cast:** Nadia Gan, Ben Thomas, Ana Valle, Paul Becker , Michael Shattner, Sarah Painter, Charles Hendricks, Kate Hess, Corey Ann Haydu, Katherine Jaeger, Lillian Medville; March 16–April 9, 2006

SLAM THEATER March 28–April 18, 2006

DREAD AWAKENING – Four short plays; Produced by Michelle Bossy, Alana Karpoff, and Eric Sanders; Design, Marcus Doshi, Mark Huang, Wilson Chin, and Candice Thompson; Stage Manager, Andy Ottoson; Production Manager, Stephanie Coulombe; Plays included: *Bloody Mary* by Roberto Aguirre-Sacasa, directed by Pat Diamond; *Pearls* by Clay McLeod Chapman directed by Arin Arbus; *Treesfall* by Justin Swain, directed by Jessica Davis-Irons; *Sleep Mask* by Eric Sanders, directed by Amanda Charlton; **Cast:** Christianna Nelson, Jedadiah Schultz, Meredith Holzman, Robert Funaro, Daniel Defarrari, Abe Goldfarb, Maggie Stokley, Jenny Gammello, Joe Plummer; April 6–23, 2006

THE DEBATE PLAYS by Mat Smart; Presented by Slant Theatre Project; Directors, Wes Grantom, Evan Cabnet, Adam Knight; Stage Manager, Kasey Campbell; **Cast:** Jeff Glafer, Chad Goodridge, Garrett Neergaard, Kathleen White; April 8–May 13, 2006

TAILS Book and lyrics by Mark Masi, music by Jess Platt; Director/Choreographer, Christopher Scott; Music Directors, Mary Feinsinger and Alex Yagupsky; Design, Peter Feuchtwanger, Cheryl McCarron, Ray Shike; **Cast:** Miguel Cervantes, William Thomas Evans, Judith Greentree, Ron Kidd, Tracey Stephens; April 27–May 14, 2006

DOROTHY STRELSIN FRESH INK READING SERIES Presented by Primary Stages; Series included: *Monostrosity* by Lucy Thurber, directed by Suzanne Agins; *In Loco Parentis* by Andrew Case, directed by Christian Parker; *Lake Effect Show* by Rogelio Martinez, directed by Sam Gold; *Dusty and the Big Bad World* by Cusi Cram, directed by Tyler Marchant; *The Archduke of Libertyville* by Brooke Berman, directed by Josh Hecht; May 16–20, 2006

59E59

EAST TO EDINBURGH FESTIVAL 15 American productions heading to the Edinburgh Fringe Festival; July 12–31, 2005

DAPH! by Le Wilhelm; Director, Merry Beamer; Produced by Orange Jumpsuit Productions; August 3–21, 2005

MAIDEN'S PROGENY: AN AFTERNOON WITH MARY CASSATT, 1906 Written and directed by Le Wilhelm; Presented by Rage Against Time; August 10–28, 2005

THE ASPHALT KISS by Nelson Rodriguez; translated by Alex Ladd; Director, Sarah Cameron Sunde; Produced by Lord Strage Company and Mike Everett; Designers, Lauren Helpern, Wade Baboissonnier, Traci Klainer, Jeremy Lee; Choreography, Melissa Riker; Production Manager, Sam Tresler; Stage Manager, Angela M. Adams; **Cast:** James Martinez, Jessica Kaye, Charles Turner, Arlene Chico-Lugo, Joe Capozzi, Paul De Sousa, Paul Klementowicz, Dawn McGee; Theater B; October 7–29, 2005

HIS ROYAL HIPNESS LORD BUCKLEY IN THE ZAM ZAM ROOM Written and performed by Jake Broder; Director, Phillip Breen; Theater C; November 30–December 31, 2005

POET IN NEW YORK Presented by Pig Iron Theatre Company, Philadelphia; Performed by Dito van Reigersberg; December 7–11, 2005

THIS WAY THAT WAY Created and directed by Mark Lonergan in collaboration with performers Joel Jeske and Ryan Kasprzak; Produced by Parallel Exit; Theatre B; December 14–31, 2005

REVERIE PRODUCTIONS WINTER REPERTORY FESTIVAL *Havana Bourgeois* by Carlos Lacámara; Director, Jocelyn Sawyer; Set, Zhanna Gurvich; Costumes, Ramona Ponce; Lighting, Colin D. Young; Sound, Paul Belger; **Cast:** Jaime Sanzez, James Martinez, Ursula Cataan, Selena Nelson, Thom Rivera, Rashaad Ernesto Green, George Bass, Alexander Alito; *Ping Pong Diplomacy* by Joe Basque; Director, David Hilder; Set, Zhanna Gurvich; Costumes, Michael Oberle; Lighting, Colin D. Young; Sound, Charles Vorce; **Cast:** Kim Donovan, Jesse Hooker, Jerzy Gwiazdowski, Robert Wu, Jeffrey Nauman, Christopher Graham, Constance Wu, David Shih; Theater C; January 8–February 5, 2006

GIVE UP! START OVER! (IN THE DARKEST TIMES I LOOK TO RICHARD NIXON FOR HOPE) Created and performed by Jessica Almasy, directed by Rachel Chavkin; **HOWL** Adapted and directed by Rachel Chakin from Allen Ginsberg's poem; Presented by TEAM; January 10–15, 2006

RIDDLELIKELOVE (WITH A SIDE OF KETCHUP) written and performed by Julie Fitzpatrick, co-written and directed by Douglas Anderson; Presented by Godlight Theater Company and Town Hall Theater of Vermont; Theater C; March 26–April 26, 2006

SCREWMACHINE/EYECANDY OR: HOW I LEARNED TO STOP WORRYING AND LOVE BIG BOB by C.J. Hopkins; Produced by Clancy Productions in association with Scamp Theatre Ltd.; Director, John Clancy; Scenery, Simon Holdsworth; Costumes, Ronnie Dorsey; Lighting, Lauren Phillips; Sound and Music, Damien Coldwell; Stage Manager, Chandra Laviolette; **Cast:** Bill Coelius, Nancy Walsh, David Calvitto, James Cleveland; Theater B; April 16–30; 2006

78TH STREET THEATRE LAB

GREETINGS FROM YORKVILLE, THE SONGWRITER MUSICAL Written and performed by Anya Turner and Robert Grusecki; Director, Thommie Walsh; Presented by Woodstock Fringe; June 8–14, 2005

VOICES FROM THE HOLY…AND NOT SO HOLY LAND Written and performed by Steve Greenstein; July 16–31, 2005

A WRINKLE IN TIME August 11–27, 2005

THE GREAT AMERICAN DESERT Book by Joel Oppenheimer, music by Joe Schlitz and Joe Jung; Director, Garrett Ayers; Produced by Try Try Again Theatre Company; Design, Lighting, Jerome J. Hoppe, Jr.; Stage Manager, Erin Albrecht; **Cast:** Brian Frank, Ben Rosenblatt, Erin Gorski, Emily Moulton, Joe Jung, Christopher T. VanDijk. Maurice Doggan, Andrew McLeod, Brian Sell; September 29–October 16, 2005

THE DEVIL OF DELANCEY STREET Written and directed by Sharon Fogarty; Produced by Making Light; **Cast:** John Cunningham, Sharon Fogarty, Patti Goettlicker, Bobbi Owens, Matthew Porter, Jeffrey Plunkett, Bradley True, Karen Christie-Ward; October 19–November 5, 2005

RECONSTRUCTION by Clifford Lee Johnson III; Director, Tom Coash; Produced by The Open Book; **Cast:** Alice King; October 27–November 19, 2005

THE LAST CHRISTMAS OF EBENEZER SCROOGE by Marvin Kaye; Costumes, RJ Lewis; Produced by The Open Book; **Cast:** Marvin Kaye, Stacey Jenson, H. Clark Kee, Nancy Temple; December 1–17, 2005

MANIGMA Created and performed by Michael Aronov; December 22–January 28, 2006

LEMKIN'S HOUSE by Catherine Filloux; Director, Jean Randich; Scenery, Sue Rees; Lighting, Matthew Adelson; Sound, Robert Murphy; Costumes, Camille Assaf; Props, Liz Maestri; Stage Manager, Joanna Jacobsen; Assistant Stage Manager, Tobias Levin; Associate Producer, Morgan Allen; **Cast:** John Daggett, Christopher McHale, Christopher Edwards, Constance Winston, and Laura Flanagan; February 3–26, 2006

BLUFF by Jeffrey Sweet; Director, Sandy Shinner; Costumes, Erin Elizabeth Murphy; Lighting, Cris Dopher; Sound, Andre Pluess and Ben Sussman; **Cast:** Michelle Best, Luke McCloskey, Kristine Niven, Ean Sheehy, Bill Tatum, Sarah Yorra; March 10–26, 2006

MRS. CALIFORNIA by Doris Baizley; Director, Megan R. Wills; Produced by River Heights Productions; Design, Viviane Galloway; Sound, Di Drago; **Cast:** Elizabeth Burke, Heather E. Cunningham, Matilda Downey, Dave DiLoreto, Jim Kilkenny, India Myone McDonald, Kristen Vaughan, and the voice talents of Jack H. Cunningham, Reginald V. Ferguson, Kimberly Greene; March 15–April 1, 2006

THE AMULET by Peretz Hirshbein; Director, Isaac Butler; Produced by New Worlds Theatre Project; Scenery, David Birn; Lighting, Sabrina Braswell; Costumes, Sydney Marseca; **Cast:** Hanna Creek, Anita Keal, David Little, Daryl Lathon; April 13–May 6, 2006

I WILL COME LIKE A THIEF Written and directed by Trish Harnetiaux and Jude Domski; Produced by Morning Line Productions; Scenery, Sarah Pearline; Lighting, Justin Partier; Costumes, Lex Liang; Sound, Simon Taufique; **Cast:** Arthur Acuna, Henry Afro-Bradley, JJ Auczkiewicz, Carey Cromelin, Loris Diran, Michael Colby Jones, Corey Tazmania, Jerry Zellers; May 13–June 4, 2006

ABINGDON THEATRE ARTS COMPLEX

JUNE HAVOC THEATRE

WALKING IN MEMPHIS: THE LIFE OF A SOUTHERN JEW Written and performed by Jonathan Adam Ross; Produced by Ontheinside Productions/Sutton Foster; November 27, 2005–January 15, 2006

FOOL FOR LOVE by Sam Shepard; Produced by Grey Productions; Directed and designed by Christopher Martin; **Cast:** Marc Menchaca, Michelle David, Laurence Cantor, Ben Wiggins; December 8–18, 2005

OTHELLO by William Shakespeare; Produced by Inner Circle Theater Company; Director, Chris Cotone; Costumes, Angel Jones; Sound, Jewels Eubanks; Stage Manager, Michael Ormand; **Cast:** Pascal Beauboeuf, Sybille Bruun, Chris Cotone, Brian Greer, Sam Chase, David Lamberton, Elizabeth C. Rosengren, Claudia Casamassimo, Brian Linden, Galway McCullough, Robert Garabedian, Charles Baker, Mick Bleyer, Shawn McLaughlin, Matt Walley, Amy Flanagan; March 17–April 2, 2006

DOROTHY STRELSIN THEATRE

EVENSONG by Mary Gage; Produced by Broad Horizons Theatre Company; Director, Lewis Magruder; **Cast:** Ruby Holbrook, Elizabeth Elson, Arthur French, Dante Giammarco, Cam Kornman, Mary Elizabeth Ashley; July 28–August 6, 2005

TAPE by Stephen Belber; Director, David Newer; Produced by Underground Artists Theatre Company; Scenery, Jay Pingree; Costumes, Sarah Frechette; **Cast:** Jayson Gladstone, Ben Schmoll, Randa Karambelas; January 19–29, 2006

LARGO DESOLATO by Vaclav Havel, translated by Tom Stoppard; Produced by Beyond the Wall Productions; February 2–11, 2006

UNCLE VANYA by Anton Chekhov; Produced by Sonnet Repertory Theatre; March 3–5, 2006

ACCESS THEATER

THE CARNIVAL OF CULTURE Produced and curated by John Tedeschi; Co-Producer, Brenda Bush, Co Curator, Greg Zukowski; June 22–July 9, 2005

BUSTED JESUS COMIX by David Johnston; Produced by Blue Coyote Theater Group; Director, Gary Shrader; Design, Evan O'Brient, Jonna McElrath; **Cast:** Bruce Barton, Michael Bell, Paul Caiola, R. Jane Casserly, Brian Fuqua, Vince Gatton, Tracey Gilbert, John Koprowski, David Lapkin, Joseph C. Yeargain; July13–August 7, 2005

MURDERING MARLOW by Charles Marowitz; Director, Jason King Jones; Produced by In Actu Theatre; Design, Aaron Spivey, Zachary Quarles, Brian J. Ruggaber, Maggie Dick; Stage Manager, Josiane M. Lemieux; **Cast:** Cedric Hayman, Patrick Hallahan, Tim McGeever, Mandy Olsen, Caralyn Kozloski, Glenn Peters, Bryan Cogman, Jeremy Beazilie, Nicholas J. Coleman; October 11–23, 2005

THE EAST END PLAYS by George F. Waker; Produced by Sightlines Theater Company; October 29–November 20, 2005; Schedule included: *Love and Anger* Director, Lee Gundersheimer; **Cast:** Bill Balzac, Ted Hannan, Michael Kuhn, Cecil MacKinnon, Jaquitq Ta'le, Rae C. Wright; *Criminals in Love* Director, Eileen Phelan; **Cast:** Franklin Clay Boyd, David Colacci, Lila Donnolo, Faryl Millet, Melanie Rey, John Taylor; *Tough!* Director, Chris Mirto; **Cast:** Mary Cavett, Nick Scoullar, Nell Teare; Readings of *Beautiful City* directed by Shelley Wyant, *Better Living* directed by Donna Linderman, *Escape from Happiness* directed by Gaye-Taylor Upchurch

FITS & STARTS: THE SACRED HEART by Vicki Caroline Cheatwood; Presented by Overlap Productions; January 10–28, 2006

A LIE OF THE MIND by Sam Shepard; Produced by thriftshop theatre workshop; Director, Alex Correia; Design, Andrew Boyce, David Withrow; Stage Manager, Sean Ryan; **Cast:** Getchie Argetsinger, Wendy Brantley, Gina DeMayo, Guil Fisher, Doug Goodenough, Kevin Kaine, Scott Laska, Pamela Tate; January 27–February 5, 2006

PARADISE by David Foley; Produced by Blue Coyote Theater Group; Director, Gary Shrader; Design, Evan O'Brient, Katherine Harber; Stage Manager, Laura Desmond; **Cast:** Nathalie Altman, Bruce Barton, Michael Bell, Robert Buckwalter, Tracey Gilbert, John Koprowski, Tom Ligon, Jonna McElrath, Lana Marks, Joseph Melendez, Gregory Northrop, Brandon Wolcott; February 6–26, 2006

HARD LOVIN' EVER AFTER: THE BALLAD OF COWBOY MONK AND HIS LADY LOVE by Lucas Hnath; Produced by Active Eye; Director, Jyana S. Gregory; Composer/Music Director, Rika Iino; Space and Light, Shaun Fillion; Costumes, Jessica Ford; Stage Manager, Betsy Ayer; **Cast:** Anna Fitzwater, Andrew Grusetskie, John Patrick Higgins, Kristine Kuroiwa, Kevin Townley, Bobby Williams; February 15–19, 2006

HELP WANTED Written and performed by Josh Lefkowitz; March 20–April 2, 2006

PAINS OF YOUTH by Ferdinand Bruckner; Produced by The 7th Sign Theatre Productions; Directors, Charles Wilson and Michael Fitzgerald; Design, Dave Powell, Katja Andreiev, Nick Kolin, Deena Selenow; Stage Manager, Maria Shaffer; **Cast:** Kari Floberg, Sheila Carrasco, Donna Lazar, Mich Lauer, Amy Ewing, Josh Heine, Michael Newman; May 6–20, 2006

ACE OF CLUBS

THE NELLIE OLESONS: OLDER! UGLIER! MEANER! Sketch comedy by The Nellie Olesons; June 3–11, 2005

JONNY MCGOVERN: I LIKES TO HAVE FUNZ Written and performed by Jonny McGovern; June 9–21, 2005

MEAT Sketch Comedy by Elizabeth Ellis, Reggan Holland, Becky Poole, Livia Scott; September 28–November 2, 2005

LET'S PLAY DOCTOR Created, written and produced by Lisa Levy, Jim Conley, Brad Steuernagel, and Mike Burns; January 13–February 17, 2006

I, CLAUDIUS LIVE Created and presented by Theatre Askew; Director, Tim Cusack and Jason Jacobs; **Cast:** Nathan Blew, Walter Brandes, Tim Cusack, Jennifer Doerr, Jonathan Green, Jason Jacobs, Bianca Leigh, Jennifer Malloy, Jerry Marsini, Stephanie Mnookin, Joanna Parsons, Paul Siemens, Erik Sherr, William Watkins, Josie Whittlesey; January 23–February 27, 2006

SPRING BLING! Comedy Variety Show presented by Billionaires For Bush; Choreography, Seamus Lee Rich; March 18–April 15, 2006

THE FACTS OF LIFE: THE LOST EPISODE by Jamie Morris, lyrics by Brooks Braselman, music by Hank Bones; Director, Chris Melohn, Scenery, Michael Lee Scott; **Cast:** Brooks Braselman, Christopher Kenney, Charlie Logan, Jamie Morris, Jaquay Thomas; April 2–May 28, 2006

HARVEY FINKLESTEIN'S SOCK PUPPET SHOWGIRLS Revised edition with new material; May 13–August 5, 2006

ACTORS THEATRE WORKSHOP

BLUE STATES by Benjamin Kessler; Director, Michael Melamedoff; Producers, Nicole Romano and Sarah DeLuca; Music, Patrick Force; **Cast:** Cass Buggé, Anna Chlumsky, DeVon Jackson, Peter Karinen; January 25–29, 2006

IPHIGENIA AND OTHER DAUGHTERS by Ellen McLaughlin; Director, Michael Perlman; Produced by the Temporary Theatre Company; Design, Laura Jellinek, Ali Cruso, Meredith Neal; Stage Manager, Andrea Morales; Production Manager, Kenneth Scott Thompson; **Cast:** Elizabeth Taylor, Claire Karpen, Charise K. Smith, Colleen Horan, Lance Rubin; March 17–26, 2006

ALTERED STAGES

BRILLIANT TRACES by Cindy Lou Johnson; Director, Steven Farmer; Produced by Creative Madness Productions; July 13–17, 2005

DEN OF THIEVES by Stephen Adly Guirgis; Director, Cecila Rubino; Presented by PossEble Theatre Company; **Cast:** J.R. Adduci, Katie Cappiello, Brandon Scott, Jonathan Meyer, Mark Mallek; September 6–18, 2005

THE CATERERS by Jonathan Leaf; Produced by the Immediate Theater Company; Director, José Zayas; Design, Ryan Elliot Kravetz, Aaron J. Mason, Mel Haley, Philip Quinaz; Stage Manager, Parys LeBron; **Cast:** Ian Blackman, Judith Hawking, Peter Reznikoff, Brian Wallace; October 6–30, 2005

FULLY PACT: ONE ACTS IN REP Produced by Playwrights/Actors Contemporary Theater; *The Exciting Life* by Anthony Pennino; Director, Don Jordan; *Theory of Heaven* by Patrick Kennedy; Director, Elizabeth London; *Issues* by Danna Call; Director, Maryna Harrison; *Train of Thought* by Craig Pospisil; Director, Chris Maring; *Tragedy (A Comedy)* by Stuart D'Ver; Director, Jody O'Neil; *Vermouth and Chicken* by P. Seth Bauer; Director, Jorelle Aronovitch; *Oh, Mister Cadhole!* Book & lyrics by Lisa Ferber, music & lyrics by Robert Firpo-Cappiello; Director, Christopher Windom; November 10–20, 2005

THE DICKENS by Michael Scott-Price; Produced by Firebrand Theory Theater Company; Director, Jaime Robert Carrillo; Design, Bill Pierce, Chris Manning, Kit Stolen, Jaime Robert Carrillo; **Cast:** Brian Shaer, Rich Renner, Johanna Bon, Shaka Malik, Jorge Luis Casanova-Alvarez, Izzy Ruiz, and Jessica Pagan; December 1–17, 2005

SHORTLY AFTER TAKEOFF Written and directed by Stuart Warmflash; Presented by The Harbor Theatre; Design, Mark Symczak, Jeffrey E. Salzberg, Peter Sylvester, Aaron Mastin; Stage Manager, Maria Cameron; **Cast:** Patricia Kalember, Lucy McMichael, Anthony Bagnetto, Adelia Suanders, Bruce Mohat, Eric Shelley; March 9–April 2, 2006

CUPID AND PSYCHE by Joseph Fisher; Director, Alex Lippard; Produced by The Themantics Group, (Jay Aubrey Artistic Director); Design, Lucas Krech, Mike Gonzalez, Michael Moore, Erin Elizabeth Murphy; Stage Manager, Jessica

Pecharsky; **Cast:** Jonathan Todd Ross, Stephanie Janssen, Nick Cearley, Lanette Ware, Kim Schultz, Jeannie Dalton, Richard Sterne, Johnny Sparks; April 7–30, 2006

DOWN THE ROAD by Lee Blessing; Produced by Black Henna Productions; Director, Malini Singh McDonald; May 18–27, 2006

AMERICAN GLOBE THEATRE

TAP ATTACK Presented by Metronome Rhythm Tap; June 23–25, 2005

THE MERCHANT OF VENICE by William Shakespeare; Director, John Basil; Composer, Scott O'Brien; Design, Mark Hankla, Shima Ushiba, Gloria Sun; Stage Manager, Marc Eardley; **Cast:** Wendy Chu, Debra Lewis, Nicole Patrick, Robert Chaney, Bill Fairbairn, Richard Fay, Deepti Gupta, David Dean Hastings, Jon Hoche, Elizabeth Keefe, Damon Kinard, Sarah Price, Rainard Rachele, Mathew J. Sanders, Graham Stevens, Robert Lee Taylor, Warren Watson; March 16–April 8, 2006

15 MINUTE PLAY FESTIVAL Twelfth Annual, Presented with the Turnip Theatre Company; April 24–May 6, 2006

AMERICAN THEATRE OF ACTORS

CHERNUCHIN THEATRE

THE WALTZ OF ELEMENTARY PARTICLES Written and directed by Jessica Lanius/**JULIE** Adapted and directed by Andrea Arden based on August Strindberg's *Miss Julie;* Produced by Theatre Lila; Design, Jeremy C. Doucette, Deirdre Wegner, John LaSala, Michael A. Reese, Alexander Bruehl; Stage Manager, Christine D. Goutmann; **Cast:** Andrea Arden, Amy Clites, Jennifer Donlin, Yvette Feurer, Quinne Mander, Jill Blythe Reimer, Susan Schuld, Travis Stroessenreuther, Kristofer Updike, Laura Walczak; Presented in repertory June 3–25, 2005

HAMLET by William Shakespeare; Produced and directed by James Jennings; **Cast:** Josh Stamell, James Wirt, Alan Hasnas, David Silberger, Mark Kinch, Jessica Jennings; June 29–July 10, 2005

JAPANESE AND WAR Readings presented by Theatre Arts Japan; September 12–25, 2005; Series included *Citizen of Seoul* by Oriza Hirata, directed by Catherine Miller; *Seifuku* by Kobo Abe, directed by Jun Kim; *Happy Lads* by Hideo Tsuchida, directed by Michael Billingsley; *Dust Storm* by Rick Foster, directed by Yukako Yamazoe

THE DARKER FACE OF THE EARTH by Rita Dove, Director, Trezana Beverley; Produced by Take Wing and Soar Productions (Debra Ann Byrd, Artistic Director) and OdD Socks Productions (Trezana Beverley and Beverley Prentice, Co-Founders); Choreography, Gelan Lambert; Musical Director, Ahmondylla Best; Scenery, Robin D. Vest; Lighting, Jane Shaw; Costumes, Ali Turns; Fight Choreography, Jim Robinson; Producing General Manager, Jackie Jeffries; Associate Producers: Flora Gillard, Brigitte Waites, Yvette Reed, Roz D. Fox; **Cast:** Michael Chenevert, Kelvin Cooper, Roz Beauty Davis, Denise Du'Maine, Charles Dumas, David Ellner, Tamu Favorite, Joe Fellman, Zaria Griffin, Julius Hollingsworh, Sharita Hunt, Kittson O'Neill, Beverley Prentice, Adesina Sampson, Traci Tolmaire, Stephanie Weeks, Yaegel T. Welch; February 4–19, 2006

WRECKED Created and directed by Andrea Arden, based on the Aeschylus' *Orestia* trilogy; Produced by Theatre Lila; Scenery, Jeremy C. Doucette; Lighting, Michael A. Reese; Costumes, Niki Hernandez-Adams; Sound/Video, Alexander Bruehl; Stage Manager, Jessica Pecharsky; **Cast:** Jill Blythe Riemer, Bashir Solebo, Jennifer Donlin, Kristofer Updike, Bess Richardson, Amy Clites, Susan Schuld, Yvette Feuer, Travis Stroessenreuther, Scott Giguere, Patrick Hogan, Jason Updike; March 3–18, 2006

SARGENT THEATRE

CHESTER HORN SHORT PLAY FESTIVAL Presented by Theatre Rats; June 21–26, 2005

GREYHOUNDS by Daryl Lisa Fazio; Produced by James Jennings; Director, Jesse Jou; **Cast:** Heather Massie, Cheri Wicks; July 13–17, 2005

AN IDEAL HUSBAND by Oscar Wilde; Director, Robert Francis Perillo; Presented by Jambalaya Productions August 31–September 17, 2005

PORN YESTERDAY with Aaron Wilton; August 17–28, 2005

THE DRUNK MONK Presented by DirtyFeet Productions; September 22–October 2, 2005

BALM IN GILEAD by Lanford Wilson; Presented by Barefoot Theatre Company; Director, Eric Nightengale; **Cast:** Anna Chlumsky, Victoria Malvagano, Diego Ajuz, Jeremy Brena, Louis Reyes Cardenas, Sabrina C. Cataudella, John Gazzale, Trey Gibbons, Jerzy Gwiazdowski, Elizabeth June, Jeff Keilhotz, David Lamberton, Luke Leonard, Michael LoPorto, Ruben Luque, Victoria Malvagano, Diane Mashburn, Joe B. McCarthy, Chiara Montalto, Roderick Nash, Luca Pierucci, Francisco Solorzano, Jennie West, Christopher Whalen; October 27–November 20, 2005

ENDGAMES by JD Edwards; Presented by Brickworks Theatre Company; Director, Baltimore Russell; November 30–December 11, 2005

BY THE SEA by Graig Stewart; Produced by James Jennings; Director, Barbara Pitcher; **Cast:** Alan Hasnas, Connie Perry, Samantha Ridge, Caroline Samaan; January 18–January 22, 2006

A QUESTION OF BALANCE by Alex Menza; Produced by James Jennings; Director, Alan Wynwroth; **Cast:** Peter Barker, Marilyn Duryea, Antoinette Gallo, George Gallo, Bill Grevel; February 15–19, 2006

BURIED CHILD by Sam Shepard; Director, Cyndy Marion; Produced by White Horse Theater Company; Design/Crew: Brendan Lee Regimbal, Debra Leigh Siegel; Kevin Paul Giordano, Caroline Abella, Michael G. Chin, Elliot Lanes; **Cast:** Bill Rowley, Rod Sweitzer, Karen Gibson, David Look, Chris Stetson, Ginger Kroll, David Elyha; January 27–February 12, 2006

FROM ISRAEL TO SEX IN THE SITY Written and performed by Iris Zieber; March 2–29, 2006

GOOD ENOUGH TO BE TRUE by Raphael Bob-Waksberg; Presented by Theatre of Mass Destruction; Director, Kielsoen Baker; **Cast:** Ali Skye Bennet, Matt Lockwood, Jake Alexander, Siobhan Doherty; March 3–19, 2006

SICKLE by Sophia Romma; Presented by First Breeze Productions; Director, Leslie Lee; **Cast:** Emily Mitchell, Stu Richel, Heather Massie, Malcolm Madera, Matt Zehnder; March 30–April 16, 2006

TOP GIRLS by Caryl Churchill; Presented by Etcetera Theatre Company; Director, Patricia McNamara; **Cast:** Marguerite Moray, Kristen Walsh, Lillian J. Small, Talia Gonzalez, Susan Faye Groberg, Ellen Reif, Colleen Summa; April 19–23, 2006

WELCOME HOME STEVE by Craig McNulty; Director, Guilherme; Produced by MADAIR Productions; Design/Crew: Nick Kolin, Ken Larson, Meredith Magoun, Teel James Glenn, Wren Sheldon; **Cast:** Melani Adair, Joseph Amato, Morgan Baker, Heather Edwards, Schuyler Yancey; April 25–May 7, 2006

BECKMAN THEATRE

VIVIEN by Rick Foster; Director, Peter Sander; Starring Janis Stevens; September 4–23, 2005

THE WAR AT DAWN by Eric Alter; Director, Rodney E Reyes; Produced by Apricot Sky Productions; Stage Manager, Jennifer Spinello; **Cast:** Sonia Tatninov, Tammy Tunyavongs, Miguel Emir, Hayden Roush, Morgan Parker; October 11–30, 2005

THANE QWAD Written and directed by James Crawford; **Cast:** Ken Coughlin, Sandi Griffith, Linda Myers; November 2–6, 2005

WIRED (A WORK IN PROGRESS) Conceived and directed by Chantel Cherisse Lucier; Presented by woken' glacier theatre company; **Cast:** Beth Manspeizer, Chantel Cherisse Lucier, Mike Neal, Ai Kiyono, Michael Billingsley; November 8–13, 2005

THE HOUSE OF YES by Wendy McLeod; Director Adam Gerdts; **Cast:** Chris Albright, Amy Heidt, Kate Middleton, Guy Olivieri, Perry Silver; November 16–20, 2005

TWELFTH NIGHT by William Shakespeare; Director, Kelly Barrett; Produced by Developing Acts; Arrangements, Kristin Carter, Set, Dave Smith; Costumes, Gemma Le; **Cast:** Rebecca Nyahay, Sri Gordon, Bob Manus, Kristin Carter, Hunter Tremayne, Andrew D. Montgomery, Wende O'Reilly, Valerie Austin, Nick Giello, Gretchen Howe, Henri Douvry, Taniya Sen, Chris Gilmer; April 20–30, 2006

OUTDOOR THEATRE

TROILOUS AND CRESSIDA by William Shakespeare; Produced and directed by James Jennings; **Cast:** Jane Bacon, Richard Davis, William Greville, Jessica Jennings, Moti Margolin, Josh Stamell June 8–26, 2005

ALL'S WELL THAT ENDS WELL by William Shakespeare; Produced and directed by James Jennings; **Cast:** Philip Bartolf, Timothy Dudek, Ken Coughlin, Marilyn Duryea, Lauren Waisbren, James Wirt; September 7–25, 2005

ARCLIGHT THEATER

RICHARD AND ANNE by Maxwell Anderson; Produced by The Mirror Repertory Company in association with Young Mirror; June 2–19, 2005

BLOOD AND HONEY Conceived and directed by Elizabeth Mozer; June 23–July 3, 2005

ZASTROZZI: THE MASTER OF DISCIPLINE by George F. Walker; Director, Adam Parrish; Produced by The 7th Sign Theatre Productions, Inc.; Scenery, Brian Cote; Costumes, Katja Andreiev; Lighting, Nick Kolin; Sound and Props, Jared Silver; Stage Manager, Caitlyn Larsson; **Cast:** Elliotte Crowell, Danny Deferrari, Matt Harrington, Emily Stern, Orion Taraban, Charlie Wilson; October 7–23, 2005

JACK AND THE BEANSTALK Produced by Pantomonium Productions; Director, Christopher Major, Music Director, Roger Ames; Lighting, Mark Heiser; **Cast:** Goerge Bleecher, Hank Crosby, Richard Saltzman, Henry Gabay, Hilary Howard, Vanessa Kai, Robert McKeon, Lara Milian, Andrew O'Brien, Alan Sanders, Anne Marcarian, Lydia DeSouza; December 9–18, 2005

APARTMENT 3A by Jeff Daniels; Director, Valentina Fratti; Produced by Traci Klainer, Lisa Dozier, and M2 Productions; Scenery, Lauren Helpern; Costumees, David Newall; Lighting, Traci Klainer; Sound, Jeremy J. Lee; Stage Manager, Jennifer Cicelsky George; **Cast:** Jonathan Teague Cook, J. Austin Eyer; Amy Landecker, Arian Moyaed, Joseph Collins; January 23–February 11, 2006

NORA Adapted by Ingmar Bergman from *A Doll's House* by Henrik Ibsen; Produced by Test Pilot Productions and Josh Coleman; Director, Pamela Moller Kareman; Scenery, Joseph J. Egan, Costumes, Kimberly Matela; Lighting, David Pentz; Sound, Matt Stine; Stage Manager Maggie Bell; Assistant Producers, Maggie Bell, Stephanie Bayliss, Melissa Javoreck; **Cast:** Sarah Bennett, Tyne Firmin, Carey Macaleer, Troy Myers, John Tyrrell; February 23–March 12, 2006

FREAK WINDS Written and directed by Marshall Napier; Produced by Hair of the Dog; Design: Jeremy Chernick, Andre Ivanov, Rie Ono, Mike Newman; **Cast:** Marshall Napier, Tamara Lovatt-Smith, Damiean de Montemas; March 28–April 22, 2006

ARTHUR SEELEN THEATRE AT THE DRAMA BOOK SHOP

THE STRIKING VIKING STORY PIRATES inspired by stories written by kids, adapted by the Cast; presented by The Striking Viking Story Pirates (Lee Overtree, Artistic Director; Benjamin Salka, Executive Director); Director, Lee Overtree; Scenery, Drew Callander, Kim Overtree and Molly Russo; Costumes, Drew Callander; Stage Manager, Heather Cohn and Dory Weiss; Musical Director, Eli Bolin; Managing Director, Jessie Salka; Choreographer, Cheryl Conkling; Interns, Gena Miller, Jenny Brown, Hanna Schwartz; **Cast:** Drew Callander, Lee Overtree, Jacob Rossmer, Chris Tuttle, Quinton Johnson, Ned Noyes, Claire Wilmouth, Sam Reiff-Pasarew, Peter Russo, Liz Bangs, Joanna Simmons, Laura Hernandez, Jess Lacher, Jesica Avellone, Amelia Zin-Rose Brown; September 17th, 2005–June 24th, 2006

MATRIX, INC by Diana Raznovich; Presented by LaMicro Theatre; November 10–20, 2005

The Cast of the *Striking Viking Story Pirates* at the Arthur Seelen Theatre PHOTO BY BETSY GROSSMAN

The Wau Wau Sisters — Tanya Gagné and Adrienne Truscott at Ars Nova

ARS NOVA

HOLY CROSS SUCKS! Written and performed by Rob Nash; Director, Jeff Calhoun; August 31–October 1, 2005

[TITLE OF SHOW] Written and performed by Jeff Bowen and Hunter Bell, with Susan Blackwell and Heidi Blickenstaff; Director, Michael Berresse; Music Director, Larry Pressgrove; September 11–27, 2005

LETTING GO OF GOD Written and performed by Julia Sweeney; October 19–26, 2005, April 28–29, 2006

STRIKING 12 Music and lyrics by Valerie Vigoda, Brendan Milburn, Gene Lewin, book by Rachel Sheinkin; Director, Ted Sperling; December 3–23, 2005

CREATION NATION Presented by Sam Forman; Director, Benjamin Salka; Hosts: Billy Willing and Robin Lord, with Eli Bolin on piano, Lee Overtree on drums and special guest stars; December 16, 2005, February 26–March 1, 2006

ANN E. WRECKSICK & THE ODYSSEY OF THE BULIMIC ORPHANS by Scott Allqauer and Damon Intrabartolo; Director, Kristin Hanggi; Choreography, Kelly Devine; **Cast:** Scott Allgauer, J. Cameron Barnett, Beth Curry, Byron St. Cyr, Joey Dudding, Matthew-Lee Erlbach, Amy Goldberger, Karen Katz, Caroline McMahon, Eddie Pendergraft, and Sandy Rustin; February 20–March 19, 2006

THE FACTS OF LIFE: THE LOST EPISODE (see credits under Ace of Clubs); March 3, 2006

NIGHTWATCHES by Victoria Stewart; Director, Susanna L. Harris; Producer, Tania Inessa Kirkman; Scenery, Evan O'Brient; Lighting, Aaron Sporer; Sound, Elizabeth Coleman; Stage Manager, Melissa Spengler; **Cast:** Lenni Benicaso, Ivanna Cullinan, Matt Jared; April 14–29, 2006

THE WAU WAU SISTERS Created and performed by Tanya Gagné and Adrienne Truscott; Opened April 21

THE IVES SIX PACK by David Ives; Director, Jay Snyder and Anthony Salerno; Produced by The Bang Theatre Collective; **Cast:** Vinnie Penna, Ted Lewis, Gregory Abbey, Marc Thompson, Kathleen McInerny, Kelly Deadmon; Ann Malloy; May 10–13, 2006

YOU WANNA PIECE OF ME? Written and performed by Joe Hernandez-Kolski; Music by DJ Jedi; May 17–18, 2006

THE JONATHAN AMES AND MOBY VARIETY SHOW May 30, 2006

BANK STREET THEATRE

SWEET LOVE ADIEU by Ryan J-W Smith; Presented by Hudson Shakespeare Company; Director, Sandy Harper; July 28–30, 2005

ON THE BANKS OF THE SURREAL by Jean Cocteau, Michel de Ghelderode, Eugene Ionesco, Rene Margritte, and Tristan Tzara; Producer, Director, and Choreography, Shela Xoregos; Co-director, David Ostwald; Music Director, Bonita Labossiere; Design, Carrie Yacono, Cris Dopher; Sound, Joe Galione; Costumes, Amy Elizabeth Bravo, Galina Kuznetsova; Stage Manager, Colleen C. Conwell; **Cast:** Jen Avray, Rupak Ginn, Niae Knight, Rachel Lu, Christopher Berryman, Peter Johnson, Rodney Sheley, Dirk Weiler, and John Rose; August 4–21, 2005

EDWARD II by Bertolt Brecht; Produced by Creative Mechanics Theatre Company; Director, Gabriel Shanks; Lighting, Erik C. Bruce; Sound, Chris Meade; Scenery, Allen Cutler; Costumes, Shannon Maddox; Original Compositions, Rob Fellman, Chris Meade; Stage Manager, Kate Scefonas; **Cast:** Willie LeVasseur, Noshir Dalal, Janice Herndon, Frank Blocker, Avi Glickstein, Joshua Marmer, Shannon Maddox, John Dohrmann, Matthew Trumbull, R.J. Foster, Josh Billig, Christopher McAllister, Jeffrey James Keyes, Christian Felix, Oscar Castillo, J. Damian Houston; September 8–25, 2005

THE BUBBLE Written and directed by Frank J. Avella; Produced by The New Cockpit Ensemble; Design, Jody C. Ratti; Original Music/Sound, Joe Morse; Art Direction, Avery Herman; Stage Manager, David Kovach; **Cast:** Wind Klaison, Marie Lazzaro, Guenia Lemos, Tom Patterson, Joe Pistone, Justin D. Quackenbush, Brian Townes; September 27–October 16, 2005

GREENER Written and directed by Frank J. Avella; Produced by The New Cockpit Ensemble; Design, Jody C. Ratti; Original Music/Sound, Joe Morse;**Cast:** Joe Pistone, Patrick Allen, Lisa Marie Gargione, Wind Kalison, Nicholas Lazzaro, Nick Mathews, Jennifer Nehila & Justin D. Quackenbush; February 14–26, 2006

COLD by Liz Blocker; Produced by Present Tense Theatre Project; Director, Cynthia Croot; Design, David M Barber; Lighting, Ken Nero; Sound, Kevin Diamond; April 7–16, 2006

BARROW GROUP ARTS CENTER

NAME DAY Presented by Immigrants Theatre Project; May 31–June 19, 2005

26 DATES…AND COUNTING…by Garth Wingfield; Director, Stacy Shane; July 1–29, 2005

THE AMERICAN DREAM AND OTHER FRACTURED FAIRY TALES Presented by Streetlight Productions; October 19–30, 2005

A CHRISTMAS CAROL by Charles Dickens, adapted and directed by Stephen Wargo with arrangements by Stephen Wargo; **Cast:** Paul Aguirre, Paul Blank, Melissa Center, Jordan D'Angelo, Kristen Duffy, Henry Evans, Sasha Friedenberg, Rich Fromm, Juliet Heller, Pamela Jane Henning, Carol Hickey, Kathleen Hinders, Colin Israel, Chris Kateff, Michelle Kinney, Nick Alexiy Little, Robert Ian Mackenzie, Bryan McElroy, Andrea McCullough, Melissa Menzie, Jenny Lee Mitchell, Adair Moran, Michael Pesce, Michael Poignand, Howard Pinhasik, Michal Salonia, Katie Zaffrann; Presented by Personal Space Theatrics; December 2–18, 2005

DOUBLE OCCUPANCY Two solo performance one acts, directed by Virginia Scott; *Bodhichitta*, written and performed by Sidse Ploug Soerensen, and *Faulty Hitch*, written and performed by Wendy Herlich; May 5–22, 2006

BLUE HERON ARTS CENTER*

BEYOND REASON by Nichol Alexander; Director, Kira Simring; Produced by Water's Edge Writers; June 11–25, 2005

THE TIMES Music by Brad Ross, book and lyrics by Joe Keenan; Produced by Sonnet Repertory Theater; Director, Jess McLeod; **Cast:** Jordan Leeds, Lisa Brescia, Jennifer Ferrin, Kevyn Morrow, Anne L. Nathan, Bill English, Michael Arkin, Robyne Parrish; July 13–17, 2005

THE MARILYN TAPES Written and performed by Lenore Zann; Original songs by Cliff Jones; with David Raleigh; October 5–23, 2005

KRANKENHAUS BLUES by Sam Forman; Produced by The Visible Theatre Company; Director, Donna Mitchell; Music, Hannah Hens-Piazza; Design, Kimi Maeda; **Cast:** Christine Bruno, Joe Sims, Bill Green, Angela DeMatteo; October 7–24, 2005

THE LONG CHRISTMAS DINNER by Thornton Wilder/**A NEW YORK CHRISTMAS CAROL** adapted from Charles Dickens; Produced by New York Theatre Experiment; Directors, Glenn Peters and Joseph Schultz; Producer, Allyson Morgan; Design, Amy Elizabeth Bravo, Scott Brodsky, Niki Hayes, Creighton James; Stage Manager, Tzipora Kaplan; **Cast:** Casey Burns, Nicholas J. Coleman, Emberli Edwards, Laura Gale, Amy Hattemer, Kevin Hoffman, Allyson Morgan, Scott Price; December 8–18, 2005

*The Blue Heron closed permanently on December 31, 2005

BOTTLE FACTORY THEATER

33 TO NOTHING by Grant James Varjas; Director, John B. Good; Produced by Argo Theater Company; **Cast:** Grant James Varjas (Gray), Preston Clarke (Bri), Ken Forman (Barry), Amanda Gruss (Alex), John B. Good (Tyler); March 8–April 29, 2006

THE BRICK

THE MORAL VALUES FESTIVAL June 3–July 3, 2005; Included: *The Absence of Magic* created and performed by Eric Davis, created and directed by Sue Morrison; *Coney Island Last Stop* written and directed by Michael Schwartz; *Dear Dubya: Patriotic Love Letters to WHITEHOUSE.ORG*, Curated and written by John A. Wooden, directed by R.J. Tolan; *eleven* Written and performed by Mikki Baloy, directed by John DeVore; *An Evening with Roberta Combs* directed by Timothy Haskell featuring Cathy McNelis, Rachelle Mendez, Mark O'Connell; *A Feast Unknown* written and performed by Jason Robert Bell, based on the book by Philip Jose Farmer; *Flat* Created by Jason Schuler, directed by Jason Schuler and Kourtney Rutherford, written by Love Ablan, Tim Cummings, Kenny Finkle, Sibyl Kempson, Kirk Marcoe, Jake Oliver, Kourtney Rutherford, Jason Schuler, Mike Taylor, Jon Leon Torn, Jennifer Zern; *The Fourth Reich* written, directed and performed by Danny Bowes with Greg Fisk; *Françoise changes her mind (the things bondage can do)* written and directed by Robert Honeywell featuring Peter Bean, Celia Montgomery, Jana Zenadeen; *Freak Out under the Apple Tree: (Some of) The Best of Tom X. Chao* by Tom X. Chao, performed by Tom X. Chao and Erin A. Leahy; *The Great Moral Values Theatre Debate* moderated by Martin Denton; *I Found Her Tied to My Bed* written and directed by Jeff Tabnick with Shannon Kirk, Talia Rubel; *It Came from New York* curated and hosted by Michele Carlo with Erik Seims, Bruce Smolanoff, Marie Mundaca, Irene Bremis, Laura Dinnebeil, Liam McEaneany, music by Eddy Martinez and Stefan Zeniuk; *The Ladies Auxiliary Telephone Bee: Moral Values Edition; Mahamudra (or Postconsumer Waste Recycled Paper)* written and performed by Chris Harcum; *Misshapen Jack, the Nebraska Hunchback* written, directed and performed by Trav SD; *Mr. Nobody* created and performed by Bidalia Albanese Hess, Steven Hess, Dan Guarino, Jen Nevergole, Mathew Sandoval and deeAnn Nelson; *My Year of Porn* written and performed by Cole Kazdin, directed by Ivanna Cullinan; *Nharcolepsy* written and performed by Richard Harrington and Chris Kauffman, directed by Patricia Buckley; *Oh Holy 'night, mother-Fucker* written and directed by Brian Fraley, choreography by Michelle Lamb, with Jill Ann Dugan, Peter Brydges, and Mikey McCue Featuring Suzy Darling, Erika Insana, Michelle Lamb; *The Perfect Girl (a Bizarre Science Fantasy)* written and directed by Jeffrey A. Lewonczyk, performed by and created with Katie Brack, Hope Cartelli, Jessi Gotta, Jay Klaitz, Jeff Lewonczyk, Robin Reed; *The Return of Toodles von Flooz* written and directed by Lisa Ferber, with Trav SD, Ivanna Cullinan, Lisa Barnes; *Sinistrality* choreographed by Jennifer Schmermund, with KC Chun, Leslie Cuyjet, Jennifer Schmermund, Sarah Wagner, Kim Young and Sarah Young; *A Song Sampling from The Banger's Flopera* by Kirk Wood Bromley and composer John Gideon, directed by Ben Yalom; *The Temperamentals* by Jon Marans, directed by Mark Ramont, with Arnie Burton, Tom Beckett, Andrew Nelson, Matthew Schneck, Michael Urie; *Third Person* written and directed by Peter S Petralia, with James Tigger Ferguson and Carlton Ward; *Visuals* by Laura Klein and James Morrison, Music by Nicole Jung; *THIS IS NOT A BURLESQUE: a surrealist burlesque* Directed by Juliet O'Brien and Rosalie Purvis, performed and choreographed by Juliet O'Brien, Clara Purvis and Rosalie Purvis; *World Gone Wrong* written and directed by Ian W. Hill, with Gyda Arber, Fred Backus, Eric C. Bailey, Gita Borovsky, Walter Brandes, Amy Caitlin Carr, Josephine Cashman, Maggie Cino, Bryan Enk, Stacia French, Matthew Gray, Ian W. Hill, Christiaan Koop, Dan Maccarone, Josh Mertz, Roger Nasser, Dina Rose Rivera, Yvonne Roen, Ken Simon, Adam Swiderski, Debbie Troche; *Zero Boy & Red Bastard* performed by Zero Boy and Eric Davis

MEMOIRS OF MY NERVOUS ILLNESS based on the book by Daniel Paul Schreber, written and directed by Michael Gardner; **Cast:** Hope Cartelli, Jessi Gotta, Ian W. Hill, Robert Honeywell, Jeff Lewonczyk; October 7–29, 2005

THAT'S NOT HOW MAHLER DIED Text, direction, scenery, and props by Ryan Holsopple; Produced by 31 Down radio theater; Set and Props, Mirit Tal; Video Keunyoung Oh; Lighting, John Luton; **Cast:** Lian Sifuentes, Ryan Holsopple, Frank Boudreaux, DJ Mendel; November 4–19, 2005

THE BABY JESUS ONE ACT JUBILEE December 1–17, 2005; Series included: *M*E*N*S*C*H* by Eric Winick; director, Christian Parker; *Humbugger* by Jon Marans; director, Arnie Burton; *Execution of a Reindeer* by Gary Winter, director, Hayley Finn; *The Christmas Suicides* by Peter S. Petralia; director, Ian W. Hill; *Damn Teddybears* by Alexis Sottile; director, Dominc d'Andrea; *A Christmas Full of Family Love* by Thomas Brashaw; director, Judson Kniffen; *An Intelligent Design* by Jeff Tabnick; director, Anthony Luciano; *Walking Shadow* by Danny Bowes, director, Ivanna Cullinan; *The Most Wonderful Time of the Year* by John DeVore, director, RJ Tolan; *Granduncle Tells the Children a Story of Kisselstrite During the War* by Jeff Lewonczyk; director, Hope Cartelli; *Christmas* by Young Jean Lee; director, Yehuda Duenyas; *Ich Liebe Jesus* by Robert Honeywell; director, Jeff Lewonczyk

NO STRINGS ATTACHED: FOREMAN FEST 4 February 9–26, 2006

TOTAL FAITH IN COSMIC LOVE by John DeVore; Director, RJ Tolan; **Cast:** Kate Sandberg, Steve Sanpietro; March 2–April 1, 2006

ADVENTURES OF CAVEMAN ROBOT Story by Jason Robert Bell and Britton Walters, book, lyrics and direction by Jeff Lewonczyk, music and lyrics by Debby Schwartz; Presented by Piper McKenzie Productions; Art direction, Jason Robert Bell; Costumes, Julz Kroboth; Lighting, James Bedell; Co-Producer, Shoshanna Weinberger; **Cast:** Jason Robert Bell, Hope Cartelli, Jorge Cordova, Kevin Draine, Chris Harcum, Ian W. Hill, Devon Ludlow, Robin Reed; April 8–May 13, 2006

CENTER STAGE, NY

ONE SOLO ARTS FESTIVAL Presented by terraNOVA Collective; Series included: *Dreaming of Kitchens* written and performed by Kate McGovern; *Snapshot* written and performed by Carmen Mitzi Sinnott; *Jazz Desert* written and performed by Rebecca Hart; *Tales from the Schminke* Tub by Steve Danziger and performed by Haskell King; *Mrs. Barry's Marriage* written and performed by Bronwen Coleman; The Peoples Improv Theater; *Meisterklasse; Pentecostal Wisconsin* original music, written and performed by Ryan Paulson; *Way to Go!; Deconstructing the Magician* written and performed by Nelson Lugo; *Without Regret, Deenie Nast* written and performed by Audrey Crabtree June 13–26, 2005

THE BIGGER MAN by Sam Marks; Producer, Partial Comfort Productions; Director, Louis Moreno; Design, Lex Liang; Lighting, Jason Jeunnette; Sound, Zach Williamson; Stage Manager, Claire M. Raper; **Cast:** Mark Alhadeff, Barnaby Carpenter, Sharon Freedman, Greg Keller, Molly Pearson; July 7–23, 2005

BILLY SLEEPYHEAD Book and lyrics by Webb Wilcoxen, music and lyrics by Webb Wilcoxen and Arthur Bacon; Produced by Bryan Billig, Heather Morris, John Richardson, and Jinn S. Kim; Director and Choreographer, Jill DeArmon; Design, Joe Powell, Nick Moore, Meghan Healey; Stage Manager, Aime Kelly; **Cast:** Alex Flores, Megan Lynch, Elijah Martinez, Andrew Mayer, Kiko Morini, Danielle Piacentile, Gabrielle Piacentile, Kristin Piacentile, Lindsey Rose, Elanna White, Charles Goforth; August 3–21, 2005

TOUCH ME/ROSA RUGOSA Two one-acts by Charles Cissel; Produced and directed by Dame Terese Hayden; Starring Jacqueline Brookes; October 5–16, 2005

Gillian Chadsey and Elisa Blynn in *Three Dollar Bill* by Kirk Wood Bromley, presented by Inverse Theater Company PHOTO BY JANE STEIN

TOUGHING SLUMARIA by Janeen Stevens; Produced by Original Intent Theater; Director, Barry Gomolka; Design, Hoyt Charles, Georgien Cooney, Hillery Makatura; **Cast:** Scott Van Tuyl, Ali Squiteri, Marie-Rose Pike, Chudney Sykes, Jahnavi Rennison, Barbara Miluski, Lane Wray, Stephanie English, Erin Fogel, Manny Liyes, Ray Wasik; October 29–November 13, 2005

GROUNDBREAKER'S READING SERIES Presented by terraNOVA Collective; November 17–19, 2005

THREE DOLLAR BILL Three short plays by Kirk Wood Bromley; Presented by Inverse Theater Company and Jane Goldstein; Director, Howard Thoesen; Included: *What Are You Thinking, Mary Cheney?, Civilization in Disco Tents, The Welcome Mask;* Design, Jane Stein, Jeff Nash, Karen Flood, John Gideon; Stage Manager, Ruthie Condie; **Cast:** Gillian Chadsey, Elisa Blynn, Bob Laine, John McConnel, Sonja O'Hara, Timothy McCown, David Nash; December 1–23, 2005

THE BIRDS AND THE BEES OR THE BIRDS AND THE BIRDS Nine short plays produced by Woman Seeking...; Writers: Rich Orloff, Tara Meddaugh, Barb Wolfe, Andrew N. Davis, Laurie Marvald, Kerri Kochanski, Ken Dashow, Judy Carlson Hulbert, Christine Mosere; Directors: Stephanie Hepburn, Kel Haney, Tzipora Kaplan, Kate Place, Ken Dashow, Nancy Larsen, Deb Guston; Design, Evan O'Brient, Ken Dashow; Choreography, Martha Cataldo-Casey; Stage Manager, Tzipora Kaplan; **Cast:** Joseph Small, Ruth Jaffe, Ken Dashow, Mark J. Foley, Jordan Auslander, Stephanie Hepburn, Jeff Wise, Nicole Winston, Christine Mosere, Wynne Anders, Laurie Marvald, Emily Alpren, Amy Bizjak, Andrew N. Davis, Vivian Meisner, Rhonda Ayers, Mary Anna Principe, Erin Roth, Jane Purcell Dashow, Robyn Hatcher, Martha Cataldo-Casey, Spring Sarvis, Kate Place, Merrick Dean; January 6–22, 2006

CRAVE by Sarah Krane; Presented by Bosley Theatrical Productions; Director, Justin Quinn Pelegano; Design, Andrew Lu; Production/Stage Manager, Devlin Goldberg; **Cast:** Heidi Armbruster, Michael Chmiel, Ryan Farley, Julie Fitzpatrick; February 22–March 4, 2006

BABY GIRL by Edith Freni; Presented by Partial Comfort Productions; Director, Padraic Lillis; Design, Lex Liang, Jason Jeunnette, Zach Williamson; Stage Manager, Christopher Munnell; **Cast:** Andrew Stewart-Jones, Chris Kipiniak, Curran Connor, John Summerour, Sarah Hayon, Trisha LaFache; March 15–April 1, 2006

CHARLIE PINEAPPLE THEATER

TRUE WEST by Sam Shepard; Director, Sarah VanDerBeets; Produced by the Charlie Pineapple Theater Company; Stage Manager, Scott Williamson; **Cast:** Robert McCarthy, Mark VanDerBeets, Ben Schiff, Joanne Joseph; June 2–25, 2005

ONE FLEW OVER THE CUCKOO'S NEST by Ken Kesey and Dale Wasserman; Director, Mark VanDerBeets; Produced by the Charlie Pineapple Theater Company; Stage Manager, Scott Williamson; **Cast:** Jerry Broome, Cidele Curo, George Stonefish, Michael Snow, Brian Leider, Michael Maher, Christopher Franklin, Kevin Pinassi, Vincent Allocca , Oscar Medina, Richard Millen, Jenn Zarine Habeck, Amy Jackson, Sarah Magnuson, Michael Glover, Jesse Perez, Rawle Williams, Timothy J. Cox; January 12–February 4, 2006

THE SNOW HEN written and performed by Hannah Bos and Paul Thureen; Director, Oliver Bulter; Produced by The Debate Society; Lighting, Mike Riggs; Costumes, Sydney Maresca; Sound, Nathan Leigh; Stage Manager, Amy Ehrenberg; Associate Producer, Vanessa Sparling; Featuring the voices of Pamela Payton-Wright and Adam Silverman

CHASHAMA

Anita Durst, Founder

OUTSIDE ARTS FESTIVAL, presented in BAM Park; July 9–31, 2005; Included: "Ha-Go-Ro-Mo" by Zeami, choreographed by Noriko Wako; Women's Voices/ Women's Visions by choreographers Cathy Richards, Abi Sebaly, Luis Gabriel Zaragoza and spoken-word artist Lenelle N. Moise; *Sleepless Solimnoquy* produced by Sacred Circle Theater; Trilok Fusion classical Indian dance; Cirque Boom Circus Theater's *Madness & Joy!*

SLAM THEATER at the Tank; September 6–27, 2005

COUCHWORKS 7 new short plays set on a couch presented by Slant Theatre Project; Included: *Museum Piece* by Rachel Axler, directed by Daniel Goldstein; *Pride and Prejudice* written & directed by Evan Cabnet; *"Rhapsody 3, or My Brother's Keeper"* by Marcus Gardley, directed by Wes Grantom; *Exposium* by Adam Knight, directed by Ellen Beckerman; *Members Only* by Adam Rapp, directed by Meredith McDonough; *Aftermath* by Theresa Rebeck, directed by Josh Hecht; *Music for a High Ceiling* by Mat Smart, directed by Steve Cosson; The Tank; September 10–October 4, 2005

CURRENCY 2005 International Performance Art; Organized by Dan McKereghan; The Tank; October 6–15, 2005

THE COLLECTION written and directed by Christina Masciotti; **Cast:** John Hagan, Jimmie James, Anna Kohler; 217 East 42nd Space; October 13–30, 2005

WILLIAM SHAKESPEARE'S HAUNTED PIER Created and directed by Mark Greenfield; Presented by chashama and The Faux-Real Theatre Company; Pier 25; October 29–31, 2005

SLAM, ACT 2 Presented by SLAM Theater; The Tank; November 7–28, 2005

AWAKENING *Reflections in Life, Death and Everything In Between…* by Karin Williams, Peter F. Langman, Dan Trujillo, November Dawn, Christine DiGiovanni, Lia Romeo, Adam Szymkowicz, Jim Dunleavy, Elizabeth Canavan, Catherine Zambri, Dale Anderson, Cristina Pippa, Laura Lewis Barr; Presented by This Woman's Work Theatre Company; Director, Christopher Goodrich; Lighting, Christopher R. Hoyt; **Cast:** Debra Kay Anderson, Jack R. Marks, Tawanna Brown, Mary E. Hodges, Mando Alvarado, Maybeth Ryan, Mollye Asher, Troy Hall, Frank Juliano, Candace Reid, Aaron Fili, Bonnie Barrios, Kevin Logie; 217 E 42nd Space; January 26–28, 2006

SILENCE IS HEALTH/SILENCIO ES SALUD by Karina Casiano; Presented by LaCriatura; **Cast:** David Storck Elodián Barbosa, José Acevedo, Antonio Pantojas; chashama @Queens; May 18–June 11, 2006

CHERRY LANE THEATRE – STUDIO THEATER

DOTTIE HOPE Written and performed by Laurie Sanderson; Director, Courtney Munch; July 20–22, 2005

PHAEDRA X 3 Part 1 bt Jean Racine, translated by Ted Hughes; Part 2 by Matthew Maguire; Part 3 by Sandra Kane; Produced by One Year Lease; Director, Ianthe Demos; Design, James Hunting, Kay Lee, Mike Riggs, Dave Chessman; **Cast:** Danny Bernardy, Jennie Hahn, Jim Kane, Christina Lind, Susannah Melone, Gregory Waller; November 22–December 22, 2005

ALL THAT FALL by Samuel Beckett; Produced by Kaliyuga Arts; Director and Designer, John Sowle; Sound, Sara Bader; Stage Manager, Jack Dyville; **Cast:** Helen Calthorpe, Guenevere Donohue, Kate Hamil, Daniel Hall Kuhn, Rand Mitchell, Steven Patterson, Erik Kever Ryle, Dan Seda, Bradley Wayne Smith, Matt Walker, Janet Ward; May 24–June 3, 2006

CHOCOLATE FACTORY THEATER

THE GUT GIRLS by Sarah Daniels; Presented by Flying Fig Theater and Heather Ondersma; Director, Michaela Goldhaber; Design/Crew: Phebe Taylor, Deb E Miner, Rebekah Bateman, Linda Jones, Judi Lewis Ockler; **Cast:** Soraya Broukhim, Twinkle Burke, Rodrigo Chazaro, Beth Wren Elliott, Tiffany Green, Janine Kyanko, Irene McDonnell, Kila Packett, Tracy Pérez, Brandt Reiter; July 17–August 7, 2005

GUN PLAY Director, Brian Rogers; Design: David Evans Morris, Beth Turomsha, Chris Peck, Maggie Dick; Timothy Haskell; Created and performed by Kanako Hiyama, Mikeah E. Jennings, Sheila Lewandowski, Elizabeth Ward, Paula Wilson; January 12–February 4, 2006

SOMEONE IN THE GHOST BOX TOLD ME IT WAS YOU Director, Kenneth Collins; Music, Andrew Elsesser; **Cast:** Ben Beckley, Alisa Burket, Gary Hogan, Anne Sorce; February 23–25, 2006

CARY FROM THE COCK Created and performed by Cary Curran; Director, Andi Stover; March 30–April 8, 2006

BURDEN Created and performed by Marissa Perel in collaboration with Kayvon Pourazar and Jon Moniaci; April 13–15, 2006

OLD TRICKS Created by Red Metal Mailbox; Design, Chloe Z Brown, Brad Kisicki, Mary McKenzie; Music, Sarah Gancher; **Cast:** Sarah Gancher, Alison Harmer, Sarah Maxfield, Rachel Tiemann; April 4–13, 2006

CLEMENTE SOTO VELEZ CULTURAL CENTER

THE MISSTEPS OF A SALSA DANCER by Candido Tirado; Director, Gloria Zelaya; Presented by The Latino Experimental Fantastic Theatre; Milagros Theater; June 17–25, 2005

KID DYNAMO Presented by Shady Glen Playas; June 23–25, 2005

LIMITLESS JOY Conceived and directed by Josh Fox; Presented by The International WOW Company; Design: Josh Fox, David Esler, Beau Allulli; Choreography, Josh Fox, Peter Schmitz and Ensemble; Flamboyán Theater; September 11–October 1, 2005

NIGHTMARE Director, Tim Haskell; October 14–31, 2005

CHEEKS Written and directed by Guillermo Gentile; Presented by The Latino Experimental Fantastic Theatre; Milagros Theater; November 11–December 11, 2005

THE MYTH CYCLE: AHRAIHSAK Written and directed by Rubén Polendo; Presented by Theater Mitu, Inc.; Design: Scott Spahr, Ryan Mueller, Miranda Hoffman, Ben Fox, Lori Petermann; Music, Todd Almond, Jef Evans; Stage Manager, Rebecca Griffin; **Cast:** Aysan Elik, Airrion Doss, Ben Fox, Carmen M. Herlihy, Jason Lew, Jenni-Lynn McMillin, Darren Pettie, Mark Schultz, Corey Sullivan, Peggy Trecker; LaTea Theatre; January 13–28, 2006

SILENCE IS HEALTH/SILENCIO ES SALUD by Karina Casiano; Presented by LaCriatura; **Cast:** David Storck Elodián Barbosa, José Acevedo, Antonio Pantojas; February 22–March 5, 2006

JERICHO by Jon Davidson; Presented by Moson Productions; March 17–31, 2006

BLOODY MARY by Rachel Shukert; Director, Stephen Brackett; Produced by Third Man Productions; Design: Anjeanette Stokes, Matt Urban, Andrew Boyce, Jacob A Climer; Composer, Cormac Bluestone; Stage Manager, Betty Hong Yiu Tung; **Cast:** Audrey Lynn Weston, Ian Unterman, Kristin Slaysman, Reginald Veneziano, Alison Tigard, Danie Streisand, James Ryan Caldwell, Edi Gathegi, Jo Hudson, Jeff Addiss, Evan Shafran, Chris Hale, Raina Wildenburg, Colin Gilroy, Adam Arian, Madeleine Maby, Sam Forman, Van Hansis; April 28–May 13, 2006

KNOWING BLISS Director, Lorca Peress; April 29–May 13, 2006

HAMLET by William Shakespeare; Director, Jose Esquea; Presented by Teatro LaTea; May 17–25, 2006

SUBURBIA by Eric Bogosian; Director, William Balzac; Presented by PossEble Theatre Company; May 18–June 4, 2006

COLLECTIVE: UNCONSCIOUS

D and **DANGER MAN** Two one-act performance pieces presented by Project D Company; June 16–26, 2005

NO ALARMS: (HEADFULLOFRADIO) Experimental theatre presented by Shifting Ambitions Theatre Company and Veritas Productions; July 21–29, 2005

BRINGING IT ALL BACK HOME by Terrence McNally; Director, Jacquie Phillips; Produced by Pravin Sathe and Solid Hang; **Cast:** Audrey Amey, Brandon Bales, Mary Guiteras, Peter Karinen, Tiffany May, Dean Storm; September 8–11, 2005

VENUS IN FURS Adapted by Michael Scott-Price from the novel by Leopold von Sacher-Masoch; Produced by Firebird Theory Theatre Company; Director, Michael Scott-Price; Sound, Javier Berzal; Set, Daniel A. Krause; Costumes, Stephanie Nichols; Lighting, Andrew Luther Glickman; Stage Manager, Mariel Matos; Choreography, Saar Harari; **Cast:** Jaime Robert Carrillo, Kim Katzberg, Amy Kersten, Carlton R. Tanis; September 30–October 16, 2005

JOSEPH HUBERTUS PILATES: AN AUTHENTIC WORK OF FICTION Written and directed by Marie Grillo; Produced by Under Construction Productions; **Cast:** Joe Carr, Dara Centonze, Delia Baseman, Mary Anna Principe, Olivia Baseman, Delia Baseman, Veronica James, Jonathan Prichard, Eric Starker, Brian Shaer; March 16–19, 2006

PAUL ZALOOM: THE MOTHER OF ALL ENEMIES Presented by Axepart; March 30–April 9, 2006

HABIB ALBI IS … NOT A MAN by Moheb Soliman; April 15, 2006

THE SHAPE OF THINGS by Neil Labute; Produced by Fine Point Theatre; Director, Kevin Dodd; Music, Tasneem Nadji; Design: Maggie Levin, Amith A Chandrashaker; Producer, Nickol Matallana; Stage Manager, Tzipora Kaplan; **Cast:** Lilly Cornell, Nickol Matallana, Cameron Ward, Noah Wunsch; May 4–7, 2006

THE NOSE Conceived and directed by Alissa Mello; adapted by Andy Roth; Puppets, Michael Kelly; Music, Joemca and Kamala Sankaram; **Cast:** Michael Kelly, Eva Lansberry, Jon Riddlegerger, Jane Catherine Shaw, Brian Snapp, Eric Wright; May 12–21, 2006

CONNELLY THEATER

KICKER by Robert Simonson; Produced by Triptych Theatre; Director, Brendan Hughes; Design, Ben Arons, Ryan Etzel, Sandra Godmark, Anne Kenney, Cat Tate; **Cast:** Jonathan Fielding, Juliet Gowing, Dalane Mason, Liam Mitchell, Lordan Napoli, Matt Pepper, James Lloyd Reynolds, Kelly Shaffer; June 9–25, 2005

NORMAL Book and lyrics by Yvonne Adrian and Cheryl Stern, music by Tom Kochan; Produced by Robyn Hussa and Transport Group; Director, Jack Cummings III; Scenery, John Story; Costumes, Kathryn Robe; Lighting, R. Lee Kennedy; Sound, Seth Guterman and Ray Schilke; Musical Director, John De Pinto; Choreography, Scott Rink; Production Manager, Matthew Trombetta; Stage Manager, Rebecca Yarsin; **Cast:** Barbara Andres, Nicholas Belton, Toni DiBuono, Adam Heller, Erin Leigh Peck, Shann Polly, Barbara Walsh; October 22–November 12, 2005

Graeme Malcolm and Jane Nichols in *Norman & Beatrice: A Marriage in Two Acts* presented by Synapse Productions PHOTO BY TONY JONES

ANIMAL FARM by George Orwell, adapted by Sir Peter Hall; Music by Richard Peaslee, lyrics by Adrian Mitchell; Produced by Synapse Productions; November 18–20

THE BROTHERS KARAMAZOV January 22–February 15, 2006

NORMAN & BEATRICE: A MARRIAGE IN TWO ACTS by Barbara Hammond; Produced by Synapse Productions; Director, David Travis; **Cast:** Jane Nichols, Graeme Malcolm; February 4–March 4, 2006

CUL-DE-SAC by John Cariani; Presented by Transport Group; Director, Jack Cummings III; **Cast:** Nicole Alifante, John Cariani, Robyn Hussa, Monica Russell, James Weber, John Wellman; April 29–May 13, 2006

CREATIVE PLACE THEATRE

THE DEVIL WINKS Written and performed by David Sirk; June 2–19, 2005

MRS. WARREN'S PROFESSION by George Bernard Shaw/ **MRS. WEINBERG'S PROFESSION** adapted by Aaron Rosenblatt; Rotating in repertory September 21–28, 2005

CRS STUDIO THEATRE

LIKE DECORATIONS IN A CEMETERY based on a poem by Wallce Stevens, created by Luminous Works; performed by Laylage Courie; June 11–12, 2005

SHIFTINGS Written, directed and performed by Joan Merwyn; October 7–16, 2005

THE MAIDS/DEATHWATCH by Jean Genet; Produced by Egress Theatre Company; Director, Andrew Bielski; **Cast:** Brendan McMahon, Nicholas Warren-Gray, William Fraser II, Kevin Dwane; Performed in repertory October 28–November 20, 2005

HANJO by Yukio Mishima; Director, Kameron Steele; **Cast:** Ivana Catanese; February 3–12, 2006

THE KIMONO LOOSENED Written and performed by Yuki Kawahisa; Director, Maureen Robinson; February 24–March 12, 2006

LITTLE EYOLF by Henrik Ibsen, Directed and adapted by David Greenwood; Produced by Fresh Look Theatre and Dharma Road Productions; Design: Casey Smith, Alex Moore, Alice Bryant; Stage Manager, Elliot Lanes; **Cast:** Christopher Michael Todd, Debbie Jaffe, Glenn Stoops, Raum-Arun, Margaret A. Flanagan, Alyssa Simon; April 14–May 7, 2006

THE CUTTING ROOM

LE SCANDAL Neo Burlesque and vaudeville with a dash of Coney Island with music by the NYC Blues Devis; Open run since January 3, 2004

BLITZKRIEG, THE HASSIDIC PROFESSIONAL WRESTLING MUSICAL Written and directed by Ron Glucksman; with Matin Friedrichs and Kelly Fraunfelder; September 7–21, 2005

CAUSE CELEB; September 12–26, 2005

THE GLAMAZONS IN DANCE OF THE SUGAR PLUMP FAIRIES December 3, 2005

A VERY BRINI CHRISTMAS featuring Brini Maxwell and The David Downing Trio; December 4, 2005

DINA MARTINA'S YULE LOG Written and performed by Dina Martina; December 5–6, 2005

MISFIT TOYS with Everett Bradley; December 11–26, 2005

NICE JEWISH GIRLS GONE BAD Comedy hosted by The Goddess Perlman with Rachel Feinstein, Rena Zager, Susie Felber, The Schlep Sisters, Dottie Lux, with Tracy Stark on piano and Eve Sicular on Drums; December 24, 2005

SHOCK & AWE A-GO-GO with Epstein and Hassan; February 24–October 27, 2006

NATALIE JOY JOHNSON in Concert March 15, 2006

DINA MARTINA: SEDENTARY LADY Written and performed by Dina Martina; April 13–29, 2006

CONFESSIONS OF A PRAIRIE BITCH Written and performed by Alison Angrim; May 12–13, 2006

JACKIE BEAT IS NOT A PEOPLE PERSON May 26–28, 2006

DILLONS

MEDIA KILLED THE VIDEO STAR Written and performed by Alex Perez; June 2–August 11, 2005

CLOSER THAN EVER Music by David Shire, lyrics by Richard Maltby, Jr.; Director, J. William Bruce; August 5–29, 2005

THE URBAN CHASE: SPRING IS SPRUNG Created and produced by Benjamin Rivers; **Cast:** Jake T. Walton, Michael Andrews, Keith Walton, Teresa Rivera, Steven Bennett; May 16–30, 2006

DIXON PLACE

SELF AT HAND: A PLAY IN 3 MODULES by Jack Hanley; Director, Christopher Eaves; June 3–11, 2005

AMERICA AIN'T READY by Pamela Sneed; June 17–18, 2005

2005 HOT! FESTIVAL June 29–August 29, 2005; Series included: *The Alice Complex* by Peter Nickowitz; Director, Bill Oliver; *The Values Horror Show* by Susana Cook; *Pride* by Perry Ojeda; *Party and Prey* by Brandon Olson and Rami Ramirez; Performances by Holly Hughes, Kate Bornstein, Murray Hill, Carmelita Tropicana, Lavinia Co-op, Miss Saturn, Jon Kinzel, Tanwi Nandini Islam, and Andy Horwitz

WARNING: NOT FOR BROADWAY 2005 Presented in conjunction with NYMF; September 22–25, 2005; Series included: *The Eggmobile* by Ricardo Ortiz; *Tuesday* by Brett Macias and Caroline Murphy, directed by Tom Wojtunik; *States of Confinement* by Lance Horne and Mark Campbell; *lovesick* by Michelle Feldman and Mames Jannucci, directed by Sarna Lapine; *BFG* by Gary Plotkin; *The Victor Woo Project* by Kevin Merritt and Kevin So; *Saddamn the Musical (Part II)* by Mitch Kess; *Deaf Man Mocking* by Jay Alan Zimmerman; *Only Children* by Michael Jackson and Rachel Peters; *Doctor Dick* by Susan Horowitz; *Pearl's*

Gone Blue by Leslie Kramer and Gabriel Gordon, directed by Sherry Teitlebaum; *Wake Her Up* by Janine MaGuire and Emily Paul, directed by Rose Ginsberg; *Olsen Terror* by Chris Wells, David May and Jeremy Bass

OLSEN TERROR by Chris Wells, David May and Jeremy Bass; Produced by Chris Mirto; January 9–March 13, 2006

HELP WANTED Written and performed by Josh Lefkowitz; January 13–21, 2006

ARABY by Chris Rael; Presented by Mondo Cane!; **Cast:** John Kelly, Gwen Snyder, Dudley Saunders, Shara Worden, Chris Rael, Rima Fand, Marla Hansen, Joe Quigley, Serena Jost, Marlon Cherry; January 26–28, 2006

THE PAINTER'S PROJECT An evening of short plays presented by Theatre Three Collaborative Company; **Cast:** Mauro Bossi, Colin Bridges, Dinh Doan, Guen Donahue, Donna Florio, Nicole Hafner & Dana Shiraki; February 2–4, 2006

BRINK Curated by Kimberly Brandt; **Cast:** Jack Ferver, Matthew Rogers, Jen Rosenblit; February 10–11, 2006

THE MAYOR OF BALTIMORE by Kristen Kosmas; Director, Kip Fagan; **Cast:** Lula Graves, Heidi Schreck, Jenny Stone, Haley Hughes, Elizabeth Latimer, Denver Latimer, Jesse Karch, Dana Olson, Forrest Gillespie, Tyler Nolan, Josh Olivera, Jane Beachy, Elizabeth Taylor, Mary Archias, Kristen Kosmas; February 17–25, 2006

CARMEN BORGIA: SOUTH Written and performed by Carmen Borgia; March 3–April 1, 2006

THE LEDGE by Jack Hanley; Director, Christopher Eaves; **Cast:** Mike Houston; March 24–April 8, 2006

VICKI WEAVER AND I... Written and performed by Rae C. Wright; Director, Merri Milwe; With Miranda Strand and Caitlin Sanders; April 20–22, 2006

THE BALLAD OF JUNK & MALFUNCTION Written and performed by Joseph Keckler and Melaena Cadiz; Director, Erin Markey; May 5–27, 2006

EVA PERON IN THE BONFIRE Written and performed by Marsha Gall; May 25, 2006

DON'T TELL MAMMA

SETH'S BROADWAY CHATTERBOX Created and hosted by Seth Rudetsky; Weekly on Thursday evenings, open run

FOLLYWOOD Sketch comedy written and performed by Walt Frasier, Laurice Fattal, Bill Beyrer, Robyn Kay, Spero Chumas, Jamie Watson, Stephanie Schreiber, Aaron Blumberg; July 7–August 25, 2005

RAGTIME JIMMIE: THE MUSIC OF JAMES V. MONACO Director, Earl Wentz; Presented by Wenhelm Productions; October 22–November 5, 2005

A VERY BETTE CHRISTMAS by Elizabeth Fuller; Director, Mark S. Graham; Starring Tommy Femia; November 17, 2005–January 8, 2006

EILEEN FULTON HOLIDAY CABARET SHOW December 9–16, 2005

UNDER THE INFLUENCE Director, Hector Coris; Musical Director, Gerry Dieffenbach; **Cast:** Marilyn Bettinger, Lana Krasnyansky, Suan Neuffer, Barbara Zaid; March 22–25, 2006

SUBURBAN GLITTER Created and performed by Paul Martin; April 21–23, 2006

REVIVAL! THE GOSPEL ACCORDING TO THE FABULOUS PINK FLAMINGOS Conceived, written and directed by Russell Taylor; Musical Director, David Snyder; April 24–May 16, 2006

DR2—THE D-LOUNGE

BIG STICKY Presented by Blue Box Productions; Shows included; *The Final Stage* by Ali Ayala and Peter Sarafin; *She Was a Real Tomato* by Lisa Ferber; *undertow* and *bridesmaid* by Clay McLeod Chapman; *30th Birthday Party* and *Candy* by Elizabeth Emmons; *Epistemology* by Ian Grody; *Showing Skin* by Rehana Mirza; *Piece by Piece* by Dennis Moritz; *Shooting the Breeze* by Chuck Orsland; *Snow* by Adam Szymkowicz; *In Between* by Jesse Wann; *ASL* by Gary Winter; Cast and directors: Adeel Akhtar, Ali Ayala, Jim Boyle, Virginia Callaway, Henry Caplan, Clay McLeod Chapman, Hanna Cheek, Jeremiah Clancy, Jarel Davidow, Elizabeth Emmons, Sarah Gliko, Jenny Greeman, Robert Hancock, Neil Hellegers, Matthew Korahais, David Marcus, Veronica Newton, Elaine O'Brien, Stacy Rock, Barry Roth, Peter Sarafin, Taniya Sen, Eve Udesky, Ana Valle; February 10–26, 2006

ASSISTED LOVING Written and performed by Bob Morris; March 1–April 30, 2006

DUO THEATRE

THE BOX Adapted and directed by Suzanne von Eck and Jeffrey Guyton; Presented by Gilgamesh Theatre Group; Music, Avram Pengas and the Noga Group; June 20–24, 2005

BUTTERFLIES ARE FREE by Leonard Gershe; Presented by No Limit Productions; Director, Joe Anania; **Cast:** Danny Araujo, Stephanie Fischer, Jane Carosiello, Andrew Whitney; October 20–30, 2005

ANGRY YOUNG WOMEN IN LOW RISE JEANS WITH HIGH CLASS ISSUES Written and directed by Matt Morillo; Presented by Kings and Desperate Men Productions; **Cast:** Jessica Durdock, Thomas J. Pilutik, Martin Friedrichs, Devon Pipars, Angelique Letitzia, Jessann Smith, Rachel Nau, Nicholas J. Coleman; January 19, 2005–February 25, 2006

THE FLEA

BOOCOCK'S HOUSE OF BASEBALL Written and performed by Paul Boocock; Director, Mary Catherine Burke; Design, David Evans Morris, Jeff Croiter, Jessica Gafney, Jake Hall; Stage Manager, Jennifer DeSimone; Downstairs at the Flea; June 30–July 23, 2005

INFILTRAGE An evening of one-acts; July 11–12, 2005

HALF LIFE by Robert Mouthrop; Director, Teresa K. Pond; Design, Dana Liebowitz, Mimi Maxen, Timothy Owen Mazur, Julie Duro; Stage Manager, Eliza Johnson; **Cast:** Cynthia Foster, Anna Chlumsky, Mark Lynch, Cameron Hughes, Michele Fulves; Extended from Fringe NYC; September 9–24. 2005

THE LIGHTNING FIELD by David Ozanich; Director, Jared Coseglia; Design, Paul Hudson, Amanda Ford; Music, Drew Brody; **Cast:** H Clark, Cory Grant, Ron McClary, Bekka Lindstrom; Extended from FringeNYC; September 12–28, 2005

GALAPAGOS ART SPACE

MONDAY NIGHT BURLESQUE Weekly ongoing variety show

CATCH XII Featuring work by Cynthia Hopkins, Myles Kane, Karinne Keithley, Sybil Kempson, Jeff Larson, David Neumann, Jenny Seastone Stern, and John Wyszniewski; August 27–October 1, 2005

DICK CHENEY'S HOLIDAY SPECTACULAR 2005 Presented by Billionaires for Bush; December 16–19, 2005

NEAL MEDLYN: SUPERSTAR DUETS March 3–31, 2006

POINT BREAK LIVE! Adapted from the film and directed by James Hook; March 17–April 2, 2006

RIP ME OPEN Created and performed by Desiree Burch, Michael Cyril Creighton, Kyle Jarrow, Brian Mullin; April 7–28, 2005

JACK AND THE BEANSTALK by Natalie Weiss; April 7, 2006

GREAT MEN OF GENIUS May 5–26, 2006

GARMENT DISTRICT THEATRE

UNDER A MONTANA MOON Written and performed by Bill Bowers; December 3–18, 2005

GOATS by Alan Berks; Presented by the Production Company; Director, Mark Armstrong, Producing Director, Kori Schneider; Design, Erica Hemminger, Jessica Gaffney, Emily Wright; Production Manager, Mary E. Leach; Stage Manager, Laura Williams; **Cast:** Michael Szeles; January 26–February 12, 2006

GENE FRANKEL THEATRE

MERRILY WE ROLL ALONG Music and lyrics by Stephen Sondheim, book by George Furth; June 3–12; 2005, Transferred to the 45th Street Theatre (see complete listing under 45th Street Theater in this section)

MEMOIRS OF A MANIC DEPRESSIVE by Gary Mizel; Director, Lorca Peress; Performed by Sexter Brown; June 27–July 9, 2005

THE QUEENS by Normand Chaurette, translated by Linda Gaboriau; Presented by Juxtaposed Theatre Company; Director, Gretchen M. Michelfeld; Stage Manager, Melissa Fendell; Design, Antoine Jermaine Thrower, Beatrice Terry; Ron Gilad, Nicole Provonsil; **Cast:** Katelyn Clark, Anna Fitzwater, Phyre Hawkins, Sarah Lemp, Nedra Morgan, Roni Yacobovitch; July 14–30, 2005

ANATHEMAVILLE by Scott Venters; Presented by The Orphanage; Director/Sound, Jess McLeod; Stage Manager, Leigh Murnane; Design, Nickey Frankel, Cecilia R. Durbin, Courtney Whipple, John D. Ivy; **Cast:** Scott Williams, Peter Dixon, Sidney Austin, Daniel Burress, Evan Rapp, Carolyn Castiglia, John D. Ivy, Mary McKenna, Paul Case, Maria Teresa Creasey; September 2–18, 2005

COP-OUT and **THE TALKING DOG** Two one-acts by John Guare; Presented by Red Radar Productions October 6–16, 2005

YOU NEVER KNOW Written and performed by Leslie Meisel; Co-conceived by Terry Jinn, Lisa Ackerman, Dan Sherman; by Manhattan Comedy Collective; February 2 and 16, 2006

I WANT TO BE A PONY Solo impov created by Topping Haggaerty; Presented by Manhattan Comedy Collective; February 9 and 23, 2006

BLACK MEN CRY TOO Presented by F.I.G. Theater Ensemble; Directors, Christopher George, Arno Austin, Marc Arnez, Cilque Brown; Company: Arno Austin, Terri Greene, Billy Collins, Andrew R. Cooksey, Saida Cooper, Nolan Edmonson, Bobby Faust, June Jefries, Jai Howard, John Menchion, Doug Powell, Vanessa Robinson, Lyle Schmerz, Vincent Shelley, Chrystal Stone, Carol Carter, Buddy Woodson, Adam Aronson; February 25–March 18, 2006

BRILLIANT TRACES by Cindy Lou Johnson; Produced by Any Old Company; Director, Marta Stout; Scenery, Zhanna Gurvich; Costumes, Julianna Bass; Lighting, Anjeanette Stokes; Sound, Jason Helias; Stage Manager, Dennis Loleng; Graphics, Bobby Kelly; **Cast:** Ben Abel Bey (Henry Harry), Katie Vaughan (Rosanna Deluce); February 28–March 11, 2006

SATURDAY NIGHT REWRITTEN Created and produced by Erik Marcisak; Writers: Rob Bates, Laura Buchhoz, Devon Coleman, Josh Drimmer, Fed Hatoum, Matt Koff, Dan McCoy, Lorie Steele, Lou Fernandez, Elliott Kalan, Brock Mahan, Anne Marie Rose, Sara Schaefer, Josh Wallach; Directed by Alan Fessenden and Eric Zuckerman; Stage Manager, Nicola Piggott; **Cast:** Christina Casa, Kibibi Dillon, Stuart Draper, Alan Fessenden, Lindsey Joy, Rick Murphy, Stacy Mayer, Phil Wedo, Rick Younger, Eric Zuckerman, Jeremiah Murphy, Ryan Stur; March 12–May 21, 2006

SHILOH RULES by Doris Baizley; Presented by Flying Fig Theater and Middle Tennessee State University; Director, Michaela Goldhaber; Design, Scott Boyd, Alisha Engle, Christopher Colucci; Fight Choreography, Chris Ockler; **Cast:** Judi Lewis Ockler, Kate Weiman, Janine Kyanko, Cordis Heard, Gwen Eyster, Samarra; March 18–April 9, 2006

AMERICAN SPIRITS Four one-acts by Amy Witting; Director, Bruce Ornstein; April 23, 2006

LOCOMOTIVE by Matthew Paul Olmos; Presented by woken'glacier theater company; Director, Nicholas Cotz; Design, Dash Barrett, Chantel Cherisse Lucier, Oscar Mendoza; **Cast:** Tim Douglas, Beth Manspeizer, Danielle Quisenberry; May 5–20, 2006

GREENWICH STREET THEATRE

NIGHTS OF WRATH by Armand Salacrou; Presented by Horizon Theatre Repertory; Director, Rafael DeMussa; Design, Ramona Ponce, Scott Aronow, Steve O'Shea, Krystin Smith; Stage Managers, Jonathan Solari, Kanako Morita; **Cast:** Alicia Adema, Gary Carlson, Rafael DeMussa, James Craft, Ed Suarez, John Gilligan, Ruth Kavanagh, Cain Perry; June 2–26, 2005

HOW YOU LIKE IT Director, Reginald Metcalf; Design, Shaun Motley, Victoria Tzykun; **Cast:** Jessica Gerono, Lilly Husbands, Jacquelyn Poplar, Kimberly Stowall; August 18–27, 2005

IDIOGLOSSIA by Mark Handley; Director, Osnat L. Greenbaum; Produced by The Absinthe-Minded Theatre Company; Producer and Designer, Ralph Scarpato;

Lighting and Videography, Paul Naclerio; **Cast:** Abi Clancey, Greta Pauley, Nina Rochelle, Ralph Scarpato; September 21–25

ARCADIA by Tom Stoppard; Presented by QED Productions; Director, Zander Teller; Producer, Michah Freedman, Martha Sparks, John McWhorter; Design, Melissa Daghini, Dov Lebowitz-Nowak, Mary Vorassi; Stage Manager, Ashley Herron; **Cast:** Michael James Anderson, Tim Astor, Mac Brydon, Tom Cleary, Michah Freedman, Lori Garrabrant, Rachel Jablin, Jennifer Lima, Shelley McPherson, John McWhorter, Michael O'Brien, Andrew Rein, Julia O'Brien; November 9–20, 2005

THE LADY CAVALIERS: SIGNATURE STORIES Written and directed by Peter Hilton; Produced by The Lady Cavalier Theatre Company, Krishna C. Nadella and Carrie Brewer; Design, Cheryl McCarron, Kevin Hardy; Stage Manager, Barbara Seifert; **Cast:** Amanda Barron, Carrie Brewer, Peter Hilton, Maggie Macdonald, Ricki G. Ravitts, Mark Silence, Nandita Shenoy; December 7–18, 2005

ANTON Written and directed by Pierre van der Spuy; Produced by VeritasLux Productions; Design, Jessica Lynn Hinkle, Sarah Phykitt, Katie Stults; Stage Manager, Sarah Ford; **Cast:** Loyita Chapel, Ana Kearin Genske, Jim Heaphy, Lee Kaplan, Kent Langloss, Shelley Phillips, Pierre van der Spuy, Jamison Vaughn; January 11–29, 2006

FOUR WOMEN by Cheever Tyler; Directed and produced by Christopher Carter Sanderson; Stage Manager, Terri K. Kohler; **Cast:** Kelly Tuohy, Ninon Rogers, Robin Benson, Debbie Stanislaus; February 5–28, 2006

THE LONG MARCH by Martin M. Maguire; March 31–April 2, 2006

LOOK BACK IN ANGER by John Osborne; Director, Don K. Williams; Produced by Wake Up, Marcon!; Design, Mark Delancy, Marion Talon, Allison Ferrier, Stage Manager, Audrey Marshall; **Cast:** Devin Delliquanti, Grace Riley, Timothy McDonough, Melissa Pinsly, Ned Cray; April 28–May 13, 2006

EXIT 13 Written, produced and directed by Frank Terranova; May 17–21, 2006

HENRY STREET SETTLEMENT — ABRONS ART CENTER AND HARRY DE JUR PLAYHOUSE

VISSI GALA CONCERT Presented by Vissi Dance Theater; Artistic Director, Courtney Ffench; **Cast:** Tonika Custalo, Kara Ffench, Juan Espinosa, Ariel Polanco, Candice Franklin Jill Rucci, Dan'te Jenifer, Erin Pride, Danielle Pizzaro, Chanel Mobley, Diedre Sears, Perdella In Baptiste, Pearl Marasigan, Erica Montalvo, Charlie Logan, September 15–18, 2005

PAUL ROBESON by Phillip Hayes Dean; Presented by Woodie King Jr.'s New Federal Theatre; Director, Shauneille Perry; Design, Shirley Prendergast, Sean O'Halloran, Patrice Andrew Davidson, Karen Perry; Stage Manager, John Eric Scutchins; **Cast:** Kevin Maynor, Cary Gant; November 17–December 11, 2005

NUTCRACKER IN THE LOWER Created and directed by Daniel Catanach; Presented by Urban Ballet Theater; November 26–December 3, 2005

BOOK OF SONGS Adapted and directed by Kuan Yu Fong and Stephen Kaplin; Presented by Chinese Theatre Works; March 4–5, 2005

CHAMPION and **THE STUTTERING PREACHER** Two one-acts presented by Woodie King Jr.'s New Federal Theater and Black Spectrum Theater; Design, Tony Davidson, Anita Ali Davis, Antoinentte Tynes, Sean O'Halloran; *Champion* by David Paladino, directed by Tommy Redmond Hicks; **Cast:** David Paladino, Ski

Cutty Carr; *The Stuttering Preacher* by Levy Lee Simon, directed by Woodie King Jr.; **Cast:** Joyce Sylvester, Levy Lee Simon; April 6–30, 2006

AUGUST IN APRIL Selections from the works of August Wilson with live performance and film documentary; Presnted by Woodie King Jr's New Federal Theatre; Director, Yvette Ganier; Design, Ashley Nicole Herring, Tameka Holmes, Jeremy Kumin, Travis Walker; Technical/Film: Dale Byam, Charles St. Clair, John Jannone, Michael Dotolo, Mark Ordway; Dramaturg, Karen Teacott; Choreography, Jacqueline Sawyer; **Cast:** Yaa Asantewa, Carmen Barika, J. Bernard Calloway, Gerard Catus, Nyasha Hatendi, Michael Fewx, Patricia R. Floyd, Tanika L.A. Harbor, Donald E. Jones II, Sally E Stewart, Sam Smith, Timothy Parham; Documentary **Cast:** Phylicia Rashad, Charles Dutton, Suzan-Lori Parks, Stephen Henderson, Viola Davis, Anthony Chisholm, Paul Carter Harrison, Ruben Santiago-Hudson, Lloyd Richards, Paul Butler, Woodie King, and Gus Edward; April 27–29, 2006

TREINTA Presented by Annabella Gonzalez Dance Theatre; Director, Choreography, Dancer, Annabella Gonzalez; Associate Choreography, Johnny Martinez; Composer, Stefania de Kenessey; **Cast:** Lucia Camboy, Juan Echazarreta, Heather Panikkar, Colin Roberts; May 12–13, 2006

HERE ARTS CENTER

DISPOSABLE MEN Written and performed by James Scruggs; Director, Kristin Marting; June 6–July 2, 2005

THE AMERICAN LIVING ROOM FESTIVAL July 20–August 20, 2005; Series included: *Still Life With Runner* by Steven Gridley; Directors, Steven Gridley and Jacob Titus; *Suadade* Created by The South Wing, Director, Kameron Steele; *Aurolac Blues* by Saviana Stanescu; Director, Nina Hein; *Drinking the Kool-Aid* Created and performed by Fernando Maneca/Manoiseca; *Yit, Ngay* Written and directed by Michael Lew; *Querrelle Quartet and Coming Forth By Day* directed by Yvan Greenber; performed by Laboratory Theater; *Is This a Gentleman?* written and directed by Kara Feely; Sound, Travis Just; Performed by Ross Beschler and Avi Glickstein; *Wound Up* choreographed and performed by Cheryl Conkling; Director, Maureen Towey; *Solo/Together* created by vibe Theater Experience; Directors, Dana Edell and Chandra Thomas; *Organized Color Intoxication* Director, Jonathan Zalben; Mixing and film, Taylor Krauss; *My Words Turn to Songs In Your Fists* Composed & conducted by John Altieri; Choreography, Daman Harun; *The Secret Face* by Elisabet Jokulsdottir; Director, Steinunn Knutsdottir; Performed by Palina Jonsdottir; *K.* Conceived and directed by Kenn Watt; Choreography, Tanya Calamneri; Created by Sean Simon, Deke Weaver, Raquel Cion, Gillian Chadsey, Sam Zuckerman; *Destruction* Adapted from Richard Foreman's notebooks; Director, Caleb Hammond; *All the Faithfully Departed* Choreography, Jeremy Laverdure; Performed by besto perfeckto; *In the Belly of the Beast With Two Backs* Conceived & directed by Lisa Jackson, with physical consulting by Matthew Morgan; *Flint, Michigan* Directed & co-conceived by Elizabeth Bourgeois, produced & co-conceived by Hays Hitzing; *State of the Union* Co-directed & created by Greg Felden, Alice Moore & Jonathan C. Green; *Fresh Kills: A Waste Is a Terrible Thing to Mind* Directed & composed by Lanny Meyers; Videos, Christine Schiavo; *Stay* Choreographed by Shannon Hummel in collaboration with dancers Vanessa Adato & Donna Costello of Cora Dance Company; *Eat Shit and Die With the Joneses!* Written & performed by Boomie Aglietti and Max Dana of The Society for Creative Dissent

BATH PARTY Written and perfomed by Meital Dohan, Karen Shefler, Ayelet Dekel; August 21–September 18, October 21–November 20, 2005

BOX OF FOOLS Created by Jessica Putnam Peskay, written by Joshua Putnam Peskay; Director, Matthew A. Peskay; Music, Stephen Jacobs and Eric Rockwin; August 21–27, 2005

THE WATER STATION (MIZU NO EKI) by Shogo Ohta; Director, Steve Pearson; Presented by Pacific Performance Project; September 7–11, 2005

BURNING BUSH: A FAITH BASED MUSICAL by Noah Diamond and Amanda Sisk; Produced by Nero Fiddled and Corey Moosa; Lighting, Chris Brown; Musical Arrangements and Sound, Death Mask (Mike Biskup, Drew Brady, Steve Dans, Boris Veysman); **Cast:** Amanda Sisk, Corey Moosa, Ellie Dvorkin, Kim Moscaritolo, Noah Diamond, Brian Louis Hoffman, Jennifer Boutell; September 15–October 16, 2005

CARNIVAL OF SAMHAIN Puppet theatre presented by Drama of Works; November 3–6, 2005

PAULSEN'S LONELY BANQUET Created and performed by John Paulsen; Director, George L. Lewis; November 25–December 17, 2005

CULTUREMART January 5–22, 2006

HEDDATRON by Elizabeth Meriwether based on Ibsen's *Hedda Gabler*; Presented by Les Freres Corbusier and Aaron Lemon-Strauss; Director, Alex Timbers; Design, Cameron Anderson, Tyler Micoleau, Jenny Mannis, Jacob Pinholster, Bart Fasbender, The Botmatrix, Mike Solomon, Stephanie Wiener, Erin Kennedy Lunsford; Dramaturgy, Anne Davison; Casting, Stephanie Klapper, Stage Manager, Kat West, Alaina Buckland; **Cast:** Carolyn Baeumler, Sam Forman, Gibson Frazier, Ryan Karels, Daniel Larlham, Julie Kake, Nina Hellman, Spenser Leigh, Michael Schulman, Ian Unterman, Jeremy Shamos; February 16–25, 2005

INSIDEOUT Created by Jason Pizzarello and Aaron Rhyne; Presented by Live Project, in association with Caden Manson; Director, Aaron Rhyne; Design, Linsey Bostwick, Aaron Rhyne, Erich Bussing, Daniel LiCalzi, Phil Christensen; **Cast:** Maria Theresa Creasey, Maria McConville, Graham Skipper, Steven Stafford; February 23–March 19, 2006

PHENOMENON by Gordon Cox; Presented by Nerve Ensemble; Director, Alyse Rothman; Design, Michael Moore, Miriam Nilofa Crowe, Dustin O'Neill; Music, Lance Horne; **Cast:** Michael Urie, Julie Jesneck, Rebecca Hart, Michael Lopez, Marshall York, Becka Vargus; March 6–25, 2006

Carolyn Baeumler in *Heddatron* by Elizabeth Meriwether presented at HERE Arts Center
PHOTO BY JOAN MARCUS

ALICE'S ADVENTURES IN WONDERLAND Adapted, directed and designed by Lake Simons and John Dyer; Lighting, James Latzel; Costumes, Carol Binion and Diane Simons; **Cast:** Deana Acheson, Mathew Acheson, Oliver Dalzell, Brendan McMahon, Yoko Myoi, Erin Orr, Lake Simons, Eric Wright, Nami Yamamoto; Musicians: Memory's Mystic Band (John Dyer, Justin Sherburn, Shera Worden, Michael Bodycomb, Adam Sorensen); March 29–April 22, 2006

THE ADVENTURES OF CHARCOAL BOY Created by Elyas Kahn, Eric Novak and Sarah Provost; Director, Sarah Provost; Music, Elyas Kahn; Puppets, Eric Novak; Lighting, James Latzel; Puppeteers: Lute Breuer, Ceili Clemens, Sam Hack, Kevin Taylor, Amanda Villalobos; April 1–23, 2006

STADTTHEATER NEW YORK — Presented by German Theatre Abroad; May 3–26, 2006; Included: *Slipped Disc – A Study of the Upright Walk* by Ingrid Lausund, translated by Henning Bochert; Director, Simon Blattner; Design, Malve Lippmann, Peter West, Elizabeth Rhodes; Stage Manager, Verity Van Tassel; Dramaturgy, Birgit Lengers; **Cast:** Sanjit De Silva, John Summerour, Danielle Skraastad, Andrea Ciannavei, Ron Domingo; *The Woman Before* by Roland Schimmelpfennig, translated by David Tushingham; Director, Daniel Fish; Design, Malve Lippman, Melissa Schlachtmeyer, Peter West, Elizabeth Rhodes; Stage Manager, Jason Kaiser; Dramaturgy, Dagmar Domros; **Cast:** Cynthia Mace, Ronald Marx, Christen Clifford, Diana Ruppe, Jeremiah Miller; *New German Voices 2006*– Staged Readings: *Electonic City* by Falk Richter, directed by Christoph M. Gosepath; *The Ballad of the Pine Tree Killer* by Rebekka Kricheldorf; *Dog Eats Grass* by Meike Hauck, directed by Daniel Brunet; *The Cold Child* by Marius von Mayenburg, directed by Johanna McKeon

HORSE TRADE THEATER GROUP

KRAINE THEATER

SERENADING LOUIE by Lanford Wilson; Produced by the If Ensemble; Director, Lisa Mitchell; **Cast:** Nate Rubin, John Samuel Jordan, Erin DePaula, Candence Allen; June 16–25, 2005

TREATY OF LONG ISLAND CITY by Ryan Tavlin; Director, Jon Rowan; July 7–9, 2005

THE ADVENTURES OF EVERYWOMAN Written and directed by Jeff Bedillion; Produced LMNO Theatre Company; Music, Ethan Hein; Choreography, Tomas Bell; Musical Director, Travis Blook; **Cast:** Stefanie Eris, Lisa McQuade, Danielle Morellino, Jennifer Susi, Margaret Spirito, Maiken Weiss; July 18–August 10, 2005

TAPE by Stephen Belber; Director, Esther Pan; Design, Nicholas Vaughan, Owen O'Malley; **Cast:** Pascal Beauboeuf, Nick Chase, Jennifer Robinson; September 8–September 17, 2005

THE SEVEN DEADLY SINS: 2005 by Dale Johnson; Presented by the Dale Johnson Creative Group; Directors, Dale Johnson and Jason Godbey; Stage Manager, Rob Signom; **Cast:** Eileen Reardon, Joshua Cherof, Allegra McBane, Ying-Yu Tan, Candace Laricci, Kyle Pierson, Ryland Shelton, Jennifer Makholm, Cindy Klaja-McLaughlin; October 4–26, 2005

WHAT WOMEN TALK ABOUT Presented by Manatee on the Couch Productions and Dragonchase; Directors, Hugh Sinclair and Wayne Parillo; **Cast:** Lauren Seikaly, Lynne Rosenberg, Katharine Heller, Brenna Palughi; October 6–November 12, 2005

A VERY NOSEDIVE CHRISTMAS CAROL Adapted by James Comtois; Produced by Nosedive Productions; Director, Pete Boisvert; Stage Manager, Stephanie Williams; Design, Patrick Shearer, Chris Daly, Catherine Culbertson; Producers, Pete Boisvert, James Comtois, Patrick Shearer, Stephanie Williams; **Cast:** Patrick Shearer, Christopher Yustin, Marsha Martinez, Scot Lee Williams, Larry Lees, Rebecca Comtois, Brian Silliman, Stephanie Williams, Shay Gines, Marc Landers, Jeremy Goren; December 8–17, 2005

GONER by Brian Parks; Produced by Word Monger Productions; Director, John Clancy; Design, Eric Southern; **Cast:** David Calvitto, Bill Coelius, Leslie Farrell, Patrick Frederic, Jody Lambert, Matt Oberg, Jona Tuck; January 5–28, 2006

TOO MUCH LIGHT MAKES THE BABY GO BLIND Created, directed and Produced by New York Neo-Futurists; Company: Desiree Burch, Regie Cabico, Chris Dippel, Molly Flynn, Sarah Levy, Rob Neill, Marta Rainer, Justin Tolley, and Yolanda Kae Wilkinson; Opened January 20, 2006 for an open run

SEVEN.11 CONVENIENCE THEATRE Fourth edition; Created and produced by Despina & Company; Director, Darron Carson; Music Director, Samrat Chakrabarti; Choreography, D.J. Salisbury; Design, Jeff McCrum, Ezekiel Kendrick, Shana Solomon, Jenny Fisher; Writers: Vishakan Jeyakumar (*Jaffna Mangoes*); Celena Cipriaso (*Homecoming*); Jackson Loo (*Kung Fu Hustle*); Samrat Chakrabarti and Sanjiv Jhaveri (*Who Killed Mr. Naidu First?*); Elizabeth Emmons (*Undone*); J.P. Chan (*The Old New World*); Rehana Mirza (*Bombay Screams*); **Cast:** Bill Caleo, Meetu Chilana, Andrew Guilarte, Sean T. Krishnan, Jerold E. Solomon, John Wu, Alicia Ying; March 30–April 16, 2006

MAN OF THE HEART Written and performed by Sudipto Chatterjee, based on the works of Lalon Phokir; Presented by East Coast Artists; Director, Suman Mukherjee April 27–May 7, 2006

THE RED ROOM

MY HEART SPLIT IN TWO by Terry Withers; Presented by Lucid Theatre; Director, Brendan Hughes; Rotating Cast including: Brenda Withers, Bob Holman, Adrianne Dunbar, Cliff Campbell, Paul Murillo; Opened July 21, 2005 for an open run

LIFE UNDER WATER by Richard Greenberg; Director, Dev Bondarin; August 8–10, 2005

IPHIGENIA AT AULIS by Euripides, adapted by W.S. Merwin; Presented by TimeSpace Theatre Company; Director, Greg Taubman; **Cast:** Anna Chlumsky, Mark Hattan, Maureen VanTrease, Rick Busser, Paul Casali, Christian Roulleau, Doug Sheppard; August 26–28, 2005

CONFERENCE ROOM A by Ben Cikanek; Produced by Kids With Guns Theater Company; Director, Mike Klar; Costumes, Heather Klar; Press, Sun Productions; **Cast:** Candice Holdorf, John Perry, Joshy Tyson; October 13–November 5, 2005

THE EIGHT: REINDEER MONOLOGUES by Jeff Goode; Presented by the Dysfunctional Theatre Company; Design, Porsha Taylor, Jason Unfried, Justin Plowman; **Cast:** Robert Brown, Jennifer Gill, Theresa Goehring, Amy Overman, Justin Plowman, Peter Schuyler, Jason Unfried, Jennifer Jill White; November 18–December 18, 2005

ON THE VERGE, OR THE GEOGRAPHY OF YEARNING by Eric Overmyer; December 2005

FAIRY TALE MONOLOGUES: FABLES WITH ATTITUDE by Paul Weissman; Director, Jeff Love; Produced by Point of You Productions; Design, Jeff Love,

Gerard J. Savoy, Karron Karr; Stage Manager, Sean Rodriguez; **Cast:** Cassandra Cooke, Evan Crook, Marlise Garde, David Holt, Melanie Kuchinski Rodriguez, Johnny Blaze Leavitt, Jeff Love, Alyssa Mann, Gerard J. Savoy, Paul Weissman; January 11–28, 2006

COWBOY MOUTH by Sam Shepard/**THICK LIKE PIANO LEGS** by Robert Attenweiler; One acts presented by Disgraced Productions; Directors, John Patrick Hayden and Robert Attenweiler; Design, Gabriel Hainer Evansohn, Graham Johnson; **Cast:** Nathan Williams, Mary Guiteras, Vina Less, Bret Haines, Becky Benhayon, Adam Groves, Keith Myers; February 21–March 1, 2006

MY HOUSE WAS COLLAPSING TOWARD ONE SIDE Conceived and designed by Christy Honigman, Conceived and directed by Charles L. Mee; Music, Myra Melford; Choreographed and performed by Myra Melford; March 2–5, 2006

THEY'RE JUST LIKE US by Boo Killebrew; Presented by CollaborationTown, a Theatre Company, Inc.; Director, Mike Doyle; Design, Ann Bartek, Meredith Neal, Ryan Trupp, Brandon Wolcott; Managing Director, Amanda Berkowitz; **Cast:** Jesica Avellone, Carly Cioffi, Geoffrey Decas O'Donnell, Boo Killebrew, Ryan Purcell, Hana Roth Seavey, Jordan Seavey, Phillip Taratula, TJ Witham; March 29–April 15, 2006

UNDER ST. MARKS

THE PERSIANS … A COMEDY ABOUT WAR WITH FIVE SONGS by Aeschylus, adapted and produced by Waterwell; Director, Tom Ridgely; Design, Sabrina Braswell, Lauren Crego, Brian McMullen, Elizabeth Payne; Choreography, Kate, Mehan, Lynn Peterson; Stage Manager, Kendall O'Neill; **Cast:** Hanna Cheek, Rodney Gardiner, Arian Moayed, Tom Ridgely; May 26–June 18, 2005

AMERICAN A-HOLE: THE SEARCH FOR THE MOST GREATEST SUPERSTAR EVER Presented by BRATPak Productions; July 7–16, 2005

HAM AND CHEESE Written and directed by Jessica Arnold and Andrew Toutain; Presented by the Rapscallions of the Periphery; October 7–22, 2005

THERE GOES THE NEIGHBORHOOD by Mari Brown; Presented by Synapse Productions; Director, Mari Brown and David Travis; Performed by Deanna Pacelli; September 26–November 7, 2005

SEQUINS FOR SATAN by Rachel Shukert; Presented by fetty productions; Director, Stephen Brackett; **Cast:** Lacey Langston, Jake Margolin, Reginald Veneziano, Justine Tante, Rachel Shukert, some other people, and ME as Grandma, Chasid Numba 1; November 15–16, 2005

CIGARETTES AND CHOCOLATE by Anthony Minghella; Presented by Emergency Theater Project; Director, Kate Pines; Design, Sarah Jakubasz, Fabio Blazina; **Cast:** Benjamin Correale, Lauren Ellman, Zarina Shea, Jesse Hooker, Erin Kunkel; December 1–5, 2005

THE UNDERSTUDIES Written and directed by Jeff Bedillion; Produced by LMNO Theatre Company, Jose Navarro; Design, Anna Peterson, Lynn Wheeler; Associate Producer, John Chatterton; **Cast:** Robert Abid, Tomas Bell, Stefanie Eris, Jennifer Susi, Maiken Wiese; January 13–29, 2006

HAM & EGG Written and performed by Pam Wilterdink and Meg Schroeder; Produced by BRATPak Productions, Dana Discordia; Design, Aaron Sporer, Stephan George, Carol Caronite; Music and Sound, Neil Benezra; Guitar, Jackson Schroeder; Graphics, Patric Kelly, Karen Kelly; Set and Prop Consultant, David Peterson; February 2–26, 2006

FROM MADISON TO MADURAI: 134 DAYS IN MOTHER INDIA Written and performed by H.R. Britton; Presented by Overcoat Theater; March 30, 2006

TWO ROOMS by Lee Blessing; Produced by Checkpoint Productions; Director, Kara-Lynn Vaeni; Design, Bryan Keller, Jessica Ford; Stage Manager, Heather Guthrie; **Cast:** Derek Lucci, Katie Tuminelly, Jaco Knowll, Emily Zeck; May 4–20, 2006

IMPACT THEATER

THE INSTITUTION by Gerald Zipper; Director, E.K. Rivera; Presented by Impact Theater Company; **Cast:** Steve Bussen, Ross Kidder, Ron Leir, Genia Morgan, Oh Rayne, Kimberly Stowell; July 21–31, 2005

THE SHADOW by Yevgeny Schvarts; Director, Oleg Barude; October 2005

SISTERS/TO DIE FOR LOVE Two one-acts by Gerald Zipper; Director, E.K. Rivera/ Greg Cucchino; **Cast:** *Sisters*: Tanya Drago, Jenna Harris; *To Die For Love*: Rosemarie Beltz, Anthony Parker, Elizabeth Poett; October 27–November 6, 2005

OUT OF THE FRYING PAN Director, Ted Mornel; December 2005

IMPACT WINTER ONE ACT FESTIVAL Presented by Impact Theater Company; Week One: *Blind Date* by Doug Beatty, directed by Vincent Reardon; *The Unexpected Visitor* by Robert Marese, directed by Dudley Craig; *…To Ashes* by Christine Conley, directed by Jonathan Whittle-Utter; *Crossing the Bar* by Christine Emmert, directed by Dudley Craig; *Audience Choice* by Brayn Clark, supervised by Lucas Peltonen; Week 2: *My Sloth* by Mark Robertson, directed by Sabrina Vajraca; *No Such Joy* by Jay Ferrari, directed by Tal Shahar; *Statues of Liberty* by Elisa Abatsis, directed by Nicole Franklin; *Dummy* by Tanya Ritchie, directed by Tal Shahar; January 19–29, 2006

THE TEMPEST by William Shakespeare; Presented by The Waterloo Bridge Theatre; Director, J. Brandon Hill; March 20–April 6, 2006

RUDY RUTABAGA & THE TERRIBLE DRAGON OF AMSTERYORK March April 2006

FEMALE BONDING by Susan Kaessinger; Director, James Alexander; **Cast:** **Cast:** Jordan Auslander, Keith Bethea, Corinna Bordewieck, Stephanie Bush, DeBorah Green, Susan Kaessinger, Anna Kull, Sonia Perez, Hannah Snyder-Beck, Jim Williams; March 22–April 1, 2006

WOUNDED HOPES based on the poetry of Gerald Zipper; Director/Designer, D.F. Ladd; May 11–21, 2006

AN EVENING OF ONE-ACTS *Overtones* by Alice Gerstenberg and *Dummy* by Tanya Ritchie; Director, Tal Shahar; May 2006

THE INDEPENDENT THEATER

SPIKE HEELS by Theresa Rebeck; Director, Jenn Bornstein; Produced by "des i am" productions; November 3–19, 2005

TWO YEATS PLAYS: THE CAT AND THE MOON/THE ONLY JEALOUSY OF EMER by William Butler Yeats; Presented by Handcart Ensemble; Director, Sam McCready; Design, Elana Zlotescu; Music, Nathan Bowen; Choreography, Andrea Homer-Macdonald; Lighting, David Kniep; **Cast:** Ron Bopst, David

D'Agostini, Marin Leggat, Jane C. Pejtersen, Brittany Pixton, Javen Tanner, Jjana Valentiner; March 30–April 15, 2006

FUNHOUSE by Eric Bogosian; Director, Jodi Smith; Produced by Native Aliens Theatre Collective; **Cast:** Cynthia Russell, Brooke Hoover, Jon Erdman, Brandon Heath, Jordan Smith, Christopher Speziale, Kenneth L. Naanep, Peter Schuyler, Liz Wisan, Philip Estera, Chandra Ratner, Rachel Grundy, Malachy Orozco; May 8–13, 2006

INTERART ANNEX

MEXICO by Peter Blomquist; Director, Molly Martin; Produced by Groove Mama Ink; Stage Manager, Kim Braun; **Cast:** Peter Blomquist, Gabriel Carter, Rachel Scott, Kara M. Tyler, Rolls Andre; July 21–30, 2005

LYING adapted by Jessica Burr and Matt Optrny from the memoir by Lauren Slater; Presented by Blessed Unrest; May 5–8, 2006

JAN HUS PLAYHOUSE

A CHRISTMAS CAROL, OY! HANNUKAH, MERRY KWANZAA, HAPPY RAMADAN Written and directed by Vit Horejs; Presented by the Czechoslovak-American Mariotnette Theatre; Design, Michelle Beshaw, Milos Kasal; **Cast:** Frances Devine, Vit Horejs, Gail Whitmore; December 1, 2005–January 1, 2006

THE MOST FABULOUS STORY EVER TOLD by Paul Rudnick; Director, Elaine Connolly; Produced by Luciano Kovacs and the Jan Hus Presbyterian Church Social Justice Committee; **Cast:** Renee Brown, Will Brown, Jim deProphetis, Robert Frink, Margaret Girouard, Luciano Kovacs, Heather Anne Smith, Caitlin Reilly, Danni Willis; March 3–11, 2006

THE KITCHEN

ROBERT MELEE'S TALENT SHOW Curated by Robert Melee; June 29–30, 2005

WISH YOU WERE HERE Created and choreographed by Beth Gill and Dkduya Ohashi; Performed by Ohashi and Miu Miu; September 29–30, 2005

DARA FRIEDMAN: SUNSET ISLAND September 15–October 22, 2005

THE END OF REALITY Written and directed by Richard Maxwell; Presented by the New York City Players; Design, Eric Dyer, Kaye Voyce; Fight Consultant, Brian Mendes; Stage Manager, Scott Sherratt; **Cast:** Jim Fletcher, Marcia Hidalgo, Thomas Bradshaw, Alex Delinois; Sibyl Kempson, Brian Mendes; January 12–28, 2006

STILL SMOKING Choreographed by Maria Hassabi; April 13–15, 2006

THE SHOW (ACHILLES' HEELS) Choreographed by Richard Move; Music, Deborah Harry; Score, Arto Lindsay; Design, Nicole Eisenmann; April 26–May 6, 2006

LARK PLAY DEVELOPMENT CENTER

PLAYWRIGHTS WEEK FESTIVAL June 10–18, 2005; Included: *Joys of Lipstick* by Layla Dowlatshahi, *Smart* by Robert Fieldsteel, *Billy Dillan Prays* by Ken Hanes, *Mother in Another Language* by Taniya Hossain, *Matka King* by Anosh Irani, *The Ruby Vector* by Karla Jennings, *Southern Cross* by Dan O'Brien, *Good Hope* by August Schulenberg, *All Fall Away* by Said Sayrafiezadeh, *The Death of A Cat* by C. Denby Swanson, *Counter Offense* by Rahul Varma

BAREBONES SERIES

BARNSTORMER Book and lyrics by Cheryl L. Davis, music by Douglas J. Cohen; Director, Jerry Dixon; Music Director, Bill Tinsley; Choreography, A.C. Ciulla; Stage Manager, Robert A. Sherrill; **Cast:** Cheryl Alexander, Erica Ash, Stu James, Andre Montgomery, Ken Prymus, David St. Louis, Gayle Turner; November 5–16, 2005

LENIN'S SHOE by Saviana Stanescu; Director, Daniella Topol; **Cast:** Amir Arison, William Carden, Walter J. Masterson, Florin Penisoara, Jessica Warner, Jennifer Dorr White, Shawn-Caulin Young; February 1–11, 2006

BREATH by Javon Johnson; Director, Rajendra Ramoon Maharaj; **Cast:** Jerome Preston Bates, Chadwick Boseman, Jed Dickson, Barbara Gulan, Trish McCall, Nick Petrie; March 15–25, 2006

AMERICAN HWANGAP by Lloyd Suh; Director, John C. Eisner; **Cast:** Michi Barall, Joel DelaFuente, Mia Katigbak, Peter Kim, Hoon Lee

STUDIO RETREATS

JIHAD JONES AND THE KALASHNIKOV BABES by Yussef El Guindi; Director, Sturgis Warner; September 15, 2005; **MISTERIOSO-119** by Koffi Kwahule; Director, Liesl Tommy; October 27, 2005; **VATTAGO** by Ian Cohen; Director, Steven Williford; November 17, 2005; **MAURITIUS** Written and directed by Theresa Rebeck; December 8, 2005; **AMERICAN HWANGAP** by Lloyd Suh; Director, John C. Eisner; December 15, 2005; **SMART** by Robert Fieldsteel; Director, Linnet Taylor; January 19, 2006; **PLEASURE AND PAIN** by Chantal Bilodeau; Director, Jessica Heidt; February 16, 2006; **SOMETHING ELSE AGAIN** by Brian Dykstra; Director, Margarett Perry; April 6, 2006

PUBLIC READINGS

THE FACE OF JIZO by Hisahshi Inoue; Director, John C. Eisner; September 12, 2005

THE MISFORTUNE OF OUR FRIENDS by Sandi Goff; Director, Steven Williford; September 26, 2005

LOOKING GLASS THEATRE SPACE

HELP ME HELP MYSELF: THE NEW YORK GUIDE TO LOVE, FAME, FORTUNE AND EVERYTHING YOU'VE EVER DREAMT OF IN 30 DAYS OR LESS by Jenna Bans; Produced by Off the Leash Productions; Director, Matthew G. Rashid; Designer, Dianna Whitten; Costumes, Jessica Jahn; **Cast:** Jessica Arinella, Marina Kotovnikov, Joffre Myers, Matthew G Rashid, Julie Tortorici; November 9–19, 2005

AVALON Director, Glory Sims Bowen; Produced by FHB Productions; Scenery, Carolyn Mraz; Costumes, Irma L. Escobar; Lighting, Amanda Woodward; Sound, Christopher Brooks; Fight Choreography, Ryan Bartruff; Choreography, Hana Mori Taylor; **Cast:** Randi Sobol, Matthieu Cornillon, Linda Blackstock, Michael Whitney, Ali Baynes, John Bertrand, Jordana Oberman, Maggie Surovell, Sarah Jebian, Jesse May, Randy Howk, Matthew Sholler, Cameron Peterson, Susan Rankus, J. Dolan Byrnes, Yvonne Roen, Joe Sevier, Jess Cassidy White, Andrew Beattie, Amy Dannenmueller; February 2–25, 2006 in repertory with *Babies With Rabies* and *Winter*

BABIES WITH RABIES by Jonathan Calindas; Produced by Cuchipinoy Productions; Director, Rodney E. Reyes; Scenery, Mario Corrales; Music, Mickey Zetts; Stage Manager, Lisa Hataf; **Cast:** Erwin Falcon, Tami Gebhardt, Dennis Lemoine, Tom McCartan, Rob Moretti, Kelly Rauch, and Andrew Rothkin; February 3–26, 2006 in repertory with *Avalon* and *Winter*

WINTER by A.J. Raath based on Shakespeare's *The Winter's Tale*; Produced by 2B and Wrash Theatre Company; Director, W. Allen Wrede; **Cast:** Michael Beaman, Sarah Brynne, Andrew Carter, Anthony Ciccotelli, R.J. Foster, Felicia Graybeal, Topping Haggerty, Suzanne Hall, Jeffrey Kitrosser, Stephanie Roman, Daniela Tedesco; February 4–26, 2006 in repertory with *Avalon* and *Babies With Rabies*

MANHATTAN REPERTORY THEATRE

ENDINGS Five short plays written and directed by John Capo; Presented by Etcetera in association with John Capo Productions; **Cast:** Sean Patrick Monahan, R. Ross Pivec, Mark Souza, Joseph Kopyt, Jack Moran, Gillian Sheffler, Hunter Treymayne, Deborah Radloff, Emily Mitchell, John Capo; February 21–26, 2006

ONE GOOD MARRIAGE by Sean Reycraft; Produced by diy theater/Kneeling Buss Theatre; Director, Diana Belshaw; **Cast:** Justin Conley, Siobhan Power; April 6–23, 2006

THE MERRY MONTH OF MAY FESTIVAL

THE DENTIST (OR BE CAREFUL WHAT YOU PUT IN YOUR MOUTH) by Jason Kendall, Director, Blake Bradford; **Cast:** Evan Alboum, Barbara Charlene, Melissa Macleod Herion, John Carey, Steven Ungar, Wyatt Keuther, Joel Bischoff, Maggie Lauren, Amanda Garry, Jared R. Lopatin, Emma Gordon; May 4–27, 2006

DONNA'S LATE NIGHT CABARET Written and performed by Donna Steams; Produced by Jason Kendall; Choreography, Ria Binaoro; May 5–26, 2006

A MIDSUMMER NIGHT'S DREAM Produced by Jason Kendall; Director, Lon Blais; **Cast:** Jason Adamo, Ashton Crosby, Sarah Silk, Chella Ferrow, Michael Vaccaro, Stephen A. Long, Marty Keiser, Dusty McKellan, Robert Dioguardi, Matthew R. Staley, Paul Pakler Brett Maughan, Emily Gerstell, Erica Francis, Judith Kilzer, Christina Lynn Vinsick; April 30–May 3, 2006

MUCH ADO ABOUT NOTHING Produced by Jason Kendall; Director, Jerry Marco; Musical Director, Talia Segal; **Cast:** Marisa Marquez, Rob Tode, Uma Incrocci, Kevin Davis, Justin Ness, Taras Berezowsky, Paul Weissman, Rainbow Dickerson, Michael J. Muldoon, Krista Peterson, Sabrina Colie, Eveline Tseng, Mateo Moreno, Kenny Wade Marshall, Paul Hufker, Rawle Williams, Andrea Cosley, Miriam Morales, Tammy Tunyavongs; May 7–10, 2006

ALL'S WELL THAT ENDS WELL Produced by Jason Kendall; Director, Stephen Wargo; **Cast:** Navida Stein, Collin Biddle, Richard Fromm, Carol Hickey, Michael Poignand, Hank Davies, Alex Pappas, Chris Kateff, Melissa Menzie, Nicholas Alexiy Moran, Matt Mullin; May 14–17, 2006

TWELFTH NIGHT Produced by Jason Kendall; Director, James Alexander Bond; Music, Donna Stearns; **Cast:** Elizabeth G. Wilson, Gavin Hoffman, Shashanah Newman, Brandon Wardell, Erik Sherr, Charles J. Roby, Erik Sherr, Charles J. Roby, Erin Caldwell, Michael Bernstein, Adam Raynen, Marc Improta, Christopher James Reed, Adam David Jones;May 21–24, 2006

MANHATTAN THEATRE SOURCE

JUNE REP Three one-acts presented by Working Man's Clothes: *The Audition, Lost, Found, and Remembered,* and *Playoff Picture;* June 5–7, 2005

AND BABY MAKES SEVEN by Paula Vogel; Director, Lila Rose Kaplan; Produced by the Temporary Theatre Company; Design, Laura Jellinek, Jay Scott, Mikaela Holmes, Todd Lincoln; Stage Manager, Kate Scefonas; Production Manager, Margaret E. Hall; **Cast:** Olywyn Conway, Claire Karpen, Jordan Seavey; June 23–25, 2005

ELIZA'S WINDOW Presented by Paper City Productions; July 9–August 27, 2005

SAINT FRANCES OF HOLLYWOOD by Sally Clark; Produced and directed by Daryl Boling; Design, Stephen Arnold, Andrew Bellware, Michael Bevins; Stage Manager, Leslie Cloninger; **Cast:** Sarah Ireland, Sharon Fogarty, Hank Davies, Dave Bachman, Jeff Broitman, Fiona Jones, Kendra Kohrt, Lex Woutas, Michael Shattner, Jeffrey Plunkett; July 13–August 6, 2005

MIDNIGHT Written and directed by David Epstein; Presented by the Invisible City Theater Company; Lighting, Jason J. Rainone; Stage Manager, Maggie Bell; **Cast:** Gerry Lehane, Rob Armstrong, Dan Patrick Brady, Nicholas Warren-Gray, Kathleen Wallace, Jeff Galfer, Douglas Goodrich, Elizabeth Horn; August 10–27, 2005

FINDING PEDRO Written by and starring James Heatherly; Co-written and directed by Lisa Gay Gardner; Produced by Saturday Players; Lighting, Trent Armstrong; Sound, Aaron David Blank; Set and Costumes, Jared B. Leese; Production Manager, Juanita Schwartz; August 30–September 10, 2005

ESTROGENIUS FESTIVAL 2005 September 21–October 15, 2005; Series included: Week 1– *Rearview Mirror* by Laura Schlachtmeyer, directed by Daryl Boling; *A Left at Happily Ever After* by Cathrine Goldstein, directed by Anna Guttormsgaard; *Fix Me, Please and Thank You* by Catherine Zambri, directed by Alison Talis; *Reunion* by Daryl Boling, directed by Paula D'Alessandris; *Challenged* by Fiona Jones, directed by Betsy Sanders; Stage Manager, Ben Sulzbach; Design, Alex Senchak, Paul Maaz, K.B. Sanders; Week 2– *Baggage* by Michael Ramirez, directed by Johanna Gruenhut; *Ladies of the Lake* by Stuart D'Ver, directed by Synge Maher; *The Wedding* by Lucia Del Vecchio, directed by Jocelyn Sawyer; *Take Care of Yourself* by Diana Fithian, directed by Miriam Eusebio; *Strange Bedfellows* by Peggy Dougherty, directed by Laura Henry; Stage Manager, Matt Quint; Design, Alex Senchak, Paul Mazza, Aaron Meadows; Week 3– *Blood White* by Brian Blake, directed by Heidi Handelsman; *The One That Got Away* by Lissa Brennan, directed by Joan Murray; *Remind Me Again* by Sharyn Rothstein, directed by Rachael Evans; *Rewind* by Renee Fleming, Directed by Kelly Haydon; *Purity and the Prince* by Robin Rice Lichtig, directed by Handan Ozbilgin; Stage Manager, Alexis

Hadsall; Design, Alex Senchak, Ann Sandoval, Paul Mazza, Kevin Hardy; Week 4– *Awake* by Meryl Cohn, directed by Alexandra De Suze; *Haunted* by Stephanie Zadravec, directed by Amber Estes; *Oh Hell No!* by Vanessa A. Spencer, directed by Esther Pan; *Love, Joel* by Jennifer J. Katz, directed by Maura Kelley; *You Look Really Hot* by Mac Rogers, directed by Jordana Davis Williiams; *Ice, Rock and Dust* by Kim Kolarich, directed by Kathleen O'Neill; Stage Manager, Amber Estes; Design, Alex Senchak, Annie Simon, Paul Mazza, Stephen Arnold

SCREWUPS by Justin Warner; Directors, Courtney Birch, Michael D. Jackson, Ari Laura Kreith; November 9–19, 2005

CORONADO by Dennis Lehane; Director, David Epstein; Presented by the Invisible City Theater Company; Design, Michael Carnahan, Michael Bevins, Driscoll A. Otto; **Cast:** Maggie Bell, Dan Patrick Brady, Elizabeth Horn, Gerry Lehane, Jason MacDonald, Rebecca Miller, Lance Rubin, Kathleen Wallace; November 30–December 17, 2005

IT'S A WONDERFUL (ONE MAN SHOW) LIFE! Directed and adapted by Sharon Fogarty, featuring Jason Grossman; Produced by Funny…Sheesh and Making Light; December 5–29, 2005

A CHRISTMAS CAROL Adapted and performed by Greg Oliver Bodine; Produced by Sharon Fogarty and Making Light Productions; Director, Shana Solomon; December 11–30, 2005

THE MANDRAKE by Niccolo Machiavelli, translated by Vinne Marano and Ollie Rasini; Director, Daryl Boling; Design, Stephen Arnold, Maruti Evans, Michael Bevins, Mari Kenny, Drew Bellware; Stage Manager, Laura Schlactmeyer; **Cast:** Steve Deighan, Cynthia Foster, Ridley Parson, Jeffrey Plunkett, Kathy Searle, Michael Shattner, Clare Stevenson, Benjamin Thomas; January 5–28, 2006

MACHIAVELLI by Richard Vetere; Director, Andrew Frank; Design, Maruti Evans, Michael Bevins; **Cast:** Jason Howard, Lex Woutas, Jim Wetzel, Liza Vann; January 12–February 5, 2006

PROOF by David Auburn; Director, Adam Gerdts; Presented by Groud Up Productions; **Cast:** Kate Middleton, Amy Heidt, Stuart Marshall, Guy Olivieri; February 8–18, 2006

TEMPLE by Tim Aumiller; Produced by Bridge Club Productions and Working For Tips Productions, Laura Camien, James McNeel, John Ort; Director, Greg Foro; Design, Marc Jnowitz, Chase Tyler; Stage Manager, Will Geisler; Production Manager, Emilia Goldstein; **Cast:** Audrey Amey, Tom Baran, Phil Burke, Tom Macy, Lesley Miller, David Rudd, Joshua Seidner; February 22–March 11, 2006

GOOD by C.P. Taylor; Director, Jennifer Gordon Thomas; Produced by Sharon Fogarty and Making Light Productions; Musical Director, Charles Geizhals; Design, Stephen Arnold, Renee M. Bell; Choreography, Melissa Riker; Stage Manager, Ben Sulzbach; **Cast:** Daryl Boling, Waltrudis Buck, Jason Grossman, Stephanie Kovacs, Chip Phillips, Danielle Quisenberry, Christian Rummel, Laura Schwenninger, G. Ivan Smith, Jeff Wills; March 15–April 1, 2006

EAST VILLAGE WRITER'S BLOC by Arthur Nersesian; Director, Paul Mazza; April 19–22, 2006

PUMP BOYS AND DINETTES by John Foley, Mark Hardwick, Debra Monk, Cass Morgan, John Schimmel, and Jim Wann; Directors, Adam Gerts and Laura Standley; Produced by Ground Up Productions; Design, Rachel Gilmore, Christopher Baine; Stage Manager, Devan Hibbard; **Cast:** Franklin Golden, Amy Heidt, Michael Hicks, Zeb Holt, Kate Middleton, Mitch Rothrock; May 10–27, 2006

MEDICINE SHOW THEATRE

PILGRIMS by Jamie Carmichael; Produced by Babel Theatre Project, Jeremy Blocker; Director, Geordie Broadwater; Design, Josh Randall, Anthony Gabriele, Melissa Goldman, Meredith James, Asta Hostetter; Fight Choreographers, Dan Renkin, Brad Lemons; Stage Manager, Sarah Curtis; **Cast:** Catherine Gowl, Eric Murdoch, Rufus Tureen, Emily Young; July 8–31, 2005

THE LAST BOHEMIANS by Stelios Manolakakis; Presented by Princes' Kisses Theatre Group; September 8–October 2, 2005

THE SWORD POLITIK Presented by The Hudson Skakespeare Company; September 12–17, 2005

CONFESSIONS OF A PT&A MOM Created and written by Carole Montgomery; October 5, 2005

THE CHANGELING by Thomas Middleton and William Rowley; Presented by the Theatre Rats; Director, Lauren Reinhard; **Cast:** Sarah Tilson, Vince Phillip, Anna Chlumsky, Jess C. White, Jamie Askew, Robert Haufrecht, Cedric Jones, Joshua Price, Zac Springer, Eric Bailey, Dalane Mason, Malachy Orozco, Michael Freeland, Brooke Hoover, Chris Speziale, Amy Kersten, Kenneth Naanep, Jen Cintron; March 2–11, 2006

JOAN'S VOICES *Joan of Lorraine* by Maxwell Anderson, *The Lark* by Jean Annoulih, *St. Joan* by George Bernard Shaw; Presented by Malvern Players; Director, Ron Parrella; Design, Christopher Jensen, Sam Joseph; Stage Manager, Lara Buck; **Cast:** Steven Ackerman, Ed Avila, Charlotte Balibar, Michael Blanc, Michael Bordwell, Steve Bovch, Lara Buck, Jill Butterfield, Christopher Currie, Michael Donaldson, Brian Hagerty, Sam Joseph, Mark Lobene, Harriet Parker Mann, John Rawlinson, Jillian Smith, Len Weiss; May 25–June 4, 2006

MICHAEL WELLER THEATRE

ONE MONKEY DON'T STOP NO SHOW Director, Khary Wilson; Design, Cathy Beals, Shoshana Solomon, Allison May; Stage Manager, Vincent Allen; **Cast:** Gil Charleston, Jessica Jackson, Donald Gilmore, Alicia Jones, Zay Pierre-Louis, Nisha Beech, Angela Lewis, Jacquelyne Wade George; October 12–16, 2005

JUST HAPPY TO BE HERE? Written and performed by Damien D. Smith, directed by Jason Summers; and **SKINPOPPIN** Written and performed by Basil Scrivens, directed by Ozzie Jones; Two solo shows presented by Arch Productions; November 17–20, 2005

FISH BOWL Written and produced by Simona Berman and Andrew Thomas Pitkin; Presented by I Ate What? Theatre Company; Director, Chris Henry; Choreography, Jenny Rocha; Stage Manager, Lanita Ward; Composer, Stephen Pitkin; Design, Jian Jung, Sarah James, Ted Sullivan, Matthew Lebe, Sherry Ann Danna; **Cast:** Jeff Edgerton, Simone Harrison, James Huffman, Pamela Stewart, Michael Borrelli, Simona Berman, Shevaun Smythe-Hiler, Anna Farkas, Christine Poland, Reiko Yamanaka; January 7–22, 2006

GIRL IN HEAT by Nelson Avidon; Director, Robert Walden; Design, Maya Kaplun, Hillery Makatura; Stage Manager, Charles Casano; **Cast:** Cheryl Leibert, Nelson Avidon; January 27–February 19, 2006

L.A & PITCHING TO THE STAR by Donald Marguiles; Director, Jessica Dermody; March 26–27, 2006

THE MONSTER CABARET

2005 SPOTLIGHT ON HALLOWEEN FESTIVAL Presented by Spotlight On Productions (Frank Calo, Artistic Director); October 8–November 3, 2005; Included: *Somebody Else's Life* by Jerry Rabushka, directed by Greg Hunsaker, presented by Ragged Blade Productions; *Knife Assassin* by Alan Kanevsky, directed by Mike Strozier and Scott R. Weigand; *Unlikely Conversations* (*Helga Schmidt's Pussy* by Edward Crosby Wells/*Sisters of Little Mercy* by Edward Crosby Wells/*Fairy Tales Can Come True* by Richard Lay/*Sitting Across from God* by David Occhino) directed by Steven Thornburg and Frank Calo; *Booooo! Threeee!* by The Mistake, directed by Ken Scudder; *Babies with Rabies* by Jonathan Calindas, presented by Cuchipinoy Productions; *The Mysteries of the Castle of the Monk of Flaconara* by James Armstrong, directed by Ken Kaisser; *Alice on the Edge* by Andrew Rothkin; *Requiem for Adrian Bayle* by Drew David Sotomayer, directed by Jonathan Tessero; *The Cobra Lady Strikes* by Todd Michaels, directed by Neal Sims, presented by Grayce Productions; *Avalon* by Glory Sims Bowen, presented by FHB Productions; *Vintage Halloween-Stories and Songs* by Grant Barrett and Eugene Nicks, directed by Charles Catanese; *Apathy—the Gen X Musical in CONCERT* by Mickey Zetts, directed by Paula D'alessandris; *Stage Kiss* by Mike Koleman, directed by Leecia Manning; *Evening of One Acts: Shake Your Do Do Crack* by Marjorie Edwards, directed by Karen Wilson-Mack/*Mystic TV* by Mary Beth Shannahan, directed by Geeta Citygirl/*Broadway Baby* by Carol Hollenbeck; *Prince Trevor Amongst the Elephants* by Duncan Pflaster, presented by Cross Eyed Bear Productions; *LaContessa's Halloween Variety Show* by Hector Lugo, presented by the Gay and Lesbian Acting Company; *The Sisterhood* by Contance Clark, directed by Daniel Haben Clark, presented by Loop Ltd.; *Dressing Up is Hard to Do* by Robert Vest; *Timeless* by John Luke, musical direction by Jerry Scott; *Theatre of the Dead* five one-acts by David Occhino, Georgette Moger, Justin Ambrosino; directed by Justin Ambrosino

TACIT AGREEMENT by Brian Saxe; Presented by Spotlight On and Saxe Appeal Productions; Director, Sarah Loabonte; **Cast:** Peter Mannion, Jonty Valentine, Lindsay Curcio, Stephen James Longo, Adam Zuniga; Frankie J. Alvarez, Joshua Seidner; December 3–12, 2005

NEIGHBORHOOD PLAYHOUSE

MANHATTAN BOUND Conceived by Lawrence Feeney, written by Michael Lazan and Erica Silberman, music and lyrics by Jeremy Schonfeld; Director, Gregory Simmons; Choreography, Tricia Brouk; July 21–25, 2005

THE ATRAINPLAYS, VOL. XX Conceived by Lawrence Feeney; September 13–24, 2005

NEW VICTORY THEATRE

BLACK GRACE Dance Troupe from Auckland, New Zealand; September 16–October 9, 2005

THE MOUSE QUEEN Presented by London's Little Angel Theatre; October 14–23, 2005

CATHAY: 3 TALES OF CHINA Presented by Ping Chong & Company; (see listing in Off-Off-Broadway Company Series in this volume); October 28–November 13, 2005

GOLDEN DRAGON ACROBATS November 18, 2005–January 1, 2006

THE STONES Presented by Zeal Theatre of Melbourne, Austrailia; January 6–22, 2006

BARON RABINOVITSJ February 17–26, 2006

THE FROG BRIDE Presented by RainArt Productions; March 3–12, 2006

COMPLEXIONS Dance Troupe; March 17–26, 2006

COMEDY 4 KIDS with James Campbell; March 31–April 16, 2006

BRUNDIBAR & COMEDY ON THE BRIDGE Adapted by Tony Kushner, designed by Maurice Sendak; Director, Tony Tacone; Music, Hans Krasa & Bohuslav Martinu; April 28–May 21, 2006

4–ISH Hip Hop and dance troupe from Amsterdam; June 2–18, 2006

NUYORICAN POETS CAFÉ

GOD, SWAP, AND BASQUIAT by Frank Perez, Steve Cannon and Melanie Marie Goodreuax; August 26–September 4, 2005

MOMMA'S BOYZ Written and directed by Cándido Tirado; Presented by Experimental Play Productions; **Cast:** Janio Marrero, Jesœs Mart'nez, Flaco Navaja; October 6–29, 2005

BOXES AND BOUNDARIES Written and presented by Girlstory; Directors, Ellen Hagan and Lisa Ascalon; **Cast:** Asia Ceasar, Chasity Seda, Ellen Hagan, Jasmin Morales, Mauricia Mullings, Menaka Menon, Lisa Ascalon, Tara Betts, and Zaedryn Meade; April 6–16, 2006

ULTERIOR SIDE DISHES by Lori Payne; Director, Kim Weston-Moran; **Cast:** Tom Martone, Kiersten D. Terrell, Ebony Coles, Chrystal Stone, Casandra Kate Escobar, Anthony Harper, Robert Starks, Garrett Lee Hendricks, Tashawn Jackson; May 11–June 3, 2006

OHIO THEATRE

ICE FACTORY 2005 Presented by Solto Think Tank; June 28–August 13, 2005; Schedule included: *Fathom* presented by Sabooge Theatre; *The Position* written and directed by Kevin Doyle, presented by Sponsored By Nobody; *Switch Triptych* created and presented by The Riot Group; *Psyche* presented by Favored Nations Theatre; *Major Bang* presented by The Foundry Theatre; *In a Hall in the Palace of Pyrrhus* presented by Witness Relocation Company

COMMEDIA DELL SMARTASS by Sonya Sobieski; Presented by New Georges, Susan Benfield and Sarah Cameron Sunde; Director, Jean Randich; Design, Garin Marschall, Robert Murphy, Sue Rees; Production Manager, Samuel C. Tresler; Stage Manager, Kathryn Galloway; **Cast:** Jessi Campbell, Jesse Hooker, Nurit Monacelli; Debargo Sanyal; September 9–October 1, 2005

LA TEMPESTAD by Larry Loebell; Presented by Resonance Ensemble; Director, Eric Parness; Design, Martin T. Lopez, Sidney Shannon, Aaron Copp, Nick Moore; Stage Manager, Katie Kring; **Cast:** Alberto Bonilla, Brian Flegel, Vivia Font, Felipe Javier Gorostiza, Ed Jewett, Lori McNally, Patrick Melville, Ray A. Rodriguez, Gordon Stanley, Frank Tamez, James T. Ware; October 13–30, 2005

THE TEMPEST by William Shakespeare, adapted and directed by Victor Maog; Presented by Resonance Ensemble; Associate Director, Daniel Brunet; Mentor, Brian Kulick; Design, Martin T. Lopez, Aaron Copp, Elizabeth Rhodes; **Cast:** Rashaad Ernesto Green, Daniel Larlham, Orlando Pabotoy; October 14–29, 2005 in repertory with *LaTempestad*

THE BARBIE PROJECT Presented by White Bird Productions; Director, Michael Schiralli; Design, Kelly Hanson; Artistic Director, Kathryn Dickinson; Performers: Stephanie Bok, Julie Pittman, Paul Boocock, Kathryn Dickinson, Cindy Hanson, Lorrie Harrison, the Jones Twins and Janice Lowe, the RedWall Dance Theatre; November 10–19, 2005

HELENA Translated by Douglas Langworthy; Presented by Target Margin; Director, David Herskovits; Design, Carol Bailey, Susan Barras, David Zinn, Lenore Doxsee, John Collins; Stage Manager, Brenna St. George Jones; **Cast:** Will Badgett, Daphne Gaines, David Greenspan, Nicole Halmos, Lian-Marie Holmes, Wayne Alon Scott, Eunice Wong; December 1–17, 2005

THE EXPENSE OF SPIRIT Written and directed by Josh Fox; Presented by the International WOW Company; December 19–24, 2005

WHAT THEN by Rinne Groff; Director, Hal Brooks; Produced by Clubbed Thumb, Inc. (Arne Jokola, Producer/Founder; Michael Levinton, Meg MacCary, Maria Striar, Producers); Scenery, Jo Winiarski; Costumes, Kirche Leigh Zeile; Lighting, Kirk Bookman; Sound, Jill BC DuBoff; Music, Joe Popp; Stage Manager, Jessica Percharsky; Press, Publicity Outfitters; **Cast:** Andrew Dolan, Meg MacCary, Piter Marek, Merritt Wever; January 7–28, 2006

.22 CALIBER MOUTH by Lauren Robert; Presented by PREMIERES; Director, Diane Paulus; Music Director, Ray Fellman; Artistic Director, Paulette Haupt; Associate Producer, Matt Cowart; Stage Manager, Randy Lawson; Design, Randy Weiner, Jason Fitzgerald; Technical Director, Ben Struck; Casting, Dave Clemmons; **Cast:** Lauren Robert, Tim Warmen, Laura Jordan, Ted Brunetti, Paul Oakley Stovall; February 22–26, 2006

FATBOY Written and directed by John Clancy; Presented by SoHo Think Tank; Music, Jody Lambert; Costumes, Michael Oberle; Sets, Kelly Hanson; Stage Manager, Brendan Turk; **Cast:** Dave Calvitto, Jody Lambert, Matt Oberg, Del Pentecost, Nancy Walsh; March 6–25, 2006

LITTY WILLY by Mark Kassen; Presented by Rude Mechanicals Theater Company; Director, John Gould Rubin; Design, Clint Ramos, Niicole Pearce, Elizabeth Rhodes, Molly Schwartz; Stage Manager, Jeff Benish; **Cast:** Mark Kassen, Roxanna Hope; April 6–30, 2006

THE NECKLACE by Lisa D'Amour, Ellen Maddow, Lizzie Olesker, Paul Zimet; Presented by The Talking Band; Directors, Anne Kauffman, Melissa Kievman; Music, Peter Gordon; Design, Anna Kiraly, Mark Barton, Olivera Gajic; Choreography, Johanna Meyer; **Cast:** David Brooks, Tina Shepard, Paul Zimet, Katie Pearl, Gibson Frazier, Ian Holloway, Jodi Lin; May 6–28, 2006

ONTOLOGICAL THEATER AT ST. MARK'S CHURCH

GRAVEDIGGERS Written and directed by Karly Maurer; Presented by Wreckio Ensemble; Scenery, Dechelle Damien; Costumes, Oana Botez Ban; Lighting, Lucrecia Brinceno; Production Manager, Tamera Cone; **Cast:** Dechelle Damien (Gravedigger 1), Michelle Diaz (Gravedigger 2), Nick Bixby (Son), Randi Berry (Mother), Demitra Bixby (Corpse), Tara Greico (Phoe); June 2–25, 2006

PANEL.ANIMAL by Jason Craig; Produced by Banana Bag & Bodice in association with the Ontological-Hysteric Theatre; Director, Miranda Hardy; Sound, Jamie McElhinney; Music, Dave Malloy; Ensemble and co-creators, Peter Blomquist, Jason Craig, Sarah Egelke, Rod Hipskind, Jessica Jelliffe, Heather Peroni; July 1 – 9, 2005

AGE LESS Written, directed and performed by Beth Kurkjian; Produced by the Ontological Theatre; Presented with the short piece *Glimpse* performed by Leigh Garrett; July 12 – 17, 2005

THE EISTEDDFOD Developed by Lally Katz; Presented by Stuck Pigs Squealing of Melbourne, Austailia; Director, Chris Kohn; Design, Adam Gardnir; Sound, Jethro Woodward; Stage Managers, Martina Murray, Julie Wright; **Cast:** Luke Mullins, Jessamy Dyer; August 31 – September 10, 2005

OUTSIDE/INPUT April 26 – 28, 2006

PLAYS ON WORDS May 11 – 15, 2006

BRIDE May 18 – 21, 2006

EVOKE MEMORIES OF A GOLDEN AGE May 25 – 28, 2006

PARADISE FACTORY

BROTHER Written and directed by Lisa Ebersole; Produced by Luke Rosen; July 21 – August 21, 2005

ESCAPE FROM BELLEVUE AND OTHER STORIES Written and performed by Christopher John Campion; Director, Horton Foote, Jr.; December 2, 2005 – February 25, 2006

PAYAN THEATRE

METAMORPHOSES Conceived, translated, adapted and performed by Todd Conner; October 3 – 24, 2005

DESSERT WITH DURANG Short plays by Christopher Durang; Director, Michael Raimondi; Produced by TimeSpace Theatre; **Cast:** Paul Casali, Linda Comess, Eric Deskin, Kim Douthit, Michelle Enfield, Justin Lamb, Cecelia Martin, Allison Niedermeier, Richard Rella Jr., Emily Sandack, Maureen Van Trease; February 23 – 25, 2006

GHETTO CHRONICLES Written, choreographed and directed by D. Whit; Produced by Wabi Sabi Productions and Whit Pick Entertainment; March 23 – June 11, 2006

IN PURSUIT OF JUSTICE by Wendy Jones and **RED ROSE** by Christine Emmert, two solo performance plays performed by Ida B. Wells; Produced by Wabi Sabi Productions; Director, Emmitt Thrower; March 23 – April 2, 2006

GRAND ILLUSIONS: THE LADY IS A TRAMP Performed by Kit Holiday; Produced by Wabi Sabi Productions; Director, Emmitt Thrower; March 25 – April 2, 2006

THE PEOPLE'S IMPROV THEATRE

CHAMPAGNE Written and performed by Troy Fischnaller and Dusty Warren; August 26, 2005

THE ISRAELI-PALESTINIAN CONFLICT: A ROMANTIC COMEDY Written and performed by Negin Farsad and Alexander Zalben; Presented by Madame Funnypants; Director, Bob Wiltfong; September 16 – October 14, 2005

LIVESTOCK with Rachel Biello, Carla Briscoe, Michelle Fix, Sara J., Stephen Ruddy, Beth White; January 5 – 26, 2006

YOU MUST TAKE THE A TRAIN Written and performed by Lindsay Brandon Hunter; March 16, 2006

UNACCESSORIZED Written and performed by Rich Kiamco; Director, Dan Bacalzo; April 6 – 27, 2006

EVERYBODY WANTS A PIECE OF BRAESON Director, Virginia Scott; April 11 – 25, 2006

PERFORMANCE SPACE 122 (PS 122)

Anne Dennin, Artistic Director

AT SAID by Gary Winter; Presented by 13P (Thirteen Playwrights-Gary Winter, Artistic Director; Rob Handel, Managing Director); Director, Tim Farrell; Sets, Sue Rees; Costumes, Meghan Healey; Lighting, Andrew Hill; Sound, Jody Elff; Stage Manager, Danielle Monica Long; Producer for *At Said*, Mariana Newhard; Producer for 13P, Maria Goyanes; **Cast:** Lia Aprile, Gilbert Cruz, Marisa Echeverria, Vedant Gokhale, Anita Hollander; May 13 – June 4, 2006

YOUNG LADIES OF... Written and performed by Taylor Mac; Presented by Schoolhouse Roxx; Director, Tracy Trevett; June 2 – 4, 2005

THE REJECTION SHOW Hosted by Jon Friedman; Presented Monthly

THE WYSIWYG TALENT SHOW A monthly all-blogger series of readings and performances; Created by Chris Hampton, Andy Horwitz, and Dan Rhatigan

THE GOTOUR ROAD SHOW Presented by The Field; July 8 – 9, 2005

FRINGENYC August 12 – 28th, 2005 (See Listings in Off-Off-Broadway Company Series)

FORGET ME NOT Presented by Praxis (Brainard Carey and Delia Bajo); September 7 – 13, 2005

CHRISTINA OLSON: AMERICAN MODEL Created by Tamar Rogoff Performance Projects; Video, Harvey Wang and Andrew Baker; Lighting, David Ferri; Costumes, Liz Prince; Performed by Claire Danes; September 21 – October 2, 2005

PASTORALIA by George Saunders, adapted and performed by Yehuda Duenyas; September 21 – October 9, 2005

JOHN MORAN AND HIS NEIGHBOR SAORI Presented by Schoolhouse Roxx; October 6 – 8, 2005

DEAR LAND Director, Lydia Steier; Presented by International Contemporary Ensemble; October 27 – 30, 2005

HERD OF BULLS Presented by Saar Harari Company; October 18–23, 2005

MURDER by Hanoch Levin; Presented by Personal Space Theatrics; Adapted and directed by Michael Weiselberg; **Cast:** Nathalya Bey, Kyrian Freidenberg, Yafit Hallely, Brandon Jones, Sarah Matthay, Eric Miller, Gina Shmukler, Jarrad Skiner, Gilbert Vela, Bradley Wells, Jerry Zellers, Rochelle Zimmerman; October 15–30, 2005

DANCEOFF With Terry Dean Bartlett, Katie Workum, and featuring David Neumann, Andrew Dinwiddie, Leigh Garrett, Nicholasleichterdnace, Christopher Williams, Tehreema Mitha Dance, Pig Iron Theatre, Julian Barnett; October 11–12, 2005, March 21–22, 2006

AVANT-GARDE-ARAMA Performance Space 122's longest-running series; Hosted by Susan Blackwell, Hunter Bell, Jeff Bowen, and Heidi Blickenstaff; October 14–15, 2005; Avant-Garde-Arama for the Family presented October 16

HELEN STRATFORD'S SUICIDE, THE MUSICAL Presented by Schoolhouse Roxx; Director, Julie Atlas Muz; Musical Director, Joe McCanta; **Supporting Cast:** Taylor Mac, Machine Dazzle, Hattie Hathaway, James Ferguson; Armen Ra; November 3–5, 2005

PUSH: AN AMPLIFIED READING adapted and performed by Alexia Monduit and Thomas Rannou from the novel by Sapphire; translated by Jean-Pierre Carasso; November 3–13, 2005

ITCHING OF THE WINGS Conceived by Philippe Quesne; Performed by Gaëtan Vourc'h, Sébastien Jacobs, Rodolphe Auté, Tristan Varlot, Zinn Atmane; November 9–13, 2005

PUPPY-SKILLS Presented by Sally Silvers & Dancers; Music, Iris DeMent, Bruce Andrews, and Michael Schumacher; Lighting, David Fritz; Costumes, Elizabeth Hope Clancy; Design, Yumi Kori; **Cast:** Sally Silvers, Vicky Shick, Paige Martin, Julie Atlas Muz, Jamie Di Mare, Marion Ramirez, Liz Filbrun, Pooh Kaye, Cydney Wilkes; Featuring: sculptor Anne Katrin Grotepass and musician Carolyn Hall; November 17–20, 2005

PROPHET by Thomas Bradhaw; November 30–December 17, 2005

…IT'S ONLY A REHEARSAL Presented by Zero Visibility Corp; Choreography, Ina Christel Johannessen; Music, Murcof; Design, Jens Sethzman; Text, Ovid; **Cast:** Line Tormoen, Dimitri Jourde; November 30–December 1, 2005

UN-DO-THREE Presented by Baktruppen Company of Norway; December 3–4, 2005

BUT, WHAT'S IT ALL ABOUT? Created by Ole Mads Velve; December 3–4, 2005

VERDENSTEATERET: CONCERT FOR GREENLAND December 7–8, 2005

WE FAILED TO HOLD THIS REALITY IN MIND Written and performed by Hooman Sharifi; December 10–11, 2005

TRACHTENBURG FAMILY SLIDESHOW PLAYERS ON ICE December 18–23, 2005

'TWAS THE NIGHT BEFORE THE TWELVE DAYS OF A NUT CRACKER CHRISTMAS CAROL by Ken Nintzel; **Cast:** David Neumann, Johanna Meyer, Beth Kurkjian, Leigh Garret, Eric Dyer, Richard Foreman; December 15–23, 28–30, 2005

SCOTTY THE BLUE BUNNY—THE END IS HERE: ENJOY! Presented by Schoolhouse Roxx; Director, Eric Wallach; December 29–30, 2005

ABSN:RJAB or Abacus Black Strikes Now! The Rampant Justice of Abacus Black; Presented by The National Theater of the United States of America; **Cast:** Ryan Bronz, Mark Doskow, Yehuda Duenyas, Jesse Hawley, Jonathan Jacobs, Normandy Sherwood, James Stanley; January 19–February 12, 2006

COIL A WINTER DANCE FESTIVAL Featuring Saar Harari, BalletLab, Adrienne Truscott, Helen Herbertson; January 19–24, 2006

NO GREAT SOCIETY Presented by Elevator Repair Service; **Cast:** Susie Sokol and Ben Williams; February 2–18, 2006

THE MONEY CONVERSATION Written and performed by Sara Juli; Director, Chris Ajemian; February 15–19, 2006

SUSAN SONTAG'S A PARSIFAL Presented and directed by John Jahnke and The Hotel Savant; Featuring Black Eyed Susan, Gardiner Comfort and Okwui Okpokwasili; February 23–March 5, 2006

THOUSAND YEARS WAITING by Chiori Miyagawa; conceived and directed by Sonoko Kawahara; Music, Bruce Odland; Presented by Crossing Jamaica Avenue; featuring Otome Bunraku Puppet Master Masaya Kiritake; February 23–March 12, 2006

NO DIRECTION HOMO Created and performed by Dan Fishback; Presented by Schoolhouse Roxx; March 9–11, 2006

SINNER Created and performed by Liam Steel and Ben Wright; Presented by Stan Won't Dance; Directors, Rob Tannion and Liam Steel; March 15–19, 2006

JUNTA HIGH Created and performed by Clay McLeod Chapman; Presented by the Pumpkin Pie Show; Music, the Hungry March Band; March 16–26, 2006

AVANT-GARDE-ARAMA Performance Space 122's longest-running series; *Love Insurgency* Hosted by Mark Mitton with James Godwin; March 24–25; Avant-Garde Arama for the Whole Family presented March 26, hosted by Ulysses S. Dee and Booker Dee

DANGEROUS WOMEN A performance art double-bill, with Nao Bustamante and Dynasty Handbag; Presented by Schoolhouse Roxx; March 30–April 1, 2006

HELL Created by Eileen Myles, music by Michael Webster, inspired by Dante's *Inferno;* Presented by The People's Opera and Beth Morrison Projects; March 31–April 9, 2006

RED TIDE BLOOMIN Performed by Taylor Mac; Puppets, Basil Twist; Choreography, Julie Atlas Muz; April 13–23, 2006

FLUKE Presented by Radiohole; April 21–May 7, 2006

ABSENCE AND PRESENCE Created and performed by Andrew Dawson; April 27–May 7, 2006

THE SPRING GALA 2006 Performances by Jonathan Ames, Eric Bogosian, Hazelle Goodman, Judith Ivey, Jay McInerney, Rosie O'Donnell and James Urbaniak; May 4, 2006

THROW PEOPLE Choreography, Chris Elam; Presented by Misnomer Dance Theater; May 11–14, 2006

AT SAID by Gary Winter; Director, Tim Farrell; Presented by 13P (Supervising Producer, Maria Goyanes; Producer for P#4, Mariana Newhard); Scenery, Sue Rees; Costumes, Meghan Healey; Lighting, Andrew Hill; Sound, Jody Elff; **Cast:** Lia Aprile, Gilbert Cruz, Marisa Echeverria, Vedant Gokhale, Anita Hollander; May 13–June 4, 2006

CLEANSING THE SENSES Created and performed by Peter Rose; May 18–28, 2006

LEFTOVER STORIES TO TELL: A TRIBUTE TO SPALDING GRAY Created and co-directed by Kathleen Russo and Lucy Sexton; **Cast:** James Urbaniak, Bob Holman, Ain Gordon, Jonathan Ames, Hazelle Goodman; Guest performances by Olympia Dukakis, David Strathair, Steve Buscemi, Aidan Quinn, Fisher Stevens, Debra Winger, Joel Grey; May 31–June 4, 2006

PHIL BOSAKOWSKI THEATRE

THE FANTASTICKS by Tom Jones and Harvey Schmidt; Produced by Beth Alson and White Star Productions; Director, Brady Amoon; Musical Director, Sheldon Forrest; Choreogrpahy Ericka Crocco; Stage Manager, David Rigano; **Cast:** Doglas Cochran, Bekah Vega, Joel Maki, Laurence Cantor, Alexander Cassanovas, Tana Hinz, Gregg Lauterbach, Douglas LeLand; August 19–28, 2005

PENNSYLTUCKY by Sloan McRae; Director, Amy Kaissar; Presented by Epiphany Theater Company; September 9–24, 2005

THE DUMB WAITER by Harold Pinter; Presented by Ward 10 Theatre Company; Director, Tlaloc Rivas; Design, Stephen Petrilli, Gabe Wood, Susan Zeeman Rogers, Amelia Dombrowski; Fight Director, David Anzuelo; Stage Manager, Karen Hergesheimer; **Cast:** Tim Kang, John Krupp; May 17–27, 2006

THE PRODUCERS CLUB

CO-OP Written and directed by John Cecil; presented by PraHaHa; **Cast:** Josh Meindertsma, Jeanette Bonner, Chiko Méndez, Jenn Marie Jones, Orion Simprini, Paul Cabrelli, Rachel Lee, John Cecil; June 2–17, 2005

PASTA & PIGSKIN by Joseph A. Mileto; Director, Bob Foley; produced by 4/10 of a Mile Productions, Michael Aparo, and Chris Raffaele; **Cast:** Jeremy Bohen, Danny Doherty, Matt Laspata, Rob Ruvolo, Jason Arthur Russo; June 13–19, 2005

THE FIRST DAY OF SCHOOL Written and performed by Brian Hopson, Ross Beshear, and Stephen Radochia; presented by The Little Bus Sketch Comedy Brigade; June 15, 2005

BLUES IN A BROKEN TONGUE by Leslie Lee; Presented by Negro Ensemble Company; Director, Barbara Montgomery; June 20–24, 2005

OLD MAN PETE by Randoph Edmonds; Presented by The Diversity Players of Harlem; **Cast:** Shawn Luckey; June 22–26, 2005

LA NENA SE CASA by Carlos Ferrari; Director, Emil Cruz; **Cast:** Patricia Chacon, Omar Cruz, Michelle Cruz, Buena Ventura, Wendy Garcia, Bruno Aponte; June 30–July 1, 2005

COME AWAY: THE STORY OF RUTH Director, Roberto Munoz; Producers Club II; June 30–July 3, 2005

THE TEMPEST by William Shakespeare; Presented by Manhattan Repertory Theater; Director, Ken Wolf; July 8–25, 2005

IT HAD TO BE YOU by Renee Taylor and Joe Balogna; Presented by IAAM Productions; Producers Club II; July 13–24, 2005

PROPS by Michael Roderick; Director, Moira K. Costigan; Presented by Small Pond Entertainment; Crowne Theatre; July 18–27, 2005

THE FERTILITY FACTOR by Mara Lesemann; Director, Carlo Fiorletta; **Cast:** Marc DiNunzio, Carlo Fiorletta, Rachel Kalusner, Vikki Massulli, Lou Nargi, Michelle Pucci; Doug Schneider; July 22–24, 2005

BREAK THROUGH Produced by Joe Loera and kamp NYC; Director, Kate Marks, Vocal Director, Richard Lissemore; Musical Director, Robert Grusecki; Choreography, Joey Dowling; **Cast:** Lauren Molina, Allie Peterson, Jaclyn Joseph, Sam Lips, Adam Luhrs, Chelsea Swanderski, Travis Harris, Becca McArthur, Emily Luhrs, Jacqlyn Conte, Jamie Billings, Chanel Odell, Emily Fisher, Carly Seyler, Lauren Sarno, Patterson Floberg, Tori Senicki, Ashley Streichert; July 30–31, 2005

THE STRAWBERRY ONE-ACT FESTIVAL Produced by the Riant Theatre; August 5–21, 2005

OH SISTER! Written and performed by Daniel Stone; August 17, 2005

A One Act Play Showcase presented by Under the Spell Productions and Teresa Lasley; **THE FALLEN ANGEL** by Elois Beasley, directed by Patricia White; **Cast:** Teresa Michelle Lasley, Sandie Luna, **FANTASY, GIRL** by LyaNisha Gonzalez; directed by Rhonney Greene; Cast Lya Nisha Gonzalez, Sharif Gordon, Robin Lowman, Traci M. Tolmarire, Apphia Campbell; Crowne Theatre; August 18–21, 2005

STAND CLEAR OF THE CLOSING DOORS Director, Eric Sydnor, Musical Director, Jeff Caldwell; September 6–7, 2005

TVIZKA THE SOLDIER Written and performed by Avi Levi; September 10, 2005

THE MERCHANT OF VENICE by William Shakespeare; September 9–17, 2005

REVENGE OF A KING A hip hop retelling of Shakespeare's *Hamlet;* Choreography, Carly Hughes; Presented by DAP Ensemble, the Loaves and Fish Traveling Repertory Company in association with H. Newsome and Jean Marie Donnelly; **Cast:** Rory Clarke, Jason Fernandez, Camille Gaston, Ryan Hollis, Martha Ighodaro, Joe Albert Lima, Riddick Marie, Samuel Muniz, Herb Newsome, Channie Waites, Lisa-Roxanne Walters, Bill White, Meibaka Yohannes; September 13–18, 2005

TWO BY TENN *Lord Byron's Love Letter* and *Talk to Me Like the Rain and Let Me Listen* Two one-acts by Tennessee Williams; Produced by Royalrich Productions; September 22, 2005

GAY SLAVE HANDBOOK Written and directed by Blake Bradford; Produced by Phare Play Productions; **Cast:** Vincent Giardina, Melissa Macleod Herion, Nate Steinwachs; Royal Theatre; September 21–24, 2005

JESUS CHRIST SUPERSTAR Music by Andrew Lloyd Webber, lyrics by Tim Rice; Presented by LiveStage Performance; Director, Doug Thoms; Design, Niklas Anderson, Derrick Bonnet, Kyrst Hogan, Sherry Gallant; Music Director, Joseph Charles Reina; Stage Manager, J. Armen; **Cast:** Mike Faraci, Bridget Beirne, Timothy Quinlan, Kyrst Hogan, Jay Pierce, Melissa Robinette, TJ Moss, Richard Kent Green, Akiko Hiroshima, Heidi Suhr, Joseph Torello, Juson Williams; September 23–October 2, 2005

500 RUMMY by Joanne DeSimone; and **PARLOR TRICKS** by Christina Jannell; Two one-acts presented by Under the El Productions, Inc.; October 5–8, 2005

NAKED MACBETH: THE STRIPPED-DOWN RETELLING OF A CLASSIC Adapted and directed by Russell Taylor; Producer, Dan Maceyak; Stage Manager, Michael Janney; **Cast:** Jack McGowan, Victor FIschbarg, Ryan Metzger, Gary Patent, Mike Skillern, Moti Margolin, Adam Zuniga, Cameron Caley, Nathan Perry, Jonty Valentine, Matthew Park, Tanner Max; Sonnet Theatre; October 9–30, 2005

BLACK FOLKS GUIDE TO BLACK FOLKS Written and performed by Hanifah Wlidah; Produced by Emmitt Thrower and Wabi Sabi Productions; October 14–30, 2005

AMERICAN COLORS Scenes from Ibsen's *A Doll's House* and *When We Dead Awaken*; Directors, Noah Burger and Mike Hidalgo; Presented by Eyeblink Entertainment; October 22, 2005

...FOUR ONE-LEGGED MEN! Written and performed by Gary Corbin; Presented by The Arts Den; October 5–23, 2005

I AM A LATINO DAMNIT AND MY SKIN IS BLACK! Written, performed and produced by Luis Lassen; Producers Club II; October 6–23, 2005

A MIDSUMMER NIGHT'S DREAM by William Shakespeare; Presented by Wench Productions; Artistic Directors, Patti Azzara, Crysstal Hubbard, Nicholas Martin-Smith: **Cast:** Cidele Curo, Anna Hanson, Sarah Francios, Maria Hurdle, Annie Keating, Becky Lake, Paige Lussier, Taryn Matusik, Kristin Mellian, Jordana Oberman, Ana Parsons, Andrea Pinyan, Melissa Rhoads, Heather Waghlestein; October 26–31, 2005

AFTER THE FALL by Arthur Miller; Presented by Rose Bud Productions; **Cast:** Jeff Todesco, Robin Long, Nitzan Koshet, Anna Guttormsgaard, Ryan Farrell, Pat Ceasar, Matthew Healy, Trayn Matusik, Stacey Kelleher, Chris Bischoff; November 2–6, 2005

MY SUPER EVIL INFERIOR COMPLEX by Steven William; November 2–6, 2005

DRUMMERS, DREAMS, AND FAMILY MATTERS Written and directed by Norman Weinstein; Stage Manager, Elliot Lanes; Design, Laura Williams, Scott Williams; **Cast:** Deborah Hope, Clyde Kelley, Colleen Kennedy, Alex Kosma, Tom Thornton, George Trahanis, Laura Williams; Crowne Theatre; November 7–20, 2005

RAPTURE by Ruth Tyndall Baker; Director, Cat Parker; November 17–19, 2005

THE SCREWTAPE LETTERS by C.S. Lewis, adapted by Nigel Ford; Director, Ralph Irizarry; Produced by Cornergate Productions; **Cast:** Steven Wargo, Maria Bellantoni, Kevin O'Bryan, Justin Stoney, David Esteve, Holly Hurley, Paul Parker, Sheila Simmons, David Arthur Bachrach; November 9–20, 2005

WE HAVE A BODY by Claire Chaffe; Presented by Apple Girl Productions; Director, Valerie Davenport; Design, Patrick Smith, Beau Edmondson; Stage Manager, Merdith Kaufman; **Cast:** Laila Ayad, Stefanie Black, Natasha Malinsky, Julie Lynn Stump; November 3–22, 2005

THE LIZARD BRAIN VARIETY HOUR II Produced and directed by Lucas Peltoner; **Cast:** Damani Rivers, Lisa Lyons, Raniah Al-sayed, Sarah Chaney; Producers Club II; December 2–3, 2005

FIVE DAYS WITH DYLAN by Pamela Scott; Director, Nye Heron; Lighting, Paul Jones, Wavetek Productions; Produced by Aching Dogs Theatre; **Cast:** Beth Anderson, Vance Clemente, Brenda Crawley, Rose Courtney, Sandra Cummings, Walter DeForest, Chris Dugger, Edgar Felix, Alicia Frank, Sultan Mahmud,

Michael McGuire, Jenn Neumann, Lisa Marie Reisenweber, Nina Rochelle, Magdalena Rogowski; December 7–18, 2005

THROUGH THE EYES OF AN ABUSED MALE by Brenda Allman-Dow; December 10–11, 2005

WHAT LIFE MAY BRING Written and directed by Christan Narvaez; December 14–18, 2005

CHAMPIONS by Michael Turner; Produced by Joe Loera and kamp NYC; Director, Jessica Redish; Vocal Director, Richard Lissemore; Choreography, Jacki Ford and Joey Dowling; December 31, 2005–January 1, 2006

WINTERKILL Written and performed by Denise B. Flemming; **THANGS YOU DON'T SAY OUTDOORS** by Dawn Winkler, performed by "Aba"; Two one-act solo plays presented by Wabi Sabi Productions; January 13–21, 2006

PARADISE LOST Music and lyrics by Benjamin Birney, lyrics and direction by Rob Seitelman; Produced by Jordan Grossman/Niaterra Arts and Entertainment; Additional lyrics, Seth Magoon; Music Director, Seth Bisen-Hersh; Choreography, Jason Summers; Design, Sarah Levine, David Jordan Nestor; Press, Brett Singer; **Cast:** Adia, Seth Baird, Kyle Barisch, Ashleigh Chilton, Darryl Calmese, Felicity Claire, Kevin T. Collins, Ashleigh Davidson, Tynan Davis, Michelle Dyer, Chris Gleim, Patrick Lutdt, Sarah Madej, Al Pagano, Andrew Giarolo, Danielle Erin Rhodes, Tim Roberts, Melissa Robinette, Paul A. Schaefer, Margaret M. Spirito; Producers Club II; February 23–March 18, 2006

TWENTY BROKEN LEGS by Meny Beririo; Presented by Mid Life Crisis Productions; Director, Mitch Poulos; **Cast:** Nina Burns, Hank Davies, John Gray, David Michael Holmes, Bekka Lindstrom, Jordan Wishner; March 12–13, 2006

ONLY YOU by Timothy Mason; Director, Jeffrey Kurtz; **Cast:** Michael Benjamin, Kathryn Forsatz, Michael Henry Harris, Ken Matthews, Tom Mazur, Whitnie Wood, Jeffrey Kurtz; March 22–25, 2006

THE MERCY SEAT by Neil LaBute; Director, Terry Berliner; March 24–27, 2006

AVEN'U BOYS by Frank Pugliese; Director, Anthony Frisina; Design, Grace Uffner; **Cast:** Tricia Alexandro, Hillary Bettis, Joey Calveri, VInny Duwe, Lolita Foster; March 31–April 11, 2006

SHOOT THEM IN THE CORNFIELDS by Sophia Murashkovsky; Presented by Cinema Anastasia Productions; Producers Club II; April 2–23, 2006

LYRICAL ARTS Created by Strife's Way Productions; Directed and produced by Rashawn Strife; **Cast:** Jacqueline Hankins, Rashawn Strife, Jonna Stark, Ausar English, Joseph Romanoff, Timothy Dark, Andre Ivory, Amando James, Aurelia Lavizzo, Elizabeth Hammett, Lauren Hoyte, Cherish Duke, Casandra Kate Escobar, Cortes, Zay Pierre-louise; April 5–9, 2006

61 DEAD MEN Conceived and directed by Janus Surratt; Produced by Beyond the Wall Productions; April 19–23, 2006

HELL'S KITCHEN — THE MUSICAL Book by Jon Montgomery, music by Jon Montgomery and Toby Kasavan; Presented by Bridge Across Productions; April 21, 2006

THE BALTIMORE WALTZ by Paula Vogel; Presented by Tongue in Cheek Theater; Director, Heather Guthrie; **Cast:** Jake Lipman, Joel Peterson, Brian W. Seibert, Royal Theatre; April 25–29, 2006

TRIPTYCH Three new plays by Brian Trzeciak; Director, Donna Scheer; Presented by Stickboy Productions; **Cast:** Michele McNally, Jason Jacoby, Meryl

Bezructczyk, Angelo Miliano, Josh Mertz, Dapne Peterson-Van Kangegan, Kim Douthit; May 3, 2006

BURKE by Manny Liyes; May 10 – 12, 2006

IN SIGHT 12 Festival presented by The Puerto Rican Traveling Theatre; Included: *The Last of Bernada* by Oscar A. Colon, directed by Sturgis Warner; *Phomph!!* by Fred Crecca, directed by Mary Keefe; *Three Men on a Base* by Maria Elna Torees, directed by Shawn Rozsa; Producers Club II; May 11 – 28, 2006

BACKSTAGE AT DA FONKY B Written, directed and produced by Alycya K. Miller; Presented by Diversity Players of Harlem; Music, Darlyne Cain; Choreography, Hana Ginsburg, Meredith Miller, Nedra NeQuan, Rill Oji; Producer, Shawn Luckey, Dwight A. Williams; Costuems, Katy Simola; **Cast:** Miho Sato, Zakiyyah Modeste, Sancha Durham, Jay Ward, Nedra Ne'Quan, The Genie; May 17 – 27, 2006

DANCE AT BATAAN Written and directed by Blake Bradford; Produced by Etcetera Theatre Company; **Cast:** James Heaphy, Christine Vinh, Casey Duncan, Tim Kondrat, Phil Horton, Alicia Green, Kevin Josephson; Crowne Theatre; May 17 – 24, 2006

A FAMILY'S PLAY Written and directed by Shawn Luckey; Presented by Diversity Players of Harlem; May 18 – 27, 2006

SPRING ONE ACTS Presented by Love Creek Productions; Crowne Theatre; Series B, May 18 – 21, 2006: *Mr. Paradise* by T. Williams, directed by Marcus Jones; *The Jaycee Wives of Mammoth Spring Arkansas Discuss Thomas Mann's "Death in Venice"* by Le Wilhelm, directed by Kymm Zuckert; *Vintage* by Steve Monroe, directed by Kymm Zuckert; *Gene Tierney's Hat* by Harlene Goodrich, directed by Rob Aloi; Series C, May 22 – 24, 2006: *Why Do You Smoke So Much, Lily?* By T. Williams, directed by Kelly Barrett; *Horse Tails* by Melinda Bowles, directed by Carla Torgrimson; *Passed Hordes* by Mark Harvey Levine, directed by Gregg David Shore; *Sun Tea with Bagels* by Le Wilhelm, directed By Erin Smiley; *The Art of Dating* by Jeffrey Elwell, directed By Gregg David Shore

SAGE THEATER

THE GREGOR & OLGA SHOW Written and created by Gregory Levine and Gabi Hegan; Director, Monica Rodriguez; Costumes, Emily Taradash; Sound and Lighting, Thomas Honeck; **Cast:** Gregory Levine and Gabi Hegan; Miss Ruby Valentine, Jonathan Holtzman; June 23 – 25, 2005

EAT AND GET GAS HERE Presented by Cleo's Comedy Players; October 29 – December 17, 2005

ONE NIGHT I MET AN AUSTRALIAN Written and performed by Daria; May 6 – June 10, 2006

SANDE SHURIN THEATRE

THE FAN THE SH*T HIT Written and produced by Anthony Gelsomino; Director, Greg Alkalay; Presented by Lucky Devil Theatre Company, Vicki Warivonchik; Design, Laura Corby Lundgren, Amie Kolb, Raymond Richardson, Dennis Shinners, Andy Hill; **Cast:** Anthony Gelsomino, George Hahn, Hassan Sayyed, Scott Shincick; July 21 – 31, 2005

REVOLUTION ROW by Edward Miller; August 18 – September 11, 2005

OUT, OUT DAMNED CLOCK: FAUST MEETS MACBETH by Nathaniel Green; November 3 – 13, 2005

SANFORD MEISNER THEATRE

LITTLE MARY by William Leavengood; Director, Jessica Kubzansky; Produced by Diana Lucas Leavengood and Will Knot Di Productions; Scenery, Steve Mitchell; Costumes, Carla Bellisio; Lighting, Brian Lilienthal; Original Music and Sound, Leon Rothenberg; Stage Manager, Michelle Clark; **Cast:** Ron Orbach (Archbishop Tivoli), Jeremy Lawrence (Cardinal Gian), Robyn Hatcher (Mother Lulit), Kaipo Schwab (Jose Navarez), Monica Raymond (Christina Navarez), Nelson Avidon (Cardinal Savici); June 2 – 26, 2005

TOP TEN by Peter Gil-Sheridan; Director, Jeff Stanley; Produced by Working for Tips Productions (Artistic Director, John Ort; Managing Director, Elizabeth Huber); Associate Producer, Tim Aumiller; **Cast:** Dionne Audain, Aaron Clayton, Kim Grogg, David Michael Holmes, Lian-Marie Holmes, Lauren Milberger, John Ort, Navida Stein, Daniel Zaitchik, Chris Bester; July 7 – 31, 2005

FIRES by Marguerite Yourcenar; Produced by Tali Friedman; Director, Gisela Cardenas; Design, Akiko Nishijima, Oana Botez-Ban, Lucrecia Briceno, Josephine Kukla, Mark Valadez; Chreography, Irina Constantine Poulos; Associate Producer, James O'Donnell; **Cast:** Tali Friedman, Joanna Bonnaro, Catherine Friesen, Laura Heidinger, Marco Prado; August 16 – 28, 2005

THE ROOF by Suzanne Bradbeer; Presented by The Blue Collar Theater Company; Director, Maggie Low; Design, Shaun Motley, Pamela Kupper, Laura Bowman, Ryan Maeker; Stage Manager, Jonathan A. Gershon; **Cast:** Lucas Blondheim, Andrew Lawton, Denise Lute; September 15 – October 1, 2005

THE UNSPEAKABLE ACT Created and presented by 23 Elephants Theatre Company (Steven Hess and Bidalia F. Albanese-Hess, Artistic Directors); Director, Steven Hess; Choreography, deeAnn Nelson; Originally presented in the HELL Festival at the Brick July 7 – 21, 2005 and the 2001 Fringe Festival; October 14 – 16, 2005

THE DEATH OF LITTLE IBSEN Written, directed and presented by Wakka Wakka Productions; Lighting, Andrew Dickey; Music, Lars Petter Hagan; Sound, Karl Schwarz; Stage Manager, Gabrielle Brechner; **Cast:** David Arkema, Kirjan Waage, Gwendolyn Warnock; April 29 – June 11, 2006

THE SLIPPER ROOM

RED LIGHT NIGHT: AN EVENING OF SHORT PLAYS ABOUT SEX Presented by Firecracker Productions; Featuring the talents of Jenny Ricciardi, Noa Gottlieb, Kate Kolendo and Ian Marks; June 21, July 26, August 30, 2005

WHAT IS LEGITIMATE THEATER Presented by The Legitimate Theater Company; August 12 – September 9, 2005

TWELFTH NIGHT, OR WHAT YOU WILL: THE DRINKING GAME adapted from William Shakespeare; Director, Richard Lovejoy; Presented by The Legitimate Theater Company; January 6 – February 10, March 31 – April 8, 2006

SHIT & CHAMPAGNE by D'arcy Drollinger; Presented by Back It Up Productions and Kirsten Caufield; Director, Greg Ayres; Costumes, Ramona Ponce, Sound, Gregory Kage, Stage Manager, Lance A. Michel; **Cast:** D'arcy Drollinger, Clayton Dean Smith, Adreas Kookino, Anne Gaynor, Brandon Olson, Camille Habacker, Kat Ventura; February 17 – May 12, 2006

SNUG HARBOR CULTURAL CENTER

BLOOD BROTHERS by Willy Russell; Director, Christopher Catt; Presented by Sundog Theatre Company; August 5 – 14, 2005

THE MYSTERY OF EDWIN DROOD by Rubert Holmes; October 14 – 23, 2005

A CHRISTMAS CAROL by Charles Dickens; Presented by Sundog Theatre Company; December 2 – 11, 2005

A DICKENS FESTIVAL December 2 – 31, 2005

SCENES FROM THE STATEN ISLAND FERRY '06 Presented by Sundog Theatre Company; March 2006

SOHO PLAYHOUSE

MAXIMUM RISK Created, written and starring Chris McDaniel; Co-created and produced by David Adamovich; Co-written and directed by Simon Lovell; Guest Artists: Ravi Seepersad, The Graeat Throwdini, Ekaterina, Charon Queen of Swords, Matthew Cassiere (Matt The Knife), Ula the Painproof Rubber Girl; June 6 – July 11, 2005

D'arcy Drollinger in *Shit & Champagne* at the Slipper Room

SYSTEM ETERNAL by Chance D. Muehleck; Director, Melanie S. Armer; Presented by LIVE Theater Company; August 13 – 21, 2005

UNSPEAKABLE: AN UNAUTHORIZED EXPLORATION OF THE LIFE OF RICHARD PRYOR! by James Murray Jackson, Jr. and Rod Gailes; Director, Rod Gailes; **Cast:** Benja K, Deborah Keller, Dominique Morisseau, Michelle Wilson, Steve Ramshur, Richard Carroll, Paris Campbell, James Murray Jackson, Jr.; Extension from the Fringe Festival; September 9 – 12, 2005

HAM LAKE by Sam Rosen and Nat Bennett; Director, Ian Morgan; Produced by Jefferson Bjoraker, Paddy Mulloy, and Josh Hartnett; **Cast:** Sam Rosen; April 27 – June 24, 2006

BELLY OF A DRUNKEN PIANO Written and performed by Stewart D'Arrietta; August 8 – October 9, 2005; Revived May 25 – July 1, 2006

STELLA ADLER STUDIO THEATRE

PHILIP HEART PRIVATE EYE: IN A CASE FOR DEATH … OOOH! Written and performed by David Tyson and presented by David Tyson's Weaver of Tales Theatre; July 8 – 24, 2005

BOOK OF DAYS by Lanford Wilson; Produced by New World Theatre; Director and Producer, Robert A. Zick, Jr.; Producer, Karron Korr, Meghan Dickerson; Design, J Gerard J. Savoy, Keri Thibodeau; **Cast:** Michael Boland, David Cooper, Meghan Dickerson, Douglas Gowland, D.H. Johnson, Karron Karr, Tarek Khan, Kelly Miller, Pamela Paine, Michael Tranzilli, Tina Trimble, Tashya Valdevit; August 10 – 27, 2005

BETRAYAL by Harold Pinter; Presented by theatre1050; Director, Don Miller; January 21 – 28, 2006

HAROLD CLURMAN FESTIVAL OF THE ARTS Created by Tom Oppenheim and the Stella Adler Studio, Featuring seminars, readings, performances and lectures by Zoe Caldwell, Lois Smith, Elaine Stritch, Roy Scheider, Derek Walcott, Grace Schulman, Marian Seldes, John Guare, Harold Bloom, Ronald Rand, David Amram, Cynthia Adler, Holland Taylor, Charles Wright, Martha Serpas, Nina Capelli, Marian Bell, Shannon Sutherland, Elizabeth Parrish, Horton Foote, Edward Albee, George C. White May 5 – 8, 2006

TADA! THEATER

SLEEPOVER by Philip Freedman and Jim Beloff; Director, Emmanuel Wilson; July 8 – 30, 2005

RELATIONSHIPS by Alastair King; January 23 – February 7, 2006

THE GIFT OF WINTER Music by David Evans, lyrics by Faye Greenberg; book by Michael Slade; January 20 – February 20, 2006

THE TROJAN WOMEN by Euripides; Directed by Linnet Taylor; Choreography, Karinne Keithley; Presented by Chekhov Theatre Ensemble; Design: Russel Drapkin, G L Aundry, Amanda Embry, Kristine Koury; **Cast:** Joy Barrett, Russell Barnes, Kevin Cardenas, Albert Elias, Max Evjen, Rajeeyah Finnie, Sebastian Iturregui-Shelton, Maria Kelly, Chris Kline, T. Scott Lilly, Dana Panepinto, Andrea Seigel, Jennifer Shirley, Anne Sorce, Jennifer Wintzer; March 15 – April 1, 2006

THEY CHOSE ME! Music and lyrics by Ned Paul Ginsberg and Michael Colby; April 21 – May 7, 2006

THEATRE ROW THEATRES

BECKETT THEATRE

INDIA AWAITING by Anne Marie Cummings; Director, Tyler Marchant; Scenery, Narelle Sissons; Lighting, Peter West; Sound, Bart Fasbender; Music, Deep Singh; Producers, Immediate Vision, Sudhir Vaishnav, Madhur Jaffrey; Aroon Shivdasani; **Cast:** Maulik Pancholy, Margot White, Yolande Bavan, Robert Ian Mackenzie, Patricia Mauceri, Alok Tewari; October 15 – Novmeber 6, 2005

HAYMARKET by Zayd Dorn; Produced by Alchemy Theatre Company of Manhattan, Inc.; Director, Robert Saxner; Scenery, Heidi Meisenhelder; Costumes, Victoria Tzykun; Lighting, Stephen Sakowski; Sound, Haddon Kime; Stage Manager, Noel Webb; **Cast:** Morgan Baker, Birgit Huppuch, Judson Jones, Dennis McNitt, Squeaky Moore, D. Zhonzinsky; December 8 – 23, 2005

CLURMAN THEATRE

BAG FULLA MONEY by Scott Brooks; Director, Sam Viverito; Produced by SunnySpot Productions in association with Second Life Productions and Badlands Theatre Company; Set, Michael Hotopp; Lighting, Andrew Grant; Costumes, Vito Lenza; **Cast:** Dina DeLe Cruz, Amber Dow, Heather Dilly, Jon Ecklund, Richard Mazda, Stu Richel, Darius Stone, Christopher Wisner, David White; January 16 – 29, 2006

3 TO A SESSION One-acts presented by the Immediate Theater Company; Included: *Play>* written and directed by Paul Siemens; *See the World* written and directed by Jeremy McCarter; *A Monster's Tale* by Desi Moreno-Penson, directed by José Zayas; February 1 – 5, 2006

ALL-IN-ONE One-acts presented by Oberon Theatre Company; Included: *Village Wooing* by George Bernard Shaw, directed by Rachel Wood; *Lion Tamer* by Rich Orloff, directed by Walter Brandes; *The Mystery at Twicknam Vicarage* by David Ives, directed by Philip Emoett; *Well-Laid Desert* by Walter Brandes, directed by Eric Parness; February 8 – 12, 2006

LION THEATRE

QUIET CRY Book by Adam Dick, music and lyrics by Paul Dick; Produced by PASSAJJ Productions; Director/Chroreography, Andrea Andresakis; Music Director, Jonathan Smith; Scenery, Brittany Fahner; Costumes, Arnulfo Maldonado; Lighting, Tony Marques; Stage Manager, Jessica Forella; **Cast:** David Gillam Fuller, Alex Greenshields, Shea Hess, Robert Kane, Eric S. Kuhn, Will Perez, Kwame Michael Remy, Natalie Silverlieb, Flenna Stauffer, Kit Williams; June 10 – 26, 2005

REBEL WITHOUT A CAUSE by James Fuller, adapted from Stewart Stern's screenplay, originally adapted by Irving Shulman from a story by Nicholas Ray; Presented by Barely Balancing Artists Group; Directors, Brian Stites and Joshua Colmean; **Cast:** Allie Mulholland, Joshua Coleman, Erin Cunningham, Stan Andrew, Adeline Drescher, Selena C. Dukes, Gio Crisafulli, Jamie Effros, Jonathan Maccia, Major Dodge, Peter Bongiorno, Swann Gruen, Valerie Cirillo; October 6 – 30, 2005

JANE HO by John Palotta, Director, Arian Blanco;Presented by the Hudson Exploited Theater Company, Inc.; Score, Andy Cohen; Design, Gregg Bellon; Sound, Joe DiSanzo; Production Manager, Amber Estes; **Cast:** Liche Ariza, Mikaela Kafka, Daina Michelle Griffith, A.B. Lugo, Heather Male; November 4 – 18, 2005

'TIS THE F@#$%–ING SEASON Presented by kef Productions and Rachel Neuburger; Included: *The First Annual St. Ignatius Chanukah Pageant* by Mac Rogers and Sean Williams; co-written and directed by Jordana Williams; *Why Am I Attracted to Narcissists? – A Christmas Story* by Kelly Stuart, directed by Adam Fitzgerald; **Cast:** Amy Goldberger, Brian M. Golub, David Gurland, Robert Hoyt, Rob Maitner, Laura Perloe, Byron St. Cyr; December 8 – 21, 2005

GREYHOUNDS by Daryl Lisa Fazio; Produced by James Jennings; Director, Jesse Jou; Set, Hal Tiné; Lighting, Thomas Fowlkes; Sound, Ross Jeffcoat; Stage Manager, Sarah Ford; Produced by Cheri Wicks, John Shaw and Maria Gamboni; **Cast:** Heather Massie, Cheri Wicks; February 2 – 19, 2006

SAVAGES by Anne Nelson; Presented by Back House Productions; Director, Chris Jorie; Set, Lauren Helpern; Costumes, Rebecca J. Bernstein; Lighting, Betsy Adams; Sound, Jill BC DuBoff; **Cast:** Julie Danao-Salkin, James Matthew Ryan, Jim Howard, Brett Holland; March 9 – April 1, 2006

NEW VOICES PLAY FESTIVAL April 13 – 29, 2006; Presented by Columbia University's School of the Arts; Directors, Rebecca Brown, Mary Catherine Burke, Mariana Carreno, Daniel Jaquez, Alex Lippard, Eduardo Machado, Cecil Mackinnon, Lou Moreno, Margarett Perry

PRIME TIME by Alex DeWitt; Produced by Cosmic Breez, Inc. and David Marantz; Director, Fern R. Lopez; Set, Josh Zangen; Lighting, Jennifer Schriever; Costumes, Ruby Randig; Video Geoff Watland; Sound, Fire Team; Stage Manager, Susan Lee; Casting, Stark Naked Productions/Elsie Start Casting; Graphics, FABS Group; Press, Brett Singer; **Cast:** Teve Beauchamp, Vance Bradford, Julia Montgomery Brown, Aquarius Cheers, Alex DeWitt, Dudley F Findlay Jr., David F. Gandy, Peyton List, Spencer List, David Marantz; May 5 – 27, 2006

STUDIO THEATRE

JEWSICAL—THE CHOSEN MUSICAL Book, lyrics and direction by Joel Paley, music by Marvin Laird; Choreography, A.C. Ciulla; **Cast:** Toni Carington, April Henry, David Ruffin, Craig Sculli, Adam Shapiro; Presented by Entertainment Events Inc. and Robert Dragotta; January 13, 2006

MINE and **THEY TOLD ME THAT YOU CAME THIS WAY** by David Epstein; Presented by Briar Patch Pictures; April 6 – 11, 2006

GAUGUIN/SAVAGE LIGHT by George Fischoff; **Cast:** Jeff Nardone, Kelly Dynan, Joseph Martin Guidera, Sylvianne Chebance, Jennifer Sanchez; April 25 – May 21, 2006

TAPE by Stephen Belber; Presented by You Are Here Productions; Director, Tammy Tunyavongs; Designers, John Lencovic, David Barr, Drew Padrutt; Stage Manager, Josh Kauffman; **Cast:** Greg Cayea, Blaire Carson, Duane Langley; May 31 – June 11, 2006

THEATRE THREE

FOUR ONE-ACT PLAYS Presented by Our Time Theatre Company, An artistic home for people who stutter; *So You Think You Know Me* written and directed by Angelina Bruno-Metger, performed by Taro Alexander; E. Donisha Brown, Noah Cornman, Julie Glickman, Laurel Steinhauser; *If You Got It … Flaunt It!* written and directed by Naudia Vivienne Jones; performed by Linda Gjonbalaj, Chelsea Lacatena, David Nachman, Alysia Reiner; *Body Language* written and directed by Yoni Messing; performed by Dashiell Eaves, Amanda Jornov, Kimmarie

Lynch; *I, Man On Stage* written and directed by Donny Sethi; performed by Everett Bradley and Dashiell Eaves; December 16–18, 2005

CANDY & DOROTHY by David Johnston; Director, Kevin Newbury; Design, Robert Monaco, D.M. Wood, Jessica Jahn, Jared Coseglia; General Manager, Matthew Principe; Press, David Gersten; Stage Management, Mary Kathryn Blazek, Jessica D'Alosio, Lauren A. Duffy; **Cast:** Sloane Shelton, Vince Gatton, Amir Arison, Nell Gwynn, Brian Fuqua; January 9–28, 2006

IN TUNE WITH THE UNIVERSE by Erika Stadtlander; May 17–21, 2006

THEATRE 315

EGG AND CHIPS FOR WINSTON by Paula Danhom and Emmy Wilde; Director, Paula Danhom; August 23–27, 2005

THE FALLEN 9/11 by Robert Masrese; Director, Dunsten J. Cormack; **Cast:** Tim Davis, Robb Hurst, Heather McHugh, Aaron Walters; September 6–24, 2005

THE SCREWTAPE LETTERS by C.S. Lewis, adapted by Jeffrey Fiske and Mx McLean, inspired by Tony Lawton's stage adaptation; Produced by FPA Theatre Company; Director, Jeffrey Fiske; Set, Scott Aronow; Costumes, Jessica Lustig; Lighting, Charles Foster, Sound, John Duncan; Stage Manager, Laurel Stinson; **Cast:** Max McLean, Jenny Savage; January 26–April 10, 2006

THEATRE 5

TAM LIN Written and directed by N.G. McClernan; Costumes, Cheri Cunningham; Lighting, Karen Sweeney; Puppets, Talaura Harms; Sound, Rich Baker; Stage Manager, Suzanne Apicella; **Cast:** Christina Dunham, Nick Lowe, Talaura Harms, Nancy Nagrant, Skid Maher, Troy Acree, Randi Sobol, Mike Durell, Jason Hare, Len Childers; October 8–30 2005

SIZE ATE. ONE WOMAN'S SEARCH FOR THE PERFECT FIT Written and performed by Margaux Laskey; Director, Steven McElroy; Design, Julie Walker, Graham Kindred, Laurie Brown; November 5–19, 2005

OF LOSS AND GRACE by Joey Brenneman; Director, Donna Jean Fogel; Scenery, Robert Monaco; Lighting, Renée Molina; Costumes, Hillary Pace Bradley; Sound, Terrance Taylor; **Cast:** Joey Brenneman, Hoon Lee, Amanda Schill, Hallie Claire Waletzko; December 1–18, 2005

NEUROFEST Presented by Untitled Theater Company #61; January 5–29, 2006; Included: *CJD* written and directed by James Jordan, presented by The Boondogglers; *Impostors* by Justin Warner, directed by Ari Laura Kreith, presented by Buffalo Bridge Productions; *Stranges* and *Linguish* written and directed by Edward Einhorn, presented by Untitled Theater Company #61; *Syndrome* by Kirk Wood Bromley, performed and directed by Timothy McCown Reynolds, presented by Inverse Theatre Company; *Tabula Rasa* words by Robert Lawson, music and direction by Henry Akona, music direction by Ekaterina Stanislavskaya, presented by High Fidelity Theater; *Welcome to Tourettaville!* by Jonathan Ospa, June Rachelson-Ospa, and Daniel Neiden, music by Jody Gray, Doug Katsaros, and Daniel Neiden; *Cincinatti* by Don Nigro, directed by John Clancy; NEUROshorts: *The Boy Who Wanted to be a Robot* by Edward Einhorn, directed and performed by Barry Weil; *Vestibular* by Kelly R. Haydon, director, Jolie Tong; *The Taste of Blue* by Alexandra Edwards, directed by Julia Martin; *Doctors Jane and Alexander* by Edward Einhorn, directed by Ian Hill

RAGAMUFFINS Book, music and lyrics and direction by Erika Stadtlander; Arrangements/Musical Director, Lon Lonescu; Choreography, Raluca Georgiana; March 30–April 9, 2006

TRIAD THEATRE

THE GREAT DIVIDE Written and directed by Charles Messina; Produced by Bruce Robert Harris, Scott Brooks, and Gina Ferranti; **Cast:** Ernie Curcio, Gina Ferranti, Johnny Tammaro, Barbie Insua; June 6–29, 2005

LA CONTESSA'S STARS AND STARS EXTRAVAGANZA June 18–July 4, 2005

PERMISSION, A ROCK MYTHOLOGY Composed and Music Directed by L.R. Heffter; Director, John Tedeschi; Choreography, Ann Robideaux; Art Direction, Adam Stroncone; Costumes, Sylvester Ceecon; Produced by Edward Berk; Sound, Peter Fitgerald; Stage Manager, Sherry Ann Danna; Lighting, Guy Smith; **Cast:** Evan Andrews, Lisa Hugo, Marcus Collins, Kellee Knighten, Angela Arnold, Logan Tracey, John Tedeschi July 13–25, 2005

ONE MAN'S WAR written and directed by Sammy Dallas Bayes; Presented by New Century Productions in association with Steffles Productions, LLC., The Triad Theatre and James Van Hook; **Cast:** Ed Bergtold, Jeremy Eric Feldman, James Gagne, Max Hambleton, Daniel Kipler, Aubrey Levy, Mike Marinaccio, Brian Nemiroff, Chris Perry, Andrew Smith, Mark Thomas, Lane Wray; February 25–April 19, 2006

KABBALAH by Tuvia Tenenbom; Presented by The Jewish Theater; **Cast:** Emily Stern; November 15–December 31, 2005

THE ACCIDENTAL PERVERT Written and performed by Andrew Goffman; Director, Charles Messina; February 2–24, 2006

TAP DANCING THROUGH THE BOARDROOM Written and performed by Neale S. Godfrey; Director, Kate Lyn Reiter; Produced by Christopher E. Lanni; March 3–5, 2006

UCB THEATRE

FLAMING BOX OF STUFF August 25–27, 2005

SHOWGIRLS: THE BEST MOVIE EVER MADE. EVER! February 9–May 25, 2006

WE USED TO GO OUT by Jason Mantzoukas and Jessica St. Clair; March 9–April 27, 2006

FREE TO BE FRIENDS Written and performed by Sue Galloway and Julie Klausner; May 12–26, 2006

URBAN STAGES

THE GERANIUM ON THE WINDOW SILL JUST DIED Based on the book by Albert Culluim; adapted and directed by Michael Lluberes; Music and Sound, Eric Shim; Scenery, Seth Easter; Lighting, Carrie Wood; Original Song, Wally Pleasant; Associate Producer, Gregory Bonsignore and Ashley Gates; Stage Manager, Alissa Zulvergold; **Cast:** Megan Cook, Molly Feingold, Carly Lukas, Ted Schneider, Carrie Specksgoor; August 10–14, 2005

THE SNOW QUEEN by Hans Christian Andersen, adapted by Stanton Wood; Produced by Urban Stages; Director, Daniella Topol; Costumes, Nadia Fadeeva, Scenery, Mikiko Suzuki, Puppets, Eric Wright, Sound, Allison Leyton-Brown; **Cast:** Utkarsh S. Ambudkar, Susan Heyward, Lanna Joffrey, Ned Massey; December 11, 2005 – January 15, 2006

SAFETY by Chris Thorpe; Produced by Crash Landing Productions; Director, Daisy Walker; Scenery, Kevin Judge; Costumes, Kevin Christiana; Lighting, Patricia Nichols; Sound, Samuel Scott Doerr; **Cast:** David Wilson Barnes, Katie Firth, Susan Molloy, Jeffrey Clarke; January 23 – February 12, 2006

DEVIL LAND by Desi Moreno-Penson; Produced by the Immediate Theatre Company; Director, José Zayas; Scenery, Ryan Elliot Kravetz; Lighting, Jorge Arroyo; Costumes, Mel Haley; Sound, David Lawson; Stage Manager, Sarah Locke; **Cast:** Desi Moreno-Penson, Miguel Sierra, Paula Ehrenberg, DJ Thacker; April 14 – May 7, 2006

WORTH by Suzanne Lee; Director, Marc Parees; May 15 – June 3, 2006

WALKERSPACE

BIG TIMES Written and performed by Mia Barron, Maggie Lacey and Danielle Skraastad; Produced by Sasha Eden, Victoria Pettibone, and Marla Ratner; Director, Leigh Silverman; June 18 – July 16, 2005

ROMEO AND JULIET by William Shakespeare; Produced by Cry Havoc; Director, Kitt Lavoie; Design, Gabriel Evansohn; Costumes, Jennifer Reichert; Associate Director, Jennifer Curfman; Fight Director, Jeff Bender and Keith Conway; Associate Designer, Carl Faber; Production Manager, Russell Hankin; **Cast:** Jenny Kirlin, Jane Pfitsch, Will Harper, Libby Kelly, Jack M. Hartman, Kerry Flanagan, Graeme Gillis, Christopher Cooper, Ewan Ross, Benjamin Sands, Jeb Toms, Tom Lapke, Mary Cavett, Eric Aschenbrenner, Laura Johnson, Russell Hankin, Francisco Valera, Matthew Johnson, Ryan Schira, Lillian Meredith; July 21 – August 6, 2005

STROM THURMOND IS NOT A RACIST by Thomas Bradshaw; Director, Eliza Hittman; August 11 – 21, 2005

EINSTEIN'S SECRET LETTERS (A LOVE STORY) by J.B. Edwards; Director, G. Beaudin; **Cast:** Marvin Starkman, Robert Kya-Hill, Memory Contento, Waltrudis Buck; September 23 – October 2, 2005

THE GIRL IN THE FLAMMABLE SKIRT Adapted and directed from Aimee Bender's short stories by Bridgette Dunlap; Produced by the Ateh Theater Group; Sets, Amanda Rehbein and Emily French; Lighting, Cris Dopher; Costumes, Asta Hostetter; Illustrations, Manny Silva; Stage Manager, Hannah Miller; Publicist, Michelle Brandon; **Cast:** Jeff Addiss, Cormac Bluestone, Ryan Canfield, Alexis Grausz, Jeff Hughes, Kathryn Ekblad, Madeleine Maby, Sara Montgomery, Elizabeth Neptune; October 15 – 29, 2005

TAMING OF THE SHREW by William Shakespeare; Presented by The Queen's Company; Director, Rebecca Patterson; Set, Jeremy Woodward, Costumes, Sarah Iams, Lighting, Aaron Copp; Sound, Jane Shaw; Fight Director, Rachel Scott; Stage Manager, Rebecca Sealander, **Cast:** Karen Berthel, Amy Driesler, Natlie Lebert, Terri Power, Beverley Prentice, Smarra, Gisele Richardson, Carey Urban; November 5 – 20, 2005

BEAST WITH TWO BACKS by Don Nigro; Presented by Specter Theatre Company in association with M2M Communications; Director, Ann Bowen; Stage Manager, Russ Marisak; Lighting, Stephen Sakowski; Costumes, Cheryl McCar-

ron; **Cast:** Heather Anthony, Alison Costine, Ashley Davies, Tom Pavey, Peter Picard, Sam Reich, Chapin Springer; December 1 – 17, 2005

THE RED BOX by Jason Mitchell; Produced by Sara Katz in association with the Miranda Theatre Company; Director, Tesha Buss; Stage Manager, Alix Claps; Scenery, Ted LeFevre; Lighting, Graham Kindred; Sound, Kristyn Smith; Costumes, Jessa-Raye Court; **Cast:** Lawrence Merritt, Marilyn O'Connell, Jonathan Monk, Ryan Andes, Susan Ferrara, Cobey Mandarino, Eli Kranski, Aubrey Levy, Dave Droxler; March 2 – 12, 2006

THE PRIVATE LIFE OF THE MASTER RACE by Bertolt Brecht, translated by Binyamin Shalom; Director, James Phillip Gates; Presented by Roust Theatre Company; Set, Richard Hoover; Costumes, Heather Klar; Lighting, Andy Smith; Sound, Susan Small; Composer, Giovanni Spinelli; **Cast:** Kristen Barnett, Tracy Hostmyer, Betty Hudson, David Beck, Nicholas Daniele, Peter Levine, Khris Lewin, Brad Russell; March 20 – April 22, 2006

BONE PORTRAITS by Deborah Stein; Director, Lear deBessonet; Presented by Still Point Productions; Co-Created and performed by Michael Crane, Gian-Murray Gianino, Adam Green, Miriam Silverman, Jessica Wortham; Design, Justin Townsend; Video and Film, Gregory King; Costumes, Kirche Leigh Zelle; Sound, Mark Huang; Production Manager, Ben Sterling; Stage Manager, Dave Polato; Assistant Director, Michael Perlman; May 9 – 20, 2006

WHERE EAGLES DARE THEATRE

ABNORMAL STEW by King Talent, Daniel Guyton and Laz Viciedo; Director, King Talent; Produced by Baby Hippopotamus Productions; **Cast:** King Talent, Giselle Talent, Laz Viciedo, Jillyn McKittrick, Andy Jacobs, Matt Talent, Melissa Jo Talent, Kimberly Conzo; August 22 – December 5 ,2005

THE KNIFE ASSASSIN by Alan Kanevsky; Director, M. Stefan Strozier; August 13 – September 15, 2005

THE FALL MINI-FEST November 3 – 20, 2005; Series included: *Return of the Native or the Wages of Sin* with book, music and lyrics by John Taylore Thomas; *Only His Knees* and *Losin' Mannie* by Eddie Betz, presented by La Muse Vénale Acting Troupe; *Last Day* by Jesse Schmitt; *RE: Mr.Stanley* and *Séance at Fountainebleau* by Michael Kalmen, presented by Xoregos Performing Company; *Simply Selma* by Jonathan Joy; *The Spy Surfs* a multimedia work

Ned Massey and Utkarsh S. Ambudkar in Urban Stages' *The Snow Queen* PHOTO BY PAVEL ANTONOV

DEAD POET COME ALIVE Director, Bryan Kern; December 15–18, 2005

THE WHALES Written and directed by M. Stefan Strozier; January 5–29, 2006

BEYOND THE VEIL Written and directed by John Chatterton; Produced with La Muse Vénale Acting Troupe; February 2–26, 2006

SERVY-N-BERNICE 4EVER by Seth Zvi Rothesfeld; Presented by BOFA Productions; March 30–April 8, 2006

SECRETS by Gerald Zipper; Director, Ted Mornel; April 13–2006

THE TRAGEDY OF ABRAHAM LINCOLN by M. Stefan Strozier; Produced with La Muse Vénale Acting Troupe; Director, Alan Kanvesky; April 13–May 7, 2006

WINGS THEATRE

TRANSIT: THREE ONE-ACT PLAYS by Adam Beechen; Director, Nate Dushku; Produced by Kori Schneider and Kia Graves; Lighting, Mark Mudo; Costumes, Korine Lightsmith; **Cast:** *On Approach:* Kia Graves, Billy Covert, Andrea A. McCullough; *Pacifica:* Kori Schneider, Livia Scott, Charlotte Hampden, Jeffrey Cutaiar; *A Whole New Ballgame*: Jack Caputo, Smeralda Abel, Adriean Dlaney; June 2–25

THE AUDITION Written and directed by Betsy Head; Stage Manager, Dora Naughton; Produced by Page 10 Productions; September 7–October 1, 2005

JIGSAW Written and directed by Jayson McDonald; Produced by Stars & Hearts; Lighting, Michael O'Connor; Sound, Sookie Mei; Production Design, Kathryn Immonen; **Cast:** Lil Malinich, Anthony Crep, Paola Grande, Mark Lawrence, Shannon Black, Hanna Hayes; October 31–November 16, 2005

THE DELUXE ILLUSTRATED BODY by Jayson McDonald and Lil Malinich; Produced by Sprial, Inc.; November 3–16, 2005

RACHEL Book and lyrics by Bernice Lee, music by Lou Greene; Director, Scott Pegg; Musical Director, Richard Sterne; Design, Nadine Charlson; Costumes, Tom Claypool; **Cast:** Kay Arnold, James Bormann, Karen Dillie, John Kelly, Susan Jerfome, Geany Masi, Leslie Shreve, Mark Silberg; December 1–10, 2005

SUV: THE MUSICAL by Gersh Kuntzman and Marc Dinkin; Produced by NeoShtick Theater; Director, Eric Oleson; Choreography, Katie Workum; Stage Manager, Hollie Rosenberg; **Cast:** Adam Wofsdorf, Jen Kersey, Dina Plotch, Kenny Wade Marshall, Stephanie Roy, Jerry Miller, Chris Griggs, Christian Maurice, Derek Roland, Matt Knight; Originally presented at the 2005 FringeNYC; January 1–21, 2006

GALILEO: FATHER DEAREST Written and directed by Barbara Bregstein; Presented by Forum Theatre; Designers, Nestor Rodriguez, Colin Huggins, Bunn Mateosian; **Cast:** Jack Drucker, Margot Staub, Marguerite Moral, Devin Moriarity, Laura Johnson, Warren Katz, Isaac Scranton, Michael Muldoon; January 25–March 18, 2006

WORKSHOP THEATRE SPACE

THE WINTER'S TALE by William Shakespeare; Produced by Love Street Theatre; Director, Julie S. Halpern; Lighting, Josh Cohen; Costumes, Jenn Dugan; Stage Manager, Courtney Sweeting; **Cast:** David Mead, Julie S. Halpern, Nora Hummel, Christopher Grubbs Leavell, Tony White, Sean Eager, Tom Cleary, Carrie Edel, Jody Christopherson, Chris M. Allport, Brian Silliman, Paige J. Lussier; Jewel Box Theater, August 31–September 18, 2005

MISS JULIE by August Strindberg; Director, Mhari Sandoval; Lighting, Alyssa Humphries; **Cast:** Brie Eley, Rachel Hollon, Brad Lee Thomason; April 12–15, 2006

ADDITIONAL OFF-OFF BROADWAY PRODUCTIONS AND EVENTS

ACCOMPLICE: NEW YORK Created by Tom Salamon and Betsy Salamon-Sufott; **Cast:** James Feuer, Joseph Tomasini, Alan Steele, Joe Luongo, Roland Uruci, Brendan Irving, Lauren Potter, John Cannatella; Mystery locations throughout the city; June–November 2005

TARA'S CROSSING by Jeffrey Solomon; Director, Steve Satta; Presented by the LES Tenement Museum, Houses on the Moon Theater Company, in conjunction with the American Friends Service Committee Immigrant Rights Program; Tenemant Theater; June 2–26, 2005

BLITZKRIEG: THE HASSIDIC PROFESSIONAL WRESTLING MUSICAL by Ron Glucksman; Director, Dan Carlton; Design, Stephanie Leonard, Kevin Harkins, Wendy Wincentsen; Musical Director, John Z; Choreography, Stephanie Beauchamp; **Cast:** Ryan Link, Jill Pakuski, Eric Storm, Dan Truman, Cash Tilton, KB Nau, Dan Carlton; Uncle Ming's; June 7–23, 2005

1776 by Peter Stone, music and lyrics by Sherman Edwards; Director, Bruce Biggins; Music Director, Philip McCarthy; Choreography, Elisa DiSimone; **Cast:** Joe Tarulli, Michael Edmund, Bruce Biggins, Robert Zanfini, David Thomas Crowe, John D'Arcangelo, Marc Crawford Leavitt, Frank Manzi, Tom Zainea, Richard Zaltzman, J. Dolan Byrnes, Brandon deSpain, Chadwick Vogel, Walter Mantani, Nicholas Barnes, Peter R. Thewes, Robert Scott Denny, Scott Van Tuyl, Richard Binder, Robert Driemeyer, Arthur Atkinson, Jarrod Simons, Elisa DiSimone, Michele Maugeri; Trent Ballard Franco, Dennis Hearn, Robert Resnikoff, Kerry Watterson; Fraunces Tavern Restaurant; June 3–July 2, 2005

BOUNDLESS AS THE SEA *The Tempest* and *Twelfth Night* by William Shakespeare presented in repertory; Director, Marc Silberschatz; Produced by Twenty Feet Productions; West Park Church; June 7–26, 2005

CARCASS by Peretz Hirshbein, translated and adapted by Mark Altman and Ellen Perecman; Presented by Diaspora Drama Group; Common Basis Theatre; June 9–26, 2005

FOR COLORED GIRLS WHO HAVE CONSIDERED SUICIDE WHEN THE RAINBOW IS ENUF by Ntozake Shange; Director, Arnold Beauchamp; Producer, Dr. Josephine English; Artistic Director, Micheal "Scorp" Sheppard; **Cast:** Suzanne M. Harvin, Candice Hassell, Marlana Marie, Derika Abraham, Velvet A. Ross, Natasha Lowery, Tish Harper; Paul Robeson Theatre; June 18–July 30, 2005

THE NEST by Franz Xaver Kroetz; Director, Marcia Haufrect; **Cast:** Roxana Alonso, Christopher Kerson; Mint Space Theatre; July 5–23, 2005

ROMEO AND JULIET by William Shakespeare; Director, Janicza M. Bravo; Presented by Real Theatre Works; Designer, Ted Walter; Choreographer: Jennie Liu, Hannah Heller; Composer, Heather Christian; Costumes, Andrea Gastelum, Melinda Relyea; **Cast:** Brandon Bales, Malcolm I. Barrett, Frank Boyd, Sebastian Calderon-Bentin, David Call, Sean Donovan, Nicholas Gorham, Carmen M. Herlihy, Ben Kerrick, Alexandria Kryzaniwsky, Mireya Lucio, Charlotte Miller, Prentice Onayemi, Laura Stinger; St. John's Church; July 6–16, 2005

BAYSIDE! THE UN-MUSICAL! Produced by Incredio Productions; Apocalypse Lounge; July 17–19, October 18–23, 2005

THE PECULIAR PATRIOT Written and performed by Liza Jessie Peterson; Produced by INBOND Management; The Gallery; July 18–September 19, 2005

TO ONE I SAW SMALL Written and directed by Cristina Septien; Presented by South Pleasant Company; **Cast:** Diana Buirski, Chris Corporandy; Merce Cunningham Studio; July 22–30, 2005

MY YEAR OF PORN written and performed by Cole Kazdin, directed by Ivanna Cullinan; Magnet Theatre; August 5, 12, 19, September 23, 30, 2005

WALK! WITH GREGORY DEETZ AND MUFFY LAGUARDIA Conceived by Richard Olmstead; Sara Roosevelt Park; August 6–29, 2005

DON QUIJOTE: HIS LAST ADVENTURE based on the the novel by Cervantes, adapted by Margarita Galban and Lina Montalvo; Director, Gloria Zelaya; Choreography Adolfo Vasquez; Presented by the Puerto Rican Traveling Theatre; Various locations in New York and New Jersey; August 19–28, 2005

HOWL! FESTIVAL Presented by Federation of East Village Artiists; Series included: *Miller vs. Williams, Bath Party, Inside/Outside, Way the F**K Off-Broadway;* Bowery Poetry Club, Tompkins Sqauare Park, and other East Village locations; August 21–28, 2005

MISS JULIE by August Strindberg; Director, Mercedes Murphy; Presented by Théâtre Trouvé; Design, D.M. Wood, Bailey Heck, Anthony Gabriel; Stage Manager, Elizabeth Kegley; **Cast:** Danielle Fink, David Ian Lee, Peggy Trecker; Théâtre Trouvé; August 17–September 10, 2005

PLAY OUTSIDE! FESTIVAL OF FREE OUTDOOR THEATRE 2005; Various locations; September 4–26, 2005; Included: *Twelfth Night: Illyrium Delirium* presented by Aisling Arts; *Buckaroo Bindlestiff's Wild West Jamboree* presented by Bindlestiff Family Cirkus; *Princess* presented by Circus Amok; Dominican Folk Dances presented by Conjunto Folklorico de Alianza Dominicana; *Opera Buffonia* presented by Culture Connection Theatre; *The Winter's Tale* presented by Magis Theatre Company; *Romeo and Juliet* presented by New Perspectives Theatre Company; *The Time Cycle* presented by NaCl; *Nice Hat* presented by 3 of Clubs; *Field of Schemes* presented by Under the Table

BLUES FOR MISTER CHARLIE by James Baldwin; Presented by Turtle Shell Productions; Director, Brad Malow; Producer, John W. Cooper; Stage Manager, Norva Bennett; Design, Gino Ng, Dennis Ballard, Lance Darcy; **Cast:** Marcia Berry, Michael Carlsen, Frances Chewning, Brian Cooper, Ron Crawford, Evander Duck, Jr., Mika Duncan, Jason Drumwright, Mark Hairston, Zoey Martinson, Nia McGovern, Madalyn McKay, Matthew S. Morgan, Bristol Pomeroy, W.D. Richardson, Jessica Taylor, Lloyd Watts, Page Hearn, Kamahl Palmer, Justin Stevens; Marjorie S. Deane Little Theatre; September 8–26,2005

THE CAUCASIAN CHALK CIRCLE by Bertolt Brecht; Presented by The Mettawee River Theatre Company; Director and Design, Ralph Lee; Costumes, Casey Compton, Music, Neal Kirkwood and Harry Mann; **Cast:** Bruce Connelly, Kim Gambino, Kevin Lawler, Tom Marion, Joe Osheroff, Clea Rivera; Outdoor Garden at St. John the Divine; September 9–18, 2005

MACBETH by William Shakespeare; Presented by Shakespeare in the Industrial Park; Director, Peach Paulison; **Cast:** Cory Solar, Mim Granahan, Richard Bolster, Jack Perry, Joseph Miller, Vic DiMonda, Peach Paulison, Kyle Hansen, Rachel McKinney, Daniel Cecil, Carlos Fernandez, Saysha Heinzman, Shawn Renfro, Delia Baseman, Amelia Henderson, James D. Jacobus, Jonas Amadeus Barranca; Rooftop at OfficeOps; September 10–October 2, 2005

STILL-LIFE (WITH RUNNER) by Steven Gridley; previously presented at HERE as part of the American Living Room festival; Produced by Spring Theatreworks (Jeffrey Horne, Artistic Director); Direction and design by Steven Gridley and Jacob Titus; Costumes, Rabiah Troncellliti; **Cast:** Sharon Floyd, Doug Simpson, Erin Treadway, Jesse Erbel, David Wylie, Eric McGregor, Jeffrey Horne; Presented with a short dance-theatre piece entitled *Waking Up* by Jacob Titus; Spring Theatreworks Studio at 25 Jay Street; September 15–October 22, 2005

MOSCOW CATS THEATRE Tribeca Performing Arts Center; September 16–December 29, 2005 (Transferred Off-Broadway to the Lamb's Theatre-see "Off Broadway Plays that Opened" in this volume for production credits)

TO KILL A MOCKINGBIRD by Harper Lee; Produced by Brave New World Repertory; Director, Claire Beckman; **Cast:** Claire Beckman (Jean Louise), Taylor Morgan (Scout), Kristin Janine (Calpurnia), Jeremy White (Jem), Zak Stevens (Dill), Henry Brown (Young boy), Baz Snider (Judge Taylor), Doug Barron (Heck Tate), Christine Siracusa (Miss Maudie), Cynthia Babak (Miss Stephanie), Sara Elsen (Mayella Ewell), John Morgan (Bob Ewell), Ezra Barnes (Atticus Finch), Lynn Brown (Walter Cunningham), Eleanor Ruth (Mrs Dubose), Damon Pooser (Tom Robinson), Ghylian Bell (Helen Robinson), Gary Cowling (Mr. Gilmer), Karl Greenberg (Boo Radley), Roy Eaton (Reverend Sykes), Juanita Fleming (Mrs. Robinson); Performed on 5 porches and the sidewalks on Wesminster Road in Brooklyn; September 18, 2005

LENZ A theatrical environmental play created, presented and performed by bluemouth, inc. of Toronto (Stephen O'Connell, Sabirna Reeves, Lucy Simic, Richard Windeyer); Ye Old Carlton Arms Hotel; September 29–October 8, 2005

'TIS PITY SHE'S A WHORE by John Ford; Produced by Les Gutman and Friendly Fire Theatre Company; Director, Alex Lippard; Set, Michael V. Moore; Costume, Martin T. Lopez ; Lighting, Scott Bolman; Sound and Original Music, Allison Leyton-Brown; Fight Director, Rick Sordelet; Production Stage Manager, Elyzabeth Gorman; Dramaturg, Ben Nadler; Associate Producers, Helena Webb and Danielle Muniz; Assistant Producer, Jack Trinco, Jay Sullivan; Press, Sam Rudy Media Relations; **Cast:** Craig Baldwin, Rachel Matthews Black, Craig Braun, Colby Chambers, Sam Chase, Mel Cobb, Helmar Augustus Cooper, Catherine Curtin, Cameron Folmar, Jan Leslie Harding, Mauricio Tafur Salgado, John Douglas Thompson, Betsy Winchester; Storm Theatre; September 29–October 21, 2005

PLATINUM TRAVEL CLUB by Franca Miraglia; Presented by New Perspectives Theatre Company and Melody Brooks; Director, Anne Beaumont; Design, Casey Smith, Eric Larson, Coleen Scott, Anne Beaumont; Fight Director, E. Calvin Ahn; Stage Manager, Rosela Moseng; **Cast:** Christiane Amorosia, Jed Dickson, Andrew Platner, Joanie Schumacher, Tony Neil, Anne Winkles; October 4–22, 2005

WOYZECK by Georg Buchner; Presented by Flying Pig Collective and Boston Directors' Lab; Rifstone Arch in Central Park; October 14–23, 2005

4PLAY ... SEX IN A SERIES An play presented in four episodes by Graham Brown, Nathan Faudree, and Lisa Roth; Director, Graham Brown; Presented by trip.; **Cast:** Graham Brown, Nathan Faudree, Corey Ann Haydu, Jessica Jolly, Emily Merryn, Aaron Sandler, Phil Wilcox, Kira Blaskovich; Lucky Jack's; November 2–December 17, 2005

AUTOMATIC SUPERSTAR Written, directed and produced by Bob Weidman; Co-Producer, Neil Nathan; Design, Dana Sterling, Jason Candler, Melanie Swersey, Andrewa R. Lenci; Video, Michael Burlingame; Stage Manager, Stephanie Bashall, **Cast:** Zachary Mordechai, Franky Paul, Tracie Hendricks, Bryan Matland, Steve Hoevertsz, Frank Caira, Isaac Everett, Howard Alper, Eliane, Moxie Block, Zorikh Lequidre, Michael Cramer, Miriam Kushnir, Victoria Smalc; Show Nightclub; November 4–18, 2005; Reopened May 12–June 23, 2006

LETTERS FROM THE EARTH based on the writings of Mark Twain; Created and performed by Collapsable Giraffe Company; Collapsable Hole; November 2–December 17, 2005

ESTRELLA, MY REFUGEE by Kate Bell; Presented by Committed Theatre Company; Director, Thomas G. Waites; **Cast:** Mayte Arguello, Shelly Ebner, Luciana Magnoli, Diane Love, Mihaela Mihut, Robert Mobley, Stephen Savona, Hank Sage, Geoff Schmith, Lauren Stocks; Bernie West Theatre at Baruch College; November 4–20, 2005

THE EVOLUTION OF A SEXY MUTHA FUCKA!! Written and performed by Sue Costello; Zipper Theater; November 4–12, 2005

BLOCKING OUT THE SYMPTOMS One-act plays by Stanford Pritchard; Presented by New Media Repertory Theater; Director, Miranda McDermott; **Cast:** Ken Schwarz; December 13–17, 2005

KILLA DILLA by OyamO; Director, Andre DeShields; Produced by The Working Theatre; **Cast:** Kim Brockington, Leland Gantt, Laura E. Johnston, Angela Lewis, Gil Pritchett, Roslyn Ruff, Dan Teachout, Joan Valentina, Bill Weeden; Players Theatre; January 5–15, 2006

WHAT MAKES SAMMY RUN? Based on the novel by Budd Schulberg, music and lyrics by Ervin Drake, book by Budd Schulberg and Stuart Schulberg, revised and directed by Robert Armin; Costumes, Joanne Hess; Lighting, Jeffrey Salzberg; Arrangements and Musical Direction, Richard Danley; Choreography, Jack Dyville; **Cast:** Carl Anthony-Tramon, Selby Brown, Darron Cardosa, Larry Daggett, Jeffrey Farber, Jessica Luck, Kristin McLaughlin, Matthew Napoli, Steven Patterson, Moira Stone; West End Theatre at the Church of St. Pauls; January 19–29, 2006

DEATH MIGHT BE YOUR SANTA CLAUS Created and directed by Lear deBessonet, additional text by Juliana Francis; Presented by Still Point Productions; Scenery, Michael Casselli; Costumes, Sarah Majorino; Lighting, Beth Turomsha; Sound, Raul Enriquez; **Cast:** Sara Barker, Gillian Chadsey, Jonathan Green, Nicholas Job, Jamie King, David Laufgraben, Anne Robinson, Robert Saietta, Lucy Smith; 15 Nassau; February 18–21, 2006

LORCA FEDERICA LORCA Written and directed by Luis Caballero; Teatro Circulo; March 2–April 9, 2006

ILLUMINATE Conceived and directed by Joe Doran; Presented by Equliaterial Theatre Company; Choreograpy, Tony Guglietti; Music, Nick Moore; Performers: Tony Guglietti, Amanda Page, Ellen Guglietti, Laura Sculco, Danny Mitsios; Mulberry Street Theater; March 22–25, 2006

KRAPP'S LAST TAPE by Samuel Beckett; Director and Design, Mercedes Murphy; Presented by Théâtre Trouvé; Sound, Anthony Gabriele; Lighting, DM Wood; **Cast:** Philip Graeme; Performed in an undisclosed, site specific location; March 23–April 9, 2006

THE COOKIE CUTTER'S CLUB by Alec Coiro; The Dactyl Foundation; March 23–April 1, 2006

HASTY PUDDING THEATRICALS #158—SOME LIKE IT YACHT! Book and lyrics by Josh Brener and Sam Gale Rosen; Director, Tony Parise; Music, Ben Green, Music Supervision, Allen Feinstein; Arrangements, Dan Ring and Danny Percefull; Music Director, Manny Dayao and Matt Corriel; Choreography, Karen Pisani; Design, Peter Miller, Joahn Cuff, Heidi Hermiller; Producers, Mary Kate Burke, Ashley Zolta; **Cast:** Josh C. Phillips, Alan D. Zackheim, David W. Ingber, John P. Blickstead, Sean R. Fredricks, Michael B. Hoagland, Toby W. Burns, Ben K. Kawaller, Justin V. Rodriguez, Peter A. Dodd, David J. Anderson, Kaye Playhouse at Hunter College; March 24–25, 2006

HEARING VOICES (SPEAKING IN TONGUES) Written and performed by Michael Mack; Director, Daniel Gidron; Stage Manager, Marina Morrow; Matthew Corozine Studio Theater, Time Square Arts Center; April 9–May 14, 2006

FOR CHRIST'S SAKE...THE MUSICAL Written and directed by Richard Fowler; Presented by C3M Producions (Christian City Church Manhattan); Executive Producer, Stephen Hickson; Associate Producer, Marlyne Afflack; Musical Director, Hugh Wilson; Performers: Maria Christensen, Randel Duk Kim, Annie Occhiorgrosso; New World Stages, April 12–15, 2006

SIDEWAYS STORIES FROM WAYSIDE SCHOOL by Louis Sachar, adapted by John Olive; Philip Coltoff Center; April 20–May 21, 2006

ANGELS FALL by Arthur Miller; Director, Russell Taylor; Producer, Ellen Seltz; Design, Andrew Seltz, Ginny Hack, Bernard Fox; Stage Manager, Danielle Campbell; **Cast:** Jeff Farber, Frankie Ferrara, June Flanagan, Kathryn Barnhardt, Andrew Reaves, Tim Moore; Church for All Nations; April 21–May 7, 2006

FOREVER PLAID Conceived by Stuart Ross, Arrangements by James Raitt; Director, Brian Swasey; Scenery, Ryan D. Lee; Lighting, Erik J. Michael; Music Director, Jeffrey Campos; Stage Manager, Megan Schwarz; **Cast:** Frederick Hamilton (Frankie), Shad Olsen (Sparky), Ryan J. Ratliff (Jinx), Joseph Torello (Smudge); Astoria Performing Arts Center; April 28–May 14, 2006

LITTLE RED: LOST IN THE WOODS Composed by Nate Farrar; Presented by The Toy Box Theatre; Director, David (Michael) Holmes; Assistant Director, Jonathan Barsness; Film Direction, Alex P. Baack; Technical Director, Ross Johnson; Cinematographer, Serko Artinian; Lighting Designer, Chris Kay; Production Manager, Mandy Pouliot; Scenic Design, Robert Monaco, Stage Manager, Michelle Salerno; **Cast:** Doug Bellitto, Ashleigh Beyer, Julie Ferrell, Joanne Joseph, Matthew Landfield, Larry Mitchell, Matthew Simon, Diane Tyler, Daniel Zaitchik; Morocco Studio; April 28–May 8, 2006

BLANCO by Pablo Garcia-Gámez; Presented by Instituto Arte Teatral International; Theatre IATI; May 4–21, 2006

Off-Off-Broadway Company Series

13TH STREET REPERTORY

Edith O'Hara, Artistic Director/Founder

Short Play Festival-July 21–30, 2005; Laura Cosentino and Troy Miller, Executive Producers; Menu A: *Red Roses* by Lisa Soland; *Love, Joel* by Jennifer J. Katz; *Coming Out of the Closet* by John Zygmunt; *A Hillside in Hell* by Maurice Martin; *It's a Dog's Life* by Fran Handman; *Public Service* by Ralph Tropf; *Zoloft or Zofia* by Michael Stockman; *The Death of My Own Family* by David L. Meth; Menu B: *Siren Song* by Ellen Koivisto; *We and the Queen* by Phil Keeling; *Hypothermia* by Alex Dremann; *Virgin Rock* by Kevin Christopher Snipes; *Shoe Polish* by Scott T. Barsotti

JJ Baron Concert performance; June 18, 2005; September 10, 2005–March 19, 2006

Radio Mirth & the Third Reich by Sharon Wajswol & Jack Kelly; January 11–March 8, 2006

Conversations with a Kleagle by Rudy Gray; Director, Cristina Alicea; February 16–April 7, 2006

Troika: God, Tolstoy & Sophia by Peter Levy; Director, Karen Raphaeli; April 27–June 17, 2006

PRODUCTIONS FROM PREVIOUS SEASONS

New Voices in Poetry and Music Closed February 4, 2006

Let's Be Frank (Old Blue Eyes Is Back!) Written and directed by Hootch Hoolahan; Opened October 1, 2004; Closed March 19, 2006

Line by Israel Horovitz; Director, Michael Whitney in association with Edith O'Hara; 32nd year; still running as of May 31, 2006

READINGS

Pageant by Daniel MacDonald; Director, Karen Raphaeli; June 2005

Kill My Wife with a Knife by Brent Carlsberg; Director, Lisa Maley; June 2005

Radio, Mirth, and the Third Reich by Sharon Wajswol and Jack Kelly; July 2005

Dragon Fly Tale by Lorey Hayes and Bobby Crear; Director, Imani; July 2005

The Turtle Gets There Too by Arni Ibsen; Director, Lisa Maley; July 2005

Troika: God, Tolstoy & Sophia by Peter Levy; Director, Karen Raphaeli; September 2005

Seven Year Clause by Sharon Wajswol; Director, Karen Raphaeli; October 2005, March 2006

Conversations with a Kleagle by Rudy Gray; Director, Cristina Alicea; November 2005

All Happy Families by Ted Tinling; Director, Syeus Mottel; December 2005

Exposure by Michael Stockman; Director, Karen Raphaeli; January 2006

Road's End by Greg Foote; Director, June Rachelson-Ospa; January 2006

Why Are We in Iraq? By Heny Meyerson; Direcotr, Jennifer Blevins; February 2006

Triangle Book and lyrics by June Rachelson-Ospa; Music by Mark Barkan; Director, Robert W. McMaster; April 2006

Nazo Fast! by Sharon Wajswol; Director, Mack Gilbert; April 2006

Death by Visitation of God by Lowrie Fawley; Directors, Lowrie Fawley and Christian St. John; May 2006

29TH STREET REP

David Mogentale, Artistic Director

PLAYS IN MOTION-READING SERIES

Post-Mortem by J.B. Miller; **Men of Tortuga** by Jason Wells; **The Blood Red Hand or How a Borstal Stayed True** by Patrick Kennedy; **Where the Sky Begins** by Mark Farnen; September 2005

MAINSTAGE

Lenny & Lou by Ian Cohen; Director, Sturgis Warner; Scenery, Ryan Scott; Costumes, Isabel Rubio; Lighting, Charles Foster; Sound, David Margolin Lawson; Fight Director, J. David Brimmer; Stage Mangager, Cesar Malantic; Production Manager, Patrick Kennedy; **Cast:** David Mogentale (Lenny Feinstein), Todd Wall (Lou Feinstein), Suzanne Toren (Fran Feinstein), Heidi James (Julie Riggio), Carolyn Michelle Smith (Sabrina DuChamp); January 26–February 26, 2006; 24 performances

3GRACES THEATRE COMPANY

Chelsea Silverman, Executive Director; Elizabeth Bunnell and Annie McGovern, Artistic Directors; Kelli Lynn Harrison, Managing Director

Ladyhouse Blues by Kevin O'Morrison; Director, Marc Weitz; Producer, Chelsea Silverman and Elizabeth Bunnell; Music Director/Composer, John D. Ivy; Scenery, Alexis Distler; Costumes, Veneda Truesdale; Lighting, Patrick T. Cecala II, Stage Manager, Bill Kuhrt; **Cast:** Dorothy Abrahams, Kathleen Bishop, Kelli Lynn Harrison, Nitra Gutiérrez, Annie McGovern; Linhart Theater at 440 Studios; June 16–July 1, 2005

The Lower East Side Project by Kayla S. Cagen; Adapted and directed by Karen Sommers; Scenery, Alexis Distler; Lighting, Patrick T. Cecala II; **Cast:** Pete Sander, Gayle Robbins, Greg Dubin, Brian Sack, Suzanne Barbetta, Goldie Zweibel, Amy Broder, Jordanna Oberman, Joseph Cordaro; Linhart Theatre at 440 Studios; June 19–July 3, 2005

Flyer by Kate Aspengren; Director, Karen Sommers; Producer, Kelli Lynn Harrison; Scenery, Michael P. Kramer; Costumes, Sylvie Marc-Charles; Lighting, Cris Dopher; Sound, John D. Ivy; Stage Manager, Jennifer B. Harvey; **Cast:** Dorothy Abrahams, Elizabeth Bunnell, Cherelle Cargill, Paul de Cordova, Richard Ferrone, John Kaisner, Brian McFadden, Annie McGovern, Chelsea Silverman, Hal Smith Reynolds; Bank Street Theater; October 21–November 6, 2005

Finding Happy Written and performed by Cate Smit; Director, Judith Searcy; Bank Street Theater, October 25–November 1, 2005

The Portable Dorothy Parker by Annie Lux; Director, Lee Costello; **Cast:** Margot Avery; October 25–November 1, 2005

The Cabaret, A Tribute to the U.S.O. Director, Kathleen Bishop; Bank Street Theater; October 23–November 4, 2005

ABINGDON THEATRE COMPANY

Jan Buttram and Pamela Paul, Artistic Directors; Samuel J. Bellinger, Managing Director

STAGE II PRODUCTIONS — DOROTHY STRELSIN THEATRE

In the Arms of Baby Jesus by Michéle Raper Rittenhouse; Director, Carole Mansley; **Cast:** Patti Mariano; September 9–25, 2005

Daniella Uses Dirty Words by Matthew Moses; Director, Kim T. Sharp; Scenery, Ryan Scott; Costumes, Susan Scherer; Lighting, Gabriel Hainer Evansohn; Original Music, Carlton DeWoody and Tyler Burba; Stage Manager, Katie Raben; **Cast:** Teddy Bergman, Dan Cordle, Kevin Curtis, Donna Marie Rose, Jennifer Rubins, Shelley Karen Molad; November 4–20, 2005

My Deah by John "Lypsinka" Epperson; Director, Mark Waldrop; Scenery and Costumes, Mark Simpson; Costumes, David Kaley; Sound, Matt Berman; **Cast:** Nancy Opel; Bryan Batt, Philip Clark; Lori Gardner, Michael Hunsaker, Geoffrey Molloy, Jay Rogers, Kevin Townley; April 21–May 7, 2006

STAGED READINGS

Acting Alone by David M. Korn; Director, Kim T. Sharp; June 2005

Distant Music by James McLindon; Director, Elliot J. Cohen; July 2005

The Death Bite by Hal Corley; Director, Taylor Brooks; August 2005

The Fire Box by Ian Strasfogel; Director, Charles Maryan; September 2005

Hostage Wife by Nancy Moss; Director, Peter Brouwer; October 2005

The President and Her Mistress by Jan Buttram; Director, Rob Ubinati; November 2005

Trailer Park Propehcies by James Farrell; Director, Edward J. McKeaney; December 2005

Innocence by Bruce J. Robinson; Director, Marvin Starkman; January 2006

The Lives of Bosie by John Wolfson; Director, Austin Pendleton; February 2006

Beachwood Drive by Steven Leigh Morris; Director, Cat Parker; March 2006

Out of Isak by Laura Edmondson; Director, Jocelyn Sawyer; April 2006

Test Drive by Jean Reynolds; Director, Sturgis Warner; May 2006

ACT FRENCH FESTIVAL

A Season of New Theatre from France; Conceived by the Cultural Services of the French Embassy and Association Française d'Artistique; July–December 2005

59E59 THEATERS

Adramelech's Monologue by Valère Novarina, translated by Guy Bennett; **Cast:** Hilario Saavedra; Theater C; November 18–20 **A.W.O.L** based on *Colonel Zoo* by Olivier Cadiot, translated by Cole Swensen; Presented by In Parentheses, Director, Marion Schoevaert; **Cast:** Steven Rattazzi and All Male Chrous; Composer Adam Silverman; Theater B; November 8–27; **Colonel Zoo** by Olivier Cadiot; Director, Compagnie Ludovic Lagarde; Presented by In Parentheses; starring Laurent Poitrenaux; Theater B; November 2–3; **Fairy Queen** by Olivier Cadiot; translated by Cole Swenson; Director, Compagnie Ludovic Lagarde; Presented by In Parentheses; **Cast:** Laurent Poitrenaux; Valerie Dashwood, Philippe Duquesne; Theater B; November 4–5; **Hilda** by Marie Ndiaye; Theater A; November 11–December 11 (see "Off Broadway Openings"); **Marie Ndiaye: Public Readings** *Papa doit manger* translated by Erika Rundle; *Rosie Carpe* read by Marie Ndiaye; Produced by The Play Company; Theater C; November 16; **Take No Survivors** by Gérard Bagardie; Director, Elysabeth Kleihans, translated by Arnold Slater; presented by Animated Theaterworks; Theater C; October 27–30, November 1–13

The Life and Death of Pier Paolo Pasolini by Michel Azama; Director, Elisabeth Williamson; June Havoc Theater at Abingdon Theatre Complex; November 22–December 4

BROOKLYN ACADEMY OF MUSIC HARVEY THEATRE

4.48 Psychose by Sarah Kane, translated by Evelyne Pieiller; Director, Claude Régy; **Cast:** Isabelle Huppert and Gérard Watkins; October 19–30; **Bright Abyss** written and directed by James Thiérrée, **Cast:** Gaëlle Bisellach-Roig, Raphaëlle Boitel, Niklas Ek, Thiago Martins, James Thiérrée, Una Ysamat; November 9–13

…She Said Adaptation from Marguerite Duras' "Destroy, She Said" by Ivan Talijancic; Presented by WaxFactory; The Brooklyn Lyceum; November 3–13

Paradis (Unfolding Time) Written and directed by Pascal Rambert; Dance Theater Workshop; December 7–10

FLORENCE GOULD HALL AT FRENCH INSTITUTE ALLIANCE FRANÇAISE

Commentaire D'Amour by Jean-Marie Besset; **Cast:** Josh Hamilton, Mary Stuart Masterson; November 11–13; **Liaison Transatlantique: Letters of Simone de Beauvoir to Nelson Algren** by Fabrice Rozié; Director, Sandrine Dumas; performed by Marie-France Pisier; September 30–October 2

Old Clown Wanted by Matei Visniec; Director, Gregory Fortner; Presented by Trap Door Theatre; HERE Arts Center; November 29–December 4

BIG: Episode #2 (Show/Business) by Superamas; The Kitchen; November 2–5

Misterioso-119 by Koffi Kwahulé, translated by Chantal Bilodeau; Director, Liesl Tommy; New York Theatre Workshop (October 24); Lark Theatre Play Development Center (October 27)

Le Dernier Caravansérail Created by Théâtre du Soleil with music by Jean-Jacques Lemêtre; Director, Ariane Mnouchkine; Lincoln Center Festival/Damrosch Park; July 17–31

Situating Sartre 2005; September 29–October 1; Symposium of Francophone African and Caribbean Theater and Readings; Maison Française of NYU; October 28

The Workroom by Jean-Claude Grumberg, translated by Daniel A. Stein and Sarah O'Connor; Director Moni Yakim, Presented by The Unbound Theatre; Manhattan Theatre Source; November 23–26

Carte Blanche: French-American Theater Dialogue Series; Martin E. Segal Theatre at The Graduate Center, CUNY; October 11, 24; November 1, 5, 7, 21, 28; December 12

NEW YORK PUBLIC LIBRARY FOR THE PERFORMING ARTS

An Afternoon with Lucien and Micheline Attoun: Supporters of New Dramatic Writing since 1971 October 22; *A Festival of Arte: Theatre Programming from Europe's Premier Culture Channel* December 5–10; *Lectures by Emmauel Wallon On The Historical & Current Contexts Of French Theater* November 18–19; *Listening Means Seeing More: The Unique World of French Radio Theater* December 12–13

The Island of Slaves and **Actors of Good Faith** by Marivaux, adapted by Neil Bartlett; Director, Marc Paquien; New York Theater Workshop; October 3

OHIO THEATER

The José Pliya Project: A Celebration of Francophone African Playwright José Pliya Conceived by Philippa Wehle in association with Ellen Lampert-Gréaux; Presented by Soho Think Tank; Readings included: *Cannibals, We Were Sitting on the Shores of the World, An Ordinary Family,* November 1–5; and a full production of **Trapped (Le Complexe de Thénardier),** directed by Vincent Colin; **Cast:** Sylvie Chenus and Hyam Zaytoun; November 4–6

P.S. 122

The Itching of the Wings conceived and directed by Philippe Quesne; November 9–13 **PUSH: An Amplified Reading** Based on the novel by Sapphire, translated by Jean-Pierre Carasso; Directors, Alexia Monduit and Thomas Rannou; November 3–6, 9–13

Playwrights' Symposium with Jean-Claude Carrière, Marie Ndiaye, Jean-Marie Besset and several leading American playwrights; The Public Theater; November 14

Notes From Underground by Fyodor Dostoyevsky; translated by André Markowicz; Read by Patrice Chéreau; Symphony Space; October 11

THE ALTERNATE THEATRE

Kareem Fahmy, Founder/Artisic Director

Lion in the Streets by Judith Thompson; Produced with Derek Butler; Director, Kareem Fahmy; Scenery, Brian Ireland; Costumes and Makeup, Anne K. Wood; Lighting, Andrew Lu; Sound, Andrew Papadeas; Stage Manager, Andrea Wales; Dramaturg, Courtney Todd; **Cast:** Nathan Blew; Amanda Boekelheide, James Ryan Caldwell, Jeffrey Clarke, Tania Molina, Rachel Schwartz, Tracy Weller; June Havoc Theatre in Abingdon Arts Complex; September 8–25, 2005

The Collected Works of Billy the Kid by Michael Ondaatje; Director, Kareem Fahmy; Scenery, Jeffery Eisenmann; Costumes, Lisa Renee Jordan; Lighting, Scott Bolman; Sound and Music, Andrew Papadeas; Dramaturgy, Courtney Todd; Choreography, Nicole Holst; Musical Director, Rob Evans; Stage Manager, Andrew Wales; General Manager, Elizabeth Reed; **Cast:** Nathan Blew, Rob Evans, Vivia Font, Steven French, G.R. Johnson, Kyle Knauf, Melissa Miller, Tony Neil, Ryn O'Connor, Doug Simpson; Theater at Riverside Church; April 19–22, 2006

AMAS MUSICAL THEATRE

Donna Trinkoff, Producing Director

SIX O'CLOCK MUSICAL THEATRE LAB SERIES

Sheba Book and lyrics by Sharleen Cooper Cohen; music by Gary William Friedman; Director, Iona Morris; Music Director, Debra Barsha; **Cast:** Rob Evan, Brandy Chavonne Massey, Ana Marie Andricain, Sean Curley, Brett Glazer, Kevin Free, Danielle Greaves, Alan Green, Dequina Moore, Lyn Philistine, Manley Pope, Gerard Salvador, Stacey Scotte, Kacie Sheik, Peter Matthew Smith, Jodi Stevens, Bruce Winant; Barrow Group Theatre space; September 27–28, 2005 (presented in conjunction with the New York Musical Theatre Festival)

Magpie Book by Steven M. Jacobson, lyrics by Edward Gallardo, music by Gary William Friedman; Director, Rajendra Ramoon Marharaj; Players Theatre; February 22–23, 2006

Preto Change-O! Book by Barbara Gordon, book, music and lyrics by Mel Mandel and Norman Sachs; Director, Dan Siretta; Players Theatre; April 4–6, 2006

3RD ANNUAL BLAST FROM THE PAST BENEFIT

Damn Yankees Book by George Abbott and Douglass Wallop, music by Richard Adler and Jerry Ross and Lyrics by Mr. Adler and Mr. Ross; Director and Choreography, Rajendra Ramoon Maharaj; Music Director, Charles Creath; **Cast:** Sara Ramirez and Tamara Tunie (Lola), Rodney Hicks and Darius de Haas (Joe Hardy), Alton F. White (Applegate), Chuck Cooper (Coach), Ken Prymus (Older Joe), Vivian Reed (Meg), Tina Fabrique (Sister), Rob Evan (Mr. Welch); Ensemble: Wayne W. Pretlow, Raun Ruffin, Eric Anthony, Carmen Ruby Floyd, Rob Evan, Stacey Sargeant, Christine Clemons, Amber Efe, Britton Jones, Kevin Anthony, Michael A. Blackmon, Delance Minefee; November 14, 2005

WORKSHOP PRODUCTION

DogMusic Book and lyrics by Mark Masi, music by Jess Platt; Director, Alex Lippard; Music Director, Andrew Gerle; **Cast:** Deven May, Kay Walbye, Sarah Dacey Charles, Miguel Cervantes, Ryan Hillard; The Players Theatre; October 20–22, 2005; 4 performances

ROSETTA LENOIRE MUSICAL THEATRE ACADEMY PRODUCTION

On The Town by Betty Comden, Adolph Green, and Leonard Bernstein; Director, Christopher Scott; Choreography, Monica Johnson; Music Director, Marshall Keating; Scenery, Michael V. Moore; Lighting, Herrick Goldman; Costumes, Cheryl A McCarron; Sound, SFX Producitons; Hudson Guild Theatre; May 12–21, 2006; 9 performances

ANDHOW! THEATRE COMPANY

Jessica Davis-Irons, Artistic Director; Andrew Irons, Producing Director

Little Suckers by Andrew Irons; Director, Jessica Davis-Irons; Scenery, Meganne George; Costumes, Becky Lasky; Lighting, Owen Hughes Sound, Jill BC DuBoff; **Cast:** Arthur Aulisi, Ryan Bronz, Erin Quinn Purcell, Margie Stokley; Ohio Theatre; June 4–30, 2005

GARDEN PLAYS AT THE WEST 104TH STREET GARDEN

A Lightening of Fireflys by John-Richard Thompson; July 7 – 16, 2005

You Can Fish All You Want But the Sea Always Wins in the End by Brian PJ Cronin; July 7 – 30, 2005

READINGS AND BENEFITS

Dialogue 05: a reading series *Angel Mountain* by John-Richard Thompson; *That's Life* by Rebecca Chianese; *Purple Creek* by Andrew Irons; Blue Heron Arts Center Studio Theater; October 30 – November 20, 2005

Torch Songs at the Torch Club, featuring Margie Stokley, Arthur Aulisi, Peter Bernstein, Erin Quinn Purcell, Andrew Sherman; February 8, 2006

WORKSHOPS

Wonderdam by Margie Stokley, music and lyrics by Emily Curtis, Ethan Eubanks, Teddy Goldstein, and Jodi Sheeler; The Great Room at ART/NY; December 12, 2005

Purple Creek by Andrew Irons; Director, Jessica Davis-Irons; The Great Room at ART/NY; March 26, 2006

ATLANTIC THEATRE COMPANY

Neil Pepe, Artistic Director; Andrew D. Hamingson, Executive Director

ATLANTIC 453 / ATLANTIC STAGE 2

OTMA by Kate Moira Ryan; Director, Karen Kohlhaas; **Cast:** Ellen Crowley-Etten, Katherine Emmer, ElizaBeth Malone, Carla Rzeszewski; June 14 – July 3, 2005

10X20 – Ten ten-minute plays by twenty playwrights celebrating ATC's 20th Anniversary and Atlantic Theatre's new space, Atlantic Stage 2 at 330 W. 16th Street

June 14 – 17, 2006: **Three Little Words** by Hilary Bell; Director, Karen Kohlhaas; **Cast:** Kathryn Erbe and Kate Blumberg; **Leavings** by Jez Butterworth; Director, Neil Pepe; **Cast:** Peter Maloney; **Milos** by John Guare; Director, Neil Pepe; **Cast:** Patrick Breen; **Our Favorite Child** by Rolin Jones; Director, Christian Parker; **Cast:** Linda Gehringer, Jonathan Rossetti, Ray Anthony Thomas; **Home** by David Mamet; Director, Hilary Hinckle; **Cast:** Jordan Lage, Kathryn Erbe; **The Muse** by Quincy Long; Director, Dave Mowers; **Cast:** Kate Blumberg, Brennan Brown; **On Story** by Bill Wrubel; Director, Robert Bella; **Cast:** Patrick Breen, Brennan Brown, Jim Frangione, Peter Maloney, Emily Peck Patrick Taylor

June 21 – 24, 2006: **Master Disaster** by Kia Corthron; Director, Jackson Gay; **Cast:** Donna Duplantier, Zabryna Guevara; **It Takes an Orchard** by Tom Donaghy; Director, Neil Pepe; **Cast:** Carolyn McCormick; **Maybe 21** written and directed by Peter Hedges; **Cast:** Kristen Johnston, John Benjamin Hickey; **Quotidian** by Howard Korder; Director, Neil Pepe; **Cast:** Ted Danson; **He's Come to Take the Children Home** by Craig Lucas; Director, Neil Pepe; **Cast:** Ryan King, Mark Webber; **The Burning** by Joe Penhall; Director, Karen Kohlhaas; **Cast:** Alex Draper, Steven Hawley; **Mutterliebe** by Keith Reddin; Director, Christian Parker; **Cast:** Jen Albano, Matt Dawson, Jan Maxwell

June 28 – July 1, 2006: **The Compassioneer** by Kevin Heelan; Director, Carl Forsman; **Cast:** Christian Parker, Steven Skybell; **Through a Glass Darkly** by Tina Howe; Director, Christian Parker; **Cast:** Kate Blumberg, Peter Jacobson;

Untitled by David Pittu; **Cast:** David Pittu, Peter Bartlett; **Hello. Northwood Mental Health Center** by David Rabe; Director, Robert Bella; **Cast:** Ronnie Butler, Robert Maxwell, Christa Scott-Reed; **Jody's Mother** by Edwin Sanchez; **Cast:** Roberta Maxwell; **The Intervention** by Jeff Whitty; Director, Dave Mowers; **Cast:** Susan Pourfar, Christa Scott-Reed, Ronnie Butler, Mike Doyle

ATLANTIC FOR KIDS

You're a Good Man, Charlie Brown Book, music and lyrics by Clark Gesner, based on the comic strip *Peanuts* by Charles M. Schulz; Additional material by Michael Mayer, additional music and lyrics by Andrew Lippa; Director, Brandon Thompson; Music Director, Adam Gwon; Choreography, Alison Beatty; September 24 – October 16, 2005

The Big Stew by Kimberly Foster; Director, Paul Urcioli; Scenery/Lighting, Eric Southern; Costumes, Catherine Backhole; Choreography, Alison Beatty; Production Director, Geoff Berman; **Cast:** Damon Cardasis, Lauren Hines, Laura Hughes, Maggie Jeary, Cassie Newman, Christina Joy Walton; March 11 – April 2, 2006

AXIS COMPANY

Jeffrey Resnick, Executive Producer

Hospital 2005 A serial play by Axis Company; Director/Music and Lyrics, Randy Sharp; Design, Kate Aronsson-Brown; Lighting, David Zeffren; Sound, Steve Fontaine; Production Stage Manager, Jared Abramson; **Cast:** Wren Arthur, David Balutanski, Paul Marc Barns, Brian Barnhart, David Crabb, George Demas, Joe Fuer, Jason Kaufman, Laurie Kilmartin, Ciarán McCarthy, Sue Ann Molinell, Edgar Oliver, Marc Palmieri, Margo Passalaqua, Sayra Player, Abigail Savage, Brian Sloan, Randy Spence, Ian Tooley, Peterson Townsend; Episode One: July 15 – 23; Episode Two: July 29 – August 6; Episode 3: August 12 – 20; Episode 4: August 26 – 27

Seven in One Blow, or The Brave Little Kid by the Brothers Grimm; Director and Original Music, Randy Sharp; **Cast:** Marc Palmieri, David Crabb, Abigail Savage, Jim Sterling, Brian Barnhart, Randy Sharp, Joe Fuer, Margo Passalaqua, Sue Ann Molinell, Edgar Oliver, Laurie Kilmartin, Kate Aronsson-Brown, August Aronsson-Brown; December 2 – 18, 2005 (Fourth Annual presentation)

BLUE HERON THEATRE*

Ardele Striker, Artistic Director

Trailerville by John Dufresne; Director, Wayne Maugans; Scenery, Daniel Ettinger, Costumes, Martin T. Lopez, Llighting, Jessica Hinkle,Sound, Vera Beren; Dramaturge, Kimberly Megna; Associate Producer, Dean Gray; Production Stage Manager, Isaac Scranton; **Cast:** Ann Hillary (Merdelle Harris), Ron Faber (Bobby), Peter Waldren (Arlis Bryant), Michele Ammon (Kitty Bit), Christian Kohn (Bromo), Miles Purinton (Theron), Erik Kever Ryle (Willis), Greta Sleeper (Kristie), Lenore Zann (Pug); June 3 – 26, 2005

Bartleby the Scrivener by R.L. Lane, adapted from the story by Herman Melville; Director, Alessandro Fabrizi; Scenery and Lighting, Harry Feiner; Costumes, Dennis Ballard; Sound, David Lawson; Production Stage Manager, Sarah Ford; **Cast:** Gerry Bamman, Marco Quaglia, Jeff Burchfield, Sterling Coyne, Hunter Gilmore, Robert Grossman, Christian Haines, and Brian Linden; November 4 – 27, 2005

*The Blue Heron Arts Center closed December 30, 2005.

THE BINDLESTIFF FAMILY CIRKUS

Stephanie Monseu, Artistic Director; Keith Nelson, Managing Director

Kinko the Clown's Trash Can Dreams Written, designed and directed by Keith Nelson; **Cast:** Keith Nelson (Kinko the Clown); North American Cultural Laboratories; July 29–30, 2005; 2 performances

Buckaroo Bindlestiff's Wild West Jamboree by Keith Nelson and Stephanie Monseu; Co-produced by Play Outside Festival; Director, Stephanie Monseu; Scenery Keith Nelson and Stephanie Monseu; Costumes, Stephanie Monseu; Sound, Sean Condron; Stage Manager, Matthew Zimmerman; **Cast:** Stephanie Monseu (Miss Philly), Keith Nelson (Gentleman Jack Pennygaff), Sean Condron (Professor Fruit Jar); Karl Meyers (Commander Karl); Parks of New York City; September 1–October 4, 2005; 11 performances in 9 parks

Bindlestiff Family Cirkus Cabaret; Director, Stephanie Monseu; Stage Manager, Matthew Zimmerman; Production Manager, Ellia Bisker; **Cast:** Stephanie Monseu (Philomena, ringmistress), Keith Nelson (Mr. Pennygaff and Kinko the Clown), Tanya Gagne (aerialist), Scott Gravell (Scotty the Blue Bunny), Dee Norris (Baby Dee), Peter Bufano (musician), and a number of other variety acts making one night appearances; Galapagos Art Space, Brooklyn; Fridays from March 24–April 28, 2006; 7 performances

Bindlestiff's Cavalcade of Youth Director, Viveca Gardiner; Stage Manager, Matthew Zimmerman; Circus Consultant: Keith Nelson, Stephanie Monseu, Sean Blue; Henry Street Settlement/Abrons Arts Center, NYC; March 26, April 2, 2006; 2 performances

Bindlestiff Family Cirkus and Magic Hat Summer Variety Show Tour Director, Stephanie Monseu; Production Manager, Keith Nelson; Musical Director, Sxip Shirey; Stage manager: Maisy Metrix; Co-sponosors, Magic Hat Brewing Company; **Cast:** Stephanie Monseu (Philomena), Keith Nelson (Kinko the Clown and Mr. Pennygaff); Scott Grabell (Scotty the Blue Bunny); Elizabeth Gifford (Dizzy Lizzy); David Hunt (Slack Rope walker), Sxip Shirey (Musician); Adam Kuchler (Clown), Ariele Ebacher (Tight wire dancer); Opened May 31, 2006; toured 25 towns June to August 2006

BOOMERANG THEATRE COMPANY

Tim Errickson, Artistic Director

Two Gentlemen of Verona by William Shakespeare; Director, Kate Ross; Stage Manager, Sue Abbott; Costumes, Marion Talon; **Cast:** Jeremy Beck, Mac Brydon, Patrick Connolly, Benjamin Ellis Fine, Henry Martone, Ron McClary, Dennis McNitt Peter Morr, Jessica Myhr, Sharon Paige, Sara Thigpen, Bill Weeden; Performed in Central Park, Riverside Park, Prospect Park, and Astoria Park; June 18–July 31, 2005

Artist Descending a Staircase by Tom Stoppard; Director, John Hurley; Scenery, Scott Orlesky; Costumes, Cheryl McCarron; Lighting, Carrie Wood; Sound, Ann Warren; Stage Manager, Jessica Poludin; **Cast:** Ronald Cohen, Tom Knutson, Mary Murphy Michael Poignand, Ed Schultz, Joe Whelski, Aaron Michael Zook; CenterStage/NY; September 10–October 2, 2005

Giant 'n Variation by Francis Kuzler; Director, Eric Amburg; Scenery, Scott Orlesky; Costumes, Cheryl McCarron; Lighting, Carrie Wood; Sound, Ann Warren; Stage Manager, Monika Tandon; **Cast:** Zack Calhoon, Dante Giammarco, Jennifer Larkin, Barbara Drum Sullivan, Carsey Walker Jr., Christopher Yeatts; CenterStage/NY; September 15–October 1, 2005

All For Love by John Dryden; Director, Cailin Heffernan; Scenery, Scott Orlesky; Costumes, Cheryl McCarron; Lighting, Carrie Wood; Sound, Ann Warren; Stage Manager, Carol A. Sullivan; **Cast:** Taylor Nicole Adams, Steven Bari, Heather Braverman, Dylan Carusona, Ursula Cataan, Alexandra Crisco, Kirk Gostkowski, Ingrid Griffith, Andrew Harriss, Bram Heidinger, Mark Light-Orr, Gregory Mikell, Sheryl McCallum, Peter Picard, Stephanie Rosenberg, Melissa Haley Smith; CenterStage/NY; September 9–30, 2005

FIRST FLIGHT READINGS

Places by Mike Folie, Katharine Clark-Gray, Steven Gridley, Francis Kuzler, and Kelly McAllister; November 30, 2005

Love in the Insecurity Zone by Mike Folie; December 1, 2005

An Intervention for Isaac by Noah Smith; December 2, 2005

Untitled Freedom Play by Francis Kuzler; December 3, 2005

American Mercy by Sharyn Rothstein; December 4, 2005

THE BRIDGE THEATRE COMPANY

Esther Barlow and Dustin Olson, Artistic Directors

Making Marilyn by Ken Cameron; Director, Robin A. Paterson; **Cast:** Ashlie Atkinson, Patrick Costello, Robin Mervin, Devin Scott, Reyna deCourcy; Theatre 54 at Shetler Studios; November 23–December 8, 2005

Lone Star/Laundry & Bourbon by James McLure; Director, Janice Goldberg; Set, Robin A. Paterson; **Cast:** Jason Fraser, Avi Glickstein, Dustin Olson; Jennifer Laine Williams, Robin Suzukawa, Ellen Dolan; February 12–19, 2006

Zarathustra Said Some Things, No? by Trevor Ferguson; Director, Robin A. Paterson; **Cast:** Lina Roessler, Brett Watson; April 25–May 21, 2006

Lina Roessler in *Zarathustra Said Some Things, No?* by Trevor Ferguson, presented by Bridge Theatre Company

BROADWAY BY THE YEAR

Scott Siegal, Creator and Host; Barbara Siegel, Advisor; Ross Patterson, Musical Director/Arranger; Michael Lavine, Sheet Music Consultant; Ross Patterson Little Big Band, Accompanist

The Broadway Musicals of 1962 Starring: Liz Callaway, Scott Coulter, Felicia Finley, Danny Gurwin, Brad Oscar, Christine Pedi; Special Guest: Robert Goulet; Featuring: Will Taylor, Eric Stretch; Town Hall; June 13, 2005

The Broadway Musicals of 1938 Director, Marc Kudisch; Starring: Nancy Anderson, Celia Keenan-Bolger, Sean Martin Hingtson, Marc Kudisch, Douglas Ladnier, Shannon Lewis, Deven May, Miles Phillips, Jennifer Simard, Emily Skinner, Mary Testa and Michael Winther; Town Hall; March 6, 2006

The Broadway Musicals of 1956 Director, Emily Skinner; Starring: Christine Andreas, Brent Barrett, Ashley Brown, Brandon Cutrell, Marc Kudisch, Connie Pachl, Rachelle Rak, Devin Richards, Emily Skinner and John Treacy Egan; Town Hall; April 3, 2006

The Broadway Musicals of 1968 Director, Brad Oscar; Starring: Scott Coulter, Annie Golden, Adam Grupper, Lisa Howard, Lorinda Lisitza, Bill Nolte, Jack Noseworthy, Jeffry Denham, Christina Norrup, Brad Oscar, Kim Shriver, Shayna Steele and Courtney Young; Town Hall; May 1, 2006

BROKEN WATCH THEATRE COMPANY

Drew DeCorleto, Aristic Director

THE STAGE READING SERIES — JUNE 2005

Splendid by J. Holtham; Director, Stephen Brumble, Jr

Pluto's Listening by David Parr; Director, Leo Lauer

The Good Red Road by Robert Vaughan; Director, Austin Pendleton

Quarter Life by Sam Foreman; Driector, Drew DeCorleto

Jason Pugatch and Tinashe Kajese in Broken Watch Theatre Company's production of Christopher Kyle's *The Safety Net* PHOTO BY THOMAS HINTON

MAINSTAGE

The Safety Net by Christopher Kyle; Director, Martha Banta; Scenery, J. Wiese; Costumes, Cora Levin; Lighting, Miriam Nilofa Crowe; Sound, Jill BC DuBoff; **Cast:** Jason Pugatch, Tinashe Kajese, Eve Kaminsky, Maren Perry, Peggy Scott, Mark Setlock; Sande Shurin Theatre; September 16–October 9, 2005

A Broken Christmas Carol by James Christy, J. Holtham, and Kendra Levin; Director, Drew DeCorleto; Scenery, Joshua A Robinson; Costumes, Barrett Hall, Jenny Rodriguez, Sandra Schobel, Teresa Goding; Lighting, Barrett Hall; Sound, Drew DeCorleto, Barrett Hall; Music, Drew Sarich; **Cast:** J. Clint Allen, Janine Barris, Keith Arthur Bolden, Chaz Brewer, Ellen Daschbach, Daneille Davenport, Guil Fisher, William Jackson Harper, Leo Lauer, Aly Wirth; Michael Weller Theatre; December 8–30, 2005

COLLABORATIVE ARTISTS PROJECT 21 (CAP 21)

Frank Ventura, Executive Artistic Director; Eliza Ventura, Artistic Director

Workshop Productions **The 60's Project** Conceived and written by Janet Brenner; Director, Richard Maltby, Jr. Musical Supervision, Don York; Choreography, Lisa Shriver; **Cast:** Cameron Adams, Jeb Brown, Mark Bush, Dwayne Clark, Tonya Doran, J. D. Goldblatt, Steven Goldsmith, Demond Green, Kevin Hale, Rodney Hicks, Claire Karpen, Chad Kimball, Anika Larsen, Megan Lewis, Amy McAlexander, Jason Poole, Lois Robbins, Idara Victor, Max von Essen, Andy Whaley and Angela Williams; November 9–19, 2005

Unlock'd Book and lyrics by Sam Carner, music by Derek Gregor; Director, Selda Sahin; Musical Director, Nicole Zuratis; Producer, Lindsay Gibbs and Rick Cekovsky; **Cast:** Leah Johnston, Katrina Art, Dave Perlow, Ryan Neller, TJ Black, Jabari Brisport, Brad Broman, Elena Fichtel, Sean Galvin, Hannah Ginsberg, Christina Giordano, Michael Montalbano, Jennafer Newberry, Frank Paiva, Renee Rakel, Aaron Schroeder, Elisabeth Sprague, Emma Tattenbaum-Fine, Alexandra Weaverling, Nathan Zebede; Players Theatre; December 3–5, 2005

The Classics Professor by John Pielmeier; Director, Clayton Phillips; **Cast:** Elaine Anderson, Peggy Cosgrave, Bram Heidinger, Steve Liebman, Christina Morrell; June 1–17, 2006

MONDAY NIGHT READING SERIES

Pages, a new musical Music by Will Van Dyke, lyrics byJosh Halloway and Will Van Dyke, book, Josh Halloway; Director, Larry Arancio; **Lady Alice, a new musical** Music by Steven Schoenberg, book and lyrics by Diane Seymour; Musical Director, David Loud; **The Classics Professor** by John Pielmeier; Director, Clayton Phillips; **The Times** Book and lyrics, Joe Keenan, music by Brad Ross; Director, Greg Ganakas; **Sapphisto Summers** by Mary Fengar Gail; Director, Aimee Francis; **My Bernhardt Summer** by Mark St. Germain; Director, Will Pomerantz

CONSERVATORY PRODUCTIONS

Goddess Wheel Music by Galt MacDermot, book and lyrics, Matty Selman; Director, Frank Ventura; November 31–December 10, 2005; **Radiant Baby** Book by Stuart Ross, music by Debra Barsha, lyrics by Ira Gasman, Stuart Ross, and Debra Barsha; Director, Frank Ventura; March 1–10, 2006; **Starmites** Music and lyrics by Barry Keating, Book by Stuart Ross and Barry Keating; Directors, Barry Keating and Jeremy Quinn; March 29–April 2, 2006

CASTILLO THEATRE

Artistic Director, Dan Friedman; Managing Director, Diane Stiles

License to Dream Conceived by David Parsons and Fred Newman; Performed by The Parsons Dance Company and Young Performers of the All Stars Project; June 10–19, 2005

This is Your Ridiculous Life! Director, David Nackman (ongoing)

Rules for Good Manners in the Modern World by Jean-Luc Lagarce; Director, Zeljko Djukic; Presented by The Utopian Theatre Asylum of Chicago; August 25–28, 2005

Sally and Tom (The American Way) Book and lyrics, Fred Newman, Music by Annie Roboff; Directors, Fred Newman and Gabrielle L. Kurlander; **Cast:** Jonathan Frank, Kalia Lynne, Johnnie Moore, Melvin Shambry, Jr., J.T. Michael Taylor; October 7–December 4, 2005

Our City Inspired by Thornton Wilder's *Our Town*; Presented by All Stars' Youth Onstage! Experimental Theatre Workshop; November 11–December 4, 2005

Have You Ever Seen a Dream Rapping? Conceived by Fred Newman; Directors, Pamela A. Lewis and David Nackman; Performed by the All Stars Talent Show Network; February 3–19, 2006

Rudimentary by August Stramm; February 12, 2006

Left of the Moon by Fred Newman; Director, Dan Friedman; Choreography, Franceli Chapman; Presented by members of the All Stars' Youth Onstage!; April 7–22, 2006

CHERRY LANE THEATRE

Angelina Fiordellisi, Founder/Artistic Director; James King, Managing Director

Huck and Holden by Rajiv Joseph; Director, Giovanna Sardelli; Scenery, Regina Garcia; Costumes, Rebecca Bernstein; Lighting, Pat Dignan; Sound, Bart Fasbender; Stage Manager, Libby Steiner; Production Manager, Janio Marrero; **Cast:** Cherise Boothe, Nick Choksi, Arjun Gupta, LeRoy McClain, Nilaja Sun; Cherry Lane Studio Theater; January 17–February 25, 2006; originally produced in the Mentor Project 2005

TONGUES: READING SERIES 2005–2006

Post 9/11: A Community Celebrates Its Resilience *Three Weeks After Paradise* by Israel Horovitz with Matthew Arkin; *Speaking Well of the Dead* by Israel Horovitz with Lisa Emery, Marin Ireland, Matthew Arkin; September 8–10; *Breathing Time* by Beau Willimon with Patch Darragh, Angela Gaylor, Marin Ireland, Keira Naughton, Patrick Sarb, Paul Sparks; September 9

Those Left Behind by Benjamin Bettenbender; Director, Judith Ivey; **Cast:** Kenny Bonavitacola, Christian Corp, Ron Orbach, Jenny Sterlin, Clarke Thorell

Soccer Moms by Kathleen Clark; Director, Judith Ivey; **Cast:** Nancy Ringham, Deborah Sonenberg, Allison White; June 5, 2006

MENTOR PROJECT 2006–STUDIO THEATRE

Scenery, Kerry Chipman; Costumes, Rebecca Bernstein; Lighting, Ian Grunes; Sound, Bill Bowen

Lascivious Something by Sheila Callaghan; Mentor, Michael Weller; Reading: January 30, 2006; Showcase: Director, Suzanne Agins; Stage Manager, Scott Earley; **Cast:** Charles Borland, Jessi Campbell, Christina Lind, Danielle Skraastad; March 14–25, 2006

Hoodoo Love by Katori Hall, Mentor: Lynn Nottage; Reading: January 23, 2006; Showcase: Director, Lucie Tiberghien; Stage Manager, Sara Kmack; **Cast:** Eric Abrams, Marjorie Johnson, Angela Lewis, Postell Pringle; April 4–15, 2006

Girl by Megan Mostyn-Brown; Mentor: Theresa Rebeck; Reading: February 6, 2006; Showcase: Director, Joshua Hecht; Stage Manger, Jeff Meyers; **Cast:** Flora Diaz, Susan Hunt, Jennifer Regan, Maggie Siff, Max Woertendyke; April 25–May 6, 2006

INTERN PROJECT 2005–2006

Life Under Water by Richard Greenberg; Director, Sarah Wansley; **Cast:** Alex Fine, Meghan Griffin, Carolyn Holding, Dani Tufano; June 29–July 1, 2005

MASTER CLASSES

Edward Albee, November 22; Theresa Rebeck, November 28; A.R. Gurney, February 13; David Henry Hwang, March 6; Emily Mann, May 22

CELEBRATING WOMEN PLAYWRIGHTS

Bhutan by Daisy Foote; Director, Amy Redford; November 8–19, 2005

CHERRY PIT LATE NITE

Please Stop Talking by Sam Forman; Director, Erwin Maas; featuring Heather Hollingsworth, Bridgett Ane Lawrence and Leah Lawrence October 13–29, 2005

Too Much Light Makes the Baby Go Blind The New York Neo-Futurists present 30 plays in 60 minutes; November 4–December 17, 2005

Screwing Rachel by Desi Moreno-Penson; Director, Don Johanson; **Cast:** Peter Donato, Cedric Jones, Joshua Kingdon, Jon Arthur, Jenny Perdomo and Leah Sari Sparkes; November 17, 2005

Black Girl You've Been Gentrified Written and performed by Nichole Thompson-Adams; Director, John Church III; December 8, 2005 and January 26–February 11, 2006 **The Passion of the FUCT** performed by the underground comedy troupe FUCT; February 24–25, 2006

DJM PRODUCTIONS

Dave McCracken, Artistic Director

Body and Soul by John Glines; Produced in association with The Glines; Director, Dave McCracken; **Cast:** Michael Bianco, Dale Church, Christian Sebastian, Shawn Willett, Blake Young-Fountain; Dionysus Theatre's Lil' Peach; May 12–June 12, 2005

Chicken Delight by John Glines; Produced in association with The Glines; Director, Dave McCracken; **Cast:** Gil Bar-Sela (Splash), Will Barrios (Neil), Dale Church (Brockley), Michael Eisenbrown (Harry), Brett Parks (Randy), Doug Spangnola (Jesus); Dionysus Theatre's Lil' Peach; June 21–August 27, 2005

Ghosts by Henrik Ibsen, adapted by Dave McCracken; Director, Karen Case Cook; Assistant Director, Doug Spangnola; **Cast:** Melanie Boland, Dale Church, Curtis Harwell; Dionysus Theatre's Lil' Peach; November 17–December 18, 2005

DRAMA DEPARTMENT

Douglas Carter Beane, Artistic Director; Michael S. Rosenberg, Executive Director

The Big Time Book by Douglas Carter Beane, music and lyrics by Douglas J. Cohen; Presented as part of the New York Musical Theatre Festival; Director, Christopher Ashley; Musical Director, Jonathan Smith; Choreography, Daniel Pelzig; Scenery, Robert Bissinger; Costumes, David Zinn; Lighting, Jeff Croiter; Stage Manager, Adam Grosswirth; **Cast:** David Beach, Raymond Bokhour, Bradley Dean, Joanna Glushak, Debbie Gravitte, Jackie Hoffman, Michael McCormick, Patrick Quinn, Sal Viviano; Lion Theatre; September 16–28, 2005

THE DRILLING COMPANY

Hamilton Clancy, Producing Artistic Director; Karen Kitz, Associate Producer

Revenge Seven new short American plays on something oft desired; Scenery, Paul Gelinas; Lighting, Dan Sheehan; Sound, Michel Graetzer; Stage Manager, Billie Davis; Visual Artists, John Riveaux and John Pollack; Dramaturgy, Megan Sher, Percussion, Thom Garvey; Shows included: *A Play* by Scott Baker, with Tom Cleary; *Youngsters* by Brian Dykstra, Director, Peter Bretz, **Cast:** Karen Kitz and Eirik Gislasson; *A Luncheon* by Vincent Delaney, Director, Richard Harden, **Cast:** Stacy Wallace, Kathleen O'Grady and Keith Elijah Fasciani; *Ms. Santos' Dream After Reading Medea* by Sheri Graubert, Director, Nancy Chu, **Cast:** Anna Klein, Michelle Maxson, Tom Cleary and Andrew Dolan; *The Black Paintings* by Neil Olson, Director, Bradford Olson, **Cast:** Hamilton Clancy and Brigitte Barnett; *Bruce* by C. Denby Swanson, Director, Kate Moloy, **Cast:** Colleen Cosgrove, Kim Donovan and Dave Marantz; *The Agenda* by Paul Siefken, Director, Tom Demenkoff, **Cast:** Ben Masur, Mike Dressel, Douglas Taurel and Eirik Gislasson; *The Dorsal Striatum* by Trish Harnetiaux, Director, Jude Domski, **Cast:** Dave Marantz and Don Carter; 78th Street Theatre Lab; June 3–19, 2005

Mutant Sex Party by Edward Manning; Director, Hamilton Clancy; Scenery, Paul Gelinas; Lighting, Jerry Browning; Sound, Robert Siefken; Visual Artists, John Pollack, John Riveaux; Stage Manager, Adam Erdossey; **Cast:** Erik Van Wyck (Clay), Tom Demenkoff (John); 78th Street Theatre Lab; June 6–25, 2005

The Taming of the Shrew by William Shakespeare; Co-Produced with Ludlow Ten; Director, Leonard McKenzie; **Cast:** Hamilton Clancy (Petruchio) Karen Kitz (Kate), Carrie Rachel Ellman (Bianca), Stuart Luth (Gremio), Jason Munt (Lucentio), Richard Davis (Biondello), Derrick Peterson (Baptista), Patrick Pizzolorusso (Tranio), Joel Stigliano (Grumio), William B. Torres (William), Jeff Cureton (Hortensio); Shakespeare in the Parking Lot, the corner of Ludlow and Broome; July 14–August 6, 2005

Ah Wilderness! by Eugene O'Neil; produced in collaboration with Youth Theatre Project's professional program for young people; Director, Isaiah Cazares; Scenery, Zhanna Gurvich; Costumes, Angela Kahler; Stage Manager, Billie Davis; **Cast:** Hamilton Clancy (Mr. Miller), Karen Kitz (Mrs. Essie Miller), Kezia Bernard (Tommy), Trevor Brown (Sid), Danea Robinson (Muriel), Anthony Thompson (Mr. McComber/ Salesman), Leon Peterson (Arthur), Erin Napoleon, Simone Medley (Muriel), Steve Delice (Richard), Paige Donaldson (Mildred), Shayna Cacho (Belle), Jimmy Zephyr (Wint), Nakia Duffy (Belle); 59E59 Theatre C; August 7–13, 2005

Revenge 2 Ten more short plays on something often sought and seldom found; Set Design, Rebecca Lord; Lighting, Miriam Crowe; Original Music, Thom Garvey; Production Stage Manager, Billie Davis; Program included: *Served Cold* by Katharine Clark Gray; Director, Adam Eisenstein; **Cast:** Brigitte Barnett, Michael Gnat, Laura Johnston, Geoffrey Warren Barnes II, Sharon Hope; *Medea Unharnessed* by Molly Rice; Director, Kara-Lynn Vaeni; **Cast:** Heather Anderson, John Giampetro, James Lloyd Reynolds; *The Deal* by Kate McCamy; Director, Richard Mover; **Cast:** Richard Mover, Michael Ornstein, Randy Noojin; *Still Life #2* by Tom Strelich; Director, Peter Bretz; **Cast:** Bradford Olson, Adam Erdossey, Brian Linden, Kelly Jeanne Grant, Tom Cleary; *Bee* by Stephen Bittrich; Director, Dan Teachout; **Cast:** Karen Tsen Lee, Ron Dreyer, Kelly Jeanne Grant; *Thor's Hammer* by Nicholas Gray; Director, Matt Cowart; **Cast:** Bill Homan, Don Carter; *Stop the Lawns* by P. Seth Bauer; Director, Gabriele Forster; **Cast:** Tobias Segal, Alessandro Colla, Michael Schreiber; *Blue Christmas* by Scott Baker; Director, James Davis; **Cast:** Stephen Bittrich, Bill Green, Kelly Jeanne Grant, Mike Dressel, Alyssa Simon, Billie Davis; 78th Street Theatre Lab; December 3–17, 2005

The Refinery – short plays presented late nights: *The Offenses of Cacti* by Matthew I. Swaye; Director, Zoe Aja Moore; **Cast:** Bill Green (Barton) , Rebecca Darke (Marci), Rob Skolits(Barton), Melora Griffis (Marci); *Last Word* by Sheri Graubert; Director, Hamilton Clancy; **Cast:** Karen Kitz (Pearl), Colleen Cosgrove (Flo), Tom Demenkoff (Charlie); 78th Street Theatre Lab; December 12–14, 2005

DISCOVERY SERIES – DEVELOPING FULL-LENGTH WORKS

The Karma Cookie by P. Seth Bauer; Director, Eric Nightengale; Stage Manager, Billie Davis; **Cast:** Hamilton Clancy (Alistair), Phillip Douglas(Barry); September 29–October 8, 2005

Atomic Farmgirl by C. Denby Swanson; Director, Brooke Brod; **Cast:** Karen Kitz, Hamilton Clancy, Kathleen O'Grady, Dave Marantz, Jeremy Bobb, Ana Parea; February 1–17, 2006

Exit Strategy by Tom Strelich; Director, Hamilton Clancy; **Cast:** Darrell Larson, Edwind Owens, Karen Kitz, Hamilton Clancy, William Green, Alessandro Colla; May 9, 2006

EMERGING ARTISTS THEATRE COMPANY

Artistic Director, Paul Adams; Associate Artistic Director, Derek Jamison

Fall Eatfest 2005 Scenery Robert Monaco; Costumes, Melanie Blythe; Lighting, Jennifer Granrud; Sound, Aaron David Blank; Stage Manager, Darren Maurer; Props, Stephanie Weisner; Theatre 5; November 1–20, 2005; Series included: **Wally and Jesus** by Christopher Heath; Director, Dylan McCullough; **Cast:** Glory Gallo (Judy), Graeme Gillis (Wally), Wayne Henry (Jesus); **Laughing All the Way** by Carol Mullen; Director, Deb Guston; **Cast:** Amy Bizjak (Joanne), Stacy Mayer (Erin), **Cloudy** by Michael Griffo; Director, Derek Jamison; **Cast:** Brian Letscher (Dan), Danielle Quisenberry (Georgia), **All the Details** by Cary Pepper; Director, Troy Miller; **Cast:** Desmond Dutcher (Jerry etc), Erin Hadley (Melanie etc), Danae Hanson (Pierre etc), Peter Herrick (Charles) , Mariah Sage (Daphne), Matt Stapleton (Bill etc); **Reunion** by William Borden; Director, Paul Adams; **Cast:** Peter Levine (Merritt), Vivian Meisner (Margaret); **Final Answer** by Marc Castle; Director, Kevin Dodd; **Cast:** John Beebout (Man), Lee Kaplan (Host), Hershey Miller (Mrs. Seidelman), Kristin Wilkins (Wendy), **Cupid's Beau** by Barbara Lindsay; Director, Ian Streicher; **Cast:** Aimee Howard (Lacey), Steve

Zilliax (Peter); **A Touching Story** by Rich Orloff; Director, Jeffrey Lawhorn; William Reinking (Jeff), Karen Stanion (Niki), Greg Skura (Dennis); **How Can Love Survive?** by Kevin Brofsky; Director, Caden Hethorn; **Cast:** Blanche Cholet (Mother), Steven Hauck (Son); **Park Bench** by Kristyn Leigh Robinson; Director, Yana Landowne; **Cast:** Tom Greenman (Young Man), Ryan Hilliard (Old Man); **Larry Gets the Call** by Matt Casarino; Director, Melissa Attebery; **Cast:** Ron Bopst (Larry), Christine Bruno (God), Rebecca Nyahay (Petra)

Triple Threat 2006 Scenery Bill Pollock; Costumes Sarah Stubble (*Edenville*) Ellen Reilley (*Rock the Line, The Kitchen Table*); Lighting Jenny Granrud; Sound Aaron David Blank; Props Casey Smith; Fight Director Ian Marshall; Theatre 5 February 7–26, 2006; Series included: **Edenville** by Gregory Fletcher; Director, Tom Wojtunik; Stage Manger Jennifer Russo; Assistant Director Ryan Kasprzak; **Cast:** Adrian Anchondo (Roberto), Josh Berresford (David etc), Gary Cowling (C.E.O.), Sebastian La Cause (Jules), Nick Ruggeri (Dad, Peterson); **Rock the Line** by Kathleen Warnock; Director, Steven McElroy; Stage Manager David Bishop; **Cast:** Roberto Cambeiro (Mickey), Stephanie Deliani (Lucy), Erin Hadley (Kelly), Jamie Heinlein (Joanne), Noelle Holly (Leslie), Rebecca Nyahay (Nancy), Karen Stanion (Candy); **The Kitchen Table** by Peter Levine; Director, Troy Miller; Stage Manager Marc Eardley; **Cast:** Bob Adrian (Narrator/Old Peter), Michael Cuomo (Jon) Robert L. Haber (Sam), Brian Louis Hoffman (Peter), Geany Masai (Louise), Lué McWilliams (Pearl), Jacqueline Sydney (Aunt Harriet)

Spring Eatfest 2006 Scenery Robert Monaco; Costumes, Melanie Blythe; Lighting, Jennifer Granrud; Sound, Aaron David Blank; Props, Casey Smith; Stage Manager, Tzipora Kaplan; Production Manger, Darren Maurer; Theatre 5; March 7–26, 2006; Series included: **My Sister the Cow** by Gregory Fletcher; Director, Paul Adams; **Cast:** Amy Bizjak (Jackie), Jason Hare (Carl), Lué McWilliams (Pearl); **Blackout** by Vladimir Maicovski; Director, Anthony Luciano; **Cast:** Danny Mullock (Elliot), Maureen Sebastian (Amanda); **Star Train** by Susan Merson; Director, Melissa Attebery; **Cast:** Ryan Hilliard (Ed), Yvonne Roen (Judy), Jarret Summers (Porter); **A Perfectly Normal Family Dinner** by Matthew J. Hanson; Director, Deb Guston; **Cast:** Ron Bopst (Tiberius), Jack Herholdt (Bradley), Irene Longshore (Lynne), Christine Mosére (Penelope), Matt Stapleton (James); **The Secret of Our Success** by Staci Swedeen; Director, Derek Jamison; **Cast:** Patrick Arnheim (Barry), A.J. Handegard (Paul), Aimee Howard (Christy); **Nagasaki** by Kevin Brofsky; Director, Kel Haney; **Cast:** Irene Glezos (Ann), Steven Hauck (Darren); **Mr. Company** by Marc Castle; Director, Max Montel; **Cast:** Deb Armelino (Dee Dee), Christopher Borg (Mr. Company), Sarah Dacey Charles (Lorna); **What We Talk About** by Emily Mitchell; Director, Ian Streicher; **Cast:** Blanche Cholet (Virginia), Betty Hudson (Evelyn), Vivian Meisner, (Peg) Jenny Lee Mitchell (Maggie); **The Test** by Caitlin Mitchell, Director, Chris Maring; **Cast:** Brian Louis Hoffman (Mikey), Kyle T. Jones (Charles), Maya Rosewood (Frances), Kelly Scanlon (Claire); **Mom, Stoned** by Bekah Brunstetter; Director, Kevin Dodd; **Cast:** Michele Fulves (Jodie), Stacy Mayer (Bess), Rhoda Pauley (Bev)

ENSEMBLE STUDIO THEATRE

Curt Dempster, Artistic Director

OCTOBERFEST 2005

October 5–30, 2005

Mountains in the Bering by Sean Sutherland, directed by Deborah Hedwall

THICKER THAN WATER 2006 — YOUNGBLOOD PRODUCTIONS

Henrietta Hermaline's Fall From Great Heights, by Maggie Smith; Director, Abigail Zealey Bess; **Cast:** Nicol Zanzarella-Giacalone, Denny Bes, Brendan McMahon; January 23–February 12, 2006; **Hungry** by Amy Herzog; Director, Christine Farrel; **Cast:** Lucia Brizzi, Erin McMonagle, Rebecca Pace; January 23–February 12, 2006; **A Bitter Taste** by Kevin Christopher Snipes; Director, R.J. Tolan; **Cast:** Paul Clark, Haskell King, Peter O'Connor; January 30–February 12, 2006; **The Traveling Lady** by Horton Foote; Director, Dr. Marion Castleberry; Scenery, Maruti Evans; Costumes, Maggie Lee-Burdorff; Lighting, Jason Jeunnette; Sound, Graham Johnson; Stage Manager, Angrette McCloskey; Producer, Peter Marsh; **Cast:** Jamie Bennett, Margot White, Rochelle Oliver, Frank Girardeau, Lynn Cohen, Stan Denman, Carol Goodheart, Matthew Conlin, Quincy Confoy, Alice McLane; March 3–19, 2006

FIRST LIGHT 2006

April 4–May 20, 2006

Readings: **Ephemeris** by Dominic Taylor, April 4; **Constant** by David Valdes Greenwood, April 5; **Unnatural History** by Judith Montague, April 6; **Fishing With Tony & Joe** by Jeffrey Stanley, April 7

Workshops: **Monkey's Uncle** by Matthew Wells; Director, Robert Ross Parker; April 10; **Serendib** by David Zellnik; Director, Carlos Armesto; Puppetry, Gretchen van Lente; April 14; **Galois** by Sung Rno; Director, Will Pomerantz; April 17; **Progress in Flying** by Lynn Rosen; Director, Daniella Topol; April 21–23; **Infinite Potential** by Samara Kanegis; Director, Abigail Zealey Bess; April 27; **Moving Picture** by Dan O'Brien; Director, Carlos Armesto, May 1

Cabaret Scientifique, featuring Eric Davis, Alec Duffy, Les Freres Corbusier, Noah Tarnow & The Big Quiz Thing, The Organ Donors & The Percodettes, Silent Voice; April 10

Satellite Event: **Bone Portraits** Conceived by Deborah Stein and Lear DeBessonet; text by Deborah Stein; Director Lear DeBessonet; Presented at Walkerspace, May 5–20

EST MARATHON 2006

May 23–June 25, 2006

Scenery and Lighting, Maruti Evans; Costumes, Amela Baksic; Sound, Brian Petway; Fight Director, Qui Nguyen; Stage Manager, Carol A. Sullivan

Series A (May 23–June 10): **Breakfast and Bed** by Amy Fox; Director, Abigail Zealey Bess; **The Other Woman** by David Ives; Director, Walter Bobbie; **Davy and Stu** by Anton Dudley; Director, Jordan Young; **Not All Korean Girls Can Fly** by Lloyd Suh; Director, RJ Tolan

Series B (May 30–June 19): **Bone China** by David Mamet; Director, Curt Dempster; **100 Most Beautiful Names of Todd** by Julia Cho; Director, Jamie Richards; **On the Sporadic** by James Ryan; Director, Charles Richter; **Intermission** by Will Eno; Director, Michael Sexton

Series C (June 13–25): **The Night That Roger Went to Visit the Parents of His Old High School Girlfriend** by Ann Marie Healy; Director, Andrew McCarthy; **The Bus to Buenos Aires (A Musical)** by Thomas Mizer and Curtis Moore; Director, Carlos Armesto; **Detail** by Michael Louis Wells; **Lila on the Wall** by Edward Allan Baker; Director, Kevin Confoy; **Dominica: The Fat, Ugly 'Ho** by Stephen Adly Guirgis; Director, Adam Rapp

THE FLEA THEATER

Jim Simpson, Artistic Director; Todd Rosen, Managing Director; Carol Ostrow, Producing Director

MAINSTAGE

Screen Play by A.R. Gurney; Director, Jim Simpson; Scenery, Jim Simpson; Costumes, Melissa Schlachtmeyer; Lighting, Joe Novak; Musical Director, Kris Kukul; Assistant to the Director, Deborah Wolfson; Technical Director, Joe Novak; **Cast:** John Fico (Sen. Abner Patch), Drew Hildebrand (Nick), Meredith Holzman (Sally), Nedra McClyde (Myrna), Dave McKeel (Charley Washington), Kevin T. Moore (Swing), Brian Morvant (Walter Wellman); July 6–30, 2005; extended September 8–30, 2005 (see "Off-Broadway Plays That Opened" in this volume).

Ashley Montana Goes Ashore in the Caicos — or: What Am I Doing Here? — by Roger Rosenblatt; October 6 – November 19, 2005; 36 performances (see "Off-Broadway Plays That Opened" in this volume)

[W] hole created and performed by LAVA conceived by Sarah East Johnson; Director, Sarah East Johnson; Visual Design, Nancy Brooks Brody; Costumes, Liz Prince; Lighting, Chloe Brown; Music, Steve Hamilton; Video, Heather Delaney; Words, Sini Anderson and Capital B; **Cast:** Natalie Agee, Molly Chanoff, Eugenia Chiappe, Diana Y. Greiner, Sarah East Johnson, Rebecca Stronger; January 5 – February 19, 2006; 28 performances

Mercy on the Doorstep by Gip Hoppe; March 14 – May 6, 2006; 48 performances; (see "Off-Broadway Plays That Opened" in this volume)

DOWNSTAIRS

Sister and Miss Lexie adapted for stage by David Kaplan and Brenda Currin; Produced in association with Edwin Schloss; Director, David Kaplan; Scenery, Sue Rees; Costumes, Ellen Pittman Stockbridge; Lighting, Megan Tracy; Musical Supervisor, Philip Fortenberry; Stage Manager, Gwendolyn Gilliam; Technical Director, Erik Fulk; Makeup Consultant, Christopher Halladay; Headpieces by, Jerry Stacy; Assistant to the Director, Andrew Gilchrist; **Cast:** Brenda Currin (performer), Ayako Morino (Pianist); October 27 – December 18, 2005; 32 performances

Back of the Throat by Yussef El Guindi; Director, Jim Simpson; Scenery, Michael Goldsheft; Costumes, Erin Elizabeth Murphy; Lighting, Benjamin C. Tevelow; Choreography, Mimi Quillin; Stage Manager, Lindsay Stares; Assistant to the Director, Sherri Kronfeld; Facilities Manager, Joshua Higgason; **Cast:** Adeel Akhtar (Khaled), Bandar Albuliwi (Asfoor), Jamie Effros (Carl), Jason Guy (Bartlett), Erin Roth (Beth/Ms. Shelly/Jean); February 2 – March 8, extended March 17 – April 22 and May 11 – July 1, 2006; 60 performances

READINGS AND WORKSHOPS

Crazy Mary by A.R. Gurney; Director, Jim Simpson; August 4, 2005 **Calcutta Kosher** by Shelley Silas; Director, Rita Wolfe; August 31, 2005

Maria Kizito by Erik Ehn; Director, Jim Simpson; December 5–7, 2005

Post Mortem by A.R. Gurney; Director, Jim Simpson; March 16, 2006

P.O. Box by Alice Tuan; Director, Jim Simpson; March 29–31, 2006

FRESH FRUIT FESTIVAL 2005

Carol Polcovar, Artistic Director

July 7–31, 2005

MUSICALS, MUSICAL REVUES, CABARET PERFORMANCE

Ain't We Got Fun Written and directed by Micheal McFaden; Produced by Ron Sanford; **Cast:** Robert M. Bowden, Shawn Carnes, L.t. Kirk, Vernon Kreun, Melissa Landry, Bryan Lelek, Mark Middleton, Steve Mogck, Danny Proctor, Ron Sanford, Layne Sasser, Daniel Vincent; Blue Heron Arts Center; July 28–31

What's Your Problem by Hector Coris and Paul L. Johnson; featuring Hector Coris, Dawn Trautman, Travis Bloom and Matthew Myers; Blue Heron Arts Center; July 25–27

Fresh Fruit Cocktail Curated and directed by Bob Ost; The Duplex Cabaret; July 13

The Girl That I Marry Starring Elaine St. George; Duplex Cabaret; July 13–14

PLAYS-BLUE HERON ARTS CENTER

Waafrika by Nanna Mwaluko; July 21–24

Pen Pals by Barbara Kahn; July 21–24

Somewhere in Between by Ronny Almog; July 24–27

PERFORMANCE PIECES AND SHORT PLAYS

Diagnosis: Jew Pain Written and performed by Michael Feldman; Blue Heron Arts Center; July 27–30

Low Brow Written and performed by Pedro Angel Serrano; Blue Heron Arts Center; July 28–31

Cocktails with Coward by Daniel Lavender; Bowery Poetry Club; July 15–17

Friut Melange An evening of short works by women: *Calamity Jane Writes a Letter To Her Daughter* by Carolyn Gage with Leslie Bernadini; *The Pamachene Belle* by Carolyn Gage featuring Leslie Bernadini; *From Brooklyn to Maui* written and performed by Aiyan Adams; *Tender Hooks* written and performed by Paige Collette; Blue Heron Arts Center; July 29–30

FUGLY PRODUCTIONS

Founder, Joe DeFeo

Titus X by Shawn Northrip ; Director, Peter Sanfilippo; Music Director, Christian Imboden; Costumes, Peter Sanfilippo; Lighting, Zaheed Essack; Sound, Andy Sarroff; Stage Manager, Jessica Levin; Projections, Frank Luna; Hair and Makeup, Harmony Chamberlain; Press, Brett Singer; **Cast:** Francile Albright (Tamora), Laurie Davis (Lavinia), Joe Pindelski (Saturninus, et al.), Ben Pryor (Lucius, et al.), Peter Schuyler (Titus), Dwayne Thomas (Aaron), Sharon Fischman (drums), Jacob Jackovich (bass), Billy Bob Bonson (guitar); The Tank; July 27 – August 24, 2005; 5 performances

Lunch by Shawn Northrip; Director, Shirley Serotsky; Music Director, Seth Bisen-Hersh; Choreography, Jim Augustine; Scenery, Klyph Stanford; Costumes, Peter

Sanfilippo; Lighting, Klyph Stanford; Sound, Andy Sarroff; Wigs, Erin Kennedy Lundsford, Fight Choreographer, Kenneth Cahall; Stage Manager, Lizzie Cheslock; Co-Producer, Caehlin Bell; Press, Brett Singer; **Cast:** Bryan Davis (Dmitry/Mr. Birdbaum), Matt Doyle (Mophead), Tara Giordano (Brynn/Vanessa/Ms. Parker), Leo Goodman (John/Coach Johnson), Rich Hollman (Ben/Brian), Alessandra Migliaccio (Misty/Diana), Hollis Scarborough (Kelly/Heather), Bryant Sullivan (Magic Box), Kelly Tighe (Britney/Ms. Jane), Correy West (Anton/Charles), Andy Welchel (keyboard), Nate Bonfiglio (drums), Jacob Jackovich (bass), Billy Bob Bonson (guitar); 45th Street Theatre; September 13–24, 2005; 6 performances

GALLERY PLAYERS

Heather Siobhan Curran, Board President; Matt Schicker, Board Vice-President

8th Annual Black Box New Play Festival Producers, Heather Siobhan Curran and René Poplaski; June 2–26, 2005

Box 1: Brooklyn Plays-Brooklyn Playwrights (June 2–5) *Only the Dead Know Brooklyn* by Michael Bettencourt; Director, Elfin Vogel; *Cat and Dick* by Andrea Alton; Director, Stacy Mayer; *Anxiety and Grandma* by Judd Lear Silverman; Director, Steve Velardi ; *The Me That's Me* by Maggie Lehrman, Director; Brooke Delaney; *Goode's Books and Press* by Allan Lefcowitz; Director, Scott Brocious

Box 2: The Sex Box (June 9–12) *Bibbity Bobbity Boo* by Charlotte Winters; Director, Bradley Campbell; *Sporting Goods* by Michael Bettencourt; Director, Ray Zilberberg; *The Poison Party* by John Paul Porter; Director, Martin Miller; *The Sex of Our Lives* by Erik Cristian Hanson; Director, Matthew Calhoun

Box 3: Heaven and Earth (June 16–19) *Bon Voyage Mr. Phelps!* by Daniel Damiano; Director, Heather S. Curran; *The Green Angel* by Joe Lauinger; Director, Erin Kate Howard; *Her Favorite Color and Grandma's Blue Sweater* by Joe Lauinger; Director, Erin Kate Howard; *Chasing the Deal* by Staci Swedeen; Director, Ray Zilberberg

Box 4: The Sandbox-Plays for Families and Children (June 23–26) *The Runaway Birthday* and *Melvin the Meek* by Jennifer Palumbo; Director, Dominic Cuskern

The Laramie Project by Moises Kaufmann; Director, Neal Freeman; Producer, M.R. Goodley; Costumes, David Thompson; Lighting, Jennette Kollmann; Technical Advisor, Edward Hodge; Stage Manager, Jessica Urtecho; **Cast:** Kathy Cortez, Daniel Damiano, Flannery Foster, Jill Michael, Steve Nagle, Joe Rux, Stephen Tyrone Williams, Anna-Elise Wincorn; September 10–25, 2005

The Fantasticks Music by Tom Jones, lyrics by Harvey Schmidt; Directors, Tina Marie Casamento, Dominic Cuskern; Producers, Robert Doxsey, Ken Dray; Scenery, Timothy J. Amrhein; Costumes, Sara Rizza; Lighting, Jeffrey E. Salzberg; Musical Director, David Libby; Stage Manager, Erica Omundson; **Cast:** Bonnie Fraser, Jason Robert Winfield, Paul Niebank, Dominic Cuskern, Mike Durkin, Tom Corbisiero; Darron Cardosa, Julia Kelly, October 15–November 6, 2005

The Marriage of Bette and Boo by Christopher Durang; Director, Heather Siobhan Curran; Producer, Matt Schicker; Scenery, Cully Long; Lighting, Ben Swope; Costumes, Amy Elizabeth Bravo; Stage Manager, Jennifer Russo; **Cast:** Mike Durkin, Daniel Haggard, Erin Kate Howard, Matt Jared, E.C. Kelly, Patricia Lavin, Laura Livingston, Jill Michael, Maria Ryan, Tom Weyburn; November 26–December 11, 2005

As You Like It by William Shakespeare; Director, Neal Freeman; Producer, Martin Miller; Scenery, Ann Bartek, Costumes, David Thompson; Lighting, Alison Cherry; Stage Manager, Jessica V. Urtecho; **Cast:** Daniel Damiano, Wesley Turner-Harris, Alex Domeyko, Jeffrey Woodard, E.C. Kelly, Nat Cassidy, Jared Mercier, Anna Olivia Moore, Alisha R. Spielmann, Jennifer Russo, Elizabeth Devlin, David Harrison, Colin Pritchard, Patrick Yeoman, Angela Hamilton, Heather Rodgers; January 14–29, 2006

Side Show Book and lyrics by Bill Russell, music by Henry Krieger; Director, Matt Schicker; Producer, Robin Michik-Jett; Scenery, Joseph Trainor; Costumes, Melanie Swersey; Lighting, Kevin Hardy; Musical Director, Cindy Gerlach; Choreography, Joe Barros; Stage Manager, Norva Bennett; **Cast:** Greg Horton, Traci Skoldberg, Lorraine Cink, Emily Battles, Melvin Shambry, Jimmy Hays Nelson, Matt Witten, Jeff Bush, Christopher Yee, Anthony Daniel, Dennis Lue, Jonathan Brian, Suzanne Pilzer, Tauren Hagans, William Cabrera, Minami Yusui, Adam MacLean, Kathryn Gerhardt, Tiffany Diane Smith, Kristen Sergeant; February 18–March 12, 2006

Take Me Out by Richard Greenberg; Director, Tom Wojtunik; Producer, Katie Adams; Scenery, Cully Long; Costumes, David Withrow; Lighting, Travis I. Walker; Sound, Aaron David Blank; Stage Manager, Jennifer Russo; **Cast:** Ron Brice, Noshir Dalal, Peter Hawk, Nobuo Inubushi, Jonathan Kaplan, John Kudan, Jamil Mena, Scott McGowan, Joe Moretti, Miguel Romero, Kit Wannen; April 1–16, 2006

Once on This Island Music by Stephen Flaherty, lyrics and book by Lynn Ahrens; Director/Choregrapher, Steven Smeltzer; Producer, Heather Siobhan Curran; Musical Director, Steve Przybylski; Scenery, Joseph Trainor; Costumes, Amy Elizabeth Bravo; Lighting, Niklas J.E. Anderson; Puppets, Jill Michael; Stage Manager, Caroline Listul; **Cast:** Alicia Christian, Anthony Wayne, Lisa Nicole Wilkerson, Dann B. Black, Debra Thais Evans, Monica Quintanilla, Michael C. Harris, Katherine Emily Mills, Rashad Webb, Ashley Marie Arnold, Lincoln Cochran, Daralyn Adams, Holden Berryman, Bella Bertram, Kevin Bradley Jr., Jayson Kerr, Kako Kitano, Mabel Jose, Ben Tostado; May 6–28, 2006

GINGOLD THEATRICAL GROUP: PROJECT SHAW

David Staller, Founder and Artistic Director

Innaugural season of montly public readings of the complete works of George Bernard Shaw

The Players Club, Grammercy Park South; produced and directed by David Staller; Associate Producers, Jerry Wade, Theresa Diamond, Anita Jaffe, Kate Ross

Arms and the Man Host: Howard Kissel; **Cast:** Nancy Anderson (Raina Petkoff), Malcolm Gets (Captain Bluntschli), Cynthia Harris (Catherine Petkoff), Alison Fraser (Louka), Nick Wyman (Nicola), George S. Irving (Major Paul Petkoff), Marc Kudish (Major Sergius Saranoff), Victor Slezak (Narrator One), Evalyn Baron (Narrator Two); January 23, 2006

Fanny's First Play Additional Producer, Bill Barbanes; Host: Charles Isherwood; **Cast:** Marc Kudisch (Juggins), Patrick Quinn (Savoyard), Jonathan Freeman (Count O'Dowd), Kate Baldwin (Fanny), George S. Irving (Mr. Gilby), Evalyn Baron (Mrs. Gilby), Sally Wilfert (Dora), James Murtaugh (Mr. Knox), Cynthia Harris (Mrs. Knox), Rebecca Luker (Margaret), Max von Essen (Bobby), Graham Rowat (Duvallet), Maureen Mueller (Narrator); Critics: Howard Kissel (Trotter), Michael Riedel (Vaughn), David Cote (Bannal), Patrick Pacheco (Gunn); February 27, 2006

Heartbreak House Host: John Simon; **Cast:** Fritz Weaver (Captain Shotover), Charlotte Moore (Lady Utterword), Michele Pawk (Hesione Hushabye), Ciaran O'Reilly (Boss Mangan), Malachy McCourt (The Burglar), Laura O'Deh (Ellie

Dunn), Jack Gilpin (Hector Hushabye), Simon Jones (Mazzini Dunn), George Dvorsky (Randall Utterword), Lynn Cohen (Nurse Guinness), David Cote (Narrator one), Margaret Hall (Narrator two); March 20, 2006

You Never Can Tell Host: Howard Kissel; **Cast:** James Ludwig (Mr. Valentine), Liz Morton (Dolly Clandon), Simon Kendall (Philip Clandon), Elena Shaddow (Gloria Clandon), Tovah Feldshuh (Mrs. Clandon), Paxton Whitehead (Fergus Crampton), George S. Irving (Waiter), Nick Wyman (Finch McComas), Allen Fitzpatrick (Bohun), John Martello (Narrator One), Charlotte Moore (Narrator Two); April 17, 2006

Overruled and **Augustus Does His Bit** Two one-acts; Host: Howard Kissel; **Cast:** *Overruled:* Kathleen Widdoes (Mrs. Juno), Paxton Whitehead (Gregory Lunn), George S. Irving (Sibthrope Juno), Charlotte Moore (Mrs. Lunn), Howard Kissel (Narrator); *Augustus Does His Bit:* George S. Irving (Lord Augustus Highcastle), Paxton Whitehead (Horatio Floyd Beamish), Charlotte Moore (A Lady), Kathleen Widdoes (Narrator); May 8, 2006

HARLEM REPERTORY THEATER

Keith Lee Grant, Artistic Director

Aaron Davis Hall at City College; June 24–August 13, 2005

Cabaret Book by Joe Masteroff, lyrics by Fred Ebb, music by John Kander

For Colored Girls Who Have Considered Suicide/ When the Rainbow Is Enuf by Ntozake Shange

Once on This Island Book and lyrics by Lynn Ahrens, music by Stephen Flaherty

HIP HOP THEATER FESTIVAL

Danny Hoch, Founder

5th Annual; June 11–18, 2005; Venues included New York Theatre Workshop, Apollo Studio Theater, Dance Theater Workshop, Joe's Pub, and the Zipper Theater

5th Anniversary Celebration Special performances by Danny Hoch, Ben Snyder, Full Circle

Big Voices Presented by Russell Projects; with PattyDukes, QueenGodis, Shaun Redwood, BJ, Abigail Nessen, and Ruby Pan

What You Say White Boy? presented by Playback NYC

Solo Series I—Witness to War: *From Tel Aviv to Ramallah* by Yuri Lane and *Live From the Front Lines: Petrol & Protein* by Jerry Quickley

Breathe by Javon Johnson, co-presented by Lark Play Development Center

Needle to Da' Groove Directed by Tracy Thomas

Solo Series II—Tales From the Hood: *Reminiscence of the Ghetto (and other things that Raized Me)* by Angela Kairiotis and *NE 2nd Avenue* by Teo Castellanos

Welcome to Arroyo's Written and performed by Kristoffer Diaz; Director, Margarett Perry

Benji Reid: 13 Michs and **Niels "Storm" Robitzky: Solo For Two** Double bill solo performances

Deep Azure by Chadwick Boseman; Director, Derrick Sanders; Presented by Congo Square Theater

Her Holy Water: A Black Girl's Rock Opera by Imani Uzuri

HORSE TRADE THEATER GROUP

Erez Ziv, Managing Director; Morgan Lindsey Tachco, Associate Producer

EDGE OF INSANITY COMPANY

Galaxy Video 2 Written and directed by Marc Morales; Scenery, Bradd Baskin; Sound, Kari O'Donnell; Producer, Morgan Lindsey Tachco; **Cast:** Susan Atwood, Nicole Benisch, Joanna Clay, Brian DePetris, Elizabeth Dominguez, Clay Drinko, Joe Edison, Lenny Gallo, Vinnie Kay, Alexandra Lemosle, Deondra Lyonne, Melanie Maras, Alfred Pagano, Jon Pogash, Mei Sakamoto, Barnet Senegal, Kevin Shaffer, Lucas Wotkowski, Rob Yang, Lynn Sher; UNDER St. Marks; October 12, 2005–November 4, 2005

HANDWRITTEN THEATRE COMPANY

Sodom: The Musical Book and Lyrics by Kevin Laub; Composer, Adam David Cohen; Director, Ben Rimalower; Scenery, Jason Courson; Lighting Designer, Shane Mongar; Production Stage Manager, Katherine Geers; Music Director, Marcus Baker; **Cast:** Jonathan Kaplan, Randy Jones, Brian Munn, Blythe Gruda, Amy Barker, Stanley Bahorek, Matt Owen, David Abeles, Jake Manabat, Ryan Kelly, Stephanie Kovacs, Patrick Gallagher and Galit Sperling; Kraine Theater; November 4, 2005–December 5, 2005

THE STOLEN CHAIR THEATRE COMPANY

The Man Who Laughs by Kiran Rikhye; Director, Jon Stancato; Scenery, David Bengali; Costumes, May Elbaz; Lighting, David Bengali; Stage Manager, Aviva Meyer; Music Composed and Performed by Emily Otto; **Cast:** Jon Campbell, Cameron J. Oro, Ariana Seigel, Alexia Vernon, Dennis Wit, Jennifer Wren; The Red Room; October 31, 2005–November 12, 2005

Stage Kiss by Kiran Rikhye; Director, Jon Stancato; Scenery, David Begali; Costumes, May Elbaz; Lighting, David Begali; Stage Manager, Aviva Meyer; Created by The Stolen Chair Theatre Company; **Cast:** Jon Campbell, Layna Fisher, Cameron J. Oro, and Alexia Vernon; The Red Room; May 3, 2006–May 27, 2006

THE JOHN MONTGOMERY THEATRE COMPANY:

Flirting with Reality by Suzanne Bachner; Conceived by Felicia Scarangello, Director, Trish Minskoff; Scenery, Nadia Volvic; Costumes, Deborah Alves; Lighting, John Tees, III;; Sound, Alexander R. Warner; Stage Manager, Jeff Goldschmidt; Producer, Suzanne Bachner; **Cast:** Felicia Scarangello, Alexander R. Warner; The Red Room; October 14, 2005–November 14, 2005

Run to the Roar by Sonia Sanchez; Director, Indira Etwaroo; Costumes, Deborah Alves; Lighting, Douglas Shearer; Sound, Thaddeus Daniels; Stage Manager, Douglas Shearer; Producers, Suzanne Bachner and Indira Etwaroo; **Cast:** Tamela Aldridge, Nicoye Banks, Henry Afro-Bradley, Karen Armatrading, Shani Borden, Ju-Yeon Ryu, Baraka de Soleil, Eric Sosa, Margaret Stockton, Alexander R. Warner; The Red Room; December 12, 2005–December 13, 2005

Alexander R. Warner and Felicia Scarangello in the John Montgomery Theatre Company's production of Suzanne Bachner's *Flirting with Reality* PHOTO BY SCOTT WYNN

DYSFUNCTIONAL THEATRE COMPANY

The Eight Reindeer Monologues by Jeff Goode; Director, The Ensemble; Scenery, Jason Unfried; Costumes, Porsha Taylor; Lighting, Jason Unfried; Sound, Justin Plowman; **Cast:** Robert Brown, Jennifer Gill, Theresa Goehring, Amy Overman, Justin Plowman, Pete Schuyler, Jason Unfried, Jennifer Jill White; The Red Room, November 18, 2005 – December 17, 2005

WORKSHOPS

Ensemble Studio Theatre and Gang of Four

Time/Unstuck A Time Piece by Neal Bell; Director, Jordan Young; **Cast:** JJ Kandell, Marguerite Stimpson, Jeffrey Nauman; The Red Room; April 20 – 30, 2006

2 Soldiers by Bathsheba Doran; Director, Dominic D'Andrea; **Cast:** Sturgis Adams, Johnny CO Green; The Red Room; April 20 – 30, 2006

Solo Performance Shows

Naked Trampoline Hamlet Written and performed by Andres du Bouchet; UNDER St. Marks; October 5 – 19, 2005

Madison to Madurai Written and performed by H.R. Britton; UNDER St. Marks; March 16 – 30, 2006

Toasted Written and performed by Elisa DeCarlo; The Red Room; June 17, 2006 – July 15, 2006

HOURGLASS GROUP

Elyse Singer, Artistic Director; Carolyn Baeumler and Nina Hellman, Associate Directors

Wellspring by Ruth Margraff; Director, Elyse Singer; Composer, Nikos Brisco; Scenery, Zhanna Gurvich; Costumes, Angela M. Kahler; Lighting, Anjeanette Stokes; Music by the Café Antarsia Ensemble (Nikos Brisco, Rami El-Aasser, Ruth Margraff, Ron Riley); Music Director, Jill Brunelle; **Cast:** Karen Lynn Gorney, Piter Marek, Tony Naumovski, John Schumacher, Jelena Stuplijanin, Carol Tammen; The Century Center for the Performing Arts Ballroom Theatre, December 4 – 6, 2005

READINGS

Killing Women by Marisa Wegrzyn; Director, Elyse Singer; November 2005

Dishes for Artists by Kate Moira Ryan; Director, Elyse Singer; April 2006

IMPETUOUS THEATER GROUP

James David Jackson, Artistic Director; Josh Sherman, Managing Director

Venezuela by Guy Helminger, translated by Penny Black; Director, James David Jackson; Scenery, Joe Powell; Costumes, Meryl Pressman, Lighting, George Gountas; Sound, Bill Kirby; Stage Manager, Amy Rubin; Fight Choreography, Qui Nguyen; Associate Director, Tim Errickson; **Cast:** Brendan Bradley, Hasnai Issa, Jamie Klassel, Joe Sousa, Jason Zimbler; Players Theatre; August 21 – 27, 2005 in conjunction with the FringeNYC

Office Sonata by Andy Chmelko; Director, Jason Zimbler; Scenery, Rachel Gordon; Costumes, Kara Harmon; Lighting, George Gountas; Sound, Ryan Dowd; Consultant, James Carter; Fight Director, Qui Nguyen; Video, Andrew Gaines; Stage Manager, Nancy Valladares; Production Stage Manager, Shuhei Seo; Production Manager, Joe Powell; **Cast:** Brendan Bradley, Bryce Gill, Beth Jastroch, DH Johnson, Steve Lavner, Shashanah Newman, Heidi Niedermeyer, Rose O'Hara, Brian MacInnis Smallwood, Justin Swain; Irish Arts Center; December 2 – 14, 2005

12th Night of the Living Dead Adapted from Shakespeare by Brian MacInnis Smallwood; Director, John Hurley; Design, Rachel Gordon, Laura Eckelman, Lilli Rhiger, Ryan Down, Donna Delmas, Allison Getz, Joe Powell; Stage Manager, Nancy Valladares; **Cast:** David Berent, Anna Chlumsky, Timothy J. Cox, Jonathan Desley, Meimh Djourabchi, Benjamin Ellis Fine, Justin Jain, Erin Jerozal, Tom Knutson, Rebecca McHugh, Shashanah Newman, Kristen Nolan, Alok Tewari, Akyiaa Wilson, Richard Zekaria; Center Stage NY; February 16 – 17, 2006

47:59 Play Festival-2nd Annual; 6 plays written and produced in less that two days; Produced by Jamie Klassel and Amanda Haley; Stage Manager, Tzipora Kaplan; Program included: *The Death of Chivalry?* by Jay Twitchell & Janet Zarecor, directed by Allison Juszkiewicz; featuring Jessica Asch and Liz Maestri; *Beautiful Stranger* by Michael Eisenstein & Jay Twitchell, directed by Corey Ann Haydu, featuring Manish Baliga & Devin Shayla Rudd; *Drunken Lesbian Homebuilding* by Janet Zarecor & Rob O'Hare, directed by James David Jackson, featuring Andy Chmelko, Dolores Diaz & Lindsay Wolf; *The Genuine Article* by Rob O'Hare & Michael Eisenstein, directed by Ivy Baldwin, featuring Bryce T. Gill, Nick Monroy & Jerielle Morwitz; *Number 4* by Adam David Jones & James Carter, directed by Josh Sherman, featuring Rebeka Pinon-Cassidy,

Meghan Reilly & Joseph Yeargain; *Billy's Bad Behavior or Mommy & Daddy & the Principal* by James Carter & Adam David Jones, directed by Michael Bottomley, featuring Bo Gorman, DH Johnson & Jennifer Loryn; Center Stage NY; February 18–19, 2006

A Night Near the Sun by Don Zolidis; Director, James David Jackson; Scenery, Joe Powell; Lighting, George Gountas; Costumes, Melissa Haley; Sound, Ryan Dowd; Stage Manager, Brian MacInnis Smallwood; **Cast:** Cidele Curo; Reyna De Courcy, Zachary Fletcher, Brian Linden, Michael Rudez; Black Box at 440 Studios; May 12–27, 2006

FUNDRAISERS AND SPECIAL EVENTS

The Beautiful Freak Show Produced by Joe Powell and Eliza Jane Bowman; Featuring Lisa Jackson and Girl Friday; Strange Aeons, and DJ Dirty Danchez; Siberia Bar; July 21, 2005

Mischief Night Produced by Josh Sherman and Brian MacInnis Smallwood; Featuring Devils Dancebelt and The Late Night Players; The Limerick House; October 28, 2005

The Sugahtown Brothel by Josh Sherman and Brian MacInnis Smallwood; **Cast:** Joseph Mathers, Joseph Yergain, Lindsay Wolf; Center Stage NY benefit hosted with Boomerang Theatre Company, Partial Comfort Productions, terraNova Collective, and Vampire Cowboys; October 30, 2005

Open All Night hosted by John Patrick Shanley; Produced by James David Jackson and Tim Errickson; with family and friends from LAByrinth; Boomerang Theatre Company, Partial Comfort Productions, terraNova Collective, and Vampire Cowboys; Center Stage NY; December 5, 2005

Nights Without the Sun-Readings May 2006; *The Chair* by Edwin Hansen Nelso, Director, Tim Errickson; May 16; *The Chronological Secrets of Tim* by Janet Zarecor; Director, Jamie Klassel; May 17; *Hope Suppressant Therapy* by Andy Chmelko; Director, Brendan Bradley; May 22; *The World's Largest Rodent* by Don Zolidis; Director, Brian MacInnis Smallwood; May 23

JEAN COCTEAU REPERTORY

Off Off Bowery Festival July 12–31, 2005; Series included: Barefoot Theatre Company's *Kingdom Come* written and directed by Francisco Solorzano; KEF Productions' *Corpus Christi* by Terrence McNally, directed by Adam Fitzgerald; The Lady Cavalier Theatre Company's *Fighting the Clock* by Peter Hilton, James Armstrong, Mariana Elder, Kelly DePuis and Qui Nguyen; directed by Nandita Shenoy, Gita Reddy, Nathan Lemoine and Dawn Elane; Quest Theatre Ensemble's *Twelfth Night* by William Shakespeare, directed by Tim Browning; Odyssey Theatre Ensemble's *Othello* by William Shakespeare, directed by Rachel Macklin; Geek Ink's *Desire Caught by the Tail* by Pablo Picasso, directed by Meredith Zolty; Mark Singer's *Headliners and One-Liners*

Sucker Fish Messiah by Ryan Michael Teller; Director, Taylor Brooks; **Cast:** Jennifer Sanders, Shannon Jones, Darren Ryan, May 12–June 4, 2006

KEEN COMPANY

Carl Forsman, Artistic Director; Wayne Kelton, Producer

6TH SEASON–Performances at the Connelly Theater

The Breadwinner by W. Somerset Maugham; Director, Carl Forsman; Scenery, Nathan Heverin; Costumes, Theresa Squire; Lighting, Josh Bradford; Sound, Samuel Doerr; **Cast:** Joe Delafield (Patrick), Jack Gilpin (Charles), Virginia Kull (Judy), Margaret Laney (Diana), Robert Emmet Lunney (Alfred), Alicia Roper (Margery), David Standish (Timothy), Jennifer Van Dyck (Dorothy); September 6–October 2, 2005

Children of a Lesser God by Mark Medoff; Director, Blake Lawrence; Scenery, Nathan Heverin; Costumes, Theresa Squire; Lighting, Josh Bradford; Sound, Matthew Given; ASL Translation and coach, Jackie Roth; **Cast:** Alexandria Wailes (Sarah Norman), Jeffry Denman (James Leeds), Guthrie Nutter (Orin Dennis), Ian Blackman (Mr. Franklin), Lee Roy Rogers (Mrs. Norman), Tami Lee Santimyer (Lydia), Makela Spielman (Edna Klein); March 14–April 9, 2006

In the Matter of J. Robert Oppenheimer by Heinar Kipphardt; Director, Carl Forsman; Scenery, Nathan Heverin; Costumes, Theresa Squire; Lighting, Josh Bradford; **Cast:** Dan Daily (Ward V. Evans), Peter Davies (Thomas A. Morgan), Matt Fischel (Hans Bethe), Wilbur Edwin Henry (Gordon Gray), Jonathan Hogan (John Lansdale), DJ Mendel (Colonel Boris Pash), Matthew Rauch (C.A. Rolander), Keith Reddin (Edward Teller), Steve Routman (Herbert S. Marks), Thomas Jay Ryan (J. Robert Oppenheimer), Rocco Sisto (Roger Robb), Ian Stuart (Lloyd Garrison); May 30–June 25, 2006

LABYRINTH THEATRE

Philip Seymour Hoffman and John Ortiz, Artistic Directors; Oliver Dow, Executive Director

THE BARN SERIES 2005 Shiva Theater at the Public - December 2-19, 2005

Pretty Chin Up by Andrea Ciannavei; Director, Michele Chivu; **Cast:** Buzz Bovshow, Andrea Cinnavei, Beth Cole, Alexis Croucher, Sal Inzirello; December 2 and 3; **City of Palms** by Raul Castillo; Director, Mariana Hellmund; **Cast:** Carlo Alban, Vanessa Aspillaga, Maggie Bofill, Alexis Croucher, Felix Solis, Doug Stender; December 4 and 11; **All the Bad Things** by Cusi Cram; Director, Paula Pizzi; **Cast:** Vanessa Aspillaga, Jen Grant, Justin Reinsilber, Phyllis Somerville, Alexa Scott-Flaherty, David Zayas; December 6 and 8; **1+1** written and directed by Eric Bogosian; **Cast:** Katie Nehra, Michael Puzzo, Justin Reinsilber; December 5 and 7; **Intringulis** written and performed by Carlo Alban; Director, David Anzuelo; December 10 and 18; **Going After Alice** by Megan Mostyn-Brown; Director, Chris McGarry; **Cast:** Renee Brown, Lauren Hodges, Laura Hughes, Stephen Payne, Portia and Marshall Sharer; December 12-13; **A Small Melodramatic Story** by Stephen Belber; Director, Lucie Tiberghien; **Cast:** Carlo Alban, Ron Cephas Jones, Chris McGarry, Portia; December 14 and 16; **She Talks to Rainbows** by Michael Puzzo; Director, Padraic Lillis; **Cast:** Mark Hammer, Sal Inzirello, Portia and David Zayas; December 15; **No Viet Cong Ever Called Me Nigger** written and directed by Brett C. Leonard; **Cast:** Ron Cephas Jones, Chris Chalk and Trevor Long; December 17; **The Little Flower of East Orange** written and directed by Stephen Adly Guirgis; **Cast:** Elizabeth Canavan, Jeff DeMunn, Richie Petrocelli, Lauren Velez, David Zayas; December 19

LA MAMA EXPERIMENTAL THEATRE CLUB (ETC)

Ellen Stewart, Founder and Director

FIRST FLOOR THEATRE

Three Sisters by Anton Chekhov, Director, design, and translation, Arthur Adair; Costumes, Karen Anselm; Composer, Richard Cohen, Stefano Zazzera; **Cast:** Ben Pirtle, Michele Cuomo, Caesar Del Trecco, Alana DiMaria, Sara Elsen, Jason Grechanik, Chris Oden, Rick Redondo, Andrew Rothkin, Jessica Marie Smith, Joseph Sousa, Pierre van der Spuy, Liza Bryn, Wendy Callard-Booz, Joe McGee; June 16–26

Seekers based on poetry of Hafiz; Presented by DAH Theatre Research Centre's Jadranka Andjelic Project; October 7–8

Saint Oedipus Written and directed by Piotr Tomaszuk; Presented by Wierszalin Theatre of Poland; October 13–30

Hamlet Adapted and directed by Kanako Hiyama; Design, Ryo Onodera; Puppets, Tom Lee; **Cast:** Joseph C. Yeargain, Erin Treadway, Brendan Bradley, Ivo Velon, Tony Naumovski, Roger Dale Stude, David Gochfeld, Morteza Tavakoli, Neimah Djourabchi; November 3–20

Dreaming the Sea Written and directed by Dario D'Ambrosi; with Lorenzo Alessandri and Dario D'Amborsi; Presented by Pathological Theatre in association with Italian Cultural Institute; November 25–27

The Curse of Mami Wata Written and directed by Prisca Ouya; Choreography, Prisca Ouya and Kiazi Malonga; December 1–4

Einstein by Gabriel Emanuel; Director, Howard Rypp; **Cast:** Victor Attar; December 7–11

Golgotha by Shmuel Refael, adapted by Haim Idissis, translated by Howard Rypp; Director, Geula Jeffet-Attar; **Cast:** Victor Attar; December 14–22

Harvest by Manjula Padmanabhan; Director, Benjamin Mosse; Scenery, Lee Savage; Lighting, Scott Bolman; Costumes, Chloe Chapin; **Cast:** Zina Anaplioti, Diksha Basu, Sam Chase, Rupak Ginn, Naheed Khan, Christianna Nelson, Debargo Sanyal, Jeffrey Wither. Video, Matt Bockelman; January 19–February 5

Death and the Ploughman by Der Ackermann aus Böhmen; Adapted and Directed by Peter Case; Music, Storm Garner; **Cast:** Rob Howard, Robert Yang, Elli Stefanidi; Storm Garner, Bridget Clark; February 9–26

The Last Night of Salome by Emanuele Vacchetto; Director, Maria Luisa Bigai; Presented by Istituto di Studi dello Spettacolo-Teatro Studio of Rome; **Cast:** Lydia Biondi, Carla Cassola, Avner Kam; March 2–19

Travels, Tours and One-Night Stands Conceived by Kim Imma & Onni Johnson Directed and Choreographed by Kim Imma; **Cast:** Chris Wild, Duane Boutté, Onni Johnson, Kim Ima, and rotating special guests; March 23–April 9

The Dragon Princess & the Scholar Director, Liang Tee Tue; Performed by Juliana and Danny Lau; April 19–23

Sundown Written and directed by Watoku Ueno; presented by Yara Arts Group; April 28–May 14

Sister by Mario Fratti; Director, Pamela Billig; **Cast:** Eleanor Ruth, Brian Voelcker, Shân Willis; May 18–June 4

THE ANNEX

Universe Expanding Conceived by Jane Cathy Shaw; Music, David Patterson Lighting, Jeff Nash; **Cast:** Frank Dowd, Michael Kelly, Elisa Hevia, Eva Lansberry, Alissa Mello, Jon Riddleberger, Priscilla Siregar, Bethany Sullivan; June 9–26

It's a Dance Thing, Two!! Curated by Nicky Paraiso; June 30–July 10

Caracolas de un Mar de Fuego Presented by the Maria Elena Anaya Dance Company; October 13–23

Transience Performed by Kumi Kuwahata and White Art Dance Group; November 7–8

Sultan Kudarat Conceived and choreographed by Potri Ranka Manis; Presented by Kinding Sindaw; November 10

Balletto Stiletto Written and directed by Mary Fulham; Produced by Watson Arts; Music, Benjamin Marcantoni; Choreography, Heidi Latsky; December 1–18

Mami Wata Written and Directed by Prisca Ouya; Choreographed by Prica Ouya and Kiazi Malonga; January 5–8

Major Barbara by George Bernard Shaw; Director, Brooke O'Harra Music, Brendan Connelly; Produced by The Theatre of a Two-Headed Calf; **Cast:** David Brooks, Lula Graves, Laryssa Husiak, Bob Jaffe, Johnny Klein, Tom Lipinski, Nadia Mahdi, Mike Mikos, Tatiana Pavela, Slaney Ross, Tina Shepard, Heidi Schreck; January 12–29

The Emperor Jones by Eugene O'Neill; Director, Arthur Adair; **Cast:** Xander Gaines, Sheila Dabney, Brian P. Glover; February 2–12

Passing Away Created and Directed by Leszek Madzik from the text by Tadeusz Rozewicz; Music, Marek Kucznski; Presented by Poland's Scena Plastyczna KUL; February 16–March 5

Operetta by Witold Gombrowicz; Director, Zishan Ugurlu; presented by New School University, the Eugene Lang College; March 9–12

Trilogy-Iphigenia, Helen, Odyssey Conceived, designed and directed by Theodora Skipitares; Music, Arnold Dreyblatt, Tim Schellenbaum, and Yukio Tsuji; March 16–April 2

Let's Crack Some Eggs by Michael Dinwiddie; Music, Mark Ballora; Choreography, Errol Grimes; April 6–16

What I Heard About Iraq Adapted by Simon Levy from the article by Eliot Weinberger; Presented in association with Theatre Eighty Eight; **Cast:** Rich Brown, Mahmood Karimi-Hakak, Lary Opitz, Jacquelyn Roberts, Yvonne Perry. Director, John Benitz April 18

Women in Confinement Written and directed by Maria Morett; Presented by Mxteatro; April 20–30

Herakles via Phaedra Conceived and Directed by Ellen Stewart; Music by Genji Ito, Michael Sirotta, Heather Paauwe and Ellen Stewart; May 18–June 11

THE CLUB

Moodswings or The Journey of a Hair Choreographed by Evelyna Dann; Presented by Company Gojico; June 2–12

Scottish Music Night Presented by Clann an Uabhair G.L.S.A; Featuring Uncle Moon, Antie Angus, The Highland Shatners; June 20

The Whore of Sheridan Square Written and directed by Michael Baron; Dramaturgy by Joe E. Jeffreys; **Cast:** Ken Barnett, Doug Brandt, Harris Doran, Ginger Eckert, Vanessa Hidary and Eric McNaughton; June 16–July 3

Fresh Meat Presented by Alien Comic Tom Murrin; October 3

Why Hanna's Skirt Won't Stay Down by Tom Eyen; Director, George Ferencz; Design, Gian Marco LoForte, Tom Schellenbaum, Jeff Tapper; **Cast:** Helen Hanft, Christopher Zorker; October 7–16

Club Riot Choreographed by Heidi Latsky; Musical Director, Frank Ponzio; **Cast:** Christina Briggs, Jeffery Freeze, Matt Henley, Jillian Hollis, Johari Mayfield, Kerry Nicholson, Christine Poland, Terrence Poplar, Jenny Rocha; October 21–30

Request Programme by Franz Xavier Kroetz; Director, Zishan Ugurlu; Music, Josua Fried; **Cast:** Raina von Waldenburg, Presented by Actors Without Borders; November 4–13

A Full Blown Blast! The Adventures of Richard See Concept, music and text by Richard Cohen; Choreography, Evelyna Dann; November 18–20

I Wanna Be Rosie by Bev Petty; Director, Valerie Gardner Rives; Music, Ricky Ritzle; December 2–18

The Victor Woo Showcase Conceived and performed by Soce; Director, Kevin Merritt; Music, Kevin So; featuring Taiyo Na, Kevin So, Risa Binder; December 5

Tomorrow's House featuring Wayne Barker, Suzanne Hevner, Greg Carter with George Rush and Brandon Seabrook; January 10

RrrrrrrrrrrrrrrrrrRKILLKILLKILL ... to infinity (MAKE IT LOOK REAL) Created by Chris Yon, in collaboration with Jeanine Durning, Taryn Griggs and John Scott; Music design, Justin Jones; January 19 & 21

Delicious Rivers Written & Composed by Ellen Maddow Director, Paul Zimet; Featuring The Talking Band; January 13–February 5

Wrequiem Conceived and performed by Benjamin Marcantoni and Armen Ra; January 23

Particular People Director, Pablo Vela; Choreography, Meredith Monk; featuring the music of Donald Ashwander; February 10–19

The Rule of Capture by Charles Case; February 15

Banished to Siberia Variety show featuring Ashley "Fishbone" Strand, Joey Defeo, Ian Ghent, Benny Mailman, sketches from Jolly Llamas and Edutainment Inc!; Music by Baboon Ass; February 24–25

For Bill An evening of music and performance dedicated to Bill Rice; Hosted by Nicky Paraiso & Ron Jones; February 27

In Dire Circumstances Created and performed by Wallie Wolfgruber and friends; March 3–5

Quentin & I Written and performed by David Leddick; Music, Andrew Sargent, Director, David Kingery; March 6–7

Pinchas, the Fish-People and the Great Flood Created and presented by Tami Stronach Dance, text by Jason Lindner, music, Jacob Lawson, Sound, Jeff Lorenz, Puppets, Kevin Augestine; **Cast:** Richard Crawford, Jessica Green, Jason Lindner, Lindsey Dietz Marchant, Jason Dietz Marchant, David Tirosh, Tami Stronach, Meghan Williams; March 10–12

Gazpacho Andalu Created and performed by Arturo Martinez, Alfonso Cid, Gary Raheb, Tony De Vivo, Barbara Martinez, Sol Koeraus, May de Silva; March 24–26

Mediterranean Voices Conceived and Choreographed by Nicola Iervasi Director, Kevin Albert; March 31–April 2

Mammamiro Conceived and performed by Virginia Virilli; April 1

Pear Cowboy Planet Conceived and performed by Chris Yon, Justin Jones, Jeff Larson, Zach Steel and the Zambonis; April 7–9

Odysseus and Ajax Director, Tom Lee; Music, Martin Halpern; Puppets, Tom Lee; April 14–23

The Fancy Stitch Machine Listening Hour by Karinne Keithley; April 24

Mustard Written and directed by Mitchell Polin; Music, Tungsten 74; **Cast:** Kristopher Kling, Jessie Richardson, The Philly, Kimberly Brandt, Michael Burke Ben Horner; April 28–May 14

Past Escape Performed by Christopher Wild; Director, Cate Hirst; May 1

Alien Comic's Performance Art Workshop Show with Tom Murrin; May 16

Swell Music of Daniel Zaitchik, featuring Jeremy Bass and Christina Courtin; May 21

Fe-Mail Written and Directed by N.C. Heikin; Featuring Tovah Feldshuh; May 22

LINCOLN CENTER FESTIVAL 2005

Nigel Redden, Director

July 12–31, 2005

Le Dernier Caravansérail Created by Le Theatre du Soleil; Director, Ariane Mnouchkine; North American premiere performed in Damrosch Park, 19 performances

Arlecchino, Servant of Two Masters by Carlo Goldoni; Director, Giorgio Strehler; Presented by Teatro di Milano; Alice Tully Hall; 4 performances

Modern Noh Plays by Yukio Mishima; Director, Yukio Ninagawa; Rose Theatre; 3 performances

I La Galigo Conceived, directed, and designed by Robert Wilson; New York State Theater, 4 performances

My Life as a Fairy Tale Music and lyrics by Stephin Merritt; Book by Erik Ehn; Director, Chen Shi-Zheng; **Cast:** Fiona Shaw, Mia Maestro, Blair Brown, Qian Yi, Mary Lou Rosato; Gerald W Lynch Theater at John Jay College; 3 performances

LOOKING GLASS THEATRE

Justine Lambert, Artistic Director; Jenn Boehm, Managing Director

The Girlhood of Shakespeare's Heroines by Don Nigro; Co Produced with Urban Enchantment; Director, Rachel Axelrod; Lighting, James Bedell; **Cast:** Raquel Florim, Sarah Antelek, Evy Ortiz, Kelli Bragdon, Jessie Coleman; July 13–17, 20–24, 2005

Not Enough Princesses Adapted and directed by Shari Johnson; Scenery, Bokyoung Youn; Costumes, Brenda Renfroe; Lighting, James Bedell; Stage Manager, Nikki Rothenberg, Julia Martin; **Cast:** Megan Raye Manzi (Alva/Goblin Princess), Sam Rolen (Troll King/Bear), Jeremy Procopio (Jerker), Amber Ford (Johanna), Daniel Meredith (Ole), Marissa Michaels (Percussionist), Jonas Dickson (Prince), Christie Booker (Troll Mother/Forest Hag/Tomte/Troll Servant); Weekend matinees September 24–November 6, 2005

Measure for Measure by William Shakespeare; Director, Glory Bowen; Choreography, Julia Hart; Scenery, Bokyoung Youn; Costumes, David Thompson; Lighting, James Bedell; Sound, Christopher Brooks; Stage Manager, Ain Rashida Sykes; **Cast:** Amanda Bailey, Peter Bean, Emily Begin, Christine Bokhour, Orion Delwaterman, Nicole DiGaetano, Megan Ferguson, Paula Galloway, Ethan Gomez, Tania Jeudy, Jesse May, Duncan Pflaster, Susan Rankus, Caroline Samaan, Dax Valdes, Marya Wegman, Jess Cassidy White, Michael Whitney; October 13–November 6, 2005

Spring's Awakening Based on the play by Frank Wedekind, adapted by Kennedth Nowell; Director, Charmian Creagle; Scenery, Inseung Park; Costumes, Jessa-Raye Court; Lighting, Ryan Metzler; Sound, Sean P. Doran; Movement, Amanda Boekelheide; Stage Manager, Nick Monroy; Film, Christopher Romero; Photography/Editor, Daryl Lathon; **Cast:** Melissa Coleman, Kevin Coyle, Christina DeRosier, Will Ellis, Hana Nora McGrath, Annie Reilly, Josh Silverman, Ben Sumrall; March 9–April 2, 2006

Spring 2006 Writer/Director Forum May 25–28: *Medea* by Euripides; Director, Candace O'Neil Cihocki; *Hollywood Lights* by Suzanne Wesley; Director, Emily Plumb; June 8–11: *Population Growth* by Aoise Stratford; Director, Nikki Rothenberg; *Muncie & Mayhem in "Rats" and "Tea"* by Laylage Courie; Director, Rose Ginsberg; *Aquarium* by Lila Rose Kaplan; Director, Aliza Shane; June 15–18: *Things That GO Hump in the Night* by Peggy Dougherty; Director, Ain Rashida Sykes; *Richard III* by William Shakespeare; Director, Kelly R. Haydon; June 22–25: *The Patriots* by Kate Marks; Director, Tzipora Kaplan; *Dick 'n Spooner* by Melissa Fendell; Director, Jill Landaker; *Swimming in the Ocean* by Kato McNickle; Director, Elizabeth Sturrus; Casts included: Francile Albright, Satomi Blair, Enid Cortés, Carolyn Demisch, Drummond Doroski, Sofia Dubrawsky, Rob Esris, Leigh Feldpausch, Dain Geist, Lara Gold, Dayna Graber, Robert Grossman, Annette Guarrasi, M. Alan Haley, Tara Henderson, Erinn Holmes, Kelly Hummert, Don Jeanes, Lane Keough, Sarah Kozinn, Margot Littlefield, April Grace Lowe, Lauren Maxwell, Katie Mazzola, Tom McCartan, Carolyn Morrison, Heidi Niedermeyer, Christie Oakes, Glenn Peters, Kirsta Peterson, Patrick Pizzolorusso, Gretchen Poulos, Candice Renee, Andrew Rothkin, Aaron Sandler, Josh Silverman, Scott Simpson, Frank Tamburin, Shane Wallis, Bradley Wells, Akilah Williams, Lindsay Wolf, Rob Yang, Nick Zelletz

MANHATTAN CLASS COMPANY (MCC)

THEATER FOR THOUGHT SERIES

Assisted Loving by Bob Morris; Director, Josh Hecht; September 26, October 2, 10, 16–17, 2005

SPECIAL READINGS

Wit by Margaret Edson; Director, Leigh Silverman; November 21, 2005

Nixon's Nixon by Russell Lees; Director, Jim Simpson; January 9, 2006

Beirut by Alan Bowne; Director, Jimmy Bohr; April 17, 2006

MANHATTAN CHILDREN'S THEATRE

Laura Stevens, Executive Director/Producer; Bruce Merrill, Artistic Director

Sideways Stories from the Wayside School Adapted by John Olive, from the novels by Louis Sachar; September 24–November 6

The Snow Maiden Adapted and directed by Bruce Merrill; November 12–December 18, 2005

Brave Irene Book, music and lyrics by Joan Cushing, adapted from the original book by William Steig; Director, Bruce Merrill; December 31, 2005–February 12, 2006

Last of the Dragons by Kristin Walter, adapted from the story by Edith Nesbit; February 18–April 2, 2006

Jack & the Beanstalk April 8–May 21, 2006

THE MEDICINE SHOW THEATRE ENSEMBLE

Barbara Vann, Artistic Director

35th Season

The Republic of Poetry Conceived and directed by Barbara Vann; Co-conceived by Aaron Beall, Nicole Colbert and Stelios Manolakakis; Contributors: Martin Espada, Arnold Weinstein, Harry Matthews, Bayard, Denise Duhamel, Vincent Katz, Roy Lisker, Filip Marinovich, Simon Pettet, Miram Sagan, Bruce Weber; **Cast:** Alex Bilu, Jasha Bilan, Mark Dempsey, Mark Gering, Jason Alan Griffin, Beth Griffith, Kirt Harding, Amanda Ifrah, Monica Lynch, Ward Nixon, Kip Potharas, Ken Scudder, Lisa Shred, Ayanna Siverls, Barbara Vann; June 9–26, 2005

Undercover Lover by Arnold Weinstein, Frank O'Hara and John Gruen; Director, Barbara Vann; **Cast:** Morton Banks, Sarah Engelke, Mark Dempsey, Diana Dunbar, Beth Griffith, Kirt Harding, Mike Still, Barbara Vann, Monrico Ward, David Weitzer, Andrew York; November 3–December 4, 2005

Don Juan in Hell by George Bernard Shaw; Director, Alec Tok; Design, Blythe Pittman; Music, Noah Creshevsky; Costumes, Uta Bekaia; Choreography, Ernesto Corvino; **Cast:** Mark J. Dempsey, Monica Lynch, Peter Judd, Barbara Vann; February 2–26, 2006

Fire Exit: Vaudeville for Eurydice by V.R. Lang; Director, Barbara Vann; Design, Susan Nicholson, Sandra Sprecher, Uta Bekaia; Choreography, Nicole Colbert; **Cast:** Barbara Vann, Lora Lee Ecobelli, Beth Griffith, Elana Zazanis, Mark J. Dempsey, Sarah Nuffer, John Crefeld, Alex Bilu, Greg Vorob, Jason Alan Griffin, Constantine Montana, Amy Kersten, Julia Granacki, Morty Banks, Joel Bernstein; April 27–May 21, 2006

MELTING POT THEATRE COMPANY

Larry Hirschhorn, Founding Artistic Director; Sean Patrick Flahaven, Managing Director

9TH SEASON

All About Eve 1951 Lux Radio Theatre adaptation of the film by Joseph L. Mankiewicz; Director, Nick Corley; Music Director, Jono Mainelli; **Cast:** Gregg Edelman, Tovah Feldshuh, Jonathan Hadary, Adam Heller, Jackie Hoffman, Fred Newman, Christine Pedi, Patrick Quinn, Jennifer Rae Beck, David Ogden Stiers, Emily Skinner, Tamara Tunie, Greg Carter, Suzanne Hevner, Vanessa A. Jones, Barrow Street Theatre; November 7, 2005

Terezin Book by Peter Ullian, music by Joel Derfner, lyrics by Len Schiff; Director, Jeremy Dobrish; Music Director, Andrew Wilder; **Cast:** Danny Gurwin, Zac Halley, David Hibbard, Carolann Page, Donna Vivino, Kathy Voytko, Blake Whyte, Stuart Zagnit; Leonard Nimoy Thalia Theatre at Symphony Space; February 23–25, 2006

In This House Music and book by Mike Reid, lyrics and book by Sarah Schlesinger, book and direction by Jonathan Bernstein; Music Director, Andrew Wilder; **Cast:** George Lee Andrews, Stephanie J. Block, Mary Beth Peil, Charlie Pollock; Leonard Nimoy Thalia Theatre at Symphony Space; April 26–28, 2006

METROPOLITAN PLAYHOUSE

Alex Roe, Artistic Director; Michael Bloom, Associate Artistic Director

Herman Melville's Moby Dick Written and performed by Christopher Moore; Director, Alex Roe; Scenery, Ryan Scott; Lighting, Maryvel Bergen; June 2–19, 2005

Alphabet City...III Written and featuring Tod Mason, Mario Quesada, and Deborah Johnstone; Director, Derek Jamison; Design, Nicole Hersey, Ryan Scott; Stage Manager, Michael Bloom; August 17–28, 2005

The Scarecrow Adapted by Percy MacKaye from Nathaniel Hawthorne's *The Feathertop*; Director, Alex Roe; Design, Ryan Scott; **Cast:** Avery Clark, Sidney Fortner, Ian Gould, Paul Jackel, Deborah Johnstone, Andy MacDonald, Melissa Miller; September 30–October 30, 2005

Inheritors by Susan Glaspell; Director, Yvonne Conybeare; Stage Manager, Pamela Hybridge; Design, Ryan Scott, Rebecca Lustg, Alexander C. Senchak, Ben Ruby; Fight Director, Scott Barrow; **Cast:** Matthew Trumbull, Sue Glausen Smith, David Fraioli, Tod Mason, Jeff Pagliano, Sean Dill, Samantha Needles, Margaret Loesser Robinson, David Lally, Peter Judd, November 11–December 11, 2005

Poe-Fest Readings and plays based of the works of Edgar Allen Poe; January 16–29, 2006 Included: *Elanora* by Tara Bahna-James and Jonathan Portera; *101 Ways* by Stephen Peace; *Quoth the Raven* by Dan Evans; *POE* a musical by Jack Aaronson and Gil Varod; *The Tell-Tale Heart: a Musicabre* by Danny Askhenasi; *Curese of the Neckrophreniac* by Tras S D; *Masque of the Red Death* by Wander-

ing Rom Players; *The Raven Prepares* by Patrick Blake; *Mr E.A. Poe's New Year's Bash* by Jeremy Halpern; *Somewhat Damaged* by Alexander Poe, Presented by Redux Theatre Company; Director, Joseph Varca; **Cast:** Cort Garretson, Emilee Dupre, Ben Correale, Jeff Addiss, Jonathan Kells Phillips; *Blackheart* by Dick St. George and Susan Hopkins; *The Black Cat* and *The Telltale Heart* readings; *Raving* by Peter Lobdell and Charles Ditto

The Melting Pot by Israel Zangwill; Director, Robert Kalfin; Design, Andrew C. Boyce, Douglas Filomena, Gail Cooper-Hecht; **Cast:** Daniel Shevlin, Kendall Rileigh, Ronnie Newman, Suzanne Toren, Frau Quixano, Steve Sterner; March 3–April 2, 2006

Haunted Written, directed, and designed by Alex Roe; **Cast:** Andrew Firda, Teresa Kelsey, Charlotte Hampden, Tod Mason; April 28–May 28, 2006

MICHAEL CHEKHOV THEATRE COMPANY

Michael Horn, Producing Artistic Director

SAM SHEPARD FESTIVAL SERIES AT THE BIG LITTLE THEATRE

Series 1

Buried Child Director, Tom Herman; **Cast:** Kristin Carter, Brian Lee Elder, Patricia Elisar, James Glenn, Jason Griffith, Thomas Francis Murphy, Tom Pavey; March 15–April 15, 2006

Simpatico Director, Ann Bowen; **Cast:** Heather Anthony, Alison Costine, Gary Iamadore, Jennifer Lee, Tom Pavey, Peter Picard, Talia Thelen; March 17–April 8, 2006

A Lie of the Mind Director, Kathy Curtiss; **Cast:** Susan Capra, Ali Costine, Frieda Lipp, Thomas Francis Murphy, Curtis Nielsen, Adrian O'Donnell, Anna Podolak, Will Schneider; March 19–April 10, 2006

Series 2

Red Cross and **Cowboy Mouth** Two one-acts; Directors, Cyndy A. Marion and Alisha Silver; **Cast:** Michelle Comba, David C. Marshall, Jaime Sheedy, Moti Margolin, Daniel C. O'Brien; April 19–May 11, 2006

Action, Chicago, and **Cowboys 2** Three one-acts; Director, Tom Amici; **Cast:** Nadia Asencio, Penny Bittone, Julianna Bloodgood, Jason Kalus, Adrian O'Donnell, Stas May, Liz Sanders, Kristen Schneider, Tim Scott, Ali Stover; April 21–May 13, 2006

Series 3

Icarus's Mother/Chicago Director, Dennis Gleason; **Cast:** Kate Campbell, Mark Stevens, Liz Sanders, Jason Kalus, Jean Noel Ruhland, Will Schnieder, Tim Scott; May 17–June 2, 2006

MIDTOWN INTERNATIONAL THEATRE FESTIVAL

John Chatterton, Founder and Executive Producer

Sixth Annual; July 18–August 7, 2005; Venues included the WorkShop Theatre Mainstage and Jewel Box; Where Eagles Dare Theatre and Studio

21 Stories: A Broadway Tale by G.W. Stevens

Actor.Comedian.Negro Written, directed and performed by Baron Vaughn

Apathy: The Gen X Musical Music and lyrics by Mickey Zetts; Director, Paul D'Alessandria; **Cast:** Fiona Choi, Ethan Gomez, Samantha Leigh Josephs, Ryan G. Metzger, Matt Miniea, Duncan Pflaster, Sami Rudnick

The Baby Is Blue by Matt Schatz; Director, S. Caden Hethorn; Presented by Incumbo Theater Company; **Cast:** Ethan Baum, Ayelet Blumberg, Mark Montgomery, Elizabeth Schmidt

Black Panther Women

Cervix with a Smile Written and performed by Elisa DeCarlo; Additional music by Ellen Mandel

Cex and the Sity Created and Produced by Robin Ackerman and Marjorie Suvalle; Written by Rick Suvalle; Director, Michael Ormond; Music, Joshua Rosali; **Cast:** Elizabeth Bowden, Sam Dingman, Chris Flynn, Theresa Fowle, Jim Longo, Jay Spece, Marjorie Suvalle

Charles and Diana: The Musical Music and Book by Lewis Papier, lyrics by Mary Sullivan Struzi; Director, Clyde Baldo; **Cast:** Michael Digioia, Amanda Ladd, Rob Resnick, Kate Greer, Tracy Rosten, Kenneth Garner, Natalie Delena, Kiirsten Kuhi, Amy Russ, Monica Russell, Alan Ostroff

Cosmos/Ethos: From Bris to Abyss Two solo performaces: *A Cosmic Mishap in an Accidental Universe in America* written and performed by Aaron Petrovich; *The Ethics of Rav Hymie Goldfarb* written and performed by Robin Goldfin

The Criminal Perspective/No Parole Written, directed and performed by Carlo D'Amore

Dreamhouse Conceived by Ari Laura Kreith and David Wolfson, music by David Wolfson, lyrics by Barbara DeCesare; Director, Ari Laura Kreith; **Cast:** Jennie Eisenhower, Amy Hutchins, Maree Johnson, Gayla D. Morgan, Suzan Postel

End Caligula Presented by Unartistically Frustrated Productions

Feasting on Cardigans by Mark Eisman; Director, Amy Henault; **Cast:** Ian Pfister, Kate Sandberg, Katie Barrett, Andrea Gallo, Tyler Samuel Lee; Presented by the Oberon Theatre Ensemble

Fell in Love with a Girl by Samara Siskind; Director, Ryan Brown; Produced by the WAIT Company; **Cast:** Amanda Clayton, Meagan Gordon, Mike Kulbieda, Anthony Saracino

Flyers and Other Tales by Kate Marks; Director, Heidi Handelsman

Four for the Office Three short plays and a monologue

The Girls Who Wore Black Adapted by JoEllen Notte from the writings of Elise Cowen, Diane di Prima, Joyce Johnson, Hettie Jones, Leo Skir and Anne Waldman; Director, JoEllen Notte; **Cast:** Nicole Carpino, Anna Howland, Margaux Laskey, Michele Weiss, Beth White

Glory Road Book and Lyrics by Greg Senf, Music by Gregory Max, based on an idea by Jamie Heck; Director, George Wolf Reily; Musical Director, Jeremy Rosen; **Cast:** Chet Carlin, Beth Chiarelli, Michael Finkelstein, Kristen Hammer, Barbara Litt, Jeannine Otis, Eric Petersen, Jessie Thatcher

The Goat Song by Kimberly Patterson, Director, Jill Jichetti; Produced by Lifeblood Theater Company; **Cast:** Sarah Doudna, Megan Hutten, Ingrid Nuñez, Bryan Ponemon

Good Opinions by Anne Fizzard; Director, Katrin Hilbe; **Cast:** Nicole Taylor, Marc Geller, Stephen Morfesis, Andrew Dawson, Oliver Conant, Kevin Stapleton, Joan Pelzer, Wende O'Reilly

Grieving for Genevieve by Kathleen Warnock; Director, Peter Bloch; **Cast:** Derin Altay, Karen Stanion, Susan Barnes Walker, Jo Anne Bonn

Guns, Shackles and Winter Coats by M. Stefan Strozier; Director, Alan Kanevsky; Artistic Director, Jean-Claude Villareal; Produced by La Muse Venale, Inc.; **Cast:** Chris Sorensen, Anita Anthonj, Penny Bittone, Johnpaul, Damian Ladd, Yza Shady, Joe Wissler

How to Ride Roller Coasters Written and performed by Tina Lee; Music, Darryl Gregory; Director, David Godbey

Inside Cherry Pitz Written and performed by Cyndi Freeman; Co-Written and created by Zack Stratis; Director, Cheryl King

Invisible Child Written and performed by Lisa Barri; Director/Choreographer, Don Johanson; Original Score, William Catanzaro; Dancers: Tabitha Boulding, Robera Mathes, Karlen Schreiber

It's Only a Play by Terrence McNally; Produced by Dack Dowd with John Capo Productions; Director, John Capo; **Cast:** Yuval David, Frederick Hamilton, Cynthia Henderson, Betty Hudson, Sheila Mart, Charles Marti, Glenn Peters, John Squire

Jackie Undressed Written and performed by Andree Stolte; Director, Michael Schiralli; Wig and Make up, Jason Hayes

Leftovers by Vincent Caruso; Director, James Martinelli

MentalPause Written, choreographed, and performed by Margaret Liston; Director, Merri Milwe; Producer, Jane Dubin and Margaret Liston

A Musical Journey ... with the songs of Jacques Brel, Kurt Weill and Charles Aznavour; Written and directed by Bob Ost; Starring Vickie Phillips and Gerry Dieffenbach

not a nice girl/Rights of Man Written and performed by Cheryl King/Aaron Petrovich

Old Words, New Words by Mary E. Goulet; Director, Jesse L. Kearney, Jr., **Cast:** Sarah M. Wilson; Jesse L. Kearney, Jr.; Danielle Fisk; Laura Heidinger; Corey Jay Moran

On the Couch With Nora Armani Written and performed by Nora Armani; Director, François Kergourlay

Passin' Time & Just Short of a Beauty *Passin Time:* Written and performed by Khemali Murray; Director, Chuck Patterson; *Just Short of A Beauty:* Written and performed by Diane Gioseffi; Director, Cheryl King

Peace Now Written and directed by Tom Peterson; Produced by Exit 69 Productions; **Cast:** Michael C. Maronna, Frank Harts, Carter Jackson, Genia Michaela, Cameron Blair, Cameron Peterson, Matthew Decapua, Christian Pedersen, Adrianne Rae-Rodgers, Kim Shaw

Penny-4-Eyes Rock N' Roll Show with Christiana Anbri, Vachelle Gil, Sasha Toro, Lady Altovise, Chris Reed and Lucia Giannetta; The Band: Jimi K. Bones, Andy Galore, Andrew Shantz, Aaron Brooks, Brendan Peck

Revolutionary Chickens Created and performed by Rob Lok; Visual/Sounds, Kris Anton; Design Consultant, Spencer Moy

Santa Claus IS Coming Out...or How the Gay Agenda Came Down My Chimney Written and performed by Jeffrey Solomon

Savior by Daniel R. O'Brien; Director, Christopher Carter Sanderson; Produced by Tragicomic Theatre; **Cast:** Jy Murphy, Hilary Howard, Jeff Barry

Sex & Sealing Wax by Adam Burns and Romy Nordlinger; Director, Julie Troost; Performed by Romy Nordlinger

Sex, Cellulite & Large Farm Equipment Written and performed by River Huston; Director, Cheryl King

Shakespeare Is Dead by Orran Farmer; Director, Chris Chaberski; **Cast:** Chelsea Lagos, Luke Rosen

The Soldier's Fiddle by Stephen Rosenfield and Ribeau; Performed by Ribeau

Soul to Keep Written, co-produced, and performed by Joyia D. Bradley; **Cast:** BJ Wheeler a.k.a."Priest"; Co-produced by Joan Liman; Director, Alexandra Lopez

Spit It Out! by Amy Coleman and Valerie Smaldone; Director, Sarah Gurfield; Musical Director, Donna Kelly; **Cast:** Amy Coleman, Valerie Smaldone, Stephen Bienskie, The Spit it Out! Blues Band: Andy Bassford, Donna Kelly

Under My Apron Written and directed by Debbie Williams; Produced by RealArts; **Cast:** Ron Williams, Kristen Egan, Jessa Watson, Corey Greenan, Debbie Williams, Kevin Starzynski, Maria Couch

When Silence Explodes: Fetus/Don't Break Your Egg *When Silence Explodes: Fetus* Written and performed by Rada Angelova; Creative consultant: Cheryl King; *Don't Break Your Egg* Written and performed by Christine Fall

MILK CAN THEATRE COMPANY

Julie Fei-Fan Balzer, Artistic Director; Bethany Larsen, Managing Director

The Paperback Musical Music by Nick Moore, book and lyrics by Jack Dyville, Dyan Flores, Travis Kramer, Bethany Larsen, Selda Sahin, Susannah Pearse; Directors, Habib Azar, Melissa Fendell, Jake Hirzel, Russell Kaplan, Lauren Reinhard; Musical Director, Marcus Baker; **Cast:** Kerry Flanagan, Thomas Lash, Matthew Naclerio, Ruben Ramos, Sarah Hubbard, Kate Tellers, Kenneth Scott Thompson, Cotton Wright; Michael Weller Theatre; December 5, 2005

The Hamlet Plays *The Player King Musical* by Anne Phelan, music by Bill Tinsley; Director, Terry Berliner; **Cast:** Carrie Ann Champlin and Dennis Clark; *Baloney* written and directed by ML Kinney; **Cast:** Byron Blevins and Timothy Cole; *The Match* by Sharon E. Cooper; Director, Pat Diamond; **Cast:** Derek Peith and Nick Fondulis; *The Lamp's Lit* by Cheryl Davis; Director, Kate Marks; **Cast:** TJ Morton, Roya Shanks, and Andrew Zimmerman; *Maybe He's Just Not That Into You...* by Bethany Larsen; Director, Tom Nondorf; **Cast:** Lauren Mary Gleason, Cynthia Rice, and Katie Northlich; *Decisive* by Susannah Pearse, music by Nick Moore; Director, Selda Sahin; **Cast:** John Buxton, Jennifer Stackpole, Reza Jacobs, and Jared Dembbowski; Scenery, Michael Ostaszewski; Costumes, Marija Djordjevic; Lighting, Marty Vreeland; Sound, Nick Moore; Stage Manager, Riv Massey; Michael Weller Theatre; April 29 – May 14, 2006; 8 performances

Rosencrantz and Guildenstern Are Dead by Tom Stoppard; Director, Julie Fei-Fan Balzer; Scenery, Michael Ostaszewski; Costumes, Marija Djordjevic; Lighting, Marty Vreeland; Sound, Nick Moore; Stage Manager, John Simmons; Assistant Director, Amanda Weir; Composer, Nick Moore; **Cast:** Walter Brandes (Guildenstern), Avery Clark (Rosencrantz), Zack Calhoon (The Player), Tom Cleary (Polonius), Noah Crowe (Player), Charles Drexler (Player), David A. Ellis (Dusty), Jessi Gtta (Ophelia), Catherine Gowl (Gertrude), Chris Kloko (Alfred), Lawrence Merritt (Claudius), Aaron Mize (Corduroy/Horatio), Matt Stapleton (Hamlet); Michael Weller Theatre; May 3 – 14, 2006; 10 performances

SCENE HERD UDDERED: WORKSHOP SERIES

The Uncertainty Principle by Bethany Larsen; Director, Julie Fei-Fan Balzer; October 24, 2005

The Paperback Musical by Jack Dyville, Dyan Flores, Travis Kramer, Bethany Larsen, Selda Sahin, and Susannah Pearse, Music by Nick Moore; Directors, Habib Azar, Melissa Fendell, Jake Hirzel, Russell Kaplan, and Lauren Reinhard; December 5, 2005

Impossible Lorca: A Theatrical Hat-Trick by Federico Garcia Lorca; Director, Melissa Fendell; March 6, 2006

MOOSE HALL THEATRE COMPANY/ INWOOD SHAKESPEARE FESTIVAL

Ted Minos Producing Artistic Director

Henry V by William Shakespeare; Director, Ted Minos; Technical Director, Catherine Bruce; Costumes, Marie Gallas-Suissa; Stage Manager, Polly Solomon; Fight Choreographer, Ray A. Rodriguez; Music, Luke St. Francis; Graphics, Lee Kaplan; General Manager, Frank Zilinyi; **Cast:** E. Calvin Ahn, Joel Bischoff, Craig Clary, Benjamin Curns, Morganne Davies, Bernardo De Paula, David A. Ellis, Chaya Gordon, Ian Gould, Garth Guibord, Greg Horton, Roxann Kraemer, Marca Leigh, Jay Longan, Omar Robinson, Gael Schaefer, Kevin G. Shinnick, Aaron Simms, Tom Steinbach, Amanda Weeden, Max Woertendyke; Outdoors in Inwood Hill Park Peninsula, Upper Manhattan; June 8 – 25, 2005

The Three Musketeers by Victor Hugo adapted by Ted Minos; Director, Ted Minos; Technical Director, Catherine Bruce; Costumes, Marie Gallas-Suissa; Stage Manager, Polly Solomon; Fight Choreographer, Ray A. Rodriguez; Music, Luke St. Francis; Graphics, Lee Kaplan; General Manager, Frank Zilinyi; **Cast:** E. Calvin Ahn, Bob Armstrong, Sam Bailer, Nicole Benisch, Michael Bernstein, Samantha Bruce, Alexandra Devin, Esmeralda, Nicole Godino, Ian Gould, Greg Horton, Roxann Kraemer, David Lamb, Marca Leigh, Michael M. McGuire, Devin Moriarity, Dina Prioste, Ray A. Rodriguez, Aaron Simms, Polly Solomon, Matthew R. Staley, Tom Steinbach, Steven Ungar, Frank Zilinyi; Outdoors in Inwood Hill Park Peninsula, Upper Manhattan; July 20 – August 6, 2005

The Cast of *Henry V* presented by Moose Hall Theatre Company/Inwood Shakespeare Festival PHOTO BY TED MINOS

MUSICALS TONIGHT

Mel Miller; Producer and Artistic Director

The High Life by Arthur Schwartz and Howard Dietz; 45th Street Theatre; October 18–30, 2005

Good News by Ray Henderson, Laurence Schwab, B.G. DeSylva, and Lew Brown; Director, Thomas Mills; Music Director, Rick Hip-Flores; **Cast:** Selby Brown, Ryan Dunkin, Leo Ash Evens, Katy Frame, Ben Franklin, Adam Mac-Donald, Missy Matherne, Patrick Maubert, Erik McEwen, Emily Mixon, Noel Molinelli, Jonathan Osborne, Annie Ramsey, Roger Rifkin, Sandie Rosa, Adam Shonkwiler, Tad Wilson, Dana Zihlman; 45th Street Theatre; November 1–13, 2005

Mademoiselle Modiste by Victor Herbert; 45th Street Theatre; March 21–April 2, 2006

Oh Lady! Lady! by Jerome Kern, P.G. Wodehouse, and Guy Bolton; Director and Choreography, Thomas Mills; Music Director, Rick Hip-Flores; **Cast:** Amy Bils, Christopher Corts, Elizabeth DeRosa, Maxime Alvarez de Toledo, Katherine Harber, Genevieve Koch, John O'Creagh, Megan Opalinski, Robyne Parrish, Trip Plymale, George Psomas, Roger Rifkin, Marc Schaeffer, Eyal Sherf, Jennifer Winegardner; 45th Street Theatre; April 25–May 7, 2006

Let's Face It by Cole Porter, Dorothy and Herbert Fields; Director, Thomas Mills; Music Director, James Stenborg; **Cast:** Amy Barker, David M. Beris, Steve Brady, Ari Butler, Roseanne Colosi, Donna Coney Island, Ben Franklin, Amy Griffin, Hannah Knowlton, Erik McEwen, Rachel Alexa Norman, Tripp Pettigrew, Sandie Rosa, Sam Sagenkahn, Jessica Scholl, Blake Whyte; 45th Street Theatre; May 9–21, 2006

NAKED ANGELS

Jenny Gersten, Artistic Director

The Mag-7: Seven Short Plays from Naked Angels' Writers Group Scenery, Faye Armon; Costumes, Daphne Javitch; Lighting, Benjamin C. Tevelow; Sound, Brittany O'Neill; Production Stage Manager, Rhonda Picou; Scenic Painter, John Bonafede; Producer, Patricia McGuire; The Flea, February 16–March 12, 2006. Plays included: *Waning Poetic* by Chip Dunnigan; Director, Jonathan Bernstein; **Cast:** Bill Cwikowski (Poet), with an appearance by Erik Jensen; *Orange Alert* by John Kim; Director, Kerry Whigham; **Cast:** Kelly Hutchinson (Molly), Sam Breslin Wright (George); *Waiting* by Heather by Lynn MacDonald; Director, Julia Gibson; **Cast:** Erin McMonagle (Jen), Eric Miller (Dan), Tom Riis Farrell (Phil); A *Twist So Shocking You Have To See It To Believe It* by Hugh Murtagh; Director, Dave Dalton; **Cast:** Michael Crane (Telly), Abbie Kileen (Miranda); *Penicillin* by Deirdre O'Connor; Director, Dave Dalton; **Cast:** Nancy McNulty (Jen), James McMenamin (John); *The Handlers* by Louis Cancelmi; Director, Glynis Rigsby; **Cast:** Bill Cwikowski (Stan), Tim Cummings (Dale); *Untitled Short Play* by Itamar Moses; Director, Michelle Tattenbaum; **Cast:** Michael Crane (Man), Erin McMonagle (Woman), Gideon Banner (Reader)

READINGS AND WORKSHOPS

His Girl Friday, adapted by John Guare, from "The Front Page" by Ben Hecht and Charles MacArthur and the Columbia Pictures Film; Director, Christopher Ashley; The Mahaiwe Performing Arts Center; October 8, 2005

The Gospel According to Adam An Angels in Progress New Play Workshop by Geoffrey Nauffts; Director, Sheryl Kaller; The Studio Theater on Theater Row; January 16–17, 2006

NATIONAL ASIAN-AMERICAN THEATRE COMPANY (NAATCO)

Jennifer Wah, President; Mia Katigbak, Founder/Vice-President

Cowboy v. Samurai by Michael Golamco, adapted from Rostrand's *Cyrano de Bergerac*; Director, Lloyd Suh; Scenery, Sarah Lambert; Lights, Stephen Petrilli; Costumes, Elly van Horne; **Cast:** Timothy Davis, Joel de la Fuente, C.S. Lee, Hana Moon; Rattlestick Playwrights Theatre at 224 Waverly; November 8–27, 2005

THE NEW GROUP (NAKED)

Scott Elliott, Artistic Director; Geoffrey Rich, Executive Director

A Spalding Gray Matter Written and performed by Michael Brandt; Director, Ian Morgan; Clurman Theatre; May 3–May 27, 2006

Jayson with a Y by Darci Picoult; Director, Sheryl Kaller; **Cast:** Kevin Geer, Marin Hinkle, Daniel Oreskes, Maryann Plunkett, Miles Purinton, Alysia Reiner; Lion Theatre; June 1–24, 2006

NEW YORK ARTISTS UNLIMITED

Melba LaRose, Artistic Director

Bad Play Festival Director, Melba LaRose; Downeast Arts Center; August 10–27, 2005; Included: **Bad Plays, Good Times** featuring *Safecracking* by Chuck Spoler, *Blood Astounds Me* by Don Chan Mark, *Expletives Deleted* by Crystal D. Langley; **Foreign Bodies & Sexual Furniture** featuring *Space Sluts Are Hotties* by Jay Boyer, *A Friendly Fiasco* by Frederick Timm, *Screwing Rachel* by Desi Moreno-Penson; **So Bad, It's Good** featuring *die gefahrliche Dunkelheit* (The Dangerous Dark) by Mark Ginocchio, *Film Noix* by Ed Malin, *The Hotter Crucible* by Con Chapman, *Punchlines* by Bob Ost, *The Unblackening of the Black Heart of King David, Who Had a Black Heart* by Steven Pinto

A Jingle From St. Nick Written and directed by Melba LaRose; Music, Michele Carlo; **Cast:** Megan McCoy, Frances Eldred, Briana Packen, Michael Smith-Rivera, Brendan Rothman-Hicks, Goldie Zwiebel, and Patrick Egan; December 17–24, 2005

World's First Bad Musicals Festival Three evenings of bad musicals; Downeast Arts Center; April 20–May 14, 2006; Included: **Something to Offend Everyone**: *Tamponville* by CJ Critt & Ralph Cole, Jr., directed by Hans Friedrichs; *My Mouse is Not a Rat* By Don Chan Mark, directed by Melba LaRose; *Best Little Crackhouse in Philly (or…Crackwhore…the Musical!)* by Stan Peal, directed by Melba LaRose; **Out of this World:** *We Met the Space People* by Con Chapman; *Virgo Ascending* by Fran Handman, directed by Robert W. McMaster; *Finding the Wonder* by Gwynne Watkins, lyrics Betina Hershey, music Denver Casado, directed by Nick Fondulis; *Love.com* by Chris Widney, music David Christian Azarow; **It Ain't Kansas Anymore:** *Desiree of Beverly Hills* by Peter Morris, music Mat Eisenstein, directed by Rob Cardazone; *The*

Beautiful Brown Danube by Charles Lupia, music Johann Strauss, Jr., directed by Shana Soloman; *The Sound of Wizards* by K. Knapp (from Canada), directed by Jack Dyville; **Sex, Thugs, and Rock 'n Roll: *Music is my Fist*** (an Audience with the Pope of Pop, Nicholas Albert Sobella) by Bill Squier, Scott Blakeman, Robert Taub, music Jerold Goldstein, directed by Michael Shiffer; *The Devil's Music: The True History of Rock N' Roll* (A CAUTIONARY TALE) by Brock Mahan & Elliott Kalan, music by Keith Burgun, directed by Gustavo Alonso

NEW YORK INTERNATIONAL FRINGE FESTIVAL

Elena K. Holy, Producing Artistic Director

Ninth Annual; August 12–28, 2005; Performances at Access Theater, Ace of Clubs, Collective: Unconscious, Connelly Theater, Dixon Place, Flea Theater, FringeCENTRAL 125 W 3rd, Linhart Theater at 440 Studios, Lucille Lortel Theatre, Mazer Theater, P.S. 122, Players Theatre, SoHo Playhouse, Theater at the Center for Architecture, 13th Street Repertory Company, Village Theatre

A Certain Level of Commitment (an actor prepares) Written, directed and performed by Brandon Wolcott; Producer, First Person Productions

A Different Woman: A True Story of a Texas Childhood by Veronica Rulssell, adapted from *My First Thirty Years* by Gertrude Beasley; Director, Perry Martin; Producer, Texpatriate Productions

A Family of Women Written and directed by Karlton Parris; Producer, Skint Productions

A Lesbian in the Pantry Book, music, lyrics by Joe Latessa, Director, Spike Kunetz, Music Director, Jeff Bouthiette; Producer, Fashionatrix in Association with Cabinet Theatre

A Play with Myself Written and performed by Marina Lutz; Director, David G. Armstrong; Music, Mick Harvey; Producer, Coraggio Productions

A.F.R.A.I.D (as Reported by Fanny Fern) Adapted, music, lyrics by Susan Stoderl based on text by Fanny Fern; Lyrics, Director, Charmaine Chester; Music Director, Mary Bopp; Producer, Susan Stoderl Music

Amerika adapted by Alex Poe from Kafka's novel; Directors, Alex Poe and Joe Varca; Producer, Redux Theatre Company

Anaerobic Respiration by Krista Knight; Director, Alex Torra; Producer, The Shifting Company

Animal Farm Project 1 — Version White: Funny Pigs Adapted from Orwell's text and directed by Park, Kwang Tae; Producer, Theater Sang Sang

Aquarium by Robin Maguire; Director, Tim Redmond; Producer, Left Eye Productions

Arias for the Mundane Written and performed by James Junio; Director, Melanie T. Morgan; Proudcer, (Parenthetically Speaking Productions)

As Much As You Can by Paul Oakley Stovall; Director, Krissy Vanderwarker; Producer, Dog & Pony Theatre Company

Basura! Created and directed by Colette Searls of Searls Puppetry; Choreography, Carol Hess

Beautiful Words by Michael Arquilla, music by Stephen Barnett; Director, Al Sgro; Producer, JEM Productions

Beyond Book by Helga Krauss, music, direction, and translation by Danny Ashkenasi; Producer, Fredrick Byers Productions

Big, Black & Under the Bed by Kimberly Rosenstock; Director, Antonia Grilikhes-Laskey; Producer, A Valentine From The Dogs

Billionaires For Bush — The Musical Book by Marc Brodsky, music and lyrics by Clifford J. Tasner; Director, Mahayana Landowne; Choreography, DJ McDonald; Producer, Huzzah! Productions

Bridezilla Strikes Back! Written and performed by Cynthia Silver, co-written by Kenny Finkle; Director, Paul Urcioli; Producer, Pink Lemonade Productions

Bronx Express by Osip Dymov, translated by Nahma Sandrow, lyrics by Glen Berger and Joseph Goodrich, music by Jonathan David, conceived and directed by Miriam Weiner; Choreography, Darren Lee; Producer, The Bornx Express Company

By Oscar Micheaux by Cheryl L. Davis; Director, Chuck Patterson; Producer, Parker Entertainment and Hinton Battle Laboratory

Byuioo by Nate Weida; Director, Jimmy Kilduff; Producer, Commander Squish Productions

Byzantium: A New Musical Music by Steven Jamail, lyrics by Troy Scheid, book by John Kaiser; Director, Cailín Heffernan; Music Director, Steven Jamail; Producer, Theatre Collinde

Cemetery of Lips Written and produced by Nancy Ancowitz; Director, Barbara Rubin; featuring Jaye Austin Williams

Channel Rat Written and performed by Tara Clancy; Director, Kel O'Neill; Producer, The East Queens Trading Company

Confessions of a Dope Dealer Written, produced and performed by Sheldon Norberg; Director, Bill Allard

Crossing Currents Written and directed by Jorge C. Perez; Producer, 2 Tilt at Windmills Productions

Dance With Me, Harker Written and directed by Eileen Connolly; Chreography, Richard Omar and Eileen Connolly; Producer, Wallis Knot Inc.

Dark Deceptions: The Séance Experience Written, directed, produced and performed by Todd Robbins

Dependent Study Written, directed and produced by Andrew Schneider; Co-produced by big|picture|group

Dykapalooza Written, directed, produced and performed by Jeanie Antonlini; Music, Ruth Wyand

Edna St. Vincent Millay Speaks to the Committee on Immortality Written and performed by Jennifer Gibbs; Producer, Firt Fig Productions

Electra Votes by Sheila Morgan; Producer, Blunt Theater Company

Elements of Style by Wend Weiner; Producer, Give Me Shelter Productions

Extra Virgin by Howard Walters; Director, Michael Melamedoff; Producer, Extra Virgin Productions

Extraordinary Book, lyrics, and direction by Dante Russo, music by David F.M. Vaughn; Choreography, Lindsay Rogan; Producer, Ruso Famiglia in association with Vital Theatre Company

Faker Book and lyrics by Karen Weinberg, co-composed by Karen Weinberg and Jonathan Wagner; Director, Norm Holly; Choreography, Scott Ferguson; Producer, Bully Productions

Feud: Fire on the Mountain Written and directed by Creighton James; Producer, New York Theatre Experiment

Film Noix by Ed Malin; Director, John DeBenedetto; Producer, Temerity Theatre

Finger Love Written and directed by Anna Sobel; Producer, Talking Hands Theatre

Fleet Week: The Musical Music by Sean Williams, book by Mac Rogers, lyrics by Jordana Williams; Director, Eric Pilner; Producer, Gideon Productions and Lindsay Brown

Fluffy Bunnies in a Field of Daisies Written and directed by Matt Chaffee; Choreography, Sangini Majmadar; Producer, The Subtle Bliss Theater Company

Frida and Herself Created by Brandy Leary and Prashant Gupta; Director and choreography, Brandy Leary; Producer, Anadam

Fucking Ibsen Takes Time by Erick Herrscher; Director, Benjamin Mosse; Producer, carbs & dairy

Genius Famous Book, music, and lyrics Jason Atkinson; Director, Ryan J. Davis; Staging, Seth Sikes; Producers, Neil and Richelle Trivedi, spurn producions

Gift by Mark Schultz; Director, Daniel Talbott; Producer, Rising Phoenix Repertory

God's Waiting Room by Ashlin Halfnight; Director, Alexis Poledouris; Producer, Performance Lab 115

Go-Go Kitty, Go Written and performed by Greg Jackson and Erin Quinn Purcell; Director, Samuel Buggein; Producer, Theatre B

Good Fences Make Good Neighbors by Adam Klasfield; Director, Sherri Kronfeld; Producer, Amphibian Productions

Good Luck With It Written, directed, and produced by Will Franken

Grandmotherfucker & the Seducers by Desiree Burch, Pat Candaras, Michael Cyril Creighton, Jack Kukoda; Director, Rusty Owen; Producer, Anonymous Allies

Half Life by Robert Moulthrop; Producer, The Seeking an Extended Run Company

Help! Created, directed and performed by Ariel de Man, Adam Fristoe, Maia Knispel, Justin Welborn, Steve Yockey; Producer, Out of Hand Theater

Hercules in High Suburbia Written and directed by Mary Fulham, music, lyrics, and musical direction by Paul Foglino; Producer, Watson Arts

Hit By Shanon Weaver; Director, Melissa Livingston; Producer, a chick & a dude productions

Icarus Created and directed by Nina Hein; collaboration with Elyssa Dole, Jonette Ford, music by Katharina Rossenberger

It's Phuc Tap! Written and produced by Eileen Fogarty; Directors, Jean Collins and Christine Schoenwald

Jesus in Montana: Adventures in Doomsday Cult Written and performed by Barry Smith; Director, Lynn Aliya; Producer, Aspen Stage

Johnny Got His Gun by Dalton Trumbo; Director, Gerritt Turner; Producer, Sleepless Theatre Company

Jigsaw Nation by Marjorie Louis, Malachy Walsh, Gary Winter; Director, Hayley Finn; Producer, The Relentless Theatre Company

Lady Convoy by Ken Gallo; Director, Robert Ross Parker; Producer BRATPak Productions

Legend of the Gypsy Bride Book and lyrics by David Jenness, music and dances by Gypsies of Transylvania; Director, Koby Benevenesti; Choreography, Ken Roberson, Andrea Kalan Chemda

Letter From Poland by Michael Wrynn Doyle; Director, Peter Schmitz; Producer, Altfel Spus Productions

Little House on the Parody by Becky Eldridge and Amy Petersen, music, lyrics, and direction by Andy Eninger; Choreography, Erica Reid

LOL by Tony Sportiello; Director, Jerry Less; Producer, Algonquin Productions

Love is in the Air by Dustin Helmer; Producer, Pig Brooch, Inc

Love Sick by Gabriel McKinley; Director, Marc Fratello; Producer, Shoot First Theatre

Lynndie England Followed No Space Written and directed by David G. Tretiakoff, Charlotte Schioler; Producer, Compagnie de L'entorse

Magician by Katherine Knowles; Director, Todd Lundquist; Producer, The RCB

Manatee by Alex Moggridege; Director, Patrick McNulty; Producer, SeaCow Productions

Marlowe by Harlan Didrickson; Director, David Zak; Choreography, Erik Pearson; Producer, Balliwick Repertory Theatre of Chicago

Match Me by Aurin Squire, concept by Niketa Calame and Kerry-Jayne Wilson; Director, Denyse Owens; Producer, Under the Skin

Movie Geek Written and co-conceived by Dylan Dawson; directed and co-conceived by Andy Donald; Producer, The Charlie B. Theater Company

Muriel Vanderbilt Goes Walking Written and directed by Dan Shanahan, with music by Paul Kozlowski; Producer, Torn Space Theater

My Father's Son by Jennnie Contuzzi; Director, Adam R. Perlman; Producer, Not a Toaster Productions

My Pony's in the Garage by Eileen Kelly; Director, Kimmy Gatewood; Producer, Stichie Productions

No Return by Carolyn Connelly, Heather Daniels, Laura Reyna; Directors, Rosaleen Knoepfel, Linsey Bostwick

Not Dead Yet by Aaron Samson; Director, Paul Nicolai Stein; Producer, The Next Arena

Out of Body and Out of Mind by Matt Yeager; Director, Alexa Polmer; Producer, Lucid Theater

Patty Cake Written and directed by Ken Prestininzi; Producer, Identity Crisis Productions

Payment by Donna Fiumano; Director, Amber Estes

Pierrot Le Quin by Sylvia Manning, based on a story by Guy de Muapassant; Producer, Me, You, and Eli Productions in association with The Waterfront Ensemble

Pipe Dreams by Mickey and Nicole Blaine; Director, Mickey Blaine; Producer, 717 Productions

Places Like Here Written and directed by Robert Attenweiler; Producer, Disgraced Productions

Ponzi Man by Gary Morgenstein; Producer, Women Seeking . . . a theatre company

Pride and Soul Written and performed by Stephanie Marshall and Keith Wild Child Middleton; Director, Allison Easter; Producer, Black 33 Productions

Professor Dilexi Presents Dramatis Personae of the Apocryphal Menagerie Written and directed by Rebecca Fullan; Producer, Uncut Pages Theater Company

Ratface by j. Snodgrass; Director, Adrienne Willis; Producer, Wall Street Productions

Ricardo Jamon: Mastermentalist—The Heavy Metal Tour by Ricardo C. Jamon; Producer, TAP

Rock Out by Gregory Jones; Producer, The Tickly Cheeks Group

Roller Skates and Mary Jane by Caroline Liadakis; Director, Ted Anderson; Producer, Wabi Productions in association with Corky Productions

Sandy Takes a Break by Christopher Lee and Ben Seeder; Director, Ed Illades; Producer, The Leeder Company

Screwball by Douglas McFerran; Director, Aaron Mullen; Producer, Tony Lepore

Seduction by Jack Heifner; Director, Peter Bull; Producer, Shamelessboyz Theatre Company

Sex with Jake Gyllenhaal and Other Fables of the Northeast Corridor by Anthony Giunta; Director, Mark Harborth; Producer, toyboy

Shakedown Street Book by Michael Norman Mann, music and lyrics by Jerry Garcia and Robert Hunter; Director, Jeff Griffin; Musical Director, George Croom; Choreography, Christine O'Grady; Producer, A2E Musicals

She Wears a Peacock Crown Adapted by Taniya Sen and Sakti Sengupta from stories by Rabindranath Tagore and Mahasweta Devi; Director, Sakti Sengupta; Producer, Epic Actors' Workshop and Choir

Shutter Created and produced by LightBox; Director, Ellen Beckerman

Silence! The Musical Music and lyrics by Jon and Al Kaplan; book adapted by Hunter Bell form the screenplay *Silence of the Lambs;* Director and Choreograpy, Christopher Gattelli; Music Director, Brian J. Nash; Producer, Tesseract Theatre, John Pinckard, Brian J. Nash, Mark Hartman

Sitchaassadown Written and directed by Kanene Holder; Producer, Urbintel/QBR

Slow Children Playing Written, directed, produced, performed and choreographed by Anna Marie Agniel

Soirée Dada: Neue Weltaffen Based on a concept by Joe Janes and Joel Jeske; Director, Don Hall; Producer, WNEP Theater

Some Unfortunate Hour by Kelly McAllister; Director, Christopher Grabowski; Producer, hope theatre, inc

Supposedly Written and directed by Barbara Cassidy; Producer, Wax Lips

Surviving David by Kathryn Graf; Director, Tony Sears; Producer, Whacky World Productions

SUV: The Musical! by Gersh Kuntzman and Marc Dinkin; Director, Eric Oleson; Producer, Neo-Shtick Theater

Swimming Upstream: A Sex-Ed Escapade of Genetic Proportions Music and book by Marshall Pailet, lyrics and book by Al Pailet; Director and Choreographer, Marlo Hunter; Music Supervisor, Ben Cohn

System Eternal by Chance D. Muehleck; Director, Melanie S. Armer; Producer, LIVE Theater Company

Tarot Reading: Love, Sex, and Mommy Produced and written by Kimberlee Auerbach; Director, Eric Davis

The Comedy of Terrors by Larry Brenner; Director, Jay Michaels; Producer, Genesis Repertory

The Consolation of Poetry (Becoming Elizabeth Barrett Browning) Researched, written and directed by Barbara Neri; Producer, Khoros, Inc

The Crazy Locomotive by Stanislaw I Witkiewicz; Director, Beata Pilch; Producer, Trap Door Theatre

The Cross by Toby Wherry; Director, Laura Strausfled; Producer, Pom Pom Productions

The Day the World Went Queer! Book by Jonathan Matthew Gilbert, music by Lavell V. Blackwell, lyrics by Joshua H. Cohen; Producer, Moral Decay, Inc

The Dirty Talk by Michael Puzzo; Director, Padraic Lillis; Producer, Escapist Productions

The Eisteddfod by Lally Katz; Director, Chris Kohn; Producer, Stuck Pigs Squealing

The Friar and the Nurse by Stan Peal; Director, Lon Baumgarner; Producer, Epic Arts Repertory Theatre

The Great God Money Written and directed by Emily Davis; Producer, Messenger Theatre Company

The Great Official Subway Musical Written and produced by Victor Verhaeghe; Director, Robert Petkoff

The Greatest B-Movie Ever Told by Todd Michael; Director, Neal Sims; Producer, Peter Steinman

The Importance of Marrying Wells by Dana Slamp; Director, Nancy S. Chu; Producer, DRD Productions

The Information She Carried by David L. Williams; Director, Ann Carroll; Producer, W&W Productions

The Irish Curse by Martin Casella; Director, Matt Lenz; Producer, Side Of The Road Entertainment

The Kimono Loosened by Yuki Kawahisa; Director, Maureen Robinson; Producer, Atelier Tsukiko

The Last Black Cowboy Written, produced, and directed by Jimonn Cole

The Last Castrato by Andy Eninger; Director, Brad McEntire; Producer, Audacity Productions

The Last Days of Cleopatra Music and lyrics by Charlie Barnett, book by Charlie Barnett and John Morogiello; Director, Christopher Gerken; Choreography, Daniel Haley; Producer, Light! Camera! Love…

The Last Silver Zephyer by Bill Svanoe; Director, Blake Bradford; Producer, Zephyer Productions

The Lightning Field by David Ozanich; Director, Jared Coseglia; Producer, BANNER, NY

The Lives of Young Black Folk: Young Sistas & Bang! Bang! Bang! by Lorna Littleway; Directors, Sue Lawless and Lorna Littleway; Producer, Juneteenth Legacy Theatre

The Lizards by Alan Bowne; Director, Damon W. Arrington; Producer, Exposed Brick Productions

The Magnificent Hour by Jamil Ellis, Anne Johnson, Gene Perelson, Chris Chan Roberson; Producer, Experimental Troupe Comedy

The Mayor Who Would Be Sondheim by John Doble; Producer, B. Dash Productions

The Metaphysics of Breakfast Written and directed by Eli Clark; Producer, The Crowded Muffin

The Miss Education of Jenna Bush Written and created by Melissa Rauch and Winston Beigel; Co-created and directed by Tom Wojtunik; Producer, Lucky Dawg Productions

The Monster Under My Bed Drank My Vodka by Lisa David Dean; Director, Anthony Rich; Producer, Puddytat Productions

The New Bohemia by Patrick Bonomo and Shelly Watson; Director, Dennis Hinson; Choreography, Julie Atlas Muz; Producer, Epicurean Productions

The Philomel Project: A Barbarous Pleasure Conceived and directed by Sonnet Blanton and Julia M. Smith; Producer, Refraction Arts Project

The Redemption Written and directed by Sudipta Bhawmik; Procucer, Ethnomedia LLC

The Rude Pundit in the Year of Living Rudely by Lee Papa; Director, Mark H. Creter; Producer, The Rude Pundit

The Salacious Uncle Baldrick by Sean Kent nad Kenan Minkoff; Producer, The Salacious Company

The Silent Concerto by Alejandro Morales; Director, Scott Ebersold; Producer, Packawallop Productions

The Social Affair Created and presented by Comedy Social LLC

The Suffrajets Present a Musical Séance Created by Stephanie Gill, Laurie Norton and Dia Shepardson; Music, Tom Bartos; Director, Dia Shepardson; Producer, Woodhull & Claflin Co.

The Three of Clubs Written, directed, and choreographed by Gila Sand; Co-choreography, Jen Slaw

The True Tragedy of the Mortician by Daniel Diamond; Director, Jason Alan Carvell; Producer, Odyssesy Productions

The Typist's Nightmare by J. Snodgrass; Director, Greg Allen; Producer, Cityworks Theater Company

The Velocity of Things Written, directed, choreographed, and produced by Regina Jejman

Thick by Rick Bland; Director, Mark Bruce; Producer, Blandino Productions and Downstairs Cabaret Theatre

This Isn't Working by Francesco Marciuliano; Director, Jefferson Jowdy; Producer, Rule of 3

Three Ring Circus: Israel, the Palestinians and My Jewish Identity by Daniel Thau-Eleff and Chris Gerrard-Pinker; Director, Chris Gerrard-Pinker; Producer, Moving Target Theatre Company

Toby by Anthony P. Pennino; Director, Don Jordan; Producer, Pilot House, The Theater Company

Tolyo Nostalgia Presented by Theatre Arts Japan; Director, Eriko Ogawa

Trash Company: Immanent Eye Productions by David M. White; Director, Eric Love

Travis Tanner Libretto by Melanie N. Lee, music by Robert Stephens; Director, DJ McDonald; Producer, Patiotic Jesters Productions

Treaty 321! A Musical Book and lyrics by Christopher Buckley, music by Steve Murphy and Lenny; Director, Sam Scalamoni; Choreography, Jennifer DiMinni; Producer, Jon Loves Suzie Productions

Uncle Sam's Satiric Spectacular: On Democracy and Other Fictions, Featuring Patriotism Acts and Blue Songs From a Red State by Greg Allen, Sheila Callaghan, Bridget Carpenter, Eric Coble, Richard Dressler, Hilly Hicks Jr; Songs, Michael Friedman; Director, Wendy McClellan; Producer, The 2005 Apprentice Company from Actors Theatre of Louisville

Unexceptional Tricks Created and directed by Max rada dada; Producer, rada dada Sideshow

Unholy Secrets of the Theremin Conceived, written and directed by Kip Rosser and Jef Anderson

Unspeakable: Richard Pryor Live & Uncensored, A Dramatic Fantasia by Rod Galiles OBC, James Murray Jackson Jr; Director, Rod Gailes OBC; Producer, Peoria Stroker, LLC

Vicarious Written and directed by Justin Quinn Pelegano; Producer, Bosley Productions

Wade Written, directed and produced by Steve Barney

Warfield, USA: The Musical Written and produced by Jazz Hands Across America; Director, Michael Descoteaux

Weddings of Mass Destruction Created and Produced by GayCo Productions, additional material by Matt Elwell and Mary Beth Burns; Director, Jim Zulevic; Musical Director, Stephanie McCullough; Choreography, Elizabeth Lentz

Weight by Melanie Hoopes; Director, Jamie Sherman; Producer, Magnet Theater

Widow of Abraham by David Valdes Greenwood; Director, Jennifer O'Donnell; Producer, Wilde Stage

Word Infirmia: The Criminal Perspectives Project Developed and performed by Perri Ynaiv; Director, Glynis Rigsby; Producer, The Black Cat Group

Yes, We have No Bananas! Written and directed by Charlotte Schiøler; Assistant directors, Marianne Ilum Sørensen and David Tretiakoff; Producer, Tarzan's Wife

You Again, A Musical About Cloning Book, lyrics and direction by Bill Gullo; music and musical direction by Rob Wagner; Producer, thirty hunting films

You Mutha! A One-Mother Show by Jennie Fahn with music by Daryl Archibald, lyrics by Jennie Fahn; Director and choreography, Larry Sousa; Producer, Fahn Field

You Wanna Piece of Me? Written and performed by Joe Hernandez-Kolski; Director, Benjamin Byron Davis; Producer, Venice Theatre Works

NEW YORK CLASSICAL THEATRE

Stephen Burdman, Artistic Director

As You Like It by William Shakespeare; Director, Stephen Burdman; Design, Lora LaVon; Vocal Coach, Barbara Adrian; Associate Producer/Fight Director, Jen Nelson; Stage Manager, Jennifer Russo; Publicity, Laurie Sheppard; **Cast:** Adam Devine, Bob Armstrong, Christine Albright, Corey Behnke, Dustin Sullivan, Hunter Gallagher, Jenn Schulte, Jennifer Tober, Joshua Decker, Michael Marion, Taylore Mahogany Scott, Torsten Hillhouse; Central Park; June 2 – 26, 2005

Scapin by Moliere; Director, Stephen Burdman; Design, Amelia Dombrowski; Voice Coach, Barbara Adrian; Stage Manager, Jennifer Russo; Publicist, Laurie Sheppard; **Cast:** Alexis Hyatt, Birgit Huppuch, Erik Gratton, Grant Neale, Johnny Sparks, Michael Marion, Paco Lozano, Taylore Mahogany Scott, William Greville; Central Park; August 4 – 28, 2005

NEW YORK MUSICAL THEATRE FESTIVAL (NYMF)

Kris Stewart, Founder and Executive Director; Isaac Robert Hurwitz, Producing Director; Geoff Cohen, Executive Producer

Second Annual; September 12 – October 2, 2005; Performances at Makor, 59E59 Theatre B, BMI, Neighborhood Playhouse, York Theatre, Donnell Library, Museum of Television and Radio, Snapple Theatre Center, Theatre at St. Clements, 45th Street Theatre, New Dramatists, Birdland, Beckett Theatre-Lion Theatre-Studio Theatre on Theatre Row, The Barrow Group Theatre, Where Eagles Dare Theatre, The Duplex, CUNY Graduate Center, Upright Citizen's Brigade Theatre, The Marquee, Virgin Megastore Union Square

NEXT LINK PRODUCTIONS

The Banger's Flopera by Kirk Wood Bromley and John Gideon; Director, Ben Yalom

But I'm a Cheerleader by Andy Abrams and Bill Augustin; Director, Daniel Goldstein

Don Imbroglio by Matt Boresi and Peter Hillard; Director, Jenny Lord

Isabelle and the Pretty-Ugly Spell by Steven Fisher and Joan Ross Sorkin; Director, David G. Armstrong

It Came From Beyond by Cornell Christianson, Stephen M. Schwartz, and Norman Thalheimer; Director, Jeff Calhoun

The Mistress Cycle by Beth Blatt and Jenny Giering; Director, Joe Calarco

Monica! The Musical by Adam Blau, Daniel J. Blau, and Tracie Ptochnik; Director, Casey Hushion

No Boundaries by Liz Oliver, Sam Brisbee, Pamela Laws, Laura Love, Marcus Miller, Speech, The Spooks; Director, Liz Oliver

Orphan Train by L.E. McCullough, Michael Barry Greer, and Doug Katsaros; Director, Pat Birch

Plane Crazy by Suzy Conn; Director, Jamibeth Margolis

The Shaggs: Philosophy of the World by Joy Gregory and Gunnar Madsen; Director, John Langs

Tom Jones by Paul Leigh and George Stiles, with Daniel D. Brambilla, Vera Guerin, John Doyle; Director, Gabriel Barre

Uncle Jed's Barbershop by Kenneth Grimes and David Wohl; Director, Susan Einhorn

The Unknown by Janet Allard, Jean Randich, and Shane Rettig; Director, Jean Randich

Wild Women of Planet Wongo by Steve Mackes, Dave Ogrin, and Ben Budick; Director, Doug Moser

Yank! by David and Joseph Zellnik; Director, Igor Goldin

You Might As Well Live by Norman Mathews based on the writings of Dorothy Parker; Director, Guy Stroman

INVITED PRODUCTIONS

The Ballad of Bonnie and Clyde by Michael Aman, Oscar E. Moore, and Dana P. Rowe; Director, Michael Bush

The Big Time by Douglas Carter Beane and Douglas J. Cohen; Director, Christopher Ashley

Feeling Electric byBrian Yorkey and Tom Kitt; Director, Peter Askin

Nerds:// A Musical Software Satire by Jordan Allen-Dutton, Erik Weiner, and Hal Goldberg; Director, Andy Goldberg

People Like Us by Todd Almond and Gus Kaikkonen; Director, Gus Kaikkonen

Reluctant Pilgrim by Stephen Schwartz; conceived and directed by Jamie McGonnigal

Richard Cory by Ed Dixon, adapted from a play by A.R. Gurney; Director, James Brennan

Rooms by Paul Scott Goodman and Miriam Gordon; Director, Scott Schwartz

Serenade the World by Oscar Brown, Jr. and Genovis Albright

Six Women With Brain Death by Mark Houston, Cheryl Benge, Christy Brandt, Rosanna E. Coppedge, Valerie Fagan, Ross Freese, Sandee Johnson, and Peggy Pharr Wilson; Director, Marcia Milgrom Dodge

Soon of a Mornin' by Andrea Frierson-Toney; Director, Gerry McIntyre

The View From Here by Timothy Huang and Elizabeth Lucas; Director, Elizabeth Lucas

NYMF-UCBT MUSICAL/COMEDY SERIES

Project Footlight developed by NYMF and Upright Citizens Brigage Theatre; **Dances With Pitchforks** written and performed by John Flynn; **Listen, Kid** by Peter Gwinn and Stpehanie McCullough; **Guttenberg! The Musical!** Written and performed by Scott Brown and Anthony King; **Baby Wants Candy** an improvised musical; **I Eat Pandas & Friends** an improvised musical; **The Pearl Brunswick** an all female musical improvisation

SPECIAL EVENTS

06880 the Musical by Lawrence Rosen; **Camille** (Broadway USA! production) by Julia Gregory and Renato R. Birbin, Jr.; **Dorian Gray** (Broadway USA! production) by Charles Chilton, Joan Littlewood, and Theatre Workshop, Inc. **Drift**

by Jeremy Schonfeld and Craig Pospisil; **Fairies** by Thomas Gustafson and Cory Krueckeberg, and Jessica Fogle, based on William Shakespeare's lyrics

READINGS AND PRESENTATIONS

Bump in the Road by Carole Lonner and Brenda Earle; **The Big Ending & The Big Beginning** by Peter Shrubshall, Richard Free, Scott Guy, and Ross Kalling; **Campaign of the Century** by Robert L. Freedman and Steven Lutvak; **Jubillee** by Mark Smollin and Kelly Dupuis; **Liberty Smith** by Michael Weiner, Adam Abraham, Marc Madnick, and Eric R. Cohen; **Oh What a Lovely War** by Joan Littlewood; **Seagull: The Musical** by Nancy Weber, Vadim Zhuk, and Alexander Zhurbin; **Sheba** by Sharleen Cooper and Gary William Friedman; **War Brides** by Ron Sproat, Christopher Berg, and Frank Evans

CONCERT SERIES

Dagmar by Jim Bauer; **Guilty Pleasures**-Broadway performers sing Rock; **Dan Lipton and David Rossmer; Whiskers on Kittens** starring John Hill; **Stephen Weiner: Songs of Love & Aggravation** featuring Michael Arden, Norm Lewis, and Evan Pappas; **BMI Songwriters Showcase; The Music of Michael Longoria; NYU Songwriters Concert**

MUSICALS IN OTHER MEDIA

Musicals on Television: **Trouble in Tahiti; The Music of Harold Arlen; Once Upon a Mattress; Sondheim at 75; Our Town, Ruggles of Red Gap**

Movie Musical Series: **Open House; Best of RIPFEST: Movie Musicals; Broadway Sing Alongs**-Mary Poppins, The Wizard of Oz, Grease

PARTNER EVENTS

The Tutor by Maryrose Wood and Andrew Gerle; **The A-Train Plays; LaPlaya; Jim Caruso's Cast Party; Lonely Rhymes** by Peter Mills and Cara Reichel; **Bingo City** by Alan Cancelino, Jenne Wason, and Lance Sticksel; **Discovered Treasures; Dixon Place "Warning: Not for Broadway" Series; Trunk Songs; Broadway Curtain Calls**

Thea McCartan and Alvaro Sena in Nicu's Spoon's production of *Stumps* by Mark Medoff

NICU'S SPOON

Stephanie Barton-Farcas, Founder and Artistic Director

The Little Prince by Rick Cummins and John Scoullar, adapted from the book by Antoine de St. Exupery; Director, Stephanie Barton-Farcas; Lights, James Bedell; Original Music, Damon Law; Costumes, Elynne Whaley; Mural Design, Ruel Wallace; ASL Interpreters, Pamela Mitchell and Gerald Small; **Cast:** Bart Mallard, Alvaro Sena, Sheena Gersberg, Erwin Falcon, Jyotsna Du Ciel, Ani Mandara, Hannah Briendel, Clarice Allee, Maria, Angela Popovic; Pelican Theatre; July 6–31, 2005; 20 performances

Stumps by Mark Medoff; Director/Scenery/Sound, Stephanie Barton-Farcas; Lighting, Steven Wolf; Stage Manager, David Vandervliet; **Cast:** Kate Breen, Darren Frazier, Tyson Jennette, Paul Savas, Thea McCartan, Jovinna Chan, Pamela Mitchell, Karam Puri, Alvaro Sena, T.J. Mannix; Pelican Theatre; October 26–November 13, 2005; 15 performances

Skin Tight by Gary Henderson; Director, Pamela Butler; Lighting, Steven Wolf; Sound, Sarah Gromko; Stage Manager, Kodi McLachlan; **Cast:** James Jacobus, Stephanie Barton-Farcas, Douglas Gowland; The Looking Glass Theatre; April 5–23, 2006; 15 performances

READINGS

Love in the Veins by Raymond Luczak; Director, Frank Datallo; **Cast:** Lewis Merkin, Anne Tomasetti, Scott Nogi, Pamela Mitchell; Pelican Theatre; Novmeber 1&8, 2005; 2 performances

Three short plays (*The Offenses of Cacti, The Common Cold, Horses for Sale and Hay*) by Matthew Swaye; Director, Brett Maugham; Pamela Mitchell and Russell Waldman; **Cast:** Douglas Gowland, Rebecca Challis, Erwin Falcon, Steven Wolf, Jim Williams; The Looking Glass Theatre; April 2006, 2 performances

ONTOLOGICAL-HYSTERIC THEATER

Richard Foreman, Founder and Artistic Director; Shannon Sindelar, Managing Director

SUMMER SERIES — 2005

Is This a Gentleman? Written and directed by Kara Feely; Sound, Travis Just; Performed by Ross Beschler and Avi Glickstein; July 27–30

That's Not How Mahler Died Presented by 31 Down Radio Theater; Created and performed by Ryan Holsopple, Lian Sifuentes, Frank Boudreaux; with DJ Mendel; August 10–13

Tea with the Twins or the End of the World Written, directed, designed and performed by Normandy Sherwood and Jenny Seastone Stern; August 10–13

Last Year in the Universe—It Came to me in a Dream Presented by Temporary Distortion; Written, directed and designed by Kenneth Collins; performed by Brian Greer and Lorraine Mattox; August 17–20

Veils/Vestiges: the aesthetics of hidden things Written, directed, and performed by Annie Kunjappy and Temple Crocker, with Daniel Nelson, Will Waghorn, Barb Lancier; August 24–27

ORIGIN THEATRE COMPANY

George C. Heslin, Artistic Director

Crestfall by Mark O Rowe; Director, George C. Heslin; Scenery, Lex Liang; Costumes, Elizabeth Flauto; Lighting, Jason Junette; Sound, Zachary Williams; Stage Manager, Carol A Sullivan; **Cast:** Fianna Toibin (Olive), Barbara J Spence (Alison Ellis), Mari Howells (Tilly); 59E59 Theatre C; October 6–23, 2005

Clocks and Whistles by Samuel Adamson; Director, Talya Klein; Scenery, Lex Liang; Costumes, Elizabeth Flauto; Lighting, Jesse Belsky; Sound, Zachary Williamson; Stage Manager, Pam Salling; **Cast:** Meghan Andrews (Anne), Jerzy Gwiazdowski (Trevor), David Mawhinney (Henry); Catherine Eaton (Caroline), Christopher Randolph (Alec); Chashama; May 9–21, 2006

READINGS AND WORKSHOPS

The Gist of It by Rodney Lee; Director, Jim Culleton; May 2006

Swansong by Conor MacDermott Roe; Director, George C Heslin; May 2006

Our Bad Magnet by Douglas Maxwell; Director, Alyse Rothman; May 2006

PAGE 73 PRODUCTIONS

Artistic Director/Managing Director Liz Jones, Asher Richelli, Nicole Fix, Daniel Shiffman

Monica, the Musical by Adam Blau (music), Dan Blau & Tracie Potochnik (book and lyrics); Presented as part of the 2005 New York Musical Theatre Festival; Director, Casey Hushion; Musical Supervision, Nadia DiGiallonardo; Music Director, W. Brent Sawyer, Set/Costumes, Seth Sklar-Heyn; Lighting, Jason Lyons; Stage Manager, Tzipora Kaplan; Line Producer, R. Erin Craig; **Cast:** Frenchie Davis (Betty Currie), Christine DiGiallonardo (Monica Lewinsky), Duke Lafoon (Bill Clinton), Megan Lawrence (Hillary Clinton), Ray McLeod (Tom Jones), Rashad Naylor (Vernon Jordan), Charlie Pollock (Ken Starr), Kristie Dale Saunders (Janet Reno), Josh Walden (George Stephanopolous).; UCB Theatre; September 21–October 2, 2005; 6 performances

James Martinez in Page 73 Productions' *Elliot, A Soldier's Fugue* by Quiara Alegria Hudes
PHOTO BY EVAN SUNG

The Unknown by Shane Rettig (music), Janet Allard & Jean Randich (book and lyrics); Presented as part of the 2005 New York Musical Theatre Festival; Director, Jean Randich; Scenery, Sue Rees; Costumes, Dan Urlie; Lighting, Joel E. Silver; Sound, Ken Travis; Stage Manager, Mary Lesnik; Choreography, Sally Dean. Line Producer, Robert Sherrill; **Cast:** Joel Garland (Malibar Absolut), Brook Sunny Moriber (Joan), Manu Narayan (Alonzo), Piter Marek (Fell), Dale Soules (The Ostracized Doctor), Steve Rattazzi (Detective); TBG Theatre; September 22–October 1, 2005; 6 performances

Elliot, A Soldier's Fugue by Quiara Alegria Hudes; Director, Davis McCallum; Scenery, Sandra Goldmark; Costumes, Chloe Chapin; Lighting, Joel Moritz; Sound, Walter Trarbach and Gabe Wood; Stage Manager, Jenn Grutza; Assistant Stage Manager, Tiffany Tillman; Music, Michael Friedman; **Cast:** Armando Riesco (Elliot), Zabryna Guevara (Ginny), Mateo Gomez (Grandpop), Triney Sandoval (Pop); 45 Bleecker Below at Culture Project; January 28–February 9, 2006; 16 performances

READINGS

This Storm Is What We Call Progress by Jason Grote; Director, Andrew Grosso; March, 2006

1001 by Jason Grote; Director, Liesl Tommy; May 2006

PHOENIX THEATRE ENSEMBLE

Craig Smith, Elise Stone, Michael Surabian, Angela Madden, Jason Crowl, Founders

Broken Journey by Glyn Maxwell; Director, Ted Altschuler; Scenery, Narelle Sissons; Costumes, Nicole Frachiseur; Lighting, Tony Mulanix; Sound, Elizabeth Rhodes; Production Stage Manager, Amy Wagner; **Cast:** Sheila O'Malley (Mrs. Millwod), Joe Rayome (Paul), Craig Smith (Troy), Elise Stone (Chloe), Michael Surabian (André); Theatre Three; November 12–December 10, 2005

Wolfpit by Glyn Maxwell; Director, Robert Hupp; **Cast:** Craig Smith, Elise Stone, Angela Madden, Jason Crowl, John Lenartz, Joe Menino, Jason O'Connell, Nicole Raphael, Margo Passalaqua, Jonathan Tindle; Theatre Three, April 7–May 6, 2006

The Complete Works of William Shakespeare (abridged) by Adam Long, Daniel Singer, and Jess Winfield; Director, Michael Surabian; Scenery, Robert Klingelhoefer; Costumes, Nicole Frachiseur; **Cast:** Brian A. Costello, Matt Neely, Scott D. Phillips; Theatre Three; April 15–May 6, 2006

PING CHONG & COMPANY

Ping Chong, Artistic Director; Bruce Allardice, Managing Director

Cathay: Three Tales of China by Ping Chong & Company and The Shaanxi Folk Art Theater; Director, Ping Chong; Assistant Director and Dramaturge, Liang Jun; Scenery, Randy Ward; Costumes, Stefani Mar; Lighting, Randy Ward; Sound, Christopher Walker; Puppet Designs, Stephen Kaplan & Wang Bo; Projections, Ruppert Bohle; Stage Manager, Claire Zawa; Produced in association with The John F. Kennedy Center for the Performing Arts and Seattle Repertory Theater; **Cast:** Performed by members of The Shaanxi Folk Art Theater & Carter Family Puppet Theater; Seattle Repertory Theatre (Seattle), The John F. Kennedy Center for the Performing Arts (Washington, DC), The New Victory Theater (New York City), Vienna Festival (Austria); Sept 10, 2005 – June 4, 2006; 64 performances

Secret History: Journeys Abroad, Journeys Within by Ping Chong and Leyla Mordirzadeh in collaboration with Talvin Wilks and Sara Zatz; Director, Ping Chong and Leyla Mordirzadeh; Lighting/Production Manager, Darren McCroom; Stage Manager, Courtney Golden; Project Manager, Sara Zatz; **Cast:** Sagno Alseny, Saul Avina, Tiffany Miller, Leyla Mordirzadeh, Dalia Ruiz-Palumbo; Clark Studio Theater, Lincoln Center For The Performing Arts; October 17 – November 6, 2005; 25 performances

PUBLIC THEATER

New Work Now! (readings) September 9 – 18, 2005; Included: *The End of It All* by Cusi Cram, Directed by Margaret Whitton; *Love Child* by Luther Goins, Directed by Billy Porter; *Life, Love and E.B.I.T.D.A.* by Anuvab Pal, Directed by John Dias; *Autobiography of a Terrorist* by Saïd Sayrafiezadeh, Directed by Anne Kauffman; *Durango* by Julia Cho, Directed by Chay Yew; *Kingdom* Music by Ian Williams, Words by Aaron Jafferis, Directed by Michael John Garcés; *Stockholm Brooklyn* Written and directed by Desmond Hall; *All We Can Handle* by Andrew Dainoff, Directed by Alex Lippard; *Paris Commune* by Steven Cosson and Michael Friedman, Directed by Steve Cosson; *The Poor Itch* by John Belluso, directed by Lisa Peterson; *Untitled* by Sunil Kuruvilla, directed by Liz Diamond; *Rants* written and performed by Eric Bogosian, Lea Delaria, Florencia Lozano, Billy Porter, Jennifer Miller, Pamela Sneed and Mike Daisey

New Work Then! (readings) September 23 – October 3, 2005; Included: *Top Girls* by Caryl Churchill; *for colored girls who have considered suicide, when the rainbow is enuf* by Ntozake Shange; *Curse of the Starving Class* by Sam Shepard

UNDER THE RADAR 2006 (INTERNATIONAL EDITION)

Shadows by William Yang (Austrailia); January 20 – 23

Rehearsal.Hamlet by Cia dos Atores (Brazil); January 19 – 23

Big 2nd Episode (show/business) by Superamas (France/Austria); January 19 – 22

Kommer by Kassys (The Netherlands); January 20 – 23

Amajuba: Like Doves We Rise by Yael Farber (South Africa); January 20 – 22

Five Streams conceived and created by Ibrahim Quraishi (South Asia); Produced by the Asia Society

My Arm by Tim Crouch (UK); January 20 – 23

The Days of the Sledgehammer Have Gone by Lone Twin (UK), January 20

The Seven by Will Power (US), directed by Jo Bonney (see Off Broadway Company Series in this volume)

The End of Reality by Richard Maxwell; presented by the NYC Players; January 12 – 28 (See Listing in Off-Off-Broadway Openings, The Kitchen, in this volume)

Major Bang Or: How I Learned to Stop Worrying and Love the Dirty Bomb Presented by Arts at St. Ann's, Produced by the Foundry Theatre (see Off Broadway Plays That Opened in this volume)

The Myth Cycle: Ahraihsak written and directed by Rubén Polendo, produced by Theater Mitu (see Off-Off-Broadway Plays That Opened, Clemente Soto Velez Cultural Center, in this volume)

The Public Sings: A 50th Anniversary Celebration January 30, 2006 at New York City Center; This one-night-only event celebrated the rich history of musicals produced by The Public Theater, including *Hair, A Chorus Line, Bring in 'Da Noise, Bring in 'Da Funk, Caroline, or Change*; Produced in association with David Binder; Director, James Lapine; Musical Director, Todd Ellison; Choreography, Baayork Lee and Jonathan Buttrell; Scenery, Beowulf Borritt; Costumes, Tom Broecker; Lighting, David Lander; Sound, Dan Moses Schreier; **Cast:** Jolly Abraham, Alicia Albright, Glenn Seven Allen, Mathias Anderson, Bridget Berger, David Bonanno, Graham Bowen, Patrick Boyd, Zach Braff, Michelle Bruckner, Betty Buckley, David Burnham, Paul Buschman, Katie Cameron, Kate Chapman, Tracy Nicole Chapman, Maurice Chestnut, Kimberly Chesser, Chuck Cooper, Zahif Corkidi, Michelle Liu Coughlin, Jared (JR) Crawford, Kayce Davis, Marshall Davis, Jr., Aisha De Haas, Lea DeLaria, Christiane DiGiallonardo, Joey Dudding, Eric Dysart, Benjamin Eakeley, Adam Elsberry, Parker Esse, Shakiem Evans, Jesse Tyler Ferguson, Ruben Flores, Lindsay Gee, Savion Glover, Jessica Goldyn, Cheyenne Gross, Elena Gutierrez, Blake Hammond, Marva Hicks, Richard J. Hinds, Dell Howlett, Mary Illes, Nadine Isenegger, Cheyenne Jackson, Joanne Javien, Capathia Jenkins, Matt Johnson, Nehal Joshi, Ramona Keller, Kurt Kelly, Logan Keslar, Raymond King, Peter King-Yuen, James Kinney, Eartha Kitt, Bryan Knowlton, Marc Kudisch, Catherine La Valle, Nicole Leach, Mark Ledbetter, Adriane Lenox, Norm Lewis, Sean Mamola, Cindy Marchionda, Ryan McCallum, Idina Menzel, Dustienne Miller, Mark Moreau, Donna Murphy, Kathryn Mowet Murphy, Maurice Murphy, Mike Nichols, Cynthia Nixon, Clifton Oliver, Rebecca K. Overton, Destan Owens, Rosie Perez, Beth Polito, Billy Porter, Natalie Portman, Shane Rhodes, Daphne Rubin-Vega, Stacey Sargeant, Kim Shriver, Ben Stiller, Amber Stone, Meryl Streep, Elaine Stritch, Dormeisha Sumbry-Edwards, Mary Testa, Gregory Treco, Rickey Tripp, Robert Tunstall, Joshua Weidenmiller, Noah Weisberg, Lillias White, Brynn Williams, George C. Wolfe

JOE'S PUB-SELECTED PERFORMANCES

Dance-mOpolitan Presented by Dancenow/NYC; June 3 – 4, 2005, March 3, 2006

John Tartaglia: AD-Liberty June 13 – July 5, 2005

Jesse Tyler Ferguson in Adios Pantalones: The Music of William Finn and Michael John LaChiusa; Director, Jason Eagan; Music Director, Vadim Feichtner; June 13 – July 4, 2005

Her Holy Water: A Black Girl's Rock Opera with Imani Uzuri; June 17, 2005

Sam Harris June 27, 2005

The Kinsey Sicks: I Wanna Be a Republican July 6, 2005

Lillias White: 21st Annual Birthday Party July 18 – 23, 2005

Bob Stillman Cabaret by Bob Stillman; August 7, 2005

Flopz Produced and directed by Jamie McGonnigal; Musical Director, Michael Lavine; performances by Shoshana Bean, Jenn Colella, Celia Keenan-Bolger, Sara Gettelfinger, Tyler Haynes, Cady Huffman, Natalie Joy Johnson, Jai Rodriguez; August 7, 2005

Penny Arcade: The Essential Penny Arcade August 24, 2005

Klea Blackhurst: Autumn in New York: Vernon Duke's Broadway August 28–29, 2005

Sara Krame Debut Cabaret; September 5, 2005

The Music of Frank Wildhorn With Frank Wildhorn, Rob Evan, Kate Shindle, Michael Lanning, Tracy Miller; September 5–19, 2005

Donna McKechnie: Here's to the Public! The Music of Joe Papp's Public Theater; October 3–24, 2005

With Love, From Broadway to the Bayou Hosted by Bryan Batt; Directed and produced by Jamie McGonnigal; Music Director, Seth Rudetsky; With: Shoshana Bean, Kerry Butler, Ann Hampton Callaway, Liz Callaway, Matt Cavenaugh, Nikki Renee Daniels, Natascia Diaz, Melissa Errico, Max von Essen, Sara Gettelfinger, Judy Gold, Danny Gurwin, Cady Huffman, Tina Maddigan, Judy McLane, Julia Murney, Kelli O'Hara, Randy Redd, Brooke Tansley, Patrick Wilson; October 23, 2005

Steven Pasquale November 7, 2005

Jackie Hoffman: Chanukah at Joe's Pub December 5, 2005–January 15, 2006

Varla Jean Merman: I'm Not Paying For This! by Jeffery Roberson with Jacques Lamarre, Director, Michael Schiralli; December 6–7, 2005

Daphne Rubin-Vega January 9, 2006

Lea DeLaria's Big Gay Comedy Show January 15, 2006

Sutton Foster: June in January January 16, 2006

Lesley Gore Cabaret; January 31–March 7, 2006

Natalie Joy Johnson Debut Cabaret; February 1, 2006

The Lights of Piazza With Aaron Lazar, Sarah Uriarte Berry, Patti Cohenour, Glenn Seven Allen, Jennifer Hughes, Joe Siravo, Laura Griffith, Katie Clarke, Catherine LaValle, David Bonanno; Music Director, Sam Davis; February 6, 2006

Euan Morton: NewClear March 30–April 3, 2006

Franc D'Ambrosio's Broadway Written and directed by Abe Reybold; Music Director, John Boswell; April 30, 2006

Become: The Music of Pasek & Paul Presented by Jamie McGonnigal; Music and lyrics by Benj Pasek and Justin Paul; May 14, 2006

PROSPECT THEATER COMPANY

Cara Reichel, Producing Artistic Director; Melissa Huber, Managing Director

The Tutor Music by Andrew Gerle, book and lyrics by Maryrose Wood; Director, Sarah Gurfield; Music Director, Ray Fellman; Choreography, Christine O'Grady; Scenery, Nick Francone; Costumes, Naomi Wolff; Lighting, Aaron J. Mason; Sound, Jeffrey Yoshi Lee; Stage Manager, Nathan Williams; **Cast:** Eric Ankrim (Edmund), Meredith Bull (Sweetie), Gayton Scott (Esther), Richard Pruitt (Richard), Rafael Fetta (Sean/Bo), Lucy Sorenson (Hildegarde/Pippi); 59E59 Theater B; September 10–October 2, 2005

Lonely Rhymes Book, music and lyrics by Peter Mills; Presented as part of the New York Musical Theatre Festival; 59E59 Theater B; September 24–27, 2005

The Book of the Dun Cow Music and lyrics by Randy Courts, book by Mark St. Germain, adapted from the novel by Walter Wangerin, Jr.; Director, Cara Reichel; Scenery, Paulo Seixas; Costumes, David Withrow; Lighting, Stacey Boggs; Sound, Sara Bader; Choreography, Jessica Hendricks; Music Director, Marcus Baker; **Cast:** Micah Bucey (Cockatrice), Alexander Elisa (Lord Russel/Wyrm), David Foley Jr. (Mundo Cani), Jacob Grigolia-Rosenbaum (Narrator), Carol Hickey (Beryl/Dun Cow), Suzanne Houston (Hen/Mouse Child/Basilisk), Amy Hutchins (Hen/Mouse Child/Five Pin/Basilisk), Jesse Kearney (Ant/Scarce), Thadd Krueger (Ant/Senex/One Pin/Basilisk), Susan Maris (Widow Mouse), Vaness June Marshall (Pertelote), Brian Munn (Chauntecleer), Jessica Ordman (Hen/Mouse Child/Ten Pin/Basilisk), Bo Ranney (Tick Tock/Nimbus), Robby Sharpe (John Wesley), David Stallings (Ant/Ebeneezer/Basilisk), Esther Triggs (Hen/Mouse Child/Basilisk); West End Theatre at Chuch of St. Paul; February 4–26, 2006

Iron Curtain Music by Stephen Weiner, lyrics by Peter Mills, book by Susan Dilallo; Director, Cara Reichel; Music Director, Daniel Feyer; Choreography, Christine O'Grady; Scenery, Nick Francone; Costumes, Sidney J. Shannon; Lighting, Stephen Arnold; Sound, Yoshi D. Lee; **Cast:** Jeff Edgerton (Murray), Marcus Neville (Howard), Gordon Stanley (Onanov), Larry Brustofski (Schmearnov), Maria Couch (Shirley), Bethe B. Austin (Hildret), Jessica Grové (Masha), Amber Dow (Olga/Ensemble), Dara Seitzman (Ticket Agent/Ensemble), Doug Shapiro (Producer/Underling/Ensemble), Brad York (Khrushchev/Cop/Ensemble), Robby Sharpe (Desk Clerk/Ensemble), David S. Miller (Super/Ensemble), Rich Silverstein (Border Guard/Ensemble); West End Theatre at Chuch of St. Paul; April 8–30, 2006

PROSEPECT'S DARK NIGHTS SERIES

Album Playwrights: Zakiyyah Alexander, Andrew Case, Michael John Garces, Rogelio Martinez, Lucy Thurber. Directors: Adam Arian, Isaac Butler, Shoni Currier, Eliza Hittman, Chris Maring; West End Theatre; February 5–11, 2006

Steve by Stephen Belber; Director, Michael Lew; **Cast:** Jason Liebman, Jackson Loo, Paco Tolson; West End Theatre; February 12–15, 2006

Last Call by Michael John Garces; Director, Dominic D'Andrea; **Cast:** Lethia Nall, Jeff Pucillo, Veronica; West End Theatre; February 18–25, 2006

DAY Eight New 10 minute plays based on one 3-hour period; featured playwrights: Kristoffer Diaz, Graeme Gillis, J. Holtham, Kyle Jarrow, Marisol Ling, Qui Nguyen, Sonya Sobieski, and Lloyd Suh; Featured directors: dam Arian, Kate Pines-Schwartz, Christopher Maring, Dylan McCullough, Andrew Rothschild, Awoye Timpo, Catherine Ward, and Kerry Whigham; West End Theatre; April 11–22, 2006

New PROSPECTives *45 Blows* written and directed by Donald Butchko; *Leap* by Morgan Allen, directed by Sarah Cameron Sunde; *The Duck Variations* by David Mamet, directed by Merete Muenter; *The Proposal* by Anton Chekhov, directed by Dev Bondarin; West End Theatre; April 15–25, 2006

PULSE ENSEMBLE THEATRE

Alexa Kelly; Artistic Director Brian Richardson, Managing Director

A Midsummer Night's Dream by William Shakespeare; Director, Alexa Kelly; Scenery, Ruben Arana Downs; Costumes, Kathryn Rohe; Lighting, Zhanna Gurvich; Sound, Louis Lopardi; Stage Manager, Russ Marisak; **Cast:** Actors:

Christine Amorosia, Alyssa Ashley, Phylicia Ashley, Shirine Babb, Cornelius Bates, Robert Bellsey, Rajesh Bose, Nicloe Bowman, Michael Gilpin, Terrence Kirkland, Steve Lloyd, Courtney Lugo, Michael Marrinaccio, Darnell Mcgee, Lawrence Merritt, Tiffany O'Bannon, Nailah Pressley, Brian Richardson, Charles Roby, Cassandra Ruiz, Andre Stanford, Sarah Zorn; Riverbank State Park; August 3–28, 2005; 16 performances

READINGS

Chaos Theory by Anuvab Pal, November 2005

QUEENS PLAYERS

Richard Mazda, Founder and Artistic Director

All the Wild Horses by Richard Mazda; Director, Rebecca A Trent; **Cast:** Billy Staples, Richard Mazda, Gary Soldati, Kate Frederic, Rick Benson, Lars Drew, Phaea Crede, Josh Rivedal, Craig D. Murphy, Ross Mason, Sara Haley, Asher Grodman, Traci Redmond, Alain LaForest, Tany Farifoot; June 21–30, 2005

Cyrano de Bergerac by Edmond Rostand; Adapted and directed by Richard Mazda; **Cast:** Rick Benson, Jeanette Bonner, Joel Bischoff, Lars Drew, Traci Redmond, Christa Savery, Deirdre Flynn, Alain LaForest, Brett Ryan, Isaac Schinazi, Mike Duff, Robert Glasser, Sabrina Head, Richard Mazda; August 31–September 17, 2005

Lysistrata: Revenging the Bush by Aristophanes, adapted by Shanara Teumba Mckeever; Director, Rebecca A. Trent; **Cast:** Amanda Beale, Rick Benson, Kate Frederic, Rob Glasser, Shanara McKeever, Melissa Menzie, John Morton, Trci Redmond, Nicky Savage, Isaac Schinazi, Erin Stegeman, Ben Turner; October 5–22, 2005

That Way Madness Lies Adapted from stories by Poe, King, Ogden, Shakespeare, and Euripides; Director, Christa Savery; **Cast:** Salvatore Brienik, Brian Lee Elder, Deirdre Flynn, Timothy Gore, Jennifer Harder, Meredyth Holmes, Savannah Mazda, Sabrina Head, Alain Laforest, Fred Urfer; Creek Theatre and La Nacional Central Espanol and Creek Theatre; October 23–30, 2005

Cinderella—An English Pantomime Written and directed by Richard Mazda; Choreography, Sara Haley; Costumes, Grace Koh; Scenery, Alexis Achilles, Grey Jewtt, Jacquelyn Poplar; **Cast:** Linda Johnson, Berda Gilmore, Jennifer Danielle, Tarek Khan, Randall Marquez, Ali Silva, Holly Vanesse, Richard Mazda, Dana DiAngelo, Savannah Mazda, Alyssa Van Gorder; December 7–18, 2005

Sextangle by Robert Leets and Jacquelyn Poplar; Director, Jacquelyn Poplar; Scenery, Alexis Achilles and Grey Jewett; Costumes, Grace Koh; Stage Managers, Savanna Mazda, Emma Wisniewski; **Cast:** John Albano, Jennifer Danielle, Rob Glasser, Alain Laforest, Brian Lukas, Max Ferguson, Richard Mazda, Ali Silva, Jennifer Vaillancourt, Alyssa Van Gorder, Holly Vanasse, Alex Shannon Wilburn, Sarah Wood; March 9–25, 2006

Return to the Grand Guignol Directors, Richard Mazda and Max Ferguson; May 4–20, 2006

RADIOTHEATRE

Dan Bianchi, Creator

The War of the Worlds by H.G. Wells; Adaptation, direction, and sound by Dan Bianchi; Music, Gary Anderson; Stage Manager, Amber Estes; Sound Operator, Graham Johnson; **Cast:** Collin Biddle, Charles Wilson, John Nolan, Keith Chandler, Adam Murphy, Rhe DeVille, Ryan Kelly, Joe Sevier; Kraine Theater; May 18–June 15, 2005

Hardboiled Text, Direction, Scenery, and Sound by Dan Bianchi; Composer, Gary Anderson; Production Manager, Brad Lane; Piano, Brian Cashwell; Bass, Jimmy Sullivan; **Cast:** Ryan Kelly, Adam Murphy, Dan Truman, Elizabeth Bianchi, John Nolan, Charles Wilson; Sarah Stephens, Rhe DeVille; Dillons;

King Kong Adapted, directed, music and sound by Dan Bianchi; **Cast:** John Nolan, Charles Wilson, Donna Heffernan, Jason Grossman, Collin Biddle; Kraine Theater; November 30–December 21, 2005

The Pigman of Delancy Street Written, directed, music and sound by Dan Bianchi; **Cast:** Jamie Jackson; Dillons; May 20–June 25, 2006

RAW IMPRESSIONS

David Rodwin, Producing Artistic Director; Masi Asare, Associate Artistic Director

Raw Impressions Music Theatre Marathon 2006 Events Produced by Jane Abramson & Laura Penney; Casting, Kevin Kennison; Press, Russell Kodoly

RIMT #19 – Guitar Based Music Theatre Directors, Victor Maog, Erik Bryan Slavin; Guitarist, Brian Silvoy; Event Manager, Alexa McAllister; Writers: Dan Basila, Sammy Buck, Cheryl Davis, Kristoffer Diaz, Brian Fountain, Alison Loeb, Aoise Stratford, Craig Weiner; Composers: Carl Danielsen, Jessica del Vecchio, Paul Scott Goodman, Andrew Ingkavet, Josh Joplin, Max Klau, Bert Lee, Aimee Norwich; Performers: Ashley Bliss, Kate Chadwick, John Flynn, Adam Harper, Victor Hawks, Jason Howard, Colleen Longshaw, Leannis Maxwell, Benjamin Schrader, Mariama Whyte; Greenwich Street Theatre; March 19–20, 2006

RIMT #20 – Contemporary Music Theatre Directors, David Glenn Armstrong, Sarah Gurfield; Music Directors, Douglas Maxwell, Amy Southerland; Event Manager, Samantha Tella; Writers: Chantal Bilodeau, Chris Kipiniak, Jack Lechner, Andrea Lepcio, Joshua Levine, Barry Putt, Robin Rothstein, Ken Urban; Composers: Charles Bloom, Jeff Blumenkrantz, Denver Casado, Sam Davis, Natalie Kajs, Ilann Maazel, Douglas Maxwell, Peter Yarin; Performers: Josh Davis, James Donegan, Thursday Farrar, Erin Krom, Orville Mendoza, Glenn Peters, Stacey Scotte, Eric Sosa, Alysha Umphress, Mollie Vogt-Welch; Flea Theatre; March 26–27, 2006

RIMT #21 – Triple Threat Music Theatre Directors, Stephen Nachamie, Jessica Redish; Music Directors, Seth Bisen-Hersh, Stephanie Johnstone; Event Manager, Jared Cohen; Writers: Jay Boyer, J.P. Chan, John Ekizian, Annie Kessler, Shannon Morrison, Roger Nasser, Owen Robertson, Joshua Rebell; Composers: Dan Acquisto, Robert Terrell Bledsoe, Lisa DeSpain, Dan Furman, Michael Hicks, David Ogrin, Ryan Scott Oliver, Matt Vinson; Performers: Rheaume Crenshaw, Reed Davis, Andrew Fitch, Lyndy Franklin, Michael Hunsaker, Karen Hyland, Daniel Keeling, Brian Munn, Alena Watters, Lisa Wilkerson; Flea Theatre; April 2–3, 2006

THE REGROUP THEATRE

Dana Lynn Bennett, Nancy Medina, Patricia Runcie, Founders

Blackouts by J. Anthony Roman; Director, Nancy Medina; **Cast:** Jon Castro, Sarah Nuffer, Sarah Politis, Patricia Runcie, Robert Taylor; The Next Stage Theater; January 20, 2006

Nature Boy by Yesi T. Mills; Directors, Nancy Medina and Patricia Runcie: **Cast:** J. Anthony Roman and Leah Yanathom; Siberia Bar; February 8, 2006

Hair Pieces Part of the Collision Festival; The Next Stage Theater; May 2–9, 2006; Included: *Jeannie With The Light Brown Hair* by Jerry McGee, directed by Elizabeth Bove; *Recreation* by David Michael Downey, directed by Greg Campbell, *Coupe de Cheveux* by Jon Steinhagan, directed by Nancy Medina; *My Yeti Dreams* by Lisa Dillman, directed by Bob Simonello; *Nerve of Some People* by Allison Orr Block, directed by Marie Pendolino; *Houseplay* by J. Anthony Roman, directed by David Mitnowsky; *What's This Hair Doing in My Vita?* By Bill Johnson, directed by David Mitnowsky, *Love & Nappiness* by Dominique Morrisseau, directed by Leah Michele Yananton; *Blond is Better* by Lindsay Price, directed by Katie Raben; *Between the Dog and Wolf* by Adam Rivera, directed by Bob Simonello; *Blue Hats* by Claudia Turbides, directed by Patricia Runcie; *Indoctrination* by Brian St. John Brooks, directed by Brandon Kalbaugh; *Soap Operetta* by Betty Pink, directed by Nancy Medina

RISING SUN PERFORMANCE COMPANY

Akia, Artistic Director; David Anthony, Executive Director

Lysistrata written and directed by Jason Tyne; Costumes, Jessa Raye Court; **Cast:** Liz Burke, Steve Gribben, Josh Hyman, Julie Bain, Di Drago, Anna Gorman, Sandra Chan, Courtney Boddie, Ton-essa La'Rocque; Summit Rock in Central Park; September 3–25; 8 performances

HellCab by Will Kern; Director, Akia; Scenery, Laura Jellinek; Costumes, Jessa Raye Court; Lighting, David Anthony and P. William Pinto; Sound, Di Drago; Stage Manager, Anna Gorman; **Cast:** Nic Mevoli, David Anthony, Adam Purvis, Elizabeth Burke, Nicole Watson, Reagan Wilson, John Patrick Bray, Steve Gribben, Lindsey Smith, Sarah Sirota, Renee Valenti, Crystal Francishini, Sahadev Poudel, Robert Richardson, Reginald Ferguson, Anna Gorman; UNDER St. Marks; November 4, 2005–January 26, 2006; 21 performances

Adam Purvis and Nic Melvoli in Rising Sun Performance Company's *HellCab* by Will Kern
PHOTO BY DAVID ANTHONY

The Crucible by Arthur Miller; Director, Melissa Attbery; Lighting, G. Ben Swope; Scenery, Jeremy Rosenstein; Costumes, Katherine Stebbins; Stage Manager Dallas Bird; **Cast:** John Hart, Jarret Summers, Prentiss Marquis, Lorraine Thompson, Alessia Siniscalchi, Patrick Egan, Kelly Scanlon, Sarah Sirota, Nic Mevoli, Akia, Reginald Ferguson, Jared Mercier, William Greville, Anna Gorman, Adam Purvis, Brian Trybom, Rey Oliver Bune, Elizabeth Burke, Barbara Lifton, Jenn Schatz, Seth Abrams; Kraine Theatre; May 11–21, 2006; 10 performances

MUSICAL CABARET SERIES AT DANNY'S SKYLIGHT ROOM FEATURING RISING SUN ENSEMBLE MEMBERS

Beneficial Bawdiness Director, Anna Gorman & Courtney Hebert; August 29, 2005

Let's Just Be Friends Driectors, Anna Gorman & Peter Pinto; September 12, 2005

Full Moon Follies Director, Courtney Hebert; October 18, 2005

Love Me! Love Me! Director, Anna Gorman & Peter Pinto; February 13, 2006

READINGS AND WORKSHOPS

Amerikan Mine by John Patrick Bray; Director, Anna Gorman; Beckett Theater; July 12, 2005

The Rule of Thumb Written and directed by Akia; The Red Room; March 21, 2006

Cover Magnets by John Patrick Bray; Director, Rachel Klein; The Red Room; March 21, 2006

THE SACKETT GROUP

Robert J. Weinstein, Artistic Director, Dov Lebowitz-Nowak, Producing Director; Dan Haft, Managing Director

Suddenly Last Summer by Tennessee Williams; Director, Robert J. Weinstein; Brooklyn Music School Playhouse; July 14–August 6, 2005

The American Clock by Arthur Miller; Director, Robert J. Weinstein; Design, John Scheffler, Dallas Williams, Michael Hairston, Michael Pheiffer; Choreography, Joan Murray, Music Director, Steve Velardi; Stage Manager, Corinne J. Sagle; **Cast:** Val Balaj, Dashiell Barrett, Steven W. Bergquist, Bernard Bosio, Paul Falcetta, James Feurer, Tiandra Gayle, Susan Faye Groberg, Dawn Marie Hale, Malena Hougen, Kristen Keim, Allan Mirchin, Charles J. Roby, Lillian J. Small, David B. Sochet, Thomas Sullivan, Penny Frank-White, Audrie Zerui; Brooklyn Music School Playhouse; January 26–February 19, 2006

One Big Happy Family Written and directed by Joe Costanza; Brooklyn Music School Playhouse; April 27–May 21, 2006

SHAKESPEARENYC

Board of Directors: Beverly Bullock, Geoffrey Dawe, Marcus Dean Fuller, Douglas Johnson, Vanessa Vozar

Julius Ceasar Director, Beverly Bullock; Stage Manager, Christina Martinez; **Cast:** Shari Paige Acker, C. Daniel Barr, Wayne Preston Chambers, Corey Cicci, Eric Conley, Geoffrey Dawe, Marcus Dean Fuller, Susanna Harris, Peter Herrick,

Gretchen Howe, Douglas Clark Johnson, Matt Mercer, John Montague, Jeff Riebe, Ellen Seltz, Lillian Small, Nicholas Stannard, Jared Waltzer, Melon Wedick; Lion Theatre on Theatre Row; August 8–20, 2005

Romeo and Juliet Lion Theatre on Theatre Row; January 12–28, 2006

SIX FIGURES THEATRE COMPANY

Kimberly Kefgen and Cris Buchner, Artistic Directors; Loren Ingrid Noveck, Literary Manager

ARTISTS OF TOMORROW '05 SERIES OF DEVELOPING WORK; WEST END THEATRE; SEPTEMBER 14–OCTOBER 9, 2005

Parable by Monica Raymond; Director, Marcy Arlin

Nayana's Passing by Tanwi Nandini Islam; Director, Tanwi Nandini Islam

The Fan-Maker's Inquisition by Anushka Carter and Andy Paris; Director, Andy Paris

Dark Deceptions by Todd Robbins; Director, Todd Robbins

My Year of Porn by Cole Kazdin; Director, Ivanna Cullinan

The Clown Pageant Created by the ensemble; Director, Kendall Cornell

Devil's Dancebelt Improv Troupe; Director, Ben Hauck

If You Take One Elf off the Shelf by Francesca Sanders; Director, Jocelyn Sawyer

Where's My Cue by Suzanne Dottino; Director, Jeff Griffiths

Fish by Bryce Weinert; Director, Bryce Weinert

Pink Salome conceived by Kendall Cornell

Show Ho by Sara Moore; Director, Peter Sampieri

Seens from the Unexpectedness of Love by Pamela S. Booker; Director, Anita Gonzalez

Too Much Light Makes the Baby Go Blind by NY NeoFuturists

Like Decorations in a Cemetery by Laylage Courie

Premises for Sale by Lisa Biggs; Director, Alycia Smith-Howard

Pressing Beyond In Between by Soha al-Jurf; Director, Dalia Basouny

Seen by the Dog by Andrea Moon; Director, Brooke Brod

The Territory by Tanya Krohn; Director, Dean Parker

Any Distance Home Created by the ensemble; Director, Melissa Riker

The Morons Don't Have to Laugh by CLUNK

Not a Dream by Regina Robbins; Director, Regina Robbins

Cemetery of Lips by Nancy Ancowitz; Director, Barbara Rubin

The Water Principle by Eliza Anderson; Director, Shoshana Gold

Becoming Natasha by Anna Klein; Director, Nancy S. Chu and Anna Klein

Eve Descending; Director, Abena Koomson

ONCE by Misa Ogasawara; Director, Misa Ogasawara

The Great Divorce by David Chapman; Director, Laurie Sales

The Second Amendment Club by Peter Morris; Director, Elizabeth Williamson

Free Space by Tara Medaugh; Director, Anya Martin

The Territory by Tanya Krohn; Director, Cris Buchner; Scenery Nick Francone; Costumes, Jessica Wegener; Lighting, Alison Cherry; Sound/Composer, Dean Parker; Stage Manager, Greg LoProto; Choreographer, Juan Borona; Featuring: Kit Bihun, George Demas, Andrew Firda, Christopher Illing, Alana McNair, Lethia Nall, Sarah Nedwek, Debargo Sanyal; West End Theatre; March 11–April 1, 2006

SPRING FLING–WORKSHOP SERIES, WEST END THEATRE; MARCH 11–APRIL 1, 2006

Bareback Montage by Patrick Wilcox and Rick White

Clown Pageant Director, Kendall Cornell

Pieces of Myth American by Pam Wilterdink

Girl Blog from Iraq: Baghdad Burning by Kimberly Kefgen and Loren Noveck; Director, Kimberly Kefgen

Two Men Talking by Murray Nossel and Paul Browde

The Should Dream by Victoria Libertore; Director, Ryan Migge

TraumNovela by Cris Buchner and Juan Borona; Director, Cris Buchner and Juan Borona

Achtung Grimm by Renee Philippi; Director, Renee Philippi

The Wolf's Response to the Shepherd's Call by Matthew Bukovac; Director, Laurie Sales

NotePlay Director, Ari Laura Kreith

YY by Justin Deabler; Director, Mahayana Lansdowne

Seaside Theater Festival by Sara Moore; Director, Peter Sampieri

SOHO REP

Sarah Benson, Artistic Director; Alexandra Conley, Executive Director

MAINSTAGE

Peninsula Written and directed by Madelyn Kent; Scenery, Narelle Sissons; Costumes, Theresa Squire; Lighting, Matt Frey; Sound, Kenta Nagai; Stage Manager, Ryan Parow; **Cast:** Louis Cancelmi, Tim Cummings, David Chandler, Curzon Dobell, Marielle Heller; January 12–February 4, 2006

Not Clown by Steve Moore and Carlos Treviño; Produced in association with Physical Plant; Director, Carlos Treviño; Lighting/Stage Manager, Natalie George; Sound, Robert Pierson; **Cast:** Robert Deike, Elizabeth Doss, Lee Eddy, Matt Hislope, Josh Meyer, Robert Pierson, Mark Stewart, Rommel Sulit; March 16–25, 2006

WRITER/DIRECTOR LAB READING SERIES

Purity by Thomas Bradshaw; Director, Mallory Catlett

Somewhere Fun by Jenny Schwartz; Director, Sarah Cameron Sunde

Creature by Heidi Schreck; Director, Sarah Benson

Marie Antoinette by David Adjmi; Director, Shana Gold

Hamilton Township by Jason Grote; Director, Maria Goyanes

ST. BART'S PLAYERS

Making a Scene Conceived and directed by Brad Harlan; **Cast:** Martha Armes, Katherine Beitner, Shana Costa, Faith Elliott, Leslie Engel, Alexandra Kane, Steven Platt, Laura Raines, Penny Robb, Richard Spector, Lana Taradash, Anne Watters, Michael Weems, Barbara Zaid; September 9–10, 2005

Guys and Dolls Music and lyrics by Frank Loesser, music by Abe Burrows and Jo Swerling, based on stories by Damon Runyon; Director and Choreographer, Kathleen Conry; Music Director, Scott Ethier; Design, Heather Wolensky, Jason Scott, David Withrow; Stage Manager, Natalya Brook; **Cast:** Noah Aberlin, Truly Ager, David Pasteelnick, Elizabeth Gravitt, Ulises Giberga, Chazmond Peacock, Dan Grinko, Bradford Harlan, Alan Budoff, Nick Walkonis, John Shubeck, Erich Werner, Jim Mullins, Joe Gambino, Wendy Valdez, Martha Armes, Neal Jones, Gary Kurnov, Lynette Morse, Jack Molyneaux, Lana Krasnyansky, Shana Costa, Laura Loveless, Shani Barrett, Nick Nerio, Lauren Mazer; November 10–20, 2005

Whose Life Is It Anyway? by Brian Clark; Director, Melanie Sutherland; Composer, Valerie Pielski; Design, Andrew Boyce, Michael Gugliotti, Kim Gill; Stage Manager, Deirdre Mullins; Producer, Bob Berger; **Cast:** Martin Zwerling, Dolores Rogers, Allison Mazer, David Kurnov, Leslie Engel, Bob Oliver, Veronica Shea, Joe Gambino, Dan Grinko, Bill McEnaney, Brian Haggerty, Katherine Beitner, Penny Robb, Mariel Matero; February 23–March 5, 2006

Merrily We Roll Along Music and lyrics by Stephen Sondheim, book by George Furth, based on the play by George S. Kaufman and Moss Hart; Director/Staging, Amy Rogers; Music Director, Nancy Evers; Design, David Evans Morris, Jay Scott, Anne Lommel; Stage Manager, Ellen Marks; **Cast:** Brad Negbaur, Hope Landry, Greg Halpen, Merrill Vaughn, Harley Diamond, Reanna Muskovitz, Tammy Williams, Jill Conklin, David Pasteelnick, Aili Venho, Daniel Burke, Lesley Berry, Mikey LoBalsamo, Nick Walkonis, Kenny D'Elia, Spencer Langerman; April 27–May 7, 2006

Straight Up With a Twist Produced by Bonnie Berens and Dan Grinko; Benefit Cabaret featuring Bonnie Berens, Rich Berens, Lesley Berry, Ulises Giberga, Dan Grinko, Chazmond J. Peacock, Veronica Shea, Victor Van Etten, Barbara Zaid, Grace Grinko, Campbell Hester; June 24, 2006

THE STORM THEATRE

Board of Directors: Peter Dobbins (President), Thomas Gray, Carl Pasbjerg, Jim Scully; Chance Michaels, Producing Director

The Salvage Shop by Jim Nolan; Director, Peter Dobbins; Scenery, Todd Ivins; Costumes, Erin Murphy; Lighting, Michael Abrams; Sound, Scott O'Brien; Stage Manager, Sarah Myers; **Cast:** Karen Eke; Roland Johnson, David Little, Ted McGuinness, Paul Anthony McGrane, Caitlin Mulhern; October 28–November 19, 2005

The House of Desires by Sor Juana Inés de la Cruz, translated by Catherine Boyle; Director, Peter Dobbins; Scenery, Todd Ivins; Costumes, Erin Murphy; Lighting, Michael Abrams; Sound, Scott O'Brien; Stage Manager, Joe Danbusky; Fight Director, Michael Daly; **Cast:** Mark Cajigao, Amanda Cronk, Michael Daly; Christopher Kale Jones, Jamil Mena, Caitlin Mulhern, Jessica Myhr, Joshua Vasquez, Gabriel Vaughan; January 6–28, 2006

SUMMER PLAY FESTIVAL (SPF)

Arielle Tepper, Founder and Executive Producer

SECOND SEASON

July 5–31, 2005; Performances at the Theatre Row Theatres (Lion, Clurman, Beckett, Kirk, Acorn)

The Adventures of Barrio Grrrl! by Quiara Hudes; Director, Liesl Tommy

Courting Vampires by Laura Schellhardt; Director, Lou Jacob

crooked by Catherine Trieschmann; Director, Linsay Firman

Ephemera by John Yearley; Director, Erma Duricko

How Love Is Spelt by Chloë Moss; Director, Michael Sexton

Indoor/Outdoor by Kenny Finkle; Director, Daniel Goldstein

Madagascar by J. T. Rogers; Director, Gus Reyes

The Map Maker's Sorrow by Chris Lee; Director, Stefan Novinski

Messalina by Gordon Dahlquist; Director, David Levine

Mimesophobia by Carlos Murillo; Director, Matt August

Sick by Zakiyyah Alexander; Director, Daniella Topol

Split Wide Open by Christina Gorman; Director, Lisa Rothe

Ted Kaczynski Killed People With Bombs by Michelle Carter; Director, Jeremy Dobrish

tempOdyssey by Dan Dietz; Director, Randy White

Welcome to Arroyo's by Kristoffer Diaz; Director, Jaime Castaneda

Wildlife by Victor Lodato; Director, Michael Sexton

THE ACTORS COMPANY THEATRE (TACT)

Scott Alan Evans, Cynthia Harris, and Simon Jones, Co-Artistic Directors; Cathy Bencivenga, General Manager

Watch on the Rhine by Lillian Hellman; Director, Scott Alan Evans; Lighting, Mary Louise Geiger; Costumes, David Toser; Stage Manager, Dawn Dunlop; **Cast:** Darrie Lawrence, Cynthia Harris, Scott Schafer, Kyle Fabel, Margaret Nichols, Terry Layman, Francesca DiMauro, Daniel Oreskes, Leah Morales, Travis Walters, Sean J. Moran; Musicians: Kamako Koyama, David Gale, Jessie Marino, Youn Joo Lee; Florence Gould Hall; October 15–17, 2005

Both Your Houses by Maxwell Anderson; Director, Michael Pressman; Lighting, Stacey Boggs; Stage Manager, Dawn Dunlop; Music, Marcus Paus; **Cast:** Tara Falk, Jenn Thompson, Curzon Dobell, James Murtaugh, Terry Layman, Tuck Milligan, Scott Schafer, James Prendergast, Darrie Lawrence, Kyle Fabel, Richard Ferrone, Anthony Crane, Scott Schafer; Musicians: Yoni Levyatov, Dan Urness; Florence Gould Hall; November 11–13, 2005

He and She by Rachel Crothers; Director, Kyle Fabel; Lighting, Steve O'Shea; Costumes, Steven Cozzi; Stage Manager, Dawn Dunlop; **Cast:** Greg McFadden, Paul DeBoy, Angela Reed, Rachel Fowler, Eve Bianco, Gloria Moore, James Murtaugh; Musicians: Jonathan Faiman, David Gale, Mary Wing, Russell Bonifede; Florence Gould Hall; November 19–21, 2005

The HOT L Baltimore by Lanford Wilson; Director, Victor Pappas; Costumes, Suzanne Chesney; Lighting, Mary Louise Geiger, Stage Manager, Jamie Rose Thoma; **Cast:** Scott Schafer, Adina Verson, Delphi Harrington, Cynthia Darlow, Elizabeth Meadows Rouse, James Prendergast, Kelly Hutchinson, Bob Braswell, Eli Ganias, Ashley West, Richard Ferrone; Jamie Bennett, Nora Chester; Musicians: Seth Fruyterman, Rupert Boyd; Florence Gould Hall; May 6–8, 2006

SALON SERIES

Come Back Little Sheba by William Inge; Director, Michael Pressman; January 8–9, 2006

Dear Liar by Jerome Kilty; Director, Scott Alan Evans; January 29–30, 2006

A Handsome Man by Alexander Ostrovsky; Adapted by Scott Alan Evans and Greg McFadden; February 12–13, 2006

The Cherry Sisters Revisited by Dan O'Brian; Director, Andrew Leynse; April 2–3, 2006

THEATER FOR THE NEW CITY

Crystal Field, Executive Director

Ren, Ah Ren (You, Oh You Humans) adapted and directed by Joanna Chan, (see listing under Yangtze Repertory Company in this section); June 2–19, 2005

Pier 13 by Juan Riquelme; Director, Yuji Takematsu; Scenery, Mark Marcante, Lighting, Tamiko Komatsu; Stage Manager, Charlene Blades; **Cast:** Susan Charett, Izzy Durakovic, Hamilton Meadows, Ron Palais, Cristina Sanjuan; June 2–19, 2005

The Scaffolding Composed, written and directed by Martin Halpern, Design, Judith Barnes; **Cast:** Jacqueline Thompson, Mark Womack, Vincent Chambers, Wendy Brown; June 23–26, 2005

The Real Inspector Hound by Tom Stoppard; Produced by Performers Access Studio; Director, Ron Jones; Design, Jason Sturm; Stage Manager, Jill Strykowski; **Cast:** Kenneth Stewart, Frank Senger, Anthony Scott, Laurel Sanborn, Todd Schmidt, Mary Theresa Archibold; Erin Clancy, Lawrence Merrit, Nicholas Viselli; July 13–24, 2005

A Man Died by Saleque Kahn; Presented by Bangladesh Theater of America; June 24–July 2, 2005

Social Insecurity by Crystal Field; Music, Joseph Vernon Banks; Presented by Theater for a New City's Street Theater Tour; August 6–September 18, 2005

You Should Have Your Own HBO Special Written and performed by Steve Epstein and Naimah Hassan (The Black and the The Jew); August 12–September 2, 2005

Soul Searching Music and lyrics by Avi Kunstler; Book, additional music and lyrics and direction by Matt Okin; Music Director, Ytizy Glickman; Producer, Michael Gurin; Design, Jason Norris; Stage Manager, Susan Erenberg; **Cast:** Shelly Dague, Danielle Faith Leonard, Faye Meyer, Elizabeth Woodard, Avery Pearson, Max Roll, Stewart Shneck, Russell Feder, Aaron Grant, Richard Lurie, Eytan Bayme; September 8–October 2, 2005

Homeland by Gene Ruffini; September 8–25, 2005

We Are the Sperm Cells by Daisuke Koshikawa; October 5–23, 2005

Shock and Awe A-Go-Go Hosted by Epstein and Hassan (The Black and the Jew); November 4–25, 2005

My Juilliard by Gloria J. Browne; Director, David Sheppard; Produced by TNC and Frank Silvera Writers Workshop; November 10–December 4, 2005

Legend of the Siguanaba Presented by Imaginationexplosion and the Latin American Community Art Project; November 10–20, 2005

Beyond the Mirror Presented by Bond Street Theater and Exile Theater of Kabul; November 17–December 4, 2005

2nd Annual VOICE 4 VISION Puppet Festival Curated by Sarah Provost and Jane Catherine Shaw; Shows included: *The Adventures of Charcoal Boy* by Sarah Provost, Eric Novak and Elyas Khan; *Portraits-Night & Day; Mrs Wright's Escape* by Amanda Maddock; and Nikolai Gogol's *The Nose*; December 1–11, 2005

Bread and Puppet Theater presents The National Circus & Passion of the Correct Movement; Cardboard Celebration Circus; December 8–23, 2005

Fear Itself by Jean-Claude van Italie; Director, George Ferencz; Lighting, Federico Restrepo; Sound, Tim Schellenbaum; Costumes, Sally Lesser; **Cast:** Ken Perlstein, Susan Patrick, Joe Gioco, Roland Sanchez, Leslie Ann Hendricks, Jason Howard, Jean-Claude van Itallie, Rene Anderson, Timothy Doyle, Eric Goss, Jenn Vath; December 10, 2005–January 8, 2006

Your Town by Walter Corwin; December 15–30, 2005

The Art of Love by Robert Kornfeld; Director, Tom Thornton; Scenery, Mark Mercante, Costumes, Carolyn Adams, Lighting, Alex Moore, Sound, Elliot Lanes; Stage Manager, Janice Dekoff; **Cast:** James Nugent, Laura Lockwood, Stephen Francis, Doug Stone, Samantha Payne, Nina Covalesky, Tom Thornton; January 12–February 5, 2006

Trouble by Michael T. Smith; January 12–February 5, 2006

The Funniest Show in the World About the History of Comedy Performed by Two Brothers in Less Than Two Hours for Under Twenty Bucks Written and performed by Josh and Danny Bacher; Director, Dom J. Buccafusco; Scenery, Robert Monaco; Costumes, Mama Jean; Lighting, Randy Glickman; January 12–February 4, 2006

The Love Show by Angela Harriell; January 12–29, 2006

Follies of Grandeur by Ross MacLean; Director, Mark Finley; Scenery, Michael Muccio; Lighting, Igor Goldin; **Cast:** Daryl Brown, Melissa Center, Brian Hoover, Kevin Kelleher, Jolie Meshbesher, Mary Louise Mooney, Bobbi Owens, McGregor Wright, Jennifer Dominguez; February 2–19, 2006

Republic of Iqra Written and directed by Bina Sharif; February 23–March 4, 2006

Rue by August Schulenburg; Director, Kelly O'Donnell; Scenery, Jared Klein; Lighting, Jared Klein and Rebecca Marzalek-Kelly; Sound, Matt Given, Costumes, Jessa-Raye Court; **Cast:** Rachel Bauder, Ian Bedford, Kacy Christensen, Tiffany Clementi, Jessica Conrad, David Crommett, Liz Dailey, Will Ditterline, Candice Holdorf, Joseph Mathers, Michelle O'Connor, Jason Paradine, Colleen Raney, August Schulenburg, Rodman Spilling, Isaiah Tanenbaum, Victor Truro, Adina Verson, Laura Walczak, Gregory Waller; Cotton Wright; March 1–19, 2006

Long Time Passing Written and directed by Barbara Kahn; Music, Alicia Svigals; Puppets, Harry Rainbow, Scenery, Mark Marcante; Lighting, David Ullman; Costumes, Carla Grant; Sound Elliot Lanes; Stage Manager, Janice Dekoff; **Cast:** Evan Bass, Karla Bruning, Alexandra Gutierrez, Maria Hansen, Brian Morvant, Matthew Rappaport, Erin Leigh Schmoyer, Steph Van Vlack; March 9–April 2, 2006

What Do I Know About War? Written and performed by Margo Lee Sherman; Director, Crystal Filed; March 9–26, 2006

Allende: The Death of a President by Rodolfo C. Quebleen; Director, German Jaramillo; Performed by Ramiro Sandoval; April 6–23, 2006

Desert Sunrise Written and directed by Misha Shulman; Music, Yoel Ben-Simhon; Choreography, Dalia Carella; Lighting, Itai Erdal; Art Director, Celia Owens; Stage Manager, Melissa Robison; **Cast:** Yoel Ben-Simhon, Dalia Carella, Alice Borman, Haythm Noor, Jared Miller, Yifat Sharabi, Morteza Tavakoli; April 6–23, 2006

The Adventures of the Aesthetic Presented by Imaginationexplosion; April 6–16, 2006

Suck Sale…and Other Indulgences Written, directed and produced by Evan Laurence; Lighting, Mi Sun Choi and Heejung Noh; Costumes, Mary-Anne Buyondo, Corinne Darroux, and Josefin Sandling; Stage Manager, Jason Bogdan; **Cast:** Dan Almekinder, Lindsay Brill, Andie Cartwright, Wendy Charles, Tanya Everett, Brian Ferrari, Evan Laurence, David Slone; May 4–21, 2006

SPECIAL EVENTS

Grand American Traveling Dime Museum Presented by Circus Contraption; September 1–October 1, 2005

Village Halloween Costume Ball; October 31, 2005

Times Square Angel Written and performed by Charles Busch; Director, Carl Andress; December 19, 2005

Thunderbird American Indian Dancers; February 10–19, 2006

Love 'n Courage Benefit for Theater for a New City's Emerging Playwrights Program; February 13, 2006

Wendy Osserman Dance Company; May 3–14, 2006

New York Uke Festival; April 27–30, 2006

The 11th Annual Lower East Side Festival of the Arts; May 26–28, 2006

THEATRE TEN TEN

Judith Jarosz, Producing Artistic Director

A Month in the Country by Ivan Tergenev; Director, David Scott; Scenery, Jennifer Columbo; Lighting, Jay Scott; Costumes, Jeanette Aultz Look; Assistant Director/Dramaturg, DeLisa White; Production Stage Manager, Lisa Hataf; Stage Manager, Jack Kyte; **Cast:** Greg Oliver Bodine, Elizabeth Fountain, Beth Ann Leone, Annalisa Loeffler, Paula Hoza, Timothy McDonough, Tim McMurray, Lisa Riegel, Ron Sanborn, and David Tillistrand; October 21–November 20, 2005

Kiss and Cry by Tom Rowan; Director, Kevin Newbury; Scenery, Robert Monaco; Costumes; Joanne Haas; Lights, Diana Kesselschmidt; Sound, Robert Gould; Production Stage Manager, Taylor Hanson; **Cast:** Julie Leedes (Fiona), David Lavine (Stacy), Nell Gwynn (Lauren), Timothy Dunn (Trent), Reed Prescott (Ethan), Elizabeth Cooke (Brittany); February 10–March 12, 2006

The Singapore Mikado Book and Lyrics by W.S. Gilbert, music by Arthur Sullivan, conceived by David Fuller and Gharles Berigan; Director, David Fuller; Scenery, Katherine Day; Costumes, Viviane Galloway; Lighting, Robert Eberle; Choreography, Judith Jarosz; Production Stage Manager, Sarah Ford; **Cast:** David Arthur Bachrach, Beth Kirkpatrick, Andrew Clateman, Joel Gelpe, Emily Grundstad, Martin Fox, David Tillistrand, Timothy Dunn, Greg Horton,, Jane Brendler Buchi, Kristopher Monroe, Bianca Carragher, Heather Mieko, Rebecca Pace, Nicholas Mongiardo-Cooper, Andrea Schmidt, John Burns, Sara Jeanne Asselin, Allen Hale, Cristiane Young; April 28–May 28, 2006

TOSOS II (THE OTHER SIDE OF SILENCE II)

Doric Wilson, General Director; Mark Finley, Artistic Director; Barry Childs, Administrative Director

Lady in Question by Charles Busch; Directors, Jason Bowcutt, Christopher Borg; Pianist, Seth Bisen-Hersh; Costumes, Ellen Reilly, Chris Weikel; Producers, Doric Wilson, Mark Finley, Barry Childs; **Cast:** Wynne Anders, Christopher Borg, Desmond Dutcher, Shay Gines, Ashley Green, Steven Hauck, Jamie Heinlein, Rebecca Hoodwin, Matthew Rashid, Ellen Reilly, Chris Weikel; Downstairs at The Monster; Dec 5–7, 2005; 3 performances.

The Billy Blackwell Musical Theatre Project, Igor Golden, director

Musically Speaking: The World of John Wallowitch, a revue conceived and directed by Mark Finley; Musical Director, Jason Loffredo; Stage Manager, Mark Barranco; Scenery, Michael Muccio; Graphic Design, Doric Wilson; Producers, Barry Childs, Doric Wilson; **Cast:** Robert Locke, Heather Olt, Chris Weikel; The Duplex Cabaret Theatre; February 17–March 19, 2006; 8 performances

New York Minutes, a revue of the songs of John Wallowitch conceived and directed by Mark Finley; Musical Director, Ray Fellman; Stage Manager, Mark Barranco; Scenery, Michael Muccio; Graphic Design, Doric Wilson; Producers, Barry Childs, Doric Wilson; **Cast:** Robert Locke, Jolie Meshbesher, Chris Weikel; The Duplex Cabaret Theatre; April 1–29, 2006; 5 performances

The Madness of Lady Bright, by Lanford Wilson; Director, Mark Finley; Assistant Director, Frederic Gravenson; Stage Manager, Jesse Greene; Set design, Michael Muccio; Graphic Design, Doric Wilson; Producers, Barry Childs, Doric Wilson (in association with The Peculiar Works Project); **Cast:** Melissa Center, Marlon Hurt, Michael Lynch; The Duplex Cabaret Theatre; April 11–May 3, 2006; 8 performances

T. SCHREIBER STUDIO

Terry Schreiber, Founder

Last Summer at Bluefish Cove by Jane Chambers; Director, Pamela Scott; Design, Anne Goetz, Karen Anne Ledger; Stage Manager, Brad Gore; **Cast:** Kate Foley, Sharon Maguire, Susan Montez, Summer Moore, Meg Pickrell, Darcy Reed, Emily Sproch, Karyn Plonsky; September 29–October 30, 2005

Love! Valour! Compassion! by Terrence McNally; November 10–December 11, 2005

How I Learned to Drive by Paula Vogel; March 2–April 2, 2006

Marvin's Room by Scott McPherson; Director, Peter Jensen; April 13–May 14, 2006

UNOFFICIAL NEW YORK YALE CABARET

Pun Bandhu, Joseph Barna, George Tynan Crowley, Artistic Directors

Most Happy Written and directed by George Tynan Crowley; Set, Evan Adamson; Costumes, Frank Scaccia; Lighting, Jared Goldstein; **Cast:** Dana Watkins, Nicole Alifante, Sheryl Moller; Upstairs at Bennigan's; October 7 – 24, 2005

Three Children by Puay Tin Leow; Director, Alec Tok; **Cast:** Rob Lok, Charlotta Mohlin, Tijuana Ricks; Upstairs at Bennigan's; November 4 – 21, 2005

Separating the Men From the Bull by Neal Learner and Michael Heintzman; Director, Becky London; **Cast:** Daniel Jenkins, Neal Lerner; Laurie Beechman Theatre; January 28 – February 19, 2006

Valiant by Lanna Joffrey; Director, Tamilla Woodard; Design, Dan Urlie; Lighting, Michael Boll; Projections, Nya Gerasimenko; Sound, Sabrina McGuigan; Stage Manager, Andrew Haas; **Cast:** Lanna Joffrey, Tami Dixon, Sharahn LaRue; Laurie Beechman Theatre; February 24 – March 11, 2006

VAMPIRE COWBOYS THEATRE COMPANY

Qui Nguyen and Robert Ross Parker, Artistic Directors; Abby Marcus, Managing Director

Living Dead in Denmark by Qui Nguyen; Director, Robert Ross Parker; Fight Director, Marius Hanford; Scenery & Lighting, Nick Francone; Costumes, Jessica Wegener; Zombie Masks/Blood & Gore Effects, Chuck Varga; Puppet Design, David Valentine; Graphic Media, Nathan Lemoine; Composer, Dan Deming; Additional Sound, Jeff Lorenz; Producer, Abby Marcus; **Cast:** Carlo Alban, Jason Liebman, Maggie Macdonald, Tom Myers, Melissa Paladino, Jason Schumacher, Maureen Sebastian, Andrea Marie Smith, Temar Underwood, Amy Kim Waschke; Center Stage NY; May 4 – 21, 2006

Amy Kim Waschke, Maureen Sebastian, Melissa Paladino, Maggie MacDonald, and Carlo Alban in Vampire Theatre Cowboy's production of *Living Dead in Denmark* by Qui Nguyen

VARIANT THEATRE COMPANY

Peter Sanfilippo, Artistic Director

The Ends of the Earth by Morris Panych; Director, Peter Sanfilippo; Scenery, Bobby Riggs; Costumes, Peter Sanfilippo; Lighting, Zaheed Essack; Projections, Frank Luna; Stage Manager, Dallas Bird; **Cast:** David Jacks (Frank), Leslie Loggans (Walker), Kelly Miller (Clayton, ensemble.), Mary Aufman (Willie, ensemble) Elizabeth Alice Murray (Alice, ensemble), Amy Broder (Astrid, ensemble); Sanford Meisner Theater; March 16 – 26, 2006

VITAL THEATRE COMPANY

Stephen Sunderlin, Producing Artistic Director; Suzu McConnell-Wood, Director of Vital Children's Theatre; Cynthia Thomas, General Manager

Rebound and Gagged by Aaron Ginsburg; Director, ; Scenery, Jess Hooks; Costumes, Colleen Kesterson; Lighting, Rie Ono; Sound, Lauren Areneson; Producer, Teresa K. Pond, General Manager, Cynthia Thomas; Stage Manager, Eliza Johnson; **Cast:** Jason Gilbert, Matt Hobby, Jeff Meacham, Nia McGovern, Sara Beth-Lee Williams; McGinn/Cazale Theatre; October 15 – November 6, 2005

Vital Signs 10-New Works Festival December 1 – 4, 2005: **Relationtrip** by Sharyn Rothstein; Director, Catherine Ward; **Norman!** By D.T. Arcieri; Director, Alexis Williams; **Passed Hordes** by Mark Harvey Levine, Director, Brad Caswell; **Sorrento** by Lucile Lictblau; Director, Cynthia Thomas; **All in the Miming** by Qui Nguyen; Director, Alexandra Hastings; December 8 – 11, 2005: **Sandlot Ball** by Michael John Garces; Director, Mary Kate Burke; **Harper Lee's Husband** by Thomas H. Diggs; Director, S. Caden Hethorn; **Last Stop: Neverland** by Jackie Maruschak; Director, Christopher Fessenden; **American Soil** by Ellen Margolis; Director, Teresa K. Pond; **The Prisoner's Dilemma** by Michael Wolfson; Director, Mahayana Landowne; **Giblet: A Nightmare** by Ian Finley; Director, David Hilder; December 15 – 18, 2005-Arts Pass In Process-Ten minute plays: **Reading List** by Susan Miller; Director, Cynthia Croot; **Notes** by Kate Moira Ryan; Director, Marya Cohn; **Ride** by Eric Lane; Directory Daisy Walker; **Second Kiss** by Andrea Lepcio; Director, Stephanie Gilman; **Please Have a Seat and Someone Will Be With You Shortly** by Garth Wingfield; Director, Laura Josepher

A Midsummer Night's Dream by William Shakespeare; Co-produced in association with HoNkBarK! Productions; Director, John Ficarra; Scenery, Scott Aronow; Costumes, Carl A. Ruckdeschel; Music, Dana Haynes; Lighting, Steve O'Shea; Producer, Laura LeBleu, Associate Producer, Kristin Price Stage Manager, Susan Manikas; **Cast:** Kristin Price, Sorsha Miles, Linda Jones, Aaron Simms, Earle Hugens, Sara Moore, Laura LeBleu, Neil Hellegers, Todd Faulkner, Tyler Woods, Richard Bolster, Jo Mei, Shauna Miles, Bridgette Shaw, Sarah Mathews, Katie Knipp, Janna Kefalas, Sam Swartz, Rachel Holmes, Dana Haynes, Rich Renner, Mark Ungar, Alexander Merinov; January 6 – 28, 2006

Full Bloom by Suzanne Bradbeer; Director, Linda Ames Key; Scenery, Michael Moore; Costumes, Colleen Kesterson; Lighting, Rie Ono; Sound, Zachary Williamson; Stage Manager, Susan Manikas; **Cast:** Jennifer Blood, Jason Furlani, William Jackson Harper, LeeAnne Hutchisonn, Jennifer Dorr White; March 11 – April 2 , 2006

Vital Drama League Alumni Directors Fest April 27–May 7, 2006; Scenery, Brian Prather, Lighting, Alison Cherry; Stage Manager, Korey Kent, Producers, Danny Martin, Julie Westilin-Naigus; Festival Curator, Julie Hamberg; **Blue Period-Still Into Life** conceived and directed by Mahayana Landowne; **Cast:** Jenny Vath, Bronwin Proser, Karim Sekou, Gerritt Turner, Jenny Weaver, Melody Bates, Jaime Hardy, Jennifer Loryn; **Bumping Heads** by Brian Sloan; Director, Andrew Volkoff; **Cast:** Nancy Beard, Jimmy Owens, Eric Sand; **Poor Ophelia** by Sahem B. Hirbayashi; Director, Julie Hamberg; Choreography, Danielle Quisenberry; Scenery, Susan Woldman; **Cast:** Julian Elfer, Jenna Kalinowski, Laura LeBleu; R. Paul Hamilton; **Swan Lake Calhoun** by Yehuda Hyman; Director, Pesha Rudnick; **Cast:** Megan Gaffney, Ryan Good, Luke Rosen; **Dearborn Heights** by Cassandra Medley; Director, Gregory Lamont Allen; **Cast:** Amber Gray, Felicia Wilson; **Push It** by Maria Gabriele; Director, Tom Rowan; **Cast:** Julie Leedes, Robert Libetti, Mitch Poulos; Jeff Riebe, Christine Verleny, Alison Watrous; **Tell Her That** by Michael John Garcés; Director, Moritz von Stuelpnagel; **Cast:** Moria McDonald, Jane Ray, Thom Rivera; **The Older Gentleman** by Max Sparber; Director, Rob Urbinati; Costumes/Hair, Richard Kathlean; **Cast:** Peter Brauwer, Teddy Bergman; Gary Cowling, Anne DuPont, Steven Hauck, Jane Nichols, Andy Phelan.

VITAL CHILDREN'S THEATRE

The Nastiest Drink in the World Book and Lyrics by Mark Loewenstern, music by John Gregor; Director, Linda Ames Key; Scenery, Jess Hooks, Costumes, Sylvie Marc Charles; Lighting, Graham Kindred, Stage Manager, Amy Gargan; **Cast:** Julie Brooks, Brooke Hetrick, Michael Huber, Chris Janssen, Dan Kalodny; September 10–October 16, 2005

Radiant Ruby Book and Lyrics by Dante Russo, music by Rob Baumgartner; Director and Chreography, Jason Summers; Music Director, Jad Bernardo; Scenery, Jess Hooks; Costumes, Sylvie Marc Charles; Lighting, Rie Ono; Stage Manager, Kanako Morita; **Cast:** Darcie Champagne, Lindsay Gordon, Carrie McCrossen, David Perlman, Eric Peterson, Stephanie E. Seidell; October 29–December 4, 2005

The Bully Music and lyrics by John Gregor, book by David L. Williams; Director, Suzu McConnell-Wood; Choreography, Marco Jo Clate; Music Director, John Gregor; Scenery, Eric Everett; Costumes, Amy Kitzhaber; Lighting, Carrie Yacono; Production Stage Manager, Kanako Morita; **Cast:** Laura Binstock, Jeanette Bonner, Katherine Boynton, Shane Camp, Miron Gusso, Brian Charles Rooney, Jere Williams; December 17, 2005–February 5, 2006

Out of Orbit Music, book, and lyrics by Ren Casey, book by Brianna Tyson; Director, Catherine Ward; Choreography, Michelle Marie Traina; Music Director, Jad Bernardo; Scenery, Katy Tucker; Costumes, Amy Kitzhaber; Lighting, Amith Chandrashker; Stage Manager, Susan Manikas; **Cast:** Katherine Boynton, Ashley Brooke, Amanda-Adair Brown, Shane Camp, Dustin Tyler Moore, Shawn Shafner, Kenneth Scott Thompson; February 18–March 26, 2006

Cinderella's Mice Music and lyrics by Ben Morss, book and lyrics by Justin Warner; Director, David Hilder; Choreography, Danielle Quisenberry; Music Director, Rick Hip-Flores; Scenery, Zhanna Gurvich; Costumes, Amy Kithaber; Lighting, Eric Larson; Stage Manager, Susan Manikas; **Cast:** Andrew Biggs; Bridget Harvey, Marc De La Concha, Kyle Minshew, Mary McLellan, Kara Schwartz, Justin Stoney; April 8–May 14, 2006

VORTEX THEATRE COMPANY

Joshua Randall, Artistic Director; Allison Glenzer, Managing Director

Deviant by A. Rey Pamatmat; Director, Kara-Lynn Vaeni; Co Produced by TheatREX, Ryan King, and Joshua Randall; Scenery, Mikiko Suzuki; Costumes, Daniel Urlie; Lighting, S. Ryan Schmidt; Sound, John Ivy; **Cast:** Jacob Blumer, Jennifer Lim; Courtnie Sauls, Daniel Zaitchik; Sandford Meisner Theater; October 7–23, 2005

Agamemnon Adapted and directed by Gisela Cardenas; Produced by Joshua Randall; Scenery, Jian Jung; Costumes, Oana Botez-Ban; Lighting, Lucrecia Briceno; Sound, Elizabeth Coleman; Puppets, Andrea Gastelum; Stage Manager, Paul Kowalewski; **Cast:** Linda Park, Jonathan Co Green, David Arkema, Seth Powers, Catherine Friesen, Raniah Al-Sayed, Irene Antoniazzi, Sebastian Calderon-Bentin, Vivian Chiu, Trevor Dallier, Gus Danowski, Brandon deSpain, Amelia Henderson, Rebecca Lingafelter, Lucy Alibar, Sara Buffamanti, Andrea Gastelum; St. Veronica's Church; October 19–November 11, 2005

Dog in the Manger Adapted by Quinnopolis, NY; Director, David Dalton; Design, Peter Ksander; Costumes, Jessica Wegener; **Cast:** Jeremy Beck, Robert M Johanson, Abbie Killeen; Sanford Meisner Theater; January 6–February 4, 2006

The Northern Quarter Adapted from the Dutch play by Alex van Warmerdam; Director, Erwin Maas; Design: Oana Botez-Ban, Lucrecia Briceno, Tim Cryan, Andrea Gastelum; **Cast:** Joy Barrett, Michael Downing, Heather Hollingsworth, Adam Gallo, Dave Gueriera, Justin Krauss, Noah Trepanier, Vincent van der Valk, Matt Walter; Sanford Meisner Theater, January 7–22, 2006

In Delirium: (after) the sorrows of young werther Created and performed by Joshua Randall, co created and directed by Gisela Cardenas; adapted from von Goethe's novel; Scenery, Jian Jung; Costumes, Oana Botez-Ban; Lighting, Lucrecia Briceno; Sound, John Ivy; Sandford Meisner Theatre; March 31–April 23, 2006

WINGS THEATRE COMPANY

Jeffrey Corrick, Artistic Director; Robert Mooney, Managing Director

Skating on Thin Ice by Robert Canning; Director, Robert Crest; **Cast:** Robert Stoeckle, Andrew Towler, Jack R. Marks, Al Gordon, Steve Pudenz; June 24–July 23, 2005

Repo! The Genetic Opera by Terrance Zdunich and Darren Smith; Director, Terrance Zdunich; Music Director, C.J. DeAngeles, Jr.; Stage Manager, Walter Guzman; Costumes, Roberta Moreno; Choreography, Marco Puente; Lighting, Steven Wolf; **Cast:** Kathryn Lawson, Tony Perry, Robert Grossman, Annie Lee Moffett, Marie-France Arcilla, Enrique Cruz DeJesus, Marcus Montoya, Terrance Zdunich, Melody Moore, Man Ting Chan, Ellie Diez, Alisa Burkett, Kia Lee, Marco Puente, Stephanie Klemons, Tracy McDowell; August 4–27, 2005

Through A Naked Lens by George Barthel; Co-Director, Co-Scenery, Costumes, L.J. Kleeman; Co-Director, Multi Media, Richard Bacon; Scenery, Ray Wagner; Lighting, Sean Linehan; Media, Jas McDonald; Stage Manager, Parys LeBron; Fight Director, Kymberli E. Morris; **Cast:** Stephen Smith, JoHary Ramos, Richard Bacon, Shay Coleman, Tracy M Gaillard, Heather Murdock, Tom Patterson, Joe Pepe, Sheila Shaignay, Raymond O. Wagner, Laura Beth Wells, December 16, 2005–January 21, 2006

Tiger by the Tail by Frawley Becker; Co-produced by Firehouse Theatre Project; Director, Jules Ochoa;; Scenery, Josh Zangen; Lighting, Rachel Eichorn; Sound, Di Drago; **Cast:** Steven Hauck, Matthew Wilkas, Christian Rummel, John Leonard Thompson, Terrence Michael McCrossan, Franklin John Westbrooks, Nick Marcotti; March 24 – April 22, 2006

Cowboys! Book and lyrics by Clint Jefferies, music and music direction by Paul L. Johnson; Director, Jeffrey Corrick; Scenery, Elisha Shaefer; Costumes, Tom Claypool; Lighting, Colin Huggins; Choreography, Kate Swan; Production Manager, L.J. Kleeman; Stage Manager, Vanessa Wendt; **Cast:** Brian Ogilvie, Rory Hughs, Jesse Factor, Jeff Sheets, Brynn Neal, Stephen Cabral, David Tacheny, Jennifer Fagundes, James Bullard; Musicians: Paul L. Johnson, Daniel Reyes, Richard Shapiro; April 28 – June 10, 2006

WORKING MAN'S CLOTHES PRODUCTIONS

Isaac Byrne, Co-Founder and Artistic Director, Jared Culverhouse, Co-Founder and Executive Director

Pulling Teeth by Brandon Koebernick; Director, Jared Culverhouse; American Place Theatre; July 21 – August 7, 2005

To Ninevah — A Modern Miracle Play by Bekah Brunstetter; Director, Isaac Byrne; American Place Theatre; October 28 – November 13, 2005

More for Your Money Festival Series included: *Boop* and *Hill* by John Paul DeSena and Amy Schulz; *Arms* and *Ocean Side Parkway* by Bekah Brunstetter and Eric Sanders; American Place Theatre; April 28 – May 18, 2006

WORKSHOP THEATRE

Timothy Scott Harris and Elysa Marden, Artistic Directors; Riley Jones-Cohen, Executive Director

Pineapple and Henry by Linda Segal Crawley; Director, Scott C. Sickles; **Cast:** Ellen Dolan, Frank Piazza, Harry Pearce, DeeDee Friedman, David Pincus, Ray Alvin, Brian Voelcker; Mainstage Theatre; June 17 – July 9, 2005

The Mentee Written and directed by Steven Fechter; **Cast:** Kathy Gail MacGowan, Michael Reilly; Jewel Box Theatre; June 23 – 25, 2005

Stealing Home by Ray Alvin; Director, Holli Harms; **Cast:** Ray Alvin; Mainstage Theatre; September 15 – October 8, 2005; Performed in repertory with *Raisins, Not Virgins*

Shaking the Goose Egg Written and told by Jane Gennaro; Director, Christopher Cartmill; Jewel Box Theatre; September 22 – 24, 2005

Raisins Not Virgins by Sharbari Ahmed; Director, Thomas Cote; **Cast:** Sharbari Ahmed, Marc Geller, Anna Itty, Nelson Lugo, Harry Peerce, Anar Vilas; Mainstage Theatre; September 23 – October 22, 2005; Performed in repertory with *Stealing Home*

Anthony and Cleopatra by William Shakespeare; Director, Jerry Less; **Cast:** Debra Whitfield, Christopher Graham, Brian C. Homer, Jeffrey Swann Jones, Marie-Pierre Beausejour, Jeff Paul, C.K. Allen; Jewel Box Theatre; October 6 – 28, 2005

A View From the Bridge by Arthur Miller; Director, Dominick Feola; **Cast:** David Copeland, Dee Dee Friedman, Rebecca Welles, Nate Chura, Jack Luceno, Greg Adair, Andrew Fitzsimmons, G.W. Reed; Jewel Box Theatre; November 2 – 4, 2005

Cold Snaps — One Act Festival: *Down The Shaw* by Gary Giovannetti; Director, Kathy Gail MacGowan; **Cast:** Mary Murphy, Marci Occhino, Marta Reiman, Peter Stoll; *Stone Soup* by Dana Leslie Goldstein; Director, Moira Boag; **Cast:** Jennifer Kathryn Marshall, Ben Sumrall, Susan Wallack; *The Last Seder* by Allan Knee; Director, Thomas Cote; **Cast:** Chris Stack, Dana Watkins; *The Aquatic Ape* by Joy Wilkinson; Director, Elysa Marden; presented with London's Unrestricted View Company; **Cast:** Marc Geller, Wende O'Reilly; Jewel Box Theatre; December 8 – 17, 2005

Steal Away: The Living History of Harriet Tubman by Rick Balian; Director, Melody Brooks; Produced in association with New Perpectives Theatre Company; **Cast:** James Blanshard, Natalie Lehert, Denise Lock, Miebaka Yohannes; Mainstage Theatre; February 4 – March 11, 2006

Caseload by Levy Lee Simon; Director, Mary Beth Easley; **Cast:** Ellen Barry, Sandflower Dryson, Brian Homer, Erik Kilpatrick, Madeline McCray, Gary Mink, Rob Morgan, Terrance Mueller, Darcie Siciliano, Ayanna Siverls; Mainstage Theatre; April 28 – May 20, 2006

Will-A-Thon 6 Nights of Shakespeare conceived and directed by Charles E. Gerber; Candide, Ron Crawfore, Alexandra Devin, Letty Ferrer, Audrey Maeve Hager, David M. Mead, Sandy Moore, Joan Pelzer, Brian Silliman, Ben Sumrall, L.B. Williams, Charles E Gerber; Jewel Box Theatre; May2 – 7, 2006

PLAYS IN PROGRESS SERIES

Bettinger's Luggage by Albert M. Tapper; Director, Timothy Scott Harris; Mainstage Theatre; August 19 – 27, 2005

M is for the Million Things: Plays About Mothers and Motherhood by Scott C. Sickles; *The Anticque Shop* directed by Kathy Gail MacGowan; **Cast:** David Palmer Brown, Burt Edwards, Patricia O'Ocnnell, Marta Reiman; *The Man in 119* directed by David Gautschy; **Cast:** Peter Farrell, Joanie Schumacher; *The Mother Lode* directed by Harry Peerce; **Cast:** C.K. Allen, Bob Manus, Linda Segal; *Yea, Though I Walk* directed by Paula D'Alessandris; **Cast:** Greg Adair, C.K. Allen, Maggie Fales, Leslie Gwyn, Anne Fizzard, Gerrianne Raphael, Marta Reiman; Jewel Box Theatre; February 2 – 11, 2006

Messiah by Martin Sherman; Director, David Gautschy; **Cast:** Ron Cohen, Carrie Edel, Letty Ferrer, Martin Fox, Jenny Greeman, Tobi Kanter, Duncan Pflaster, Anna Roberts; Jewel Box Theatre; March 30 – April 8, 2006

The Jazz Age by Allan Knee; Director, Thomas Cote; **Cast:** Marta Meiman, P.J. Sosko, Dana Watkins; Jewel Box Theatre; April 13 – 22, 2006

STAGED READINGS-JEWEL BOX THEATRE

Messiah by Martin Sherman; Director, David Gautschy; November 18 – 20, 2005

Love Me Knots by Dave Riedy; Director, Holli Harms; January 19 – 21, 2006

Desire in the Suburbs by Frederic Glover; Director, Timothy Scott Harris; January 13 – 14, 2006

The Mentee by Steven Fechter; Director, Elysa Marden; March 9 – 11, 2006

Appetites by Owa; Director, Jason Jacobs; March 16 – 18, 2006

The Astonished Heart by Noel Coward; Director, Richard Kent Green; May 11 – 13, 2006

YANGTZE REPERTORY THEATRE OF AMERICA, INC.

Joanna Chan, Artistic Director; Scott Shi, Executive Director

Ren, Ah Ren (You, Oh You Humans) Adapted and directed by Joanna Chan, from the novel by Dai Hou Ying; Presented by Yangtze Repertory Theater Company, Scenery, Peter Spack; Lighting, Dana Sterling, Costumes, Harrison Xu; **Cast:** Arthur Kwan, Dinh Q. Doan, Vivian Chiu, Nadia Gan, David Chen, Erik Strongbowe, Jo Mei, Kathleen Kwan, John Wu, Nelson Ando; Theater For The New City; June 2–19, 2005

 Variations in a Foreign Land VI; Choreographers, Cha-Lee Chan, Kun-Yang Lin and Sridhar Shanmugam; Lighting, Alberto Edwin Bohl; Stage Manager, Luis Garbiel Zaragoza; Merce Cunningham Studio; September 22–25, 2005; 4 performances.

Teahouse by Lao She Beijing; New York debut of the People's Art Theater's national tour; Director, Jiao JuYin and Xia Chun; Artistic Director, Lin ZhaoHua; Scenery, Gao Qiang, Li Yan and Zhang ZhiJin; Lighting, Wang JianHua, Li Cong and Fang Yi; Costumes, Wang HongYi and Wang WeiWei; Sound, Zheng Chen; Stage Manager, Yang Tiezhu; **Cast:** Pu CunXin (Master Chang), Yang LiXin (Qin ZhongYi), He Bing (Pock-Mark Liu), Wu Gang (Tang the Oracle), Song DanDan (Kang Shunzi), FenYuanZheng (Master Song); Schimmel Center For The Arts at Pace University; November 26–December 1, 2005; 6 performances.

Luo Shen (The Legend of the River Luo) by Joanna Chan; Director, Joanna Chan; set, Peter Spack; Lighting, Joe Hodge; Costumes, Harrison HouJian Xu; Movements, Zhao NaiYi and David ChienHui Shen; Stage Manager, Kristen Aveis; **Cast:** William YueKun Wu (Cao Zhi), YiLing Li (Zhen Mi), Andrei Drooz English Chorus Master), Xiao YunFei (Chinese Chorus Master), Shuang Deng (Cao Pi), Fang YuLin (General Cao Cao), Jenny Hsia (Lady Cui); Theater For The New City, June 8–25, 2006; 12 performances.

A scene from *Luo Shen (The Legend of the River Luo)* by Joanna Chan presented by Yangtze Repertory Theatre of America PHOTO BY JONATHAN SLAFF

YORK THEATER COMPANY

James Morgan, Artistic Director; Tom Smedes and Carl White, General Managers; Founding Director, Janet Hayes Walker

DEVELOPMENTAL READING SERIES

Gauguin: A Musical Sketchbook by George Fischoff; June 19, 2005

War Brides by Ron Sproat, Christopher Berg, and Frank Evans; August 23, 2005

Friends Like These by John McMahon and Jay Jeffries; September 15, 2005

Fairest of Them All by Tyler M. Phillips; September 22, 2005

Murder on Broadway by Bryan D. Leys and James Campodonico; September 24, 2005

Noah and the Gremlins by Bill Banett and Howard Kilik; September 29, 2005

Love, Incorporated by Marc Castle; October 6, 2005

Oh, Progeny! By Diane Sampson; October 24, 2005

The Hunchback of Notre Dame by Anthony Scully, Hal Hackady, and Joseph Gianono; November 11, 2005

Dorian Gray: The Musical by Barry Gordon and Andrew Steven Ross; November 14, 2005

Black Silk by P.J. Barry; November 21, 2005

Saratoga Trunk Songs by David Arthur; December 5–6, 2005

Bye, Bye Big Guy by Michael Slade, David Evans, and Faye Greenberg; December 12, 2005

Trouble in Shameland by Bryan Putnam; December 13, 2005

Green Gables by Janet Yates Vogt and Mark Friedman, February 7, 2006

Cyclone and the Pig-Faced Lady by Dana Goldstein and Rima Fand; February 24, 2006

The Enchanted Cottage by Thomas Edward West, Kim Oler, Allison Hubbard; February 28, 2006

Faraway Bayou by Michael Milton, Margaret Dorn, Janie Barnett; February 28, 2006

The Strange Case of Mary Lincoln by June Bingham and Carmel Owen; March 7, 2006

Bad Ideas by Joshua Z. Kant; March 13, 2006

Delilah by Frederick S. Rossman and Neil Middleton; March 14, 2006

Mongrel by Cornelia Cody; April 25, 2006

Ethan Frome by Michael Ruby and Adam Gwon; May 9, 2006

Kiss a Mad Dog by P.J. Barry; May 22, 2006

Gone to Texas by Steve Warren, Tom Masinter, and June Rachelson-Ospa; May 25, 2006

PROFESSIONAL REGIONAL COMPANIES

ACT THEATRE

Seattle, Washington
FORTY-SECOND SEASON

Artistic Director, Kurt Beattie

THE PILLOWMAN by Martin McDonagh; Directed by Kurt Beattie; Scenic Designer, Matthew Smucker; Costume Designer, Marcia Dixcy Jory; Lighting Designer, Mary Louise Geiger; Sound Designer, Dominic CodyKramers; Composer, Adam Stern; Fight Director, Geoffrey Alm; Stage Manager, Jeffrey K. Hanson; Assistant Stage Manager, Lisa Ann Chernoff; Assistant Lighting Designer, Robert J. Aguilar; March 17–April 16, 2006; **Cast:** Denis Arndt (Tupolski), Ian Bell (Father), Corina Boettger (Girl), Julie Briskman (Mother), Joshua Froebe (Boy), Matthew Floyd Miller (Katurian), Shawn Telford (Michal), R. Hamilton Wright (Ariel)

MISS WITHERSPOON by Christopher Durang; Directed by M. Burke Walker; Scenic Designer, Bill Forrester; Costume Designer, Frances Kenny; Lighting Designer, Rick Paulsen; Sound Designer, Jim Ragland; Stage Manager, JR Welden; Assistant Stage Manager, Lori Amondson Flint; Assistant Lighting Designer, Lynne Ellis; April 28–May 28, 2006; **Cast:** Anne Allgood (Veronica), Christine Calfas (Maryamma), Demene E. Hall (Teacher/Woman in a Hat), Terry Edward Moore (Fathers #1 and #2/Man in the Playground/Dog Owner/Wise Man), Mari Nelson (Mothers #1 and #2)

WINE IN THE WILDERNESS by Alice Childress; Directed by Valerie Curtis-Newton; Scenic Designer, Matthew Smucker; Costume Designer, Melanie Taylor Burgess; Lighting Designer, Kathy A. Perkins; Sound Designer, Dominic CodyKramers; Stage Manager, Jeffrey K. Hanson; Assistant Stage Manager, Stina Lotti; Assistant Lighting Designer, Lynne Ellis; June 9–July 9, 2006; **Cast:** Anthony Leroy Fuller (Sonny-Man), William Hall, Jr. (Oldtimer), Lakeetra Knowles (Cynthia), Shanga Parker (Bill Jameson), April Yvette Thompson (Tommy)

MITZI'S ABORTION by Elizabeth Heffron; Directed by Kurt Beattie; Scenic Designer, Narelle Sissons; Costume Designer, Sarah Nash Gates; Lighting Designer, Chris Reay; Sound Designer, Dominic CodyKramers; Stage Manager, JR Welden; Assistant Stage Manager, Nora Menkin; Media and Lighting Design Assistant, L.B. Morse; Dialect Coach, Alyssa Keene; July 21–August 20, 2006; **Cast:** Eric Ray Anderson (Thomas Aquinas/Tim/Geneticist), Sean Cook (Chuck/The Expert/Sergei), Kit Harris (Vera), Leslie Law (Reckless Mary/Sheila Luffington), Sharia Pierce (Mitzi), Shelley Reynolds (Nita/Nurse), Richard Ziman (Rudolfo/Dr. Block/Uncle Tub)

A NUMBER by Caryl Churchill; Directed by John Kazanjian; Scenic Designer, Carey Wong; Costume Designer, Deb Trout; Lighting Designer, Rick Paulsen; Sound Designer, Lindsay Smith; Stage Manager, Jeffrey K. Hanson; Assistant Stage Manager, Lisa Ann Chernoff; Dialect Coach, Judith Shahn; Assistant Lighting Designer, Ben Zamora; September 1–October 1, 2006; **Cast:** Peter Crook Bernard 1/Bernard 2/Michael Black), Kevin Tighe (Salter)

THE UNDERPANTS by Steve Martin; Directed by Kurt Beattie; Scenic Designer, Carey Wong; Costume Designer, Marcia Dixcy Jory; Lighting Designer, Mary Louise Geiger; Sound Designer, Eric Chappelle; Stage Manager, JR Welden; Assistant Stage Manager, Nora Menkin; Assistant Lighting Designer, Robert J. Aguilar; October 13–November 12, 2006; **Cast:** Julie Briskman (Louise Maske), Matthew Floyd Miller (Frank Versati/The King), Marianne Owen (Gertrude Deuter), David Pichette (Benjamin Cohen), Wesley Rice (Klinglehoff), Richard Ziman (Theo Maske)

A CHRISTMAS CAROL by Charles Dickens; Adapted by Gregory A. Falls; Directed by R. Hamilton Wright; Music Composed and Conducted by Adam Stern; Scenic Designer, Shelley Henze Schermer; Costume Designer, Deb Trout; Lighting Designer, Michael Wellborn; Sound Designer/Music Director, Eric Chappelle; Original Sound Design, Steven M. Klein; Choreographer, Wade Madsen; Dialect Coach, Alyssa Keene; Stage Manager, Jeffrey K. Hanson; Assistant Stage Manager, JR Welden; Production Assistant, Nora Menkin; Assistant Lighting Designer, Ann Ciecko; November 24–December 24, 2006; **Cast:** Hans Altwies (Fred/DickWilkins/Bread Lady/Spirit #3), Ian Bell (Gentleman #1/Mr. Fezziwig/Grocer/Topper/Businessman #1), Julie Briskman (Mrs. Dilber/Mrs. Fezziwig/Sugar Plum Seller/Sister), Alban Dennis (Bob Cratchit/Dancer), David Drummond (Marley/Poor Man/Old Joe), Britt Flatmo (Elizabeth Cratchit/Fan/Lil Fezziwig/Want), Emjoy Gavino (Belle/Niece), Langston Guettinger (Tiny Tim/Ignorance), Emma Kelley (Martha Cratchit/Dancer), Charles Leggett (Gentleman #2/Spirit #2/Ragpicker), Jane May (Spirit #1/Party Guest/Charwoman), Tallis Moore (Peter Cratchit), Terry Edward Moore (Scrooge), Galen Joseph Osier (Middle Scrooge/Robin Crusoe/Beggar/Party Guest/Businessman #2), David Pichette (Scrooge), Nick Robinson (Singing Thief/Undertaker's Assistant/Turkey Boy), Morgan Rowe (Mrs. Cratchit/Dancer), Jeremy Weizenbaum (Charles Cratchit/Young Scrooge/Master Fezziwig), Waverley Woodley (Belinda Cratchit), DeLancey Grace Zeller Lane (Tiny Tim/Ignorance), Erika Godwin (Female Understudy), Dennis Kleinsmith (Male Understudy)

ACTORS THEATRE OF LOUISVILLE

Louisville, Kentucky
FORTY-SECOND SEASON

Artistic Director, Marc Masterson

LOVE, JANIS Conceived, Adapted and Directed by Randal Myler; Inspired by the book "Love, Janis" by Laura Joplin; Music Direction, Sam Andrew; Scenic Designer, Paul Owen; Costume Designer, Lorraine Venberg; Lighting Designer, Don Darnutzer; Sound Designer, Eric Stahlhammer; Properties Designer, Doc Manning; Stage Manager, Debra Anne Gasper; August 16–September 10, 2005; **Cast:** Morgan Hallett (Janis), Katrina Chester and Lauren Dragon (Janis Joplin), Fred Major (Interviewer)

Cast of *The Crucible* PHOTO BY HARLAN TAYLOR

TOO MUCH LIGHT MAKES THE BABY GO BLIND Created by Greg Allen; Written, Directed, and Performed by The Neo-Futurists; September 13–25, 2005; **Cast:** Sean Benjamin, Kristie Koehler, Noelle Krimm, Steve Mosqueda, Jay Torrence

TWELFTH NIGHT by William Shakespeare; Adapted and Directed by Aaron Posner; Scenic Designer, Paul Owen; Costume Designer, Lorraine Venberg; Lighting Designer, Deb Sullivan; Sound Designer, Matt Callahan; Properties Designer, Mark Walston; Production Stage Manager, Paul Mills Holmes; Original Music, Craig Wright and Peter Lawton; September 20–October 15, 2005; **Cast:** Eric Hissom (Feste), Jessica Wortham (Viola), Scott Greer (Sea Captain/Valentine), Matt Schwader (Sebatian), Craig Wallace (Antonio), Ian Merrill Peakes (Orsino), Zabryna Guevara (Olivia), James Gale (Malvolio), Shona Tucker (Maria), David Marks (Sir Toby Belch), James Sugg (Sir Andrew Aguecheek), Isaac Gardner (Curio)

DRACULA Adapted by Hamilton Deane and John L. Balderston from Bram Stoker's Novel; Directed by William McNulty; Scenic Designer, Paul Owen; Costume Designer, Laura Patterson; Lighting Designer, Tony Penna; Sound Designer/Original Music, Benjamin Marcum; Properties Designer, Doc Manning; Dialect Coach, Rinda Frye; Fight Director, Drew Fracher; Stage Managers Nancy Pittelman and Heather Fields; September 27–October 30, 2005; **Cast:** Sarah Augusta (Ms. Wells), Tyler Pierce (Jonathan Harker), Mark Sawyer-Dailey (Dr. Seward), Graham Smith (Van Helsing), Oliver Wadsworth (Renfield), Cliff Williams III (Butterworth), Kim Stauffer (Lucy), Misha Kuznetsov (Count Dracula), Ashanti Brown, Michael C. Schantz, Lily Stark and Stephanie Thompson (Undead Ensemble)

THE CRUCIBLE by Arthur Miller; Directed by Marc Masterson; Scenic Designer, Paul Owen; Costume Designer, Lorraine Venberg; Lighting Designer, Ben Stanton; Sound Designer, Matt Callahan; Properties Designer, Mark Walston; Fight Director, Drew Fracher; Production Stage Manager, Paul Mills Holmes; October 25–November 19, 2005; **Cast:** Madison Cyr (Betty Parris), James Sugg (Reverend Samuel Parris), Shona Tucker (Tituba), Gardner Reed (Abigail Williams), Keira Keeley (Susanna Wallcott), Lynne Perkins (Mrs. Ann Putnam, Sarah Good, Martha Corey), Drew Fracher (Thomas Putnam), Robin Grace Thompson (Mercy Lewis), Olivia Keister (Mary Warren), Ian Merrill Peakes (John Proctor), Adale O'Brien (Rebecca Nurse), Larry John Meyers (Giles Corey), Rex Young (Reverend John Hale), Deanne Lorette (Elizabeth Proctor), Pete Webb (Francis Nurse), David Marks (Ezekiel Cheever), Toby Knops (John Willard), Tom Dahl (Marshall Herrick), Martin Giles (Judge Hathorne), William McNulty (Deputy Governor Danforth)

A TUNA CHRISTMAS by Jaston Williams, Joe Sears and Ed Howard; Directed by Russell Treyz; Scenic Designer, Paul Owen; Costume Designer, John P. White; Lighting Designer, Tony Penna; Sound Designer, Benjamin Marcum; Properties Designer, Ann Marie Werner; Stage Manager, Ben Royer; November 3, 2005–January 5, 2006; **Cast:** Dan McCleary (Thurston Wheelis/Elmer Watkins/Bertha Bumiller/R.R. Snavely/Aunt Pearl Burras/Sheriff Givens/Ike Thompson/Inita Goodwin/Leonard Childers/Phoebe Burkhalter and Joe Bob Lipsey), John Leonard Thompson (Arles Struvie/Didi Snavely/Petey Fisk/Jody Bumiller/Charlene Bumiller/Stanley Bumiller/Vera Carp/Dixie Deberry/Helen Bedd/Farley Burkhalter and Garland Poteet)

A CHRISTMAS CAROL by Charles Dickens; Adapted by Barbara Field; Directed by Wendy McClellen; Scenic Designer, Paul Owen; Costume Designer, Lorraine Venberg; Lighting Designer, Deb Sullivan; Sound Designer, Matt Callahan; Properties Designers, Doc Manning and Mark Walston; Dialect Coach, Rinda Frye; Production Stage Manager, Paul Mills Holmes; November 25–December 23, 2005; **Cast:** William McNulty (Ebenezer Scrooge), Bryan Davis (Grasper/Dick

Jessica Wortham, Zabryna Guevara in *Twelfth Night* PHOTO BY HARLAN TAYLOR

Wilkens/Poulterer), Oliver Wadsworth (Snarkers/Marley/Young Marley/Topper), Drew Fracher (Bob Cratchit), Jeff Cribbs (Fred/Krookings), Shona Tucker (Mrs. Blakely/Mrs. Dilber), Fred Major (Forrest/Undertaker), Ann Hodapp (Mrs. Grigsby/Mrs. Fezziwig), Olivia Deister (Ghost of Christmas Past/Dorothea), Tyrone Mitchell Henderson (Schoolmaster/Ghost of Christmas Present), A.J. Glaser (Billy/Fezziwig Kid/Peter Cratchit), Joseph Benjamin Glaser (Jeremiah/Fezziwig Kid/Tom Cratchit), Luke Craven Glaser (Boy Scrooge/Simon), Ben Friesen (Ali Baba/Ghost of Christmas Future/Fazziwig Guest/Second Man), Hannah Davenprot (Fan/Basil/Belinda Cratchit), Jenn Miller Cribbs (Belle/Mrs. Fred), Mark Sawyer-Dailey (Mr. Fezziwig/Old Joe), Lynne Perkins (Cook/Mrs. Cratchit), Eva Gil (Petunia Fezziwig/Sophia), Stephanie Thompson (Marigold Fezziwig/Martha Cratchit), Drew Koch (Tiny Tim/Ignorance), Ashanti Brown, Tom Coiner, Lee Dolson, Cindy Kawasaki, Grace Maddox, Michael C. Schantz and Sean Sullivan (Carolers/Children)

INTIMATE APPAREL by Lynn Nottage; Directed by Timothy Bond; Scenic Designer, Paul Owen; Costume Designer, Lorraine Venberg; Lighting Designer, Darren W. McCroom; Sound Designer, Matt Callahan; Properties Designer, Mark Walston; Dialect Coach, Don Wadsworth; Stage Manager, Debra Anne Gasper; January 3–28, 2006; **Cast:** Gwendolyn Mulamba (Esther), Perri Gaffney (Mrs. Dickson), Denise Cormier (Mrs. Van Buren), Joe Hickey (Mr. Marks), Tiffany Adams (Mayme), Erik LaRay Harvey (George)

BAD DATES by Theresa Rebeck; Directed by William McNulty; Scenic Designer, Paul Owen; Costume Designer, Lorraine Venberg; Lighting Designer, Deb Sullivan; Sound Designer, Benjamin Marcum; Properties Designer, Mark Walston; Production Stage Manager, Paul Mills Holmes; February 2–25, 2006; **Cast:** Susan Riley Stevens (Haley Walker)

I AM MY OWN WIFE by Doug Wright; Directed by D. Lynn Meyers; Scenic Designer, Paul Owen; Costume Designer, Rebecca Senske; Lighting Designer, Brian C. Mehring; Sound Designer, Fitz Patton; Properties Designer, Doc Manning; Stage Manager, Brady Ellen Poole; January 19–February 5, 2006; **Cast:** Todd Almond (Charlotte von Mahlsdorg, et al)

CROWNS by Regina Taylor; Adapted from the book by Michael Cunningham and Craig Marberry; Directed by Andrea Frye; Choreographed by Mercedes Ellington; Scenic Designer, Marjorie Bradley Kellogg; Costume Designer, Reggie Ray; Lighting Designer, Dawn Chiang; Sound Designer, Brian Jerome Peterson; Production Stage Manager, Paul Mills Homes; April 19–May 14, 2006; **Cast:** Thomas Jefferson Byrd (Man), Crystal Fox (Yolanda), Pat Bowie (Mother Shaw), April Nixon (Jeanette), Angela Karol Grovey (Wanda), Erika LaVonn (Velma), Julia Lema (Mabel)

HUMANA

SIX YEARS by Sharr White; Directed by Hal Brooks; Scenic Designer, Paul Owen; Costume Designer, Catherine F. Norgren; Lighting Designer, Tony Penna; Sound Designer, Matt Callahan; Video Content Designer, Joanna K. Donehower; Properties Designer, Mark Walston; Fight Director, Cliff Williams III; Stage Manager, Nancy Pittelman; March 7–April 1, 2006; **Cast:** Michael J. Reilly (Phil Granger), Kelly Mares (Meredith Granger), Harry Bouvy (Tom Wheaton), Frank Deal (Jack Muncie), Marni Penning (Peg Muncie), Stephanie Thompson (Dorothy), Isaac Gardner (Michael Granger)

ACT A LADY by Jordan Harrison; Directed by Anne Kauffman; Scenic Designer, Kris Stone; Costume Designer, Lorraine Venberg; Lighting Designer, Deb Sullivan; Sound Designer, Benjamin Marcum; Properties Designer, Doc Manning; Stage Manager, Debra Anne Glaser; Original Music by Michael Friedman; Dialect Coach, Rinda Frye; March 7–April 1, 2006; **Cast:** Paul O'Brien (Miles/Lady Romola), Matt Seidman (True/The Countess Roquefort), Steven Boyer (Casper/Greta the Maid), Suzanna Hay (Dorothy/Miles), Cheryl Lynn Bowers (Lorna/True), Sandra Shipley (Zina/Casper)

THE SCENE by Theresa Rebeck; Directed by Rebecca Bayla Taichman; Scenic Designer, Paul Owen; Costume Designer, Catherine F. Norgren; Lighting Designer, Tony Penna; Sound Designer, Matt Callahan; Properties Designer, Jennifer Dums; Stage Manager, Brady Ellen Poole; Fight Director, Cliff Williams III; March 11–April 2, 2006; **Cast:** Stephen Barker Turner (Charlie), David Wilson Barnes (Lewis), Anna Camp (Clea), Carla Harting (Stella)

NATURAL SELECTION by Eric Coble; Directed by Marc Masterson; Scenic Designer, Kris Stone; Costume Designer, Lorraine Venberg; Lighting Designer, Deb Sullivan; Sound Designer, Martin R. Desjardins; Video Designer, Jason Czaja; Properties Designer, Doc Manning; Fight Director, Mark Mineart; Production Stage Manager, Paul Mills Holmes; March 16–April 8, 2006; **Cast:** Jay Russell (Henry Carson), Mark Mineart (Ernie Hardaway/Mr. Neiberding), Heather Dilly (Yolanda Pastiche/Penelope/Ms. Fjeldstad), Melinda Wade (Suzie Carson), Javi Mulero (Zhao Martinez), Joseph Benjamin Glaser (Terrance)

HOTEL CASSIOPEIA by Charles L. Mee; Directed by Anne Bogart; Created and Performed by SITI Company; Scenic Designer, Neil Patel; Costume Designer, James Schuette; Lighting Designer, Brian H. Scott; Sound Designer, Darron L West; Properties Designer, Mark Walston; Projection Designer, Gregory King; Company Stage Manager, Elizabeth Moreau; March 21–April 2, 2006; **Cast:** Barney O'Hanlon (Joseph), Michi Barall (Waitress), Stephen Webber (Astronomer), Leon Ingulsrud (Herbalist), J. Ed. Araiza (Pharmacist), Ellen Lauren (Allegra), Akiko Aizawa (Mother)

LOW Written, Produced and Performed by Rha Goddess; Directed by Chay Yew; Sound Designers/Composers, Baba Israel, Darrin Ross, Marcel Wierckx; Choreographer, Rennie Harris; Stage Manager/Production Director, Sarah Goshman; March 25–April 2, 2006; **Cast:** Rha Goddess (Lowquesha, et al)

NEON MIRAGE by Liz Duffy Adams, Dan Dietz, Rick Hip-Flores, Julie Jensen, Lisa Kron, Tracey Scott Wilson and Chay Yew; Directed by Wendy McClellan; Scenic Designer, Paul Owen; Costume Designer, John P. White; Lighting Designer, Nick Dent; Sound Designer, Benjamin Marcum; Properties Designer, Joe Cunningham; Stage Manager, Megan Schwarz; **Cast:** Sarah Augusta, Lauren Bauer, Ashanti Brown, Kim Carpenter, Tom Coiner, Bryan Manley Davis, Lee Dolson, Melissa Dowty, Ben Friesen, Isaac Gardner, Eva Gil, Cindy N. Kawasaki, Keira Keeley, Toby G. Knops, Aaron Alika Patinio, Michael C. Schantz, Robin Grace Thompson, Stephanie Thompson, Elizabeth Truong, Cliff Williams III

TEN-MINUTE PLAYS

Scenic Designer, Paul Owen; Costume Designer, John P. White and Stacy Squires; Lighting Designer, Paul Werner; Sound Designer, Benjamin Marcum; Properties Designer, Mark Walston; Stage Manager, Debra Anne Gasper; April 1 and 2, 2006

SOVEREIGNTY by Rolin Jones; Directed by Shirley Serotsky; **Cast:** Heather Dilly (Mrs. Elsbeth), Sandra Shipley (Mrs. Merriweather), James B. Seiler, Jr. (Boy), Matt Seidman (Boy's Father)

THREE GUYS AND A BRENDA by Adam Bock; Directed by Frank Deal; **Cast:** Suzanna Hay (Joe), Keira Keeley (Bob), Cheryl Lynn Bowers (Randall), Sarah Augusta (Brenda)

LISTENERS by Jane Marin; Directed by Jon Jory; **Cast:** Melinda Wade (Eleanor), Mark Mineart (Ralph), Jay Russell (Walter), Tom Coiner, Lee Dolson, Ben Friesen, Aaron Alika Patinio (Listeners)

Katrina Chester in *Love, Janis* PHOTO BY HARLAN TAYLOR

ALLEY THEATRE

Houston, Texas
FIFTY-NINTH SEASON

Artistic Director, Gregory Boyd

DEATHTRAP by Ira Levin; Directed by James Black; Scenic Design, Kevin Rigdon; Costume Design, Linda Ross; Lighting Design, Michael Lincoln; Sound Design, Joe Pino; Fight Direction, Brian Byrnes; Stage Manager, Elizabeth M. Berther; Assistant Stage Manager, Terry Cranshaw; June 24–July 10, 2005; Alley Theatre Hubbard Stage; **Cast:** Elizabeth Heflin (Myra Bruhl), Ty Mayberry (Clifford Anderson), David Rainey (Porter Milgrim), Carole Seitz (Helga Ten Dorp), Todd Waite (Sidney Bruhl)

SPIDER'S WEB by Agatha Christie; Directed by Gregory Boyd; Scenic Design, Kevin Rigdon; Costume Design, Linda Ross; Lighting Design, Michael Lincoln; Sound Design, Joe Pino; Fight Direction, Brian Byrnes; Stage Manager, Elizabeth M. Berther; Assistant Stage Manager, Terry Cranshaw; July15–31, 2005, Alley Theatre Hubbard Stage; **Cast:** Jeffrey Bean (Sir Royland Delahaye), James Belcher (Elgin), Bettye Fitzpatrick (Mildred Peake), Elizabeth Heflin (Clarissa Hailsham-Brown), Paul Hope (Henry Hailsham-Brown), Philip Lehl (Oliver Costello), Ty Mayberry (Jeremy Warrender), Lauren Opper (Pippa Hailsham-Brown), David Rainey (Giles Corey), John Tyson (Hugo Birch), Todd Waite (Inspector Lord), Timothy Wrobel (Constable Jones)

HAPGOOD by Tom Stoppard; Directed by Gregory Boyd; Scenic Design, Jeff Cowie; Costume Design, Linda Ross; Lighting Design, Chris Parry; Original Music and Sound Design, John Gromada; Associate Sound Design, Ryan Rumery; Stage Manager, Elizabeth M. Berther; Dramaturg, Amy Steele; September 23–October 23, 2005; Alley Theatre Neuhaus Stage; **Cast:** Josie De Guzman (Hapgood), John Tyson (Blair), Todd Waite (Kerner), Jeffrey Bean (Ridley), David Rainey (Wates), Paul Hope (Maggs), Chris Hutchinson (Merryweather), Philip Lehl (The Russian), Andrew Chennisi or Terran Swonke (Joe)

BE MY BABY by Ken Ludwig; Directed by John Rando; Scenic Design, Alexander Dodge; Costume Design, David C. Woodlard; Lighting Design, Donald Holder; Sound Design, John Gromada; Production Stage Manager, Terry Cranshaw; Stage Manager, Richard Constable; September 30–October 23, 2005; Alley Theatre Hubbard Stage; **Cast:** Elizabeth Bunch (Gloria Nance), Dixie Carter (Maud Kinch), Ty Mayberry (Christy McCall), Hal Holbrook (John Campbell), James Black (Male Ensemble), Robin Moseley (Female Ensemble)

A CHRISTMAS CAROL: A GHOST STORY OF CHRISTMAS by Charles Dickens; Adapted and Directed by Michael Wilson; Scenic Design, Tony Straiges; Costume Design, Alejo Vietti; Lighting Design, Rui Rita; Original Music and Sound Design, Max Williams; Choreography, Hope Clark; Dance Captain, Michael Tapley; Music Director, Deborah Lewis; Associate Director, Max Williams; Stage Manager, Elizabeth M. Berther; Stage Manager, Terry Cranshaw; Assistant Stage Manager, Sara Elida Mills; November 22–December 28, 2005; Alley Theatre Hubbard Stage; **Cast:** James Black (Ebenezer Scrooge), Jeffrey Bean (Mrs. Dilber), Chris Hutchinson (Bob Cratchit), Philip Lehl (Fred), James Belcher (First Solicitor), Paul Hope (Second Solicitor), Bettye Fitzpatrick (Mary Pidgeon), Melissa Pritchett (Rich Lady), David Rainey (Bert), Todd Waite (Mr. Marvel), Charles Krohn (Undertaker), Jeffrey Bean (Jacob Marley), Bettye Fitzpatrick (Spirit of Christmas Past), Charles Swan (Scrooge at Fourteen), Philip Lehl (Scrooge at Twenty One), Paul Hope (Mr. Fezziwig), Shelley Calene-Black (Mrs. Fezziwig), Natalie Arneson or Loren Thornton (Wendy), Particia (Melissa Pritchett), James Belcher (Fiddler), Ezequiel Guerra Jr. (Dick Wilkins), Michael Tapley (Travis), Elizabeth Bunch (Belle), David Rainey (Spirit of Christmas Present), Shelley Calene-Black (Mrs. Cratchit), Natalie Arneson (Martha Cratchit), Elizabeth Bunch (Fred's Wife), Michael Tapley (Mr. Topper), Robin Terry (Fred's Sister-in-Law), Charles Krohn (Old Joe), Michael Tapley/Natalie Arneson/Ezequiel Guerra Jr./Melissa Pritchett/Charles Swan/Robin Terry (Ghostly Apparitions/Citizens of London), Jeremiah Pratt or Sydney Welling (Tim Cratchit), Katerina Pasat or Victoria Van Sickle (Spoiled Child), Destin Leo Bourgeois/Julian Brashears/Ty Doran/Joseph Kilian Wolf (School Boys), Jennifer Laporte or Aurora Dawn Silva (Belinda Cratchit/School Boy), Chase I. Duffin or Robert Liam Wolf (Boy Scrooge), Gabi Chennisi or Maureen Fenninger (Fan), Jade Gilbo or Sara Elizabeth Ortega (Claire), Andrew Chennisi or Cole Thompson (Peter Chratchit), Breanna Presley or Evan Thompson (Cider Kid/Ignorance), Caylin Falcon or Rissa Medlenka (Cider Kid/Want), Jack Delac or Ty Doran (Turkey Boy)

CULTURE CLASH IN AMERICCA: Created, Written and Performed by Culture Clash, Richard Montoya, Ric Salinas and Herbert Sigüenza; Directed by Clash Collective; Costume Design, Herbert Sigüenza; Lighting Design, Clint Allen; Sound Design, Richard Montoya; Choreography, Ric Salinas; Company Stage Manager, Francisco Hernandez; Stage Manager, Elizabeth M. Berther; Assistant Stage Manager, Sara Elida Mills; January 6 -29, 2006, Alley Theatre Hubbard Stage

THE PILLOWMAN by Martin McDonagh; Directed by Gregory Boyd; Scenic & Lighting Design, Kevin Rigdon; Costume Design, Linda Ross; Original Music and Sound, John Gromada; Fight Direction, Brian Byrnes; Stage Manager, Terry Cranshaw; Assistant Director, Alex Harvey; January 27–February 26, 2006; Alley Theatre Neuhaus Stage; **Cast:** Jeffrey Bean (Michal), Chris Hutchison (Father), Melissa Pritchett (Mother), David Rainey (Ariel), Rick Stear (Katurian), John Tyson (Tupolski)

JOURNEY'S END by R.C. Sherriff; Directed by Gregory Boyd; Scenic Design, Hugh Landwehr; Costume Design, Linda Fisher; Lighting Design, Pat Collins; Sound Design, John Gromada, Ryan Rumery; Stage Manager, Elizabeth M. Berther; Dialect Coach, Stephen Gabis; Assistant Stage Manager, Sara Elida Mills; Dramaturg, Joe Luis Cedillo; February 24–March 19, 2006; Alley Theatre Hubbard Stage; **Cast:** Daniel Freedom Stewart (Captain Hardy), James Black (Lieutenant Osborne), Noble Shropshire (Private Mason), Joe Delafield (2nd Lieutenant Raleigh), Mark Shanahan (Captain Stanhope), Jeffrey Bean (2nd Lieutenant Trotter), Avery Clark (2nd Lieutenant Hibbert), Daniel Freedom Stewart (The Company Sergeant–Major), James Belcher (The Colonel), Brandon Hearnsberger (A German Soldier), Ezequiel Guerra Jr., Brandon Hearnsberger and John R. Johnston (Soldiers)

ORSON'S SHADOW by Austin Pendleton; Directed by David Cromer; Conceived by Judith Auberjonois; Scenic Design, Takeshi Kata; Costume Design, Miguel Angel Huidor; Lighting Design, Kevin Rigdon; Sound Design, Philip T. Cassidy; Choreography, Michael Tapley; Stage Manager, Terry Cranshaw; March 31–April 30, 2006; Alley Theatre Neuhaus Stage; **Cast:** Jeffrey Bean (Ken), Chris Hutchison (Sean), Wilbur Edwin Henry (Orson), James Black (Larry), Elizabeth Bunch (Joan), Elizabeth Heflin (Vivien)

THE MISER by Molière; Adapted by David Ball; Conceived by Steven Epp and Dominique Serrand; Directed by Dominique Serrand; Scenic Design, Richard Hernandez; Costume Design, Sonya Berlovitz; Lighting Design, Marcus Dilliard; Sound Design, David Remedios; Production Stage Manager, Glenn D. Klapperich; Assistant Stage Manager, Sarah Elida Mills; Assistant Director, Kevin Bitterman; April 7–April 30, 2006; Alley Theatre Hubbard Stage; **Cast:** Jess Akin (Ensemble), Sarah Agnew (Elise), Stephen Cartmell (Cleante), Maggie Chestovich (Mariane/Dame Claude), Michelle Edwards (Ensemble), Steven Epp (Harpagon), Ezequiel Guerra, Jr. (Ensemble), Nathan Keepers (La Fleche), Barbara Kingsley (Frosine), Charles Krohn (Anselme), Jim Lichtscheidl (Valere), Melissa Pritchett (Ensemble), David Rainey (Master Jacques), Santry Rush (Ensemble), Brooke E. Wilson (Ensemble)

WITNESS FOR THE PROSECUTION by Agatha Christie; Directed by Gregory Boyd; Scenic Design, Hugh Landwehr; Costume Design, Linda Ross; Lighting Design, Clifton Taylor; Original Music and Sound, John Gromada; Dramaturg, Joe Luis Cedillo; Stage Manager, Elizabeth M. Berther; Assistant Stage Manager, Terry Cranshaw; May 13–June 4, 2006, Alley Theatre Hubbard Stage; **Cast:** Jeffrey Bean (Mr. Myers, Q.C.), James Belcher (Sir Wilfrid Robards, Q. C.), Elizabeth Bunch (Greta), Shelley Calene-Black, Bettye Fitzpatrick (Janet Mackenzie), Elizabeth Heflin (Romaine), Paul Hope (Carter), Chris Hutchison (Clerk of the Court), John R. Johnston (Plain-Clothes Detective/Barrister), Charles Krohn (Mr. Justice Wainwright), Philip Lehl (Mr. Clegg), Mike Lovell (Barrister), Taavi Mark (Barrister), Patrick Mitchell (Dr. Wyatt), Darwin Miller (Barrister), Melissa Pritchett (The Other Woman), Santry Rush (Warder), Mark Shanahan (Leonard Vole), Noble Shropshire (Detective Inspector Hearne), Ron Solomon (Barrister), John Tyson (Mr. Mayhew), Timothy Wrobel (Courtroom Policeman)

ALLIANCE THEATRE

Atlanta, Georgia
THIRTY-SEVENTH SEASON

Artistic Director, Susan V. Booth

MOONLIGHT AND MAGNOLIAS by Ron Hutchinson; Directed by Lynne Meadow; Scenic Designer, Santo Loquasto; Costume Designer, Jane Greenwood; Lighting Designer, Rui Rita; Sound Designer, Jason Romney; Projection Designer, Sage Marie Carter; Original Sound Designer, Obadiah Eaves; Associate Director, Hilary Adams; Associate Lighting Designer, Ben Krall; Production Stage Manager, Pat A. Flora; September 14–October 9, 2005; **Cast:** Tess Malis Kincaid (Miss Poppenghul), Kevin O'Rourke (Victor Fleming), David Pittu (Ben Hecht), Thomas Sadoski (David O. Selznick)

TICK, TICK…BOOM! Book, Music and Lyrics by Jonathan Larson; Script Consultant, David Auburn; Vocal Arrangements and Orchestrations by Stephen Oremus; Direction and Musical Staging by Kent Gash; Scenic Designer, Emily Jean Beck; Costume Designer, Alvin B. Perry; Lighting Designer, Liz Lee; Sound Designer, Clay Benning; Musical Director, Michael Fauss; Associate Director, Byron Easley; Production Stage Manager, lark hackshaw; Dramaturg, Freddie Ashley; September 7–October 2, 2005; **Cast:** Dwayne Clark (Michael), Soara-Joye Ross (Susan/Karessa), Matthew Scott (Jonathan)

EINSTEIN IS A DUMMY by Karen Zacarías; Music by Deborah Wicks La Puma; Directed by Rosemary Newcott; Scenic Designer, Rochelle Barker; Costume Designer, English Toole; Lighting Designer, Ken Yunker; Video Designer, Sabina Maja Angel; Production Stage Manager, Colleen Janich; Dramaturg, Freddie Ashley; November 5–December 10, 2005; **Cast:** Kylie Brown (Elsa), David de Vries (Herr Schloppnoppdinkerdonn), Jahi Kearse (The Cat), Derek Manson (Albert), Justin Tanner (Constantin)

A CHRISTMAS CAROL by Charles Dickens; Adapted by David H. Bell; Directed by Rosemary Newcott; Scenic Designer, D. Martyn Bookwalter; Costume Designer, Mariann Verheyen; Lighting Designer, Diane Ferry Williams; Sound Designer, Clay Benning; Musical Director, Michael Fauss; Assistant Director, Freddie Ashley; Choreographer, Celeste Miller; Production Stage Manager, Pat A. Flora; December 2–24, 2005; **Cast:** Elizabeth Wells Berkes (Belle/Ensemble), Chandra Currelley (Ensemble), Brandon J. Dirden (Dick Wilkins/Ensemble), Neal A. Ghant (Bob Cratchit), Eddie Gillot (Peter Cratchit/Ensemble), Bart Hansard (Mr. Fezziwig/Christmas Present/Ensemble), Denitra

Isler (Mrs. Fezziwig/Mrs. Dilber/Ensemble), Jordan Jackson (Daniel Cratchit/Turkey Boy/Ensemble), Kelly M. Jenrette (Martha Cratchit/Fan/Ensemble), Chris Kayser (Ebenezer Scrooge), Katie Kneeland (Bess/Ensemble), Tendal Jaret Mann (Tiny Tim/Ensemble), Daniel Thomas May (Marley/Ensemble), Megan McFarland (Christmas Past/Peg/Ensemble), Tessa Lene Palisoc (Want/Ensemble), Thomas Piper (Young Scrooge/Ensemble), Ken Robinson (Topper/Ensemble), Keenan Rogers (Wyatt Cratchit/Ignorance/Ensemble), David Rossetti (Ensemble), Morgan Saylor (Belinda Cratchit/Ensemble), India Scandrick (Melinda Cratchit/Ensemble), Brad Sherrill (Fred/Ensemble), Shontelle Thrash (Mrs. Cratchit/Ensemble)

PRIDE AND PREJUDICE by Jane Austen; Adapted and Directed by Jon Jory; Scenic Designer, Robert A. Dahlstrom; Costume Designer, Michael Krass; Lighting Designer, Michael Philippi; Sound Designer, Stephen LeGrand; Choreographer, Daniel Pelzig; Production Stage Manager, Pat A. Flora; January 11–February 12, 2006; **Cast:** Adele Bruni (Kitty Bennet), Julia Dion (Elizabeth Bennet), Jennifer Erdmann (Lydia Bennett/Georgiana), Douglas B. Giorgis (Dancer/Officer/Manservant), Krista Hoeppner (Jane Bennet), Joe Knezevich (Lt. Wickham), Anthony Marble (Mr. Darcy), Pat Nesbit (Lady Catherine de Bourgh/Housekeeper), David Pichette (Mr. Bennet), Peggity Price (Mrs. Bennet), Amy Resnick (Miss Bingley/Mrs. Gardiner), Sarah Roberts (Mary Bennet/Charlotte Lucas), Remi Sandri (Mr. Lucas/Gardiner/Collins), Liam Vincent (Mr. Bingley/Fitzwilliam)

THE STINKY CHEESE MAN AND OTHER FAIRLY STUPID TALES Based on the book by Jon Scieszka and Lane Smith; Adapted by John Glore; Directed by Rosemary Newcott; Scenic Designer, Kat Conley; Costume Designer, Sydney Roberts; Lighting Designer, Michael Philippi; Sound Designer, Thom Jenkins; Production Stage Manager, Colleen Janich; Dramaturg, Celise Kalke; February 18–March 5, 2006; **Cast:** Rob Cleveland (Cocky Locky/Prince/Frog/Wolf/Stepsister), Wendy Melkonian (Goosey Loosey/Bowling Ball Princess/Red Riding Shorts/Rabbit/Old Man/Crowd), Chris Moses (Jack/Rumplestiltskin), Courtney Patterson (Red Hen/Chicken Licken/Tortoise/Crowd), Scott Warren (Cow Patty Boy/Foxy Loxy/Ugly Duckling/Stepsister/Fox/Crowd), Sharisa Whatley (Ducky Lucky/Frog Princess/Cinderella/Owl/Old Lady)

BLUISH by Janece Shaffer; Directed by Susan V. Booth; Scenic Designer, Joseph P. Tilford; Costume Designer, Rachel Anne Healy; Lighting Designer, Ken Yunker; Sound Designer, Clay Benning; Production Stage Manager, Kate McDoniel; Dramaturg, Celise Kalke; February 10–March 12, 2006; **Cast:** Karen Uchida Beyer (Lane), Kati Brazda (Beth), Suehyla El-Attar (Ilene), Howard Elfman (Manny), Todd Gearhart (Ben), Joyce Reehling (Lillian)

JELLY'S LAST JAM Book by George C. Wolfe; Music by Jelly Roll Morton; Lyrics by Susan Birkenhead; Musical Adaptation and Original Music Composed by Luther Henderson; Orchestral Reduction by Darryl G. Ivey; Directed by Kent Gash; Choreographed by Kent and Byron Easley; Scenic Designer, Emily Jean Beck; Costume Designer, Austin K. Sanderson; Lighting Designer, William H. Grant III; Sound Designer, Clay Benning; Musical Director, Darryl G. Ivey; Production Stage Manager, lark hackshaw; Dramaturg, Celise Kalke; March 15–April 9, 2006; **Cast:** Eric B. Anthony (Young Jelly), Rodrick Covington (Jack The Bear), Karole Foreman (Anita), LaVon Fisher (Gran Mimi/Ensemble), J.D. Goldblatt (Jelly Roll Morton), Dell Howlett (Three Finger Jake/Ensemble), Billy Porter (The Chimney Man), Alecia Robinson (Hunnie/Nick), Ken Robinson (Foot in Yo Ass Sam/Gus/Ensemble), Alexis Sims (Hunnie/Too Tight Nora/Al Melrose), Allison Upshaw Spragin (Miss Mamie), André Ward (Buddy Bolden/Ensemble), Andrea Washington (Ensemble), Daniel J. Watts (Ensemble), Laurie Williamson (Hunnie/Frank Melrose), Melissa Lola Youngblood (Ensemble)

...," SAID SAID by Kenneth Lin; Directed by Sharon Ott; Scenic and Lighting Designer, Kent Dorsey; Costume Designer, Deborah L. Trout; Sound Designer, Stephen LeGrand; Fight Choreographer, Jason Armit; Production Stage Manager, Robert Allen Wright; Dramaturg, Freddie Ashley; April 7–30, 2006; **Cast:** Jacqueline Antaramian (Sarah Said), Kate Donadio (Emily), David Limbach (Guard), Michael Santo (Andre Said), Victor Slezak (Michel Garcet)

INTIMATE APPAREL by Lynn Nottage; Directed by Susan V. Booth; Scenic Designer, Scott Bradley; Costume Designer, Mariann Verheyen; Lighting Designer, Robert Wierzel; Sound Designer and Original Music Composer, Lindsay Jones; Producer Stage Manager, Kate McDoniel; Dramaturg, Celise Kalke; April 19–May 14, 2006; **Cast:** Quincy Tyler Bernstine (Mayme), Andrea Frye (Mrs. Dickson), Rhoda Griffis (Mrs. Van Buren), Tyrone Mitchell Henderson (George), Tzahi Moskovitz (Mr. Marks), Roslyn Ruff (Esther)

STEVE MARTIN'S THE UNDERPANTS by Steve Martin; Adapted from the play by Carl Sternheim; Directed by Aaron Posner; Scenic Designer, Kris Stone; Costume Designer, Linda Roethke; Lighting Designer, Ken Yunker; Sound Designer, Clay Benning; Music Composer, Dr. Greg Wilder; Production Stage Manager, lark hackshaw; Dramaturg, Freddie Ashley; May 24–June 18, 2006; **Cast:** Elizabeth Wells Berkes (Louise Maske), David de Vries (Visitor), Lori Larsen (Gertrude Deuter), Eddie Levi Lee (Klinglehoff), Jeff Portell (Theo Maske), Ariel Shafir (Frank Versati), Todd Weeks (Benjamin Cohen)

Ariel Shafir, Elizabeth Wells Berkes in *Steve Martin's The Underpants* PHOTO BY GREG MOONEY

AMERICAN CONSERVATORY THEATER

San Francisco, California
THIRTY-NINTH SEASON

Artistic Director, Carey Perloff

THE OVERCOAT Created and directed by Morris Panych and Wendy Gorling; Scenic Designer, Ken MacDonald; Costume Designer, Nancy Bryant; Lighting Designer, Alan Brodie; Stage Manager, Jan Hodgson; Production Coordinator/Advance Electrician, Jim Brett; August 25–September 25, 2005; **Cast:** Peter Anderson (The Man), Victoria Adilman (Office Worker/Whore/Fabric Worker), Manon Beaudoin (Landlady's Old Mom/Tailor's Assistant/Inmate/Office Worker), Matt Bois (Inmate/Sweatshop Runner/Office Boy), Mark Christmann (Tailor/Bartender/Doctor), Judi Closkey (New Girl), Diana Coatsworth (Office Worker/Whore/Fabric Worker/Nurse/Boss's Wife), Monica Dottor (Office Worker/Fabric Worker/Whore), Tracey Ferencz (Landlady), Peter Grier (Architect/Sweatshop Worker/Inmate), Colin Heath (Office Manager/Tailor's Assistant/Inmate), Ryan Hollyman (Architect/Sailor/Sweatshop Worker/Inmate), Matthew Hunt (Sweatshop Worker/Waiter/Bike Guy), Darren Hynes (Tenant/Orderly/Butler/Sweatshop Worker), Cyndi Mason (Secretary to the Head of the Firm), Allan Morgan (Head of the Firm/Police Chief/Inmate), Graham Percy (Architect/Thug/Fabric Worker), Avi Phillips (Inmate/Office Boy/Sweatshop Runner/Waiter), Derek Scott (Office Janitor/Orderly/Fabric Customer), Sal Scozzari (Thug/Sweatshop Foreman/Waiter/Party Guest), Courtenay Stevens (Architect/Sweatshop Worker/Sailor/Inmate), Brahm Taylor (Inmate/Fabric Worker)

CAT ON A HOT TIN ROOF By Tennessee Williams; Directed by Israel Hicks; Scenic Designer, Ralph Funicello; Costume Designer, Sandra Woodall; Lighting Designer, Russell H. Champa; Sound Designer, Fitz Patton; Dramaturg, Michael Paller; Casting, Meryl Lind Shaw; Assistant Director, Dave Sikula; Dialect Coach, Deborah Sussel; October 13–November 13, 2005; **Cast:** René Augesen (Margaret), Michael James Reed (Brick), Katherine McGrath (Big Mama), Jack Willis (Big Daddy), Anne Darragh (Mae), Rod Gnapp (Gooper), Julian López-Morillas (Reverend Tooker), James Carpenter (Doctor Baugh), Fannie Lee Lowe (Sookey), Austin Greene/William Halladey Lanier/Kevin Matthew Maltz/Tobiah Rickind (Buster/Sonny [alternating]), Devyn Hocevar-Smith/Anya Jessie Richkind (Dixie [alternating])

A CHRISTMAS CAROL by Charles Dickens, Adapted by Carey Perloff and Paul Walsh; Directed by Carey Perloff; Music, Karl Lundeberg; Choreography, Val Caniparoli; Musical Direction, Laura Burton; Scenic Designer, John Arnone; Costume Designer, Beaver Bauer; Lighting Designer, Nancy Schertler; Sound Designer, Jake Rodriguez; Associate Director, Domenique Lozano; Casting, Meryl Lind Shaw and Greg Hubbard; Dramaturg, Michael Paller; November 26–December 26, 2005; **Cast:** Giles Havergal (Ebenezer Scrooge), Ken Ruta (Ghost of Jacob Marley), Jud Williford (Bob Cratchit), Jamila Webb (Anne Cratchit), Carly Cozad (Sally Cratchit), Duke Butterfield (Peter Cratchit), Jack Indiana (Tiny Tim Cratchit), Elizabeth Perry (Belinda Cratchit), Aidan Mehmet (Ned Cratchit), Nina Freeman (Martha Cratchit), Drew Hirshfield, Andrew McClain (Clerks), Joel Rainwater, Deontay Wilson (Charitables), David Gross, Steve Irish, Julian Stetkevych, Mark Watson (Businessmen), G. D. Kimble (Fred), Sharon Lockwood (Mrs. Dilber), Allison Youngberg (Ghost of Christmas Past), Julian Stetkevych (Schoolmaster), David Perle McKenna (Davey), Jack Lundquist (Edward), Evan Bass (Boy Dick), Sam Pritzker (Boy Scrooge), Vanessa Anderson (Little Fan), Cindy Goldfield (Woman in the Street), Laura Sanders (Beggar Girl), Steve Irish (Mr. Fezziwig), Sharon Lockwood (Mrs. Fezziwig), Morgan Spector (Young Scrooge), Drew Hirshfield (Dick Wilkins), Puja Lalmalani (Belle), Nina Freeman (Ermengarde), Ann Farrar (Felicity), Caroline Sharman (Dorothy),

Andrew McClaine (Jim), G. D. Kimble (Burt), Mark Watson (Giles the Fiddler), Joel Rainwater (Alan), Claire Brownell (Ruth), Gianluca Balestra (Alfred), Dylan Ames, Tobi Jane Moore, Lisa Marie Woods (Children of Alan and Ruth), Tobi Jane Moore (Precious Wilkins), Lisa Marie Woods (Sarah Wilkins), Dylan Ames (Rory Wilkins), Velina Brown (Ghost of Christmas Present), Monica Gibbons, Jack Lundquist (Onions), Dylan Ames, Lisa Marie Woods (Figs), Juliana Cressman, Jackeline Warner (Plums), Cindy Goldfield, Drew Hirschfield (Produce Sellers), Claire Brownell (Mary), Ann Farrar (Beth), David Gross (Topper), Caroline Sharman (Annabelle), Andrew McClain (Thomas), Deontay Wilson (Ignorance), Ann Farrar (Want), Evan Bass, David Perle McKenna, Joel Rainwater, Morgan Spector (Gang Members), Caroline Sharman (Mrs. Filcher), Sam Pritzker (Boy in Sunday Clothes), Puja Lalmalani (Belle Wilkins).

SEXUAL PERVERSITY IN CHICAGO by David Mamet; Directed by Peter Riegert; Scenic Designer, Kent Dorsey; Costume Designer, Christine Dougherty; Lighting Designer, Alexander V. Nichols; Sound Designer, Lindsay Jones; Casting, Bernard Telsey Casting and Meryl Lind Shaw; Stage Manager, Elisa Guthertz; January 5–February 5, 2006; **Cast:** David Jenkins (Danny), Elizabeth Kapplow (Joan), Marjan Neshat (Deborah), Gareth Saxe (Bernie)

GEM OF THE OCEAN by August Wilson; Directed by Ruben Santiago-Hudson; Scenic Designer, Chuck Patterson; Cosutme Designer, Karen Perry; Lighting Designer, Jane Cox; Sound Designer, Garth Hemphill; Music by Bill Sims, Jr. and Broderick Santiago; Casting by Laura Stanczyk and Meryl Lind Shaw; Additional Percussion by Stephen O'Neal; Assistant Director, Jade King Carroll; Stage Manager, Dick Daley; February 10–March 12, 2006; **Cast:** Chuck Patterson (Eli), Owiso Odera (Citizen Barlow), Michele Shay (Aunt Ester), Roslyn Ruff (Black Mary), Raynor Scheine (Rutherford Selig), Steven Anthony Jones (Solly Two Kings), Gregory Wallace (Caesar)

THE RIVALS by Richard Brinsley Sheridan; Directed by Lillian Groag; Scenic Designer, Donald Eastman; Costume Designer, Beaver Bauer; Lighting Designer, Nancy Schertler; Sound Designer, Jake Rodriguez; Hair and Makeup Designer (Jeanna Hurd); Dramaturg, Michael Paller; Fight Director, David Maier; Dialogue Coach, Deborah Sussel; Movement and Dance Coach, Christine Mattison; Casting, Meryl Lind Shaw; Assistant Director, Mike Ward; Stage Manager, Joseph Smelser; March 23–April 23, 2006; **Cast:** Mark D. Watson (Thomas), T. Edward Webster (Fag), Claire Brownell (Lucy), René Augesen (Lydia Languish), Stacy Ross (Julia), Jill Tanner (Mrs. Malaprop), Charles Dean (Sir Anthony Absolute), Anthony Fusco (Captain Jack Absolute), Gregory Wallace (Faulkland), Dan Hiatt (Bob Acres), Ann Farrar (Errand Boy), Andy Murray (Sir Lucius O'Trigger), Jud Williford (David), Django (Princess)

A NUMBER by Caryl Churchill; Directed by Anna D. Shapiro; Scenic Designer, David Korins; Costume Designer, Callie Floor; Lighting Designer, Russell H. Champs; Sound Designers, Rob Milburn and Michael Bodeen; Casting, Meryl Lind Shaw; Assistant Director, Laley Lippard; Elisa Guthertz, Stage Manager; April 28–May 28, 2006; **Cast:** Bill Smitrovich (Salter), Josh Charles (Bernard, Bernard, Michael)

HAPPY END. A MELODRAMA WITH SONGS Lyrics by Bertolt Brecht; Music by Kurt Weill; Original German Play by Dorothy Lane (Elisabeth Hauptmann and Bertolt Brecht); Book and Lyrics Adapted by Michael Feingold; Directed by Carey Perloff; Choreographer, John Carrafa; Music Director/Conductor, Constantine Kitsopoulos; Scenic Designer, Walt Spangler; Costume Designer, Candice Donnelly; Lighting Designer, Robert Wierzel; Sound Designer, Jeff Curtis; Dramaturg, Michael Paller; Casting, Meryl Lind Shaw; New York Casting, Telsey + Company; Assistant Director, Nathan Baynard; Stage Manager, Kimberly Mark Webb; June 8–July 9, 2006; **Cast:** Peter Macon (Bill Cracker), Jack Willis (Sam

"Mammy" Wurlitzer), Sab Shimono (Dr. Nakamura ["The Governor"]), Charles Dean (Jimmy Dexter ["The Reverend"]), Rod Gnapp (Bob Marker ["The Professor"]), Justin Leath (Johnny Flint ["Baby Face"]), Linda Mugleston (A Lady in Grey ["The Fly"]), Celia Shumann (Miriam, the barmaid), Joan Harris-Gelb (Major Stone), Steven Anthony Jones (Captain Hannibal Jackson), Charlotte Cohn (Lieutenant Lillian Holiday ["Hallelujah Lil"]), René Augesen (Sister Mary), Lianne Marie Dobbs (Sister Jane), Jud Williford (Brother Ben Owens), Dan Hiatt, Jud Williford (Cops), Jackson Deavis, Dan Hiatt, Drew Hirshfield, Wendy James, Stephanie Saunders, Colin Thompson (Ensemble)

AMERICAN REPERTORY THEATRE

Cambridge, Massachusetts
TWENTY-SEVENTH SEASON

Artistic Director, Robert Woodruff

CARMEN by Georges Bizet; Libretto by Henri Meilhac and Ludovic Halevy; Music adaptation by Bradley Greenwald; Directed by Dominique Serrand; Music Director, Barbara Brooks; Scenic Designer, Dominique Serrand; Costume Designer, Sonya Berlovitz; Lighting Designer, Marcus Dilliard; Stage Manager, Amy James; Subtitles, Steven Epp; September 3–October 8, 2005; **Cast:** Christina Baldwin (Carmen), Bradley Greenwald (Don Jose), Jennifer Baldwin Peden (Micaela/Frasquita), Bill Murray (Escamillo/soldier), Thomas Derrah (Zuniga/The Guide), Justin Madel (Dancaire/Soldier), Kelvin Chan (Remendado/soldier), Corissa White (Mercedes/cigarette girl), Momoko Tanno (Frasquita/cigarette girl), Madeline Cieslak (Pastia/cigarette girl), Dieter Bierbrauer (Morales), Fred Metzger (child), Chorus: Donna Bareket, Neal Ferreira, Hayley Thompson-King, Robert Shtter, Christine Teeters

THE KEENING by Humberto Dorado; English Translation by Joe Broderick and Ryan McKittrick; Directed by Nicolas Montero; Set and Lighting Designer, Alejandro Luna; Costume Designer, David Reynoso; Sound Designer, David Remedios; Dramaturg, Ryan McKittrick; Stage Manager, Peter Braasch Dean; Voice and Speech Coach, Nancy Houfek; October 14 -November 14, 2005; **Cast:** Marissa Chibas

THREE SISTERS from a play by Anton Chekhov; Adapted by Krystian Lupa; Based on a Translation by Paul Schmidt; Directed by Krystian Lupa; Scenic Design, Krystian Lupa; Costume Designer, Piotr Skiba; Lighting Designer, Scott Zielinski; Sound Designer, David Remedios; Original Music by Jacek Ostaszewski; Video Design, Zbyszek Bzymek; Assistant Director, Marcin Wierzchowski; November 26, 2005–January 1, 2006; **Cast:** Sean Dugan (Andrei Prozorov), Kelly McAndrew (Olga), Molly Ward (Masha), Sarah Grace Wilson (Irina), Julienne Hanzelka Kim (Natasha), Will LeBow (Kulygin), Frank Wood (Vershinin), Jeff Biehl (Baron Tuzenbach), Chris McKinney (Solyony), Thomas Derrah (Chebutykin), Sean Sibro (Fedotik), Patrick Mapel (Rohde), Jeremy Geidt (Ferapont/messanger), Mikki Lipsey (Anfisa), Freddy Franklin (Soldier), Elbert Joseph (Soldier), Mason Sand (Soldier)

NO EXIT by Jean-Paul Sartre; Translated by Stuart Gilbert; Directed by Jerry Mouawad; Scenic Designer, Jerry Mouawad; Costume Designer, Rafael Jaen; Sound Designer, David Remedios; Dramaturg, Mark Poklemba; Stage Manager, Darren Brannon; January 7–January 29, 2006; **Cast:** Remo Airaldi (Valet), Will Le Bow (Garcin), Karen MacDonaold (Estelle), Paula Plum (Inez)

ROMEO AND JULIET by William Shakespeare; Directed by Gadi Roll; Scenic Designer, Riccardo Hernandez; Costume Designer, Kasia Maimone; Lighting Designer, DM Wood; Sound Designer, David Remedios; Fight Choreographer, Rod Kinter; Movement, Doug Elkins; Production Stage Manager, Chris De Camillis; Dramaturg, Ryan McKittrick; Dramaturg, Rachael Rayment; Voice and Speech Coach, Nancy Houfek; February 4–March 25, 2006; **Cast:** John Campion (Escales), Tony Roach (Paris), Jeremy Geidt (Montague), Will LeBow (Capulet), Remo Airaldi (Peter), Mickey Solis (Romeo), Che Ayende (Mercucio), Molly Ward (Benvolio), Marc Aden Gray (Tybalt), James Ryen (Petruchio), Thomas Derrah (Friar Lawrence), James T. Alfred (Friar John, Sampson), Mara Sidmore (Balthazar), Scott MacArthur (Abram), Edward Tournier (Gregory), Matthew Shawlin (Page to Paris), Scott MacArthur (Apothecary), Mikki Lipsey (Lady Montague), Elizabeth Hess (Lady Capulet), Annika Boras (Juliet), Karen MacDonald (Nurse), James Ryen (First Watch) Santio Cupon (Ensemble), Melissa Ham-Ellis (Ensemble), Tenile Pritchard (Ensemble), Caitlin Shaub (Ensemble), Matthew Shawlin (Ensemble), Will Weaver (Ensemble)

ORPHEUS X Music and text by Rinde Eckert; Video by Denise Marika; Directed by Robert Woodruff; Scenic Designer, David Zinn and Denise Marika; Costume Designer, David Zinn; Lighting Designer, Christopher Akerlind; Sound Designer, David Remedios; Stage Manager, Peter Braasch Dean; Dramaturg, Ryan McKittrick; Voice and Speech Coach, Nancy Houfek; March 25–April 23, 2006, **Cast:** Rinde Eckert (Orpheus), Suzan Hanson (Eurydice), John Kelly (John/Persephone)

ISLAND OF SLAVES by Pierre Marivaux; Translation by Gideon Lester; Directed by Robert Woodruff; Scenic Designer, David Zinn; Lighting Designer, Christopher Akerlind; Sound Designer, David Remedios; May 13–June 11, 2006; **Cast:** John Campion (Iphicrate), Remo Airaldi (Arlequin), Karen MacDonald (Euphrosine), Fiona Gallagher (Cleanthis), Thomas Derrah (Trivelin), Ryan Carpenter (Fena Barbitall), Airline Inthyrath (JuJu Bee), Adam Shanahan (Raquel Blake), Freddy Franklin (Mohogoney Brown), Santio Cupon (Landa Plenty)

ARENA STAGE

Washington, District of Columbia
FIFTY-FIFTH SEASON

Artistic Director, Molly Smith

CROWNS by Regina Taylor; adapted from the book by Michael Cunningham and Craig Marberry; Directed and choreographed by Marion J. Caffey; Music Director, Marcus Harper; Scenic and Lighting Designer, Dale F. Jordan; Costume Designer, Emilio Sosa; Original Sound Design, Rick Menke; Casting, Elissa Myers, Paul Fouquet; Dance Captain, LaVon D. Fisher; Stage Manager, Marianne Montgomery; Assistant Stage Manager, Kurt Hall; Technical Director, Jim Glendinning; July 5–August 7, 2005; **Cast:** Rob Barnes (Man/Preacher/Teddy/Elegba–Orisha of Crossroads), Gretha Boston (Velma/Oya–Orisha of Storms), Roz Beauty Davis (Yolonda/Ogun–Orisha of Iron, War & Labor), LaVon D. Fisher (Jeanette/Yemaya–Orisha of Seas), Angela Karol Grovey (Mabel/Shango-Orisha of Fire), Joy Lynn Matthews (Wanda/Oshun–Orisha of Rivers & Waters), Barbara D. Mills (Mother Shaw/Obatala–Orisha of Wisdom & Creativity)

PASSION PLAY, A CYCLE by Sarah Ruhl; Directed by Molly Smith; Scenic Designer, Scott Bradley; Costume Designer, Linda Cho; Lighting Designer, Joel Moritz; Sound Design and Original Music, André Pluess; Dramaturg, Mark Bly; Stage Manager, Amber Dickerson; Assistant Stage Manager, Angie O. Moy; Production Manager, Carey Lawless; Technical Director, Jim Glendinning; Properties Manager, Chuck Fox; Master Electrician, Christopher V. Lewton; Master Sound Technician, Timothy M. Thompson; Costume Shop Manager, Joseph P.

Salasovich; September 2–October 16, 2005; **Cast:** Kelly Brady (Mary 1/Ensemble), Parker Dixon (Ensemble), Robert Dorfman (Queen Elizabeth/Hitler/Reagan/Nixon/Ensemble), Leo Erickson (Director/Ensemble), Carla Harting (Mary 2/Ensemble), Edward James Hyland (Visiting Friar/Visiting Englishman/VA1/Ensemble), Karl Miller (Machinist/German Officer/Young Director/Ensemble), Polly Noonan (Village Idiot/Violet/Ensemble), Howard W. Overshown (John/Eric/J/Ensemble), Lawrence Redmond (Carpenter #2/Ensemble), J. Fred Shiffman (Carpenter #1/VA 2/Ensemble), Felix Solis (Pontius/Foot Soldier/P/Ensemble)

BORN YESTERDAY by Garson Kanin; Directed by Kyle Donnelly; Scenic Designer, Kate Edmunds; Costume Designer, Michael Krass; Lighting Designer, Nancy Schertler; Sound Designer, Timothy M. Thompson; Hair/Wigs, Jon Aitchison; Speech and Vocal Coach, Kim Bey; Fight Director, Rick Sordelet; Dramaturg, Michelle T. Hall; Casting, Eli Dawson; Stage Manager, Brady Ellen Poole; Assistant Stage Manager, Kurt Hall; Production Manager, Carey Lawless; Technical Director, Jim Glendinning; Properties Manager, Chuck Fox; Master Electrician, Christopher V. Lewton; Master Sound Technician, Timothy M. Thompson; Costume Shop Manager, Joseph P. Salasovich; September 30–November 6, 2005; **Cast:** Susan Lynskey (Helen), Michael Bakkensen (Paul Verrall), Matt Dunphy (Bellhop/Bootblack), Jesse Terrill (Bellhop/Barber), Hugh Nees (Eddie Brock), Jonathan Fried (Harry Brock), James Konicek (Assistant Manager), Suli Holum (Billie Dawn), Rick Foucheux (Ed Devery), Kerri Rambow (Manicurist), Terrence Currier (Senator Norval Hedges), Nancy Robinette (Mrs. Hedges)

CUTTIN' UP Written and directed by Charles Randolph-Wright; adapted from the book by Craig Marberry; Scenic Designer, Shaun L. Motley; Costume Designer, Emilio Sosa; Lighting Designer, Michael Gilliam; Sound Designer, Timothy M. Thompson; Hair/Wigs, Jon Aitchison; Speech and Vocal Coach, Kim Bey; Dramaturg, Mark Bly; Casting, Eli Dawson; Stage Manager, Lloyd Davis Jr.; Assistant Stage Manager, Audra L. Roberson; Production Manager, Carey Lawless; Technical Director, Jim Glendinning; Properties Manager, Chuck Fox; Master Electrician, Christopher V. Lewton; Master Sound Technician, Timothy M. Thompson; Costume Shop Manager, Joseph P. Salasovich; November 4, 2005–January 1, 2006; **Cast:** Peter Jay Fernandez (Andre), Ed Wheeler (Howard), Psalmayene 24 (Rudy), Duane Boutté (Wheeler Parker/Dr. Pressley/Otis and others), Carl Cofield (Lou/Eddie/Howard Jr. and others), Bill Grimmette (Vernon Winfrey/Rev. Jenkins/Uncle and others), Marc Damon Johnson (Kenny/Silas/Rev. Carson and others), Marva Hicks (Karen/Jean/Brenda and others)

DAMN YANKEES Lyrics and music by Richard Adler and Jerry Ross; book by George Abbott and Douglass Wallop; based on the novel by Douglass Wallop The Year the Yankees Lost the Pennant; Directed by Molly Smith; Choreographer, Baayork Lee; Music Director, George Fulginiti-Shakar; Scenic Designer, Rachel Hauck; Costume Designer, Martin Pakledinaz; Lighting Designer, John Ambrosone; Sound Designer, Timothy M. Thompson; Hair and Wig Designer, Jon Aitchison; Assistant Director/Dialect Coach, Anita Maynard-Losh; Assistant Music Director, Jose C. Simbulan; Assistant Choreographer/Dance Captain, Parker Esse; Dramaturg, Michelle T. Hall; Casting, Eli Dawson; Stage Manager, Susan R.White; Assistant Stage Manager, Amber Dickerson; Production Manager, Carey Lawless; Technical Director, Jim Glendinning; Property Master, Chuck Fox; Master Electrician, Christopher V. Lewton; Master Sound Technician, Timothy M. Thompson; Costume Shop Manager, Joseph P. Salasovich; December 9, 2005–February 5, 2006; **Cast:** Lawrence Redmond (Joe Boyd), Kay Walbye (Meg Boyd), Brad Oscar (Mr. Applegate), Rayanne Gonzales (Sister), Lynn Mcnutt (Doris/Ensemble), Matt Bogart (Joe Hardy), Michael L. Forrest (Van Buren), Cindy Marchionda (Gloria Thorpe), J. Fred Shiffman (Welch), Stephen F. Schmidt (Lynch/Ensemble), Meg Gillentine (Lola), Tracy Lynn Olivera (Miss Weston), Christopher Bloch (Commissioner/Ensemble), Harry A. Winter (Postmaster/Ensemble), Stephen Gregory Smith (Bryan-Reporter/

Ensemble), Philip Michael Baskerville (Mark/Ensemble), Kevin M. Burrows (Henry/Ensemble), Michelle Liu Coughlin (Maxine/Ensemble), Steven Cupo (Smokey/Ensemble), Drew Distefano (Del/Ensemble), Parker Esse (Linville/Ensemble), Michael S. Goddard (Rocky/Ensemble), Deanna Harris (Frankie/Ensemble), Ellyn Marie Marsh (Frankie/Ensemble), Christina Lynn Phillips (Gracie/Ensemble), Diego Prieto (Vernon/Ensemble), Kim Shriver (Viv/Ensemble), John Leslie Wolfe (Sohovik/Ensemble), Kate Arnold, Shaun R Parry (Swings), Philip R. Hochberg (Announcer)

AWAKE AND SING! by Clifford Odets; Directed by Zelda Fichandler; Scenic Designer, Andromache Chalfant; Costume Designer, Linda Cho; Lighting Designer, Allen Lee Hughes; Sound Designer, Marc Gwinn; Hair and Wig Designer, Jon Aitchison; Vocal/Speech/Dialect Coach, Deborah Hecht; Dramaturg, Laurence Maslon; Cultural and Historical Consultant, Irving Jacobs; Stage Manager, Martha Knight; Assistant Stage Manager, Kurt Hall; Production Manager, Carey Lawless; Technical Director, Jim Glendinning; Property Master, Chuck Fox; Master Electrician, Christopher V. Lewton; Master Sound Technician, Timothy M. Thompson; Costume Shop Manager, Joseph P. Salasovich; January 20–March 5, 2006; **Cast:** Adam Green (Ralph), Steve Routman (Myron Berger), Miriam Silverman (Hennie), Robert Prosky (Jacob), Jana Robbins (Bessie Berger), Hugh Nees (Schlosser), Adam Dannheisser (Moe Axelrod), Brian Reddy (Uncle Morty), Richard J. Canzano (Sam Feinschreiber)

THE RAINMAKER by N. Richard Nash; Directed by Lisa Peterson; Scenic Designer, Michael Yeargan; Costume Designer, Ilona Somogyi; Lighting Designer, James F. Ingalls; Sound Design and Additional Music by Mark Bennett; Speech and Vocal Consultant, Lynn Watson; Fight Choreographer, Brad Waller; Dramaturg, Mark Bly; Casting, Eli Dawson; Stage Manager, Susan R. White; Assistant Stage Manager, Angie O. Moy; Production Manager, Carey Lawless; Technical Director, Jim Glendinning; Property Master, Chuck Fox; Master Electrician, Christopher V. Lewton; Master Sound Technician, Timothy M. Thompson; Costume Shop Manager, Joseph P. Salasovich; March 3–April 9, 2006; **Cast:** William Parry (H.C. Curry), Graham Winton (Noah Curry), Ben Fox (Jim Curry), Jesse Hooker (Jim Curry), Johanna Day (Lizzie Curry), Frank Wood (File), Delaney Williams (Sheriff Thomas), Michael Laurence (Bill Starbuck)

LADY DAY AT EMERSON'S BAR AND GRILL by Lanie Robertson; Directed by Wendy C. Goldberg; Music Director, William Foster McDaniel; Scenic Designer, Shaun L. Motley; Costume Designer, Austin K. Sanderson; Lighting Designer, Michael Gilliam; Sound Designer, Timothy M. Thompson; Wig Designer, Jon Aitchison; Dramaturg, Martin Kettling; Casting, Eli Dawson; Stage Manager, Amber Dickerson; Assistant Stage Manager, Kurt Hall; Production Manager, Carey Lawless; Technical Director, Jim Glendinning; Property Master, Chuck Fox; Master Electrician, Christopher V. Lewton; Master Sound Technician, Timothy M. Thompson; Costume Shop Manager, Joseph P. Salasovich; March 31–June 4, 2006; **Cast:** Lynn Sterling (Lady Day), William Foster McDaniel (Jimmy Powers), Musicians: Eric Kennedy (Drums), Thomas E. Short Jr. (Bass)

ON THE VERGE: OR THE GEOGRAPHY OF YEARNING by Eric Overmyer; Directed by Tazewell Thompson; Scenic Designer, Donald Eastman; Costume Designer, Carrie Robbins; Lighting Designer, Robert Wierzel; Sound Designer/Original Music, Fabian Obispo; Wig Designer, Sara Jean Landbeck; Vocal Production, Lynn Watson; Dialect Coach, Deena Kaye; Dramaturg, Michelle T. Hall; Casting, Eli Dawson; Stage Manager, Linda Harris; Assistant Stage Manager, Angie O. Moy; Production Manager, Carey Lawless; Technical Director, Jim Glendinning; Property Master, Chuck Fox; Master Electrician, Christopher V. Lewton; Master Sound Technician, Timothy M. Thompson; Costume Shop Manager, Joseph P. Salasovich; May 5–June 11, 2006; **Cast:** Laiona Michelle (Mary),

Molly Wright Stuart (Fanny), Susan Bennett (Alex), Tom Beckett (Alphonse, Grover, Yeti, Gorge Troll, Mr. Coffee, Madame Nhu, Gus, Nicky Paradise)

ARIZONA THEATRE COMPANY

Tucson, Phoenix and Mesa, Arizona
THIRTY-NINTH SEASON

Artistic Director, David Ira Goldstein

PRIDE AND PREJUDICE by Jane Austen; Adapted and directed by Jon Jory; Scenic Designer, Robert A. Dahlstrom; Costume Designer, Michael Krass; Lighting Designer, Michael Philippi; Composer, Peter Eckstrom; Sound Designer, Stephen LeGrand; Choreographer, Daniel Pelzig; Assistant Director, Tamara Fisch; Dialect Coach, Dianne J. Winslow; Production Stage Manager, Glenn Bruner; Stage Manager, Bruno Ingram; Assistant Stage Manager, John Kingsbury; Assistant to the Stage Manager, Stacey Flores; Tucson: September 10–October 1, 2005; Phoenix: October 6–23, 2005; Mesa: October 28–November 6, 2005; **Cast:** Adele Bruni (Kitty Bennet), Julia Dion (Elizabeth Bennet), Jennifer Erdmann (Lydia Bennet/Georgiana), Douglas B. Giorgis (Dancer/Officer/Manservant), Krista Hoeppner (Jane Bennet), Joe Knezevich (Lt. Wickham), Anthony Marble (Mr. Darcy), Pat Nesbit (Lady Catherine de Bourgh/Housekeeper), David Pichette (Mr. Bennet), Peggity Price (Mrs. Bennet), Amy Resnick (Miss Bingley/Mrs. Gardiner), Sarah Roberts (Mary Bennet/Charlotte Lucas), Remi Sandri (Mr. Lucas/Gardiner/Collins), Liam Vincent (Mr. Bingley/Fitzwilliam)

BAD DATES by Theresa Rebeck; Directed by Aaron Posner;; Scenic Designer, William Bloodgood; Costume Designer, Sam Fleming; Lighting Designer, Rick Paulsen; Sound Designer, Brian Jerome Peterson; Production Stage Manager, Glenn Bruner; Assistant Stage Manager, Bruno Ingram; Tucson: October 22–November 12, 2005; Phoenix: November 17–December 4, 2005; **Cast:** Erika Rolfsrud (Haley)

HANK WILLIAMS: LOST HIGHWAY by Randal Myler and Mark Harelik; Directed by Randal Myler; Musical Director, Dan Wheetman; Scenic Designer, Vicki Smith; Costume Designer, Robert Blackman; Lighting Designer, Don Darnutzer; Sound Designer, Eric Stahlhammer; Stage Manager, Bruno Ingram; Assistant Stage Managers, Glenn Bruner and Elizabeth Lohr, Assistant to the Stage Manager, Stacey Flores; Tucson: November 26–December 17, 2005; Phoenix: December 29, 2005–January 22, 2006; Mesa: February 3–12, 2006; **Cast:** Stephen G. Anthony (Hoss), Mississippi Charles Bevel (Tee-Tot), Margaret Bowman (Mama Lilly), Patricia Dalen (The Waitress), H. Drew Perkins (Leon Loudmouth), Mike Regan (Fred "Pap" Rose), Regan Southard (Audrey Williams), Myk Watford (Jimmy Burrhead), Russ Wever (Shag), Van Zeiler (Hank Williams)

CROWNS by Regina Taylor; Directed by Andrea Frye; Musical Director, James M. Calhoun; Choreographer, Mercedes Ellington; Scenic Designer, Marjorie Bradley Kellogg; Costume Designer, Reggie Ray; Lighting Designer, Dawn Chiang; Sound Designer, Brian Jerome Peterson; Stage Manager, Elizabeth Lohr; Assistant Stage Manager, Bruno Ingram; Assistant to the Stage Manager, Cheryl Hanson; Assistants to the Director, Stephen Sposito and Jerusha Rubi; Tucson: January 14–February 4, 2006; Phoenix: February 9–26, 2006; **Cast:** Pat Bowie (Mother Shaw), Thomas Jefferson Byrd (Man), Crystal Fox (Yolanda), Angela Karol Grovey (Wanda), Erika LaVonn (Velma), Julia Lema (Mabel), April Nixon (Jeanette)

SHERLOCK HOLMES: THE FINAL ADVENTURE by Steven Dietz; Directed by David Ira Goldstein; Scenic Designer, Bill Forrester; Costume Designer, David Kay Mickelsen; Lighting Designer, Dennis Parichy; Composer, Roberta Carlson; Sound

Designer, Brian Jerome Peterson; Fight Director, Kenneth Merckx, Jr.; Production Stage Manager, Glenn Bruner; Assistant Stage Managers, John Kingsbury and Bret Torbeck; Assistant to the Stage Manager, Stacey Flores; Tucson: March 4–25, 2006; Phoenix: March 30–April 16, 2006; **Cast:** Laurence Ballard (Professor Moriarty), Erin Bennett (Madge Larrabee), Mark Capri (Sherlock Holmes), H. Michael Croner (Ensemble), Roberto Guajardo (Sid Prince), Jonathan Hicks (Ensemble), Preston Maybank (The King of Bohemia), Kenneth Merckx, Jr. (James Larrabee), Victor Talmadge (Doctor John Hamish Watson), Libby West (Irene Adler)

TUESDAYS WITH MORRIE by Jeffrey Hatcher and Mitch Albom; Directed by Samantha K. Wyer; Scenic Designer, Robin Sanford Roberts; Costume Designer, Kish Finnegan; Lighting Designer, T. Greg Squires; Composer, Michael Koerner; Sound Designer, Brian Jerome Peterson; Production Stage Manager, Glenn Bruner; Assistant Stage Manager, John Kingsbury; Assistant to the Stage Manager, Cheryl Hanson; Tucson: April 15–May 6, 2006; Phoenix: May 11–28, 2006; Mesa: June 2–11, 2006; **Cast:** Mark Chamberlain (Mitch), Clayton Corzatte (Morrie)

ARKANSAS REPERTORY THEATRE

Little Rock, Arkansas
THIRTIETH SEASON

Artistic Director, Robert Hupp

STEEL MAGNOLIAS by Robert Harling; Directed by Robert Hupp; Scenic Designer, Mike E. Nichols; Costume Designer, Robert A. Pittenridge; Lighting Designer, James Japhy Weideman; Sound Designer, M. Jason Pruzin; Properties Designer, Christina Gould; Production Manager, Rafael Colon Castanera; Stage Manager, Julie Stemmler; Style Consultant, Grady Smith; September 9–25, 2005; **Cast:** Lori Fischer (Truvy), Erin Moon (Annelle), Judy Trice (Clairee), Kelly Mares (Shelby), Laurie Dawn (M'Lynn), Harold Nichols (DJ)

OF MICE AND MEN by John Steinbeck; Directed by Robert Hupp; Set Designer, Mike E. Nichols; Costume Designer, Margaret A. McKowen; Lighting Designer, Andrew Meyers; Sound Designer, M. Jason Pruzin; Properties Designer, Christina Gould; Fight Choreographer, D.C. Wright; Production Manager, Rafael Colon Castanera; Stage Manager, Tara Kelly; Musical Arrangements, Nick Plakias; October 14–30, 2005; **Cast:** Michael Stewart Allen (George), Joseph Graves (Lennie), Harris Berlinsky (Candy), Nick Plakias (The Boss), Brad Thomason (Curley), Amber C. Irvin (Curley's Wife), Peter Bretz (Slim), Roger M. Eaves (Carlson), Mark Hansen (Whit), Jasper McGruder (Crooks)

DISNEY'S BEAUTY AND THE BEAST Music by Alan Menken; Lyrics by Howard Ashman and Tim Rice; Book by Linda Woolverton; Orginally Directed by Robert Jess Roth; Originally Produced by Disney Theatrical Productions; Directed by Brad Mooy; Musical Director, Kristy L. Nicholson; Choreographer, Ron Hutchins; Set Designer; Christopher C.McCullom, Costume Designer, Rafael Colon Castanera; Lighting Designer, Andrew Meyers; Sound Designer, M. Jason Pruzin; Properties Designer, Christina Gould; Hair and Wig Designer, Christina Grant; Fight Choreographer, Dan O'Driscoll; Stage Manager, Christine Lomaka; Assistant Stage Manager, Tara Kelly; December 2, 2005–January 1, 2006; **Cast:** Holly O'Brien (Belle), Ian Scott (Baker/Ensemble), Ross David Crutchlow (Bookseller/Monsieur D'Arque/Ensemble/Voice of the Narrator), Courter Simmons (LeFou), Jonathan "Goose" Burgard (Gaston), Sheridan Essman (Silly Girl/Ensemble), Kate Fahrner (Silly Girl/Ensemble), Liz O'Donnell (Silly Girl/Ensemble), Ron Lee Savin (Maurice), Dennis J. Clark (Wolf/Ensemble), Edgar Contreras (Wolf/Ensemble), Joshua Gibby (Wolf/Ensemble), Dick Decareau (Cogsworth), Ron Wisniski (Lumiere), Hillary Elliott (Babette), Leslie Becker (Mrs. Potts), Charlie Askew (Chip), Matthew Ponder (Chip), Mika Duncan (Beast), Linda Lane

Smith (Madame de la Grande Bouche), Lacy J. Dunn (Ensemble), Mary Finnie (Ensemble), Peter Eli Johnson (Ensemble), Erick Price (Ensemble), Ragan Renteria (Ensemble), Mickey Toogood (Ensemble), Alex Bush (Young Ensemble), Libby Cathey (Young Ensemble), Shelby Kirby (Young Ensemble), Caroline McCormick (Young Ensemble), Molly Rosenthal (Young Ensemble), Gracie Stover (Young Ensemble)

TOWNS FACING RAILROADS by Jo McDougall; Directed by Eve Adamson; Scenic Designer, Mike E. Nichols; Costume Designer, Olivia Koach; Lighting Designer, Matthew Webb; Sound Designer, M. Jason Pruzin; Production Manager, Rafael Colon Castanera; Stage Manager, Julie Stemmler; January 20–February 5, 2006; **Cast:** Nancy Eyermann (Girl), Joseph Graves (Man), JoAnn Johnson (Woman)

CROWNS by Regina Taylor; Adapted from the book by Michael Cunningham and Craig Marberry; Directed by Lawrence Hamilton; Musical Director, Gayle King; Scenic Designer, Mike E. Nichols; Costume Designer, Trish Clark; Lighting Designer, David Neville; Sound Designer, M. Jason Pruzin; Production Manager, Rafael Colon Castanera; Stage Manager, Tara Kelly; January 27–February 19, 2006; **Cast:** Barbara D. Mills (Mother Shaw), Joilet F. Harris (Mabel), NaTasha Yvette Williams (Velma), Chaundra Cameron (Wanda), Lumiri Tubo (Jeanette), Chandra Thomas (Yolanda), C. Mingo Long (The Man)

BAD DATES by Theresa Rebeck; Directed by Brad Mooy; Set and Properties Designer, Christina Gould; Costume Designer, Stephanie Crenshaw; Lighting Designer, Katharine Lowery; Sound Designer, M. Jason Pruzin; Production Manager, Rafael Colon Castanera; Stage Manager, Christine Lomaka; March 3–19, 2006; **Cast:** Mary Proctor (Haley)

TUESDAYS WITH MORRIE by Jeffrey Hatcher and Mitch Albom; Original New York Production Produced by David Singer and Elizabeth I. McCann; Directed by David Grapes; Scenic Designer, Mike E. Nichols; Costume Designer, Olivia Koach; Lighting Designer, Eric Larson; Sound Designer, M. Jason Pruzin; Properties Designer, Christina Gould; Production Manager, Rafael Colon Castanera; Stage Manager, Julie Stemmler; March 10–26, 2006; **Cast:** Christopher Cass (Mitch), Frank Lowe (Morrie)

THE RETREAT FROM MOSCOW by William Nicholson; First Produced at the Chichester Festival in October 1999; Directed by Brad Mooy; Scenic Designer, Mike E. Nichols; Costume Designer, Olivia Koach; Lighting Designer, Matthew Webb; Sound Designer, M. Jason Pruzin; Properties Designer, Christina Gould; Production Manager, Rafael Colon Castanera; Stage Manager, Christine Lomaka; April 14–30, 2006; **Cast:** Samuel Maupin (Edward), Tom Bateman (Jamie), JoAnn Johnson (Alice)

INTIMATE APPAREL by Lynn Nottage; Commissioned and First Produced by South Coast Repertory and Center Stage; Originally Produced in New York by Roundabout Theatre Company, Todd Haimes, Artistic Director; Directed by Rajendra Ramoon Maharaj; Scenic Designer, Mike E. Nichols; Costume Designer, Leslie Bernstein; Lighting Designer, James Japhy Weideman; Sound Designer, M. Jason Pruzin; Properties Designer, Christina Gould; Production Manager, Rafael Colon Castanera; Stage Manager, Tara Kelly; April 21–May 7, 2006; **Cast:** Sandra Mills Scott (Mrs. Dickinson), Kellie Turner (Esther), Margot Ebling (Mrs. Van Buren), Hisham Tawfiq (George), Michael Kaplan (Mr. Marks), Sherry Boone (Mayme)

A CHORUS LINE Conceived and Originally Directed and Choreographed by Michael Bennett; Music by Marvin Hamlisch; Book by James Kirkwood and Nicholas Dante; Lyrics by Edward Kleban; Co-Choreographer by Bob Avian; Directed by Cliff Fannin Baker; Choreographer, Lynne Kurdziel-Formato; Musical Director, Kristy L. Nicholson; Set Designer, Mike E. Nichols, Costume Designer, Yslan Hicks; Lighting Designer, Ken White; Sound Designer, M. Jason Pruzin;

Properties Designer; Production Manager, Rafael Colon Castanera; Stage Manager, Tara Kelly; Assistant Stage Manager, Melissa Goldhamer; June 2–July 1, 2006; **Cast:** Steven Baker (Mark), Matthew D. Brooks (Butch), Darryl Calmese, Jr. (Richie), DJ Chase (Mike), Joi Chen (Connie), Case Dillard (Bobby), Tony Falcon (Al), Lauren Farrell (Lois), Bob Gaynor (Zack), Matt Gibson (Don), Dennis Glasscock (Larry), Colleen Hawks (Val), Hollie Howard (Sheila), Kolina Janneck (Bebe), Christine LaDuca (Diana), Deborah Leamy (Maggie), Eric T. Mann (Frank), Kathryn Mowat Murphy (Cassie), Joey Murray (Roy), Miguel A. Romero (Paul), Allison Stodola (Kristine), Michael Susko (Greg), Cameron Wade (Tricia), Melanie Waldron (Judy); Kim Scott (Additional Vocals)

BARTER THEATRE

Abingdon, Virginia
SEVENTY-THIRD SEASON

Producing Artistic Director, Richard Rose

LYING IN STATE by David C. Hyer; Directed by Nicholas Piper; Assistant Director, Frank Taylor Green; Scenic Designer, Cheri Prough DeVol; Costume Designer, Karen Brewster; Lighting Designer, Craig Zemsky; Sound Designer, Bobby Beck; Stage Manager, Karen N. Rowe; February 1–April 15, 2006; **Cast:** Melissa Owens (Edna), Michael Poisson (Herb), Scot Atkinson (Wally), Seana Hollingsworth (Buttons), John Hedges (Fred), Mary Lucy Bivins (Margo), Gill Braswell (Harry)

Mike Ostroski, Meredith Autry Holcomb in *Murderer* PHOTO BY BETSY TROYER

FOUR HEARTS AND A CLUB by Jennifer Jarrett; Music and lyrics by Nick Plakias; Directed by Richard Rose; Musical Director, James Hollingsworth; Scenic Designer, Monica-Marie Coakley; Costume Designer, Amanda Aldridge; Lighting Designer, Cheri Prough DeVol; Sound Designer, Logan Kilburn; Stage Manager, Cindi A. Raebel; February 9–April 22, 2006; **Cast:** Mike Ostroski (Spunky Deerbourne), Amy Baldwin (Mavis Deerbourne), Matt Greenbaum (Larry Setzer); Amelia Ampuero (Peaches Brinkley)

GREATER TUNA by Jaston Williams, Joe Sears, Ed Howard; Directed by John Hardy; Scenic Designer, Derek Smith; Costume Designer, Amanda Aldridge; Lighting Designer, Cheri Prough DeVol; Sound Designer, Logan Kilburn; Stage Manager, Cindi A. Raebel; February 18–May 13, 2006; **Cast:** Rick McVey (Thurston/Elmer/Bertha/Yippy/Leonard/RR/Rev. Spikes/Sheriff/Hank), Ben Corbett (Arles/Didi/Harold Dean/Petey/Jody/Stanley/Charlene/Chad/Phineas/Vera)

SECOND SAMUEL by Pamela Parker; Directed by Mary Lucy Bivins; Scenic Designer, Cheri Prough DeVol; Costume Designer, Amanda Aldridge; Lighting Designer, Craig Zemsky; Sound Designer, Logan Kilburn; Stage Manager, Karen N. Rowe; February 23–April 15, 2006; **Cast:** Matt Greenbaum (B Flat), Nicholas Piper (Frisky), Frank Taylor Green (U.S.), John Hedges (Mansel Deanne), Gill Braswell (Mr. Mozel), Seana Hollingsworth (Omaha), Amelia Ampuero (Jimmy Deanne), Amy Baldwin (Ruby), Melissa Owens (Marcela Deanne), Michael Poisson (Doc), Scot Atkinson (June)

MAN OF CONSTANT SORROW by Douglas Pote; Directed by Richard Rose; Scenic Designer, Cheri Prough DeVol; Costume Designer, Amanda Aldridge; Lighting Designer, Craig Zemsky; Sound, Bobby Beck and Rosa Bott; Stage Manager, Karen N. Rowe; April 21–May 27, 2006; **Cast:** Gill Braswell (Ralph Stanley), Nicholas Piper (Carter Stanley), Ed Snodderly, Brandon Story and Buddy Woodward (The Clinch Mountain Boys), Janee Reeves (Jimmie Rodgers), Ed Snodderly (Mr. Nathan), Kimberly Mays (Lucy Stanley), Buddy Woodward (WCYB Manager), Ed Snodderly (Orderly/Bus Driver)

ROMEO AND JULIET by William Shakespeare, adapted by John Hardy; Directed by John Hardy; Scenic Designer, Mark J. DeVol; Costume Designer, Holly Battrum; Lighting Designer, Cheri Prough DeVol; Sound Designer, Bobby Beck & John Hardy; Stage Manager, Cindi A. Raebel; April 28–May 27, 2006; **Cast:** Katy Brown (Chorus), Matt Greenbaum (Romeo), Melissa Owens (Montague), Amelia Ampuero (Juliet), Michael Poisson (Capulet), Amy Baldwin (Lady Capulet), Scot Atkinson (Tybalt), Mary Lucy Bivins (Juliet's Nurse), Melissa Owens (Peter), Frank Taylor Green (Mercutio), John Hedges (Count of Paris), Katy Brown (Prince of Verona), Seana Hollingsworth (Friar Laurence), Scot Atkinson (An Apothecary), Seana Hollingsworth (First Citizen)

MY RIVER, MY VALLEY by Ron Osborne; Directed by Katy Brown; Scenic Designer, Cheri Prough DeVol; Costume Designer, Amanda Aldridge; Lighting Designer, Michael Nowak; Sound Designer, Rosa Bott; Stage Manager, Karen N. Rowe; May 19–July 30, 2006; **Cast:** Mary Lucy Bivins (Viola Cummings), Tricia Matthews (Bessie Brown), Michael Poisson (Sheriff Hankins)

THOROUGHLY MODERN MILLIE by Richard Morris and Dick Scanlan; Directed by Richard Rose; Musical Director, James Hollingsworth. Scenic Designer, Daniel Ettinger; Costume Designer, Amanda Aldridge; Lighting Designer, Craig Zemsky; Sound Designer, Bobby Beck; Stage Manager, Cindi A. Raebel; June 2–August 13, 2006; **Cast:** Jessica Phillips (Millie Dillmount), Brianne Bassler, Sean Campos, Chad Harlow, John Hedges, Seana Hollingsworth, Landen Jones, Sarah Nischwitz, Mary Elizabeth Williams (Moderns), Nicholas Piper (Jimmy Smith), Seana Hollingsworth (Ruth), Amelia Ampuero

(Alice), Janee Reeves (Gloria), Mary Elizabeth Williams (Lucille), Sarah Nischwitz (Rita), Brianne Bassler (Cora), Anne Butler (Ethel Peas), Gilda Ball (Mrs. Meers), Amy Baldwin (Miss Dorothy), Eugene Wolf (Ching Ho), Ben Corbett (Bun Foo), Seana Hollingsworth (Miss Flannery), Rick McVey (Trevor Graydon), Brianne Bassler, Sarah Nischwitz, Janee Reeves, Mary Elizabeth Williams (Stenographers), Sean Campos, Frank Taylor Green, Matt Greenbaum, Ben Greenstone, Chad Harlow, John Hedges, Landen Jones (File Clerks), Brianne Bassler, Sean Campos, Frank Taylor Green, Ben Greenstone, Chad Harlow, John Hedges, Landen Jones, Sarah Nischwitz, Mary Elizabeth Williams (At the Speakeasy), Matt Greenbaum (Policeman), Melissa Owens (Muzzy), Sean Campos (George Gershwin), Ben Greenstone (Ira Gershwin), Mary Elizabeth Williams (Dorothy Parker), Frank Taylor Green (Rodney), Landen Jones (F. Scott Fitzgerald), Sarah Nischwitz (Zelda Fitzgerald), Brianne Bassler, Anne Butler, Chad Harlow, John Hedges, Seana Hollingsworth, Landen Jones, Janee Reeves (Other Guests), Matt Greenbaum (The Butler), Amelia Ampuero (Mathilde, Muzzy's Maid), Sean Campos, Chad Harlow, John Hedges, Landen Jones, Brianne Bassler, Frank Taylor Green, Ben Greenstone (Muzzy's Boys), Seana Hollingsworth (Daphne), Matt Greenbaum (Daphne's Husband)

I'LL NEVER BE HUNGRY AGAIN by Catherine Bush; Music by Gary Bartholomew; Directed by Nicholas Piper. Musical Director, James Hollingsworth. Scenic Designer, Cheri Prough DeVol; Costume Designer, Karen Brewster; Lighting Designer, Michael Nowak; Sound Designer, Bobby Beck; Stage Manager, Karen N. Rowe; June 14–September 16, 2006; **Cast:** Frank Taylor Green (David/ Sissy), Seana Hollingsworth (Starlett O'Hara), Tom Angland (Emerald O'Hara, Ghastly Wilkes, Stank Kennedy), John Hedges (Whet Butler/Whammy), Melissa Owens (Smelanie Hamilton/Swell Watling)

THE PHILADELPHIA STORY by Philip Barry; Directed by Mary Lucy Bivins; Scenic Designer, Daniel Ettinger; Costume Designer, Karen Brewster; Lighting Designer, Craig Zemsky; Sound Designer, Bobby Beck; Stage Manager, Cindi A. Raebel; June 23–August 12, 2006; **Cast:** Amy Baldwin (Tracy Lord), Gwen Edwards (Dinah Lord), Tricia Matthews (Margaret Lord), Ben Corbett (Alexander [Sandy] Lord), Matt Greenbaum (Thomas), Eugene Wolf (William [Uncle Willie] Tracy), Janee Reeves (Elizabeth [Liz] Imbrie), Gill Braswell (Macaulay [Mike] Connor), Rick McVey (George Kittredge), Scot Atkinson (C.K. Dexter Haven), Michael Poisson (Seth Lord)

ALMOST HEAVEN: SONGS OF JOHN DENVER by John Denver and Others; Original Concept by Harold Thau; Directed by John R. Briggs; Muscial Director, Darren Ledbetter. Scenic Designer, Cheri Prough DeVol; Costume Designer, Amanda Aldridge; Lighting Designer, Todd O. Wren; Sound Designer, Bobby Beck; Stage Manager, Karen N. Rowe, Assistant Stage Manager, Jessica Borda; August 18–September 17, 2006; **Cast:** Jill Anderson, Shirine Babb, Sean Campos, Ben Mackel, Kim Mays, Trevor Southworth

MURDERER by Anthony Shaffer; Directed by Richard Rose; Scenic Designer, Cheri Prough DeVol; Costume Designer, Amanda Aldridge; Lighting Designer, Michael Nowak; Sound Designer, Bobby Beck; Stage Manager, Cindi A. Raebel; September 7–November 12, 2006; **Cast:** Mike Ostroski (Norman Bartholomew), Meredith Autry Holcomb (Millie Sykes), Frank Taylor Green (Sergeant Stenning), Carrie Smith (Elizabeth Bartholomew)

GREEN GABLES, THE NEW MUSICAL by Janet Yates Vogt and Mark Friedman; Directed by Katy Brown; Musical Director, James Hollingsworth. Scenic Designer, Cheri Prough DeVol; Costume Designer, Amanda Aldridge; Lighting Designer, E. Tonry Lathroum; Sound Designer, Bobby Beck; Stage Manager, Karen N. Rowe; Assistant Stage Manager, Jessica Boorda; September 22–November 18, 2006; **Cast:** Amelia Ampuero (Anne Shirley), Michael Poisson (Matthew

Tricia Matthews, Mary Lucy Bevins in *My River, My Valley* PHOTO BY BETSY TROYER

Cuthbert), Amy Baldwin (Mrs. Spencer), Ben Corbett (Station Master), Tricia Matthews (Marilla Cuthbert), Mary Lucy Bivins (Rachel Lynde), Melissa Owens (Mrs. Thomas), Eugene Wolf (Mrs. Hammond), Alexandra Eleas (Young Anne), Eugene Wolf (Mrs. Blewett), Maxey Whitehead (Josie Pye), Scot Atkinson (Gilbert Blythe), Matt Greenbaum (Moody Spurgeon), Anne Butler (Jane Andrews), Ezra Colon (Charlie Sloan), Melissa Owens (Mrs. Barry), Seana Hollingsworth (Diana Barry), Alexandra Eleas (Minnie May Barry), John Hedges (Mr. Philips), Tom Angland (Doctor), Rick McVey (Minister), Ben Corbett, Tom Angland (Professors), Rebecca Reinhardt (Lucilla Harris)

THE SUGAR BEAN SISTERS by Nathan Sanders; Directed by Ben Corbett; Scenic Designer, Cheri Prough DeVol; Costume Designer, Amanda Aldridge; Lighting Designer, Michael Nowak; Sound Designer, Rosa Bott; Stage Manager, Karen N. Rowe; September 29–November 11, 2006; **Cast:** Tricia Matthews (Faye Clementine Nettles), Mary Lucy Bivins (Willie Mae Nettles), Melissa Owens (Miss Videllia Sparks), Mike Ostroski (The Bishop Crumley), Frank Taylor Green (The Reptile Woman)

JANE EYRE adapted by Richard Rose from the novel by Charlotte Bronte. Directed by Richard Rose; Scenic Designer, Richard Finkelstein; Costume Designer, Amanda Aldridge; Lighting Designer, E. Tonry Lathroum; Sound Designer, Bobby Beck; Stage Manager, Cindi A. Raebel; October 6–November 18, 2006; **Cast:** Maxey Whitehead (Young Jane), Meredith Autry Holcomb (Jane Eyre), Tom Angland (Mrs. Reed), Carrie Smith (Bessie), Eugene Wolf (Mr. Brocklehurst), Carrie Smith (Miss Temple), Amelia Ampuero (Helen Burns), Seana Hollingsworth (Mrs. Fairfax), Maxey Whitehead (Adele Varens), Carrie Smith (Grace Poole), John Hedges (Rochester), Amy Baldwin (Blanche Ingram), Michael Poisson (Richard Mason), Eugene Wolf (Carter), Michael Poisson (John Eyre), Amy Baldwin (Woman), Eugene Wolf (Clergyman), Tom Angland (St. John Rivers)

IT'S A WONDERFUL LIFE A new adaptation of the Capra film by Richard Rose; Directed by Richard Rose; Musical Director, James Hollingsworth; Scenic Designer, Daniel Ettinger; Costume Designer, Amanda Aldridge; Lighting Designer, E. Tonry Lathroum; Sound Designer, Bobby Beck; Stage Manager, Karen N. Rowe, Assistant Stage Manager, Jessica Borda. November 24–December 30, 2006. **Cast:** Rick McVey (George Bailey), Tom Angland (Mr. Gower), Eugene Wolf (Mr. Martini), Tricia Matthews (Ma Bailey), Matt Greenbaum (Bert), Scot Atkinson (Ernie), Seana Hollingsworth (Mary Hatch Bailey), Hunter E. Wilson (Michael Bailey), Rachel Boyd (Janie Bailey), Gabriel Gounaris (Pete Bailey),

Catie Lott (Beth Anne Bailey), Sydney Gounaris (ZuZu), Frank Taylor Green (Clarence Odbody), Hunter E. Wilson (Young George Bailey), Gabriel Gounaris (Young Harry Bailey), Michael Ostroski (Voice of Young Sam Wainwright), Rachel Boyd (Young Mary Hatch), Catie Lott (Young Violet Bick), Michael Poisson (Uncle Billy), Tricia Matthews (Cousin Tilly), Michael Ostroski (Mr. Tom Bailey), Eugene Wolf (Mr. Potter), Ben Corbett (Potter's Man), Amelia Ampuero (Violet Bick), Nicholas Piper (Harry Bailey), Ben Corbett (A Cop), Tom Angland (Mr. Campbell), Amelia Ampuero (Ruth Dakin), Amelia Ampuero (Mrs. Hatch), Michael Ostroski (Voice of Sam Wainwright),Customers in Building and Loan: Tom Angland (Ed), Ben Corbett (Tom), Matt Greenbaum (Joe), Amelia Ampuero (Mrs. Thompson), Nicholas Piper (Randall), Michael Ostroski (Charlie), Tricia Matthews (Woman with Children), Sydney Gounaris, Catie Lott (Children), Tricia Matthews (Mrs. Martini), Tom Angland (Potter's Agent), Michael Ostroski (Carter), Nicholas Piper (Horace), Devan Stevens (Reporter), Catie Lott, Gabriel Gounaris (Mary's Children), Michael Ostroski (Art Jenkins)

JACOB MARLEY'S CHRISTMAS CAROL by Tom Mula; Directed by Susanne Boulle; Scenic Designer, Cheri Prough DeVol; Costume Designer, Heather Fleming; Lighting Designer, Cheri Prough DeVol; Sound Designer, Bobby Beck; Stage Manager, Cindi A. Raebel; November 21–December 23, 2006; **Cast:** John Hedges (Jacob Marley), Mary Lucy Bivins (The Bogle), Melissa Owens (Ebenezer Scrooge), Amy Baldwin (Record Keeper and others)

BERKELEY REPERTORY THEATRE

Berkeley, CA
THIRTY-EIGHTH SEASON

Artistic Director, Tony Taccone

OUR TOWN by Thornton Wilder; Directed by Johnathan Moscone; Scenic Designer, Neil Patel; Costume Designer, Lydia Tanji; Lighting Designer, Scott Zielinski; Sound Designer & Additional Music, Mark Bennett; Production Stage Manager, Michael Suenkel; Stage Manager, Katherine Riemann; Movement Coach, Mary Beth Cavanaugh; Dramaturg, Amy Utstein; Dialect Coach, Lynne Soffer; Choir Director, Susan Swerdlow; Casting, Amy Potozkin; September 9–October 23, 2005; **Cast:** Trevor Cheitlin (Joe Crowell, Jr./Si Crowell), Jacob Cohen (Wally Webb), Julie Eccles (Mrs. Gibbs), Bill Heck (George Gibbs), Alex Kaplan (Wally Webb), Gideon Lazarus (Joe Crowell, Jr./Si Crowell), Sharon Lockwood (Mrs. Soames), Jarion Monroe (Professor Willard/Constable Warren/Joe Stoddard), Paul Vincent O'Connor (Mr. Webb), Barbara Oliver (Stage Manager), Emma Roberts (Emily Webb), Charles Shaw Robinson (Dr. Gibbs), Ken Ruta (Simon Stimson), Sarah Smithton (Rebecca Gibbs), Emily Trumble (Rebecca Gibbs), T. Edward Webster (Howie Newsome/Sam Craig), Nance Williamson (Mrs. Webb)

FINN IN THE UNDERWORLD by Jordan Harrison; Directed by Les Waters; Scenic Designer, David Korins; Costume Designer, Annie Smart; Lighting Designer, Matt Frey; Sound Designer, Darron L. West; Stage Manager, Kevin Johnson; Dramaturg, Scott Horstein; Casting, Amy Potozkin, Janet Foster; October 6–November 6, 2005; **Cast:** Randy Danson (Rhoda), Lorri Holt (Gwen), Clifton Guterman (Finn), Reed Birney (Carver)

COMEDY ON THE BRIDGE & BRUNDIBAR *Comedy on the Bridge* Libretto by Tony Kushner; Adapted from Václav Kliment Klicpera; Music by Bohuslav Martin; *Brundibar* English adaptation by Tony Kushner after Adolf Hoffmeister's libretto; Music by Hans Krasá; Directed by Tony Taccone; Production Designer, Maurice

Sendak with Kris Stone; Music Director & Conductor, Valerie Gebert; Scenic Designer, Kris Stone; Costume Designer, Robin I. Shane; Lighting Designer, Donald Holder; Sound Designer, Rob Milburn, Michael Bodeen; Movement Director, Kimi Okada; Production Stage Manager, Michael Suenkel; Assistant Stage Manager, Cynthia Cahill; Casting, Janet Foster, Amy Potozkin; Presented in collaboration with Yale Repertory Theatre; November 11–December 28, 2005; **Cast:** Anjali Bhimani (Popelka/The Sparrow), Henry DiGiovanni (Captain Ladinsky/The Ice-Cream Seller), Matt Farnsworth (Sykos/The Milkman), Aaron Simon Gross (Pepicek), Geoff Hoyle (The Strokopounkutnik Sentry/The Baker/The Dog), Euan Morton (The Liskovite Sentry/Brundibar), Devynn Pedell (Aninku), Angelina Réaux (Eva/The Cat), Martin Vidnovic (Bedronyi/The Policeman) William Youmans (Professor Ucitelli), Ensemble: Faith Bowman, Nikaela Bradford, Misha Brooks, Matia Emsellem, Maggie Franks, Julia Franks, Lia Friedman-Salaverry, Elena Garrido-Shaqfeh, Elizabeth Goings, Mason Heller, Gideon Lazarus, Brigette Lundy-Paine, Alec Mathieson, Allison McCoy, Forest McMillin, Evan Neiman, Amanda Neiman, Yael Platt, Nicole Raynor, Brendan Reilly, Erin Reilly, Michelle Roginsky, Oriana Schaaf, Ariele Scharff, Madeline Silverman, Sophia Sinsheimer, Amber Solberg, Gabriel Vergez, Marnina Wirtschafter; Alternates: Debriana Cannon, Sadie Hazelkorn, Sabra Jaffe, Kelty Morash, Ariella Neckritz, Alison Thvedt

9 PARTS OF DESIRE by Heather Raffo; Directed by Joanna Settle; Scenic Designer, Antje Ellerman; Costume Designer, Kasia Walicka Maimone; Lighting Designer, Peter West; Sound Design, Obadiah Eaves; Stage Manager, Nicole Dickerson; January 20–March 5, 2006; **Cast:** Mozhan Marnò

CULTURE CLASH'S ZORRO IN HELL Created, written & performed by Culture Clash: Richard Montoya, Ric Salinas, Herbert Siguenza; Directed by Tony Taccone; Scenic Designer, Christopher Acebo; Costume Designer, Christal Weatherly; Lighting Designer, Alexander V. Nichols; Sound Designer, Robbin E. Broad; Stage Manager, Kimberly Mark Webb; Fight Director, Dave Maier; Movement Director, Mary Beth Cavanaugh; Dramaturg, Shirley Fishman; Casting, Amy Potozkin; Presented in association with La Jolla Playhouse; March 3–April 2, 2006; **Cast:** Richard Montoya (Clasher/Ensemble), Ric Salinas (Kyle [the Bear]/Ensemble), Herbert Sigüenza (Don Ringo/Ensemble), Joseph Kamal (Diego/Zorro/Ensemble), Sharon Lockwood (200 Year Old Woman/Ensemble), Vincent Christopher Montoya (El Musico/Ensemble)

THE GLASS MENAGERIE by Tennessee Williams; Directed by Les Waters; Scenic Designer, Scott Bradley; Costume Designer, Lydia Tanji; Lighting Designer, Matt Frey; Composer, Peter Golub; Dramaturg, Madeleine Oldham; Assistant Dramaturg, Laura Brueckner; Dance Consultant, Mary Beth Cavanaugh; Dialect Coach, Lynne Soffer; Casting, Amy Potozkin; April 6–June 4, 2006; **Cast:** Emily Donahoe (Laura Wingfield), Erik Lochtefeld (Tom Wingfield), Rita Moreno (Amanda Wingfield), Terrence Riordan (Jim O'Connor)

THE MISER by Moliere; Adapted by David Ball; Directed by Dominique Serrand; Scenic Designer, Riccardo Hernandez; Costume Designer, Sonya Berlovitz; Lighting Designer, Marcus Dilliard; Sound Designer, David Remedios; Stage Manager, Glenn D. Klapperich; Assistant Director, Kevin Bitterman; Local Castng, Amy Potozkin; Produced in association with Theatre de la Jeune Lune, American Repertory Theatre, and Actors Theatre of Louisville; May 12–June 25, 2006; **Cast:** Sarah Agnew (Élise), Stephen Cartmell (Cléante), Maggie Chestovich (Mariane/Dame Claude), Steven Epp (Harpagon), Nathan Keepers (La Flèche), Barbara Kingsley (Frosine), Jim Lichtscheidl (Valère), David Rainey (Master Jacques), GreyWolf (Anselme), Kate Austin-Gröen (ensemble), Larkin Boero (ensemble), Brianne Kostielney (ensemble), Brian Stevens (ensemble), Marian Wagner (ensemble), Clive Worlsey (ensemble)

BERKSHIRE THEATRE FESTIVAL

Stockbridge, Massachusetts
SEVENTY-SEVENTH SEASON

Executive Director, Kate Maguire

SIDE BY SIDE BY SONDHEIM Music and lyrics by Stephen Sondheim; Music by Jule Styne, Leonard Bernstein, Mary Rodgers, Richard Rodgers; Continuity by Ned Sherrin; Directed by Gary English; Musical Director, Steven Freeman; Choreography, Gerry McIntyre; Scenic Designer, Yoshi Tankura; Costume Designer, David Murin; Lighting Designer, Daniel J. Kotlowitz; Sound Designer, Ray Schilke; Casting Director, Alan Filderman; June 21–July 9, 2005; **Cast:** Allison Briner, Marcus Neville, Michele Ragusa, Jessica Walter; Pianist: Steven Freeman

EQUUS by Peter Shaffer; Directed by Scott Schwartz; Costume Design, Jess Goldstein; Set Design, Beowulf Boritt; Lighting Design, Kevin Adams; Sound Design, Ray Schilke; Movement Consultant, Gus Solomons Jr.; Production Stage Manager, Marjorie Hanneld; July 12–July 23, 2005; **Cast:** John Curless (Frank Strang), Tara Franklin (Jill Mason), Randy Harrison (Alan Strang), Roberta Maxwell (Hesther Salomon), Jill Michael (Nurse), Pamela Payton-Wright (Dora Strang), Victor Slezak (Dr. Martin Dysart), Don Sparks (Harry Dalton), Steve Wilson (Horseman/Nugget); Richie duPont, Joe Jung, Brad Kilgore, Ryan O'Shaughnesey, Brian Sell (Horse Chorus)

AMERICAN BUFFALO by David Mamet; Directed by Anders Cato; Scenic Designer, Carl Sprague; Costume Designer, Olivia Gajic; Lighting Designer, Jeff Davis; Sound Designer, Scott Killian; Casting Director, Alan Filderman; July 26–August 13, 2005; **Cast:** Chris Noth (Teach), Jim Frangione (Don Dubrow), Sean Nelson (Bobby)

SOUVENIR by Stephen Temperley; Co-production with Ted Snowdon; Directed by Vivian Matalon; Scenic Designer, R. Michael Miller; Costume Designer, Tracy Christensen; Lighting Designer, Ann G. Wrightson; Sound Designer, David Budries; Casting Director, Alan Filderman; August 17–September 3, 2005; **Cast:** Judy Kaye (Florence Foster Jenkins); Donald Corren (Cosme McMoon)

CALDWELL THEATRE COMPANY

Boca Raton, Florida
THIRY-FIRST SEASON

Artistic Director, Michael Hall

MODERN ORTHODOX by Daniel Goldfarb; Directed by Michael Hall; Scenic Designer, Tim Bennett; Costume Designer, Susan Stowell; Lighting Designer, Thomas Salzman; Sound Designer, Steve Shapiro; Production Stage Manager, Jeffry George; June 18–July 10, 2005; Held over to July 31, 2005; **Cast:** Benim Foster (Ben Jacobson), Jason Schuchman (Hershel Klein), Rachel Jones (Hannah Ziggelstein), Margery Lowe (Rachel Feinberger)

WHERE'S CHARLEY? Music & Lyrics by Frank Loesser; Book by George Abbott; Based on the play *Charley's Aunt* by Brandon Thomas; Directed by Michael Hall; Scenic Designer, Tim Bennett; Costume Designer, Susan Stowell; Lighting Designer, Kirk Bookman; Sound Designer, Steve Shapiro; Choreographer, Barbara Flaten; Musical Director, Kevin Wallace; Scenic Artist, Cindi Taylor; Production Stage Manager, Jeffry George; November 6–December 18, 2005; **Cast:** Terrell Hardcastle (Brassett), Bruce Linser (Jack Chesney), Josh

Grisetti (Charley Wykeham), Lauren Shealy (Kitty Verdun), Irene Adjan (Amy Spettigue), Dennis Creaghan (Sir Francis Chesney), John Felix (Mr. Spettigue), Lourelene Snedeker (Donna Lucia D'Alvadorez), Emily Clark, Chris Gleim, Joe Kokofsky (Chorus)

BLITHE SPIRIT by Noel Coward; Directed by Michael Hall; Scenic Designer, Tim Bennett; Costume Designer, Erin Amico; Lighting Designer, John Hall; Sound Designer, Steve Shapiro; Production Stage Manager, Marci A. Glotzer; December 30, 2005–February 12, 2006; **Cast:** Margery Lowe (Edith), Laura Turnbull (Ruth), Dennis Creaghan (Charles), John Felix (Doctor Bradman), Angie Radosh (Mrs. Bradman), Elizabeth Dimon (Madame Arcati), Jacqueline Knapp (Elvira)

UNDER THE BED by Susan Sandler; Directed by Michael Hall; Scenic Designer, Tim Bennett; Costume Designer, Erin Amico; Lighting Designer, Thomas Salzman; Sound Designer, M. Anthony Reimer; Production Stage Manager, Jeffry George; February 19–April 2, 2006; **Cast:** Sylvia Kauders (Various), Ben Hammer (Various), Rosemary Prinz (Various), Kathleen Emrich (The Voice)

THE IMPRESSIONISTS by Michael McKeever; Directed by Michael Hall; Scenic Designer, Tim Bennett; Costume Designer, Erin Amico; Lighting Designer, John D. Hall; Sound Designer, Steve Shapiro; Video Projection Programmer, Sean Lawson; Production Stage Manager, Marci A. Glotzer; April 9–May 21, 2006; **Cast:** Deanna Henson (Berthe Morisot), George Kapetan (Camille Pissarro), Terrell Hardcastle (Claude Monet), Tim Burke (Edgar Degas), Bruce Linser (Pierre-Auguste Renoir), Eric Martin Brown (Edouard Manet), Peter Haig (Charles Gleyre, a waiter, various critics), Kathryn Lee Johnston (Edma Morisot, Camille Doncieux, Lissette, various critics)

CAPITAL REPERTORY THEATER

Albany, NY
TWENTY-FIFTH SEASON

Producing Artistic Director, Maggie Mancinelli-Cahill

BREAKING UP IS HARD TO DO Book by Erik Jackson & Ben H. Winters, Music by Neil Sedaka, Conceived by Marsh Hanson & Gordon Greenberg; Directed by Gordon Greenberg; Scenic Designer, Tobin Ost; Costume Designer, Thom Heyer; Lighting Designer, Jeffrey Croiter; Sound Designer, Christopher St. Hilaire; Choreographer, Lisa Shriver; Production Stage Manager, Diane McLean; WORLD PREMIÈRE July 15–August 21, 2005; **Cast:** Jill Abramovitz (Marge Gelman), Jamie LaVerdiere (Gabriel Green), Nora Mae Lyng (Esther Simopwitz), Edward Staudenmayer (Del Delmonaco), Laura Woyasz (Lois Warner), Stuart Zagnit (Harvey Feldmann)

MEDEA IN JERUSALEM by Roger Kirby; Directed by Maxwell Williams; Scenic Designer, Roman Tatarowicz; Costume Designer, Denise Dygert; Lighting Designer, Annmarie Duggan; Sound Designer, Jeremy Wilson; Production Stage Manager, Liz Reddick; July 15–August 21, 2005; **Cast:** Judith Lightfoot Clarke (Medea), Michael Gotch (Jason's brother), Sean Haberle (Jason), Jennifer McCabe (Medea's sister), Peter Reardon (O'Malley)

SYNCOPATION by Allan Knee, Directed by Maggie Mancinelli-Cahill; Scenic Designer, Roman Tatarowicz; Costume Designer, Thom Heyer; Lighting Designer, Annmarie Dugan ; Sound Designer, Jane Shaw; Choreographer, Susan Cicarelli Caputo; Production Stage Manager, Liz Reddick; October 7–November 6, 2005; **Cast:** Stacey Harris (Anna Bianchi), Adam Pelty (Henry Ribolow)

YOU CAN'T TAKE IT WITH YOU by George S. Kaufman & Moss Hart; Directed by Maggie Mancinelli-Cahill; Scenic Designer, Michael Heil; Costume Designer, Denise Dygert; Lighting Designer, Deborah Constantine; Sound Designer, Christopher St Hilaire; Production Stage Manager, Diane McLean; November 18–December 18, 2005; **Cast:** Kris Anderson (Ed Carmichael), Stephen Bradbury (Mr. Kirby), Tug Coker (Tony Kirby), Meghan Doherty (Alice Sycamore), Iris M. Farrugia (Rheba), James Keil (Wilbur C. Henderson), Richard Mawe (Martin Vanderhof), John Noble (Paul Sycamore), Terry Rabine (Boris Kolenkov), Pat Reilly (Mrs. Kirby), Eileen Schuyler (Penny Sycamore), Nicola Sheara (Gay Wellington, Grand Dutchess Olga Katrina), Rachel Sullivan (Essie Carmichael), Shawn Williams, (Donald), Ted Zeltner (Mr. DePinna)

8-TRACK — THE SOUNDS OF THE 70's Conceived & Directed by Rick Seeber; Costume Designer, Barbara Wolfe; Lighting Designer, Stephen Quandt; Production Design Consultant, Mark Derryberry; Choreographer, Tonya Phillips; Production Stage Manager, Liz Reddick; January 13–February 18, 2006; **Cast:** Teddey Brown (Tenor), Tonya Phillips (Soprano), Nik Rocklin (Baritone), Liana Young (Alto)

LOOKING OVER THE PRESIDENT'S SHOULDER by James Still; Directed by Regge Life; Scenic Designer, S. Anthony Panfili; Costume Designer, Tirza Chappelle; Lighting Designer, Andi Lyons; Sound Designer, Christopher St. Hilaire; Production Stage Manager, Katharine M. Hanley; March 3–March 31, 2006; **Cast:** Larry Marshall (Alonzo Fields)

METAMORPHOSES — by Mary Zimmerman; Based on the Myths of Ovid; Directed by Maggie Mancinelli–Cahill; Scenic Designer, Ted Simpson; Costume Designer, Barbara Wolfe; Lighting Designer, Brian J. Lilienthal; Sound Designer, Christopher St. Hilaire; Production Stage Manager, Liz Reddick; April 28–May 27, 2006; **Cast:** Tiffany Anne Carrin (Scientist/Erysichthon's mother/Nursemaid/Therapist), Parker Cross (Erysichthon/Poseidon/Narrator/Zeus), Nick Gabriel (Orpheus/Philemon/Singer/servant), David Girard (Silenus/Buyer/Phaeton), Lanna Joffrey (Alcyone/Ceres/Persephone/Pomona), Ericka Kreutz (Aphrodite/Harp/Baucis), Christina Bennett Lind (Pandora/Eurydice/Myrrah), Heather Lind (Eurydice/Pandora/Psuche), Kevin Craig West (Bacchus/Ceyx/Hermes/Eros), Craig Wroe (Midas/Hades/Cinyras/Apollo)

ALWAYS … PATSY CLINE Written and originally directed by Ted Swindley; Directed by Maggie Mancinelli-Cahill; Original Set Designer, Katherine McCauley; Costume Designer, Tirza Chappelle; Original Lighting Designer, Stephen Quandt; Sound Designer, Christopher St, Hilaire; June 16–July 2, 2006; **Cast:** Shelly Stephens (Patsy Cline), Diana Rogers (Louise Seger)

Trey Lyford, Geoff Sobelle in *All Wear Bowlers* PHOTO BY CRAIG SCHWARTZ

CENTER THEATRE GROUP

Los Angeles, California
THIRTY-NINTH SEASON

Artistic Director, Michael Ritchie

MARK TAPER FORUM

ROMANCE by David Mamet; Directed by Neil Pepe; Scenic Designer, Robert Brill; Costume Designer, Sarah Edwards; Lighting Designer, James F. Ingalls; Sound Designer, Obadiah Eaves; Fight Director, Rick Sordelet; Casting, Bernard Telsey Casting and Amy Lieberman, CSA; Production Stage Manager, Matthew Silver; Stage Manager, David S. Franklin; September 29–November 13, 2005; **Cast:** Noah Bean (Bernard), Ed Begley, Jr. (The Defense Attorney), Larry Bryggman (The Judge), Jim Frangione (The Prosecutor), Steven Goldstein (The Defendant), Steven Hawley (The Bailiff), Todd Weeks (The Doctor)

LEWIS AND CLARK REACH THE EUPHRATES by Robert Schenkkan; Directed by Gregory Boyd; Scenic Designer, Jeff Cowie; Costume Designer, Judith Dolan; Lighting Designer, Howell Binkley; Music and Sound Designer, John Gromada; Projection Designer, Marc I. Rosenthal, Fight Director, Steve Rankin; Casting, Amy Lieberman, CSA; Production Stage Manager, Mary K Klinger; Stage Manager, Michelle Blair; December 1, 2005–January 22, 2006; **Cast:** Roy Abramsohn (Jefferson Aide/Corps Member), Tony Amendola (Corps Member/Black Buffalo/Charbonneau), James Barbour (Captain Meriwether Lewis), Rubén C. González (Corps Member/Warrior/Crow at Rest), Eugene Lee (York), Tess Lina (Sally Hemmings/Crow's Wife/Sacagawea), Ty Mayberry (Jefferson Aide/Corps Member), Jeffrey Nordling (Captain William Clark), Randy Oglesby (Durien/Hugh McCracken/Corps Member), Morgan Rusler (Thomas Jefferson/Big White/Corps Member)

THE CHERRY ORCHARD by Anton Chekhov; Adapted by Martin Sherman; Directed by Sean Mathias; Scenic Designer, Alexander Dodge; Costume Designer, Catherine Zuber; Lighting Designer, James F. Ingalls; Sound Designer, Jon Gottlieb; Casting, Amy Lieberman, CSA; Production Stage Manager, David S. Franklin; Stage Manager, Anna Belle Gilbert; February 2–March 19, 2006; **Cast:** Annette Bening (Ranyevskaya), Lothaire Bluteau (Gaev), Peter Cambor (Yasha), Tom Costello (Post Office Clerk), Jennifer Dundas (Dunyasha), Frances Fisher (Carlotta), Jeanine Hackett (Ensemble), Jason Butler Harner (Trofimov), Heidi Johanningmeier (Ensemble), Lyle Kanouse (Simeonov-Pishchik), Alan Mandell (Firs), Alfred Molina (Lopakhin), Tim Monsion (Ensemble), Rebecca Mozo (Anya), Sarah Paulson (Varya), Reed Ruby (Ensemble), Raphael Sbarge (Yepikhodov), Don Oscar Smith (Station Master), Alison Weller (Ensemble), Alexander Zale (A Stranger)

iWITNESS by Joshua Sobol; Adapted by Barry Edelstein from an English Language version by Joshua Sobol; Directed by Barry Edelstein; Scenic Designer, Neil Patel; Costume Designer, Robert Blackman; Lighting Designer, Russell Champa; Sound Designer, Jon Gottlieb; Projection Designer, Jan Hartley; Cinematographer, Alice Brooks; Casting, Amy Lieberman, CSA; Production Stage Manager, James T. McDermott; Stage Manager, Elizabeth Atkinson; March 30–May 21, 2006; **Cast:** JB Blanc (General Mussof, Sgt. Bastian), Christina Burdette (Maria), Seamus Dever (Hans/General Ranft/Warden), Katrina Lenk (Margaret), Rebecca Lowman (Franca), Joan McMurtrey (Vice-Admiral Arps/Dr. Raps), James Joseph O'Neil (Martin/Feldmann), Michael Rudko (Schreiber/Fr. Jochmann), Gareth Saxe (Franz Jägerstätter)

WITHOUT WALLS by Alfred Uhry; Directed by Christopher Ashley; Scenic Designers, Thomas Lynch and Charlie Corcoran; Costume Designer, David C. Woolard; Lighting Designer, Donald Holder; Sound Designer and Additional Music, Mark Bennett; Casting, Erika Sellin, CSA, and Amy Lieberman, CSA; Production Stage

Manager, Alex Lyu Volckhausen; Stage Manager, Michelle Blair; June 1–July 16, 2006; **Cast:** Laurence Fishburne (Morocco Hemphill), Matt Lanter (Anton McCormick), Amanda MacDonald (Lexy Sheppard)

WATER & POWER by Richard Montoya for Culture Clash; Directed by Lisa Peterson; Scenic Designer, Rachel Hauck; Costume Designer, Christopher Acebo; Lighting Designer, Alexander V. Nichols; Music and Sound Designer, Paul James Prendergast; Dramaturg, John Glore; Fight Director, Steve Rankin; Choreographer, Jennifer Sanchez; Casting, Erika Sellin, CSA; Production Stage Manager, James T. McDermott; Stage Manager, Susie Walsh. July 27–September 17, 2006; **Cast:** Moises Arias (Deer Dancer/Gibby/Gabby), Dakin Matthews (The Fixer), Richard Montoya (Water), Emilio Rivera (El Musico/Vendor), Winston J. Rocha (Asunción Garcia), Ric Salinas (Norte/Sur), Herbert Siguenza (Power)

AHMANSON THEATRE

DEAD END by Sidney Kingsley; Directed by Nicholas Martin; Scenic Designer, James Noone; Costume Designer, Michael Krass; Lighting Designer, Kenneth Posner; Sound Designer, Kurt Kellenberger; Music Composition, Mark Bennett; Fight Director, Rick Sordelet; Casting, Amy Lieberman, CSA, and Erika Sellin; Production Stage Manager, Grayson Meritt; Stage Managers, James T. McDermott and Elizabeth Atkinson; August 28–October 16, 2005; **Cast:** Carol Androsky (Governess), Ian Barford (Patrolman Mulligan), Walter Beery (Wealthy Gentleman), Beck Bennett (Policeman), Scott Burman (G-Man), Dennis Cockrum (Hunk), Nick Dazé (Intern), Ryan Eggold (2nd Ave. Boy), Wyatt Fenner (Young Man), Ben Giroux (2nd Ave. Boy), Shiloh Goodin (Young Girl), Pamela Gray (Francey), Kathryn Hahn (Drina), Megan Marie Harvey (Tenement Girl), Sarah Hudnut (Kay), Jeffrey Hutchinson (Mr. Jones), Charley Lang (Mr. Griswald), Clay Larsen (2nd Ave. Boy), Geoffrey E. Lind, Jr. (G-Man), Melanie Lora (Street Girl), Leo Marks (Jack Hilton), Luce Morgan (Wealthy Lady), Cole Morgen (Boy), Sam Murphy (Spit), Dohn Norwood (Doorman), Trevor Peterson (T.B.), Donna Pieroni (Lady With Dog), Benjamin Platt (Philip Griswald), Greg Roman (Dippy), Adam Rose (Angel), Tom Everett Scott (Gimpy), Jeremy Sisto (Baby-Face Martin), Ed Sorrell (Ed), Barry Squitieri (Mr. Tranche), Josh Sussman (Milty), Juliana Long Tyson (Young Girl), Ricky Ullman (Tommy), Danielle Van Beest (Tenement Girl), Joyce Van Patten (Mrs. Martin), Teddy Vincent (Lady With Broom), Craig Matthias Vogeley (Boy), Ryan Wilkins (G-Man)

THE DROWSY CHAPERONE. Music and Lyrics, Lisa Lambert and Greg Morrison; Book, Bob Martin and Don McKellar; Directed and Choreographed by Casey Nicholaw; Scenic Designer, David Gallo; Costume Designer, Gregg Barnes; Lighting Designer, Ken Billington and Brian Monahan; Sound Designer, Acme Sound Partners; Casting, Bernard Telsey Casting and Amy Lieberman, CSA; Orchestrations, Larry Blank; Dance and Incidental Music Arrangement, Glen Kelly; Music Direction and Vocal Arrangements, Phil Reno; Technical Supervision, Brian Lynch; Production Stage Manager, Karen Moore; Stage Managers, Joshua Halperin and Susie Walsh; November 10–December 24, 2005; **Cast:** Danny Burstein (Aldolpho), Georgia Engel (Mrs. Tottendale), Sutton Foster (Janet), Edward Hibbert (Underling), Troy Britton Johnson (Robert), Eddie Korbich (George), Garth Kravits (Gangster # 2), Jason Kravits (Gangster #1), Beth Leavel (Drowsy), Kecia Lewis-Evans (Trix), Bob Martin (Man in Chair), Angela Pupello (Servant/Reporter/Dream Janet), Jennifer Smith (Kitty), Joey Sorge (Servant/Reporter/Super), Patrick Wetzel (Servant/Reporter/Dream Robert), Lenny Wolpe (Feldzieg)

THE IMPORTANCE OF BEING EARNEST by Oscar Wilde; Directed by Sir Peter Hall; Production Designers, Kevin Rigdon and Trish Rigdon; Sound Designers, Rob Milburn and Michael Bodeen; Casting, Deborah Brown; Production Stage Manager, John McNamara; Assistant Stage Manager, Brian j. L'Ecuyer; Theatre Royal Bath production–Producer, Danny Moar, and Associate Director/Producer, Trish Rigdon; January 17–March 5, 2006; **Cast:** Bianca Amato (Gwen-

dolen Fairfax), Greg Felden (Footman), Miriam Margolyes (Miss Prism), Charlotte Parry (Cecily Cardew), Robert Petkoff (Algernon Moncrieff), Lynn Redgrave (Lady Bracknell), Terence Rigby (Reverend Canon Chasuble), Geddeth Smith (Merriman), James A. Stephens (Lane). James Waterston (Jack Worthing)

THE BLACK RIDER, THE CASTING OF THE MAGIC BULLETS by Robert Wilson, Tom Waits and William S. Burroughs; Direction, Scenic and Lighting Designer, Robert Wilson; Music and Lyrics, Tom Waits; Text, William S. Burroughs; Original Musical Arrangements, Greg Cohen and Tom Waits; Costume Designer, Frida Parmeggiani; Dramaturg, Wolfgang Wiens; Associate Director, Ann-Christin Rommen; Stage Manager, Lorna Earl; Assistant Stage Managers, Penelope Foxley and Sue Karutz; April 22–June 11, 2006; **Cast:** Vance Avery (Pegleg), Sona Cervena (Bird, Messenger, Ghost), Joan Mankin (Anne), Matt McGrath (Wilhelm), Mary Margaret O'Hara (Käthchen), Nigel Richards (Robert/Man on Stag/Georg Schmid), Dean Robinson (Bertram), Gabriella Santinelli (Bridesmaid/Ghost), Richard Strange (Kudo), Monika Tahal (Attendant/Warden/Bird/Ghost), Jake Thornton (Young Kuno/Warden/Bird/Ghost), John Vickery (Wilhelm's Old Uncle/Duke)

CURTAINS Book by Rupert Holmes; Music by John Kander; Lyrics by Fred Ebb; Original Book and Concept, Peter Stone; Additional Lyrics, John Kander and Rupert Holmes; Directed by Scott Ellis; Choreographer, Rob Ashford; Orchestrations, William David Brohn; Music Director/Vocal Arrangements, David Loud; Scenic Designer, Anna Louizos; Costume Designer, William Ivey Long; Lighting Designer, Peter Kaczorowski; Sound Designer, Brian Ronan; Dance Arrangements, David Chase; Fight Director, Rick Sordelet; Aerial Effects Designer, Paul Rubin; Casting, Jim Carnahan; Production Supervisor, Beverley Randolph; Technical Supervisor, Peter Fulbright; Stage Managers, Scott Taylor Rollison and David S. Franklin; July 25–September 10, 2006; **Cast:** Nili Bassman (Arlene Barucca), Ward Billeisen (Brick Hawvermale), John Bolton (Daryl Grady), Jason Danieley (Aaron Fox), Jennifer Dunne (Jan Setler), David Eggers (Detective O'Farrell/Roy Stetson), Matt Farnsworth (Marv Fremont), Patty Goble (Jessica Cranshaw/Connie Subbotin), Edward Hibbert (Christopher Belling), Mary Ann Lamb (Mona Page), Brittany Marcin (Peg Prentice), Michael X. Martin (Johnny Harmon), Michael McCormick (Oscar Shapiro), Debra Monk (Carmen Bernstein), Jim Newman (Randy Weinstein), Jill Paice (Niki Harris), David Hyde Pierce (Lieutenant Frank Cioffi), Noah Racey (Bobby Pepper), Joe Aaron Reid (Ronnie Driscoll), Darcie Roberts (Roberta Wooster), Megan Sikora (Bambi Bernstein), Christopher Spaulding (Russ Cochran), Robert Walden (Sidney Bernstein), Karen Ziemba (Georgia Hendricks)

Bonus Productions at the Ahmanson Theatre

Matthew Bourne's **SWAN LAKE** March 7–19, 2006
DAME EDNA: BACK WITH A VENGEANCE March 28–April 9, 2006

KIRK DOUGLAS THEATRE

all wear bowlers created and performed by Trey Lyford and Geoff Sobelle; Directed by Aleksandra Wolska; Scenic Designer, Jarek Truczynski; Costume Designer, Tara Webb; Lighting Designer, Randy "Igleu" Glickman; Sound Designer, James Sugg; Film, Michael Glass; Film Music Composer, Michael Friedman; Production Stage Manager, Michelle Blair; September 23–October 28, 2005; **Cast:** Trey Lyford (Wyatt R. Levine), Geoff Sobelle (Earnest Matters)

A VERY OLD MAN WITH ENORMOUS WINGS based on a short story by Gabriel García Márquez; Adapted by Nilo Cruz; Directed by Andrew Tsao; Scenic Designer, Yael Pardess; Costume Designer, Allison Leach; Lighting and Projection Designer, Shaun Fillion; Sound Designer and Original Music, Nathan Wang; Movement Direction, Nick Erickson; Casting, Erika Sellin; Production Stage Manager, Elizabeth Atkinson; November 13–December 18, 2005; **Cast:**

Christian Barillas (Juan Jose/Don Galante), Liam Craig (Pelayo), Gloria Garayua (Girl With Box of Prayers/Peddler), Lena Gwendolyn Hill (Fefé), Ameenah Kaplan (Justina, Worker 3), Matthew Yang King (Momó), Damian D. Lewis (Afar), Elisa Llamido (Elisenda/Bonafacia); Christopher Michael Rivera (Cirilo/Showman), Dreya Weber (La Luna/Spider Woman)

PERMANENT COLLECTION by Thomas Gibbons; Directed by Dwain Perry; Scenic Designers, James Eric and Victoria Bellocq; Costume Designer, Naila Aladdin-Sanders; Lighting Designer, Ian Garrett; Sound Designer/Composer, Joshua Horvath; Production Stage Manager, Sammie Wayne IV; Stage Manager, Sue Karutz; The Robey Theatre Company and Greenway Arts Alliance production; January 8–February 12, 2006; **Cast:** Doug Cox (Paul Barrow), Ben Guillory (Sterling North), Kent Minault (Alfred Morris), Kiersten Morgan (Gillian Krane), Elayn J. Taylor (Ella Franklin), LaFern Watkins (Kanika Weaver)

THE STONES by Tom Lycos and Stefo Nantsou; Directed by Corey Madden; Choreographer, Jacques Heim; Scenic Designer, Sibyl Wickersheimer; Costume Designer, Audrey Fisher; Lighting Designer, Shaun Fillion; Original Music Composition and Sound Designer, Paul James Prendergast; Casting, Erika Sellin; Production Stage Manager, Anna Woo; **Cast:** Joe Hernandez-Kolski (Yahoo/Russo), Justin Huen (Shy Boy/Quinn)

SOLOMANIA! A Repertory Festival of Solo Performances. **¡GAYTINO!** Written and Performed by Dan Guerrero; Directed by Diane Rodriguez; Choreographer, Kay Cole; Music Arrangement and Production, David De Palo, Joseph Julian Gonzalez, Germaine Franco; **LIVE FROM THE FRONT** Written and Performed by Jerry Quickley; Directed by reg e gaines; **TAKING FLIGHT** Written and Performed by Ariana Sevan; Directed by Giovanna Sardelli; **THE WATTS TOWERS PROJECT** Written and Performed by Roger Guenveur Smith; Composer, Mark Anthony Thompson; For the Festival: Scenic Designer, Edward E. Haynes Jr.; Costume Designer, Candice Cain; Lighting Designer, José López; Sound Designer, Adam Phalen; Production Stage Manager, David S. Franklin; Stage Managers, Scott Harrison, Young Ji. April 26–June 11, 2006. World premieres.

PYRENEES by David Greig; Directed by Neel Keller; Scenic Designer, Mark Wendland; Costume Designer, Allison Leach; Lighting Designer, Geoff Korf; Sound Designers, Robbin E. Broad and Michael Hooker; Casting, Erika Sellin; Production Stage Manager, Sue Karutz; July 2–30, 2006; **Cast:** Frances Conroy (Vivienne), Tom Irwin (The Man), Tessa Thompson (Anna), Jan Triska (The Proprietor)

CENTERSTAGE

Baltimore, Maryland
FORTY-THIRD SEASON

Artistic Director, Irene Lewis

KING LEAR by William Shakespeare; Directed by Irene Lewis; Scenic Designer, Robert Israel; Costume Designer, Catherine Zuber; Lighting Designer, Rui Rita; Sound Designer, David Budries; Composer, Karen Hansen; Fight Director, J. Allen Suddeth; Speech Consultant, Deena Burke; Production Dramaturg, Gavin Witt; Casting Director, Judy Dennis; Stage Manager, Debra Acquavella; Assistant Stage Manager, Mike Schleifer; September 23–November 6, 2005; **Cast:** David Adkins (Albany), Heidi Armbruster (Cordelia), Rod Brogan (Facilitator), Jon David Casey (Edmund), David Cromwell (Gloucester), Jay Edwards (Facilitator), Karen Hansen (Musician), Sarah Knowlton (Goneril), Diana LaMar (Regan), Stephen Markle (Lear), Conan McCarty (Oswald), Laurence O'Dwyer (Fool), James Joseph O'Neil (Cornwall), Michael Rudko (Kent), Tony Ward (Edgar)

Stephen Markle, Tony Ward in *King Lear* PHOTO BY RICHARD ANDERSON

HAY FEVER by Noël Coward; Directed by Will Frears; Scenic Designer, Alexander Dodge; Costume Designer, Linda Cho; Lighting Designer, Matthew Richards; Sound Designer, Vincent Olivieri; Speech Consultant, Gillian Lane-Plescia; Fight Director, J. Allen Suddeth; Production Dramaturg, James Magruder; Casting Director, Judy Dennis; Stage Manager, Mike Schleifer; Assistant Director, Kate Pines-Schwartz; Assistant Stage Manager, Debra Acquavella; November 3–December 4, 2005; **Cast:** Lisa Altomare (Clara), Harry Barandes (Simon Bliss), Cheryl Lynn Bowers (Sorel Bliss), Anna Camp (Jackie Coryton), Brad Heberlee (Richard Greatham), Nicholas Hormann (David Bliss), Pamela Payton-Wright (Judith Bliss), Charles Daniel Sandoval (Sandy Tyrell), Sara Surrey (Myra Arundel)

ONCE ON THIS ISLAND by Lynn Ahrens (book/lyrics) & Stephen Flaherty (music); Based on the novel *My Love, My Love* by Rosa Guy; Directed & Choreographed by Kenneth Lee Roberson; Musical Director, Darryl G. Ivey; Scenic Designer, Neil Patel; Costume Designer, Emilio Sosa; Lighting Designer, David Weiner; Sound Designer, Garth Hemphill; Assistant Choreographer, Byron Easley; Speech Consultant, Scott Whitehurst; Production Dramaturg, Otis Ramsey-Zöe; Casting Director, Mark Simon; Orchestra Contractor, Edward Goldstein; Stage Manager, Debra Acquavella; Assistant Stage Manager, Mike Schleifer; December 16, 2005–January 22, 2006; **Cast:** Lakisha Anne Bowen (Andrea), E. Faye Butler (Erzulie), LaVon Fisher (Asaka), J.D. Goldblatt (Daniel), Heaven Leigh Horton (Little Ti Moune), Trisha Jeffrey (Ti Moune), Christopher L. Morgan (Papa Ge), Erick Pinnick (Armand), C.E. Smith (Tonton Julian), David St. Louis (Agwe), Gayle Turner (Mama Euralie), Miah Marie Patterson (Little Ti Moune–Alternate)

THE MURDER OF ISAAC by Motti Lerner; Translated by Anthony Berris; Directed by Irene Lewis; Composer/Musical Director, Eric Svejcar; Scenic Designer, Christopher Barreca; Costume Designer, Candice Donnelly; Lighting Designer, Mimi Jordan Sherin; Sound Designer, David Budries; Fight Director, J. Allen Suddeth; Speech Consultant, Deena Burke; Choreographer, Kenneth Lee Roberson; Production Dramaturg, Gavin Witt; Casting Directors, Eli Dawson & Judy Dennis; Stage Manager, Mike Schleifer; Assistant Musical Director, Daniel Feyer; Assistant Stage Manager, Debra Acquavella; February 3–March 12, 2006; **Cast:** Lise Bruneau (Shulamit), Charlotte Cohn (Talia), Kelli Danaker (Female Guard), Mia Dillon (Lola), Daniel Feyer (Musician), Olek Krupa (Yuda), Dan Manning (Boris), David Margulies (Binder), Chaz Mena (Avi), Tzahi Moskovitz (Avner), Benjamin Pelteson (Yigal), Jeffrey Ware (Eliahu), Gordon Joseph Weiss (Mendel), Joe Zaloom (Natan)

RADIO GOLF by August Wilson Directed by Kenny Leon; Scenic Designer, David Gallo; Costume Designer, Susan Hilferty; Lighting Designer, Donald Holder; Composer, Kathryn Bostic; Sound Designer, Amy C. Wedel; Dramaturg, Todd Kreidler; Vocal Coach, Erin Annarella; Casting Director, Harriet Bass; Dramaturg, Otis Ramsey-Zöe; Stage Manager, Marion R. Friedman; Stage Manager, Debra Acquavella; March 24–April 30, 2006; **Cast:** Denise Burse (Mame Wilks), Rocky Carroll (Harmond Wilks), Anthony Chisholm (Elder Joseph Barlow), John Earl Jelks (Sterling Johnson), James A. Williams (Roosevelt Hicks); Ron Cephas Jones (Elder Joseph Barlow; Mar 30, Apr 4–7)

CRUMBS FROM THE TABLE OF JOY by Lynn Nottage; Directed by David Schweizer; Scenic Designer, James Noone; Costume Designer, David Burdick; Lighting Designer, Alexander Nichols; Sound Designer, Mark Bennett; Speech Consultant, Gillian Lane-Plescia; Production Dramaturg, Liana Thompson; Casting Director, Judy Dennis; Stage Manager, Mike Schleifer; Assistant Director, Adrian Wattenmaker; Assistant Stage Manager, Debra Acquavella; May 5–June 11, 2006; **Cast:** Patricia Ageheim (Gerte Schulte), Edwina Findley (Ermina Crump), LeLand Gantt (Godfrey Crump), Amina S. Robinson (Ernestine Crump), Kelly Taffe (Lily Ann Green)

CINCINNATI PLAYHOUSE IN THE PARK

Cincinnati, Ohio
FORTY-SIXTH SEASON

Producing Artistic Director, Edward Stern

A FUNNY THING HAPPENED ON THE WAY TO THE FORUM Book by Burt Shevelove and Larry Gelbart, Music and lyrics by Stephen Sondheim; Directed by Edward Stern; Choreographer, Janet Watson; Musical Director, Darren R. Cohen; Scenic Designer, John Ezell; Costume Designer, David Kay Mickelsen; Lighting Designer, Peter E. Sargent; Sound Designer, Chuck Hatcher; First Stage Manager, Jenifer Morrow; Second Stage Manager, Bruce E. Coyle; September 6–October 7, 2005; **Cast:** Bob Walton (Pseudolus), John Seidman (Senex), Jared Gertner (Protean), Bryan Lefeber (Protean), Dominic Roberts (Protean), Lynn Eldredge (Domina), Jeff Skowron (Hysterium), Eric Ulloa (Hero), Keith Jochim (Marcus Lycus), Jaclyn Minerva (Tintinabula), Karen Hyland (Geminae), Hayley Nelson (Geminae), Carol Schuberg (Vibrata), Erika Lynn Rominger (Gymnasia), Lynette Knapp (Philia), Nat Chandler (Miles Gloriosus), Whit Reichert (Erronius)

LOVE, JANIS Conceived and adapted by Randal Myler; Directed by Randal Myler; Music Director, Sam Andrew; Scenic Designer, Paul Owen; Costume Designer, Lorraine Venberg; Lighting Designer, Don Darnutzer; Sound Designer, Eric Stahlhammer; Conductor, Joel Hoekstra; Stage Manager, Suann Pollock; September 22–November 6, 2005; **Cast:** Morgan Hallett (Janis), Katrina Chester (Janis Joplin, alternating), Lauren Dragon (Janis Joplin, alternating), Fred Major (Interviewer)

CAT ON A HOT TIN ROOF by Tennessee Williams; Directed by Marshall W. Mason; Scenic Designer, David Potts; Costume Designer, David R. Zyla; Lighting Designer, Phil Monat; Composer, Peter Kater; Assistant Director, Rand Mitchell; First Stage Manager, Andrea L. Shell; Second Stage Manager, Bruce E. Coyle; October 18–November 18, 2005; **Cast:** Molly Schaffer (Maggie), Jason Kuykendall (Brick), Mary Proctor (Mae), Jo Twiss (Big Mama), John Lepard (Gooper), Edwin J. McDonough (Reverend Tooker), Michael McCarty (Big Daddy), Joneal Joplin (Doctor Baugh)

THE COMPLETE HISTORY OF AMERICA (ABRIDGED) by Adam Long, Reed Martin and Austin Tichenor; Scenic Designer; Phil Englehardt; General Manager, Megan Loughney; Technical Director, Matt McClane; November 15, 2005–January 15, 2006; Cast (of three, alternating): Dominic Conti, Michael Faulkner, Jerry Kernion, Reed Martin and Austin Tichenor

ALL THE GREAT BOOKS (ABRIDGED) by Reed Martin and Austin Tichenor; Additional material by Matthew Croke and Michael Faulkner; Directed by Reed Martin and Austin Tichenor; Scenic Designer; Phil Englehardt; General Manager, Megan Loughney; Technical Director, Matt McClane; November 15, 2005–January 15, 2006; Cast (of three, alternating): Dominic Conti, Michael Faulkner, Jerry Kernion, Reed Martin and Austin Tichenor

A CHRISTMAS CAROL by Charles Dickens, Adapted by Howard Dallin; Director, Michael Evan Haney; Scenic Designer, James Leonard Joy; Costume Designer, David Murin; Lighting Designer, Kirk Bookman; Sound Designer and Composer, David B. Smith; Lighting Contractor, Susan Terrano; Costume Coordinator, Cindy Witherspoon; Music Director, Rebecca N. Childs; Choreographer, Dee Anne Bryll; Production Stage Manager, Bruce E. Coyle; First Stage Manager, Jenifer Morrow; Second Stage Manager, Andrea L. Shell; December 1–30, 2005; **Cast:** Bruce Cromer (Ebenezer Scrooge), Stephen Skiles (Mr. Cupp/Percy/Rich Father at Fezziwig's), Ron Simons (Mr. Sosser/Tailor at Fezziwig's/Topper/Man with Shoe Shine), Andy Prosky (Bob Cratchit/Schoolmaster Oxlip), Jay Stratton (Fred), Gregory Procaccino (Jacob Marley/Old Joe), Dale Hodges (Ghost of Christmas Past/Rose/Mrs. Peake), Evan Martin (Boy Scrooge/Boy at Fezziwig's/Bootblack), Corri Elizabeth Johnson (Fan/Guest at Fezziwig's), Keith Jochim (Mr. Fezziwig/Ghost of Christmas Present), Amy Warner (Mrs. Fezziwig/Patience), Mike Anthony (Dick Wilkins/Streets), Allison McLemore (Mary at Fezziwig's/Streets), Todd Lawson (Young and Mature Scrooge/Ghost of Christmas Future), Shannon Koob (Belle/Catherine Margaret), Alex Dittmer (Rich Caroler/Constable at Fezziwig's), Regina Pugh (Mrs. Cratchit/Laundress), Cullen Cornelius Arbaugh (Peter Cratchit/Gregory/Apprentice at Fezziwig's), Jo Ellen Pellman (Belinda Cratchit/Guest at Fezziwig's), K. McKenzie Miller (Martha Cratchit/Guest at Fezziwig's), John Michael Griffith (Tiny Tim), Ann Marie Siegwarth (Rich Caroler/Guest at Fezziwig's), Renee Franck-Reed (Poor Caroler/Rich Wife at Fezziwig's), Daniel Winters (Poor Caroler/Guest at Fezziwig's), Jarred Kjack (Man with Pipe/Streets), Jack Bender (Matthew/Ignorance), Emmye Kearney (Want/Guest at Fezziwig's), Courtney Bell (Mrs. Dilber/Streets), Rob Riley (Guest at Fezziwig's/Undertaker/Streets), Gregory Boglin (Charles/Apprentice at Fezziwig's/George), David Bunch (Poulterer/Streets)

THE CLEAN HOUSE by Sarah Ruhl; Directed by Michael Evan Haney; Scenic Designer, Narelle Sissons; Costume Designer, Gordon DeVinney; Lighting Designer, David Lander; Sound Designer, Jill BC Du Boff; First Stage Manager, Andrea L. Shell; Second Stage Manager, Suann Pollock; January 24–February 24, 2006; **Cast:** Michele Vazquez (Matilde), Priscilla Shanks (Lane), Susan Greenhill (Virginia), Paul DeBoy (Charles/A Man), Lynn Milgrim (Ana/A Woman)

YELLOWMAN by Dael Orlandersmith; Directed by Harold Scott; Scenic Designer, Hugh Landwehr; Costume Designer, Gordon DeVinney; Lighting Designer, Clifton Taylor; Production Stage Manager, Jenifer Morrow; February 11–March 12, 2006; **Cast:** Tamela Aldridge (Alma), Spencer Scott Barros (Eugene)

COMPANY Music and lyrics by Stephen Sondheim, Book by George Furth; Directed and choreographed by John Doyle; Music Supervisor/Orchestrator Mary-Mitchell Campbell; Scenic Designer, David Gallo; Costume Designer, Ann Hould-Ward; Lighting Designer, Thomas C. Hase; Sound Designer, Andrew Keister; First Stage Manager, Suann Pollock; Second Stage Manager, Erica Briggs;

March 14–April 14, 2006; **Cast:** Keith Buterbaugh (Harry), Matt Castle (Peter), Robert Cunningham (Paul), Angel Desai (Marta), Raul Esparza (Robert), Kelly Jeanne Grant (Kathy), Kristin Huffman (Sarah), Amy Justman (Susan), Heather Laws (Amy), Leenya Rideout (Jenny), Fred Rose (David), Bruce Sabath (Larry), Elizabeth Stanley (April), Barbara Walsh (Joanne)

STONE MY HEART by Joseph McDonough; Directed by Edward Stern; Scenic Designer, Joseph P. Tilford; Costume Designer, Claudia Stephens; Lighting Designer, Thomas C. Hase; Composer, Douglas Lowry; Stage Manager, Andrea L. Shell; April 1–30, 2006; **Cast:** Todd Lawson (Robby), Sean Haberle (Terrence), Lanie MacEwan (Jessica), Tim Altmeyer (Zach), Kevyn Morrow (Marcus)

WITNESS FOR THE PROSECUTION by Agatha Christie; Directed by Michael Evan Haney; Scenic Designer, Paul Shortt; Costume Designer, Elizabeth Covey; Lighting Designer, Phil Monat; Production Stage Manager, Jenifer Morrow; Stage Manager, Suann Pollock; May 2–June 4, 2006; **Cast:** Richert Easley (Carter/Dr. Wyatt), Tarah Flanagan (Greta), Robert Langdon Lloyd (Mr. Mayhew), Christopher Kelly (Leonard Vole), Joneal Joplin (Sir Wilfrid Robarts, Q.C.), Mark Leydorf (Inspector Hearne), Deanne Lorette (Romaine), Stephen Skiles (Clerk), Julian Gamble (Mr. Myers, Q.C.), Michael Rothhaar (Mr. Justice Wainwright), Courtney Bell (The Stenographer), Rob Riley (Warder), Alex Dittmer (Barrister), David Bunch (Barrister/Clegg), Jarred Kjack (Barrister/Clegg), Dale Hodges (Janet MacKenzie), Mike Anthony (Policeman), Ann Marie Siegwarth (The Other Woman)

SQUEEZE BOX by Ann Randolph; Directed by Alan Bailey; Lighting Designer, Susan Terrano; Stage Manager, Andrea L. Shell; May 20–June 25, 2006; **Cast:** Ann Randolph (Ann)

CITY THEATRE COMPANY

Pittsburgh, Pennsylvania
THIRTY-FIRST SEASON

Artistic Director, Tracy Brigden

CROWNS by Regina Taylor; book by Michael Cunningham and Craig Marberry; Directred by Timothy Douglas; Scenic Designer, Tony Ferrieri; Costume Designer, Susan Tsu; Lighting Designer, Lap-Chi Chu; Sound Designer, Joe Pino; Choreographer, Greer A. Reed; Music Director/Accompanist, Cliff Barnes; Music Supervisor, Timothy Wesley Douglas; Production Stage Manager, Patti Kelly; September 22–October 16, 2005; **Cast:** Khaliah Adams (Yolanda), Inga Ballard (Mabel), Maria Becoates Bey (Velma), Etta Cox (Wanda), Garbie Dukes (Man), Linda Haston (Jeanette), Avery Sommers (Mother Shaw)

TUESDAYS WITH MORRIE by Jeffrey Hatcher and Mitch Albom; Directed by Alice Jankell; Scenic Designer, Tony Ferrieri; Costume Designer, Pei-Chi Su; Lighting Designer, Andrew David Ostrowski; Sound Designer, Elizabeth Atkinson; Production Stage Manager, Patti Kelly; November 17–December 11, 2005; **Cast:** Maria Becoates Bey (Voice of Janine), Daniel Krell (Mitch), Bernie Passeltiner (Morrie)

HEARTS ARE WILD Music and Lyrics by George Griggs, Book by Darrah Cloud; Directed by Tracy Brigden; Scenic Designer, Michael Olich; Costume Designer, Pei-Chi Su; Lighting Designer, Andrew David Ostrowski; Sound Designer, Keith Bates; Choreographer, Danny Herman; Music Director, Douglas Levine; Dramaturg, Carlyn Aquiline; Associate Director, Kellee Van Aken; Production Stage Manager, Patti Kelly; January 25–February 19, 2006; The Band: Craig "Izzy"

Arlet (Guitar), Tom Early (Drums), Brian Stahurski (Bass); **Cast:** Katie Allen (Brianna), Ben Evans (Steve's Dad (past)/Steve), Julie Dingman Evans (Steve's Mom/Sharon), Billy Hartung (The Oracle/Steve's Dad (present)/Rob/Daphne/Skater Dude/Lonny/The Shrink)

PYRETOWN by John Belluso; Directed by Diane Rodriguez; Scenic Designer, Victoria Petrovich; Costume Designer. Angela M. Vesco; Lighting Designer, C. Todd Brown; Sound Designer, Elizabeth Atkinson; Production Stage Manager, Alison Paleos; March 2–April 2, 2006; **Cast:** Tobias Forrest (Harry), Chandler Vinton (Louise)

OPUS by Michael Hollinger; Directed by Terrence J. Nolen; Scenic Designer, James Kronzer; Costume Designer, Michael McAleer; Lighting Designer, Andrew David Ostrowski; Sound Designer, Jorge Cousineau; Dramaturg, Carlyn Aquiline; Assistant Director, Georgia Schlessman; Production Stage Manager, Patti Kelly; March 17–April 9, 2006; **Cast:** Erika Cuenca (Grace), Patrick McNulty (Elliot), Douglas Rees (Carl), David Whalen (Dorian), Greg Wood (Alan)

TALKING HEADS by Alan Bennett; Directed by Tracy Brigden; Scenic Designer, Anne Mundell; Costume Designer, Michael McAleer; Lighting Designer, Andrew David Ostrowski; Sound Designer, Elizabeth Atkinson; Wig Design, Elsen Associates; Stage Manager, Amy Monroe; Production Stage Manager, Alison Paleos; April 13–May 14, 2006; **Cast:** Program A: Patricia Kilgarriff (Irene Ruddock/Celia), Helena Ruoti (Lesley); Program B: Patricia Kilgarriff (Miss Fozzard), Helena Ruoti (Rosemary/Susan)

HONUS AND ME by Steven Dietz; Adapted from the novel by Dan Gutman; Directed by Lou Jacob; Scene Designer, Tony Ferrieri; Costume Designer, Paul Tazewell; Lighting Designer, Andrew David Ostrowski; Sound Designer, Joe Pino; Wig Design, Elsen Associates; Production Stage Manager, Patti Kelly; May 4–28, 2006; Jeffrey Carpenter (Birdie), Martin Giles (Coach/Mr. Mendoza), Patrick Jordan (Chuck/Ty Cobb), Daniel Krell (Dad), Randall Newsome (Honus Wagner), Mary Rawson (Miss Young/Lady Fan), Marcus Stevens (Joey Stoshack), Robin Walsh (Mom/Lady Fan)

CLEVELAND PLAYHOUSE

Cleveland, Ohio
NINETIETH SEASON

Artistic Director, Michael Bloom

ROOM SERVICE by John Murray and Allen Boretz; Directed by Jeff Steitzer; Scenic Designer, Ursula Belden; Costume Designer, David Kay Mickelsen; Lighting Designer, Victor En Yu Tan; Sound Designer, James C. Swonger; Production Stage Manager, Corrie Purdum; October 7–30, 2005; **Cast:** Tom Beckett (Joseph Gribble), Craig Bockhorn (Harry Binion), Elizabeth A. Davis (Hilda Manney), Todd Gearhart (Gordon Miller), Mark Alan Gordon (Simon Jenkins/Senator Blake), Samuel Holloway (Bank messenger), Joshua John McKay (Leo Davis), Jason Michael Miller (Timothy Hogarth), Larry Paulsen (Faker Englund), Allen Lewis Rickman (Gregory Wagner), Greg Thornton (Sasha Smirnoff), Ivy Vahanian (Christine Marlowe), Ronald Thomas Wilson (Dr. Glass)

I AM MY OWN WIFE by Doug Wright; Directed by Anders Cato; Scenic Designer, Hugh Landwehr; Costume Designer, Jeffrey van Curtis; Lighting Designer, Howell Binkley; Sound Designer, James C. Swonger; Stage Manager, John Godbout; Dialect Coach, Deborah Hecht; November 4–27, 2005; **Cast:** Mark Nelson (Charlotte von Mahlsdorf)

A CHRISTMAS STORY by Philip Grecian, based on the motion picture written by Jean Shepherd, Leigh Brown and Bob Clark; Directed by Seth Gordon; Scenic Designer, Michael Ganio; Costume Designer, David Kay Mickelsen; Lighting Designer, Richard Winkler; Sound Designer, James C. Swonger; November 25–December 18, 2005; **Cast:** Angela Holecko (Esther Jane Alberry), Louie Rosenbaum (Flick), Elizabeth Ann Townsend (Mother), Christopher McHale (Ralph), Cody Swanson (Ralphie), Billy Lawrence (Randy), Peggy Scott (Mrs. Shields), Alex Biats (Schwartz), Charles Kartali (The Old Man), Carolyn Williams (Heather Weathers)

A STREETCAR NAMED DESIRE by Tennessee Williams; Directed by Michael Bloom; Scenic Designer, Todd Rosenthal; Costume Designer, Susan Tsu; Lighting Designer, Michael Lincoln; Sound Designer, James C. Swonger; Composer, Larry Delinger; Dialect Coach, Chuck Richie; Fight Choreographer, Ronald Thomas Wilson; Stage Manager, John Godbout; January 13–February 5, 2006; **Cast:** Kelly Mares (Stella), Jason Paul Field (Stanley), Lucas Caleb Rooney (Mitch), Starla Benford (Eunice), Hollis Resnik (Blanche), Doug Jewel (Steve), Jason Miller (Pablo), Elizabeth A. Davis (Townsperson), Joshua John McKay (A young collector), Lelund Durond Thompson (Townsperson), Nicole Fitzpatrick (Flower woman), Mark Alan Gordon (Doctor), Bailey Varness (Nurse)

INTIMATE APPAREL by Lynn Nottage; Directed by Timothy Bond; Scenic Designer, Paul Owen; Costume Designer, Lorraine Venberg; Lighting Designer, Darren McCroom; Sound Designer, Matt Callahan; Dialect Coach, Don Wadsworth; Stage Manager, Corrie Purdum; February 7–March 5, 2006; **Cast:** Tiffany Adams (Mayme), Denise Cormier (Mrs. Van Buren), Perri Gaffney (Mrs. Dickson), Erik LaRay Harvey (George), Joe Hickey (Mr. Marks), Gwendolyn Mulamba (Esther Mills)

Mark Nelson in *I Am My Own Wife* PHOTOS BY ROGER MASTROIANNI

WELL by Lisa Kron; Directed by Michael Bloom; Scenic Designer, Michael Raiford; Costume Designer, Jennifer Caprio; Lighting Designer, David Nancarrow; Sound Designer, James C. Swonger; Stage Manager, John Godbout; March 3–26, 2006; **Cast:** Alicia Roper (Lisa), Denny Dillon (Ann), Zandy Hartig, Jason Miller, Lelund Durond Thompson, Bailey Varness (Ensemble)

DREAM A LITTLE DREAM by Denny Doherty and Paul Ledoux; Directed by Randal Myler; Scenic Designer, Vicki Smith; Costume Designer, Kevin Copenhaver; Lighting Designer, Don Darnutzer; Sound Designer, James C. Swonger; Video Director: Gabreal Franklin; Instrumental Arrangements, David Smyth; Vocal Arrangements, Doris Mason; Stage Manager, Corrie Purdum; March 31–April 29, 2006; **Cast:** Denny Doherty, Lisa MacIsaac, Doris Mason, Graham Shaw

CUSTODY OF THE EYES by Anthony Giardina; Directed by Michael Butler; Scenic Designer, Russell Parkman; Costume Designer, Charlotte Yetman; Lighting Designer, Nancy Schertler; Sound Designer, James C. Swonger; Stage Manager, John Godbout; April 28–May 21, 2006; **Cast:** Alexander Timothy Biats (Riley Rosenthal), Joseph Collins (Edmond LeBlanc), Paula Duesing (Mrs. Callahan), Jan Leslie Harding (Sheila Rosenthal), JR Horne (Donald Leger), Mark Mayo (Gary Burger/Ferryman), Kenneth Tigar (Robert Sullivan)

DALLAS THEATER CENTER

Dallas, Texas
FORTY-SEVEN SEASON

Artistic Director, Richard Hamburger

CROWNS by Regina Taylor; Adapted from the book by Michael Cunningham and Craig Marberry; Directed by Regina Taylor; Associate Director, René Moreno; Scenic Designer, Randel Wright; Costume Designer, Reggie Ray; Lighting Designer, Marcus Doshi; Sound Designer, Bruce Richardson; Choreographer, Dianne McIntyre; Musical Director and Pianist, Sanford Moore; Percussionist, S-Ankh Rasa; October 5–30, 2005; **Cast:** Miche Braden (Mother Shaw), Roz Beauty Davis (Yolanda), M. Denise Lee (Velma), Liz Mikel (Mabel), Wayne W. Pretlow (Man), Pt sha Storey (Jeanette), Vickie Washington (Wanda)

A CHRISTMAS CAROL by Charles Dickens; Adapted by Richard Hellesen; Original Music by David de Berry; Directed and Choreographed by Joel Ferrell; Scenic Designer, Bob Lavallee; Costume Designer, Wade Laboissonniere; Lighting Designer, Matthew Richards; Sound Designer, Brian Branigan; Musical Director, Lindy Heath Cabe; November 25–December 24, 2005; **Cast:** Robin Chadwick (Ebenezer Scrooge), Laurie Bulaoro (Fred's Wife/Ensemble), Jon Paul Burkhart (Topper/Ensemble), Chamblee Ferguson (Bob Cratchit/Ensemble), Brian Gonzales (Second Subscription Gentleman/Ensemble), Ron Gonzalez (Fred/Ensemble), Jennifer Green (Ensemble), Chelsea Erin Jones (Martha Cratchit/Ensemble), Shannon J. McGrann (Mrs. Cratchit/Ensemble), Liz Mikel (The Ghost of Christmas Present/Ensemble), Matt Moore (Ebenezer the Apprentice/Ensemble), Dean Nolen (The Ghost of Jacob Marley), Bob Reed (Fezziwig/Ensemble), Joanna Schellenberg (The Ghost of Christmas Past/Ensemble), Jessica D. Turner (Belle/Ensemble), Phillip Cole White (Peter Cratchit/Ensemble)

JOE EGG by Peter Nichols; Directed by Richard Hamburger; Scenic Designer, Michael Yeargan, Costume Designer, Linda Fisher; Lighting Designer, Mark McCullough; Original Music and Sound Design, Fitz Patton; January 18–February 12, 2006; **Cast:** James Crawford (Freddie), David Manis (Bri), Clara Peretz (Joe), Sandra Shipley (Grace), Wendy Rich Stetson (Shelia), Jessica D. Turner (Pam)

I AM MY OWN WIFE by Doug Wright; Directed by David Kennedy; Scenic Designer, Lee Savage; Cosutme Designer, Claudia Stephens; Lighting Designer, Matthew Richards; Sound Designer, Fitz Patton; March 1–26, 2006; **Cast:** Damien Atkins (Charlotte von Mahlsdorf, et al.)

HANK WILLIAMS: LOST HIGHWAY by Randal Myler and Mark Harelik; Directed by Randal Myler; Music Director, Dan Wheetman; Scenic Designer, Vicki M. Smith; Costume Designer, Robert Blackman; Lighting Designer, Don Darnutzer; Sound Designer, Eric Stahlhammer; April 12–May 4, 2006; **Cast:** Stephen J. Anthony (Hoss), Mississippi Charles Bevel (Tee-Tot), Margaret Bowman (Mama Lilly), Patricia Dalen (Waitress), H. Drew Perkins (Leon "Loudmouth"), Mike Regan (Fred "Pap" Rose), Regan Southard (Audrey Williams), Myk Watford (Jimmy "Burrhead"), Russ Wever (Shag), Van Zeiler (Hank Williams)

THE ILLUSION by Pierre Corneille; Freely adapted by Tony Kushner; Directed by Richard Hamburger; Scenic Designer, Michael Yeargan, Costume Designer, Wade Laboissonniere; Lighting Designer, Stephen Strawbridge; Sound Designer, David Budries; Fight Director, Brian Byrnes; May 31–June 25, 2006; **Cast:** Brad Bellamy (Matamore), Brienin Bryant (Elicia/Lyse/Clarina), Jakie Cabe (Pleribo/Adraste/Prince Florilame), Al Espinosa (Calisto/Clindor/Theogenes), Chamblee Ferguson (The Amanuensis/Geronte), Keith Jochim (Pridamant of Avignon), James McDonnell (Alcandre), Kathryn Meisle (Melibea/Isabelle/Hippolyta)

DELAWARE THEATRE COMPANY

Wilmington, Delaware
TWENTY-SEVENTH SEASON

Producing Director, Anne Marie Cammarato

THE NERD by Larry Shue; Directed by Anne Marie Cammarato; Assistant Director, Susan Schaeffer; Scenic Designer, Eric Schaeffer; Costume Designer, Mattie Ullrich; Costume Design Assistant, Darolyn D. Robertson; Lighting Designer, Rebecca G. Frederick; Sound Designer, Shannon Zura; Stage Manager, Sara J. Tantillo; Assistant Stage Manager, Mara B. Hyatt; September 14–October 2, 2005; **Cast:** Ben Cherry (Willum Cubbert), Ericka Kreutz (Tansy McGinnis), Keith Powell (Axel Hammond), John Grassilli (Warnock Waldgrave), Diane Robinson (Clelia Waldgrave), Alex Cook and Josh Zimmerman (Thor Waldgrave), Jeffrey M. Bender (Rich Steadman)

UNDERNEATH THE LINTEL by Glen Berger; Directed by David Stradley; Scenic and Lighting Designer, Michael Philippi; Costume Designer, Mattie Ullrich; Sound Designer, Fabian Obispo; Dialect Coach, Deena Burke; Stage Manager, Sara J. Tantillo; October 19–November 6, 2005; **Cast:** Christopher Coucill (The Librarian)

WINTER WONDERETTES Created and Directed by Roger Bean; Vocal Arrangements, Roger Bean and Brian Baker; Musical Arrangements, Brian Baker; Musical Director, Jim Ryan; Choreographer, Kevin Ramsey; Scenic Designer, Vicki R. Davis; Costume Designer, Susan Schaeffer; Lighting Designer, Eileen Smitheimer; Sound Designer, P. J. Stasuk; Stage Manager, Sara J. Tantillo; November 30, 2005–January 1, 2006; **Cast:** Tracey Conyer Lee (Betty Jean), Inuka Nyota (Cindy Lou), Adia (Missy), Taifa Harris (Suzy)

THE PRICE by Arthur Miller; Directed by John Grassilli; Scenic and Costume Designer, Marie Chiment; Lighting Designer, Mark O'Maley; Assistant Lighting Designer, Caitlin Smith Rapoport; Sound Designer, Josh Schmidt; Stage Manager, Sara J. Tantillo; January 25–February 12, 2006; **Cast:** John Wojda (Victor Franz), Dee Pelletier (Esther Franz), Joel Friedman (Gregory Solomon), Bob Ari (Walter Franz)

THE SYRINGA TREE by Pamela Gien; Directed by C. Michael Wright; Scenic and Lighting Designer, Shannon Zura; Costume Designer, Devon Painter; Dialect Coach, Stanton Davis; Stage Manager, Sara J. Tantillo; March 8–26, 2006; **Cast:** Lia Aprile (Elizabeth), Erica Bradshaw (Salamina)

A MURDER, A MYSTERY AND A MARRIAGE by Mark Twain; Book and Lyrics by Aaron Posner; Music by James Sugg; Directed by Aaron Posner; Assistant Director, Meredith McDonough; Composer, James Sugg; Music Director, Jay Ansill; Choreographer, Karma Camp; Scenic Designer, Tony Cisek; Costume Designer, Kate Turner-Walker; Lighting Designer, James Leitner; Sound Designer, Matthew M. Neilson; Stage Manager, Sara J. Tantillo; Dramaturg, Michael Hollinger; April 26–May 14, 2006; **Cast:** Dan Manning (Clem & Reverend Hurley), Anthony Lawton (John Gray), Sherri L. Edelen (Sally Gray), Erin Weaver (Mary Gray), Ben Dibble (Hugh Gregory), Scott Greer (The Mysterious Stranger), Thomas Adrian Simpson (David Gray/Sheriff Thwacker) Musicians: Jay Ansill, Larry Cohen, Wanamaker Lewis, Andrew Nelson

DENVER CENTER THEATRE COMPANY

Denver, Colorado
TWENTY-SEVENTH SEASON

Artistic Director, Kent Thompson

ALL MY SONS by Arthur Miller; Directed by Bruce K. Sevy; Scenic Designer, Bill Forrester; Costume Designer, Bill Black; Lighting Designer Charles R. MacLeod; Sound Designer, Matthew C. Swartz; Production Manager, Edward Lapine; Stage Manager, Lyle Raper; September 29–November 5, 2005; **Cast:** Mike Hartman (Joe Keller), Jeanne Paulsen (Kate Keller), David Furr (Chris Keller), Rachel Fowler (Ann Deever), David Ivers (George Deever), James Michael Reilly (Dr. Jim Bayliss), Leslie O'Carroll (Sue Bayliss), Steven Cole Hughes (Frank Lubey), Eileen Little (Lydia Lubey), Sam Van Wetter (Bert)

A FLEA IN HER EAR by Georges Feydeau; Translated by John Mortimer; Directed by Kent Thompson; Scenic Designer, Scott Weldin; Costume Designer, Susan Branch; Lighting Designer, Rachel Budin; Sound Designer, Craig Breitenbach; Dramaturg, Sylvie Drake; Production Manager, Edward Lapine; Stage Manager, Christopher C. Ewing; Assistant Stage Manager, Christi B. Spann; October 6–November 5, 2005; **Cast:** Douglas Harmsen (Camille Chandebise), Stephanie Cozart (Antoinette Plucheux), Erik Sandvold (Etienne Plucheux), Randy Moore (Dr. Finache), Angela Pierce (Lucienne Homenides de Histangua), Kathleen McCall (Raymonde Chandebise), Jamie Horton (Victor Emmanuel Chandebise, Poche), John Hutton (Romain Tournel), Sam Gregory (Carlos Homenides de Histangua), Amber Voiles (Eugénie), Bill Christ (Augustin Feraillon), Kathleen M. Brady (Olympe), Philip Pleasants (Baptistin), Mark Rubald (Herr Schwarz), John Behlmann, Rachel Duvall, Rob Karma Robinson, Justin Walvoord (Hotel Guests)

SEPTEMBER SHOES by José Cruz González; Directed by Amy González; Scenic & Costume Designer, Christopher Acebo; Lighting Designer, Don Darnutzer; Sound Designer, Iæden Hovorka; Music Composer, Daniel Valdez; Production Manager, Edward Lapine; Stage Manager, Erock; October 20–December 17, 2005; **Cast:** Luís Saguar (Hulio/Juan), Karmín Murcelo (Gail), Wilma Bonet (Cuki/Lily Chu), John Herrera (Alberto), Adriana Gaviria (Ana)

A CHRISTMAS CAROL by Charles Dickens; adapted by Richard Hellesen; Directed by Bruce K. Sevy; Music by David de Berry; Musical Direction by Gregg Coffin; Dances Choreographed by Gina Cerimele-Mechley; Orchestrations by Thom Jenkins; Scenic Designer, Vicki Smith; Costume Designer, Kevin Copenhaver; Lighting Designer, Liz Lee; Sound Designer, Craig Breitenbach; Production

Manager, Edward Lapine; Stage Manager, Lyle Raper; Assistant Stage Managers, Christopher C. Ewing, Christi B. Spann; November 25–December 24, 2005; **Cast:** Leslie Alexander (Mrs. Cratchit/Ensemble), Madisen Beaty (Belinda/Ensemble), John Behlmann (Suitor/Belle's Husband/Ghost of Christmas Yet to Come/Ensemble), Kathleen M. Brady (Mrs. Fezziwig/Laundress/Ensemble), Colton Castañeda (Ebenezer the Child/Edward/Ensemble), Rachel Duvall (Fezziwig Daughter/Martha/Ensemble), Ruth Eglsaer (Belle/Ensemble), Sam Gregory (Bob Cratchit/Ensemble), Karl Hanover (Dick Wilkins/Fred's Party Guest/Ensemble), Jamie Horton (Subscription Gentleman/Old Joe/Ensemble), John Hutton (Ghost of Jacob Marley/Ensemble), David Ivers (Fred/The Undertaker's Man/Ensemble), David Allen James (Peter/Ensemble), Karen LaMoureaux (Fezziwig Daughter/Ensemble), Eileen Little (Fred's Party Guest/Ensemble), Kathleen McCall (Ghost of Christmas Past/Fred's Wife/Charwoman/Ensemble), Randy Moore (Ebenezer Scrooge), Rachel Obering (Fan/Want/Ensemble), Robert Ousley (Subscription Gentleman/Ghost of Christmas Present/Ensemble), Philip Pleasants (Ebenezer Scrooge), Jeffrey Roark (Ensemble), Rob Karma Robinson (Fiddler/Merchant from the Exchange/Ensemble), Brent Rose (Ebenezer the Young Man/Merchant form the Exchange/Ensemble), Christine Rowan (Fezziwig Daughter/Street Singer/Ensemble), Mark Rubald (Fezziwig/Ensemble), Jasper Ryckman (Ignorance/Boy in the Street/Ensemble), Randy St. Pierre (Suitor/Ensemble), Harrison Steele (Tiny Tim/Ensemble), Nicholas Thorne (Ensemble), Sam Van Wetter (Beggar Child/Ensemble), Amber Voiles (Wife's Sister/Ensemble), Justin Walvoord (Suitor/Topper/Merchant from the Exchange/Ensemble)

JESUS HATES ME by Wayne Lemon; Directed by David McClendon; Scenic Designer, Robert Mark Morgan; Costume Designer, Kevin Copenhaver; Lighting Designer, Jane Spencer; Sound Designer, Iæden Hovorka: Fight Director, Geoffrey Kent; Production Manager, Edward Lapine; Stage Manager, Erock; January 12–March 11, 2006; **Cast:** Justin Adams (Ethan), Marlon Morrison (Trane), Kathleen McCall (Annie), Craig Pattison (Boone), Chelsey Rives (Lizzy), Michael Keyloun (Georgie)

GEM OF THE OCEAN by August Wilson; Directed by Israel Hicks; Scenic Designer, Michael Brown; Costume Designer, David Kay Mickelsen; Lighting Designer, Charles R. MacLeod; Sound Designer, Matthew C. Swartz; Production Manager, Edward Lapine; Stage Manager, Christopher C. Ewing; January 19–February 25, 2006; **Cast:** Marlene Warfield (Aunt Ester), Terrence Riggins (Caesar), Kim Staunton (Black Mary), Charles Weldon (Solly Two Kings), Michael Eaddy (Citizen Barlow), Harvy Blanks (Eli), Jamie Horton (Rutherford Selig)

MEASURE FOR MEASURE by William Shakespeare; Directed by Kent Thompson; Music Composed by Gregg Coffin; Scenic & Costume Designer, G. W. Mercier; Lighting Designer, Don Darnutzer; Sound Designer, Craig Breitenbach; Vocal Coach, Michael Cobb; Production Manager, Edward Lapine; Stage Manager, Lyle Raper; Assistant Stage Manager, Christi B. Spann; January 26–February 25, 2006; **Cast:** John Behlmann (Gentleman in the Duke's Court and Ensemble), Kathleen M. Brady (Mistress Overdone), Bill Christ (Elbow/Barnardine), Stafford Clark-Price (Claudio), Ruth Eglsaer (Isabella), Rachel Fowler (Francesca, Mariana/Ensemble), Sam Gregory (Lucio), Karl Hanover (Froth/Ensemble), Brent Harris (Angelo), Steven Cole Hughes (Friar), John Hutton (The Duke), David Ivers (Pompey), Eileen Little (Juliet/Ensemble), Randy Moore (Escalus), Philip Pleasants (Abhorson), Rob Karma Robinson (Ensemble), Brent Rose (Ensemble), Mark Rubald (Provost), Amber Voiles (Ensemble), Justin Walvoord (Gentleman in the Duke's Court/A Justice, Ensemble)

THE CLEAN HOUSE by Sarah Ruhl; Directed by Wendy C. Goldberg; Scenic Designer, Alexander Dodge; Costume Designer, Anne Kennedy; Lighting Designer, Jane Cox; Sound Designer, Craig Breitenbach; Dialect Coaches, Kathryn G. Maes, Douglas W. Montequin; Fight Director, Robert Davidson; Produc-

tion Manager, Edward Lapine; Stage Manager, Christopher C. Ewing; Assistant Stage Manager, Christi B. Spann; March 23–April 22, 2006; **Cast:** Caitlin O'Connell (Lane), Romi Dias (Matilde), Charlotte Booker (Virginia), Jamie Horton (Charles/A Man), Judith Delgado (Ana/A Woman)

THE LADIES OF THE CAMELLIAS by Lillian Groag; Directed by Casey Stangl; Scenic Designer, Vicki Smith; Costume Designer, Devon Painter; Lighting Designer, Charles R. MacLeod; Sound Designer, Matthew C. Swartz; Dialect Coaches, Kathryn G. Maes, Douglas W. Montequin; Fight Director, Geoffrey Kent; Production Manager, Edward Lapine; Stage Manager, Lyle Raper; March 16–April 22, 2006; **Cast:** Beverly Leech (Sarah Bernhardt), Monique Fowler (Eleonora Duse), Stephanie Cozart (Girl), Randy Moore (M. Benoit), Philip Pleasants (Alexandre Dumas, FILS), Bill Christ (M. Worms), John Hutton (M. Andò), James Knight (Ivan), Mark Rubald (Benoit Constant Coquelin)

AFTER ASHLEY by Gina Gionfriddo; Directed by Anthony Powell; Scenic Designer, Lisa M. Orzolek; Costume Designer, David Kay Mickelsen; Lighting Designer, Charles R. MacLeod; Sound Designer, Iæden Hovorka; Production Manager, Edward Lapine; Stage Manager, Erock; April 6–June 3, 2006; **Cast:** Tobias Segal (Justin Hammond), Angela Reed (Ashley Hammond), Sam Gregory (Alden Hammond), John G. Preston (David Gavin), Ruth Eglsaer (Julie Bell), David Ivers, (Roderick Lord), Susanna Florence, Eric Laurits, Anne Marie Nest, Bradford Shreve, Moses Villarama (Ensemble)

CROWNS by Regina Taylor; Based on the book *Crowns: Portraits of Black Women in Church Hats* by Michael Cunningham and Craig Marberry; Directed and Choreographed by Kent Gash; Musical Direction by Ron Metcalf; Associate Director/Choreographer, Byron Easley; Scenic Designer, Emily Beck; Costume Designer, Kevin Copenhaver; Lighting Design, William H. Grant III; Sound Design by Craig Breitenbach; Production Manager, Edward Lapine; Stage Manager, Lyle Raper; Assistant Stage Manager, Christopher C. Ewing; May 11–June 18, 2006; **Cast:** Barbara D. Mills (Mother Shaw), B.J. Crosby (Mabel), Gretha Boston (Velma), Rosa Curry (Wanda), Karole Foreman (Jeanette), Uzo Aduba (Yolanda), C.E. Smith (Man), Ron Metcalf (Piano), Sherman Arnold (Percussion)

FORD'S THEATRE

Washington, D.C.
THIRTY-EIGHTH SEASON

Producing Director, Paul R. Tetreault

LEADING LADIES by Ken Ludwig; Directed by Mark Rucker; Scenic Designer, John Coyle; Costume Designer, Judith Dolan; Lighting Designer, Michael Gilliam; Original Sound Designer, John Gromada; Co-Sound Designer, Steven Severson; Hair and Wig Designer, Tom Watson; Choreographer, Michele Lynch; Fight Choreographer, Brad Waller; Dialect Coach, Ellen O'Brien; Casting, Liz Woodman; Production Stage Manager, Craig A. Horness; Associate Producer-General Manager, Christine Dietze; Associate Producer-Artistic, Mark Ramont; September 23–October 23, 2005; **Cast:** John Astin (Doc), JD Cullum (Jack), Daniel Frith (Butch), Ian Kahn (Leo), Patrick Kerr (Duncan), Lacey Kohl (Audrey), Charlotte Rae (Florence), Karen Ziemba (Meg)

A CHRISTMAS CAROL by Charles Dickens; Adapted by Michael Wilson, Directed by Matt August, Scenic Designer, G. W. Mercier; Costume Designer, Fabio Toblini; Lighting Designer, Pat Collins; Original Music, Mark Bennett; Sound Designer, Michael Creason; Choreographer, Karma Camp; Choral Direction, George Fulginiti-Shakar; Wig and Hair Designer, Tom Watson; Vocal Coach,

Deborah Hecht; Casting, Liz Woodman; Production Stage Manager, Craig A. Horness; Associate Producer-General Manager, Christine Dietze; Associate Producer-Artistic, Mark Ramont; November 16–December 31, 2005; **Cast:** Clinton Brandhagen (Nephew Fred/Young Scrooge), Michael Bunce (1st Solicitor), Michael John Casey (Bob Crachit), Teresa Castracane (Mrs. Fred), Elliot Dash (Fruit Vendor/Ghost of Christmas Present), Carlos Gonzalez (Clock Vendor/Ghost of Christmas Future), Michael Goodwin (Jacob Marley), Kimberly Parker Green (Belle), Bill Hensel (Mr. Fezziwig), Iliana Inocencio (Fred's Sister), Kathleen Kulikowski (Martha), Amy McWilliams (Mrs. Cratchit), Claudia Miller (Ensemble), Kip Pierson (Ensemble), Martin Rayner (Scrooge), Suzanne Richard (Doll Vendor/Ghost of Christmas Past), Todd Scofield (2nd Solicitor)

TRYING by Joanna McClelland Glass; Directed by Gus Kaikkonen; Scenic Designer, Jeff Bauer; Costume Designer, Pamela Scofield; Lighting Designer, Rui Rita; Sound Designer, Tony Angelini; Casting, Liz Woodman; Production Stage Manager, Allison Deutsch; Assistant Stage Manager, Craig A. Horness; Associate Producer-General Manager, Christine Dietze; Associate Producer-Artistic, Mark Ramont; January 20–February 19, 2006; **Cast:** Karron Graves (Sarah), James Whitmore (Jude Francis Biddle)

SHENANDOAH Music by Gary Geld; lyrics by Peter Udell; book by James Lee Barrett, Peter Udell and Philip Rose; based on the original screenplay by James Lee Barrett; Directed by Jeff Calhoun; Musical Direction, Arrangements and Orchestration by Steven Landau; Scenic and Costume Designer, Tobin Ost; Lighting Designer, Michael Gilliam; Sound Designer, David Budries; Hair and Wig Design, Tom Watson; Fight/Military Choreography, David Leong; Dialects Coach, Gary Logan; Assistant Director/Choreographer, Noah Riley; Casting, Jim Carnahan; Production Stage Manager, Craig A. Horness; Assistant Stage Manager Dana DePaul & Myra Coffield; Choreography, Jeff Calhoun & Chase Brock; Associate Director, Coy Middlebrook; Associate Producer-General Manager, Christine Dietze; Associate Producer-Artistic, Mark Ramont; April 1–May 21, 2006; **Cast:** Scott Bakula (Charlie Anderson), Cherry Harth Baumbusch (Ensemble), Christopher Bloch (Reverend Bryd/Carol), Peter Boyer (Sergeant Johnson), Evan Casey (Lieutenant), Kevin Clay (Robert), Rick Faugno (Nathan), Richard Frederick (Drifter), Ryan Jackson (Henry), Megan Lewis (Jenny), Timothy Dale Lewis (Confederate Sniper), Garrett Long (Anne), Mike Mainwaring (Gabriel), Tracy Lynn Olivera (Ensemble), Geoff Packard (Corporal), Richard Pelzman (Engineer), Noah Racey (Sam), Aaron Ramkey (Jacob), Andrew Samonsky (James), Stephen F. Schmidt (Tinkham), Anna Marie Sell (Ensemble), Bret Shuford (John), Rachel Zampelli (Ensemble)

GEORGE STREET PLAYHOUSE

New Brunswick, New Jersey
THIRTY-FIRST SEASON

David Saint, Artistic Director

2 LIVES by Arthur Laurents; Directed by David Saint; Scenic Designer, James Youmans; Lighting Designer, David Lander; Costume Designer, Theoni V. Aldredge; Sound Designer, Christopher J. Bailey; Stage Managers: Tom Clewell and C. Renee Alexander; **Cast:** Tom Aldredge (Matt), James Sutorius (Howard), Matt Cavenaugh (Scooter), Jessica Dickey (Mary Anne), Joanne Camp (Willi), Jim Brachitta (Leo), Helen Gallagher (Eloyse), Dee Hoty (Nerissa)

INSPECTING CAROL by Daniel Sullivan and the Seattle Repertory Company; Directed by David Saint; Scenic Designer, R. Michael Miller; Costume Designer, Brenda King; Lighting and Sound Designer, Christopher J. Bailey; Stage Managerer, Tom Clewell; **Cast:** Dan Lauria (Larry), Wally Dunn (Kevin), Randy Donald-son (Walter), Michael Mastro (Phil), Peter Scolari (Wayne), MacIntyre Dixon (Sidney), Catherine Cox (Zorah), Peggy Cosgrave (Dorothy), Mary-Catherine Wright (M.J.), John Keller (Bart), Aaron Wilton (Spike), Christopher J. Stewart (Luther)

UNDERNEATH THE LINTEL by Glen Berger; Directed by Maria Mileaf; Scenic Designer, Neil Patel; Lighting Designer, David Lander; Sound Designer, Fabian Obispo; Costume Designer, Katherine Roth; Stage Manager, C. Renee Alexander; **Cast:** Richard Schiff (The Librarian)

THE PILLOWMAN by Martin McDonagh; Directed by Will Frears; Scenic Designer, Sandra Goldmark; Lighting Designer, Paul Whitaker; Sound Designer, Christopher Bailey; Costume Designer, Anne Kenney; Original Music by Michael Friedman; Stage Manager, Tom Clewell; **Cast:** Scott Ferrara (Katurian), Daniel Oreskes (Ariel), Michael Mastro (Michal), Lee Sellars (Tupolski)

GUNMETAL BLUES by Marion Adler and Scott Wentworth; Directed by David Saint; Scenic Designer, Michael Anania; Costume Designer, by David Murin; Sound Designer, Tom Morse; Lighting Design, Christopher J. Bailey; Stage Manager, C. Renee Alexander; **Cast:** Alison Fraser (The Blonde), Daniel Marcus (The Piano Player), Patrick Quinn (Sam)

GEORGIA SHAKESPEARE

Atlanta, Georgia
TWENTIETH SEASON

Producing Artistic Director, Richard Garner

SHAKE AT THE LAKE: MACBETH by William Shakespeare; Directed by Drew Fracher; Scenic Designer, Kat Conley; Costume Designer, Sydney Roberts; Lighting Designer, Liz Lee; Sound Desnger, Mita Beach; Resident Dramaturg, Dr. Andrew H. Hartley; Fight Choreography, Drew Fracher; Stage Manager, Karen S. Martin; **Cast:** Brik Berkes (Macduff), Chris Ensweiler (Malcolm), Ishmal Ibn Connor (Witch/Old Man/Seyton/Murderer), Rachel Craw (Witch/Gentlewoman/Murderer), Alison Hastings (Witch/Murderer/Macbeth Servant), Jesse Hinson (Angus/Soldier), Chris Kayser (Duncan/Porter/Siward), Daniel May (Macbeth), Allen O'Reilly (Banquoe/Doctor), Kate Donadio (Lady Macduff/Party Guest/Soldier), Joanna Mitchell (Lady Macbeth), Barry Stoltze (Ross), Thomas Ward (Lennox), Hannah Rose Adams (Young Macduff), Alex Miller (Fleance), Jason Watkins (Donalbain, Young Siward, Party Guest)

THE COMEDY OF ERRORS by William Shakespeare; Directed by Richard Garner; Scenic Designer, Kat Conley; Costume Designer, Sydney Roberts; Lighting Designer, Mike Post; Composer, Klimchak; Sound Designer, Clay Benning; Text & Vocal Coach, Allen O'Reilly; Resident Dramaturg, Dr. Andrew J. Hartley; Stage Manager, Margo Kuhne; **Cast:** Chris Kayser (Antipholus of Syracuse/Antipholus of Ephesus), Chris Ensweiler (Dromio of Syaracuse/Dromio of Ephesus), Bruce Evers (Egeon of Syracuse), Hudson Adams (Duke Solinus of Ephesus), Brandon J. Dirden (Angelo), Crystal Dickinson (Andriana), Courtney Patterson (Luciano), Daniel May (First Merchant), Bradley Sherrill (Second Merchant), Joe Knezevich (Balthazar), Park Krausen (Courtesan), Rob Cleveland (Dr. Pinch), Megan McFarland (Abbess), Stanton Nash (Duke's Officer), Robert Wells III (Executioner), Diane Rodriquez (Pinch's Assistant), Jennifer Henry (Pinch's Assistant), Klimchak (Musician of Ephesus)

A STREETCAR NAMED DESIRE by Tennessee Williams; Directed by Karen Robinson; Scenic Designer, Leslie Taylor; Costume Designer, Mark Pirolo; Lighting Designer, Liz Lee; Fight Choreographer, Jason Armit; Sound Designer, Clay Benning; Dialect Coach, Cynthia Barrett; Dramaturg, Freddie Ashley; Stage Manager, Robert Schultz; **Cast:** Carolyn Cook (Blanche DuBois), Courtney Patterson (Stella Kowalski), Daniel May (Stanley Kowalski), Allen O'Reilly (Mitch), Crystal Dickinson (Eunice), Brandon J. Dirden (Steve), Rob Cleveland (Pablo), Jennifer Henry (Eunice's Friend), Stanton Nash (Young Collector), Diany Rodriguez (Mexican Woman), Chris Kayser (Doctor), Megan McFarland (Nurse)

THE CHERRY ORCHARD by Anton Chekhov; Directed by Sabin Epstein; Scenic Designer, Angela Calin; Costume Designer, Christine Turbitt; Lighting Designer, Liz Lee; Composer, Laura Karpman; Sound Designer, Mimi Epstein; Text & Vocal Coach, Elisa Carlson; Resident Dramaturg, Dr. Andrew J. Hartley; Stage Manager, Margo Kuhne; **Cast:** Carolyn Cook (Lyubov Ranyeskaya), Diany Rodriquez (Anya), Park Krausen (Varya), Allen O'Reilly (Leonid Gayev), Bruce Evers (Yermolai Lopakhin), Bradley Sherrill (Petya Trofimov), Hudson Adams (Boris Semeonov-Pishchik), Megan McFarland (Charlotta), Crystal Dickinson (Dunyasha), Chris Kayser (Firs), Joe Knezevich (Yasha), Daniel May (Homeless Man), Rob Cleveland (The Stationmaster), Brandon J. Dirden (The Postmaster), Jennifer Henry (Ensemble), Stanton Nash (Ensemble), Robert Wells III (Ensemble)

ROMEO AND JULIET by William Shakespeare; Directed by Richard Garner; Scenic Designer, Rochelle Barker; Costume Designer, Sydney Roberts; Lighting Designer, Liz Lee; Composer, Klimchak; Fight Director, Jacki Blakeney; Text Coach, Allen O'Reilly; Consulting Dramaturg, Dr. Andrew J. Hartley; Stage Manager, Margo Kuhne; **Cast:** Tony Vaugn (Lord Capulet), Joan Pringle (Lady Capulet), Lakeisha Woodard (Juliet), Crystal Dickinson (Nurse/Lady Montegue), Theroun Patterson (Tybalt/Friar John), Jesse Hinson (Peter), Henry Bazemore (Lord Montegue/Paris), Eugene Russel IV (Romeo), Enoch King (Benvolio), Neal Ghant (Mercutio/Apothecary), Chris Kayser (Friar Laurence/Montague Kinsman)

GOODMAN THEATRE

Chicago, Illinois
EIGHTY-FIRST SEASON

Artistic Director, Robert Falls; Managing Director, Roche Schulfer; General Manager, Kathy Murphy

DOLLHOUSE by Henrik Ibsen; Adapted by Rebecca Gilman; Directed by Robert Falls; Scenic Designer, Robert Brill; Costume Designer, Mara Blumenfeld; Lighting Designer, James F. Ingalls; Sound Designer, Richard Woodbury; Production Stage Manager, Alden Vasquez; June 18–July 24, 2005; **Cast:** Maggie Siff (Nora), Anthony Starke (Terry), Lance Stuart Baker (Pete), Elizabeth Rich (Kristine), Firdous Bamji (Raj Patel), Charin Alvarez (Marta), Maritza Cervantes (Iris), Melody Hollis, Allison Sparrow (Skyler), Ryan Cowhey, Matthew Gerdisch (Max), Jordyn Knysz, Emily Leahy (Macey)

PURLIE Music by Gary Geld; lyrics by Peter Udell; book by Ossie Davis, Philip Rose, and Peter Udell; Directed by Sheldon Epps; Scenic Designer, James Leonard Joy; Costume Designer, Paul Tazewell; Sound Designer, Frederick W. Boot; Lighting Designer, Allen Lee Hughes; Choreographer, Kenneth Lee Roberson; Music Director, Ronald (Rahn) Coleman; Stage Manager, T. Paul Lynch; Production Stage Manager, Joseph Drummond; September 17–October 30, 2005; **Cast:** Jacques C. Smith (Purlie Victorious Judson); Joyce "Peaches" Faison (Idella Landy); Paulette Ivory (Lutiebelle Gussie Mae Jenkins); E. Faye Butler (Aunt Missy Judson); Harrison White (Gitlow Judson); Billy Gill (Charlie Cotchipee); Lyle Kanouse (Ol' Cap'n Cotchipee); Sean Blake, Meloney Collins, Ronald Duncan, Mamie Duncan-Gibbs, Derric Harris, Edwin Henry, Danielle Alvergia Hobb, Sara Beth Lane, Elaine McLaurin, Rocklin Thompson, Timothy Ware, Byron Glenn Willis (Ensemble); Band: Ronald (Rahn) Coleman (Pianist/

Conductor); Tim Gant (Keyboards); Tim Tobias (Keyboards); Felton Offard (Acoustic and Electric Guitar); Bill Dickens (Upright and Electric Bass); Y.L. Douglas (Drums); Leddy Garcia (Percussion); Derric Harris (Dance Captain)

BEYOND GLORY by Stephen Lang; From the book by Larry Smith; Directed by Mr. Lang; Scenic Designer, Tony Cisek; Lighting Designer, Dan Covey; Sound Designer, Cecil Averett; Original Music Composers, Robert Kessler and Ethan Neuberg; Projections Designer, John Boesche; Production Stage Manager, Kimberly Osgood; Assistant Director, Michael Fosberg; **Cast:** Stephen Lang; September 10–October 9, 2005

A CHRISTMAS CAROL by Charles Dickens; adapted by Tom Creamer; Directed by Kate Buckley; Scenic Designer, Todd Rosenthal; Costume Designer, Heidi Sue McMath; Lighting Designer, Robert Christen; Sound Designer, Lindsay Jones; Original Music and Traditional Carols Arranger, Joe Cerqua; Musical Director, Joe Cerqua; Choreographer, Susan Hart; Voice and Dialect Coach, Linda Gates; Production Stage Manager, Alden Vasquez; Stage Manager, Sascha Connor; Flying Effects by ZFX, Inc.; November 19–December 26, 2005; **Cast:** Justin Amolsch (Musician); LaShawn Banks (Mr. Crumb); William Brown (Ebenezer Scrooge); Christine Bunuan (Ghost of Christmas Past/Martha Cratchett); Wayne T. Carr (Dick Wilkins/Young Man); Lisa Dodson (Mrs. Cratchit); Glynis Gilio (Fan/Emily Cratchit); Allen Gilmore (Chestnut Seller/By Scrooge); Dennis Grimes (Wreathseller/Young Scrooge); Matthew D. Heffernan (Turkey Boy/Pratt/Ignorance); Steven Hinger (Fred); Gregory Hirte (Musician/Ghost of Christmas Future); Bethany Jorgensen (Musician/Maid); John Lister (Ghost of Jacob Marley/Old Joe/Undertaker); Bradley Mott (Poulterer/Mr. Fezziwig/Ghost of Christmas Present); William J. Norris (Mr. Ortle); Grace Parker (Johnston/ Belinda Cratchit/ Want); Elijah Roberts (Tiny Tim); Malcolm Ruhl (Musician); Sharon Sachs (Mrs. Fezziwig/Philomena/ Charwoman); Tiffany Scott (Belle/Young Woman); Edward Stevens (Ensemble); Kevin Theis (Undertaker/Topper); Penelope Walker (Abby/ Mrs. Dilber); Jonathan Weir (Bob Cratchit/ Schoolmaster)

John LaGuaradia and Steve Pickering in *Romance* PHOTO BY LIZ LAUREN

PERICLES by William Shakespeare; Directed by Mary Zimmerman; Scenic Designer, Daniel Ostling; Costume Designer, Mara Blumenfeld; Lighting Designer, T.J. Gerckens; Sound Designer, Andre Pluess and Ben Sussman; Choreographer, Daniel Pelzig; Production Stage Manager, Joseph Drummond; Stage Manager, T. Paul Lynch; January 7–February 12, 2006; **Cast:** Glenn Fleshler (Antiochus/Pander); Ryan Artzberger (Pericles); Laura Scheinbaum (Daughter to Antiochus); Dan Kenney (Thaliard); Craig Spidle (Helicanus); Gary Wingert (Escanes/1st. Fisherman); Berwick Haynes (Lord of Tyre/3rd. Fisherman); Joseph Costa (Cleon); Michelle Shupe (Dionyza/Diana); Evan Zes (Leonine); Erik Steele (2nd Fisherman, Lysimachus); Joel Hatch (Simonides); Colleen Delany (Thaisa); Naomi Jacobson (Lychorida/Bawd); Glory Kissel (Cerimon); Marguerite Stimpson (Marina); Jesse J. Perez (Boult); JR Drew, Katherine Foster, Stephen Grush, Bethany Hubbard, Kenneth Z. Kendall, Akili Moore, Meghan Murphy, Dillon Porter, Dan Sanders-Joyce, Laura Scheinbaum, Kevin V. Smith (Ensemble)

A LIFE IN THE THEATRE by David Mamet; Directed by Robert Falls; Scenic Designer, Mark Wendland; Costume Designer, Birgit Rattenborg Wise; Lighting Designer, Michael Philippi; Sound Designer, Richard Woodbury; Production Stage Manager, Alden Vasquez; Stage Manager, Sascha Connor; March 4–April 9, 2006; **Cast:** David Darlow (Robert); Matt Schwader (John)

ROMANCE by David Mamet; Directed by Pam MacKinnon; Scenic Designer, Todd Rosenthal; Costume Designer, Rachel Anne Healy; Lighting Designer, Robert Christen; Sound Designer, Cecil Averett; Dramaturg, Tanya Palmer; Production Stage Manager, Kimberly Osgood; Stage Manager, Dana M. Nestrick; March 17–April 23, 2006; **Cast:** Matt DeCaro (Judge); Matthew Krause (Doctor); John LaGuardia (Bernard); David Pasquesi (Defendant); Steve Pickering (Prosecutor); Christian Stolte (Defense Attorney)

THREE PROGRAMS OF ONE-ACT PLAYS by David Mamet; Scenic Designer, Todd Rosenthal; Lighting Designer, Robert Christen; Sound Designer, Cecil Averett; Costume Designer, Rachel Anne Healy (Daughters, Sisters, Mothers); Costume Designer, Tatjana Radisic (Homecomings, Ghost Stories); April 7–April 23, 2006; **Homecomings/The Duck Variations** Directed by Louis Contey; Stage Manager, Andrea J. Collignon; **Cast:** Maury Cooper (Emil Varec); Howard Witt (George S. Aronvitz); **Homecomings/The Disappearance of the Jews** Directed by Rick Snyder; Stage Manager, Adam Ford; **Cast:** Joe Dempsey (Bobby Gould); Keith Kupferer (Joey); **Homecomings/Home** Directed by Louis Contey; Stage Manager, Andrea J. Collignon; **Cast:** Darrell W. Cox (Robert); Laura T. Fisher (Claire); **Daughters, Sisters, Mothers/Almost Done** Directed by Ann Filmer; Stage Manager, Kristi J. Martens; **Cast:** Bethany Caputo (A Woman); **Daughters, Sisters, Mothers/Reunion** Directed by Ann Filmer; Stage Manager, Kristi J. Martens; **Cast:** Bethany Caputo (Carol Mindler); Danny Goldring (Bernie Cary); **Daughters, Sisters, Mothers/Jolly** Directed by Rick Snyder; Stage Manager: Adam Ford; **Cast:** Rengin Altay (Jolly); Joe Dempsey (Bob); Todd Lahrman (Carl); **Daughters, Sisters, Mothers/Dark Pony** Directed by Ann Filmer; Stage Manager, Kristi J. Martens; **Cast:** Danny Goldring (The Father); Bethany Caputo (The Daughter); **Ghost Stories/No One Will Be Immune** Directed by Steve Scott; Stage Manager, Ellen Hay; **Cast:** Chistian Stolte (A); Steve Pickering (B); **Ghost Stories/The Shawl** Directed by Mike Nussbaum; Stage Manager, Ellen Hay; **Cast:** Matt DeCaro (John); Laura T. Fisher (Miss A); Darrell W. Cox (Charles)

THE REVENGE OF THE SPACE PANDAS, or BINKY RUDICH AND THE TWO-SPEED CLOCK by David Mamet; Directed by Steve Scott; Scenic Designer, Todd Rosenthal; Costume Designer, Tatjana Radisic; Lighting Designer, Robert Christen; Sound Designer, Cecil Averett; Composer and Music Director, Alaric "Rokko" Jans; Production Stage Manager, Ellen Hay; March 25–April 22, 2006; **Cast:** Gary Alexander (George Topax); Sean Blake (Retainer/Ensemble); McKinley Carter (Mrs. Rudich); Jose Antonio Garcia (Buffy); Blaine Hogan (Leonard "Binky" Rudich); Maribeth Monroe (Vivian Mooster); Ron Rains (Court Jester/Ensemble); Eric Slater (Bob); Edward Stevens (Newsman/Ensemble); Kevin Theis (Edward Farpis); Jamie Vann (Boots)

THE CLEAN HOUSE by Sarah Ruhl; Directed by Jessica Thebus; Scenic Designer, Todd Rosenthal; Costume Designer, Linda Roethke; Lighting Designer, James F. Ingalls; Original Music and Sound Designer, Andre Pluess and Ben Sussman; Dramaturg, Tanya Palmer; Production Stage Manager, Joseph Drummond; Stage Manager, T. Paul Lynch; Choreographer, Marla Lampert; April 29–June 4, 2006; **Cast:** Patrick Clear (Charles); Marilyn Dodds Franks (Ana); Christine Estabrook (Virginia); Mary Beth Fisher (Lane); Guenia Lemos (Matilde)

CRUMBS FROM THE TABLE OF JOY by Lynn Nottage; Directed by Chuck Smith; Scenic Designer, Linda Buchanan; Costume Designer, Birgit Rattenborg Wise; Lighting Designer, Robert Christen; Sound Designers, Ray Nardelli and Joshua Horvath; Dramaturg, Tom Creamer; Production Stage Manager, Kimberly Osgood; Dialect Coach, Linda Gates; May 27–June 25, 2006; **Cast:** John Steven Crowley (Godfrey Crump); Ella Joyce (Lily Ann Green); Nambi E. Kelley (Ernestine Crump); Bakesta King (Ermina Crump); Karen Janes Woditsch (Gerte)

GUTHRIE THEATER

Minneapolis, Minnesota
FORTY-THIRD SEASON

Artistic Director, Joe Dowling

HIS GIRL FRIDAY adapted by John Guare from *The Front Page* by Ben Hecht and Charles MacArthur and the Columbia Pictures film; Directed by Joe Dowling; Scenic Designer, John Lee Beatty; Costume Designer, Jess Goldstein; Lighting Designer, Brian MacDevitt; Sound Designer, Scott W. Edwards; Dramaturg, Carla Steen; Voice and Dialect Coach, Deborah Hecht; Movement, Marcela Lorca; Stunt Choreographer, Peter Moore; Stage Manager, Martha Kulig; Assistant Stage Manager, Ann K. Terlizzi; July 2–July 31, 2005; **Cast:** Matthew Amendt (Sweeney), Angela Bassett (Hildy Johnson), Raye Birk (Buddy "Mac" McCue), Barbara Bryne (Mrs. Baldwin), Bryan Clark (Carl), Zach Curtis (Diamond Louie), Bob Davis (Jack Wilson), Katie Eifrig (Mollie Malloy), Wayne A. Evenson (Woodenshoes), Joel Friedman (Rev. Cyrus Pickett), Peter Michael Goetz (Mayor), Jonas Goslow (Frank), Shawn Hamilton (Mike Endicott), Terry Hempleman (Ernie Kruger), Reginald Vel Johnson (Sheriff Percival B. Hartman), Karl Kenzler (Bruce Baldwin), Jim Lichtscheidl (Roy V. Bensinger), Bill McCallum (Eddie Schwartz), Kris L. Nelson (Earl Holub), Mark Rosenwinkel (Silas F. Pinkus), Courtney B. Vance (Walter Burns)

THE CONSTANT WIFE by W. Somerset Maugham; Directed by John Miller-Stephany; Scenic Designer, Patrick Clark; Costume Designer, Mathew J. LeFebvre; Lighting Designer, Matthew Reinert; Sound Designer, Scott W. Edwards; Dramaturg, Michael Lupu; Voice, Speech and Dialect Coach, Lucinda Holshue; Movement, Marcela Lorca; Stage Manager, Chris A. Code; Assistant Stage Manager, Michele Harms; August 13–September 11, 2005; **Cast:** Patricia Conolly (Mrs. Culver), Megan Gallagher (Constance Middleton), Charity Jones (Barbara Fawcett), Colin McPhillamy (Mortimer Durham), Michelle O'Neill (Martha Culver), Stacia Rice (Marie-Louise Durham), Armand Schultz (John Middleton), Peter Gregory Thomson (Bentley), Jeff Yagher (Bernard Kersal)

INTIMATE APPAREL by Lynn Nottage; Directed by Timothy Bond; Scenic Designer, Scott Bradley; Costume Designer, Helen Q. Huang; Lighting Designer, Ann G. Wrightson; Composer/Music Director, Michael Keck; Sound Designer, Scott W. Edwards; Dramaturg, Jo Holcomb; Voice, Speech and Dialect Coach, Elisa Carlson; Movement, Marcela Lorca; Production Stage Manager, Russell

W. Johnson; Assistant Stage Manager, Ann K. Terlizzi; September 24–October 23, 2005; **Cast:** Sterling K. Brown (George Armstrong), Cassandra F. Freeman (Mayme), Ron Menzel (Mr. Marks), Isabell Monk O'Connor (Mrs. Dickson), Michelle O'Neill (Mrs. Van Buren), Sharon Washington (Esther)

A CHRISTMAS CAROL by Charles Dickens; Adapted by Barbara Field; Directed by Gary Gisselman; Scenic Designer, Neil Patel; Costume Designer (1996), Jess Goldstein; Additional Costume Designs, David Kay Mickelsen; Lighting Designer, Marcus Dilliard; Composer, Victor Zupanc; Musical Director, Anita Ruth; Sound Designer, Scott W. Edwards; Dramaturgy, Michael Lupu; Voice and Dialect Coach, Elisa Carlson; Associate Director/Movement Coach, Myron Johnson; Stage Manager, Martha Kulig; Assistant Stage Manager, Theresa Schatz; November 19–December 24, 2005; **Cast:** Lauren Asheim (Marigold Fezziwig), Megan A. Bartle (Belle/Ella), Raye Birk (Ebenezer Scrooge), Michael Booth (Bob Cratchit), Laura Esping (Mrs. Dilber/Dorothea), Nathaniel Fuller (Joe), Jonas Goslow (Young Scrooge/Cecil), Jon Andrew Hegge (Ghost of Christmas Yet to Come), Kathleen Humphrey (Jane), Richard S. Iglewski (Jacob Marley/Topper/Ghost of Christmas Past), Charity Jones (Mrs. Fred), Michael Kissin (Fiddler/Krookings), Tracey Maloney (Petunia Fezziwig/Mr. Grub/Mr.Queeze), Bill McCallum (Blackings Foreman), Kris L. Nelson (Blakely, Snarkers), Lee Mark Nelson (Fred), Stephen Pelinski (Ghost of Christmas Present), Randy Reyes (Albert Hall, Edwards, Grasper), Doug Scholz-Carlson (Young Jacob Marley, Squeeze), Vern Sutton (Mr. Fezziwig, Elliott), Suzanne Warmanen (Sophia), Sally Wingert (Forrest, Mrs. Cratchit)

THE PEOPLE'S TEMPLE written by Leigh Fondakowski with Greg Pierotti, Stephen Wangh and Margo Hall; Directed by Leigh Fondakowski; Scenic Designer, Sarah Lambert; Costume Designer, Gabriel Berry; Lighting Designer, Betsy Adams; Sound Designer, Jake Rodriguez; Head Writer, Greg Pierotti; Project Researcher/Archivist, Denice Stephenson; Project Dramaturg, Jo Holcomb; Musical Arrangements/Direction, Miche Braden; Vocal Coach, Lucinda Holshue; Original Movement, Jean Issacs; Additional Movement, Randy Reyes; Stage Manager, Cynthia Cahill; Assistant, Chris A. Code; January 7–February 5, 2006; **Cast:** Will Badgett (Hue Fortson/Odell Rhodes/Pop Jackson), Colman Domingo (Eugene Smith/Jim Jones, Jr./Willie Brown, Jr.), Margo Hall (Shanette Oliver/Zipporah Edwards/Janet Williamson), Mike Hartman (Phil Tracy/Congressman Leo J. Ryan/Rev. John Moore), Lauren Klein (Barbara Moore/Liz Forman Schwartz/Neva Sly), John McAdams (Stephan Jones/Rev. Jim Jones/Jack Beam), Novella Nelson (Hyacinth Thrash/Nell Smart/Woman in White), Greg Pierotti (Vernon Gosney/Dick Tropp/Danny Curtain), Barbara Pitts (Meredith Reese/Julie Smith/Carolyn (Moore) Layton), Kelli Simpkins (Annie Moore/Juanite Bogue/Grace (Stoen) Jones), Regina Marie Williams (Ollie Smith/Deanna Wilkinson/Elsie Bell), Michael Winther (Tim Carter/Garry Lambrev)

HAMLET by William Shakespeare; Directed by Joe Dowling; Scenic Designer, Richard Hoover; Costume Designer, Paul Tazewell; Lighting Designer, Matthew Reinert; Composer, Mel Marvin; Sound Designer, Scott W. Edwards; Voice and Language Consultant, Andrew Wade; Dramaturg, Michael Lupu, Carla Steen; Movement, Marcela Lorca; Fight Director, John Stead; Production Stage Manager, Russell W. Johnson; Assistant Stage Manager, Martha Kulig; March 4–May 7, 2006; **Cast:** Matthew Amendt (Guildenstern), Raye Birk (Francisco/First Gravedigger), Leah Curney (Ophelia), Nathaniel Fuller (Ghost/Priest), Peter Michael Goetz (Polonius), Jonas Goslow (Rosencrantz), Matthew Greer (Claudius), Santino Fontana (Hamlet), Shawn Hamilton (Cornelius/Captain), Richard S. Iglewski (Player King), Ron Menzel (Barnardo/Fortinbras), Kris L. Nelson (Reynaldo), Lee Mark Nelson (Marcellus/Osric), Isabell Monk O'Connor (English Ambassador), Kevin O'Donnell (Horatio), Richard Ooms (Voltemand/Second Gravedigger), Markus Potter (Laertes), Randy Reyes (Sailor), Christina Rouner (Gertrude), Sally Wingert (Player Queen/Gentlewoman), Stephen Yoakam (First Player)

ILLINOIS THEATRE CENTER

Park Forest, Illinois
THIRTIETH SEASON

Producing Director, Etel Billig

PICNIC by William Inge; Directed by Etel Billig; **Cast:** Christian Castro, Mackenzie Kyle, Jennifer Haering, Judy Rossignuolo-Rice, Maris Hudson, Bernard Rice, Ted Jonas, Michele Lazowski, Amanda Claire Gray, Nancy Greco, Reid O'Connell

A MOON FOR THE MISBEGOTTEN by Eugene O'Neill; Directed by Etel Billig; **CAST:** Becca McCoy, John Tomlinson, Christopher Merrill, Scott Stangland, Brad Sandefur.

THE GIFTS OF THE MAGI by Mark St. Germain & Randy Courts; Directed by Etel Billig; **Cast:** Scott Sowinski, Joe Lehman, Cara Scott, George Andrew Wolff, Mary Jane Guymon, Frank Roberts

ART by Yasmina Reza, translated by Christopher Hampton; Directed by Judy Rossignuolo-Rice; **Cast:** David Perkovich, Bernard Rice, Dan LaMorte

PRETTY FIRE by Charlayne Woodard; Directed by Etel Billig; **Cast:** Inda Craig-Galvan

MESHUGAH by Emily Mann, based on the story by Isaac Bashevis Singer; Directed by Etel Billig; **Cast:** Alan Ball, Michele Kline, Andy Gwyn, Garrett Matheson, Etel Billig

BY JEEVES by Alan Ayckbourn & Andrew Lloyd Webber, based on the P.G. Wodehouse stories; Directed by Frank Roberts; **Cast:** Joe Lehman, David Perkovich, David Boettcher, Mary Jane Guymon, Ed Rutherford, David Lipshutz, Jeny Wasilewski, David Tibble, Paige Jarvie, Billy Vitucci

KANSAS CITY REPERTORY THEATRE

Kansas City, Missouri
FORTY-SECOND SEASON

Producing Artistic Director, Peter Altman

CARTER'S WAY Written and directed by Eric Simonson; Musical Director, Darrell Leonard; Scenic Designer, Neil Patel; Costume Designer, Karin Kopischke; Lighting Designer, Michelle Habeck; Sound Designer, Barry G. Funderburg; Production Stage Manager, Chad Zodrow; Assistant Stage Manager, Nancycaroline Cubine; June 3–26, 2005; **Cast:** Walter Coppage (Peewee Abernathy/Cedric), Damon Gupton (Oriole Carter), Gary Neal Johnson (Jack Thorpe/Porter), Danny Mastrogiorgio (Johnny Cozollo/Dutch), Kelly Sullivan (Eunice Fey), Dean Vivian (Corky/Billings/Henry/Andy/Indiana), Nikki E. Walker (Marilyn Stokes); Band: Johnnie Bowls, George Forbes, Elijah Murray

MAN AND SUPERMAN by George Bernard Shaw; Directed by Sharon Ott; Scenic Designer, Hugh Landwehr; Costume Designer, David Murin; Lighting Designer, Peter Maradudin; Sound Designer, Steve LeGrand; Dialect Coach, Louis Colaianni; Movement Coach, Jennifer Martin; Production Stage Manager, Mary R. Honour; Assistant Stage Manager, Christine M. Dotterweich; September 23–October 16; **Cast:** Christine Marie Brown (Violet Robinson), Lindsay Erika Crain (Maid), Ruth Eglsaer (Ann Whitefield), Ian Fraser (Octavius Robinson), Peggy Friesen (Mrs. Whitefield), Jim Gall (Henry Straker), Kaleo Griffith (Jack Tanner), James Knight (Hector Malone), Dan Kremer (Roebuck Ramsden), Merle Moores (Miss Ramsden), Mark Robbins (Hector Malone, Sr.)

GIVE 'EM HELL, HARRY by Samuel Gallu, Directed by Larry Carpenter, Scenic Designer, Michael B. Raiford; Costume Designer, Antonia Ford-Roberts; Lighting Designer, Rick Paulsen; Sound Designer, John Story; Dialect and Voice Coach, Louis Colaianni; Production Stage Manager, Lori Lundquist; October 7 – November 6, 2005 and March 24 – April 23, 2006; **Cast:** Gary Neal Johnson (Harry Truman)

A CHRISTMAS CAROL by Charles Dickens; Adapted by Barbara Field and originally produced by the Guthrie Theater; Directed by Linda Ade Brand; Scenic Designer, John Ezell; Costume Supervisor and Additional Costume Designer, Antonia Ford-Roberts; Lighting Designer, Shane Rowse; Sound Designer, John Story; Musical Director, Molly Jessup; Choreographer, Jennifer Martin; Production Stage Manager, November 19 – December 26, 2005; **Cast:** Jeanne Averill (Mrs. Fezziwig), Craig Benton (Bob Cratchit), Robert Gibby Brand (Charles Dickens), Peggy Friesen (Ghost of Christmas Past), Charles Fugate (Fred), Jim Gall (Ghost of Christmas Present), Griffin Galley (Tiny Tim), Larry Greer (Marley), Gary Neal Johnson (Scrooge), Amy Lewis (Belle), Jennifer Mays (Mrs. Fred), Emilee S. Minnick (Fan), Michael Linsley Rapport (Mr. Fezziwig), Brad Shaw (Ghost of Christmas Future), Michael Andrew Smith (Scrooge as a young man), Cameron Benton Stout (Tiny Tim), Kathleen Warfel (Mrs. Cratchit); Ensemble: Caroline Adams, Daniel Bateman, Tia Battle, Leah Darby, Alexandra Duncan, Elizabeth Ernst, Chloe Michelle Fey, Garrison Galley, Christian Gamble, Evan Michael Haas, David Tyler Horseman, Jeremy Ims, Jessica Ims, Kelly Kitchens, Sarah LaBarr, Brock Lorenzen, Kelcie Nicole Marquardt, Alex Montgomery, Kyle L. Mowry, Alex Petersen, Casi Riegle, Laure Ronnebaum, Nolyn Rutherford, Rusty Sneary, Ashley Soper, Sylvia Stoner, Richard Stubblefield, Daniel Robert Sullivan, Carson Lee Teague, Brandin Tolbert, Joshua Tolbert, Jake Walker, Spencer Wilson

A RAISIN IN THE SUN by Lorraine Hansberry; Directed by Lou Bellamy; Scenic Designer, Vicki M. Smith; Costume Designer, Mathew J. LeFebvre; Lighting Designer, Michelle Habeck; Production Stage Manager, Chad Zodrow; Assistant Stage Manger, Christine M. Dotterweich; January 20 – February 12, 2006; **Cast:** Adeoye (Joseph Asagai), David Alan Anderson (Walter), Damron Russel Armstrong (Bobo), Francelle Stewart Dorn (Lena Younger), George Forbes (Moving Man), Kyle Haden (George), Bakesta King (Beneath), Larry Paulsen (Karl Lindner), Ralph Prosper (Moving Man), Shané Williams (Ruth), Rasson Wofford (Travis).

HANK WILLIAMS: LOST HIGHWAY by Randal Myler and Mark Harelik, directed by Randal Myler; Musical Director, Dan Wheetman; Scenic Designer, Vicki M. Smith; Costume Designer, Robert Blackman; Lighting Designer, Don Darnutzer; Sound Designer, Eric Stahlhammer; Production Stage Manager, Bruno Ingram; Assistant Stage Manager, Mary R. Honour, February 25 – March 19, 2006; **Cast:** Stephen G. Anthony (Hoss), Mississippi Charles Bevel (Tee Tot), Margaret Bowman (Mama Lilly), Patricia Dalen (Waitress), H. Drew Perkins (Leon "Loudmouth"), Mike Regan (Fred "Pap" Rose), Regan Southard (Audrey Williams), Myk Watford (Jimmy "Burrhead"), Van Zeiler (Hank Williams)

David Perkovich, Joe Lehman in *By Jeeves* PHOTO BY WARREN SKALSKI

THE TRIP TO BOUNTIFUL by Horton Foote, directed by Eric Rosen; Scenic Designer, Geoffrey M. Curley; Costume Designer, Nan Cibula-Jenkins; Lighting Designer, Joel Moritz; Sound Designer and Original Music, Andre Pluess; April 28 – May 21, 2006; **Cast:** Kailey Bell (Thelma), Darrie Lawrence (Carrie Watts); John McAdams (Ludie); Michael Linsley Rapport (Harrison Ticket Man); John Sterchi (Houston Ticket Man/Sherrif); Cheryl Weaver (Jessie Mae)

MCCARTER THEATRE CENTER

Princeton, New Jersey
SEVENTY-SEVENTH SEASON

Artistic Director, Emily Mann

MISS WITHERSPOON, a world premiere by Christopher Durang; Directed by Emily Mann; Scenic Designer, David Korins; Costume Designer, Jess Goldstein; Lighting Designer, Jeff Croiter; Sound Designer, Darron L West; Dramaturg, Janice Paran; Production Stage Manager, Alison Cote; Assistant Stage Manager, Christine Whalen; World Premiere; A co-production with Playwrights Horizons; September 9 – October 16, 2005; **Cast:** Kristine Nielsen (Veronica), Mahira Kakkar (Maryamma), Colleen Wethmann (Mother 1 and 2), Jeremy Shamos (Father 1 and 2/Man in the Playground/ Dog Owner/ Wise Man) and Lynda Gravatt (Teacher/Woman in a Hat).

GEM OF THE OCEAN by August Wilson; Directed by Ruben Santiago-Hudson; Scenic Designer, Michael Carnahan; Costume Designer, Karen Perry; Lighting Designer, Jane Cox; Sound Designer, Garth Hemphill; Composer, Bill Sims, Jr.; Additional Music, Broderick Santiago; Production Stage Manager, Cheryl Mintz; Assistant Stage Manager, Kasey Ostopchuck; Casting Director, Laura Stanczyk, CSA; October 11 – October 30, 2005; **Cast:** Chuck Patterson (Eli), Russell Hornsby (Citizen Barlow), Phylicia Rashad (Aunt Ester), Roslyn Ruff (Black Mary), Raynor Scheine (Rutherford Selig), John Amos (Solly Two Kings), Keith Randolph Scott (Caesar)

A CHRISTMAS CAROL by Charles Dickens; Adapted by David Thompson; Directed by Michael Unger; Choreographer, Rob Ashford; Scenic Designer, Ming Cho Lee; Costume Designer, Jess Goldstein; Lighting Designer, Stephen Strawbridge; Sound Designer, Brian Ronan; Original Music and Lyrics by Michael Starobin; Musical Director, Charles Sundquist; Dialect Coach, Stephen Gabis; Supervising Stage Manager, Cheryl Mintz; Production Stage Manager, Mindy Richardson; Assistant Stage Manager, Kasey Ostopchuck; Casting Director, Laura Stanczyk, CSA; December 4 – December 24, 2005; **Cast:** David Cromwell (Ebenzer Scrooge), Price Waldman (Bob Cratchit), Nick Toren (Fred), Angela Lin (Lily), Susan Pellegrino (Mrs. Dilber), Peter Cambor (Jacob Marley), Garrett Long (Mrs. Bonds/Fan), Anne O'Sullivan (Mrs. Stocks/Mrs. Fezziwig), Count Stovall (Mr. Fezziwig/Old Joe), Cherise Boothe (Christmas Present), Susan Knight (Mrs. Cratchit), Simon Kendall (Young Scrooge)

A MOON FOR THE MISBEGOTTEN by Eugene O'Neill; Directed by Gary Griffin; Scenic Designer, Eugene Lee; Costume Designer, Jess Goldstein; Lighting Designer, Jane Cox; Sound Design, Andre Pluess and Ben Sussman; Fight Director, J. Steven White; Production Stage Manager, Cheryl Mintz; Assistant Stage Manager, Kasey Ostopchuck; Casting Director, Laura Stanczyk, CSA; January 13 – February 19, 2006; **Cast:** Kathleen McNenny (Josie Hogan), Peter Scanavino (Mike Hogan), Jack Willis (Phil Hogan), Andrew McCarthy (James Tyrone, Jr.), Jeremiah Wiggins (T. Stedman Harder)

A MIDSUMMER NIGHT'S DREAM by William Shakespeare; Directed by Tina Landau; Original Music Composed and Performed by GrooveLily; Scenic Designer,

Louisa Thompson; Costume Designer, Michael Krass; Lighting Designer, Scott Zielinski; Sound Design, Michael Bodeen and Rob Milburn; Aerial Design, Christopher Harrison; Dramaturg, Douglas Langworthy; Vocal Coach, Deena Burke; Production Stage Manager, Alison Cote; Assistant Stage Manager, Christine Whalen; Casting, Laura Stanczyk, CSA and Alison Franck; A co-production with Paper Mill Playhouse; March 21–April 9, 2006; **Cast:** Jay Goede (Theseus/Oberon), Ellen McLaughlin (Hippolyta/Titania), Stephen Payne (Egeus/Peter Quince), James Martinez (Lysander), Will Fowler (Demetrius), Stacey Sargeant (Hermia), Brenda Withers (Helena), Guy Adkins (Philostrate, Puck), Lea DeLaria (Bottom), Demond Green (Flute), Karl Christian (Peaseblossom/Attendant), Reginald Holden Jennings (Mustardseed), Jesse Nager (Cobweb), Gene Lewin (Snug/GrooveLily), Brendan Milburn (Tom Snout/GrooveLily), Valerie Vigoda (Starveling/GrooveLily).

RIDICULOUS FRAUD, by Beth Henley; Directed by Lisa Peterson; Scenic Designer, Michael Yeargan; Costume Designer, Jess Goldstein; Lighting Designer, Peter Kaczorowski; Sound Designer, Martin Desjardins; Dramaturg, Janice Paran; Dialect Coach, Gillian Lane-Plescia; Fight Consultant, Rick Sordelet; Production Stage Manager, Cheryl Mintz; Assistant Stage Manager, Kasey Ostopchuck; Casting Director, Laura Stanczyk, CSA; World Premiere May 5–June 11, 2006; **Cast:** Daniel London (Lafcad Clay), Reg Rogers (Andrew Clay), Ali Marsh (Willow Clay), Tim DeKay (Kap Clay), Charles Haid (Baites), Heather Goldenhersh (Georgia), Barbara Garrick (Maude Chrystal), John Carroll Lynch (Ed Chrystal)

MERRIMACK REPERTORY THEATRE

Lowell, Massachusetts
TWENTY-SEVENTH SEASON

Artistic Director, Charles Towers

THE BREADWINNER by W. Somerset Maugham; Directed by Carl Forsman; Scenic Designer, Nathan Heverin; Costume Designer, Theresa Squire; Lighting Designer, Josh Bradford; Sound Designer, Sam Doerr; Production Stage Manager, Emily F. McMullen; October 7–October 30, 2005; **Cast:** Joe Delafield (Patrick Battle), Jack Gilpin (Charles Battle), Virginia Kull (Judy Battle), Margaret Laney (Diana Granger), Robert Emmet Lunney (Alfred Granger), Alicia Roper (Margery Battle), David Standish (Timothy Granger), Jennifer Van Dyck (Dorothy Granger)

THE ART OF SACRIFICE by Anthony Clarvoe; Directed by Charles Towers; Scenic Designer, David Evans Morris; Costume Designer, Jane Alois Stein; Lighting Designer, Juliet Chia; Production Stage Manager, Emily F. McMullen; November 10–December 4, 2005; **Cast:** Nesbitt Blaisdell (Will), Jeremiah Wiggins (Aron)

SQUEEZE BOX Written and performed by Ann Randolph; Directed by Alan Bailey; Lighting Designer, Brian Lilienthal; Production Stage Manager, Emily F. McMullen; December 29, 2005–January 22, 2006

INTIMATE APPAREL by Lynn Nottage; Directed by Jane Page; Scenic Designer, Bill Clarke; Costume Designer, Nanzi Adzima; Lighting Designer, Stephen Quandt; Sound Designer, Kevin Dunayer; Production Stage Manager, Emily F. McMullen; February 9–March 5, 2006; **Cast:** Howard Kaye (Mr. Marks), Tracey Conyer Lee (Mayme), Nadine Mozon (Esther Mills), Kennedy Reilly-Pugh (George Armstrong), Kristie Dale Sanders (Mrs. Van Buren), Elizabeth Van Dyke (Mrs. Dickson)

AUNTIE & ME by Morris Panych; Directed by Munson Hicks; Scenic Designer, Richard Wadsworth Chambers; Costume Designer, Jane Alois Stein; Lighting Designer, Daniel Meeker; Sound Designer, Jamie Whoolery; Production Stage Manager, Emily F. McMullen; Assistant Stage Manager, Adam C. Scarano; March 16–April 9, 2006; **Cast:** Nancy E. Carroll (Grace), Tim Donoghue (Kemp)

REAL HUSH-HUSH by John Corwin; Directed by Charles Towers; Scenic Designer, Bill Clarke; Costume Designer, Deb Newhall; Lighting Designer, John Ambrosone; Production Stage Manager, Emily F. McMullen; April 20–May 14, 2006; **Cast:** Dennis Creaghan (Shaw), Christian Kohn (Larry), Caitlin Mueulder (Anna), Sean Patrick Reilly (Wilson)

SANDERS FAMILY CHRISTMAS Written by Connie Ray; conceived by Alan Bailey; Directed by Alan Bailey; Scenic Designer, Peter Harrison; Costume Designer, Jeanette deJong; Lighting Designer, Brian Lilienthal; Sound Designer, Production Stage Manager, Emily F. McMullen; December 9–December 18, 2005; **Cast:** Constance Barron (Vera Sanders), David Hemsley Caldwell (Mervin Oglethorpe), Tess Hartman (June Sanders), Angela Brinton Mack (Denise Sanders), B. Hayben Oliver (Dennis Sanders), Bob Payne (Burl Sanders), Bobby Taylor (Stanley Sanders)

Nesbitt Blaisdell and Jeremiah Wiggens in *The Art of Sacrifice*

OREGON SHAKESPEARE FESTIVAL

Ashland, Oregon
SEVENTIETH SEASON

Artistic Director, Libby Appel

ANGUS BOWMER THEATRE

RICHARD III by William Shakespeare; Directed by Libby Appel; Scenic Designer, Rachel Hauck; Costume Designer, Mara Blumenfeld; Lighting Designer, Robert Peterson; Assistant Director, Bill Fennelly; Dramaturg, Barry Kraft; Voice and Text Director, Scott Kaiser; Resident Movement and Fight Director, John Sipes; Assitant Fight Director, U. Johnathan Toppo; Stage Manager, Gwen Turos; Assistant Stage Manager, Amy Miranda Warner; February 18–October 30 2005; **Cast:** Richard Elmore (King Edward IV), Suzanne Irving (Queen Elizabeth), Travis Bond (Edward), Kyle Barnes (Richard), Robert Vincent Drake (George), James Newcomb (Richard), Linda Alper (Duchess of York), Robynn Rodriguez (Duchess of York), Robin Goodrin Nordli (Queen Margaret), Laura Morache (Lady Anne), Kyle Haden (Thomas Grey), Chris Erric Maddox (Lord Richard Grey), Matt McTighe (Anthony Woodville, Earl Rivers), Jason McBeath (Sir thomas Vaughan), Michael Elich (Duke of Buckingham), Jonathan Haugen (Lrd Hastings), Brad Whitmore (Lord Stanley), Tyrone Wilson (Sir William Catesby), Juan Rivera LeBron (Sir Richard Ratcliffe), Chris Maslen (Sir Thomas Lovel), Sandy McCallum (Sir Robert Brakenbury), Richard Elmore (Cardinal), Robert Vincent Frank (John Morton), Matt McTighe (Lord Mayor of London), Jason McBeath (Sir James Tyrrell), Paul Michael Garcia (First Murderer), Danforth Comins (Second Murderer), Danforth Comins (Henry), Ensemble: Danforth Comins, Paul Michael Garcia, Kyle Haden, Chris Erric Maddox, Chris Maslen, Jason McBeath, Matt McTighe, Brandon St. Clair Saunders, Rafael Untalan

ROOM SERVICE by John Murray & Allen Boretz; Directed by J.R. Sullivan; Scenic Designer, Richard L. Hay; Costume Designer, Joyce Kim Lee; Lighting Designer, Robert Jared; Composer, Todd Barton; Assistant Sound Designer, David K. Weberg; Dramaturg, Lue Morgan Douthit; Voice and Text Director, Scott Kaiser; Resident Movement and Fight Director, John Sipes; Stage Manager, Susan L. McMillan; Production Assistant, Melissa Wanke; February 20–October 29, 2005; **Cast:** Eileen DeSandre (Sasha Smirnoff), David Kelly (Gordon Miller), Richard Howard (Joseph Gribble), Tony DeBruno (Harry Binion), Michael J. Hume (Faker Englund), Tyler Layton (Christine Marlowe), Christopher DuVal (Leo Davis), Linda K. Morris (Hilda Manney), Jeffrey King (Gregory Wagner), John Pribyl (Simon Jenkins), Danforth Comins (Timothy Hogarth), Richard Farrell (Dr. Glass), Jake Street (Bank Messenger), Robert Sicular (Senator Blake)

THE PHILANDERER by George Bernard Shaw; Directed by Penny Metropulos; Scenic Designer, William Bloodgood; Costume Designer, Christina Poddubiuk; Lighting Designer, Michael Chybowski; Music Designer, Sterling Tinsley; Dramaturg, Scott Horstein; Voice and Text Director, David Carey; Resident Movement and Fight Director, John Sipes; Stage Manager, Jill Rendall; Assistant Stage Manager, Mandy Younger; Assistant Director, Clinton Johnston; February 19–July 10, 2005; **Cast:** Derrick Lee Weeden (Leonard Charteris), Vilma Silva (Grace Tranfield), Miriam A. Laube (Julie Craven), Aisha Kabia (Sylvia Craven), Mark Murphey (Colonel Daniel Craven), James Edmondson (Joseph Cuthburtson), Jeff Cummings (Doctor Paramore), John Tufts (Pageboy)

NAPOLI MILIONARIA by Eduardo De Filippo; adapted by Linda Alper and Beatrice Basso; Director, Libby Appel; Scenic Designer, Michael Dempsey; Costume Designer, Robert Morgan; Lighting Designer, Robert Peterson; Sound Designer, Irwin Appel; Dramaturg, Beatrice Basso; Voice and Text Director, Evamarii Johnson; Resident Movement and Fight Director, John Sipes; Stage Manager, Jeremy Eisen; Production Assistant, Melissa Wanke; Assistant Director, Stefanie Sertich; April 19–October 30 2005; **Cast:** Richard Elmore (Gennaro), Linda Alper (Amalia), Juan Rivera LeBron (Amedeo), Heather Robison (Maria Rosaria), Armando Duran (Errico Settebellizze), Shad Willingham (Peppe the Jack), Richard Howard (Riccardo Spasiano), Judith-Marie Bergan (Adelaide), Terri McMahon (Assunta), Brad Whitmore (Miezo Prevete), John Pribyl (Pascalino, Doctor), Tony DeBruno (Ciappa), Jason McBeath (Federico), Catherine E. Coulson (Donna Peppenella), Laura Morache (Margherita), Sarah Rutan (Teresa), Matt McTighe (Wine Man/Guard)

THE BELLE'S STRATAGEM by Hannah Cowley; Directed by Davis McCallum; Scenic Designer, William Bloodgood; Costume Designer, Deborah M. Dryden; Lighting Designer, Ann G. Wrightson; Composer, Todd Barton; Dramaturg, Melinda C. Finberg; Voice and Text Director, Ursula Meyer; Resident Movement and Fight Director, John Sipes; Choreographer, Suzanne Seiber; Stage Manager, Amy Miranda Warner; Assistant Stage Manager, Mandy Younger; Production Assistant Intern, Kaitlyn Johnson; Assistant Director, Deanna Downes; July 28–October 30, 2005; **Cast:** Gregory Linington (Doricourt); Heather Robison (Latitia Hardy), Michael J. Hume (Old Hardy), David Kelly (Sir George Touchwood), Miriam A. Laube (Lady Frances Touchwood), Shad Willingham (Saville), Demetra Pittman (Mrs. Racket), Terri McMahon (Miss Ogle), Mark Murphey (Villers), John Tufts (Flutter), Mirron E. Willis (Courtall), Aisha Kabia (Kitty Willis), Jake Street (Tony), Caroline Crocker (Servant), Adam Cuppy (Servant), Sean Kelly (Servant), Caroline Crocker (Ensemble) Adam Cuppy (Ensemble), Aisha Kabia (Ensemble), Sean Kelly (Ensemble), Jake Street (Ensemble)

NEW THEATRE

BY THE WATERS OF BABYLON by Robert Schenkkan; Directed by Bill Rauch; Scenic Designer, Michael Ganio; Costume Designer, Denise Damico; Lighting Designer, James Ingalls; Sound Designer, Jeremy J. Lee; Dramaturg, Lue Morgan Douthit; Voice and Text Director, David Carey; Resident Movement and Fight Director, John Sipes; Choreograper, Janis Rosenthal; Stage Manager, Jeremy Eisen; Production Assistant, Jonathan Dickey; Assistant Director, Clinton Johnston; February 24–June 24, 2005; **Cast:** Catherine E. Coulson (Catherine), Armando Duran (Arturo)

MA RAINEY'S BLACK BOTTOM by August Wilson; Directed by Timothy Bond; Scenic Designer, William Bloodgood; Costume Designer, Helen Qizhi Huang; Lighting Designer, Darren McCroom; Composer and Music Director, Michael Keck; Dramaturg, Lue Morgan Douthit; Assistant Director, Bill Fennelly; Voice and Text Director, Evamarii Johnson; Resident Movement and Fight Director, John Sipes; Assistant Fight Director, U. Jonathan Toppo; Choreographer, Suzanne Seiber; Stage Manager, D. Christian Bolender; Production Assistant, S.A. Rogers; March 30–October 30, 2005; **Cast:** Bill Geisslinger (Mel Strdyvant), U. Jonathan Toppo (Irvin), Josiah Phillips (Cutler), Abdul Salaam El Razzac (Toledo), Frederick Charles Canada (Slow Drag), Kevin Kenerly (Levee), Greta Oglesby (Ma Rainey), Mark Peterson (Sylvester), Julia Pace Mitchell (Dussie Mae), James J. Peck (Policeman)

GIBRALTAR by Octavio Solis; Directed by Liz Diamond; Scenic Designer, Richard L. Hay; Costume Designer, Deborah M. Dryden; Lighting Designer, Chris Parry; Sound Designer, Jeremy J. Lee; Dramaturg, Douglas Langworthy; Voice and Text Director, Scott Kaiser; Resident Movement and Fight Director, John Sipes; Asistant Fight Director, U. Jonathan Toppo; Stage Manager, Jill Rendall; Production Assistant, S.A. Rogers; Assistant Director, Isis Sartial Misdary; July 5–October 30, 2005; **Cast:** Vilma Silva (Amy), Rene Millan (Palo), Kevin Kenerly (Steven), Dee Masske (Francesca), U. Jonathan Toppo (Taylor), Julie Oda (Sharon), Bill Geisslinger (Jackson), Judith-Marie Bergan (Dot), Alicia Rendall (Lila)

ELIZABETHAN STAGE/ALLEN PAVILION

TWELFTH NIGHT by William Shakespeare; Directed by Peter Amster; Scenic Designer, William Bloodgood; Costume Designer, Shigeru Yaji; Lighting Designer, Robert Peterson; Composer, Joseph Cerqua; Dramaturg, Lue Morgan Douthit; Voice and Text Director, Ursula Meyer; Resident Movement and Fight Director, John Sipes; Assistant Fight Director, U. Jonathan Toppo; Stage Manager, Gwen Turos; Assistant Stage Manager, Amy Miranda Warner; Assistant Director, Peter Reynolds; June 7–October 9, 2005; **Cast:** Michael Elich (Orsino), Robin Goodrin Nordli (Olivia), Linda K. Morris (Viola), Gregory Linington (Sebastian), Mirron E. Willis (Antonio), Kyle Haden (Valentine), Jake Street (Curio), Robert Sicular (Sir Toby Belch), Christopher DuVal (Sir Andrew Aguecheek), Kenneth Albers (Malvolio), Suzanne Irving (Maria), Robert Vincent Frank (Fabian), Richard Farrell (Feste), James Newcomb (Sea Captain), Jose Luis Sanchez (Priest); Ensemble: Caroline Crocker, Robert Vincent Frank, Paul Michael Garcia, Kyle Haden, Christ Erric Maddox, Chris Maslen, Jose Luis Sanchez, Jake Street, Rafael Untalan, Jaclyn Williams, Edward Condon (Musician)

THE TRAGICAL HISTORY OF DOCTOR FAUSTUS by Christopher Marlowe; Directed by James Edmondson; Scenic Designer, Richard L. Hay; Costume Designer, Marie Anne Chiment; Lighting Designer, Robert Peterson; Composer, Todd Barton; Dramaturg, Barry Kraft; Voice and Text Director, Ursula Meyer; Resident Movement and Fight Director, John Sipes; Assistant Fight Director, U. Jonathan Toppo; Stage Manager, D. Christian Bolender; Assistant Stage Manager, Mandy Younger; Assistant Director, Peter Reynolds; June 8–October 7, 2005; **Cast:** Demetra Pittman (Chorus), Jonathan Haugen (Dr. Faustus), Ray Porter (Mephostophilis), Shad Willingham (Wagner), Juan Rivera LeBron (Robin), Julia Pace Mitchell (Good Angel), Catherine C. Lynne Davis (Evil Angel), Kenneth Albers (Valdes), Abdul Salaam El Razzac (Cornelius), Matt McTighe (First Scholar), Tyrone Wilson (Second Scholar), Chris Maslen (Third Scholar), Brent Harris (Lucifer), James J. Peck (Belzebub), Andrea Ferraz (Pride), Matt McTighe (Covetousness), Sarah Rutan (Envy), Jaclyn Williams (Wrath), Tyrone Wilson (Gluttony), Brandon St.Clair Saunders (Sloth), Laura Morache (Lechery), Josiah Phillips (Pope Adrian), Mark Peterson (Pope Bruno), Frederick Charles Canada (Emperor Charles), Matt McTighe (Frederick), Jason McBeath (Benvolio), Chris Maslen (Alexander the Great), Jaclyn Williams (Alexander's Paramour), Chris Erric Maddox (Duke of Vanholt), Nicole Marie Strykowski (Dutchess of Vanholt), Brandon St.Clair Saunders (Vintner's Boy), Sarah Rutan (Old Woman), Laura Morache (Helen of Troy); Ensemble: Andrea Ferraz, Juan Rivera LeBron, Chris Erric Maddox, Chris Maslen, Jason McBeath, Matt McTighe, Laura Morache, James J. Peck, Mark Peterson, Sarah Rutan, Brandon St. Claire Saunders, Nicole Marie Strykowski, Jaclyn Williams, Tyrone Wilson

LOVE'S LABOR'S LOST by William Shakespeare; Directed by Kenneth Albers; Scenic Designer, Marjorie Bradley Kellogg; Costume Designer, Susan E. Mickey; Lighting Designer, Robert Peterson; Composer, John Tanner; Dramaturg, Barry Kraft; Voice and Text Director, Scott Kaiser; Resident Movement and Fight Director, John Sipes; Choreographer, Suzanne Seiber; Stage Manager, Susan L. McMillan; Production Assistant, Melissa Wanke; Production Assistant Intern, James Standley; June 9–October 8, 2005; **Cast:** Brent Harris (Ferdinand), Jeff Cummings (Berowne), Jose Luis Sanchez (Longaville), Christopher DuVal (Dumaine), Catherine Lynn Davis (The Princess of France), Tyler Layton (Rosaline), Andrea Ferraz (Maria), Sarah Rutan (Katherine), Derrick Lee Weeden (Boyet), Robert Sicular (Forester), John Pribyl (Don Adriano de Armado), Julie Oda (Moth), Ray Porter (Costar), Jeffrey King (Dull), Jaclyn Williams (Jaquenetta), Eileen DeSandre (Holofernes), James Edmondson (Sir Nathaniel), Robert Sicular (Marcade/Ensemble), Jeris Schaefer (Aramis/Ensemble)

PAPER MILL PLAYHOUSE

Millburn, New Jersey
SEVENTY-FIRST SEASON

President and CEO, Michael Gennaro

CINDERELLA by Rodgers and Hammerstein; Directed by Gabriel Barre; Musical Director, Tom Helm; Choreographer, Jennifer Paulson Lee; Scenic Designer, James Youmans; Costume Designer, Pamela Scofield; Lighting Designer, Tim Hunter; Sound Designer, Randy Hansen; Hair and Wig Design, Gerard Kelly and Jason P Hayes; Production Stage Manager, Gail P. Luna; October 19–December 4, 2005; **Cast:** Suzanne Douglas (Fairy Godmother), Angela Gaylor (Cinderella), Nora Mae Lyng (Stepmother), Janelle Anne Robinson (Grace), Jen Cody (Joy), Paolo Montalban (Prince Christopher), Stanley Wayne Mathis (Lionel, Royal Steward), Joy Franz (Queen Constantina), Larry Keith (King Maximillian); Ensemble: James Bulleri, Ron DeStefano, Lauren Brim, Jacqueline Colmer, Daisy Hobbs, Paul Jackel, Karina Michaels, Skie Ocasio, Diane Veronica Phelan, Jason Robinson, Dante Russo, Leah Sprecher, Tina Stafford, David Tankersley, Erin Webley, Jason Weston; Understudies: Joseph Cullinane (Dove/Cat/Mice), Daisy Hobbs (Fairy Godmother), Paul Jackel (King Maximillian), Karina Michaels (Grace), Skie Ocasio (Prince Christopher), Diane Veronica Phelan (Cinderella), Tina Stafford (Queen/Stepmother), Erin Webley (Joy), Jason Weston (Lionel); Swings: Joseph Cullinane, Lael Van Keuren; Dance Captain: Karina Michaels

THE DIARY OF ANNE FRANK Written by Frances Goodrich and Albert Hackett; Newly adapted by Wendy Kesselman, Directed by Carolyn Cantor; Scenic Designer, David Korins; Costume Designer, Ilona Somogyi; Lighting Designer, Kevin Adams; Sound Designer, Randy Hansen; Hair and Wig Design, Charles LaPointe; Production Stage Manager, Gail P. Luna; January 18–February 26, 2006; **Cast:** Shana Dowdeswell (Anne Frank), Peter Kybart (Otto Frank), Isabel Keating (Edith Frank), Dana Powers Acheson (Margot Frank), Christa Scott-Reed (Miep Gies), Michael Stahl-David (Peter van Daan), Jeff Talbott (Mr. Kraler), Nancy Robinette (Mrs. van Daan), David Wohl (Mr. van Daan), Michael Rupert (Mr. Dussel), Peter Bretz (First Man), Steve Brady (Second Man), Seamus Mulcahy (Third Man), Voiceovers: Steve Brady (Bolkestein/ other voices), Peter Bretz (Rauter/other voices), Jeff Talbot (BBC Announcer/other voices);Understudies: Steve Brady (Mr. Frank, Mr. van Daan), Peter Bretz (Mr. Dussel/Mr. Kraler), Donna Davis (Mrs. Frank, Mrs. van Daan), Seamus Mulcahy (Peter van Daan), Dana Powers Acheson (Anne Frank), Rachel Schwartz (Margot Fram, Miep Gies)**.**

Tovah Feldshuh and Company in *Hello, Dolly!* PHOTO BY GERRY GOODSTEIN

Ellen McLaughlin and Jay Goede in *A Midsummer Night's Dream* PHOTO BY T. CHARLES ERICKSON

CARNIVAL Music and lyrics by Bob Merrill, book by Michael Stewart; Directed by Erica Schmidt; Musical Director, Tom Helm; Choreographer, Peter Pucci; Scenic Designer, Christopher Barreca; Costume Designer, Michelle R. Phillips; Lighting Designer, Donald Holder; Sound Designer, Randy Hansen; Hair and Wig Design, Gerard Kelly and Jason P Hayes; Puppets Designed and built by Jesse Mooney-Bullock; Production Stage Manager, Gail P. Luna; March 8–April 9 2006; **Cast:** Eric Michael Gillett (Jacquot/Henry), Nick Wyman (B. F. Schlegel), Alexandra Cassens (Greta Schlegel), Julia Sann (Greta's Sister), Albert Christmas, Jim Corti, David Garry, Vinson German (Roustabouts), Jennifer Allen (The Incomparable Rosalie), Paul Schoeffler (Marco The Magnificent), Krissy Richmond (Princess Olga), Nikka Graff Lanzarone (Gladys Zuwicki), Sarah Lin Johnson (Gloria Zuwicki/Bluebird), Mam Smith (Aerialist/Acrobat), Richard Pruitt (Grobert), Charlie Pollack (Paul Berthalet/Carrot Top), Elena Shaddow (Lili), Jason Babinsky (Roustabout/Acrobat/Bluebird/ Cracher du feu), Michael H. Fielder (Roustabout/Acrobat/ Bluebird), Hector Flores (Roustabout/Acrobat/ Bluebird), Nikka Graff Lanzarone (Bluebird), Mindy Wallace (Bluebird), Drew Cortese (Renardo/Dr. Glass), Benjie Randall (Marguerite); Understudies: Noah Aberlin (Dr. Glass), Jason Babinsky (Renardo/Marguerite) Alexandra Cassens (Lili); Albert Christmas (Grobert), Jim Corti (Jacquot/Henry), Michael H. Fielder (Aerialist), David Garry (Paul/Carrot Top), Vinson German (Marco), Nikka Graff Lanzarone (Olga), Richard Pruitt (Schlegel), Krissy Richmond (Rosalie), Allison Stodola (Gladys/Greta); Swings: Noah Aberlin, Allison Stodola; Aerial Choreographer: Mam Smith; Dance Captain: Jim Corti

A MIDSUMMER NIGHT'S DREAM by William Shakespeare; music by GROOVELILY, Co- Produced with the McCarter Theater in Princeton, NJ.; Directed by Tina Landau; Scenic Designer, Louisa Thompson; Costume Designer, Michael Krass; Lighting Designer, Scott Zielinski; Sound Designer, Michael Bodeen and Rob Milburn; Hair and Wig Design, Bettie O. Rogers; Production Stage Manager, Alison Cote; April 19–May 21, 2006; **Cast:** Valerie Vigoda, Brendan Milburn, Gene Lewin (GrooveLily), Guy Adkins (Puck), Ellen McLaughlin (Hippolyta/Titania), Karl Christian, Christopher Mai, Ryan Overberg (Attendants), Jay Goede (Theseus/Oberon), Guy Adkins (Philostrate), Stephen Payne (Egeus), Stacey Sargeant (Hermia), William Fowler (Demetrius), James Martinez (Lysander), Stephen Payne (Peter Quince), Lea DeLaria (Nick Bottom), Demond Green (Francis Flute), Brendan Milburn (Tom Snout), Valerie Vigoda (Robin Starveling), Gene Lewin (Snug), Jesse Nager (Fairy Cobweb), Reginald Holden Jennings (Fairy Mustardseed), Karl Christian (Fairy Peaseblossom), Ryan Overberg (Fairy Moth), Adam Lobato and Christopher Mai (Additional Faries)

HELLO, DOLLY! by Michael Stewart; Music and lyrics by Jerry Herman; Directed by Mark S. Hoebee; Musical Director, Tom Helm; Choreographer, Mia Michaels; Scenic Designer, Michael Anania; Costume Designer, James Schuette; Lighting Designer, Charlie Morrison; Sound Designer, Randy Hansen; Hair and Wig Design, Bettie O. Rogers; Production Stage Manager, Gail P. Luna; September 2–October 2, 2005; **Cast:** Tovah Feldshuh (Mrs. Dolly Gallagher Levi), Anna McNeely (Ernestina), Andrew Gehling (Ambrose Kemper), Walter Charles (Horace Vandergelder), Lauren Marcus (Ermengarde), Jonathan Rayson (Cornelius Hackl), Brian Sears (Barnaby Tucker), Kate Baldwin (Irene Molloy), Jessica-Snow Wilson (Minnie Fay), Leisa Mather (Mrs. Rose), Willlam Solo (Rudolph), Denis Lambert (Stanley), Roger Preston Smith (Judge), Christopher Noffke (Court Clerk), Townspeople, Waiters: Jennifer Allen, Brian Barry, Nova Bergeron, Margot de La Barre, Heather Carino, Nigel Columbus, Marissa Joy Ganz, Ben Hartley, Denis Lambert, Leisa Mather, Anna McNeely, Christopher Noffke, Benjie Randall, Eric Daniel Santagata, Roger Preston Smith, William Solo, Brandon Tyler, Mindy Wallace, Ryan Worsing; Understudies: Margot de La Barre (Minnie Fay/Mrs. Rose), Marissa Joy Ganz (Emangarde), Denis Lambert (Ambrose), Leisa Mather (Ernestina/Irene Malloy), Anna McNeely (Dolly Levi), Benjie Randall (Cornelius), Roger Preston Smith (Rudolph), William Solo (Horace), Ryan Worsing (Barnaby), Swings: Dennis O'Bannion, Lael Van Keuren; Dance Captain: Ben Hartley

PEOPLE'S LIGHT & THEATRE COMPANY

Malvern, Pennsylvania
THIRTY-FIRST SEASON

Artistic Director, Abigail Adams

THE MEMBER OF THE WEDDING by Carson McCullers; Directed by Abigail Adams; Scenic Designer, James F. Pyne, Jr; Costume Designer, Marla J. Jurglanis; Lighting Designer, Dennis Parichy; Sound Designer, Charles T. Brastow, Production Stage Manager, Charles T. Brastow; Sept. 14–Oct. 23, 2005; **Cast:** Anne Berkowitz (Frankie Adams), Melanye Finister (Berenice Sadie Brown), Jerrell Henderson (Honey Camden Brown), Michael LiDondici (Jarvis), Stephen Novelli (Royal Addams), Kathryn Petersen (Mrs. West), Kalev Rudolph (John Henry West), Franklin John Westbrooks (T.T. Williams), Julianna Zinkel (Janice), Emily Berkowitz (Helen), Rebecca Berkowitz (Doris)

JASON AND THE GOLDEN FLEECE by John Olive; Directed by Shannon O'Donnell; Scenic Designer, James F. Pyne Jr.; Costume Designer, Marla J. Jurglanis; Lighting Designer, Dennis Parichy; Sound Designer/Composer, Christopher Colucci; Production Stage Manager, Kate McSorley; Oct. 13–Nov. 20, 2005; **Cast:** Michael Cruz (Jason), Peter DeLaurier (Ensemble), Mark del Guzzo (Ensemble), Joanna Liao (Ensemble), Benjamin Lloyd (Ensemble), Ahren Potratz (Ensemble), Mary Elizabeth Scallen (Ensemble)

JACK & THE BEANSTALK, AN AMERICAN PANTO Book & lyrics by Kathryn Petersen; original music by Vince di Mura; Directed by David Bradley; Scenic Designer, Lewis Folden; Costume Designer, Rosemarie E. McKelvey; Lighting Designer, John Stephen Hoey; Musical Direction, Vince di Mura; Movement Director, Samantha Bellomo; Sound Designer/Stage Manager, Charles T. Brastow; Nov. 23, 2005–Jan. 8, 2006; **Cast:** Anne Berkowitz (Ensemble), Scott Boulware (Horatio the Harp/Ensemble), Alda Cortese (Madame Vermillion), Joilet Harris (Hester the Hen/Ensemble), Matthew Hultgren (Ensemble), Mark Lazar (The Widow Trot), Susan McKey (Fern Fiddlehead), Christopher Patrick Mullen (Clive Bungy), Stephen Novelli (Carpal the Carniverous), Tom Teti (Percival/Pierre), Erin Weaver (Jack)

FABULATION—OR THE RE-EDUCATION OF UNDINE by Lynn Nottage; Directed by Abigail Adams; Scenic Designer, Scott Weldin; Costume Designer, Rosemarie E. McKelvey; Lighting Designer, Dennis Parichy; Original Music/Soundscape, Michael Keck; Stage Manager, Kate McSorley; Jan. 11 – Feb. 19, 2006; **Cast:** Rob Barnes (Yoruba Priest/Father), Kevin Bergen (Richard/Addict/Gregory), Melanye Finister (Allison/Mother/Inmate), Clark Jackson (Herve/Guy), Chantal Jean-Pierre (Undine), Edward O'Blenis (Flow/Agent Duva/Lance), Mary Elizabeth Scallen (Stephie/Inmate/Rosa), Cathy Simpson (Grandma/Addict)

THE CRUCIBLE by Arthur Miller; Directed by David Bradley; Scenic Designer, James F. Pyne Jr.; Costume Designer, Marla J. Jurglanis; Lighting Designer, Dennis Parichy; Stage Manager/Sound Designer, Charles T. Brastow; Feb. 22 – Apr. 9, 2006; **Cast:** Claire Inie-Richards (Betty Parris), Peter DeLaurier (Rev. Parris), Lenny Daniels (Tituba), Julianna Zinkel (Abigail Williams), Anne Berkowitz (Susanna Wallcott), Marcia Saunders (Ann Putnam/Sarah Good), Mark Lazar (Thomas Putnam/Ezekial Cheever), Kimberly Carson (Mercy Lewis), Kristyn Chouiniere (Mary Warren), Christopher Patrick Mullen (John Proctora), Ceal Phelan (Rebecca Nurse), Tom Teti (Giles Corey), Benjamin Lloyd (Rev. Hale), susan McKey (Elizabeth Proctor), Robert Toperzer (Francis Nurse), Jeb Kreager (Marshall Willard), Stephen Novelli (Judge Hathorne), Graham Smith (Deputy Governor Danforth)

YEMAYA'S BELLY by Quiara Alegría Hudes; Directed by Shannon O'Donnell; Scenic Designer, Regina Garcia; Costume Designer, Rosemarie E. McKelvey; Lighting Designer, John Stephen Hoey; Composer/Sound Designer, Christopher Colucci; Movement Choreographer, Jen Schoonover; Stage Manager, Kate McSorley; March 30 – May 7, 2006; **Cast:** Michael Cruz (Jelin), Mark Del Guzzo (Jesús/Mulo), Joe Guzmán (Tico), Joanna Liao (Maya/Yemaya), Mary Elizabeth Scallen (Mami/Lila)

THE MAN FROM NEBRASKA by Tracy Letts; Directed by Ken Marini; Scenic Designer, Arthur R. Rotch; Costume Designer, Rosemarie E. McKelvey; Lighting Designer, Dennis Parichy; Sound designer/Stage Manager, Charles T. Brastow; May 24 – June 25, 2006; **Cast:** Kevin Bergen (Harry Brown), Tom Byrn (Reverend Todd), Peter DeLaurier (Ken Carpenter), Miriam Hyman (Tamyra), Karen Peakes (Ashley Kohl), Kathryn Petersen (Pat Monday), Ceal Phelan (Cammie Carpenter), Marcia Saunders (Nancy Carpenter)

Grant Goodman in *Front Page* PHOTO BY JON GARDINER

THE FOREIGNER by Larry Shue; Directed by David Ingram; Scenic Designer, James F. Pyne, Jr.; Costume Designer, Marla J. Jurglanis; Lighting Designer, Gregory Scott Miller; Sound Designer, Charles T. Brastow; Dialect Coach, Stanton Davis; Stage Manager, Kate McSorley; June 28 – July 23, 2006; **Cast:** Alda Cortese (Betty Meeks), Lenny Haas (Rev. David Marshall Lee), Jeb Kreager (Ellard Simms), Mark Lazar (Sgt. Froggy LeSeuer), Pete Pryor (Charlie Baker), Graham Smith (Owen Musser), Elizabeth Webster (Catherine Simms)

PLAYMAKERS REPERTORY COMPANY

Chapel Hill, North Carolina
THIRTIETH SEASON

Artistic Director, David Hammond

THE FRONT PAGE by Ben Hecht and Charles MacArthur; Directed by Gene Saks; Scenic Designer, Narelle Sissons; Costume Designer, James Scott; Lighting Designer, Allen Hahn; October 5 – 30, 2005; **Cast:** Nikolas Priest (Wilson), Ray Dooley (Endicott), Matt Patterson (Murphy), Jeffrey Blair Cornell (McCue/Mr. Pincus), Estes Tarver (Schwartz), David zum Brunnen (Kruger), Ronn Carroll (Bensinger), Julie Fishell (Mrs. Schlosser/Mrs. Grant), Kenneth P. Strong (Woodenshoes), John Feltch (Diamond Louie), Grant Goodman (Hildy), Lori Prince (Jennie/Peggy), Marla Yost (Mollie Malloy), Rand Bridges (Sherrif), Sam Maupin (Mayor), Ken Jennings (Earl Williams), Mike Genovese (Walter Burns), William Stutts (Carl – Deputy), Wes Schultz (Frank – Deputy), Marshall Spann (Policeman 1), Chris Taylor (Policeman 2)

STRING OF PEARLS by Michele Lowe; Directed by Trezana Beverley; Scenic Designer, Robin Vest; Costume Designer, Tracy Christensen; Lighting Designer, Peter West; Sound Designer, Michèl Marrano; Composer, M. Anthony Reimer; November 16 – December 11, 2005; **Cast:** Susan Barrett (Woman #3), Diane Ciesla (Woman #2), Allison Reeves (Woman #4), Kathryn Hunter Williams (Woman #1)

FROZEN by Bryony Lavery; Directed by Drew Barr; Scenic Designer, Narelle Sissons; Costume Designer, Kim Krumm Sorenson; Lighting Designer, Justin Townsend; Sound Designer, Michèl Marrano; Composer, M. Anthony Reimer; January 18 – February 12, 2006; **Cast:** Julie Fishell (Nancy), James Kennedy (Ralph), Deborah Hazlett (Agnetha Gottmundsdottir)

GOD'S MAN IN TEXAS by David Rambo; Directed by Anthony Powell; Scenic Designer, Robin Vest; Costume Designer, Anne Kennedy; Lighting Designer, Peter West; Sound Designer, Michèl Marrano; Composer, M. Anthony Reimer; March 1 – 26, 2006; **Cast:** Philip Davidson (Dr. Philip Gottschall), Sean Hennigan (Hugo), Kenneth P. Strong (Dr. Jeremiah "Jerry" Mears)

CYRANO DE BERGERAC by Edmund Rostand; Directed by Joseph Haj; Scenic Designer, McKay Coble; Costume Designer, Marion Williams; Lighting Designer, Justin Townsend; Sound Designer, Michèl Marrano; Composer, M. Anthony Reimer; April 12 – May 7, 2006; **Cast:** Matthew Baldiga (2nd Cavalier/young Marquis/Spaniard), Robert Barr (Burgher/3rd Poet/Bertrandou the Fifer), Joseph Bowen (Ragueneau), Michael Brislin (Cuigy/Spanish Officer), Janie Brookshire (Buffet-girl/Sister Martha), Jeffrey Blair Cornell (Le Bret), Ray Dooley (Cyrano), John Feltch (De Guiche), Julie Fishell (Duenna/Mother Marguerite), Justin Flexen (Drunkard/Man of Letters/Spaniard), David Friedlander (1st lackey/5th Cadet), Kate Gleason (Roxane), Grant Goodman (Christian), David McClutchey (Marquis/Musketeer/2nd Cadet), Matthew Patterson (Montfleury/8th Cadet/Sentry), Nikolas Priest (1st Cavalier/4th Cadet), Allison Reeves (Actress/lackey(Act 3)/Sister Claire), Wes Schultz (Brissaille/1st Page/

Spaniard), Marshall Spann (2nd Lackey/2nd Poet/7th Cadet), Heaven Stephens (1st Lady/Nun), William Stutts (Porter/4th Poet/The Poet/2nd Page/Spaniard), Estes Tarver (Valvert/3rd Cadet), Chris Taylor (Guardsman/6th Cadet), Danika Williams (2nd Lady/Nun), Marla Yost (Lise/Theatre Lady/Nun), Steven Green (Burgher's son/A Child/Boy w/troops), Kristian Marceno (Burgher's son/A Child/Boy w/troops).

PORTLAND CENTER STAGE

Portland, Oregon
EIGHTEENTH SEASON

Artistic Director, Chris Coleman

UNDERNEATH THE LINTEL by Glen Berger; Director/Scene Design, Nancy Keystone; Costume Designer, Jeff Cone; Lighting Designer, Justin Townsend; Sound Designer, Jen Raynak; Stage Manager, Marcella Y. Crowson; Production Assistant, Jacob Fenston; Casting, Julia Flores Casting; September 27 – August 30, 2005; **Cast:** Time Winters (The Librarian)

PRIDE AND PREJUDICE adapted from Jane Austen's novel by Marcus Goodwin; Directed by Jane Jones; Scenic Designer, Greg Carter; Costume Designer, Deb Trout; Lighting Designer, Diane Williams; Sound Designer, Jen Raynak; Stage Manager, Mark Tynan; Assistant Stage Manager, Marcella Y. Crowson; Period Dance & Movement Consultant, Laura Ferri; Assistant to the Director, Jessica Wallenfels; Dramaturg, Jennifer Lee Taylor; Dialect Coach, Teresa Thuman; Production Assistant, Jamie Hill; Casting, Rose Riordan and Harriet Bass Casting; October 25 – November 20, 2005; **Cast:** Tobias Anderson (Sir William Lucas/Mr. Gardiner), Spencer Conway (Jenkins/Officer Denny/Col. Fitzwilliam/Jacob), Stephanie Danna (Lydia Bennet), Andrew DeRycke (Mr. Darcy), Kimberly King (Mrs. Bennet/Lady Catherine de Bourgh), Maya Lawson (Kitty Bennet/Miss de Bourgh, Geiorgiana Darcy), Debera-Ann Lund (Mrs. Hurst/Charlotte Lucas/Mrs. Gardiner), Alex Podulke (Mr. Wickham/Captain Carter), Laura Faye Smith (Mary Bennet), Mollyl Wright Stuart (Jane Bennet), Jennifer Lee Taylor (Elizabeth Bennet), Brian Thompson (Mr. Bennet), Tim True (Rev. Collins/Mr. Hurst), Kelsey Tyler (Mr. Bingley), Alison Weller (Miss Bingley/Housekeeper)

THIS WONDERFUL LIFE World premiere of an adaptation of the screenplay *It's a Wonderful Life*, conceived and performed by Mark Setlock, written by Steve Murray; Directed by Martha Banta; Performed by Mark Setlock; Scenic Designer, Dex Edwards; Costume Designer, Jeff Cone; Lighting Designer, Matt Frey; Sound Designer, Jen Raynak; Stage Manager, Marcella Y. Crowson; Assistant Stage Manager, Mark Tynan; Production Assistant, Jacob Fenston; Casting, Rose Riordan; November 29 – December 24, 2005; **Cast:** Mark Setlock (George Bailey and others)

THE FANTASTICKS Book and lyrics by Tom Jones, music by Harvey Schmidt; Directed by Chris Coleman; Music Director/Conductor, Rick Lewis; Assistant Director, Eric Skinner; Scenic Designer, Dex Edwards; Fight Choreographer, John Armour; Costume Designer, Jeff Cone; Lighting Designer, Peter Maradudin; Sound Designer, Jen Raynak; Stage Manager, Mark Tynan; Assistant Stage Manager, Creon Thorne; Production Assistant, Jamie Hill; Casting, Rose Riordan, Harriet Bass Casting; January 10 – February 5, 2006; **Cast:** Adrian Bailey (El Gallo), Rebecca Stanley (Luisa), Raymond J. Lee (Matt), Ron Daum (Hucklebee), ;Michael Mandell (Bellamy), Tim True (Mortimer/The Mute), Brian Thompson (Henry), Brian T. Wilson, Kurt Conroyd (Stage Hands), Rick Lewis, Ross Seligman, Will Amend (Musicians)

THE INTELLIGENT DESIGN OF JENNY CHOW by Rolin Jones; Directed by Kim Rubenstein; Assistant Director, Johanna Gruenhut, Scenic Designer, G.W. Mercier; Cosutme Designer, Nephelie Andonyadis; Lighting Designer, Peter Maradudin; Sound Designer, Daniel Baker; Composer, Matthew Suttor; Stage Manager, Nicole Olson; Assistant Stage Manager, Mark Tynan; Production Assistant, Jacob Fenston; Casting, Laura Richin Casting, Rose Riordan, Bruce Elsperger; Co-produced with San Jose Repertory Theatre, (Timothy Near, Artistic Director; David Jobin Managing Director); February 14 – March 5, 2006; **Cast:** Ka-Ling Cheung (Jenny Chow), Sue Jean Kim (Jennifer Marcus), Craig W. Marker (Todd), Kevin Rich (Preston/Terrence/Col. Hubbard/Dr. Yakunin/computer translator), Valerie Stevens (Adele), Tim True (Mr. Marcus)

CROWNS by Regina Taylor, adapted from the book *Crowns: Portraits of Black Women in Church Hats* by Michael Cunningham and Craig Marberry; Directed by Andrea Frye; Musical Director, James M. Calhoun; Choreographer, Mercedes Ellington; Scenic Designer, Marjorie Bradley Kellogg; Costume Designer, Reggie Ray; Lighting Designer, Dawn Chiang; Sound Designer, Brian Jerome Peterson; Stage Manager, Bret Torbeck; Production Assistant, Jacob Fenston; Casting, Elissa Myers Casting, Rose Riordan, Samantha Wyer, Zan Sawyer-Daily; Co-produced with Arizona Theatre Company (David Ira Goldstein, Artistic Director; Jessica L. Andrews, Managing Director) and Actors Theatre of Louisville (Marc Masterson, Artistic Director; Alexander Speer, Executive Director); March 14 – April 9, 2006; **Cast:** Pat Bowie (Mother Shaw), Thomas Jefferson Byrd (Man), Crystal Fox (Yolanda), Angela Karol Grovey (Wanda), Erika LaVonn (Velma), Julia Lema (Mabel), April Nixon (Jeanette)

CELEBRITY ROW by Itamar Moses; Directed by Chris Coleman; Scenic Designer, Daniel Ostling; Costume Designer, Jeff Cone; Lighting Designer, Daniel Ordower; Sound Designer, Casi Pacilio; Dialect Coach, Teresa Thuman; Dramaturg, Mead Hunter; Stage Manager, Mark Tynan; Production Assistant, Jamie Hill; Casting by Harriet Bass and Rose Riordan; World Premiere March 21 – April 16, 2006; **Cast:** Leslie Kalarchian (Maze Carroll and others), Daniel Thomas May (Timothy McVeigh and others), Jesse J. Perez (Luis Felipe and others), Ariel Shafir (Ramzi Yousef and others), Ebbe Roe Smith (Ted Kaczynski and others)

THE REPERTORY THEATRE OF ST. LOUIS

St. Louis, Missouri
THIRTY-NINTH SEASON

Artistic Director, Steven Woolf

MAINSTAGE

CAT ON A HOT TIN ROOF by Tennessee Williams; Directed by Marshall W. Mason; Scenic Designer, David Potts; Costume Designer, David Zyla; Lighting Designer, Phil Monat; Composer, Peter Kater; Casting, Rich Cole & Julia Flores; Assistant Director, Rand Mitchell; Stage Manager, Glenn Dunn; Assistant Stage Manager, Shannon B. Sturgis; September 7 – October 7, 2005; **Cast:** Molly Schaffer (Maggie), Jason Kuykendall (Brick), Mary Proctor (Mae), Jo Twiss (Big Mama), John Lepard (Gooper), Edwin McDonough (Reverend Tooker), Michael McCarty (Big Daddy), Joneal Joplin (Doctor Baugh)

A FUNNY THING HAPPENED ON THE WAY TO THE FORUM Book by Burt Shevelove and Larry Gelbart; music and lyrics by Stephen Sondheim; Directed by Edward Stern; Choreographed by Janet Watson; Music Director, Darren R. Cohen; Scenic Designer, John Ezell; Costume Designer, David Kay Mickelsen; Lighting Designer, Peter E. Sargent; Casting, Rich Cole; Stage Manager, T.R. Martin; Assistant Stage Manager, Tony Dearing; October 12–November 11, 2005; **Cast:** Bob Walton (Pseudolus), John Seidman (Senex), Jared Gertner (Protean), Bryan Lefeber (Protean), Dominic Roberts (Protean), Lynn Eldredge (Domina), Jeff Skowron (Hysterium), Eric Ulloa (Hero), Keith Jochim (Marcus Lycus), Jaclyn Minerva (Tintinabula), Karen Hyland & Hayley H. Nelson (Geminae), Carol Schuberg (Vibrata), Stefanie Cedro (Vibrata) Erika Lynn Rominger (Gymnasia), Lynette Knapp (Philia), Nat Chandler (Miles Gloriosus), Whit Reichert (Erronius)

ALL THE GREAT BOOKS (ABRIDGED) by Reed Martin & Austin Tichenor; additional material by Matthew Croke & Michael Faulkner; Directed by Reed Martin; Scenic & Costume Designer, Dorothy Marshall Englis; Lighting Designer, Peter E. Sargent; Casting, Rich Cole; Stage Manager, Glenn Dunn; Assistant Stage Manager, Shannon B. Sturgis; November 30–December 30, 2005; **Cast:** Adam Richman (Coach), Craig Baldwin (Professor), Dustin Sullivan (Dustin)

I AM MY OWN WIFE by Doug Wright; Directed by John Going; Set & Costume Designer, Marie Anne Chiment; Lighting Designer, F. Mitchell Dana; Sound Designer, Joe Payne; Stage Manager, T.R. Martin; Assistant Stage Manager, Tony Dearing; January 4–February 3, 2006; **Cast:** Arnie Burton (Charlotte von Mahlsdorf and others)

PIRANDELLO'S HENRY IV by Luigi Pirandello; In a new version by Tom Stoppard; Directed by Steven Woolf; Scenic Designer, Narelle Sissons; Costume Designer, Elizabeth Covey; Lighting Designer, Mary Jo Dondlinger; Casting, Rich Cole; Stage Manager, Glenn Dunn; Assistant Stage Manager, Shannon B. Sturgis; February 8–March 10, 2006; **Cast:** Alex Burkart (Landolf), Nathan Lee Burkart (Harold), Will Davis (Ordulf), Matt Timme (Bertold), Keith Perry (Giovanni), Dan Domingues (Di Nolli), Lori Prince (Frida), Jerry Vogel (Belcredi), John Thomas Waite (Doctor), Susan Wands (Matilda), Andrew Long (Henry IV)

WITNESS FOR THE PROSECUTION by Agatha Christie; Directed by Michael Evan Haney; Scenic Designer, Paul Shortt; Costume Designer, Elizabeth Covey; Lighting Designer, Phil Monat; Casting, Rich Cole; Stage Manager, Glenn Dunn; Assistant Stage Manager, Tony Dearing; March 15–April 14, 2006; **Cast:** Richert Easley (Carter), Tarah Flanagan (Greta), Robert Langdon Lloyd (Mr. Mayhew), Christopher Kelly (Leonard Vole), Joneal Joplin (Sir Wilfrid Robarts, Q.C.), Mark Leydorf (Inspector Hearne), Deanne Lorette (Romaine), Whit Reichert (Clerk), Julian Gamble (Mr. Myers, Q.C.), Michael Rothhaar (Mr. Justice Wainwright), Erin Anderson (The Stenographer), Christopher Harris (Warder), Chuck Lavazzi (Barrister), Dan McGee (Barrister), Richert Easley (Dr. Wyatt), Dale Hodges (Janet MacKenzie), Alain Pierre (Policeman), Charles Heuvelman (Clegg), Kelslan Scarbrough (The Other Woman)

STUDIO

COMPLETELY HOLLYWOOD (ABRIDGED) by Reed Martin and Austin Tichenor; General Manager, Megan Loughney; Creative Consultant, Steve Smith; RSC Founder, Daniel Singer; Stage Manager, Sara C. Bubenik; October 26–November 13, 2005; **Cast:** The Reduced Shakespeare Company–Dominic Conti, Michael Faulkner, Reed Martin, Austin Tichenor

YELLOWMAN by Dael Orlandersmith; Directed by Susan Gregg; Scenic & Lighting Designer, Michael Philippi; Costume Designer, Clyde Ruffin; Casting Director, Rich Cole; Stage Manager, Champe Leary; January 18–February 5, 2006; **Cast:** Julia Pace Mitchell (Alma and others), Carsey Walker, Jr. (Eugene and others)

HUMBLE BOY by Charlotte Jones; Directed by Steven Woolf; Scenic Designer, John Ezell; Costume Designer, Elizabeth Covey; Lighting Designer, Mary Jo Dondlinger; Composer/Sound Designer, Joe Payne; Sound Design Adapted by Tori Meyer; Casting Director, Rich Cole; Stage Manager, Champe Leary; March

22–April 9, 2006; **Cast:** Chris Hietikko (Felix Humble), Carolyn Swift (Mercy Lott), Patricia Hodges (Flora Humble), Dane Knell (Jim, the gardener), Anderson Matthews (George Pye), Rachel Fowler (Rosie Pye)

OFF-RAMP

TAKE ME OUT by Richard Greenberg; Directed by Rob Ruggiero; Scenic Designer, Adrian W. Jones; Costume Designer, Michael J. McDonald; Lighting Designer, John Lasiter; Original Sound Designer, Janet Kalas; Sound Design Adapted by Lee Buckalew; Casting, Rich Cole; Stage Manager, Champe Leary; Assistant Stage Manager, Jenni Bowman; September 21–October 9, 2005; **Cast:** Tim Altmeyer (Kippy Sunderstrom), Philip Anthony-Rodriguez (Darren Lemming), Michael Balsley (Shane Mungitt), Jorge Oliver (Martinez), Jose Joaquin Perez (Rodriguez), Tony Hoty (The Skipper/William Danziger), Jake Schneider (Jason Chenier), Matthew Montelongo (Toddy Koovitz), Shawn T. Andrew (Davey Battle), Nat DeWolf (Mason Marzac), Ikuma Isaac (Takeshi Kawabata)

BUG by Tracy Letts; Directed by Susan Gregg; Scenic & Costume Designer, Marie Anne Chiment; Lighting Designer, Mark Wilson; Sound Designer, Doug Gardner; Fight Choreographer, Bruce Longworth; Casting, Rich Cole; Stage Manager, Champe Leary; Assistant Stage Manager, Jenni Bowman; October 19–November 6, 2005; **Cast:** Bernadette Quigley (Agnes White), Effie Johnson (R.C.), Jay Stratton (Peter Evans), Steve Isom (Jerry Goss), Gary Wayne Barker (Dr. Sweet)

THIS IS OUR YOUTH by Kenneth Lonergan; Directed by John Ruocco; Scenic Designer, John Ezell; Costume Designer, Curtis Hay; Lighting Designer, John Wylie; Sound Designer, Zena Yeatman; Casting, Rich Cole; Stage Manager, Champe Leary; Assistant Stage Manager, Jenni Bowman; November 16–December 4, 2005; **Cast:** Brian Petersson (Dennis Ziegler), Will Rogers (Warren Straub), Kristina Valada-Viars (Jessica Goldman)

THE IMAGINARY THEATRE COMPANY

BAH! HUMBUG! Adapted by Jack Herrick from Charles Dickens' *A Christmas Carol*; Directed by Bruce Longworth; Music Direction, Joe Dreyer; Scenic Design, Lou Bird; Costume Design by Lou Bird; Stage Manager, Brian Peters; Director of Education, Marsha Coplon; Artistic Supervisor, Jeffery Matthews; 2005–2006; **Cast:** Jason Contini (Do-Gooder/Scroogette/Bob Cratchit/Marley's Ghost/Ghost of Christmas Past (Young Scrooge)/Announcer/Doctor); Anna Blair (Little Beggar Girl/Scroogette/Mama/Ghost of Christmas Present/Ma Cratchit/Nurse); Alan Knoll (Scrooge); Meghan Brown (Do-Gooder/Scroogette/Little Polly/Tiny Tim/Ghost of Christmas Future)

THE BOX WARS by Kim Esop Wylie; music by Neal Richardson; Directed by Kat Singleton; Music Direction, Neal Richardson; Scenic and Costume Design, Dorothy Marshall Englis; Stage Manager, Brian Peters; Director of Education, Marsha Coplon; Artistic Supervisor, Jeffery Matthews; 2005–2006; **Cast:** Meghan Brown (Milly), Jason Contini (Ben), Alan Knoll (Sven, Mrs. Svenson), Anna Blair (Silvia, Mother)

MACBETH Adapted by Bruce Longworth from William Shakespeare's *Macbeth*; Directed by Jeffery Matthews; Scenic and Costume Design, Dorothy Marshall Englis; Stage Manager, Brian Peters; Director of Education, Marsha Coplon; Artistic Supervisor, Jeffery Matthews; 2005–2006; **Cast:** Jason Contini (Macbeth, Bloody Sergeant); Alan Knoll (First Witch/Ross/Macduff/Servant/First Murderer); Meghan Brown (Lady Macbeth/Second Witch/Malcolm/Fleance/Porter); Anna Blair (Third Witch/Duncan/Banquo/First Murderer/Gentlewoman)

SHAKESPEARE THEATRE COMPANY

Washington, DC
TWENTIETH SEASON

Artistic Director, Michael Kahn

OTHELLO by William Shakespeare; Directed by Michael Kahn; Scenic Designer, James Noone; Costume Designer, Jess Goldstein; Lighting Designer, Charlie Morrison; Composer, Adam Wernick; Sound Designer, Martin Desjardins; Fight Director, Paul Dennhardt; Vocal & Text Coach, Ralph Zito; Movement Consultant, Michael Bobbitt; August 30–October 30, 2005; **Cast:** Patrick Page (Iago), Erik Steele (Roderigo), David Sabin (Brabantio), Avery Brooks (Othello), Colleen Delany (Desdemona), Gregory Wooddell (Cassio), Ralph Cosham (Duke of Venice), W. Alan Nebelthau (Gratiano), Michael John Casey (Senator of Venice), Laurence Drozd (Lodovico), Joris Stuyck (Montano), Lise Bruneau (Emilia), Andrea Cirie (Bianca); Gentlemen, Messengers, Sailors, Officers and Attendants played by the Ensemble: Dacyl Acevedo, Michael John Casey, Jordan Coughtry, Blake Ellis, Stephen Graybill, Tony Nam, Nicholas Urda, Jeremy West, Ryan Young

THE COMEDY OF ERRORS by William Shakespeare; Directed by Douglas C. Wager; Set/Costume Designer, Zack Brown; Lighting Designer, Allen Lee Hughes; Composer, Fabian Obispo; Sound Designer, Martin Desjardins; Illusions and Pyrotechnics, David M. Glenn, MD; Resident Voice and Text Consultant, Ellen O'Brien; Fight Director, Brad Waller; Choreographer, Karma Camp; November 15, 2005–January 8, 2006; **Cast:** David Sabin (Solinus), Ralph Cosham (Egeon), Gregory Wooddell (Antipholus of Syracuse), Paul Whitthorne (Antipholus of Ephesus), Daniel Breaker (Dromio of Syracuse), LeRoy McClain (Dromio of Ephesus), Bill Hamlin (Balthazar), Walker Jones (Angelo), Floyd King (Doctor Pinch), Ted Feldman (First Merchant/Officer), Don Mayo (Second Merchant), Tana Hicken (Emilia), Chandler Vinton (Adriana), Marni Penning (Luciana), Sandra L. Murphy (Nell), Victoire Charles (Courtesan); Jailer, Officers, Citizens and Attendants: Dacyl Acevedo, Jordan Coughtry, Blake Ellis, Stephen Graybill, Katie Mazzola, Nicholas Urda, Ryan Young

DON JUAN by Molière; Translated, adapted and directed by Stephen Wadsworth; Scenic Designer, Kevin Rupnik; Costume Designer, Anna R. Oliver; Lighting Designer, Joan Arhelger; Sound Consultant, Christopher Walker; Resident Sound Designer, Martin Desjardins; Choreographer, Daniel Pelzig; Fight Director, Geoffrey Alm; Resident Voice and Text Consultant, Ellen O'Brien; January 24–March 19, 2006; **Cast:** Laurence O'Dwyer (Prologue Player/Don Luis), Gilbert Cruz (Gusman/The Statue), Michael Milligan (Sganarelle), Jeremy Webb (Don Juan), Francesca Faridany (Donna Elvira/Don Alonso), Laura Heisler (Charlotte/Ragotin), Burton Curtis (Pierrot/Pauper/La Violette), Laura Kenny (Mathurine/Dimanche), Daniel Harray (Don Carlos/La Ramée), Ensemble: Dacyl Acevedo, Jordan Coughtry, Nicholas Urda, Ryan Young

THE PERSIANS by Aeschylus; Adaptation by Ellen McLaughlin; Directed by Ethan McSweeny; Set Designer, James Noone; Costume Designer, Jess Goldstein; Lighting Designer, Kevin Adams; Composer/Musical Director/Sound Score, Michael Roth; Projection Designer, Michael Clark; Choreographer, Marcela Lorca; Resident Voice and Text Consultant, Ellen O'Brien; April 4–May 21, 2006; **Cast:** Don Mayo (Counselor), John Livingstone Rolle (Counselor), David Sabin (Counselor), Emery Battis (Counselor), John Seidman (Counselor), David Emerson Toney (Counselor), Floyd King (Counselor), Ed Dixon (Counselor), Helen Carey (Atossa), Scott Parkinson (Herald), Ted van Griethuysen (Darius), Erin Gann (Xerxes), Ensemble: Dacyl Acevedo, Jordan Coughtry, Blake Ellis, Stephen Graybill, Nicholas Urda, Ryan Young; Musicians: N. Scott Robinson (Percussionist), Orlando Cotto (Percussionist), Caroline Kang (Cellist)

LOVE'S LABOR'S LOST by William Shakespeare; Directed by Michael Kahn; Set Designer, Ralph Funicello; Costume Designer, Catherine Zuber; Lighting Designer, Mark Doubleday; Composer, Adam Wernick; Sound Designer, Martin Desjardins; Resident Voice and Text Coach, Ellen O'Brien; June 6–July 30, 2006; **Cast:** Amir Arison (King Ferdinand of Navarre), Hank Stratton (Berowne), Erik Steele (Longaville), Aubrey Deeker (Dumaine), Claire Lautier (Princess of France), Sabrina LeBeauf (Rosaline), Angela Pierce (Maria), Colleen Delany (Katherine), Floyd King (Boyet), Geraint Wyn Davies (Don Adriano de Armado), Nick Choksi (Moth), Ted van Griethuysen (Holofernes), David Sabin (Sir Nathaniel), Rock Kohli (Anthony Dull), Michael Milligan (Costard), Jolly Abraham (Jaquenetta), James Rana (Forester), Leo Erickson (Monsieur Marcadé), Brian Q. Silver (Sitar Player), Servants and others: Jordan Coughtry, Blake Ellis, Kunal Nayyar, Nicholas Urda, Ryan Young

PERICLES by William Shakespeare; Directed by David Muse; Original Direction by Mary Zimmerman; Set Designer, Daniel Ostling; Costume Designer, Mara Blumenfeld; Lighting Designer, TJ Gerkens; Composer, André Pleuss; Choreographer, Daniel Pelzig; Resident Voice and Text Consultant, Ellen O'Brien; May 25–June 4, 2006; **Cast:** Rick Foucheux (Antiochus/Pander), Thomas M. Hammond (Pericles), Jaclyn DiLauro (Daughter to Antiochus), James Ricks (Thaliard), Bernard Burak Sheredy (Helicanus), Hugh Nees (Escanes/First Fisherman), Joseph Costa (Cleon), Michelle Shupe (Dionyza/Diana), Evan Zes (Leonine), Jeff Cribbs (Second Fisherman/Lysimachus), Stephen Conrad Moore (Third Fisherman), John Tillotson (Simonides), Julia Coffey (Thaisa), Naomi Jacobson (Lychorida/A Bawd), Sarah Marshall (Cerimon), Marguerite Stimpson (Marina), Jesse J. Perez (Bolt), Dori (Daisy the dog), Lords, Ladies, Gentlemen, Knights, Pirates, Sailors, Messengers, Servants, Attendants and Virgins: Dacyl Acevedo, Jaclyn DiLauro, Clifton Duncan, Daniel Eichner, Tiffany Fillmore, Leo Goodman, Ian Lockhart, Thomas Matthews, Tony Nam, Elaine Qualter, Darius Suziedelis

SEATTLE REPERTORY THEATRE

Seattle, Washington
FORTY-THIRD SEASON

Artistic Director, David Esbjornson

CATHAY: THREE TALES OF CHINA Conceived, written and directed by Ping Chong; Made in collaboration with The Shaanxi Folk Art Theater of Xian China; Assistant Director/Dramaturge, Liang Jun; Puppet Designer, Stephen Kaplin; Puppet Co-Designer, Wang Bo; Set & Lighting Designer, Randy Ward; Costume Designer, Stefani Mar; Projection Designer, Ruppert Bohle; Sound Designer, Christopher Walker; September 10–October 9, 2005; **Cast:** Shaanxi Folk Art Theater: Liang Jun, Liang Yunru, Feng Mei, Song Dongqing, Wang Bo, Yang Qing; Carter Family Marionettes: Dmitri Carter, Heather Carter, Yang Xie Zheng

THE KING STAG A new adaptation by Shelley Berc and Andrei Belgrader from the original play by Carlo Gozzi; Director, Andrei Belgrader; Scenic Designer, Kelly Hanson; Costume Designer, Melanie Watnick; Sound Designer, Dominic Codykramers; Lighting Designer, Marcus Doshi; September 24–October 22, 2005; **Cast:** Sean G. Griffin (Durandarte), Caroline Hall (Angela), Daoud Heidami (Truffaldino), Charles Leggett (Brighella), Kelly Mak (Clarice), Sarah Rudinoff (Smeraldina), Nathan Smith (Leandro), Todd Waring (Deramo), Michael Urie (Cigolotti/Pantalone), R. Hamilton Wright (Tartaglia)

PURGATORIO by Ariel Dorfman; Directed by David Esbjornson; Scenic and Projection Designers, Nick Schwartz-Hall and David Esbjornson; Costume Designer, Elizabeth Hope Clancy; Lighting Designer, Scott Zielinski; Sound Designer, Steve LeGrand; October 29–November 26, 2005; **Cast:** Dan Snook (Man), Charlayne Woodard (Woman)

RESTORATION COMEDY by Amy Freed; Directed by Sharon Ott; Scenic Designer, Hugh Landwehr; Costume Designer, Anna R. Oliver; Lighting Designer, Peter Maradudin; Sound Designer, Stephen LeGrand; Period Movement Coach, Art Manke; Dialect Coach, Louis Colaianni; December 3, 2005–January 7, 2006; **Cast:** Laurence Ballard (Old Coupler Manlove/Parson Bull/Sir Tunbelly/Sly), Gabriel Baron (Lory), Suzanne Bouchard (Berinthia), Melissa Brown (Ensemble), Stephen Caffrey (Mr. Loveless), Jonathan Freeman (Sir Novelty Fashion/ Lord Foppington), Laura Kenny (Nurse/Hillaria), Caralyn Kozlowski (Amanda), Neil Maffin (Mr. Worthy), Rebecca Olson (Ensemble), Garlyn Punao (Ensemble), Bhama Roget (Fistula/Hoyden/ Narcissa), Matthew Schneck (Young Fashion/Snap)

RADIO GOLF by August Wilson; Directed by Kenny Leon; Scenic Designer, David Gallo; Costume Designer, Susan Hilferty; Lighting Designer, Donald Holder; Dramaturg, Todd Kreidler; Original Music Composed and Arranged by Kathryn Bostic; January 19–February 18, 2006; **Cast:** Denise Burse (Mame Wilks), Rocky Carroll (Harmond Wilks), James A. Williams (Roosevelt Hicks), John Earl Jelks (Sterling Johnson), Anthony Chisholm (Elder Joseph Barlow)

PRIVATE LIVES by Noel Coward; Directed by Gabriel Barre; Scenic Designer, Walt Spangler; Costume Designer, Elizabeth Hope Clancy; Lighting Designer, Howell Binkley; Sound Designer, Christopher R. Walker; Dialect Coach, Judith Shahn; Fight Director, Rick Sordelet; March 2–April 1, 2006; **Cast:** Suzanne Bouchard (Amanda Prynne), Rob Breckenridge (Elyot Chase), Allen Fitzpatrick (Victor Prynne), Nikki Coble (Sibyl Chase), Lori Larsen (Louise)

NINE PARTS OF DESIRE by Heather Raffo; Directed by Joanna Settle; Scenic Designer, Antje Ellerman; Costume Designer, Kasia Walicka Maimone; Lighting Designer, Peter West; Sound Designer, Obadiah Eaves; March 18–April 15, 2006; **Cast:** Najla Said

TUESDAYS WITH MORRIE by Jeffrey Hatcher and Mitch Albom; Directed by David Esbjornson; Scenic Designer, Robert Brill; Costume Coordinator, Julia Collins; Lighting Designer, Jane Cox; Original Sound Designer, John Kilgore; April 8–May 7, 2006; **Cast:** Alvin Epstein (Morrie), Lorenzo Pisoni (Mitch)

SOUTH COAST REPERTORY

Costa Mesa, CA
FORTY-SECOND SEASON

Producing Artistic Director, David Emmes; Artistic Director, Martin Benson

THE CAUCASIAN CHALK CIRCLE by Bertolt Brecht; Translated by W.H. Auden, James Stern and Tania Stern; Directed by Kate Whoriskey; Original Music by Rob Milburn and Michael Bodeen; Scenic Designer, Walt Spangler; Costume Designer, Ilona Somogyi; Lighting Designer, Christopher Akerlind; Musical Directors and Sound Designers, Rob Milburn and Michael Bodeen; Choreographer, Randy Duncan; Assistant Director, Magdalena Zira; Stage Manager, Jamie A. Tucker; September 2–October 9, 2005; **Cast:** Cyrus Alexander (Ironshirt), Daniel Breaker (Singer), Josh Campbell (Ironshirt), Daniel Chaffin (Ironshirt), Assaf Cohen (Shauva), Matt D'Amico (Fat Prince), Richard Doyle (Governor), Jamie Hebert (Ironshirt), Nina Hellman (Natella/Sister-in-Law), Michael Irish (Ironshirt), Liam Kraus (Ironshirt), Hal Landon Jr. (Doctor), Katrina Lenk (Gru-

sha), Martha McFarland (Exiled Woman), Alex Mendoza (Simon), Lynn Milgrim (Mother-in-Law), Adriana Sevan (Nurse), William Seymour (Corporal), Elaine Tse (Doctor), Frank Wood (Azdak), Ogie Zulueta (Adjutant)

DUMB SHOW by Joe Penhall (American Premiere); Directed by David Emmes; Scenic and Costume Designer, Angela Balogh Calin; Lighting Designer, Tom Ruzika; Musical Arrangement and Sound Designer, Dennis McCarthy; Dramaturg, Megan Monaghan; Stage Manager, Scott Harrison; September 25–October 16, 2005; **Cast:** Heidi Dippold (Liz), John Rafter Lee (Greg), Micheal McShane (Barry)

BORN YESTERDAY by Garson Kanin; Directed by Warner Shook; Scenic Designer, Michael Ganio; Costume Designer, Frances Kenny; Lighting Designer, York Kennedy; Composer and Sound Designer, Jim Ragland; Stage Manager, Randall K. Lum; October 14–November 20, 2005; **Cast:** Derek Armstrong (Bellhop/Bootblack/Waiter), Alan Blumenfeld (Eddie Brock), Kacie Brown (Manicurist), Richard Doyle (Ed Devery), Dale Jones (Bellhop/Barber), Hal Landon Jr. (Senator Hedges/Ass't Hotel Manager), Jennifer Lyon (Billie Dawn), Jane Macfie (Mrs. Hedges/Helen), Paul Morgan Stetler (Paul Verrall), Richard Ziman (Harry Brock)

BUNNICULA (Part of the Theatre for Young Audiences series) Book by Deborah and James Howe; Adapted for the stage by Jon Klein; Lyrics by Jon Klein; Music by Chris Jeffries; Directed by Stefan Novinski; Scenic Designer, Donna Marquet; Costume Designer, Angela Balogh Calin; Lighting Designer, Lonnie Rafael Alcaraz; Musical Director, Tim Horrigan; Sound Designer, Drew Dalzell; Stage Manager, Jamie A. Tucker; November 4–20, 2005; **Cast:** Mauri Bernstein (Bunnicula), Diana Burbano (Chester), Louis Lotorto (Harold), Robert Negron (Toby), Jennifer Parsons (Mrs. Monroe), Tom Shelton (Mr. Monroe), Travis Vaden (Pete)

A CHRISTMAS CAROL by Charles Dickens; Adapted by Jerry Patch (26th Anniversary Production); Directed by John-David Keller; Scenic Designer, Thomas Buderwitz; Costume Designer, Dwight Richard Odle; Lighting Designer, Donna and Tom Ruzika; Musical Arrangement and Composer, Dennis McCarthy; Sound Designer, Drew Dalzell; Vocal Director, Dennis Castellano; Choreographer, Linda Kostalik; Assistant Director, Laurie Woolery; Stage Manager, Erin Nelson; November 26–December 24, 2005; **Cast:** Cyrus Alexander (Constable/Wreath Seller/Young Jacob Marley/Poulterer), Sara Bashor (Elizabeth Shelley/Fan/Pursued Maiden), Megan Blanco (Martha Cratchit, in rotation), Daniel Blinkoff (Bob Cratchit), Lauren Buangan (Girl About Town/Want, in rotation), Joshua Campbell (Puppeteer/Mr. Topper), Matt Cardoza (Oliver Shelley/Ebenezer as a Boy/Ignorance, in rotation), Richard Doyle (Solicitor/The Spirit of Christmas Past/Gentleman), Madison Dunaway (Lena/Belle/Scavenger), Chas Hume (Peter Cratchit, in rotation), Michael Irish (Thomas Shelley), John-David Keller (Mr. Fezziwig/Gentleman), Art Koustik (Joe/Ensemble), Timothy Landfield (The Spirit of Christmas Present/Ensemble), Hal Landon Jr. (Ebenezer Scrooge), Zach Martin (Oliver Shelley/Ebenezer as a Boy/Ignorance, in rotation), Alexandra McCue (Belinda Cratchit, in rotation), Martha McFarland (Mrs. Fezziwig/Solicitor), Chloe Mercado (Martha Cratchit, in rotation), Alexandra Mullin (Belinda Cratchit, in rotation), Jennifer Parsons (Mrs. Cratchit), Will Peterson (Peter Cratchit, in rotation), Cheryl Robinson (Teen Girl About Town, in rotation), Howard Shangraw (Fred/Gentleman), Akshay Sharma (Boy on the Street, in rotation), Mandy Shold (Teen Girl About Town, in rotation), Elisabeth Smith ("Tiny" Tim Cratchit, in rotation), Edward Swanson ("Tiny" Tim Cratchit, in rotation), Hisa Takakuwa (Toy Lady/Sally/Scavenger), Rachel Teague (Girl About Town/Want, in rotation), Don Took (Jacob Marley/The Spirit of Christmas Yet-To-Come), Travis Vaden (Undertaker/Young Ebenezer), Joel Wagner (Boy on the Street, in rotation)

LA POSADA MÁGICA: THE MAGICAL JOURNEY Written and Directed by Octavio Solis; Music by Marcos Loya (12th Anniversary Production); Scenic Designer, Christopher Acebo; Costume Designer, Shigeru Yaji; Lighting Designer,

Lonnie Rafael Alcaraz; Musical Director, Marcos Loya; Choreographer, Linda Kostalik; Stage Manager, Jamie A. Tucker; December 9–24, 2005; **Cast:** Christine Avila (Caridad/Widow), Denise Blasor (Consuelo/Widow), Danny Bolero (Papi/Jose Cruz), Sol Castillo (Refugio/Buzzard), Crissy Guerrero (Mom/Mariluz), Marcos Loya (Musician/Ensemble), Lorenzo Martinez (Musician/Ensemble), Miguel Najera (Horacio), Kevin Sifuentes (Eli/Bones/Lauro), Tiffany Ellen Solano (Gracie)

THE FURTHER ADVENTURES OF HEDDA GABLER by Jeff Whitty (World Premiere); Directed by Bill Rauch; Scenic Designer, Christopher Acebo; Costume Designer, Shigeru Yaji; Lighting Designer, Geoff Korf; Composer and Sound Designer, Paul James Prendergast; Choreographer, Art Manke; Assistant Director, Brian J. Sivesind; Dramaturg, Megan Monaghan; Stage Manager, Randall K. Lum; January 8–29, 2006; **Cast:** Dan Butler (Patrick and Others), Patrick Kerr (Steven and Others), Preston Maybank (Eilert Lovborg and Others), Christopher Liam Moore (George Tesman), Kate A. Mulligan (Their Neighbor and Others), Susannah Schulman (Hedda Gabler), Kimberly Scott (Their Servant), Bahni Turpin (Woman in Pink and Others)

HITCHCOCK BLONDE Written and Directed by Terry Johnson (American Premiere); Scenic, Costume and Video Designer, William Dudley; Lighting Designer, Chris Parry; Composer and Sound Designer, Ian Dickinson; Video Realization, Ian Galloway for Mesmer; Assistant Director, Magdalena Zira; Stage Manager, Jamie A. Tucker; February 3–March 12, 2006; **Cast:** Sarah Aldrich (Blonde), Adriana DeMeo (Jennifer), Dakin Matthews (Hitch), Martin Noyes (Husband), Robin Sachs (Alex)

THE ADVENTURES OF PØR QUINLY (Part of the Theatre for Young Audiences series) by Quincy Long; Music by Michael Silversher; Directed by John-David Keller; Scenic Designer, Haibo Yu; Costume Designer, Angela Balogh Calin; Lighting Designer, Tammy Owens Slauson; Musical Director, Michael Silversher; Stage Manager, Erin Nelson; February 10–26, 2006; **Cast:** Christine Avila (Scattermonger), Allison Case (Little Dippa), Sol Castillo (Lobster/Mel), Richard Doyle (Macbirthday/King of Tears/Gnumptious the Deep/Quinly the Elder), Alex Miller (Pør Quinly), Tom Shelton (Mister River/Big Dippa), Jodee Thelen (Mother Quinly/Mermaid/Gilly Galloo)

MAN FROM NEBRASKA by Tracy Letts (West Coast Premiere); Directed by William Friedkin; Scenic Designer, Christopher Barreca; Costume Designer, Nephelie Andonyadis; Lighting Designer, Lonnie Rafael Alcaraz; Sound Designer, Drew Dalzell; Assistant Director, Craig J. George; Stage Manager, Randall K. Lum; March 12–April 2, 2006; **Cast:** Kathy Baker (Nancy Carpenter), Susan Dalian (Tamyra), Jane A. Johnston (Cammie Carpenter), Brian Kerwin (Ken Carpenter), Hal Landon Jr. (Bud Todd), Ben Livingston (Reverend Todd), Laura Niemi (Pat Monday), Susannah Schulman (Ashley Kohl), Julian Stone (Harry Brown)

THE STUDIO Written, Directed and Choreographed by Christopher d'Amboise (World Premiere); Scenic Designer, Christopher Barreca; Costume Designer, Angela Balogh Calin; Lighting Designer, Peter Maradudin; Composer, Karl Fredrik Lundeberg; Sound Designer, B.C. Keller; Assistant Director, Kelly Crandall; Dramaturg, Megan Monaghan; Stage Manager, Erin Nelson; March 31–May 7, 2006; **Cast:** Nancy Lemenager (Lisa), Terrence Mann (Emil), John Todd (Jackie), Seth Belliston (Understudy: Jackie), Yvette Tucker (Understudy: Lisa)

BLUE DOOR by Tanya Barfield (World Premiere); Directed by Leah C. Gardiner; Scenic Designer, Dustin O'Neill; Costume Designer, Naila Aladdin Sanders; Lighting Designer, Lonnie Rafael Alcaraz; Sound Designer, Jill BC DuBoff; Dramaturg, John Glore; Stage Manager, Randall K. Lum; April 23–May 14, 2006; **Cast:** Reg E. Cathey (Lewis), Larry Gilliard, Jr. (Simon/Rex/Jesse)

THE REAL THING by Tom Stoppard; Directed by Martin Benson; Scenic Designer, Ralph Funicello; Costume Designer, Angela Balogh Calin; Lighting Designer, Peter Maradudin; Composer and Sound Designer, Karl Fredrik Lundeberg; Assistant Director, Nicholas C. Avila; Stage Manager, Jamie A. Tucker; May 19–June 25, 2006; **Cast:** Bill Brochtrup (Henry), McCaleb Burnett (Brodie), Amanda Cobb (Debbie), David Barry Gray (Billy), Pamela J. Gray (Charlotte), Martin Kildare (Max), Natacha Roi (Annie)

THE STINKY CHEESE MAN AND OTHER FAIRLY STUPID TALES (Part of the Theatre for Young Audiences series) by Jon Scieszka and Lane Smith; Adapted by John Glore; Directed by Anne Justine D'Zmura; Scenic and Costume Designer, Nephelie Andonyadis; Lighting Designer, Christina L. Munich; Sound Designer and Music Director, Tim Horrigan; Stage Manager, Erin Nelson; June 9–25, 2006; **Cast:** Larry Bates (Cow Patty Boy/Cocky Locky/Prince/Stepsister #1/Owl/Stinky), John Cabrera (Jack/Tortoise), Allison Case (Ducky Lucky/Princess #2/Cinderella/Cow Butt), Jennifer Chu (Chicken Licken/Princess #1/Little Red/Rabbit), Michael Faulkner (Foxy Loxy/Ugly Duck/Wolf/Giant/ Rumpelstiltskin/Fox), Kevin Sifuentes (Surgeon General/King/Frog/Stepsister #2/Little Old Man/Cow Head/Legal Guy), Jodee Thelen (Red Hen/Goosey Loosey/Queen/Stepmother/Little Old Lady)

VIRGINIA STAGE COMPANY

Norfolk, Virginia
TWENTY-SEVENTH SEASON

Artistic Director, Chris Hanna

THE TASTE TEST by Frank Higgins; (World Premiere); Directed by Chris Hanna; Scenic Designer, Bill Clarke; Costume Designer, Jeni Schaefer; Lighting Designer, Victor En Yu Tan; Sound Designer, Michael Boso; Production Stage Manager, Bradley C. Cooper; Production Assistant, Dawn M. Choat; September 13–October 2, 2005; **Cast:** Nadine Mozon (Frances), Susan Wands (Mary), Doris Belack (Clair)

ROUNDING THIRD by Richard Dresser; Directed by Charles Towers; Scenic Designer, David Evans Morris; Costume Designer, Polly Byers; Lighting Designer, Juliet Chia; Sound Designer, Jeffrey Alan Jones; Production Stage Manager, Karen Oberthal; Production Assistant, Dawn M. Choat; October 18–November 6, 2005; **Cast:** Ed Hodson (Don), Frank Deal (Michael)

A CHRISTMAS CAROL by Charles Dickens, Adapted by David McCann; Directed by Neal Easterling–Based on Original Staging by Aaron Cabell; Musical Director, Joseph Walsh; Set Designer, Anita Tripathi Easterling; Costume Designer, Jeni Schaefer; Lighting Designer, Lynne Koscielniak; Sound Designer, Michael Boso; Original Sound Designer, Walter Tillman; Production Stage Manager, Bradley C. Cooper; Production Assistant, Dawn M. Choat; December 7–23, 2005; **Cast:** Jesse Hanna (Tiny Tim), John-Patrick Driscoll (Christmas Present/Ensemble), Amy Kim Washke (Mrs. Cratchit/Ensemble), Robert Ruffin (Marley/Ensemble), Mia Ulibarri (Mrs. Dilber/Ensemble), Saeed Wilkins (Fred/Ensemble), Michael Kroeker (Bob Cratchit/Ensemble), Shannon Murphy (Belle/Ensemble), Chaney Tullos (Christmas Past/Ensemble), Peter Moore (Scrooge)

INTIMATE APPAREL by Lynn Nottage; Directed by Jane Page; Set Designer; Bill Clarke, Costume Designer, Nanzi Adzima; Lighting Designer, Dan Kotlowitz and Darren McCroom; Sound Designer, Kevin Dunayer; Production Stage Manager, Karen Oberthal; Production Assistant, Dawn M. Choat; January 17–February 5, 2006; **Cast:** Elizabeth Van Dyke (Mrs. Dickerson), Nadine Mozon (Esther Mills), Kennedy Pugh (George Armstrong), Kristie Dale Sanders (Mrs. Van Buren), Howard Kaye (Mr. Marks), Laiona Michelle (Mayme)

OF MICE AND MEN by John Steinbeck; Directed by Chris Hanna; Set Designer, Anita Tripathi Easterling; Costume Designer, Jeni Schaefer; Lighting Designer, A. Nelson Ruger IV; Sound Designer, Walter Tillman; Production Stage Manager, Bradley C. Cooper; Production Assistant, Dawn M. Choat; February 28 – March 19, 2006; **Cast:** Tony Ward (George), Jefferson Breland (Lennie), Robert Nelson (Candy), Dave Hobbs (The Boss), Sean Meehan (Curley), Kristin Fiorella (Curley's Wife), David Sitler (Slim), Terry Jernigan (Carlson), Chaney Tullos (Whit), Ernest Perry, Jr. (Crooks)

CONTACT by Susan Stroman and John Weidman; Original Direction by Susan Stroman; Original Direction Recreated by Tomé Cousin; Scenic Designer, Thomas Lynch; Costume Designer, William Ivey Long; Lighting Designer, Andrew David Ostrowski; Sound Designer, Michael Boso, Based on the Broadway Sound Design by Scott Stauffer; Scenic Coordinator, Anita Tripathi Easterling; Costume Coordinator, Jeni Schaefer; Associate Choreographer, Leeanna Smith; Production Stage Manager, Karen Oberthal; Production Assistant, Dawn M. Choat; April 4 – 23, 2006; **Cast:** Sean Ewing (Servant), Danny Herman (Aristocrat), Ariel Shepley (Girl on a Swing), Tina Moya (a Wife), Jonathan Manning (a Husband/a Bartender), Thom Graham (a Headwaiter), Fletcher McTaggart (an Advertising Executive), Sheri Griffith (a Girl in a Yellow Dress), Dan Crowley (Ensemble), Julia Hubara (Ensemble), Dennis Lue (Ensemble), Ami Price (Ensemble), Marcos Santana (Ensemble), Leeanna Smith (Ensemble), Mary Lynn Tiep (Ensemble), Rocker Verastique (Ensmble)

YALE REPERTORY THEATRE

New Haven, CT
FORTIETH SEASON

James Bundy, Artistic Director

THE CHERRY ORCHARD adapted by Alison Carey from Anton Chekhov as translated by Maria Amadei Ashot; Directed by Bill Rauch; Scenic Designer, Christopher Acebo; Costume Designer, Shigeru Yaji; Lighting Designer, Michael Chybowski; Sound Designer, Andrew Nagel; Choreographer, Peter Pucci; Production Stage Manager, James Mountcastle; October 7 – 29, 2005; **Cast:** Alec Beard (the personal valet who has an attitude), James Chen (ensemble), Carson Elrod (The clerk who has squeaky boots), Rubén Garfias (The businessman who wears shined shoes), Patrick Garner (The brother who loves candies and billiards), Tom Golden (ensemble), Lisa Harrow (The estate owner who wears a magenta dress), Gustave Johnson (The neighbor who has a daughter that sends her regards), Bridget Jones (The maid who uses a powder puff), Daniel John Kelley (ensemble), Laura Odeh (The daughter who went up in a hot air balloon), Jesse J. Perez (The student who wears glasses), Sarayu Rao (The adopted daughter who carries the keys), Brenda Thomas (The governess who owns a dog), and Peter Van Wagner (the butler who carries a cane)

SAFE IN HELL by Amy Freed; Directed by Mark Wing Davey; Scenic Designer, Leiko Fuseya; Costume Designer, Emily Rebholz; Lighting Designer, Gina Scherr; Sound Designer, David Budries; Special Character Effects Designer, Aleksandra Maslik; Choreographer, Peter Pucci; Stage Manager, Glenn J. Sturgis; November 11 – December 3, 2005; Katie Barrett (Maggie Smurt), Chad Callaghan (Young Man of Salem), Adam Dannheisser (Reverend Doakes), Sean Dougherty (Indian Roger), Sofia Gomez (Abigail), Erik Lochtefeld (Cotton Mather), Graeme Malcolm (Increase Mather), Alexis McGuinness (Little Mary), Jeff Steitzer (Townsman/Judge/Mrs. Smurt), Myra Lucretia Taylor (Tituba), and Welker White (Mrs. Doakes/Mr. Smurt)

THE PEOPLE NEXT DOOR by Henry Adam; Directed by Evan Yionoulis; Set Designer, Kanae Heike; Costume Designer Kate Cusack; Lighting Designer, Cat Tate; Sound Designer and Original Music Composer, Sharath Patel; Dialect Coach, Stephen Gabis; Fight Director, Rick Sordelet; Stage Manager, Shawn Senavinin; January 13 – February 4, 2006; **Cast:** Christopher Innvar (Phil), Marcia Jean Kurtz (Mrs. McCallum), James Miles (Marco), Manu Narayan (Nigel).

COMEDY ON THE BRIDGE AND BRUNDIBAR. Co-production with Berkeley Repertory Theatre, presented in association with Yale School of Music. COMEDY ON THE BRIDGE: libretto by Tony Kushner adapted from Václav Kliment Klicpera and music by Bohuslav Martinu; BRUNDIBAR: English adaptation by Tony Kushner after Adolf Hoffmeister's libretto and music by Hans Krása. Production Designer, Maurice Sendak with Kris Stone; Scenic Designer, Kris Stone; Costume Designer, Robin I. Shane; Lighting Designer, Donald Holder; Sound Designers, Rob Milburn and Michael Bodeen; Musical Director, Greg Anthony; February 10 – March 5, 2006; **Cast:** Anjali Bhimani (Popelka/The Sparrow), Henry DiGiovanni (The Liskovite Sentry/The Ice-Cream Seller), Matt Farnsworth (Sykos/The Milkman), Joe Gallagher (Captain Ladinsky/Brundibar), Aaron Simon Gross (Pepicek), Geoff Hoyle (The Strokopounkutnik Sentry, The Baker/The Dog), Devynn Pedell (Aninku), Angelina Reáux (Eva/The Cat), Martin Vidnovic (Bedronyi/The Policeman), William Youmans (Professor Ucitelli). Youth Ensemble: Malka Alexandra Berro, Nathalya Rose Bey, Celina M. Burgueño, Helena M. Burgueño, Christina Celone, Melissa Anne DeChello, Charlotte Dillon, Sophie Dillon, Jordyn Rakel DiNatale, Risa Duff, Meaghan Ashley Elliot, Garrett Michael Erff, Abby Mae Erwin, Mark Esposito, Emma E. Gannon-Salomon, Deanna Giulietti, Madison Hayes, Daniel Matthew Humphrey, Delaney Louise Jordan, John Jorge, Eliza-Lynne Kanner, Miranda Card Lampke, Caroline B. Lellouche, Alexander Marmor, Nicholas Marmor, Russell Moore, Rishi Mutalik, Gianna Michelle Petrillo, Talvin Anton Rodgers, Jamall Sancho, Samantha Solomon, Ashlee Woods

dance of the holy ghosts: a play on memory by Marcus Gardley; Directed by Liz Diamond; Original Music Composer Scott Davenport Richards; Musical Director XY Eli; Choreographer Peter Pucci; Scenic Designer Aleksandra Maslik; Costume Designer Jennifer Moeller; Lighting Designer, Jennifer Tipton; Sound Designer, Arielle Edwards; Stage Manager, Adam Ganderson; March 17 – April 8, 2006; **Cast:** Pascale Armand (Mother Morningpew, Precious Parquett, Earma Who Be Drivin the Bus, Norma Who Be on the Phone); La Tonya Borsay (Darlene, Princess Parquett); Chuck Cooper (Oscar Clifton); Harriett D. Foy (Viola Eaton, Tanisha Taylor); Brian Henry (Marcus G.); Paul J. Medford (Big Ass Willie Smalls, Father Michael, The Bluesy Tusedo, The Paramour)

ALL'S WELL THAT ENDS WELL by William Shakespeare; Directed by James Bundy and Mark Rucker; Choreographer, John Carrafa; Original Music and Arrangements, Matthew Suttor; Scenic Designer, Zane Pihlstrom; Costume Designer Mike Floyd; Lighting Designer, Matthew Frey; Sound Designer, Andrew Nagel; Fight Director, Rick Sordelet; Vocal Coach, Beth McGuire; Music Director, Erika Schroth; Stage Manager, Sarah Bierenbaum; April 21 – May 20, 2006; **Cast:** Lisa Birnbaum (Ensemble); Michael Braun (First Lord Dumain/Ensemble); Kathleen Chalfant (Countess of Rossillion); Helmar Augustus Cooper (Lafew); Nick Corley (Lavatch); John Cunningham (King of France); Erin Felgar (Diana, Ensemble); Christopher Grant (First Soldier, Ensemble); Dana Green (Helena); Nicholas Heck (Bertram); Ayano Kataoka (Ensemble); Brian O'Neill (Reynaldo, Ensemble); Gamal J. Palmer (Ensemble); Bryce Pinkham (Ensemble); Richard Robichaux (Parolles); Tom E. Russell (Ensemble); Susannah Schulman (Mariana); Dale Soules (Widow/Ensemble); Elliot Villar (Second Lord Dumain/Ensemble); Amanda Warren (Ensemble); Walton Wilson (Duke of Florence)

2005–2006 THEATRICAL AWARDS

2006 THEATRE WORLD AWARD WINNERS

Harry Connick, Jr. of *The Pajama Game*

Felicia P. Fields of *The Color Purple*

Maria Friedman of *The Woman in White*

Richard Griffiths of *The History Boys*

Mamie Gummer of *Mr. Marmalade*

Jayne Houdyshell of *Well*

Bob Martin of *The Drowsy Chaperone*

Ian McDiarmid of *Faith Healer*

Nellie McKay of *The Threepenny Opera*

David Wilmot of *The Lieutenant of Inishmore*

Elisabeth Withers Mendes of *The Color Purple*

John Lloyd Young of *Jersey Boys*

62ND ANNUAL
THEATRE WORLD AWARDS PRESENTATION

Tuesday, June 6, 2006 at Studio 54

Originally dubbed *Promising Personalities* in 1944 by co-founders Daniel Blum, Norman MacDonald, and John Willis to coincide with the first release of *Theatre World*, the now sixty-two-year-old definitive pictorial and statistical record of the American theatre, the Theatre World Awards, as they are now known, are the oldest awards given for debut performances in New York City, as well as one of the oldest honors bestowed on New York actors.

Administered by the Theatre World Awards Board of Directors, a committee of current New York drama critics chooses six actors and six actresses for the Theatre World Award who have distinguished themselves in Broadway and Off Broadway productions during the past theatre season. Occasionally, Special Theatre World Awards are also bestowed on performers, casts, or others who have made a particularly lasting impression on the New York theatre scene.

The Theatre World Award "Janus" statuette is an original bronze sculpture in primitive-modern style created by internationally recognized artist Harry Marinsky. It is adapted from the Roman myth of Janus, god of entrances, exits, and all beginnings, with one face appraising the past and the other anticipating the future. It is cast and mounted on marble in the Del Chiaro Foundry in Pietrasanta, Italy.

Theatre World Awards Board of Directors:

Peter Filichia, President
Walter Willison, Vice President
Patricia Elliott, Secretary
Douglas Holmes, Treasurer
Tom Lynch
Ben Hodges
Leigh Giroux
Jamie deRoy
Kati Meister

The Theatre World Awards are voted on by the following committee of New York drama critics: Peter Filichia (Theatermania.com), Harry Haun (*Playbill*), Matthew Murray (TalkinBroadway.com), Frank Scheck (*New York Post*), Michael Sommers (Newhouse Papers), Doug Watt (Critic Emeritus, *New York Daily News*), and Linda Winer (*Newsday*).

Ceremony Highlights

Written by Peter Filichia; Directed by Walter Willison; Executive Producers, Ben Hodges and Kati Meister; Musical Director, Fred Barton; Associate Producers, Scott Denny and Shane Frampton Wolters; Presented on the set of the Roundabout Theatre Company's production of *The Threepenny Opera* designed by Derek McLane; Staff for the Roundabout Theatre Company: Event Manager, Jetuan Dobbs; Stage Manager, Elisa R. Kuhar; Production Electrician, Josh Weitzman; Sound Engineer, Greg Peeler; House Head Properties, Lawrence Jennino; Head Carpenter, Dan Hoffman; Theatre Manager, Tina Beck Carlson; House Manager, LaConya Robinson; Maintenance, Ralph Mohan; Security, Gotham Security; Photographers: Henry Grossman, Michael Riordan, Michael Viade, Jack Williams; Video Photographers, Richard Ridge and Bradshaw Smith

Host: Peter Filichia

Presenters

Lucie Arnaz, *They're Playing Our Song*, 1979
Kate Burton, *Present Laughter/Alice in Wonderland/Winners*, 1983
Maxwell Caulfield, *Class Enemy*, 1980
Ralph Fiennes, *Hamlet*, 1995
Tammy Grimes, *Look After Lulu*, 1959
Harry Groener, *Oklahoma!*, 1980
La Chanze, *Once On This Island*, 1991
Andrea McArdle, *Annie*, 1977
Liza Minnelli, *Best Foot Forward*, 1963
Patricia Neal, *Another Part of the Forest*, 1947
Ken Page, *Guys and Dolls*, 1977
John Rubinstein, *Pippin*, 1973
Jonathan Pryce, *The Comedians*, 1977

2006 Theatre World Award Janus presenter: Beth Johnson, *Spamalot*

Musical Numbers: "Kansas City" (Harry Groener), "Tomorrow" (Andrea McArdle), "Sit Down, You're Rockin' the Boat" (Ken Page), "Corner of the Sky" (John Rubenstein). The ceremony concluded with winners, presenters and past winners gathering on stage to sing an early "Happy Birthday" to John Willis who was to turn 90 on October 16, 2006.

Special Thanks: Allen Arrow, Dan Aquisto, Britt Augenfeld, Baruch/Viertel/Routh/Frankel Group, Miriam Berman, Mark Birch, Brian Black, Broadway Beat, Lisa Bruno, Sammy Buck, Michael Buckley, Victoria Bundonis, Karen Carzo, Pearl Chang, Ted Chapin, Michael Che, Barbara Custer, Kim D'Armond, Tim Deak, Dan Debenport, Vanessa Elese, Darl Fowkes, Richard Frankel Productions, Ira Fronk, Allison Graham, Karlene Lamnle, Holli Leggett, Jack Lenz, The Marketing Group, Eric Martin, Michael Messina, Chase Mishkin, David Montalvo, Matthew Murray, Lucy Nathanson, Peter Neufeld, O'Keefe Productions, Inc., Danny O'Keefe, Nancy Owens, Kelley and Ken Perlstein, Kay Radthke, Rapid Copy Center, Richard Ridge, Sculpture House Casting, Inc., Lonnie Sill, Jeffrey Silverman, Joan Slavin, Bradshaw Smith, Eleanor Steert/The Drama Book Shop, Don Stobbs, Trump Ice, Tom Viola, The Roundabout Theatre Company, and especially Jonathan Pryce

Gift Bag Promotions supplied by Applause Theatre and Cinema Books, Columbia Artists, iSi North America, JB Cumberland Public Relations, Lenz Entertainment, Mundial, Inc., Original Cast Records, The Producers of *The Color Purple*, Vollrath Co., LLC

Special Contributors: The Learning Theatre Inc., Theatermania.com, and Susan Stroman

Theatre Awards After-Party generously sponsored by **Trattoria Dopo Teatro,** 125 West 44th Street between 6th Avenue and Broadway

The Theatre World Awards, Inc. is a 501 (c)(3) nonprofit organization, and our annual presentation is made possible by the generous contributions of previous winners and friends. For more information please visit the website at www.theatreworldawards.org.

TAX DEDUCTIBLE CONTRIBUTIONS CAN BE SENT TO:

Theatre World Awards, Inc.
Box 246 Radio City Station
New York, NY 10101-0246

Pajama Game actress Joyce Chittick, 1990 winner Michael McKean (*Accomplice*) with actress Annette O'Toole

Theatre World co-editor/Theatre World Awards executive producer Ben Hodges with founder/co-editor John Willis

2006 performers/presenters Harry Groener (*Oklahoma!* 1980) and Ken Page (*Guys and Dolls*, 1977)

Theatre World Awards post-ceremony celebration at Trattoria Dopo Teatro

2006 Theatre World Awards venue Studio 54

Theatre World Awards president/host Peter Filichia with Theatre World Awards secretary and 1973 winner Patricia Elliott (*A Little Night Music*)

Liza Minnelli, Harry Connick Jr., Felicia P. Fields, John Lloyd Young

Theatre World associate editor Allison Graham

2006 recipient Jayne Houdyshell with 2006 presenter Patricia Neal

2006 presenter Tammy Grimes (*Look After Lulu*, 1959)

Theatre World founder/co-editor John Willis is surprised by audience with a rendition of *Happy 90th Birthday*

2006 presenter Lucie Arnaz (*They're Playing Our Song*, 1979) with 2006 recipient Bob Martin

2006 presenter Kate Burton (*Present Laughter/Alice in Wonderland/Winners*, 1983)

2006 presenter La Chanze (*Once on This Island*, 1991)

PREVIOUS THEATRE WORLD AWARD RECIPIENTS

1944–45: Betty Comden (*On the Town*), Richard Davis (*Kiss Them For Me*), Richard Hart (*Dark of the Moon*), Judy Holliday (*Kiss Them for Me*), Charles Lang, Bambi Linn (*Carousel*), John Lund (*The Hasty Heart*), Donald Murphy (*Signature* and *Common Ground*), Nancy Noland (*Common Ground*), Margaret Phillips (*The Late George Apley*), John Raitt (*Carousel*)

1945–46: Barbara Bel Geddes (*Deep Are the Roots*), Marlon Brando (*Truckline Café* and *Candida*), Bill Callahan (*Call Me Mister*), Wendell Corey (*The Wind is Ninety*), Paul Douglas (*Born Yesterday*), Mary James (*Apple of His Eye*), Burt Lancaster (*A Sound of Hunting*), Patricia Marshall (*The Day Before Spring*), Beatrice Pearson (*The Mermaids Singing*)

1946–47: Keith Andes (*The Chocolate Soldier*), Marion Bell (*Brigadoon*), Peter Cookson (*Message for Margaret*), Ann Crowley (*Carousel*), Ellen Hanley (*Barefoot Boy With Cheek*), John Jordan (*The Wanhope Building*), George Keane (*Brigadoon*), Dorothea MacFarland (*Oklahoma!*), James Mitchell (*Brigadoon*), Patricia Neal (*Another Part of the Forest*), David Wayne (*Finian's Rainbow*)

1947–48: Valerie Bettis (*Inside U.S.A.*), Edward Bryce (*The Cradle Will Rock*), Whitfield Connor (*Macbeth*), Mark Dawson (*High Button Shoes*), June Lockhart (*For Love or Money*), Estelle Loring (*Inside U.S.A.*), Peggy Maley (*Joy to the World*), Ralph Meeker (*Mister Roberts*), Meg Mundy (*The Happy Journey to Trenton and Camden* and *The Respectful Prostitute*), Douglass Watson (*Antony and Cleopatra*), James Whitmore (*Command Decision*), Patrice Wymore (*Hold It!*)

1948–49: Tod Andrews (*Summer and Smoke*), Doe Avedon (*The Young and Fair*), Jean Carson (*Bravo!*), Carol Channing (*Lend an Ear*), Richard Derr (*The Traitor*), Julie Harris (*Sundown Beach*), Mary McCarty (*Sleepy Hollow*), Allyn Ann McLerie (*Where's Charley?*), Cameron Mitchell (*Death of a Salesman*), Gene Nelson (*Lend an Ear*), Byron Palmer (*Where's Charley?*), Bob Scheerer (*Lend an Ear*)

1949–50: Nancy Andrews (*Touch and Go*), Phil Arthur (*With a Silk Thread*), Barbara Brady (*The Velvet Glove*), Lydia Clarke (*Detective Story*), Priscilla Gillette (*Regina*), Don Hanmer (*The Man*), Marcia Henderson (*Peter Pan*), Charlton Heston (*Design for a Stained Glass Window*), Rick Jason (*Now I Lay Me Down to Sleep*), Grace Kelly (*The Father*), Charles Nolte (*Design for a Stained Glass Window*), Roger Price (*Tickets, Please!*)

1950–51: Barbara Ashley (*Out of This World*), Isabel Bigley (*Guys and Dolls*), Martin Brooks (*Burning Bright*), Richard Burton (*The Lady's Not For Burning*), Pat Crowley (*Southern Exposure*), James Daly (*Major Barbara and Mary Rose*), Cloris Leachman (*A Story for a Sunday Evening*), Russell Nype (*Call Me Madam*), Jack Palance (*Darkness at Noon*), William Smithers (*Romeo and Juliet*), Maureen Stapleton (*The Rose Tattoo*), Marcia Van Dyke (*Marcia Van Dyke*), Eli Wallach (*The Rose Tattoo*)

1951–52: Tony Bavaar (*Paint Your Wagon*), Patricia Benoit (*Glad Tidings*), Peter Conlow (*Courtin' Time*), Virginia de Luce (*New Faces of 1952*), Ronny Graham (*New Faces of 1952*), Audrey Hepburn (*Gigi*), Diana Herbert (*The Number*), Conrad Janis (*The Brass Ring*), Dick Kallman (*Seventeen*), Charles Proctor (*Twilight Walk*), Eric Sinclair (*Much Ado About Nothing*), Kim Stanley (*The Chase*), Marian Winters (*I Am a Camera*), Helen Wood (*Seventeen*)

1952–53: Edie Adams (*Wonderful Town*), Rosemary Harris (*The Climate of Eden*), Eileen Heckart (*Picnic*), Peter Kelley (*Two's Company*), John Kerr (*Bernardine*), Richard Kiley (*Misalliance*), Gloria Marlowe (*In Any Language*), Penelope Munday (*The Climate of Eden*), Paul Newman (*Picnic*), Sheree North (*Hazel Flagg*), Geraldine Page (*Mid-Summer*), John Stewart (*Bernardine*), Ray Stricklyn (*The Climate of Eden*), Gwen Verdon (*Can-Can*)

1953–54: Orson Bean (*John Murray Anderson's Almanac*), Harry Belafonte (*John Murray Anderson's Almanac*), James Dean (*The Immoralist*), Joan Diener (*Kismet*), Ben Gazzara (*End as a Man*), Carol Haney (*The Pajama Game*), Jonathan Lucas (*The Golden Apple*), Kay Medford (*Lullaby*), Scott Merrill (*The Threepenny Opera*), Elizabeth Montgomery (*Late Love*), Leo Penn (*The Girl on the Via Flaminia*), Eva Marie Saint (*The Trip to Bountiful*)

1954–55: Julie Andrews (*The Boy Friend*), Jacqueline Brookes (*The Cretan Woman*), Shirl Conway (*Plain and Fancy*), Barbara Cook (*Plain and Fancy*), David Daniels (*Plain and Fancy*), Mary Fickett (*Tea and Sympathy*), Page Johnson (*In April Once*), Loretta Leversee (*Home is the Hero*), Jack Lord (*The Traveling Lady*), Dennis Patrick (*The Wayward Saint*), Anthony Perkins (*Tea and Sympathy*), Christopher Plummer (*The Dark is Light Enough*)

1955–56: Diane Cilento (*Tiger at the Gates*), Dick Davalos (*A View From the Bridge*), Anthony Franciosa (*A Hatful of Rain*), Andy Griffith (*No Time for Sergeants*), Laurence Harvey (*Island of Goats*), David Hedison (*A Month in the Country*), Earle Hyman (*Mister Johnson*), Susan Johnson (*The Most Happy Fella*), John Michael King (*My Fair Lady*), Jayne Mansfield (*Will Success Spoil Rock Hunter?*), Sarah Marshall (*The Ponder Heart*), Gaby Rodgers (*Mister Johnson*), Susan Strasberg (*The Diary of Anne Frank*), Fritz Weaver (*The Chalk Garden*)

1956–57: Peggy Cass (*Auntie Mame*), Sydney Chaplin (*Bells Are Ringing*), Sylvia Daneel (*The Tunnel of Love*), Bradford Dillman (*Long Day's Journey Into Night*), Peter Donat (*The First Gentleman*), George Grizzard (*The Happiest Millionaire*), Carol Lynley (*The Potting Shed*), Peter Palmer (*Li'l Abner*), Jason Robards (*Long Day's Journey Into Night*), Cliff Robertson (*Orpheus Descending*), Pippa Scott (*Child of Fortune*), Inga Swenson (*The First Gentleman*)

1957–58: Anne Bancroft (*Two for the Seesaw*), Warren Berlinger (*Blue Denim*), Colleen Dewhurst (*Children of Darkness*), Richard Easton (*The Country Wife*), Tim Everett (*The Dark at the Top of the Stairs*), Eddie Hodges (*The Music Man*), Joan Hovis (*Love Me Little*), Carol Lawrence (*West Side Story*), Jacqueline McKeever (*Oh, Captain!*), Wynne Miller (*Li'l Abner*), Robert Morse (*Say, Darling*), George C. Scott (*Richard III*)

1958–59: Lou Antonio (*The Buffalo Skinner*), Ina Balin (*A Majority of One*), Richard Cross (*Maria Golovin*), Tammy Grimes (*Look After Lulu*), Larry Hagman (*God and Kate Murphy*), Dolores Hart (*The Pleasure of His Company*), Roger Mollien (French Theatre National Populaire), France Nuyen (*The World of Suzie Wong*), Susan Oliver (*Patate*), Ben Piazza (*Kataki*), Paul Roebling (*A Desert Incident*), William Shatner (*The World of Suzie Wong*), Pat Suzuki (*Flower Drum Song*), Rip Torn (*Sweet Bird of Youth*)

1959–60: Warren Beatty (*A Loss of Roses*), Eileen Brennan (*Little Mary Sunshine*), Carol Burnett (*Once Upon a Mattress*), Patty Duke (*The Miracle Worker*), Jane Fonda (*There Was a Little Girl*), Anita Gillette (*Russell Patterson's Sketchbook*), Elisa Loti (*Come Share My House*), Donald Madden (*Julius Caesar*), George Maharis (*The Zoo Story*), John McMartin (*Little Mary Sunshine*), Lauri Peters (*The Sound of Music*), Dick Van Dyke (*The Boys Against the Girls*)

1960–61: Joyce Bulifant (*Whisper to Me*), Dennis Cooney (*Every Other Evil*), Sandy Dennis (*Face of a Hero*), Nancy Dussault (*Do Re Mi*), Robert Goulet (*Camelot*), Joan Hackett (*Call Me By My Rightful Name*), June Harding (*Cry of the Raindrop*), Ron Husmann (*Tenderloin*), James MacArthur (*Invitation to a March*), Bruce Yarnell (*The Happiest Girl in the World*)

1961–62: Elizabeth Ashley (*Take Her, She's Mine*), Keith Baxter (*A Man for All Seasons*), Peter Fonda (*Blood, Sweat and Stanley Poole*), Don Galloway (*Bring Me a Warm Body*), Sean Garrison (*Half-Past Wednesday*), Barbara Harris (*Oh, Dad, Poor Dad, Mamma's Hung You in the Closet and I'm Feeling So Sad*), James Earl Jones (*Moon on a Rainbow Shawl*), Janet Margolin (*Daughter of Silence*), Karen Morrow (*Sing, Muse!*), Robert Redford (*Sunday in New York*), John Stride (*Romeo and Juliet*), Brenda Vaccaro (*Everybody Loves Opal*)

1962–63: Alan Arkin (*Enter Laughing*), Stuart Damon (*The Boys from Syracuse*), Melinda Dillon (*Who's Afraid of Virginia Woolf?*), Robert Drivas (*Mrs. Dally Has a Lover*), Bob Gentry (*Angels of Anadarko*), Dorothy Loudon (*Nowhere to Go But Up*), Brandon Maggart (*Put It in Writing*), Julienne Marie (*The Boys from Syracuse*), Liza Minnelli (*Best Foot Forward*), Estelle Parsons (*Mrs. Dally Has a Lover*), Diana Sands (*Tiger Tiger Burning Bright*), Swen Swenson (*Little Me*)

1963–64: Alan Alda (*Fair Game for Lover*), Gloria Bleezarde (*Never Live Over a Pretzel Factory*), Imelda De Martin (*The Amorous Flea*), Claude Giraud (*Phédre*), Ketty Lester (*Cabin in the Sky*), Barbara Loden (*After the Fall*), Lawrence Pressman (*Never Live Over a Pretzel Factory*), Gilbert Price (*Jerico-Jim Crow*), Philip Proctor (*The Amorous Flea*), John Tracy (*Telemachus Clay*), Jennifer West (*Dutchman*)

1964–65: Carolyn Coates (*The Trojan Women*), Joyce Jillson (*The Roar of the Greasepaint – The Smell of the Crowd*), Linda Lavin (*Wet Paint*), Luba Lisa (*I Had a Ball*), Michael O'Sullivan (*Tartuffe*), Joanna Pettet (*Poor Richard*), Beah Richards (*The Amen Corner*), Jaime Sanchez (*Conerico Was Here to Stay* and *The Toilet*), Victor Spinetti (*Oh, What a Lovely War*), Nicolas Surovy (*Helen*), Robert Walker (*I Knock at the Door* and *Pictures in the Hallway*), Clarence Williams III (*Slow Dancing on the Killing Ground*)

1965–66: Zoe Caldwell (*Slapstick Tragedy*), David Carradine (*The Royal Hunt of the Sun*), John Cullum (*On a Clear Day You Can See Forever*), John Davidson (*Oklahoma!*), Faye Dunaway (*Hogan's Ghost*), Gloria Foster (*Medea*), Robert Hooks (*Where's Daddy?* and *Day of Absence*), Jerry Lanning (*Mame*), Richard Mulligan (*Mating Dance* and *Hogan's Ghost*), April Shawhan (*3 Bags Full*), Sandra Smith (*Any Wednesday*), Leslie Ann Warren (*Drat! The Cat!*)

1966–67: Bonnie Bedelia (*My Sweet Charlie*), Richard Benjamin (*The Star-Spangled Girl*), Dustin Hoffman (*Eh?*), Terry Kiser (*Fortune and Men's Eyes*), Reva Rose (*You're A Good Man, Charlie Brown*), Robert Salvio (*Hamp*), Sheila Smith (*Mame*), Connie Stevens (*The Star-Spangled Girl*), Pamela Tiffin (*Dinner at Eight*), Leslie Uggams (*Hallelujah, Baby*), Jon Voight (*That Summer – That Fall*), Christopher Walken (*The Rose Tattoo*)

1967–68: David Birney (*Summertree*), Pamela Burrell (*Arms and the Man*), Jordan Christopher (*Black Comedy*), Jack Crowder – aka Thalmus Rasulala (*Hello, Dolly!*), Sandy Duncan (*Ceremony of Innocence*), Julie Gregg (*The Happy Time*), Stephen Joyce (*Stephen D.*), Bernadette Peters (*George M*), Alice Playten (*Henry, Sweet Henry*), Michael Rupert (*The Happy Time*), Brenda Smiley (*Scuba Duba*), Russ Thacker (*Your Own Thing*)

1968–69: Jane Alexander (*The Great White Hope*), David Cryer (*Come Summer*), Blythe Danner (*The Miser*), Ed Evanko (*Canterbury Tales*), Ken Howard (*1776*), Lauren Jones (*Does a Tiger Wear a Necktie?*), Ron Leibman (*We Bombed in New Haven*), Marian Mercer (*Promises, Promises*), Jill O'Hara (*Promises, Promises*), Ron O'Neal (*No Place to Be Somebody*), Al Pacino (*Does a Tiger Wear a Necktie?*), Marlene Warfield (*The Great White Hope*)

1969–70: Susan Browning (*Company*), Donny Burks (*Billy Noname*), Catherine Burns (*Dear Janet Rosenberg, Dear Mr. Kooning*), Len Cariou (*Henry V* and *Applause*), Bonnie Franklin (*Applause*), David Holliday (*Coco*), Katharine Houghton (*A Scent of Flowers*), Melba Moore (*Purlie*), David Rounds (*Child's Play*), Lewis J. Stadlen (*Minnie's Boys*), Kristoffer Tabori (*How Much, How Much*), Fredricka Weber (*The Last Sweet Days of Isaac*)

1970–71: Clifton Davis (*Do It Again*), Michael Douglas (*Pinkville*), Julie Garfield (*Uncle Vanya*), Martha Henry (*The Playboy of the Western World, Scenes From American Life,* and *Antigone*), James Naughton (*Long Days Journey Into Night*), Tricia O'Neil (*Two by Two*), Kipp Osborne (*Butterflies Are Free*), Roger Rathburn (*No, No, Nanette*), Ayn Ruymen (*The Gingerbread Lady*), Jennifer Salt (*Father's Day*), Joan Van Ark (*School for Wives*), Walter Willison (*Two by Two*)

1971–72: Jonelle Allen (*Two Gentlemen of Verona*), Maureen Anderman (*Moonchildren*), William Atherton (*Suggs*), Richard Backus (*Promenade, All!*), Adrienne Barbeau (*Grease*), Cara Duff-MacCormick (*Moonchildren*), Robert Foxworth (*The Crucible*), Elaine Joyce (*Sugar*), Jess Richards (*On The Town*), Ben Vereen (*Jesus Christ Superstar*), Beatrice Winde (*Ain't Supposed to Die a Natural Death*), James Woods (*Moonchildren*)

1972–73: D'Jamin Bartlett (*A Little Night Music*), Patricia Elliott (*A Little Night Music*), James Farentino (*A Streetcar Named Desire*), Brian Farrell (*The Last of Mrs. Lincoln*), Victor Garber (*Ghosts*), Kelly Garrett (*Mother Earth*), Mari Gorman (*The Hot l Baltimore*), Laurence Guittard (*A Little Night Music*), Trish Hawkins (*The Hot l Baltimore*), Monte Markham (*Irene*), John Rubinstein (*Pippin*), Jennifer Warren (*6 Rms Riv Vu*), Alexander H. Cohen (Special Award)

1973–74: Mark Baker (*Candide*), Maureen Brennan (*Candide*), Ralph Carter (*Raisin*), Thom Christopher (*Noel Coward in Two Keys*), John Driver (*Over Here*), Conchata Ferrell (*The Sea Horse*), Ernestine Jackson (*Raisin*), Michael Moriarty (*Find Your Way Home*), Joe Morton (*Raisin*), Ann Reinking (*Over Here*), Janie Sell (*Over Here*), Mary Woronov (*Boom Boom Room*), Sammy Cahn (Special Award)

1974–75: Peter Burnell (*In Praise of Love*), Zan Charisse (*Gypsy*), Lola Falana (*Dr. Jazz*), Peter Firth (*Equus*), Dorian Harewood (*Don't Call Back*), Joel Higgins (*Shenandoah*), Marcia McClain (*Where's Charley?*), Linda Miller (*Black Picture Show*), Marti Rolph (*Good News*), John Sheridan (*Gypsy*), Scott Stevensen (*Good News*), Donna Theodore (*Shenandoah*), Equity Library Theatre (Special Award)

1975–76: Danny Aiello (*Lampost Reunion*), Christine Andreas (*My Fair Lady*), Dixie Carter (*Jesse and the Bandit Queen*), Tovah Feldshuh (*Yentl*), Chip Garnett (*Bubblin' Brown Sugar*), Richard Kelton (*Who's Afraid of Virginia Woolf?*), Vivian Reed (*Bubblin' Brown Sugar*), Charles Repole (*Very Good Eddie*), Virginia Seidel (*Very Good Eddie*), Daniel Seltzer (*Knock Knock*), John V. Shea (*Yentl*), Meryl Streep (*27 Wagons Full of Cotton*), A Chorus Line (Special Award)

1976–77: Trazana Beverley *(for colored girls…)*, Michael Cristofer (*The Cherry Orchard*), Joe Fields (*The Basic Training of Pavlo Hummel*), Joanna Gleason (*I Love My Wife*), Cecilia Hart (*Dirty Linen*), John Heard (*G.R. Point*), Gloria Hodes (*The Club*), Juliette Koka *(Piaf…A Remembrance)*, Andrea McArdle (*Annie*), Ken Page (*Guys and Dolls*), Jonathan Pryce (*Comedians*), Chick Vennera (*Jockeys*), Eva LeGallienne (Special Award)

1977–78: Vasili Bogazianos (*P.S. Your Cat Is Dead*), Nell Carter (*Ain't Misbehavin'*), Carlin Glynn (*The Best Little Whorehouse in Texas*), Christopher Goutman (*The Promise*), William Hurt (*Ulysses in Traction, Lulu, and The Fifth of July*), Judy Kaye (*On the 20th Century*), Florence Lacy (*Hello, Dolly!*), Armelia McQueen (*Ain't Misbehavin'*), Gordana Rashovich (*Fefu and Her Friends*), Bo Rucker (*Native Son*), Richard Seer (*Da*), Colin Stinton (*The Water Engine*), Joseph Papp (Special Award)

1978–79: Philip Anglim (*The Elephant Man*), Lucie Arnaz (*They're Playing Our Song*), Gregory Hines (*Eubie!*), Ken Jennings (*Sweeney Todd*), Michael Jeter (*G.R. Point*), Laurie Kennedy (*Man and Superman*), Susan Kingsley (*Getting Out*), Christine Lahti (*The Woods*), Edward James Olmos (*Zoot Suit*), Kathleen Quinlan (*Taken in Marriage*), Sarah Rice (*Sweeney Todd*), Max Wright (*Once in a Lifetime*), Marshall W. Mason (Special Award)

1979–80: Maxwell Caulfield (*Class Enemy*), Leslie Denniston (*Happy New Year*), Boyd Gaines (*A Month in the Country*), Richard Gere (*Bent*), Harry Groener (*Oklahoma!*), Stephen James (*The 1940's Radio Hour*), Susan Kellermann (*Last Licks*), Dinah Manoff (*I Ought to Be in Pictures*), Lonny Price (*Class Enemy*), Marianne Tatum (*Barnum*), Anne Twomey (*Nuts*), Dianne Wiest (*The Art of Dining*), Mickey Rooney (Special Award)

1980–81: Brian Backer (*The Floating Light Bulb*), Lisa Banes (*Look Back in Anger*), Meg Bussert (*The Music Man*), Michael Allen Davis (*Broadway Follies*), Giancarlo Esposito (*Zooman and the Sign*), Daniel Gerroll (*Slab Boys*), Phyllis Hyman (*Sophisticated Ladies*), Cynthia Nixon (*The Philadelphia Story*), Amanda Plummer (*A Taste of Honey*), Adam Redfield (*A Life*), Wanda Richert (*42nd Street*), Rex Smith (*The Pirates of Penzance*), Elizabeth Taylor (Special Award)

1981–82: Karen Akers (*Nine*), Laurie Beechman (*Joseph and the Amazing Technicolor Dreamcoat*), Danny Glover (*Master Harold…and the Boys*), David Alan Grier (*The First*), Jennifer Holliday (*Dreamgirls*), Anthony Heald (*Misalliance*), Lizbeth Mackay (*Crimes of the Heart*), Peter MacNicol (*Crimes of the Heart*), Elizabeth McGovern (*My Sister in This House*), Ann Morrison (*Merrily We Roll Along*), Michael O'Keefe *(Mass Appeal)*, James Widdoes *(Is There Life After High School?)*, Manhattan Theatre Club (Special Award)

1982–83: Karen Allen (*Monday After the Miracle*), Suzanne Bertish (*Skirmishes*), Matthew Broderick (*Brighton Beach Memoirs*), Kate Burton *(Winners)*, Joanne Camp (*Geniuses*), Harvey Fierstein (*Torch Song Trilogy*), Peter Gallagher (*A Doll's Life*), John Malkovich (*True West*), Anne Pitoniak (*'Night Mother*), James Russo (*Extremities*), Brian Tarantina (*Angels Fall*), Linda Thorson (*Streaming*), Natalia Makarova (*On Your Toes* Special Award)

1983–84: Martine Allard (*The Tap Dance Kid*), Joan Allen (*And a Nightingale Sang*), Kathy Whitton Baker (*Fool For Love*), Mark Capri (*On Approval*), Laura Dean (*Doonesbury*), Stephen Geoffreys (*The Human Comedy*), Todd Graff (*Baby*), Glenne Headly (*The Philanthropist*), J.J. Johnston (*American Buffalo*), Bonnie Koloc (*The Human Comedy*), Calvin Levels (*Open Admissions*), Robert Westenberg (*Zorba*), Ron Moody (Special Award)

1984–85: Kevin Anderson (*Orphans*), Richard Chaves (*Tracers*), Patti Cohenour (*La Boheme* and *Big River*), Charles S. Dutton (*Ma Rainey's Black Bottom*), Nancy Giles (*Mayor*), Whoopi Goldberg (*Whoopi Goldberg*), Leilani Jones (*Grind*), John Mahoney (*Orphans*), Laurie Metcalf (*Balm in Gilead*), Barry Miller (*Biloxi Blues*), John Turturro (*Danny and the Deep Blue Sea*), Amelia White (*The Accrington Pals*), Lucille Lortel (Special Award)

1985–86: Suzy Amis (*Fresh Horses*), Alec Baldwin (*Loot*), Aled Davies (*Orchards*), Faye Grant (*Singin' in the Rain*), Julie Hagerty (*House of Blue Leaves*), Ed Harris (*Precious Sons*), Mark Jacoby (*Sweet Charity*), Donna Kane (*Dames at Sea*), Cleo Laine (*The Mystery of Edwin Drood*), Howard McGillin (*The Mystery of Edwin Drood*), Marisa Tomei (*Daughters*), Joe Urla (*Principia Scriptoriae*), Ensemble Studio Theatre (Special Award)

1986–87: Annette Bening (*Coastal Disturbances*), Timothy Daly (*Coastal Disturbances*), Lindsay Duncan (*Les Liaisons Dangereuses*), Frank Ferrante (*Groucho: A Life in Revue*), Robert Lindsay (*Me and My Girl*), Amy Madigan (*The Lucky Spot*), Michael Maguire (*Les Misérables*), Demi Moore (*The Early Girl*), Molly Ringwald (*Lily Dale*), Frances Ruffelle (*Les Misérables*), Courtney B. Vance (*Fences*), Colm Wilkinson (*Les Misérables*), Robert DeNiro (Special Award)

1987–88: Yvonne Bryceland (*The Road to Mecca*), Philip Casnoff (*Chess*), Danielle Ferland (*Into the Woods*), Melissa Gilbert (*A Shayna Maidel*), Linda Hart (*Anything Goes*), Linzi Hateley (*Carrie*), Brian Kerwin (*Emily*), Brian Mitchell (*Mail*), Mary Murfitt (*Oil City Symphony*), Aidan Quinn *A Streetcar Named Desire*), Eric Roberts (*Burn This*), B.D. Wong (*M. Butterfly*), Tisa Chang and Martin E. Segal (Special Awards)

1988–89: Dylan Baker (*Eastern Standard*), Joan Cusack (*Road* and *Brilliant Traces*), Loren Dean (*Amulets Against the Dragon Forces*), Peter Frechette (*Eastern Standard*), Sally Mayes (*Welcome to the Club*), Sharon McNight (*Starmites*), Jennie Moreau (*Eleemoysynary*), Paul Provenza (*Only Kidding*), Kyra Sedgwick (*Ah, Wilderness!*), Howard Spiegel (*Only Kidding*), Eric Stoltz (*Our Town*), Joanne Whalley-Kilmer (*What the Butler Saw*); Pauline Collins (*Shirley Valentine* Special Award), Mikhail Baryshnikov (Special Award)

1989–90: Denise Burse (*Ground People*), Erma Campbell (*Ground People*), Rocky Carroll (*The Piano Lesson*), Megan Gallagher (*A Few Good Men*), Tommy Hollis (*The Piano Lesson*), Robert Lambert (*Gypsy*), Kathleen Rowe McAllen (*Aspects of Love*), Michael McKean (*Accomplice*), Crista Moore (*Gypsy*), Mary-Louise Parker (*Prelude to a Kiss*), Daniel von Bargen (*Mastergate*), Jason Workman (*Jason Workman*), Stewart Granger and Kathleen Turner (Special Awards)

1990–91: Jane Adams (*I Hate Hamlet*), Gillian Anderson (*Absent Friends*), Adam Arkin (*I Hate Hamlet*), Brenda Blethyn (*Absent Friends*), Marcus Chong (*Stand-up Tragedy*), Paul Hipp (*Buddy*), LaChanze (*Once on This Island*), Kenny Neal (*Mule Bone*), Kevin Ramsey (*Oh, Kay!*), Francis Ruivivar (*Shogun*), Lea Salonga (*Miss Saigon*), Chandra Wilson (*The Good Times Are Killing Me*); Tracey Ullman (*The Big Love* and *Taming of the Shrew*), Ellen Stewart (Special Award)

1991–92: Talia Balsam (*Jake's Women*), Lindsay Crouse (*The Homecoming*), Griffin Dunne (*Search and Destroy*), Larry Fishburne (*Two Trains Running*), Mel Harris (*Empty Hearts*), Jonathan Kaplan (*Falsettos and Rags*), Jessica Lange (*A Streetcar Named Desire*), Laura Linney (*Sight Unseen*), Spiro Malas (*The Most Happy Fella*), Mark Rosenthal (*Marvin's Room*), Helen Shaver (*Jake's Women*), Al White (*Two Trains Running*), *Dancing at Lughnasa* cast (Special Award), Plays for Living (Special Award)

1992–93: Brent Carver (*Kiss of the Spider Woman*), Michael Cerveris (*The Who's Tommy*), Marcia Gay Harden (*Angels in America: Millennium Approaches*), Stephanie Lawrence (*Blood Brothers*), Andrea Martin (*My Favorite Year*), Liam Neeson (*Anna Christie*), Stephen Rea (*Someone Who'll Watch Over Me*), Natasha Richardson (*Anna Christie*), Martin Short (*The Goodbye Girl*), Dina Spybey (*Five Women Wearing the Same Dress*), Stephen Spinella (*Angels in America: Millennium Approaches*), Jennifer Tilly (*One Shoe Off*), John Leguizamo (Special Award), Rosetta LeNoire (Special Award)

1993–94: Marcus D'Amico (*An Inspector Calls*), Jarrod Emick (*Damn Yankees*), Arabella Field (*Snowing at Delphi* and *4 Dogs and a Bone*), Aden Gillett (*An Inspector Calls*), Sherry Glaser (*Family Secrets*), Michael Hayden (*Carousel*), Margaret Illman (*The Red Shoes*), Audra Ann McDonald (*Carousel*), Burke Moses (*Beauty and the Beast)*, Anna Deavere Smith (*Twilight: Los Angeles, 1992*), Jere Shea (*Passion*), Harriet Walter (*3Birds Alighting on a Field*)

1994–95: Gretha Boston (*Show Boat*), Billy Crudup (*Arcadia*), Ralph Fiennes (*Hamlet*), Beverly D'Angelo (*Simpatico*), Calista Flockhart (*The Glass Menagerie*), Kevin Kilner (*The Glass Menagerie*), Anthony LaPaglia (*The Rose Tattoo*), Julie Johnson (*Das Barbecu*), Helen Mirren (*A Month in the Country*), Jude Law (*Indiscretions*), Rufus Sewell (*Translations*), Vanessa Williams (*Kiss of the Spider Woman*), Brooke Shields (Special Award)

1995–96: Jordan Baker (*Suddenly Last Summer*), Joohee Choi (*The King and I*), Karen Kay Cody (*Master Class*), Viola Davis (*Seven Guitars*), Kate Forbes (*The School for Scandal*), Michael McGrath (*Swinging on a Star*), Alfred Molina (*Molly Sweeney*), Timothy Olyphant (*The Monogamist*), Adam Pascal (*Rent*), Lou Diamond Phillips (*The King and I*), Daphne Rubin-Vega (*Rent*), Brett Tabisel (*Big*), *An Ideal Husband* cast (Special Award)

1996–97: Terry Beaver (*The Last Night of Ballyhoo*), Helen Carey (*London Assurance*), Kristin Chenoweth (*Steel Pier*), Jason Danieley (*Candide*), Linda Eder (*Jekyll & Hyde*), Allison Janney (*Present Laughter*), Daniel McDonald (*Steel Pier*), Janet McTeer (*A Doll's House*), Mark Ruffalo (*This Is Our Youth*), Fiona Shaw (*The Waste Land*), Antony Sher (*Stanley*), Alan Tudyk (*Bunny Bunny*), *Skylight* cast (Special Award)

1997–98: Max Casella (*The Lion King*), Margaret Colin (*Jackie*), Ruaidhri Conroy (*The Cripple of Inishmaan*), Alan Cumming (*Cabaret*), Lea Delaria (*On the Town*), Edie Falco (*Side Man*), Enid Graham (*Honour*), Anna Kendrick (*High Society*), Ednita Nazario (*The Capeman*), Douglas Sills (*The Scarlet Pimpernel*), Steven Sutcliffe (*Ragtime*), Sam Trammel (*Ah, Wilderness!*), Eddie Izzard (Special Award), *Beauty Queen of Leenane* cast (Special Award)

1998–99: Jillian Armenante (*The Cider House Rules*), James Black (*Not About Nightingales*), Brendan Coyle (*The Weir*), Anna Friel (*Closer*), Rupert Graves (*Closer*), Lynda Gravátt (*The Old Settler*), Nicole Kidman (*The Blue Room*), Ciáran Hinds (*Closer*), Ute Lemper (*Chicago*), Clarke Peters (*The Iceman Cometh*), Toby Stephens (*Ring Round the Moon*), Sandra Oh (*Stop Kiss*), Jerry Herman (Special Award)

1999–2000: Craig Bierko (*The Music Man*), Everett Bradley (*Swing!*), Gabriel Byrne (*A Moon for the Misbegotten*), Ann Hampton Callaway (*Swing!*), Toni Collette (*The Wild Party*), Henry Czerny (*Arms and the Man*), Stephen Dillane (*The Real Thing)*, Jennifer Ehle (*The Real Thing*), Philip Seymour Hoffman (*True West*), Hayley Mills (*Suite in Two Keys*), Cigdem Onat (*The Time of the Cuckoo*), Claudia Shear (*Dirty Blonde*), Barry Humphries (Special Award)

2000–2001: Juliette Binoche (*Betrayal*), Macaulay Culkin (*Madame Melville*), Janie Dee (*Comic Potential*), Raúl Esparza (*The Rocky Horror Show*), Kathleen Freeman (*The Full Monty*), Deven May (*Bat Boy*), Reba McEntire (*Annie Get Your Gun*), Chris Noth (*The Best Man*), Joshua Park (*The Adventures of Tom Sawyer*), Rosie Perez (*References to Salvador Dali Make Me Hot*), Joely Richardson (*Madame Melville*), John Ritter (*The Dinner Party*), Seán Campion and Conleth Hill (*Stones in His Pocket* Special Awards)

2001–2002: Justin Bohon (*Oklahoma!*), Simon Callow (*The Mystery of Charles Dickens*), Mos Def (*Topdog/Underdog*), Emma Fielding (*Private Lives*), Adam Godley (*Private Lives*), Martin Jarvis (*By Jeeves*), Spencer Kayden (*Urinetown*), Gretchen Mol (*The Shape of Things*), Anna Paquin (*The Glory of Living*), Louise Pitre (*Mamma Mia!*), David Warner (*Major Barbara*), Rachel Weisz (*The Shape of Things*)

2002–2003: Antonio Banderas (*Nine*), Tammy Blanchard (*Gypsy*), Thomas Jefferson Byrd (*Ma Rainey's Black Bottom*), Jonathan Cake (*Medea*), Victoria Hamilton (*A Day in the Death of Joe Egg*), Clare Higgins (*Vincent in Brixton*), Jackie Hoffman (*Hairspray*), Mary Stuart Masterson (*Nine*), John Selya (*Movin' Out*), Daniel Sunjata (*Take Me Out*), Jochum ten Haaf (*Vincent in Brixton*), Marissa Jaret Winokur (*Hairspray*), Peter Filichia (Special Award), Ben Hodges (Special Award)

2003–2004: Shannon Cochran (*Bug*), Stephanie D'Abruzzo (*Avenue Q*), Mitchel David Federan (*The Boy From Oz*), Alexander Gemignani (*Assassins*), Hugh Jackman (*The Boy From Oz*), Isabel Keating (*The Boy From Oz*), Sanaa Lathan (*A Raisin in the Sun*), Jefferson Mays (*I Am My Own Wife*), Euan Morton (*Taboo*), Anika Noni Rose (*Caroline, or Change*), John Tartaglia (*Avenue Q*), Jennifer Westfeldt (*Wonderful Town*), Sarah Jones (*Bridge and Tunnel* Special Award)

2004–2005: Christina Applegate (*Sweet Charity*), Ashlie Atkinson (*Fat Pig)*, Hank Azaria (*Spamalot*), Gordon Clapp (*Glengarry Glen Ross)*, Conor Donovan (*Privilege*), Dan Fogler (*The 25th Annual Putnam County Spelling Bee*), Heather Goldenhersh (*Doubt*), Carla Gugino (*After the Fall)*, Jenn Harris (*Modern Orthodox)*, Cheyenne Jackson (*All Shook Up*), Celia Keenan-Bolger (*The 25th Annual Putnam County Spelling Bee)*, Tyler Maynard (*Altar Boyz*)

MAJOR THEATRICAL AWARDS

AMERICAN THEATRE WING'S ANTOINETTE PERRY "TONY" AWARDS

Sunday, June 11, 2006 at Radio City Music Hall

The 60th annual Tony Awards are presented in recognition of distinguished achievement in the Broadway theatre. The 2005–2006 Tony Awards Nominating Committee (appointed by the Tony Awards Administration Committee), included: Victoria Bailey, executive; Joe Benincasa, executive; Susan Birkenhead, lyricist; Edward Burbridge, scenic designer; Robert Cally, executive; Ben Cameron, executive; Bettie Corwin, executive; John Dias, producer/dramaturg; Mercedes Ellington, choreographer;   Sue Frost, producer/company manager; Joanna Gleason, actor; David Henry Hwang, playwright; Andrew Jackness, scenic designer; Betty Jacobs, historian/script consultant; Robert Kamlot, manager; Todd London, artistic director; Brian Stokes Mitchell, actor; John Nakagawa, producer; Lynn Nottage, playwright; Gilbert Parker, executive; Jonathan Reynolds, playwright/screenwriter; Steve Suskin, author; Jac Venza, producer; Tom Viola, executive; Franklin Weissberg, judge.

BEST PLAY (award goes to both author as well as producer): *The History Boys* by Alan Bennett; produced by Boyett Ostar Productions, Roger Berlind, Debra Black, Eric Falkenstein, Roy Furman, Jam Theatricals, Stephanie P. McClelland, Judith Resnick, Scott Rudin, Jon Avnet/Ralph Guild, Dede Harris/Mort Swinsky, The National Theatre of Great Britain

Nominees: *The Lieutenant of Inishmore* by Martin McDonagh; produced by Randall L. Wreghitt, Dede Harris, Atlantic Theater Company, David Lehrer, Harriet Newman Leve & Ron Nicynski, Zavelson Meyrelles Greiner Group, Mort Swinsky & Redfern Goldman Productions, Ruth Hendel; *Rabbit Hole* by David Lindsay-Abaire; produced by Manhattan Theatre Club, Lynne Meadow, Barry Grove; *Shining City* by Conor McPherson; produced by Manhattan Theatre Club, Lynne Meadow, Barry Grove, Scott Rudin, Roger Berlind, Debra Black

BEST MUSICAL (award goes to producer): *Jersey Boys* produced by Dodger Theatricals, Joseph J. Grano, Pelican Group, Tamara and Kevin Kinsella, Latitude Link, Rick Steiner/Osher/Staton/Bell/Mayerson Group

Nominees: *The Color Purple* produced by Oprah Winfrey, Scott Sanders, Roy Furman, Quincy Jones, Creative Battery, Anna Fantaci & Cheryl Lachowicz, Independent Presenters Network, David Lowy, Stephanie P. McClelland, Gary Winnick, Jan Kallish, Nederlander Presentations, Inc., Bob & Harvey Weinstein, Andrew Asnes & Adam Zotovich, Todd Johnson; *The Drowsy Chaperone* produced by Kevin McCollum, Roy Miller, Boyett Ostar Productions, Stephanie P. McClelland, Barbara Freitag, Jill Furman; *The Wedding Singer* produced by Margo Lion, New Line Cinema, The Araca Group, Roy Furman, Douglas L. Meyer/James D. Stern, Rick Steiner/The Staton Bell Osher Mayerson Group, Jam Theatricals, Jujamcyn Theaters, Jay Furman, Michael Gill, Dr. Lawrence Horowitz, Rhoda Mayerson, Marisa Sechrest, Gary Winnick, Dancap Productions, Inc., Élan V. McAllister/Allan S. Gordon/Adam Epstein

BEST BOOK OF A MUSICAL: Bob Martin and Don McKellar, *The Drowsy Chaperone*

Nominees: Chad Beguelin and Tim Herlihy, *The Wedding Singer*; Marshall Brickman and Rick Elice, *Jersey Boys*; Marsha Norman, *The Color Purple*

BEST ORIGINAL SCORE (music and/or lyrics): Lisa Lambert and Greg Morrison, *The Drowsy Chaperone*

Nominees: Brenda Russell, Allee Willis and Stephen Bray, *The Color Purple*; Matthew Sklar and Chad Beguelin, *The Wedding Singer*; Andrew Lloyd Webber and David Zippel, *The Woman in White*

BEST REVIVAL OF A PLAY (award goes to producer): *Awake and Sing!* produced by Lincoln Center Theater, André Bishop, Bernard Gersten

Nominees: *The Constant Wife* produced by Roundabout Theatre Company, Todd Haimes, Ellen Richard, Julia C. Levy; *Edward Albee's Seascape* produced by Lincoln Center Theater, André Bishop, Bernard Gersten; *Faith Healer* produced by Michael Colgan & Sonia Friedman Productions, The Shubert Organization, Robert Bartner, Roger Berlind, Scott Rudin, Spring Sirkin, Gate Theatre Dublin

BEST REVIVAL OF A MUSICAL (award goes to producer): *The Pajama Game*, produced by Roundabout Theatre Company, Todd Haimes, Harold Wolpert, Julia C. Levy, Jeffrey Richards, James Fuld, Jr., Scott Landis

Nominees: *Sweeney Todd*, produced by Tom Viertel, Steven Baruch, Marc Routh, Richard Frankel, Ambassador Theatre Group, Adam Kenwright, Tulchin/Bartner/Bagert; *The Threepenny Opera*, produced by Roundabout Theatre Company, Todd Haimes, Harold Wolpert, Julia C. Levy

BEST PERFORMANCE BY A LEADING ACTOR IN A PLAY: Richard Griffiths, *The History Boys*

Nominees: Ralph Fiennes, *Faith Healer*; Zeljko Ivanek, *The Caine Mutiny Court-Martial*; Oliver Platt, *Shining City*; David Wilmot, *The Lieutenant of Inishmore*

BEST PERFORMANCE BY A LEADING ACTRESS IN A PLAY: Cynthia Nixon, *Rabbit Hole*

Nominees: Kate Burton, *The Constant Wife*; Judy Kaye, *Souvenir*; Lisa Kron, *Well*; Lynn Redgrave, *The Constant Wife*

BEST PERFORMANCE BY A LEADING ACTOR IN A MUSICAL: John Lloyd Young, *Jersey Boys*

Nominees: Michael Cerveris, *Sweeney Todd*; Harry Connick, Jr., *The Pajama Game*; Stephen Lynch, *The Wedding Singer*; Bob Martin, *The Drowsy Chaperone*

BEST PERFORMANCE BY A LEADING ACTRESS IN A MUSICAL: LaChanze, *The Color Purple*

Nominees: Sutton Foster, *The Drowsy Chaperone*; Patti LuPone, *Sweeney Todd*; Kelli O'Hara, *The Pajama Game*; Chita Rivera, *Chita Rivera: The Dancer's Life*

BEST PERFORMANCE BY A FEATURED ACTOR IN A PLAY: Ian McDiarmid, *Faith Healer*

Nominees: Samuel Barnett, *The History Boys*; Domhnall Gleeson, *The Lieutenant of Inishmore*; Mark Ruffalo, *Awake and Sing!*; Pablo Schreiber, *Awake and Sing!*

BEST PERFORMANCE BY A FEATURED ACTRESS IN A PLAY: Frances de la Tour, *The History Boys*

Nominees: Tyne Daly, *Rabbit Hole*; Jayne Houdyshell, *Well*; Alison Pill, *The Lieutenant of Inishmore*; Zoë Wanamaker, *Awake and Sing!*

BEST PERFORMANCE BY A FEATURED ACTOR IN A MUSICAL: Christian Hoff, *Jersey Boys*

Nominees: Danny Burstein, *The Drowsy Chaperone*; Jim Dale, *The Threepenny Opera*; Brandon Victor Dixon, *The Color Purple*; Manoel Felciano, *Sweeney Todd*

BEST PERFORMANCE BY A FEATURED ACTRESS IN A MUSICAL: Beth Leavel, *The Drowsy Chaperone*

Nominees: Carolee Carmello, *Lestat*; Felicia P. Fields, *The Color Purple*; Megan Lawrence, *The Pajama Game*; Elisabeth Withers-Mendes, *The Color Purple*

BEST SCENIC DESIGN OF A PLAY: Bob Crowley, *The History Boys*

Nominees: John Lee Beatty, *Rabbit Hole*; Santo Loquasto, *Three Days of Rain*; Michael Yeargan, *Awake and Sing!*

BEST SCENIC DESIGN OF A MUSICAL: David Gallo, *The Drowsy Chaperone*

Nominees: John Lee Beatty, *The Color Purple*; Derek McLane, *The Pajama Game*; Klara Zieglerova, *Jersey Boys*

BEST COSTUME DESIGN OF A PLAY: Catherine Zuber, *Awake and Sing!*

Nominees: Michael Krass, *The Constant Wife*; Santo Loquasto, *A Touch of the Poet*; Catherine Zuber, *Edward Albee's Seascape*

BEST COSTUME DESIGN OF A MUSICAL: Gregg Barnes, *The Drowsy Chaperone*

Nominees: Susan Hilferty, *Lestat*; Martin Pakledinaz, *The Pajama Game*; Paul Tazewell, *The Color Purple*

BEST LIGHTING DESIGN OF A PLAY: Mark Henderson, *The History Boys*

Nominees: Christopher Akerlind, *Awake and Sing!*; Paul Gallo, *Three Days of Rain*; Mark Henderson, *Faith Healer*

BEST LIGHTING DESIGN OF A MUSICAL: Howell Binkley, *Jersey Boys*

Nominees: Ken Billington and Brian Monahan, *The Drowsy Chaperone*; Natasha Katz, *Tarzan*; Brian MacDevitt, *The Color Purple*

BEST CHOREOGRAPHY: Kathleen Marshall, *The Pajama Game*

Nominees: Rob Ashford, *The Wedding Singer*; Donald Byrd, *The Color Purple*; Casey Nicholaw, *The Drowsy Chaperone*

BEST DIRECTION OF A PLAY: Nicholas Hytner, *The History Boys*

Nominees: Wilson Milam, *The Lieutenant of Inishmore*; Bartlett Sher, *Awake and Sing!*; Daniel Sullivan, *Rabbit Hole*

BEST DIRECTION OF A MUSICAL: John Doyle, *Sweeney Todd*

Nominees: Kathleen Marshall, *The Pajama Game*; Des McAnuff, *Jersey Boys*; Casey Nicholaw, *The Drowsy Chaperone*

BEST ORCHESTRATIONS: Sarah Travis, *Sweeney Todd*

Nominees: Larry Blank, *The Drowsy Chaperone*; Dick Lieb and Danny Troob, *The Pajama Game*; Steve Orich, *Jersey Boys*

Special Tony Award for Lifetime Achievement in the Theatre: Harold Prince

Regional Theatre Tony Award: Intiman Theatre, Seattle, Washington

Special Tony Award: Sarah Jones

PAST TONY AWARD WINNERS

Awards listed are Best Play followed by Best Musical, and as awards for Best Revival and the subcategories of Best Revival of a Play and Best Revival of a Musical were instituted, they are listed respectively.

1947: No award given for musical or play **1948:** *Mister Roberts* **1949:** *Death of a Salesman, Kiss Me, Kate* **1950:** *The Cocktail Party, South Pacific* **1951:** *The Rose Tattoo, Guys and Dolls* **1952:** *The Fourposter, The King and I* **1953:** *The Crucible, Wonderful Town* **1954:** *The Teahouse of the August Moon, Kismet* **1955:** *The Desperate Hours, The Pajama Game* **1956:** *The Diary of Anne Frank, Damn Yankees* **1957:** *Long Day's Journey into Night, My Fair Lady* **1958:** *Sunrise at Campobello, The Music Man* **1959:** *J.B., Redhead* **1960:** *The Miracle Worker, Fiorello!* tied with *The Sound of Music* **1961:** *Becket, Bye Bye Birdie* **1962:** *A Man for All Seasons, How to Succeed in Business Without Really Trying* **1963:** *Who's Afraid of Virginia Woolf?, A Funny Thing Happened on the Way to the Forum* **1964:** *Luther, Hello, Dolly!* **1965:** *The Subject Was Roses, Fiddler on the Roof* **1966:** *The Persecution and Assassination of Marat as Performed by the Inmates of the Asylum of Charenton Under the Direction of the Marquis de Sade, Man of La Mancha* **1967:** *The Homecoming, Cabaret* **1968:** *Rosencrantz and Guildenstern Are Dead, Hallelujah Baby!* **1969:** *The Great White Hope, 1776* **1970:** *Borstal Boy, Applause* **1971:** *Sleuth, Company* **1972:** *Sticks and Bones, Two Gentlemen of Verona* **1973:** *That Championship Season, A Little Night Music* **1974:** *The River Niger, Raisin* **1975:** *Equus, The Wiz* **1976:** *Travesties, A Chorus Line* **1977:** *The Shadow Box, Annie* **1978:** *Da, Ain't Misbehavin', Dracula* **1979:** *The Elephant Man, Sweeney Todd* **1980:** *Children of a Lesser God, Evita, Morning's at Seven* **1981:** *Amadeus, 42nd St., The Pirates of Penzance* **1982:** *The Life and Adventures of Nicholas Nickelby, Nine, Othello* **1983:** *Torch Song Trilogy, Cats, On Your Toes* **1984:** *The Real Thing, La Cage aux Folles, Death of a Salesman* **1985:** *Biloxi Blues, Big River, Joe Egg* **1986:** *I'm Not Rappaport, The Mystery of Edwin Drood, Sweet Charity* **1987:** *Fences, Les Misérables, All My Sons* **1988:** *M. Butterfly, The Phantom of the Opera, Anything Goes* **1989:** *The Heidi Chronicles, Jerome Robbins' Broadway, Our Town* **1990:** *The Grapes of Wrath, City of Angels, Gypsy* **1991:** *Lost in Yonkers, The Will Rogers' Follies, Fiddler on the Roof* **1992:** *Dancing at Lughnasa, Crazy for You, Guys and Dolls* **1993:** *Angels in America: Millenium Approaches, Kiss of the Spider Woman, Anna Christie* **1994:** *Angels in America: Perestroika, Passion (musical), An Inspector Calls, Carousel* **1995:** *Love! Valour! Compassion!, Sunset Boulevard, Show Boat, The Heiress* **1996:** *Master Class, Rent, A Delicate Balance, The King and I* **1997:** *Last Night of Ballyhoo, Titanic, A Doll's House, Chicago* **1998:** *Art, The Lion King, View from the Bridge, Cabaret* **1999:** *Side Man, Fosse, Death of a Salesman, Annie Get Your Gun* **2000:** *Copenhagen, Contact, The Real Thing, Kiss Me, Kate* **2001:** *Proof, The Producers, One Flew Over the Cuckoo's Nest, 42nd Street* **2002:** *Edward Albee's The Goat, or Who Is Sylvia?, Thoroughly Modern Millie, Private Lives, Into the Woods* **2003:** *Take Me Out, Hairspray, Long Day's Journey Into Night, Nine the Musical* **2004:** *I Am My Own Wife, Avenue Q, Henry IV, Assassins* **2005:** *Doubt, Monty Python's Spamalot, Glengarry Glen Ross, La Cage aux Folles*

VILLAGE VOICE OBIE AWARDS

Monday, May 15, 2006 at the Skirball Center

51st annual; For outstanding achievement in Off-and Off-Off-Broadway theater:

Performance: Michael Cumpsty, *Hamlet;* Christine Ebersole, *Grey Gardens;* Ari Fliakos and Scott Shepherd, *Poor Theater: A Series of Simulacra;* Edwin Lee Gibson, *The Seven;* Peter Francis James and Byron Jennings, *Stuff Happens;* Marin Ireland, *Cyclone;* Dana Ivey, *Mrs. Warren's Profession;* Meg MacCary, *What Then;* S. Epatha Merkerson, *Birdie Blue;* Euan Morton, *Measure for Pleasure;* Sherie Rene Scott, *Landscape of the Body;* Lois Smith, *The Trip to Bountiful;* Julie White, *The Little Dog Laughed;* Gary Wilmes, *Red Light Winter;* Reed Birney, sustained excellence of performance

Direction: Daniel Sullivan, *Stuff Happens*; John Clancy, sustained excellence of direction

Playwriting: Rolin Jones, *The Intelligent Design of Jenny Chow;* Martin McDonagh, *The Lieutenant of Inishmore*

Design: The National Theater of the United States of America, *Abacus Black Strikes Now! The Rampant Justice of Abacus Black*; Allen Moyer, sustained excellence of set design; Anita Yavich, sustained excellence of costume design

Special Citations: Hunter Bell, Michael Berresse and Jeff Bowen, *[title of show]*; Ricky Ian Gordon, Jane Moss, Jon Nakagawa and Doug Varone, *Orpheus and Eurydice*; Danai Gurira, Robert O'Hara and Nikkole Salter, *In the Continuum*; Adam Rapp, *Red Light Winter*

Theater Grants: Billie Holiday Theatre, Edge Theater Company, Red Bull Theater

Emerging Playwright Grants: Neena Beber, Rinne Groff

Ross Wetzsteon Memorial Award: Soho Repertory Theater

Lifetime Achievement: Eric Bentley

PAST OBIE BEST NEW PLAY WINNERS

1956: *Absalom, Absalom* **1957:** *A House Remembered* **1958:** no award given **1959:** *The Quare Fellow* **1960:** no award given **1961:** *The Blacks* **1962:** *Who'll Save the Plowboy?* **1963:** no award given **1964:** *Play* **1965:** *The Old Glory* **1966:** *The Journey of the Fifth Horse* **1967:** no award given **1968:** no award given **1969:** no award given **1970:** *The Effect of Gamma Rays on Man-in-the-Moon Marigolds* **1971:** *House of Blue Leaves* **1972:** no award given **1973:** *The Hot L Baltimore* **1974:** *Short Eyes* **1975:** *The First Breeze of Summer* **1976:** *American Buffalo, Sexual Perversity in Chicago* **1977:** *Curse of the Starving Class* **1978:** *Shaggy Dog Animation* **1979:** *Josephine* **1980:** no award given **1981:** *FOB* **1982:** *Metamorphosis in Miniature, Mr. Dead and Mrs. Free* **1983:** *Painting Churches, Andrea Rescued, Edmond* **1984:** *Fool for Love* **1985:** *The Conduct of Life* **1986:** no award given **1987:** *The Cure, Film Is Evil, Radio Is Good* **1988:** *Abingdon Square* **1989:** no award given **1990:** *Prelude to a Kiss, Imperceptible Mutabilities in the Third Kingdom, Bad Benny, Crowbar, Terminal Hip* **1991:** *The Fever* **1992:** *Sight Unseen, Sally's Rape, The Baltimore Waltz* **1993:** no award given **1994:** *Twilight: Los Angeles 1992* **1995:** *Cryptogram* **1996:** *Adrienne Kennedy* **1997:** *One Flea Spare* **1998:** *Pearls for Pigs and Benita Canova* **1999:** no award given **2000:** no award given **2001:** *The Syringa Tree* **2002:** no award given **2003:** no award given **2004:** *Small Tragedy* **2005:** no award given **2006:** no award given

DRAMA DESK AWARDS

Sunday, May 21, 2006 at LaGuardia Concert Hall-Lincoln Center

51st annual, for outstanding achievement in the 2005–2006 season, voted on by an association of New York drama reporters, editors and critics including Barbara Siegel (Theatermania.com and TalkinBroadway.com), William Wolf (WolfEntertainmentGuide.com, Drama Desk President); Michael Buckley (*Playbill* On-Line), Christopher Byrne (*Gay City News*), Matthew Murray (TalkinBroadway.com, *Stage Directions*), Andrew Propst (American Theater Web, XM Satellite Radio), and Richard Ridge (Broadway Beat TV)

New Play: *The History Boys*

New Musical: *The Drowsy Chaperone*

Revival of a Play: *Awake and Sing!*

Revival of a Musical: *Sweeney Todd*

Book: Bob Martin and Don McKellar, *The Drowsy Chaperone*

Composer: Lisa Lambert and Greg Morrison, *The Drowsy Chaperone*

Lyricist: Lisa Lambert and Greg Morrison, *The Drowsy Chaperone*

Actor in a Play: Richard Griffiths, *The History Boys*

Actress in a Play: Lois Smith, *The Trip to Bountiful*

Featured Actor in a Play: Samuel Barnett, *The History Boys*

Featured Actress in a Play: Frances de la Tour, *The History Boys*

Actor in a Musical: John Lloyd Young, *Jersey Boys*

Actress in a Musical: Christine Ebersole, *Grey Gardens*

Featured Actor in a Musical: Jim Dale, *The Threepenny Opera*

Featured Actress in a Musical: Beth Leavel, *The Drowsy Chaperone*

Solo Performance: Antony Sher, *Primo*

Director of a Play: Nicholas Hytner, *The History Boys*

Director of a Musical: John Doyle, *Sweeney Todd*

Choreography: Kathleen Marshall, *The Pajama Game*

Orchestrations: Sarah Travis, *Sweeney Todd*

Set Design of a Play: Michael Yeargan, *Awake and Sing!*

Set Design of a Musical: David Gallo, *The Drowsy Chaperone*

Costume Design: Gregg Barnes, *The Drowsy Chaperone*

Lighting Design: Richard G. Jones, *Sweeney Todd*

Sound Design: Steve Canyon Kennedy, *Jersey Boys*

Unique Theatrical Experience: *Christine Jorgensen Reveals*

Outstanding Ensemble Performances: *Stuff Happens, Awake and Sing!*

Career Achievement Award: Horton Foote for his bountiful body of work that sensitively explores the human condition

Special Awards: BMI-Lehman Engel Musical Theater Workshop, The York Theatre Company, Sh-K-Boom and Ghostlight Records

OUTER CRITICS CIRCLE AWARDS

Thursday, May 25, 2006 at Sardi's

56th annual; For outstanding achievement in the 2005–2006 season, voted on by critics in out-of-town periodicals and media:

Broadway Play: *The History Boys*

Off-Broadway Play: *Stuff Happens*

Revival of a Play: *Awake and Sing!*

Actor in a Play: Gabriel Byrne, *A Touch of the Poet*

Actress in a Play: Lois Smith, *The Trip to Bountiful*

Featured Actor in a Play: Richard Griffiths, *The History Boys*

Featured Actress in a Play: Frances de la Tour, *The History Boys*

Director of a Play: Nicholas Hytner, *The History Boys*

Broadway Musical: *Jersey Boys*

Off-Broadway Musical: *Grey Gardens*

Outstanding New Score: *The Drowsy Chaperone*

Revival of a Musical: *Sweeney Todd*

Actor in a Musical: John'Lloyd Young, *Jersey Boys*

Actress in a Musical: Christine Ebersole, *Grey Gardens*

Featured Actor in a Musical: Jim Dale, *The Threepenny Opera*

Featured Actress in a Musical: Beth Leavel, *The Drowsy Chaperone*

Director of a Musical: John Doyle, *Sweeney Todd*

Choreography: Kathleen Marshall, *The Pajama Game*

Scenic Design: David Gallo, *The Drowsy Chaperone*

Costume Design: Gregg Barnes, *The Drowsy Chaperone*

Lighting Design: Howell Binkley, *Jersey Boys*

Solo Performance: Antony Sher, *Primo*

John Gassner Playwriting Award: Danai Gurira and Nikkole Salter, *In the Continuum*

PULITZER PRIZE AWARD WINNERS FOR DRAMA

1918: *Why Marry?* by Jesse Lynch Williams **1919:** no award **1920:** *Beyond the Horizon* by Eugene O'Neill **1921:** *Miss Lulu Bett* by Zona Gale **1922:** *Anna Christie* by Eugene O'Neill **1923:** *Icebound* by Owen Davis **1924:** *Hell-Bent for Heaven* by Hatcher Hughes **1925:** *They Knew What They Wanted* by Sidney Howard **1926:** *Craig's Wife* by George Kelly **1927:** *In Abraham's Bosom* by Paul Green **1928:** *Strange Interlude* by Eugene O'Neill **1929:** *Street Scene* by Elmer Rice **1930:** *The Green Pastures* by Marc Connelly **1931:** *Alison's House* by Susan Glaspell **1932:** *Of Thee I Sing* by George S. Kaufman, Morrie Ryskind, Ira and George Gershwin **1933:** *Both Your Houses* by Maxwell Anderson **1934:** *Men in White* by Sidney Kingsley **1935:** *The Old Maid* by Zoe Atkins **1936:** *Idiot's Delight* by Robert E. Sherwood

1937: *You Can't Take It with You* by Moss Hart and George S. Kaufman **1938:** *Our Town* by Thornton Wilder **1939:** *Abe Lincoln in Illinois* by Robert E. Sherwood **1940:** *The Time of Your Life* by William Saroyan **1941:** *There Shall Be No Night* by Robert E. Sherwood **1942:** no award **1943:** *The Skin of Our Teeth* by Thornton Wilder **1944:** no award **1945:** *Harvey* by Mary Chase **1946:** *State of the Union* by Howard Lindsay and Russel Crouse **1947:** no award **1948:** *A Streetcar Named Desire* by Tennessee Williams **1949:** *Death of a Salesman* by Arthur Miller **1950:** *South Pacific* by Richard Rodgers, Oscar Hammerstein II, and Joshua Logan **1951:** no award **1952:** *The Shrike* by Joseph Kramm **1953:** *Picnic* by William Inge **1954:** *The Teahouse of the August Moon* by John Patrick **1955:** *Cat on a Hot Tin Roof* by Tennessee Williams **1956:** *The Diary of Anne Frank* by Frances Goodrich and Albert Hackett **1957:** *Long Day's Journey Into Night* by Eugene O'Neill **1958:** *Look Homeward, Angel* by Ketti Frings **1959:** *J.B.* by Archibald MacLeish **1960:** *Fiorello!* by Jerome Weidman, George Abbott, Sheldon Harnick, and Jerry Bock **1961:** *All the Way Home* by Tad Mosel **1962:** *How to Succeed in Business Without Really Trying* by Abe Burrows, Willie Gilbert, Jack Weinstock, and Frank Loesser **1963:** no award **1964:** no award **1965:** *The Subject Was Roses* by Frank D. Gilroy **1966:** no award **1967:** *A Delicate Balance* by Edward Albee **1968:** no award **1969:** *The Great White Hope* by Howard Sackler **1970:** *No Place to Be Somebody* by Charles Gordone **1971:** *The Effect of Gamma Rays on Man-in-the-Moon Marigolds* by Paul Zindel **1972:** no award **1973:** *That Championship Season* by Jason Miller **1974:** no award **1975:** *Seascape* by Edward Albee **1976:** *A Chorus Line* by Michael Bennett, James Kirkwood, Nicholas Dante, Marvin Hamlisch, and Edward Kleban **1977:** *The Shadow Box* by Michael Cristofer **1978:** *The Gin Game* by D.L. Coburn **1979:** *Buried Child* by Sam Shepard **1980:** *Talley's Folly* by Lanford Wilson **1981:** *Crimes of the Heart* by Beth Henley **1982:** *A Soldier's Play* by Charles Fuller **1983:** *'night, Mother* by Marsha Norman **1984:** *Glengarry Glen Ross* by David Mamet **1985:** *Sunday in the Park with George* by James Lapine and Stephen Sondheim **1986:** no award **1987:** *Fences* by August Wilson **1988:** *Driving Miss Daisy* by Alfred Uhry **1989:** *The Heidi Chronicles* by Wendy Wasserstein **1990:** *The Piano Lesson* by August Wilson **1991:** *Lost in Yonkers* by Neil Simon **1992:** *The Kentucky Cycle* by Robert Schenkkan **1993:** *Angels in America: Millenium Approaches* by Tony Kushner **1994:** *Three Tall Women* by Edward Albee **1995:** *Young Man from Atlanta* by Horton Foote **1996:** *Rent* by Jonathan Larson **1997:** no award **1998:** *How I Learned to Drive* by Paula Vogel **1999:** *Wit* by Margaret Edson **2000:** *Dinner with Friends* by Donald Margulies **2001:** *Proof* by David Auburn **2002:** *Topdog/Underdog* by Suzan Lori-Parks **2003:** *Anna in the Tropics* by Nilo Cruz **2004:** *I Am My Own Wife* by Doug Wright **2005:** *Doubt* by John Patrick Shanley **2006:** No Award

NEW YORK DRAMA CRITICS' CIRCLE AWARD WINNERS

2006 New York Drama Critics' Circle Committee: President, Adam Feldman (*Time Out*), Clive Barnes (*The New York Post*), David Cote (*Time Out New York*), Michael Feingold (*The Village Voice*), Robert Feldberg (*The Bergen Record*), Elysa Gardner (*USA Today*), John Heilpern (*The New York Observer*), Howard Kissel (*Daily News*), Michael Kuchwara (The Associated Press), Jacques le Sourd (*Gannett Newspapers*), Jeremy McCarter (*The New York Sun*), David Rooney (*Variety*), Frank Scheck (*The Hollywood Reporter, New York Post*), David Sheward (*Back Stage*), John Simon (*Bloomberg news*), Michael Sommers (*The Star-Ledger/Newhouse* Newspapers), Terry Teachout (*The Wall Street Journal*), Linda Winer (*Newsday*), Richard Zoglin (*Time*)

Awards listed are in the following order: Best American Play, Best Foreign Play, Best Musical, and Best Regardless of Category, which was instituted during the 1962–1963 award season:

1936: *Winterset* **1937:** *High Tor* **1938:** *Of Mice and Men, Shadow and Substance* **1939:** *The White Steed* **1940:** *The Time of Your Life* **1941:** *Watch on the Rhine, The Corn Is Green* **1942:** *Blithe Spirit* **1943:** *The Patriots* **1944:** *Jacobowsky and the Colonel* **1945:** *The Glass Menagerie* **1946:** *Carousel* **1947:** *All My Sons, No Exit, Brigadoon* **1948:** *A Streetcar Named Desire, The Winslow Boy* **1949:** *Death of a Salesman, The Madwoman of Chaillot, South Pacific* **1950:** *The Member of the Wedding, The Cocktail Party, The Consul* **1951:** *Darkness at Noon, The Lady's Not for Burning, Guys and Dolls* **1952:** *I Am a Camera, Venus Observed, Pal Joey* **1953:** *Picnic, The Love of Four Colonels, Wonderful Town* **1954:** *Teahouse of the August Moon, Ondine, The Golden Apple* **1955:** *Cat on a Hot Tin Roof, Witness for the Prosecution, The Saint of Bleecker Street* **1956:** *The Diary of Anne Frank, Tiger at the Gates, My Fair Lady* **1957:** *Long Day's Journey into Night, The Waltz of the Toreadors, The Most Happy Fella* **1958:** *Look Homeward Angel, Look Back in Anger, The Music Man* **1959:** *A Raisin in the Sun, The Visit, La Plume de Ma Tante* **1960:** *Toys in the Attic, Five Finger Exercise, Fiorello!* **1961:** *All the Way Home, A Taste of Honey, Carnival* **1962:** *Night of the Iguana, A Man for All Seasons, How to Succeed in Business without Really Trying* **1963:** *Who's Afraid of Virginia Woolf?* **1964:** *Luther, Hello Dolly!* **1965:** *The Subject Was Roses, Fiddler on the Roof* **1966:** *The Persecution and Assassination of Marat as Performed by the Inmates of the Asylum of Charenton under the Direction of the Marquis de Sade, Man of La Mancha* **1967:** *The Homecoming, Cabaret* **1968:** *Rosencrantz and Guildenstern Are Dead, Your Own Thing* **1969:** *The Great White Hope, 1776* **1970:** *The Effect of Gamma Rays on Man-in-the-Moon Marigolds, Borstal Boy, Company* **1971:** *Home, Follies, The House of Blue Leaves* **1972:** *That Championship Season, Two Gentlemen of Verona* **1973:** *The Hot L Baltimore, The Changing Room, A Little Night Music* **1974:** *The Contractor, Short Eyes, Candide* **1975:** *Equus, The Taking of Miss Janie, A Chorus Line* **1976:** *Travesties, Streamers, Pacific Overtures* **1977:** *Otherwise Engaged, American Buffalo, Annie* **1978:** *Da, Ain't Misbehavin'* **1979:** *The Elephant Man, Sweeney Todd* **1980:** *Talley's Folly, Evita, Betrayal* **1981:** *Crimes of the Heart, A Lesson from Aloes, Special Citation to Lena Horne, The Pirates of Penzance* **1982:** *The Life and Adventures of Nicholas Nickleby, A Soldier's Play,* (no musical) **1983:** *Brighton Beach Memoirs, Plenty, Little Shop of Horrors* **1984:** *The Real Thing, Glengarry Glen Ross, Sunday in the Park with George* **1985:** *Ma Rainey's Black Bottom,* (no musical) **1986:** *A Lie of the Mind, Benefactors,* (no musical), Special Citation to Lily Tomlin and Jane Wagner **1987:** *Fences, Les Liaisons Dangereuses, Les Misérables* **1988:** *Joe Turner's Come and Gone, The Road to Mecca, Into the Woods* **1989:** *The Heidi Chronicles, Aristocrats, Largely New York* (special), (no musical) **1990:** *The Piano Lesson, City of Angels, Privates on Parade* **1991:** *Six Degrees of Separation, The Will Rogers Follies, Our Country's Good,* Special Citation to Eileen Atkins **1992:** *Two Trains Running, Dancing at Lughnasa* **1993:** *Angels in America: Millenium Approaches, Someone Who'll Watch Over Me, Kiss of the Spider Woman* **1994:** *Three Tall Women,* Anna Deavere Smith (special) **1995:** *Arcadia, Love! Valour! Compassion!,* Special Award: Signature Theatre Company **1996:** *Seven Guitars, Molly Sweeny, Rent* **1997:** *How I Learned to Drive, Skylight, Violet, Chicago* (special) **1998:** *Pride's Crossing, Art, The Lion King, Cabaret* (special) **1999:** *Wit, Parade, Closer,* David Hare (special) **2000:** *Jitney, James Joyce's The Dead, Copenhagen* **2001:** *The Invention of Love, The Producers, Proof* **2002:** *Edward Albee's The Goat, or Who is Sylvia?,* Special citation to Elaine Stritch for *Elaine Stritch at Liberty* **2003:** *Take Me Out, Talking Heads, Hairspray* **2004:** *Intimate Apparel* (Special citation to Barbara Cook for her contribution to the musical theatre) **2005:** *Doubt, The Pillowman* **2006:** *The History Boys, The Drowsy Chaperone,* John Doyle, Sarah Travis and the cast of *Sweeney Todd* (special), Christine Ebersole (special)

LUCILLE LORTEL AWARDS

Monday, May 1, 2006 at New World Stages

Presented by the League of Off-Broadway Theatres and Producers. The 2005–2006 awards committee consisted of Barrack Evans, Kurt Everhart, David Finkle, George Forbes, Walt Kiskaddon, Patrick Lee, Barbara Pasternack, Victor Pappas, Zachary Pincus-Roth, Jo Porter, Mark Rossier, Donald Saddler, David Savran, Tom Smedes, Barbara Wolkoff.

Play: *The Lieutenant of Inishmore,* by Martin McDonagh

Musical: *The Seven,* by Will Power

Outstanding Revival: *The Trip to Bountiful,* by Horton Foote

Actor: Tie: Christopher Denham, *Red Light Winter;* David Wilmot, *The Lieutenant of Inishmore*

Actress: Lois Smith, *The Trip to Bountiful*

Featured Actor: Charles Durning, *Third*

Featured Actress: Hallie Foote, *The Trip to Bountiful*

Direction: Harris Yulin, *The Trip to Bountiful*

Choreography: Bill T. Jones, *The Seven*

Scenery: Eugene Lee, *The Ruby Sunrise*

Costumes: Eric Becker, *Abigail's Party*

Lighting: Aaron Black, *Funnyhouse of a Negro*

Sound: Darron L. West, *The Seven*

Body of Work: Atlantic Theater Company

Edith Olivier Award: Betty Corwin

Playwrights Sidewalk Award: John Patrick Shanley

Lifetime Achievement Award: Wendy Wasserstein

PAST LUCILLE LORTEL AWARD WINNERS

Awards listed are Outstanding Play and Outstanding Musical, respectively, since inception

1986: *Woza Africa!;* no musical award **1987:** *The Common Pursuit;* no musical award **1988:** no play or musical award **1989:** *The Cocktail Hour;* no musical award **1990:** no play or musical award **1991:** *Aristocrats; Falsettoland* **1992:** *Lips Together, Teeth Apart; And the World Goes 'Round* **1993:** *The Destiny of Me; Forbidden Broadway* **1994:** *Three Tall Women; Wings* **1995:** *Camping with Henry & Tom; Jelly Roll!* **1996:** *Molly Sweeney; Floyd Collins* **1997:** *How I Learned to Drive; Violet* **1998:** (tie) *Gross Indecency* and *The Beauty Queen of Leenane;* no musical award **1999:** *Wit;* no musical award **2000:** *Dinner With Friends; James Joyce's The Dead* **2001:** *Proof; Bat Boy. The Musical* **2002:** *Metamorphoses; Urinetown* **2003:** *Take Me Out, Avenue Q* **2004:** *Bug; Caroline or Change* **2005:** *Doubt; The 25th Annual Putnam County Spelling Bee*

AMERICAN THEATRE CRITICS/STEINBERG NEW PLAY AWARDS AND CITATIONS

NEW PLAY CITATIONS

1977: *And the Soul Shall Dance* by Wakako Yamauchi **1978:** *Getting Out* by Marsha Norman **1979:** *Loose Ends* by Michael Weller **1980:** *Custer* by Robert E. Ingham **1981:** *Chekhov in Yalta* by John Driver and Jeffrey Haddow **1982:** *Talking With* by Jane Martin **1983:** *Closely Related* by Bruce MacDonald **1984:** *Wasted* by Fred Gamel **1985:** *Scheherazade* by Marisha Chamberlain

NEW PLAY AWARDS

1986: *Fences* by August Wilson **1987:** *A Walk in the Woods* by Lee Blessing **1988:** *Heathen Valley* by Romulus Linney **1989:** *The Piano Lesson* by August Wilson **1990:** *2* by Romulus Linney **1991:** *Two Trains Running* by August Wilson **1992:** *Could I Have This Dance* by Doug Haverty **1993:** *Children of Paradise: Shooting a Dream* by Steven Epp, Felicity Jones, Dominique Serrand, and Paul Walsh **1994:** *Keely and Du* by Jane Martin **1995:** *The Nanjing Race* by Reggie Cheong-Leen **1996:** *Amazing Grace* by Michael Cristofer **1997:** *Jack and Jill* by Jane Martin **1998:** *The Cider House Rules, Part II* by Peter Parnell **1999:** *Book of Days* by Lanford Wilson

ATCA/STEINBERG NEW PLAY AWARDS AND CITATIONS

2000: *Oo-Bla-Dee* by Regina Taylor; Citations: *Compleat Female Stage Beauty* by Jeffrey Hatcher; *Syncopation* by Allan Knee **2001:** *Anton in Show Business* by Jane Martin; Citations: *Big Love* by Charles L. Mee; *King Hedley II* by August Wilson **2002:** *The Carpetbagger's Children* by Horton Foote; Citations: *The Action Against Sol Schumann* by Jeffrey Sweet; *Joe and Betty* by Murray Mednick **2003:** *Anna in the Tropics* by Nilo Cruz; Citations: *Recent Tragic Events* by Craig Wright; *Resurrection Blues* by Arthur Miller **2004:** *Intimate Apparel* by Lynn Nottage; Citations: *Gem of the Ocean* by August Wilson; *The Love Song of J. Robert Oppenheimer* by Carson Kreitzer **2005:** *The Singing Forest* by Craig Lucas; Citations: *After Ashley* by Gina Gionfriddo; *The Clean House* by Sarah Ruhl; *Madagascar* by J.T. Rogers **2006:** *A Body of Water* by Lee Blessing; *Red Light Winter* by Adam Rapp; *Radio Golf* by August Wilson

CARBONELL AWARDS

Due to a change in the calendar season, The Carbonell Awards for 2006 were slated for April, 2007 to honor performances from September, 2005 – December, 2006. The 2006 awards will be listed in *Theatre World* Volume 63.

CLARENCE DERWENT AWARDS

61st annual; given to a female and male performer by Actors Equity Association, based on work in New York that demonstrates promise.

Felicia P. Fields; Jason Ritter

CONNECTICUT CRITICS' CIRCLE AWARDS

16th annual; For outstanding achievement in Connecticut theater during the 2005 – 2006 season:

Production of a Play: Long Wharf Theatre, *Underneath the Lintel*

Production of a Musical: Downtown Cabaret Theatre, *Sweet Charity*

Actress in a Play: Lynda Gravátt, *A Raisin in the Sun* (Hartford Stage)

Actor in a Play: Mark Nelson, *Underneath the Lintel* (Long Wharf Theatre)

Actress in a Musical: Ernestine Jackson, *Lady Day at Emerson's Bar and Grill* (Long Wharf Theatre)

Actor in a Musical: Bruce Connelly, *A Funny Thing Happened on the Way to the Forum* (Seven Angels Theatre)

Direction of a Play: Eric Ting, *Underneath the Lintel* (Long Wharf Theatre)

Direction of a Musical: Owen Thompson, *The Mikado* (River Rep)

Choreography: Scott Thompson, *Sweet Charity* (Downtown Cabaret Theatre)

Set Design: Tony Straiges, *The Learned Ladies of Park Avenue* (Hartford Stage)

Lighting Design: Clifton Taylor, *Journey's End* (Westport Country Playhouse)

Costume Design: Linda Fisher and Randall E. Klein, *David Copperfield* (Westport Country Playhouse)

Sound Design: Arielle Edwards, *dance of the holy ghosts* (Yale Rep)

Ensemble Performance: Curtis Billings, Mike Boland, Leon Addison Brown, Natalie Brown, Kevin Cutts, Robert Hannon Davis, Susan Fay, William Jay Marshall, Chandler Parker, Erica Tazel in *The Exonerated* (TheaterWorks)

Road Show: Hartford Stage, *2 Pianos 4 Hands* (Yale Rep)

Debut Award: Glenn Lawrence, *Li'l Abner* (Goodspeed Musials)

Tom Killen Memorial Award: The Connecticut Commission on Culture and Tourism

DRAMA LEAGUE AWARDS

72nd annual; For distinguished achievement in the American theater:

Play: *The History Boys*

Musical: *Jersey Boys*

Revival of a Play: *Awake and Sing!*

Revival of a Musical: *Sweeney Todd*

Performance: Norbert Leo Butz, *Dirty Rotten Scoundrels*

Julia Hansen Award for Excellence in Directing: Des McAnuff

Achievement in Musical Theatre: Patti LuPone

Unique Contribution to Theater: Marian Seldes

DRAMATIST GUILD AWARDS

Elizabeth Hull-Kate Warriner Award (to the playwright whose work deals with social, political or religious mores of the time): Adam Guettel and Craig Lucas, *The Light in the Piazza*

Frederick Loewe Award for Dramatic Composition: Harvey Schmidt

Flora Roberts Award: Robert Waldman

Lifetime Achievement: August Wilson

ELLIOTT NORTON AWARDS

24th annual; For outstanding contribution to the theater in Boston, voted by a Boston Theater Critics Association selection committee comprising Terry Byrne, Carolyn Clay, Iris Fanger, Joyce Kullhawik, Jon Lehman, Bill Marx, Ed Siegel and Caldwell Titcomb.

Sustained Excellence: Spiro Veloudos

Visiting Company: *Monty Python's Spamalot,* produced by Broadway in Boston

Large Resident Company: *Olly's Prison,* produced by American Repertory Theatre

Midsized Resident Company: *Five By Tenn,* produced by SpeakEasy Stage Company

Small Resident Company: *Arcadia,* Publick Theatre

Local Fringe Company: *P.S. Page Me Later,* produced by Alarm Clock Theatre Company

Actor: Large company: Bill Camp, *Olly's Prison;* Midsized company: Allyn Burrows, *The Homecoming, King Lear* and *Five By Tenn*

Actress: Large company: Karen McDonald, *Olly's Prison, No Exit;* Midsized company: Sandra Shipley, *Long Day's Journey Into Night*

Musical Production: *On the Twentieth Century,* produced by Overture Productions

Solo Performance: Jefferson Mays, *I Am My Own Wife*

Director: Large company: Brian McEleney, *Hamlet;* Small/Midsized company: Scott Edmiston, *Five By Tenn*

Set Design: Janie E. Howland, *Urinetown, Talley's Folly, True West* and *Five By Tenn*

Special Citations: Boston Conservatory for training musical theatre stars of tomorrow; CityStage for 30 years of work with children

Guest of Honor: William Finn

GEORGE FREEDLEY MEMORIAL AWARD

For the best book about live theater published in the United States the previous year; 2005 winner: *Charlotte: Being a True Account of An Actress's Flamboyant*

Adventures in Eighteenth-Century London's Wild and Wicked Theatrical World, by Kathryn Shevelow

Special Jury Prize: *Susan Glaspell: Her Life and Times,* by Linda Ben-Zvi

GEORGE JEAN NATHAN AWARD

For dramatic criticism; 2005–2006 winner: Charles Isherwood, The New York Times

GEORGE OPPENHEIMER AWARD

To the best new American playwright, presented by *Newsday*

2005–2006 winner: Elizabeth Meriwether for her play *Heddatron*

HELEN HAYES AWARDS

22nd annual; Presented by the Washington Theatre Awards Society in recognition of excellence in Washington, D.C.'s Warner Theater.

RESIDENT PRODUCTIONS

Play: *The Clean House,* produced by Woolly Mammoth Theatre Company

Musical: *Urinetown,* produced by Signature Theatre

Lead Actress, Musical: (tie) Erin Driscoll, *Urinetown;* Meg Gillentine, *Damn Yankees*

Lead Actor, Musical: Will Gartshore, *Urinetown*

Lead Actress, Play: Eunice Wong, *The Intelligent Design of Jenny Chow*

Lead Actor, Play: (tie) Rick Foucheux, *Take Me Out;* Patrick Page, *Othello*

Supporting Actress, Musical: Jenna Sokolowski, *Urinetown*

Supporting Actor, Musical: Stephen F. Schmidt, *Urinetown*

Supporting Actress, Play: Franca Barchiesi, *The Clean House*

Supporting Actor, Play: Bruce R. Nelson, *The Violet Hour*

Director, Play: Jay Zinoman, *A Number*

Director, Musical: Joe Calarco, *Urinetown*

Set Design, Play or Musical: Simon Higlett, *Lady Windermere's Fan*

Costume Design, Play or Musical: Robert Perdziola, *Lady Windermere's Fan*

Lighting Design, Play or Musical: Charlie Morrison, *Othello*

Sound Design, Play or Musical: Martin Desjardins, *columbinus*

Musical Direction, Play or Musical: Jay Crowder, *Urinetown*

Choreography: Karma Camp, *Urinetown*

NON-RESIDENT PRODUCTIONS

Production: *I Am My Own Wife* produced by The National Theatre

Lead Actress: Stephanie J. Block, *Wicked*

Lead Actor: Jefferson Mays, *I Am My Own Wife*

Charles MacArthur Award for Outstanding New Play: *Starving* by S. M. Shepherd-Massat

HENRY HEWES DESIGN AWARDS

For outstanding design originating in the U.S., selected by a committee comprising of Jeffrey Eric Jenkins (chair), Tish Dace, Michael Feingold, Glenda Frank, Mario Fratti, Randy Gener and Joan Ungaro; 2006 winners:

Scenic Design: Allen Moyer, *Grey Gardens*

Lighting Design: Howell Binkley, *Jersey Boys*

Costume Design: Anita Yavich, *Measure for Pleasure*

Notable Effects: Rupert Bohle (production design), *Cathay: Three Tales of China*; Stephen Kaplan, Wang Bo (puppetry), *Cathay: Three Tales of China*

JOSEPH JEFFERSON AWARDS

RESIDENT PRODUCTIONS

38th annual; for achievement in Chicago theater during the 2005–2006 season, given by the Jefferson Awards Committee in 28 competitive categories.

New Work, Play: *Voyeurs de Venus* by Lydia R. Diamond

New Work, Musical: *Loving Repeating: A Musical of Gertrude Stein* by Stephen Flaherty and Frank Galati

New Adaptation: (tie) *A Flea in Her Ear* by Chicago Shakespeare Theater; *The Old Curiosity Shop* by Raymond Fox, Heidi Stillman and Laura Eason

Production of a Play: Court Theatre, *Fences*

Production of a Musical: Court Theatre, *Man of La Mancha*

Production of a Revue: Northlight Theatre and Geva Theatre Center, *A Marvelous Party: The Noel Coward Celebration*

Director of a Play: Ron OJ Parson, *Fences*

Director of Musical: Charles Newell, *Court Theatre*

Director of a Revue: David Ira Goldstein, *A Marvelous Party: The Noel Coward Celebration*

Actor in a Principal Role, Play: A.C. Smith, *Fences*

Actress in a Principal Role, Play: Tie: Jacqueline Williams, *Fences*; Kristen Fitzgerald, *The Sea Horse*

Actor in a Supporting Role, Play: Rick Boynton, *A Flea in Her Ear*

Actress in a Supporting Role, Play: Ella Joyce, *Crumbs From the Table of Joy*

Actor in a Principal Role, Musical: Michael Buchanan, *Urinetown The Musical*

Actress in a Principal Role, Musical: Cindy Gold, *Loving Repeating: A Musical of Gertrude Stein*

Actor in a Supporting Role, Musical: Jeff Kuhl, *Grand Hotel, The Musical*

Actress in a Supporting Role, Musical: Barbara Robertson, *Grand Hotel, The Musical*

Actress in a Revue: Anna Lauris, *A Marvelous Party: The Noel Coward Celebration*

Actor in a Revue: Carl Danielsen, *A Marvelous Party: The Noel Coward Celebration*

Ensemble: *Man of La Mancha*, produced by Court Theatre

Scenic Design: John Culbert, *Man of La Mancha*

Costume Design: Mara Blumenfeld, *A Flea in Her Ear*

Lighting Design: Mark McCullough, *Man of La Mancha*

Sound Design: Mikhail Fiksel and Andre Pluess, *Blind Mouth Singing*

Choreography: Brian Loeffler, *Urinetown The Musical*

Original Incidental Music: (tie) Andre Pluess and Ben Sussman, *after the quake*; Alaric Jans and Lindsay Jones, *Henry IV, Parts 1 and 2*

Musical Direction: Doug Peck, *Man of La Mancha*

Solo Performance: Michael Patrick Thornton, *The Good Theif*

CITATIONS WING AWARDS

33rd annual; for outstanding achievement in professional productions during the 2005–2006 season of Chicago theaters not operating under union contracts:

Production, Play: *The Kentucky Cycle, Parts 1 & 2*, produced by Infamous Commonwealth Theatre

Production, Musical: *Kiss of the Spiderwoman*, produced by Bailiwick Repertory

Ensemble: *The Kentucky Cycle, Parts 1 & 2*, produced by Infamous Commonwealth Theatre

Director: Play: Jason Kae & Genevieve Thompson, *The Kentucky Cycle, Parts 1 & 2*; Jonathan Wilson, *Two Trains Running*; Musical: Susan Finque, *Kiss of the Spiderwoman*

New Work: Play: Margaret Lewis, *Fellow Travelers*; William C. Kovacsik, *The Masrayana*; Musical: Christina Calvit and George Howe, *Queen Lucia*

New Adaptation: Curt Columbus, *Three Sisters*; John Hildreth, *Lifeline Theatre*

Actress in a Principal Role: Play: Donna McGough, *Death of a Salesman*; Rebekah Ward-Hays, *The Skin of Our Teeth*; Musical: Monique Whittington, *Josephine Tonight!*

Actor in a Principal Role: Play: Alfred H. Wilson, *Two Trains Running*; Jürgen Hooper, *What's Wrong with Angry?*; Paul D'Addario, *Hurlyburly*; Paul Noble, *True West*; Musical: Ryan Lanning, *Kiss of the Spiderwoman*; Stan Q. Wash, *Kiss of the Spiderwoman*

Actress in a Supporting Role: Play: Millie Hurley Spencer, *Dancing at Lughnasa*; Musical: Danielle Brothers, *A Jacques Brel Revue: Songs of Love and War*

Actor in a Supporting Role: Play: Eric Hoffmann, *Loose Knit*; Rian Jairell, *The Kentucky Cycle, Parts 1 & 2*; Musical: Stephen Feder, *I Sing!*

Scenic Design: Brian Sidney Bembridge, *Three Sisters*; Jack Magaw, *Two Trains Running*

Costume Design: Alison Siple, *Time and the Conways*; Laura M. Dana, *Seascape*

Lighting Design: Jared Moore, *Kiss of the Spiderwoman*

Sound Design: Michael Griggs and Mikhail Fiksel, *Angels in America, Part One: Millennium Approaches*

Projections Design: Mike Tutaj, *Martin Furey's Shot*

Choreography: Brenda Didier, *Kiss of the Spiderwoman*

Original Incidental Music: Nikhil Trivedi, *The Masrayana*

Musical Direction: Kevin O'Donnell, *Valentine Victorious*; Robert Ollis, *Kiss of the Spiderwoman*

Fight Design: Geoff Coates, *The Talisman Ring*

JOSEPH KESSELRING PRIZE

National Arts Club member Joseph Otto Kesselring was born in New York in 1902. He was an actor, author, producer, and playwright. Mr. Kesselring died in 1967, leaving his estate in a trust which terminated in 1978 when the life beneficiary died. A bequest was made to the Nation Arts Club "on condition that said bequest be used to establish a fund to be known as the Joseph Kesselring Fund, the income and principal of which shall be used to give financial aid to playwrights, on such a basis of selection and to such as the National Arts Club may, in its sole discretion, determine."

A committee appointed by the president and the governors of the National Arts Club administers the Kesselring Prizes. It approves monetary prizes annually to playwrights nominated by qualified production companies whose dramatic work has demonstrated the highest possible merit and promise and is deserving of greater recognition, but who as yet has not received prominent national notice or acclaim in the theater. The winners are chosen by a panel of judges who are independent of the Club. In addition to a cash prize, the first prize winner also receives a staged reading of a work of his or her choice. The Kesselring Prize Committee: O. Aldon James, Stanley Morton Ackert III, Arnold J. Davis, Michael Parva, Jason deMontmorency, Dary Derchin, Alexandra Roosevelt Dworkin, John T. James, Raymond Knowles.

2006: Mark Schultz **2005:** Deb Margolin **2004:** Tracey Scott Wilson **2003:** Bridget Carpenter **2002:** Melissa James Gibson **2001:** David Lindsay-Abaire **2000:** David Auburn **1999:** Heather McDonald **1998:** Kira Obolensky **1997:** No Award **1996:** Naomi Wallace **1995:** Amy Freed, Doug Wright **1994:** Nicky Silver **1993:** Anna Deavere Smith **1992:** Marion Isaac McClinton **1991:** Tony Kushner **1990:** Elizabeth Egloff, Mel Shapiro **1989:** Jo Carson **1988:** Diane Ney **1987:** Paul Schmidt **1986:** Marlane Meyer **1985:** Bill Elverman **1984:** Philip Kan Gotanda **1983:** Lynn Alvarez **1982:** No Award **1981:** Cheryl Hawkins **1980:** Susan Charlotte

HONORABLE MENTIONS

2006: Bruce Norris **2005:** Tanya Barfield **2004:** John Borello **2003:** Lynn Nottage **2002:** Lydia Diamond **2001:** Dael Orlandersmith **2000:** Jessica Hagedorn **1999:** Stephen Dietz **1998:** Erik Ehn **1997:** Kira Obolensky, Edwin Sanchez **1996:** Nilo Cruz **1993:** Han Ong **1992:** JosÈ Rivera **1991:** Quincy Long, Scott McPherson **1990:** Howard Korder **1989:** Keith Reddin **1988:** Jose Rivera, Frank Hogan **1987:** Januzsz Glowacki **1986:** John Leicht **1985:** Laura Harrington **1983:** Constance Congdon **1981:** William Hathaway **1980:** Carol Lashof

KENNEDY CENTER

HONORS

28th annual; For distinguished achievement by individuals who have made significant contributions to American culture through the arts: Tony Bennett, Suzanne Farrell, Julie Harris, Robert Redford and Tina Turner

MARK TWAIN PRIZE

9th annual; For American humor:

Neil Simon

M. ELIZABETH OSBORN AWARD

Presented to an emerging playwright by the American Theatre Critics Association; 2005 winner: Steven Tomlinson, *American Fiesta*

MUSICAL THEATER HALL OF FAME

This organization was established at New York University on November 10, 1993.

Harold Arlen; Irving Berlin; Leonard Bernstein; Eubie Blake; Abe Burrows; George M. Cohan; Betty Comden; Dorothy Fields; George Gershwin; Ira Gershwin; Adolph Green; Oscar Hammerstein II; E.Y. Harburg; Larry Hart; Jerome Kern; Burton Lane; Alan Jay Lerner; Frank Loesser; Frederick Loewe; Mary Martin; Ethel Merman; Cole Porter; Jerome Robbins; Richard Rodgers; Harold Rome.

NATIONAL MEDALS OF THE ARTS

For individuals and organizations who have made outstanding contributions to the excellence, growth, support, and availability of the arts in the United States, selected by the President of the United States from nominees presented by the National Endowment; 2005 winners:

Louis Auchincloss, James DePreist, Paquito D'Rivera, Robert Duvall, Leonard Garment, Ollie Johnston, Wynton Marsalis, Dolly Parton, Pennsylvania Academy of the Fine Arts, Tina Ramirez

NEW YORK INNOVATIVE THEATRE AWARDS

Given annually to honor individuals and organizations who have achieved artistic excellence in the Off-Off-Broadway theatre. The New York IT Awards committee recognizes the unique and essential role Off-Off-Broadway plays in contributing to American and global culture, and believes that publicly recognizing excellence in independent theatre will expand audience awareness and appreciation of the full New York theatre experience. Staff: Jason Bowcutt, Executive Director; Shay Gines, Executive Director; Nick Micozzi, Executive Director; Awards Committee: Paul Adams (Artistic Director, Emerging Artists Theatre), Dan Bacalzo (Managing Editor, TheatreMania), Christopher Borg (Actor, Director), Jason Bowcutt (Executive Director, New York IT Awards), Tim Errickson (Artistic Director, Bommerang Theatre Co.), Thecla Farrell (Outreach Coordinator, Castillo Theatre Co.), Constance Congdon (Playwright), Shay Gines (Executive Director, New York IT Awards), Ben Hodges (Executive Producer, Theatre World Awards, Inc.), Leonard Jacobs (National Theatre Editor, Back Stage), Ron Lasko (Public Relations, Spin Cycle), Blake Lawrence, Bob Lee, Nick Micozzi (Executive Director, New York IT Awards), Risa Shoup, (Programming Director, Chashama), Nicky Paraiso (Curator for Performance, LaMaMa), Jeff Riebe (The January Initiative), Akia Squiterri (Artistic Director, Rising Sun Performance Company).

Outstanding Actor in a Featured Role: Trey Gibbons, *How I Learned to Drive,* produced by T. Schreiber Studio

Outstanding Actress in a Featured Role: Summer Crockett Moore, *Last Summer at Bluefish Cove,* produced by T. Schreiber Studio

Outstanding Solo Performance: Margaux Laskey, *size ate,* produced by size ate productions

Outstanding Original Short Script: Vishakan Jeyakuma, *Jaffna Mangoes,* produced by Seven 11 Convenience Theatre, Desipina & Compnay

Outstanding Original Full-Length Script: Bekah Brunstetter, *To Nineveh: A Modern Miracle,* produced by Working Man's Clothes

Outstanding Original Music: Brendan Connelly, *Major Barbara,* produced by La MaMa E.T.C. in association with Two-Headed Calf

Outstanding Choreography/Movement: Marius Hanford, *Living Dead In Denmark,* produced by Vampire Cowboys Theatre Company

Outstanding Sound Design: Paul John DeSena, *To Nineveh: A Modern Miracle,* produced by Working Man's Clothes

Outstanding Costume Design: Sidney Shannon, *Iron Curtain,* produced by Prospect Theater Company

Outstanding Lighting Design: Arthur Adair, *The Emperor Jones,* produced by La MaMa E.T.C.

Outstanding Set Design: Eddy Trotter, *Love! Valour! Compassion!,* produced by T. Schreiber Studio

Outstanding Actress in a Lead Role: Ellen David, *To Nineveh: A Modern Miracle,* produced by Working Man's Clothes

Outstanding Actor in a Lead Role: Greg Horton, *The Singapore Mikado,* produced by Theatre Ten Ten

Outstanding Director: Isaack Byrne, *To Nineveh: A Modern Miracle,* produced by Working Man's Clothes

Outstanding Ensemble: *To Nineveh: A Modern Miracle,* produced by Working Man's Clothes-David Carr-Berry, Jared Culverhouse, Ellen David, Paul Fears, Andaye' Hill, Julian James, Gregory Porter Miller, Brian Schlanger

Outstanding Performance Art Production: *Too Much Light Makes The Baby Go Blind,* produced by New York Neo-Futurists

Outstanding Production of a Musical: *Iron Curtain,* produced by Prospect Theater Company

Outstanding Production of a Play: *To Nineveh: A Modern Miracle,* produced by Working Man's Clothes

2006 HONORARY AWARDS

The 2006 Artistic Achievement Award for significant artistic contribution to the Off-Off-Broadway community was presented to Tom O'Horgan

The 2006 Stewardship Award for significant contribution to the Off-Off-Broadway community through service, support and leadership was presented to The Field

The Caffe Cino Fellowship Award for consistent production of outstanding work includes a grant of $1,000 to be used toward an Off-Off-Broadway production, was presented to The Vampire Cowboys Theatre Company

NEW DRAMATISTS LIFETIME ACHIEVEMENT AWARD

To an individual who has made an outstanding artistic contribution to the American theater; 2006 winner: Chita Rivera

OVATION AWARDS

Established in 1989, the L.A. Stage Alliance Ovation Awards are Southern California's premiere awards for excellence in theatre; 2006 winners:

World Premiere Play: *Zero Hour,* Jim Brochu, produced by West Coast Jewish Theatre

World Premiere Musical: *The Break Up Notebook: The Lesbian Musical,* by Patricia Cotter, Lori Scarlett, and Rose Marcario

Lead Actor in a Play: Charlie Robinson, *Fences*

Lead Actress in a Play: Laurie Metcalf, *All My Sons*

Lead Actor in a Musical: Bob Martin, *The Drowsy Chaperone*

Lead Actress in a Musical: Sutton Foster, *The Drowsy Chaperone*

Featured Actor in a Play: Dakin Matthews, *Water & Power*

Featured Actress in a Play: Dale Dickey, *Southern Baptist Sissies*

Featured Actor in a Musical: Stephen Breithaupt, *It Came From Beyond*

Featured Actress in a Musical: Harriet Harris, *On The Town*

Solo Performance: Jay Johnson, *Jay Johnson: The Two and Only!*

Ensemble Performance: *The Trials and Tribulations of a Trailer Trash Housewife,* Del Shores, Jason Dottley and Zephyr Theatre

Director of a Play: Ben Bradley, *Joe Turner's Come and Gone*

Director of a Musical: Casey Nicholaw, *The Drowsy Chaperone*

Choreographer: Dana Solimando, *Swing!*

Musical Direction: Gerald Sternbach, *Zorba*

Play: (intimate theatre): *Joe Turner's Come and Gone*; (large theatre): *All My Sons*

Musical: (intimate theatre): *Gorey Stories*; (large theatre): *The Drowsy Chaperone*

Set Design: (intimate theatre): Dana Moran Williams, *Elizabeth Rex*; (large theatre): James Noone, *Dead End*; David Gallo, *The Drowsy Chaperone*

Lighting Design: (intimate theatre): Luke Moyer, *Elizabeth Rex*; (large theatre): Robert Wilson, *The Black Rider: The Casting of the Magic Bullets*

Sound Design: (intimate theatre): Christopher Burns, *The Lion in Winter*; (large theatre): David O, *Ubi Roi*

Costume Design: (intimate theatre): A. Jeffrey Schoenberg, *Elizabeth Rex*; (large theatre): Leon Wiebers, *Ubi Roi*

The Career Achievement Award: Jerry Herman

Community Outreach Award: California Institute of the Arts Community Arts Partnership (CAP)

RICHARD RODGERS AWARDS

For staged readings of musicals in nonprofit theaters, administered by the American Academy of Arts and Letters and selected by a jury including Stephen Sondheim (chairman), Lynn Ahrens, John Guare, Sheldon Harnick, Jeanine Tesori, and John Weidman

2006 winners: *Grey Gardens,* Scott Frankel, Michael Korie and Doug Wright; *The Yellow Wood,* Michelle Elliott and Danny Larsen; *True Fans,* Chris Miller, Bill Rosenfield and Nathan Tysen

ROBERT WHITEHEAD AWARD

For outstanding achievement in commercial theatre producing, bestowed on a graduate of the fourteen-week Commercial Theatre Institute Program who has demonstrated a quality of production exemplified by the late producer, Robert Whitehead.

The Commercial Theatre Institute, Frederic B. Vogel, director, is the nation's only formal program which professionally trains commercial theatre producers. It is a joint project of the League of American Theatres and Producers, Inc., and Theatre Development Fund.

2005: No Award **2004:** David Binder **2001–2003:** No Award **2000:** Anne Strickland Squadron **1999:** Eric Krebs **1998:** Liz Oliver **1997:** Marc Routh **1996:** Randall L. Wreghitt **1995:** Kevin McCollum **1994:** Dennis Grimaldi **1993:** Susan Quint Gallin; Benjamin Mordecai

SUSAN SMITH BLACKBURN PRIZE

28th annual; For women who have written works of outstanding quality for the English-speaking theater: Amelia Bullmore, *Mammals*

WILLIAM INGE THEATRE FESTIVAL AWARD

25th annual, presented in Independence, Kansas, April 26–29, 2006

For distinguished achievement in American theater: Reunion of all past honorees: Tina Howe (2005), Arthur Laurents (2004), Romulus Linney (2003), John Kander and Fred Ebb (2002), Lanford Wilson (2001), A.R. Gurney (2000), John Guare, (1999), Stephen Sondheim (1998), Neil Simon (1997), August Wilson (1996), Arthur Miller (1995), Terrence McNally (1994), Wendy Wasserstein (1993), Peter Shaffer (1992), Edward Albee (1991), Betty Comden and Adolph Green (1990), Horton Foote (1989), Sidney Kingsley (1988), Garson Kanin (1987), John Patrick (1986), Robert Anderson (1985), William Gibson (1984), Jerome Lawrence (1983), William Inge (1982)

New Voice: Melanie Marnich

THE THEATER HALL OF FAME

The Theater of Hall of Fame was created in 1971 to honor those who have made outstanding contributions to the American theater in a career spanning at least twenty-five years, with at least five major credits.

The following were honorees inducted January 30, 2006:

Graciela Daniele; Ben Edwards; William Gibson; Sir Peter Hall; John Lithgow; William Ivey Long; Dorothy Loudon; Sada Thompson

George Abbott; Maude Adams; Viola Adams; Stella Adler; Edward Albee; Theoni V. Aldredge; Ira Aldridge; Jane Alexander; Mary Alice; Winthrop Ames; Judith Anderson; Maxwell Anderson; Robert Anderson; Julie Andrews; Margaret Anglin; Jean Anouilh; Harold Arlen; George Arliss; Boris Aronson; Adele Astaire; Fred Astaire; Eileen Atkins; Brooks Atkinson; Lauren Bacall; Pearl Bailey; George Balanchine; William Ball; Anne Bancroft; Tallulah Bankhead; Richard Barr; Philip Barry; Ethel Barrymore; John Barrymore; Lionel Barrymore; Howard Bay; Nora Bayes; John Lee Beatty; Julian Beck; Samuel Beckett; Brian Bedford; S.N. Behrman; Norman Bel Geddes; David Belasco; Michael Bennett; Richard Bennett; Robert Russell Bennett; Eric Bentley; Irving Berlin; Sarah Bernhardt; Leonard Bernstein; Earl Blackwell; Kermit Bloomgarden; Jerry Bock; Ray Bolger; Edwin Booth; Junius Brutus Booth; Shirley Booth; Philip Bosco; Alice Brady; Bertolt Brecht; Fannie Brice; Peter Brook; John Mason Brown; Robert Brustein; Billie Burke; Abe Burrows; Richard Burton; Mrs. Patrick Campbell; Zoe Caldwell; Eddie Cantor; Len Cariou; Morris Carnovsky; Mrs. Leslie Carter; Gower Champion; Frank Chanfrau; Carol Channing; Stockard Channing; Ruth Chatterton; Paddy Chayefsky; Anton Chekhov; Ina Claire; Bobby Clark; Harold Clurman; Lee. J. Cobb; Richard L. Coe; George M. Cohan; Alexander H. Cohen; Jack Cole; Cy Coleman; Constance Collier; Alvin Colt; Betty Comden; Marc Connelly; Barbara Cook; Katherine Cornell; Noel Coward; Jane Cowl; Lotta Crabtree; Cheryl Crawford; Hume Cronyn; Russel Crouse; Charlotte Cushman; Jean Dalrymple; Augustin Daly; E.L. Davenport; Gordon Davidson; Ossie Davis; Ruby Dee; Alfred De Liagre Jr.; Agnes DeMille;

Colleen Dewhurst; Howard Dietz; Dudley Digges; Melvyn Douglas; Eddie Dowling; Alfred Drake; Marie Dressler; John Drew; Mrs. John Drew; William Dunlap; Mildred Dunnock; Charles Durning; Eleanora Duse; Jeanne Eagles; Fred Ebb; Florence Eldridge; Lehman Engel; Maurice Evans; Abe Feder; Jose Ferber; Cy Feuer; Zelda Fichandler; Dorothy Fields; Herbert Fields; Lewis Fields; W.C. Fields; Jules Fischer; Minnie Maddern Fiske; Clyde Fitch; Geraldine Fitzgerald; Henry Fonda; Lynn Fontanne; Horton Foote; Edwin Forrest; Bob Fosse; Rudolf Friml; Charles Frohman; Robert Fryer; Athol Fugard; John Gassner; Larry Gelbart; Peter Gennaro; Bernard Gersten; Grace George; George Gershwin; Ira Gershwin; John Gielgud; W.S. Gilbert; Jack Gilford; William Gillette; Charles Gilpin; Lillian Gish; John Golden; Max Gordon; Ruth Gordon; Adolph Green; Paul Green; Charlotte Greenwood; Jane Greenwood; Joel Grey; Tammy Grimes; George Grizzard; John Guare; Otis L. Guernsey Jr.; A.R. Gurney; Tyrone Guthrie; Uta Hagen; Lewis Hallam; T. Edward Hambleton; Oscar Hammerstein II; Walter Hampden; Otto Harbach; E.Y. Harburg; Sheldon Harnick; Edward Harrigan; Jed Harris; Julie Harris; Rosemary Harris; Sam H. Harris; Rex Harrison; Kitty Carlisle Hart; Lorenz Hart; Moss Hart; Tony Hart; June Havoc; Helen Hayes; Leland Hayward; Ben Hecht; Eileen Heckart; Theresa Helburn; Lillian Hellman; Katharine Hepburn; Victor Herbert; Jerry Herman; James A. Herne; Henry Hewes; Gregory Hines; Al Hirschfeld; Raymond Hitchcock; Hal Holbrook; Celeste Holm; Hanya Holm; Arthur Hopkins; De Wolf Hopper; John Houseman; Eugene Howard; Leslie Howard; Sidney Howard; Willie Howard; Barnard Hughes; Henry Hull; Josephine Hull; Walter Huston; Earle Hyman; Henrik Ibsen; William Inge; Bernard B. Jacobs; Elise Janis; Joseph Jefferson; Al Jolson; James Earl Jones; Margo Jones; Robert Edmond Jones; Tom Jones; Jon Jory; Raul Julia; Madeline Kahn; John Kander; Garson Kanin; George S. Kaufman; Danny Kaye; Elia Kazan; Gene Kelly; George Kelly; Fanny Kemble; Jerome Kern; Walter Kerr; Michael Kidd; Richard Kiley; Sidney Kingsley; Kevin Kline; Florence Klotz; Joseph Wood Krutch; Bert Lahr; Burton Lane; Frank Langella; Lawrence Langner; Lillie Langtry; Angela Lansbury; Charles Laughton; Arthur Laurents; Gertrude Lawrence; Jerome Lawrence; Eva Le Gallienne; Ming Cho Lee; Robert E. Lee; Lotte Lenya; Alan Jay Lerner; Sam Levene; Robert Lewis; Beatrice Lillie; Howard Lindsay; Frank Loesser; Frederick Loewe; Joshua Logan; Santo Loquasto; Pauline Lord; Lucille Lortel; Alfred Lunt; Charles MacArthur; Steele MacKaye; Judith Malina; David Mamet; Rouben Mamoulian; Richard Mansfield; Robert B. Mantell; Frederic March; Nancy Marchand; Julia Marlowe; Ernest H. Martin; Mary Martin; Raymond Massey; Elizabeth Ireland McCann; Ian McKellen; Siobhan McKenna; Terrence McNally; Helen Menken; Burgess Meredith; Ethel Merman; David Merrick; Jo Mielziner; Arthur Miller; Marilyn Miller; Liza Minnelli; Helena Modjeska; Ferenc Molnar; Lola Montez; Victor Moore; Robert Morse; Zero Mostel; Anna Cora Mowatt; Paul Muni; Brian Murray; Tharon Musser; George Jean Nathan; Mildred Natwick; Nazimova; Patricia Neal; James M. Nederlander; Mike Nichols; Elliot Norton; Sean O'Casey; Clifford Odets; Donald Oenslager; Laurence Olivier; Eugene O'Neill; Jerry Orbach; Geraldine Paige; Joseph Papp; Estelle Parsons; Osgood Perkins; Bernadette Peters; Molly Picon; Harold Pinter; Luigi Pirandello; Christopher Plummer; Cole Porter; Robert Preston; Harold Prince; Jose Quintero; Ellis Rabb; John Raitt; Tony Randall; Michael Redgrave; Ada Rehan; Elmer Rice; Lloyd Richards; Ralph Richardson; Chita Rivera; Jason Robards; Jerome Robbins; Paul Robeson; Richard Rodgers; Will Rogers; Sigmund Romberg; Harold Rome; Lillian Russell; Donald Saddler; Gene Saks; William Saroyan; Joseph Schildkraut; Harvey Schmidt; Alan Schnider; Gerald Shoenfeld; Arthur Schwartz; Maurice Schwartz; George

C. Scott; Marian Seldes; Irene Sharaff; George Bernard Shaw; Sam Shepard; Robert F. Sherwood; J.J. Shubert; Lee Shubert; Herman Shumlin; Neil Simon; Lee Simonson; Edmund Simpson; Otis Skinner; Maggie Smith; Oliver Smith; Stephen Sondheim; E.H. Sothern; Kim Stanley; Jean Stapleton; Maureen Stapleton; Frances Sternhagen; Roger L. Stevens; Isabelle Stevenson; Ellen Stewart; Dorothy Stickney; Fred Stone; Peter Stone; Tom Stoppard; Lee Strasburg; August Strindberg; Elaine Stritch; Charles Strouse; Jule Styne; Margaret Sullivan; Arthur Sullivan; Jessica Tandy; Laurette Taylor; Ellen Terry; Tommy Tune; Gwen Verdon; Robin Wagner; Nancy Walker; Eli Wallach; James Wallack; Lester Wallack; Tony Walton; Douglas Turner Ward; David Warfield; Ethel Waters; Clifton Webb; Joseph Weber; Margaret Webster; Kurt Weill; Orson Welles; Mae West; Robert Whitehead; Richard Wilbur; Oscar Wilde; Thorton Wilder; Bert Williams; Tennessee Williams; Landford Wilson; P.G. Wodehouse; Peggy Wood; Alexander Woollcott; Irene Worth; Teresa Wright; Ed Wynn; Vincent Youmans; Stark Young; Florenz Ziegfeld; Patricia Zipprodt

FOUNDERS AWARD

Established in 1993 in honor of Earl Blackwell, James M. Nederlander, Gerald Oestreicher and Arnold Weissberger, the Theater Hall of Fame Founders Award is voted by the Hall's board of directors to an individual for his of her outstanding contribution to the theater:

1993: James M. Nederlander **1994:** Kitty Carlisle Hart **1995:** Harvey Sabinson **1996:** Henry Hewes **1997:** Otis L. Guernsey Jr. **1998:** Edward Colton **1999:** no award **2000:** Gerard Oestreicher, Arnold Weissberger **2001:** Tom Dillon **2002:** No Award **2003:** Price Berkley **2004:** No Award **2005:** Donald Seawell

MARGO JONES CITIZEN OF THE THEATER MEDAL

Presented annually to a citizen of the theater who has made a lifetime commitment to theater in the United States and has demonstrated an understanding and affirmation of the craft of playwriting:

1961: Lucille Lortel **1962:** Michael Ellis **1963:** Judith Rutherford Marechal; George Savage (university award) **1964:** Richard Barr, Edward Albee, and Clinton Wilder; Richard A. Duprey (university award) **1965:** Wynn Handman; Marston Balch (university award) **1966:** Jon Jory; Arthur Ballet (university award) **1967:** Paul Baker; George C. White (workshop award) **1968:** Davey Marlin-Jones; Ellen Stewart (workshop award) **1969:** Adrian Hall; Edward Parone and Gordon Davidson (workshop award) **1970:** Joseph Papp **1971:** Zelda Fichandler **1972:** Jules Irving **1973:** Douglas Turner Ward **1974:** Paul Weidner **1975:** Robert Kalfin **1976:** Gordon Davidson **1977:** Marshall W. Mason **1978:** Jon Jory **1979:** Ellen Stewart **1980:** John Clark Donahue **1981:** Lynne Meadow **1982:** Andre Bishop **1983:** Bill Bushnell **1984:** Gregory Mosher **1985:** John Lion **1986:** Lloyd Richards **1987:** Gerald Chapman **1988:** no award **1989:** Margaret Goheen **1990:** Richard Coe **1991:** Otis L. Guernsey Jr. **1992:** Abbot Van Nostrand **1993:** Henry Hewes **1994:** Jane Alexander **1995:** Robert Whitehead **1996:** Al Hirschfeld **1997:** George C. White **1998:** James Houghton **1999:** George Keathley **2000:** Eileen Heckart **2001:** Mel Gussow **2002:** Emilie S. Kilgore **2003–2004:** Christopher Durang and Marsha Norman **2005-2006:** Jerome Lawrence and Robert E. Lee

Longest-Running Shows on **Broadway**

LONGEST-RUNNING SHOWS ON BROADWAY

*Production is still running as of May 31, 2006, and performance count includes performances up to that date.
Phantom of the Opera became the longest running show in Broadway history on Monday, January 9, 2006.

PHANTOM OF THE OPERA*
7,649 performances
Opened January 26, 1988

CATS
7,485 performances
Opened October 7, 1982; Closed September 10, 2000

LES MISÉRABLES
6,680 performances
Opened March 12, 1987; Closed May 18, 2003

A CHORUS LINE
6,137 performances
Opened July 25, 1975; Closed April 28, 1990

OH! CALCUTTA (REVIVAL)
5,959 performances
Opened September 24, 1976; Closed August 6, 1989

BEAUTY AND THE BEAST*
4,978 performances
Opened April 18, 1994

RENT*
4,211 performances
Opened April 29, 1996

MISS SAIGON
4,097 performances
Opened April 11, 1991; Closed January 28, 2001

CHICAGO (REVIVAL)*
3964 performances
Opened November 19, 1996

THE LION KING*
3,596 performances
Opened November 13, 1997

42ND STREET
3,486 performances
Opened August 25, 1980; Closed January 8, 1989

GREASE
3,388 performances
Opened February 14, 1972; Closed April 13, 1980

FIDDLER ON THE ROOF
3,242 performances
Opened September 22, 1964; Closed July 2, 1972

LIFE WITH FATHER
3,224 performances
Opened November 8, 1939; Closed July 12, 1947

TOBACCO ROAD
3,182 performances
Opened December 4, 1933; Closed May 31, 1941

HELLO, DOLLY!
2,844 performances
Opened January 16, 1964; Closed December 27, 1970

MY FAIR LADY
2,717 performances
Opened March 15, 1956; Closed September 29, 1962

CABARET (1998 REVIVAL)
2,378 performances
Opened March 19, 1998; Closed January 4, 2004

ANNIE
2,377 performances
Opened April 21, 1977; Closed January 22, 1983

MAN OF LA MANCHA
2,328 performances
Opened November 22, 1965; Closed June 26, 1971

ABIE'S IRISH ROSE
2,327 performances
Opened May 23, 1922; Closed October 21, 1927

THE PRODUCERS*
2,129 performances
Opened April 19, 2001

OKLAHOMA!
2,212 performances
Opened March 31, 1943; Closed May 29, 1948

SMOKEY JOE'S CAFÉ
2,036 performances
Opened March 2, 1995; Closed January 16, 2000

MAMMA MIA!*
1,934 performances
Opened October 12, 2001

PIPPIN
1,944 performances
Opened October 23, 1972; Closed June 12, 1977

SOUTH PACIFIC
1,925 performances
Opened April 7, 1949; Closed January 16, 1954

THE MAGIC SHOW
1,920 performances
Opened May 28, 1974; Closed December 31, 1978

AIDA
1,852 performances
Opened March 23, 2000; Closed September 5, 2004

GEMINI
1,819 performances
Opened May 21, 1977; Closed September 6, 1981

DEATHTRAP
1,793 performances
Opened February 26, 1978; Closed June 13, 1982

HARVEY
1,775 performances
Opened November 1, 1944; Closed January 15, 1949

DANCIN'
1,774 performances
Opened March 27, 1978; Closed June 27, 1982

LA CAGE AUX FOLLES
1,761 performances
Opened August 21, 1983; Closed November 15, 1987

HAIR
1,750 performances
Opened April 29, 1968; Closed July 1, 1972

THE WIZ
1,672 performances
Opened January 5, 1975; Closed January 29, 1979

BORN YESTERDAY
1,642 performances
Opened February 4, 1946; Closed December 31, 1949

THE BEST LITTLE WHOREHOUSE IN TEXAS
1,639 performances
Opened June 19, 1978; Closed March 27, 1982

CRAZY FOR YOU
1,622 performances
Opened February 19, 1992; Closed January 7, 1996

AIN'T MISBEHAVIN'
1,604 performances
Opened May 9, 1978; Closed February 21, 1982

MARY, MARY
1,572 performances
Opened March 8, 1961; Closed December 12, 1964

HAIRSPRAY*
1,571 performances
Opened August 15, 2002

EVITA
1,567 performances
Opened September 25, 1979; Closed June 26, 1983

THE VOICE OF THE TURTLE
1,557 performances
Opened December 8, 1943; Closed January 3, 1948

JEKYLL & HYDE
1,543 performances
Opened April 28, 1997; Closed January 7, 2001

BAREFOOT IN THE PARK
1,530 performances
Opened October 23, 1963; Closed June 25, 1967

BRIGHTON BEACH MEMOIRS
1,530 performances
Opened March 27, 1983; Closed May 11, 1986

42ND STREET (REVIVAL)
1,524 performances
Opened May 2, 2001; Closed January 2, 2005

DREAMGIRLS
1,522 performances
Opened December 20, 1981; Closed August 11, 1985

MAME
1,508 performances
Opened May 24, 1966; Closed January 3, 1970

GREASE (REVIVAL)
1,503 performances
Opened May 11, 1994; Closed January 25, 1998

SAME TIME, NEXT YEAR
1,453 performances
Opened March 14, 1975; Closed September 3, 1978

ARSENIC AND OLD LACE
1,444 performances
Opened January 10, 1941; Closed June 17, 1944

THE SOUND OF MUSIC
1,443 performances
Opened November 16, 1959; Closed June 15, 1963

ME AND MY GIRL
1,420 performances
Opened August 10, 1986; Closed December 31, 1989

HOW TO SUCCEED IN BUSINESS WITHOUT REALLY TRYING
1,417 performances
Opened October 14, 1961; Closed March 6, 1965

HELLZAPOPPIN'
1,404 performances
Opened September 22, 1938; Closed December 17, 1941

THE MUSIC MAN
1,375 performances
Opened December 19, 1957; Closed April 15, 1961

FUNNY GIRL
1,348 performances
Opened March 26, 1964; Closed July 15, 1967

MUMMENSCHANZ
1,326 performances
Opened March 30, 1977; Closed April 20, 1980

MOVIN' OUT
1,303 performances
Opened October 24, 2002; Closed December 11, 2005

ANGEL STREET
1,295 performances
Opened December 5, 1941; Closed December 30, 1944

LIGHTNIN'
1,291 performances
Opened August 26, 1918; Closed August 27, 1921

PROMISES, PROMISES
1,281 performances
Opened December 1, 1968; Closed January 1, 1972

THE KING AND I
1,246 performances
Opened March 29, 1951; Closed March 20, 1954

CACTUS FLOWER
1,234 performances
Opened December 8, 1965; Closed November 23, 1968

SLEUTH
1,222 performances
Opened December 8, 1965; Closed October 13, 1973

TORCH SONG TRILOGY
1,222 performances
Opened June 10, 1982; Closed May 19, 1985

1776
1,217 performances
Opened March 16, 1969; Closed February 13, 1972

EQUUS
1,209 performances
Opened October 24, 1974; Closed October 7, 1977

SUGAR BABIES
1,208 performances
Opened October 8, 1979; Closed August 28, 1982

GUYS AND DOLLS
1,200 performances
Opened November 24, 1950; Closed November 28, 1953

AVENUE Q*
1,182 performances
Opened July 31, 2003

AMADEUS
1,181 performances
Opened December 17, 1980; Closed October 16, 1983

CABARET
1,165 performances
Opened November 20, 1966; Closed September 6, 1969

MISTER ROBERTS
1,157 performances
Opened February 18, 1948; Closed January 6, 1951

ANNIE GET YOUR GUN
1,147 performances
Opened May 16, 1946; Closed February 12, 1949

GUYS AND DOLLS (1992 REVIVAL)
1,144 performances
Opened April 14, 1992; Closed January 8, 1995

THE SEVEN YEAR ITCH
1,141 performances
Opened November 20, 1952; Closed August 13, 1955

BRING IN 'DA NOISE, BRING IN 'DA FUNK
1,130 performances
Opened April 25, 1996; Closed January 19, 1999

BUTTERFLIES ARE FREE
1,128 performances
Opened October 21, 1969; Closed July 2, 1972

PINS AND NEEDLES
1,108 performances
Opened November 27, 1937; Closed June 22, 1940

PLAZA SUITE
1,097 performances
Opened February 14, 1968; Closed October 3, 1970

FOSSE
1,092 performances
Opened January 14, 1999; Closed August 25, 2001

THEY'RE PLAYING OUR SONG
1,082 performances
Opened February 11, 1979; Closed September 6, 1981

WICKED*
1,079 performances
Opened October 30, 2003

GRAND HOTEL (MUSICAL)
1,077 performances
Opened November 12, 1989; Closed April 25, 1992

KISS ME, KATE
1,070 performances
Opened December 30, 1948; Closed July 25, 1951

DON'T BOTHER ME, I CAN'T COPE
1,065 performances
Opened April 19, 1972; Closed October 27, 1974

THE PAJAMA GAME
1,063 performances
Opened May 13, 1954; Closed November 24, 1956

SHENANDOAH
1,050 performances
Opened January 7, 1975; Closed August 7, 1977

ANNIE GET YOUR GUN (1999 REVIVAL)
1,046 performances
Opened March 4, 1999; Closed September 1, 2001

THE TEAHOUSE OF THE AUGUST MOON
1,027 performances
Opened October 15, 1953; Closed March 24, 1956

DAMN YANKEES
1,019 performances
Opened May 5, 1955; Closed October 12, 1957

CONTACT
1,010 performances
Opened March 30, 2000; Closed September 1, 2002

NEVER TOO LATE
1,007 performances
Opened November 26, 1962; Closed April 24, 1965

BIG RIVER
1,005 performances
Opened April 25, 1985; Closed September 20, 1987

THE WILL ROGERS FOLLIES
983 performances
Opened May 1, 1991; Closed September 5, 1993

ANY WEDNESDAY
982 performances
Opened February 18, 1964; Closed June 26, 1966

SUNSET BOULEVARD
977 performances
Opened November 17, 1994; Closed March 22, 1997

URINETOWN
965 performances
Opened September 20, 2001; Closed January 18, 2004

**A FUNNY THING HAPPENED
ON THE WAY TO THE FORUM**
964 performances
Opened May 8, 1962; Closed August 29, 1964

THE ODD COUPLE
964 performances
Opened March 10, 1965; Closed July 2, 1967

ANNA LUCASTA
957 performances
Opened August 30, 1944; Closed November 30, 1946

KISS AND TELL
956 performances
Opened March 17, 1943; Closed June 23, 1945

SHOW BOAT (1994 REVIVAL)
949 performances
Opened October 2, 1994; Closed January 5, 1997

DRACULA (1977 REVIVAL)
925 performances
Opened October 20, 1977; Closed January 6, 1980

BELLS ARE RINGING
924 performances
Opened November 29, 1956; Closed March 7, 1959

THE MOON IS BLUE
924 performances
Opened March 8, 1951; Closed May 30, 1953

BEATLEMANIA
920 performances
Opened May 31, 1977; Closed October 17, 1979

PROOF
917 performances
Opened October 24, 2000; Closed January 5, 2003

THE ELEPHANT MAN
916 performances
Opened April 19, 1979; Closed June 28, 1981

KISS OF THE SPIDER WOMAN
906 performances
Opened May 3, 1993; Closed July 1, 1995

THOROUGHLY MODERN MILLIE
904 performances
Opened April 18, 2002; Closed June 20, 2004

LUV
901 performances
Opened November 11, 1964; Closed January 7, 1967

THE WHO'S TOMMY
900 performances
Opened April 22, 1993; Closed June 17, 1995

CHICAGO
898 performances
Opened June 3, 1975; Closed August 27, 1977

APPLAUSE
896 performances
Opened March 30, 1970; Closed July 27, 1972

CAN-CAN
892 performances
Opened May 7, 1953; Closed June 25, 1955

CAROUSEL
890 performances
Opened April 19, 1945; Closed May 24, 1947

I'M NOT RAPPAPORT
890 performances
Opened November 19, 1985; Closed January 17, 1988

HATS OFF TO ICE
889 performances
Opened June 22, 1944; Closed April 2, 1946

FANNY
888 performances
Opened November 4, 1954; Closed December 16, 1956

CHILDREN OF A LESSER GOD
887 performances
Opened March 30, 1980; Closed May 16, 1982

FOLLOW THE GIRLS
882 performances
Opened April 8, 1944; Closed May 18, 1946

KISS ME, KATE (REVIVAL)
881 performances
Opened November 18, 1999; Closed December 30, 2001

CITY OF ANGELS
878 performances
Opened December 11, 1989; Closed January 19, 1992

CAMELOT
873 performances
Opened December 3, 1960; Closed January 5, 1963

I LOVE MY WIFE
872 performances
Opened April 17, 1977; Closed May 20, 1979

THE BAT
867 performances
Opened August 23, 1920; Unknown closing date

MY SISTER EILEEN
864 performances
Opened December 26, 1940; Closed January 16, 1943

NO, NO, NANETTE (REVIVAL)
861 performances
Opened January 19, 1971; Closed February 3, 1973

RAGTIME
861 performances
Opened January 18, 1998; Closed January 16, 2000

SONG OF NORWAY
860 performances
Opened August 21, 1944; Closed September 7, 1946

CHAPTER TWO
857 performances
Opened December 4, 1977; Closed December 9, 1979

A STREETCAR NAMED DESIRE
855 performances
Opened December 3, 1947; Closed December 17, 1949

BARNUM
854 performances
Opened April 30, 1980; Closed May 16, 1982

COMEDY IN MUSIC
849 performances
Opened October 2, 1953; Closed January 21, 1956

RAISIN
847 performances
Opened October 18, 1973; Closed December 7, 1975

BLOOD BROTHERS
839 performances
Opened April 25, 1993; Closed April 30, 1995

YOU CAN'T TAKE IT WITH YOU
837 performances
Opened December 14, 1936; Unknown closing date

LA PLUME DE MA TANTE
835 performances
Opened November 11, 1958; Closed December 17, 1960

THREE MEN ON A HORSE
835 performances
Opened January 30, 1935; Closed January 9, 1937

THE SUBJECT WAS ROSES
832 performances
Opened May 25, 1964; Closed May 21, 1966

BLACK AND BLUE
824 performances
Opened January 26, 1989; Closed January 20, 1991

THE KING AND I (1996 REVIVAL)
807 performances
Opened April 11, 1996; Closed February 22, 1998

INHERIT THE WIND
806 performances
Opened April 21, 1955; Closed June 22, 1957

ANYTHING GOES (1987 REVIVAL)
804 performances
Opened October 19, 1987; Closed September 3, 1989

TITANIC
804 performances
Opened April 23, 1997; Closed March 21, 1999

NO TIME FOR SERGEANTS
796 performances
Opened October 20, 1955; Closed September 14, 1957

FIORELLO!
795 performances
Opened November 23, 1959; Closed October 28, 1961

WHERE'S CHARLEY?
792 performances
Opened October 11, 1948; Closed September 9, 1950

THE LADDER
789 performances
Opened October 22, 1926; Unknown closing date

FIDDLER ON THE ROOF (2004 REVIVAL)
781 performances
Opened February 26, 2004; Closed January 8, 2006

FORTY CARATS
780 performances
Opened December 26, 1968; Closed November 7, 1970

LOST IN YONKERS
780 performances
Opened February 21, 1991; Closed January 3, 1993

THE PRISONER OF SECOND AVENUE
780 performances
Opened November 11, 1971; Closed September 29, 1973

M. BUTTERFLY
777 performances
Opened March 20, 1988; Closed January 27, 1990

THE TALE OF THE ALLERGIST'S WIFE
777 performances
Opened November 2, 2000; Closed September 15, 2002

OLIVER!
774 performances
Opened January 6, 1963; Closed November 14, 1964

THE PIRATES OF PENZANCE (1981 REVIVAL)
772 performances
Opened January 8, 1981; Closed November 28, 1982

THE FULL MONTY
770 performances
Opened October 26, 2000; Closed September 1, 2002

WOMAN OF THE YEAR
770 performances
Opened March 29, 1981; Closed March 13, 1983

MY ONE AND ONLY
767 performances
Opened May 1, 1983; Closed March 3, 1985

SOPHISTICATED LADIES
767 performances
Opened March 1, 1981; Closed January 2, 1983

BUBBLING BROWN SUGAR
766 performances
Opened March 2, 1976; Closed December 31, 1977

INTO THE WOODS
765 performances
Opened November 5, 1987; Closed September 3, 1989

STATE OF THE UNION
765 performances
Opened November 14, 1945; Closed September 13, 1947

STARLIGHT EXPRESS
761 performances
Opened March 15, 1987; Closed January 8, 1989

THE FIRST YEAR
760 performances
Opened October 20, 1920; Unknown closing date

BROADWAY BOUND
756 performances
Opened December 4, 1986; Closed September 25, 1988

YOU KNOW I CAN'T HEAR YOU WHEN THE WATER'S RUNNING
755 performances
Opened March 13, 1967; Closed January 4, 1969

TWO FOR THE SEESAW
750 performances
Opened January 16, 1958; Closed October 31, 1959

JOSEPH AND THE AMAZING TECHNICOLOR DREAMCOAT
747 performances
Opened January 27, 1982; Closed September 4, 1983

DEATH OF A SALESMAN
742 performances
Opened February 10, 1949; Closed November 18, 1950

FOR COLORED GIRLS WHO HAVE CONSIDERED SUICIDE/WHEN THE RAINBOW IS ENUF
742 performances
Opened September 15, 1976; Closed July 16, 1978

SONS O' FUN
742 performances
Opened December 1, 1941; Closed August 29, 1943

CANDIDE (1974 REVIVAL)
740 performances
Opened March 10, 1974; Closed January 4, 1976

GENTLEMEN PREFER BLONDES
740 performances
Opened December 8, 1949; Closed September 15, 1951

THE MAN WHO CAME TO DINNER
739 performances
Opened October 16, 1939; Closed July 12, 1941

NINE
739 performances
Opened May 9, 1982; Closed February 4, 1984

CALL ME MISTER
734 performances
Opened April 18, 1946; Closed January 10, 1948

VICTOR/VICTORIA
734 performances
Opened October 25, 1995; Closed July 27, 1997

WEST SIDE STORY
732 performances
Opened September 26, 1957; Closed June 27, 1959

HIGH BUTTON SHOES
727 performances
Opened October 9, 1947; Closed July 2, 1949

FINIAN'S RAINBOW
725 performances
Opened January 10, 1947; Closed October 2, 1948

CLAUDIA
722 performances
Opened February 12, 1941; Closed January 9, 1943

THE GOLD DIGGERS
720 performances
Opened September 30, 1919; Unknown closing date

JESUS CHRIST SUPERSTAR
720 performances
Opened October 12, 1971; Closed June 30, 1973

CARNIVAL!
719 performances
Opened April 13, 1961; Closed January 5, 1963

THE DIARY OF ANNE FRANK
717 performances
Opened October 5, 1955; Closed June 22, 1955

**A FUNNY THING HAPPENED
ON THE WAY TO THE FORUM (REVIVAL)**
715 performances
Opened April 18, 1996; Closed January 4, 1998

I REMEMBER MAMA
714 performances
Opened October 19, 1944; Closed June 29, 1946

TEA AND SYMPATHY
712 performances
Opened September 30, 1953; Closed June 18, 1955

JUNIOR MISS
710 performances
Opened November 18, 1941; Closed July 24, 1943

FOOTLOOSE
708 performances
Opened October 22, 1998; Closed July 2, 2000

LAST OF THE RED HOT LOVERS
706 performances
Opened December 28, 1969; Closed September 4, 1971

THE SECRET GARDEN
706 performances
Opened April 25, 1991; Closed January 3, 1993

COMPANY
705 performances
Opened April 26, 1970; Closed January 1, 1972

SEVENTH HEAVEN
704 performances
Opened October 30, 1922; Unknown closing date

GYPSY (MUSICAL)
702 performances
Opened May 21, 1959; Closed March 25, 1961

THE MIRACLE WORKER
700 performances
Opened October 19, 1959; Closed July 1, 1961

THAT CHAMPIONSHIP SEASON
700 performances
Opened September 14, 1972; Closed April 21, 1974

THE MUSIC MAN (2000 REVIVAL)
698 performances
Opened April 27, 2000; Closed December 30, 2001

DA
697 performances
Opened May 1, 1978; Closed January 1, 1980

CAT ON A HOT TIN ROOF
694 performances
Opened March 24, 1955; Closed November 17, 1956

LI'L ABNER
693 performances
Opened November 15, 1956; Closed July 12, 1958

THE CHILDREN'S HOUR
691 performances
Opened November 20, 1934; Unknown closing date

PURLIE
688 performances
Opened March 15, 1970; Closed November 6, 1971

DEAD END
687 performances
Opened October 28, 1935; Closed June 12, 1937

THE LION AND THE MOUSE
686 performances
Opened November 20, 1905; Unknown closing date

WHITE CARGO
686 performances
Opened November 5, 1923; Unknown closing date

DEAR RUTH
683 performances
Opened December 13, 1944; Closed July 27, 1946

EAST IS WEST
680 performances
Opened December 25, 1918; Unknown closing date

COME BLOW YOUR HORN
677 performances
Opened February 22, 1961; Closed October 6, 1962

THE MOST HAPPY FELLA
676 performances
Opened May 3, 1956; Closed December 14, 1957

DEFENDING THE CAVEMAN
671 performances
Opened March 26, 1995; Closed June 22, 1997

THE DOUGHGIRLS
671 performances
Opened Dec. 30, 1942; Closed July 29, 1944

THE IMPOSSIBLE YEARS
670 performances
Opened October 13, 1965; Closed May 27, 1967

IRENE
670 performances
Opened November 18, 1919; Unknown closing date

BOY MEETS GIRL
669 performances
Opened November 27, 1935; Unknown closing date

THE TAP DANCE KID
669 performances
Opened December 21, 1983; Closed August 11, 1985

BEYOND THE FRINGE
667 performances
Opened October 27, 1962; Closed May 30, 1964

WHO'S AFRAID OF VIRGINIA WOOLF?
664 performances
Opened October 13, 1962; Closed May 16, 1964

BLITHE SPIRIT
657 performances
Opened November 5, 1941; Closed June 5, 1943

A TRIP TO CHINATOWN
657 performances
Opened November 9, 1891; Unknown closing date

THE WOMEN
657 performances
Opened December 26, 1936; Unknown closing date

BLOOMER GIRL
654 performances
Opened October 5, 1944; Closed April 27, 1946

THE FIFTH SEASON
654 performances
Opened January 23, 1953; Closed October 23, 1954

RAIN
648 performances
Opened September 1, 1924; Unknown closing date

WITNESS FOR THE PROSECUTION
645 performances
Opened December 16, 1954; Closed June 30, 1956

CALL ME MADAM
644 performances
Opened October 12, 1950; Closed May 3, 1952

JANIE
642 performances
Opened September 10, 1942; Closed January 16, 1944

THE GREEN PASTURES
640 performances
Opened February 26, 1930; Closed August 29, 1931

AUNTIE MAME
639 performances
Opened October 31, 1956; Closed June 28, 1958

A MAN FOR ALL SEASONS
637 performances
Opened November 22, 1961; Closed June 1, 1963

JEROME ROBBINS' BROADWAY
634 performances
Opened February 26, 1989; Closed September 1, 1990

THE FOURPOSTER
632 performances
Opened October 24, 1951; Closed May 2, 1953

THE MUSIC MASTER
627 performances
Opened September 26, 1904; Unknown closing date

TWO GENTLEMEN OF VERONA (MUSICAL)
627 performances
Opened December 1, 1971; Closed May 20, 1973

THE TENTH MAN
623 performances
Opened November 5, 1959; Closed May 13, 1961

THE HEIDI CHRONICLES
621 performances
Opened March 9, 1989; Closed September 1, 1990

IS ZAT SO?
618 performances
Opened January 5, 1925; Closed July 1926

ANNIVERSARY WALTZ
615 performances
Opened April 7, 1954; Closed September 24, 1955

THE HAPPY TIME (PLAY)
614 performances
Opened January 24, 1950; Closed July 14, 1951

SEPARATE ROOMS
613 performances
Opened March 23, 1940; Closed September 6, 1941

AFFAIRS OF STATE
610 performances
Opened September 25, 1950; Closed March 8, 1952

OH! CALCUTTA!
610 performances
Opened June 17, 1969; Closed August 12, 1972

STAR AND GARTER
609 performances
Opened June 24, 1942; Closed December 4, 1943

THE MYSTERY OF EDWIN DROOD
608 performances
Opened December 2, 1985; Closed May 16, 1987

THE STUDENT PRINCE
608 performances
Opened December 2, 1924; Unknown closing date

SWEET CHARITY
608 performances
Opened January 29, 1966; Closed July 15, 1967

BYE BYE BIRDIE
607 performances
Opened April 14, 1960; Closed October 7, 1961

RIVERDANCE ON BROADWAY
605 performances
Opened March 16, 2000; Closed August 26, 2001

IRENE (REVIVAL)
604 performances
Opened March 13, 1973; Closed September 8, 1974

SUNDAY IN THE PARK WITH GEORGE
604 performances
Opened May 2, 1984; Closed October 13, 1985

ADONIS
603 performances
Opened circa. 1884; Unknown closing date

BROADWAY
603 performances
Opened September 16, 1926; Unknown closing date

PEG O' MY HEART
603 performances
Opened December 20, 1912; Unknown closing date

MASTER CLASS
601 performances
Opened November 5, 1995; Closed June 29, 1997

STREET SCENE (PLAY)
601 performances
Opened January 10, 1929; Unknown closing date

FLOWER DRUM SONG
600 performances
Opened December 1, 1958; Closed May 7, 1960

KIKI
600 performances
Opened November 29, 1921; Unknown closing date

A LITTLE NIGHT MUSIC
600 performances
Opened February 25, 1973; Closed August 3, 1974

ART
600 performances
Opened March 1, 1998; Closed August 8, 1999

AGNES OF GOD
599 performances
Opened March 30, 1982; Closed September 4, 1983

DON'T DRINK THE WATER
598 performances
Opened November 17, 1966; Closed April 20, 1968

WISH YOU WERE HERE
598 performances
Opened June 25, 1952; Closed November 28, 1958

SARAFINA!
597 performances
Opened January 28, 1988; Closed July 2, 1989

A SOCIETY CIRCUS
596 performances
Opened December 13, 1905; Closed November 24, 1906

ABSURD PERSON SINGULAR
592 performances
Opened October 8, 1974; Closed March 6, 1976

A DAY IN HOLLYWOOD/A NIGHT IN THE UKRAINE
588 performances
Opened May 1, 1980; Closed September 27, 1981

THE ME NOBODY KNOWS
586 performances
Opened December 18, 1970; Closed November 21, 1971

THE TWO MRS. CARROLLS
585 performances
Opened August 3, 1943; Closed February 3, 1945

KISMET (MUSICAL)
583 performances
Opened December 3, 1953; Closed April 23, 1955

GYPSY (1989 REVIVAL)
582 performances
Opened November 16, 1989; Closed July 28, 1991

BRIGADOON
581 performances
Opened March 13, 1947; Closed July 31, 1948

DETECTIVE STORY
581 performances
Opened March 23, 1949; Closed August 12, 1950

NO STRINGS
580 performances
Opened March 14, 1962; Closed August 3, 1963

BROTHER RAT
577 performances
Opened December 16, 1936; Unknown closing date

BLOSSOM TIME
576 performances
Opened September 29, 1921; Unknown closing date

PUMP BOYS AND DINETTES
573 performances
Opened February 4, 1982; Closed June 18, 1983

SHOW BOAT
572 performances
Opened December 27, 1927; Closed May 4, 1929

THE SHOW-OFF
571 performances
Opened February 5, 1924; Unknown closing date

SALLY
570 performances
Opened December 21, 1920; Closed April 22, 1922

JELLY'S LAST JAM
569 performances
Opened April 26, 1992; Closed September 5, 1993

GOLDEN BOY (MUSICAL)
568 performances
Opened October 20, 1964; Closed March 5, 1966

ONE TOUCH OF VENUS
567 performances
Opened October 7, 1943; Closed February 10, 1945

THE REAL THING
566 performances
Opened January 5, 1984; Closed May 12, 1985

HAPPY BIRTHDAY
564 performances
Opened October 31, 1946; Closed March 13, 1948

LOOK HOMEWARD, ANGEL
564 performances
Opened November 28, 1957; Closed April 4, 1959

MORNING'S AT SEVEN (REVIVAL)
564 performances
Opened April 10, 1980; Closed August 16, 1981

THE GLASS MENAGERIE
561 performances
Opened March 31, 1945; Closed August 3, 1946

I DO! I DO!
560 performances
Opened December 5, 1966; Closed June 15, 1968

WONDERFUL TOWN
559 performances
Opened February 25, 1953; Closed July 3, 1954

THE LAST NIGHT OF BALLYHOO
557 performances
Opened February 27, 1997; Closed June 28, 1998

ROSE MARIE
557 performances
Opened September 2, 1924; Unknown closing date

STRICTLY DISHONORABLE
557 performances
Opened Sept. 18, 1929; Unknown closing date

SWEENEY TODD, THE DEMON BARBER OF FLEET STREET
557 performances
Opened March 1, 1979; Closed June 29, 1980

THE GREAT WHITE HOPE
556 performances
Opened October 3, 1968; Closed January 31, 1970

A MAJORITY OF ONE
556 performances
Opened February 16, 1959; Closed June 25, 1960

THE SISTERS ROSENSWEIG
556 performances
Opened March 18, 1993; Closed July 16, 1994

SUNRISE AT CAMPOBELLO
556 performances
Opened January 30, 1958; Closed May 30, 1959

TOYS IN THE ATTIC
556 performances
Opened February 25, 1960; Closed April 8, 1961

JAMAICA
555 performances
Opened October 31, 1957; Closed April 11, 1959

STOP THE WORLD—I WANT TO GET OFF
555 performances
Opened October 3, 1962; Closed February 1, 1964

FLORODORA
553 performances
Opened November 10, 1900; Closed January 25, 1902

NOISES OFF
553 performances
Opened December 11, 1983; Closed April 6, 1985

ZIEGFELD FOLLIES (1943)
553 performances
Opened April 1, 1943; Closed July 22, 1944

DIAL "M" FOR MURDER
552 performances
Opened October 29, 1952; Closed February 27, 1954

GOOD NEWS
551 performances
Opened September 6, 1927; Unknown closing date

PETER PAN (REVIVAL)
551 performances
Opened September 6, 1979; Closed January 4, 1981

HOW TO SUCCEED IN BUSINESS WITHOUT REALLY TRYING (REVIVAL)
548 performances
Opened March 23, 1995; Closed July 14, 1996

LET'S FACE IT
547 performances
Opened October 29, 1941; Closed March 20, 1943

MILK AND HONEY
543 performances
Opened October 10, 1961; Closed January 26, 1963

WITHIN THE LAW
541 performances
Opened September 11, 1912; Unknown closing date

PAL JOEY (REVIVAL)
540 performances
Opened January 3, 1952; Closed April 18, 1953

THE SOUND OF MUSIC (REVIVAL)
540 performances
Opened March 12, 1998; Closed June 20, 1999

WHAT MAKES SAMMY RUN?
540 performances
Opened February 27, 1964; Closed June 12, 1965

THE SUNSHINE BOYS
538 performances
Opened December 20, 1972; Closed April 21, 1974

WHAT A LIFE
538 performances
Opened April 13, 1938; Closed July 8, 1939

CRIMES OF THE HEART
535 performances
Opened November 4, 1981; Closed February 13, 1983

DAMN YANKEES (REVIVAL)
533 performances
Opened March 3, 1994; Closed August 6, 1995

THE UNSINKABLE MOLLY BROWN
532 performances
Opened November 3, 1960; Closed February 10, 1962

THE RED MILL (REVIVAL)
531 performances
Opened October 16, 1945; Closed January 18, 1947

RUMORS
531 performances
Opened November 17, 1988; Closed February 24, 1990

A RAISIN IN THE SUN
530 performances
Opened March 11, 1959; Closed June 25, 1960

GODSPELL
527 performances
Opened June 22, 1976; Closed September 4, 1977

FENCES
526 performances
Opened March 26, 1987; Closed June 26, 1988

THE SOLID GOLD CADILLAC
526 performances
Opened November 5, 1953; Closed February 12, 1955

BILOXI BLUES
524 performances
Opened March 28, 1985; Closed June 28, 1986

IRMA LA DOUCE
524 performances
Opened September 29, 1960; Closed December 31, 1961

THE BOOMERANG
522 performances
Opened August 10, 1915; Unknown closing date

FOLLIES
521 performances
Opened April 4, 1971; Closed July 1, 1972

ROSALINDA
521 performances
Opened October 28, 1942; Closed January 22, 1944

THE BEST MAN
520 performances
Opened March 31, 1960; Closed July 8, 1961

CHAUVE-SOURIS
520 performances
Opened February 4, 1922; Unknown closing date

BLACKBIRDS OF 1928
518 performances
Opened May 9, 1928; Unknown closing date

DIRTY ROTTEN SCOUNDRELS*
518 performances
Opened March 3, 2005

THE GIN GAME
517 performances
Opened October 6, 1977; Closed December 31, 1978

SIDE MAN
517 performances
Opened June 25, 1988; Closed October 31, 1999

SUNNY
517 performances
Opened September 22, 1925; Closed December 11, 1926

VICTORIA REGINA
517 performances
Opened December 26, 1935; Unknown closing date

FIFTH OF JULY
511 performances
Opened November 5, 1980; Closed January 24, 1982

HALF A SIXPENCE
511 performances
Opened April 25, 1965; Closed July 16, 1966

THE VAGABOND KING
511 performances
Opened September 21, 1925; Closed December 4, 1926

THE NEW MOON
509 performances
Opened September 19, 1928; Closed December 14, 1929

THE WORLD OF SUZIE WONG
508 performances
Opened October 14, 1958; Closed January 2, 1960

THE ROTHSCHILDS
507 performances
Opened October 19, 1970; Closed January 1, 1972

ON YOUR TOES (REVIVAL)
505 performances
Opened March 6, 1983; Closed May 20, 1984

SUGAR
505 performances
Opened April 9, 1972; Closed June 23, 1973

MONTY PYTHON'S SPAMALOT*
504 performances
Opened March 17, 2005

SHUFFLE ALONG
504 performances
Opened May 23, 1921; Closed July 15, 1922

UP IN CENTRAL PARK
504 performances
Opened January 27, 1945; Closed January 13, 1946

CARMEN JONES
503 performances
Opened December 2, 1943; Closed February 10, 1945

SATURDAY NIGHT FEVER
502 performances
Opened October 21, 1999; Closed December 30, 2000

THE MEMBER OF THE WEDDING
501 performances
Opened January 5, 1950; Closed March 17, 1951

PANAMA HATTIE
501 performances
Opened October 30, 1940; Closed January 13, 1942

PERSONAL APPEARANCE
501 performances
Opened October 17, 1934; Unknown closing date

BIRD IN HAND
500 performances
Opened April 4, 1929; Unknown closing date

ROOM SERVICE
500 performances
Opened May 19, 1937; Unknown closing date

SAILOR, BEWARE!
500 performances
Opened September 28, 1933; Unknown closing date

TOMORROW THE WORLD
500 performances
Opened April 14, 1943; Closed June 17, 1944

Longest-Running Shows **Off-Broadway**

LONGEST-RUNNING SHOWS OFF-BROADWAY

*Production is still running as of May 31, 2006, and performance count includes performances up to that date.

THE FANTASTICKS
17,162 performances
Opened May 3, 1960; Closed January 13, 2002

PERFECT CRIME*
7,774 performances
Opened April 5, 1987

BLUE MAN GROUP*
7,621 performances
Opened November 17, 1991

TONY 'N' TINA'S WEDDING*
5,402 performances
Opened May 1, 1987

STOMP*
5, 149 performances
Opened February 27, 1994

I LOVE YOU, YOU'RE PERFECT, NOW CHANGE*
4,090 performances
Opened August 1, 1996

NUNSENSE
3,672 performances
Opened December 12, 1985; Closed October 16, 1994

THE THREEPENNY OPERA
2,611 performances
Opened September 20, 1955; Closed December 17, 1961

DE LA GUARDA
2,475 performances
Opened June 16, 1998; Closed September 12, 2004

NAKED BOYS SINGING*
2,398 performances
Opened July 22, 1999

FORBIDDEN BROADWAY 1982–87
2,332 performances
Opened January 15, 1982; Closed August 30, 1987

LITTLE SHOP OF HORRORS
2,209 performances
Opened July 27, 1982; Closed November 1, 1987

GODSPELL
2,124 performances
Opened May 17, 1971; Closed June 13, 1976

VAMPIRE LESBIANS OF SODOM
2,024 performances
Opened June 19, 1985; Closed May 27, 1990

JACQUES BREL IS ALIVE AND WELL AND LIVING IN PARIS
1,847 performances
Opened January 22, 1968; Closed July 2, 1972

FOREVER PLAID
1,811 performances
Opened May 20, 1990; Closed June 12, 1994

VANITIES
1,785 performances
Opened March 22, 1976; Closed August 3, 1980

THE DONKEY SHOW
1,717 performances
Opened August 18, 1999 ; Closed July 16, 2005

MENOPAUSE THE MUSICAL
1,712 performances
Opened April 4, 2002; Closed May 14, 2006

YOU'RE A GOOD MAN, CHARLIE BROWN
1,597 performances
Opened March 7, 1967; Closed February 14, 1971

THE BLACKS
1,408 performances
Opened May 4, 1961; Closed September 27, 1964

THE VAGINA MONOLOGUES
1,381 performances
Opened October 3, 1999; Closed January 26, 2003

ONE MO' TIME
1,372 performances
Opened October 22, 1979; Closed 1982–83 season

GRANDMA SYLVIA'S FUNERAL
1,360 performances
Opened October 9, 1994; Closed June 20, 1998

LET MY PEOPLE COME
1,327 performances
Opened January 8, 1974; Closed July 5, 1976

LATE NITE CATECHISM
1,268 performances
Opened October 4, 1995; Closed May 18, 2003

DRIVING MISS DAISY
1,195 performances
Opened April 15, 1987; Closed June 3, 1990

THE HOT L BALTIMORE
1,166 performances
Opened September 8, 1973; Closed January 4, 1976

I'M GETTING MY ACT TOGETHER AND TAKING IT ON THE ROAD
1,165 performances
Opened May 16, 1987; Closed March 15, 1981

LITTLE MARY SUNSHINE
1,143 performances
Opened November 18, 1959; Closed September 2, 1962

STEEL MAGNOLIAS
1,126 performances
Opened November 17, 1987; Closed February 25, 1990

EL GRANDE DE COCA-COLA
1,114 performances
Opened February 13, 1973; Closed April 13, 1975

THE PROPOSITION
1,109 performances
Opened March 24, 1971; Closed April 14, 1974

OUR SINATRA
1,096 performances
Opened December 8, 1999; Closed July 28, 2002

BEAU JEST
1,069 performances
Opened October 10, 1991; Closed May 1, 1994

TAMARA
1,036 performances
Opened November 9, 1989; Closed July 15, 1990

ONE FLEW OVER THE CUCKOO'S NEST (REVIVAL)
1,025 performances
Opened March 23, 1971; Closed September 16, 1973

THE BOYS IN THE BAND
1,000 performances
Opened April 14, 1968; Closed September 6, 1970

FOOL FOR LOVE
1,000 performances
Opened November 27, 1983; Closed September 29, 1985

FORBIDDEN BROADWAY: 20TH ANNIVERSARY CELEBRATION
994 performances
Opened March 20, 2002; Closed July 4, 2004

OTHER PEOPLE'S MONEY
990 performances
Opened February 7, 1989; Closed July 4, 1991

THE THREEPENNY OPERA

Jerry Orbach (left), C. James
Mitchell (center), and the Company

PHOTO BY FRIEDMAN-ABLES

**I'M GETTING MY ACT TOGETHER
AND TAKING IT ON THE ROAD**

Lee Grayson, Dean Swenson, and Gretchen Cryer

PHOTO BY SUSAN COOK

CLOUD 9
971 performances
Opened May 18, 1981; Closed September 4, 1983

SECRETS EVERY SMART TRAVELER SHOULD KNOW
953 performances
Opened October 30, 1997; Closed February 21, 2000

SISTER MARY IGNATIUS EXPLAINS IT ALL FOR YOU & THE ACTOR'S NIGHTMARE
947 performances
Opened October 21, 1981; Closed January 29, 1984

YOUR OWN THING
933 performances
Opened January 13, 1968; Closed April 5, 1970

CURLEY MCDIMPLE
931 performances
Opened November 22, 1967; Closed January 25, 1970

LEAVE IT TO JANE (REVIVAL)
928 performances
Opened May 29, 1959; Closed 1961–62 season

THE MAD SHOW
871 performances
Opened January 9, 1966; Closed September 10, 1967

HEDWIG AND THE ANGRY INCH
857 performances
Opened February 14, 1998; Closed April 9, 2000

FORBIDDEN BROADWAY STRIKES BACK
850 performances
Opened October 17, 1996; Closed September 20, 1998

WHEN PIGS FLY
840 performances
Opened August 14, 1996; Closed August 15, 1998

SCRAMBLED FEET
831 performances
Opened June 11, 1979; Closed June 7, 1981

THE EFFECT OF GAMMA RAYS ON MAN-IN-THE-MOON MARIGOLDS
819 performances
Opened April 7, 1970; Closed June 1, 1973

OVER THE RIVER AND THROUGH THE WOODS
800 performances
Opened October 5, 1998; Closed September 3, 2000

A VIEW FROM THE BRIDGE (REVIVAL)
780 performances
Opened November 9, 1965; Closed December 11, 1966

THE BOY FRIEND (REVIVAL)
763 performances
Opened January 25, 1958; Closed 1961–62 season

TRUE WEST
762 performances
Opened December 23, 1980; Closed January 11, 1981

FORBIDDEN BROADWAY CLEANS UP ITS ACT!
754 performances
Opened November 17, 1998; Closed August 30, 2000

SLAVA'S SNOW SHOW*
742 Performances
Opened September 8, 2004

ISN'T IT ROMANTIC
733 performances
Opened December 15, 1983; Closed September 1, 1985

DIME A DOZEN
728 performances
Opened June 13, 1962; Closed 1963–64 season

THE POCKET WATCH
725 performances
Opened November 14, 1966; Closed June 18, 1967

THE CONNECTION
722 performances
Opened June 9, 1959; Closed June 4, 1961

THE PASSION OF DRACULA
714 performances
Opened September 28, 1977; Closed July 14, 1979

LOVE, JANIS
713 performances
Opened April 22, 2001; Closed January 5, 2003

ADAPTATION & NEXT
707 performances
Opened February 10, 1969; Closed October 18, 1970

OH! CALCUTTA!
704 performances
Opened June 17, 1969; Closed August 12, 1972

JEWTOPIA*
698 performances
Opened October 21, 2004

SCUBA DUBA
692 performances
Opened November 11, 1967; Closed June 8, 1969

THE FOREIGNER
686 performances
Opened November 2, 1984; Closed June 8, 1986

THE KNACK
685 performances
Opened January 14, 1964; Closed January 9, 1966

FULLY COMMITTED
675 performances
Opened December 14, 1999; Closed May 27, 2001

THE CLUB
674 performances
Opened October 14, 1976; Closed May 21, 1978

THE BALCONY
672 performances
Opened March 3, 1960; Closed December 21, 1961

PENN & TELLER
666 performances
Opened July 30, 1985; Closed January 19, 1992

DINNER WITH FRIENDS
654 performances
Opened November 4, 1999; Closed May 27, 2000

AMERICA HURRAH
634 performances
Opened November 7, 1966; Closed May 5, 1968

COOKIN'
632 Performances
Opened July 7, 2004; Closed August 7, 2005

OIL CITY SYMPHONY
626 performances
Opened November 5, 1987; Closed May 7, 1989

THE COUNTESS
618 performances
Opened September 28, 1999; Closed December 30, 2000

THE EXONERATED
608 performances
Opened October 10, 2002; Closed March 7, 2004

HOGAN'S GOAT
607 performances
Opened March 6, 1965; Closed April 23, 1967

BEEHIVE
600 performances
Opened March 30, 1986; Closed August 23, 1987

CRISS ANGEL MINDFREAK
600 performances
Opened November 20, 2001; Closed January 5, 2003

THE TROJAN WOMEN
600 performances
Opened December 23, 1963; Closed May 30, 1965

THE SYRINGA TREE
586 performances
Opened September 14, 2000; Closed June 2, 2002

THE DINING ROOM
583 performances
Opened February 24, 1982; Closed July 17, 1982

MUSICAL OF MUSICALS THE MUSICAL!
(COMPANY AND COMMERCIAL RUNS)
583 Performances
Opened December 16, 2003; Closed January 25, 2004
Reopened June 10, 2004; Closed October 3, 2004
Reopened February 10 2005; Closed November 13, 2005

KRAPP'S LAST TAPE & THE ZOO STORY
582 performances
Opened August 29, 1960; Closed May 21, 1961

THREE TALL WOMEN
582 performances
Opened April 13, 1994; Closed August 26, 1995

THE DUMBWAITER & THE COLLECTION
578 performances
Opened January 21, 1962; Closed April 12, 1964

FORBIDDEN BROADWAY 1990
576 performances
Opened January 23, 1990; Closed June 9, 1991

DAMES AT SEA
575 performances
Opened April 22, 1969; Closed May 10, 1970

THE CRUCIBLE (REVIVAL)
571 performances
Opened 1957; Closed 1958

THE ICEMAN COMETH (REVIVAL)
565 performances
Opened May 8, 1956; Closed February 23, 1958

FORBIDDEN BROADWAY 2001: A SPOOF ODYSSEY
552 performances
Opened December 6, 2000; Closed February 6, 2002

THE HOSTAGE (REVIVAL)
545 performances
Opened October 16, 1972; Closed October 8, 1973

WIT
545 performances
Opened October 6, 1998; Closed April 9, 2000

**WHAT'S A NICE COUNTRY LIKE YOU
DOING IN A STATE LIKE THIS?**
543 performances
Opened July 31, 1985; Closed February 9, 1987

FORBIDDEN BROADWAY 1988
534 performances
Opened September 15, 1988; Closed December 24, 1989

**GROSS INDECENCY:
THE THREE TRIALS OF OSCAR WILDE**
534 performances
Opened September 5, 1997; Closed September 13, 1998

FRANKIE AND JOHNNY IN THE CLAIRE DE LUNE
533 performances
Opened December 4, 1987; Closed March 12, 1989

**SIX CHARACTERS IN SEARCH OF AN AUTHOR
(REVIVAL)**
529 performances
Opened March 8, 1963; Closed June 28, 1964

ALL IN THE TIMING
526 performances
Opened November 24, 1993; Closed February 13, 1994

ALTAR BOYZ*
522 performances
Opened March 1, 2005

OLEANNA
513 performances
Opened October 3, 1992; Closed January 16, 1994

MAKING PORN
511 performances
Opened June 12, 1996; Closed September 14, 1997

THE DIRTIEST SHOW IN TOWN
509 performances
Opened June 26, 1970; Closed September 17, 1971

HAPPY ENDING & DAY OF ABSENCE
504 performances
Opened June 13, 1965; Closed January 29, 1967

FORBIDDEN BROADWAY SVU*
504 performances
Opened December 16, 2004

GREATER TUNA
501 performances
Opened October 21, 1982; Closed December 31, 1983

A SHAYNA MAIDEL
501 performances
Opened October 29, 1987; Closed January 8, 1989

THE BOYS FROM SYRACUSE (REVIVAL)
500 performances
Opened April 15, 1963; Closed June 28, 1964

OBITUARIES

June 1, 2005 – May 31, 2006

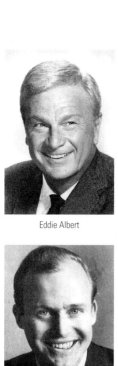

Eddie Albert

Anne Bancroft

Barbara Bel Geddes

Jocelyn Brando

Johnny Carson

Franklin Cover

Constance Cummings

Joan Diener

Geraldine Fitzgerald

Anthony Franciosa

Don Knotts

Paula Laurence

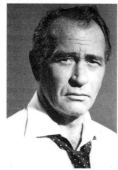

Darren McGavin

Priscilla Gillette Perrone

Brock Peters

Nipsey Russell

Maureen Stapleton

Frederic B. Vogel

Dennis Weaver

Shelley Winters

Eddie Albert (Edward Albert Heimberger), 99, Rock Island, IL-born screen, stage, and television actor, died May 26, 2005, of pneumonia in Pacific Palisades, CA. Broadway credits include *O Evening Star, Brother Rat, Room Service, The Boys from Syracuse, Miss Liberty, The Seven Year Itch, The Music Man, Say, Darling, No Hard Feelings,* and *You Can't Take It With You.* Receiving Oscar nominations for his performances in *Roman Holiday* and *The Heartbreak Kid,* he made his film debut in 1938 in *Brother Rat,* with other film credits including *On Your Toes, Four Wives, A Dispatch from Reuters, The Wagons Roll at Night, Thieves Fall Out, Out of the Fog, Eagle Squadron, Strange Voyage, Smash Up: The Story of a Woman, Every Girl Should Be Married, Carrie* (1952), *Actors and Sin, The Girl Rush, Oklahoma!, I'll Cry Tomorrow, Attack, The Teahouse of the August Moon, The Sun Also Rises, The Joker is Wild, The Roots of Heaven, The Young Doctors, The Longest Day, Captain Newman M.D., Miracle of the White Stallions, The Longest Yard* (1974), *Escape to Witch Mountain,* and *Yes, Giorgio.* On television he was best remembered for the sitcom *Green Acres,* as well as for co-starring with Robert Wagner in *Switch.* He was married for forty years to actress Margo, who died in 1985. He is survived by his son, actor Edward Albert, a daughter, and two granddaughters.

Jay Presson Allen (aka Jay Presson, aka Jay Allen), 84, Fort Worth, TX-born writer/director, died May 1, 2006, in Manhattan, New York, of a stroke. Making her breakthrough with a stage adaptation of Muriel Spark's *The Prime of Miss Jean Brodie,* which originated as a London stage production starring Vanessa Redgrave in 1966, productions eventually encompassed incarnations including Zoe Caldwell in a Tony-winning 1968 New York performance, as well as an adaptation for the screen for which Maggie Smith won an Academy Award as Best Actress for her portrayal of Jean. In 1968 Ms. Allen penned an English adaptation of *Forty Carats,* originally a French play about a forty-year old divor-cée who begins a relationship with a twenty-two year-old man, which won Julie Harris a 1969 Tony Award for Best Actress in a Play. In 1972, she adapted the musical *Cabaret* for the screen, gaining an Academy Award nomination for Best Adapted Screenplay and for which Liza Minnelli also won an Academy Award for Best Actress. Other Broadway stage adaptations include *A Little Family Business* in 1982, as well as the original scripts for *Tru* in 1989, which she created out of Truman Capote's own writings, and which garnered star Robert Morse a Tony Award for Best Leading Actor in a Play, and the Tracy Ullman vehicle *The Big Love* in 1991, for which Ullman won a Theatre World Award. Other screen credits include 1972's *Travels with My Aunt* (from Graham Greene's novel), 1981's *Prince of the City* (co-written with Sidney Lumet), and 1982's *Deathtrap,* adapted from the Broadway play and starring Michael Caine, Christopher Reeve, and Dyan Cannon. Further credits include the screenplay for Alfred Hitchcock's *Marnie* in 1964, 1975's *Funny Lady,* the sequel to *Funny Girl,* and *Just Tell Me What You Want,* starring Alan King, in 1980. In 1948 she published the novel *Spring Riot,* and worked on several television dramas in the 1950s. On television, she created the drama *Family,* which ran four seasons. She was married to producer Lewis Allen for forty-eight years, until his death in 2003, who was also the producer of two of her plays, *Tru* and *The Big Love.* She is survived by daughter, Brooke Allen, and two grandchildren.

Keith Andes (John Charles Andes), 85, Ocean City, NJ-born screen, stage, and television actor was found dead at his home in Santa Clarita, CA, Nov. 11, 2005, having committed suicide by asphyxiation. He had been suffering from blad-der cancer and other ailments. Broadway credits include *The Chocolate Soldier* (for which he won a 1947 Theatre World Award), *Kiss Me, Kate, Maggie,* and *Wildcat.* Among his movies were *The Farmer's Daughter* (1947), *Clash by Night, Blackbeard the Pirate, Away All Boats, Tora! Tora! Tora!* (as Gen. George C. Mar-shall), and *…And Justice for All.* A marriage to actress Shelah Hackett ended in divorce. He is survived by his two sons and three grandchildren.

Leon Askin, (Leo Aschkenasy), 97, Vienna, Austria-born character player died June 1, 2005, in Vienna, Austria, of natural causes. Broadway credits include *A Temporary Island* and *Twentieth Century.* He was seen in such movies as *Road to Bali, South Sea Woman, The Robe, Knock on Wood, Valley of the Kings, One, Two, Three, John Goldfarb Please Come Home, What Did You Do in the War Daddy?, The Maltese Bippy, The World's Greatest Athlete,* and *Young Frankenstein.* He also played Gen. Albert Burkhalter in the 1960s television comedy *Hogan's Heroes.*

Anne Bancroft (Anna Maria Louisa Italiano), 73, Bronx, NY-born screen, stage, and television actress, died of uterine cancer June 6, 2005, in Manhattan, New York. The 2004 volume of *Screen World* is dedicated: "To Anne Bancroft—An impassioned, clever, and gifted actress who has been equally brilliant in drama and comedy, emerging as one of the most enduring and respected performers of her generation." Broadway credits include her debut in *Two for the Seesaw,* for which she won a 1958 Theatre World Award as well as Tony Award for Best Featured Actress in a Play, *The Miracle Worker,* for which she won a Tony Award for Best Actress in a Play, *Mother Courage and Her Children, The Devils, The Little Foxes, A Cry of Players, Golda* (Tony Nomination), and *Duet for One.* She won an Academy Award for playing Annie Sullivan in *The Miracle Worker,* and became one of the iconic figures of the 1960s with her Oscar-nominated performance as Mrs. Robinson in *The Graduate.* Following her 1952 film debut in *Don't Bother to Knock,* she was seen in such films as *The Kid from Left Field, Demetrius and the Gladiators, Gorilla at Large, A Life in the Balance, Walk the Proud Land, The Girl in Black Stockings, The Pumpkin Eater* (Oscar nomination), *The Slender Thread, 7 Women, Young Winston, The Prisoner of Second Avenue, The Hindenburg, The Turning Point* (Oscar nomination), *Fatso* (which she also wrote and directed), *The Elephant Man, To Be or Not to Be* (1983), *Garbo Talks, Agnes of God* (Oscar nomination), *'night, Mother; 84 Charing Cross Road, Torch Song Trilogy, Honeymoon in Vegas, Point of No Return, Malice, How to Make an American Quilt, G.I. Jane, Great Expectations* (1998), *Keeping the Faith,* and *Up at the Villa.* She won Emmy Awards for performances in *Annie: The Women in the Life of a Man* as well as for *Deep in My Heart,* in 1999. She is survived by her husband, director/writer Mel Brooks to whom she was married since 1964, a son, Maxmillian, her mother, Mildred, and two sisters.

Marji Bank, 82, Dallas, TX-born doyenne of *Shear Madness,* Chicago's Black-stone Theater's production which became the longest-running non-musical play in American theatre history and in which Ms. Bank appeared as Mrs. Shubert for 3,300 performances (a record at the time), died May 19, 2006, in Chicago, IL, of complications of an illness. She worked in the play off an on during its run from 1982–1999. She won a Joseph Jefferson Award for her performance as Grandma Kurnitz in *Lost in Yonkers,* and was nominated for that award four additional times. She also appeared in Chicago with the Old Town Players, Lin-coln Park Theater, and the Hull House Theater. She also appeared in *Driving Miss Daisy, One Flew Over the Cuckoo's Nest, Plaza Suite,* and *Man in the Moon Marigolds,* among several other plays. She appeared on stages at the Goodman, Ivanhoe, Drury Lane, Body Politic, Victory Gardens, and Candlelight theaters, among many others. She is survived by two daughters and two grandchildren.

Barbara Bel Geddes, 82, New York City, NY-born screen, stage, and televi-sion actress, Aug. 8, 2005, in Northeast Harbor, ME, of lung cancer. Broadway credits include *Out of the Frying Pan, Little Darling, Nine Girls, Mrs. January and Mr. X, Deep Are the Roots* (for which she won a 1946 Theatre World Award), *Burning Bright, The Moon Is Blue, The Living Room, Cat on a Hot Tin Roof* (Tony nomination), *The Sleeping Prince, Silent Night, Lonely Night, Mary, Mary* (Tony nomination), *Luv, Everything in a Garden,* and *Finishing Touches.* She earned an Oscar nomination for playing Katrin Hanson in the 1948 film *I Remember*

Mama. Following her 1947 film debut in *The Long Night*, she was seen in such other pictures as *Blood on the Moon, Panic in the Streets, Fourteen Hours, Vertigo, The Five Pennies, 5 Branded Women,* and *Summertree.* Best known for her role as Miss Ellie in the television series *Dallas* in which she appeared from 1978 – 1990 (with the exception of the 1984 – 85 season, when Bel Geddes underwent heart surgery; actress Donna Reed substituted for her). She won a 1980 Best Actress Emmy Award for the role. In 1993 She was inducted into the Theater Hall of Fame, and was the author of two children's books, *I Like to be Me* (1963), and *So Do I* (1972), as well as the creator of a line of greeting cards. She was the daughter of noted and prolific theatrical designer Norman Bel Geddes. She is survived by two daughters, Susan and Betsy.

Lloyd Bochner, 81, Toronto, Ontario, Canada-born character actor died Oct. 29, 2005, in Santa Monica, CA, of cancer. Broadway credits include *Tamburlaine the Great*, in addition to performing with the Stratford Festival of Canada from 1953 – 1959, where roles included Horatio *Hamlet*, Orsino in *Twelfth Night*, and Vincentio in *Measure for Measure*. His film credits include *The Night Walker, Sylvia* (1965), *Point Blank, Tony Rome, The Detective, Ulzana's Raid, The Man in the Glass Booth*, and *The Lonely Lady*. Survivors include his wife; two sons, one of whom is actor Hart Bochner; and a daughter.

Joseph Bova, 81, Cleveland, OH-born actor, died March 12, 2006, at the Actors' Fund retirement home in Englewood, N.J., of emphysema. Broadway credits include *Once Upon A Mattress, The Rape of the Belt, Hot Spot, The Chinese and Dr. Fish* (Tony nomination), *An American Millionaire, Saint Joan*, and *42nd Street* (entire nine-year run of 1980 production). A program director for an NBC outlet in Cleveland and, as Uncle Joe Bova, host of a children's television program, he brought the character to ABC's local station in New York. His many later theatrical appearances included New York Shakespeare Festival productions in Central Park and at The Public Theater, including *King Richard III, The Comedy of Errors, Troilus and Cressida, Love's Labour's Lost*, and *Twelfth Night*. Other credits include numerous movies and television series episodes, as well as hundreds of voice-overs. He was a veteran of W.W. II. He is survived by his wife; two daughters, Gabriella Bova of Beverly Hills, CA, and Leslie Bova of Boulder, CO.; a stepson, Christopher Boal of Manhattan; a brother, Phillip Bova of Lyndhurst, OH; and a sister, Barbara Losik, of Russell, OH.

Jocelyn Brando, 86, San Francisco, CA-born actress, the older sister of screen legend Marlon Brando, died Nov. 27, 2005, in Santa Monica, CA, of natural causes. Broadway credits include *The First Crocus, Mister Roberts, The Golden State, Desire Under the Elms*, and *Mourning Becomes Electra*. Her films include *China Venture* (1953), *The Big Heat* (1953), *Ten Wanted Men, The Explosive Generation* (1961), *Bus Riley's Back in Town* (1965), *Movie Movie, Why Would I Lie?* (1980), *Mommie Dearest* (1981), and two in support of her brother, *The Ugly American* (1963) and *The Chase* (1966). She also made many television appearances. Survivors include her son.

Donald Brooks (Donald Marc Blumberg), 77, New Haven, CT-born fashion designer, died Aug. 1, 2005, in Stony Brook, NY. Broadway credits include *No Strings* (Tony nomination), *Barefoot in the Park, Fade Out-Fade In, Beekman Place, Poor Bitos, Diamond Orchid, Flora, The Red Menace, On a Clear Day You Can See Forever, Promises, Promises, Last of the Red Hot Lovers, Minnie's Boys, Night Watch, Holiday, Good News, The Member of the Wedding, Summer Brave, A Musical Jubilee, A Party with Betty Comden & Adolph Green, Monteith & Rand, Carmelina*, and *Dance a Little Closer*. Designing windows for Lord & Taylor department stores, he was hired by Dorothy Shaver, the store's president,

to design a clothing line. Opening his first store in 1963, he was cited by *The New York Times* as one of "the three B's of fashion" along with Bill Blass and Geoffrey Beane. He was the recipient of three Coty Awards for fashion and the Parsons Medal for Distinguished Achievement. A founding member of the Council Design of America, he also received The New York Drama Critics Award, an Emmy Award (*The Letter*, 1982), and another Emmy nomination (*The Two Mrs. Grenvilles*, 1987), and three Academy Award nominations, for *The Cardinal* (1963), *Star!* (1968), *Darling Lili* (1970).

Susan Browning, 65, Baldwin, NY-born actress died April 26, 2006, in New York, NY, after a brief illness. Twice nominated for Tony Awards, she is best remembered for the originating the role of the flight attendant "April" in Stephen Sondheim and George Furth's *Company*, for which she received her first nomination. Other Broadway credits include *Love and Kisses, Shelter, Sondheim: A Musical Tribute, Thieves, Goodtime Charley* (her second Tony nod), *Chapter Two*, the original production of *Big River*, and the concert revival of *Company*. Other stage credits include Goodspeed Musicals' *Lucky in the Rain*. She appeared on film and television in *Sister Act, The World According to Garp, First Ladies' Diaries: Martha Washington, Mary Hartman, Mary Hartman*, and had roles on the daytime dramas *One Life to Live* and *Love Is a Many Splendored Thing*.

Hamilton Camp (Hamid Hamilton Camp), 70, London, England – born character player died of a heart attack in Los Angeles on Oct. 2, 2005, of a heart attack. Broadway credits include *The Committee, Kelly, On a Clear Day You Can See Forever, Paul Sills' Story Theatre*, and *Ovid's Metamorphoses*. He appeared in such movies as *My Cousin Rachel, Nickelodeon, American Hot Wax, Heaven Can Wait* (1978), *S.O.B., Eating Raoul, No Small Affair*, and *Dick Tracy*. Survivors include six children and thirteen grandchildren.

Jean Carson, 82, West Virginia-born screen, stage, and television actress died of complications from a stroke on Nov. 2, 2005, in Palm Springs, CA. Broadway credits include her debut in *Bravo!* (for which she won a 1948 Theatre World Award), *Metropole, The Bird Cage, Men of Distinction*, and *Anniversary Waltz*. Among her numerous movie credits are *The Phoenix City Story, I Married a Monster from Outer Space, The Sound and the Fury, Gunn, The Party*, and *Fun with Dick and Jane* (1977). Survived by two sons.

Johnny Carson (John William Carson), 79, Corning, Iowa-born actor/comedian/writer/talk show host, died Jan. 23, 2005, in Los Angeles, CA, of complications from emphysema. His lone Broadway credit was *The Tunnel of Love* (1957). But it was as the incomparable host of *The Tonight Show*, the reigns of which he took in 1962 and held until 1992, that he will forever be remembered. *The Tonight Show* is the single biggest money-maker in television history, and Carson's influence on television, those who appeared on it, and its entertainment value to the American public is immeasurable. Beginning with a Sunday afternoon comedy show called *Carson's Cellar*, he was eventually hired by Red Skelton to write for *The Red Skelton Show*, for whom he filled in when Skelton injured himself at the last minute, resulting in CBS offering Carson his own show. He then appeared on numerous television shows, ultimately hosting *Do You Trust Your Wife?* and then *The Tonight Show*. He was a veteran of the U.S. Navy, serving from 1943 – 46, and received a star on the Hollywood Walk of Fame. With three marriages ending in divorce, to Jody Wolcott, Joanne Copeland, and Joanna Holland, respectively, his last was to Alexis Maas, who survives him, as do sons Chris and Corey; his brother, Richard; and sister, Catherine. Another son, Ricky, died in a car accident in 1991.

Franklin Cover, 77, Cleveland, OH-born actor, died Feb. 5, 2006, at the Lillian Booth Actor's Fund of America home in Englewood, NJ, of pneumonia, where he had been at recuperating from a heart condition. Broadway credits include *Giants, Sons of Giants, Calculated Risk, Abraham Cochrane, The Investigation, A Warm Body, The Freaking Out of Stephanie Blake, Forty Carats, Applause, Wild Honey,* and *Born Yesterday*. In his nearly six decades in show business, Cover made numerous appearances on television shows, including *The Jackie Gleason Show, All in the Family, Will & Grace, Living Single, Mad About You,* and *ER,* but was best known for his role as Tom Willis in the long-running *The Jeffersons,* for ten years playing one half of one of the first interracial couples on prime-time television. He also appeared in the films *The Stepford Wives* and *Wall Street,* among others.

Constance Cummings (Constance Halverstadt), 95, Seattle, WA-born Hollywood screen actress who later moved to London and became one of England's prominent stage performers, died on Nov. 23, 2005, in Oxfordshire. A Tony Award-winner for Best Actress in a Play as well as Drama Desk Award winner for her work in *Wings* (1979). Her other Broadway credits include *Treasure Girl, This Man's Town, Accent on Youth, Young Madame Conti, Madame Bovary, If I Were You, One-Man Show, The Rape of the Belt,* and *Hamlet*. She was also nominated for a Drama Desk Award for Outstanding Actress in a Play for her work in 1982's *The Chalk Garden* Off-Broadway. Her motion pictures include *The Criminal Code, The Guilty Generation, Behind the Mask, Movie Crazy, Washington Merry-Go-Round, Night After Night, The Mind Reader, Haunted Honeymoon* (*Busman's Honeymoon*), *Blithe Spirit, John and Julie, The Battle of the Sexes,* and *A Boy Ten Feet Tall* (*Sammy Going South*). Her forty-year marriage to playwright Benn Levy ended with his death in 1973. She is survived by her son and daughter.

Joan Diener, 76, Columbus, OH-born actress, died May 13, 2006, in Manhattan, New York, of complications from cancer. Best known for originating the role of Dulcinea in *The Man of La Mancha* in 1965. Her other Broadway credits include *Small Wonder, Season in the Sun, Kismet* (for which she won a 1954 Theatre World Award), *Cry for Us All,* and *Home Sweet Homer.* Diener left a London production of *Kismet* in 1955 under disputed circumstances, and after a twelve year absence from Broadway joined *La Mancha,* which began at the ANTA Washington Square Theater and then moved to Broadway. In the last weeks of a 1992 Broadway revival, she succeeded Sheena Easton, the pop singer, who had left the show. She is survived by her husband, director Albert Marre, of Manhattan, who had directed her in both *Kismet* and *Man of La Mancha,* son, Adam Marre of Manhattan, as well as by her daughter Jennifer Marre and three grandsons, all of Brooklyn.

Katherine Dunham, 96, Chicago, IL-born choreographer, director, performer, and producer, died May 21, 2006, in New York, NY. Called alternately *Matriarch* and *Queen Mother of Black Dance*. Her Broadway credits in any number of multi-hyphenated capacities include *Cabin in the Sky, Tropical Revue, Blue Holliday, Concert Varieties, Carib Song, Bal Negre, Katherine Dunham* and *Her Company*. An author and civil rights activist in addition to pioneering dancer and choreographer, she left Broadway to teach culture most of every year after 1967 in East St. Louis, IL., a high crime area. Dunham was perhaps best known for bringing African and Caribbean influences to the European-dominated dance world. Her dance company toured internationally from the 1940s to the '60s, visiting fifty-seven nations on six continents. In the late 1930s, she established the nation's first self-supporting all-black modern dance group. Dunham also choreographed *Aida* for the Metropolitan Opera. She appeared in the films *Stormy Weather* and *Carnival of Rhythm*. Dunham received 10 honorary doctorates, the National Medal of the Arts, the Albert Schweitzer Prize at the Kennedy Center Honors, and membership in the French Legion of Honor, as well as major honors from Brazil and Haiti. She additionally published *A Touch of Innocence*, in 1958, *Possessed*, in 1969, and *Kasamance*, in 1974, all autobiographical works based on her experiences. Dunham was married to theater designer John Thomas Pratt for forty-nine years before his death in 1986.

Stephen Elliott, 86, New York City, NY-born screen, stage, and television character actor, died May 21, 2005, in Los Angeles, CA, of congestive heart failure. A Drama Desk Award Winner for Outstanding Performance for *A Whistle in the Dark*, as well as a 1967 Tony Award nominee as Best Featured Actor in a Play for his performance in 1973's *Marat/Sade*. Other Broadway credits include *The Tempest, Command Decision, The Shrike, Roman Candle, The Gay Life, Photo Finish, Traveller Without Luggage, King Lear, A Cry of Players, In the Matter of J. Robert Oppenheimer, The Miser, Georgy, The Good Woman of Setzuan, The Playboy of the Western World, An Enemy of the People, Mary Stuart, The Crucible,* and *The Creation of the World and Other Business*. Off-Broadway credits include *Livin the Life, Henry IV Part I, Henry IV Part II, Twelfth Night, A Whistle in the Dark, Purple Dust, I Knock at the Door,* and *Pictures in the Hallway*. Perhaps best known for playing Jill Eikenberry's dad in the 1981 comedy hit *Arthur*. Among his other movies are *Three Hours to Kill, The Hospital, Death Wish, The Hindenburg, Cutter and Bone, Kiss Me Goodbye,* and *Beverly Hills Cop*. Survived by his wife, a daughter, a son, two stepsons, and three grandchildren.

Cy Feuer (Seymour Arnold Feuer), 95, Brooklyn, NY-born producer/director/theatre owner-operator/writer, died May 17, 2006, in Manhattan, NY, of bladder cancer. Partnered with Ernest H. Martin for more than half a century. Broadway credits on his own or with Martin include *Where's Charley, Guys and Dolls* (1951, Tony Award, Best Musical), *Can-Can, The Boy Friend, Silk Stockings, Whoop-Up, The Sound of Music, How to Succeed in Business Without Really Trying* (Tony Award, Best Musical), *Little Me* (Tony nominations, Best Musical, Best Direction of a Musical, Best Producer of a Musical), *Arturo Ui, Hamlet, Skyscraper* (Tony nomination, Best Musical, Best Direction of a Musical), *Walking Happy* (Tony nomination, Best Musical), *Marlene Dietrich, The Goodbye People, The Act,* and *I Remember Mama* (1979). His 2003 autobiography was entitled *I Got the Show Right Here*. Rising to the rank of captain in W.W. II, he spent the duration of the war making training films. A prolific director and composer. His credits include an Academy Award for *Cabaret* (1972) and the film version of *A Chorus Line* (1985). He is survived by sons Robert and Jed, as well as two grandchildren. Broadway dimmed its lights in his honor on May 18, 2006.

John Fiedler (John Donald Fiedler), 80, Plateville, WI-born actor, died June 25, 2005, in Englewood, NJ, of cancer. His Broadway credits include *One Eye Closed, Howie, A Raisin in the Sun, Harold, The Odd Couple, Our Town, The Crucible,* and *A Little Hotel on the Side*. Off-Broadway credits include *The Terrible Swift Sword* and *The Sea Gull*. Perhaps best known as the nervous patient Mr. Peterson on television's *The Bob Newhart Show*, he made many appearances in that medium, including a notable appearance on the original *Star Trek* series. He is also known for his role as the voice of Piglet in the *Winnie-the-Pooh* productions, with other screen roles including *Twelve Angry Men, Stage Struck, A Raisin in the Sun* (repeating his Broadway role), *That Touch of Mink, The World of Henry Orient, Kiss Me Stupid, A Fine Madness, The Odd Couple* (repeating his Broadway role), *True Grit,* and *Sharky's Machine,* among forty or so other films. He was a US Navy veteran of W.W. II. Survivors include his brother, James Fiedler, of Madison, WI, and sister, Mary Dean, of Milwaukee, WI.

Geraldine Fitzgerald, 91, Greystones, County Wicklow, south of Dublin, Ireland-born actress of stage and screen and theatre director, died July 17, 2005, in New York, NY, following a long battle with Alzheimer's disease. Her Broadway credits include *Heartbreak House, Sons and Soldiers, Hide and Seek, Ah, Wilderness!,* the special performances of *Geraldine Fitzgerald in Songs of the Street* (Drama Desk nomination), *A Touch of the Poet,* and *Mass Appeal* (Tony Award and Drama Desk Award Best Direction of a Play nominations). Off-Broadway credits include *The Cave Dwellers, Theatre 1965 New Playwrights Second Program, Long Day's Journey Into Night* (for which she received a 1971 Drama Desk Vernon Rice Award), *Danger: Memory!,* and *Sharon.* She earned an Academy Award nomination for playing Isabella Linton in the 1939 film *Wuthering Heights,* and her other films include *Dark Victory, Watch on the Rhine, The Pawnbroker, Rachel Rachel, Harry and Tonto, Arthur, Arthur II, Poltergeist II,* and *Easy Money.* Her numerous television appearances include those on *Alfred Hitchcock Presents, Robert Montgomery Presents, Naked City, St. Elsewhere, Cagney and Lacey, Mabel and Max,* and *The Golden Girls* (for which she received an Emmy Award nomination). Her star on the Hollywood Walk of Fame is located at 6353 Hollywood Boulevard, and she is a member of the Theater Hall of Fame. She is survived by her son, film director Michael Lindsay-Hogg; her daughter, actress Angelica Torn (from her marriage to actor Rip Torn); two grandchildren; and one step-grandchild.

Phil Ford, 85, San Francisco, CA-born comedian/performer who gained fame as half of a performing team with his wife Mimi Hines, died June 15, 2005, in Las Vegas, NV, of natural causes. Starting out in vaudeville at age twelve after having received dance training from his aunt, Ivy Ford, he also performed in bands as a clarinetist. In World War II, he served with the 84th Infantry Division and fought in the Battle of the Bulge. Following the end of the war, he moved into standup comedy. In 1952, he teamed with Mimi Hines and they formed Ford & Hines. Working in nightclubs and other venues throughout Canada and the US, they married in 1954. A booking on *The Jack Paar Show* led to many more on that show as well as to appearances on *The Ed Sullivan Show,* which kept them in demand in nightclubs throughout the country. In 1965, Ford played Eddie Ryan opposite Hines when she succeeded Barbra Streisand as Fanny Brice in the original Broadway production of *Funny Girl.* Other Broadway credits include *This Was Burlesque* (1981). The team appeared together in the first national tour of *I Do, I Do* and several productions of *Sugar Babies.* Though they divorced in 1972, they remained close friends and continued to work together, including a 1998 production of *Hello, Dolly!* at the Gateway Playhouse in Long Island, as well as many benefit performances. He played clarinet and piano every day until his death and was also an accomplished songwriter, bandleader, singer, and actor. Film appearances include *Saturday Night Bath in Apple Valley* (1965) and *Fake-Out* (1982). Television credits including *Love, American Style* and *Quincy.* Ford was married three times, once before and once after his marriage to Hines. He is survived by a daughter, Sally Ford, and a sister, Treasure Ford (another one time vaudevillian), both of Las Vegas, NV. His son, Gary, preceded him in death.

Henderson Forsythe, 88, Macon, MO-born actor of stage, film, and television, died April 17, 2006, in Williamsburg Landing, VA. A Tony Award winner as Best Supporting Actor in a Musical, as well as a Drama Desk Award winner as Outstanding Actor in a Musical for *The Best Little Whorehouse in Texas* (1978). His other Broadway credits include *The Cellar and the Well, Miss Lonelyhearts, Who's Afraid of Virginia Woolf?, The Right Honourable Gentleman, Malcolm, A Delicate Balance, The Birthday Party, Harvey, The Engagement Baby, The Freedom of the City, A Texas Trilogy: The Last Meeting of the Knights of the White Magnolia, A Texas Trilogy: The Oldest Living Graduate,* and *Some Americans Abroad.* Off-Broadway credits include *Cry the Beloved Country, A Fig Leaf in her Bonnet, The Pinter Plays, Dark Corners/Mr. Grossman, The New Pinter Plays,*

The Happiness Cage, Waiting for Godot, Krapp's Last Tape/Not I, Other Places, After the Fall, and *Cliffhanger.* Perhaps best known for his thirty-one year stint on *As The World Turns* as Dr. David Stewart until 1991, his other television appearances include *Law & Order* and *Eisenhower and Lutz.* Film roles include *Silkwood* (1983) and *End of the Line* (1988). A veteran of W.W. II, he spent nine years with the Erie Playhouse in Pennsylvania before moving to Manhattan. He is survived by his wife, actress Dorothea Carlson Forsythe; sons Eric, of Iowa; and Jason, of New Jersey; and four grandchildren.

Anthony Franciosa, 77, New York, NY-born actor of stage and screen, died Jan. 19, 2006, in Los Angeles, CA, of a stroke. A 1956 Theatre World Award winner as well as Tony nominee for his role in *A Hatful of Rain.* His other Broadway credits include *End as a Man* and *Wedding Breakfast.* His first three marriages, including one to actress Shelley Winters (his *Hatful of Rain* co-star), from 1957–1960, ended in divorce. His numerous film and television credits include *City Hall, Julie Darling, Fame is the Name of the Game, The Pleasure Seekers, Period of Adjustment, The Long, Hot Summer, A Face in the Crowd,* as well as appearances in a number of Italian films. He is survived by his fourth wife Rita, as well as his children Nina, Marco, and Christopher.

Christopher Fry (Christopher Fry Harris), 97, Bristol, England-born playwright/adapter/translator, died June 30, 2005, in Chichester, Sussex, England, of natural causes. A 1956 Tony nominee for his translation of *Tiger at the Gates,* his other Broadway credits include *A Phoenix Too Frequent/Freight, The Lady's Not For Burning, Ring Round the Moon* (and 1999 revival), *Venus Observed, The Dark is Light Enough, The Firstborn* and *Duel of Angels.* He also worked on the screenplays for *The Beggar's Opera, Ben-Hur* (uncredited), *Barabbas,* and *The Bible,* and later in his career turned to television production. Having joined the British Non-Combatant Corps during W.W. II, he was a director of the Oxford Repertory Players from 1940 to 1945, and in 1947 he became a director and later staff dramatist at London's Arts Theatre. He won the Queen's Gold Medal for Poetry in 1962. Survivors include his son.

Michael Gibson, 60, musician/orchestrator, died July 15, 2005, in New Jersey, of lung cancer. A Tony as well as Drama Desk Award nominee for *Steel Pier* (1997) and *Cabaret* (1998). Other Broadway credits include *Over Here, Man on the Moon, Truckload, Pal Joey, Onward Victoria, Woman of the Year, My One And Only* (Drama Desk Award, Outstanding Orchestration), *The Rink, Roza, Anything Goes* (Drama Desk nomination, Best Orchestration), *Mail, Chu Chem, Meet Me in St. Louis, Guys and Dolls, My Favorite Year, Kiss of the Spider Woman, A Grand Night for Singing, You're a Good Man, Charlie Brown, Anything Goes, The Boy From Oz,* and *All Shook Up.* Off-Broadway credits include *The Wild Party* (MTC production, Drama Desk nomination), *Ionescopade, Splendora,* and *Zombie Prom.* Survivors include his wife, Ellen, and son, Andrew. Frequently working with the famous composer-lyricist partnership of John Kander and Fred Ebb, he also worked for the Merchant Ivory film *Roseland* (1976), and orchestrated Kander's score in *Still of the Night.*

Frank Goodman, 89, press agent/producer, died Feb. 3, 2006, in New York, NY, of congestive heart failure. Working for the Federal Theater Project under the Works Projects Administration in the Great Depression as well as Orson Welles and John Houseman at the Mercury Theatre. His later abundant credits on Broadway include *Margin for Error, My Dear Children, Charley's Aunt, Something for the Boys, The Naked Genius, Around the World, Command Decision, Music in My Heart, Look, Ma, I'm Dancin'!, Edward, My Son, Private Lives, Along Fifth Avenue, King Richard III, Clutterbuck, Gentlemen Prefer Blondes, The Cocktail Party, Come Back, Little Sheba, The Relapse, Ring Around the Moon, Bless You*

All, The Moon Is Blue, A Tree Grows in Brooklyn, Seventeen, Gigi, Caesar and Cleopatra, Dial "M" for Murder, The Children's Hour, Men of Distinction, Me and Juliet, A Girl Can Tell, In the Summer House, The Magic and The Loss, Reclining Figure, Lunatics and Lovers, Witness for the Prosecution, The Wooden Dish, Middle of the Night, Romanoff and Juliet, The Body Beautiful, The World of Suzie Wong, L Plume de Ma Tante, Gypsy, The Sound of Music, The Andersonville Trial, Roman Candle, Caligula, The Tumbler, One More River, Christine, The World of Carl Sandburg, Irma La Douce, Critic's Choice, From the Second City, Sail Away, A Shot in the Dark, Kwamina, Daughter of Silence, The Night of the Iguana, No Strings, Tchin-Tchin, Photo Finish, Danny Kaye, Funny Girl, Beekman Place, Luv, Ready When You Are, C.B.!, I Had a Ball, Do I Hear a Waltz?, The Impossible Years, The Lion in Winter, Under the Weather, Here's Where I Belong, George M!, Fire!, The Mother Lover, Zelda, The Dozens, Hamlet, Two By Two, Tricks, Full Circle, Mister Lincoln, and *Broadway* (as producer). Off-Broadway credits include *Measure for Measure, The Taming of the Shrew, Garden District, Dark of the Moon, U.S.A., One Way Pendulum, The Tragical History of Dr. Faustus, The Secret Life of Walter Mitty, Hooray! It's a Glorious Day … and all that, To Clothe the Naked, Love and Let Love, Tea Party/The Basement, In the Bar of a Tokyo Hotel*, and *JFK*. His personal clients included Jerome Robbins, Audrey Hepburn, and writers William Inge and Clifford Odets.

Peter Halasz, 62, Hungary-born playwright/actor/director, died March 10, 2006, in Brooklyn, NY, of liver cancer. Desiring of the experience of his own funeral, he staged it a month before his death. Enclosing himself in a glass coffin before family and friends, he listened to the eulogies among a crowd of several hundred. Founder of the Squat/Love Theater collective, an Off-Off-Broadway ensemble of the 1980s, he was considered a pioneer of the free-spirited theater scene in Hungary. Barred from performing in public in Hungary in 1972, he took his players underground to perform, mostly in private homes. The ensemble left Hungary in 1976, and eventually arrived in New York City in 1977, embodying conceptual art and "happenings" of the time. The collective became known as Squat and was known for *Mr. Dead and Mrs. Free, Pig, Child, Fire!*, and *Andy Warhol's Last Love*. In 1987, Mr. Halasz presented his play *Ambition*, adapted from the André Maurois story *Palace Hotel Thanatos*, at La MaMa in Manhattan. Other stage credits include *She Who Once Was the Helmet-Maker's Beautiful Wife*, by Mr. Halasz and Seth Tillett, first staged in 1992 at the Performing Garage in SoHo. More welcome in his own country after the fall of Communism there, he spent more time there in the theater and, in recent years, won prizes in independent European film productions. He is survived by his wife, Agnes Santha of Staten Island; two daughters, Judith Halasz of Brooklyn, and Cora Fisher of Long Island City, Queens; two sons, Gabor and David, of Budapest, Hungary; and a brother, Andras, also of Budapest.

T. Edward "T" Hambleton, 94, Maryland-born producer/theatre manager, died Dec. 17, 2005, in Cockeysville, MD. Founded the Phoenix Theatre with partner Norris Houghton in 1953 on 2nd Avenue and 12th Street in New York City. It moved to a 300-seat theatre on East 74th Street in 1961. Its final home was at the Marymount Manhattan Theater. His numerous Broadway credits include *Robin Landing, I Know What I Like, The First Crocus, The Great Campaign, Galileo, Pride's Crossing, The Golden Apple, Sandhog, Phoenix '55, Marcel Marceau, Six Characters in Search of an Author, Saint Joan, The Great God Brown, Once Upon a Mattress* (Tony nomination), *Oh Dad, Poor Dad, Mama's Hung You in the Closet and I'm Feeling so Sad, You Can't Take It With You* (1965 & 1967), *The School for Scandal, Right You Are If You Think You Are, We, Comrades Three, The Wild Duck, War and Peace, Pantagleize, The Show Off* (1967 & 1968), *Exit the King, The Cherry Orchard, Pantagleize, The Cocktail Party, The Misanthrope, Cock-A-Doodle Dandy, Hamlet, Harvey, The School for Wives, The Trial of the Catonsville Nine, Murderous Angels, The Great God Brown, Don Juan, The Visit,*

Chemin de Fer, Holiday, Love for Love, The Rules of the Game, The Member of the Wedding, A Memory of Two Monday/27 Wagons Full of Cotton (Drama Desk Award nomination), *They Knew What They Wanted* (Drama Desk Award nomination) *Secret Service, Boy Meets Girl*, and *Beyond Therapy*. Off-Broadway credits include *The Carefree Tree, Diary of a Scoundrel, The Good Woman of Setzuan, Measure for Measure, The Taming of the Shrew, The Duchess of Malfi, Livin' the Life, Mary Stuart, The Makropoulos Secret, The Transposed Heads, Two Gentleman of Verona, The Broken Jug, Le Malade Imaginaire, An Evening of Three Farces, The Pirates of Penzance, Androcles the Lion/The Policeman, Who'll Save the Plowboy, Abe Lincoln in Illinois, The Dragon, Morning Sun, Next Time I'll Sing to You, The Brontes, Too Much Johnson, The Tragical Historie of Doctor Faustus, The Criminals, The Persians, Ladyhouse Blues, Marco Polo, A Sorrow Beyond Dreams, G.R. Point, Scribes, Hot Grog, The Elusive Angel, City Sugar, One Crack Out, Getting Out, Later, Says I, Says He, Big and Little, The Winter Dancers, Shout Across the River, The Trouble with Europe, Save Grand Central, Second Avenue Rag, Bonjour, La, Bonjour, The Captivity of Pixie Shedman, Meetings*, and *Two Fish in the Sky*. Phoenix received a Special Tony Award in 1968; he received a Special Tony Award in 2000, and the T Fellowship at Columbia was created in his honor "to support and develop emerging theatrical producers."

Martha Nell Hardy, 79, died Oct. 14, 2005, in Chapel Hill, NC, of cancer. She racked up 2,000 performances spanning thirty-three years as Mrs. Perkins in *Unto These Hills*, one of the oldest outdoor historical dramas in the nation, which depicts the Cherokee Indians being driven out of the Great Smoky Mountains and marched onto the Trail of Tears. She was also was a former chairwoman of the Department of Communications Studies at University of North Carolina at Chapel Hill, where in 2000. The Martha Nell Hardy Professorship was begun in her honor. In 2002 she received the state of North Carolina's highest civilian award, the North Carolina Medal, for her work as an actor and educator.

Peter Hamilton, 90, Trenton, NJ-born performer/choreographer, died Jan. 31, 2006, in New York, NY, of complications from Parkinson's disease. His Broadway credits include *Sing Out Sweet Land*, for which he received a Donaldson Award as promising young performer, *Angel in the Wings*, and *Beg, Borrow or Steal*. Credits also include solo performances at Radio City Music Hall and the Rainbow Room on Broadway. He is survived by his companion of sixty-two years, Don Liberto.

Carl Harms, 94, Chicago, IL-born actor, puppeteer, and Equity administrator, died Aug. 11, 2005, in New York, NY, following a brief illness. He made his Broadway debut in 1951 in *Flahooley*, followed by *Much Ado About Nothing* (with Clare Booth Luce), *The Girl on the Via Flaminia*, and *Man in the Moon*. He joined Equity in 1946 and served on numerous negotiating committees, including the historic first negotiation between Equity and the League of Resident Theatres in 1966. Helping also to establish a pension fund in 1960, it caused Broadway to shut down for seven days. He was also a member of Equity's governing body, the Council, as recording secretary for twelve years, and then as first vice president. He was a founder and president of the Actors Equity Foundation. Learning to carve, construct, and use puppets in the 1930s as a part of the core group of actors whose work formed the basis of the WPA Federal Theater, he eventually worked with Bill Baird, joining his Marionettes in 1940. As puppeteer he worked on such television shows as *The Adventures of Snarky Parker, Johnny Jupiter, Howdy Doody, The Tempest, Your Show of Shows*, and *The Ed Sullivan Show*. A conscientious objector during W.W. II, he still served his country in the Merchant Marines, providing support during D-Day and the Battle of the Bulge. Two daughters survive him.

Joel Hirschhorn, 67, Bronx, NY-born composer/writer/lyricist, died Sept. 17, 2005, in Thousand Oaks, CA, of a heart attack. He received two Tony Awards for his Broadway credits *Copperfield* (1981) and *Seven Brides for Seven Brothers* (1982), and received two Academy Awards for "The Morning After" from *The Poseidon Adventure* and "We May Never Love Like This Again" from *The Towering Inferno*. He and collaborator Al Kasha also received another Academy Award nomination for "Candle on the Water" from *Pete's Dragon*. He is survived by his wife, two stepsons, a sister, his mother, and a grandson.

Endesha Ida Mae Holland, 61, Greenwood, MS-born playwright, died Jan. 25, 2006, in Santa Monica, CA, of complications of ataxia, a degenerative neurological condition. Partially financed by Oprah Winfrey, *From the Mississippi Delta* premiered Off-Broadway in 1991 at the Circle in the Square. An autobiographical play about her experiences emerging from poverty, prostitution, shoplifting, and street-fighting to earn three college degrees (including a doctorate) and a successful career in academia, *From the Mississippi Delta*, is one among six plays she penned. It has been performed by the Negro Ensemble Company, the Goodman Theater in Chicago, and at the Young Vic in London. Her 1997 memoir was also titled *From the Mississippi Delta*. She taught at the University of Buffalo from 1985–1993, as well as at the University of Southern California until her retirement in 2003. She is survived by a sister, Jean Beasley; brother, Charlie Nellums; son, Cedric; and granddaughter.

Betty Lee Hunt, 85, Brooklyn, NY-born publicist/producer whose career spanned four decades, died Oct. 11, 2005, in New York, NY, of non-Hodgkins lymphoma. Beginning her career as an assistant to Dorothy Ross, mainly a nightclub publicist, in her twenties she became publicity director for Music Corporation of America, then worked for several other companies, and eventually formed Bett Lee Hunt Associates in 1950. Her Broadway credits alone or with partner Maria Christina Pucci include *Remains to Be Seen, Point of No Return, Wish You Were Here, Picnic, The Prescott Proposals, House of Flowers, There Was a Little Girl, A Second String, Advise and Consent, New Faces of 1962, Hot Spot, Rehearsal, Double Dublin, Roar Like a Dove, Sweet Charity, Paris Is Out!, All Over, Earl of Ruston, To Live Another Summer, To Pass Another Winter, On the Town, The Grass Harp, Grease, A Funny Thing Happened on the Way to the Forum, Don't Bother Me, I Can't Cop, Lysistrata, The Last of Mrs. Lincoln, Let Me Hear You Smile, Warp, The Desert Song, Rachael Lily Rosenbloom and Don't You Ever Forget It, Noël Coward in Two Keys, Over Here!, Candide, The Hashish Club, Seascape, P.S. Your Cat Is Dead!, Truckload, The Skin of Our Teeth, Yentl, Hello, Dolly!, The Norman Conquests: (Table Manners, Round and Round the Garden,* and *Living Together), Murder Among Friends, Home Sweet Homer, Rockabye Hamlet, Who's Afraid of Virginia Woolf?, The Heiress, Legend, Fiddler on the Roof, Caesar and Cleopatra, The Shadow Box, Cheaters, Stages, Working, The Grand Tour, Are You Now of Have You Ever Been, The Utter Glory of Morrissey Hall, Up in One, Lone Star & Pvt. Wars, West Side Story, Clothes for a Summer Hotel, Goodbye Fidel, Hide and Seek, Fearless Frank, Tintypes, The Philadelphia Story, Macbeth, The Floating Light Bulb, Crimes of the Heart, Pump Boys and Dinettes, Agnes of God, Solomon's Child, Moose Murders, 'night Mother, Passion, The Octette Bridge Club, As Is,* and *Execution of Justice.* She also represented *Liza Minnelli at the Winter Garden* and Peter Allen's *Up in One.* As an associate producer, she won a Tony Award for Best Play for 1983's *Torch Song Trilogy*, which also won a 1983 Drama Desk Award for Outstanding New Play. Her sometimes extensive personal client list included Lena Horne and Bobby Short, whom she represented for thirty-five years. She is survived by Pucci, a sister, Aileen, and brother, Saul.

Justine Johnston, 84, Evanston, IL-born actress, died Jan. 13, 2006, in West Hollywood, CA, of a stroke. With Broadway credits including *The Pajama Game, I Remember Mama, Follies, Sondheim: A Musical Tribute, Irene, Molly, Angel,* and *Me and My Girl*, her touring credits include *Milk and Honey, Lend Me a Tenor,* and *A Funny Thing Happened on the Way to the Forum* (the role of Domina she played off and on for over thirty years). Her final stage show was in a 2002 revival of *Follies*, which starred Patty Duke, Carol Lawrence, and Stella Stevens. Her film credits include *Arthur, 9 1/2 Weeks, Fatal Attraction,* and *Running on Empty* (with River Phoenix). She was on the governing body of Actors Equity for thirty-nine years. She also performed throughout the Mid-Pacific during W.W. II with Overseas Unit 860. She is survived by numerous nieces and nephews.

Roger Kachel, 44, Minnesota-born actor/dancer, died April 5, 2006, in Florida, of undisclosed causes. Best known for appearing in the musical *Cats* for eleven years, most notably as Mungojerrie, he was with the production on its final performance on Sept. 10, 2000. Other Broadway credits include *Starlight Express*. His film and video credits include *Tuff Turf, Girls Just Want to Have Fun,* and *Teenage Mutant Ninja Turtles: Coming Out of Their Shells Tour,* as well as *Sesame Street Live*. His second career was as a baker, joining Ron Ben Israel Cakes.

Don Knotts (Jesse Donald Knotts), 81, Morgantown, WV-born television, film, and stage actor, died Feb. 24, 2006, in Los Angeles, CA, of lung cancer. A five-time Emmy Award winner as Best Supporting Actor for his immortal role as Deputy Barney Fife on *The Andy Griffith Show* from 1960–1968, his lone but memorable Broadway credit was *No Time For Sergeants*, the film version of which he would also appear in. Other films include *The Incredibly Mr. Limpet* (1964), *The Ghost and Mr. Chicken* (1966), *The Reluctant Astronaut, The Shakiest Gun in the West* (1968), *The Love God?* (1969), *The Apple Dumpling Gang, The Apple Dumpling Gang Rides Again, Pleasantville,* and *Chicken Little* (2005). He started on television on *The Steve Allen Show*; other memorable television credits following *The Andy Griffith Show* include the swinging landlord Mr. Ralph Furley of *Three's Company* and *Matlock*, as well as *Return to Mayberry*, the latter two seeing him reunited with Griffith. He was a veteran of W.W. II, serving as an entertainer, and two marriages, to Kay Knotts and Loralee Knotts, ended in divorce. He is survived by his wife, actress Francey Yarborough, a son, and a daughter.

Frances Langford, 91, Lakeland, FL-born singer/actress, died July 11, 2005, at her home in Jensen Beach, FL, of congestive heart failure. Broadway credits include *Here Goes the Bride* and *The Pure in Heart*. Perhaps best known for introducing the classic song "I'm in the Mood for Love" in the 1935 film musical *Every Night at Eight*, She was also seen in such other pictures as *Broadway Melody of 1936, Collegiate, Born to Dance, Hollywood Hotel, Too Many Girls, Yankee Doodle Dandy, Cowboy in Manhattan, This Is the Army, The Girl Rush,* and *The Glenn Miller Story*. She was also well known on radio for the series *The Bickersons*. Survived by her husband, Harold Stuart.

Paula Laurence, (born circa 1913–1916), Brooklyn, NY-born actress/singer, died Oct. 29, 2005, in New York, NY, after having suffered a fractured hip the previous month. She made her theatrical debut in 1927 in director Orson Welles's Federal Theatre Project production of *Horse Eats Hat* (playing the girl whose hat was eaten). Later she played Helen of Troy (the only woman in the ensemble) in Welles' *Doctor Faustus*. Her last show with the group was the 1939 musical revue *Sing For Your Supper*. In 1941, Paula originated the role of the wisecracking maid in *Junior Miss*, directed by Moss Hart (to whom she was engaged at the time). In 1943, Paula was featured as Ethel Merman's stripper cousin Chiquita in the premiere of the Cole Porter musical *Something for the Boys*. The show's most memorable sequence "By the Mississiniwah" was a comedy duet by Laurence and Merman, dressed as native squaws. Later in 1943, Paula was featured in the premiere of the Kurt Weill musical *One Touch of Venus*, as the snappy secretary Molly who sings the title number. During the 1930s and 1940s, Paula also performed a supper club act of a satirical nature, appearing at Le Ruban Bleu and The Blue Angel, among other clubs. Until the last year of her life, Paula continued to sing in places like the Algonquin and in cabaret and symphony concerts at Carnegie Hall, Town Hall, and the John Drew Theatre. Other Broadway credits include *Cyrano de Bergerac* (as the Duenna with Jose Ferrer, in 1946), *Inside U.S.A.* (she succeeded Beatrice Lillie), *The Liar*, Wolcott Gibbs' comedy *Season in the Sun, The Night of the Iguana, Have I Got a Girl For You!, Hotel Paradiso* (with Bert Lahr), *Ivanov* (with Vivien Leigh and John Gielgud), *Black Comedy/White Lies*, and she replaced Jean Stapleton as Mrs. Strakosh in *Funny Girl*. During the late 1940s, Paula was a founding member of Ferrer's City Center Theatre Company and performed in its *Volpone* and *The Insect Comedy* among others. During the 1980s, Paula was a key figure in the late Bill Tynes' New Amsterdam Theatre Company (a forerunner of Encores) and performed leading roles in *Sweet Adeline, Jubilee*, and *One Touch of Venus* (her same role forty years later). She also enjoyed extensive credits in stock, regional stages, and television, including a recurring role in the cult classic *Dark Shadows*. She was married for more than forty years to the late producer-manager Charles Bowden, and together they ran the Westport Country Playhouse through the 1950s. Among his Broadway shows, Bowden produced the *The Night of the Iguana*, and he and Laurence were close friends of Tennessee Williams, so much so that the couple became the guardians of his sister Rose Williams upon his death. In recent years Paula was a source of information to biographers of Williams, Hart, Merman, Weill, the Lunts, Elia Kazan, Al Hirschfield, Ruth Draper, and Lucille Lortel, among others. As a writer, Paula contributed many articles over the years to *Madamoiselle, Vogue, Harpers Bazaar,* and *Playbill*. Up until the last months of her life and for many years, Paula was an active board member of the New Dramatists. Its artistic director Todd London termed her the organization's spiritual godmother. (In fact she was actually actress Stephanie Zimbalist's godmother.) Paula left no family but many close friends ranging from Lily Tomlin and Simon Callow to Steve Ross and Jean-Claude Baker.

Marc Lawrence, 95, New York, NY-born character actor, who specialized in villains and gangster roles over a seventy-year period, died Nov. 26, 2005, in Palm Springs, CA, of heart failure. His Broadway credits include *Romeo and Juliet* (1930, revival), *The Tree*, and *The Survivors*. Best known for his work in film, his many roles in that medium are *G Men, San Quentin, Murder in Greenwich Village, Invisible Stripes, Johnny Apollo, The Monster and the Girl, Blossoms in the Dust, Hold That Ghost, This Gun for Hire, The Ox-Bow Incident, Dillinger* (1945), *Key Largo, The Asphalt Jungle, My Favorite Spy, Helen of Troy, Krakatoa East of Java, The Man with the Golden Gun, Marathon Man, Foul Play, The Big Easy, Newsies, The Shipping News,* and *Looney Tunes: Back in Action*. Survived by his wife, a daughter, and a son.

Ernest Lehman, 89, screenwriter and producer, died July 2, 2005, in Los Angeles, CA, after a heart attack. Screenwriting credits include *The King and I, West Side Story, The Sound of Music, Who's Afraid of Virginia Woolf*, and *Hello, Dolly!*, He received Academy Award nominations for the screenplays of *West Side Story, Virginia Woolf*, and *Sabrina*, which was based on the 1953 Broadway play *Sabrina Fair* by Samuel Taylor. He was also Oscar-nominated as a producer of *Virginia Woolf* and *Hello, Dolly!*, both of which were nominated for Best Picture. Lehman co-wrote the screenplay for the 1957 film *Sweet Smell of Success*,

based on his own novella, and he was a co-producer of the 2002 Broadway musical version starring John Lithgow. His other credits include writing, producing, and directing the 1972 film *Portnoy's Complaint*, based on the Philip Roth novel; and writing *North by Northwest*, the Alfred Hitchcock film starring Cary Grant and Eva Marie Saint. In 2001, Lehman received an honorary Academy Award for Lifetime Achievement. He is survived by his second wife, Laurie Sherman, and three children: Roger, Alan, and Jonathan.

Ann Loring, 90, died July 10, 2005, in New York, NY, of complications from a stroke. Her Broadway credits include *Bright Rebel* and *Brooklyn Biarritz*. She played Tammy Forrest on the soap opera *Love of Life* for thirteen years, winning Emmy Awards for daytime actress in 1961, 1962, and 1963. She also worked in television and film, her credits in that media including *The Robin Hood of Eldorado*. For seven years she served as president of the New York local of AFTRA, and continued on the local and national boards. She was a governor and trustee of the National Academy of Television Arts and Sciences. She taught writing at the New School Of Social Research for more than twenty years, and penned books including *Mark of Satan, Thirteenth Doll, Emergency* and *Write and Sell your TV Drama*. She produced and was a panelist on *The Barry Farber Show* for 2000 airings. She is survived by two sons.

Sid Luft (Sidney Luft), 89, New York, NY-born producer/director, died Sept. 15, 2005, in Santa Monica, CA, of a heart attack. Credited with reviving wife Judy Garland's fledgling career in the 1950s, his Broadway credits are three starring Garland (for whom he was for thirteen years third husband): *Judy Garland* (1956–57), *Judy Garland* (1959), and *Judy Garland: A Home at the Palace* (1967). Perhaps best known for the 1954 film remake of *A Star is Born,* also starring Garland, his other film credits include *Kilroy Was Here* and *French Leave*. Survivors include his third wife, Camille Keaton (grandniece of Buster Keaton), son, Bari, and his two children with Garland, singer/actress Lorna Luft and Joey Luft. A marriage to Patti Hemingway in 1970 also ended in divorce.

Anne Meacham, 80, Chicago, IL-born actress, died Jan. 12, 2006, in Canaan, NY. Broadway credits include *The Long Watch* (for which she received a Clarence Derwent Award), *Ondine* (opposite Audrey Hepburn and directed by Alfred Lunt), *Eugenia* (with Tallulah Bankhead), *The Legend of Lizzie, Moonbirds, A Passage to India, The Seagull, The Crucible,* and *Rosencrantz and Guildenstern Are Dead*. She won an OBIE Award for her work Off-Broadway in *Suddenly, Last Summer* (1958), written by her close friend Tennessee Williams, as well as for *Hedda Gabler* (1961). She also appeared Off-Broadway in the Williams' plays *The Gnädiges Fraulein* (1966) and *In the Bar of a Tokyo Hotel* (1969), *The Immortal Husband, Garden District, The Lady Akane,* and *The Wives*. She toured with Eva LeGalliene's National Repertory Theatre in *The Seagull, The Crucible,* and *Ring Round the Moon*. On television she is best known for her role as the eccentric Cory family maid, Louise Goddard, on *Another World*, playing the role from 1972–1982. She is survived by a sister, Jane Brower.

Susan MacNair (aka Sue MacNair), 65, died Aug. 31, 2005, in New York, NY, following a lengthy illness. Broadway credits include *Ballroom* (1978 Tony Award nomination), *Hurlyburly, Social Security,* and *Death and the Maiden*. She also worked on *A Chorus Line* and *Seesaw* as an assistant to Michael Bennett, and worked as an assistant as well for Edward Villella and Lauren Bacall. In addition to Ms McNair's work on Broadway, she was Mike Nichols' assistant on films including *Heartburn* and *Working Girl*. She was also an associate producer on Nichols' films *Regarding Henry* and *Postcards From the Edge*, as well as having worked on *Silkwood, Heartburn, Gilda Radner*, and Monte Helmman's *Two-Lane Blacktop*. She is survived by her husband, Arthur P. Siccardi.

Darren McGavin, 83, Spokane, WA-born actor of stage, screen, and cinema, died Feb. 25, 2006, in Los Angeles, CA, of natural causes. Studying at the Neighborhood Playhouse and the Actors Studio before working in live television drama and on Broadway, his credits there include *My 3 Angels, The Rainmaker, The Innkeepers, The Lover, The Tunnel of Love, Two for the Seesaw, Blood, Sweat, and Stanley Poole, Dinner at Eight*. Off-Broadway credits include *No Rhyme, No Reason*, as well as numerous regional, summer stock, and national tour credits, including *Death of a Salesman*. Climbing off a ladder in 1945 while painting a movie set when he learned of an opening for a small role in a show, he got the part, and went on to a prolific career in television and film, starring in five series, including *Riverboat, Kolchak: The Night Stalker*, and *Mike Hammer*. He won a 1990 Emmy Award for his work in that medium as Murphy Brown's father on *Murphy Brown*. He also portrayed General George Patton in the television biography *Ike*. He made a lasting mark as the cantankerous dad in *A Christmas Story* (1983). In a career in all media that spanned over fifty years, other film credits include *Summertime* (1955, with Katharine Hepburn and Rosanno Brazzi), *The Man with the Golden Arm* (1955), *The Delicate Delinquent* (1957), *No Deposit, No Return* (1976, with Don Knotts), and *The Natural*. He is survived by his four children – York, Megan, Bridget, and Bogart – from a previous marriage to Melanie York McGavin. His second marriage was to Kathie Brown.

Fayard Nicholas, 91, Mobile, AL-born performer/dancer/choreographer, who along with brother Harold was part the tap dancing team The Nicholas Brothers, known for their amazing athleticism and who became role models for dancers including Fred Astaire and Savion Glover, died Jan. 24, 2006, in Toluca Lake, CA, of pneumonia and complications of a stroke he suffered in November 2005. Broadway credits include *Ziegfeld Follies of 1936, Babes in Arms, St. Louis Woman, Sammy*, and *Black and Blue* (1989, for which he shared a Tony Award for Best Choreography). Some of the first to break the color barrier, the Nicholas Brothers' film debut was in *Pie, Pie, Blackbird* (1928). Other film credits include *Kid Millions* (1934), *The Big Broadcast of 1936, My Son Is Guilty, Down Argentine Way, Tin Pan Alley*, a notable "Jumpin' Jive" dance sequence in *Stormy Weather* (1943) with Gene Kelly (groundbreaking interracial dance sequence), and *The Pirate* (1948). Beginning in vaudeville in 1928, their first act was as The Nicholas Kids. Fayard was 18 and Harold was 11 when they became the featured act at the Cotton Club in Harlem in 1932, known as The Show Stoppers! Their trademark was no-hands splits – in which they not only went down but sprang back up again without the use of hands. Before he fell ill, Fayard tap-danced and lectured at dance festivals across the world. His two granddaughters, calling themselves the Nicholas sisters, would perform his old steps. He was the recipient of the Kennedy Center Honors in 1991, along with his brother. His first two marriages ended in divorce, and his third wife, dancer Katherine Hopkins-Nicholas, survives him, as do sons Tony and Paul; sister, Dorothy Nicholas Morrow of Los Angeles, CA; and a great-granddaughter. His brother Harold died in 2000.

David Nillo, 89, Goldsboro, NC-born performer/choreographer/assistant/arranger and founding member of American Ballet Theater, died Sept. 28, 2005, in Los Angeles, CA, following a stroke. He began his career in Chicago, IL, with the Page-Stone Ballet, the Graff Ballet, and Federal Theater Dance Project. His Broadway credits include *Call Me Mister, Great to Be Alive!, Out of This World, Maggie, My Fair Lady, Goldilocks, Double Dublin*, and *The Desert Song*. Ballets with Ballet Theater include *Giselle* and Eugene Loring's *Billy the Kid*. Film credits include *The Vagabond King*. He was a veteran of W.W. II, serving from 1943 – 45 as a radio operator for the US Maritime Service, and was honored by former Los Angeles, CA, mayor Tom Bradley for his community service. He is survived by longtime friend, Christina Babst.

Sheree North (Dawn Shirley Crang, aka Dawn Bethel), 72, Hollywood, CA-born screen, stage, and television actress, died Nov. 4, 2005, in Los Angeles, CA, of complications from cancer surgery. Beginning a dancing career at age ten and touring with USO shows during W.W. II, she may be best remembered as Lou Grant's girlfriend on television's *The Mary Tyler Moore Show*, as well as for portraying Kramer's mother Babs on *Seinfeld*. Her Broadway credits include *Hazel Flagg*, for which she won a 1953 Theatre World Award, and *I Can Get It for You Wholesale*. She starred in such 20th Century Fox films of the 1950s as *How to Be Very, Very Popular* and *The Lieutenant Wore Skirts*. Her other movies include *Living It Up, The Best Things in Life Are Free, No Down Payment, In Love and War, Mardi Gras, Madigan, The Gypsy Moths, Lawman, Charley Varrick, The Shootist*, and *Defenseless*. She is survived by her fourth husband, two daughters, and a grandchild.

Louis Nye (aka Lewis Nye), 92, Hartford, CT-born comedian/actor, perhaps best known for his appearances on *The Steve Allen Show*, died on Oct. 9, 2005, in Los Angeles, CA, following a long battle with lung cancer. His Broadway credits include *Inside U.S.A., Touch and Go, Flahooley*, and *Charley's Aunt* (1970). He was seen in such movies as *The Facts of Life, Sex Kittens Go to College, The Wheeler Dealers, Good Neighbor Sam, A Guide for the Married Man, Won Ton Ton the Dog Who Saved Hollywood*, and *Harper Valley PTA*. He appeared in other television shows such as the recurring role of Sonny Drysdale in *The Beverly Hillbillies, Make Room for Daddy, Burke's Law, The Munsters, Love, American Style, Laverne & Shirley, Starsky and Hutch, Police Woman, Fantasy Island, St. Elsewhere, The Cosby Show*, and *Curb Your Enthusiasm*. He also recorded two comedy LPs. Survivors include his wife, Anita Leonard, to whom he was married for near fifty years, and son, artist Peter Nye.

Jean Parker (Lois May Green), 90, Deer Lodge, MT-born actress, perhaps best known for playing Beth in the 1933 film version of *Little Women*, died of a stroke Nov. 30, 2005, in Woodland Hills, CA, at the Motion Picture and Television Country House, where she had lived since 1998. Broadway credits include *Born Yesterday, Loco*, and *Burlesque*. She appeared in other films such as *Gabriel Over the White House, Lady for a Day, Operator 13, A Wicked Woman, Murder in the Fleet, The Ghost Goes West, The Texas Rangers, Penitentiary, The Flying Deuces, No Hands on the Clock, Minesweeper, One Body Too Many, Those Redheads from Seattle*, and *Apache Uprising*. Survived by her son, Robert Lowery, Jr., and two granddaughters, Katie and Nora Lowery.

Priscilla Gillette Perrone, 80, Tenafly, NJ-born actress/singer, died Feb. 2, 2006, in New York, NY, following a period of declining health. When she made her debut in the lead role of Fiona in the first national tour of *Brigadoon* in 1947 – 48, the operatic quality of her voice convinced producer Cheryl Crawford to call her back to New York from the tour to take the role of Alexandra Giddens (Zan) in *Regina*, Marc Blitzstein's 1949 opera/musical adaptation of Lillian Hellman's *The Little Foxes*. Her appearance in *Regina* earned her a Theatre World Award in 1950. She was then tapped for Cole Porter's mythological musical *Out of This World*, which ran from 1950 – 51. Mythology figured again in what was perhaps her best remembered role in the noted but ill-fated John LaTouche adaptation of the *Odyssey, The Golden Apple*, in 1954. A coming presence in early television, Priscilla starred with Charlton Heston in *The Willow Cabin*, a production of Westinghouse Studio in 1950. She was a regular in many productions of *Studio One*, including *The Legend of Jenny Lind*, in which her soaring vocal abilities were again a feature. She was also a familiar figure, in various roles over the years, on *The Edge of Night*. She is survived by her daughter, Alexandra Lowell Gifford (named for her character in *Regina*) from her marriage to John Gifford; daughter Jeane Rose Perrone; and son Andrew David Perrone, from her marriage to Dr. Francis Perrone, from whom she was divorced, but who survives her, as do her grandchildren, Jasmine and Jordan.

Brock Peters (George Fisher), 78, New York, NY-born actor, perhaps best known for portraying Tom Robinson in the 1962 classic film *To Kill a Mockingbird*, died Aug. 23, 2005, in Los Angeles, CA, of pancreatic cancer. Broadway credits include *Mister Johnson*, *The Body Beautiful*, *Kwamina*, *The Caucasian Chalk Circle*, and *Lost in the Stars* (1973, Tony nomination, Drama Desk Award for Outstanding Performance). Other films include *Carmen Jones*, *Porgy and Bess*, *Heavens Above!*, *The L-Shaped Room*, *Major Dundee*, *The Pawnbroker*, *The Incident*, *Ace High*, *Black Girl*, *Soylent Green*, *Lost in the Stars* (repeating his stage role), *Two Minute Warning*, and *Star Trek IV: The Voyage Home*. Television roles included Captain Benjamin Sisko's father on *Star Trek: Deep Space Nine*. He is survived by his companion, Marilyn Darby, and daughter, Lise Jo Peters.

Ford Rainey 96, Mountain Home, ID-born character actor, died July 25, 2005, in Santa Monica, CA, following a series of strokes. Broadway credits include *The Possessed*, *Twelfth Night*, *The Wanhope Building*, *Long Day's Journey Into Night*, and *J.B.* Other stage credits include *The Crucible* and a national tour of *King Lear*. He could be seen in such pictures as *White Heat*, *3:10 to Yuma*, *John Paul Jones*, *Flaming Star*, *Parrish*, *Two Rode Together*, *Kings of the Sun*, *The Sand Pebbles*, and *The Traveling Executioner*. He also made television appearances, including on *The King of Queens* in the 1990s. He is survived by his wife, two sons, a daughter, and five grandchildren.

Ron Randell, 86, Sydney, Australia-born screen, stage, and television actor, died June 11, 2005, in Los Angeles, CA, of complications of a stroke. Broadway credits include *The Browning Version/Harlequinade*, *Candida*, *The World of Suzie Wong*, *Butley*, *Sherlock Holmes*, *Mrs. Warren's Profession*, *No Man's Land*, *Bent*, *Duet for One*, and *The School for Scandal*. His movies include *Bulldog Drummond Strikes Back* (as Drummond), *The Sign of the Ram*, *The Loves of Carmen*, *China Corsair*, *The Mississippi Gambler*, *Kiss Me Kate* (as Cole Porter), *I Am a Camera*, *The She-Creature*, *The Story of Esther Costello*, *Davy*, *King of Kings*, *The Longest Day*, and *The Seven Minutes*. He is survived by his wife of forty-eight years, actress Laya Raki.

Dana Reeve, 44, Teaneck, NJ-born actress/singer/advocate, and devoted caretaker to her husband, actor Christopher Reeve, died March 6, 2006, in Manhattan, NY, of lung caner, which had been diagnosed in 2005. She lived in Pound Ridge, NY. Mr. Reeve, best known as the title hero in the *Superman* movie franchise, was paralyzed after a 1995 horseback riding accident in Virginia. He died Oct. 10, 2004, in New York, NY, at age 52. Ms. Reeve's Broadway credits include *More to Love*. Off-Broadway credits include *Portraits*. She also acted at such regional theaters as the Yale Repertory Theater and the New Jersey Shakespeare Festival. On television she appeared in shows including *Law and Order*, *Oz*, and *All My Children*, and was a co-host for *Lifetime Live*, a program on the Lifetime network. Ms. Reeve will be seen on March 29 in a PBS program, *The New Medicine*, which was taped in November 2005. On Jan. 12, 2006, she sang *Now and Forever* to a Sold Out crowd at Madison Square Garden on behalf of a friend, the former Rangers hockey captain Mark Messier, who was being honored in a retirement ceremony. Upon her husband's injury, she turned her attention to becoming an advocate for research into spinal cord injuries, succeeded her husband as chairman of the Christopher Reeve foundation, and established the Christopher and Dana Reeve Paralysis Resource Center, an infor-

mation clearinghouse. The couple met in 1987 in Williamstown, Mass., where Christopher saw Dana performing in a cabaret act at the Williamstown Theater Festival. They were married on April 11, 1992, in an outdoor ceremony at a farm in South Williamstown. She is survived by her son, Will, by Christopher Reeve; father, Dr. Charles Morosini; sisters, Deborah Morosini and Adrienne Morosini Heilman; and two stepchildren, Matthew and Alexandra.

Maurice Rosenfield, 91, Chicago, IL-born attorney/producer, died Oct. 30, 2005, of heart failure. In a career that spanned sixty-five years marked by advocacy of first amendment rights including defense of Lenny Bruce and *Playboy* magazine, Broadway credits include *The Goodbye People*, *Barnum* (Tony and Drama Desk Award nominations), *The Glass Menagerie* (1983, with Jessica Tandy), *Singing in the Rain*, *Falsettos*, and *The Song of Jacob Zulu* (Tony nomination). Off-Broadway credits include *The Road to Mecca* (Drama Desk Award nomination) and *Falsettoland*. Film credits include *Bang the Drum Slowly* (with an unknown Robert DeNiro, whom he cast himself), and *Wavelength*. He was also founding partner and general manager of WAIT 820 AM, one of Chicago's top-rated radio stations throughout the 1960s and early 1970s. His wife and partner (with whom he founded Rosenfield Productions in 1972), Lois F. Rosenfield, died May 25, 2003. He is survived by sons James and Andrew, daughter-in-law Betsy, and four grandchildren, Zak, Alex, Lannie, and Jake.

Nipsey Russell, 81, Atlanta, GA-born comedian-actor, who came to be dubbed "The Poet Laureate of Television," for his humorous rhyming poetry (usually in four lines), died Oct. 2, 2005, in New York, NY, following a long battle with cancer. Having appeared at such clubs as Baby Grand, Small's Paradise, and other cabarets, he parlayed his burgeoning success into a series of television appearances—in regular roles such as Officer Anderson in *Car 54 Where Are You?* and in television game shows *Match Game*, *What's My Line?*, and *Hollywood Squares*. Variety show appearances included *The Tonight Show* (with both Jack Paar and Johnny Carson), *The Dean Martin Show*, and *The Jackie Gleason Show*. His movie roles include *The Wiz* (1978, as the Tin Man), *Nemo* (1984), *Wildcats* (1986), *Posse* (1993), *Car 54, Where are You?* (1994, repeating his role from the early 1960s TV series). Survived by his cousins.

John Seitz, 67, Louisville, KY-born character actor and theatre advocate, died July 4, 2005, in Baltimore, MD, of congestive heart failure. Well known for his downtown performances, the actor won Obie Awards for his work in Maria Irene Fornes' *Abingdon Square* (1988) and Carl Hancock Rux's *Talk* (2001). His Broadway credits include Harold Pinter's *No Man's Land* (with Jason Robards and Christopher Plummer), Arnold Wesker's *The Merchant*, and Victor Gialanella's *Frankenstein*. Seitz appeared in the Public Theater productions of *Machinal*, *Casanova*, and *Talk*. He also played the title role in Richard Foreman's staging of Moliere's *Don Juan*. Other highlights included CSC productions of *Krapp's Last Tape* and *The Merchant of Venice*, the BAM Repertory's *Gorky's Barbarians*, and revivals of Samuel Beckett's *Endgame* and Sam Shepard's *Fool for Love*. A lifetime supporter of emerging artists and not-for-profit theater, Seitz received the New Dramatists' Charles Bowden Award in 1997 and the Spencer Cherashore award in 2002 for his work in these areas. Recently, he developed the New Harmony (Indiana) Project and a play project at Robert Redford's Sundance Institute. In the interest of bridging post-Cold War cultural understanding, he worked extensively with Russian artists in the U.S. and abroad as a participant in the Russian/U.S. Foundation for Mutual Trust. He is survived by a daughter, Becca Seitz, of Baltimore, Maryland; a granddaughter, Genevieve Grace Schuh, also of Baltimore; and two sisters, Lillie Hutto of Spring Hill, Florida, and Nora Manning of Louisville, Kentucky.

Diane Shalet, 71, actress, died Feb. 23, 2006, in Palm Springs, CA. Her Broadway credits include *After the Fall*, *But for Whom Charlie*, *The Changeling*, and *Tartuffe*. Television credits include *Matlock*, *The Waltons*, and *Perry Mason*. She is the author of the novel *Grief in a Sunny Climate*. Film roles include *The Last Tycoon* and *The Reivers*. A founder of the Actors and Writers Lab in Manhattan, she was also a charter member of the Lincoln Center Repertory Theatre under the direction of Robert Whitehead and Elia Kazan. She taught at UCLA for fourteen years. She was preceded in death by her husband, actor Michael Strong.

Jane Lawrence Smith (aka June Lawrence), Bozeman, MT-born actress/singer, died Aug. 5, 2005, in New York, NY. Broadway credits include *Oklahoma!*, *Inside U.S.A.*, and *Where's Charley*. A very close friend of playwright Tennessee Williams (best man at her wedding), she was married to sculptor/architect Tony Smith from 1943 until his death in 1980. Film credits include *Sailor's Holiday*. She was preceded in death by her daughter Beatrice Smith Robinson and survived by Kiki and Seton Smith and granddaughter Antonia Smith Robinson.

Lane Smith (Walter Lane Smith), 69, Memphis, TN-born screen, stage, and television character actor, died June 13, 2005, in in Northridge, CA, of Amyotrophic Lateral Sclerosis (ALS), commonly referred to as Lou Gehrig's disease. Broadway credits include *The Leaf People* and *Glengarry Glen Ross* (1984, for which he won a Drama Desk Award for Outstanding Ensemble Work). Off-Broadway credits include *Borak*, *In the First Place*, *The Honest-to-God Schozzla*, *The Nest*, *Children in the Rain*, *Pinkville*, *One Flew Over the Cuckoo's Nest*, *Barbary Shore* and *Jack Gelber's New Play: Rehearsal*. His films include *Man on a Swing*, *Network*, *Between the Lines*, *Over the Edge*, *Resurrection*, *Prince of the City*, *Frances*, *Places in the Heart*, *Weeds*, *Air America*, *My Cousin Vinny*, *The Mighty Ducks*, *The Distinguished Gentleman*, *Son in Law*, *The Scout*, *Why Do Fools Fall in Love*, and *The Legend of Bagger Vance*. On television he was best known for playing President Richard M. Nixon on the miniseries *The Final Days* (for which he received an Emmy nomination) and Perry White on the series *Lois & Clark: The New Adventures of Superman*. Survived by his wife, his son, and a stepson.

John Spencer, 58, New York, NY-born stage, screen, and television character actor, died Dec. 16, 2005, in Los Angeles, CA, of a heart attack. An OBIE Award winner for the Off-Broadway production of *Still Life* in 1981, he also received a Drama Desk Award nomination for *The Day Room*. Other stage credits include *Lakeboat* and *The Glass Menagerie*. At the time of his death he was still continuing his Emmy-winning role of chief of staff Leo McGary on the NBC series *The West Wing*, a role for which, along with his part as Tommy Mullaney on *L.A. Law* during its final four years, he is best remembered. His movies include *WarGames*, *Sea of Love*, *Black Rain*, *Presumed Innocent*, *Forget Paris*, *Cop Land*, *Twilight*, *The Rock*, *The Negotiator*, *Albino Alligator*, *Lesser Prophets*, and *Cold Heart*. He is survived by cousins, aunts, uncles, and many friends.

Maureen Stapleton (Lois Maureen Stapleton), 80, Troy, NY-born star of stage, screen, and television who won the highest possible accolades performing in all three media, died March 13, 2006, in Lenox, MA, of chronic pulmonary disease. Volume 37, 1980–81 of *Theatre World* is dedicated: "To Maureeen Stapleton— whose humor, generosity, and friendship are as deeply appreciated and treasured as are her critically acclaimed performances." In a much lauded career that spanned over fifty years, she enrolled at the New School upon moving to New York where she studied with Herbert Berghof and joined the Actors Studio in 1947, where her colleagues included Julie Harris, Marlon Brando, Anne

Jackson, and Eli Wallach. Ms. Stapleton's numerous Broadway credits included *The Playboy of the Western World*, *Antony and Cleopatra*, *Detective Story*, *The Bird Cage*, *The Rose Tatto* (for which she won a 1951 Theatre World Award as well as the Tony Award for Best Featured Actress in Play), *The Crucible*, *The Emperor's Clothes*, *All in One*, *Orpheus Descending* (opposite Cliff Robertson as Val Xavier), *The Cold Wind and the Warm* (Tony nomination), *Toys in the Attic* (Tony nomination), *The Rose Tattoo* (1966, revival), *Plaza Suite* (directed by Mike Nichols, opposite George C. Scott, Tony nomination), *Norman, Is That You?*, *The Gingerbread Lady* (Tony Award for Best Actress in a Play, Drama Desk Award for Outstanding Performance), *The Country Girl*, *The Secret Affairs of Mildred Wild*, *The Glass Menagerie*, *The Gin Game*, the special benefit *V.I.P Night on Broadway*, and *The Little Foxes* (1981, opposite Elizabeth Taylor, Tony nomination). Off-Broadway credits include *The Sea Gull*. An Academy Award winner for her fiery performance as anarchist Emma Goldman in *Reds* (1981). Her other film credits include *Miss Lonelyhearts* (1959, Best Supporting Actress Academy Award nomination), *The Fugitive Kind*, *Airport* (1970, Academy Award nomination), *Interiors* (1978, Best Supporting Actress Academy Award nomination), *Coccoon* (1985), *Cocoon: The Return* (1988), *Nuts* (1987, opposite Barbra Streisand), *The Last Good Time* (1994). She also won an Emmy Award for an adaptation of *All the King's Men*, as well as for *Among the Paths to Eden*, an adaptation of a Truman Capote story. Other television credits include *Queen of the Stardust Ballroom* (1975, Emmy nomination) and *Last Wish* (1992). She also wrote her autobiography, *A Hell of a Life*, with Jane Scovell in 1995. Her first marriage from 1949–59 to general manager/manager/producer/production crew member Max Allentuck ended in divorce, as did her second marriage to writer David Rayfiel, from 1963–66. She is survived by her daughter, Katharine Allentuck Bambery; grandson, Max and granddaughter, Alexandra, of Lenox, MA; son, Daniel Allentuck of Manhattan; brother, John, of Troy, New York. (She was not related to the actress Jean Stapleton, as many have thought.)

Don Stewart (Donald Stewart), 70, died Jan. 9, 2006, in Santa Monica, CA, of lung cancer. Broadway credits include *Camelot*, *The Student Gypsy*, and *Anyone Can Whistle*. He played the part of Michael Bauer on *The Guiding Light* from 1968–1978. He also appeared in twenty films and in other television roles. A veteran of the US Air Force, he is survived by wife, Carol; two daughters; a stepson; and two brothers.

Harold Stone, 92, New York, NY-born screen, stage, and television character actor, died Nov. 18, 2005, in Woodland Hills, CA, of natural causes. Broadway credits include *Honeymoon*, *The World We Make*, *Morning Star*, *Counterattack*, *One Touch of Venus*, *A Bell for Adano*, *Irma La Douce*, *Abraham Cochrane*, *A Way of Life*, *Charley's Aunt*, and *Ring Around the Bathtub*. He could be seen in such motion pictures as *The Harder They Fall*, *Somebody Up There Likes Me*, *The Wrong Man*, *The Garment Jungle*, *The Invisible Boy*, *Spartacus*, *The Chapman Report*, *X: The Man with the X-Ray Eyes*, *The Greatest Story Ever Told*, *The St. Valentine's Day Massacre*, *The Big Mouth*, *The Seven Minutes*, and *Mitchell*. Survived by two sons, a daughter, and four grandchildren.

Lorna Thayer, 86, Boston, MA-born actress, died June 4, 2005, in Woodland Hills, CA, having battled Alzheimer's for five years. Broadway credits include *Comes a Day* and *Never Live Over a Pretzel Factory*. Perhaps best known as the waitress who confronted Jack Nicholson when he was ordering in the "chicken salad" scene in the film *Five Easy Pieces* (1970), she was also seen in such movies as *The Lusty Men*, *The Women of Pitcairn Island*, *Cisco Pike*, *Skyjacked*, *Buddy Buddy*, and *Nothing in Common*. She is survived by two daughters and ten grandchildren.

Frankie Thomas (Frank M. Thomas, Jr.), 85, New York, NY-born actor, died May 11, 2006, in Los Angeles, CA, of respiratory failure, following a stroke. Best known for the television show *Tom Corbett, Space Cadet*, playing a member of a space academy in training to become an elite member of the Solar Guard. Broadway credits include *Carry Nation, Little Ol' Boy, Thunder on the Left, Wednesday's Child, The First Legion, Remember the Day, Seen But Not Heard,* and *Your Loving Son*. Film credits include *A Dog of Flanders, Boys Town,* and *The Major and the Minor,* as well as four Nancy Drew movies, among thirty-five others. Following the end of the run of *Tom Corbett, Space Cadet,* over the years he worked as a television and radio writer, bridge instructor, and author of mystery novels such as *Sherlock Holmes and the Masquerade Murders.* He is survived by a stepdaughter, Julie Alexander, and stepson, James Aicholtz.

Arthur A. Tookoyan (aka Art Tookoyan), 82, actor/singer, died Aug. 19, 2005. Broadway credits include *Peter Pan* (1954), *Christine, The Happiest Girl in the World, The Sound of Music, The Unsinkable Molly Brown,* and *Milk and Honey.* He was a veteran of the US Navy.

Ted Tulchin (Stanley Tulchin), 79, Manhattan, NY-born producer/banker/credit lecturer, died Dec. 19, 2005, in Manhasset, NY, of heart failure. Founder and chairman of Stanley Tulchin Associates (which underwent a name change to STA International). He also formed theatrical partnerships that included Maidstone Productions and Tuchin/Bartner/Bagert. Alone or in partnership his Broadway credits include *Taller Than a Dwarf, Fortune's Fool, Vincent in Brixton, Sweeney Todd* (2006), and *Company* (2006). A Drama Desk Award nominee for *Dinner With Friends* in 2000 and *The Unexpected Man* in 2001, he also received Tony Award nominations for *Fortune's Fool, Vincent in Brixton,* and *Sweeney Todd* (2006), for which he won a 2006 Drama Desk Award for Outstanding Revival of a Musical. Off-Broadway credits include *Thunder Knocking on the Door, Trying, Our Lady of Sligo, Rounding Third,* and *Madame Melville.* He was instrumental in having *I Just Stopped By to See the Man* produced at Steppenwolf Theatre in Chicago, IL, and at the Geffen Playhouse in Los Angeles, CA. He was also an owner of The Playhouse and The Savoy in London, England, and was involved in London productions of *Guys and Dolls, Whose Life Is It Anyway?, Hitchcock Blonde,* and *Vincent in Brixton.* He served on the board of New Dramatists, WLIW, the suburban New York City PBS station, Playwrights Horizons, and the American Academy of Dramatic Arts (also serving there as treasurer), and participated as a lecturer at the Commercial Theater Institute. He was a member of the Jewish Community Center of Sherman, CT, and served on the boards of The Topps Co. and New York Institute of Credit. He is survived by his wife of fifty-three years, Patsy; sons Steven and Jeffrey; daughter Jill; brother Norman; and three grandchildren.

Frederic B. ("Fred") Vogel, Philadelphia, PA-born producer/actor and founder of the Commercial Theater Institute, a teaching program for prospective Broadway producers and a longtime expert on theater management, died on Nov. 29, 2005, at his home in New York, NY, of complications from lung cancer. Volume 61 of *Theatre World* is dedicated: To Frederic B. Vogel: As executive director of the Commercial Theater Institute for over twenty-three years, Fred became the leading force behind producing for the commercial theatre in America, providing the first and most comprehensive workshops ever conducted for training producers to produce commercially On Broadway, Off-Broadway, and road productions. He also created the Federation for the Extension and Development of the American Professional Theatre in 1970, which under his guidance offered organizational, development, and technical assistance to more than five hundred theaters, dance companies, performing arts centers, and other arts projects throughout the United States. Beginning his theatrical career as an actor at the age of nine, Fred appeared On Broadway, Off-Broadway, in the summer stock circuit, and in television and film before switching his creative priorities to the "front office." He invested in more than fifty Broadway productions, including Shakespeare's *R&J*, as well as the Tony nominated *Marlene*. His *Producing for the Commercial Theatre*, which he edited with *Theatre World*'s Ben Hodges and including contributions from over twenty Broadway producers, general managers, publicists, and other professionals in the industry, is anticipated as the definitive guide to commercial producing in America. It is forthcoming from Applause Theatre and Cinema Books in fall 2006, a fitting tribute to Fred's indelible mark on the theatre world. Mr. Vogel established the institute in 1982 as a seminar to teach what he had learned from years in the theatrical trenches. The Commercial Theater Institute claims many accomplished producers as alumni, including Kevin McCollum, a producer of *Avenue Q*, and Nick Scandalios, the executive vice president of the Nederlander Organization, which owns nine Broadway theaters. Broadway credits as a performer include *Romeo and Juliet* (1951, starring Olivia de Havilland) and *Take A Giant Step* (1953). In addition to those mentioned above, Broadway productions for which he served as producer and/or investor also include *Same Time, Next Year* (1975) and *Enchanted April* (2003, Tony nomination). Off-Broadway credits in those capacities include *The Cover of Life* and *Lust*. He was also the producer of the independent film *A Tale of Two Pizzas*. He was assistant director for the Performing Arts at the 1962 Seattle World's Fair, which presented more than 125 international theatrical and concert attractions. He was in charge of the International Special Events Program and served as the director of the Film Program, which premiered films from around the world, and was subsequently appointed special events director of the New York State Commission on the World's Fair for the New York State Pavilion at the World's Fair, a position he held from 1963–1965. In 1988, Mr. Vogel was a founding member of Broadway Cares and was the chair of the Broadway Cares Grants Committee which from 1988–1992 distributed over $1 million to scores of AIDS service providers in New York City and across the country. With the merger of Broadway Cares and Equity Fights AIDS in May 1992, he joined the BC/EFA Board of Trustees and continued in his role as chair of the BC/EFA National Grants Committee until his death. Over the last thirteen years, as chair of the grants committee, he has been instrumental in BC/EFA, making over $25 million in grants to hundreds of AIDS and family service providers and advocates in forty-eight states, Washington, DC, and Puerto Rico. He also lectured at leading university Arts Management graduate programs in the U.S. He served as an arts consultant for the Ford Foundation in Indonesia. He is survived by niece Kathie Packer of Chicago; nephews Daniel J. Zitin of New York, NY, and Gary M. Zitin of Philadelphia, PA; sister Naomi V. Zitin and brother-in-law Williard Zitin of Philadelphia, PA. He was a mentor, colleague, and close friend of Ben Hodges, editor of this publication, and will be greatly missed by him as well as by many.

George D. Wallace (aka G.D. Wallace), 88, New York, NY-born screen, stage and television actor, died on July 22, 2005, in Los Angeles, CA, of complications from injuries he sustained earlier in the year upon falling. Broadway credits include *Pipe Dream, New Girl in Town, Jennie, The Pajama Game,* and *The First.* He also appeared in many regional and road productions. His films include *The Big Sky, Arena, Man Without a Star, The Night of the Hunter, Forbidden Planet, Texas Across the River, The Towering Inferno, Lifeguard, Protocol, Punchline, Postcards from the Edge, Defending Your Life,* and *Minority Report.* He was a veteran of the US Navy, and is survived by his wife, the actress Jane A. Johnston.

Herta Ware, 88, Wilmington, DE-born actress, died Aug. 5, 2005, in Topanga, CA. Blacklisted along with longtime husband Will Geer (most notably "Grandpa

Walton" of *The Waltons* fame). Broadway credits include *Let Freedom Ring*, *Bury the Dead*, *200 Were Chosen*, *Journeyman*, and *Six O'Clock Theatre*. Her films include *The Black Marble*, *2010*, *Cocoon*, *Slam Dance*, *Soapdish*, *Species*, *Practical Magic*, and *Cruel Intentions*. She received a Cable ACE Award for her work in television, where she appeared frequently. She is survived by three daughters, Kate Geer and actresses Ellen Geer and Melora Marshall; a son, Thad; nine grandchildren; and one great-grandson. During her marriage to Geer she helped found the Will Geer Theatricum Botanicum in Topanga, CA, where every plant mentioned in the works of Shakespeare is grown.

Wendy Wasserstein, 55, Brooklyn, NY-born playwright, died Jan. 30, 2006, in Manhattan, New York, of complications of lymphoma. Her Broadway credits include the long-running *The Heidi Chronicles*, which opened Off-Broadway and eventually landed On Broadway, starring Joan Allen and running 622 performances, and collected the Tony and New York Drama Critics Circle Awards for Best Play, as well as the Pulitzer Prize. (It was the first time a woman won the Best Play Tony Award on her own.) It was later filmed for television starring Jamie Lee Curtis. That achievement was followed by *The Sisters Rosensweig*, which at the time had the largest advance for a play in Broadway history, opened on Broadway in 1993, ran 556 performances, and received a Best Play Tony nomination. Afterward came *An American Daughter*, which was later adapted for television, and the benefit *Escape: 6 Ways to Get Away (1)* and *(2)*. Off-Broadway her credits include *Uncommon Women and Others* (produced by Phoenix Theater in 1977 and filmed for PBS's *Great Performances*, starring Glenn Close, Swoosie Kurtz, and Meryl Streep), *Isn't It Romantic* (1981, revised 1983), *Orchards*, *Urban Blight*, *Love's Fire: Fresh Numbers by Seven American Playwrights*, *Old Money*, and *Third*. Her first play, *Any Woman Can't*, was produced by Playwrights Horizons in 1973. Her other writings included a spoof of self-help literature, *Sloth*, in 2005, and two books of essays, *Bachelor Girls*, in 1990, and *Shiksa Goddess*, in 2001. Her sole screenplay credit was for *The Object of My Affection*, a 1998 romantic comedy starring Jennifer Aniston. Her first novel, *Elements of Style*, was published in 2006. She also wrote a children's book, *Pamela's First Musical*, which she adapted for the stage in collaboration with Cy Coleman and David Zippel, and wrote the libretto for *The Festival of Regrets*, one of three one-act operas presented as *Central Park* at the New York City Opera. She had also completed a libretto for another opera with music by Deborah Drattell. A recipient of a Guggenheim Fellowship, she later served on the Guggenheim Foundation board, and she also taught playwriting at several universities. In 1998, seeking to help instill her love for theater in a new generation of New Yorkers, she was responsible for the formation of a program to bring gifted underprivileged students from New York's public high schools to the theater. Administered by the Theater Development Fund, and now officially called Open Doors, the program consists of seventeen groups (more than 100 students), who are treated to a season's worth of theater offerings by interested mentors. She is survived by her brothers, Abner and Bruce, chairman of the investment banking firm Lazard and owner of *New York* magazine, and her sister, Georgette Levis of Vermont, as well as daughter, Lucy Jane, to whom she gave birth in 1999, at age forty-eight, and who will live with her brother, Bruce. The lights on Broadway were dimmed on January 31, 2006, in her honor.

Dennis Weaver (William Dennis Weaver), 81, Joplin, MO-born actor, died Feb. 24, 2006, in Ridgway, CO, of complications from cancer. He made his Broadway debut in *Come Back, Little Sheba* in 1950. Broadway credits also include *Out West of Eigth*. Best known for his roles on television as Chester in *Gunsmoke* (which he played for nine years, and for which he won a 1959 Best Supporting Actor in a Drama Emmy Award) and as Sam McCloud in *McCloud* (two Best

Leading Actor in a Drama Emmy nominations), he also starred in *Gentle Ben* from 1967 –– 69. He made numerous film appearances, most notably in *Touch of Evil* and *The Duel*, an early Spielberg film. In 1982 with wife, Gerry, he founded the organization *Love is Feeding Everyone*, which fed more than 100,000 people in Los Angeles each week, and in 1993 he and his wife founded *The Institute of Ecolonomics* (which he coined from an amalgam of the words *ecology* and *economics*, dedicated to finding solutions to environmental problems. Since 1990, Weaver and his wife had lived in a 10,000-square-foot solar powered home constructed from 3,000 recycled tires and 30,000 tin and aluminum cans. He also released several country music albums and a one-man show in which he played nineteen Shakespearean characters. A veteran of the US Navy Air Corps, he was the president of the Screen Actors Guild from 1973–75. He received a 1984 Golden Boot Award and a 1987 Humanitarian Award from at the Women in Film Crystal Awards. For the last nine years of his life he hosted *Westerns* on the Starz television network. He received a star on the Hollywood Walk of Fame in 1986, and his 2001 autobiography was entitled *All the World's a Stage*. He is survived by his wife of over sixty years, Gerry; sons Rusty, Rick, and Rob; and three grandchildren.

August Wilson (Frederick August Kittel), 60, Pittsburgh, PA-born playwright, died Oct. 2, 2005, in Seattle, WA, of liver cancer. His epic ten-play cycle chronicling the black experience in twentieth century America remains unequaled in scope. His Broadway credits include *Ma Rainey's Black Bottom* (1984, Tony nomination), followed by *Fences* (1987 Pulitzer Prize, Tony Award, Drama Desk Award for Best Play), *Joe Turner's Come and Gone* (1988, Tony nomination), *The Piano Lesson* (1990, Pulitzer Prize for Drama, Drama Desk Award), *Two Trains Running* (1992, Tony nomination), *Seven Guitars* (1996, Tony nomination), *Jitney* (2000), *King Hedley II* (2001, Tony nomination), and *Gem of the Ocean* (2004, Tony nomination). He met his longtime collaborator, Lloyd Richards, at the National Playwrights Conference at the O'Neill Theater Center in Connecticut, who eventually would direct six of his plays on Broadway in 1968, Wilson co-founded Pittsburgh's Black Horizon Theater. The partnership he formed with producer Ben Mordecai to produce his plays was named Sageworks. On August 14, 2005, New York's Virginia Theater was renamed the August Wilson Theatre in his honor. He was also a veteran of the US Army. He is survived by his third wife, costume designer Costanza Romero, as well as his two daughters, Sakina Ansari Wilson, from his marriage to first wife Brenda Burton, and Azula Carmen (with Romero). His second marriage to Judy Oliver produced no children.

Shelley Winters (Shirley Schrift, aka Shelley Winter), 85, St. Louis, MO-born actress raised in Brooklyn, NY, from age three, died Jan. 14, 2006, in Beverly Hills, CA, of heart failure. A two-time Best Supporting Actress Academy Award winner for her roles, *The Diary of Anne Frank* and *A Patch of Blue*, her Broadway credits include *The Night Before Christmas*, *Rosalinda*, *Oklahoma!*, *A Hatful of Rain*, *Girls of Summer*, *The Night of the Iguana*, *Under the Weather*, *Minnie's Boys*, and *The Effect of Gamma Rays on Man-in-the-Moon Marigolds*. She also authored a series of one-act plays that were produced Off-Broadway in 1970 entitled *One Night Stands of a Noisy Passenger*. Off-Broadway performance credits include *Cages* at the York Playhouse in 1963. Originally billed in Hollywood as the "blonde bombshell" who shared a bedroom with Marilyn Monroe, she was a veteran of over 120 films and a major film presence in cinema for over fifty years. Her numerous and many memorable roles include *What a Woman!* (1943), *A Double Life* (1947), *Phone Call from a Stanger* (1952), A *Place in the Sun* (1953, Best Actress Academy Award nomination), *I Am A Camera* (1955), *Lolita* (1962), *Alfie* (1966), *Harper* (1966), *The Poseidon Adventure* (1972, Best Supporting Actress Academy Award nomination), *Next Stop Greenwich Village*

(1976), *Pete's Dragon* (1977), and *The Portrait of a Lady* (1996). She donated her Oscar for *The Diary of Anne Frank* to the Anne Frank museum in Amsterdam, and her two autobiographies were *Shelley: Also Known as Shirley* and *Shelley II: The Middle of My Century*. She has a star on the Hollywood Walk of Fame at 1750 Vine Street, and continued to attend Charles Laughton's Shakespeare classes and worked as well as taught at the Actors' Studio long after she was an established, successful actress. Notable on television particularly for her recurring role as Roseanne's grandmother on *Roseanne* throughout the 1990s, she also made many other television appearances. She was married to her fourth and last husband, Gerry DeFord (with whom she had lived for nineteen years), just hours before her death by actress Sally Kirkland, an ordained minister of the Movement of Spiritual Inner Awareness. Her second husband was Italian actor Vittorio Gassman, with whom she had her only child, Vittoria, who survives her, as does DeFord. Her third marriage was to her *A Hatful of Rain* co-star, Anthony Franciosa.

Robert Wright (Robert Craig Wright), 90, Dayton Beach, FL-born lyricist and composer, died July 27, 2005, in Miami, Florida, as a result of undiagnosed normal pressure hydrocephalus. His seventy-year partnership with George "Chet" Forrest (1915–1999) stands unchallenged as "The Longest Running Songwriting Collaboration in Show Business History." Forever called "The Boys" by their peers, Wright and Forrest wrote eighteen musicals, songs, or scores for sixty-one films, over 2,000 songs, and produced and directed for the theatre, nightclubs, film, television, radio, and recordings. They received three Academy Award nominations for Best Song: *Always and Always* (1938), *It's a Blue World* (1940), and *Pennies for Peppino* (1942). Their standards include *The Donkey Serenade, Stranger in Paradise, And This Is My Beloved, Baubles, Bangles and Beads, Sweet Danger,* and *Strange Music.* "The Boys" met at ages 14 and 15, while attending Miami High School in 1929, and wrote their first song, *Hail To Miami High.* During his teens,

Wright played piano in nightclubs for such stars as the legendary Helen Morgan and fan dancer Sally Rand. And, with Forrest, toured the US with notorious comedian/female impersonator Ray Bourbon. Wright and Forrest, arriving in Hollywood in 1935, at ages 20 and 21, respectively, became the youngest songwriters under contract at MGM, and created a series of box-office bonanzas for Jeannette MacDonald and Nelson Eddy, including *Maytime, Rosalie, Sweethearts,* and *New Moon.* They segued to Broadway in 1943 with the acclaimed *Song of Norway.* Adapting themes by Borodin, Wright and Forrest received Tony Awards for Best Music and Best Lyrics for *Kismet,* book by Luther Davis, which also won Best Musical. Their landmark *Grand Hotel: The Musical,* book by Luther Davis, additional music and lyrics by Maury Yeston, directed by Tommy Tune, garnered five Tony Awards (and Tony nods for Best Music and Lyrics), and ran for more than 1,000 performances. In 2004, London's Donmar Theatre production received the Olivier Award for Best Musical Revival. Their other musicals include *Thank You, Columbus, Spring in Brazil, Gypsy Lady, Magdelena,* with Hector Villa Lobos, *The Great Waltz, The Carefree Heart, At the Grand, The Love Doctor, Kean, Anya, Dumas & Son, A Song for Cyrano, Timbuktu!* (Geoffrey Holder's African-based restaging of *Kismet*), and *Anastasia: The Musical,* the 1989 revival of *Anya,* book by Jerome Chodorov, starring their protégé, Judy Kaye. Mr. Wright's final stage project was as supervisor of The York Theatre's revival of *Kean,* with Walter Willison and Susan Watson, in 2000. Still active at the time of his death, he had completed work on four unproduced projects: *La Vie,* book by Jerome Chodorov; *The Incompatibles: A Molieresque Musical,* book by Walter Willison; *Betting On Bertie: The Original Jeeves Musical,* with lyrics by the legendary P.G. Wodehouse; and *Whirlygig,* a musical version of *The Ponder Heart,* both with books by Walter Willison and Douglas Holmes. In 1995, the American Society of Composers, Authors and Publishers presented Wright and Forrest with the Richard Rodgers/ASCAP Award for Outstanding Lifetime Contributions to the American Musical Theater. He is survived by his brother, Jack Wright.

INDEX

Fischer, Kurt 82
Fischer, Lori 268
Fischer, Stephanie 193
Fischman, Sharon 226
Fischnaller, Troy 203
Fischoff, George 209, 256
Fish 249
Fish Bowl 201
Fish, Daniel 196
Fishback, Dan 204
Fishburne, Laurence 274
Fishell, Julie 290
Fisher, Audrey 275
Fisher, Aurélia 181
Fisher, Barry 112
Fisher, Emily 205
Fisher, Frances 273
Fisher, Guil 184, 222
Fisher, Ian Marshall 99
Fisher, Jason 117
Fisher, Jenny 197
Fisher, John 98
Fisher, Joseph 184
Fisher, Jules 42
Fisher, Laura T. 283
Fisher, LaVon 263, 266, 275
Fisher, Layna 228
Fisher, Linda 262, 278
Fisher, Mary Beth 283
Fisher, Rob 71, 168
Fisher, Steven 242
Fishing With Tony & Joe 225
Fishman, Alan H. 152
Fishman, Carol 104, 107
Fishman, Lisa 106
Fishman, Shirley 271
Fisichella, Christine 97
Fisichella, Jeanne-Marie 115
Fisk, Danielle 235
Fisk, Greg 188
Fiske, Jeffrey 210
Fitch, Andrew 247
Fitch, Robert 154
Fitgerald, Peter 210
Fithian, Diana 200
Fits & Starts: the Sacred Heart 184
Fitzgerald, Adam 209, 230
Fitzgerald, Christopher 84
Fitzgerald, Geraldine 338, 342
Fitzgerald, Jason 202
Fitzgerald, Kathy 81
Fitzgerald, Michael 156, 184
Fitzgerald, Peter 31, 49, 93, 101, 124
Fitzgerald, Ron 122
Fitzgerald, T. Richard 28, 70, 97, 106, 117
Fitzpatrick, Allen 228, 294
Fitzpatrick, Bettye 262, 263
Fitzpatrick, Colleen 56, 92
Fitzpatrick, Julie 182, 189
Fitzpatrick, Nicole 278
Fitzsimmons, Andrew 255
Fitzsimmons, James 160
Fitzwater, Anna 184, 194
Fiumano, Donna 239
Five Course Love 105
Five Days With Dylan 206
Five Lesbian Brothers 162
Five Streams 245
Fix Me, Please and Thank You 200
Fix, Michelle 203
Fix, Nicole 244
Fizzard, Anne 235, 255

Flahaven, Sean Patrick 234
Flaherty, Peter 152
Flaherty, Stephen 42, 227, 228, 275
Flair, Nicholas 91
Flaming Box of Stuff 210
Flanagan, Amy 183
Flanagan, Bob 156
Flanagan, James 163
Flanagan, June 214
Flanagan, Kerry 211, 236
Flanagan, Laura 176, 183
Flanagan, Margaret A. 192
Flanagan, Tarah 277, 292
Flat 188
Flaten, Barbara 272
Flatmo, Britt 259
Flatow, Paula 114
Flauto, Elizabeth 98, 106, 244
Flea in Her Ear, A 279
Flea, The 193
Flea Theatre 105, 123, 226
Fleck, Charlotte 29
Fleet Week: the Musical 239
Flegel, Brian 202
Fleisher, Julian 114, 128
Fleitz, Jason 117
Fleming, Adam 74, 84
Fleming, Heather 271
Fleming, Juanita 213
Fleming, Mark 124
Fleming, Renee 200
Fleming, Sam 164, 267
Flemming, Denise B. 206
Fleshler, Glenn 104, 169, 283
Fletcher, Gregory 225
Fletcher, Jim 198
Fletcher, Kelly 77
Fletcher, Zachary 230
Flexen, Justin 290
Fliakos, Ari 121
Flight 145
Flink, Michael 112
Flinn, Lewis 166, 173
Flint, Lori Amondson 259
Flint, Michigan 195
Flirting with Reality 228
Floberg, Kari 184
Floberg, Patterson 205
Flood, Karen 189
Floor, Callie 265
Flopz 245
Flora, Pat A. 263
Florence, Susanna 280
Flores, Alex 189
Flores, Dyan 236
Flores, Elizabeth 131
Flores, Hector 289
Flores, Julia 291
Flores, Rory 141
Flores, Ruben 168, 245
Flores, Stacey 267, 268
Flores, Wally 22
Florianai, Vincent 142
Floriani, Victor 142
Florim, Raquel 233
Florin, Jacki Barlia 178
Florio, Donna 193
Florio, Kristen 181
Flower, Beth 70
Flowers, Ramón 59, 76
Floyd, Carmen Ruby 69, 219
Floyd, Mike 296
Floyd, Patricia R. 195

Floyd, Ramona 157
Floyd, Sharon 213
Fluffy Bunnies in a Field of Daisies 239
Fluitt, Keith Anthony 59
Fluke 204
Fly 225
Flyer 217
Flyers and Other Tales 235
Flying Fig Theater 190
Flying Pig Collective 213
Flying Sequences 84
Flynn, Chris 235
Flynn, Deirdre 247
Flynn, James 132
Flynn, John 242, 247
Flynn, Matthew 152
Flynn, Molly 197
Flynn, Peter 70, 108
Flynt, Mary Kathryn 78, 166
Foa, Barrett 69, 77, 83
Foard, Merwin 32, 70
Fogarty, Eileen 239
Fogarty, Sharon 100, 183, 200
Fogarty, Tara 95
Fogel, Bryan 139
Fogel, Donna Jean 210
Fogel, Erin 189
Fogle, Jessica 243
Fogler, Dan 83
Foglino, Paul 239
Foh, Julie 165
Folden, Lewis 289
Foldesi, Julie 108
Foley, Bob 205
Foley, David 184
Foley, David, Jr. 246
Foley, John 200
Foley, Kate 252
Foley, Mark J. 189
Foley, Scott 150
Foley, Siobhan 170
Folie, Mike 221
Folksbiene Yiddish Theatre 105
Follies of Grandeur 251
Follywood 193
Folmar, Cameron 213
Folmer, Jeremy 114
Folts, Barbara 70
Fondakowski, Leigh 284
Fondulis, Nick 236, 237
Fong, Kuan Yu 195
Font, Vivia 202, 219
Fontaine, Jeff 140
Fontaine, Steve 220
Fontana, Santino 284
Fool for Love 183
Fools in Love 95
Foote, Daisy 223
Foote, Greg 217
Foote, Hallie 174
Foote, Horton 174, 208, 225, 285
Foote, Horton, Jr. 203
Foote, Jenifer 72
For Bill 232
For Christ's Sake...the Musical 214
For Colored Girls Who Have Considered Suicide 212, 228, 245
Forakis, Gia 118
Forand, Eric 181
Forbach, Jason 162
Forbes, George 284, 285
Forbes, Kate 118

Forbidden Broadway: Special Victims Unit 138
Forbrich, Joe 172
Force, Patrick 184
Ford, Adam 283
Ford, Alden 181
Ford, Amanda 194
Ford, Amber 233
Ford, David 132
Ford, Jacki 206
Ford, Jennie 74
Ford, Jessica 164, 184, 198
Ford, John 213
Ford, Jonette 239
Ford, Mark Richard 26, 82
Ford, Nigel 206
Ford, Phil 342
Ford-Roberts, Antonia 285
Ford, Sarah 195, 209, 220, 252
Ford's Theatre 280
Foreign Bodies & Sexual Furniture Space Sluts Are Hotties 237
Foreigner, The 290
Forella, Jessica 209
Foreman, Karole 263, 280
Foreman, Richard 116, 195, 204, 243
Foreman, Sam 222
Forever Plaid 214
Forget Me Not 203
Forlenza, Louise 26
Forman, Ken 103, 188
Forman, Sam 187, 188, 191, 196, 223
Foro, Greg 200
Forrell, Lisa 91, 93
Forrest, George 153
Forrest, Michael 97
Forrest, Michael L. 266
Forrest, Sheldon 205
Forrest, Tobias 277
Forrester, Bill 259, 267, 279
Forsatz, Kathryn 206
Forsman, Carl 220, 230, 286
Forster, Gabriele 224
Forsythe, Henderson 342
Fortenberry, Philip 226
Fortner, Gregory 218
Fortner, Kelly 70
Fortner, Sidney 234
Forum Theatre 212
Fosberg, Michael 282
Fosse, Bob 42, 43, 71
Fosse, Nicole 79
Foster, Benim 46, 272
Foster, Charles 210, 217
Foster, Cynthia 193, 200
Foster, Dan 107
Foster, David 59
Foster, David J. 141
Foster, Flannery 227
Foster, Herb 155, 168
Foster, Hunter 81
Foster, Janet 26, 75, 271
Foster, Katherine 283
Foster, Kimberly 220
Foster, Lolita 206
Foster, R.J. 187, 199
Foster, Rick 91, 185, 186
Foster, Sutton 15, 60, 61, 183, 274
Foubert, David 130
Foucheux, Rick 266, 293
Foundry Theatre 116, 202
Fountain, Brian 247
Fountain, Elizabeth 252

Fouquet, Paul 105, 266
Four for the Office 235
Four Hearts and a Club 269
Four One-act Plays 209
Four One-legged Men! 206
Four Women 195
Fournier, Tim 109
Fourth Reich, The 188
Fowle, Theresa 235
Fowler, Alison 93
Fowler, Beth 70
Fowler, Bruce 76
Fowler, C.H. 96
Fowler, Monique 161, 280
Fowler, Rachel 250, 279, 280, 292
Fowler, Richard 214
Fowler, Robert H. 70, 81
Fowler, Will 286
Fowler, William 289
Fowlkes, Thomas 209
Fox, Alan 109
Fox, Amy 225
Fox, Ben 64, 103, 191, 267
Fox, Bernard 214
Fox, Chuck 266, 267
Fox, Crystal 261, 267, 291
Fox, Elliot 110, 167
Fox, Josh 191, 202
Fox, Lori Haley 77
Fox, Martin 252, 255
Fox, Roz D. 185
Foxley, Penelope 274
Foy, Harriett D. 77, 103, 296
Foy, Ken 109
FPA Theatre Company 210
Fracchiolla, Chris 142
Fracher, Drew 260, 281
Frachiseur, Nicole 157, 244
Fragment 155
Fraioli, David 234
Fraley, Brian 188
Frame, Katy 237
Fran's Bed 165
Franc D'ambrosio's Broadway 246
France, Wesley 152
Francios, Sarah 206
Franciona, Anthony 338, 342
Francis, Aimee 222
Francis, Erica 199
Francis, Jeff 162
Francis, Juliana 155, 214
Francis, Stephen 251
Francishini, Crystal 248
Franck, Alison 286
Franck-Reed, Renee 276
Franco, Germaine 275
Franco, Trent Ballard 212
Françoise Changes Her Mind 188
Francone, Nick 182, 246, 249, 253
Frangione, Jim 220, 272, 273
Frank, Alicia 206
Frank, Andrew 121, 200
Frank, Brian 183
Frank, Jonathan 223
Frank, Laura 78
Frank, Lawrence 182
Frank, Robert Vincent 287, 288
Frank Silvera Writers Workshop 251
Frank-White, Penny 248
Frankel-Baruch-Viertel-Routh Group 81
Frankel, Ed 46, 97
Frankel, Elizabeth 107
Frankel, Jennifer 71, 78

Royal, Bert V. 112
Royal Shakespeare Company 152
Royal Theatre 205, 206
Royalrich Productions 205
Royer, Ben 260
Royle, Abby 102
Rozanski, Kristen 123
Rozewicz, Tadeusz 231
Rozié, Fabrice 119, 218
Roznowski, Robert 139
Rozsa, Shawn 207
Rrrrrrrrrrrrrrkillkillkill ... to Infinity 232
Rubald, Mark 279, 280
Rubel, Talia 188
Rubenstein Communications 96, 108, 112, 124
Rubenstein, Kim 291
Rubi, Jerusha 267
Rubie, Melody 80
Rubin, Amy 229
Rubin, Barbara 238, 249
Rubin, John Gould 124, Gould 202
Rubin, Lance 184, 200
Rubin, Lisa 106
Rubin, Marla 51
Rubin, Nate 196
Rubin, Paul 84, 274
Rubin, Tara 55, 77, 78, 83
Rubin-Vega, Daphne 82, 158, 245
Rubino, Cecila 184
Rubins, Jennifer 218
Rubinstein, Fran 162
Rubio, Isabel 217
Ruby, Ben 234
Ruby, Michael 256
Ruby, Reed 273
Ruby Sunrise, The 169
Ruby Vector, The 199
Rucci, Jill 195
Ruck, Alan 29, 81
Ruckdeschel, Carl A. 253
Ruckel, Taylor 114
Rucker, Mark 280, 296
Rudall, Nichols 164
Rudd, David 200
Rudd, Devin Shayla 229
Rudd, Paul 11, 53
Ruddy, Stephen 203
Ruddy, Tim 156, 157
Rude Mechanicals Theater Company 202
Rude Pundit in the Year of Living Rudely, The 241
Rudetsky, Seth 177, 193, 246
Rudez, Michael 230
Rudimentary 223
Rudin, Scott 22, 50, 55, 63, 65, 73, 93, 117
Rudinoff, Sarah 293
Rudko, Michael 273, 275
Rudnick, Paul 198
Rudnick, Pesha 254
Rudnick, Sami 235
Rudolph, Kalev 289
Rudy Rutabaga & The Terrible Dragon of Amsteryork 198
Rudy, Sam 175
Rue 251
Rueben, Charles 126
Ruede, Clay C. 40
Ruff, Roslyn 214, 264, 265, 285
Ruffalo, Mark 52
Ruffin, Clyde 292

Ruffin, David 209
Ruffin, Raun 219
Ruffin, Robert 295
Ruffini, Gene 251
Ruger, A. Nelson, IV 296
Ruggaber, Brian J. 183
Ruggeri, Nick 225
Ruggiero, Holly-Anne 34
Ruggiero, Rob 292
Ruggles of Red Gap 243
Ruhl, Malcolm 282
Ruhl, Sarah 266, 276, 280, 283
Ruhland, Jean Noel 234
Ruiz, Cassandra 247
Ruiz, Izzy 184
Ruiz-Palumbo, Dalia 245
Ruiz, Richard 168
Rukov, Mogens 51
Rule, Charles 79
Rule of Capture, The 232
Rule of Thumb, The 248
Rules for Good Manners in the Modern World 223
Rulssell, Veronica 238
Rumery, Ryan 160, 173, 262
Rumierk, Shirley A. 28
Rummel, Christian 200, 255
Run to the Roar 228
Runaway Birthday, The 227
Runcie, Patricia 248
Runda, Erika 109
Rundle, Erika 109, 218
Runolfsson, Anne 80
Runyon, Damon 250
Ruocco, John 292
Ruoti, Helena 277
Rupert, Michael 288
Rupnik, Kevin 293
Ruppe, Diana 150, 196
Rusconi, Ellen 138
Rush, Cindi 103, 124
Rush, Deborah 29
Rush, George 232
Rush, Santry 262, 263
Rusinek, Roland 80, 153, 178
Rusler, Morgan 273
Russ, Amy 235
Russek, Jim 115
Russel, Eugene, IV 282
Russell, Aaron 107
Russell, Andrew, 119
Russell, Baltimore 185
Russell, Bethany 151, 156
Russell, Bill 227
Russell, Brad 118, 211
Russell, Brenda 39
Russell, Brian, 64
Russell, Catherine 140
Russell, Cynthia 198
Russell, Francesca 65, 101, 168
Russell, Henny 104
Russell, Jay 261
Russell, Kimberly 56
Russell, Monica 192, 235
Russell, Neno 42
Russell, Nipsey 338, 347
Russell Projects 228
Russell, Ron 104, 130
Russell, Rupert 95
Russell, Susan 80
Russell, Tom E. 296
Russell, Willy 208
Russi, Celeste 142

Russo, Dante 238, 254, 288
Russo, Jason Arthur 205
Russo, Jennifer 225, 227, 242
Russo, Kathleen 205
Russo, Molly 186
Russo, Peter 186
Russo, William 165
Rustin, Sandy 139, 187
Ruta, Ken 264, 271
Rutan, Sarah 287, 288
Ruth, Anita 284
Ruth, Eleanor 213, 231
Rutherford, Alex 66, 70
Rutherford, Ed 284
Rutherford, Kourtney 188
Rutherford, Nolyn 285
Rutigliano, Danny 76, 153
Ruvolo, Rob 205
Rux, Joe 227
Ruzika, Donna 294
Ruzika, Tom 294
Ryall, William 120
Ryan, Ashley 164
Ryan, Brett 247
Ryan, Darren 230
Ryan, Dorothy 118, 128
Ryan, James 209, 225
Ryan, Jim 279
Ryan, Kate Moira 116, 220, 229, 253
Ryan, Maria 227
Ryan, Maybeth 190
Ryan, Mickey 157
Ryan, Roz 47, 71
Ryan, Sean 184
Ryan, Thomas Jay 150, 151, 230
Rychlec, Daniel 80
Ryckman, Jasper 280
Ryen, James 266
Rylance, Mark 112, 113
Ryle, Erik Kever 190, 220
Rypp, Howard 231
Ryskind, Morrie 154
Ryu, Ju-Yeon 228
Rzeszewski, Carla 220

S

Saar Harari Company 204
Saavedra, Hilario 218
Sabath, Bruce 277
Sabaugh, Pamela 93, 133
Sabberton, Kenn 95
Sabella, D. 71
Sabella, Ernie 71
Sabella-Mills, D. 71
Sabellico, Richard 177
Sabin, David 293
Sabooge Theatre 202
Sabre, Jérôme 152
Sachar, Louis 214, 233
Sacher-Masoch, Leopold von 191
Sachon, Peter 75, 124
Sachs, Norman 219
Sachs, Robin 295
Sachs, Sharon 282
Sachter-Zeltzer, Ariel 78
Sack, Brian 217
Sack, Domonic 49
Sackett Group 248
Sacks & Company 116, 128
Sacks, Alan 116
Sacred Circle Theater 190
Saculla, Chuck 72

Saddamn the Musical, Part, II 192
Sadler, Paul B., Jr. 80
Sadoski, Thomas 173, 176, 263
Sadoski, Tom, 128
Safe Harbor for Elizabeth Bishop, A 167
Safe in Hell 296
Safety 211
Safety Net, The 222
Sagan, Miram 233
Sagardia, Elisa 109
Sage, Hank 214
Sage, Mariah 224
Sage, Raymond 70
Sage Theater 207
Sagenkahn, Sam 237
Sagle, Corinne J. 248
Saguar, Luis 279
Sahin, Selda 222, 236
Saia, Janet 80
Said, Najla 294
Said Said 264
Saietta, Robert 214
Saint, David 281
Saint Frances of Hollywood 200
Saint Oedipus 231
Sakakura, Lainie 42
Sakamoto, Mei 228
Sake With The Haiku Geisha 120
Sakong, Eunhye Grace 95
Sakowski, Stephen 209, 211
Saks, Gene 290
Sala, Ed 140
Salacious Uncle Baldrick, The 241
Salacrou, Armand 194
Salamandyk, Tim 92, 153
Salamida, Danita 59
Salamon-Sufott, Betsy 212
Salamon, Tom 212
Salamone, Louis 103
Salasovich, Joseph P. 266, 267
Saldivar, Matthew 57, 58, 155, 170
Salerno, Anthony 187
Salerno, Michelle 214
Sales, Laurie 249
Salessl, Wolde 129
Salgado, Mauricio Tafur 155, 213
Salinas, Ric 262, 271, 274
Salisbury, D.J. 197
Salka, Benjamin 186, 187
Salka, Jessie 186
Salkin, Eddie 54
Salkin, Jonathan 98
Salling, Pam 244
Salloum, Fouad 99
Sally and Tom (The American Way) 223
Salmon, Russ 113
Salomons, Ruthlyn 39
Salonia, Michael 22, 188
Salter, Nikkole 110, 167
Saltzberg, Sarah 83
Saltzman, Larry 58
Saltzman, Richard 186
Salvador, Gerard 77, 219
Salvage Shop, The 250
Salvatore, John 70
Salzberg, Jeffrey E. 184, 214, 227
Salzberg, Marc 52
Salzman, Joshua 118, 181
Salzman, Thomas 272
Sam Harris 245
Sam Rudy Media Relations 69, 102, 112, 116, 117, 119, 124, 213
Samaan, Caroline 185, 233

Samarra, 194
Samayoa, Caesar 59, 177
Samonsky, Andrew 281
Samorian, John 58
Sampieri, Peter 127, 249
Sampliner, James 57, 58
Sampson, Adesina 185
Sampson, Diane 256
Samson, Aaron 239
Samson, R.J. 141
Samuel, Peter 75, 81
Samuels, Bruce 40
Samuels, Sean 66
Sanborn, Laurel 251
Sanborn, Ron 252
Sanchez, Alex 42
Sanchez, Chris-Ian 113
Sanchez, David "Dakota" 76
Sanchez, Edwin 220
Sanchez, Jennifer 209, 274
Sanchez, Jose Luis 288
Sanchez, KJ 115
Sanchez, Nick 66, 82, 137
Sanchez, Roland 251
Sanchez, Sonia 228
Sancho, Jamall 296
Sand, Eric 140, 254
Sand, Gila 241
Sand, Mason 265
Sandack, Emily 203
Sandal, Kjersti 153
Sandberg, Kate 189, 235
Sande Shurin Theatre 207
Sandefur, Brad 284
Sander, Peter 186, 217
Sander, Ryan 77
Sanders, Alan 186
Sanders, Ann 69, 70
Sanders, Betsy 200
Sanders, Caitlin 193
Sanders, Derrick 228
Sanders, Eric 64, 182, 255
Sanders Family Christmas 286
Sanders, Francesca 249
Sanders, Jay O. 169
Sanders, Jennifer 230
Sanders, K.B. 200
Sanders, Kristie Dale 286, 295
Sanders, Laura 264
Sanders, Liz 234
Sanders, Mathew J. 185
Sanders, Naila Aladdin 295
Sanders, Nathan 270
Sanders, Pete 71, 93, 105, 119, 126, 132
Sanders, Scott 39
Sanders-Joyce, Dan 283
Sanderson, Austin K. 263, 267
Sanderson, Christopher Carter 195, 235
Sanderson, Laurie 190
Sanditen, Harold 91
Sandler, Aaron 213, 233
Sandler, Adam 57
Sandler, Susan 272
Sandling, Josefin 252
Sandlot 253
Sandoval, Ann 200
Sandoval, Charles Daniel 275
Sandoval, Mathew 188
Sandoval, Mhari 212
Sandoval, Ramiro 252
Sandoval, Triney 244
Sandow, Nick 103, 134

JOHN WILLIS | Co-Editor

John Willis has been editor-in-chief of both *Theatre World* and its companion series *Screen World* for forty-two years. *Theatre World* and *Screen World* are the oldest definitive pictorial and statistical records of each American theatrical and foreign and domestic film season, and are referenced daily by industry professionals, students, and historians worldwide.

Mr. Willis has also served as editor of *Dance World*, *Opera World*, *A Pictorial History of the American Theatre 1860–1985*, and *A Pictorial History of the Silent Screen*. Previously, he served as assistant to *Theatre World* founder Daniel Blum on *Great Stars of the American Stage*, *Great Stars of Film*, *A Pictorial History of the Talkies*, *A Pictorial History of Television*, and *A Pictorial Treasury of Opera in America*.

For over forty years he presided over the presentation of the annual Theatre World Awards, incorporated in 1997 as a 501 (c)(3) nonprofit organization and now executive produced by *Theatre World* co-editor Ben Hodges. Begun in 1945 and presented by past winners, they are the oldest awards given to actors for a Broadway or Off-Broadway debut role.

On behalf of *Theatre World*, Mr. Willis received a 2001 Tony Honor for Excellence in the Theatre, the 2003 Broadway Theater Institute Lifetime Achievement Award, a 1994 special Drama Desk Award, and in 1993, the first Outstanding Special Lucille Lortel Award. On behalf of *Screen World*, he received the prestigious 1998 National Board of Review Wiliam K. Everson Award for Film History. He has also received a Professional Excellence Award from his alma mater, Milligan College.

He has served on the Tony Award nominating committee, the New York University Musical Hall of Fame selection committee, the national board of directors for the Clarence Brown Theatre at the University of Tennessee in Knoxville, TN, and past board of directors of the National Board of Review. In addition, Mr. Willis is retired from the New York public school system.

In 1993, the auditorium in which he had performed as a student was renovated and christened the John Willis Performing Arts Center at Morristown-Hamblen High School East, in Morristown, TN.

BEN HODGES | Co-Editor

Ben Hodges has been associate editor of *Theatre World* since 1998, joining Mr. Willis as co-editor on this volume. As an actor and/or director, Mr. Hodges has appeared in New York with The Barrow Group Theatre Company, Monday Morning Productions, Strawberry One-Act Play Festival, Coyote Girls Productions, Jet Productions, New York Actors' Alliance, and Outcast Productions. Additionally, he has appeared in numerous productions presented by theatre companies he founded, including the Tuesday Group and Visionary Works. On film, he can be seen featured in *Macbeth: The Comedy*.

Between 2001 and 2004, he was director of development and then served as executive director for Fat Chance Productions, Inc., and the Ground Floor Theatre, a New York–based nonprofit theatre and film production company. *Prey for Rock and Roll* was developed by Fat Chance from the stage production — the first legitimate production to appear at the legendary CBGB's — into a critically acclaimed feature film starring Gina Gershon, Drea de Matteo, and Lori Petty. Fat Chance also presented the Off-Broadway American premiere of Award-winning playwright Enda Walsh's *Misterman*.

In 2003, frustrated with the increasingly daunting economic prospects involved in producing theatre on a small scale in New York, Mr. Hodges organized NOOBA, the New Off-Off Broadway Association, an advocacy group dedicated to representing the concerns of expressly Off-Off-Broadway producers in the public forum and in negotiations with other local professional arts organizations. He also serves on the New York Innovative Theatre Awards Committee, selecting outstanding individuals for recognition Off-Off-Broadway, and has participated as a panelist and adjudicator for Theatre Resources Unlimited.

Mr. Hodges served as an editorial assistant for many years on the 2001 Special Tony Honor Award–winning *Theatre World*, becoming the associate editor to John Willis in 1998 and co-editor in 2006. Also an assistant for many years to Mr. Willis for the prestigious Theatre World Awards, Mr. Hodges was elected to the Theatre World Awards Board in 2002 and has served as the executive producer of the ceremony since 2003. He was presented with a Special Theatre World Award in 2003 for his ongoing stewardship of the event. He also served as executive producer of the 2005 LAMBDA Literary Foundation Awards in New York.

Forbidden Acts, the first collected anthology of gay and lesbian plays of the twentieth century, edited and with an introduction by Mr. Hodges, was published by Applause Theatre and Cinema Books in 2003 and was a finalist for the 2004 LAMBDA Literary Award for Drama.

His *Commercial Theater Institute Guide to Producing Plays and Musicals*, edited with the institute's longtime director, the late Frederic B. Vogel, including contributions from over twenty-five industry professionals and released by Applause in November 2006, is the comprehensive and definitive guide to theatrical production in the United States.

Reviews and articles by Mr. Hodges or about Mr. Hodges's work as a director, producer, and/or writer have appeared in *The New Yorker*, *The New York Times*, *Time Out New York*, *Playbill*, *Towers*, *BackStage*, *The Advocate*, *Gay City News*, *HX*, *Citizen Tribune*, *Philadelphia Gay News*, *Between the Lines*, and *Houston Voice*, on PBS television and *Philly Live* with Debra D'Alessandro on radio.

Mr. Hodges currently serves as executive director of The Learning Theatre, Inc., a nonprofit organization incorporating theatre into the development of learning disabled and autistic children.

SCOTT DENNY | Associate Editor

Scott Denny is an actor and singer who has worked professionally for over twenty years. Originally from Terre Haute, Indiana, he attended Western Kentucky University in Bowling Green, Kentucky, and holds a degree in Performing Arts. His professional theatrical credits include Richard Henry Lee in the national tour of *1776*, Uncle Wes in the Las Vegas and national touring production of *Footloose*, and the assistant company manager and swing performer on the national tour of Susan Stroman's production of *The Music Man*. Regionally he has appeared at Houston's Theatre Under the Stars, Wichita's Stage One, and several summer stock and dinner theatres in productions of *Paper Moon, Silver Dollar, Evita, Me and My Girl, Gypsy, She Loves Me, The Best Little Whorehouse in Texas*, and many others. In New York he has appeared Off-Off-Broadway in *Election Day, Like You Like It, Vanity Fair*, and in several readings and workshops. Mr. Denny served as assistant editor on *Theatre World Volume 60*, and as associate editor on *Volume 61*. He also served as an associate producer for the 2006 Theatre World Awards. In the past few years Mr. Denny has been working in the cruise travel industry specializing in managing large groups. He enjoys reading, collecting show business memorabilia, and seeing as much theatre as possible, and will soon return to his acting career.

ALLISON GRAHAM | Associate Editor

Allison Graham is from Columbus, Ohio. She graduated Magna Cum Laude from Otterbein College in 2004, where she studied Music and Dance. In New York, Ms. Graham sings professionally with St. Bartholomew's Choir and St. John the Divine's "Nightwatch" program. She is also a volunteer for the New York Public Library.

SHANE FRAMPTON WOLTERS | Assistant Editor

Shane Frampton Wolters used to sing and dance and act, and was a theatre gypsy for many years. Then she met a wonderful man while she was singing and dancing on a steamboat on the Mississippi River. She currently lives in Austin, Texas, with that man—who is now her husband—and cats Elvis and Priscilla. She's also a legal advocate for Safe Place, one of the first shelters in the nation to offer safety for women and their children.

LISA KUHNEN | Assistant Editor

Lisa Kuhnen is an actor, singer, and dancer, currently living in New York City. She has performed at numerous regional theatres, including the Cleveland Playhouse, Great Lakes Theatre Festival, and Syracuse Stage. Ms. Kuhnen has a Bachelor of Fine Arts from Syracuse University, where she studied musical theatre with a concentration in dance.

CAITLIN THOMSON | Assistant Editor

Caitlyn Thomson is an aspiring producer who recently graduated from the University of Michigan with degrees in Voice Performance and Political Science. While at the university Ms. Thomson produced for the largest student theatre group on campus, mounting two full-scale musicals per year in a 1,400 seat house. Favorite credits include *Dreamgirls* (winner of the Program of the Year Award from the University of Michigan), *Cabaret, Urinetown*, and Andrew Lippa's *The Wild Party*, which she also directed. Ms. Thomson is thrilled to now be a full-time resident of New York City and is currently happily employed at The Producing Office.

ADDITIONAL ACKNOWLEDGMENTS

Theatre World would like to extend a very special thank you to all the New York and regional press agents, theatre marketing departments, and theatre photographers for their constant and steadfast support of this publication, and for the endless resources that they provide to the editorial staff: Joan Marcus, Carol Rosegg, Paul Kolnik, Monique Carboni, Michal Daniel, Richard Termine, Gerry Goodstein, Audrey Ross, John Barlow, Carol Fineman, Michael Hartman, Bethany Larson, Ryan Ratelle, Dennis Crowley, Kevin Roebak, Wayne Wolf, Leslie Baden, Matt Stapleton, Michelle Bergmann, Tom D'Ambrosio, Bill Evans, Jim Randolph, Chris Boneau, Jackie Green, Juliana Hannett, Allison Houseworth, Jessica Johnson, Shanna Marcus, Christine Olver, Joe Perrotta, Matt Polk, Matt Ross, Heath Schwartz, Susanne Tighe, Adrian Bryan-Brown, Jim Byck, Aaron Meier, Brett Singer, Bruce Cohen, Peter Cromarty, David Gersten, Ellen Jacobs, Karen Greco, Helene Davis, Irene Gandy, Jim Baldassare, Jonathan Slaff, Scott Klein, DJ Martin, Bret Oberman, Keith Sherman, Glenna Freedman, Kevin McAnarney, Max Eisen, Beck Lee, Dan Fortune, Miller Wright, Marissa Altamura, Philip Carrubba, Jon Dimond, Richard Hillman, Rick Miramontez, Tony Origlio, Barbara Carroll, Philip Rinaldi, Timothy Haskell, Carrie Friedman, Richard Kornberg, Don Summa, Billy Zavelson, Howard Rubenstein, Robert Lasko, Sam Rudy, Bill Coyle, Adrianna Douzous, Jeremy Shaffer, Dan Demello, Shirley Herz, Ron Lasko, Gary Springer, Joe Trentacosta, Stephen Sunderlin, Susan L Schulman, Judy Jacksina, Bridget Klapinski, Darron Molovinsky, Pete Sanders, Arlene Kriv, Sam Neuman, Candi Adams, Michael Borowski, Marc Thibodeau, and Shayne Miller.